Life Sciences

Fundamentals and Practice

Part - **1**

Ninth edition

PRANAV KUMAR
Former faculty,
Department of Biotechnology,
Jamia Millia Islamia (JMI),
New Delhi, India

USHA MINA
Professor,
School of Environmental Sciences,
Jawaharlal Nehru University (JNU),
New Delhi, India

Pathfinder Publication
New Delhi, India

Pranav Kumar
Former faculty,
Department of Biotechnology,
Jamia Millia Islamia (JMI),
New Delhi, India

Usha Mina
Professor,
School of Environmental Sciences,
Jawaharlal Nehru University (JNU),
New Delhi, India

Life Sciences: Fundamentals and Practice

Ninth edition

ISBN: 978-81-956333-4-0 (paperback)

Publisher : Pathfinder Publication
Illustration and layout : Pradeep Verma
Cover design : Pradeep Verma
Marketing director : Arun Kumar
Production coordinator : Murari Kumar Singh

Pathfinder Publication
A unit of Pathfinder Academy Private Limited, New Delhi, India.
pathfinderpublication.in

Preface

Life Sciences have always been a fundamental area of science. It is a science whose boundaries encompass all aspects of biology, from molecules to cells, to organisms, to ecology. Due to the exponential increase in the quantity of scientific information, this field requires very elaborated, interdisciplinary, and up-to-date information and their understanding.

New to this revised and updated edition

Like all of the previous editions of this book, we have emphasized the fundamental principles of life sciences keeping in mind the need of undergraduate and post-graduate students. With every edition, this book has evolved to meet the interests and needs of students and instructors. Most importantly, the rate at which discoveries are made in life sciences requires very elaborated and up-to-date information. By considering this fact, this new edition has been extensively updated to reflect the recent advances in all domains of life sciences. As a result, several changes mark this edition.

Focus on the fundamentals

This book covers the basic concepts and facts. It is written to promote the understanding of a subject's basic principles and concepts rather than memorization of details. Therefore, fundamentals are written in a sharply focused manner without overwhelming or excessive details.

Understanding Life Sciences as a whole

We recognize that Life Sciences is an integrated network of different disciplines such as biochemistry, cell biology, immunology, etc. Hence, we have given equal importance to all domains of life sciences and maintained an interdisciplinary approach. Therefore, the order of chapters is placed in a logical sequence. However, we recognize that a course in Life Sciences is approached differently by different experts. Therefore, we have designed each of the chapters in such a manner so that it can be read independently of one another.

Expanded and updated coverage of all chapters

This new edition is an extensive revision of the previous editions. We have attempted to provide a very large amount of information from the enormous and ever-growing field of Life Sciences in an easily retrievable form. It is written in clear and concise language to enhance the self-learning skill of the readers. Texts are re-organized for increased clarity and readability.

Accuracy and currency

It is crucial to get the right concepts as well as accurate and up-to-date facts. Hence, best efforts have been taken in preparing this book in terms of concepts and facts. The information in this book is an outcome of an extensive literature survey from very authentic and highly regarded sources.

Integration of text and illustrations

We have given equal importance to text and illustrations. This edition has a number of new and improved figures and flow charts to enhance understanding. At the same time, we avoid excess detail, which can obscure the main point of the figure. We have retained the design elements that have evolved through the previous editions to make the book easier to read. Sincere efforts have been made to support textual clarifications and explanations with the help of flow charts, figures, and tables to make learning easy and convincing.

Problem-solving tools

Our primary goal in writing this book is to help students build a conceptual framework for learning life sciences and improve problem-solving skills. Hence, each chapter in this book is supplemented with problems to help students strengthen their quantitative problem-solving skills and end-of-chapter self-tests to check one's level of understanding.

Acknowledgements

Our students were the original inspiration for the first edition of this book, and we remain continually grateful to them because we learn from them how to think about the life sciences, and how to communicate knowledge in most meaningful way. We thank Dr. Diwakar Kumar Singh, Ajay Kumar and Pramod Kumar Mittal, reviewers of this book, whose comments and suggestions were invaluable in improving the text. Any book of this kind requires meticulous and painstaking efforts by all its contributors. Several diligent and hardworking minds have come together to bring out this book in this complete form. We are much beholden to each of them and especially to Dr. Neeraj Tiwari. This book is a team effort, and producing it would be impossible without the outstanding people of Pathfinder Publication. It was a pleasure to work with many other dedicated and creative people of Pathfinder Publication during the production of this book, especially to Pradeep Verma.

Pranav Kumar

Usha Mina

Contents

Chapter 1
Biomolecules and Catalysis

Chapter 2

Metabolism

Chapter 3

Cell Structure and Functions

Chapter 4

Prokaryotes and Viruses

Chapter 5
Immunology

Chapter 6
Diversity of Life

Chapter 7

Ecology

1 Biomolecules and Catalysis

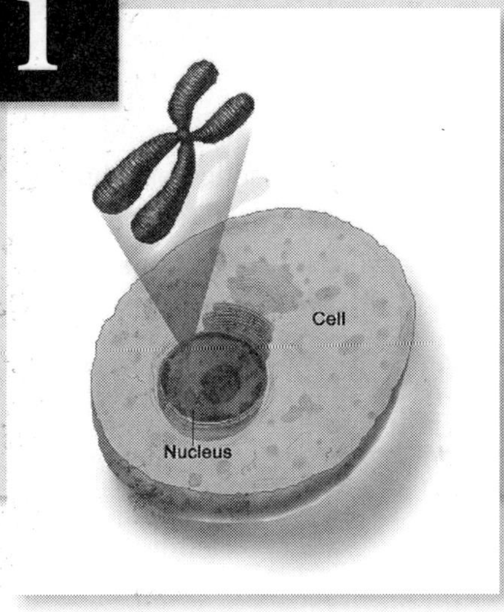

SUBJECT FOCUS

Biomolecules are **carbon-based organic compounds** that are produced by living organisms. Most biomolecules can be regarded as derivatives of hydrocarbons, with hydrogen atoms replaced by a variety of functional groups that confer specific chemical properties on the molecule. These molecules consist of a relatively small number of elements. Approximately 25 to 30 naturally occurring chemical elements are found in biomolecules, and most of these elements have a relatively low atomic number. In terms of the percentage of the total number of atoms, hydrogen, oxygen, nitrogen, and carbon together makeup over 98% of the mass of most cells. Biomolecules include both small as well as large molecules. The **small biomolecules** are low molecular weight (less than 1000) compounds which include sugars, fatty acids, amino acids, nucleotides, vitamins, hormones, neurotransmitters, primary and secondary metabolites. Sugars, fatty acids, amino acids, and nucleotides constitute the four major families of small biomolecules in cells. Each of these small biomolecules is composed of a small set of atoms linked to each other in a precise configuration through covalent bonds. **Large biomolecules** which have high molecular weight are called **macromolecules** and mostly are polymers of small biomolecules. These macromolecules are proteins, carbohydrates, and nucleic acids.

Small biomolecules	Macromolecules
Sugars	Polysaccharides
Amino acids	Polypeptides (proteins)
Nucleotides	Polynucleotides (nucleic acids)

Nucleic acids and proteins are **informational macromolecules**. Proteins are polymers of amino acids and constitute the largest fraction (besides water) of cells. The nucleic acids, DNA and RNA, are polymers of nucleotides. They store, transmit, and translate genetic information. The polysaccharides, polymers of monosaccharides, have two primary functions: serving as a storage form of energy and as extracellular structural components.

1.1 Amino acids and Proteins

Amino acids are compounds containing carbon, hydrogen, oxygen and nitrogen and serve as monomers (building block) of proteins. As the name implies, these compounds contain both an *amino group* and a *carboxyl group*. In an **α-amino acid**, the amino and carboxyl groups are attached to the same carbon atom, which is called the **α-carbon**. The various α-amino acids differ with respect to the *side chain* (**R group**) attached to their α-carbon.

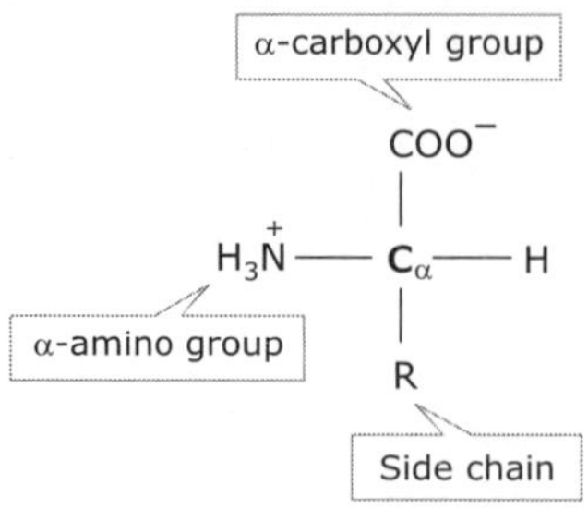

Figure 1.1 General structure of an amino acid.

The R group attached to the α-carbon is different in each amino acid. In the simplest case, the R group is a hydrogen atom and amino acid is **glycine**. With the exception of proline, all α-amino acids have the same general structure. **Proline** is unique among the α-amino acids because it is not a *primary amino acid*, but rather is a *secondary amino acid*, sometimes called an **imino acid**. Unlike the primary amino acids which contain a *primary amino group* ($-NH_2$), proline contains a *secondary amino group* (–NH–).

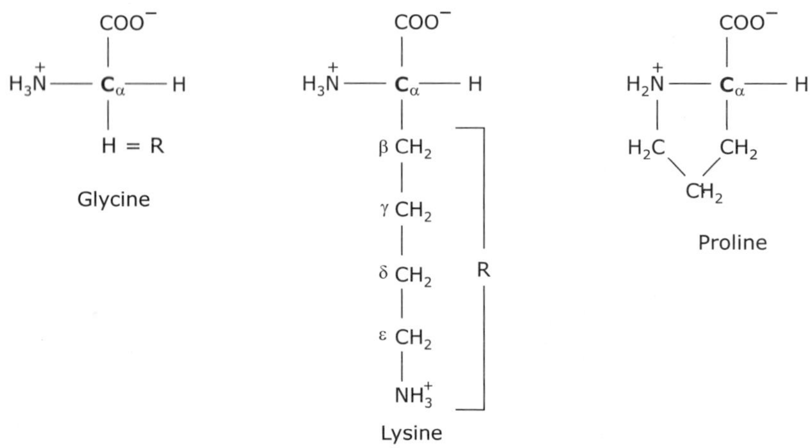

Figure 1.2 Structure of amino acids (glycine and lysine) and imino acid (proline).

In α-amino acids, both the amino group and the carboxyl group are attached to the same α-carbon atom. However, many naturally occurring amino acids not found in protein, have structures that differ from the α-amino acids. In these compounds the amino group is attached to a carbon atom other than the α-carbon atom and they are called **β, γ, δ,** or **ε**-amino acids depending upon the location of the C-atom to which amino group is attached.

Amino acids can act as acids and bases

Amino acids contain both an amino ($-NH_2$) and a carboxyl (–COOH) group. At physiological pH (~7.2), the α-amino groups are protonated ($-NH_3^+$) and the α-carboxyl groups are deprotonated ($-COO^-$). Thus, in solution at physiological pH, amino acids are present largely in their **zwitterionic** ('double ion') form. The ionization state of an amino acid varies with pH. At a very low pH (i.e. strongly acidic solution), the α-carboxyl group is protonated (–COOH) and uncharged whereas α-amino group is protonated ($-NH_3^+$) and positively charged. Thus, the overall charge on the molecule is *positive*. Similarly, at very high pH, the α-carboxyl group is deprotonated ($-COO^-$) and negatively charged whereas α-amino group is deprotonated ($-NH_2$) and uncharged. Thus, the overall charge on the molecule is *negative*. Amino acids are **amphiprotic** molecules. A molecule that can both accept and donate protons is called an amphiprotic species. Since the carboxyl group is able to lose a proton and the amino group is able to accept a proton, an amino acid can act both as an acid and a base. A substance that can act as either an acid or a base is called an **amphoteric** substance. Thus, amino acids are also amphoteric in nature.

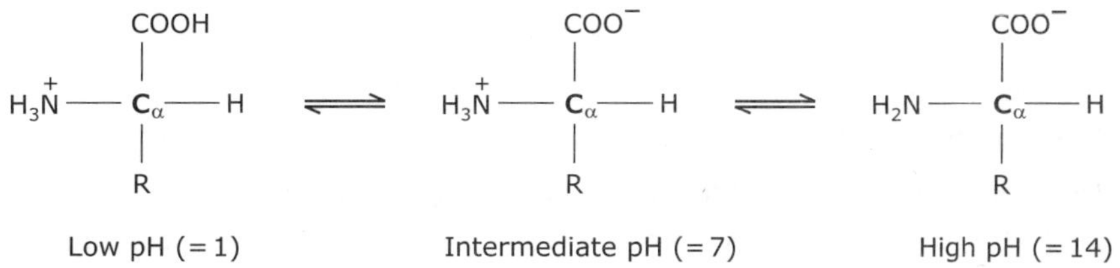

Figure 1.3 The acid-base behaviour of an amino acid in solution. The ionization state of amino acids is altered by a change in pH. At low pH, the positively charged species predominates. As the pH increases, the electrically neutral zwitterion becomes predominant. A zwitterion can act as either an acid (proton donor) or a base (proton acceptor). At higher pH, the negatively charged species predominates.

Box 1.1 Stereoisomer

Isomers are compounds that have the same molecular formula, meaning they contain the same atoms bonded together in different ways. There are two main types of isomers: **constitutional isomers,** which have different atomic connectivities, and **stereoisomers,** which have the same atomic connectivity but a different arrangement of atoms in space. Steroisomers are further classified into two types: *enantiomers* and *diastereomers*.

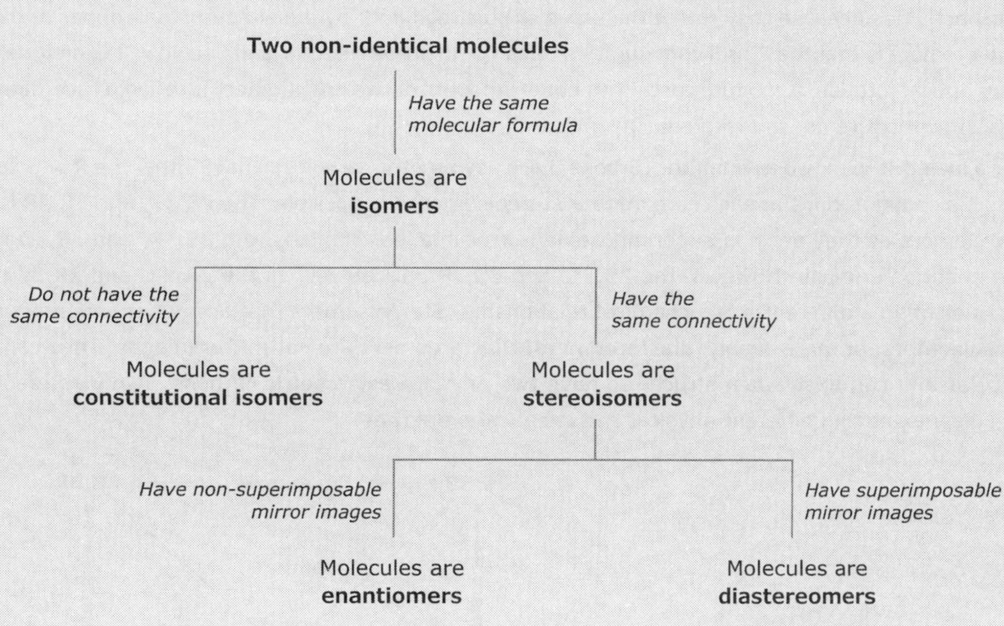

Molecules that are non-superimposable mirror images are called **enantiomers.** These molecules are **chiral,** meaning they possess the property of **chirality.** In contrast, molecules that are not chiral are said to be **achiral.** The essential difference between chiral and achiral molecules is *symmetry*. If a molecule has a plane of symmetry or a center of symmetry, it is achiral. Chiral molecules contain one or more asymmetric (chiral) carbons, which are carbon atoms bound to four different groups. A molecule with only one chiral carbon is chiral. For molecules with more than one chiral carbon, they may be either chiral or achiral, depending on their symmetry.

Nomenclature of enantiomers: Molecules that are enantiomers will have opposite absolute configurations which describes the 3-D arrangement of atoms around a chiral carbon in a molecule. There are two system for describing absolute configuration: **DL system** and **RS system.**

The **RS system** of enantiomer nomenclature is based on *priority rules*. The priority is determined by the atomic number of the four different substituents bonded to an asymmetric carbon. The higher the atomic number, the higher the priority. The arrangement of atoms at each asymmetric carbon in a molecule can be assigned using the following steps:

1. Identify an asymmetric carbon and the four different substituents (groups) bound to it.
2. Assign priorities to the four different substituents according to the **Cahn-Ingold-Prelog** (CIP) rules. Atoms with higher atomic numbers are given higher priority. The convention applied in this text dictates that the highest priority is designated as 1, while the lowest priority is denoted as 4.
3. View the molecule along the bond from the asymmetric carbon to the substituent of lowest priority.
4. Consider the clockwise or counterclockwise order of the remaining substituents. If the priorities of these substituents decrease in the *clockwise direction*, the asymmetric carbon is said to have the **R configuration** (R for *rectus*). If the priorities of these substituents decrease in the *counterclockwise direction*, the asymmetric carbon is said to have the **S configuration** (S for *sinister*).

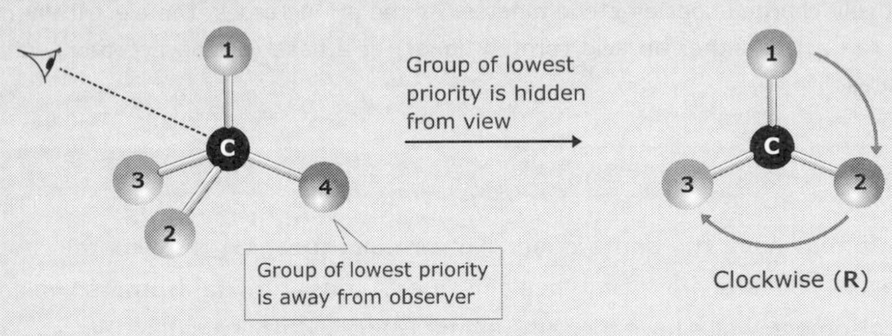

The physical and chemical properties of a pair of enantiomers are identical. However, enantiomers are distinguished by their optical activities because they rotate the plane of polarized light by equal amounts in opposite directions. An important point to note is that the R or S configuration does not indicate whether a molecule will exhibit dextrorotatory or levorotatory optical rotation. A mixture containing equal amounts of two enantiomers is called a **racemate** or **racemic mixture.** A racemic mixture doesn't rotate such light at all.

Let's consider a molecule with two asymmetric carbons. Each asymmetric carbon can have either the R or S configuration. With two possible configurations at each carbon, four stereoisomers are possible. The 2S,3S, and 2R,3R isomers form a pair of enantiomers as they are non-superimposable mirror images. Similarly, the 2S,3R, and 2R,3S isomers also constitute an enantiomeric pair. However, the 2S,3S, and 2S,3R pair, as well as the 2R,3R, and 2R,3S pair, are not enantiomers, indicating a different stereochemical relationship. Stereoisomers that are not enantiomers are referred to as **diastereoisomers,** or more simply, **diastereomers**. Diastereomers are not mirror images. They can be chiral or achiral molecules and can arise when structures have two or more asymmetric carbons. Two diastereoisomers are distinct molecules, exhibiting different physical and chemical properties.

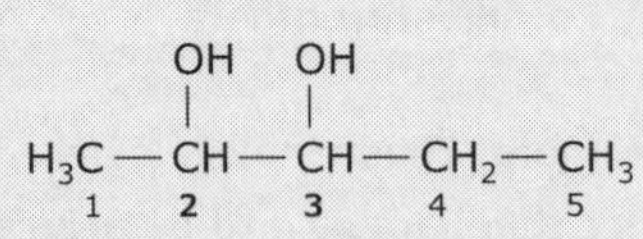

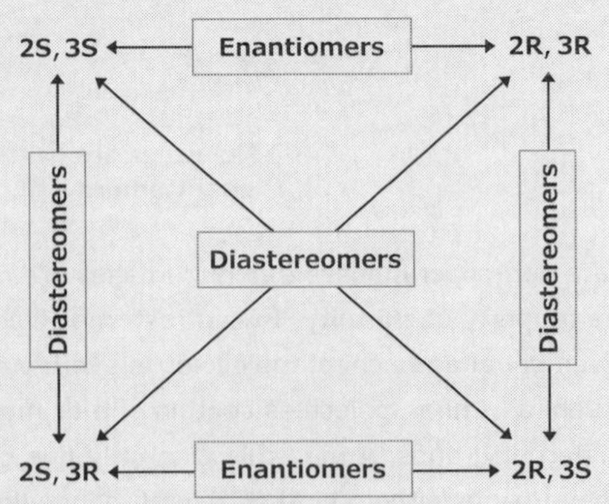

The two diastereoisomers are different compounds with different names and different properties, while the pairs of enantiomers are the same compound with the same properties, differing only in the direction in which they rotate plane polarized light.

1.1.1 Absolute configuration

All α-amino acids except glycine are *chiral* molecules. A chiral amino acid can exist in two opposite absolute configurations that are non-superimposable mirror images of each other. These two configurations are called **enantiomers**. Different systems have been developed to specify the absolute configuration of a chiral molecule. We should remember that **configuration** and **conformation** of molecules have distinct meanings. Altering the configuration of a molecule always involves breaking covalent bonds. Conversely, conformational changes refer to alterations in the geometry of a molecule without breaking any covalent bonds. These changes primarily occur due to rotation around any single covalent bonds. Conformations of a molecule are easily interconvertible and represent the same molecule.

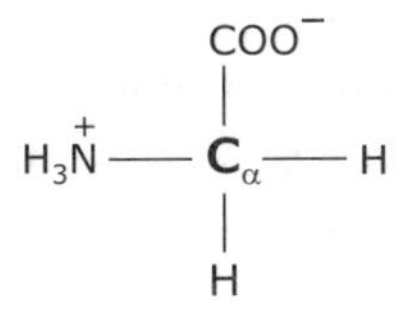

Glycine (achiral amino acid)

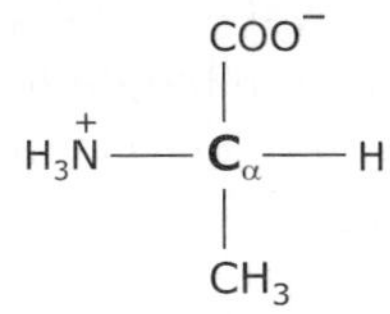

Alanine (chiral amino acid)

DL system of naming enantiomers

The 'DL system' relates the absolute configuration of the α-carbon of an amino acid to that of the 3-carbon aldose sugar *glyceraldehyde*. Glyceraldehyde has two absolute configurations. When the hydroxyl group attached to the chiral carbon is on the left in a Fischer projection, the configuration is '**L**'; when the hydroxyl group is on the right, the configuration is '**D**'. This refers *only* to the absolute configuration of the four substituents (atom or group of atoms) bonded to the chiral carbon, not to optical properties of the molecule.

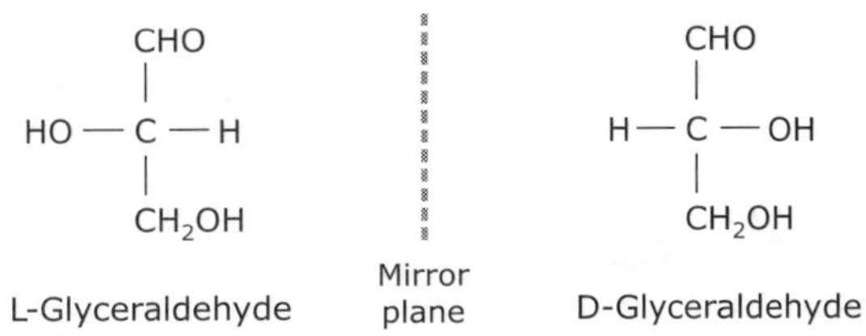

Figure 1.4 The absolute configuration of glyceraldehyde. In Fisher projection formulas, if the hydroxyl group is located on the right side of the chiral center, the molecule is D. If the hydroxyl group is on the left side, the molecule is L.

For all chiral α-amino acids, with the same configuration as that of L-glyceraldehyde are designated **L**, and configurations related to D-glyceraldehyde are designated **D**. In L-α-amino acids, the α-amino group on the left whereas in D-α-amino acids, the α-amino group is on the right.

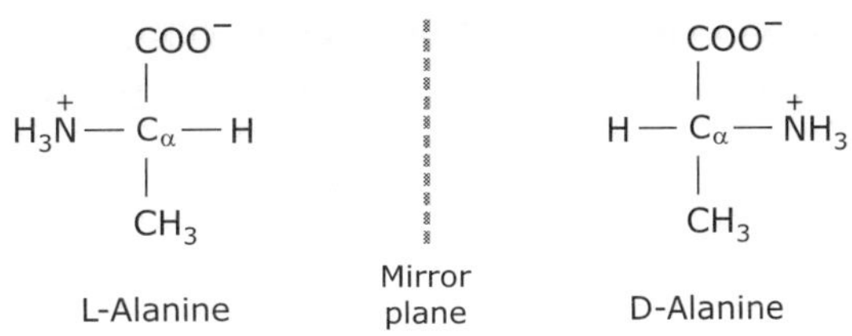

Figure 1.5 The absolute configuration of α-amino acid alanine is specified by the DL system in Fisher projection formulas.

The D- and L-designations specify the configuration of a single reference carbon. For α-amino acids, the reference carbon is the α-carbon. All amino acids except glycine exist in these two different absolute configurations. However, all the amino acids which ribosomically incorporated into proteins exhibit L-configuration. Therefore, they are all L-α-amino acids. The basis for preference for L-amino acids is not known. D-form of amino acids is *not* found in ribosomically synthesized proteins, although they exist in some peptide antibiotics and tetrapeptide chain of peptidoglycan cell wall.

RS system of naming enantiomers

For compounds with more than one chiral center, the most useful system to describe two opposite absolute configurations of enantiomers is the 'RS system'. In addition, with this system, we can define the configuration of a chiral compound in the absence of any reference compound. This approach uses **priority rules** to specify configurations. The *priority* is based on the atomic number of the four different substituents bonded to an asymmetric (chiral) carbon. The higher the atomic number, the higher the priority i.e., atoms of higher atomic number bonded to a chiral center are ranked above those of lower atomic number.

Let's use the amino acid alanine as an example to understand the prioritization of groups around a chiral carbon. In alanine, the α-carbon is bonded to one nitrogen atom (atomic number 7), two carbon atoms (atomic number 6), and one hydrogen atom (atomic number 1). To assign priorities to these groups, we consider the atomic numbers. The NH_2 group is given priority 1 since nitrogen has the highest atomic number. Priorities 2 and 3 are assigned to the COOH and CH_3 groups, respectively, while the hydrogen atom receives priority 4. When two of the atoms bonded to the chiral carbon are identical, we look at the second, third, and so on, atoms to establish priority. In this case, the COOH group has higher priority (atomic number 8) compared to CH_3 (atomic number 1).

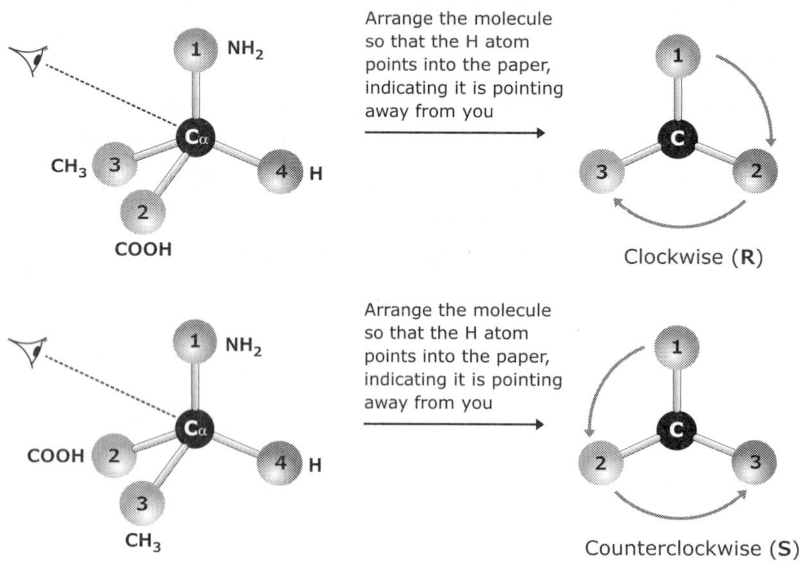

For the RS system naming, it is essential to position the lowest priority substituent away from the viewer. If the other three groups are arranged in a clockwise direction of decreasing priority, the chiral center is classified as having the **R configuration** (where R is from the Latin *rectus*, meaning 'right'). Conversely, if the three groups decrease in priority in a counterclockwise direction, the chiral center is considered to have the **S configuration** (where S is from the Latin sinister, meaning 'left').

Two opposite absolute configurations of enantiomers of the amino acids at the α-carbon is typically described by the DL system rather than the more modern RS system. According to the **DL system**, all standard amino acids from proteins have the L absolute configuration. However, in the **RS system**, all standard amino acids from proteins have the S absolute configuration, except for **cysteine**, which has the R configuration due to the presence of sulfur in its side chain.

1.1.2 Optical activity

All amino acids, except for glycine, are **chiral** molecules and, as a result, exhibit optical activity. An **optically active** compound has the ability to rotate the plane of plane-polarized light. In **unpolarized light**, the electric field vector oscillates in more than one plane; all perpendicular to the direction of propagation. If the electric field vector oscillates in single plane perpendicular to the direction of propagation, it is called **linearly** or **plane polarized light.** Optically active molecules are chiral molecules. For a molecule to be considered chiral, it must lack a plane of symmetry or a center of symmetry, or both. An optically active compound can rotate the plane of plane-polarized light either clockwise (to the right) or counterclockwise (to the left). Compounds that rotate the plane of polarized light *clockwise* are termed **dextrorotatory**, denoted by a plus sign (+) or ***d***. Those rotating *counterclockwise* are termed **levorotatory**, designated by a minus sign (–) or ***l***. The optical rotation of a sample is a quantitative measure of its optical activity, measured using a **polarimeter**. The magnitude of optical rotation indicates the extent to which the plane of polarized light is rotated, while the sign represents the direction of rotation.

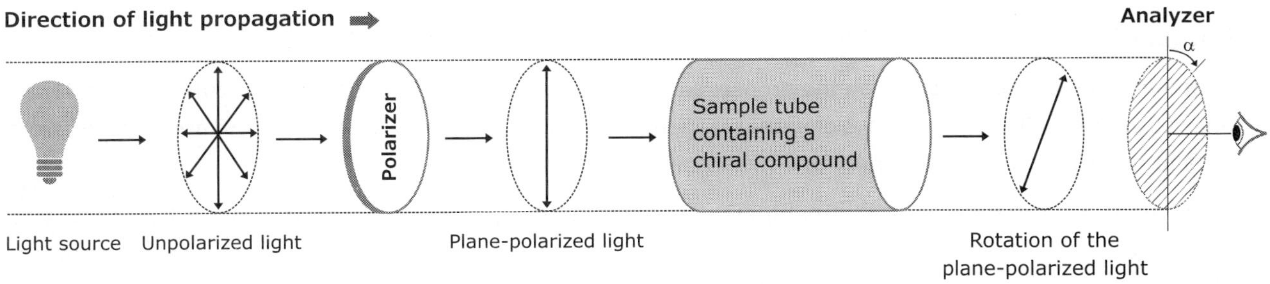

The **degree of rotation** of plane-polarized light depends on several factors: the number of optically active molecules (i.e., concentration) present in the path through which the light beam passes (i.e., path length), temperature, solvent used to dissolve the sample, and wavelength. Typically, optical rotations are measured at 20°C in a solvent such as ethanol or chloroform, using light from a sodium lamp with a wavelength of 589 nm. By convention, the concentration of the sample is expressed in *grams per milliliter*, and the path length is in *decimeters*. Dividing the observed value of optical rotation, through which the light is rotated, by the path length and concentration yields a value denoted as [α]. This value is specific to the compound in question and is known as the compound's **specific rotation**.

$$[\alpha]_\lambda^T = \frac{\text{Observed rotation}}{C \times l} \quad \text{where,}$$

$[\alpha]_\lambda^T$ = the specific rotation of compound at temperature, T (in °C) and wavelength, λ (in nm). If the wavelength of the light used is 589 nm, the symbol 'D' (the *D line* of a sodium lamp) is used, $[\alpha]_D^T$.

C = Concentration (in g/ml),

l = Path length (in decimetres)

Thus, at a particular temperature and for a given wavelength of light, **specific rotation** is defined as the observed value of optical rotation when plane-polarized light passes through a sample with a path length of 1 decimeter and a sample concentration of 1 gram per milliliter. Because the specific rotation is independent of c and l, it is used as the standard measure of optical activity.

Problem

A pure sample of the naturally occurring, chiral compound A (0.050 g) is dissolved in water (2.0 mL), and the solution is placed in a 0.5 dm cell. The observed value of the optical rotation of this compound is 0.671°. What is the value of specific rotation [α]?

Solution: $$[\alpha] = \frac{\text{Observed rotation}}{C \times l} \quad \text{where, } C = \frac{0.050}{2} = 0.025 \text{ g/mL}$$

$$= \frac{0.671°}{0.025 \times 0.5} = 53.68°$$

1.1.3 Standard and non-standard amino acids

There are hundreds of different amino acids present in the living organisms; however, only 22 different amino acids participate in protein synthesis, which are incorporated ribosomically into proteins. Such amino acids are called **standard** (or *proteinogenic*) **amino acids**. All standard amino acids are L-α-amino acids. These amino acids are specified by simple three letter. Amino acids that occur naturally in cells but are not incorporated into peptides or polypeptides through ribosomal synthesis are called **nonstandard amino acids**. Some nonstandard amino acids are constituents of ribosomically synthesized proteins, but they are generated by post-translational modification of standard amino acids which are incorporated ribosomically into proteins. Examples of some of these amino acids are **4-Hydroxyproline** (a derivative of proline), **5-Hydroxylysine** (a derivative of lysine), **desmosine** (a derivative of lysine), **N-formylmethionine** (a derivative of methionine) and γ-**carboxyglutamate** (a derivative of glutamate).

Classification of standard amino acids

Standard amino acids can be classified on the properties of their *side chain* (or R group), in particular, their polarity, or tendency to interact with water at physiological pH (near pH 7). The polarity of the side chain varies widely, from non-polar and hydrophobic to highly polar and hydrophilic.

Amino acids with non-polar side chain: Among standard amino acids, nine amino acids contain non-polar side chain. These are glycine, alanine, valine, leucine, isoleucine, proline, methionine, phenylalanine and tryptophan. *Proline* differs from other members in having its side chain bonded to both the nitrogen and the α-carbon atoms. *Phenylalanine* and *tryptophan* have aromatic side chains. The side chain of phenylalanine contains a **phenyl ring** whereas tryptophan has an **indole ring**.

Amino acids with uncharged polar side chain: Six amino acids contain uncharged polar side chain – serine, threonine, cysteine, asparagine, glutamine and tyrosine. Three amino acids, serine, threonine and tyrosine contain **hydroxyl groups** attached to a side chain. Cysteine is structurally similar to serine but contains a **sulfhydryl** or **thiol group** (–SH) in place of the hydroxyl group.

Amino acids with charged polar side chain: Some standard amino acids with polar side chains can be *positively* or *negatively* charged at neutral pH.

Positively charged side chain: Lysine and arginine have side chains that contain *positively charged groups* at neutral pH. Lysine has an **amino group** whereas arginine contains a **guanidinium group**. *Histidine* contains an **imidazole** aromatic ring (a planar five member heterocyclic ring). The imidazole ring can be uncharged or positively charged near neutral pH, depending on its local environment.

Negatively charged side chain: Amino acids aspartate and glutamate contain *acidic side chains* that contain *negatively charged* **carboxyl groups** at neutral pH.

Table 1.1 Classification of amino acids based on chemical nature of R group

Chemical nature of R group	Example
Aliphatic	Gly, Ala, Val, Leu
Aromatic	Phe, Tyr, Trp
Hydroxyl	Ser, Thr
Carboxylic	Asp, Glu
Sulphur containing	Cys, Met
Amino	Lys, Arg
Amide	Asn, Gln

The structures of the 20 standard amino acids, along with the chemical nature of their R groups, are listed in **table 1.2**. Properties of **selenocysteine** (Sec) and **pyrrolysine** (Pyl), referred to as the 21st and 22nd amino acids respectively. *Selenocysteine* is structurally similar to cysteine but contains selenium instead of sulfur in its side chain and *pyrrolysine* contains a pyrroline ring structure, making it structurally distinct from other amino acids.

Amino acids with non-polar side chain

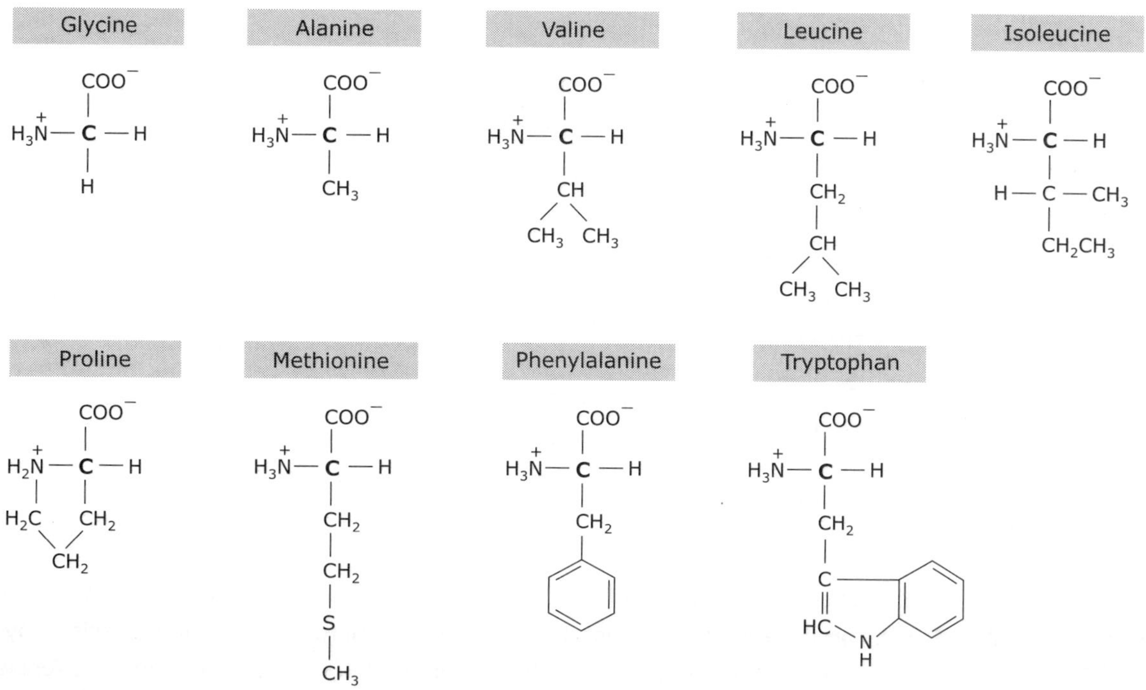

Amino acids with uncharged polar side chain at pH 7

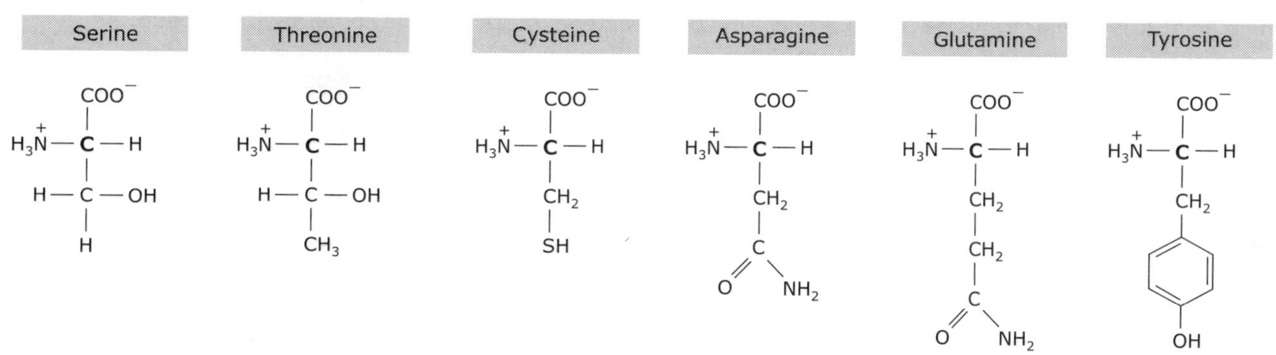

Amino acids with charged polar side chain at pH 7

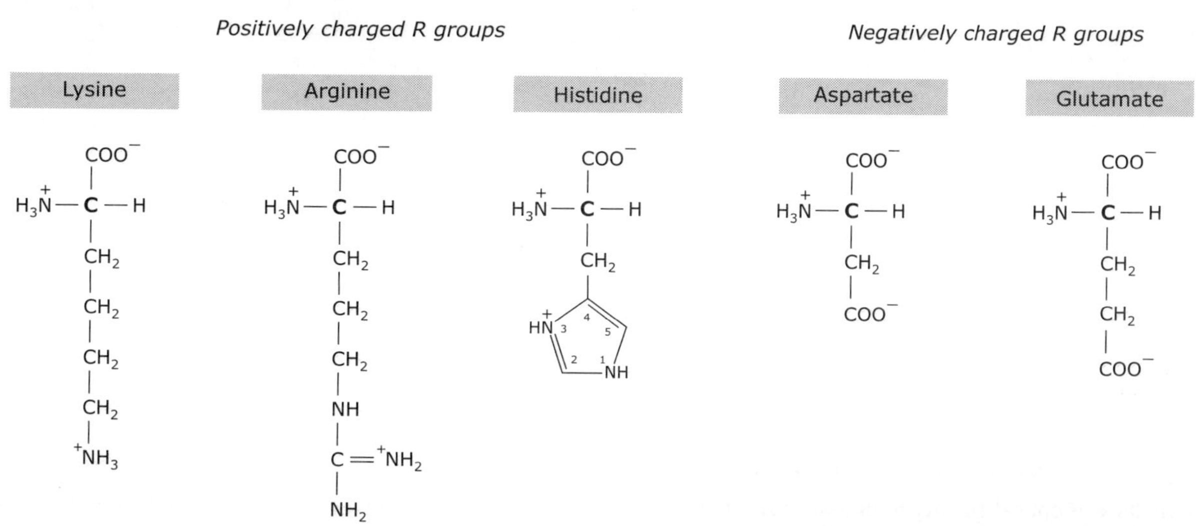

Note: Although the side chain of histidine has been shown charged, a significant fraction remains uncharged at pH 7.0.

Standard amino acids

with

- **Nonpolar side chain**
  - Glycine (Lowest MW)
  - Tryptophan (Highest MW)
  - Alanine
  - Valine
  - Leucine
  - Isoleucine
  - Proline
  - Methionine
  - Phenylalanine
- **Polar side chain**
  - **Uncharged at pH 7**
    - Serine
    - Threonine
    - Cysteine
    - Asparagine
    - Glutamine
    - Tyrosine
  - **Charged at pH 7**
    - **Negative charge**
      - Glutamate
      - Aspartate (Most acidic)
    - **Positive charge**
      - Lysine
      - Histidine
      - Arginine (Most basic)

Selenocysteine (Sec or U) is the 21st standard amino acid. It has a structure similar to that of cysteine, but it contains selenium rather than sulphur. It is incorporated into polypeptides during translation. However, it is specified by a triplet codon, UGA (a stop codon). Selenocysteine has its own tRNA containing the anticodon UCA and it is formed by modifying a *serine* that has been attached to the selenocysteine tRNA. Enzymes like *glutathione peroxidase* and *formate dehydrogenase* contain selenocysteine in their catalytic center. **Pyrrolysine** (Pyl or O) is the 22nd standard amino acid. It is similar to lysine and is present in some bacterial proteins. It is coded by UAG codon.

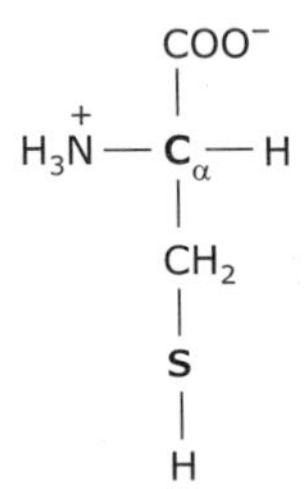

Cysteine

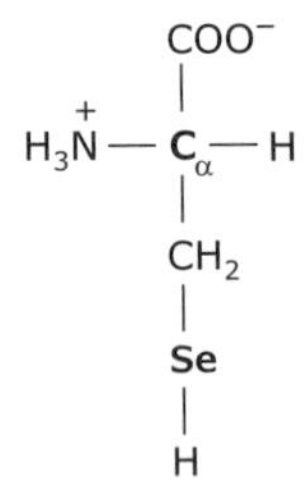

Selenocysteine

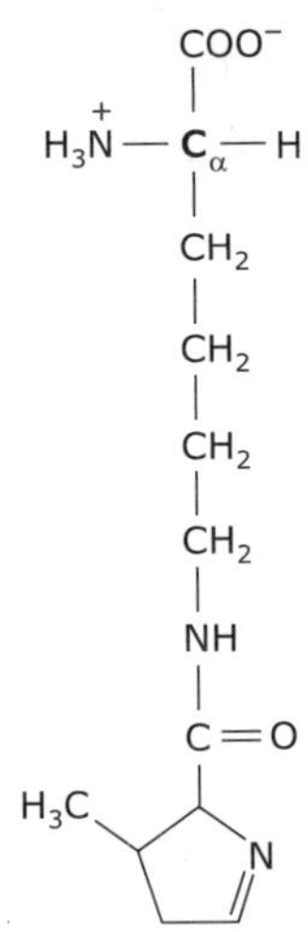

Pyrrolysine

Problem

Determine whether the following statements are true or false. If false, explain why?

1. All 20 standard amino acids found in proteins have at least one asymmetric carbon atom.
2. An equimolar mixture of D- and L-alanine does not rotate the plane of polarized light.
3. Alanine obtained from a protein hydrolysate has the same absolute configuration as D-glyceraldehyde.

Solution:

1. False; glycine has no asymmetric carbon atom.
2. True; the lack of optical activity in an equimolar mixture of D- and L-alanine (called racemic mixture) is due to the fact that the rotations caused by each enantiomer cancel each other, resulting in no net rotation of the plane polarized light.
3. False; alanine obtained from a protein hydrolysis has the same absolute configuration as L-glyceraldehyde.

1.1.4 Titration of amino acids

Because amino acids contain ionizable groups, the predominant ionic form of these molecules in solution depends on the pH. Titration of an amino acid illustrates the effect of pH on the net charge of amino acid. It involves the gradual removal of protons with increasing pH. Let us understand the titration of non-ionizable R group containing and ionizable R group containing amino acids separately.

Standard amino acids with

Non-ionizable R-group Gly, Ala, Val, Leu, Ile, Pro, Met, Phe, Trp, Ser, Thr, Asn and Gln

Ionizable R-group Asp, Glu, His, Arg, Tyr, Cys and Lys

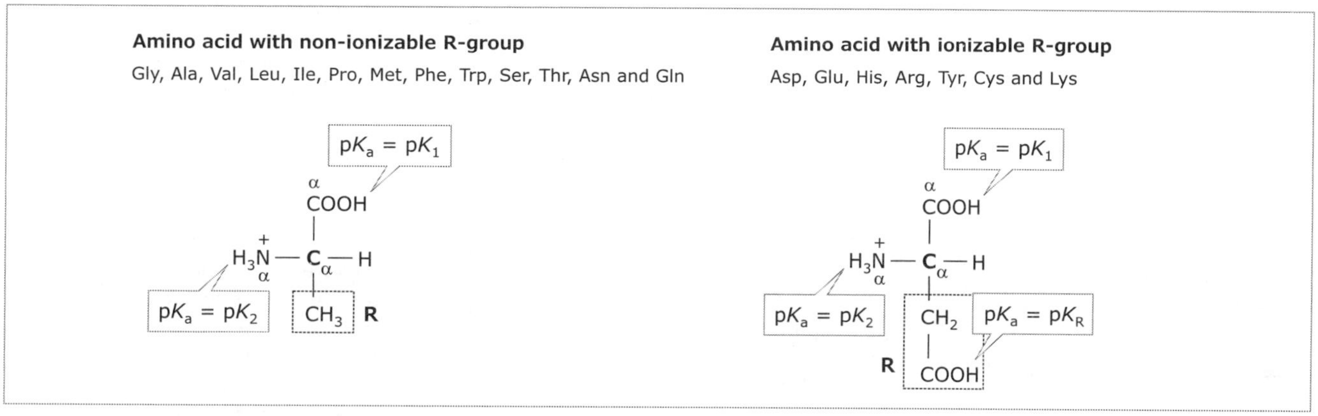

Titration of non-ionizable R group containing amino acids

Non-ionizable R groups containing amino acids (such as glycine and alanine) have two ionizable groups (α-amino and α-carboxyl group) that can undergo protonation and deprotonation. Let us understand the titration of alanine. During titration with a strong base such as NaOH, alanine loses two protons in a stepwise fashion. At a very low pH (i.e., strongly acidic solution), the predominant ionic species of alanine is the fully protonated form in which the α-carboxyl group is uncharged and α-amino group is positively charged. Under this condition, the net charge on the molecule is +1 (Ala^{+1}). However, an increase in the pH results in the deprotonation of α-carboxyl (–COOH) and α-amino ($-NH_3^+$) groups. In the first stage of the titration, the –COOH group loses its proton. After deprotonation of α-carboxyl group, the net charge on the molecule becomes zero (Ala^0). Its –COOH group has a pK_a (labeled **pK_1**) of 2.34.

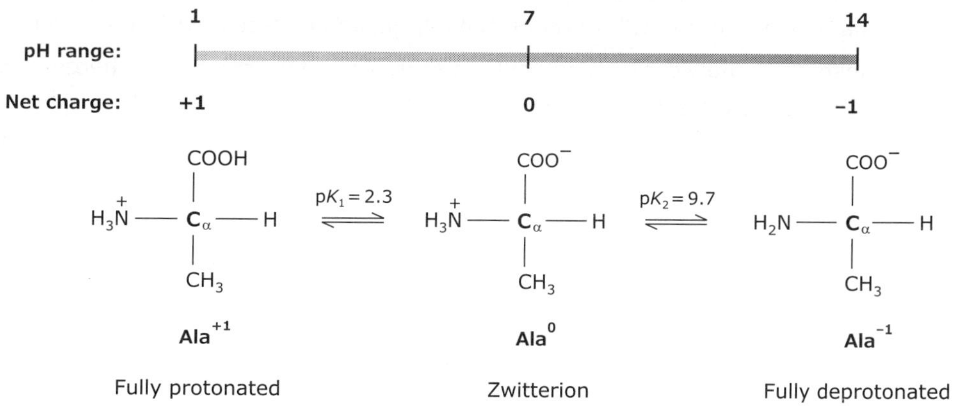

Figure 1.6 At very low pH, alanine is fully protonated, and Ala^+ is the predominant species present. As the pH is raised, the most acidic proton dissociates; this is the carboxylic acid proton, which has the lower pK_a. The fractions of Ala^{+1} and Ala^0 are equal when pH = pK_1 = 2.3. As the pH is raised further, the second dissociation occurs. This is the protonated α-amino group, which has the higher pK_a. The fractions of Ala^0 and Ala^{-1} are equal with pH = pK_2 = 9.7. As the pH is raised further, Ala^- becomes the only species present.

At pK_1, there is an equal concentration of Ala^{+1} and Ala^0. As the titration of alanine proceeds, a point is reached at pH 6.01, at which removal of the first proton is essentially complete and removal of the second has just begun. At this pH, alanine is present largely as the **dipolar ion (zwitterion)** i.e., alanine has no net charge and is electrically neutral (Ala^0). The pH at which this occurs is called the **isoelectric point** (pI). Because there is no net charge at the isoelectric point, an amino acid is electrophoretically non-mobile and least soluble at this pH. Further increase in pH results in the deprotonation of the charged α-amino group. Its $-NH_3^+$ group has a pK_a (labeled $\mathbf{pK_2}$) of 9.69. At pK_2, there is an equal concentration of Ala^0 and Ala^{-1}. At high pH (about 12), alanine is completely deprotonated and the net charge on the molecule is −1 (Ala^{-1}). The amino group is completely deprotonated and a net negative charge develops due to the presence of the carboxyl group.

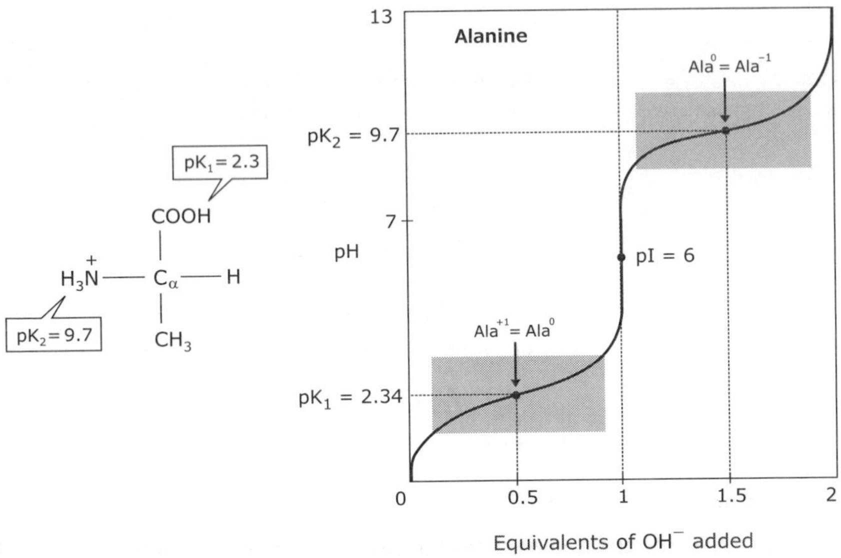

Figure 1.7
Titration of alanine. A plot of the pH of the solution versus the amount of OH^- added yields a titration curve. 1 equivalent of OH^- = 0.1 M NaOH added. At pH 1.0, for example, alanine exists almost entirely as the form Ala^{+1} with a net positive charge of 1. At pH 2.3, where there is an equal mixture of Ala^{+1} and Ala^0, the average or net positive charge is +1/2. At pH 9.7, where there is an equal mixture of Ala^0 and Ala^{-1}, the average or net negative charge is −1/2. At pH 12, alanine exists almost entirely as the form Ala^{-1} with a net negative charge.

At pH 6, alanine is present predominantly as its dipolar form, fully ionized but with no net electric charge. The characteristic pH at which the net electric charge is zero is called the **isoelectric point** or **isoelectric pH** (pI). Its isoelectric point is simply the arithmetic mean of the two pK_a values:

$$pI = \frac{pK_1 + pK_2}{2} = \frac{2.34 + 9.7}{2} = 6.0$$

At a pH value lower (more acidic) than the pI, more alanine molecules are in form Ala^{+1} than in form Ala^0; in this situation, alanine molecules has a net positive charge. At a pH value greater (more basic) than the pI, more alanine molecules are in form Ala^{-1} than in form Ala^0. In this situation, alanine molecules has a net negative charge.

Note: Although at any instant an individual amino acid molecule will have an integral charge, it is possible for a population of amino acid molecules in solution to have a fractional charge. For example, at pH 1.0 alanine exists entirely as the form Ala^{+1} with a net positive charge of 1. However, at pH 2.34, where there is an equal mixture of Ala^{+1} and Ala^0, the average or net charge on the population of alanine molecules is 0.5.

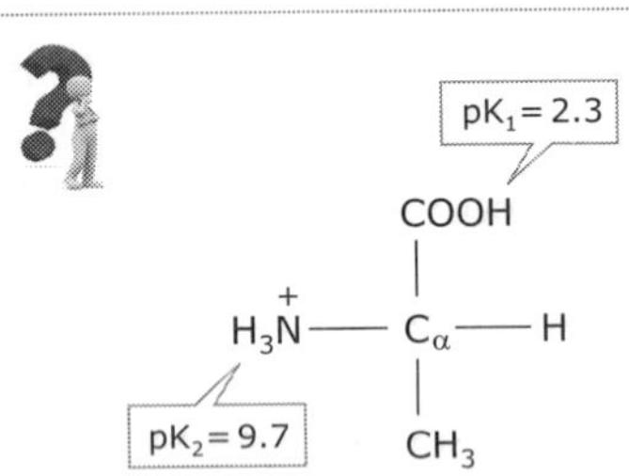

Alanine

Present predominantly as Ala^{+1}	pH less than 2.3
Average net charge is +1/2	pH equal to 2.3
Half of the amino groups are ionized	pH equal to 9.7
pH is equal to the pK_a of the carboxyl group	pH equal to 2.3
pH is equal to the pK_a of the protonated amino group	pH equal to 9.6
Present predominantly as Ala^0	pH equal to pI
Present as a 50:50 mixture of Ala^{+1} and Ala^0	pH equal 2.3
Average net charge is −1/2	pH equal to 9.7

Titration of ionizable R group containing amino acids

α-amino acids with an ionizable R group (such as glutamic acid, histidine and lysine) have three possible deprotonation steps; thus they have three pK_a values (**pK_1, pK_R** and **pK_2**). Let us understand the titration of **glutamic acid**. It has an α-COO^-, an α-NH_3^+ and a γ-COO^- group in the side chain. The pK_a of α-COOH, α-NH_3^+ and γ-COOH are pK_1, pK_2 and pK_R, respectively. At very low pH, the glutamic acid has a net positive charge of +1 (Glu^{+1}) because α-NH_3^+ group has a positive charge. During titration, as strong base such as NaOH is added and the pH increases, the α-COOH group loses its proton to become negatively charged, and the glutamic acid now has no net charge (Glu^0). As still more base is added, the γ-COOH group present in side chain loses its proton, and this is the pH at which the glutamic acid has net negative charge of –1 (Glu^{-1}). At still higher values of pH, the α-NH_3^+ group loses its proton and the glutamic acid now has a negative charge of –2 (Glu^{-2}).

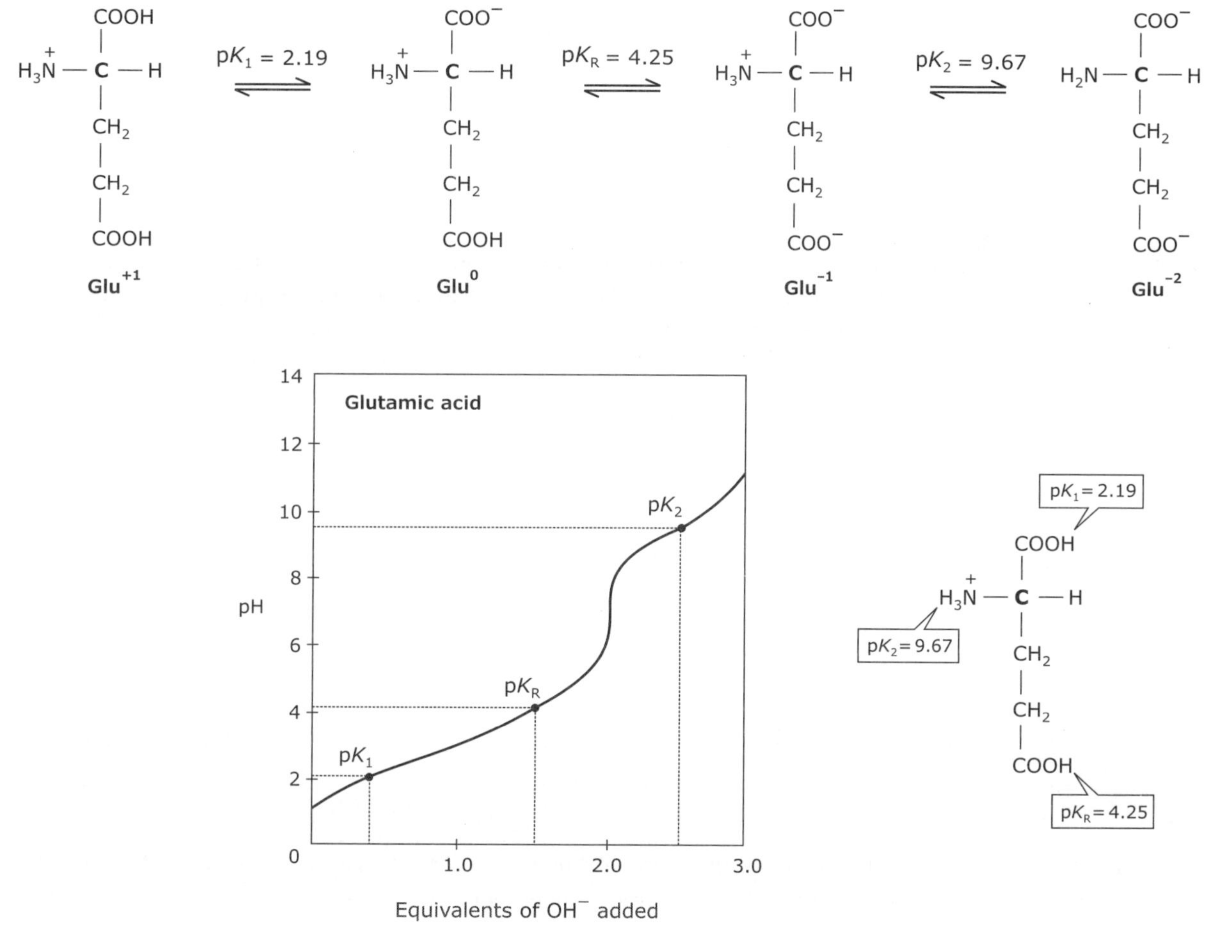

Figure 1.8 Titration of glutamic acid. At very low pH, the glutamic acid has a net positive charge of +1 because α-amino group has a positive charge. As the base is added (pH increases), the α-carboxyl group loses its proton. Glutamate now has no net charge. As still more base is added, the γ-carboxyl group loses a proton, and the molecule has a –1 charge. Adding base further results in loss of protons from ammonium ion. At this point, glutamate has a net charge of –2.

The *isoelectric point* of glutamate is simply the arithmetic mean of the two pK_a values: pK_1 and pK_R. It has a pI of 3.22, considerably lower than that of alanine. This is due to the presence of two carboxyl groups. The pI value for glutamate is the pH halfway between the pK_a values for the two carboxyl groups:

$$\text{pI} = \frac{\text{p}K_1 + \text{p}K_R}{2} = \frac{2.19 + 4.25}{2} = 3.22$$

Histidine also has three ionizable functional groups, thus has three pK_a values (pK_1 = 1.82, pK_R = 6.0 and pK_2 = 9.17). At very low pH, the histidine molecule has a net positive charge of +2 because both the imidazole and α-amino groups have positive charges (His^{+2}). As base is added and the pH increases, the α-carboxyl group loses its proton to become negatively charged, and the histidine now has a positive charge of +1 (His^{+1}). As still more base is added, the charged imidazole group loses its proton, and this is the point at which the histidine has no net charge. At still higher values of pH, the α-amino group loses its proton and the histidine molecule now has a negative charge of –1. With a pK_R value near 6, the imidazole group can be readily ionized near the physiological pH. Consequently, imidazole group can be uncharged or positively charged at physiological pH. Histidine is often found in the active sites of enzymes, where the imidazole ring can accept or release protons in the course of enzymatic reactions. Due to pK_R value near 6, only histidine provides significant buffering power near the neutral pH.

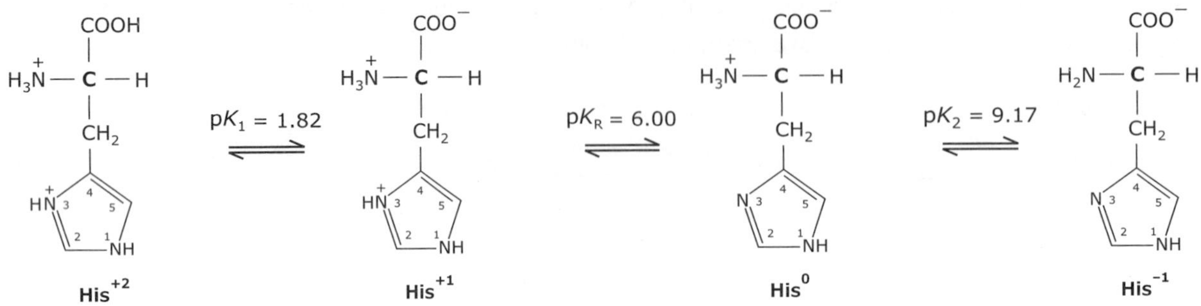

Figure 1.9 Titration of histidine. At very low pH, the histidine molecule has a net positive charge of 2 because both the imidazole and α-amino groups have positive charges. As base is added and the pH increases, the α-carboxyl group loses a proton to become negatively charged, and the histidine now has a positive charge of +1. As still more base is added, the charged imidazole group loses its proton, and this is the point at which the histidine has no net charge. At still higher values of pH, the α-amino group loses its proton and the histidine molecule now has a negative charge of –1.

Problem

An amino acid contains no ionizable group in its side chain (R). It is titrated from pH 0 to 14. Which of the following state is *not* observed during the entire titration in the pH range 0-14?

Solution: The state of amino acid mentioned in option D will not observe during the entire titration in the pH range 0-14?

Problem

An amino acid has one proton donating carboxyl group in the side chain. The pK_1, pK_2 and pK_R values for this amino acid are 2.19, 9.67 and 4.25, respectively. What will be the predominant ionization state of amino acid at pH 3, 7 and 12?

Solution: The net charge on an amino acid depends on pH. At a pH of 1, the α-carboxyl group, the carboxyl group of the side chain, and the α-amino group will remain protonated. Hence, the net charge on amino acids will be –1. However, at a pH of 3, the α-carboxyl group will lose a proton, but the remaining groups will remain protonated. Thus, a net charge will be zero. At a pH of 7, the α-carboxyl group and the carboxyl group of the side chain will lose protons, and the α-amino group will remain protonated. Hence, the net charge on amino acids will be –1. At a pH of 12, all functional groups will lose protons. Hence, the net charge on amino acids will be –2.

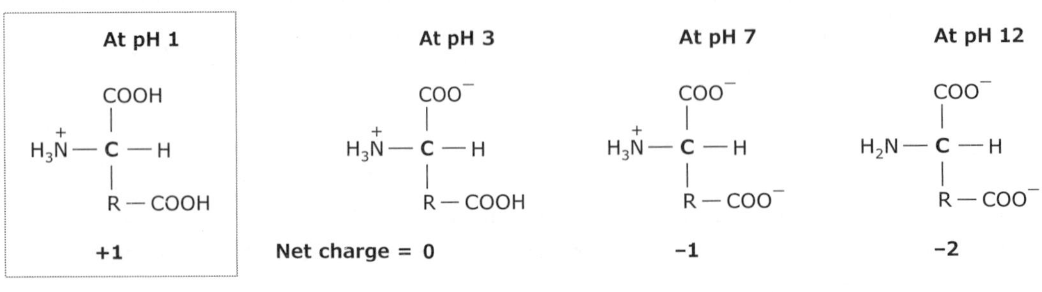

Table 1.2 pK_a values for the ionizing groups of the standard amino acids

Amino acid		MW	pK_1 (–COOH)	pK_2 (–NH_3^+)	pK_R	pI
Non-polar side chain						
Glycine	Gly, G	75	2.34	9.60		5.97
Alanine	Ala, A	89	2.34	9.69		6.01
Valine	Val, V	117	2.32	9.62		5.97
Leucine	Leu, L	131	2.36	9.60		5.98
Isoleucine	Ile, I	131	2.36	9.68		6.02
Proline	Pro, P	115	1.99	10.96		6.48
Methionine	Met, M	149	2.28	9.21		5.74
Phenylalanine	Phe, F	165	1.83	9.13		5.48
Tryptophan	Trp, W	204	2.38	9.39		5.89
Polar and uncharged side chain at pH 7						
Serine	Ser, S	105	2.21	9.15		5.68
Threonine	Thr, T	119	2.11	9.62		5.87
Asparagine	Asn, N	132	2.02	8.80		5.41
Glutamine	Gln, Q	146	2.17	9.13		5.65
Cysteine	Cys, C	121	1.96	10.28	8.18 (sulfhydryl)	5.07
Tyrosine	Tyr, Y	181	2.20	9.11	10.07 (phenol)	5.66
Polar and charged side chain at pH 7						
Positively charged						
Histidine	His, H	155	1.82	9.17	6.00 (imidazole)	7.59
Lysine	Lys, K	146	2.18	8.95	10.53 (ε-NH_3^+)	9.74
Arginine	Arg, R	174	2.17	9.04	12.48 (guanidino)	10.76
Negatively charged						
Aspartic acid	Asp, D	133	1.88	9.60	3.65 (β-COOH)	2.77
Glutamic acid	Glu, E	147	2.19	9.67	4.25 (γ-COOH)	3.22

Note: pK_a values depend on temperature, ionic strength and the microenvironment of the ionizable group. Seven amino acid side chains contain groups that ionize between pH 1 and 14. For Asp, Glu, Tyr and Cys, the ionizable groups are uncharged below their pK_R and negatively charged above their pK_R. For His, Lys and Arg, the ionizable groups are positively charged below their pK_R and uncharged above their pK_R.

All α-amino acids have pK_a of the –COOH group in the range of 1.8 to 2.4, and pK_a of the —NH_3^+ group in the range of 8.8 to 11. Amino acids with high isoelectric points are classified as *basic* amino acids. Lysine and arginine are the two most basic amino acids. The amino acids aspartic acid and glutamic acid have low isoelectric points. Amino acids with low isoelectric points are classified as *acidic* amino acids.

Table 1.3 Ionic states of standard amino acids with ionizable side chains at different pH

	pK_R	At low pH	At pH = 7	At high pH
Aspartic acid	3.65	—COOH	—COO$^-$	—COO$^-$
Glutamic acid	4.25	—COOH	—COO$^-$	—COO$^-$
Cysteine	8.18	—SH	—SH	—S$^-$
Lysine	10.53	—NH_3^+	—NH_3^+	—NH_2
Histidine	6.00	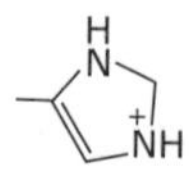	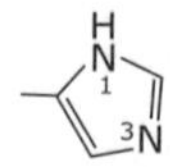	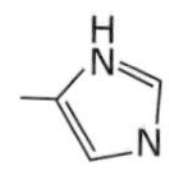
Arginine	12.48	—N(H)—C(=NH_2^+)—NH_2	—N(H)—C(=NH_2^+)—NH_2	—N(H)—C(=NH)—NH_2
Tyrosine	10.07	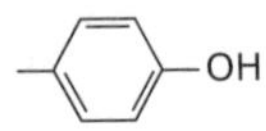	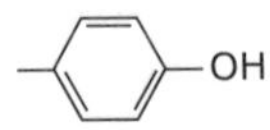	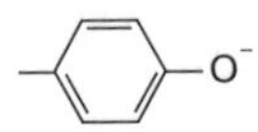

Note: Both neutral and protonated forms of histidine are present at pH 7, since its pK_R is close to 7.

Absorption of UV radiation by aromatic amino acids

Aromatic amino acids such as tryptophan, tyrosine and phenylalanine absorb ultraviolet (UV) light. The aromatic side chains of these amino acids are responsible for UV absorption. **Phenylalanine** and **tyrosine** are aromatic due to the presence of a **phenyl group** and a **4-hydroxy phenyl group**, respectively. **Tryptophan** is aromatic due to its heterocyclic **indole ring**. Tryptophan and tyrosine absorb maximum near a wavelength of 280 nm. However, phenylalanine absorbs maximum at 257.4 nm. Absorbance at 280 nm is used for detection and quantification of purified proteins. Proteins containing tyrosine and tryptophan absorb UV radiation at a wavelength of 280 nm. Phenylalanine also contributes in the absorption at this wavelength but since it is relatively insignificant, it can only be observed in the absence of both tryptophan and tyrosine. Proteins of similar molecular weight can have different absorbance values due to the difference in tryptophan and tyrosine content. UV absorbance is also affected by protein structure. Thus, conditions which affect structure (such as temperature, pH, ionic strength or the presence of detergents) can affect the ability of aromatic residues to absorb light at 280 nm.

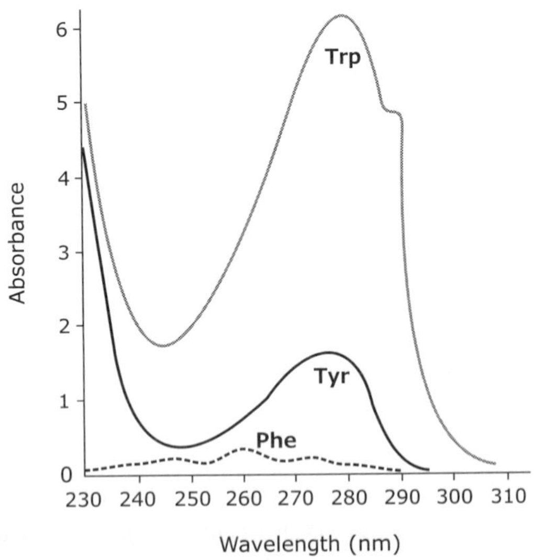

Absorbance of amino acids at neutral pH

Amino acids	Absorbance (λ_{max})
Phenylalanine (Phe)	257.4 nm
Tyrosine (Tyr)	274.6 nm
Tryptophan (Trp)	279.8 nm

Figure 1.10 Absorption of UV-light by the aromatic amino acids tryptophan, phenylalanine and tyrosine, at pH 6.0. The amino acids are present in equimolar amounts (10^{-3} M) under identical conditions. Maximum absorption for both Trp and Tyr occur near a wavelength of 280 nm and absorbance of Trp is as much as four times that of Tyr.

1.1.5 Peptide and polypeptide

Polymers of amino acids consisting of 2 to 50 amino acid residues, covalently linked by peptide bonds, are generally referred to as **peptides**. When two amino acid residues are linked through a peptide bond, then the product is called a **dipeptide**. Three amino acids can be joined by two peptide bonds to form a **tripeptide**; similarly, amino acids can be linked to form tetrapeptides, pentapeptides and so forth.

Peptides may be *ribosomically* and *non-ribosomically* synthesized. Non-ribosomically synthesized peptides (i.e., **non-ribosomal peptides**) are not specified by codons of mRNA and synthesis is not catalyzed by peptidyl transferase of ribosomes. The nature of amino acids may be standard or non-standard and their absolute configuration may be L- or D-. These peptides may be cyclic or linear in nature. Cyclic decapeptides (peptides containing 10 amino acid residues) such as **gramicidin S** and **tyrocidine** produced by the bacterium *Bacillus brevis* are examples of non-ribosomal peptides. Both peptides are antibiotics and contain both D- as well as L-amino acid residues. Ribosomically synthesized peptides (i.e., **ribosomal peptides**) are specified by codons of mRNA and their synthesis is catalyzed by peptidyl transferase of ribosomes. The nature of amino acids is always standard and with L-absolute configuration.

Small peptides, both ribosomal and non-ribosomal, play diverse roles in organisms. Some, like **oxytocin** and **vasopressin**, function as vital hormones, while others, such as **glutathione**, regulate oxidation-reduction reactions. Additionally, peptides like **enkephalins** act as natural painkillers. **Aspartame** (L-aspartylphenylalanyl methylester), a commercially synthesized dipeptide, is widely used as an artificial sweetener.

When many (generally >50) amino acid residues are joined, the product is called a **polypeptide**. Polypeptides synthesis occurs only ribosomically. Amino acids that have been incorporated into a peptide or polypeptide are termed **amino acid residues**. By convention, in a linear peptide or polypeptide, the left end is represented by the first amino acid while the right end is represented by the last amino acid. The first amino acid is also called N-terminal amino acid residue and the last amino acid is called the C-terminal amino acid residue.

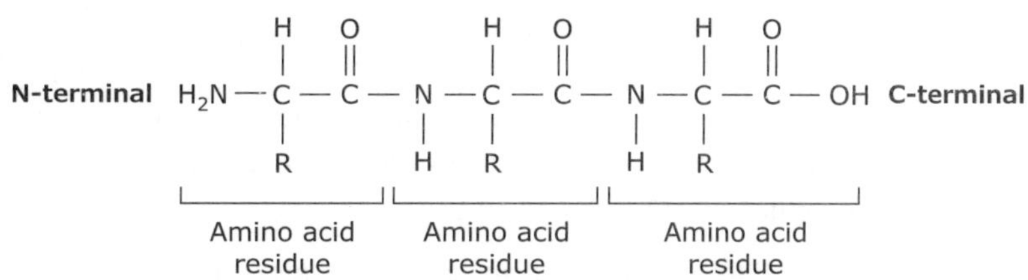

Figure 1.11 Three amino acids joined by peptide bonds form a tripeptide, and each amino acid unit in tripeptide is called a *residue*. A linear peptide or polypeptide chain has polarity because its ends are different, with an α-amino group at one end and an α-carboxyl group at the other.

The peptide bonds in proteins are formed between the α-amino and the α-carboxyl groups. But peptides do occur naturally where the peptide linkage involves a carboxyl or amino group which is attached to a carbon atom other than the α-carbon. For example, a dipeptide formed between the γ-carboxyl group of glutamic acid and the amino group of alanine is called γ-glutamylalanine.

Determination of molecular weight of peptides and polypeptides

Molecular weight (or relative molecular mass, denoted M_r) of a substance is defined as the ratio of the mass of a molecule of that substance to one-twelfth the mass of carbon-12 (^{12}C). Since molecular weight is a ratio, it is dimensionless—it has no associated units. The average molecular weight of a standard amino acid is nearer to 128. Although the average molecular weight of the 20 standard amino acids is about 138, the smaller amino acids predominate in most proteins. If we take into account the proportions in which the various amino acids occur in an average protein, the average molecular weight of protein amino acids is nearer to 128. Alternatively, this quantity may be expressed in terms of **molecular mass**. This is simply the mass of one molecule, or the molar mass divided by Avogadro's number. It is expressed in units of **daltons (Da)**. When an amino acid participates in the formation of a polypeptide one molecule of water (M_r = 18) is removed during peptide bond formation. Thus, the average molecular weight of an *amino acid residue* in a polypeptide is considered about 110 (128–18).

Problem

A protein X was fused with green fluorescent protein (GFP). The length of the protein X is 1000 amino acids and the molecular mass of GFP is 27 kDa. What is the total approximate molecular mass of the fusion protein in daltons (Da)?

Solution: The approximate molecular mass of the protein X (in Da) = 1000 × 110 = 110000 Da.

The total approximate molecular mass of the fusion protein (in Da) = 110000 Da + 27000 Da = 137000 Da.

Problem

If one arginine has a molecular mass of 174 Da, then what would be the molecular mass of a circular polymer of 38 arginines?

Solution: First, in this problem, molecular mass of amino acid is given, so we will not take the average molecular mass of amino acid residue. Second, during the formation of circular polymer of 38 arginines 38 peptide bonds will form and formation of 38 peptide bonds involve the release of 38 water molecules. So, molecular mass of circular polymer of 38 arginines = (38 × 174) − (38 × 18) = 6612 − 684 = 5928 Da.

Problem

A peptide has the sequence Glu—His—Trp—Arg—Gly. The pK_a values of the amino-terminal, carboxyl-terminal groups and those of the R groups of the Glu, His and Arg are 9.67, 2.34, 4.25, 6 and 12.48, respectively. Calculate the net charge at pH 3, 8 and 11??

Solution

	NH_3^+—	Glu—	His—	Trp—	Arg—	Gly—COOH	**Net charge**
pH 3	+1	0	+1		+1	−1	+2
pH 8	+1	−1	0		+1	−1	0
pH 11	0	−1	0		+1	−1	−1

Problem

A peptide has the sequence Glu—His—Trp—Ser—Arg—Pro—Gly. The pK_a values of the α-amino group at N-terminus, α-carboxyl group at C-terminus and those of the R groups of the Glu, His and Arg are 9.67, 2.34, 4.25, 6 and 12.48, respectively. Calculate the pI of this peptide?

Solution: To estimate the pI for this peptide, we will find net charge at pH 2.34, 4.25, 6.0, 9.67 and 12.48. The net charge at pH 1 will be +3. With increasing pH net charge on peptide will be

$$+3 \xrightleftharpoons{2.3} +2 \xrightleftharpoons{4.2} +1 \xrightleftharpoons{6.0} 0 \xrightleftharpoons{9.7} -1 \xrightleftharpoons{12.5} -2$$

Hence, pI = (9.67 + 6)/2 = 7.8.

1.1.6 Peptide bond

Ribosomal peptides and polypeptides are linear, unbranched polymers composed of amino acids linked together by **peptide bonds.** Peptide bonds are **amide bonds** formed between the α-amino group of one amino acid and the α-carboxyl group of another. This reaction is a *dehydration reaction*; that is, a water molecule is removed. The linked amino acids are referred to as **amino acid residues.** The peptide bond exhibits *partial* double bond character (approximately 40 percent) due to resonance.

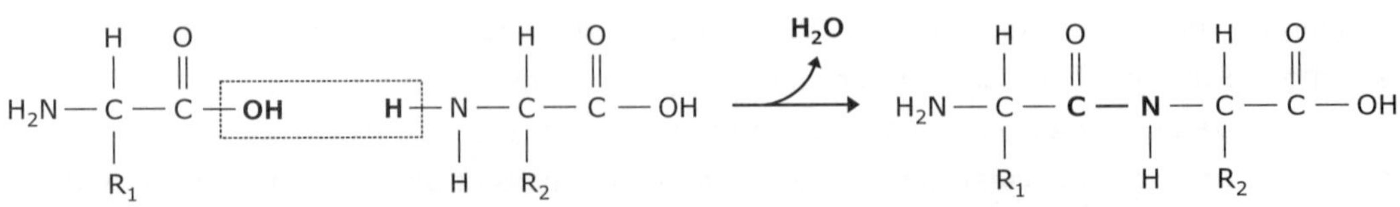

Figure 1.12 The formation of a peptide bond (also called an *amide bond*) between the α-carboxyl group of one amino acid to the α-amino group of another amino acid is accompanied by the loss of a water molecule.

This arises because nitrogen can donate its unhybridized lone pair of electrons to the carbonyl carbon, pushing electrons from the carbonyl double bond towards the oxygen, forming the oxygen anion. As a result, electrons become delocalized over nitrogen, carbon, and oxygen atoms, imparting partial double bond character to the peptide bond. This characteristic contributes to the peptide bond length being only 1.33 Å, which lies between the expected values for a C–N single bond (1.49 Å) and a C=N double bond (1.27 Å). Due to electrons delocalization, the oxygen carries a partial negative charge, while the nitrogen has a partial positive charge, creating a small **electric dipole**. The partial double bond character maintains the peptide bond in a rigid, planar configuration. In a pair of amino acids linked by a peptide bond, six atoms (C_α, C, O, N, H and C_α) lie in the same coplanar structure, known as the **amide plane.**

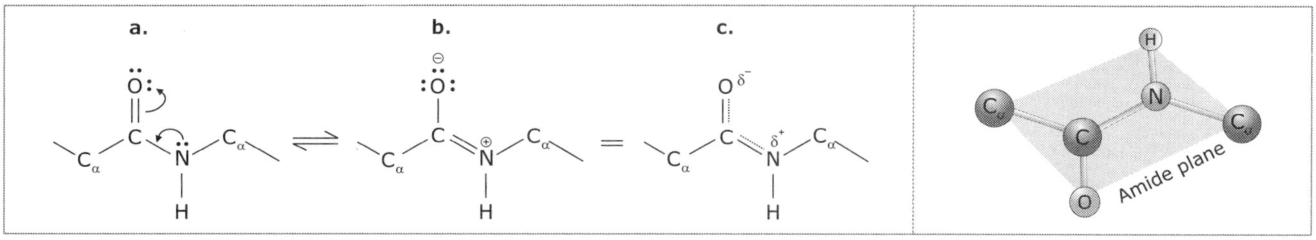

Figure 1.13 Each peptide bond possesses partial double-bond character due to resonance. The peptide bond is a resonance hybrid of two states (**a** and **b**). The resonance structure of the peptide bond is shown in (**c**). The dashed line indicates the resonance of the peptide bond. For a pair of amino acids linked by a peptide bond, the six atoms of the peptide group lie in a single plane: the α-carbon atom and CO group of the first amino acid, and the NH group and α-carbon atom of the second amino acid.

Due to the partial double-bond character, two possible configurations, *cis* and *trans*, are observed for a peptide bond in polypeptides. In the *cis* configuration, successive α-carbon atoms are on the same side of the peptide bond. In the *trans* configuration, the two successive α-carbon atoms are on opposite sides of the peptide bond (**figure 1.14**). The restricted rotation about C—N bond can be specified by torsion angle ω (**omega**). In the *trans* configuration, ω = 180° and in the *cis* configuration, ω = 0°. **Torsion angle** and **dihedral angle** are terms that are often used interchangeably. The *dihedral angle* specifically refers to the angle between two planes, each defined by three atoms in a sequence of four bonded atoms (A–B–C–D)—that is, the angle between the plane formed by atoms A–B–C and the plane formed by atoms B–C–D. In contrast, the term *torsion angle* is more commonly used when describing rotation around a bond.

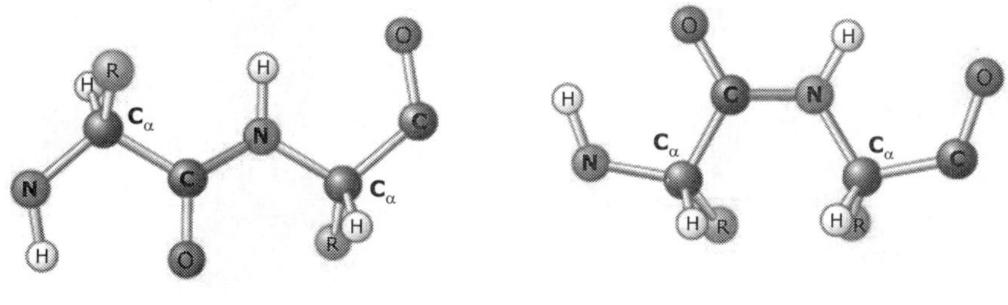

trans configuration (ω = 180°) *cis* configuration (ω = 0°)

Figure 1.14 *cis* and *trans* configuration of peptide bond. In *cis* configuration, successive C_α atoms are on the same side of the peptide bond whereas in *trans* configuration, successive C_α atoms are on opposite sides of the peptide bond joining them.

Virtually all peptide bonds in proteins adopt the *trans* configuration. The *cis* configuration is less stable due to steric clashes between the groups attached to the α-carbon atoms of adjacent amino acids. In the *trans* configuration, these clashes are minimized, making it energetically more favorable. However, in peptide bonds involving **proline** residues, steric interference is reduced because of proline's structure, allowing the *cis* configuration to occur more frequently than with other amino acids.

In contrast with the peptide bond, the bonds between the nitrogen of amino group and the α-carbon atom (i.e., N—C_α bond) and between the α-carbon atom and the carbon of carbonyl group (i.e., C_α—C bond) are pure single bonds.

The two adjacent rigid peptide units can rotate about these bonds, taking on various orientations. The rotations about these bonds can be specified by torsion angles ϕ (**phi**) and ψ (**psi**). The torsion angle about the bond between the amino nitrogen and the α-carbon atoms (**N—C**$_\alpha$ bond) is called ϕ whereas, the torsion angle about the bond between the α-carbon and the carbonyl carbon atoms (**C**$_\alpha$**—C** bond) is called ψ. ϕ and ψ can have any value between +180° and −180° (i.e., 360° of rotation for each). But not all combinations are possible due to physical clashes of atoms in 3-dimensional space. Atoms take up space and two atoms cannot occupy the same space at the same time. These physical clashes are called **steric interference**.

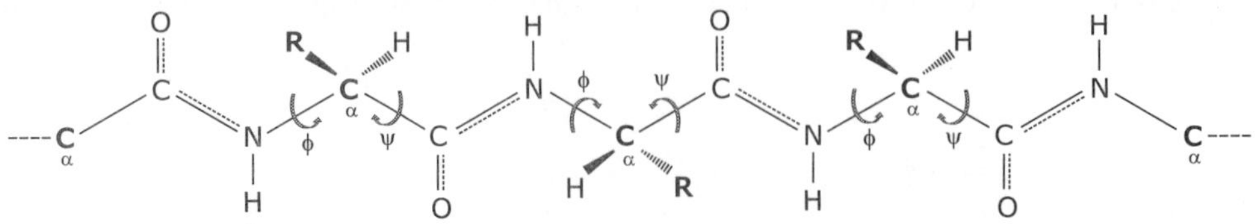

Figure 1.15 The bonds between the amino nitrogen and the α-carbon atom (i.e., N—C$_\alpha$ bond) and between the α-carbon atom and the carbonyl carbon (i.e., C$_\alpha$—C bond) are pure single bonds. Hence, rotation can occur about these bonds. The rotations about these bonds can be specified by torsion angles ϕ (phi) and ψ (psi). The torsion angle about the N—C$_\alpha$ bond of the same amino acid is called ϕ and that about the C$_\alpha$—C bond is ψ of the same amino acid. ϕ and ψ can have any value between +180° and −180°.

Ramachandran plot: Most values of ϕ and ψ are not allowed due to steric interference between atoms in the polypeptide backbone and amino acid side chains. The combinations of ϕ and ψ values that are permitted in a peptide backbone or that are not permitted due to steric constraints were first determined by G. N. Ramachandran. These permitted values can be visualized on a two-dimensional plot called a **Ramachandran plot**. Polypeptide conformations are defined by the values of ϕ and ψ. Most values of ϕ and ψ are not allowed due to steric interference between non-bonded atoms. Hence, most areas of Ramachandran plot (i.e., most combinations of ϕ and ψ) represent sterically disallowed conformations of a polypeptide chain because of steric collisions between side chains and main chain.

The ϕ and ψ torsion angles of an amino acid residue in a peptide or polypeptide depend on factor such as:

Type of amino acid: Different side chains impose varying degree of steric interference.

Absolute configuration of amino acid: This feature of an amino acid determines which ϕ and ψ torsion angles are allowed.

Nature of secondary structure: An amino acid residue that is part of a specific secondary structure is characterized by a particular range of ϕ and ψ angles.

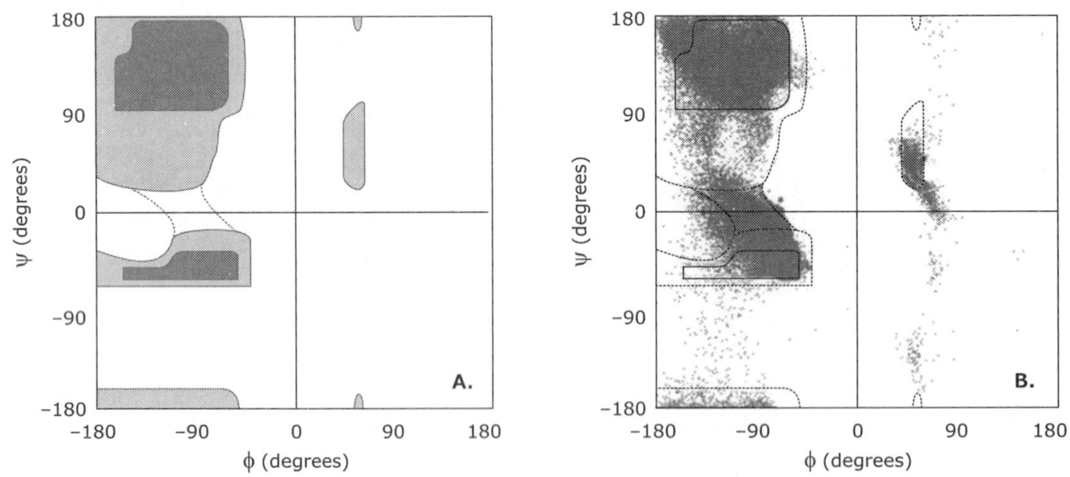

Figure 1.16 A. Ramachandran plots showing allowed combinations of the torsion angles ϕ and ψ. Most values of ϕ and ψ are not allowed due to steric interference between non-bonded atoms. The areas shaded dark black represent the sterically allowed ϕ and ψ values. The plots for L-amino acid residues with unbranched side chains are nearly identical. The allowed ranges for branched residues such as threonine are somewhat smaller than amino acids with unbranched side chains. The glycine residue, which is less sterically hindered, has a much broader allowed range. The cyclic side chain of proline limits its range of ϕ values to angles of around −60°, making it most conformationally restricted amino acid residue. **B.** Observed values for all residue types except glycine. Each point represents ϕ and ψ values for an amino acid residue in a well-refined x-ray structure to high resolution.

In the **figure 1.16**, the *white* regions correspond to sterically disallowed conformations in which any non-bonding interatomic distance is less than its corresponding van der Waals radii. These regions are sterically disallowed for all amino acids except glycine which is unique as it lacks a side chain. The *black* regions called *allowed regions* correspond to conformations where there are no steric interferences. Most of ϕ and ψ values associated with each amino acid residue of a polypeptide chain fall within these allowed regions of the Ramachandran plot. There are, however, some notable exceptions. For example, glycine (the amino acid with smallest side chain) is much less sterically restricted than the other amino acid residues. Hence, its allowed range of ϕ and ψ covers a larger area of the Ramachandran plot. In case of proline, the cyclic side chain limits its range of ϕ values to angles of around –60°, making it most conformationally restricted amino acid residue. *Grey* regions correspond to conformation having outer limit van der Waals distances i.e., the atoms are allowed to come a little closer together.

1.1.7 Protein structure

Proteins are unbranched polymers constructed from 22 standard α-amino acids. They have four levels of the structural organization. **Primary structure**, the amino acid sequence, is specified by genetic information. As the polypeptide chain folds, it forms certain localized arrangements of adjacent amino acids that constitute **secondary structure**. The overall three-dimensional shape that a polypeptide assumes is called the **tertiary structure**. Proteins that consist of two or more polypeptide chains (or subunits) are said to have a **quaternary structure**.

Primary structure

The primary structure (1° structure) of a polypeptide is its amino acid sequence. The amino acids are connected by peptide bonds. Each polypeptide has its own unique sequence of amino acids. Primary structure of polypeptide determines to a large extent the native (most frequently occurring) *secondary* and *tertiary structures*.

Problem

How many different pentapeptides from five amino acids (Gly, Asp, Tyr, Cys and Leu) are theoretically possible with no restrictions on the number of times a given residue type can be used.

Solution: Suppose, 'X' is the number of amino acids used to prepare the peptides and '*n*' is the number of amino acid residues in the peptide. If repetitions are allowed and order matters then we can calculate number of different pentapeptides by using formula = X^n. In this way, the number of different pentapeptides theoretically possible are 5^5 i.e., 625.

Problem

How many different pentapeptides are theoretically possible that contain one residue each of Gly, Asp, Tyr, Cys and Leu?

Solution: Suppose, 'X' is the number of amino acids used to prepare the peptides and '*n*' is the number of amino acid residues in the peptide. If no repetitions are allowed and order matters then we can calculate number of different pentapeptides by using formula = $X! / (X - n)!$. In this way, the number of different pentapeptides theoretically possible are $5! / (5 - 5)!$ i.e., 120.

Problem

If there are 20 different standard amino acids and they can be assembled in any order, then how many different polypeptides of 100 amino acid residues can theoretically be produced?

Solution: In general, the number of possible polypeptides for a sequence of *n* amino acids is the number of amino acids used to prepare the polypeptides raised to the power of *n* (i.e., 20^n). Hence, a polypeptide with 100 amino acid residues, the number of different polypeptides that can be made from the 20 amino acids is 20^{100}.

Secondary structure

Protein secondary structure describes the spatial arrangement of its main-chain atoms, without regard to the positioning of its side chains. These structures are stabilized by **hydrogen bonds** between the carbonyl oxygen and the amide hydrogen present in the polypeptide's backbone.

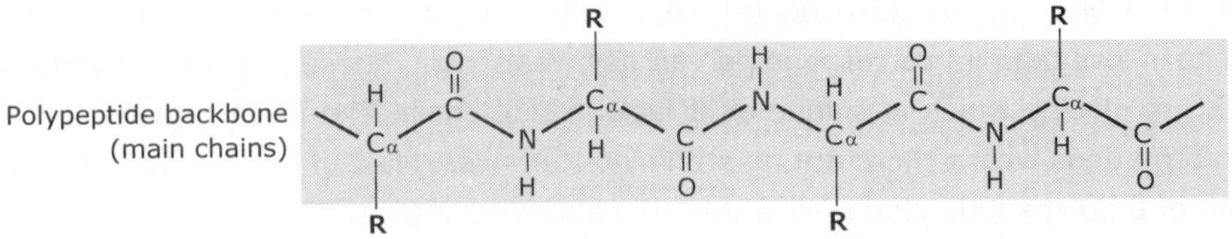

Secondary structures can be broadly categorized into **regular** and **irregular** forms, based on their backbone torsion angles (ϕ and ψ) and hydrogen bonding patterns. A secondary structure is termed **regular** if it retains the fixed or nearly the fixed torsion angles (ϕ and ψ) throughout the segment. The most common regular secondary structures are the α-helix and the β-sheet. **Irregular secondary structures** do not have consistent ϕ and ψ angles or regular hydrogen bonding patterns; these include loops and random coils.

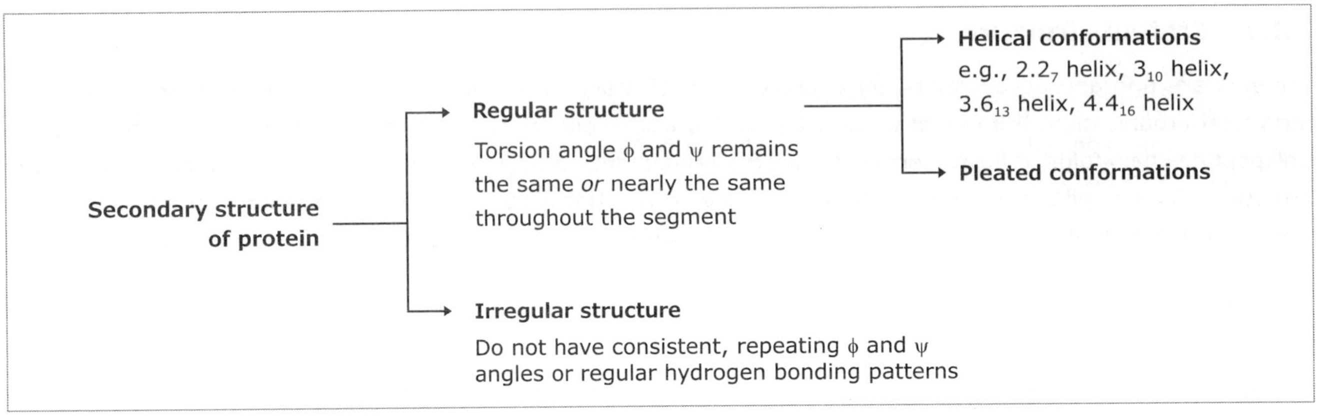

α-helix

The α-helix is a rigid, rod-like structure that forms when a polypeptide chain twists into a **helical conformation**. The *screw sense* of α-helix can be *right-handed* (clockwise) or *left-handed* (counterclockwise). **Screw sense** describes the direction in which a helical structure rotates with respect to its axis. If, viewed down the axis of a helix, the chain turns in a clockwise direction, it has a right-handed screw sense. If the turning is counterclockwise, the screw sense is left-handed. Right-handed helices are energetically more favorable because there is less steric clash between the side chains and the backbone. *Essentially all α-helices found in proteins are right-handed.* Short regions of left-handed α-helices (3-5 residues) occur only occasionally. In α-helix, there are 3.6 amino acid residues per turn of the helix and the pitch (the length of one complete turn along the helix axis) is 0.54 nm. Each residue is related to the next one by a rise of 1.5 Å (0.15 nm) along the helix axis. A single turn of α-helix involves 13 atoms from O to the H of the hydrogen-bonded loop. For this reason, the α-helix is referred to as the 3.6_{13}-helix.

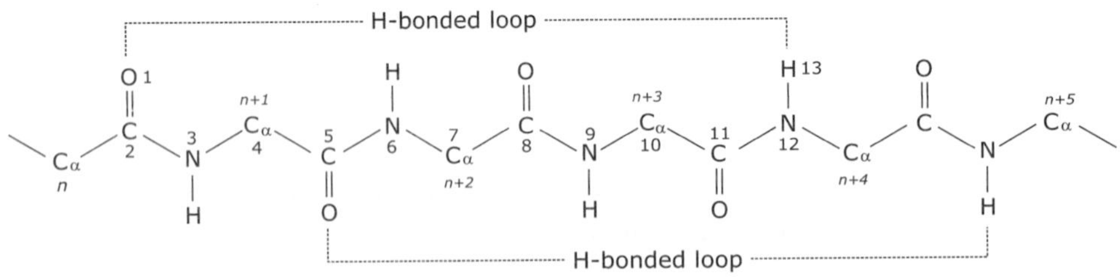

Figure 1.17 The H-bond arrangement in the α-helix. A H-bond is formed between the CO of residue n and the NH of residue n+4. The α-helix is known as the 3.6_{13}-helix, where 3.6 is the number of residues per turn and 13 is the number of atoms in the H-bonded loop.

Length of α-helix is usually 10–15 amino acid residues. In globular proteins, α-helices vary considerably in length, ranging from four or five to over forty amino acid residues. The average length is around ten residues, corresponding to three turns. The α-helix is stabilized by **intrachain** hydrogen bonds between the NH and CO groups of the main chain.

The CO group of each amino acid forms a hydrogen bond with the NH group of the amino acid that is situated four residues ahead in the sequence. Except for amino acids near the ends of an α-helix, *all the main-chain CO and NH groups are hydrogen bonded*. In a typical α-helix of n residues, there are ($\boldsymbol{n}$**-4**) hydrogen bonds. All the hydrogen bonds lie parallel to the helix axis and point in the same direction. The side chains of amino acids extend outward from the helix. The amino acid side chains project out from the α-helix and do not interfere with it, except for proline.

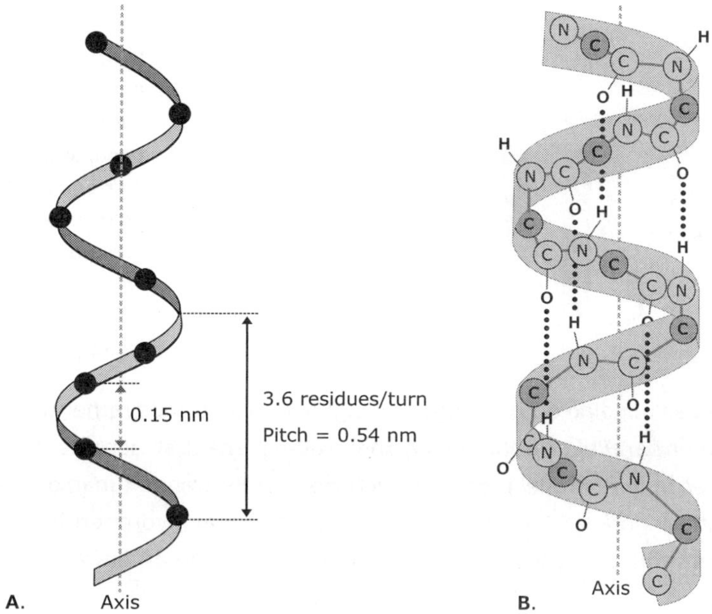

Figure 1.18 **A.** *Describing the geometry of α-helix*. The helix structure is defined by: the *pitch* (the distance along the axis between successive turns) and the rise per residue. The number of residues per helical turn is 3.6. In the right handed α-helix, a complete turn of the helix contains 3.6 amino acid residues, and the distance it rises per turn (its pitch) is 0.54 nm. **B.** The α-helix is stabilized by intrachain hydrogen bonds between the NH and CO groups of the main chain. All the hydrogen bonds lie parallel to the helix axis and point in the same direction. The R groups of each amino acid residues in an α-helix face outward (not shown in the figure).

Helices can be formed from either D- or L-amino acids, but a given helix must be composed entirely of amino acids of one configuration. The α-helix cannot be formed from a mixed copolymer of D- and L-amino acids. Amino acids also have different propensities for forming α-helices. Amino acids such as alanine, glutamine, glutamate, leucine, methionine, arginine show the higher tendency to form α-helices (**helix former**). Branching at the β-carbon atom, as in valine, threonine and isoleucine, tends to destabilize α-helices because of steric clashes (**helix breaker**). Serine, aspartate and asparagine also tend to disrupt α-helices because their side chains contain hydrogen-bond donors or acceptors in close proximity to the main chain, where they compete for main-chain NH and CO groups. Proline also is a helix breaker and least commonly found in α-helices. It is an imino acid; it has a secondary nitrogen with only one hydrogen. When participating in a peptide bond, the nitrogen no longer has hydrogen bound to it. Thus, peptide bonds in which the nitrogen is supplied by proline are incapable of functioning as hydrogen-bond donors. Secondly, its ring structure prevents it from assuming the ϕ value to fit into an α-helix.

Apart from most common α-helix (3.6_{13} helix), other helical structures (such as **2.2_7 helix**, **3_{10} helix** and **4.4_{16} helix**) are also found in proteins. The second most common helical structure is the 3_{10} helix, which has three residues per turn and 10 atoms in the hydrogen-bonded loop.

Type	**2.2_7 helix**	**3_{10} helix**	**3.6_{13} helix**	**4.4_{16} or π helix**
Residues per turn	2.2	3	3.6	4.4
Atoms in H-bonded loop	7	10	13	16
Hydrogen bonding	$n-n+2$	$n-n+3$	$n-n+4$	$n-n+5$

β-pleated sheets

β-pleated sheets (or, more simply, the **β-sheet**) form when two or more polypeptide chain segments line up side by side. Each individual segment is referred to as a **β-strand**. Rather than being coiled, each β-strand is fully extended. The distance between adjacent amino acids along a β-strand is approximately 3.5 Å, in contrast with a distance of 1.5 Å along an α-helix. β-pleated sheets are stabilized by **interchain** hydrogen bonds that form between the polypeptide backbone N—H and carbonyl groups of adjacent strands.

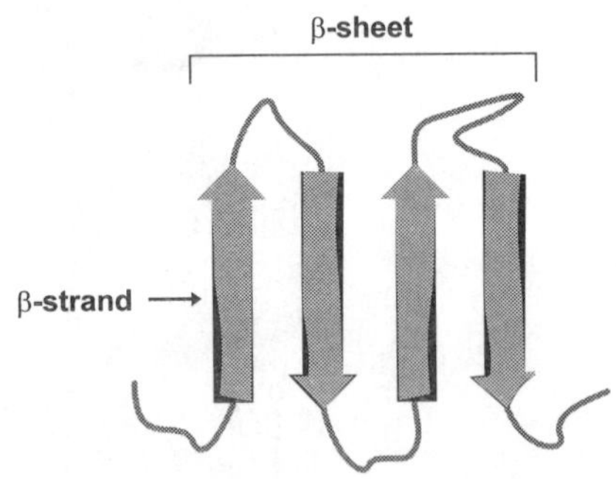

Figure 1.19
β-sheets are formed from extended β-strands. Hydrogen bonding occurs between neighboring β-strands rather than within one, as in an α-helix. β-sheets in proteins contain 2 to as many as 22 β-strands, with an average of 6 β-strands. Each strand may contain up to 15 residues, the average being 6 residues.

In β-sheets, however, hydrogen bonding occurs between neighboring β-strands rather than within one as in an α-helix. Adjacent strand can be either *parallel* or *antiparallel*. In **parallel β-sheet** structures, the β-strands are arranged in the same direction. However, in **antiparallel β-sheet** structures, the β-strands run in opposite directions. Antiparallel β-sheets are more stable than parallel β-sheets because fully collinear hydrogen bonds form. β-strands can also combine into **mixed β-sheets** with some β-strands pair parallel and some antiparallel.

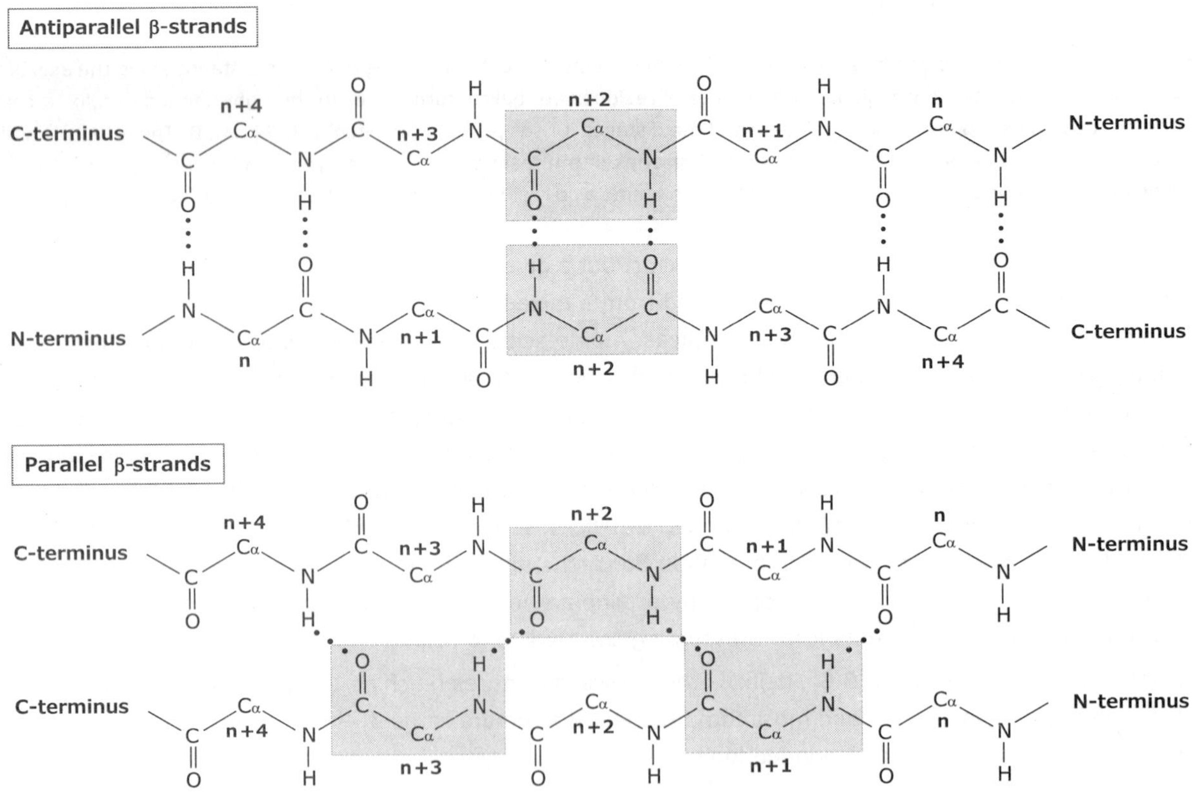

Figure 1.20 β-strands can interact in either parallel or antiparallel orientation and each of the two forms has a distinctive pattern of hydrogen bonding. In an antiparallel β-sheet, adjacent strands run in opposite directions. Hydrogen bonds between NH and CO groups connect each amino acid to a single amino acid on an adjacent strand. In the parallel β-sheet, adjacent strands run in the same direction. Hydrogen bonds connect each amino acid on one strand with two different amino acids on the adjacent strand. For each amino acid, the NH group is hydrogen bonded to the CO group of one amino acid on the adjacent strand, whereas the CO group is hydrogen bonded to the NH group on the amino acid two residues farther along the chain.

Problem

You have a polypeptide chain containing 105 amino acid residues,

1. calculate the approximate length (in nanometers) if it exists entirely in α-helical form.
2. calculate the approximate length (in nanometers) if it exists entirely in fully extended form.
3. calculate the number of H-bonds involving the backbone CO and NH if it exists entirely in α-helical form.

Solution: As we know, β-strand represents a fully extended conformation. The distance between adjacent amino acid residues along a β-strand is approximately 3.5 Å, in contrast with a distance of 1.5 Å along an α-helix.

1. 105 × 1.5 Å = 157.5 Å = 15.75 nanometers.
2. 105 × 3.5 Å = 367.5 Å = 36.75 nanometers.
3. In an α-helix, *one* amino acid residue can make a maximum of *two* H-bonds. Therefore 105 residues can make up to 2 x 105 = 210 H-bonds. In the α-helix, *four* amino acid residues at the N-terminus and *four* at the C-terminus make only 1 H-bond per residue. This makes the total number of H-bonds 210 − 8 = 202. When calculating this number, we count each H-bond twice: *one* for the donor residue and *one* for the acceptor. Hence, the actual number of H-bonds is 202/2 = 101. We can also find the value by applying the n−4 rule, where n is the number of amino acid residues.

As mentioned earlier, the ϕ and ψ values associated with each amino acid residue depend on its secondary structure of polypeptide segment. Common regular secondary structures such as α-helix, β-sheet have characteristics ϕ and ψ values. Each type of regular secondary structure can be described by the ϕ and ψ values associated with each amino acid residue. The D- and L-form of the amino acids have their side-chain oriented differently with respect to the CO group, they have different allowed ϕ and ψ angles. If polypeptides are built from D-amino acids, they have different ϕ and ψ angles than those that are exclusively made up of L-amino acids. As shown by a **Ramachandran plot** (**figure 1.21**), the torsion angles that define the α-helix and β-sheet fall within a relatively restricted range of sterically allowed regions. The backbone torsion angles for right-handed α-helix fall in the plot's lower left quadrant. In contrast, β-sheet is made up of almost fully extended strands, with ϕ and ψ angles fall in the upper left quadrant of the Ramachandran plot.

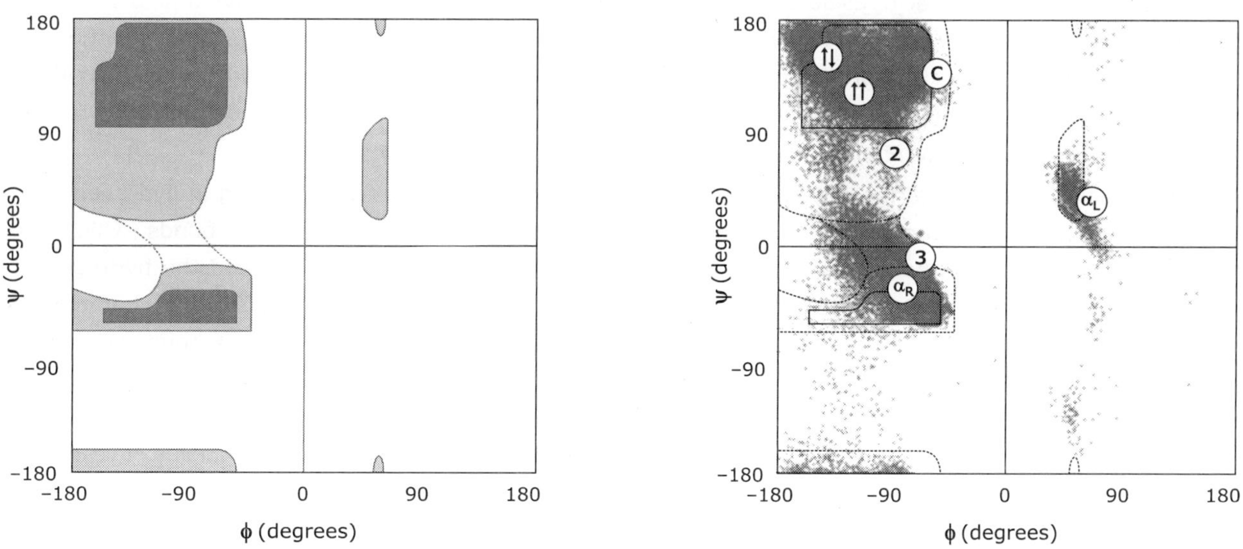

Figure 1.21 Ramachandran plots showing a variety of secondary structures. The values of ϕ and ψ for various allowed secondary structures are overlaid on the plot. The white circles represent torsion angles of several secondary structures: α_R for right-handed α-helix; α_L for left-handed α-helix; 3 for right-handed 3_{10}-helix; 2 for 2.2_7-helix; C for collagen; ↑↑ for parallel β-sheet and ↑↓ for antiparallel β-sheet.

Table 1.4 Idealized ϕ and ψ angles for common secondary structures in proteins

Secondary structure	Torsion angle (in degree)		Secondary structure	Torsion angle (in degree)	
	ϕ	ψ		ϕ	ψ
Antiparallel β-sheet	– 139	+ 135	Right-handed 3_{10}-helix	– 49	– 26
Parallel β-sheet	– 119	+ 113	Collagen	– 51	+ 153
Right-handed 3.6_{13}-helix	– 57	– 47	Left-handed α-helix	+ 57	+ 47

Note: In real proteins, the torsion angles often vary somewhat from these idealized values.

Turns

Secondary structures are usually divided into **α-helix**, **β-sheet** and **loops**. The α-helix and the β-sheet are *regular secondary structures*. These secondary structures have repetitive and regular patterns (torsion angle ϕ and ψ remains the same or nearly the same throughout the segment). As compared to α-helix and β-sheet, **loops** do not have regular, periodic structures. They have non-repetitive, nonregular secondary structure composed of sequences of residues which do not have similar ϕ and ψ values. *Loops* interconnect different secondary structures and change the direction of the polypeptide chain. They are typically found on the surface of the globular protein, which is largely responsible for its shape and dynamics.

Differences between loop and turn:

Feature	**Turn**	**Loop**
Length	4–5 residues	Variable length (often >5 residues)
Geometry	Fixed ϕ and ψ angles	No fixed ϕ and ψ torsion angles
Hydrogen bonding	Often has a specific H-bond pattern	May or may not have H-bonds

Shorter loops are usually called **turns**. Turns are composed of three to six amino acid residues. The turns can be γ-turns (consisting of 3 amino acid residues), β-turns (four amino acid residues), α-turns (five amino acid residues) and π-turns (six amino acid residues). A hydrogen bond between their end residues stabilizes these short, U-shaped secondary structures. *Glycine* and *proline* are commonly present in turns. The lack of a large side chain in glycine and stabilization of the *cis* configuration of the peptide bond by proline allow the polypeptide backbone to fold into a tight U-shape. Turns allow large proteins to fold into highly compact structures.

Turns are classified usually in terms of ϕ and ψ angles or the two end residues participating in hydrogen bonding. In an **α-turn**, the hydrogen bond donor and acceptor residues are separated by *four* peptide bonds (which involves five amino acid residues). H-bond forms between the carbonyl oxygen of residue (n) and the hydrogen of the amide group of residue (n+4). **β-turn** (or **reverse turn** or **hairpin turn**), the most common form, is characterized by hydrogen bond(s) in which the donor and acceptor residues are separated by *three* peptide bonds. The structure involves four amino acid residues, with the carbonyl oxygen of the first residue forming a hydrogen bond with the amino-group hydrogen of the fourth (n and n+3). The peptide groups of the central two residues do not participate in any hydrogen bonding. There are several types of β-turns, each defined by the ϕ and ψ angles of residues n+1 and n+2. **Type I** and **type II β-turns** are the most common, and they differ mainly in the orientation of the peptide bond between the residues n+1 and n+2.

α-turn	**β-turn**	**γ-turn**
Five amino acid residues	Four amino acid residues	Three amino acid residues
Four peptide bonds	Three peptide bonds	Two peptide bonds
H-bond between n and n+4	H-bond between n and n+3	H-bond between n and n+2

Similarly, a γ-**turn** is characterized by hydrogen bond(s) in which the donor and acceptor residues are separated by *two* peptide bonds. It is a three amino acid residue turn with a hydrogen bond between the first and third residues (n and n+2). It is a three amino acid residue turn with a hydrogen bond between the first and third residues.

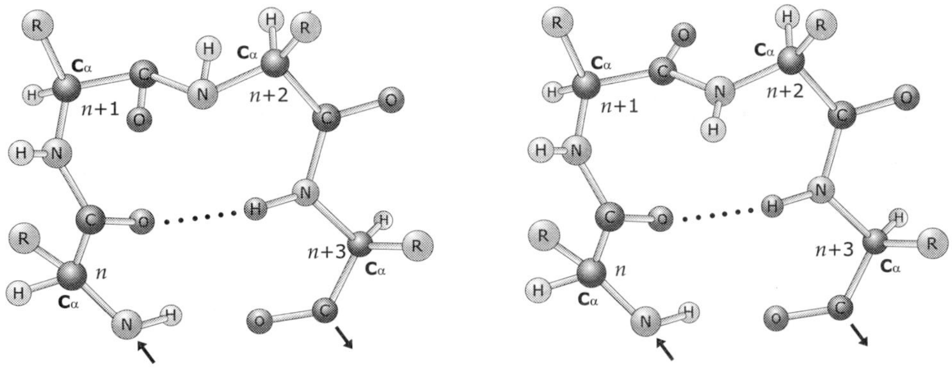

Type I β-turn

Type II β-turn

Figure 1.22 Structure of a β-turn. The CO group of residue n of the polypeptide chain is hydrogen bonded to the NH group of residue n+3 to stabilize the turn. β-turns have been classified according to the values of their central residue torsion angles, ϕ and ψ, i.e., n+1 and n+2.

Box 1.2 Motif and domain

The exact meaning of terms *motif* and *domain* is not easy to define because both are used in several, partially overlapping contexts. Certain combinations of secondary structures with a specific geometric arrangement are present in many proteins. These combinations are called **motifs** (or **supersecondary structures**). The α-helix, β-sheet and other secondary structures are combined in different ways to produce several kinds of motifs in proteins. A motif can be simple and small structure (such as two elements of secondary structure folded against each other, and represent only a small part of a protein) or a very large structure (a single motif may comprise the entire protein). Motifs are mostly associated with a particular function such as DNA binding. Motifs are of several types. These can be αα (two α-helices linked by a loop), ββ (two β-strands linked by a loop), βαβ (two antiparallel β-strands are connected by an α-helix) or more complexes structures, like β-meander, Greek-key or beta-barrel.

βαβ Greek-key motif β-meander

Figure 1.23 Structural motif is a combination of several secondary structural elements produced by the folding of adjacent sections of the polypeptide chain into a specific three-dimensional configuration.

Domain is an independently folded stable tertiary structure and shows a certain level of evolutionary conservation. It is a polypeptide chain or a part of a polypeptide chain (range in size from about 30 to 400 amino acid residues) that can fold independently into a stable three-dimensional tertiary structure. It is an independent functional and structural unit of protein. Proteins may comprise a single domain or more than one domain. A small protein often consists of only one domain. Proteins with more than a few hundred amino acid residues often have two or more domains.

Tertiary structure

The term *tertiary structure* (3° structure) refers to the unique three-dimensional conformations that globular proteins assume as a consequence of the interactions between the side chains in their primary structure. All information needed to fold the protein into its native tertiary structure is contained within the primary structure of the peptide chain itself. The following types of covalent and non-covalent interactions stabilize tertiary structure:

1. Hydrophobic interactions (major form of non-covalent interaction)
2. Ionic interactions (or salt bridges)
3. Hydrogen bonds
4. van der Waals force of interactions
5. Covalent bonds: The covalent bond present in a tertiary structure is the *intrachain disulfide bond*. A **disulfide bond** (also called an S-S bond) forms between two cysteine residues due to oxidation of their *thiol* or *sulfhydryl* groups. The oxidized dimer form of the amino acid cysteine is called **cystine**. The other sulfur-containing amino acid, *methionine*, cannot form disulfide bonds.

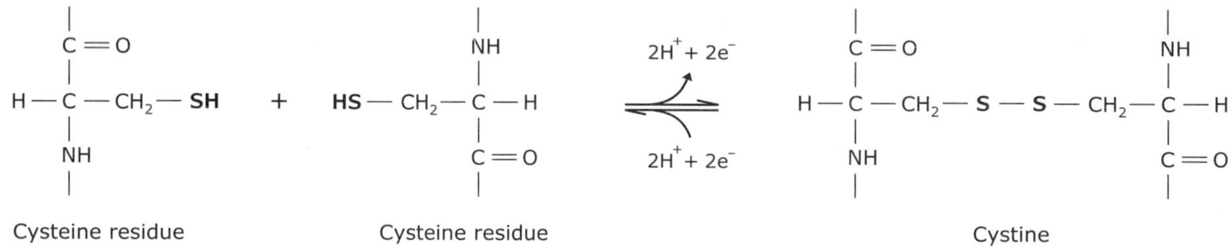

Figure 1.24 Structure of cystine.

Quaternary structure

Many proteins like hemoglobin, are composed of two or more polypeptide chains. These proteins are called **multimeric proteins** and each polypeptide chain is called a **subunit**. Subunits in a multimeric protein may be identical (**homomultimer**) or quite different (**heteromultimer**). Polypeptide subunits assemble to form quaternary structure (4° structure) and are held together by non-covalent interactions (such as hydrophobic interactions, electrostatic interactions and hydrogen bonds) as well as covalent interactions (*interchain disulfide bonds*).

1.1.8 Denaturation of proteins

Denaturation is a process in which proteins lose their **native conformation** i.e., normal, biologically active folded conformation. It includes loss of quaternary, tertiary and secondary structure of a protein which is present in the native state. Denaturation includes the breaking of *non-covalent* (electrostatic interactions, H-bonds, van der Waals force of interactions and hydrophobic interactions) and *covalent* (disulfide bonds) bonds. Denaturation usually does not include the breaking of peptide bonds. It does not affect primary structures (that is, the sequence of amino acids that make up the polypeptide chain). Denaturation results in a loss of activity. Depending on the degree of denaturation, the molecule may partially or completely lose its biological activity. Since the native conformation is usually the most water-soluble, disrupting the secondary and tertiary structures causes changes in solubility and frequently results in precipitation of the protein from solution. Reagents or conditions that can cause denaturation are called **denaturing agents**. Urea is most commonly used as denaturing agent. However, the molecular basis for urea's ability to denature protein remains unknown. Urea may exert its effect directly by making H-bonds with polar moieties of the protein, particularly peptide group or indirectly, by altering the solvent environment diminishing the hydrophobic effect.

Examples of denaturing agents

Strong acids or bases: Changes in pH result in protonation or deprotonation of the side group of amino acids of protein which alters hydrogen bonding and salt bridge patterns.

Organic solvents: Reagents such as ethanol that are capable of forming intermolecular hydrogen bonds with protein molecules disrupt the intramolecular hydrogen bonding within the molecule.

Detergents: Detergents are amphipathic molecules which may be ionic or non-ionic in nature. These agents mainly disrupt hydrophobic interactions and unfold proteins into extended polypeptide chains.

Reducing agents: Reducing agents such as β-mercaptoethanol reduces the disulfide bonds to sulfhydryl groups and breaks intra or interchain disulfide bonds.

Heavy metal ions: Heavy metals such as mercury and lead affect protein structure in several ways. They may disrupt salt bridges by forming ionic bonds with negatively charged groups. Heavy metals also bond with sulfhydryl groups.

Heat: As the temperature increases, the rate of molecular vibration increases. Eventually, weak interactions such as hydrogen bonds and van der Waals interaction are disrupted and the protein unfolds.

1.1.9 Solubilities of proteins

Solubility depends on the ability of a solvent to interact with a solute more strongly than solute particles interact with each other. The solubility of proteins in aqueous solution varies considerably in given set of conditions. It depends on several factors like pH, ionic strength, nature of solvent, temperature, etc.

Effect of pH: The isoelectric point of a protein occurs at the pH at which there are an equal number of positive and negative charges (the protein has no *net* charge). At any pH above the isoelectric point, the protein molecules have a net negative charge; at any pH below the isoelectric point, they have a net positive charge. The water solubility of proteins often depends on the repulsive forces between like charges on their surfaces. When protein molecules are at a pH at which they have a net positive or negative charge, the presence of these like charges causes the protein molecules to repel one another. These repulsive forces are smallest at the isoelectric point, when the net charges are zero. When there are no repulsive forces, the protein molecules tend to clump together to form aggregates of two or more molecules, reducing their solubility. As a consequence, *proteins are least soluble in water at their isoelectric points and can be precipitated from their solutions* (**isoelectric precipitation**).

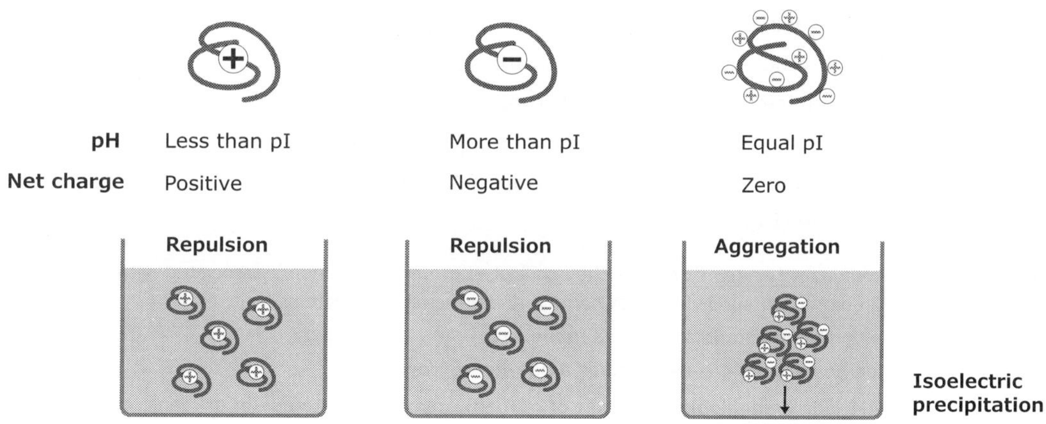

Effect of ionic strength: The solubility of a protein at low ionic strength generally increases with increasing salt concentration. This process is known as **salting in**. It occurs due to the binding of salt ions to the protein's ionizable groups which decrease the interaction between oppositely charged groups on the protein molecules. Water molecules then form solvation spheres around these groups. However, when large amounts of salt are added to a protein in solution, a precipitate forms. This process is referred to as **salting out**. The cause of insolubility in this case is different from that for isoelectric precipitation. Salting out is dependent on the hydrophobic nature of the surface of the protein. Hydrophobic groups predominate in the interior of the protein, but some are located at the surface. Water is forced into contact with these groups. When salts are added to the system, water solvates the salt ions and as salt concentration increases water is removed from around the protein, eventually exposing the hydrophobic groups. Hydrophobic groups on one protein molecule can interact with those of another, resulting in aggregation and thus precipitation.

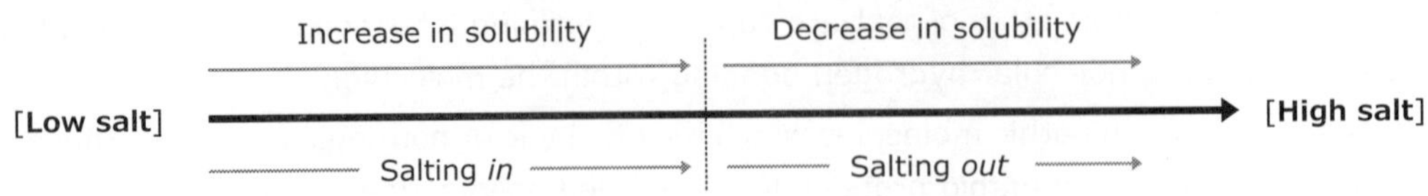

Effect of solvent: Organic solvents such as acetone, ethanol, decrease the **dielectric constant** of the aqueous solution, which in effect allows two proteins to come close together through electrostatic force of attraction. These solvents due to their low dielectric constants lower the solvating power of aqueous solutions.

1.1.10 Simple and conjugated proteins

On the basis of composition, proteins are classified as *simple* or *conjugated*. **Simple proteins**, such as serum albumin, contain only amino acids. In contrast, **conjugated protein** consists of a simple protein combined with a non-protein component. The non-protein component is called a **prosthetic group**. A conjugated protein without its prosthetic group is called an **apoprotein**. Apoprotein combined with its prosthetic group is referred to as a **holoprotein**. Conjugated proteins are further classified according to the nature of their prosthetic groups. For example, **glycoproteins** contain a carbohydrate component, while **lipoproteins** contain lipid molecules. Similarly, **metalloproteins** are proteins that contain metal ions as cofactors. These include proteins such as phosphoproteins, which contain phosphate groups, and iron proteins, which possess iron ions in either the ferrous or ferric state.

Table 1.5 Examples of few conjugated proteins

Glycoproteins	Fibronectin
	Cadherin
Lipoproteins	Chylomicron
	High density lipoprotein (HDL)
Metalloproteins	Ferritin (Iron)
	Alcohol dehydrogenase (Zinc)
	Cytochrome oxidase (Copper and Iron)
	Nitrogenase (Molybdenum and Iron)
	Hemoglobin (Iron) and Myoglobin (Iron)
	Cytochrome *c* (Iron) and Cytochrome P450 (Iron)
	Catalase (Iron)

Iron proteins are classified as *conjugated proteins* because they consist of protein components associated with iron, either in the ferrous or ferric state. These proteins can be further subdivided into *heme* and *non-heme* iron proteins:

- If the iron is present within a porphyrin ring, it is termed a **heme iron**.
- If the iron is not bound to a porphyrin ring, it is classified as a **non-heme iron**.

Examples of heme iron proteins include **hemoglobin** (transport of oxygen), **myoglobin** (storage of oxygen), **cytochrome c** (transport of electrons), and **catalase** (Degradation of hydrogen peroxide). In contrast, proteins such as **ferredoxin** and **iron-sulfur** (Fe-S) proteins are examples of non-heme iron proteins.

1.2 Fibrous and globular proteins

Proteins can be classified into two categories – fibrous and globular proteins, on the basis of shape and solubility. **Fibrous proteins** are long, rod-shaped molecules that are insoluble in water and physically tough. Fibrous proteins, such as keratins have structural and protective functions. These proteins usually consist largely of a single type of secondary structure. For example, silk fibers consist largely of the fibrous protein *fibroin*, made up largely of β-sheets whereas fibers of wool consist largely of the *keratin* protein, which is largely α-helix.

Globular proteins are compact spherical molecules that are usually water-soluble. These proteins often contain several types of secondary structure. The main driving force for folding water-soluble globular protein molecules is to pack hydrophobic side chains into the interior of the molecule, thus creating a hydrophobic core and a hydrophilic surface. In these proteins, the non-polar residues *Val*, *Leu*, *Ile*, *Met* and *Phe* largely occur in the interior of a protein, out of contact with the aqueous solvent. The charged polar residues *Arg*, *His*, *Lys*, *Asp* and *Glu* are largely located on the surface of the protein in the contact with the aqueous solvent. Uncharged polar residues *Ser*, *Thr*, *Asn*, *Gln* and *Tyr* are usually present on the protein surface.

Table 1.6 The major functions of proteins and their examples

Function	**Examples**
Structural	Collagen, Keratin and Fibrin
Catalytic	Enzymes such as Lysosomes, Proteases, Polymerase and Kinases
Membrane transport	Glucose transporter and Aquaporin
Cell recognition	MHC proteins
Osmotic regulation	Serum albumin
Gene regulation	*lac* repressor
Hormonal	Insulin, Vasopressin and Oxytocin
Transport throughout body	Hemoglobin
Ion-binding	Ferritin and Calmodulin
Contraction	Actin and Myosin
Defense	Antibodies and Snake venom

1.2.1 Collagen

Collagen is the major structural protein in the extracellular matrix and also the most abundant protein in vertebrates. A typical collagen molecule is long, inelastic, stiff, triple stranded helical structure. This molecule consists of three polypeptide chains, called **α-chains.** Each chain is generally more than 1000 residue long. In some collagens, all three chains are identical, while in others, the molecules contain two or even three different α-chains. The α-chains are *left-handed* polypeptide helices and have 3.3 amino acid residues per turn. Three α-chains wind around one another in a characteristic *right-handed* **triple helix**. Vertebrates have about 25 different kinds of α-chains, each coded by different genes and has its own unique amino acid sequence. These different types of α-chains combine in various ways to form at least 27 different types of collagen molecules. Types I, II and III represent 90% of collagens. Type I collagen predominates in bones, tendons, and skin. Type II collagen, found in cartilage, and type III collagen, found in blood vessels, consist of three identical α-chains.

The amino acid sequence in α-chain is generally a repeating tripeptide unit, **Gly–X–Y**, where *X* is often proline and *Y* is often 3- or 4-hydroxyproline or 5-hydroxylysine. Glycine constitutes approximately one-third of the amino acid residues. Proline and hydroxyproline confer rigidity on the collagen molecule. They together comprise up to 30% of the residues of collagen.

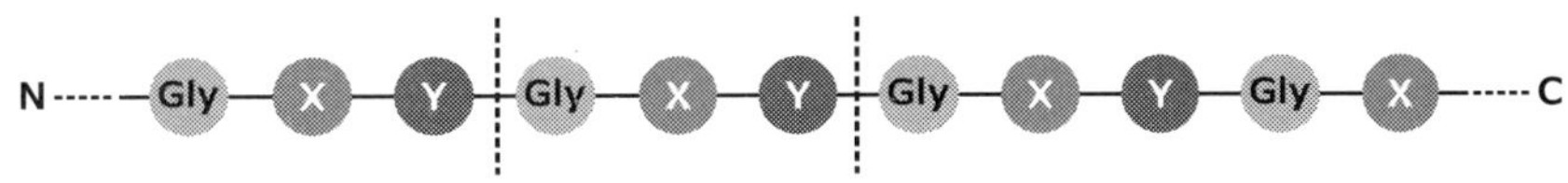

Figure 1.25 Collagen polypeptide has a distinctive amino acid composition: nearly one-third of its residues are glycine. The amino acid sequence of a typical collagen polypeptide consists of repeating triplets of sequence Gly-X-Y over a segment of ~1000 residues, where X is often proline and Y is often hydroxyproline. Hydroxylysine sometimes appears at the Y position.

The hydroxylation is carried out during post-translational modifications of α-chains by two enzymes: *prolyl hydroxylase* and *lysyl hydroxylase*. **Ascorbate** (**vitamin C**) acts as cofactors for these enzymes and hence is essential for hydroxylation of proline and lysine residues. Hydroxylation of amino acids results in the formation of interchain H-bonds. It also allows the glycosylation of hydroxylysine residues. A deficiency in vitamin C causes the formation of unstable collagen molecules and is responsible for disease **scurvy**, a disease characterized by swollen and bleeding gums and blood-vessel fragility. The triple-stranded helical structure of collagen consists of three parallel helices, in which the special type of molecular packing is contributed by the occurrence of glycine as every third residue. This prototype structure is stabilized by interchain hydrogen bonds, unlike the well-established α-helical structure for polypeptides (not to be confused with the nomenclature of α-chains used for the single chains in the collagen triple helix), which is stabilized by intrachain hydrogen bonds. In collagen, three strands wind around one another to form a superhelical cable that is stabilized by hydrogen bonds between strands. The hydrogen bonds form between the N-H groups of one α-chain and the C=O groups of the other chain. The hydroxyl groups of hydroxyproline residues also participate in hydrogen bonding.

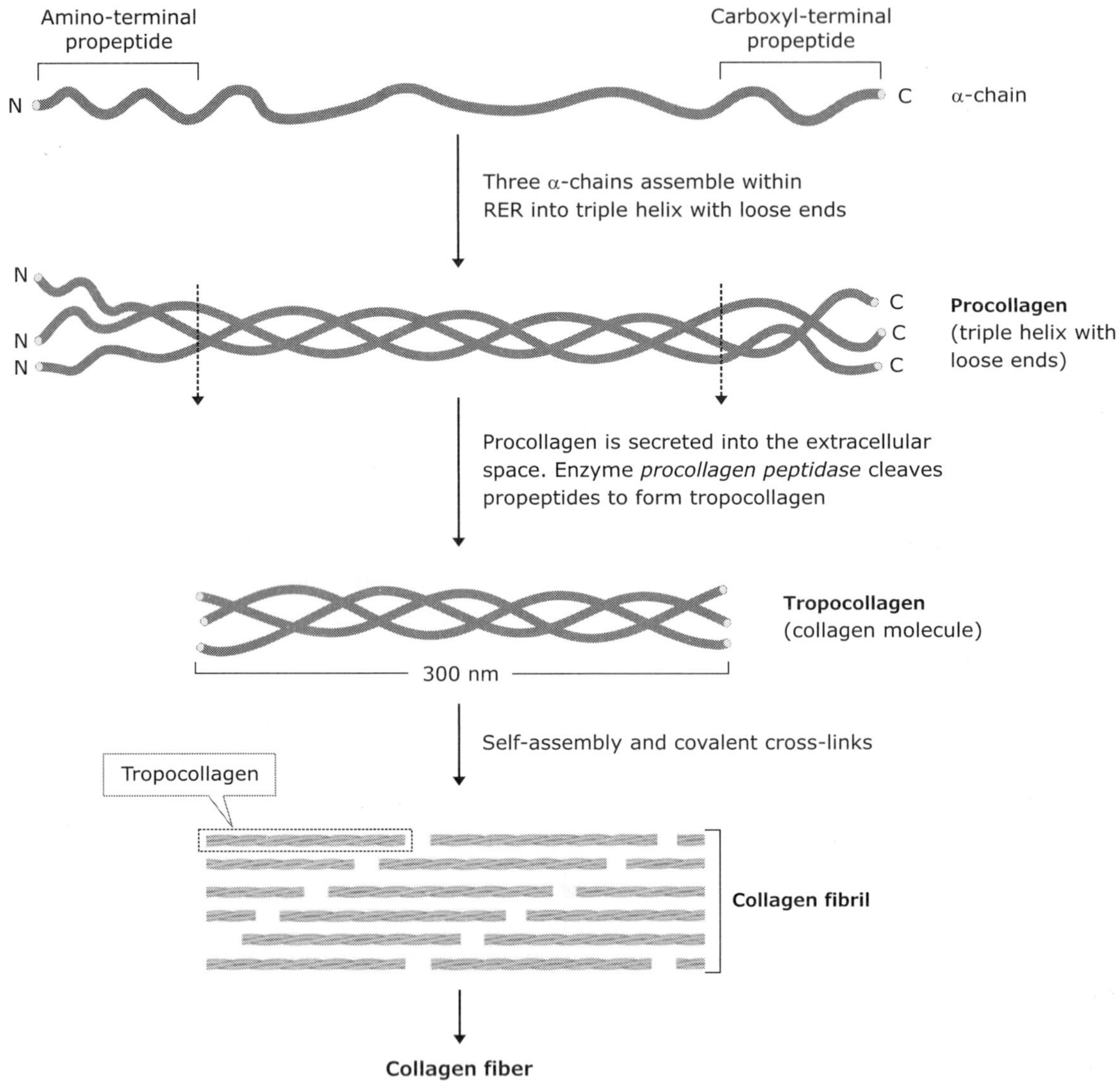

Figure 1.26 Schematic representation of the collagen structure. Nuclear transcription of collagen gene produces α-chains. The three α-chains are intracellularly assembled into the triple helix molecule called *procollagen*. Procollagen is converted into tropocollagen by the removal of the amino- and carboxyl-terminal propeptides in the extracellular space via procollagen peptidase enzymes. Self-assembly and covalent cross-linking form *collagen fibrils*. Collagen fibers are formed by the aggregation of collagen fibrils.

The α-chains are synthesized on membrane-bound ribosomes and enter into the lumen of the endoplasmic reticulum (ER). In the lumen of the ER selected proline and lysine residues are hydroxylated to form hydroxyproline and hydroxylysine, respectively, and some of the hydroxylysine residues are glycosylated.

Each α-chain then combines with two others to form a hydrogen-bonded, triple-stranded helical molecule known as **procollagen.** The procollagen is secreted into the extracellular space. Enzyme **procollagen peptidase** cleaves amino and carboxyl termini *propeptides* of α-chains to form **tropocollagen** (or **collagen molecule**). In the extracellular space, the tropocollagens assemble in to form **collagen fibrils.**

Covalent cross-linking: Several types of cross-links are formed via enzymatic and non-enzymatic pathways. The formation of a cross-linking profile varies during the maturation and ageing of collagen. Covalent cross-links are formed both within a tropocollagen molecule (**intratropocollagen cross-links**) and between different tropocollagen molecules (**intertropocollagen cross-links**). There are two major groups of cross-links based on their formation pathways, enzymatic and non-enzymatic. The biosynthesis of enzymatic covalent cross-links starts with the enzymatic oxidative deamination of the ε-amino groups of lysine and hydroxylysine residues into **allysine** and **hydroxyallysine,** respectively, by enzymes **lysyl oxidases** (copper-dependent extracellular enzymes). Then, these aldehydes undergo a series of spontaneous condensation reactions with lysine, hydroxylysine, or other aldehydes to form a variety of di-, tri-, and tetrafunctional cross-links.

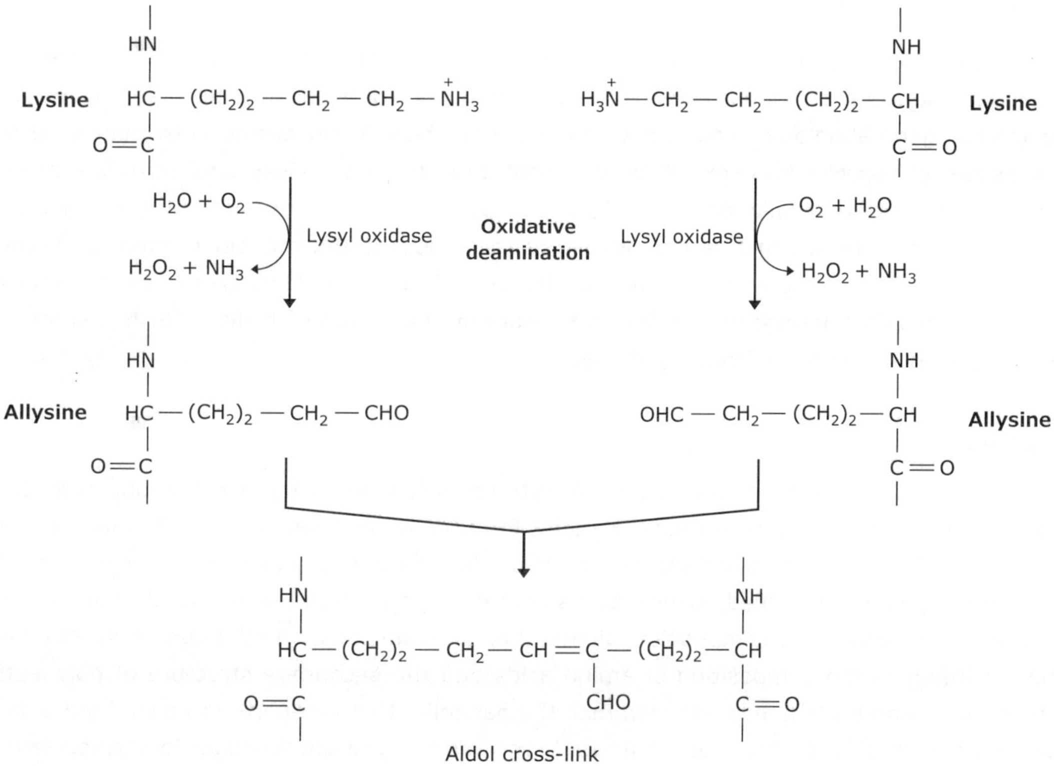

Figure 1.27 Intratropocollagen cross-links form between allysine after oxidative deamination of ε-amino groups of lysine residues. Such aldehydes of two side chains then link covalently in a spontaneous non-enzymatic aldol condensation.

1.2.2 Elastin

Elastin is a highly hydrophobic connective tissue protein that is responsible for extensibility and elasticity. It is the second major protein in the extracellular matrix, which is the main component of elastic fibers found in ligaments, large arteries, and lungs. After synthesis, a 72 kDa molecule of soluble **tropoelastin** is secreted into the matrix. This protein is rich in non-polar amino acid and unusually rich in proline and glycine. Unlike collagen it is not glycosylated and contain some hydroxyproline. The tropoelastin is composed largely of two types of short sequences that alternate along the polypeptide chain: *hydrophobic segments* rich in glycine, alanine, proline and valine and *hydrophilic segments*, contain lysine–alanine and lysine–proline motifs, which are involved in cross-linking.

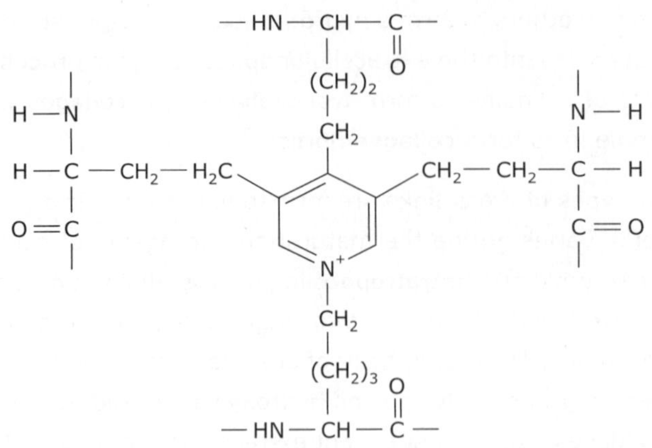

Figure 1.28 Pyridinium-containing cross-links in elastin. Enzyme lysyl oxidase catalyzes the oxidative deamination of the ε-amino group of lysine residues to the highly reactive allysine. Subsequently, covalent cross-links form spontaneously by non-enzymatic condensation of lysine and allysine residues. The four lysine groups combine to form a pyridinium nucleus.

Tropoelastin is secreted as soluble, unglycosylated protein by elastogenic cell types such as fibroblasts, smooth muscle cells, endothelial cells, or chondrocytes. After secretion, the tropoelastin molecules become highly cross-linked to one another, generating an extensive network of elastin fibers. In the extracellular matrix, certain ε-amino groups of lysyl residues of tropoelastin are oxidatively deaminated to aldehydes by **lysyl oxidase** (referred to as **allysine**). Different types of covalent cross-links are formed by the spontaneous condensation of lysine and allysine that are referred to as bi-, tri-, tetra-, and pentafunctional with respect to the number of involved lysine moieties. The condensation of three of these lysine-derived aldehydes with an unmodified lysine results in formation of a tetrafunctional cross-link called **desmosines** and its isomer **isodesmosine.** Once cross-linked in its mature, extracellular form, elastin is highly insoluble and extremely stable.

1.2.3 Keratins

Keratins are fibrous structural proteins present in the cytoplasm (intracellular) of eukaryotic cells. It refers to a group of insoluble and filament-forming proteins. Keratins form the horny layer of the epidermis and the epidermal appendages such as hair, nails, horns and feathers. Within a cell, it replaces the cytoplasmic content and transforms living and functional cells into cornified, structurally stable dead cells. There are several types of keratins. The classification depends on amino acid composition, distribution, and functions. Keratins can be classified as α-**keratin** and β-**keratin** according to the composition of amino acids and the secondary structure of polypeptide chains. α-keratin is found in mammals (there is one mammal, the pangolin, that is reported to have both α and β), and it is the primary constituent of wool, hair, nails, hooves, horns and the stratum corneum (outermost layer of skin).

The β-keratin is found in birds and reptiles as a constituent of feathers, claws and beaks of birds, and scales and claws of reptiles. Keratins are also classified as **hard keratin** and **soft keratin**-based on the cysteine content. *Hard keratins,* found in hair, nails, claws, beaks, are rich in cysteine and thus have a higher amount of sulfur. *Soft keratins* (epidermal keratins such as the stratum corneum of skin) have a lower amount of sulfur because of lesser cysteine residues. The cysteine residues play a key role in the structural stability of keratin by forming intra- or intermolecular disulfide bonds. Keratins are highly resistant to degradation by common proteases such as trypsin and pepsin. Keratins can also be distinguished according to their pI into two categories – **type I** (acidic) **keratins** and **type II** (neutral-basic) **keratins.** In humans, type I keratins have a pI of 4.9-5.4, whereas type II keratins have a pI of 6.5-8.5.

The α-keratin (found in mammals), belongs to the intermediate filament protein family. The structure of the α-keratin is dominated by right-handed α-helical segments. Two α-keratin polypeptide chains, oriented in parallel, are coiled about each other to form a heterodimeric left-handed coiled-coil structure. The heterodimer is made up of type I (acidic) and type II (neutral-basic) α-keratin polypeptide chains. Two heterodimers join in an antiparallel manner to form the fundamental tetrameric subunit (a **protofilament**). Two protofilaments constitute a **protofibril.** Four protofibrils constitute a microfibril, which associates with other microfibrils to form a **macrofibril.**

1.2.4 Myoglobin

Myoglobin (Mb), a globular protein, contains a single polypeptide chain of 153 amino acid residues (molecular weight 17,800), and a single heme group. The inside of Mb consists almost exclusively of non-polar residues, whereas the outside contains both polar and non-polar residues. About 75% of the polypeptide chain is α-helical. There are eight helical segments. These eight helical segments are commonly labeled A–H, starting from the NH_2-terminal end. The interhelical regions are designated as AB, BC, CD,..., GH, respectively. The iron atom of the heme is directly bonded to a nitrogen atom of a histidine side chain of globin.

Heme: Globin of Mb binds a single *heme* group by forming a co-ordinate bond. The heterocyclic ring system of heme is a porphyrin derivative. The porphyrin in heme is known as **protoporphyrin IX**. It is made up of 4-pyrrole ring and 4-pyrroles are linked by **methine** (=CH–) bridges to form a tetrapyrrole ring. The *Fe atom* is present either in Fe^{2+} or Fe^{3+} oxidation state in the center of the protoporphyrin IX ring.

Only Mb in Fe^{2+} state can bind O_2. The iron atom has six co-ordination bond, 4 in the plane of flat porphyrin ring and two perpendicular to it. The iron atom of the heme is directly bonded to one of the histidine called **proximal histidine** (His^{93} or His F8) of globin protein. It is 93rd amino acid residue from the amino-terminal end of the myoglobin polypeptide chain (i.e., His^{93}) or the 8th residue in helix F (i.e., His F8). The O_2-binding site is present on the other side of the heme plane, at the sixth coordination position. A second histidine residue, termed as **distal histidine**, His^{64} or His E7, (not bonded to the heme) makes H-bond with oxygen molecules. O_2 binds directly to the iron atom of the heme only.

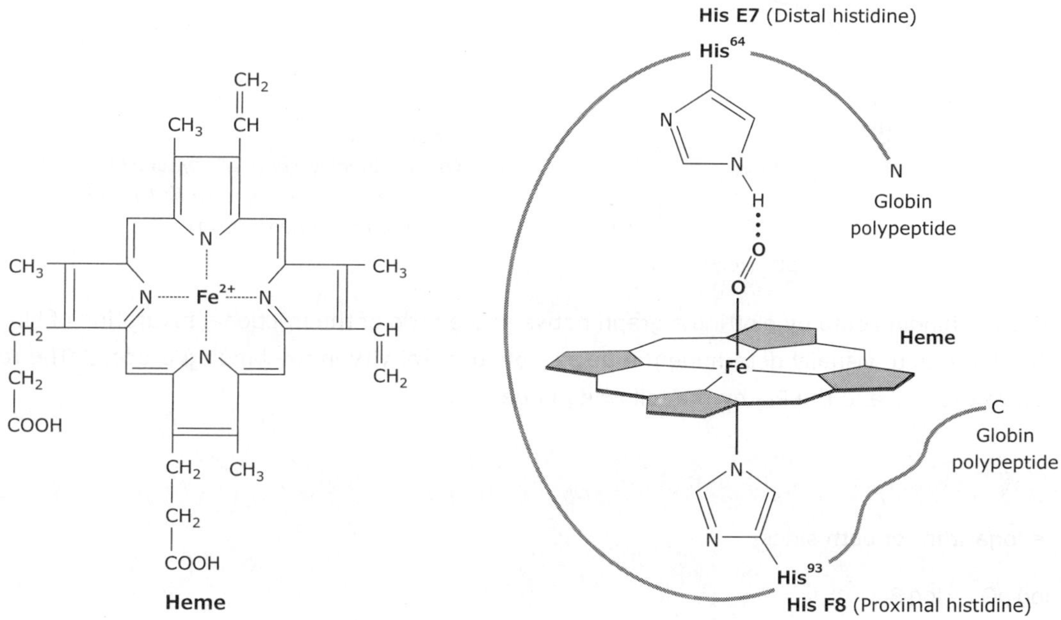

Figure 1.29 The pyrrole rings and methylene bridge carbons are coplanar, and the iron atom resides in almost the same plane. The fifth and sixth coordination positions of iron atom are directed perpendicular to—and directly above and below—the plane of the heme ring. The fifth coordination position of the iron is linked to a ring nitrogen of the proximal histidine. The distal histidine lies on the side of the heme ring opposite to proximal histidine.

Binding of oxygen to Mb: Mb, functions as an oxygen-storage protein, binds with one oxygen molecule. The dissociation of the myoglobin-oxygen complex (MbO_2) is described by

$$MbO_2 \overset{K_d}{\rightleftharpoons} Mb + O_2$$

K_d is the *dissociation constant* and used to express the affinity of a protein for a ligand. A lower value of K_d corresponds to a higher affinity of ligand for the protein. K_d is given by:

$$K_d = \frac{[Mb][O_2]}{[MbO_2]} \quad \text{or} \quad [MbO_2] = \frac{[Mb][O_2]}{K_d}$$

The **fractional saturation** (Y) of Mb

$$Y = \frac{\text{Number of binding sites occupied}}{\text{Total number of binding sites}} = \frac{[MbO_2]}{[MbO_2]+[Mb]} = \frac{[Mb][O_2]/K_d}{[Mb][O_2]/K_d+[Mb]} = \frac{[O_2]}{[O_2]+K_d}$$

When all of the Mb molecules in solution are bound to oxygen, Y = 1.0. Mb is saturated with oxygen at this point. When Y = 0.5, Mb is half-saturated with oxygen. K_d is equal to the $[O_2]$ at which half of the Mb molecules in solution are occupied or $[O_2]_{0.5}$.

$$Y = \frac{[O_2]}{[O_2]+[O_2]_{0.5}}$$

Because O_2 is gas, expressing its concentration in terms of its partial pressure is more convenient. If we define the partial pressure of oxygen at $[O_2]_{0.5}$ as P_{50}, then,

$$Y = \frac{pO_2}{pO_2 + P_{50}}$$

A plot of the fractional saturation of Mb, Y versus the partial pressure of oxygen pO_2, is *hyperbolic*. The term 'hyperbolic' refers to the shape of the curve on a graph. A hyperbolic curve indicates a simple and non-cooperative binding process. The binding of oxygen to one Mb molecule does not influence the binding affinity of other Mb molecules. Additionally, the probability of oxygen binding increases linearly with increasing partial pressure of oxygen.

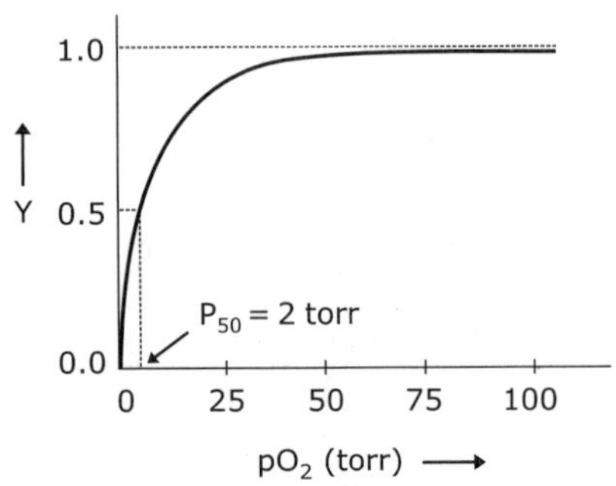

Figure 1.30
Oxygen binding curve of myoglobin.
(*1 torr equals the pressure of 1 mm Hg at 0°C and standard gravity*).

We can linearize the binding data by plotting a graph between the ratio of the fractional saturation of Mb (Y) to free Mb (1–Y). This allows us to visually determine the degree of cooperativity in the binding process. The ratio of Y to (1–Y) is related to the pO_2 and the P_{50} by the following equation:

$$\frac{Y}{1-Y} = \frac{pO_2}{P_{50}}$$

If we take the logarithm of both sides

$$\log\left(\frac{Y}{1-Y}\right) = \log pO_2 - \log P_{50}$$

This equation forms the basis for a linear plot. A plot of log (Y/[1 – Y]) versus log pO_2 for Mb is known as a **Hill plot**. In the case of Mb, this plot is a straight line with a slope of 1, reflecting that Mb has a single binding site and binds oxygen non-cooperatively. The slope of the line, also known as the **Hill coefficient** (n), indicates the degree of cooperativity in ligand binding.

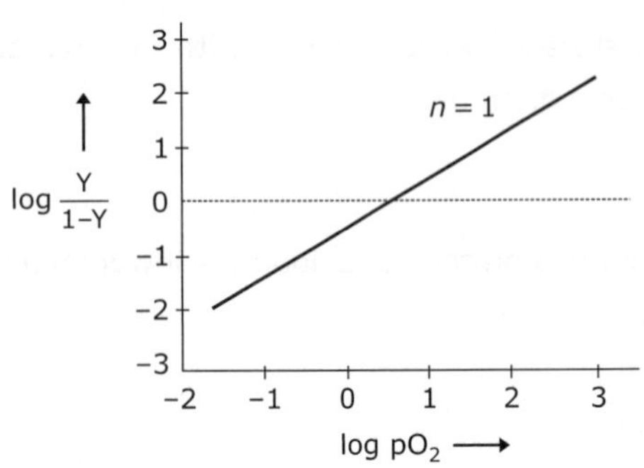

Figure 1.31
For myoglobin, which is a monomeric protein with a single oxygen binding site, the Hill plot produces a straight line with a slope (Hill coefficient, n) of 1. This means myoglobin binds oxygen non-cooperatively.

1.2.5 Hemoglobin

Hemoglobin (molecular weight of 65,450) is an oligomeric, allosteric, conjugated protein with four polypeptide chains joined by non-covalent bonds. It contains **heme** prosthetic group. *Heme* is an iron-containing porphyrin derivative. Hemoglobin (Hb) is present in all vertebrates (except Arctic fish) and in many invertebrates, including annelids, many arthropods and some molluscs. Based on the nature of globin protein, a variety of hemoglobin molecules are produced in humans. All are tetramers consisting of different combinations of globin polypeptide chains, each encoded by a separate gene.

- **Hemoglobin**
  - **Globin protein family members**
    - **α-globin subfamily**: α, ζ globins
    - **β-globin subfamily**: β, γ, ε, δ globins
  - **Prosthetic group**: Heme

HbA_1 (*or* simply HbA), which contains two α and two β-chains, represents about 98 percent of all hemoglobin found in adult RBCs. α-chains contain 141 amino acid residues and β-chains contain 146 amino acid residues. Thus, HbA_1 is designated as $\alpha_2\beta_2$. The remaining about 2 percent consists of **HbA_2**, minor adult hemoglobin. This molecule contains two α- and two δ-chains and is designated $\alpha_2\delta_2$. The δ-chain is very similar to β-chain. During embryonic and fetal development, different sets of hemoglobin are found. One type of Hb during the early embryonic state contains two ξ-chains, which are very similar to α-chains, and two ε-chains, which are very similar to β-chains ($\xi_2\varepsilon_2$). During fetal state, hemoglobin contains two α-chains and two γ-chains, which are very similar to β-chains ($\alpha_2\gamma_2$). The embryonic and fetal forms have a higher affinity for oxygen. This is necessary to obtain oxygen from the mother's blood.

Table 1.7 Different Hb expressed during different developmental stages of humans

Developmental stages	Types of globin proteins	Type of hemoglobin
Embryonic (<8 weeks)	$\xi_2\varepsilon_2$	Gower 1
Fetal (3–9 months)	$\alpha_2\gamma_2$	HbF
Adult (from birth)	$\alpha_2\beta_2$ (major)	HbA_1
	$\alpha_2\delta_2$ (minor)	HbA_2

Role of hemoglobin

Nearly all the oxygen carried by whole blood in animals is bound and transported by hemoglobin in erythrocytes (red blood cells). Its function is to transport oxygen and delivers at the level of the tissues. Hemoglobin able to binds strongly to oxygen and also releases oxygen easily, depending on conditions. In addition to carrying nearly all the oxygen required by cells, hemoglobin carries two end products of cellular respiration—H^+ and CO_2—from the tissues to the lungs and the kidneys, where they are excreted. Hemoglobin performs several parallel biological functions besides its basic function of oxygen and carbon dioxide transport. It performs an important role as a buffer. *Buffers* are aqueous systems that tend to resist changes in pH when small amounts of acid (H^+) or base (OH^-) are added. A **buffer system** consists of a weak acid (the proton donor) and its conjugate base (the proton acceptor). Hemoglobin also transports NO (the ferrous O_2 binding sites in hemoglobin also bind nitric oxide (NO), and an additional NO binding site is present on the β-chains). Hemoglobin acts as a modulator of erythrocyte metabolism and molecular heat transducer also.

Oxygen transport

Oxygen does not dissolve easily in water, so only about 1.5% of inhaled oxygen is dissolved in blood plasma, which is mostly water. About 98.5% of blood oxygen is bound to hemoglobin in red blood cells. One hemoglobin molecule binds four molecules of oxygen, one per heme. Oxygen and hemoglobin bind in an easily reversible reaction to form **oxyhemoglobin**. The reaction between Hb and O_2 is an **oxygenation**, not an **oxidation**. *Oxygenation* is the process by which oxygen molecules bind reversibly to a molecule without changing the oxidation state of the molecule. Iron in Fe^{2+} state binds oxygen molecule reversibly; in the Fe^{3+} state it does not bind oxygen. Molecules such as CO and NO also bind to the heme iron. Hemoglobin exists in two conformations or states – a **tense** or **taut** (T) and a **relaxed** (R) **states**. Oxygen binds with much higher affinity in the R-state. Oxygen binding stabilizes the R-state. T-state is predominant conformation of deoxyHb and stabilized by a greater number of ionic interactions. The binding of oxygen to a hemoglobin subunit in the T-state triggers a change in conformation to the R-state. The binding of first oxygen molecule with deoxy state occurs weakly, because it binds to a subunit in the T-state. Its binding, however, leads to conformational changes that are communicated to adjacent subunits. In effect, the T to R transition occurs more readily in the second subunit once oxygen molecule is bound to the first subunit. The last (fourth) oxygen molecule binds to a heme in a subunit that is already in the R-state, and hence it binds with much higher affinity than the first molecule.

	OxyHb	**DeoxyHb**
Conformation of Hb	R-state	T-state
Absorption spectra at 660 nm	Low	High
Absorption spectra at 940 nm	High	Low
Ionic interactions in globin	Low	High
Heme	Planar	Puckered
pI	6.6 (more acidic)	6.8 (less acidic)

Oxygen-hemoglobin binding curve: Hemoglobin does not exhibit a myoglobin-like *hyperbolic* oxygen-binding curve. Instead, oxygen binding to hemoglobin is described by a **sigmoidal** (S-shaped) **curve**. A sigmoidal binding curve indicates that a protein exhibits a special binding behavior. For hemoglobin, this shape suggests that the binding of oxygen at one site within the hemoglobin tetramer increases the likelihood that oxygen binds at the remaining unoccupied sites. Conversely, the unloading of oxygen at one heme facilitates the unloading of oxygen at the others. This sort of binding behavior is referred to as **cooperative behaviour**, because the binding reactions at individual sites in each hemoglobin molecule are not independent of one another. The binding of the first heme in the hemoglobin molecule with oxygen increases the affinity of the second heme for oxygen and oxygenation of the second increases the affinity of the third, etc., so that the affinity of hemoglobin for the fourth oxygen molecule is many times greater than that for the first.

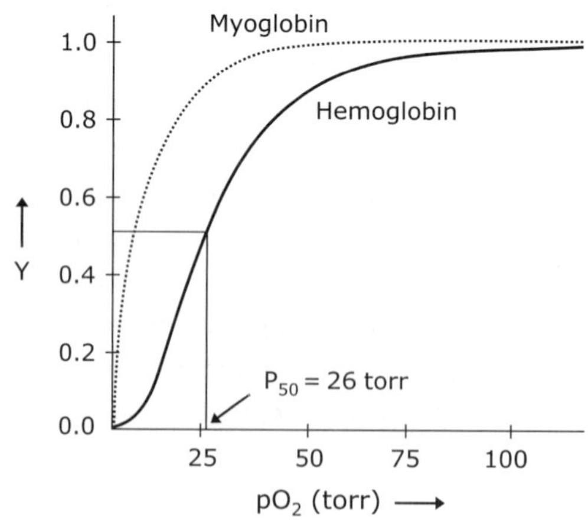

Figure 1.32 Oxygen-binding curve of Mb and Hb. A plot of the fractional saturation of Hb, Y versus the partial pressure of oxygen pO_2, is sigmoidal. The initial slope of the oxygen-Hb binding curve is low, as Hb subunits independently compete for the first oxygen. However, an oxygen molecule bound to one of hemoglobin's subunits increases the oxygen-binding affinity of its other subunits, thereby accounting for the increasing slope of the middle portion of the sigmoidal curve.

Hill equation: The *Hill equation* (developed by Archibald Hill in 1910) quantitatively describing cooperative ligand binding. This equation gives a general approach to the study of cooperative ligand binding to multisubunit proteins. For a single molecule of hemoglobin which binds up to four oxygen molecules, the equilibrium expression will be,

$$Hb + 4O_2 \rightleftharpoons Hb\,(O_2)_4$$

The equation for the fractional saturation of hemoglobin would be, $Y = \dfrac{(pO_2)^4}{(pO_2)^4 + (P_{50})^4}$

After generalizing equation by replacing the exponent 4 by n, we can write, $Y = \dfrac{(pO_2)^n}{(pO_2)^n + (P_{50})^n}$

This is known as a *Hill equation*. It describes the degree of saturation of hemoglobin as a function of pO_2. The parameter n (the **Hill coefficient**) is a measure of the degree of cooperativity in ligand binding.

If $n = 1$, equation describes a hyperbola, as in the case of Mb and oxygen binding reaction is said to be **non-cooperative**.

If $n < 1$, there is **negative cooperativity** (i.e., binding of ligand to one site *decreases* affinity of other site for ligand binding).

If $n > 1$, there is **positive cooperativity** (i.e., binding of ligand to one site *increases* affinity of other site for ligand binding).

The value of $n = 4$ would apply if oxygen binding by hemoglobin were completely cooperative. If the oxygen binding sites on hemoglobin were completely non-cooperative, that is, if the binding of one oxygen to hemoglobin had no influence on the binding of additional oxygen molecules to the same hemoglobin, n would be equal to 1.

The Hill coefficient can be graphically determined by rearranging **Hill equation.** The ratio of the fractional saturation of hemoglobin (Y) to free hemoglobin (1–Y) is related to the pO_2 and P_{50} by following equation:

$$\frac{Y}{1-Y} = \left(\frac{pO_2}{P_{50}}\right)^n$$

Taking the log of both sides yields a linear equation: $\log\left(\dfrac{Y}{1-Y}\right) = n(\log pO_2) - n \log P_{50}$

The linear plot of log Y/(1 – Y) versus log pO_2, the **Hill plot**, has a slope of n. The slope, referred to as the Hill coefficient, is a measure of the cooperativity of oxygen binding. For myoglobin, the plot is linear with a slope of 1. The Hill plot for oxygen binding to hemoglobin is not completely linear since binding is cooperative. However, the plot is approximately linear in the center with a slope of 2.8. The **Hill coefficient**, n, is equal to the slope. For normal human hemoglobin, the Hill coefficient is between 2.8 and 3.0; that is, hemoglobin's oxygen binding is highly cooperative.

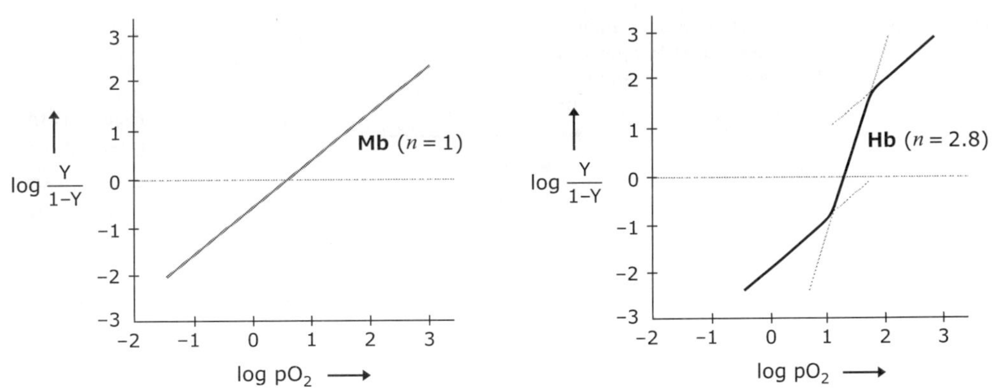

Figure 1.33 *Hill plots* for oxygen binding to Hb. The slope of a Hill plot is denoted by n, the *Hill coefficient*, which is a measure of the degree of cooperativity. If n equals 1, ligand binding is not cooperative, a situation that can arise even in a multisubunit protein if the subunits do not communicate. An n of greater than 1 indicates positive cooperativity in ligand binding. This is the situation observed in Hb, in which the binding of one molecule of oxygen facilitates the binding of others. The maximum degree of cooperativity observed for Hb corresponds approximately to n = 2.8.

Functional differences between Mb and Hb

- Hemoglobin is an allosteric protein, whereas myoglobin is not. An allosteric protein is one in which the binding of a ligand to one site affects the binding properties of another site on the same protein.
- The shape of the oxygen dissociation curve of hemoglobin is sigmoïdal, whereas that of myoglobin is rectangular hyperbolic i.e., myoglobin has a higher affinity for oxygen than does hemoglobin.
- The affinity of hemoglobin for oxygen depends on pH, whereas that of myoglobin is independent of pH.
- The binding of oxygen to hemoglobin is *cooperative* that is, as oxygen is bound to one subunit, the binding to other subunits is facilitated. The degree of cooperativity in the binding reaction is expressed by the *Hill coefficient* (n). For hemoglobin, the value of n is 2.8, whereas for myoglobin it is 1.0.

Factors affecting the affinity of Hb for oxygen

Although pO_2 is the most important factor that determines the percent oxygen saturation of hemoglobin, several other factors influence the tightness or affinity with which hemoglobin binds oxygen. In effect, these factors shift the entire curve either to the left (higher affinity) or to the right (lower affinity). Three important conditions affect the oxygen-hemoglobin dissociation curve are: pH, concentration of 2,3-bisphosphoglycerate (BPG) and temperature.

Effect of pH: Lowering of pH causes the oxygen affinity of the hemoglobin to decrease and shifts the curve to the right. When the curve is shifted in this direction, a higher pO_2 is required for hemoglobin to bind the given amount of O_2. The effect of pH on the oxygen affinity of Hb is known as the **Bohr effect**.

The molecular basis behind the Bohr effect is that the deoxyhemoglobin binds hydrogen ion more readily than the oxyhemoglobin. Under a condition of low pH (high hydrogen ion concentration), the side chain of histidine β146 becomes protonated and the quaternary structure of deoxyhemoglobin is stabilized due to the formation of ionic interaction (salt bridge). At high pH, the side chain of histidine β146 is not protonated. However, no significant change takes place in oxyhemoglobin over the same pH range. The conversion of deoxyhemoglobin to oxyhemoglobin requires the disruption of ionic interactions.

Effect of BPG: BPG is present in the RBCs of human beings and other species. It is a highly charged anion. In deoxygenated state, hemoglobin binds one molecule of BPG in the central cavity formed by its four subunits. BPG forms salt bridges with the terminal amino groups of both β-chains. It stabilizes deoxygenated (T-state) hemoglobin by forming additional salt bridges and therefore reduces the O_2 affinity of hemoglobin (by a factor of 26). It exerts its effect on O_2 affinity of hemoglobin by binding to deoxyhemoglobin but not to oxyhemoglobin. An increase in the concentration of BPG shifts the reaction to the right, causing more O_2 to be liberated.

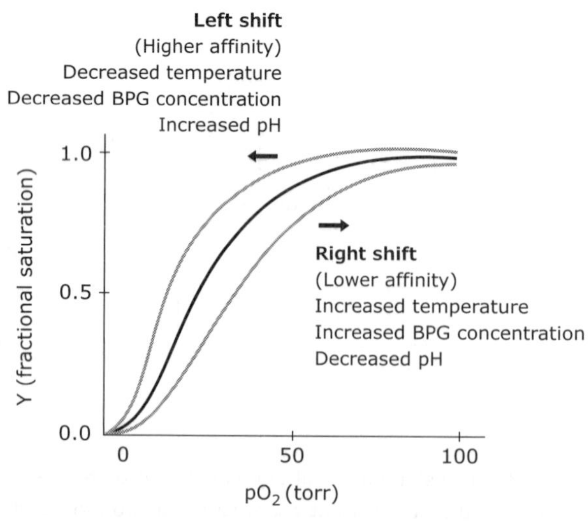

Figure 1.34 Effect of pH, BPG concentration and temperature on the oxygen affinity of hemoglobin. Change in these factors shift the entire oxygen-hemoglobin dissociation curve either to the left (higher affinity) or to the right (lower affinity).

Ascent to high altitude triggers a substantial rise in BPG concentration in red cells, with a consequent increase in the availability of oxygen to tissues. The high altitude-induced increase in BPG causes *decrease in hemoglobin's oxygen affinity*. At sea level, the arterial partial pressure of O_2 is about 100 torr and hemoglobin unloads about 38% of its bound O_2 to the tissues. However, when the arterial partial pressure of O_2 drops to about 55 torr, as it does at an altitude of 4500 m, hemoglobin would be able to unload only about 30% of its bound O_2. High-altitude adaptation has only a small effect on the binding of O_2 in the lungs but a considerable effect on the release of O_2 in the tissues. Although, it decreases the amount of O_2 that hemoglobin can bind in the lungs but, to a greater extent, increases the amount of O_2 it releases at the tissues allows hemoglobin to deliver a near-normal 37% of its bound O_2.

Carbon dioxide transport by Hb

Carbon dioxide CO_2, which is transported in the blood in three main forms: as dissolved CO_2, carbamino compounds and bicarbonate ions. The greatest percentage of CO_2—about 70%—is transported in blood plasma as *bicarbonate ions*. About 23%, transported in the form of *carbamino* compounds. CO_2 combines with the hemoglobin and forms **carbaminohemoglobin**. It combines with the amino groups of N-terminal amino acids of α- and β-globin chains to form carbamino acids.

Hemoglobin related disorders

Hemoglobin related disorders (also known as **hemoglobinopathies**) can be broadly classified into two general categories: First, those in which there is a *quantitative* defect in the synthesis of the globin polypeptide chains, either total absence or marked reduction. Second, those in which there is a *structural* defect in the globin polypeptide chains.

Disease associated with Hb
- → **Due to change in structure of Hb** → *Example*: **Sickle-cell anemia**
- → **Due to change in quantity of Hb** → *Example*: **Thalassaemia**

Sickle-cell hemoglobin and **Sickle-cell anemia**: **HbA** consists of two normal α and two normal β-chains ($\alpha_2^N \beta_2^N$). **Sickle-cell hemoglobin** (**HbS**) also contains two α and two β-chains but there is a single amino acid substitution in the β-chain. Replacement of the *glutamate* residue at sixth position in the β-chain by a *valine* residue is the only chemical difference between HbA and HbS. This residue is present on the surface of the Hb molecule. The change produces a sticky hydrophobic spot on the surface that results in abnormal quaternary association of Hb. This makes the deoxyHbS less water soluble than deoxyHbA. Insoluble deoxyHbS forms polymers that aggregate into tubular fibers. The formation of insoluble deoxyHbS fibers distorts the RBC into the elongated sickle shape structure (**sickle-shaped RBCs**). Two major effects result from the development of sickle-shaped RBCs: **Vascular blockage** (vaso-occlusion) – Rigid, sickle-shaped cells tend to clog the narrow lumen of capillaries, obstructing blood flow. This leads to reduced oxygen delivery to tissues. **Reduced RBC lifespan** (hemolytic anemia) – Sickle-shaped RBCs are fragile and undergo accelerated destruction due to mechanical stress and damage to their plasma membrane. Their average lifespan is reduced to about 20 days (compared to the normal ~120 days), leading to **chronic hemolytic anemia.**

				1	2	3	4	5	6	7	
HbA →	$\alpha_2^N \beta_2^N$ →	β^N globin →	N	Val	His	Leu	Thr	Pro	**Glu**	Glu	……C
HbS →	$\alpha_2^N \beta_2^S$ →	β^S globin →	N	Val	His	Leu	Thr	Pro	**Val**	Glu	……C

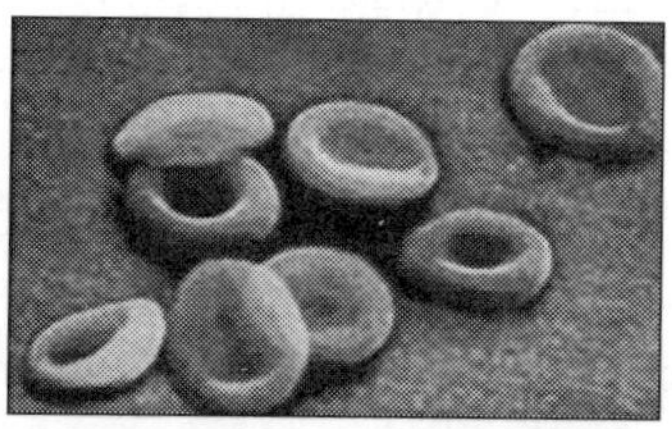

Normal red blood cells

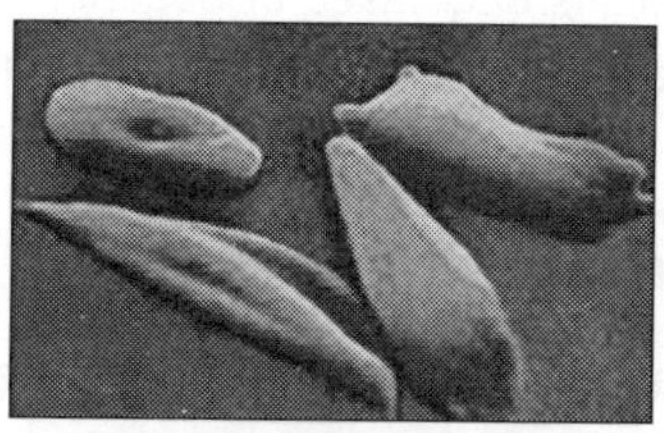

Sickled red blood cells

Box 1.3 HbA1c

Diabetes is characterized by chronic hyperglycemia. Analysis of **glycohemoglobin** (also known as **glycated hemoglobin**) in blood provides evidence of an individual's average blood glucose levels over the last two to three months. Thus, glycated hemoglobin offers a reliable measure of chronic hyperglycemia. Within the cell, proteins can undergo **glycosylation** through enzyme-catalyzed reactions and **glycation** through non-enzymatic reactions. In erythrocytes, glycation of hemoglobin occurs as a post-translational process when glucose enters the cell via a glucose transporter. In this process, glucose covalently attaches to the α-amino group of **valine** at the N-terminal of the β-chain of hemoglobin non-enzymatically. This process forms a Schiff base, resulting in the creation of a stable **Amadori product**, known as **HbA1c**. It is important to note that the clinical measurement of HbA1c is specific to the glycation of *N*-terminal valine of β-chains, although the ε-amino group of *lysine* residues on the β-chains also undergoes glycation. Due to the continuous, gradual, and irreversible nature of the non-enzymatic reaction leading to the formation of glycated hemoglobin, the concentration of HbA1c is primarily influenced by long-term blood glucose levels. HbA1c forms slowly during the 120-day lifespan of erythrocytes, and its concentration is higher in older red cells. The amount of HbA1c formed is directly proportional to the glucose concentration in the cell, and this reaction is faster in diabetics due to higher glucose concentration.

Sickle cell hemoglobin (HbS) is responsible for **sickle cell disease**, an autosomal genetic disorder. It causes deformation in RBCs, resulting in a sickle-shaped structure. **Sickle cell anemia** is the most common type of sickle cell disease, which is an umbrella term that includes a group of diseases resulting from point mutations in the gene encoding the β-polypeptide chains of hemoglobin. There's a distinction between **sickle cell anemia** and **sickle cell trait**. *Sickle-cell trait* occurs when an individual carries one abnormal allele of the β-globin gene (i.e., they are heterozygous, $\beta^N\beta^S$). On the other hand, *sickle cell anemia* arises when a person inherits two copies of the abnormal β-globin gene (i.e., they are homozygous, $\beta^S\beta^S$).

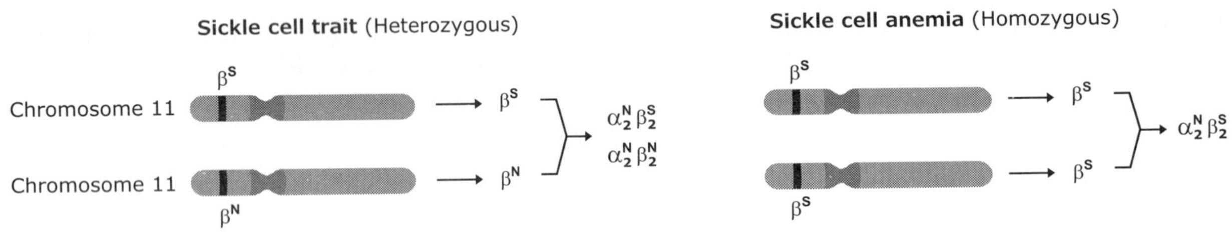

The *sickle cell trait* confers resistance to malaria caused by the mosquito-borne protozoan *Plasmodium falciparum*. How does it do so? Plasmodia increase the acidity of infected erythrocytes by ~0.4 pH units. The lower pH favors the formation of deoxyhemoglobin via the Bohr effect, thereby increasing the likelihood of sickling in RBCs that contain HbS. RBCs damaged by sickling are normally removed from the circulation by the spleen. The parasite enhanced sickling probably allows the spleen to preferentially remove infected RBCs and also parasites.

Thalassemias: The thalassemias are hereditary blood disorders. These result from the defective α or β-globin chains synthesis. There are two main types of thalassemias: α-*thalassemia* and β-*thalassemia*. In **β-thalassemia**, synthesis of β-globin chains is decreased or absent, whereas α-globin chain synthesis is normal. It includes three main forms: β-*thalassemia* major, also referred to as **Cooley's anemia**; β-*thalassemia intermedia* and *thalassemia minor* (also called β-thalassemia carrier *or* β-thalassemia trait *or* heterozygous β-thalassemia). In α-**thalassemia**, synthesis of α-globin chains is decreased or absent. The excess non-α globin chains in α-thalassemia assemble as γ_4 (γγγγ) tetramers (Hb Bart's) in intrauterine life and β_4 (ββββ) tetramers (HbH) after birth.

1.2.6 Behavior of allosteric proteins

Several models have been proposed to explain the behavior of allosteric proteins/enzymes. The **concerted model** proposed by Monod, Wyman and Changeux (**MWC**) and the **sequential model** suggested by Koshland, Nemethy and

Filmer (**KNF**) have been the most popular. Both these models explain the non-hyperbolic kinetics by assuming that the allosteric behavior is manifested by the interaction between subunits in an oligomer. Both the models proposed two distinct conformational states for the subunits. These two conformations differ with respect to their kinetic and ligand binding behavior.

Concerted model: Monod, Wyman and Changeux in 1965, proposed a concerted model to explain the behavior of allosteric proteins and enzymes. This model is based on the following postulates:

1. Allosteric proteins are oligomers composed of an even number of identical subunits.
2. Each monomer in an oligomer can exist in two conformations labeled as T (tense) and R (relaxed).
3. The binding affinities of ligand to these two conformations are different.
4. At any given time, all the monomers in an oligomeric molecule possess the same conformation.

The protein has two conformations, the R-conformation, which binds substrate tightly and the T-conformation, which binds substrate loosely. The distinguishing feature of this model is that the conformation of *all* subunits changes simultaneously. All subunits change conformation from the inactive T-conformation to the active R-conformation at the same time; that is, a concerted change of conformation occurs. The binding of the first molecule of substrate to one subunit facilitates the binding of the second substrate molecule to the other subunit. This is exactly what is meant by cooperative binding. In the absence of substrate, the enzyme exists mainly in the T-form, in equilibrium with small amounts of the R-form. The presence of substrate shifts the equilibrium to produce more of the R-form.

Sequential model: The sequential model proposes that as ligand binds to one subunit, there is a change in the conformation of the subunit, which then induces a conformational change in a contiguous subunit. The effect of ligand binding is sequentially transmitted through the interface between subunits producing increased or decreased affinity for the ligand by contiguous protomers. Hence to begin with the monomers in an oligomer exist in the T-conformation, binding of ligand to the protomer induces a conformational change from T to R and thus the conformation of the protomers in an oligomer changes sequentially to R. As for example when an oxygen molecule binds to a vacant site on one of the four subunits of Hb, the interaction causes the site to change its conformation, which in turn affects the binding constants of the three sites that are still vacant. For this reason, this model is called the *sequential model*. Unlike the *concerted model*, the sequential model can have tetramers that consist of both R- and T-state subunits.

1.3 Protein folding

Protein folding is the physical process by which a polypeptide folds into its characteristic and functional three-dimensional conformation. The correct three-dimensional structure is essential to protein function. Failure to fold into native structure produces inactive proteins. A protein molecule folds spontaneously during or after biosynthesis. However, the process also depends on the nature of solvent, the concentration of salts, the temperature, and the presence of molecular chaperones.

One of the most important experiment, which helped in understanding the process of protein folding was carried out by Christian Anfinsen and colleagues in the early 1960s. C. Anfinsen studied the refolding of protein **ribonuclease A (RNase A)**. RNase A isolated from bovine pancreas is an enzyme that has a molecular mass of 13,700 Da. It contains 124 amino acid residues and four disulfide linkages. In the presence of **urea**, a denaturant, and **β-mercaptoethanol**, a *reducing agent*, ribonuclease is denatured and the disulfide bonds are broken. When the protein is allowed to renature by removing the denaturant and the reductant, the protein regains its native conformation, including four correctly paired disulfide bonds. This finding provided the first evidence that the amino acid sequence of a polypeptide chain contains all the information required to fold the chain into its native three dimensional structure. However, when the reductant is removed while the denaturant is still present, the disulfide bonds are formed again in protein but most of the disulfide bonds are formed between incorrect partners. This indicates that weak interactions are required for correct positioning of disulfide bonds and assumption of the native conformation.

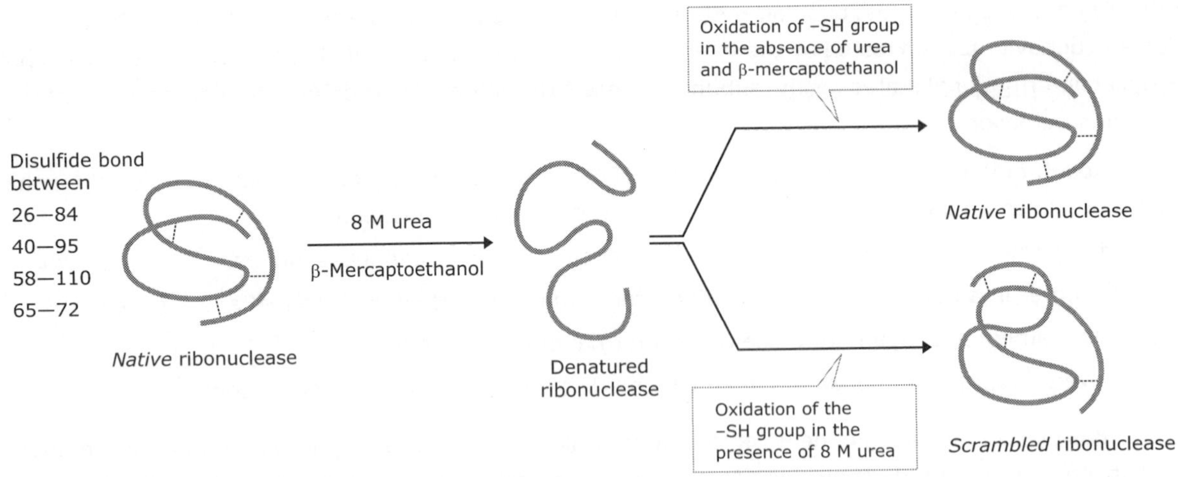

Figure 1.35 Denaturation and renaturation of ribonuclease A (RNase A). Depending on the conditions for renaturation, we obtain either native ribonuclease or scrambled ribonuclease.

The amino acid sequence of a protein determines its native conformation. But, if this is true, how do proteins find the right conformation out of the simply endless number of potential three-dimensional forms that it could randomly fold into? After all, the folding of a protein is not a chemical reaction. The folding pathway of a polypeptide is very complicated, and not all the principles that guide the process have been worked out. However, there are several models to explain folding. According to one model, folding is initiated by a spontaneous collapse of the unfolded polypeptide chain into a partly organized globular state, mediated by hydrophobic interactions among non-polar residues (**hydrophobic collapse**). The collapsed state is referred to as a **molten globule**. This state is clearly different from the native and the denatured state.

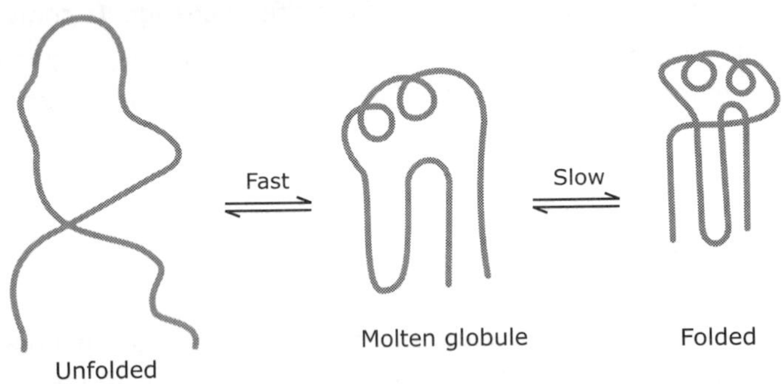

Figure 1.36
The molten globule state is an intermediate state in the folding pathway when a polypeptide chain converts from an unfolded to a folded native state.

The molten globule has most of the secondary structure of the native state but it is less compact and the proper packing interactions in the interior of the protein have not been formed. This event is very fast, usually completes within a few milliseconds. We, therefore, know almost nothing about the process that leads to the molten globule. However, we know some of the properties of this state. As mentioned above the molten globule has most of the secondary structure of the native state. It is less compact than the native structure and lacks the proper packing interactions in the interior of the protein. The interior side chains remain mobile, more closely resembling a liquid than the solid-like interior of the native state.

Folding energetics: The energetics of protein folding determine the three-dimensional structure of a folded protein. It is guided by its transition from a *high-energy state* to a *low-energy state* (a decrease in free energy) and a transition from a *high-entropy state* to a *low-entropy state*. This phenomenon is often visualized as a funnel, wherein the lowest point represents the minimum energy state—the native conformation. Thus, protein folding follows a pathway from high energy and high entropy to low energy and low entropy. This energy–entropy relationship, diagrammed in the figure 1.37, is known as a **folding funnel**. As a protein folds into an ever-decreasing number of possible conformations, its entropy and free energy decrease.

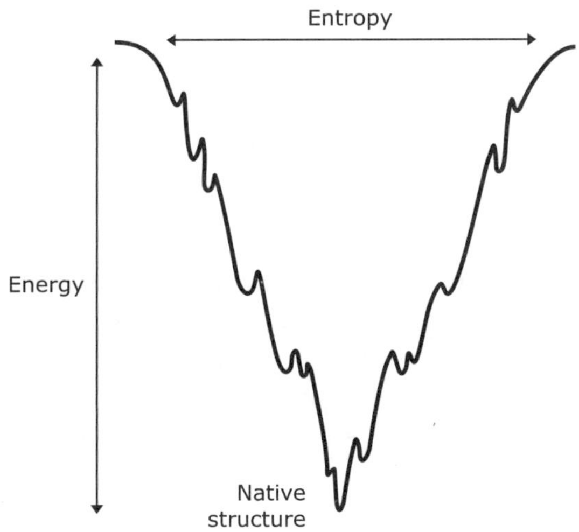

Figure 1.37
Thermodynamically, folding can be conceptualized as a free-energy funnel. Initially, the unfolded states exhibit high conformational entropy and correspondingly high free energy. However, as folding progresses, the funnel narrows, indicating a reduction in the conformational space required to reach the native state. Along the sides of this funnel, there are small depressions representing semi-stable intermediates, which momentarily impede the folding process.

Problem

The enzyme RNase A requires the formation of four disulphide bonds amongst its eight cysteine residues. If this is entirely a random phenomenon, the probability that the first correct disulphide bond will be formed is $1/7$. Following the same logic, what is the probability of formation of all four correct disulphide bonds?

Solution: There are seven possible pairings for the first disulfide bond, five for the second, and three for the third. Therefore, the probability that the correct bonds will form randomly is $1/7 \times 1/5 \times 1/3 = 1/105$.

1.3.1 Molecular chaperones

Not all proteins fold spontaneously after or during synthesis in the cell. Folding of many proteins requires molecular chaperones. A **molecular chaperone** is a protein that interacts with another protein and aids in the folding or assembly without being part of its final structure. Besides their fundamental role in *de novo* protein folding, chaperones are involved in various aspects of proteome maintenance, including assistance in macromolecular complex assembly, protein transport and degradation and aggregate dissociation and refolding of stress-denatured proteins.

The chaperones can be classified functionally into three fundamental classes based on their mode of action: *foldases*, *holdases* and *disaggregases*. **Foldases** are the chaperones that actively refold unfolded proteins. Examples for this class include the Hsp70 and Hsp60 chaperones. **Holdases** are the class of chaperones that are capable of binding the folded intermediates and prevent their aggregation. Examples for this class include the small heat-shock proteins (sHsps) and the co-chaperone Hsp40. The third class of chaperones, **disaggregases** (such as Hsp100 chaperones), primarily acts on the protein aggregates and actively digests the toxic aggregates into small peptide fragments.

Molecular chaperones were first identified in bacteria *E. coli* but are present in both prokaryotes and eukaryotes (ubiquitous). Several molecular chaperones are included among the **heat-shock proteins** (hence their designation as *Hsp*), because they are synthesized in increased amounts after brief exposure of cells to an elevated temperature (for example, 42°C for cells that normally live at 37°C). Chaperones were initially named according to their molecular weight: Hsp60s, Hsp70s, Hsp90s, Hsp100s and the small Hsps. Among many different types of chaperones, there are two major families of molecular chaperones known as the **Hsp60** and **Hsp70** families.

The members of **Hsp70 family** (such as Hsp70, Hsc70 and DnaK) act early in the life of many proteins, binding to a string of about seven hydrophobic amino acids before the protein leaves the ribosome. The Hsp70 is evolutionarily conserved and one of the most abundant chaperones. The Hsp70 polypeptide chain is divided into two functional domains–an N-terminal nucleotide-binding domain and a C-terminal substrate-binding domain connected by a highly conserved hydrophobic linker region. The substrate-binding domain binds to 5-7-residue peptide segments enriched in hydrophobic amino acids and typically flanked by positively charged residues. The substrate-binding domain is an antiparallel C-terminal region. Mammals have two primary classes of Hsp70: **Hsp70** (induced by stress) and **Hsc70** (constitutively expressed in cells). The ATP-dependent reaction cycle of Hsp70 is assisted by co-chaperone **Hsp40** in eukaryotes and **DnaJ** in eubacteria. **Co-chaperones** are proteins that assist chaperones in performing functions.

The Hsp70 chaperones participate in both – **cellular housekeeping functions** (i.e., *de novo* protein folding, protein translocation across membranes, assembly and disassembly of protein complexes, protection from proteolysis) and **stress-related activities** (i.e., protein aggregation prevention, protein refolding, protein degradation).

The **Hsp60 family** (**Hsp60** in eukaryotes and **GroEL** in eubacteria) of molecular chaperones are termed as **chaperonins**. Chaperonins are characterized by large double-ring structures with a central cavity, creating an isolation compartment in which proteins fold and are protected from aggregation. Chaperonins bind unfolded, partly folded and incorrectly folded protein molecules but not protein in their native state. This type of chaperone forms an **isolation chamber** into which misfolded proteins are fed, preventing their aggregation and providing them a favorable environment to refold. The typical structure is a ring of many subunits, forming a cylinder. Hsp60 in mitochondria forms a structure consisting of 14 subunits that are arranged in two heptameric rings stacked on top of each other in an inverted orientation. It functions in association with a **co-chaperonin**.

Chaperonins are of two types based on their phylogenetic distribution and the requirement of *co-chaperonins– group I chaperonins* and *group II chaperonins*. **Group I chaperonins** (includes Hsp60 in mitochondria, Cpn60 in chloroplasts and GroEL in eubacteria) have seven-membered rings and require the co-chaperonin (**GroES** in eubacteria, **Hsp10** in mitochondria and **Cpn10** in chloroplasts). The **group II chaperonins** in archaea and the eukaryotic cytosol usually have eight-membered rings. Their functions are independent of co-chaperonins.

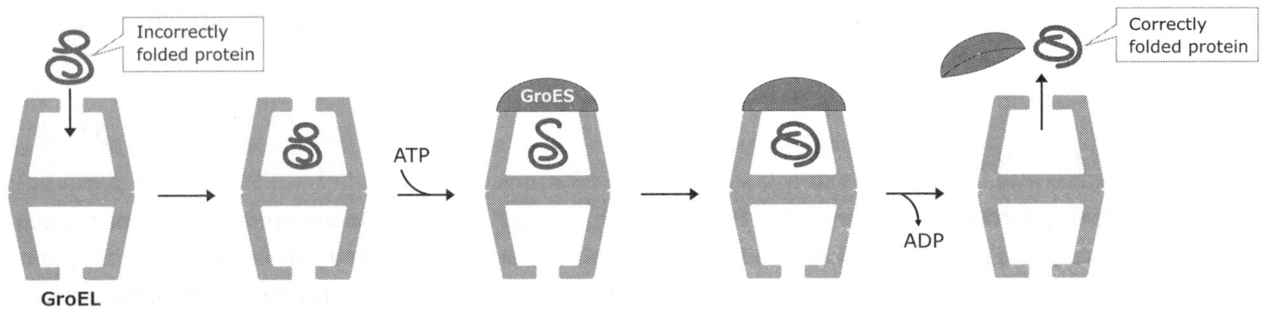

Figure 1.38 The structure and function of the chaperonin, GroEL. A misfolded protein molecule binds to one end of the GroEL. Subsequently, ATP and protein cap (GroES) bind. ATP hydrolysis occurs as the protein is folding or unfolding inside the central cavity. ATP binding and hydrolysis are required for release of GroES and the protein molecule. A new unfolded protein molecule can now bind to GroEL.

1.3.2 Amyloid

Amyloid refers to the abnormal fibrous, extra- as well as intracellular, proteinaceous deposits found in organs and tissues. It is insoluble, very resistant to degradation and is structurally dominated by β-sheet structure. Unlike other fibrous proteins, it does not commonly have a structural role but is associated with the pathology seen in a range of diseases known as the **amyloidoses**. These diseases include Alzheimer's, the spongiform encephalopathies and type II diabetes, all of which are progressive disorders.

Amyloid fibrils are insoluble and heterogeneous. Amino acid composition and sequence analysis of amyloid fibrils revealed that each amyloid disorder was associated with a particular protein or peptide. More than 20 plasma proteins have been identified that form amyloid. Interestingly, despite of the differences in amino acid sequences and native structure, these amyloidogenic peptides all appear to share a common β-sheet conformation of their polypeptide backbone. It is likely that this characteristic feature confers the proteolytic resistant and insoluble nature to all forms of amyloid.

Many proteins can take on the amyloid fibril structure as an alternative to their normal folded conformations. The proteins are secreted in an incompletely folded conformation. The core β-sheet forms before the rest of the protein fold correctly. The β-sheets from two or more incompletely folded protein molecules associate to begin forming an **amyloid fibril**. Additional protein molecules slowly associate with the amyloid and extend it to form a fibril.

1.4 Protein analysis

Protein analysis generally involves the quantification, purification, structural characterization, sequencing, and evaluation of various other properties of proteins in a sample. Some commonly used protein analysis methods are outlined.

Determination of amino acid compositions: Peptide bonds of proteins are hydrolyzed by either strong acid or strong base. In **acid hydrolysis**, the peptide can be hydrolyzed into its constituent amino acids by heating it in 6 M HCl at 110°C for 24 hours. **Base hydrolysis** of polypeptides is carried out in 2 to 4 M NaOH at 100°C for 4 to 8 hours. A mixture of amino acids in hydrolysates can be separated by ion exchange chromatography or by reversed phase HPLC. The identity of the amino acid is revealed by its elution volume and quantified by reaction with **ninhydrin.**

N-terminal analysis: Reagent *1-fluoro-2,4-dinitrobenzene* (**FDNB**) and **dansyl chloride** are used for determination of N-terminal amino acid residue. FDNB reacts in alkaline solution (pH 9.5) with the free amino group of the N-terminal amino acid residue of a peptide to form a characteristic yellow *dinitrophenyl* (DNP) derivative. It can be released from the peptide by either acid or enzymic hydrolysis of the peptide bond and subsequently identified. Sanger first used this reaction to determine the primary structure of the polypeptide hormone insulin. This reagent is often referred to as **Sanger's reagent**.

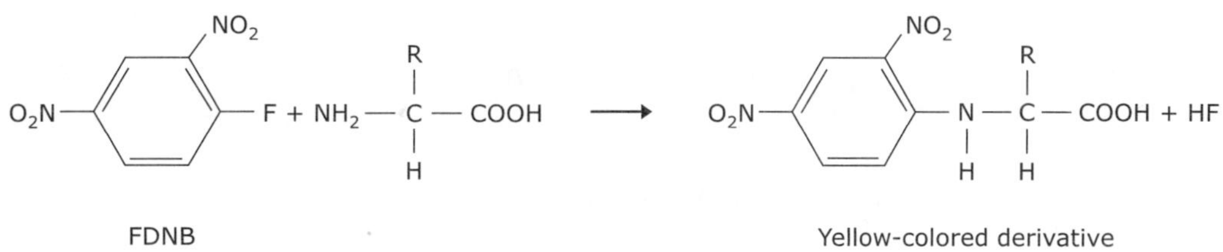

Figure 1.39 FDNB reacts with free amino group to produce dinitrophenyl (DNP) derivative of amino acid.

Similarly, **Dansyl chloride** reacts with a free amino group of the N-terminal amino acid residue of a peptide in alkaline solution to form strongly fluorescent derivatives of free amino acids and N-terminal amino acid residue of peptides.

Peptide sequencing (**Edman degradation method**): Edman degradation method for determining the sequence of amino acids in peptides from their N-terminus was developed by Pehr Edman. This chemical method uses **phenylisothiocyanate** (also termed **Edman reagent**) for sequential removal of amino acid residues from the *N-terminus* of a polypeptide chain.

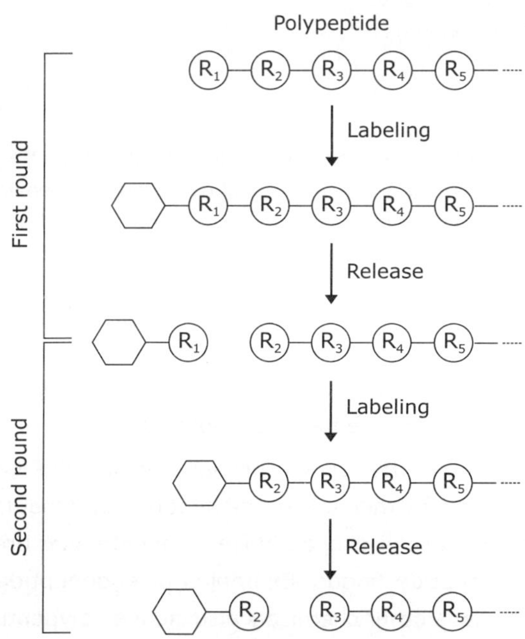

Figure 1.40
Edman degradation sequentially removes one residue at a time from the amino end of a peptide. The labeled amino-terminal residue (R_1) can be released without hydrolyzing the rest of the peptide bonds. Hence, the amino-terminal residue of the shortened peptide (R_2—R_3—R_4—R_5) can be determined in the second round.

Mechanism: Phenylisothiocyanate reacts with N-terminal amino group of polypeptide, under mildly alkaline conditions, to form the phenylthiocarbamyl-peptide derivative (**PTC-peptide**). Then, under acidic condition in the presence of anhydrous trifluoroacetic acid, this derivative of the terminal amino acid is cleaved as a **thiazolinone derivative.** The thiazolinone amino acid is then selectively extracted into an organic solvent and treated with aqueous acid to form the more stable phenylthiohydantoin-amino acid (**PTH-amino acid**) derivative that can be identified by using chromatography or electrophoresis.

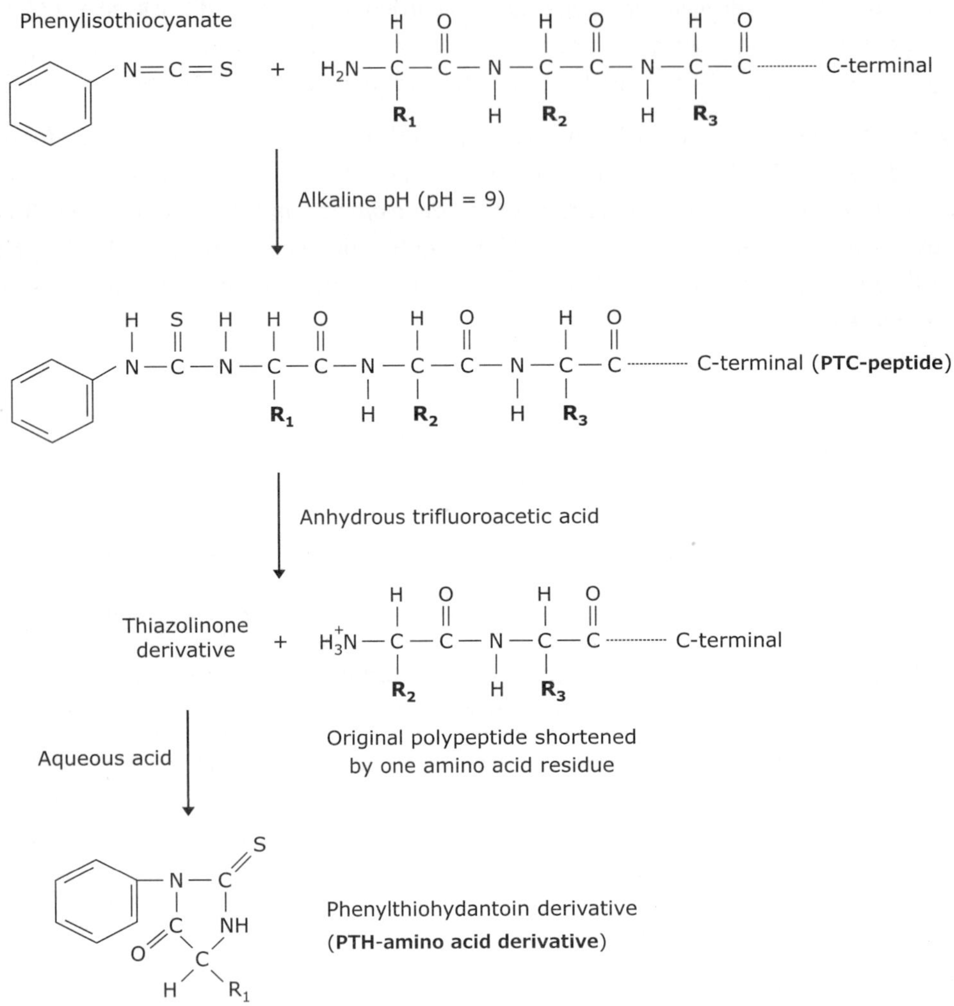

Figure 1.41 The Edman degradation. The Edman degradation sequentially removes one residue at a time from the amino end of a peptide. Phenyl isothiocyanate reacts with the uncharged terminal amino group of the peptide to form a phenylthiocarbamoyl derivative. Then, under mildly acidic conditions, a cyclic derivative of the terminal amino acid is liberated, which leaves an intact peptide shortened by one amino acid. The cyclic compound is a phenylthiohydantoin-amino acid derivative, which can be identified by chromatographic procedures.

Specific cleavage of polypeptides: Sequencing techniques currently in use cannot determine the amino acid sequence of polypeptides with more than about 50 amino acid residues. Thus, it is necessary to cleave large polypeptides into smaller peptides and to determine the amino acid sequences of the peptides individually.

Proteolytic enzymes are most commonly used, especially those that cleave proteins at specific locations. The specificities are determined by the side chains of the amino acid on either side of the peptide bond that is hydrolyzed in the polypeptide chain. Proteolytic enzymes can be endopeptidase or exopeptidase. **Exopeptidases** break terminal peptide bond. In contrast, **endopeptidases** break internal peptide bonds. Examples of endopeptidases include *trypsin*, *chymotrypsin*, *elastase*, *thermolysin* and *pepsin*. Various other chemicals also cleave polypeptide chains at specific locations. The most widely used is **cyanogen bromide** (CNBr), which cleaves peptide bond at C-terminal of Met residues. Similarly, **hydroxylamine** cleaves the polypeptide chain at Asn-Gly sequences.

Table 1.8 Specificities of proteolytic enzymes

Agents	Site of cleavage
Trypsin	Carboxyl side of Lys and Arg, $R_n \neq$ Pro
Chymotrypsin	Carboxyl side of Tyr, Phe and Trp, $R_n \neq$ Pro
Pepsin	Amino side of Tyr, Phe and Trp, $R_{n-1} \neq$ Pro
Elastase	Carboxyl side of Ala, Gly and Ser, $R_n \neq$ Pro
Thermolysin	Amino side of amino acids with bulky hydrophobic side chain like Leu, Ile, Val or Phe

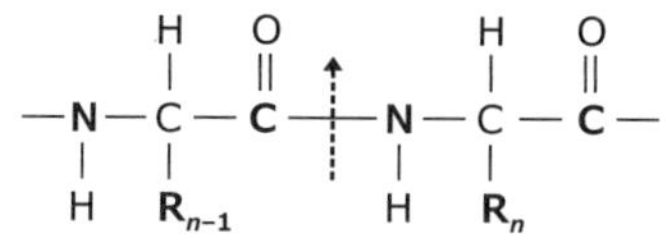

Exopeptidases are proteolytic enzymes that hydrolyze peptide bonds at the terminal ends of polypeptide chains. They differ from endopeptidases, which act within the interior of the chain. Based on the site of action, exopeptidases are classified into *carboxypeptidases* and *aminopeptidases*.

Carboxypeptidases cleave amino acid residues sequentially from the **C-terminal** (**carboxyl end**) of peptides. Most of them are **zinc-dependent metalloproteases**. They are secreted as inactive zymogens and activated in the digestive tract.

Carboxypeptidase A: Removes C-terminal amino acids except *Proline*, *Lysine*, and *Arginine*.

Carboxypeptidase B: Specifically removes basic residues, i.e., *Lysine* or *Arginine* from the *C-terminus*.

Carboxypeptidase C: Acts on any *C-terminal residue* without strong specificity.

Aminopeptidases catalyze the cleavage of amino acids from the **N-terminal** (**amino end**) of polypeptides. **Aminopeptidase M** removes all free N-terminal residues without strong specificity.

Problem

Which of the labeled bonds (a–e) is cleaved by trypsin at pH 7.0?

Lys $\underline{\ a\ }$ Arg $\underline{\ b\ }$ Pro $\underline{\ c\ }$ Lys $\underline{\ d\ }$ Arg $\underline{\ e\ }$ Gly

Solution: Trypsin is an endopeptidase that breaks internal peptide bonds. Hence, it will not cleave peptide bonds at *a* and *e*. Its cleavage site is the carboxyl side of Lys and Arg, but there should be no proline at the carboxyl side. Hence it will not cut at *b*. Thus, only the cleavage site is *d*.

Problem

A peptide was cleaved into two fragments by CNBr and into two different fragments by trypsin. The sequences of the fragments were as follows:

CNBr 1	Gly–Thr–Lys–Ala–Glu
CNBr 2	Ser–Met
Trypsin 1	Ser–Met–Gly–Thr–Lys
Trypsin 2	Ala–Glu

Determine the sequence of the parent peptide.

Solution: By arranging the sequences in an overlapping set, as follows, it is possible to determine the parent sequence:

CNBr 2	Ser–Met
Trypsin 1	Ser–Met–Gly–Thr–Lys–
CNBr 1	Gly–Thr–Lys–Ala–Glu
Trypsin 2	Ala–Glu
	Ser–Met–Gly–Thr–Lys–Ala–Glu

Problem

Enkephalins are naturally occurring opiates (pain relievers). Suppose an enkephalin has the following sequence:

Tyr–Gly–Gly–Phe–Ala–Met

a. What is the net charge of the peptide at: pH 1 and pH 7?
b. Indicate the number of bonds that could be hydrolyzed (if any) by digestion with trypsin, chymotrypsin and CNBr.

Solution:

a. The net charge of the peptide at: pH 1: +1 (N-terminus) and pH 7: 0 (zwitterion)
b. The bonds that could be hydrolyzed (if any) by digestion with:

   Trypsin: None; trypsin cleaves at carboxyl side of basic amino acid residues, Lys and Arg.

   Chymotrypsin: One; Chymotrypsin cleaves at carboxyl side of Phe, Trp, and Tyr.

   CNBr (cyanogen bromide): None; CNBr cleaves at carboxyl side of Met.

Cleavage of disulfide bonds

If protein is made up of two or more polypeptide chains and held together by noncovalent bonds then denaturing agents, such as urea or guanidine hydrochloride, are used to dissociate the chains from one another. But polypeptide chains linked by disulfide bonds can be separated by two common methods. These methods are used to break disulfide bonds and also to prevent their reformation.

Oxidation of disulfide bonds with **performic acid** produces two **cysteic acid** residues. Because these cysteic acid side chains are ionized SO_3^- groups, electrostatic repulsion prevents S-S recombination. The second method involves the reduction by β-*mercaptoethanol* or *dithiothreitol* (**Cleland's reagent**) to form cysteine residues. This reaction is followed by further modification of the reactive –SH groups to prevent reformation of the disulfide bond. Acetylation by iodoacetate serves this purpose which modifies the –SH group.

Protein assays

Protein assays are analytical methods used to determine the concentration of protein in an unknown sample. The simplest and most direct method for proteins in solution is to measure their absorbance at 280 nm in the UV range. This is because aromatic amino acids—primarily **tryptophan** and **tyrosine** (and to a lesser extent **phenylalanine**)—exhibit strong absorption at this wavelength. Because different proteins contain different proportions of aromatic residues, their absorbance at **280 nm** varies. In addition, factors that alter protein conformation—such as buffer composition, pH, or reducing agents—can influence the measured absorbance. As a very rough approximation, 1 A_{280} unit ≈ 1 mg protein/mL, but the actual value can vary significantly depending on the protein's amino acid composition (extinction coefficient).

Proteins also absorb strongly at **205 nm** due to **peptide bonds**, which are present in all proteins. Measurement at 205 nm offers greater sensitivity and less variability between proteins than 280 nm, but it requires buffers and solvents that do not absorb strongly at this wavelength.

In addition to UV absorbance, several **colorimetric, reagent-based protein assays** are widely used. In these methods, protein reacts with a specific reagent to produce a color change proportional to protein concentration. The concentration of the unknown sample is determined by comparing its absorbance to a standard curve generated from known concentrations of a purified reference protein.

Some most commonly used colorimetric, reagent-based methods are:

Biuret method: Based on the formation of a violet-colored complex between cupric ions in alkaline solution and peptide bonds of proteins. This method is not highly sensitive since the complex does not have a high extinction coefficient.

Folin method (or **Lowry method**): This method combines the **Biuret reaction** with the **Folin-Ciocalteu reaction** for enhanced sensitivity:

Biuret reaction: Under alkaline conditions, cupric ions form a complex with peptide bonds of proteins.

Folin-Ciocalteu reaction: The phosphomolybdate–phosphotungstate reagent (Folin–Ciocalteu) is reduced by certain amino acid side chains (especially tyrosine, tryptophan, and sometimes cysteine) in the cupric–peptide complex. This reduction produces a blue-colored complex whose intensity is proportional to protein concentration.

Bradford method: Based on binding of **Coomassie Brilliant Blue** dye to proteins. The dye interacts primarily with basic amino acid residues (especially lysine, arginine, and histidine) through electrostatic attraction, and also with aromatic residues via hydrophobic interactions. Upon binding to protein, the dye undergoes a shift from its red (cationic form) to blue (anionic form), with the intensity of the blue color proportional to the protein concentration.

Ninhydrin test: The Ninhydrin test is a qualitative and quantitative assay for detecting free α-amino groups in amino acids, peptides, or proteins. **Ninhydrin** (*triketohydrindene hydrate*) reacts with α-amino group of the amino acids and proteins. Ninhydrin is a strong oxidizing agent and in its presence, amino acids undergo oxidative deamination liberating ammonia, CO_2, a corresponding aldehyde and reduced form of ninhydrin.

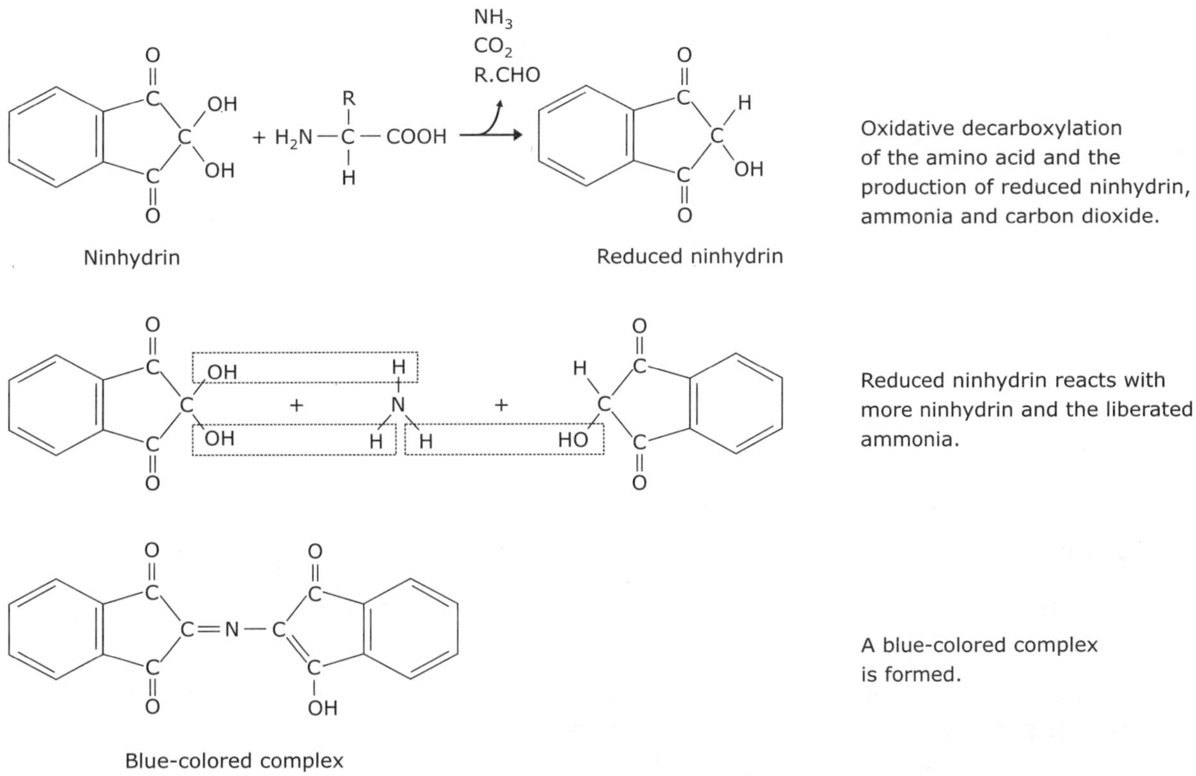

Figure 1.42 Ninhydrin test. A color reaction given by amino acids and peptides on heating with ninhydrin. Amino acids treated with ninhydrin give an intense blue color, except for proline, which gives a yellow color because it contains a secondary amino group.

Ammonia formed from α-amino group reacts with ninhydrin and its reduced product (hydrindantin) to give a blue substance called **diketohydrin** (*Ruhemann's purple*) that absorbs light at 570 nm. Proline gives a yellow color as it lacks an α-amino group. The molar absorption coefficient of the colored product can be used in the quantification of individual amino acids but this value varies from one amino acid to another. This is used for both qualitative and quantitative identification of particular amino acids.

Purification of proteins

The basic aim of purification of protein is to isolate the particular protein of interest from the mixture of proteins. Different features of proteins such as solubilities, size, charge, adsorption properties are utilized during purification process. The main separation methods used in purifying proteins based on the characteristic properties are as follows:

Properties	Method
Size or mass	Centrifugation, Gel filtration, Dialysis and ultrafiltration, Gel electrophoresis
Charge	Ion-exchange chromatography, Electrophoresis, Isoelectric focusing
Solubility	Change in pH, Change in ionic strength, Decrease in dielectric constant
Specific binding	Affinity chromatography

When scientists want to isolate a single protein from a mixture, they use several separation steps, each targeting a different property of the protein (like size, charge, etc.). After each step, they test the sample to see how pure the protein is. For enzymes (catalytic proteins), the test is usually based on the chemical reaction the enzyme normally performs in the cell. To check how well the purification is going, scientists measure something called specific activity at each step. There is a difference between activity and specific activity. The term **activity** refers to the total amount of enzyme in the sample (how much reaction it can do), whereas **specific activity** means how much enzyme activity there is per milligram of total protein.

As purification continues, specific activity increases because more of the unwanted proteins are removed, leaving mostly the enzyme. When the enzyme is completely pure, specific activity becomes constant. If the protein being purified is not an enzyme, different methods are used to measure how pure it is.

Problem

Find out of the specific activity and purification level in the table given below:

Purification procedure	Total protein (mg)	Total activity (units)
1. Crude extract*	20000	4000000
2. Salt precipitation	5000	3000000
3. DEAE-cellulose chromatography	1500	1000000
4. Size-exclusion chromatography	500	750000
5. Affinity chromatography	45	675000

* *The cells are broken open and the protein released into a solution called a crude extract.*

Solution: *Specific activity* is obtained by dividing total activity by total protein.

Purification level is a measure of the increase in purity and is obtained by dividing the specific activity, calculated after each purification step, by the specific activity of the initial extract.

Purification procedure	Total protein (mg)	Total activity (units)	Specific activity (units/mg)	Purification level
1. Crude extract	20000	4000000	200	1
2. Salt precipitation	5000	3000000	600	3
3. DEAE-cellulose chromatography	1500	1000000	667	3.3
4. Size-exclusion chromatography	500	750000	1500	7.5
5. Affinity chromatography	45	675000	15000	75

1.5 Nucleic acids

Nucleic acids, also referred to as **polynucleotides**, are polymers of nucleotides. Friedrich Meischer first identified nucleic acid as an acidic substance present in the nuclei of leukocytes obtained from surgical bandages in 1869. He named this molecule '**nuclein**,' later identified as a nucleoprotein. In 1889, Richard Altman succeeded in isolating the first protein-free material, which he termed '**nucleic acid**.' Nucleic acids are present in all living organisms, whether cellular or non-cellular. They play a fundamental role in storing and transmitting genetic information. There are two types of nucleic acids: ribonucleic acid (**RNA**) and deoxyribonucleic acid (**DNA**).

1.5.1 Nucleotides

The monomeric units of nucleic acids are called *nucleotides*. Nucleotides are *phosphate esters of nucleosides* and are made up of three components: 1. a nitrogenous base, 2. a five-carbon sugar and 3. an ion of phosphoric acid

Nitrogenous bases

Nitrogenous bases are heterocyclic structures, consisting of rings made up of carbon and nitrogen atoms. They possess a planar shape and are relatively water-insoluble aromatic compounds. There are two general types of nitrogenous bases found in both DNA and RNA: **purines** and **pyrimidines**. *Purines* consist of **9-membered rings,** whereas *pyrimidines* have **6-membered rings**.

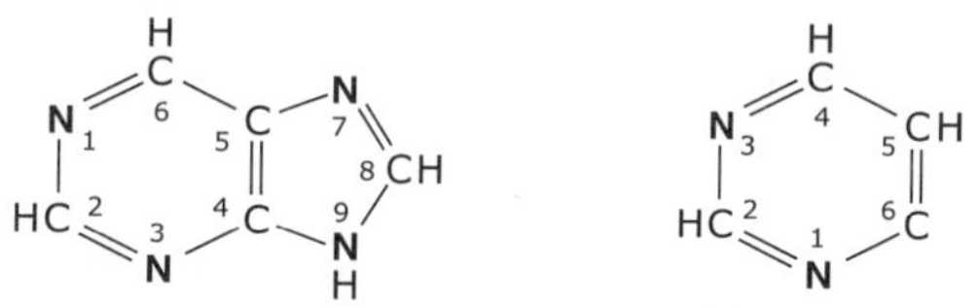

Purine **Pyrimidine**

The purines present in both DNA and RNA are **adenine** (6-aminopurine) and **guanine** (6-oxy-2-aminopurine). *Adenine* possesses an amino group ($-NH_2$) at the 6th position of the ring, while *guanine* has an amino group at the 2nd position and a carbonyl group at the 6th position.

The pyrimidines found in DNA and RNA include **thymine** (5-methyl-2,4-dioxypyrimidine), **cytosine** (2-oxy-4-aminopyrimidine), and **uracil** (2,4-dioxypyrimidine). In DNA, the pyrimidine bases consist of thymine and cytosine, while in RNA, they are uracil and cytosine. Thymine contains a *methyl group* at the 5th position with *carbonyl groups* at the 2nd and 4th positions. Cytosine contains a hydrogen atom at the 5th position and an *amino group* at 4th position. Uracil is similar to thymine but lacks the *methyl group* at the 5th position.

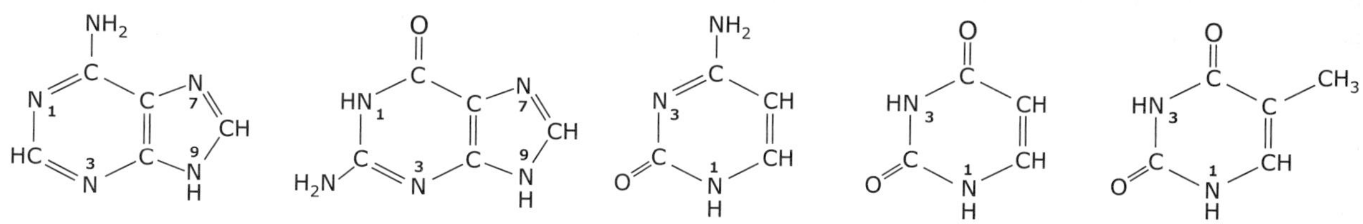

Adenine **Guanine** **Cytosine** **Uracil** **Thymine**

Sugars

The sugars present in nucleotides are **aldopentoses** with cyclic structures similar to **furan rings**. They have a β-anomeric configuration and a **non-planar** structure. They are *chiral* molecules with D-absolute configuration and are **optically active**, meaning they can rotate the plane of polarized light. These sugars are **polar molecules** with a dipole moment that is not zero and are water-soluble *hydrophilic molecules*. Naturally occurring nucleic acids have two types of pentose sugars: *ribose* and *deoxyribose sugar*.

Ribose sugar *is found in RNA*. It is a five carbon monosaccharide with a hydroxyl group (–OH) on each carbon.

Deoxyribose sugar *is found in DNA*. It is a five carbon monosaccharide, lacking one oxygen atom at 2′ position. The hydroxyl group (–OH) at 2′ position of ribose sugar is replaced by a hydrogen (–H).

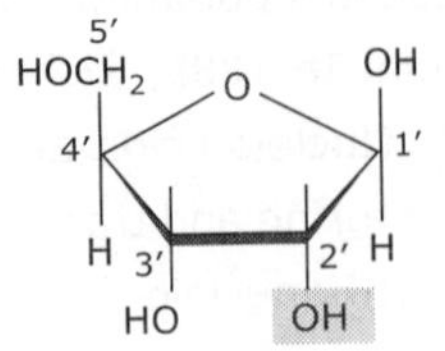

β-D-Ribose

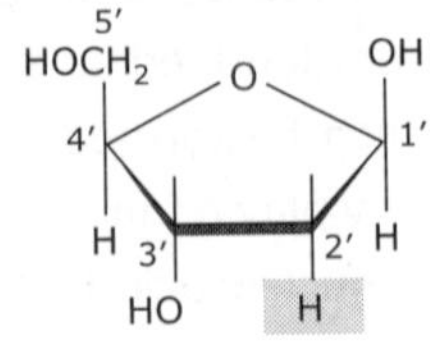

β-D-2-Deoxyribose

The carbon atoms of the ribose and deoxyribose present in nucleotides are designated with a prime (′) mark to distinguish them from the backbone numbering in the nitrogenous bases. Unprimed numbers refer to the atoms of the nitrogenous base.

The **furanose ring** of ribose or deoxyribose pentose sugar is *non-planar*. This non-planarity is termed **puckering**. The five-member furanose ring can be puckered in two basic conformations: *envelope* and *twisted*. In the **envelope form**, the four members of the furanose ring are coplanar (i.e., in the same plane) and the fifth is away from the plane. In **twisted form**, three members are coplanar and the other two lie away from the plane.

In the *envelope form* of ribose or deoxyribose sugar, the out-of-plane atom is almost always C2′ or C3′. The sugar pucker can be *endo* or *exo*. A pucker that places the C2′ or C3′ carbon atom on the same side as the base (or C5′) is termed **endo**, whereas if it places it on the opposite side of the base, it is termed **exo**. The two general classes of sugar puckers commonly seen in nucleic acids are the C2′-endo and C3′-endo puckers. These two different puckers have profound effects on the overall nucleic acid conformation. The nature of sugar puckers depends on the *type of nucleic acid* (such as dsDNA or dsRNA or DNA-RNA hybrid) and the *conformation of the nucleic acid* (such as A-DNA, B-DNA, and Z-DNA). In dsRNA, we predominantly find the C3′-endo sugar pucker. In dsDNA, it can be predominantly C3′-endo (in **A-DNA**) or C2′-endo (in **B-DNA**) or both (in **Z-DNA**). In DNA-RNA hybrids, we predominantly find C3′-endo.

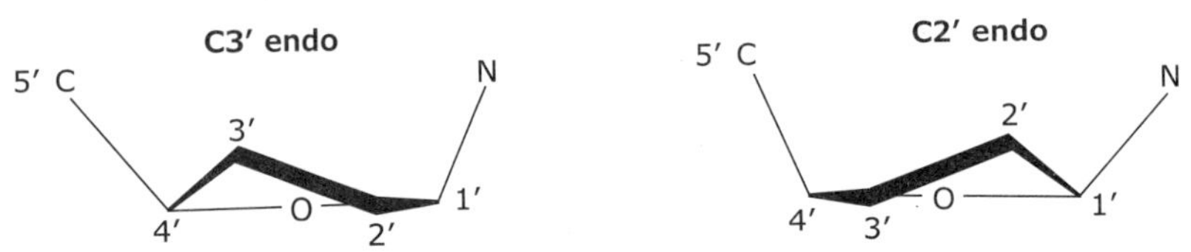

Figure 1.43 Sugar puckers. In the *envelope form* (four members of the furanose ring are in a plane and the fifth is away from the plane) of ribose or deoxyribose sugar, the out-of-plane atom is almost always C2′ or C3′. 'Endo' indicates that the displaced atom is on the same side of the ring as C5′, whereas 'exo' indicates displacement toward the opposite side of the ring from C5′. In the C3′-endo conformation, C3′ is displaced to the same side of the ring as C5′ and in C2′-endo conformation, C2′ is displaced to the same side of the ring as C5′.

Nucleoside

Sugar and nitrogenous base join to form *nucleoside*. The bond between the sugar and the base is called the ***N*-glycosidic bond**. The nitrogenous base lies above the plane of the sugar when the structure is written in the standard orientation; that is, the configuration of the *N*-glycosidic linkage is β.

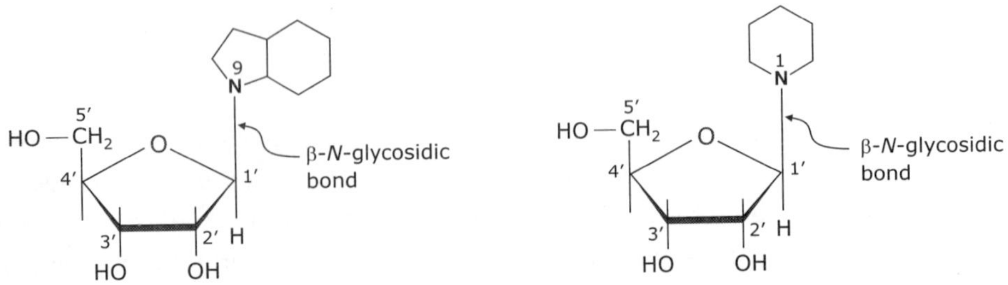

Figure 1.44 Structure of nucleoside.

The base is free to rotate around the glycosidic bond. Due to rotation of the glycosidic bond, two different conformations are possible. The two standard conformations of the base around the glycosidic bond are **syn** and **anti**. Pyrimidines tend to adopt the *anti* conformation almost exclusively, because of steric interference between O2 and C5′ in the *syn*-conformation, whereas purines are able to assume both *syn* (the purine ring is above the sugar) and *anti* (the purine ring is not above the sugar).

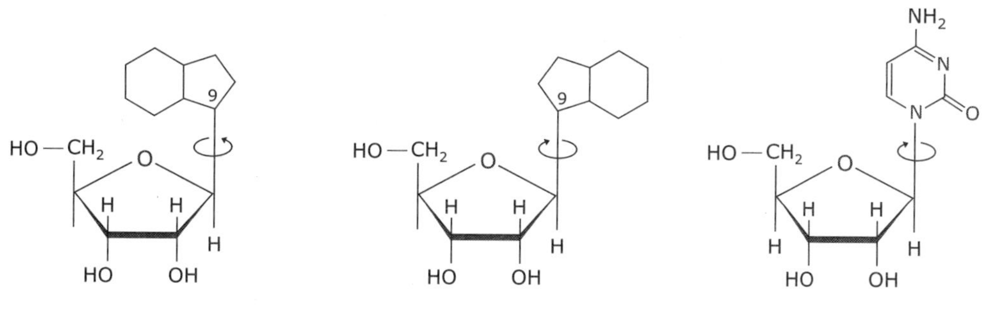

Nucleotide

The nucleotides are phosphoric acid esters of nucleosides, with phosphate at position C-5′. A nucleotide can, therefore, be called a **nucleoside-5′-phosphate**. The nucleotide can have one, two, or three phosphate groups at the C-5′ position and are called nucleoside monophosphates, diphosphates and triphosphates. In ribonucleotides, the pentose is ribose, while in deoxyribonucleotides, the sugar is 2′-deoxyribose.

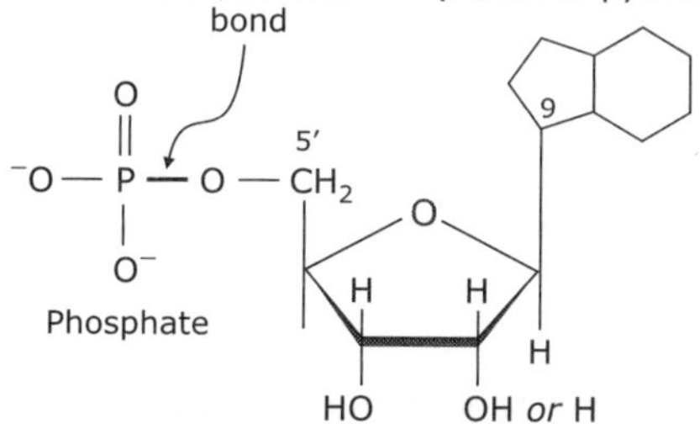

Figure 1.45
Structure of a nucleotide. A nucleotide consists of a nitrogenous base, a ribose or deoxyribose sugar, and one or more phosphate groups.

Function of nucleotides

Nucleotides are primarily responsible for the formation of polynucleotides (nucleic acids) of the cell - RNA and DNA. Polynucleotides are informational macromolecules. They store, transmit and translate genetic information. However, they also act as precursors for many important compounds that participate in a wide variety of metabolic processes. These functions include:

- Formation of **energy currency** like ATP, GTP.
- Act as a precursor for several important **coenzymes** such as NAD^+, $NADP^+$, FAD and coenzyme A.
- Serving as a precursor for **secondary messengers** like cyclic AMP (cAMP), cGMP.

ATP is the chemical link between catabolism and anabolism. It is the energy currency of the living cells. It acts as a donor of either *phosphate* or *pyrophosphate group*. ATP consists of an *adenosine* moiety to which three *phosphoryl groups* ($—PO_3^{2-}$) are sequentially linked via a **phosphoester bond** followed by two **phosphoanhydride bonds**, referred to as a 'high energy' bond. The respective phosphate groups are designated by the Greek letters α, β and γ, starting with the phosphate linked directly to the pentose sugar.

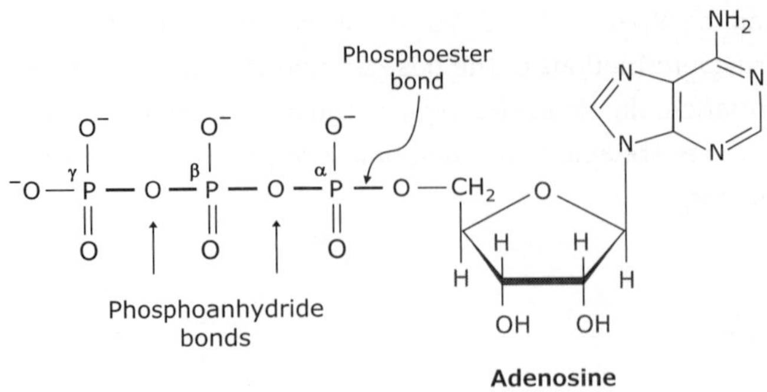

Figure 1.46 Structure of ATP indicating phosphoester and phosphoanhydride bonds. The structure of ATP is a nucleoside triphosphate, consisting of a nitrogenous base (adenine), a ribose sugar, and three serially bonded phosphate groups.

Table 1.9 Naming nucleosides and nucleotides

	Bases			
	Purines		**Pyrimidines**	
	Adenine (A)	Guanine (G)	Cytosine (C)	Uracil (U)/Thymine (T)
Nucleosides–in RNA in DNA	Adenosine Deoxyadenosine	Guanosine Deoxyguanosine	Cytidine Deoxycytidine	Uridine Deoxythymidine
Nucleotides– in RNA in DNA	Adenylate Deoxyadenylate	Guanylate Deoxyguanylate	Cytidylate Deoxycytidylate	Uridylate Deoxythymidylate
Nucleoside monophosphate	AMP	GMP	CMP	UMP/TMP
Nucleoside diphosphate	ADP	GDP	CDP	UDP/TDP
Nucleoside triphosphate	ATP	GTP	CTP	UTP/TTP

Polynucleotides

Polynucleotides are polymers of nucleotides formed by the condensation of *nucleotides*. This condensation reaction occurs between the 5′-phosphate group of one nucleotide and the 3′-hydroxyl group of a second nucleotide, resulting in the elimination of a water molecule. The linkage between two nucleotides is known as a **phosphodiester bond.** Each nucleotide that becomes a part of the polynucleotide is referred to as a **nucleotide residue.** The phosphates of polynucleotides are acidic, so at physiological pH, polynucleotides are **polyanions**. When forming phosphodiester bonds in polynucleotides, directionality is observed. By convention, the sequence of nucleotide residues in a polynucleotide is written from the 5′ end to the 3′ end, reading from left to right (e.g., 5′–pGpApTpC–3′). All nucleotides within a polynucleotide have the same relative orientation.

The order in which nucleotides occur in a polynucleotide describes its **primary structure**. The interchain or intrachain base-pairing of complementary nucleotides gives rise to the **secondary structure** of a nucleic acid. The three-dimensional arrangement of the nucleic acid, describing the molecule's spatial organization, is referred to as the **tertiary structure** of a nucleic acid.

Torsion angles that determine the conformation of a nucleotide residue in a polynucleotide: The conformation of a nucleotide in a polynucleotide chain defined by a set of torsion angles. These angles describe the rotations around specific bonds in the sugar-phosphate backbone and between the sugar and base. There are six backbone torsion angles and one glycosidic torsion angle.

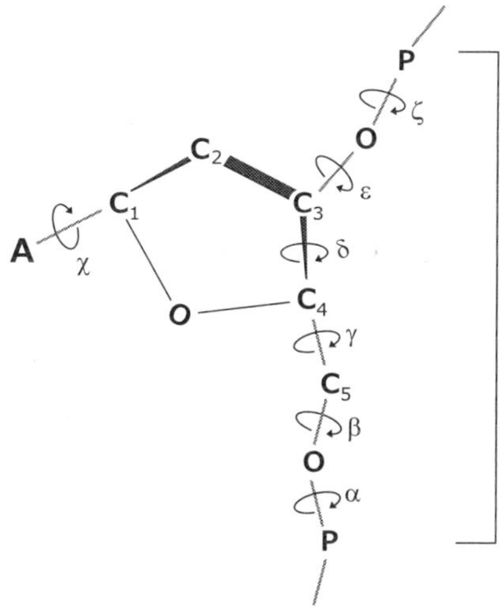

Alpha [α]	Atoms involved: O3'–**P**–**O5'**–C5′
Beta [β]	Atoms involved: P–**O5'**–**C5'**–C4′
Gamma [γ]	Atoms involved: O5'–**C5'**–**C4'**–C3′
Delta [δ]	Atoms involved: C5'–**C4'**–**C3'**–O3'
Epsilon [ε]	Atoms involved: C4'–**C3'**–**O3'**–P
Zeta [ζ]	Atoms involved: C3'–**O3'**–**P**–O5'
Chi [χ]	Rotation about the glycosidic bond linking the base to the sugar

Figure 1.47 The conformation of each nucleotide in a polynucleotide chain is governed by seven key torsion angles. These describe the rotation about specific backbone bonds and the glycosidic bond to the base.

1.5.2 Chargaff's rules

Erwin Chargaff, an Austrian biochemist, studied the base composition of DNA from a variety of sources after developing a new paper chromatography method for separating the products of hydrolysis of DNA and quantifying their relative abundance by ultraviolet spectrophotometers. Eventually, Chargaff summarized his findings on the chemistry of nucleic acids in a review in 1950. These quantitative relationships sometimes called **Chargaff's rules**. These rules played an important role in the discovery of the double helix structure of DNA.

- The base composition of DNA varies from one species to another.
- DNA isolated from different tissues of the same species have the same base composition.
- In a double-stranded DNA, the number of guanine units equals the number of cytosine units and the number of adenine units equals the number of thymine units i.e., %A = %T and %C = %G (**Chargaff's first parity rule**).
- Chargaff's first parity rule also applies, to a close approximation, to single-stranded DNA. In a single strand of a double-stranded DNA, %A ~ %T and %C ~ %G. That is if the individual strands of a dsDNA are isolated and their base compositions determined, then %A ~ %T, and %C ~ %G (**Chargaff's second parity rule**).

Chargaff's first parity rule is a property of double-stranded DNA which states that the number of A and T nucleotides, and the number of C and G nucleotides, are the same within the duplex. It arises as a result of the chemistry of dsDNA which only permits A to pair with T and C to pair with G. In contrast, Chargaff's second parity rule asserts that the same is also true within a single strand. However, unlike the first parity rule, the second is not exact but this rule has been a puzzle in molecular biology as exact reasons are still not clear. In dsDNA

1. The molar ratio of A to T equals to 1. Similarly, the molar ratio of G to C equals to 1.
2. The sum of the purines (A and G) equals that of the pyrimidines (C and T).
3. The percentage of C + G does not necessarily equal the percentage of A + T.

Problem

What would be the charge carried by **A**p**G**p**U**p**C** at neutral pH?

Solution: The tetranucleotide contains four phosphates. First phosphate contains two negative charges and the rest contains one negative charge. Thus, the total charge would be –5.

Problem

Cells were obtained from a patient with a viral infection. The DNA extracted from these cells consisted of two forms: human dsDNA and viral ssDNA. The base compositions of these two forms of DNA were as followed:

	A	C	G	T
Form 1	22.1%	27.9%	27.9%	22.1%
Form 2	31.3%	31.3%	18.7%	18.7%

Which form was the viral DNA, and which form was the human DNA? Explain your reasoning.

Solution: The single-stranded viral DNA does not have a complementary base-pairing and so one would not expect the viral DNA to follow the Chargaff's rule of base-pairing. That being the case, *Form 2* would be the viral DNA because the adenine and thymine are not present in equal proportions and the cytosine and guanine are not in equal proportions. In *Form 1*, the adenine and thymine are in equal proportions indicating that they are base-paired and the cytosine and guanine are in equal proportions indicating that they are base-paired. Therefore *Form 1* is human DNA.

Problem

A sample of purified DNA obtained from tobacco leaf contains 20.0 mole percent of cytosine. Assuming that only the four principal bases are present; calculate the approximate mole percent of purine residues in this DNA.

Solution: Adenine and guanine are the purine residues in DNA, the number of cytosine residues in dsDNA is equal to the number of guanine residues. Then, C = G = 20%. Similarly, the number of thymine residues is equal to the number of adenine residues, and the sum of purine and pyrimidine residues equal to 100 percent. Therefore,

$$(A + G) + (T + C) = 100\%$$

$$(A + 20.0) + (T + 20.0) = 100\%$$

$$(A + 20.0) + (A + 20.0) = 100\%$$

$$2A = 100\% - 40\%. \text{ Hence, } A = 30\%$$

Thus, the mole percent of purines (adenine plus guanine) present in the DNA sample is 50 percent.

1.6 Structure of dsDNA

James Watson and Francis Crick, working in the Cavendish Laboratory at Cambridge University in 1953, took advantage of Chargaff's findings and the X-ray diffraction data of DNA fibers obtained by Rosalind Franklin and Maurice Wilkins described the structure of the DNA double helix. An X-ray diffraction data of a DNA fiber provided evidence about the helical nature of a DNA molecule.

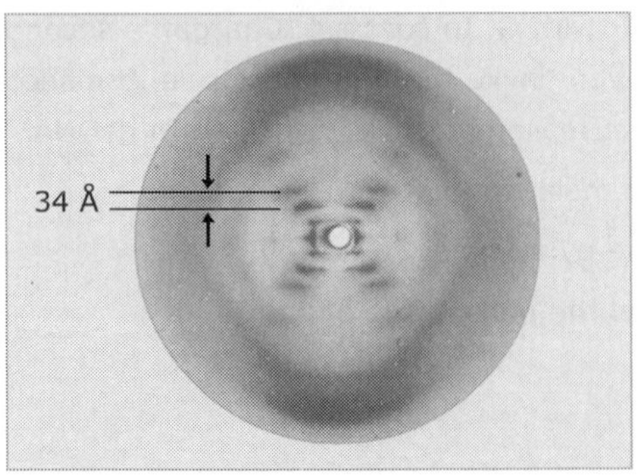

Figure 1.48
X-ray diffraction data of DNA fibers produced by Rosalind Franklin. The appearance of the pattern is characteristic of diffraction from a helix, while the location of the smears and spots give some of the helix dimensions.

Watson, *Crick* and *Wilkins* were awarded the 1962 Nobel Prize for Medicine for discovering the molecular structure of DNA. R. Franklin died of cancer before the Nobel prize was awarded. Nobel Prizes are not awarded posthumously. The *Watson-Crick* **double helix structure** describes the features of the **B-form** of DNA. However, there are many other forms or conformations of DNA (such as **A-**, **C-**, **Z-forms**), which are very distinct from the B-form. The form that DNA would adopt depends on several **intrinsic factors** such as types of nucleic acids (for example dsDNA or ds RNA), sequence of base pairs, chemical modifications of the bases, and **extrinsic factors** such as pH and ionic strength of solution. For example, under physiological conditions, dsDNA typically adopts the B-form. In contrast, dsRNA predominantly takes the A-form, which is shorter and wider B-form. Additionally, dsDNA sequences with alternating purine and pyrimidine bases can adopt the Z-form under high salt conditions, while other sequences favor the other forms under similar conditions.

1.6.1 B–DNA

The Watson-Crick double-helical structure is also referred to as **B-DNA**. It is the most stable and predominant form under physiological conditions. In this form, two long polynucleotide strands coiled around a central axis to form a **right-handed helix**. Strands are antiparallel, i.e., one strand is oriented in the 5′→3′ direction and the other in the 3′→5′ direction. Strands interact by hydrogen bonds between complementary base pairs. Base **G** forms three hydrogen bonds with **C** and **A** forms two hydrogen bonds with **T**. The bases occupy the helix core, and sugar-phosphate chains run along the periphery, minimizing the repulsions between charged phosphate groups.

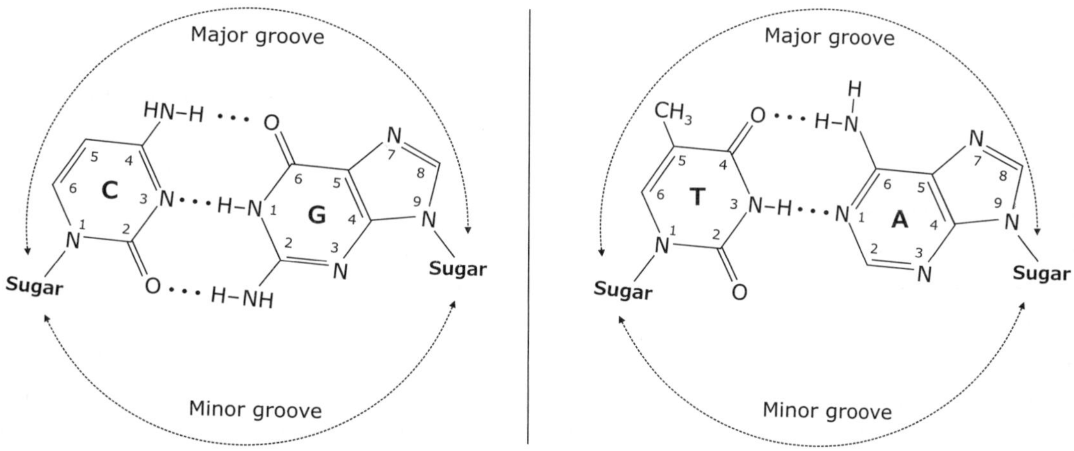

Figure 1.49 Standard base pairing (*or* Watson and Crick base pairing) between guanine and cytosine and between adenine and thymine via hydrogen bonds. The functional groups participating in H-bond formation are the amino groups of adenine, guanine and cytosine; the ring nitrogens at position 3 of pyrimidines and position 1 of purines; and the strongly electronegative oxygen atoms attached at position 4 of thymine, position 2 of cytosine and position 6 of guanine.

The sugar-phosphate backbones of the helix are not equally spaced along the helix axis, and the grooves between them are not of the same size. Instead, the intertwined chains create a **major groove** and a **minor groove.** Major groove is wide and deep, whereas the minor groove is narrow and deep. The side containing **N7** of purines represents the major groove, while the other side containing **N3** of purines is the minor groove (or major groove readout comes from C1′–N9 glycosidic bond side in purines and C1′–N1 in pyrimidines). The B-DNA is characterized by 10.4 base pairs per helical turn, and the axial height of one helical turn (i.e., helix pitch) is 33.2Å. The rise per base pair along the helix axis is 3.32 Å. The base pairs are arranged nearly perpendicular to the helix axis with anti-conformation for all glycosidic bonds and C2′-endo sugar pucker of all nucleosides. The resulting helix has a diameter of ~20 Å.

An alternative form of the right-handed double helix is **A-DNA**. A-DNA molecules differ from B-DNA molecules in a number of ways. The A-DNA is characterized by 11 base pairs per turn and the helix pitch is 24.6Å. There is a rise per base pair along the helix axis of 2.3 Å. Like B-DNA, A-DNA also has *anti*-conformation for all glycosidic bonds, but C3′-endo sugar pucker of all nucleosides. The resulting helix has a diameter of ~23 Å. The B-DNA is thus longer and thinner than A-DNA. Relatively dehydrated DNA fibers can adopt the A-conformation. Features of major groove and minor groove also differ from B-DNA. The major groove is extremely narrow but very deep, whereas the minor groove is very broad but shallow. The right-handed helical DNA-RNA hybrids and dsRNAs also adopt an A-like conformation. The 2'-OH in RNA sterically prevents double-helical regions of RNA chains from adopting the B-conformation.

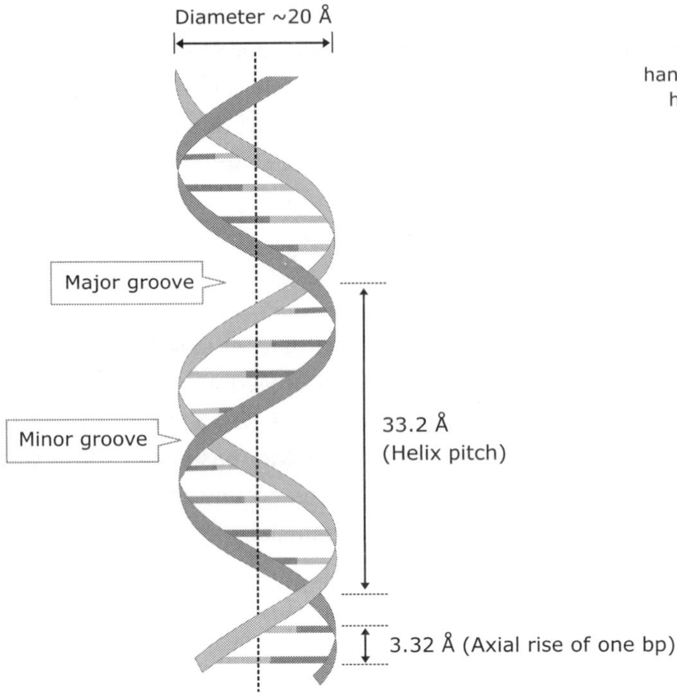

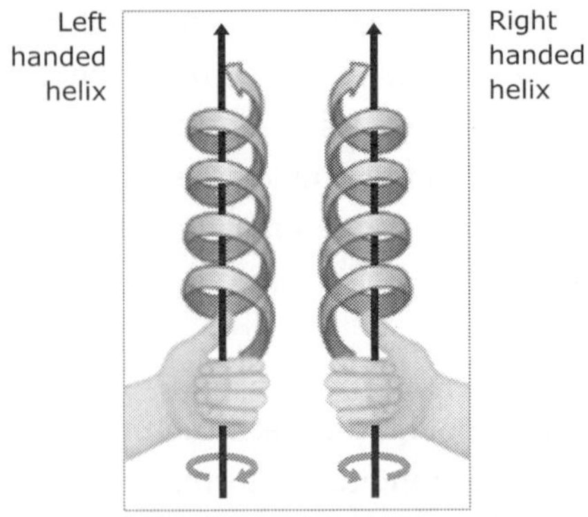

Figure 1.50
B-DNA structure. B-form of DNA is a right-handed double-helix held together by Watson-Crick type base pairing that stack directly along a helical axis, resulting in two well defined grooves.

The **helical parameters** can be categorized into two general classes to describe the absolute and relative conformations in DNA: **base-pair parameters** (translational and rotational relationships of bases in a single base pair) and **base-step parameters** (translational and rotational relationships between two stacked base pairs). Parameters such as *propeller twist*, *shear*, *stagger* and *stretch* are base-pair parameters whereas *shift*, *slide*, *rise*, *tilt*, *roll* and *twist* are base-step parameters. We can understand these parameters by considering x, y and z-axis. The x and y-axes lie in the plane of the base pair, with the y-axis lying along the long axis of the base pair. The z-axis is perpendicular to the plane of the base pair and parallel to the helix axis. Displacement of one base pair with respect to other along the x-axis, y-axis and z-axis are called **shift**, **slide** and **rise**, respectively. Three angular parameters (**tilt**, **roll** and **twist**) define the position and direction of one base pair relative to the next. **Tilt** is the rotation of base pair around the x-axis. Similarly, **roll** is the rotation of base pair around the y-axis and **twist** is the rotation of base pair around the z-axis.

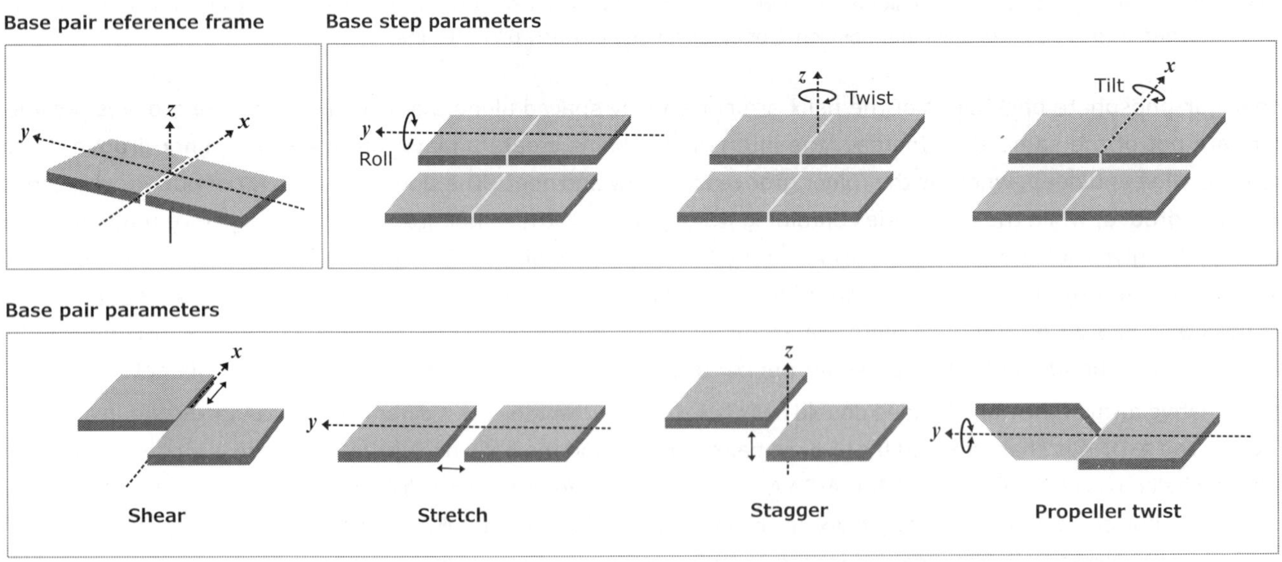

Figure 1.51 The helical parameters can be categorized into two general classes to describe the absolute and relative conformations in nucleic acids; base-pair parameters (translational and rotational relationships of bases within each base pair) and base step parameters (translational and rotational relationships between two stacked base pairs).

Problem

What is the number of hydrogen bonds in a B-DNA of 1000 base pairs with base adenine occurring 75% of the times in one strand and 10% in the other strand?

Solution: One strand of dsDNA has 1000 nucleotides. According to the question, there is 75% adenine in one strand, i.e., 750 adenine. Hence, there will be 750 thymine in the complementary second strand. Again, there is 10% adenine in the second strand, i.e., 100 adenine. So, there will be 100 thymine in the complementary strand. In this manner, the total A.T bps in dsDNA will be 850 bps, and the remaining base pairs will be G.C, i.e., 150 bps. So, total number of H-bonds = $(850 \times 2) + (150 \times 3) = 1700 + 450 = 2150$.

Problem

Molecular mass of the genomic DNA of an organism is 3.96×10^9 g/mol. The average molecular mass of base pair is 650 g/mol. If an average polypeptide in this organism consists of a chain of 400 amino acids. Calculate the maximum number of polypeptides encoded by DNA molecule.

Solution: Molecular mass of the genomic DNA is 3.96×10^9 g/mol (or dalton).

Number of base pairs = Molecular mass of DNA / Molecular mass of a base pair

= $(3.96 \times 10^9$ g/mol) / $(0.65 \times 10^3$ g/mol) = 6×10^6 base pairs

Number of nucleotides in mRNA = 6×10^6 nucleotides

Number of triplet codons possible = $6 \times 10^6/3 = 2 \times 10^6$ codons.

For synthesis of a polypeptide chain of 400 amino acids, ~400 codons of mRNA are required. From 2×10^6 codons, 2×10^6 amino acids can be encoded. Hence, the total number of polypeptide chains of 400 amino acids that can be synthesized = 2×10^6 codons/400 = 5000 polypeptides.

Problem

What is the approximate molecular mass of duplex DNA required to code for an enzyme of molecular mass 40,000 Da?

Solution: The average molecular mass of an amino acid residue in a protein is 110 Da. Thus, a protein whose molecular mass is 40,000 Da contains 40,000/110 = ~364 amino acid residues and requires a minimum dsDNA of 3×364 = ~1090 bp. Since each base pair has an average molecular mass of about 650 Da, the molecular mass of this gene would be about 1090×650 = 708,500 Da. On average, the molecular mass of coding DNA is about 18 times that of the corresponding protein.

Problem

If 80% of the base pairs of DNA in a B-conformation (12.5 kbp) and 20% are in the Z-conformation, what is the size of the DNA molecule?

Solution: Z-DNA contains 12 base pairs per turn, 0.36 to 0.38 nm rise per base pair and a pitch of 4.86 nm. If 20% of a 12.5 kbp DNA molecule is in Z-conformation and the rest is B-conformation, we can say that 2.5 kbp in Z-DNA and 10.0 kbp in B-DNA. The overall length is: 2,500 bp $\times$ 0.37 nm/bp + 10,000 bp $\times$ 0.34 nm/bp = 4,325 nm = 4.33 μm.

1.6.2 Z-DNA

Z-DNA is a **left-handed** double helical structure with two anti-parallel strands that are held together by Watson-Crick base pairing. The transition from B- to Z-DNA conformation occurs most readily in DNA segments containing alternating purines and pyrimidines, especially alternate C and G on one strand (and also in DNA segments containing alternate T and G on one strand). The existence of Z-DNA was first suggested by optical studies demonstrating that a polymer of alternating C and G in one strand in a 4 M NaCl solution. The physical reason for this finding remained a mystery until an X-ray crystallographic study of a self-complementary DNA hexamer $d(CG)_3$ revealed a left-handed double helix with two anti-parallel chains that were held together by Watson–Crick base pairing.

Z-DNA is thinner (18 Å) than B-DNA (20 Å) and there is only one deep, narrow groove equivalent to the minor groove in B-DNA. No major groove exists. In contrast to B-DNA where a repeating unit is a 1 base pair, in Z-DNA the repeating unit is a 2 base pairs. This dinucleotide repeat causes the backbone to follow a zigzag path, giving rise to the name **Z-DNA**. The glycosidic bond conformations alternate between *anti* and *syn* (*anti* for pyrimidines; *syn* for purines). Similarly, the sugar puckers alternate between C3′-endo and C2′-endo (C2′-endo for pyrimidines and C3′-endo for purines).

Z-DNA can form in regions of alternating purine-pyrimidine sequence; GCGCGC... sequences form Z-DNA most easily. TGTGTGTG... sequences also form Z-DNA but they require a greater stabilization energy. Formation of Z-DNA conformation is generally unfavourable. However, certain conditions promote Z-DNA conformation from B-DNA conformation; such as negative DNA supercoiling, high salt concentration or 5-methylated cytosine.

Table 1.10 Comparisons of A, B and Z-forms of DNA

Geometry attribute	A-form	B-form	Z-form
Helix sense	Right-handed	Right-handed	Left-handed
Diameter	23Å	20Å	18Å
Pitch (axial height of 1 helical turn)	24.6Å	33.2Å	45.6Å
Mean bp/helical turn	~11	~10.4	~12
Axial rise of one bp	2.3Å	3.32Å	3.8Å
Twist angle (rotation/bp)	33.6°	34.3°	60°/2
Base pair tilt	20°	−6°	7°
Mean propeller twist	+18°	+16°	0°
Glycosidic bond conformation	*Anti*	*Anti*	*Anti* : pyrimidines and *Syn* : purines
Sugar pucker	C3′-endo	C2′-endo	Purines: C3′-endo, Pyrimidines: C2′-endo
Repeating unit	1 bp	1 bp	2 bp
Major groove	Narrow and deep	Wide and deep	Flat
Minor groove	Wide and shallow	Narrow and deep	Narrow and deep
H-bond type	Standard	Standard	Standard

1.6.3 Triplex DNA

Triple-helical nucleic acids were first described in 1957 by Felsenfeld and Rich. In certain circumstances (e.g. low pH), a dsDNA consisting of a **homopurine** sequence in one strand and a **homopyrimidine** sequence in the complementary strand forms a **triple helical DNA** (*triplex DNA*) with either a pyrimidine-rich or a purine-rich third strand. The third strand of DNA in the triplex structure follows a path through the major groove of the duplex DNA. The triple helix will be written as *Pu*∗Pu•Py with the third strand in italics. The central strand of the triplex must be homopurine strand. The third strand bases make a **Hoogsteen** or **reverse Hoogsteen** hydrogen bonds to the homopurine strand of the duplex.

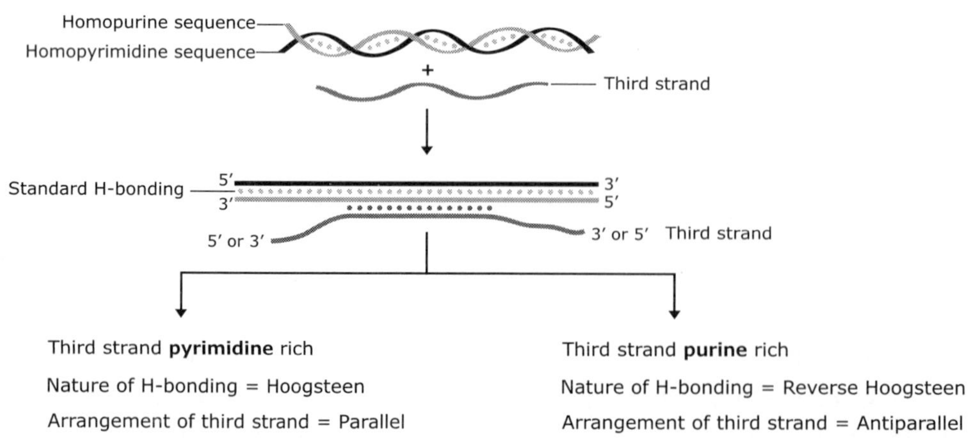

Figure 1.52 Intermolecular triplex DNA.

Typically, pyrimidine-rich third strands bind to the homopurine strand of the duplex DNA via Hoogsteen hydrogen bonding in a parallel orientation (i.e., in the same 5′ to 3′, orientation as the homopurine strand of the duplex), whereas the purine-rich third strand binds in an antiparallel orientation to the homopurine strand of the duplex via reverse Hoogsteen hydrogen bonds. Triple helix can be *intermolecular* or *intramolecular*. **Intermolecular triplexes** are formed when the triplex-forming strand originates from a second DNA molecule. In an **intramolecular triplex** (or **H-DNA**), the third strand is provided by one of the strands of the same duplex DNA molecule. Formation of both intramolecular and intermolecular triplexes depends on several factors like oligonucleotide length, base composition, pH, divalent cation and temperature. Triplexes can be built from RNA or DNA chains or their combinations.

1.6.4 G-quadruplex

G-quadruplexes (or **tetraplexes** or **G4 structures**) are four-stranded secondary structures, formed by one, two or four separate strands of DNA or RNA molecules. Nucleic acid, both DNA and RNA, containing guanine-rich sequences spontaneously fold into G-quadruplex structures. The building blocks of G-quadruplexes are **G-quartets** (also termed as **G-tetrads**) that are formed through a cyclic Hoogsteen hydrogen bonding arrangement of four guanines with each other. The planar G-quartets stack on top of one another forming four-stranded helical structures. The formation and stabilization of G-quadruplexes are dependent on monovalent cations, specifically K^+ and Na^+. The stabilization is due to the coordination of the positively charged cations with the electronegative O^6 atoms in the center channel of the adjacent stacked G-quartets.

G-quadruplex structures are topologically very polymorphic and can arise from the intra- or intermolecular folding of G-rich strands. **Intramolecular folding** requires the presence of four or more G-rich sequences in one strand, whereas **intermolecular folding** can arise from two or four strands giving rise to parallel or antiparallel structures depending on the orientation of the strands in a G-quadruplex. Quadruplexes are designated as antiparallel when at least one of the four strands is antiparallel to the others. All *parallel* quadruplexes have all guanine glycosidic bonds in an *anti* conformation. *Antiparallel* quadruplexes have both *syn* and *anti* conformations. The *in vitro* thermal stability of G-quadruplexes is dependent on features such as the number of G-quartets present in the structure and the length and composition of the loops formed by non-guanine bases.

Box 1.4 Hoogsteen base pairing

Hoogsteen (HG) base pairing is quite different from standard *Watson-Crick base pairing*. In HG base pairing, the glycosidic bond linked to purine adopts a *syn* rather than *anti* conformation. In A•T HG base pairing, there are two H-bonds, as shown in figure. The seventh position of the purine, which participates in hydrogen bonding, is often referred to as the **Hoogsteen position**. The HG base pair between guanine and cytosine can be formed only if cytosine is protonated in the N3 position. In G•C$^+$ HG base pairing, two H-bonds occur as compared to G•C Watson-Crick base pairing. Since the pK_a for the protonation of cytosine is 4.2, the formation of the HG base pair G•C$^+$ is highly unfavorable at neutral pH.

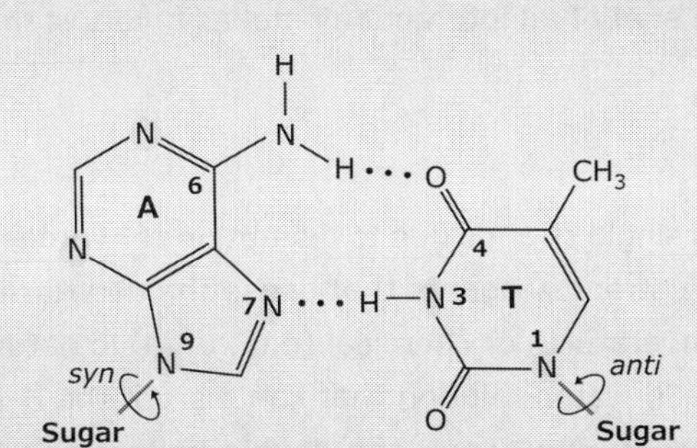

A•T Hoogsteen base pair

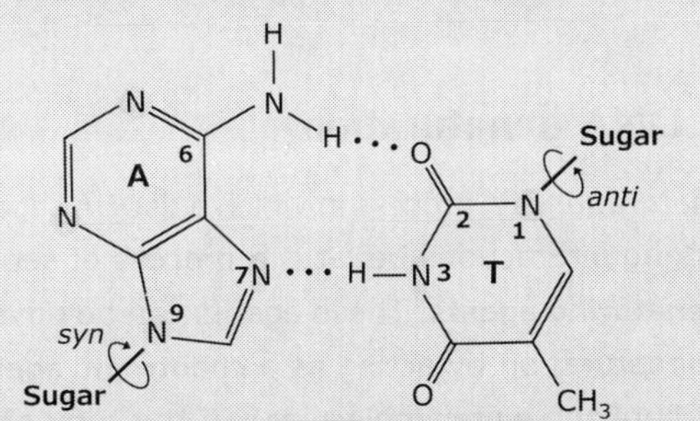

A•T Reverse Hoogsteen base pair

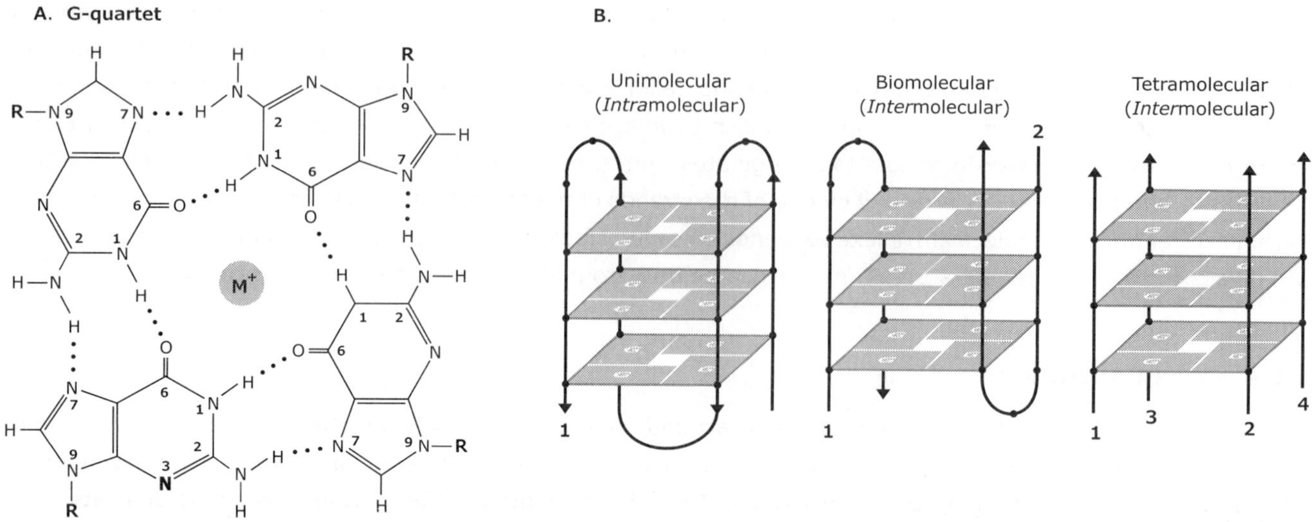

Figure 1.53 Structure of G-quadruplexes. (A) The building blocks of G-quadruplexes are G-quartets that arise from the association of four guanines into a cyclic arrangement stabilized by Hoogsteen hydrogen bonding (1–6 and 2–7). The planar G-quartets stack on top of one another, forming four-stranded helical structures. G-quadruplex formation is driven by monovalent cations such as Na^+ and K^+. (B) G-quadruplex structures are polymorphic and can be sub-grouped into different families, as for example, parallel or antiparallel according to the orientation of the strands and can be inter- or intramolecular folded.

1.6.5 Thermodynamic stability of the dsDNA helix

The helical structure of dsDNA is stabilized primarily by non-covalent interactions. These include **base-stacking interactions** between adjacent base pairs and **hydrogen bonding** between bases of complementary strands. Among these, base stacking interactions play the dominant role in maintaining the helical stability of dsDNA. The **base-stacking interactions** arises from **hydrophobic effects** and **van der Waals forces** between the planar bases. The central core of the helix is formed by base pairs that stack closely on top of one another. Base stacking minimizes the exposure of non-polar bases to water, while the nearly coplanar arrangement of the bases maximizes van der Waals interactions.

In addition, the bases of complementary strands are held together by **hydrogen bonds**: adenine pairs with thymine via two hydrogen bonds, whereas guanine pairs with cytosine via three. One point is important to note here that the contribution of hydrogen bonding to DNA stability depends solely on base composition—that is, the relative proportion of A·T and G·C pairs. In contrast, the strength of base-stacking interactions is influenced by both base composition as well as specific sequence of base pairs, since base-stacking interactions in some adjacent base pairs are more than others.

For example, a (GC).(GC) dinucleotide stack has a stacking energy of −14.59 kcal/mol/stacked pair, whereas a (TA).(TA) stack has an energy of −3.82 kcal/mol/stacked pair. Once the DNA double helix is formed, it is remarkably stable. The individual interactions stabilizing the helix are weak, but the sum of all interactions makes a very stable helix.

1.6.6 DNA denaturation

DNA denaturation is a process in which a dsDNA separates into two single strands due to disruption of hydrogen bonds and stacking interactions i.e., it is a process of separation of DNA strands. Agents that cause the denaturation are called **denaturing agents**. These agents can be physical (e.g., temperature) or chemical (e.g., urea) in nature. Urea causes denaturation by acting as a **chaotropic agent** (a molecule in water solution that can disrupt the H-bonding network between water molecules). If the temperature is the denaturing agent, the double helix is said to have *melted*. The temperature at which half of the dsDNA is denatured is called T_m (**melting temperature**). The high value of T_m is related to the higher thermodynamic stability of DNA double helix. DNA denaturation is a **cooperative process**, meaning that the denaturation of one base pair facilitates the denaturation of adjacent base pairs. This process is also associated with increases in both **enthalpy** and **entropy**. *Enthalpy*, which refers to the total heat content of a system, increases during DNA denaturation because the separation of dsDNA into single strands requires the input of heat energy. This energy is needed to break the hydrogen bonds and the base stacking interactions. *Entropy*, a measure of disorder or randomness, also increases during denaturation. The highly ordered structure of dsDNA becomes more disordered as it converts to single strands, leading to an increased entropy of the system.

Change in optical density resulting from denaturation: Denaturation increases the DNA's optical density. The denaturation process is accompanied by a change in the DNA's physical properties such as optical density, viscosity and buoyant density. The aromatic nitrogenous bases present in DNA and RNA absorb maximum at 260 nm. The absorbance at 260 nm is a consequence of the transition of delocalized π-electrons. This absorbance at 260 nm increases with the increased transition. When bases remain stacked together in dsDNA, they interact via their π-electron clouds. This interaction decreases the π-electrons transitions and thus, absorbance. Unstacking of bases increases π-electrons transition due to the diminished interactions. As a result, the absorbance at 260 nm increases. Denaturation of the dsDNA increases the absorbance (or optical density) at 260 nm. This increase in the absorbance at 260 nm is known as **hyperchromic effect**. This occurs because, in dsDNA helix, bases remain stacked, whereas denaturation causes strand separation and unstacking. Because of denaturation, the bases become mostly unstacked and thus, absorption increases at 260 nm. Conversely, when single-stranded DNA (ssDNA) renatures to form double-stranded DNA, the absorbance at 260 nm decreases, a process known as the **hypochromic effect**. The physical properties such as **viscosity** and **buoyant density** of DNA decrease during denaturation, but the underlying physical mechanisms are not fully understood.

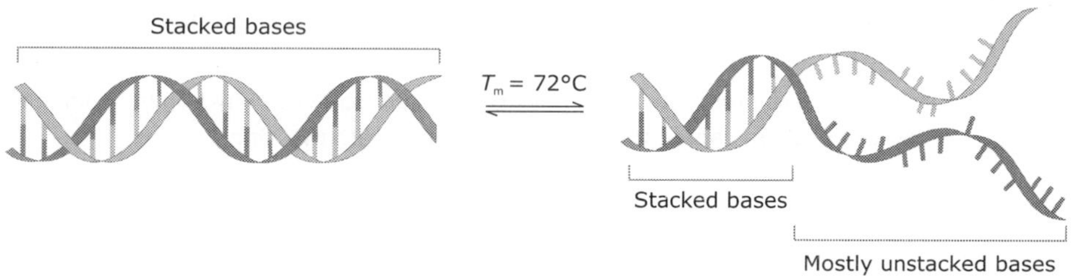

Figure 1.54 Thermal denaturation of DNA. DNA denaturation, also called DNA melting, is the process in which dsDNA separates into two single strands due to disruption of hydrogen bonds and stacking interactions. In dsDNA, all the bases are stacked together. However, during denaturation, the bases become mostly unstacked.

Factors affecting T_m

The T_m value or the thermal stability of dsDNA depends on several intrinsic and extrinsic factors. These factors are GC-content of DNA, ionic strength (the amount of the ion concentration in the solution) and pH of solution.

GC-content: dsDNA with a high GC-content has a higher T_m than DNA with a lower GC-content. This happens primarily because of high stacking interactions and greater number of H-bonds (two H-bonds in AT whereas three H-bonds in GC).

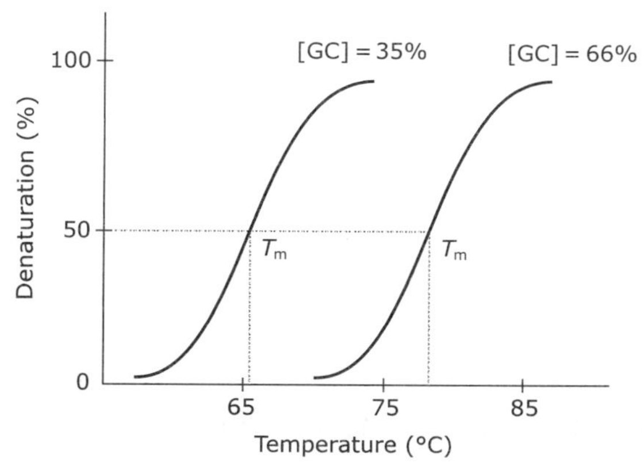

Figure 1.55 Relationship between GC content and T_m value of dsDNA. In a typical melting curve, we measure the increase in UV absorbance as the temperature increases.

Ionic strength: T_m is also dependent on the ionic strength of the solution; the lower the ionic strength, the lower the melting temperature. DNA is a polyanionic molecule. Each phosphate group in a DNA strand carries a negative charge. The negative charges on both strands of dsDNA repel each other. The magnitude of repulsion is diminished by the presence of cations such as Na^+ or Mg^{2+}. These cations interact with phosphate groups and neutralize their negative charge. When the charges are not neutralized, the electrostatic repulsion decreases the T_m of dsDNA.

pH: Change in the pH also affects the T_m. The reason behind this is the protonation and deprotonation of the bases due to the change in pH. At pH values greater than 10, extensive deprotonation of the bases occurs, destroying their hydrogen bonding potential and denaturing the DNA duplex. For example, the pK_a for the proton on N-1 of guanine is typically 9.7. When the pH approaches 10, N-1 of guanine is deprotonated. Because this proton participates in hydrogen bonding, its loss destabilizes the DNA double helix. Similarly, extensive protonation of the bases below pH 3 also disrupts base pairing. Below pH 3, some of the hydrogen bond *acceptors* that participate in base-pairing become protonated. In their protonated forms, these bases can no longer form hydrogen bonds.

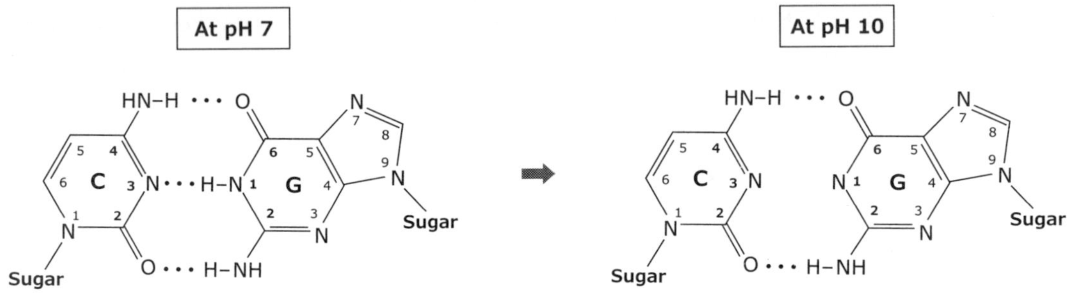

Figure 1.56 At pH 7, N-1 of guanine remains protonated, and this hydrogen participates in hydrogen bonding with N-3 of cytosine. However, after deprotonation, the N-1 position cannot form a hydrogen bond with cytosine.

1.6.7 Quantification of nucleic acids

Ultraviolet spectroscopy is used for quantification of nucleic acid. Nucleic acids show a strong absorbance in the region of 240 to 275 nm. It originates from the $\pi \rightarrow \pi^*$ transitions of the pyrimidine and purine ring systems of the nitrogenous bases. At neutral pH, the absorption maxima range from 253 nm (for guanosine) to 271 nm (for cytidine), and therefore polymeric DNA and RNA show a broad and strong absorbance near 260 nm. At this wavelength absorption is proportional to nucleic acid concentration. This relationship is so well characterized that UV absorption is used to accurately determine the concentration of nucleic acids in solution. The relationship between DNA concentration and absorption is linear. The absorbance at 260 nm is used to determine the concentration of nucleic acids. Amounts of nucleic acid are often given as A_{260} units.

For dsDNA, one A_{260} unit is equivalent to 50 μg DNA (i.e., a solution of dsDNA with a concentration of 50 μg/mL will have an absorbance at 260 nm equal to 1.0); for ssDNA, it is equivalent to 33 μg DNA; for ssRNA, it is equivalent to 40 μg RNA.

Problem

Optical density of a 400 base pair long 1 ml DNA solution was found to be 0.052. How many DNA molecules are present in the solution? [1 base pair = 650 Da, optical density of 1.0 D corresponds to 50 μg DNA/ml]

Solution: Optical density of 1 D corresponds to 50 μg/ml of dsDNA.

Hence, 0.052 corresponds to 2.6 μg/ml (= 2.6×10^{-6} g/ml) of dsDNA.

Average molecular mass of 1 base pair is 650 Da.

Hence, molecular mass of 400 bp = $650 \times 400 = 260000$ Da.

Number of moles of DNA = given mass/molecular mass = $2.6 \times 10^{-6}/260000 = 1 \times 10^{-11}$

Since, 1 mole contains 6.023×10^{23} molecules.

Thus, 1×10^{-11} moles will contain $6.023 \times 10^{23} \times 1 \times 10^{-11} = 6.023 \times 10^{12}$ molecules.

1.6.8 Supercoiled forms of DNA

Supercoiling (means the *coiling of a coil*) represents a coiling of the DNA double helix upon itself. It can occur in *covalently closed circular* DNAs and also in *linear* DNAs that are topologically constrained by being complexed with protein. In linear DNAs, if the ends of the molecule are fixed then any rotational freedom that the two backbones might have about one another is removed and as a result any local twisting or untwisting will cause a strain on the structure. DNA supercoiling is generally a manifestation of structural strain. Conversely, if there is no net bending of the DNA axis upon itself, the DNA is said to be in a **relaxed** state.

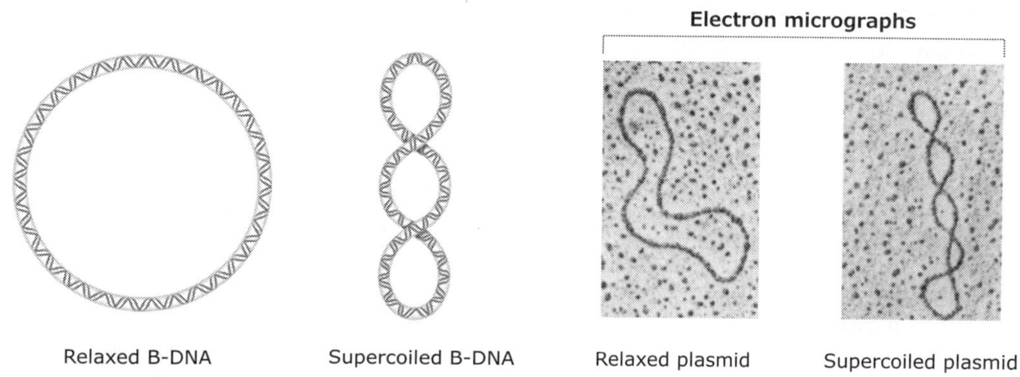

A B-DNA is considered as **relaxed** if it contains 10.4 base pairs per helical turn. If the number of base pairs in one turn is more or less than 10.4 base pairs, the B-DNA will be **supercoiled** (or *supertwist*) rather than relaxed. The increase or decrease in the number of base pairs per helical turn creates a state of torsional stress in the helix. This stress is relieved by supercoiling of the helix. The supercoiling can be positive or negative. **Positively supercoiled DNA** is *overwound* (has more helical turns than what the molecule would accommodate in relaxed state), with less base pairs per helical turn than relaxed DNA (i.e., <10.4 bp per helical turn) whereas **negatively supercoiled DNA** is *underwound* (has fewer helical turns than what the molecule would accommodate in relaxed state), with more base pairs than relaxed DNA (i.e., >10.4 bp per helical turn).

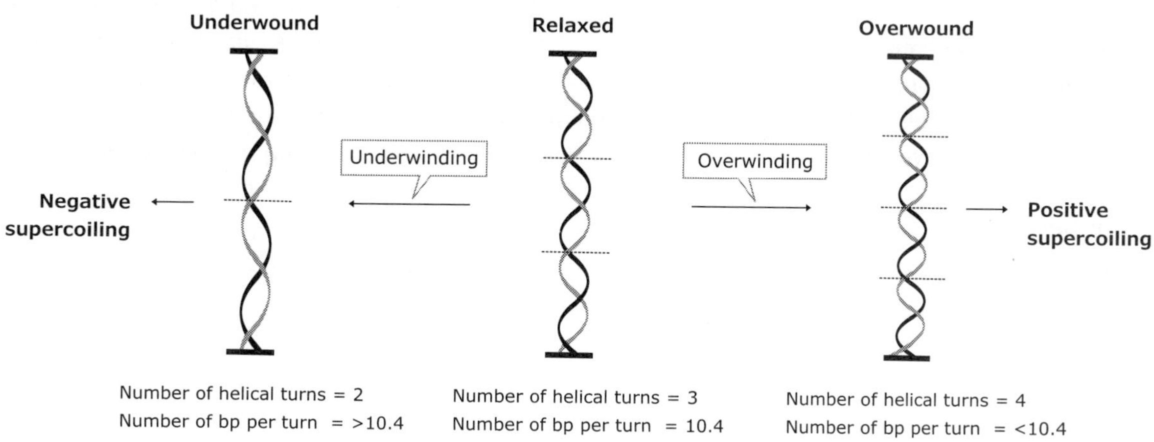

Figure 1.57 Schematic representation of B-DNA supercoiling. In a linear dsDNA molecule, the two strands of the helix are free to rotate around each other and, indeed, may unwind completely to give two separate strands. If both ends of DNA are made fixed to prevent free rotations, then the increase or decrease in the number of base pairs per helical turn creates a state of torsional stress in the helix. This stress is relieved by positive or negative supercoiling of the helix.

The supercoiling may be **plectonemic** (or *interwound*) and **solenoidal** (or *toroidal*). In *plectonemic supercoiling*, one double-helical segment winds around another. In right-handed double helix, the positive plectonemic supercoil is left-handed whereas negative plectonemic supercoil is right-handed. In *solenoidal supercoiling*, a DNA double helix is wound in a cylindrical manner.

Plectonemic supercoiling

Solenoidal supercoiling (as in nucleosome)

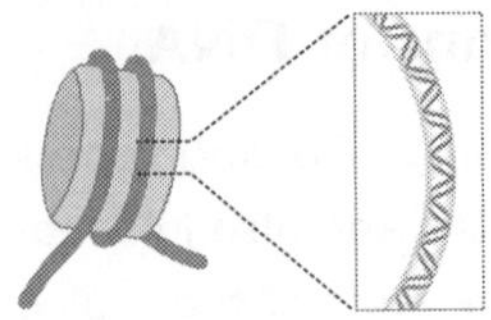

For example, wrapping of a DNA helix around the histone core to form nucleosome structure in eukaryotes. Topologically, solenoidal supercoiling and plectonemic supercoiling are equivalent. That is, negative supercoils have a *minus* sign in both cases, and positive supercoils have a *plus* sign. However, the handedness of the supercoil is opposite in the two types. In right-handed double helix, the positive solenoidal supercoil is right-handed whereas negative solenoidal supercoil is left-handed. Most DNA in organisms is found in negatively supercoiled state with a deficiency of helical turns.

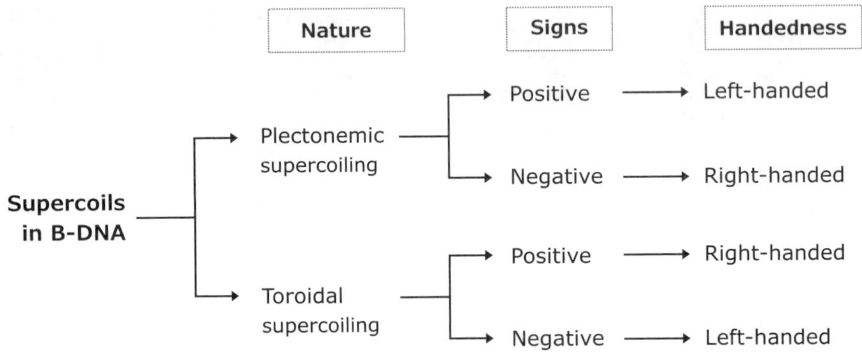

In order to understand the origin of supercoiling; imagine a circular B-DNA of 5200 base pairs. If a 5200 bp long circular B-DNA, which contains 500 helical turns with 10.4 bp per turn in the relaxed state, is twisted 50 times in right-handed direction, the DNA becomes over-coiled or overwound. It virtually means adding 50 more helical turns to the already existing 500 helical turns, making the total number of turns to 550. So the 5200 bp long DNA has to accommodate 50 more turns, which is torsionally a stressed condition. In this case, the number of base pairs per turn will be 9.4; it is a deviation from the normal and thermodynamically stable state of 10.4 bp per turn. So, in order to accommodate the excess number of turns, the helical DNA *positively* supercoils in the left-handed direction (**positive plectonemic supercoil**). Similarly, if a 5200 bp long circular DNA with 500 turns is twisted 50 times in left-handed direction, the DNA is underwound. In this case, the number of turns lost is 50 and the number of base pairs per turn will be 11.5, which is not thermodynamically stable, hence the DNA takes a right-handed supercoil on its own; the DNA helix is in the form of *negatively* supercoiled DNA (**negative plectonemic supercoil**).

Linking number

Supercoiling in covalently closed circular DNA molecules (cccDNA) is described mathematically by the **linking number** (**Lk**). Linking number defines the number of times one strand crosses over the other in space in cccDNA. The absolute value of the Lk corresponds to the minimal number of passages of one strand through the other needed to completely separate the two strands. It is a **topological quantity** and always an *integer* value.

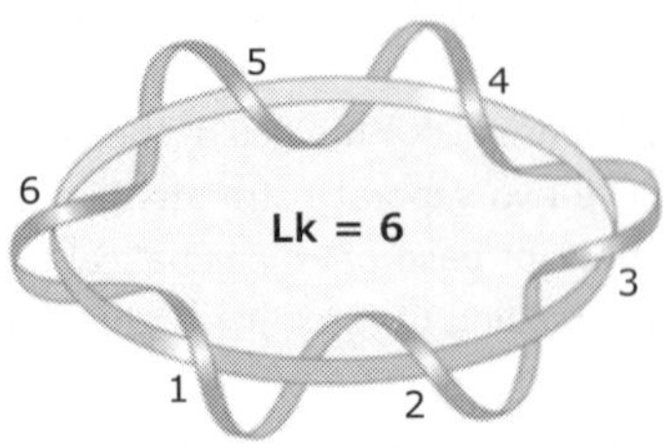

Figure 1.58
The linking number is the number of times that one DNA strand crosses the other.

Its value is independent of DNA geometry—that is, linking number does not vary with deformation of the trajectory of either strand or with changes in the characteristic geometric quantities of duplex such as pitch, roll, twist and tilt.

For a change in the linking number, phosphodiester bond must be broken in one or both strands of DNA. By convention, the linking number of a covalently closed circular DNA formed by a right-handed double helix (such as B-DNA) is positive and for a left-handed DNA helix (such as Z-DNA) is negative. Two DNA molecules differing only in linking number are called **topological isomers** (*topoisomers*) of one another. *Features related to linking number*:

1. The linking number is only defined for cccDNA and its value is fixed as long as the molecule remains covalently closed.
2. The linking number of a cccDNA can only be changed by breaking a phosphodiester bond in one or both strands, allowing the intact strand to pass through the broken strand and then rejoining the broken strand. In a cell, linking number is changed by enzymes called **topoisomerases** that transiently break and reseal the DNA double helix. Type I topoisomerases break phosphodiester bond in only one strand of the DNA, allowing one strand to rotate around the other. Type II topoisomerases break and reseal phosphodiester bonds in both DNA strands.
3. The linking number is always an **integer value** since the two strands must always be wound about each other by an integral number of times upon closure.

Twist number and Writhe number

The linking number is the sum of two components of a given covalently closed DNA molecule – **twist number**, Tw (represents the total number of helical turns in DNA or how the individual strands of DNA coil around the axis of the DNA helix) and the **writhe number**, Wr (represents the supercoiling of the helix in space). In contrast to linking number which is a topological property, the twist and writhe are geometrical quantities and need not be integers. Linking numbers can be mathematically expressed in following form:

$$\mathbf{Lk = Tw + Wr}$$

For a given covalently closed circular DNA, any change in Tw of the molecule must be accompanied by an equal and opposite change in Wr and *vice versa*. In the relaxed circular DNA, the linking number is equal to the twist number (Lk = Tw) and Wr = 0. The linking number of relaxed B-DNA, Lk_0, is equal to N/10.4; where N is the number of base pairs in the DNA molecule and 10.4 refers to the number of base pairs per helical turn. The level of supercoiling may be quantified in terms of the change in linking number (ΔLk) from that of the relaxed closed circular molecule (Lk_0). ΔLk is a measure of the extent of DNA supercoiling of DNA molecules. A DNA molecule whose Lk differs from the Lk_0 is called *supercoiled*.

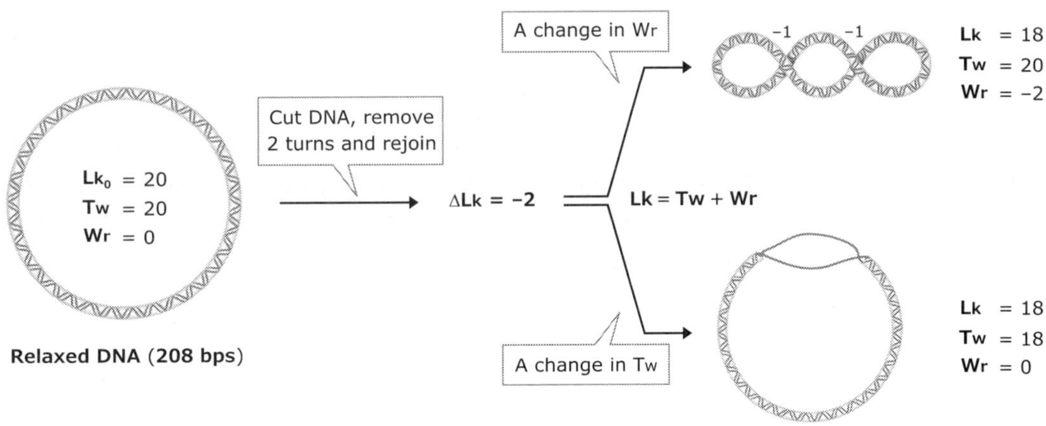

Figure 1.59 A ΔLk of 2 could be accommodated at the two extremes by a change in Tw, leading to local denaturation of 2 helical turns or a change in Wr with the formation of plectonemic supercoils.

Negatively supercoiled DNA: DNA is said to be negatively supercoiled when it has a deficiency in the linking number compared with relaxed DNA, or Lk < Lk_0 (i.e., ΔLk_0 is negative). Negatively supercoiled DNA is underwound because it has fewer helical turns than the molecule would contain in a relaxed molecule. This underwinding results in more base pairs per helical turn. If ΔLk of a given DNA molecule is –5, for example, this indicates that this molecule is underwound by 5 turns as compared to its relaxed conformation.

Positively supercoiled DNA: Most DNA isolated from natural sources is negatively supercoiled. However, DNA can exist in a positively supercoiled form when it has a greater linking number than relaxed DNA, or $Lk > Lk_0$ (i.e., ΔLk is positive). Positively supercoiled DNA is overwound in terms of the number of helical turns. This overwinding creates a situation in which there are fewer base pairs per helical turn. The tension due to overwinding of the helix is relieved by the positive supercoiling of the DNA. Few archaebacteria living at high temperature and low pH, has been shown to contain positively supercoiled DNA.

Superhelical density

Superhelical density, σ, is a quantitative measure of the intensity of supercoiling. It is independent of the length of the DNA molecule. Mathematically it can be expressed as

$\sigma = \Delta Lk/Lk_0$

ΔLk = change in linking number = $Lk - Lk_0$

Lk_0 = linking number of DNA in the relaxed state

Circular DNA from bacteria and eukaryotes are usually negatively supercoiled having the value of σ about −0.06 i.e., degree of underwinding is about 6%. The negative sign indicates that the change in linking number is due to underwinding of the DNA.

Effect of ethidium bromide on supercoiling

Ethidium bromide (**EtBr**) is a large multiringed, planar, aromatic, fluorescent molecule which is generally used to stain DNA molecules. It binds non-covalently to dsDNA by intercalating into the stacked base pairs. Intercalation of one molecule of EtBr causes the DNA to unwind by about 27°. Hence, the EtBr binding decreases the number of helical turns i.e., Tw, the twist. When EtBr binds to linear DNA, it simply causes the helical pitch to increase. But when EtBr binds to covalently circular DNA the twist decreases by 27° for each molecule of EtBr that binds to the DNA. Since Lk does not change unless the molecule is broken, this decrease in twist must be compensated for by a corresponding increase in the writhe, Wr. If, suppose the circular DNA is initially negatively supercoiled, then the addition of EtBr will increase Wr. In other words, the addition of EtBr will *relax* the DNA. If enough EtBr is added, the negative supercoiling will be brought to zero, and if even more EtBr is added, Wr will increase above zero and the DNA will become positively supercoiled.

1.6.9 DNA: A genetic material

DNA contains the genetic instructions specifying the biological development of all cellular forms of life, and many viruses. DNA acts as genetic material and used to store the genetic information of an organic life form. DNA encodes the sequence of the amino acid residues in proteins using the genetic code, a triplet code of nucleotides. For all currently known *living organisms*, the genetic material is almost exclusively DNA. Some viruses have RNA as genetic material.

The first genetic material is generally believed to have been RNA, initially manifested by self-replicating RNA molecules floating on bodies of water. This hypothetical period in the evolution of cellular life is known as the **RNA World**. This hypothesis is based on the RNA's ability to act both as genetic material and as a catalyst, known as ribozyme or a ribosome. However, once proteins, which can form enzymes, came into existence, a more stable molecule DNA became the dominant genetic material, a situation continued today. Not only does DNA's double-stranded nature allows for correction of mutations but RNA is inherently unstable. Modern cells use RNA mainly for the building of proteins from DNA instructions, in the form of messenger RNA, ribosomal RNA, and transfer RNA.

Griffith's experiment: In 1928, Griffith performed *transformation experiments* with two different strains of the bacterium *Diplococcus pneumoniae* (the organism is now named *Streptococcus pneumoniae*)– **virulent strains**, which cause **pneumonia** in certain vertebrates (such as mice, human), and **avirulent strains**, which do not cause pneumonia. The difference in virulence is related to the polysaccharide **capsule** of the bacterium. Virulent strains have this capsule, whereas avirulent strains do not. The non-capsulated bacteria are readily engulfed and destroyed by phagocytic cells. Virulent bacteria, which possess the polysaccharide capsule, are not easily engulfed. Hence, they are able to multiply and cause *pneumonia*. Encapsulated bacteria form smooth colonies (S) when grown on an agar culture plate; whereas non-encapsulated strains produce rough colonies (R). Each strain of *Diplococcus* may be of different serotypes – I*S*, II*S* and III*S* or I*R*, II*R* and III*R*. Serotypes are identified by immunological techniques. Griffith performed experiments with two different serotypes – II*R* and III*S*.

Serotype	**Morphology**	**Capsule**	**Virulence**
II*R*	Rough	Absent	Avirulent
III*S*	Smooth	Present	Virulent

Griffith injected the different strains of bacteria into mice. The III*S* strain killed the mice; the II*R* strain did not. He further noted that if the heat-killed III*S* strain was injected into a mouse, it did not cause pneumonia. When he combined heat-killed III*S* with live II*R* and injected the mixture into a mouse (remember neither alone will kill the mouse), the mouse developed pneumonia and died. From dead mouse tissue, he isolated live S-strain. Based on these information, Griffith concluded that the heat-killed III*S* bacteria were responsible for converting live avirulent II*R* cells into virulent III*S* ones and called the phenomenon **transformation**. He called the genetic information which could be passed from the dead III*S* cells to II*R* cells the **transforming principle**.

Live II*R*-strain (Avirulent, non-capsulated)	→	Injected into the mouse	→	Mouse survives		
Live III*S*-strain (Virulent, capsulated)	→	Injected into the mouse	→	Mouse dies	→	Live *S*-strains recovered from dead mouse tissues
Heat-killed III*S*-strain (Dead, avirulent)	→	Injected into the mouse	→	Mouse survives		
Heat-killed III*S*-strain and **live II*R*-strain**	→	Injected into the mouse	→	Mouse dies	→	Live *S*-strains recovered from dead mouse tissues

Figure 1.60 Griffith's demonstration of transformation in *Pneumococcus*.

Avery–MacLeod–McCarty experiment: In 1944, Oswald Avery, Colin MacLeod, and Maclyn McCarty revisited Griffith's experiment and identified DNA as the **transforming principle**. In their experiments, identical extracts from heat-killed *S*-strain bacteria were first treated with hydrolytic enzymes that specifically destroyed protein, RNA or DNA. After the enzyme treatments, the treated extracts were then mixed with live *R*-strain bacterial cells. Capsulated *S*-strain bacteria appeared in all of the cultures, except those in which the heat-killed *S*-strain bacterial extract had been treated with DNase, an enzyme that degrades DNA. These results suggested that DNA was the molecule responsible for transformation.

Extracts from heat-killed *S*-strains	RNase →	Mixed with live *R*-strains	→	Live *S*-strains appeared (Transformation)
Extracts from heat-killed *S*-strains	Protease →	Mixed with live *R*-strains	→	Live *S*-strains appeared (Transformation)
Extracts from heat-killed *S*-strains	DNase →	Mixed with live *R*-strains	→	Live *S*-strains *not* appeared (No transformation)

Figure 1.61 Avery, MacLeod, and McCarty had shown that only DNA extracts from the heat-killed *S*-strain bacteria caused transformation of live *R*-strain bacterial cells to live *S*-strain bacterial cells. To demonstrate that transforming molecule is the DNA, extracts from heat-killed *S*-strain bacteria were first treated with RNase, DNase and protease and then mixed with live *R*-strain bacterial cells.

Hershey-Chase experiment

The *Hershey-Chase experiment* was conducted in 1952 by Alfred Hershey and Martha Chase that identified *DNA as genetic material of phages*. A **phage** is a bacterial virus that infects bacteria. It consists of a protein coat that encloses the nucleic acid. Since phages consist only of nucleic acid surrounded by protein, they lend themselves nicely to the determination of whether the protein or the nucleic acid is the genetic material.

Hershey and Chase designed an experiment using radioactive isotopes of sulfur and phosphorus to keep separate track of the viral proteins and nucleic acids during the infection process. Proteins contain sulfur, but DNA does not. Conversely, DNA contains phosphate, but proteins do not. Thus, radioactive forms of phosphate (^{32}P) or sulfur (^{35}S), can be selectively incorporated into either DNA or protein. They used the **T2 phage** (genetic material is linear dsDNA) and the bacterium *Escherichia coli*. The phages were labeled by having them infect bacteria growing in culture medium containing the radioactive isotopes ^{35}S or ^{32}P. Hershey and Chase then proceeded to identify the material injected into the bacterial cell by phages. When ^{32}P-labeled phages were mixed with unlabeled *E. coli* cells, they found that the ^{32}P labeled DNA entered the bacterial cells and that the next generation of phages that burst from the infected cells carried a significant amount of the ^{32}P label. When ^{35}S-labeled phages were mixed with unlabeled *E. coli*, the researchers found that the ^{35}S labeled protein stayed outside the bacteria for the most part. Hershey and Chase thus demonstrated that the outer protein coat of a phage does not enter the bacterium it infects, whereas the phage's DNA, does enter the bacterial cell. Since the DNA is responsible for the production of the new phages during the infection process, the DNA, not the protein, must be the genetic material. Hershey shared the 1969 Nobel Prize in Physiology or Medicine for his *discoveries concerning the genetic structure of viruses*.

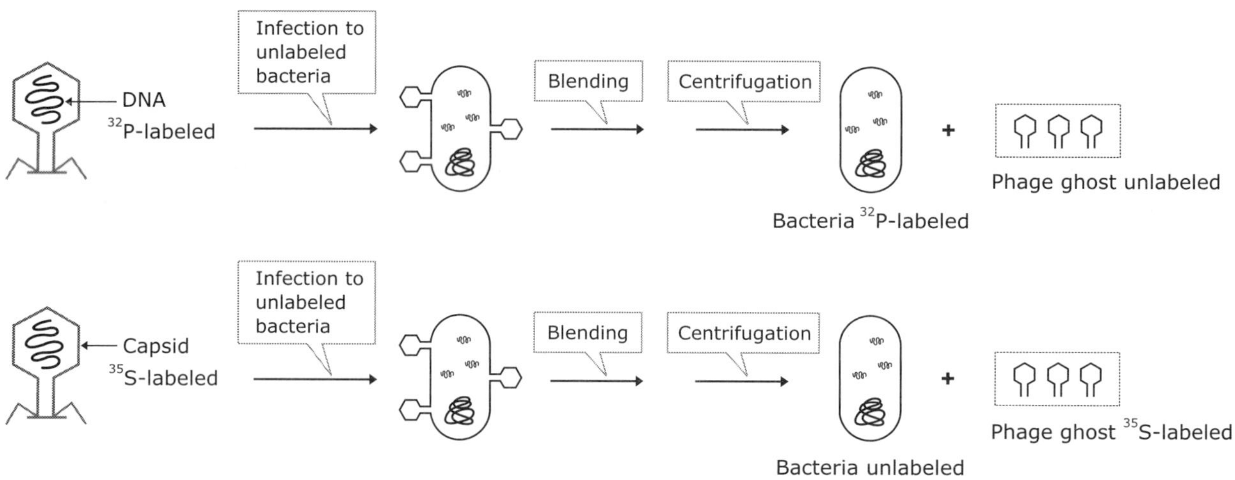

Figure 1.62 The Hershey-Chase experiment. To determine the role of DNA and protein present in T2 phage, Hershey and Chase used radioisotopes to radio-labeled protein and DNA. The radioactive forms of phosphate (^{32}P) or sulfur (^{35}S), were selectively incorporated into either DNA or protein. They prepared both ^{32}P-labeled and ^{35}S-labeled phages, which they then allowed to infect bacteria. During analysis, they discovered that almost all of the radioactive sulfur remained outside bacterial cells, while the radioactive phosphate entered the bacterial cells and could later be recovered in the next generation of phages.

1.7 RNA

Like DNA, **RNA** is composed of a long chain of nucleotides, but it differs in both structure and function. RNA is generally single-stranded and contains ribose sugar in its nucleotides. It plays diverse roles in the cell, including coding, decoding, regulating, and expressing genes. Additionally, RNA molecules can have catalytic activity and, in some cases, store genetic information (i.e., acts as genetic material and termed as **genetic RNA**). RNA with catalytic activity is termed as **ribozyme** (*ribo*nucleic acid *enzyme*). Before the discovery of ribozymes, enzymes were only the catalytic proteins. In 1989, Thomas R. Cech and Sidney Altman shared the Nobel Prize in chemistry for their discovery of catalytic properties of RNA. Most of RNA present in organisms are non-genetic in nature. The **non-genetic RNA** may be **coding** (mRNA) or **noncoding** (like tRNA, rRNA, snRNA, snoRNA, miRNA, XIST, scRNA, siRNA, tmRNA).

Brief introduction of few major RNA molecules:

tRNA (*transfer RNA*): tRNAs account for 10-15% of the total cellular RNA population. Each tRNA molecule is typically 73 to 93 nucleotides long, with the majority containing approximately 76 nucleotides. tRNAs function as **adapter molecules** that decode the mRNA codons during translation by delivering the appropriate amino acid to the ribosome. In addition to their role in translation, some tRNAs can also act as **primers** during processes like reverse transcription in retroviruses. tRNAs are found in the cytosol, where translation occurs, and also in semiautonomous organelles such as mitochondria and chloroplasts, which have their own protein synthesis machinery.

snRNA (*small nuclear RNA*): snRNAs are a class of small non-coding RNAs (typically 100-300 nucleotides long) found in the nucleus of eukaryotic cells. They play a central role in pre-mRNA splicing. snRNAs are integral components of the spliceosome, the complex responsible for removing introns from pre-mRNA. Major snRNAs include U1, U2, U4, U5, and U6 — all named for their high uridine content. Each snRNA forms a complex with proteins to create a **snRNP** (small nuclear ribonucleoprotein).

tmRNA (*transfer-messenger RNA*): tmRNA is a unique RNA molecule found in bacteria and some organelles (such as chloroplasts) that exhibits features of both tRNA and mRNA. It plays a critical role in rescuing stalled ribosomes during protein synthesis—a process known as trans-translation. tmRNA is charged with alanine and functions in association with a protein cofactor called SmpB. It contains two functional domains:

- **tRNA-like domain**: Carries alanine and enters the ribosome like a regular tRNA.
- **mRNA-like domain**: Contains a coding sequence that tags the incomplete polypeptide with a degradation signal.

rRNA (ribosomal RNA): rRNA is a type of non-coding RNA that plays a vital role in protein synthesis. It forms the structural and catalytic core of the ribosome—the cellular machinery responsible for translating mRNA into proteins. rRNA is essential for ribosome assembly and is directly involved in catalyzing peptide bond formation during translation. This catalytic function classifies rRNA as a **ribozyme** (an RNA molecule with enzymatic activity).

Types of rRNA in ribosomes

Ribosome	Small subunit	Large subunit
70S	16S rRNA	23S rRNA and 5S rRNA
80S	18S rRNA	28S rRNA, 5.8S rRNA and 5S rRNA

mRNA (*messenger RNA*): mRNA is a type of coding RNA that carries genetic information from DNA to the ribosome, where it serves as a template for protein synthesis. It consists of both translatable and non-translatable regions. The **translatable region** contains the coding sequence that is read by the ribosome to synthesize a protein. It begins with a start codon and ends with a stop codon. The **non-translatable regions** are segments of the mRNA that are not translated into protein. The **5'-UTR** (5′-untranslated region or *leader sequence*) is located upstream of the start codon. The **3'-UTR** (3′-untranslated region or *trailer sequence*) is found downstream of the stop codon. mRNAs can be either **polycistronic** or **monocistronic** – Polycistronic mRNAs, found primarily in prokaryotes, carry multiple coding sequences (cistrons), each typically encoding a different protein. Monocistronic mRNAs, predominant in eukaryotes, contain only a single coding sequence.

Thermodynamic stability of RNA secondary structure

The primary structure of RNA refers to the sequence of nucleotides. Secondary structure in RNA is mainly developed by Watson-Crick base pairing. In RNA, double-stranded helical structure adopts the **A-conformation**, which differs significantly from the canonical **B-conformation** predominantly adopted by DNA double helices at the physiological condition. Double-stranded helical RNAs are more thermodynamically stable than double-stranded helical DNAs. At physiological condition, denaturation of a double-stranded helical RNA often requires higher temperatures than those required for denaturation of a dsDNA molecule with a comparable sequence. However, the precise physical basis for these differences in thermal stability is not known. Many believe that this slightly higher energy for RNA is generally attributed to more base-stacking energy in the A-conformation, not due to differences in ribose versus deoxyribose. RNA's secondary structure is generally more stable than its tertiary structure. Thus, the formation of the secondary structure dominates the process of RNA folding. RNA tertiary structure forms through relatively weak interactions between preformed secondary structure elements.

1.7.1 Alkaline hydrolysis of RNA

RNA is susceptible to alkaline hydrolysis. Under alkaline conditions, phosphodiester bonds of RNA is hydrolyzed. This occurs because, in the presence of a hydroxide ion, the 2′-hydroxyl group of the ribose is deprotonated, forming a **2′-alkoxide ion**. The 2′-alkoxide ion then attacks and breaks the phosphodiester bond, forming a cyclic 2′,3′-nucleoside monophosphate. This cyclic intermediate subsequently yields a mixture of 2′- and 3′-nucleoside monophosphates. DNA is stable in alkaline solution because DNA lacks a 2′-hydroxyl group to carry out intramolecular catalysis.

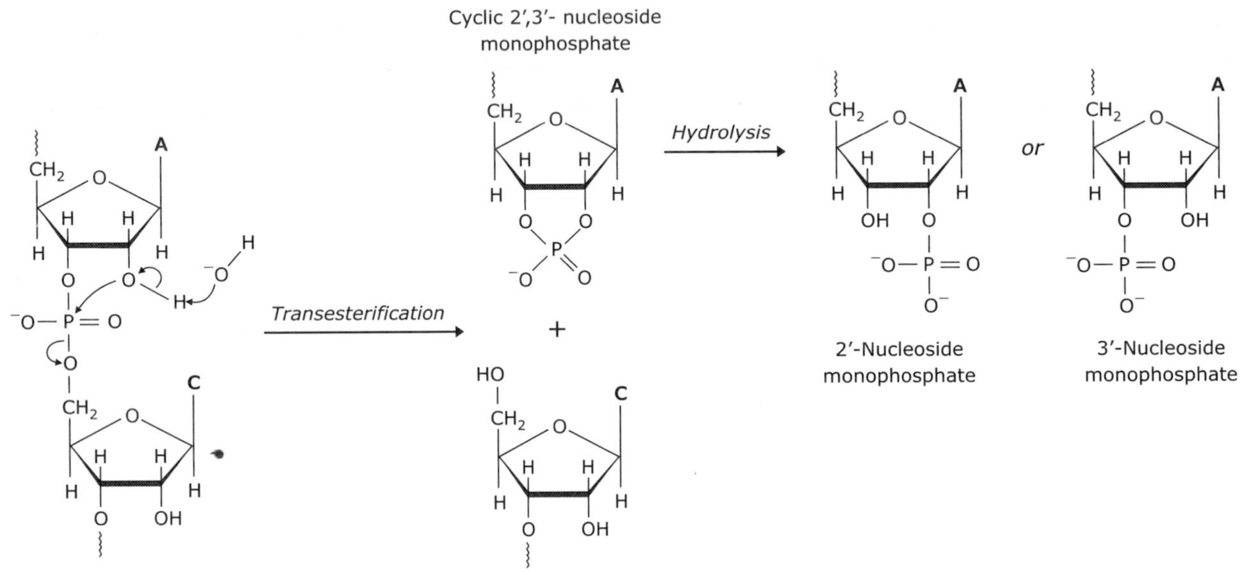

Figure 1.63 Alkali-catalyzed cleavage of RNA. The 2′ hydroxyl group of RNA becomes deprotonated under alkaline conditions leading to a nucleophilic attack on the phosphodiester bond. The resultant 2′,3′-cyclic phosphate may be further hydrolyzed to 2' or to 3' nucleoside monophosphate.

1.7.2 RNA World hypothesis

The nucleotide sequences of DNA encode proteins while DNA replication depends on the activity of proteinaceous enzymes. Now a fundamental question arises: which came first in evolution, DNA or protein? Surprisingly, it appears that neither was the initial player. The concept of an **RNA World** provides an explanation for the nature of molecules capable of performing the tasks of both genetic materials and enzymes present at the beginning of life. The term 'RNA World' was coined by Walter Gilbert in 1986. This hypothesis is supported by RNA's ability to store, transmit, and duplicate genetic information, much like DNA, as well as its capacity to catalyze chemical reactions, similar to proteins. Due to its capability to fulfill the functions of both **genetic material** and **enzymes**, it is likely that RNA served as both genetic material and enzyme in primitive cells. It was only later in evolutionary history that DNA assumed the role of genetic material, while proteins took on the role of enzymes (catalysts). However, RNA being a catalyst was reactive and hence unstable. Therefore, DNA has evolved from RNA with chemical modifications that make it more stable. DNA being double stranded and having complementary strand further resists changes by evolving a process of repair. Because RNA can perform the tasks of both genetic materials and enzymes, RNA is believed to have once been capable of independent life.

1.7.3 RNA: A genetic material

Nucleic acids function as carriers of genetic information. While DNA is the principal genetic material in most organisms, in certain organisms, particularly RNA viruses, RNA acts as the genetic material. This was a significant discovery in molecular biology, proving that DNA is not the sole hereditary molecule. One of the first experiments that established RNA as the genetic material in RNA viruses was the **reconstitution experiment** of H. Fraenkel-Conrat and B. Singer. They took two different strains of *tobacco mosaic virus* (**TMV**), separated the RNAs from their protein coats, and reconstituted **hybrid viruses** by mixing the proteins of one strain with the RNA of the second strain, and vice versa. When the *hybrid virus* was spread on tobacco leaves, the lesions that developed corresponded to the TMV from which the RNA had been obtained. Thus, it was concluded that RNA serves as the genetic material in TMV.

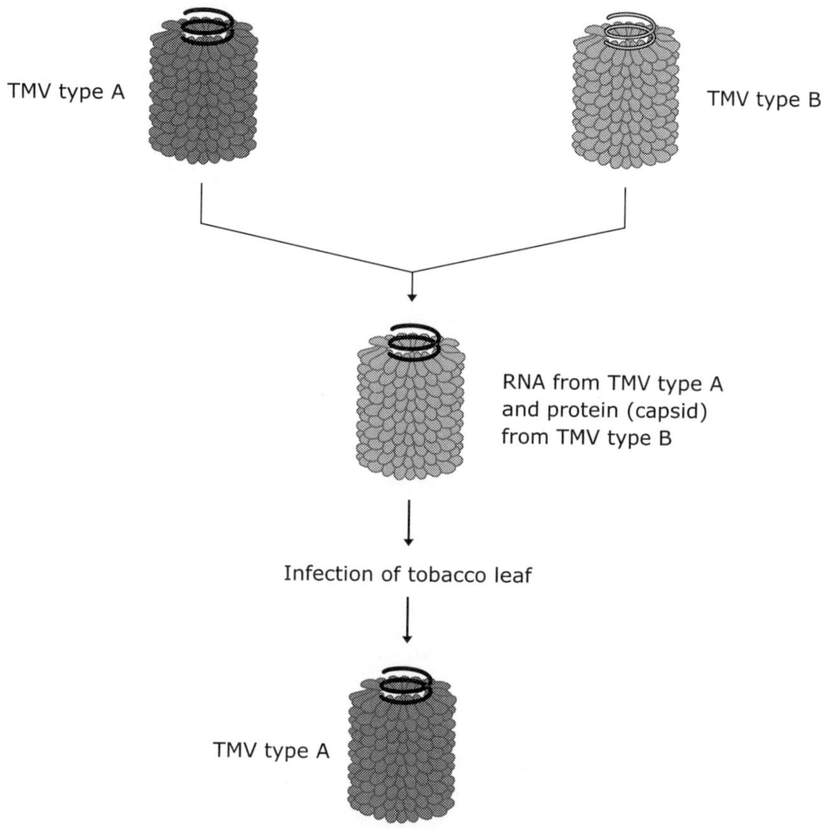

Figure 1.64 *In vivo* reconstitution of a hybrid TMV virus. There are two strains of virus (TMV type A and type B) which were separated into protein and RNA. The protein of one strain (type B) was allowed to recombine with the RNA of the other (type A). The *in vivo* progeny of this hybrid had the protein originally associated with its RNA. This proves that the genetic material of TMV is RNA, not protein.

1.8 Carbohydrates

Carbohydrates are biomolecules that are either **polyhydroxy aldehydes** or **polyhydroxy ketones**, or compounds that produce these substances upon hydrolysis. In the majority of carbohydrates, H and O are present in the same ratio as in water, hence also called as **hydrates of carbon**. Carbohydrates are the most abundant biomolecules on Earth. Carbohydrates are classified into following classes depending upon whether these undergo hydrolysis and if so on the number of products form:

Monosaccharides are simple carbohydrates that consist of a single polyhydroxy aldehyde or ketone unit.

Oligosaccharides are polymers made up of two to ten monosaccharide units joined together by glycosidic linkages. Oligosaccharides can be classified as di-, tri-, tetra- depending upon the number of monosaccharides present.

Polysaccharides are polymers with hundreds or thousands of monosaccharide units.

Note: Carbohydrates are sometimes broadly classified as **sugars** and **non-sugars**. *Sugars* are small carbohydrate molecules that typically have a sweet taste and are soluble in water. This category includes monosaccharides and disaccharides. *Non-sugars*, on the other hand, are larger carbohydrate molecules that do not taste sweet and are less soluble in water. This group includes polysaccharides and larger oligosaccharides.

1.8.1 Monosaccharides

Monosaccharides consist of a *single polyhydroxy aldehyde* or *ketone unit*. Monosaccharides are the simple sugars and they have a general formula $C_nH_{2n}O_n$. Monosaccharides are colorless, crystalline solids that are freely soluble in water but insoluble in non-polar solvents. The most abundant monosaccharide in nature is the D-glucose. Monosaccharides can be further sub-classified on the basis of:

Number of the carbon atoms

Monosaccharides can be named by a system that is based on the number of carbons with the suffix-*ose* added. The common monosaccharides have three to nine carbon atoms. The suffix -*ose* indicates that a molecule is a carbohydrate, and the prefixes tri-, tetr-, pent- and so forth indicate the number of carbon atoms in the chain. Monosaccharides with four, five, six and seven carbon atoms are called *tetroses, pentoses, hexoses* and *heptoses*, respectively.

Types of functional groups

Monosaccharides can be classified into aldoses and ketoses.

Aldoses are monosaccharides with an aldehyde group.

Ketoses are monosaccharides containing a ketone group.

For example, the monosaccharide *glucose* is an **aldohexose**; that is, it has six-carbon (-hexose) and an aldehyde group (aldo-). Similarly, *fructose* is a **ketohexose**; that is, it has six-carbon (-hexose) and a ketone group (keto-). Trioses are simplest monosaccharides. There are two trioses– dihydroxyacetone and glyceraldehyde. Dihydroxyacetone is a *ketose* because it contains a *keto* group, whereas glyceraldehyde is an *aldose* because it contains an *aldehyde group*.

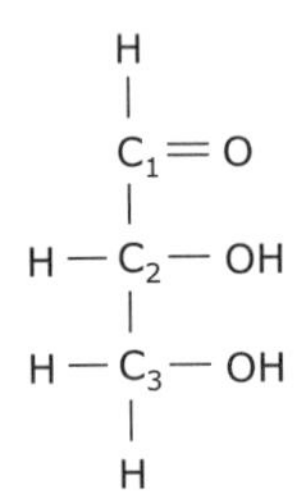

Glyceraldehyde (an aldose)

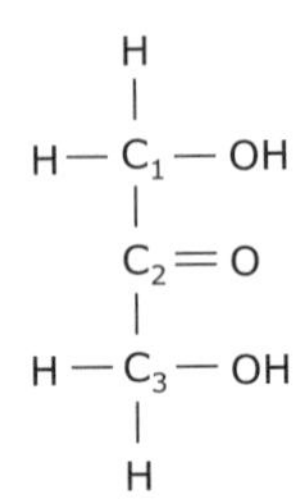

Dihydroxyacetone (a ketose)

Figure 1.65 Trioses, the simplest monosaccharides. The simplest aldose is glyceraldehyde, and the simplest ketose is dihydroxyacetone. These two simple sugars are termed trioses because they each contain three carbon atoms.

All monosaccharides, except *dihydroxyacetone*, are **chiral molecules**. Chiral molecules contain one or more chiral carbons. Glyceraldehyde, an aldotriose, has a single chiral carbon (the *second* carbon atom). The number of chiral carbons in a monosaccharide depends on the total number of carbons. In aldoses, there are ***n*–2** chiral carbons, and in ketoses, there are ***n*–3** chiral carbons, where *n* is the total number of carbons in the monosaccharide.

Chiral molecules, such as glyceraldehyde, can exist in two configurations that are non-superimposable mirror images of each other. These two absolute configurations are called **enantiomers**. An enantiomer is identified by its absolute configuration. Glyceraldehyde has two absolute configurations: when the hydroxyl group attached to the chiral carbon is on the left in a Fischer projection, the configuration is L; when the hydroxyl group is on the right, the configuration is D.

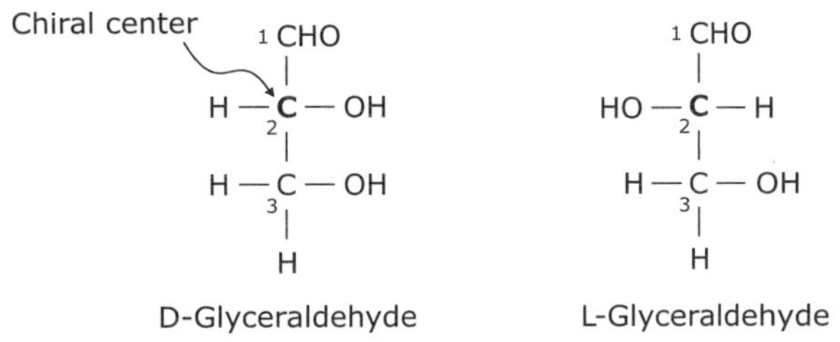

Figure 1.66 The enantiomers of glyceraldehyde. The configuration of groups around the chiral center (C_2), shown in bold, distinguishes D-glyceraldehyde from L-glyceraldehyde. The two molecules are mirror images and cannot be superimposed on one another.

D-glyceraldehyde and L-glyceraldehyde serve as reference points for the assignment of relative configurations to all other aldoses and ketoses. In case of monosaccharides with more than one chiral centers, the reference point is the penultimate carbon—that is, the next-to-the-last carbon on the chain. A **D-monosaccharide** has the same configuration at its penultimate carbon as D-glyceraldehyde (its –OH group is on the right) in a Fischer projection; an **L-monosaccharide** has the same configuration at its penultimate carbon as L-glyceraldehyde (its –OH group is on the left).

1.8.2 Epimers

Many monosaccharides are closely related and differ in configuration with respect to a single carbon atom. For example, **D-glucose** and **D-mannose** differ in configuration only at the second carbon. Stereoisomers that differ in configuration at only one carbon atom, other than the anomeric carbon, are called **epimers**. Similarly, **D-glucose** and **D-galactose** are epimers because they differ only at the fourth carbon. It is important to note that D-mannose and D-galactose are not epimers because their configurations differ at more than one carbon.

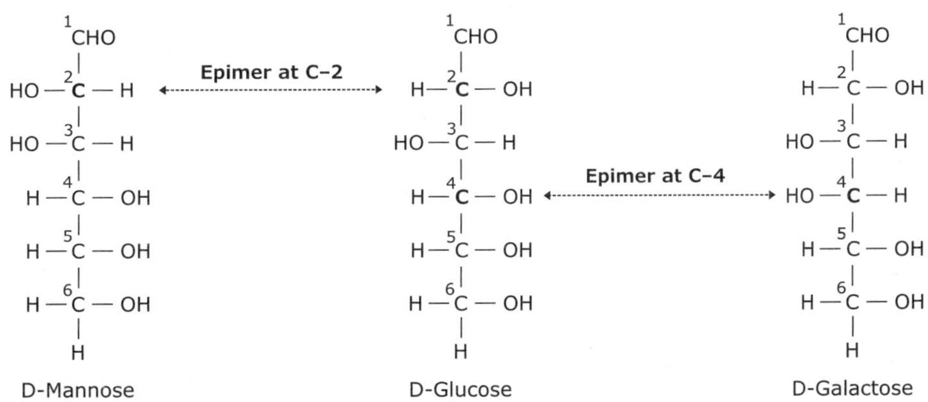

Figure 1.67 D-Glucose and two of its epimers. Two sugars that differ in configuration at only one chiral center are described as epimers. In this example, D-mannose and D-glucose are epimers and D-glucose and D-galactose are epimers, whereas D-mannose and D-galactose are not epimers.

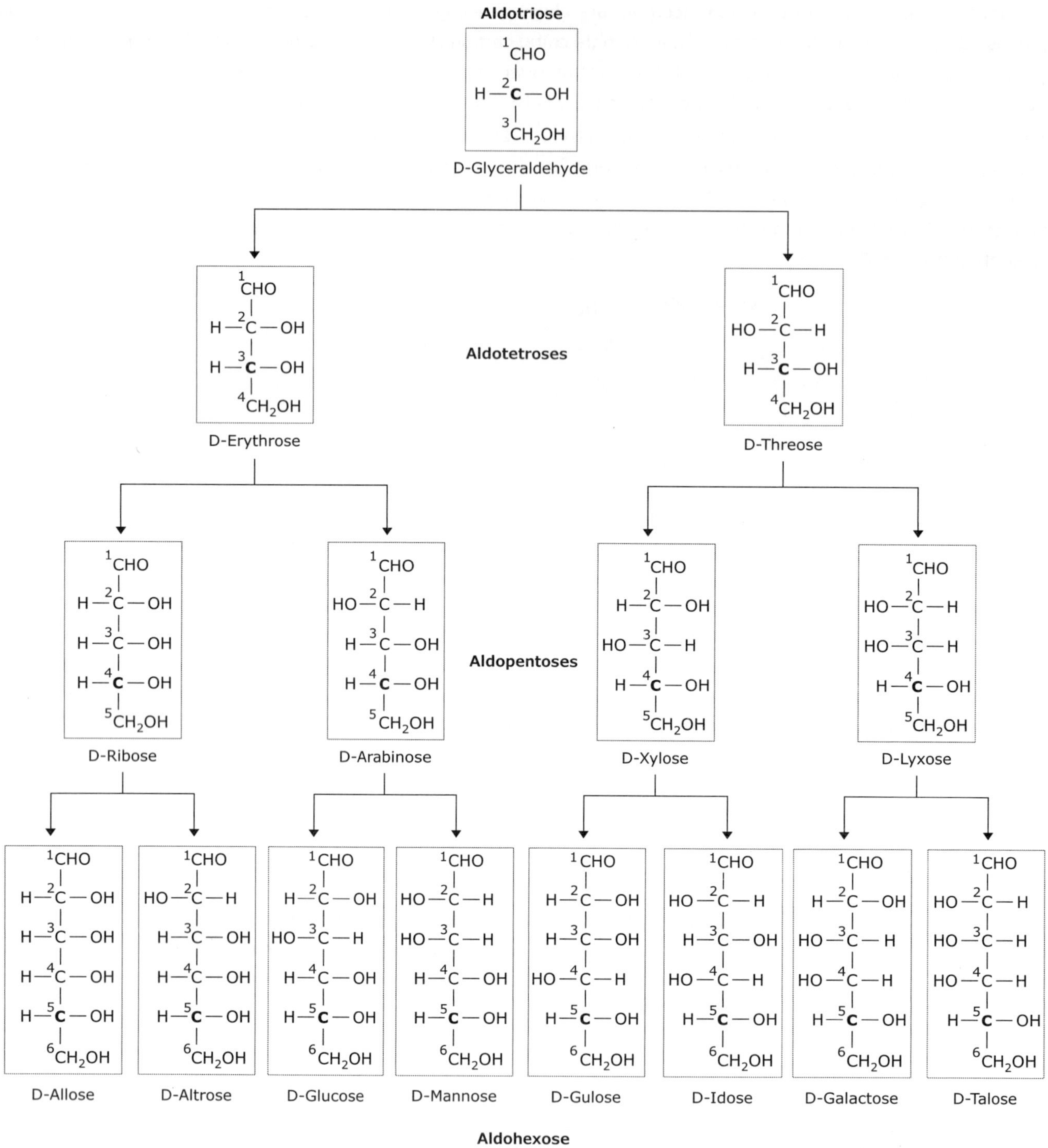

Figure 1.68 The structure of D-aldoses with three to six carbons. The configuration in each case is determined by the highest numbered asymmetric carbon (shown in bold). All of the structures shown are D-configurations, and the D-forms of monosaccharides predominate in nature, just as L-amino acids do. In all these D isomers, the chiral carbon most distant from the carbonyl carbon has the same configuration as the chiral carbon in D-glyceraldehyde. These preferences, established in apparently random choices early in evolution, persist uniformly in nature because of the stereospecificity of the enzymes that synthesize and metabolize these small molecules. Each of the eight D-aldohexoses, which differ in the stereochemistry at C-2, C-3 or C-4, has its own name: D-glucose, D-galactose, D-mannose, and so forth.

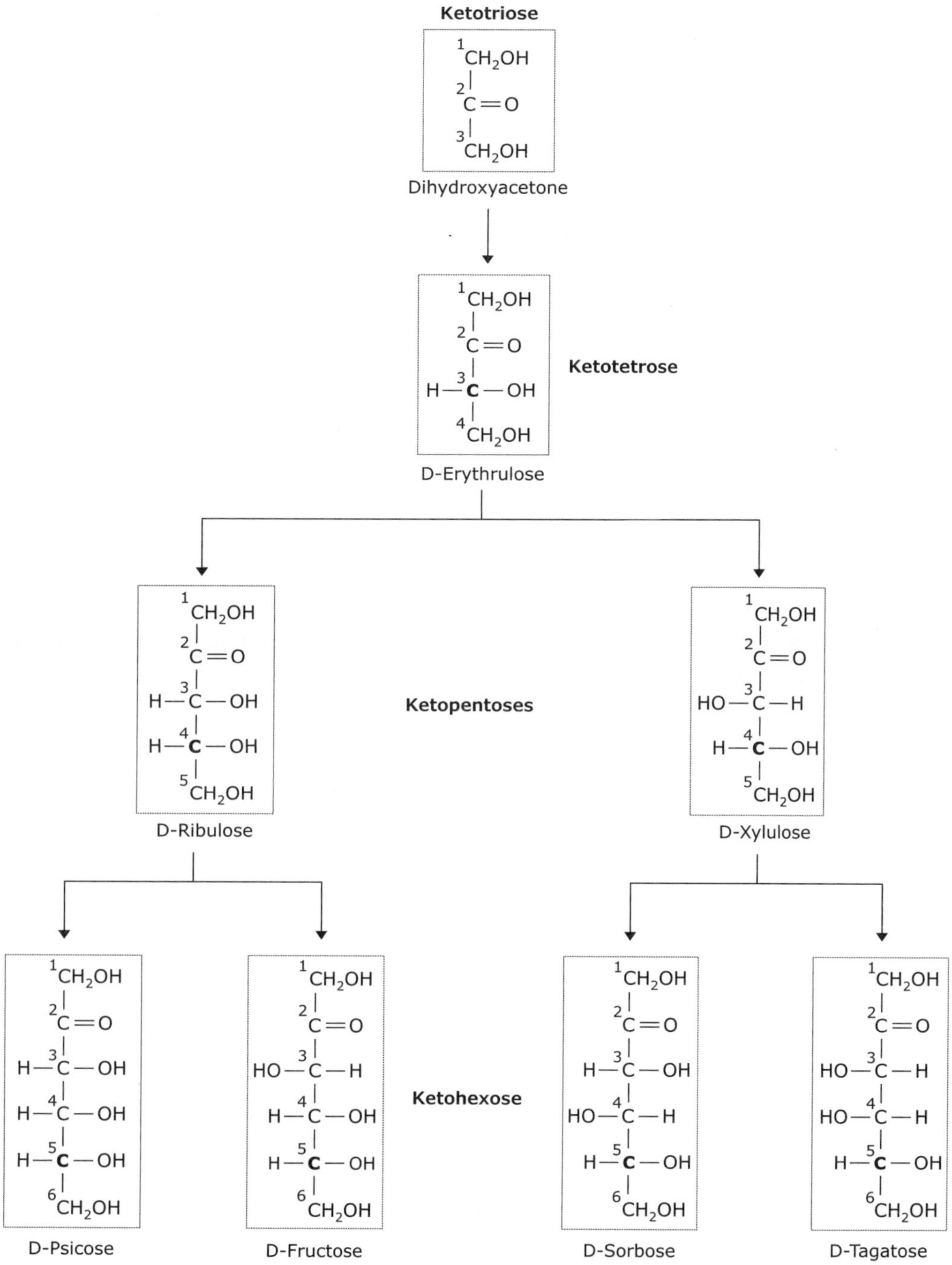

Figure 1.69 The structure of D-ketoses with three to six carbons. In all these D isomers, the chiral carbon most distant from the carbonyl carbon has the same configuration as the chiral carbon in D-glyceraldehyde.

1.8.3 Cyclic forms

In aqueous solution, monosaccharides with five or six carbon atoms predominantly exist as cyclic (ring) structures formed by an intramolecular reaction between a carbonyl group (aldehyde or ketone) and a hydroxyl group within the same molecule. This reaction produces a hemiacetal (for aldoses) or hemiketal (for ketoses) ring structure. Five- and six-membered rings are, known respectively as *furanoses* and *pyranoses.*

Hemiacetal: An aldehyde can react with an alcohol to form a *hemiacetal*.

Hemiketal: A ketone can react with an alcohol to form a *hemiketal*.

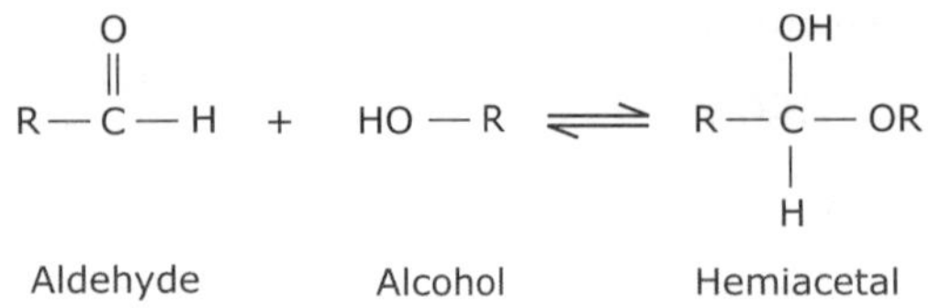

The product of the reaction between an alcohol and the carbonyl group of an aldehyde.

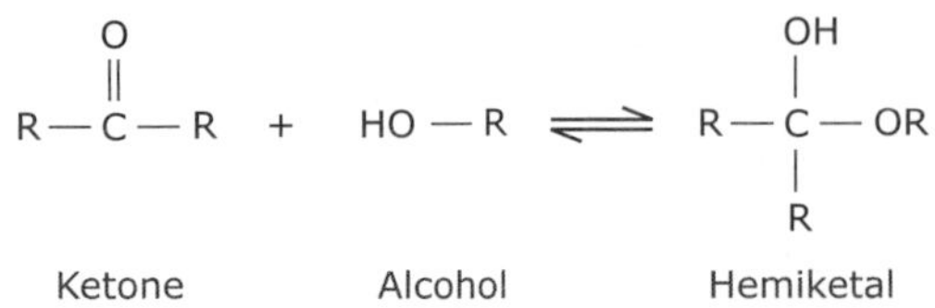

The product of the reaction between an alcohol and the carbonyl group of a ketone.

Five and six-membered cyclic structures in aqueous solution via internal hemiacetal or hemiketal formation reflect the ring size relationship to the common heterocyclic compounds **furan** and **pyran**. For an aldohexose such as glucose, the C-1 aldehyde group in the open-chain form of glucose reacts with the C-5 hydroxyl group to form an intramolecular *hemiacetal*. The resulting cyclic hemiacetal, a six-membered ring, is called **pyranose** because of its similarity to **pyran**.

Similarly, the C-2 keto group in the open-chain form of a ketohexose, such as fructose, can form an intramolecular *hemiketal* by reacting with either the C-6 hydroxyl group to form a six-membered cyclic hemiketal or the C-5 hydroxyl group to form a five-membered cyclic hemiketal. The five-membered ring is called a **furanose** because of its similarity to **furan**. Thus, fructose forms both pyranose and furanose rings. The pyranose form predominates in fructose free in solution, and the furanose form predominates in many fructose derivatives.

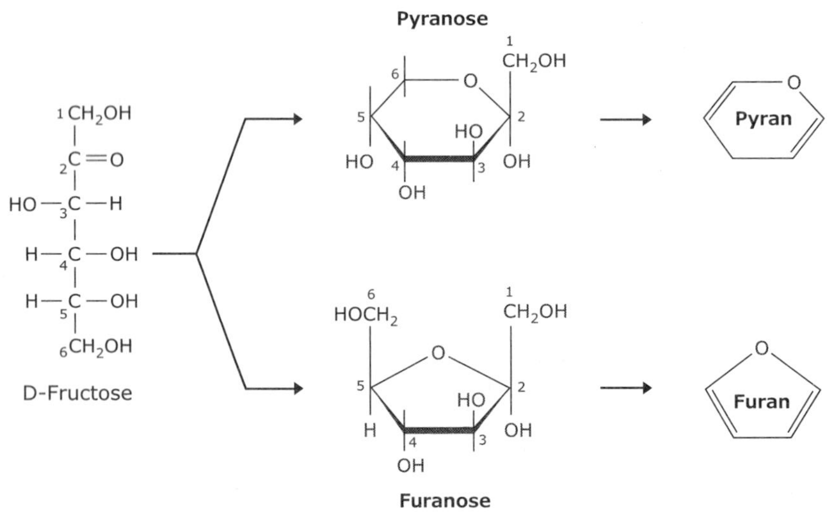

Figure 1.70 The C-2 keto group in the open-chain form of fructose, can form an intramolecular hemiketal by reacting with either the C-6 hydroxyl group to form a six-membered cyclic hemiketal or the C-5 hydroxyl group to form a five-membered cyclic hemiketal. The six-membered ring is called pyranose because of its similarity to pyran whereas the five-membered ring is called a furanose because of its similarity to furan.

Aldopentoses such as ribose can form furanose or pyranose rings. For the five carbon sugar ribose, the pyranose form arises when the carbonyl group reacts with the terminal hydroxyl group. The carbon 5 is incorporated into the ring. If cyclization occurs between the hydroxyl group on carbon 4 and the carbonyl group then the furanose ring forms. This places the carbon 5 outside the ring.

Cyclic structure exists in two different configurational forms. If the hydroxyl on the anomeric carbon is below the plane of the ring, it is said to be in the α-position; if above the plane of the ring, it is in the β-position. These two diastereoisomers are called **anomers** and the hemiacetal or hemiketal carbon is known as **anomeric carbon**. The carbonyl carbon of a monosaccharide unit, which becomes a chiral center when the sugar cyclizes to a hemiacetal or hemiketal is called *anomeric carbon*.

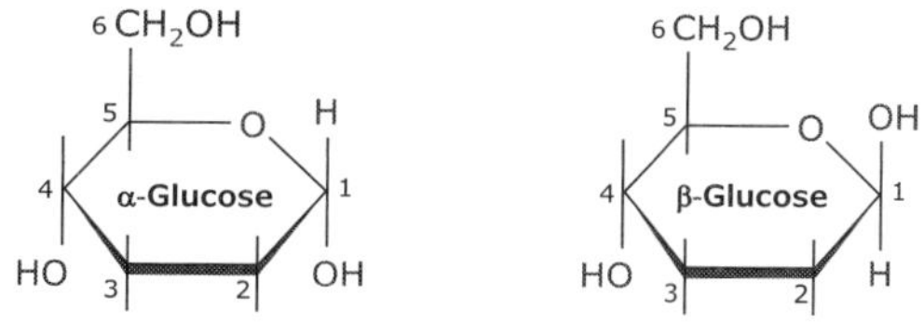

In glucose, the C-1 carbon atom is called the *anomeric carbon*, and the α and β forms are called *anomers* (as shown in the figure). An equilibrium mixture of glucose contains approximately 37% α-form and 63% β-form and less than 1% of the open chain form. The two anomers have different physical and chemical properties. For example, α-D-glucose has a specific rotation of +112° whereas the β-D-glucose form has a specific rotation of +19°. When either of these pure substances is dissolved in water, the specific optical rotation of the solution slowly changes until it reaches an equilibrium value of specific rotation of +52.7°. In aqueous solution the interconversion of α- and β-forms via the open chain structure, to give an equilibrium mixture is known as **mutarotation**. *Mutarotation is the change in specific rotation that occurs when an α or β form of a carbohydrate is converted to an equilibrium mixture of the two forms.*

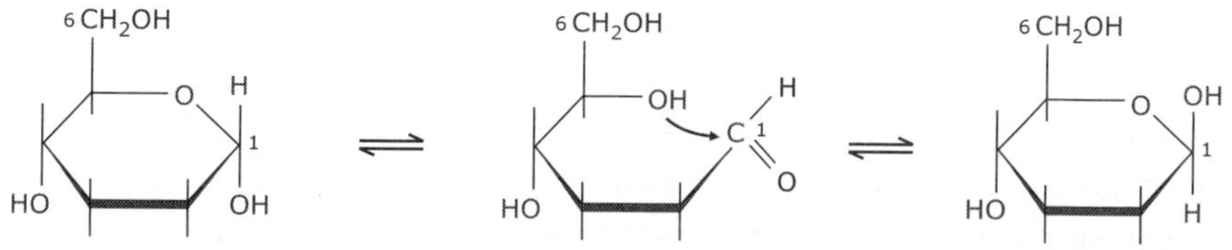

α-D-Glucose
MP = 146°C
[α] = +112°

D-Glucose

β-D-Glucose
MP = 150°C
[α] = +19°

Figure 1.71 The α and β cyclic isomers of D-glucose can interconvert, with the open-chain structure as the intermediate.

The same nomenclature applies to the ring form of **fructose**, except that α and β refer to the hydroxyl groups attached to C-2, the anomeric carbon atom. In contrast to glucose, fructose can form both five-membered furanose ring and six-membered pyranose ring.

Feature	Anomers	Epimers
Type of isomer	Differing at functional group carbon	Differing at one chiral carbon; not functional group carbon
Location of difference	Only functional group carbon	Any chiral carbon except functional group carbon
Occur in forms	Only cyclic forms	Both acyclic and cyclic forms

1.8.4 Derivatives of monosaccharide

Glycosides: A *glycoside* is a compound in which a sugar molecule (**glycone**) is bonded through its anomeric carbon to a non-sugar molecule (**aglycone**) via a glycosidic bond. The formation of glycosides exemplifies **acetal** formation, where the hemiacetal group of the glycone reacts with a hydroxyl group of the aglycone. Glycosides are a diverse group of secondary metabolites and can be classified based on the aglycone unit, the glycone unit, or the type of glycosidic bond. Glycosides are named according to the glycone unit that provides the hemiacetal group. For example, if the glycone is glucose, the resulting molecule is a **glucoside**; if it is galactose, the result is a **galactoside**. Additionally, based on the type of glycosidic bond, glycosides can be categorized as O-glycosides, C-glycosides, or S-glycosides. Examples of glycosides include ouabain, which inhibits Na^+-K^+ ATPase activity, and streptomycin, an antibiotic.

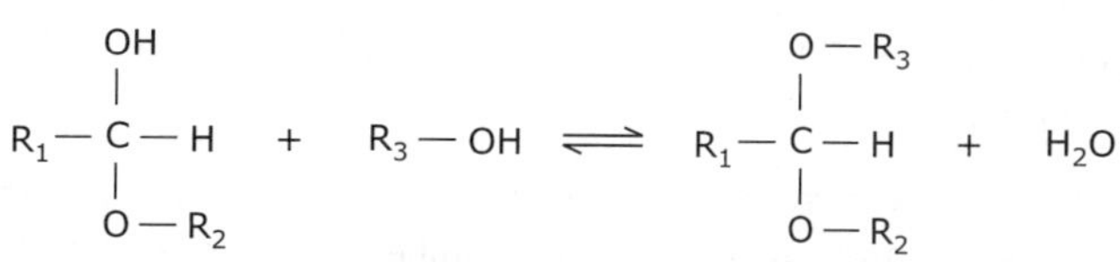

Hemiacetal Alcohol Acetal

Sugar acids: The aldehyde group in aldoses can be oxidized to produce a class of monosaccharides called **aldonic acids** (if glucose, it is gluconic acid). One important aldonic acid is L-ascorbic acid or vitamin C. Aldoses can undergo selective oxidation also. If terminal –OH group oxidizes, it produces **uronic acid** (if glucose, it is glucuronic acid). If both the aldehyde group and the terminal –OH oxidizes then **aldaric acid** (if glucose, it is glucaric acid) is produced.

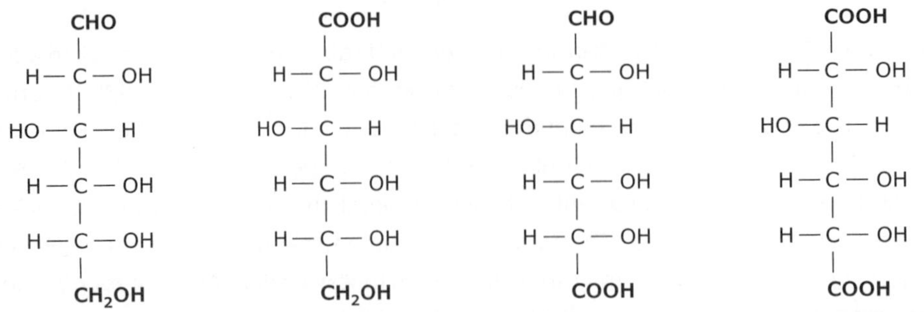

D-Glucose D-Gluconic acid D-Glucuronic acid D-Glucaric acid

Sugar alcohols: Carbonyl groups in aldoses and ketoses can be reduced to the hydroxyl group to form *sugar alcohols* (or **alditols**). Sugar alcohols are designated by the addition of *-itol* with the name of the parent sugar. The reduction of the carbonyl group of glucose and xylose produce polyhydroxy alcohols called **sorbitol** and **xylitol**, respectively. The sugar alcohols are linear molecules that cannot cyclize in the manner of aldoses.

Amino sugars: In amino sugars, a hydroxyl group is replaced by an *amino* or an *acetylamino* group. Three amino sugars are common in nature: D-glucosamine, D-mannosamine and D-galactosamine.

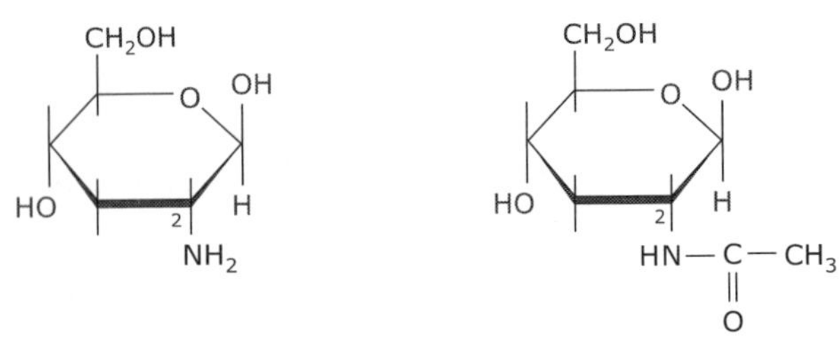

β-D-Glucosamine *N*-Acetyl-β-D-glucosamine

N-acetylglucosamine (**NAG**), a glucosamine derivative, is part of many structural polymers, including those of the bacterial cell wall. Bacterial cell walls also contain a derivative of glucosamine, *N*-acetylmuramic acid (**NAM**), in which **lactic acid** is ether-linked to the oxygen at C-3 of *N*-acetylglucosamine.

Table 1.11 Abbreviations for some common monosaccharide residues

Glucose	Glc	Xylose	Xyl
Arabinose	Ara	*N*-Acetylgalactosamine	GalNAc
Fructose	Fru	*N*-Acetylglucosamine (NAG)	GlcNAc
Ribose	Rib	*N*-Acetylmuramic acid (NAM)	MurNAc

Problem

An aqueous solution of D-galactose has an $[\alpha]_D^{25}$ of +80.2° after standing for some hours. The specific rotations of pure α-D-galactose and β-D-galactose are +150.7° and +52.8°, respectively. Calculate proportions of α-D-galactose and β-D-galactose in the equilibrium mixture.

Solution: For the equilibrium mixture, if x is the fraction of the α-anomer, then 1–x is the fraction of the β-anomer and $150.7x + 52.8(1-x) = 80.2$. Hence, x = 0.28; 1–x = 0.72. The equilibrium mixture is 28% α-anomer and 72% β-anomer.

1.8.5 Disaccharides and glycosidic bond

Disaccharides are the simplest and most common oligosaccharides. Oligosaccharides containing three or more residues are relatively rare, occurring almost entirely in plants. A *disaccharide* consists of two monosaccharides joined by an *O*-glycosidic bond. A bond formed between the anomeric carbon atom of a monosaccharide and the oxygen atom of an alcohol is called a **glycosidic bond**. Glycosidic bonds are labeled α or β depending on the anomeric configuration of the carbon involved in the glycosidic bond. For example, in **maltose** two molecules of glucose are linked by an $\alpha 1 \rightarrow 4$ glycosidic bond. The glycosidic bond forms between C-1 (the anomeric carbon) of one glucose residue and the hydroxyl oxygen atom on C-4 of the other. The configuration of the anomeric carbon atom participates in this glycosidic bond formation is α.

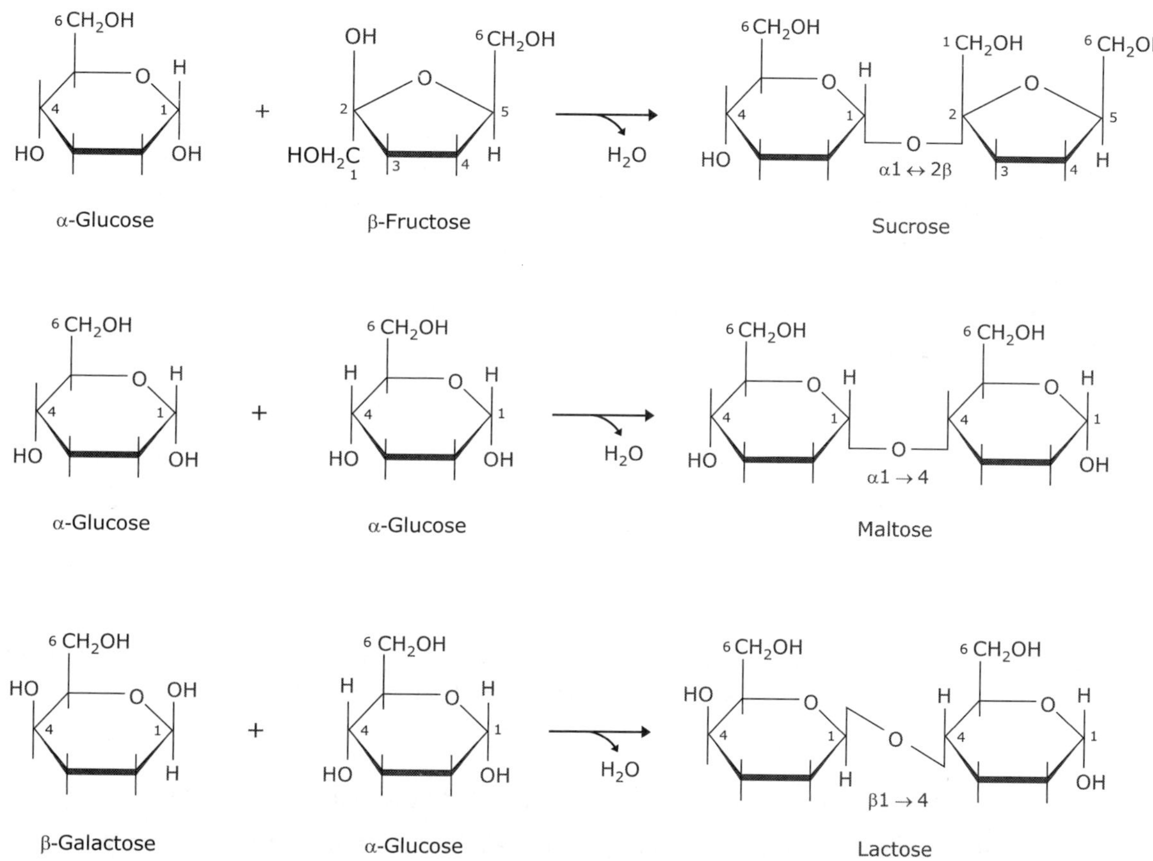

Figure 1.72 The bond connecting the anomeric carbon to the hydroxyl oxygen atom is termed a glycosidic bond. *Sucrose* is a disaccharide of glucose and fructose residues joined by $\alpha 1 \leftrightarrow 2\beta$ glycosidic bond. The disaccharide *maltose* contains two glucose residues joined by an $\alpha 1 \rightarrow 4$ glycosidic bond between C-1 (the anomeric carbon) of one glucose residue and C-4 of the other. *Lactose* is a disaccharide of galactose and glucose residues joined by a $\beta 1 \rightarrow 4$ glycosidic bond.

Similarly, **sucrose** is a disaccharide of glucose and fructose residues joined by an $\alpha 1 \leftrightarrow 2\beta$ glycosidic bond between C-1 (the anomeric carbon) of glucose residue and C-2 (the anomeric carbon) of the fructose residue. The anomeric carbons of both monosaccharide units are involved in the glycosidic bond. The configurations of the anomeric carbon atom involved in the glycosidic bond formation are α for glucose and β for fructose. The abbreviated name of sucrose is either Glc ($\alpha 1 \leftrightarrow 2\beta$) Fru or Fru ($2\beta \leftrightarrow \alpha 1$) Glc.

Oligosaccharides (as well as polysaccharides) have a directionality which is defined by their **reducing** and **nonreducing ends**. The monosaccharide unit at the *reducing end* has a free anomeric carbon atom that has reducing activity because it can form the open-chain form whereas monosaccharide unit at the *non-reducing end* has no free anomeric carbon due to its participation in the glycosidic bond formation.

Table 1.12 Occurrence and biochemical roles of some representative disaccharides

Disaccharides	Structure	Physiological role
Sucrose	Glucose (α1 $\leftrightarrow$ 2β) Fructose	A product of photosynthesis.
Lactose	Galactose (β1 $\rightarrow$ 4) Glucose	A major animal energy source.
Trehalose	Glucose (α1 $\leftrightarrow$ 1α) Glucose	A major circulatory sugar in insects; used for energy.
Maltose	Glucose (α1 $\rightarrow$ 4) Glucose	The dimer derived from the starch and glycogen.
Cellobiose	Glucose (β1 $\rightarrow$ 4) Glucose	The dimer of the cellulose polymer.
Gentiobiose	Glucose (β1 $\rightarrow$ 6) Glucose	Constituent of plant glycosides and some polysaccharides.

Hydrolysis of sucrose

Sucrose is dextrorotatory, its specific rotation being +66.5°. Hydrolysis of sucrose with hot dilute acid yields D-glucose and D-fructose. D-glucose is also dextrorotatory, $[\alpha]_\lambda^T$ = +52.7°, but D-fructose is levorotatory, $[\alpha]_\lambda^T$ = –92°. Since D-fructose has a greater specific rotation than D-glucose, the resulting mixture is levorotatory. Because of this, the hydrolysis of sucrose is known as the **inversion of sucrose**, and the equimolecular mixture of glucose and fructose is known as **invert sugar** (or invertose).

$$\underset{\substack{\text{Sucrose} \\ [\alpha]_\lambda^T = +66.5^\circ}}{C_{12}H_{22}O_{11}} \xrightarrow{+\,H_2O} \underset{\substack{\text{D-glucose} \\ [\alpha]_\lambda^T = +52.7^\circ}}{C_6H_{12}O_6} + \underset{\substack{\text{D-fructose} \\ [\alpha]_\lambda^T = -92^\circ}}{C_6H_{12}O_6}$$

$$[\alpha]_\lambda^T = (+52.7^\circ) + (-92^\circ) = -39.3^\circ$$

Problem

The enzyme invertase (sucrose) is allowed to act on a solution of sucrose until the optical rotation of the solution becomes zero. What fraction of the sucrose has been hydrolyzed?

Solution: After complete hydrolysis of sucrose, change in optical rotation = +66.5° to –39° = 106°. At zero optical rotation, the change is 66.5°. Thus, the fraction of the sucrose hydrolyzed = 66.5°/106° = 0.63.

Problem

How many different disaccharides containing D-galactopyranose plus D-glucopyranose are possible?

Solution: There are 20 possible disaccharides containing galactose plus glucose in the pyranose ring forms:

Galactosides: 1–2, 1–3, 1–4, 1–6 (linked α or β) = 4 × 2 = 8

Glucosides: 1–2, 1–3, 1–4, 1–6 (linked α or β) = 4 × 2 = 8

Nonreducing disaccharides: α–α, α–β, β–α, β–β = 4

Total: 20

1.8.6 Polysaccharides

Polysaccharides are ubiquitous in nature. They are also called **glycans**. They can be classified into two separate groups, based on their functions: *structural* and *storage polysaccharides*. Structural polysaccharides provide mechanical stability to cells, organs, and organisms. Storage polysaccharides serve as carbohydrate stores that release monosaccharides as required. Polysaccharides may be **homopolysaccharides** (contain only a single type of monomeric unit) or **heteropolysaccharides** (contain two or more different kinds of monomeric units).

Based on functions: Structural and storage polysaccharides.

Based on composition: Homopolysaccharides and heteropolysaccharides.

Homopolysaccharides

Starch is a homopolysaccharide composed of α-D-glucose units and serves as the storage form of glucose in plants. It consists of two components: a minor unbranched polymer of glucose called **amylose** and a major branched polymer of glucose called **amylopectin**. Amylose is made up of glucose units linked by $\alpha 1 \rightarrow 4$ glycosidic bonds. Amylopectin, on the other hand, is a polymer of glucose with $\alpha 1 \rightarrow 4$ glycosidic bonds and $\alpha 1 \rightarrow 6$ branching points that occur at intervals of approximately 25 to 30 glucose residues.

Iodine test: This chemical test is used to detect the presence of starch in a sample. The test uses an **iodine solution,** a solution containing elemental *iodine* and *potassium iodide* dissolved in water or alcohol. Since iodine is not very soluble in water, the reagent is prepared by dissolving iodine in water in the presence of potassium iodide. This forms a soluble linear **triiodide ion** complex. The triiodide ions interact with the helical structure of amylose. The iodine molecules become trapped within the helical structure, producing a characteristic blue-black color.

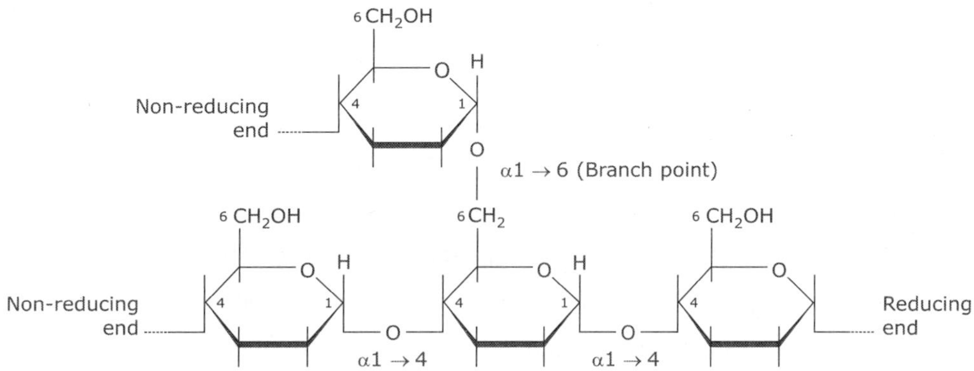

Figure 1.73 The storage polysaccharide in plants is starch. *Amylose*, the unbranched fraction of starch, consists of glucose residues joined by $\alpha 1 \rightarrow 4$ bond. *Amylopectin*, the branched fraction, has branching at intervals of 25-30 glucose residues.

Glycogen is a homopolysaccharide composed of α-D-glucose units and serves as the primary storage form of carbohydrates in animals. Similar to amylopectin, it is a branched polymer of glucose with $\alpha 1 \rightarrow 4$ glycosidic bonds and $\alpha 1 \rightarrow 6$ branching points occurring at intervals of approximately 8 to 10 glucose residues.

Cellulose is a linear, unbranched homopolysaccharide of D-glucose residues joined by $\beta 1 \rightarrow 4$ glycosidic bonds. Cellulose is a structural polysaccharide of plant cells. Although cellulose forms a part of the human diet (e.g., in vegetables and fruits), it is not hydrolyzed by human enzyme systems. *Cellulose is one of the most abundant organic compounds in the biosphere.*

Chitin is a linear homopolysaccharide composed of ***N*-acetyl-D-glucosamine** residues joined by $\beta 1 \rightarrow 4$ glycosidic bonds. The only chemical difference from cellulose is the replacement of the hydroxyl group at C-2 with an acetylated amino group. It is a structural polysaccharide present in the cell wall of fungi and also in the exoskeleton of insects and crustaceans. Chitin is the Earth's second most abundant carbohydrate polymer, following cellulose.

Heteropolysaccharides

Glycosaminoglycans (GAGs) are negatively charged, unbranched heteropolysaccharide composed of repeating disaccharide units, $[\text{Acidic sugar} — \text{Amino sugar}]_n$. **Amino sugar** is always either *N*-acetylglucosamine or *N*-acetylgalactosamine and the **acidic sugar** in most cases is a uronic acid, usually glucuronic acid. The simplest glycosaminoglycan hyaluronan (hyaluronic acid) contains alternating residues of D-glucuronic acid and *N*-acetylglucosamine. Chondroitin sulfate, keratan sulfate, heparin, heparan sulfate, dermatan sulfate and hyaluronate are the major glycosaminoglycans. These polysaccharides are unique to animals and bacteria and are not found in plants. With the exception of hyaluronic acid, all the GAGs contain sulfate groups, either as O-esters or as *N*-sulfate. All of the glycosaminoglycans except *hyaluronic acid* are found covalently attached to protein forming **proteoglycan**. The polysaccharide chain is mainly assembled on the core protein in the Golgi bodies. A specific **link tetrasaccharide** is first assembled on a serine residue. In most cases, it is not clear how the serine residue is selected. The rest of the GAG chain, consisting mainly of a repeating disaccharide unit, is then synthesized, with one sugar residue being added at a time. The covalent bond forms between serine residue of the protein and xylose sugar residue of link tetrasaccharide is *O*-glycosidic bond.

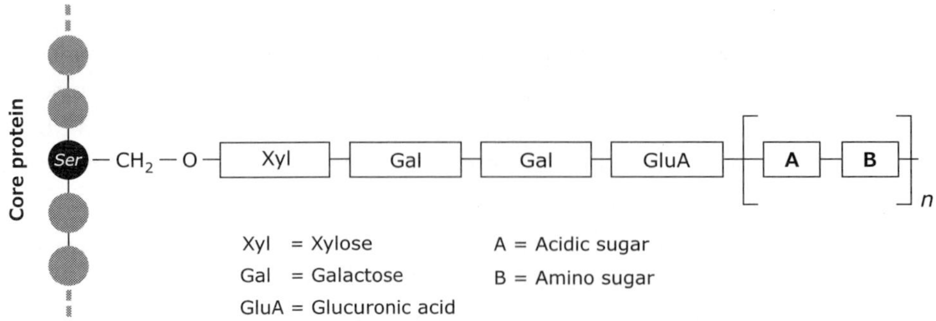

Figure 1.74 Glycosaminoglycans are made of disaccharide repeating units in which one of the two monosaccharide units is a uronic acid (*keratan sulfate is an exception*) and the other an *N*-acetylated amino sugar. Glycosaminoglycans are usually attached to proteins through link tetrasaccharide to form *proteoglycans*. In a typical link tetrasaccharide, the xylose residue at the reducing end of the linker is joined by its anomeric carbon to the hydroxyl of the Ser residue.

Table 1.13 Characteristics of Glycosaminoglycans (GAGs)

GAG	**Sugar A** (acidic sugar)	**Sugar B** (amino sugar)	Sulfates	Links to protein
Hyaluronic acid	D-Glucuronic acid	*N*-acetyl-D-glucosamine	–	–
Chondroitin sulfate	D-Glucuronic acid	*N*-acetyl-D-galactosamine	+	+
Dermatan sulfate	D-Glucuronic acid *or* L-iduronic acid	*N*-acetyl-D-galactosamine	+	+
Heparan sulfate	D-Glucuronic acid *or* L-iduronic acid	*N*-acetyl-D-glucosamine	+	+
Heparin	D-Glucuronic acid *or* L-iduronic acid	*N*-acetyl-D-glucosamine	+	+
Keratan sulfate	D-Galactose (non-acidic sugar)	*N*-acetyl-D-glucosamine	+	+

Peptidoglycan, also known as **murein**, is present in eubacterial cell walls and is composed of polymerized disaccharide units formed by alternating residues of **N-acetylglucosamine** (NAG) and **N-acetylmuramic acid** (NAM). NAG and NAM are joined through $\beta1 \rightarrow 4$ glycosidic bond. A peptide chain (termed **stem peptide**) is connected to the carboxyl group of the NAM by an *amide* linkage. Typically, the peptide chains consist of two to five amino acids.

Table 1.14 Important polysaccharides

Name	Monomer	Main linkages	Branch linkages
Murein	NAG + NAM	$\beta1 \rightarrow 4$	—
Dextran	D-glucose	$\alpha1 \rightarrow 6$	$\alpha1 \rightarrow 2$; $\alpha1 \rightarrow 3$ and $\alpha1 \rightarrow 4$
Cellulose	D-glucose	$\beta1 \rightarrow 4$	—
Starch (Amylose)	D-glucose	$\alpha1 \rightarrow 4$	—
(Amylopectin)	D-glucose	$\alpha1 \rightarrow 4$	$\alpha1 \rightarrow 6$
Inulin	D-fructose	$\beta2 \rightarrow 1$	—
Chitin	*N*-acetylglucosamine	$\beta1 \rightarrow 4$	—
Glycogen	D-glucose	$\alpha1 \rightarrow 4$	$\alpha1 \rightarrow 6$
Callose	D-glucose	$\beta1 \rightarrow 3$	—

1.8.7 Glycoproteins

Various types of compound consisting of carbohydrates covalently linked with non-carbohydrates constituent are classified under the general name called **glycoconjugates**. The major types of glycoconjugates are the glycoproteins, peptidoglycans, glycolipids and lipopolysaccharides. Carbohydrates covalently linked with proteins are called **glycoproteins**. The carbohydrate may be in the form of a monosaccharide, disaccharide, oligosaccharide, polysaccharide, or their derivatives. In glycoproteins, carbohydrates are attached either to the amide nitrogen atom in the side chain of asparagine (termed an *N-linkage*) or to the oxygen atom in the side chain of serine or threonine (termed an O-*linkage*). The term *glycoprotein* also includes **proteoglycans**, which in the past were considered as a separate class of glycoconjugates. Proteoglycans are a subclass of glycoproteins in which the carbohydrates are glycosaminoglycans. According to IUPAC, the term **glycan** is used for polysaccharides meaning a compound consists of a large number of covalently linked monosaccharides. However, in general use, this term may also be used to refer to the carbohydrate portion of a glycoconjugate, such as a glycoprotein or a glycolipid, even if the carbohydrate is only an oligosaccharide.

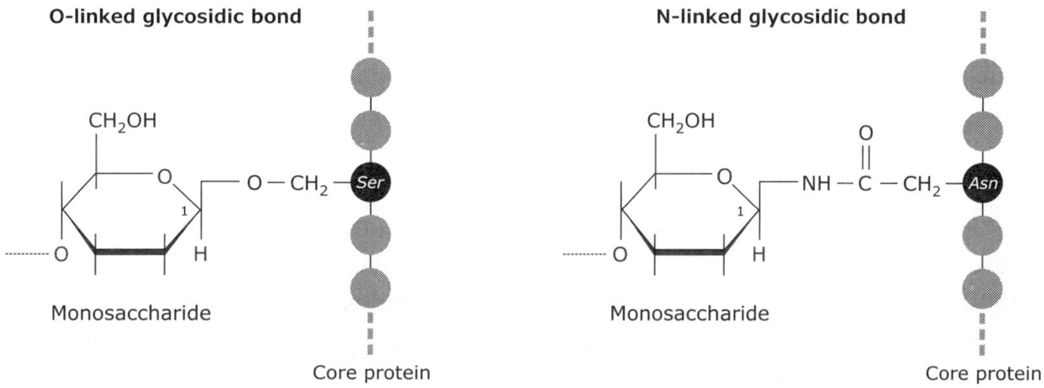

Figure 1.75 Carbohydrates are covalently attached to many different proteins to form *glycoproteins*. Carbohydrates are attached either to the amide nitrogen atom in the side chain of asparagine (termed an N-*linkage*) or to the oxygen atom in the side chain of serine or threonine (termed an O-*linkage*).

1.8.8 Reducing and non-reducing sugars

A **reducing sugar** is any sugar that can act as a **reducing agent**. A reducing sugar possesses a free aldehyde or ketone group that allows it to reduce ferric or cupric ions. All monosaccharides, whether aldoses or ketoses, are reducing sugars. Additionally, disaccharides formed through head-to-tail condensation are also reducing sugars. These disaccharides have at least one reducing end. *Reducing sugars undergo mutarotation in aqueous solution.*

Disaccharides formed through head-to-head condensation, such as sucrose and trehalose, are **non-reducing sugars**. These sugars cannot reduce ferric or cupric ions because the anomeric carbons of both monosaccharides participate in glycosidic bond formation, leaving no free anomeric carbon atoms and, therefore, no reducing end. In the context of disaccharides or polysaccharides, the end of a chain that has a free anomeric carbon (i.e., not involved in a glycosidic bond) is called the **reducing end** of the chain.

1.9 Lipids

Biological lipids are a chemically heterogeneous group of biomolecules that are:

- Insoluble or only poorly soluble in polar solvent such as water.
- Hydrophobic or amphipathic molecules.

The hydrophobic nature of lipids is due to the predominance of hydrocarbon chains ($-CH_2-CH_2-CH_2-$) in their structures. Unlike proteins and carbohydrates, lipids are not **polymeric** molecules. They comprise a highly diverse collection of molecules with varied structural and functional features. This group includes a broad range of molecules such as fatty acids, triacylglycerols, waxes, phospholipids, glycolipids, sterols, and prenols. These molecules may be derived entirely or partially from:

Carbanion-based condensations of ketoacyl thioesters.

Carbocation-based condensations of isoprene units.

Lipids have been broadly subdivided into *simple* and *complex lipids*. **Simple lipids** are those that yield two types of products on hydrolysis, while **complex lipids** yield three or more types of products on hydrolysis. For example, **triacylglycerol** is a simple lipid that yields two types of products on hydrolysis (e.g., fatty acids and glycerol), whereas glycerophospholipid is a complex lipid that yield three or more types of products on hydrolysis.

Function of lipids: Biological lipids have diverse functions. They:

- Serve as a storage form of metabolic fuel.
- Provide the structural components of membranes.
- Have protective functions in bacteria, plants, insects, and vertebrates, serving as a part of the outer coating.

Apart from these general functions, biological lipids also serve as pigments (such as carotene), hormones (vitamin D derivatives and sex hormones), signaling molecules (such as eicosanoids and phosphatidylinositol derivatives), cofactors (such as vitamin K), detergents (such as bile salts), and have many other specialized functions.

1.9.1 Fatty acids

Fatty acids are the simplest form of lipids and serve as constituents in many complex lipids. They are long-chain hydrocarbons, usually 12 to 24 carbons in length, with one carboxyl group. Fatty acids in biological systems usually contain an *even* number of carbon atoms. The alkyl chain may be **saturated** or **unsaturated**. Unsaturated fatty acids may contain one or more double bonds in the *cis*-configuration (mostly). Fatty acids are **amphipathic** by nature; that is, they have both hydrophilic and hydrophobic domains.

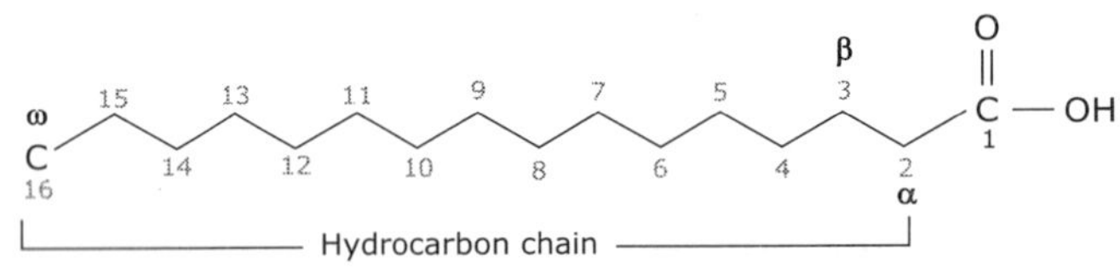

Figure 1.76 Structure of fatty acid – a carboxylic acid with a long aliphatic chain, which is either saturated or unsaturated. Most naturally occurring fatty acids have an unbranched hydrocarbon chain with an even number of carbon atoms (commonly C-14 to C-24). The carboxyl carbon is assigned the number 1 (C-1), and the carbon next to it is C-2. By an older system, in a fatty acid second carbon is referred to as the α-carbon, third carbon as the β-carbon and the end methyl carbon as the ω-carbon.

Table 1.15 Predominant naturally occurring fatty acids

Common name	Systematic name	Carbon atoms : Double bonds
Saturated fatty acid		
Lauric acid	Dodec*anoic* acid	12 : 0
Myristic acid	Tetradec*anoic* acid	14 : 0
Palmitic acid	Hexadec*anoic* acid	16 : 0
Stearic acid	Octadec*anoic* acid	18 : 0
Arachidic acid	Eicos*anoic* acid	20 : 0
Unsaturated fatty acid		
Palmitoleic acid	*cis*-Δ^{9}-Hexadec*enoic* acid	16 : 1
Oleic acid	*cis*-Δ^{9}-Octadec*enoic* acid	18 : 1
Linoleic acid	all *cis*-$\Delta^{9,\,12}$-Octadeca*dienoic* acid	18 : 2
Linolenic acid	all *cis*-$\Delta^{9,\,12,\,15}$-Octadeca*trienoic* acid	18 : 3
Arachidonic acid	all *cis*-$\Delta^{5,\,8,\,11,\,14}$-Eicosa*tetraenoic* acid	20 : 4

Saturated and unsaturated fatty acids

Saturated fatty acids have no double bonds in the chain. Their general formula is $CH_3—(CH_2)_n—COOH$ where n specifies the number of methylene groups between the methyl and carboxyl carbons. Examples of predominant saturated fatty acids are lauric, myristic, palmitic and others.

Unsaturated fatty acids have one or more double bonds, and called *monounsaturated fatty acid* (**MUFA**) or *polyunsaturated fatty acid* (**PUFA**) respectively. The double bonds in naturally occurring fatty acids are *generally* in a *cis* as opposed to a *trans* configuration. The double bonds of polyunsaturated fatty acids are almost never conjugated (alternating single and double bonds).

The **systematic name** includes the number of carbons, the number of double bonds, and the positions of the double bonds. For example, stearic acid (a saturated fatty acid) has 18 carbons and has the systematic name octadec*anoic* acid (18:0). The notation 18:0 denotes an 18 carbons fatty acid with no double bonds. Similarly, oleic acid is an 18 carbons fatty acid with one double bond and has the systematic name octadec*enoic* acid (18:1). An 18 carbons fatty acid with two double bonds is octadeca*dienoic* acid (18:2). The notation 18:1 denotes an 18 carbons fatty acid with one double bond, whereas 18:2 signifies that there are two double bonds.

Two systems are used for designating the position of double bonds in an unsaturated fatty acid. In **carboxyl-reference system**, fatty acid carbon atoms are numbered starting from the carboxyl terminus. The positions of the double bonds are described by counting from the carboxyl carbon. The position of a double bond is represented by the symbol Δ followed by a superscript number. For example, *cis*-Δ^9 means that there is a *cis* double bond between carbon atoms 9 and 10; *trans*-Δ^2 means that there is a *trans* double bond between carbon atoms 2 and 3. In this nomenclature the carboxyl carbon is designated carbon 1. For example, palmitoleic acid has 16 carbons and has a double bond between carbons 9 and 10. It is designated as 16:1:Δ^9.

In **omega-reference system**, the position of the double bond are indicated relative to the omega carbon. The carbon most distant from the carboxyl group is called the ω **carbon** and is given the number 1 (C-1) and the carboxyl carbon has the highest number. The position of the first double bond is indicated relative to the ω carbon. In this convention, PUFAs with first double bond between C-3 and C-4 are called **omega-3** (ω-3) fatty acids, and those with a double bond between C-6 and C-7 are **omega-6** (ω-6) fatty acids.

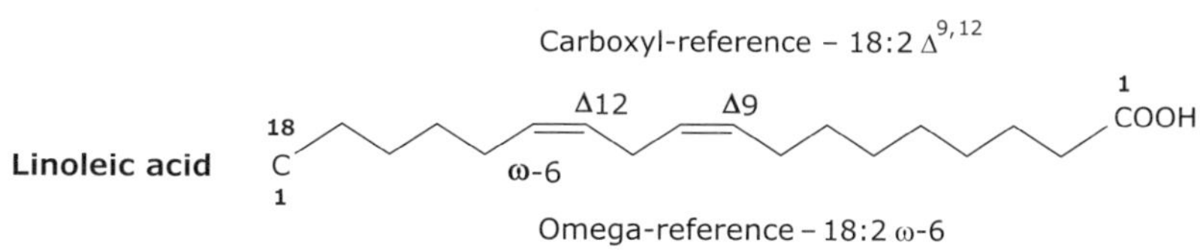

Essential fatty acids

Essential fatty acids are those fatty acids which are not synthesized by animals and must be obtained from diet. **Linoleic acid** (18:2 ω-6) and **linolenic acid** (18:3 ω-3) are the two essential fatty acids for humans and other animals. Humans lack the enzymes to introduce double bonds at carbon atoms beyond C-9 in the fatty acid chain. Hence, humans cannot synthesize linoleate and linolenate. Fatty acids that can be endogenously synthesized are termed as *nonessential fatty acids*. They are nonessential in the sense that they do not have to be obligatorily obtained from diet.

Physical properties of the fatty acids

The physical properties of fatty acids, such as solubility, melting point, and boiling point, are significantly influenced by their structure. This includes the *length of the hydrocarbon chain* (i.e., number of carbon atoms), *the presence or absence of double bond, number of double bonds* (i.e., degree of unsaturation), and the *configuration of double bond* (i.e., *cis* or *trans*). For example, the nonpolar hydrocarbon chain accounts for the poor *solubility* of fatty acids in water. The longer the hydrocarbon chain and the fewer the double bonds, the lower is the solubility of fatty acids in water. Similarly, the **melting point** (temperature at which a substance changes state from solid to liquid) of fatty acids also depends on chain length, presence or absence of double bond, configuration of double bond, and number of double bonds.

Hydrocarbon chain length: The longer the hydrocarbon chain length, the higher the melting point. Longer chains provide increased surface area for higher non-covalent interactions. This results in higher melting points.

Presence or absence of double bond: The unsaturated fatty acids have lower melting point as compared to saturated fatty acids with the same chain length. Difference in melting points is due to different degrees of packing of the fatty acid molecules. The presence of double bonds makes unsaturated chain more rigid. As a result, unsaturated chains cannot pack themselves in crystals efficiently and densely as saturated chain, so, they have a lower melting point as compared to saturated fatty acids.

Number of double bonds: Fatty acids with greater number of double bonds have lower melting point.

Configuration of double bonds: Unsaturated fatty acids with *cis* configuration have lower melting points than the unsaturated fatty acids with *trans* configuration because *cis* configuration causes more kinks in the chain compared to *trans* configuration.

Problem

Why unsaturated fatty acids have low melting points?

Solution: The presence of double bonds makes unsaturated chain more rigid. As a result, unsaturated chains cannot pack themselves in crystals efficiently and densely as saturated chain, so, they have lower melting point as compared to saturated fatty acids.

1.9.2 Triacylglycerol and Wax

Triacylglycerols (also called **triglycerides**) are triesters of fatty acids and glycerol. They are composed of three fatty acids and a glycerol molecule. Triacylglycerols are of two types – *simple* and *mixed* type. Those containing a single kind of fatty acids are called *simple triacylglycerols* and with two or more different kinds of fatty acids are called *mixed triacylglycerols*. The general formula of triacylglycerol is given below:

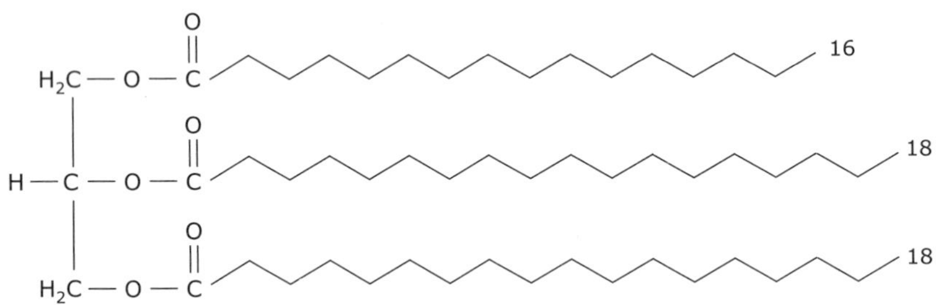

Figure 1.77 General structure of triacylglycerol.

Triacylglycerols are non-polar, hydrophobic in nature and a major form of stored lipids. Because triacylglycerols have no charge (i.e., the carboxyl group of each fatty acid is joined to glycerol through a covalent bond), they are sometimes referred to as **neutral lipid**. Triacylglycerol molecules contain fatty acids of varying lengths, which may be unsaturated or saturated. Triacylglycerols can be distinguished as **fat** and **oil** on the basis of physical state at room temperature. **Fats**, which are solid at room temperature, are mixture of triglycerides containing a high proportion of long-chain, saturated fatty acids. **Oils** are liquid at room temperature because of their relatively high proportion of unsaturated fatty acids. Triacylglycerols function as energy reserves. Because triacylglycerols are less oxidized than carbohydrates or proteins and hence yield significantly more energy per unit mass on complete oxidation. Stored triacylglycerols are virtually the sole source of energy in hibernating animals and migrating birds. In animals, adipocytes (fat cells) are specialized for the synthesis and storage of triacylglycerols.

Saponification: Hydrolysis of triacylglycerols with alkalis such as NaOH or KOH is called **saponification**. Saponification yields salts of free fatty acids (termed **soap**) and glycerol. The number of milligrams of KOH required to saponify one-gram of triacylglycerols is known as **saponification number**. The saponification number measures the average molecular weight of triacylglycerols. Similarly, the number of grams of iodine that can be added to 100 g sample of fat or oil is called **iodine number**, which is used to determine the **degree of unsaturation** (i.e., extent of unsaturation).

Waxes

Natural waxes are typically esters of fatty acids and long-chain alcohols. They are formed by esterification of long-chain fatty acids (saturated and unsaturated) and high molecular weight *monohydroxy* alcohols (C-14 to C-36). Most natural waxes are mixtures of such esters. Waxes are biosynthesized by many plants and animals. The best-known animal wax is **beeswax**. Triacontanyl palmitate (an ester of palmitic acid with the alcohol triacontanol) is the major component of beeswax. Plants also produce waxes. From the commercial perspective, the most important plant wax is **carnauba** wax, a hard wax obtained from the Brazilian palm *Copernicia prunifera*. Waxes serve as energy stores and water repellents.

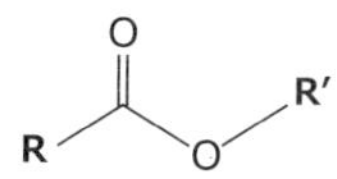

Generic wax structure
R and R' = unbranched hydrocarbon chains.

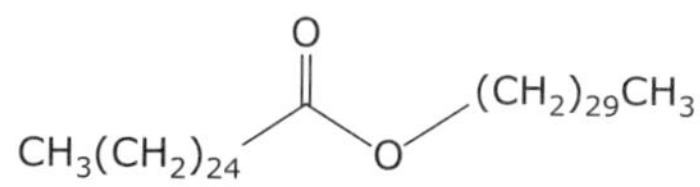

Wax myricyl cerotate

1.9.3 Phospholipids

A phospholipid is an *amphipathic molecule* composed of four components: an alcohol (glycerol or sphingosine), fatty acids, a phosphate group, and an additional alcohol attached to the phosphate. The **glycerol** or **sphingosine** serves as a platform to which the fatty acids and phosphate group are attached. The hydrocarbon chains of the fatty acids form the non-polar, hydrophobic tails, while the phosphorylated alcohol forms the polar, hydrophilic head. Based on the type of alcohol that serves as the platform, there are two main types of phospholipids: glycerophospholipids and sphingophospholipids.

Glycerophospholipids (or phosphoglycerides)

Phospholipids derived from **glycerol** are called *glycerophospholipids*. Glycerophospholipids consist of one glycerol molecule (serving as a platform), two fatty acids, and one phosphorylated alcohol. While glycerol itself has no chiral carbon, attaching a phosphate group to the first or third carbon converts it into a chiral molecule. In this case, the second carbon becomes chiral carbon, making glycerol a **prochiral molecule**. The resulting glycerol phosphate can be either **glycerol 3-phosphate** or **glycerol 1-phosphate**.

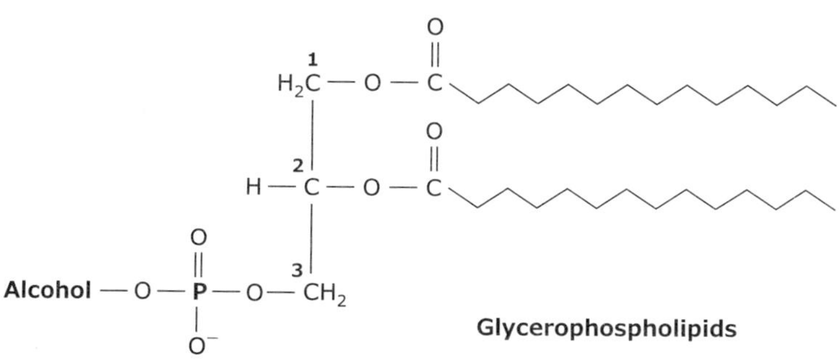

Glycerophospholipids

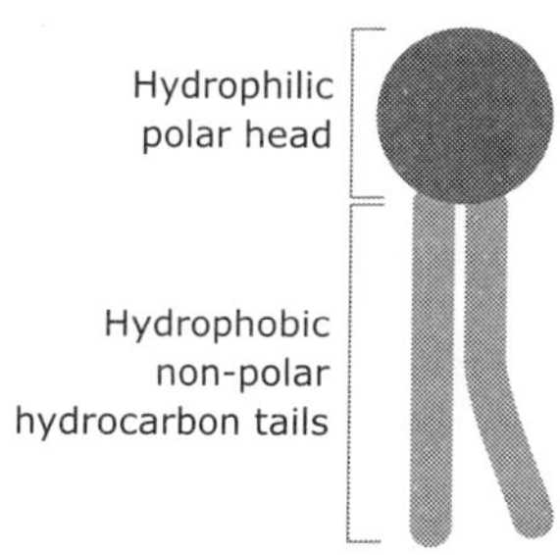

In the simplest phosphoglyceride, **phosphatidic acid,** two hydroxyl groups of glycerol are esterified to the carboxyl groups of two fatty acid chains, and one hydroxyl group of the glycerol is esterified to phosphoric acid. However, in other glycerophospholipids, an additional alcohol becomes esterified to the phosphate group. These glycerophospholipids are classified based on the type of additional alcohol attached. These alcohols include *serine*, *ethanolamine*, *choline*, *glycerol*, and *inositol*. For example, if the alcohol is **choline**, the phosphoglyceride is called **phosphatidylcholine** (also known as **lecithin**), and if the alcohol is **serine**, it is called **phosphatidylserine**.

At a physiological pH of 7, the net charge on a glycerophospholipid depends on the type of alcohol attached to the phosphate group. If no additional alcohol is attached to the phosphate, as in phosphatidic acid, the phosphate group exhibits partial protonation at pH 7, resulting in a net charge of −1. At lower pH levels (below 4.0), the phosphate group is fully protonated and carries no charge, while at higher pH levels (above 12), it is fully deprotonated with a charge of −2. Thus, at pH 7, phosphatidic acid typically carries a net charge of −1. When choline is attached to the phosphate group, as in phosphatidylcholine, the net charge is 0 at pH 7. In contrast, when serine is attached, as in phosphatidylserine, the net charge is typically −1 at pH 7.

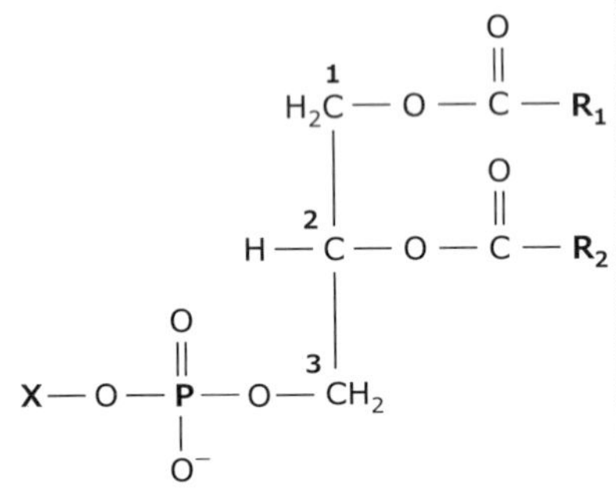

Name of X	Name of glycerophospholipid	Net charge (*at pH 7*)
Hydrogen	Phosphatidic acid	−1
Choline	Phosphatidylcholine (**Lecithin**)	0
Ethanolamine	Phosphatidylethanolamine (**Cephalin**)	0
Serine	Phosphatidylserine	−1
Glycerol	Phosphatidylglycerol	−1
Phosphatidylglycerol	Diphosphatidylglycerol (**Cardiolipin**)	−2
Inositol	Phosphatidylinositol	−1

Figure 1.78 The structure of a glycerophospholipid includes two fatty acids attached via ester bonds to the first and second carbons of glycerol, while a phosphate group is attached via a phosphoester bond to the third carbon (glycerol 3-phosphate). Additionally, the phosphate group is linked to an alcohol, represented as X. The simplest glycerophospholipids, where X is a hydrogen atom, are known as phosphatidic acids.

Ether glycerophospholipids

Ether glycerophospholipids possess an *ether linkage* instead of an acyl group at the C-1 position of glycerol. One very common example of ether glycerophospholipid found in mammals is **platelet activating factor** or **PAF**. PAF is a potent signal molecule that causes platelet aggregation and dilation of blood vessels. In ether glycerophospholipids, the ether-linked chain may be saturated or may contain a double bond between C-1 and C-2. Ether glycerophospholipids in which the alkyl moiety is *cis*-α,β-unsaturated is termed as **plasmalogen**.

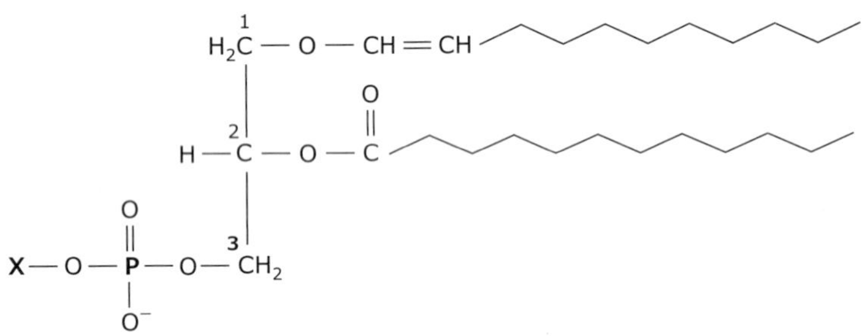

Figure 1.79
Structure of plasmalogen. One hydrocarbon group is linked to the C–1 position of glycerol as a vinyl ether.

Sphingophospholipids

Phospholipids derived from **sphingosine** are called **sphingophospholipids**. A sphingophospholipid contains an 18-carbon *amino alcohol* called sphingosine instead of glycerol. A fatty acid is joined to sphingosine via an *amide bond*, forming a **ceramide**, which is the structural unit of all sphingolipids. The addition of a phosphorylated alcohol to the C–1 position of sphingosine leads to various sphingophospholipids. One important example is **sphingomyelin**, where a phosphocholine or phosphoethanolamine group is attached to the hydroxyl group present at C-1 position. Sphingomyelin is present in the plasma membranes of animal cells and is especially prominent in the myelin sheath that surrounds some nerve cell axons.

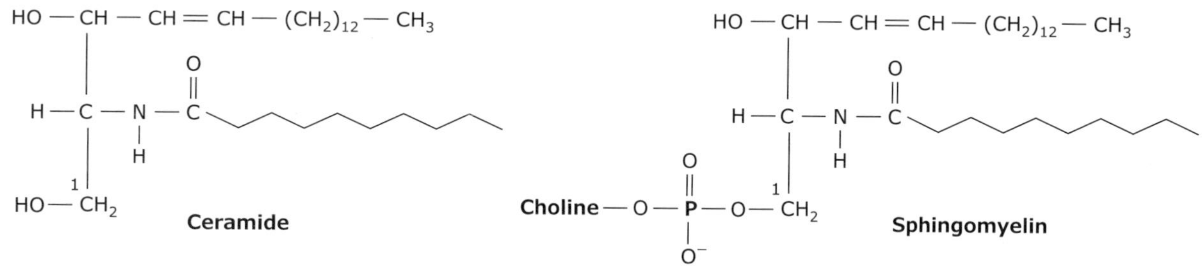

Figure 1.80 Sphingolipids are derived from sphingosine, a long-chain amino alcohol. When a fatty acid attaches to the $-NH_2$ group on C-2 via an amide linkage, the resulting compound is a ceramide. Sphingomyelin, the most common sphingophospholipid, contains either phosphocholine or phosphoethanolamine as its polar head group.

1.9.4 Glycolipids

Lipids containing carbohydrates are generally referred to as **glycolipids**. Glycolipids can be **sphingoglycolipids** and **glyceroglycolipid**. The most important type of glycolipid is the sphingoglycolipid, which constitutes the third major class of membrane lipids. In sphingoglycolipids, the head group contains mono- or oligosaccharides attached directly to the –OH group at C-1 of the ceramide moiety and does not contain phosphate. It can be:

Cerebroside: Have a single monosaccharide linked to ceramide.

Globoside: With oligosaccharide linked to ceramide.

Gangliosides: Globoside that contains complex oligosaccharides as their polar head groups with one or more residues of ***N*-acetylneuraminic acid** (NANA), a sialic acid. **Sialic acid** is a generic term for the N- or O-substituted derivatives of *neuraminic acid*, a monosaccharide with a nine-carbon backbone. Sialic acid gives gangliosides the negative charge at pH 7. More than 60 different gangliosides have been characterized. Gangliosides with one sialic acid residue are in the **GM** (M for mono-) series, those with two are in the **GD** (D for di-) series, and so on. The normal function of gangliosides is not known.

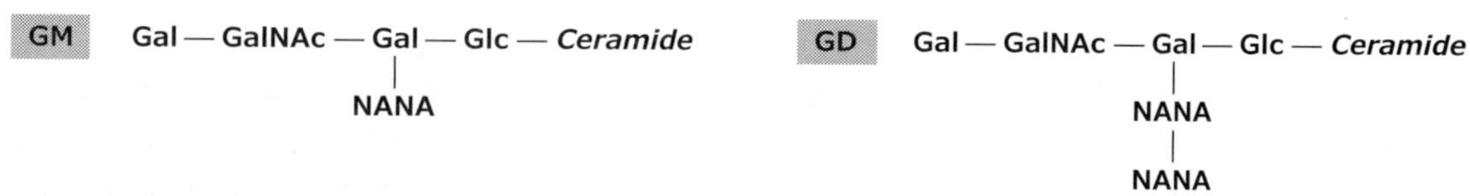

Sphingolipid storage disease

A group of inherited metabolic disorders characterized by an excessive intra-lysosomal deposition of sphingoglycolipids and sphingophospholipids. Clinical features vary with the specific subtype of the disease. Examples of selected sphingolipid storage diseases are given below:

Table 1.16 Sphingolipid storage diseases

Disease	Accumulating sphingolipid	Enzyme deficiency
Tay-Sachs	Ganglioside GM2	β-Hexosaminidase A
Gaucher's	Glucocerebroside	β-Glucosidase
Niemann Pick	Sphingomyelin	Sphingomyelinase
Fabry's	Trihexosylceramide	α-Galactosidase A
Krabbe's	Deacylated galactocerebroside	Galactocerebrosidase

1.9.5 Steroids

Steroids are a class of organic compounds characterized by the presence of a **steroid nucleus**. This nucleus is a planar structure composed of four fused rings: three six-membered rings (rings A, B, and C) and one five-membered ring (ring D). Steroids are derived from *triterpenes*, which are isoprenoid compounds consisting of six isoprene units. A **sterol** is a type of steroid that is characterized by the presence of a hydroxyl group (–OH) attached at the C-3 position of the steroid nucleus. Sterols exhibit amphipathic character. Major part of the sterol molecule consists of a rigid, four-ringed carbon skeleton. This region is highly nonpolar and hydrophobic. However, the A-ring in a sterol molecule typically has a hydroxyl group attached. This hydroxyl group exhibits polar and hydrophilic character. **Cholesterol** is an example of the sterol and an essential component in animal cell membranes. Cholesterol acts as a precursor for the biosynthesis of all **steroid hormones** and **bile salts**. Cholesterol is usually stored within cells as a fatty acid ester (*cholesteryl ester*). When cholesterol and a fatty acid are linked in a cholesteryl ester, the overall molecule becomes nonpolar and hydrophobic. Cholesterol is not found in plants and fungi. Types of sterol that is common in plants are **stigmasterol**, **sitosterol** and **campesterol**. **Ergosterol** is a sterol present in the cell membrane of fungi.

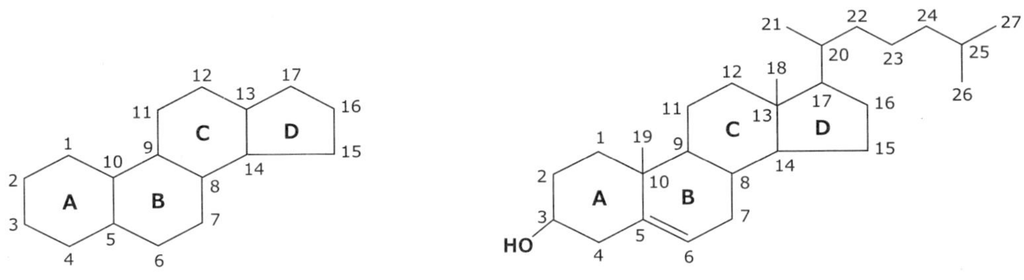

Steroid nucleus   Cholesterol

Figure 1.81 Structure of cholesterol. Cholesterol is a 27 carbon compound with a unique structure with a hydrocarbon tail, a central sterol nucleus made of four hydrocarbon rings (three hexacyclic rings and one pentacyclic ring), and a hydroxyl group.

1.9.6 Eicosanoids

Eicosanoids are paracrine signaling molecules composed of 20 carbon atoms. This group of signaling molecules includes prostanoids and leukotrienes. They are termed 'eicosanoids' due to their common origin from 20-carbon polyunsaturated fatty acids, particularly arachidonic acid.

Prostanoids and **leukotrienes** are two major groups of eicosanoids - formed via two distinct pathways, the *cyclooxygenase* and *lipoxygenase* pathways. Prostanoids, which include *prostaglandins*, *prostacyclin* and *thromboxanes*, are formed through the **cyclooxygenase pathway** (cyclic pathway) and *leukotrienes* come from the **lipoxygenase pathway** (linear pathway). The term 'cyclic pathway' in reference to the cyclooxygenase pathway denotes the formation of chemical intermediates that contain cyclic structures, such as cyclopentane rings.

Prostaglandins were first identified in human semen. Almost all mammalian cells except RBC produce prostaglandins. Prostaglandins are derivatives of the hypothetical C_{20} fatty acid **prostanoic acid** in which carbon atoms 8 to 12 comprise a *cyclopentane ring*. Individual prostaglandins are described by a system of abbreviation in which the name prostaglandin is designated PG, followed by a third letter (A to I) that indicates the nature of the substituents on the cyclopentane ring. A numerical subscript indicates the total number of double bonds in the aliphatic chains.

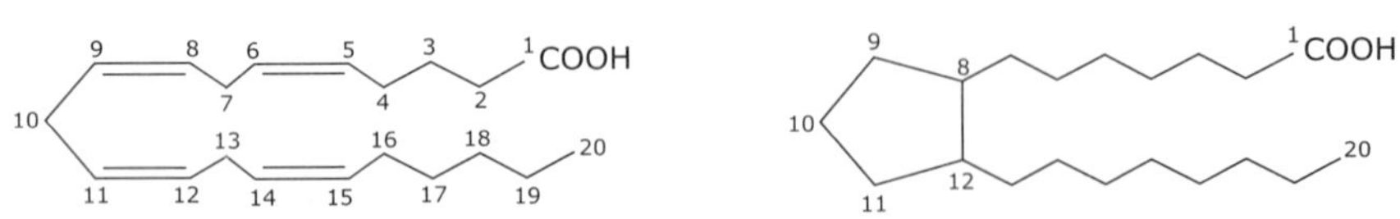

Arachidonic acid   Prostanoic acid

Figure 1.82 Structure of arachidonic acid and hypothetical C_{20} fatty acid prostanoic acid.

Synthesis of prostaglandins: In humans, the most prevalent prostaglandin precursor is 20-carbon *arachidonic acid,* (5,8,11,14-eicosatetraenoic acid). Prostaglandins are synthesized as shown in the **figure 1.83** from arachidonic acid in a metabolic pathway that begins with plasma membrane phospholipids. The enzyme **cyclooxygenase (cox)**, also called **prostaglandin G/H synthase** catalyzes the introduction of oxygen and the cyclization of the carbon chain of arachidonic acid in the region of the double-bond positions at C-8 and C-11.

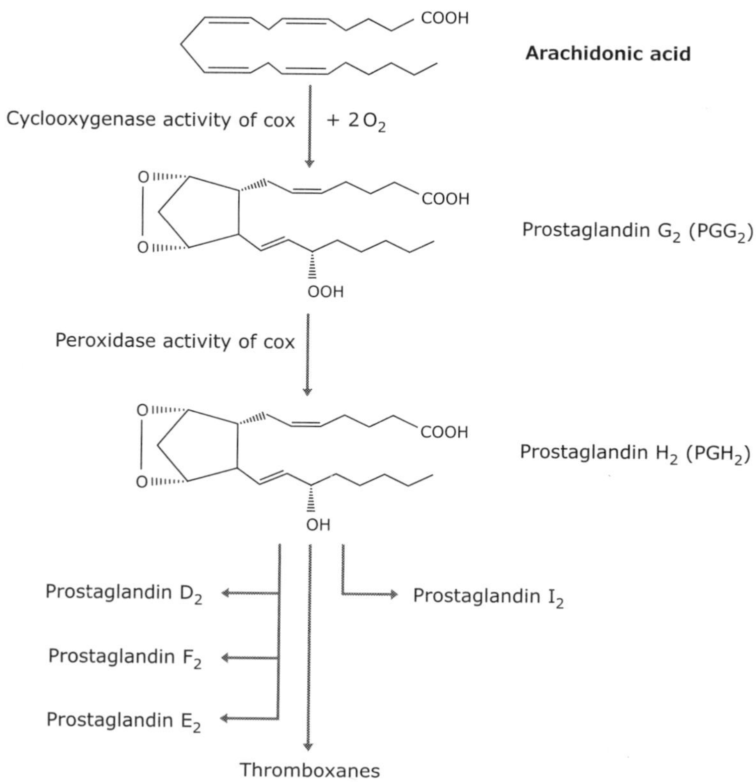

Figure 1.83
Prostaglandins and thromboxanes are formed when arachidonic acid, a 20-carbon unsaturated fatty acid, is released from the plasma membrane and metabolized by the sequential actions of prostaglandin G/H synthase, or cyclooxygenase (COX), and respective synthases. Prostaglandin production depends on the activity of prostaglandin G/H synthases, colloquially known as COXs, bifunctional enzymes that contain both cyclooxygenase and peroxidase activity.

Prostaglandin H_2 (**PGH_2**) acts as immediate precursor of other prostaglandins and thromboxanes. Mammals have two isozymes of COX, **COX-1** and **COX-2**. COX-1 is constitutively expressed in most mammalian tissues. In contrast, COX-2 is expressed only in certain tissues in response to inflammatory stimuli and hence is responsible for the elevated prostaglandin levels that cause inflammation. Prostaglandins perform diverse functions. They stimulate uterine contraction, lowering blood pressure, vasodilation, and inflammation and pain. **Aspirin** (acetylsalicylate), a *nonsteroidal anti-inflammatory drug* (**NSAID**), inhibits the synthesis of prostaglandins and used as an **analgesic** (pain-relieving), **antipyretic** (fever-reducing), and **anti-inflammatory** agent. It irreversibly inhibits COX activity by acetylating a serine residue and blocking the enzymes active site. This inhibition of COX blocks the synthesis of prostaglandins, which in turn reduces the inflammatory response. Other NSAIDs such as **ibuprofen** also inhibits COX activity after binding active site but binds non-covalently and acts as a *reversible competitive inhibitor* of COX. Aspirin and ibuprofen are non-selective NSAIDs and target both COX-1 and COX-2 whereas **coxibs** (rofecoxib and celecoxib) are selective NSAIDs and target only COX-2.

Thromboxanes are derived from prostaglandins in the **blood platelets** (thrombocytes) by the enzyme *thromboxane synthase,* which converts PGH_2 to thromboxane. They act as a vasoconstrictor and stimulator of platelet aggregation (an initial step in blood clotting). Thromboxanes have heterocyclic oxane structures. Thromboxane A (**TxA**) contains an unstable bicyclic oxygenated ring structure, while thromboxane B (**TxB**) has a stable oxane ring.

Prostacyclins (PGI_2) is generated from PGH_2 by a enzyme *prostacyclin synthase* that is particularly abundant in endothelial cells. Prostacyclin serves as a potent a potent vasodilator and inhibitor of platelet aggregation. It also promotes differentiation and inhibits proliferation in vascular smooth muscle cells.

Leukotrienes are derived from arachidonic acid via the lipoxygenase pathway and lack a ring structure. As linear eicosanoids, they contain three conjugated double bonds. Leukotriene synthesis primarily occurs in leukocytes.

Leukotrienes are classified into two main types: **leukotriene B4**, a chemoattractant that contains only hydroxyl groups, and **cysteinyl leukotrienes**, which also contain amino acid moieties. Leukotrienes play roles in chemotaxis, inflammation, and allergic reactions. Overproduction of leukotrienes can cause asthmatic attacks, making leukotriene synthesis a target for antiasthmatic drugs such as prednisone.

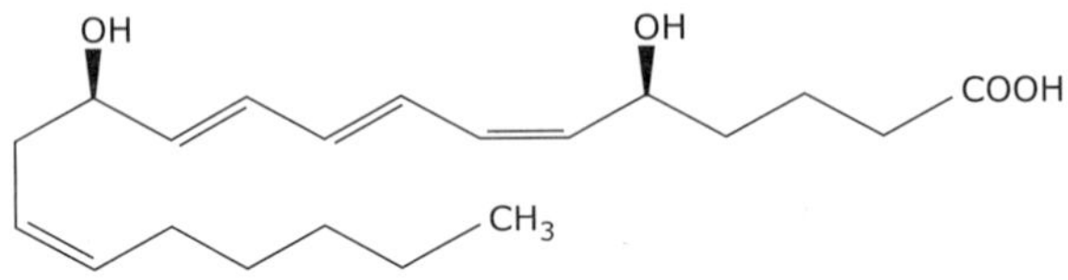

Figure 1.84 Structure of leukotriene B4.

Table 1.17 Biological effects of eicosanoids

Type	Major functions
Prostaglandins	Mediation of inflammatory response
	Regulation of nerve transmission
	Inhibition of gastric secretion
	Sensitization to pain
	Stimulation of smooth muscle contraction
Thromboxanes	Platelet aggregation
	Aorta constriction
Prostacyclins	Thromboxane antagonists
Leukotrienes	Bronchoconstriction
	Leukotaxis

1.9.7 Plasma lipoproteins

Triacylglycerols, phospholipids, cholesterol and cholesterol esters are transported in human plasma in association with proteins as **lipoproteins**. Blood plasma contains a number of soluble *lipoproteins*, which are classified, according to their densities, into five major types. These lipid-protein complexes function as a lipid transport system because isolated lipids are insoluble in blood. There are five basic types of lipoproteins in human blood: **chylomicrons**, *very low density lipoproteins* (**VLDL**), *intermediate density lipoproteins* (**IDL**), *low density lipoproteins* (**LDL**) and *high density lipoproteins* (**HDL**). A lipoprotein contains a core of neutral lipids, which includes triacylglyerols and cholesterol esters. This core is coated with a monolayer of phospholipids and cholesterols in which proteins (called **apolipoprotein**) and cholesterol are embedded.

Table 1.18 Some properties of major classes of human plasma lipoproteins

Lipoprotein	Density (g/mL)	Protein (%)	Phospho-lipids (%)	Free cholesterol (%)	Cholesterol esters (%)	Triacyl-glycerols (%)	Major apolipoprotein
Chylomicrons	<0.94	1.5–2.5	7–9	1–3	3–5	85	A-I, A-II, B-48, C-I, C-II, C-III, E
VLDL	0.95–1.006	5–10	15–20	5–10	10–15	50	B-100, C-I, C-II, C-III, E
IDL	1.006–1.019	15–20	22	8	30	22	B-100, C-I, C-II, C-III, E
LDL	1.006–1.063	20–25	15–20	7–10	35–40	7–10	B-100
HDL	1.063–1.210	50–55	20–25	3–4	15	3–4	A-I, A-II, C-I, C-II, C-III

1.10 Vitamins

Vitamins are organic compounds required in trace amounts by organisms to perform specific and essential cellular functions. These compounds play similar biological roles across nearly all forms of life. However, most animals cannot synthesize the majority of vitamins on their own—with a few exceptions—and must therefore obtain them through their diet. Plants and many bacteria can synthesize most vitamins, though not all plants or bacteria produce every vitamin. Furthermore, not all vitamins are required by all organisms; the requirement for a specific vitamin depends on the organism's metabolic and physiological needs. Vitamins can be classified according to their solubility and their roles in metabolism. Based on solubility, vitamins are categorized as **water-soluble** (e.g., B-complex and C) or **lipid-soluble** (e.g., A, D, E, and K).

Some important facts about vitamin synthesis in animals and plants

Vitamin synthesis in animals

Vitamin B3: Synthesized from tryptophan, but not in sufficient amounts to meet daily requirements.

Vitamin A: Not synthesized directly, but animals can convert β-carotene (from plant) into active vitamin A (retinol).

Vitamin D: Synthesized in the skin upon exposure to UV-B radiation from sunlight.

Vitamin C: Synthesized by most animals, except primates (including humans), guinea pigs, and some birds and fish.

Vitamin synthesis in plants

Vitamin A: Plants don't produce vitamin A directly but synthesize carotenoids, which serve as precursors of vitamin A.

Vitamin D: Not synthesized by higher plants. However, some fungi can produce **vitamin D2** when exposed to UV light.

Vitamin B12: Not produced by plants. It is synthesized exclusively by certain bacteria and archaea.

1.10.1 Water-soluble vitamins

Nine vitamins (thiamine, riboflavin, niacin, biotin, pantothenic acid, folic acid, cobalamin, pyridoxine, and ascorbic acid) are classified as *water-soluble vitamins*. Except vitamin C, water-soluble vitamins are all precursors of coenzymes.

Thiamine (Vitamin B1)

Thiamine, also known as **vitamin B1**, is an essential water-soluble vitamin that plays a crucial role in converting food into energy. It is a complex molecule composed of two main rings: an **aminopyrimidine ring** (a nitrogen-containing ring structure) and a **thiazole ring** (a sulfur-containing ring structure). These two rings are connected by a *methylene bridge*. The biologically active form of thiamine is **thiamine pyrophosphate** (**TPP**), which is formed by the transfer of a pyrophosphate group from ATP to thiamine. The thiazolium ring within TPP serves as the catalytically active functional group. TPP functions as a coenzyme in the oxidative decarboxylation of α-keto acids, a reaction catalyzed by *pyruvate decarboxylase* (an enzyme not present in animals). Additionally, TPP is an essential coenzyme for the enzyme *transketolase*.

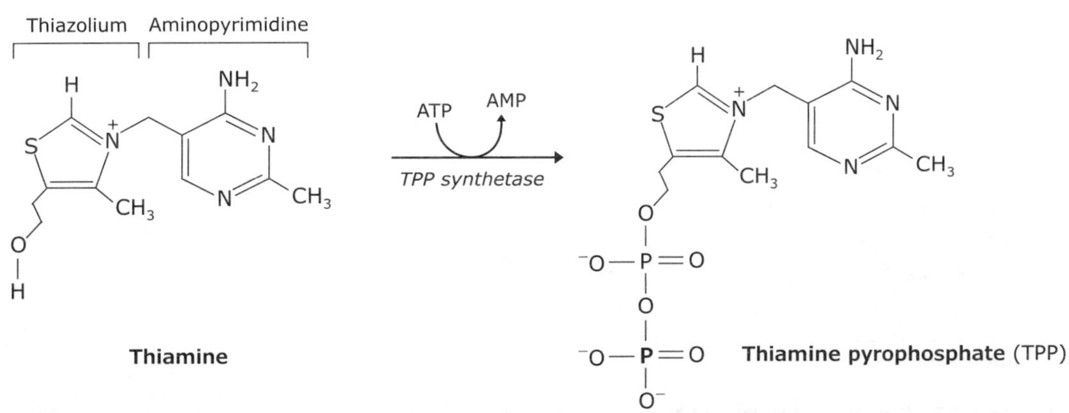

Figure 1.85 Structure of thiamine and thiamine pyrophosphate.

Vitamin B1 plays an important role in carbohydrate metabolism and neural function. Deficiency in thiamine can lead to two significant medical conditions: **Beriberi** and **Wernicke-Korsakoff syndrome.** Beriberi is often found in populations whose diet is primarily composed of polished rice (which lacks the vitamin-rich outer layers). There are two main types of beriberi: **dry beriberi** (affects the nervous system) and **wet beriberi** (affects the cardiovascular system).

Riboflavin (Vitamin B2)

Riboflavin is a component of **flavin mononucleotide** (FMN) and **flavin adenine dinucleotide** (FAD). **FMN** is synthesized by adding a phosphate group to riboflavin, while **FAD** is formed by joining an AMP moiety to FMN. Both FMN and FAD act as oxidizing agents and play crucial roles in cellular energy metabolism, as they are involved in redox reactions. As oxidizing agents both FMN and FAD can reversibly accept two hydrogen atoms, forming $FMNH_2$ or $FADH_2$, respectively. The oxidized **isoalloxazine ring** absorbs light at ~450 nm, and this absorbance disappears upon reduction.

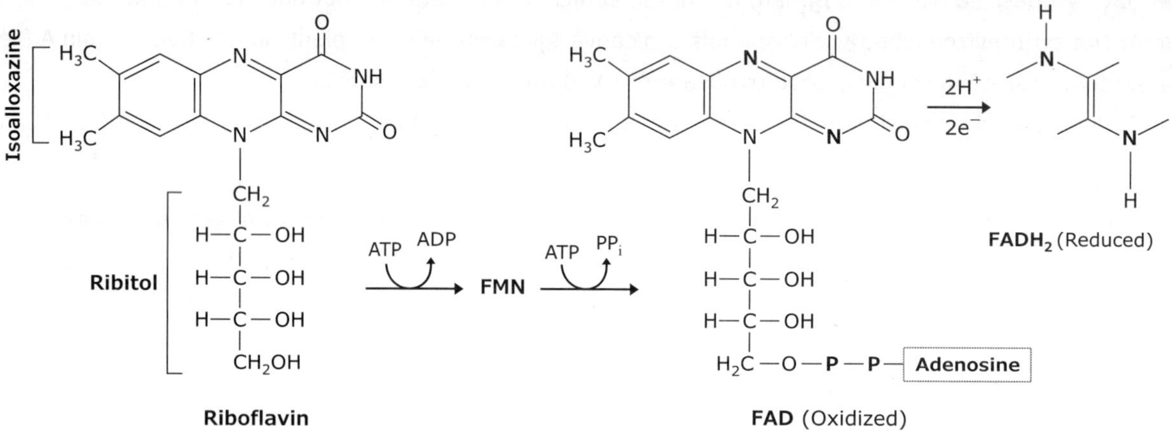

Figure 1.86 Structure of flavin mononucleotide (FMN) and flavin adenine dinucleotide (FAD).

Niacin (Vitamin B3)

Niacin, or nicotinic acid, is a substituted pyridine derivative. Its biologically active coenzyme forms are **nicotinamide adenine dinucleotide** (NAD^+) and its phosphorylated derivative, **nicotinamide adenine dinucleotide phosphate** ($NADP^+$). **Nicotinamide**, a derivative of nicotinic acid, contains an amide group instead of a carboxyl group. NAD^+ and $NADP^+$ serve as coenzymes in oxidation-reduction reactions, where they undergo reduction of the **pyridine ring** by accepting a hydride ion (H^-). The reduced forms of NAD^+ and $NADP^+$ are NADH and NADPH, respectively. Deficiency of niacin causes **pellagra,** often referred to as the 'three Ds' disease because it primarily affects the skin (**dermatitis**), digestive system (**diarrhea**), and nervous system (**dementia**).

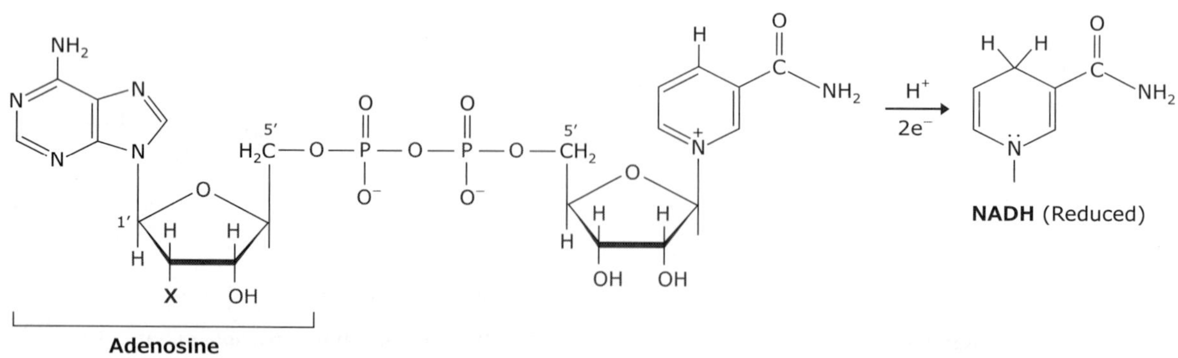

Figure 1.87 Structure of NAD^+ and $NADP^+$. In the case of NAD^+, X is –OH, and in $NADP^+$, it is $–PO_4^{2-}$.

Biotin (Vitamin B7)

Biotin, also known as **vitamin B7** or **vitamin H**, is a water-soluble vitamin. It is a bicyclic compound, consisting of a **ureido ring** fused with a **tetrahydrothiophene ring**. The molecule also includes a **valeric acid side chain**, which is crucial for its biological activity. Biotin is covalently bound to enzymes through an amide linkage between the carboxyl group of its valeric acid side chain and the ε-amino group of a lysine residue on the enzyme, forming **biocytin** (also known as **biotinyllysine**) residues. Biocytin is the biologically active form of biotin and plays a crucial role in many carboxylation reactions. It acts as a specialized carrier of one-carbon groups in their most oxidized form, CO_2. Most biotin-dependent carboxylations use bicarbonate as the carboxylating agent and transfer the carboxyl group to a substrate carbanion.

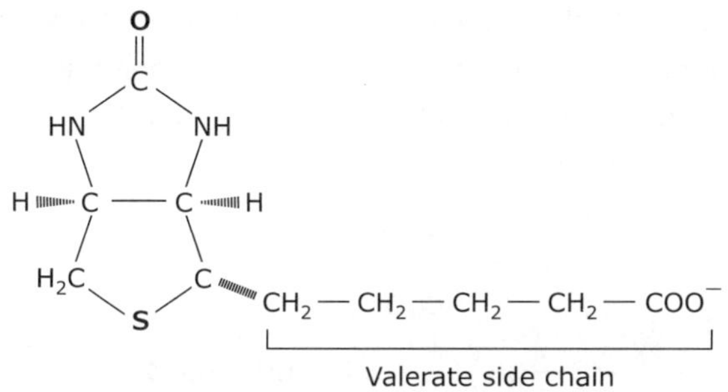

Figure 1.88
Structure of biotin. Biotin consists of three main components: the ureido ring (a five-membered ring containing nitrogen and oxygen atoms), the tetrahydrothiophene ring (another five-membered ring that includes a sulfur atom), and the valeric acid side chain. The tetrahydrothiophene ring is fused with the ureido ring to form a bicyclic structure. The valeric acid side chain extends from this bicyclic core.

Biotin deficiency is rare because the vitamin is widely distributed in foods. However, raw egg white contains a glycoprotein called **avidin**, which binds tightly to biotin and prevents its absorption in the intestine. Avidin's homolog, **streptavidin**, is a protein produced by the bacterium *Streptomyces avidinii*. Streptavidin is known for its exceptionally high affinity for biotin, forming one of the strongest known non-covalent interactions.

Pantothenic acid (Vitamin B5)

Pantothenic acid is a component of **coenzyme A**, which is responsible for the transfer of acyl groups. Coenzyme A is a complex molecule composed of adenosine 3′-phosphate, a diphosphate group, pantothenic acid, and β-mercaptoethylamine. The key functional group in CoA is the **sulfhydryl group** or a **thiol group** (–SH) that carries acyl compounds as activated thiol esters. **Pantothenic acid** is also a constituent of **acyl carrier protein** (ACP). Coenzyme A performs two main functions:

- Activation of acyl groups for transfer by nucleophilic attack.
- Activation of the α-hydrogen of the acyl group.

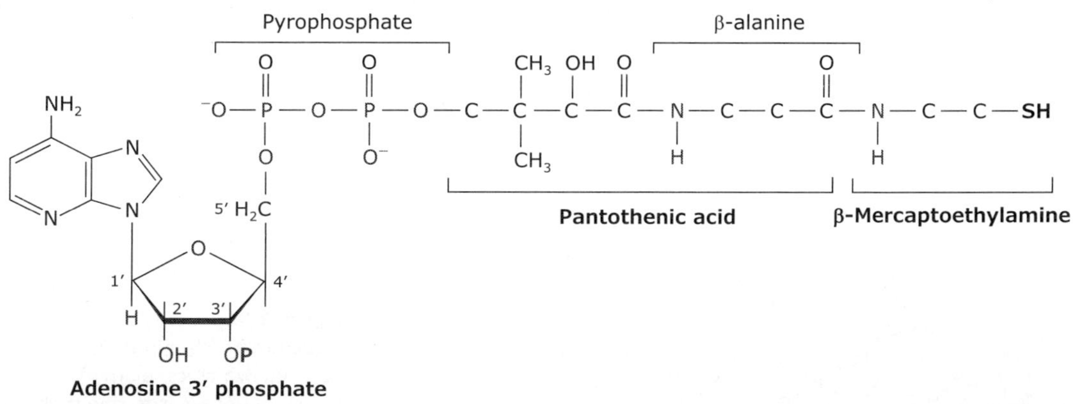

Figure 1.89 Structure of Coenzyme A (CoA-SH) – a thiol comprising a pantothenate unit in phosphoric anhydride linkage with a 3',5'-adenosine diphosphate unit; and an aminoethanethiol unit, involved in the transfer of acyl groups.

Folic acid (Vitamin B9)

Folic acid is composed of a **pterin ring** attached to **para-aminobenzoic acid** (PABA) and conjugated with one or more glutamic acid residues. A *pterin* is a 2-amino-4-oxo derivative of **pteridine**. *Sulfa drugs* or *sulfonamides* have structural similarities to PABA, an important precursor in folic acid synthesis. Hence, sulfonamides block folic acid formation by competing with PABA. The biologically active form of folate is **tetrahydrofolate** (THF). The NADPH-dependent enzyme **dihydrofolate reductase** catalyzes the reduction of the 5, 6, 7 and 8 positions of the pterin ring to produce the coenzyme tetrahydrofolate. THF plays a key role in the transfer of one-carbon units for all oxidation levels of carbon except that of CO_2 and is essential for the biosynthesis of certain amino acids, the purines and thymidylate. The one-carbon transfer reaction of THF involves the formation of a covalent bond between N-5 or N-10, or both, of THF and a one-carbon unit. **Methotrexate** (amethopterin) and **aminopterin** are two analogs of folic acid. Each binds to dihydrofolate reductase with greater affinity than folate, thus acting as a competitive inhibitor of THF formation. A primary result of folic acid deficiency is **megaloblastic anemia.** It is a condition in which the bone marrow produces unusually large, structurally abnormal, immature red blood cells (**megaloblasts**). It has several different causes - deficiencies of either *cobalamin* or *folate* are the two most common causes.

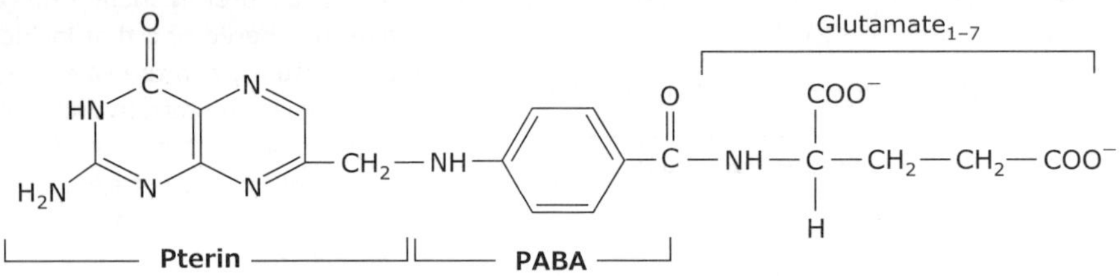

Figure 1.90 Structure of folate. The structure of folate consists of three main components: a bicyclic nitrogen-containing ring structure termed pteridine ring system (pterin), para-aminobenzoic acid (PABA) and glutamate residues.

Cobalamin (Vitamin B12)

Cobalamin has two characteristic components: the **corrin ring** system and the **5,6-dimethylbenzimidazole ribonucleotide**. Corrin ring system differs from the porphyrins. In *corrin ring system*, two pyrrole rings are linked directly rather than through a methene bridge. Second the metal that is coordinated by the four pyrrole nitrogens is **cobalt** rather than iron or magnesium. 5,6-dimethylbenzimidazole ribonucleotide, the second component of vitamin B12 is coordinated with cobalt of the corrin ring. Several groups like –CN, –OH, $–CH_3$, deoxyadenosyl group can also bind to the cobalt ion. Cobalamin is converted in the body into two coenzymes: **5′-deoxyadenosylcobalamin**, commonly referred to as **coenzyme B12** and **methylcobalamin**. The B12 coenzymes participate in two important types of reactions: **1.** Intramolecular rearrangements and **2.** Methyl group transfers.

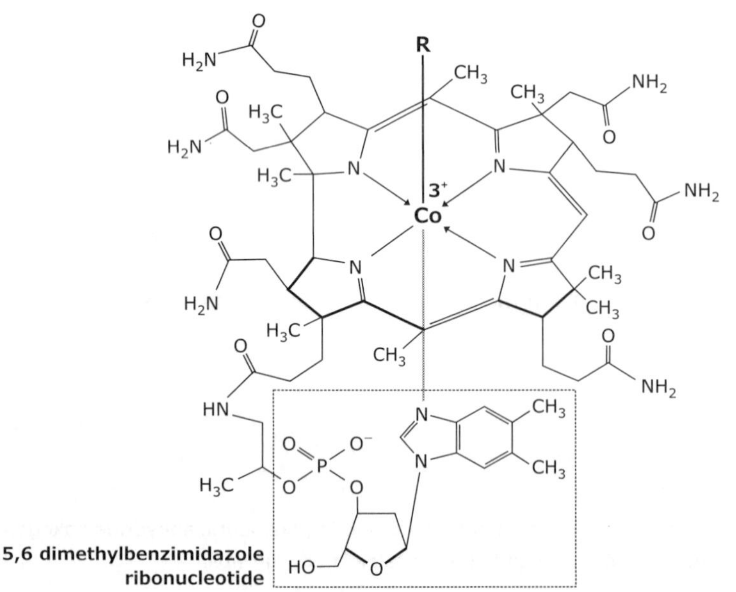

R	*Name*
CN	Cyanocobalamin
OH	Hydroxycobalamin
CH_3	Methylcobalamin
Deoxyadenosyl	Deoxyadenosylcobalamin

Figure 1.91
Structure of vitamin B12 (also known as cobalamin). It consists of a corrin ring that encircles a central cobalt ion and 5,6-dimethylbenzimidazole ribonucleotide.

Pyridoxine (Vitamin B6)

Vitamin B6 is a collective term for *pyridoxine*, *pyridoxal* and *pyridoxamine.* All are derivatives of **pyridine**, differing only in the nature of the functional group attached to the ring. Pyridoxine occurs primarily in plants, whereas pyridoxal and pyridoxamine are found in foods obtained from animals. All three compounds can serve as precursors of the biologically active coenzyme, **pyridoxal phosphate**.

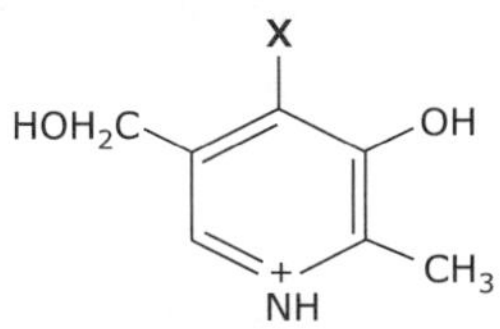

$X = CH_2NH_2$ **Pyridoxamine**
$X = CH_2OH$ **Pyridoxine**
$X = CHO$ **Pyridoxal**

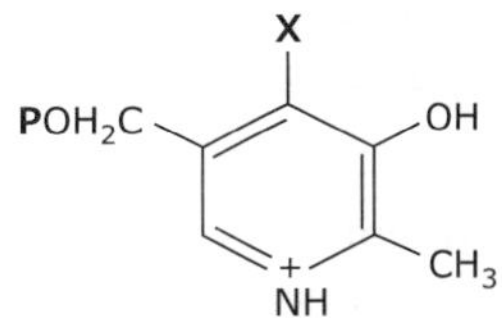

Pyridoxal phosphate

Pyridoxal phosphate participates in the wide variety of enzyme catalyzed reactions including transamination, α and β-decarboxylation, aldol reactions and β and γ-elimination.

Ascorbic acid (Vitamin C)

Ascorbic acid (*ascorbic* means anti-scurvy) is a small carbohydrate molecule which acts as a strong **reducing agent**. Its structure includes a six-carbon **lactone ring** with a double-bonded oxygen and multiple hydroxyl groups, giving it strong reducing properties. It is widely distributed in animals and plants. Vertebrates such as human and other primates, certain birds, and some fishes are unable to synthesize it due to lack of enzyme **L-gulonolactone oxidase**. Vitamin C has a well documented role in hydroxylation reactions, for example, hydroxylation of prolyl- and lysyl- residues of collagen. It acts as an important antioxidant by virtue of its water solubility and its oxidation to dehydroascorbic acid. A deficiency of ascorbic acid results in **scurvy**, a disease characterized by sore, spongy gums, loose teeth, fragile blood vessels, swollen joints, and anemia. Many of the deficiency symptoms can be explained by a deficiency in the hydroxylation of collagen, resulting in defective connective tissue.

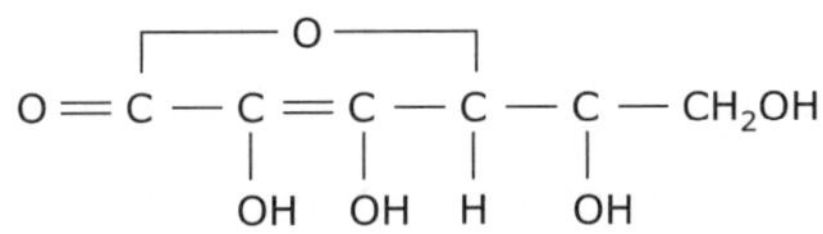

Figure 1.92 Structure of ascorbic acid.

1.10.2 Fat-soluble vitamins

Four vitamins A, D, E and K are termed *fat-soluble*. All are isoprenoid compounds synthesized by the condensation of the multiple isoprene unit. In contrast to the water-soluble vitamins, only one of the fat soluble vitamins (vitamin K) has a coenzyme function. These vitamins are released, absorbed and transported with the fat in the diet.

Vitamin A (Retinol)

Vitamin A is an **isoprenoid alcohol** and functions as hormone as well as a visual pigment. It is essential for vision, reproduction, growth, and maintenance of epithelial tissues. *Vitamin A* is often used as a collective term for several related biologically active molecules.

Retinol (vitamin A1) is a primary alcohol containing a β-ionone ring with an unsaturated side chain. Retinol is found in animal tissues as a retinyl ester with long-chain fatty acids.

β-carotene is the precursor of vitamin A1. Plant foods contain β-carotene, which can be oxidatively cleaved in the intestine to yield two molecules of retinol (Vitamin A1).

Retinal, a vitamin A derivative, derives from the oxidation of retinol. Oxidation at C-15 convert retinol to the aldehyde, retinal. Retinal and retinol can be readily interconverted. It initiates the response of rod and cone cells of the retina to light, producing a neural signal to the brain.

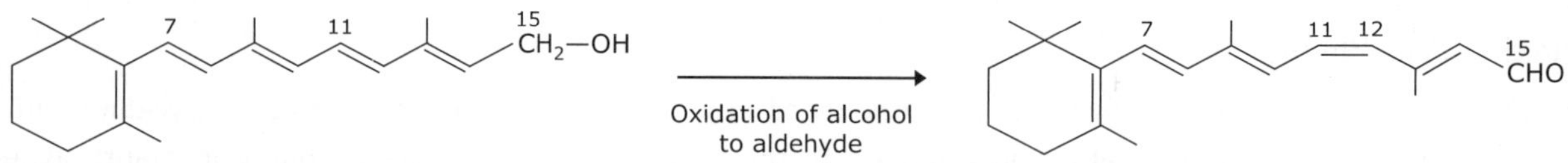

Vitamin A1 (retinol) 11-*cis*-retinal (visual pigment)

Retinal is a component of the visual pigments of rod and cone cells. **Rhodopsin**, the visual pigment of the rod cells in the retina, consists of **11-cis retinal** specifically bound to the protein **opsin**. In the dark, retinal of rhodopsin is in the *11-cis form*. When rhodopsin is exposed to light, **11-*cis* retinal** undergoes a series of photochemical reactions that convert it to **all-*trans* retinal**. This process triggers a nerve impulse that is transmitted by the optic nerve to the brain. Regeneration of rhodopsin requires the isomerization of all-trans retinal back to 11-*cis* retinal.

Retinoic acid is a vitamin A derivative, derives from the oxidation of retinal. Retinoic acid cannot be reduced in the body and therefore cannot give rise to either retinal or retinol. It regulates gene expression like steroid hormone.

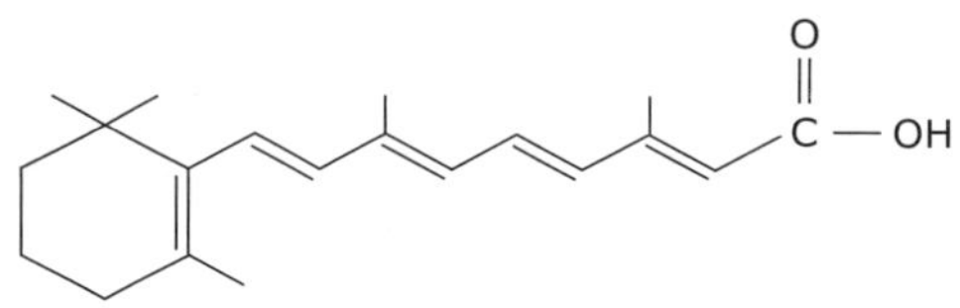

Figure 1.93 Structure of retinoic acid (all *trans*).

Vitamin D

Vitamin D serves as hormone precursors. Vitamin D_3 (also called **cholecalciferol, calciol**) is formed non-enzymatically in skin (dermis and epidermis) from 7-dehydrocholesterol (an intermediate in cholesterol synthesis) in the presence of a UV component of sunlight. Dietary forms of vitamin D are absorbed through the aid of bile salts in the small intestine. Whether absorbed in the intestine or photosynthesized in the skin, cholecalciferol is then transported to liver by **transcalciferin**. Vitamin D_3 (not biologically active) is converted by enzymes in the liver and kidney to 1, 25 dihydroxycholecalciferol, a hormone that regulates Ca^{2+} uptake in the intestine and calcium levels in kidney and bone. Like steroid hormone, 1, 25 dihydroxycholecalciferol regulates gene expression.

7-Dehydrocholesterol —UV→ → Cholecalciferol → → 1,25-Dihydroxycholecalciferol (calcitriol)

2 steps (in skin) | Absorbed into the blood | Two hydroxylation steps First hydroxylation in the liver at C-25, Second hydroxylation in the kidney at C-1

Vitamin D_2 (*ergocalciferol*) is formed by UV irradiation of the ergosterol. Vitamin D deficiency causes a net demineralization of bone resulting in **rickets** in children and **osteomalacia** in adults.

Vitamin E

Vitamin E is the most abundant lipid-soluble *antioxidant* and consists of eight naturally occurring tocopherols, with **α-tocopherol** being the most common. α-tocopherol acts as an antioxidant by donating hydrogen atoms to free radicals, thereby converting them into non-radical products. The primary function of vitamin E is to prevent the nonenzymatic oxidation of cell components by free radicals and organic peroxides. This hydrophobic molecule is incorporated into cell membranes, where it protects membrane proteins and lipids from oxidative damage. Although the exact mechanism of action of vitamin E remains unclear, its antioxidant properties are well-established. Vitamin E deficiency can lead to various neuromuscular pathologies.

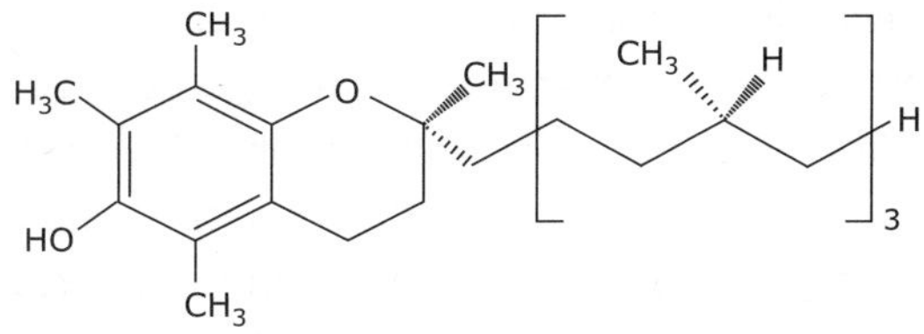

Figure 1.94 Structure of α-tocopherol. It consists of two main components: a chromanol ring (a chromane ring with a hydroxyl group on the second carbon) and a phytyl side chain (a 16-carbon isoprenoid chain attached to the second carbon of the chromanol ring).

Vitamin K

Vitamin K is a fat-soluble vitamin that exists in several forms. In plants, it is found as **phylloquinone** (vitamin K1), and in the intestinal bacterial flora, it is produced as **menaquinone** (vitamin K2). About half of the daily requirement for humans is supplied by intestinal bacteria.

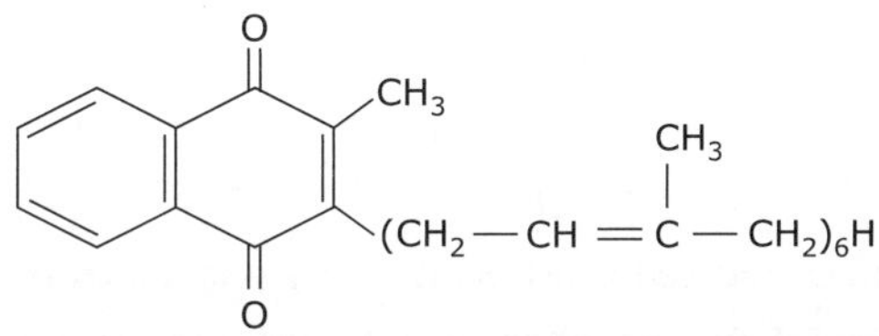

Figure 1.95 Structure of vitamin K2. The general structure of vitamin K2 consists of a 2-methyl-1,4-naphthoquinone ring (menadione) as the core structure, with an isoprenoid side chain attached at the 3-position. The length of this side chain varies depending on the number of isoprene units.

Table 1.19 Vitamins and their roles

Vitamin	Action
Water-soluble	
Thiamine (Vitamin B_1)	Cofactor in decarboxylations
	Deficiency disease: Beri-beri
Riboflavin (Vitamin B_2)	Constituent of flavoproteins.
Niacin (Vitamin B_3)	Constituent of NAD^+ and $NADP^+$
	Deficiency disease: Pellagra
Pantothenic acid (Vitamin B_5)	Constituent of CoA and acyl-group transfer
Pyridoxine (Vitamin B_6)	Group transfer to or from amino acids
Biotin (Vitamin H)	ATP-dependent carboxylation and carboxyl-group transfer
Folate (folic acid)	Coenzymes for 1-carbon transfer
	Deficiency disease: Megaloblastic anemia
Cyanocobalamin (Vitamin B_{12})	Coenzyme in amino acid metabolism
	Deficiency disease: Pernicious anemia
C (Ascorbic acid)	Antioxidant
	Deficiency disease: Scurvy
Fat soluble	
A (retinol)	Roles in vision, growth, reproduction
	Deficiency disease: Night blindness
D group	Regulation of calcium and phosphate metabolism
	Deficiency disease: Rickets (children), osteomalacia (adults)
E group	Antioxidants; cofactors in electron transport in cytochrome chain
K group	Blood coagulation, Post-translational modification of blood clotting factors

The most obvious effect of a deficiency in vitamin K in animals is delayed blood clotting due to a decrease in prothrombin activity and some clotting factors. **Prothrombin** is a proteolytic enzyme that converts **fibrinogen** to **fibrin**, the insoluble fibrous protein. The principal role of vitamin K is in the post-translational modification of blood clotting factors. It participates in the *carboxylation* of glutamate amino acid residues (the incorporation of the additional carboxyl group into the glutamate residues to form γ-carboxyglutamate) in proteins involved in blood clotting. Vitamin K deficiency prevents this carboxylation, and the resulting inactive clotting proteins lead to excessive bleeding. **Warfarin**, a structural analog of vitamin K, is a widely used rat poison that inhibits the vitamin K-dependent carboxylation of prothrombin. Warfarin is also clinically used as an anticoagulant. **Dicoumarol**, a derivative of coumarin, also acts as an anticoagulant.

1.11 Reactive oxygen species and antioxidants

Reactive Oxygen Species (**ROS**) is a phrase used to describe a number of reactive chemical species and free radicals derived from molecular oxygen. It is a collective term for species derived from O_2 that are more reactive than O_2 itself. The term includes not only oxygen radicals, but also some non-radical derivatives of O_2, such as singlet oxygen ($^1O_2$) and hydrogen peroxide (H_2O_2). Hence, *all oxygen radicals are ROS, but not all ROS are oxygen radicals.*

Ground state oxygen molecule may be converted to ROS either by **energy transfer** or by **electron transfer** reactions. The former leads to the formation of **singlet oxygen** whereas the latter results in the sequential reduction to **superoxide radical** and **peroxide ion**. Singlet oxygen is not a free radical, since it contains no unpaired electrons. In contrast, the ground-state oxygen molecule exists as **triplet oxygen**. In this state, it has two unpaired electrons located in separate degenerate antibonding orbitals with parallel spins. This parallel spin configuration is also known as the **triplet state**. Absorption of sufficient energy reverses the spin of one of its unpaired electrons leading to formation of **singlet state** in which the two electrons have opposite spin.

Oxygen (O_2) Superoxide radical ($O_2^{\bullet -}$) Peroxide ion (O_2^{2-}) Hydroxyl radical ($OH^{\bullet}$)

Free radicals are atoms or molecules that contain one or more unpaired valence electrons, which accounts for their instability and high reactivity. A **free radical** is any species capable of independent existence (hence the term 'free') that contains at least one unpaired electron. A superscript dot after the chemical formula denotes a free radical.

Many types of radicals exist, but those of greatest concern in biological systems are derived from oxygen. Oxygen readily accepts electrons from other molecules; it is a powerful oxidizing agent, and each oxygen molecule can accept a total of two electrons (one pair). However, these electrons cannot be accepted simultaneously because they would need to have parallel spins to occupy the same orbital, which violates the Pauli exclusion principle. Consequently, oxygen tends to accept electrons one at a time, leading to the formation of partially reduced, highly reactive oxygen species. If one electron is added to the ground-state oxygen molecule, it gives **superoxide radical** ($O_2^{\bullet -}$). Addition of another electron to superoxide radical gives **peroxide ion** (O_2^{2-}), a non-radical. Dismutation of superoxide radical produces hydrogen peroxide (H_2O_2), which in turn may be fully reduced to water or partially reduced to hydroxyl radical ($OH^{\bullet}$). **Dismutation** is a redox reaction in which a compound of intermediate oxidation state converts to two different compounds, one of higher and one of lower oxidation states. $OH^{\bullet}$ is the most reactive among all ROS.

$$O_2 \xrightarrow{e^-} O_2^{\bullet -} \xrightarrow{e^-} O_2^{2-} \xrightarrow{2H^+} H_2O_2 \xrightarrow{e^- + H^+} OH^{\bullet} + H_2O$$

When the level of ROS exceeds the normal level, a cell is said to be in a state of '**oxidative stress**.' The enhanced level of ROS causes peroxidation of lipids (oxidations of unsaturated fatty acids), oxidation of proteins, damage to nucleic acids, enzyme inhibition and activation of programmed cell death pathways.

Antioxidants: Free radicals derived from oxygen, nitrogen and sulphur molecules in the biological system are highly active to react with other molecules due to their unpaired electrons. These radicals are produced during cellular metabolism and have important roles in cell signaling, apoptosis, gene expression and ion transportation. However, their excessive amount causes oxidative damage to nucleic acids, proteins and lipids. Antioxidants are substances that can prevent oxidative damage. Antioxidants can include:

- Agents that catalytically remove reactive species, such as the superoxide dismutase and catalase enzymes.
- Agents that control reactive species formation e.g., transferrins and albumin.
- Quenchers of reactive species e.g., carotenoids.
- Agents that react with reactive species and stop them attacking other biomolecules e.g., GSH, α-tocopherol.

Two principle mechanisms of action have been proposed for antioxidants. The first is a chain-breaking mechanism by which they donate electrons to the free radicals present in the systems (**primary antioxidants**). The second mechanism involves removal of ROS initiators by quenching chain-initiating catalyst (**secondary antioxidants**). Cells contain multiple types of antioxidants which can broadly classified into *enzymatic* and *non-enzymatic antioxidants*. **Non-enzymatic antioxidants** include vitamin C, vitamin E, glutathione, carotenoids, flavonoids and other antioxidants. **Enzymatic antioxidant** include *superoxide dismutase* (SOD), *glutathione peroxidase* (GPx) and *catalase*. Peroxidases reduce H_2O_2 by using it to oxidize another substrate. For example, glutathione peroxidases remove H_2O_2 by reducing it to H_2O coupled with oxidation of reduced glutathione. By contrast, the catalases catalyze direct conversion of H_2O_2 to O_2.

$$O_2^{\bullet -} + O_2^{\bullet -} + 2H^+ \xrightarrow{SOD} H_2O_2 + O_2$$

$$H_2O_2 + H_2O_2 \xrightarrow{Catalase} 2H_2O + O_2$$

$$H_2O_2 + 2\,GSH \xrightarrow{GPx} 2H_2O + GSSG$$ (GSH = Reduced glutathione and GSSG = Oxidized glutathione)

1.12 Enzymes

An *enzyme* is a biocatalyst that increases the rate of chemical reaction without itself being changed in the overall process. Virtually all cellular reactions or processes are mediated by enzymes. The discovery of enzymes began with the work of Louis Pasteur, who proposed that alcoholic fermentation was carried out by living yeast cells. This view changed in 1897 when Eduard Buchner demonstrated that fermentation could occur in cell-free yeast extracts, leading to the identification of the catalytic substance **zymase**. The term **'enzyme'** was coined by Wilhelm Kühne, and in 1926 James B. Sumner provided definitive proof that enzymes are proteins by isolating and crystallizing **urease** from jack beans. Enzymes have several properties that make them unique.

- Most (but not all) enzymes are proteins (some enzymes are RNA molecules).
- Enzymes are highly specific. They are specialized proteins and have a high degree of specificity for their substrates.
- Enzymes exhibit enormous catalytic power. It increases the rate of a reaction by lowering the activation energy.
- Enzymes do not change the equilibrium state of a biochemical reaction. It changes only the rate at which equilibrium is achieved.

Proteinaceous enzymes can be divided into two general classes: **simple enzymes**, consist entirely of amino acids and **conjugated enzymes**, consist of proteins as well as non-protein components. The non-protein component is called a **cofactor**, which is required for catalytic activity. Removal of cofactor from a conjugated enzyme leaves only protein component, called an **apoenzyme**, which generally is biologically inactive. The complete, biologically active conjugated enzyme (simple enzyme plus cofactor) is called a **holoenzyme**. A cofactor can be linked to the protein portion of the enzyme either covalently or non-covalently. Some cofactors are simple metal ions and other cofactors are complex organic compounds, which are also called **coenzymes**. Many coenzymes are vitamins or contain vitamins as part of their structure. Some coenzymes are only transiently associated with a given enzyme molecule, so that they function as **cosubstrates**. Coenzymes which are tightly associated with the protein covalently or non-covalently are called **prosthetic group**. Enzymes that depend on metal ions as cofactors fall into two categories: **metal-activated enzymes** (bind metal ions weakly during catalysis) and **metalloenzymes** (enzyme binds the metal ion very tightly or requires the metal ion to maintain its stable native state).

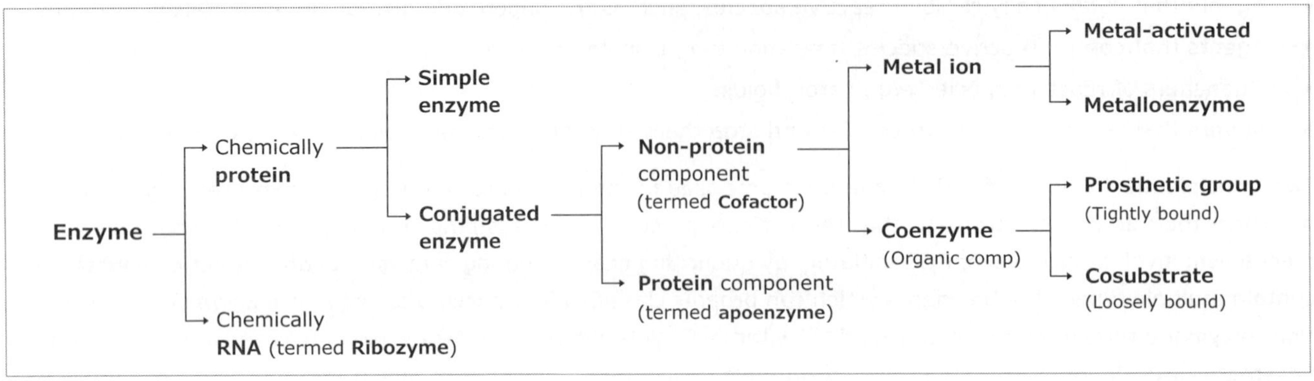

Table 1.20 Vitamin B-complex and their coenzyme forms

Vitamin	Coenzyme form	Reaction or process promoted
Thiamine (B_1)	Thiamine pyrophosphate	Decarboxylation, aldehyde group transfer
Riboflavin (B_2)	FAD and FMN	Redox reaction
Pyridoxine (B_6)	Pyridoxal phosphate	Amino group transfer
Nicotinic acid (niacin)	NAD^+ and $NADP^+$	Redox reaction
Pantothenic acid (B_5)	Coenzyme A	Acyl group transfer
Biotin	Biocytin	Carboxylation
Folic acid	Tetrahydrofolic acid	One-carbon group transfer
Vitamin B_{12}	Deoxyadenosylcobalamin	Intramolecular rearrangements

The vitamins in the human diet that are coenzyme precursors are all water-soluble vitamins.

1.12.1 Naming and classification of enzymes

Many enzymes have **trivial names**. Some enzymes were named by adding the suffix *-ase* to the name of the substrate upon which they acted, as in *urease* for the urea-hydrolyzing enzyme. Other enzymes acquired names bearing little resemblance to their activity. For example, trypsin, a proteolytic enzyme, is secreted by the pancreas. Trivial names provide little information about the reactions that enzymes catalyze. Because of the confusion that arose from these trivial names, the Enzyme Commission (EC) has given all known enzymes a **systematic name** in addition to its existing trivial name. Systematic names consist of two parts. The first contains the name of the substrate or substrates separated by a colon. The second part, ending in *-ase*, indicates the nature of the reaction. For example, malate dehydrogenase (trivial name) interconverts L-malate and oxaloacetate using NAD^+ as a coenzyme. It's systematic name 'L-malate: NAD^+ oxidoreductase'.

The Enzyme Commission has classified enzymes into six main **classes**, on the basis of type of the reaction catalyze. Within each class are **subclasses**, and under each subclass are **sub-subclasses** within which individual enzymes are listed. According to this system, the Enzyme Commission has given each enzyme a number (termed **EC number**) with four parts, like EC 2.7.1.2 (EC number for enzyme hexokinase). The first three numbers define class, subclass and sub-subclass, respectively. The last number is a serial number in the sub-subclass, indicating the order in which each enzyme is added to the list. Thus, the EC number is a numerical naming scheme for enzymes, which in strict sense, do not specify enzymes, but enzyme-catalyzed reactions.

Enzyme class	Type of reaction catalyzed
EC1 Oxidoreductases	Oxidation-Reduction reactions $A_{red} + B_{ox} \longrightarrow A_{ox} + B_{red}$
EC2 Transferases	Transfer of an atom or group between two molecules A–B + C ⟶ A + B–C
EC3 Hydrolases	Hydrolysis reactions A–B + H_2O ⟶ A–H + B–OH
EC4 Lyases	Removal of a group from substrate (not by hydrolysis) A = B + HX ⟶ A–X + B–H
EC5 Isomerases	Isomerization reactions A–B ⟶ B–A
EC6 Ligases	Catalyze synthetic reactions coupled with the hydrolysis of nucleoside triphosphate A + B + ATP ⟶ A - B + ADP

'Ligase' is the recommended name for 'synthase'. Biochemical nomenclature distinguishes *synthetases* from *synthases*. **Synthases** catalyze condensation reactions in which no nucleoside triphosphate (ATP and GTP) is required as an energy source. **Synthetases** catalyze condensations that do use nucleoside triphosphate as a source of energy for the synthetic reaction. A synthase is a lyase and does not require any energy, whereas a synthetase is a ligase and thus requires energy.

Six enzyme classes have been recognized since the first enzyme classification list was approved by the International Union of Biochemistry in 1961. These classes are Oxidoreductases (EC 1), Transferases (EC 2), Hydrolases (EC 3), Lyases (EC 4), Isomerases (EC 5) and Ligases (EC 6). However, it has become apparent that none of these could describe the important group of enzymes that catalyze the movement of ions or molecules across membranes or their separation within membranes. These enzymes have now been classified under a new EC class of **translocases** (**EC 7**). The reactions catalyzed are designated as transfers from 'side 1' to 'side 2'.

Meaning of EC number

The first digit in the EC number indicates class **oxidoreductases**. Enzymes belong to this class catalyze the oxidation-reduction reactions. The second digit (subclass) in the EC number indicates the donor of the reducing equivalents (hydrogen or electrons) involved in the reaction. The third digit (sub-subclass) refers to the hydrogen or electron acceptor.

EC	First digit	Second digit	Third digit	Fourth digit
	Class	**Subclass**	**Sub-subclass**	
	Oxidation-reduction	*Hydrogen or electron donor*	*Hydrogen or electron acceptor*	*The order in which each enzyme is added to the list*
	1	**1** Alcohol **2** Aldehyde or ketone **3** Primary amine **4** Secondary amine ⋮	**1** NAD^+ **2** Fe^{3+} **3** O_2 ⋮	

Note: *Oxidases, dehydrogenases, oxygenases* and *peroxidases* are trivial names of enzymes that belong to oxidoreductases.

Oxidases: Catalyze oxidative reactions in which oxygen acts as an electron acceptor, but oxygen atoms do not appear in the oxidized product. If oxidases oxidize two different substrates simultaneously, then are called **mixed-function oxidases.**

Dehydrogenases: Catalyze reactions in which molecules other than oxygen (e.g., NAD^+) act as electron acceptors.

Peroxidases: Catalyze oxidative reactions in which H_2O_2 acts as an electron acceptor.

Oxygenases: Catalyze oxidative reactions in which oxygen atoms are directly incorporated into the product molecules. It can be dioxygenases and monooxygenases. **Dioxygenases** catalyze reactions in which both oxygen atoms of O_2 are incorporated into the product, whereas **monooxygenases** (also called **mixed-function oxygenases**) catalyze reactions in which only one of the two oxygen atoms of O_2 is incorporated into the product, the other being reduced to H_2O.

Similarly, the first digit in the EC number (EC 5.1.1.4) indicates class **isomerases**. Enzymes belong to this class catalyze the isomerization reactions. The second digit (subclass) in the EC number indicates the type of reaction. The third digit (sub-subclass) refers to the type of molecule undergoing isomerization.

EC	First digit	Second digit	Third digit	Fourth digit
	Class	**Subclass**	**Sub-subclass**	
	Isomerization reactions	*Type of reaction*	Substrate	*The order in which each enzyme is added to the list*
	5	1 Racemization or epimerization	1 Amino acids	
		2 *cis-trans* isomerization	2 Hydroxy acids	
		⋮	⋮	

1.12.2 How enzymes operate?

An enzyme accelerates the rate of a chemical reaction several times as compared to the uncatalyzed reaction in water. It increases the rate of a chemical reaction by lowering the **activation energy**. However, an enzyme does not change the free energies of the substrate and the product. The free energy of reaction, ΔG, remains unchanged in the presence of an enzyme, so the relative amounts of reactants and products at equilibrium are unchanged. In other words, an enzyme does not change the position of equilibrium in a chemical reaction. *It only accelerates the attainment of equilibria but do not shift their positions.*

The formation of an enzyme-substrate complex is the first step in enzymatic catalysis. The region which contains the binding and catalytic sites is termed the **active site** of the enzyme. The unique physical and chemical properties of the active site limit an enzyme's activity to specific substrates. The substrate binds to the active site of an enzyme by multiple weak non-covalent interactions like hydrophobic interactions, H-bonds, ionic interactions or reversible covalent bonds. The free energy released in the formation of a large number of weak interactions between the enzyme and the substrate is termed **binding energy**. The binding between the enzyme and the substrate is highly specific. A given enzyme usually binds to only one kind of substrate. *The specificity of binding depends on the precisely defined arrangement of atoms in an active site.* The specificity of enzyme-substrate interactions arises mainly from hydrogen bonding and the shape of the active site, which rejects molecules that do not have a sufficiently complementary shape.

Two important models have been proposed to describe the binding process between substrate and enzyme. The first, the **lock-and-key model**, assumes a high degree of complementarity between the shape of the substrate and the geometry of the binding site on the enzyme. The complementarity between enzymes and their substrates is the basis of the *lock-and-key model* of enzyme function. This model was first proposed by Emil Fischer in 1894.

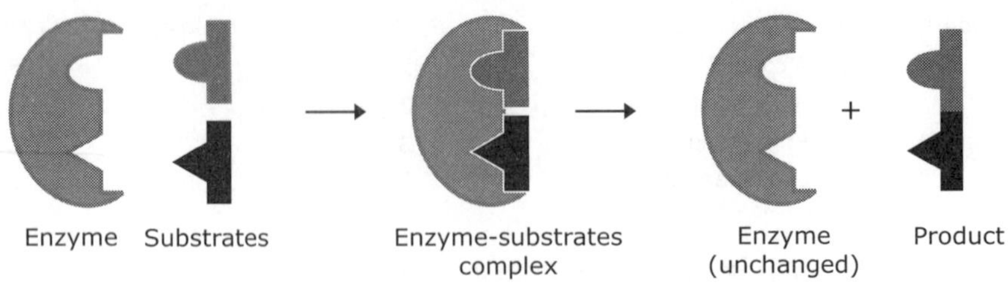

Figure 1.96 Lock-and-key model. In this model, the active site of the unbound enzyme is complementary in shape to the substrate.

According to **induced-fit model** (Daniel Koshland, 1958), enzymes are flexible and that the shapes of the active sites can be markedly modified by the binding of substrate. The binding of the substrate induces a conformational change in the enzyme that results in a complementary fit once the substrate is bound. The binding site has a different three-dimensional shape before the substrate is bound.

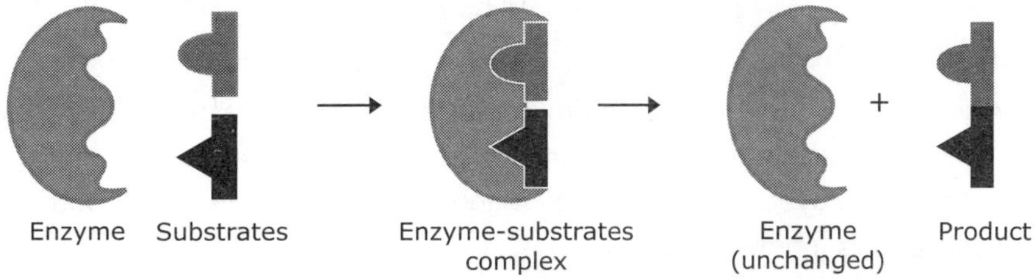

Figure 1.97 Induced-fit model. In this model, the enzyme changes shape on substrate binding. The active site forms a shape complementary to the substrate only after the substrate has been bound.

Transition-state theory and activation energy

In both uncatalyzed and enzyme-catalyzed chemical reactions, substrate changes into the product goes through a transition-state. The **transitions-state** is the intermediary state of the reaction, when the molecule is neither a substrate or product. It is unstable state and will very quickly break down to form the products (or back to substrates). It is the point of highest free energy, in which the substrates are partially converted to products.

The difference in free energy between the transition-state and the ground state of the substrate is called the *Gibbs free energy of activation* or simply the **activation energy**, symbolized by $\Delta G^{\ddagger}$. The greater the value of activation energy, the slower the reaction rate. Enzymes lower the activation energy (or we can say enzymes facilitate the formation of transition state). But there is a question – where does the energy to lower the activation energy come from? Lowering of the activation energy occurs due to the binding energy. The **binding energy** released as a result of the interactions between the enzyme and the substrate. Only the correct substrate can form maximum interactions with the enzyme and thus maximize the binding energy. Furthermore, the full complement of such interactions is formed only when the substrate is converted into the transition-state. Thus, the maximal binding energy is released when the enzyme facilitates the formation of the transition-state. The combination of substrate and enzyme creates a reaction pathway whose transition-state energy is lower than that of the reaction in the absence of enzyme. Because the activation energy is lower, more molecules have the energy required to reach the transition state. Decreasing the activation barrier is analogous to lowering the height of a high-jump bar; more athletes will be able to clear the bar.

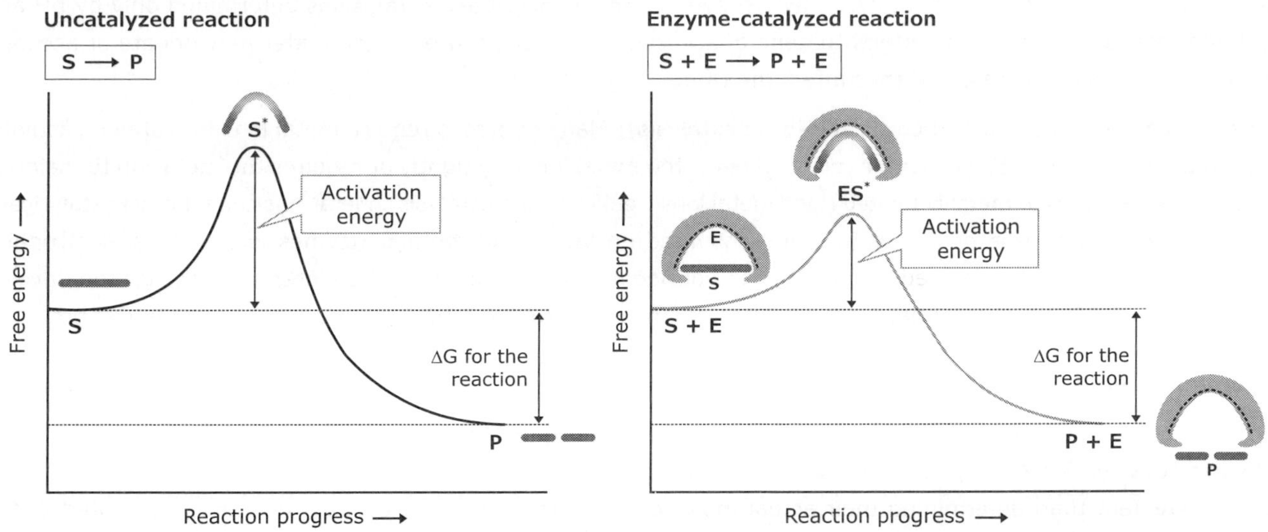

Figure 1.98 Free energy changes for a spontaneous reaction proceeding via the formation of a transition-state. An uncatalyzed and enzyme-catalyzed chemical reaction in which substrate 'S' changes into product 'P' goes through a transition state S^* ($S \rightarrow S^* \rightarrow P$). The point of highest free energy is the transition state, in which the substrates are partially converted to products. Activation energy is the difference in free energy between the substrate and the transition state. An enzyme cannot alter free energy of substrate and product; it can only decrease activation energy to allow the reaction to approach equilibrium (where the rates of the forward and reverse reactions are equal) more quickly than it would in the absence of an enzyme.

1.12.3 Catalytic strategies

Enzymes commonly employ one or more strategies to catalyze specific reactions. Among the best characterized mechanisms are *general acid-base catalysis, metal ion catalysis* and *covalent catalysis*. A combination of several catalytic strategies is usually employed by an enzyme. A good example of the use of both covalent catalysis and general acid-base catalysis occurs in chymotrypsin.

Covalent catalysis: The process of covalent catalysis involves the formation of a reversible covalent bond between the enzyme and substrate. Although the covalent interactions are temporary, the substrate is bound to the enzyme during the course of catalysis. After the completion of the reaction, the enzyme returns to its original unmodified state. The proteolytic enzyme chymotrypsin provides an excellent example of this mechanism. Enzymes performing covalent catalysis bear nucleophilic or electrophilic centers. Nucleophilic centers include negatively charged oxygen, negatively charged sulfhydryl group, carbanion and imidazole group. These groups perform **covalent nucleophilic catalysis** and readily attack electrophilic centers of substrate forming covalent intermediates. Typical electrophilic centers in substrates include phosphoryl groups, acyl groups and glycosyl groups. **Covalent electrophilic catalysis** is also observed but usually involves coenzyme adducts that generate electrophilic centers.

	Nucleophile	Electrophile
Definition	Electron donor	Electron acceptor
Electron density	High	Low
Charge	Usually negative or neutral with lone pairs	Usually positive or neutral with electron deficiency

Acid-base catalysis: Acid-base catalysis involves proton transfer. There are two kinds of acid-base catalysis – specific and general acid-base catalysis. In **specific acid-base catalysis**, hydronium ions and hydroxide ions act directly as the acid and base groups. In **general acid-base catalysis**, donors and acceptors of protons are other than hydronium and hydroxide ions. In such cases, the ionizable functional groups of aminoacyl side chains and of cofactors (if present) contribute to catalysis by acting as acids or bases. Functional groups such as imidazole, hydroxyl, carboxyl, sulfhydral, amino and phenolic group of amino acids act as acids or bases. As far as enzyme-catalyzed reactions are concerned, only general acid-base catalysis can occur. A common example of general acid-base catalysis occurs in the hydrolysis of peptidoglycan catalyzed by lysozyme. **Specific acid-base catalysis** is determined only by pH and the buffer concentration has no effect. In general acid-base catalysis, however, the buffer may donate or accept a proton in the transition state and thus affect the rate.

Metal ion catalysis (also called **Lewis acid-base catalysis**): Many enzymes require metal ions for catalytic activity. These enzymes can be **metalloenzyme** (enzyme binds the metal ion very tightly or requires the metal ion to maintain its stable native state) or **metal activated** (bind metal ions weakly during catalysis). Metal ions can function catalytically in several ways. One role of metals in metal-activated enzymes and metalloenzymes is to act as electrophilic catalysts, stabilizing the increased electron density or negative charge on a reaction intermediate that can develop during reactions. Another potential function of metal ions is to provide a powerful nucleophile at neutral pH.

Enzyme activity

The amount of an enzyme can be expressed either as a **molar quantity** (amount of substance) or in terms of its **catalytic activity**. Since enzymes are usually present in very small quantities, measuring their activity is often more convenient than determining their actual molar concentration. In such cases, the activity is related to the enzyme's concentration, and the results are reported in activity units rather than moles. Two standard units are used to express enzyme activity:

Enzyme unit (U): The amount of enzyme that catalyzes the conversion of 1 micromole (μmol) of substrate per minute at 25°C under optimal assay conditions (1 U = 1 μmol min^{-1}).

Katal (kat): The SI unit of enzyme activity. One katal is the amount of enzyme that catalyzes the conversion of 1 mole of substrate per second (1 kat = 1 mol sec^{-1}, where, 16.67 nanokat = 1U).

1.12.4 Enzyme kinetics

The study of the rates of enzyme-catalyzed reactions and affinity of enzymes for substrates and inhibitors is called **enzyme kinetics**. The general principles of chemical reaction apply to enzyme-catalyzed reactions as well. In a chemical reaction of the form A + B → P, where A and B are the reactants and P is the product, the rate of reaction can be expressed in terms of either the rate of disappearance of one of the reactants or the rate of appearance of a product. The rate of disappearance of A is $-\Delta[A]/\Delta t$, where Δ symbolizes change, [A] is the concentration of A in moles/litre, and t is the time. Likewise, the rate of disappearance of B is $-\Delta[B]/\Delta t$, and the rate of appearance of P is $\Delta[P]/\Delta t$. The rate of the reaction can be expressed in terms of any of these changes, because the rates of appearance of the product and disappearance of reactant are related by the stoichiometric equation for the reaction.

$$\text{Rate} = -\frac{\Delta[A]}{\Delta t} = -\frac{\Delta[B]}{\Delta t} = \frac{\Delta[P]}{\Delta t}$$

The negative signs for the changes in concentration of A and B indicate that A and B are being used up in the reaction, while P is being produced. It has been established that the rate of a reaction at a given time is proportional to the product of the concentrations of each reactant raised to the power of the number of molecules of that reactant taking part.

$aA + bB \rightarrow \text{Products}$

$\text{Rate} \propto [A]^a\,[B]^b$

or, as an equation, $\text{Rate} = k\,[A]^a\,[B]^b$

where k is a proportionality constant called the *rate constant*. The exponents a and b are the partial orders of reaction for A and B. The *overall order* of a reaction is the sum of all the exponents. Reactions can be first order, second order and zero order depending on the concentration of the reactants.

A **first-order reaction** is one which proceeds at a rate proportional to the concentration of one reactant. The rate is doubled when the concentration of that reactant is doubled. Thus, for a first-order reaction A → P taking place at a constant temperature and pressure in a dilute solution,

$\text{Rate} = k\,[A]^1$

A **second-order reaction** is one which proceeds at a rate proportional to the concentration of two reactants or to the second power of a single reactant. Doubling the concentration of a reactant results in a quadrupling (x4) of the reaction rate. So, for a second-order reaction A + B → P, taking place at a constant temperature and pressure in a dilute solution,

$\text{Rate} = k\,[A]^1\,[B]^1$

The reaction is said to be first order with respect to A, first order with respect to B, and *second order* overall.

Many common reactions are first or second order. It should be noted that a **zero-order reaction** is also possible. A zero-order reaction proceeds at a rate that is independent of reactant concentration. In other words, increasing or decreasing the concentration of reactants will not increase or decrease the reaction rate, respectively. This means that the rate of the reaction is equal to the rate constant, k, of that reaction. So, for a zero-order reaction A → P given by the equation:

$\text{Rate} = k\,[A]^0 = k$

Order of reaction	Rate when concentration is doubled	Rate when concentration is tripled
Zero	Does not change	Does not change
1st	Doubles (x2)	x3
2nd	Quadruples (x4)	x9

Kinetics of enzyme catalyzed reactions

When the *rate* (also called the *velocity*) of an enzyme-catalyzed reaction is measured at varying substrate concentrations, the rate depends on the substrate concentrations. At a relatively low concentration of substrate, initial velocity (V_0) increases almost linearly with an increase in a substrate concentration [S]. The reaction reaches a maximum velocity (V_{max}) with an increase in substrate concentration and it doesn't increase any further by increasing the concentration of substrate. At high substrate concentration, V_0 becomes virtually independent of substrate concentration and approaches a maximal limit. The value of V_0 at this limit is written V_{max}. This is a **saturation effect**. Since at a low concentration of the substrate, velocity is proportional to substrate concentration, the enzyme-catalyzed reaction is a **first-order reaction**. At high concentration of the substrate, velocity becomes virtually independent of substrate concentration. Since the rate is no longer dependent on at high substrate concentration, the enzyme-catalyzed reaction obeys **zero-order kinetics**. The plot based on reaction velocity versus substrate concentration shows the **substrate saturation curve**.

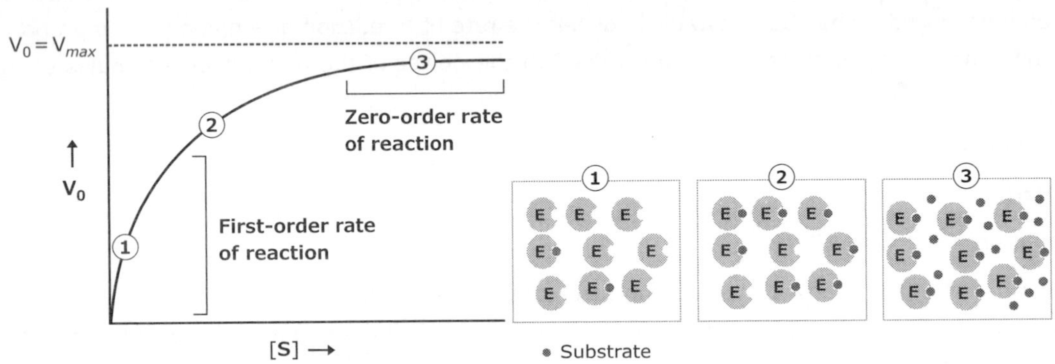

Figure 1.99 The velocity of an enzyme-catalyzed reaction depend on substrate concentration. The concentration of enzyme [E] is constant. In the lower region of the curve (at low levels of substrate), the reaction is first order, implying that the velocity (V_0) depends on substrate concentration [S]. In the upper portion of the curve (at higher levels of substrate), the reaction is zero order; the rate is independent of concentration.

At any point of time in an enzyme-catalyzed reaction, the enzyme exists in two forms, the free (E) and the enzyme-substrate complex (ES). At low substrate concentration, most of the enzyme is in the free form. The maximum velocity (V_{max}) is observed when virtually all the enzyme is present as the ES complex. Under these conditions, the enzyme is 'saturated' with its substrate, so that further increases in substrate concentration have no effect on reaction velocity. This condition exists when substrate concentration is sufficiently high that essentially all the free enzyme has been converted to the ES form. After the ES complex breaks down to yield the product (P), the enzyme is free to catalyze the reaction of another molecule of substrate.

Leonor Michaelis and Maud L. Menten proposed a general theory of enzyme action in 1913 after investigating the kinetics of an enzymatic reaction in which the enzyme **invertase** hydrolyzes sucrose, a disaccharide, into monosaccharides, glucose and fructose. Michaelis and Menten proposed the following scheme of single-substrate enzyme catalyzed reaction where there is just one substrate-binding site per enzyme.

$$\mathrm{E + S} \underset{k_{-1}}{\overset{k_1}{\rightleftharpoons}} \mathrm{ES} \underset{k_{-2}}{\overset{k_2}{\rightleftharpoons}} \mathrm{E + P}$$

If the product concentration is negligible, the formation of ES from product can be ignored.

$$\mathrm{E + S} \underset{k_{-1}}{\overset{k_1}{\rightleftharpoons}} \mathrm{ES} \xrightarrow{k_2} \mathrm{E + P}$$

In this equation, k_1 is the rate constant for the formation of the ES complex (**Michaelis complex**), from the enzyme (E) and the substrate (S); k_{-1} is the rate constant for the reverse reaction, dissociation of the ES complex to free enzyme and substrate; and k_2 is the rate constant for the conversion of the ES complex to product (P) and the subsequent release of product from the enzyme. They postulated that the enzyme first combines reversibly with its substrate to form an ES complex in a relatively fast reversible step. The ES complex then breaks down in a slower second step to yield the free enzyme (E) and the reaction product (P). When the substrate concentration becomes high enough to entirely convert the enzyme to the ES form, the second step of the reaction becomes rate-limiting and the overall reaction rate becomes insensitive to further increases in substrate concentration. Here, it has been assumed, the second reaction is irreversible; that is, no product is converted back to substrate. The interpretation of the Michaelis-Menten model were refined by Briggs and Haldane by considering the **steady-state assumption**.

According to this, [ES] remains approximately constant over time (i.e., the rate of formation of the enzyme-substrate complex equals the rate of its breakdown). So, when the enzyme and substrate are first mixed, after a very brief initial period, [ES] reaches a steady-state level ($d[ES]/dt = 0$).

To derive an expression that relates the reaction velocity of catalysis to the concentrations of substrate and enzyme, the reaction velocity can be expressed as the product of the concentration of the ES complex and k_2.

$V_0 = k_2[ES]$ (From the law of mass action)

The maximal reaction velocity (V_{max}) is attained when the catalytic sites on the enzyme are saturated with substrate. Thus, at V_{max} [ES] is equal to $[E_t]$.

$V_0 = k_2[ES]$

$V_0 = V_{max} = k_2[E_t]$

The rates of formation and breakdown of ES are given by,

Rate of formation of ES $= k_1[E][S]$

Rate of breakdown of ES $= k_{-1}[ES] + k_2[ES]$ i.e., $(k_{-1} + k_2)[ES]$

The steady-state assumption can be used to simplify matters. In a steady state, the concentrations of [ES] remain the same. This steady state is reached when the rates of formation and breakdown of the ES complex are equal.

$k_1[E][S] = (k_{-1} + k_2)[ES]$

By rearranging this equation, we obtain

$$\frac{[E][S]}{[ES]} = \frac{k_{-1} + k_2}{k_1} = K_m \text{ (Michaelis constant)}$$

In the enzyme-catalyzed reaction, the total enzyme concentration $[E_t]$ is equal to the uncombined enzyme [E] plus the concentration of the ES complex.

$[E]_t = [E] + [ES]$

$[E] = [E]_t - [ES]$

$$K_m = \frac{[E][S]}{[ES]} = \frac{[E_t]-[ES][S]}{[ES]} \qquad \text{where, } [E] = [E_t] - [ES]$$

$$K_m = \frac{[E_t][S] - [ES][S]}{[ES]} = \frac{[E_t][S]}{[ES]} - \frac{[ES][S]}{[ES]} = \frac{[E_t][S]}{[ES]} - [S]$$

$$K_m = \frac{V_{max}[S]}{k_2[ES]} - [S] \qquad \text{where, } V_{max} = k_2[E_t]$$

$$K_m = \frac{V_{max}[S]}{V_0} - [S] \qquad \text{where, } V_0 = k_2[ES]$$

$$V_0 = \frac{V_{max}[S]}{K_m + [S]}$$

This expression, the **Michaelis–Menten equation**, is the basic equation of enzyme kinetics. This equation says that the initial reaction velocity of an enzyme-catalyzed reaction (V_0), is determined by two constants, K_m (**Michaelis constant**) and V_{max} and the initial concentration of substrate. The following assumptions are made in driving the Michaelis-Menten equation:

1. The concentration of substrate [S] is much greater than the concentrations of enzyme [E].
2. The rate of formation of ES is equal to that of the breakdown of ES (the steady-state assumption).
3. Very little accumulation of P, so the formation of enzyme-substrate complex from E + P is negligible (ignored any back reaction by which EP might form ES).

The Michaelis-Menten equation is, therefore, consistent with the observed dependence of V_0 on [S]. According to this equation, the reaction velocity versus substrate concentration shows a **rectangular hyperbola**. All enzymes that exhibit a hyperbolic dependence of V_0 on [S] are said to follow **Michaelis-Menten kinetics**.

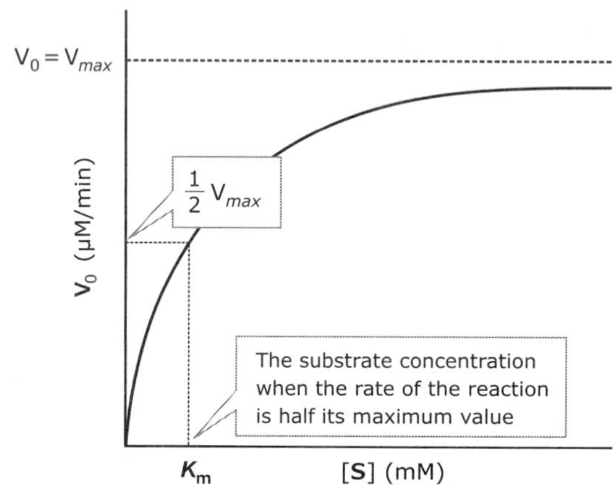

Figure 1.100 Graphical determination of V_{max} and K_m from a plot of reaction velocity (V_0), against substrate concentration, [S]. Vmax is the constant reaction velocity reached when the enzyme is completely saturated with substrate. When the reaction velocity is half its maximum value, the substrate concentration is equal to the K_m.

Case 1: [S] << K_m

At low [S], the [S] term in the denominator of the Michaelis-Menten equation becomes insignificant. The equation simplifies to $V = V_{max}[S]/K_m$ and V_0 exhibits a linear dependence on substrate concentrations i.e., $\mathbf{V_0 \propto [S]}$.

Case 2: [S] >> K_m

At high [S], the K_m term in the denominator of the Michaelis-Menten equation becomes insignificant and the equation simplifies to $V = V_{max}$; this is consistent with the plateau observed at high on substrate concentrations i.e., $\mathbf{V_0 = V_{max}}$.

Case 3: [S] = K_m

This gives the practical definition of K_m (Michaelis constant), *the substrate concentration at which the reaction velocity is half-maximal*. Therefore, if an enzyme has a small value of K_m, it achieves maximal catalytic efficiency at low substrate concentrations i.e., $\mathbf{V_0 = V_{max}/2}$.

Another interpretation of K_m relies on the assumptions of the original Michaelis–Menten scheme of reactions.

$$E + S \underset{k_{-1}}{\overset{k_1}{\rightleftharpoons}} ES \xrightarrow{k_2} E + P$$

$$K_m = \frac{k_{-1} + k_2}{k_1}$$

If k_2 is much smaller than k_{-1}, the Michaelis constant can be expressed as

$$K_m \approx \frac{k_{-1}}{k_1} = K_S$$

K_m is equal to the **dissociation constant** (K_S) of the ES complex. Since K_S is the dissociation constant of the Michaelis complex, as K_S decreases, the enzyme's affinity for substrate increases. The lower value of K_m describes the greater affinity of the enzymes for the substrate. K_m is, therefore, also a measure of the affinity of the enzyme for its substrate if k_{-1} is much greater than k_2. The K_m is expressed as a mole of substrate per liter. The K_m is unique for each enzyme-substrate pair. Different enzymes that act on the same substrate have different K_m values. For most enzymes, K_m lies between 10^{-1} and 10^{-7} M. The K_m value for an enzyme is independent of substrate and enzyme concentration but depends on the environmental conditions such as pH, temperature, and ionic strength.

Catalytic constant (k_{cat})

The *catalytic constant* is the rate of product formation when the enzyme is saturated with substrate. It defines the activity of one enzyme molecule. It is equal to the rate constant k_2. k_{cat} is also called as **turnover number**, because it is the number of substrate molecules converted into the products by an enzyme molecule in a unit time when the enzyme is fully saturated with substrate. Its unit is sec^{-1}. V_{max} is related to the k_{cat} of an enzyme. The V_{max} represents the maximum rate attainable. It depends on the concentration of the enzyme present in the system and increases as $[E_t]$ increases. Mathematically, it can be represented as

$$V_{max} = k_2 [E_t]$$

$$k_2 = k_{cat} = \frac{V_{max}}{[E_t]}$$

The term k_{cat} represents the kinetic efficiency of the enzyme. Enzyme **catalase** has the highest turnover number known; each molecule of this enzyme can degrade 40 million molecules of H_2O_2 in 1 second. At the other end of the scale, enzyme **lysozyme** requires 2 seconds to cleave a glycosidic bond in peptidoglycan cell wall.

Specificity constant

Specificity constant is a measure of how efficiently an enzyme converts substrates into products i.e., a measure of catalytic efficiency. It takes into account both the rate of catalysis with a particular substrate (k_{cat}) and the nature of the enzyme-substrate interaction (K_m). From the Michaelis-Menten equation, we can derive specificity constant of an enzyme.

$$V_0 = \frac{V_{max}\ [S]}{K_m + [S]} = \frac{k_{cat}[E_t][S]}{K_m + [S]} \qquad \text{where, } V_{max} = k_{cat}[E_t]$$

When substrate concentration is very low, the [S] term in the denominator becomes insignificant. At very low substrate concentrations, most of the enzyme is free and the concentration of free enzyme, [E], is approximately equal to $[E_t]$, so

$$V_0 = \left[\frac{k_{cat}}{K_m}\right][E][S]$$

V_0, in this case, depends on the concentration of two reactants, [E] and [S], so this is a second-order rate equation, and the constant k_{cat}/K_m is a second-order rate constant with units of $M^{-1}s^{-1}$. Thus, the rate of product formation is dependent on both how well the enzyme binds substrate and how fast the enzyme converts substrate into product once substrate is bound. Because K_m is inversely proportional to the affinity of the enzyme for its substrate and k_{cat} is directly proportional to the kinetic efficiency of the enzyme, k_{cat}/K_m provides an index of the **catalytic efficiency** of an enzyme operating at substrate concentrations substantially below saturation amounts. This parameter called the **specificity constant**, is the rate constant for the conversion of E + S to E + P. A comparison of k_{cat}/K_m for the same enzyme with different substrates, or for two enzymes with their different substrates, is widely used as a measure of enzyme catalytic efficiency.

Problem

The substrate concentration in an enzyme catalyzed reaction is equal to 1/2 K_m. What will be the initial velocity?

Solution: $$V_0 = \frac{V_{max} \cdot [S]}{K_m + [S]} = \frac{V_{max} \cdot 0.5\ K_m}{K_m + 0.5\ K_m} = \frac{V_{max} \cdot 0.5\ K_m}{1.5\ K_m} = V_{max} \cdot \frac{1}{3} = 0.33\ V_{max}$$

Problem

At what substrate concentration is the velocity (V_0) of an enzyme-catalyzed reaction is 25% of the V_{max}?

Solution: $$0.25\ V_{max} = \frac{V_{max} \cdot [S]}{K_m + [S]};\ 0.75\ [S] = 0.25\ K_m;\ [S] = \frac{0.25}{0.75} K_m = \frac{1}{3} K_m$$

Problem

What will be the fraction of the maximum velocity (V_{max}) when the substrate concentration [S] = 4K_m?

Solution: As we know that Michaelis-Menten kinetics, $V = \frac{V_{max}[S]}{K_m + [S]}$; given that [S] = 4 K_m

$$\frac{V}{V_{max}} = \frac{[S]}{K_m + [S]} = \frac{4\ K_m}{K_m + 4\ K_m} = \frac{4\ K_m}{5\ K_m} = 0.8$$

Problem

The enzyme-catalyzed reaction shown below follows Michaelis-Menten kinetics.

$$E + S \underset{k_{-1}}{\overset{k_1}{\rightleftharpoons}} ES \xrightarrow{k_2} E + P$$ where, $k_1 = 1 \times 10^8\ M^{-1}\ s^{-1}$, $k_{-1} = 4 \times 10^4\ s^{-1}$ and $k_2 = 8 \times 10^2\ s^{-1}$

From the information given above, calculate K_S and K_m.

Solution: $$K_S = \frac{K_{-1}}{K_1} = \frac{4 \times 10^4\ S^{-1}}{10^8\ M^{-1}S^{-1}} = 4 \times 10^{-4}\ M = 400\ \mu M$$

$$K_m = \frac{K_{-1} + K_2}{K_1} = \frac{4 \times 10^4 + 8 \times 10^2}{10^8} = 408 \times 10^{-6} = 408\ \mu M$$

Problem

Estimate the V_{max} and K_m of the enzyme-catalyzed reaction for which the following data were obtained.

[S] (M)	V_0 (μM/min)	[S] (M)	V_0 (μM/min)
2×10^{-6}	28	4×10^{-5}	112
4×10^{-6}	40	1×10^{-4}	128
1×10^{-5}	70	2×10^{-3}	139
2×10^{-5}	95	1×10^{-2}	140

Solution: Graphical methods are used to determine the V_{max} and K_m of an enzyme-catalyzed reaction accurately. However, these quantities can be quickly estimated by inspecting values of V_0 at increasing [S]. There is very little velocity change in the above data even though the substrate concentration increases five-fold from 2 to 10 mM. Thus, we can consider a V_{max} of 140 μM/min. K_m is defined as the substrate concentration that produces a velocity of 1/2V_{max}, i.e., 70 μM/min. The above data indicates that this V_0 occurs at [S] = 1×10^{-5} M, thus $K_m \approx 1 \times 10^{-5}$ M.

Lineweaver-Burk plot

The Lineweaver-Burk plot is a graphical representation used to analyze enzyme kinetics, specifically to determine kinetic parameters and to understand enzyme inhibition. It is very difficult to determine V_{max} directly from a hyperbolic plot of V_0 against [S]; therefore, K_m cannot readily be determined in this way either. To overcome these difficulties, the Michaelis-Menten equation can be rearranged in a number of ways to give linear graphical representations. One can transform the Michaelis-Menten equation for a hyperbolic plot into an equation for a linear plot. The **Lineweaver-Burk plot** (or **double reciprocal plot**) is a linear plot, which is plotted between the reciprocal of V_0 against the reciprocal of [S].

$$V_0 = \frac{V_{max}\,[S]}{K_m + [S]}$$

$$\frac{1}{V_0} = \frac{K_m + [S]}{V_{max}\,[S]}$$

$$\frac{1}{V_0} = \frac{K_m}{V_{max}} \times \frac{1}{[S]} + \frac{1}{V_{max}} \times \frac{[S]}{[S]}$$

$$\frac{1}{V_0} = \frac{K_m}{V_{max}} \times \frac{1}{[S]} + \frac{1}{V_{max}}$$

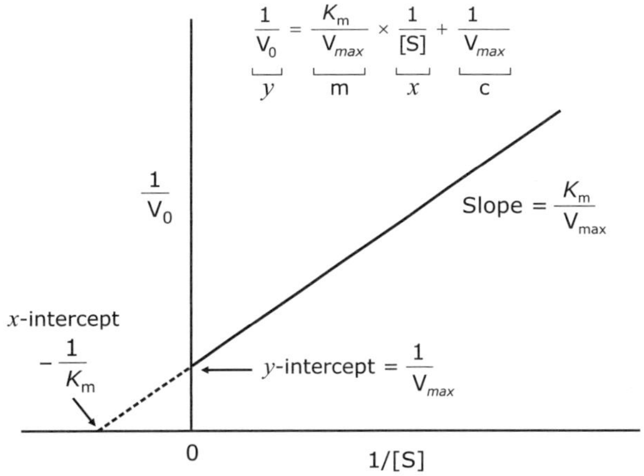

The equation now has the form of a straight line, $y = m.x + c$, where $1/V_0$ takes the place of the y-coordinate and $1/[S]$ takes the place of the x-coordinate. The slope of the line (m) is K_m/V_{max} and the y-intercept (c) is $1/V_{max}$.

The **Hanes–Woolf plot** is another rearrangement of the Michaelis–Menten equation that yields a straight line. Graph of $[S]/V_0$ versus [S] yields a straight line where the slope is $1/V_{max}$, the y-intercept is K_m/V_{max} and the x-intercept is $-K_m$

$$\frac{1}{V_0} = \frac{K_m}{V_{max}} \times \frac{1}{[S]} + \frac{1}{V_{max}}$$

Multiplying both sides of equation by [S]

$$[S] \times \frac{1}{V_0} = [S]\left[\frac{K_m}{V_{max}} \times \frac{1}{[S]} + \frac{1}{V_{max}}\right]$$

$$\frac{[S]}{V_0} = \frac{K_m}{V_{max}} \times \frac{[S]}{[S]} + \frac{[S]}{V_{max}}$$

$$\frac{[S]}{V_0} = \frac{K_m}{V_{max}} + \frac{1}{V_{max}} \times [S]$$

$$\frac{[S]}{V_0} = \frac{1}{V_{max}} \times [S] + \frac{K_m}{V_{max}}$$

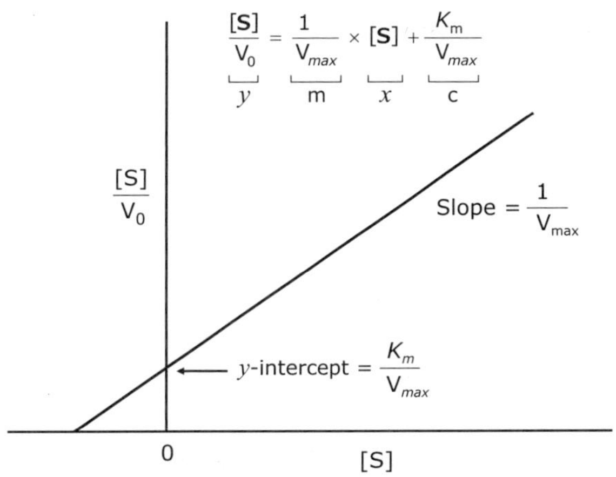

Another widely used linear form of the Michaelis-Menten equation is the **Eadie-Hofstee plot**. The plot of $V_0/[S]$ versus V_0 is linear with a slope of $-1/K_m$. The intercept on the y-axis gives V_{max}.

$$\frac{1}{V_0} = \frac{K_m}{V_{max}} \times \frac{1}{[S]} + \frac{1}{V_{max}}$$

Multiplying both sides of equation by V_{max}

$$V_{max} \times \frac{1}{V_0} = V_{max}\left[\frac{K_m}{V_{max}} \times \frac{1}{[S]} + \frac{1}{V_{max}}\right]$$

After rearranging equation

$$\frac{V_0}{[S]} = -\frac{1}{K_m} \times V_0 + \frac{V_{max}}{K_m}$$

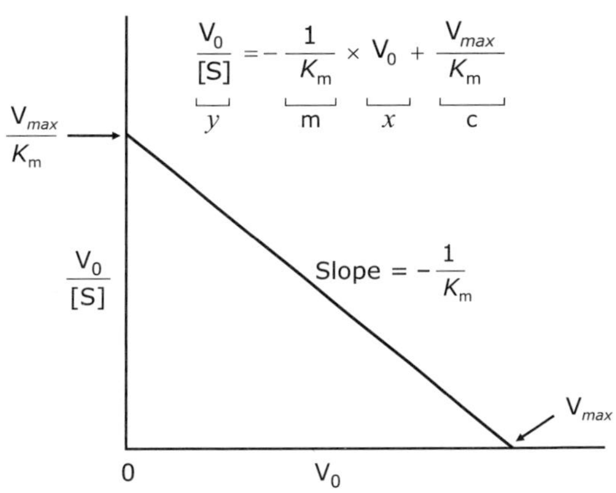

Effect of temperature and pH on enzyme's catalytic activity

Enzymes generally function in a narrow range of temperature and pH. Each enzyme shows its highest activity at the optimum temperature and optimum pH. Activity declines both below and above the optimum value. Hence, when the activity is plotted against temperature or pH, a **bell-shaped curve** is usually obtained.

Temperature: There are two general ways that rates of chemical reactions may be accelerated – increasing temperature and using catalyst. As we know that with increase in temperature, the kinetic energy of reactant molecules increase. As a result, more reactant molecules possess the energy to reach the transition state. In effect, increasing the average energy of reactant molecules makes the energy difference between the average energy and the transition-state energy smaller. The rates of chemical reactions can also be accelerated by catalysts. Catalysts work by lowering the energy of activation rather than by raising the average energy of the reactants.

The rate of most *enzyme catalyzed reactions* increases with increase in temperature. In an enzyme catalyzed reaction, enzyme and substrate have to collide with each other for the reaction to take place. The higher the temperature, the higher the kinetic energy of the molecules and thus, the more will be the collisions. As a rule of thumb, a typical reaction rate approximately doubles for every 10°C rise in temperature. But enzyme catalyzed reactions show a more complex temperature dependence because raising the temperature above certain value may cause **denaturation** (*loss of native conformation*) of proteins so, an enzyme may lose its catalytic activity. Thus, both high and low temperature influence the catalytic activity of an enzyme. The optimum temperature varies greatly from enzyme to enzyme and also from organism to organism. For example, enzyme like ***Taq* DNA polymerase** present in thermophilic bacteria *Thermus aquaticus* has optimal temperature 72°C.

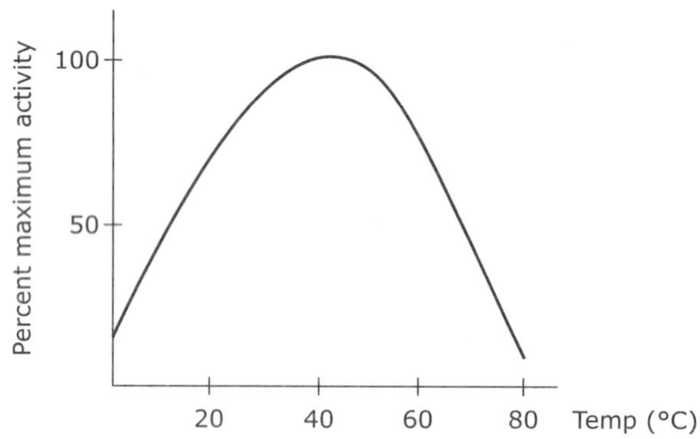

Figure 1.101
The effect of temperature on enzyme activity. The relative activity of an enzymatic reaction as a function of temperature. The decrease in the activity above 50°C is due to thermal denaturation.

pH: Enzymes are sensitive to pH. Most enzymes are active within only a narrow pH range, typically 5 to 9. This pH dependence is due to the presence of charged amino acids at the active site. Variations in pH cause changes in overall charge of amino acids. Since catalytic activity relies on a specific state of ionization of amino acid residues, enzyme activity changes as a result of change in pH. Each enzyme has its optimal pH at which maximum activity occurs.

Table 1.21 Optimum pH of some enzyme

Enzyme	Pepsin	Catalase	Trypsin	Fumarase	Ribonuclease	Arginase
Optimum pH	1.5	7.6	7.7	7.8	7.8	9.7

Kinetics of bi or multireactant system

So far, we have considered enzyme catalyzed reactions with single substrate. This situation is not common. Usually, enzymes catalyze reactions are those in which two (or more) substrates take part. Consider the case of an enzyme catalyzing a reaction involving two substrates A and B, and yielding the products P and Q:

$$A + B \rightleftharpoons P + Q$$

Such a reaction is termed as *bisubstrate reaction*. In general, bisubstrate reactions proceed by one of the two possible routes:

1. Both A and B are bound to the enzyme and then reaction occurs to give P + Q:

   $$E + A + B \rightleftharpoons E + P + Q$$

   Reactions of this type are defined as *sequential* or *single-displacement reactions*.

   Sequential reactions can be either of two distinct classes:

   a. If there is no obligatory order of addition of substrates or release of products, it is called **random sequential**.

   b. If substrates add in an obligatory order, the mechanism is called **ordered sequential**.

   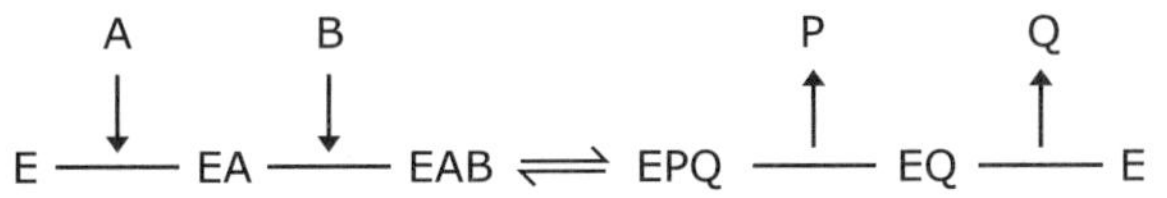

   Ordered sequential

   In ordered sequential reactions, one substrate is obligated to bind to the enzyme before a second substrate. In random sequential mechanisms, there is no preference. In practice, there is usually some degree of order in binding.

2. The other general possibility is that one substrate, A, binds to the enzyme and reacts with it to yield a chemically modified form of the enzyme (E′) plus the product, P. The second substrate, B, then reacts with E′, regenerating E and forming the other product, Q. Reactions that fit this model are called **double-displacement reactions** (or *ping-pong reaction*).

   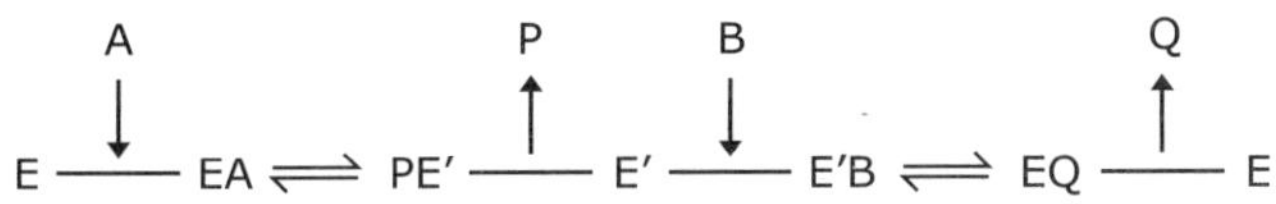

   Double-displacement

1.12.5 Enzyme inhibition

Enzyme inhibitors are molecules that interfere with catalysis, either slowing or halting enzymatic reactions. Inhibition of enzyme activity may be *irreversible* or *reversible*. In **irreversible inhibition**, an inhibitor called *irreversible inhibitor* binds tightly to the enzyme (either covalently or noncovalently). Inhibitor dissociates very slowly from the enzyme, and enzyme's catalytic activity is permanently inhibited. For example, antibiotic **penicillin** acts as an irreversible inhibitor of the enzyme **glycopeptide transpeptidase** (also known as *glycoprotein peptidase*). Penicillin covalently binds with an essential serine residue in the active site of glycopeptide transpeptidase, which acts to cross-link the polysaccharide chains of bacterial peptidoglycan cell walls. Once the cross-linking of polysaccharide chains is blocked, the bacterial cells undergo osmotic lysis, and bacterial growth is halted. Similarly, **aspirin** (acetylsalicylate) binds covalently with an enzyme **cyclooxygenase** (*prostaglandin-endoperoxide synthase*) and blocks prostaglandin synthesis. Aspirin acts as an acetylating agent and causes the covalent addition of an acetyl group to a serine residue in the active site of the enzyme.

Many irreversible inhibitors are termed **suicide inhibitors**. A suicide inhibitor binds to the enzyme as a substrate and undergoes the first few chemical steps as a normal enzymatic reaction, but instead of being transformed into the normal product, the inhibitor is converted to a very reactive intermediate compound that combines irreversibly with the enzyme (i.e., enzyme literally commits suicide). These compounds are also called **mechanism-based inhibitors** because they hijack the normal enzyme reaction mechanism to inactivate the enzyme.

Table 1.22 Examples of irreversible enzyme inhibitors

Name	Mode of action
Diisopropyl phosphofluoridate (DIPF)	Inhibits enzymes with serine at active site e.g., chymotrypsin
Sarin (nerve gas)	Like DIPF
Physostigmine	Like DIPF
Parathion (insecticide)	Like DIPF, but especially inhibitory to insect acetylcholinesterase

In **reversible inhibition**, an inhibitor called *reversible inhibitor* binds non-covalently to the enzyme and dissociates rapidly from the enzyme. The effect of a reversible inhibitor is reversed after dissociation of inhibitor from enzyme. There are three types of reversible inhibition. These are *competitive*, *uncompetitive* and *mixed inhibition*.

Competitive inhibition

The structure of a competitive inhibitor closely resembles that of the enzyme's normal substrate. Because of its structure, a competitive inhibitor binds reversibly to the enzyme's substrate binding active site. The inhibitor forms an enzyme-inhibitor complex (EI) equivalent to the enzyme-substrate complex (ES) but without leading to catalysis. The degree of competitive inhibition depends on the inhibitor's concentration and the binding affinity of the inhibitor with the enzyme. Thus, the effect of a competitive inhibitor on activity can be reversed by increasing substrate concentration. At high [S], all the active sites are filled with substrate, and reaction velocity reaches the value observed without an inhibitor.

$$\begin{array}{l} E + S \rightleftharpoons ES \longrightarrow E + P \\ + \\ I \\ \Big\downarrow\!\!\uparrow K_I \qquad K_I = \dfrac{[E][I]}{[EI]} \\ EI \end{array}$$

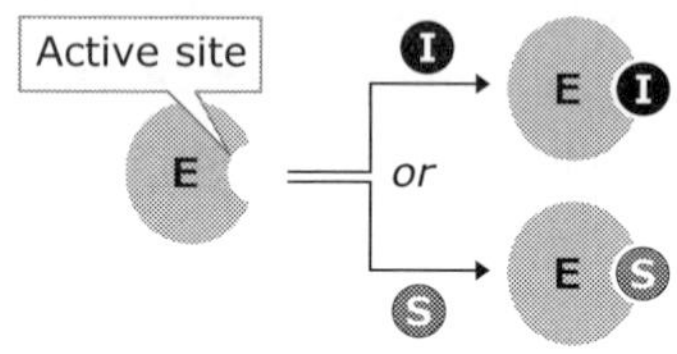

K_I is the enzyme **inhibition constant** (also known as **inhibitor dissociation constant**) is an *equilibrium constant* used to describe the binding affinity between an inhibitor and its corresponding enzyme. In the presence of a competitive inhibitor, the Michaelis-Menten equation becomes

$$V_0 = \frac{V_{max}[S]}{\alpha K_m + [S]} \qquad \text{Where, } \alpha = 1 + \frac{[I]}{K_I} \text{ and } K_I = \frac{[E][I]}{[EI]}$$

The K_m and V_{max} observed in the presence of inhibitor are often called 'apparent' K_m and 'apparent' V_{max}. As described by the equation, in the presence of a competitive inhibitor, the apparent K_m increases by a factor α, but V_{max} remains the same.

'Apparent' $K_m = \alpha K_m$ and 'Apparent' $V_{max} = V_{max}$

In a double-reciprocal form, the equation will be $\dfrac{1}{V_0} = \left[\dfrac{\alpha K_m}{V_{max}}\right]\dfrac{1}{[S]} + \dfrac{1}{V_{max}}$

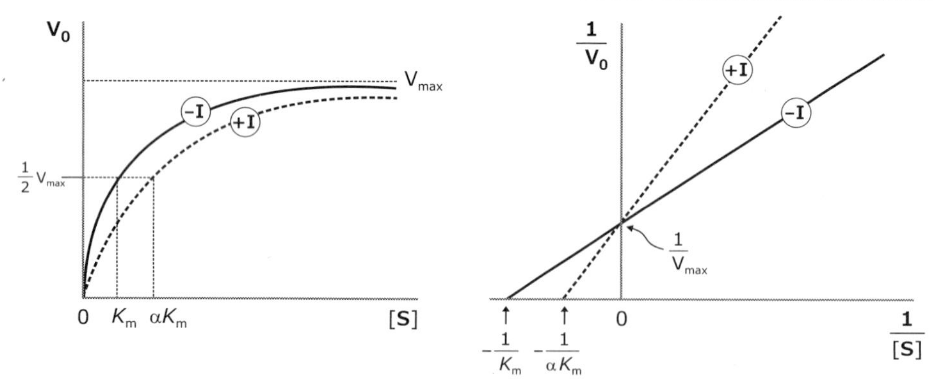

+I : with inhibitor

–I : without inhibitor

Figure 1.102 Michaelis-Menten and Lineweaver-Burk plot in the absence and presence of competitive inhibitor.

Clinical treatment of **methanol poisoning** is a typical example of exploiting a competitive inhibitory mechanism. In the case of methanol poisoning, methanol in the body is converted to harmful formaldehyde by the enzyme *alcohol dehydrogenase*. Ethanol competes effectively with methanol as an alternative substrate for alcohol dehydrogenase and is converted into non-toxic acetaldehyde. Therefore, a high dose of ethanol is used to alleviate the effect of methanol because ethanol competitively binds with the active site of the enzyme and decreases the formation of formaldehyde.

Common examples of competitive inhibitors:

Methotrexate (also called **amethopterin**) is a structural analog of **dihydrofolate** and acts as a competitive inhibitor of the enzyme *dihydrofolate reductase*. The enzyme dihydrofolate reductase catalyzes the reduction of dihydrofolate to tetrahydrofolate, an essential cofactor required for the biosynthesis of dTMP.

Allopurinol is a structural analog of **hypoxanthine** and acts as a competitive inhibitor of the enzyme *xanthine oxidase*. Xanthine oxidase converts hypoxanthine to xanthine to uric acid.

Sulfonamide (sulfa drug) is a structural analog of *para-aminobenzoic acid* (**PABA**) and competitively inhibits *dihydropteroate synthase*, an enzyme that binds PABA as a substrate for the synthesis of *dihydrofolate* (a folic acid derivative). Dihydrofolate acts as a precursor of tetrahydrofolate, an essential component of the coenzymes responsible for single carbon metabolism in cells.

Malonate is a structural analog of **succinate** and acts as a competitive inhibitor of the enzyme *succinate dehydrogenase*, a citric acid cycle enzyme that converts succinate to fumarate.

Uncompetitive inhibition

In uncompetitive inhibition, an inhibitor binds at a site distinct from the substrate binding site. However, unlike a competitive inhibitor which binds with only free enzyme, an uncompetitive inhibitor binds only to the ES complex.

$$\mathrm{E + S \rightleftharpoons ES \longrightarrow E + P}$$

$$\mathrm{ES + I} \underset{K_I'}{\rightleftharpoons} \mathrm{ESI}$$

$$K_I' = \frac{[\mathrm{ES}][\mathrm{I}]}{[\mathrm{ESI}]}$$

In the presence of uncompetitive inhibitor, the Michaelis-Menten equation becomes

$$V_0 = \frac{V_{max}\,[S]}{K_m + \alpha'[S]} = \frac{\left[\frac{V_{max}}{\alpha'}\right][S]}{\left[\frac{K_m}{\alpha'}\right] + [S]} \qquad \text{Where, } \alpha' = 1 + \frac{[I]}{K_I'}$$

As described by the equation, in the presence of uncompetitive inhibitor, both the apparent K_m and apparent V_{max} decrease.

'Apparent' $K_m = \frac{K_m}{\alpha'}$ and 'Apparent' $V_{max} = \frac{V_{max}}{\alpha'}$

In a double-reciprocal form, the equation will be $\frac{1}{V_0} = \left[\frac{K_m}{V_{max}}\right]\frac{1}{[S]} + \frac{\alpha'}{V_{max}}$

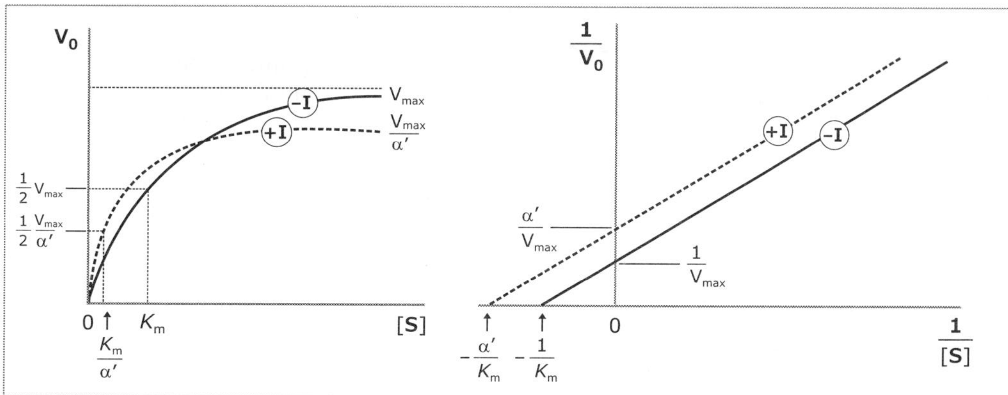

+I : with inhibitor

–I : without inhibitor

Figure 1.103 Michaelis-Menten and Lineweaver-Burk plot in the absence and presence of uncompetitive inhibitor.

Non-competitive inhibition

In *non-competitive inhibition*, an inhibitor binds at a site other than the substrate binding active site. A non-competitive inhibitor can bind to *either* the free enzyme (E) *or* the enzyme-substrate complex (ES), unlike an *uncompetitive inhibitor* that binds *only* to the enzyme-substrate complex. Compared to *competitive inhibition*, this inhibition is not reversed by increasing substrate concentration. Non-competitive inhibition can be **pure non-competitive inhibition** or **mixed non-competitive inhibition**. In *pure non-competitive inhibition*, substrate and inhibitor bind at different sites, and the binding of the inhibitor does not affect the binding of the substrate. On the other hand, in *mixed non-competitive inhibition*, substrate and inhibitor bind at different sites, but the binding of inhibitor with enzyme influences the binding of the substrate. It may be due to two regions – either the binding sites for inhibitor and substrate are near one another or conformational changes in enzyme caused by inhibitor affect substrate binding.

$$\begin{array}{ccccc} E + S & \rightleftharpoons & ES & \longrightarrow & E + P \\ + & & + & & \\ I & & I & & \\ \Big\updownarrow K_I & & \Big\updownarrow K_I' & & \\ EI & & ESI & & \end{array}$$

$$K_I = \frac{[E][I]}{[EI]} \qquad K_I' = \frac{[ES][I]}{[ESI]}$$

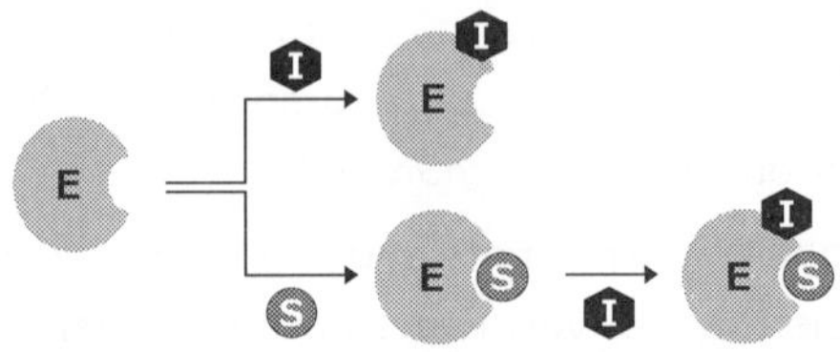

In the presence of non-competitive inhibitor, the Michaelis-Menten equation becomes

$$V_0 = \frac{V_{max}\,[S]}{\alpha K_m + \alpha'[S]} \qquad \text{Where, } \alpha' = 1 + \frac{[I]}{K_I'} \text{ and } \alpha = 1 + \frac{[I]}{K_I}$$

In **pure non-competitive inhibition** (*simple linear non-competitive inhibition*), substrate and inhibitor bind at different sites on enzyme and binding of inhibitor does not affect the binding of substrate (i.e., substrate-binding and inhibitor-binding are completely independent). Under this condition, $E + I \rightleftharpoons EI$ and $ES + I \rightleftharpoons ESI$ have an identical inhibitor constant. As a result, K_I is equal to K_I'. Hence, α is equal to α'. In this case, the Michaelis-Menten equation becomes

$$V_0 = \frac{V_{max}\,[S]}{\alpha K_m + \alpha'[S]} = \frac{V_{max}}{\alpha K_m + \alpha[S]} = \frac{\left[\frac{V_{max}}{\alpha}\right][S]}{K_m + [S]} \qquad \text{Since, } \alpha' = \alpha$$

As described by the equation, in the presence of inhibitor, 'apparent' V_{max} decreases and 'apparent' K_m remain same.

'Apparent' $K_m = K_m$ and 'Apparent' $V_{max} = \frac{V_{max}}{\alpha}$

In a double-reciprocal form, the equation will be $\frac{1}{V_0} = \left[\frac{K_m}{\frac{V_{max}}{\alpha}}\right]\frac{1}{[S]} + \frac{1}{\left[\frac{V_{max}}{\alpha}\right]} = \left[\frac{\alpha K_m}{V_{max}}\right]\frac{1}{[S]} + \frac{\alpha}{V_{max}}$

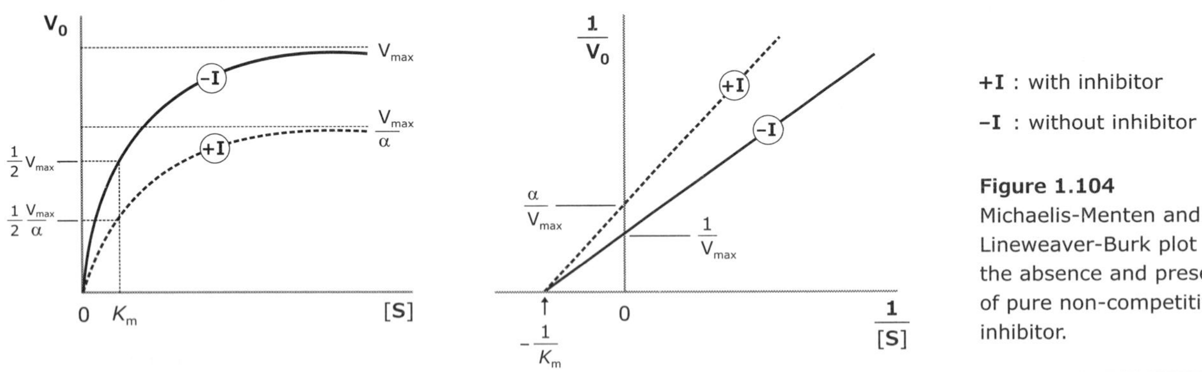

Figure 1.104 Michaelis-Menten and Lineweaver-Burk plot in the absence and presence of pure non-competitive inhibitor.

In the case of **mixed non-competitive inhibition**, the binding of inhibitor by enzyme influences the binding of substrate by enzyme (i.e., substrate-binding and inhibitor-binding are *not* completely independent). As a result, K_I and K_I' (hence, α and α') are not equal. In this case, the Michaelis-Menten equation becomes

$$V_0 = \frac{V_{max}\,[S]}{\alpha K_m + \alpha'[S]} = \frac{\left[\frac{V_{max}}{\alpha'}\right][S]}{\left[\frac{\alpha K_m}{\alpha'}\right] + [S]} \qquad \text{Here, } \alpha' \neq \alpha$$

As described by the equation, the factor α multiplying K_m as in *competitive* inhibition and the factor α' multiplying [S] as in *uncompetitive* inhibition. Hence, it is termed as **mixed inhibition**. If $K_I < K_I'$, the pattern observed lies between those of *competitive* and *non-competitive inhibition* (termed **non-competitive-competitive inhibition**) and if $K_I > K_I'$, the pattern is intermediate between those of *non-competitive* and *uncompetitive inhibition* (termed **non-competitive-uncompetitive inhibition**). In this type of inhibition, both the 'apparent' K_m and the 'apparent' V_{max} are altered by the presence of inhibitor. The apparent K_m may increase or decrease depending on whether the inhibitor binds more strongly to the free enzyme or the enzyme-substrate complex, whereas the apparent V_{max} always decreases.

'Apparent' $K_m = \frac{\alpha K_m}{\alpha'}$ and 'Apparent' $V_{max} = \frac{V_{max}}{\alpha'}$

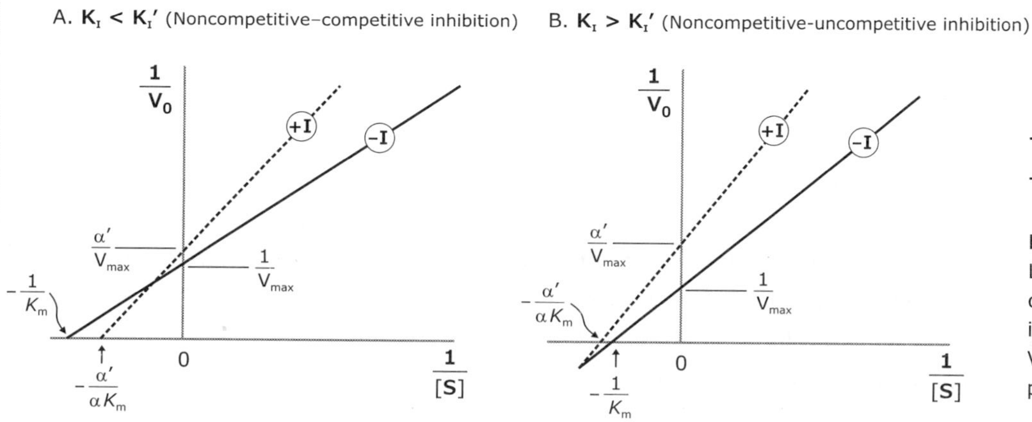

+I : with inhibitor

–I : without inhibitor

Figure 1.105
Lineweaver–Burk plot of mixed noncompetitive inhibition – both K_m and V_{max} change in the presence of inhibitor.

Table 1.23 Effects of inhibitors on the parameters of the Michaelis-Menten equation

Type of inhibition	Michaelis–Menten equation	Lineweaver–Burk equation	Effect of inhibitor
None	$V_0 = \frac{V_{max}[S]}{K_m + [S]}$	$\frac{1}{V_0} = \left[\frac{K_m}{V_{max}}\right]\frac{1}{[S]} + \frac{1}{V_{max}}$	None
Competitive	$V_0 = \frac{V_{max}\ [S]}{\alpha K_m + [S]}$	$\frac{1}{V_0} = \left[\frac{\alpha K_m}{V_{max}}\right]\frac{1}{[S]} + \frac{1}{V_{max}}$	App. $K_m = \alpha K_m$ App. $V_{max} = V_{max}$
Pure non-competitive	$V_0 = \frac{V_{max}\ [S]}{\alpha K_m + \alpha'[S]} = \frac{V_{max}\ [S]}{\alpha K_m + \alpha[S]} = \frac{(V_{max}/\alpha)[S]}{K_m + [S]}$	$\frac{1}{V_0} = \left[\frac{\alpha K_m}{V_{max}}\right]\frac{1}{[S]} + \frac{\alpha}{V_{max}}$	App. $K_m = K_m$ App. $V_{max} = V_{max}/\alpha$
Uncompetitive	$V_0 = \frac{V_{max}\ [S]}{K_m + \alpha'[S]} = \frac{(V_{max}/\alpha')[S]}{K_m/\alpha' + [S]}$	$\frac{1}{V_0} = \left[\frac{K_m}{V_{max}}\right]\frac{1}{[S]} + \frac{\alpha'}{V_{max}}$	App. $K_m = K_m/\alpha'$ App. $V_{max} = V_{max}/\alpha'$

Problem

The kinetics of an enzyme in the presence (+I) or absence (–I) of a reversible inhibitor is described in the following graph. If the concentration of the reversible inhibitor in +I experiment was equal to 3.0×10^{-3} M, then what will be the dissociation constant for the enzyme-inhibitor complex?

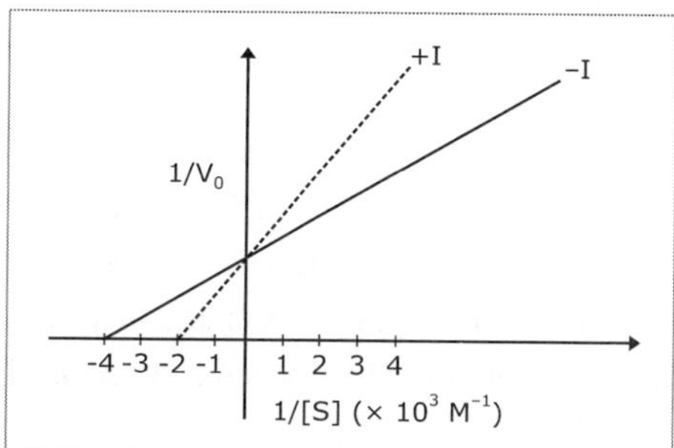

Solution: In the absence of competitive inhibitor, $-1/K_m = -4$.

In the presence of competitive inhibitor, $-1/\alpha K_m = -2$.

Hence, the value of α is 2.

Since, $\alpha = 1 + [I]/K_I$

$\Rightarrow 2 = 1 + (3 \times 10^{-3}/K_I)$

$\Rightarrow K_I = 3 \times 10^{-3}$ M.

1.12.6 Regulatory enzymes: Control of enzyme activity

In cellular metabolism, regulation of enzyme-catalyzed reactions occurs in two different ways: **control of enzyme availability** and **control of enzyme activity**. Availability of a given enzyme in a cell is regulated by its rate of synthesis and rate of degradation whereas an enzyme's catalytic activity can be modulated—either negatively or positively—through structural alterations that influence the enzyme's substrate-binding affinity or turnover number.

Enzymes whose catalytic activity can be modulated are termed as **regulatory enzymes**. These enzymes exhibit increased or decreased catalytic activity in response to specific signals. The catalytic activities of regulatory enzymes can be modulated through reversible *non-covalent binding* by regulatory compounds or by reversible *covalent modification*. Regulation through non-covalent interaction of the enzyme with regulatory compounds is termed **allosteric regulation** because the modulator binds to the enzyme at a site other than the active site.

Allosteric regulation

Allosteric enzymes (Greek words: '*allo*' meaning other and *steric* meaning place or site) are a class of regulatory enzymes which increase or decrease catalytic activities in response to certain signals. These enzymes function through reversible, non-covalent binding of regulatory compounds called **allosteric modulators** (or **allosteric effectors**). Modulator molecules are of two types: **positive modulator** (called **activators**) that enhance enzyme's catalytic activity and **negative modulator** (or **inhibitors**) which inhibit enzyme's catalytic activity. The binding of modulator causes conformational changes in the allosteric enzymes, which influence their catalytic activity.

Most allosteric enzymes are oligomeric (consisting of multiple subunits). Allosteric enzymes for which substrate and the modulator are identical are called **homotropic**. When the modulator is a molecule other than the substrate, the enzyme is said to be **heterotropic**. Allosteric enzymes of heterotropic nature have two functionally different binding sites. One of the sites, the **catalytic site**, binds with the substrate and catalyzes the reaction. The other site, known as **allosteric site** (or **regulatory site**), binds with an allosteric modulator. Enzymes with several modulators generally have different specific binding sites for each.

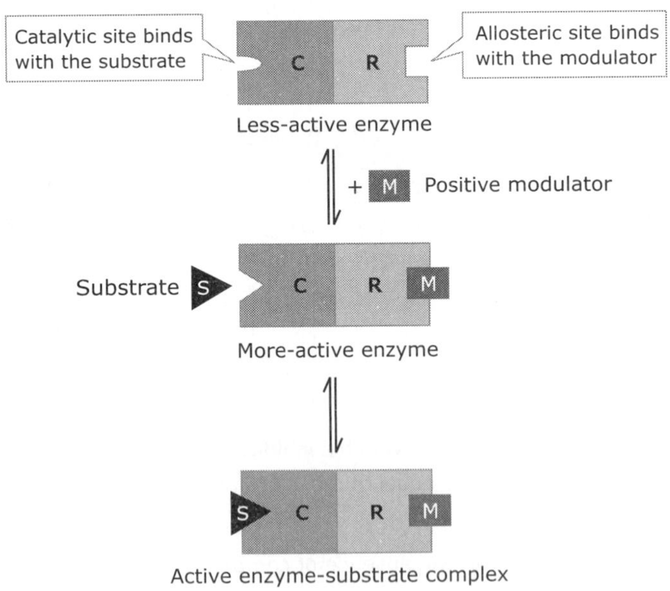

Figure 1.106
Allosteric enzymes are a class of regulatory enzymes which increases or decreases catalytic activities in response to modulators.

Allosteric enzymes don't obey Michaelis-Menten kinetics. These enzymes show relationships between V_0 and [S] that differ from Michaelis-Menten kinetics. They do exhibit saturation with the substrate when (S) is sufficiently high, produce a sigmoid saturation rather than the hyperbolic curve typical of non-regulatory enzymes. Sigmoid kinetic behaviour generally reflects cooperative interactions between protein subunits. The principles are particularly well illustrated by a noncatalytic O_2 binding protein hemoglobin. These behaviour is explained by the *concerted* and *sequential* models for subunit interaction.

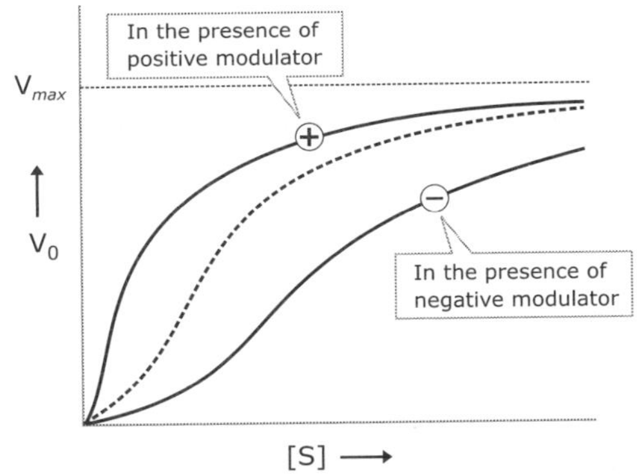

Figure 1.107
The effects of a positive modulator (+) and a negative modulator (–) on heterotropic allosteric enzyme. The central curve shows the substrate-activity relationship without a modulator.

Regulation by reversible covalent modification

Activity of some regulatory enzymes is modulated by *reversible covalent modification*. Covalent modification includes **phosphorylation** (addition of phosphate), **adenylylation** (addition of AMP), **methylation** (addition of methyl group), **uridylylation** (addition of UMP) and **ADP-ribosylation** (addition of ADP-ribose). Phosphorylation is the most common type of covalent modification. Phosphorylation is accomplished by *protein kinases*; phosphoprotein *phosphatases* act in the reverse direction to remove the phosphate group. An important example of regulation by phosphorylation occurs in *glycogen phosphorylase* of muscle and liver, which catalyzes the glycogenolysis. Glycogen phosphorylase occurs in two forms: Glycogen phosphorylase *a* (active form) and glycogen phosphorylase *b* (less active form). In glycogen phosphorylase *a*, specific *Ser* residues, one on each subunit, are phosphorylated. Glycogen phosphorylase *a* is converted to the less active glycogen phosphorylase *b* by the enzymatic loss of these phosphoryl group. Glycogen phosphorylase *b* can be reconverted to glycogen phosphorylase *a* by the action of phosphorylase kinase.

Table 1.24 Some enzymes whose activity can be controlled by reversible covalent modification

Enzyme	Modification
Glycogen phosphorylase	Phosphorylation
Glycogen synthase	Phosphorylation
Acetyl-CoA carboxylase	Phosphorylation
Glutamine synthetase (*E. coli*)	Adenylylation
Nitrogenase	ADP-ribosylation

Enzymatic activity is also regulated through **proteolytic activation** and **isozymes**. Proteolytic activation strategy is used to convert an inactive enzyme into an active one irreversibly. Many enzymes are activated by the hydrolysis of the peptide bond (s) in inactive precursors called **zymogens** (or **proenzymes**). Isozymes provide an avenue for varying regulation of the same reaction to meet the specific physiological needs in the particular tissue at a specific time.

Feedback inhibition and feedback repression

In **feedback inhibition** (or **end product inhibition**), the end product of a biosynthetic pathway inhibits the *activity* of the first enzyme that is unique to the pathway, thus controlling production of the end product. The first enzyme in the pathway is an allosteric enzyme. Its allosteric site will bind to the end product of the pathway which alters its active site so that it cannot mediate the enzymatic reaction. It is a negative regulation. It prevents enzyme from acting. Enzymes can also be subject to positive regulation, in which the enzyme's activity is stimulated by regulatory molecule rather than being suppressed.

The feedback inhibition is different from feedback repression. *Feedback inhibition* is related to enzyme's activity whereas *feedback repression* is related to enzyme synthesis. In case of **feedback repression**, negative regulation occurs at the level of enzyme synthesis mainly at the level of transcription. In this inhibitory feedback system, the end product produced in a metabolic pathway acts as a co-repressor and represses the synthesis of an enzyme at the level of transcription that is required at an earlier stage of the pathway.

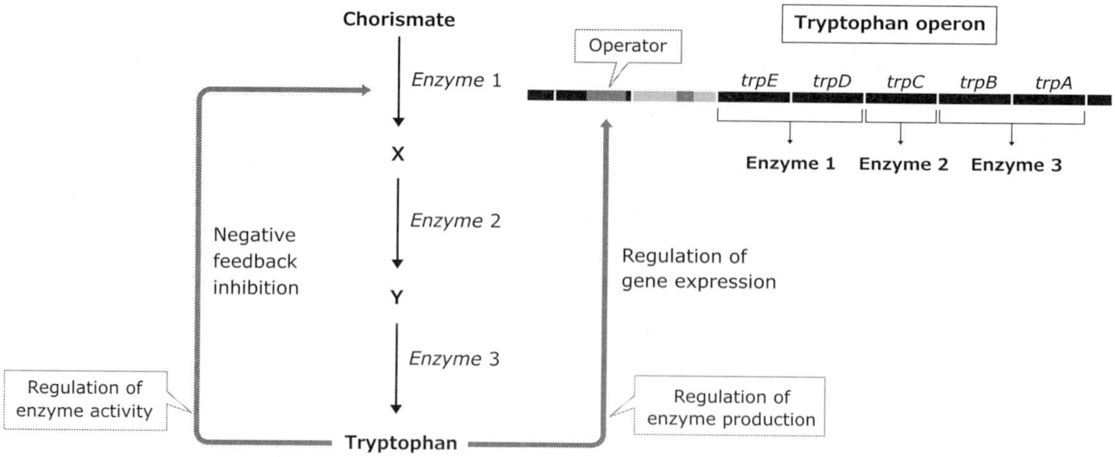

Figure 1.108 The pathway is regulated by the process of feedback inhibition and feedback repression. Tryptophan the end product of the pathway is the effector molecule that binds to the allosteric site of enzyme 1, the first enzyme in the pathway. When tryptophan is bound to the enzyme, the catalytic site of enzyme 1 is altered so that it is unable to react with its substrates and the synthesis of X is inhibited. In the case of feedback repression, negative regulation of tryptophan synthesis occurs at the level of transcription, where it acts as a co-repressor.

1.12.7 Isozymes

Isozymes (also known as **isoenzymes**) are enzymes that differ in amino acid sequence but catalyze the same chemical reaction. They are encoded by different genes located at different loci. These enzymes usually display different kinetic parameters or different regulatory properties. Isozymes differ from **allozymes**, which are enzymes that arise from alternative forms of the same gene i.e., alleles. A common example of isozyme is **lactate dehydrogenase** (**LDH**) which catalyzes the reversible conversion of pyruvate to lactate. Human beings have two isozymic polypeptide chains for this enzyme: **H polypeptide** and **M polypeptide**. The functional enzyme is tetrameric (homo– or heterotetramer). Two different subunits combine randomly with each other forming *five* isozymes. The kinetic properties of the various LDH isozymes differ in terms of their relative affinities for the various substrates and their sensitivity to inhibition by product. Different tissues express different isozyme forms, as appropriate to their particular metabolic needs.

Isozyme	Nature of subunits	Location
LDH1	HHHH (H_4)	In the heart and RBCs
LDH2	HHHM (H_3M)	In the reticuloendothelial system
LDH3	HHMM (H_2M_2)	In the lungs
LDH4	HMMM (HM_3)	In the kidneys, placenta
LDH5	MMMM (M_4)	In the liver and striated muscle

Isozymes of hexokinase: Similarly, there are four important mammalian **hexokinases** that vary in subcellular locations and kinetics with respect to different substrates and conditions. They are designated hexokinases I, II, III and IV or hexokinases A, B, C and D. Hexokinases catalyze the phosphorylation of hexose (such as glucose). While hexokinases I, II and III are capable of phosphorylating several hexoses, **hexokinase IV** (also referred to as **glucokinase**) acts only on glucose as hexose. Glucokinase is mainly expressed in liver cells and pancreatic β-cells and is characterized by a low affinity to its substrate glucose. Hexokinases I, II and III are referred to as 'low-K_m' isozymes because of a high affinity for glucose even at low concentrations (below 1 mM) and all three are strongly inhibited by their product, glucose 6-phosphate. Glucokinase can only phosphorylate glucose if the concentration of this substrate is high enough (its K_m for glucose is 100 times higher than that of hexokinases I, II and III) and is not allosterically inhibited by its product, glucose 6-phosphate.

1.12.8 Zymogen

An inactive precursor of an enzyme is called *zymogen*. Zymogen is cleaved to form the active enzyme. Many proteolytic enzymes like chymotrypsin and trypsin are initially synthesized as inactive precursor chymotrypsinogen and trypsinogen. Specific cleavage causes conformational changes in the inactive precursor that expose the enzyme active site. The activation by specific proteolysis is an irreversible process. In the duodenum, the pancreatic zymogens, *trypsinogen, chymotrypsinogen, proelastase* and *procarboxypeptidase* are converted into active enzymes by enteropeptidase and trypsin.

Origin	Zymogen	Active Protease
Pancreas	Trypsinogen	Trypsin
Pancreas	Chymotrypsinogen	Chymotrypsin
Pancreas	Procarboxypeptidase	Carboxypeptidase
Pancreas	Proelastase	Elastase
Stomach	Pepsinogen	Pepsin

Chymotrypsinogen, a single polypeptide chain of 245 amino acid residues, is converted to α-chymotrypsin, which has three polypeptide chains linked by two of the five disulfide bonds present in the primary structure of chymotrypsinogen. Chymotrypsinogen is first converted to an enzymatically active form called π-**chymotrypsin** when *trypsin* cleaves the peptide bond joining Arg^{15} and Ile^{16}. The enzymatically active π-chymotrypsin acts upon other π-chymotrypsin molecules. The end product of this processing pathway is the mature protease α-**chymotrypsin**.

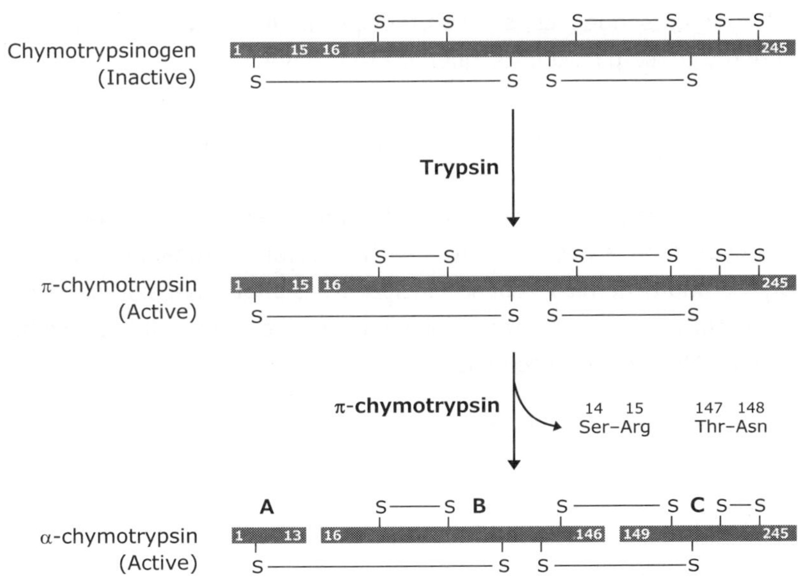

Figure 1.109
Formation of chymotrypsin (active) from chymotrypsinogen (inactive). The numbering of amino acid residues represent their positions in the primary sequence of the zymogen, chymotrypsinogen. The three polypeptide fragments (A, B and C) of chymotrypsin are linked by disulfide bonds.

1.12.9 Nucleic acids as catalysts

Ribozyme: RNA as catalyst

A *ribozyme* (term introduced by Kelly Kruger, also called RNA enzyme) is an RNA molecule that catalyzes a chemical reaction. Both natural and synthetic ribozymes are known. Before the discovery of ribozymes, proteins were the only known biological catalysts. In 1967, Carl Woese, Francis Crick, and Leslie Orgel were the first to suggest that RNA could act as a catalyst based upon findings that it can form complex secondary structures. The first ribozyme was discovered in the 1980s by Thomas R. Cech, who was studying RNA splicing in the ciliated protozoan *Tetrahymena thermophila* and Sidney Altman, who was working on ribonucleoprotein, **RNase P**. These ribozymes were found in the intron of an RNA transcript and RNA component of RNase P, which is involved in the processing of pre-tRNAs. In 1989, Thomas R. Cech and Sydney Altman won the Nobel prize in chemistry for their *discovery of the catalytic properties of RNA*. Ribozymes often require divalent metal ions such as Mg^{2+} as cofactors.

Although ribozymes are quite rare in the cell, their roles are sometimes essential for life. For example, the functional part of the ribosome, the molecular machine that translates RNA into proteins, is fundamentally a ribozyme. Some known ribozymes include RNase P, Group I and Group II introns, hairpin ribozyme, hammerhead ribozyme, hepatitis delta virus ribozyme, and tetrahymena ribozyme.

Biochemical reactions catalyzed by ribozymes: Many natural ribozymes catalyze either their own cleavage or the cleavage of other RNAs, but they have also been found to catalyze the formation of peptide bonds through peptidyl transferase activity. Ribozymes that are known today catalyze two types of biochemical reactions:

1. Cleavage of phosphodiester bonds (RNase P, group I intron and group II intron).
2. Synthesis of peptide bonds (Peptidyl transferase activity of 23S rRNA in 70S and 28S rRNA in 80S ribosomes).

However, in the test tube, synthetic RNA molecules have been shown to carry out other biochemical reactions, such as the synthesis of ribonucleotides and RNA molecules.

DNAzyme: DNA as catalyst

In nature, DNA acts as a genetic material i.e., act as a long-term repository of genetic information. Nevertheless, many experiments have shown that DNA can be a catalyst. The single-stranded DNA molecules with catalytic activity are called **deoxyribozymes** (also called **catalytic DNAs** or **DNA enzymes** or **DNAzymes**). While deoxyribozymes are unknown in nature, synthetic catalytic DNA molecules have been identified *in vitro selection* methods. *In vitro selection* is an experimental process by which random sequences, such as those of DNA or RNA nucleotides, are examined in parallel (not one at a time) to identify those particular sequences that have a desired function, such as binding or catalysis.

Natural duplex DNA is unlikely to be catalytic because a DNA duplex is a structurally regular structure and enzymatic activity requires irregular tertiary conformations that can bind substrates for catalysis. The first report of a deoxyribozyme was published in December 1994 by Breaker and Joyce. Since the initial report of an RNA-cleaving deoxyribozyme, many other catalytic activities of DNA have been reported, such as divalent metal ion-dependent DNA and RNA ligation. An unusual DNA-catalyzed photochemical reaction includes the photoreversion of thymine dimers. DNAzyme-based molecular catalysts generally depend on a metal ion cofactor for catalysis. It has also been reported that DNAzyme-mediated catalysis follows Michaelis-Menten kinetics.

1.12.10 Abzyme

Antibodies are **glycoproteins** known as **immunoglobulins** (**Igs**) that bind with high specificity to **antigens**. An antibody can be designed to recognize a molecule that structurally resembles the transition state of a specific chemical reaction. When this occurs, the antibody can bind to and stabilize the transition state, similar to how an enzyme functions. This stabilization lowers the activation energy of the reaction, thereby catalyzing it. An antibody with such catalytic activity is referred to as an **abzyme** (short for **antibody enzyme** or **catalytic antibody**).

The concept was first proposed in 1969 by William Jencks, who suggested that if an antigen mimicked a reaction's transition state, it could stimulate the immune system to produce catalytic antibodies. This hypothesis was experimentally confirmed in 1986 by Richard Lerner and Peter Schultz, who independently demonstrated that antibodies could catalyze the hydrolysis of aryl esters and carbonates, respectively. These antibodies were produced by immunizing animals with transition state analogs—stable molecules that mimic high-energy intermediates of chemical reactions.

1.12.11 Examples of enzymatic reactions

Lysozyme

Lysozyme (EC 3.2.1.17) is a hydrolytic enzyme. It cleaves the β(1–4) glycosidic bond that connects *N*-acetyl muramic acid (**NAM**) with the fourth carbon atom of *N*-acetylglucosamine (**NAG**) of peptidoglycan cell wall present in eubacteria. It does this by binding to the peptidoglycan molecules in the binding site. Lysozyme's binding site accommodates a segment of six residues (designated A to F in the figure). The reaction catalyzed by lysozyme is *hydrolysis*: a molecule of water is added to a covalent bond between two adjacent sugar molecules in the polysaccharide chain, thereby causing the bond to break. The reaction is energetically favorable because the free energy of the cleaved polysaccharide chain is lower than the free energy of the intact chain. The amino acids Glu^{35} and Asp^{52} have been found to be critical to the activity of this enzyme. Glu^{35} acts as a proton donor to the glycosidic bond, cleaving the C–O bond between NAM and NAG, whilst Asp^{52} stabilizes the carbonium ion intermediate until it reacts with a free water molecule, extracting a hydroxyl group and freeing a proton that binds to Glu^{35}, leaving the enzyme unchanged. **Figure 1.110** shows the central steps in this enzymatically catalyzed reaction.

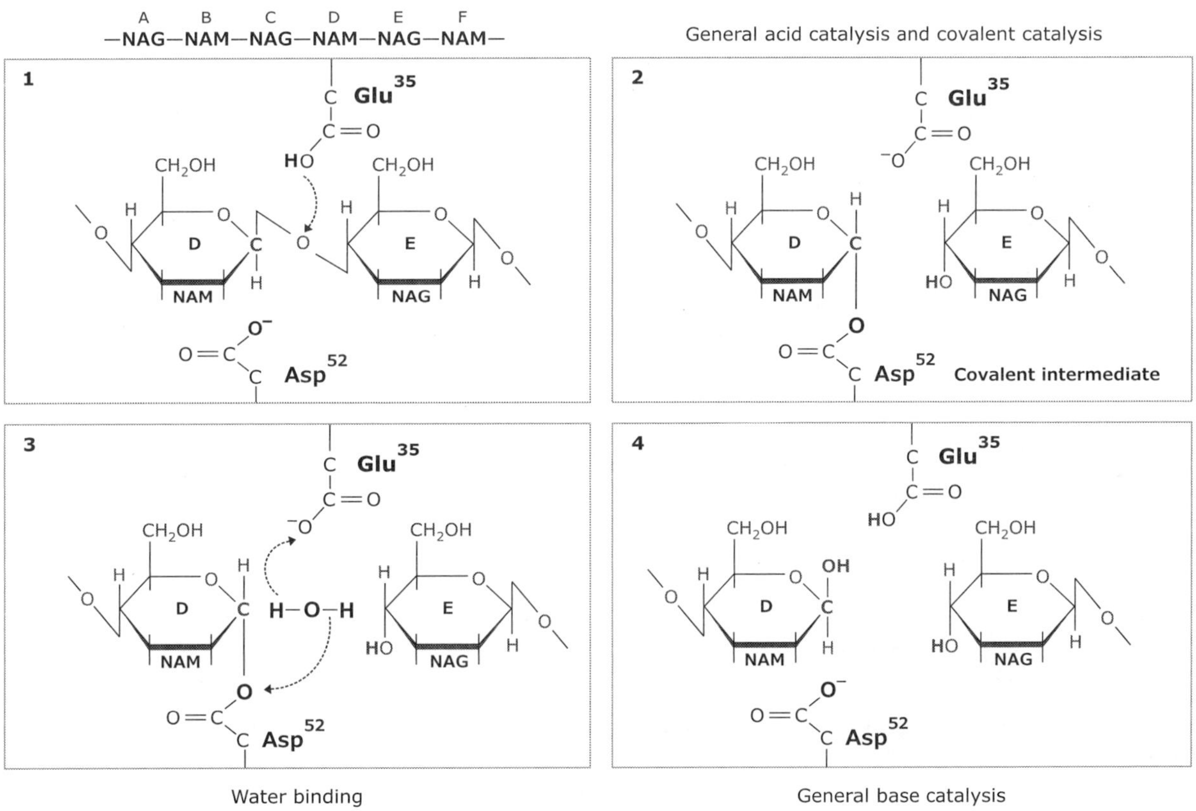

Figure 1.110 Mechanism of action of lysozyme. In the enzyme-substrate complex, Glu^{35} acts as an acid that attacks the glycosidic bond by donating a proton to sugar E. Asp^{52} attacks the C1 carbon atom and forms a covalent bond with the C1 carbon atom of sugar D. The Glu^{35} then polarizes a water molecule, so that its oxygen can readily attack and break the covalent bond with Asp^{52}. The reaction of the water molecule completes the hydrolysis and returns the enzyme to its initial state.

Chymotrypsin

Chymotrypsin is synthesized in the pancreas as a precursor called **chymotrypsinogen**, which is catalytically inactive. The active chymotrypsin (generated from cleavage) is three polypeptide fragments interconnected via disulfide bonds. This enzyme catalyzes the hydrolysis of peptide bonds of proteins in the small intestine. It is an *endopeptidase* and makes selective cleavage. It cleaves peptide bonds on the carboxyl side of aromatic or large hydrophobic side chains containing amino acids (Tyr, Trp, Phe, Met). It also catalyzes the hydrolysis of ester bonds.

Chymotrypsin is a **serine protease**. Serine proteases are a class of proteolytic enzymes whose catalytic mechanism is based on an active site serine residue. This family also includes *trypsin, elastase, thrombin, subtilisin, acetylcholinesterase* and other related enzymes. Chymotrypsin cleaves peptide bonds by attacking the unreactive carbonyl group with a powerful nucleophile, the Ser^{195} residue located in the active site of the enzyme, which briefly becomes covalently bonded to the substrate, forming an enzyme-substrate intermediate. Treatment with organofluorophosphates such as *diisopropylphosphofluoridate* (**DIPF**) inactivates the enzyme irreversibly because DIPF reacts with hydroxyl group of Ser^{195} present in the active site of the enzyme. This *chemical modification* with DIPF suggested that this unusually reactive serine residue plays a central role in the catalytic mechanism of chymotrypsin. Serine is part of a **catalytic triad** that also includes histidine and aspartic acid. The highly reactive Ser^{195}, forms a **charge-relay network** with His^{57} and Asp^{102}. The side chain of Ser^{195} is H-bonded to the imidazole ring of His^{57}. The –NH group of this imidazole ring is, in turn, H-bonded to the carboxylate group of Asp^{102}. This grouping has been found in a whole group of enzymes called serine proteases.

In the first step, a general base catalysis reaction occurs. In this reaction, His^{57} acts as a general base to withdraw a proton from Ser^{195}, facilitating nucleophilic attack by Ser^{195} on the substrate's carbonyl carbon of the peptide bond to be cleaved. This is probably a concerted step because proton transfer leaves a relatively unstable negative charge on the serine oxygen prior to the Ser^{195} attack on the carbonyl carbon. Asp^{102} stabilizes the positive charge acquired by His^{57}. Nucleophilic attacks on the carbonyl carbon create a **tetrahedral intermediate** (a transition state).

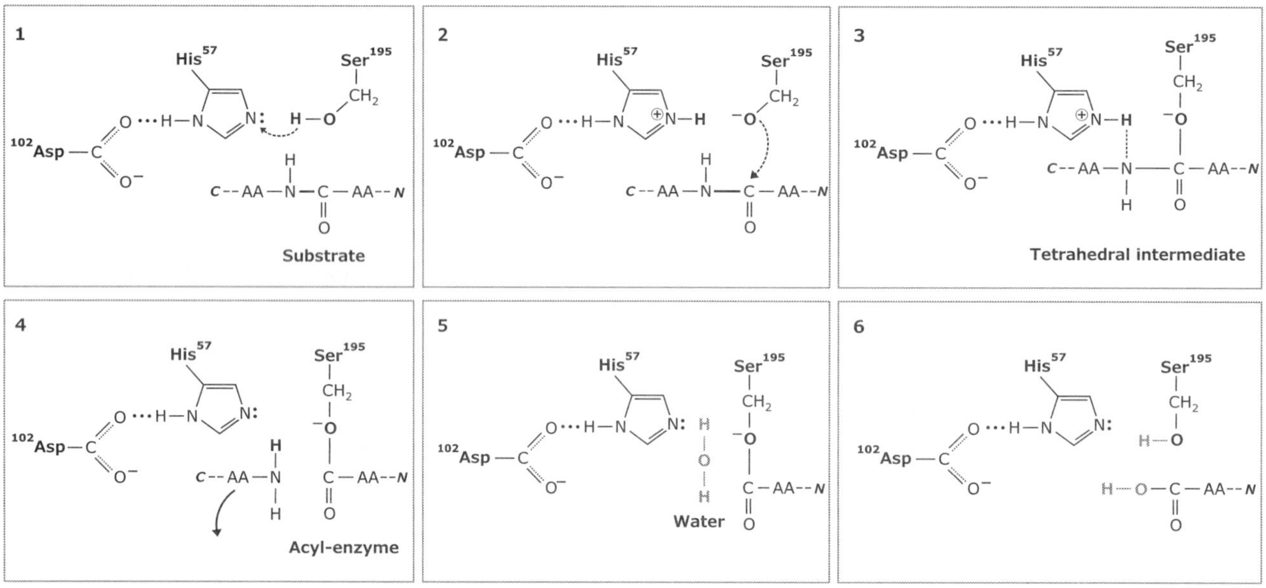

Figure 1.111 Three polar amino acid residues—His^{57}, Asp^{102}, and Ser^{195}—form a catalytic triad at the active site. The imidazole group of His^{57} is located next to the –OH group of Ser^{195} and is able to form an H-bond to it. The second nitrogen atom of His^{57} is H-bonded to the carboxylate group of Asp^{102}. It creates a *charge-relay system*. Removal of the proton from serine by histidine (*a base catalyst*) allows the resulting nucleophilic oxygen (*a covalent catalyst*) to attack the carbonyl carbon of the peptide bond. This results in the formation of the tetrahedral intermediate (transition state). Breakdown of the tetrahedral intermediate occurs when histidine acts as an *acid catalyst* and donates a proton to the nitrogen of the peptide bond. This step cleaves the peptide bond and results in the formation of the acyl-enzyme. The C-terminal fragment of the substrate (*first product*) is released. Water (*second substrate*) binds to the active site. A proton is transferred from water to His^{57}, leading to the formation of the second tetrahedral intermediate. Deacylation is the reverse of acylation. Water molecule attacks the carbonyl carbon of the acyl-enzyme. His^{57} then donates its extra proton to the Ser^{195} as it leaves the substrate acyl carbon, forming the *second product* and completing the peptide bond hydrolysis.

General acid catalysis by His^{57} aids breakdown of the tetrahedral intermediate to the **acyl-enzyme intermediate**. The transient, protonated form of His^{57} transfers its proton to the amine leaving group. The form of the enzyme in which Ser^{195} is covalently attached to the *N*-terminal fragment of the cleaved substrate by an ester linkage is termed the **acyl-enzyme**. Once the acyl-enzyme is formed, the *C*-terminal fragment of the substrate (*first product*) is released. Water, as a *second substrate*, binds the active site. A proton is transferred from water to His^{57}, leading to the formation of the second tetrahedral intermediate. His^{57} acts as a general base in this step, accepting a proton from the attacking water molecule. The subsequent collapse of the tetrahedral intermediate is assisted by proton donation from His^{57} to the serine oxygen in a concerted manner.

RNase A

Ribonucleases (or RNases) are a group of enzymes that catalyze the hydrolysis of the phosphodiester bonds in RNA molecules. Various types of RNases, such as RNase N, RNase II, RNase III, RNase H and RNase A, are reported in prokaryotes and eukaryotes. Bovine pancreatic RNase A, the most studied RNase, catalyzes the hydrolysis of phosphodiester bonds (in an ssRNA) between the phosphate group of a pyrimidine nucleotide and an adjacent nucleotide to give 3′-phosphate and an RNA fragment with 5′-hydroxyl terminus.

The imidazole group of **His^{12}**, acting as a *general base catalyst*, abstracts a proton from the 2′-OH group of sugar, forming a nucleophilic alkoxide anion. This alkoxide anion attacks neighboring phosphorus atoms. Cleavage of the P–O bond in the substrate 5′-3′ phosphodiester bond yields a cyclic 2′-3′ nucleoside monophosphate intermediate. The released 5′-alkoxide anion picks up a proton from His^{119}. Thus, **His^{119}** acts as a **general acid catalyst**. The 2′-3′ phosphodiester intermediate hydrolyzes in the next steps. The role of histidine 119 and 12 are reversed in the hydrolysis reaction. Thus, His^{119}, whose imidazole group is now unprotonated, abstracts a proton from water. The hydroxide ion created in this step attacks the phosphorus atom of the intermediate. In this step, the 2′-oxygen, the leaving group, retrieves a proton from the imidazolium ion group of His^{12}.

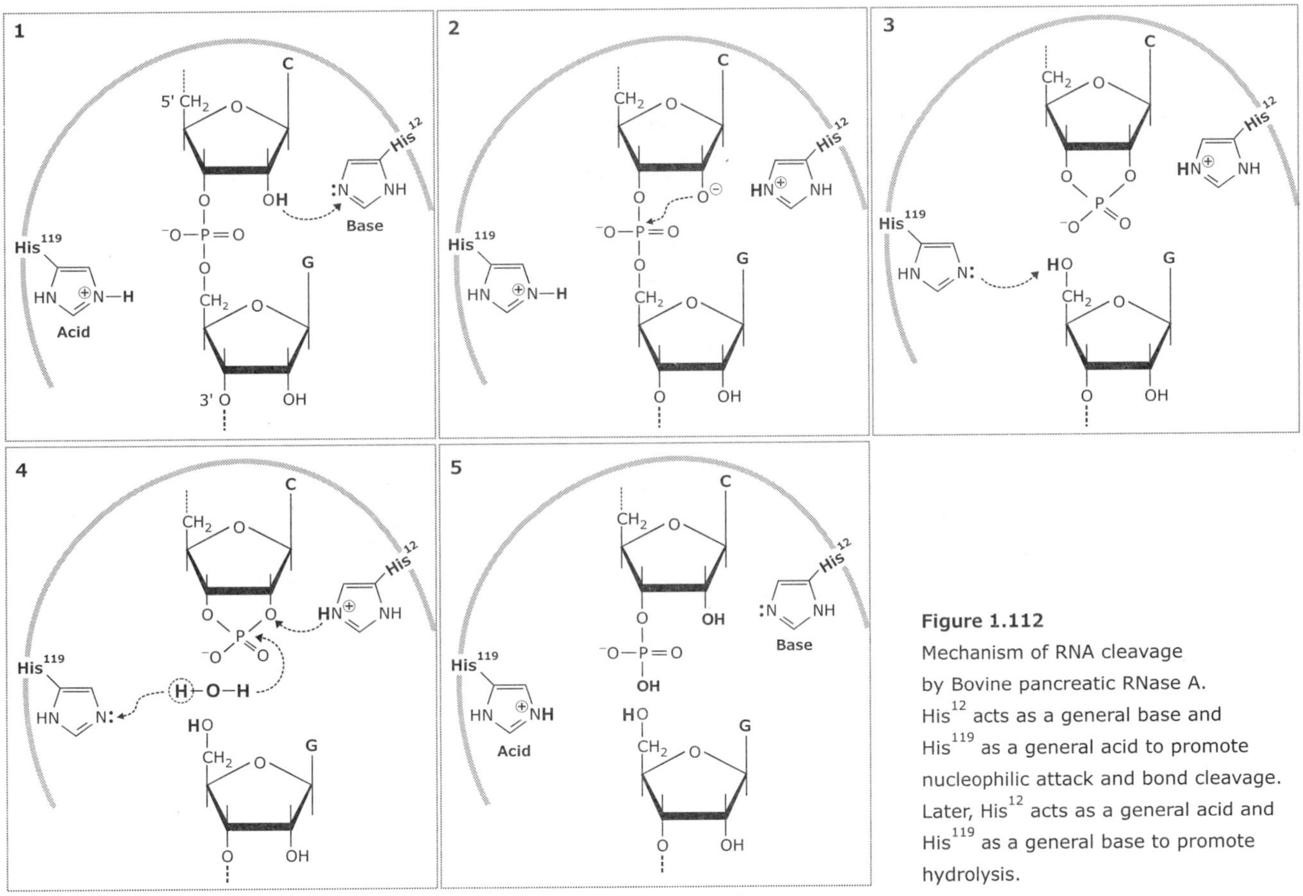

Figure 1.112
Mechanism of RNA cleavage by Bovine pancreatic RNase A. His^{12} acts as a general base and His^{119} as a general acid to promote nucleophilic attack and bond cleavage. Later, His^{12} acts as a general acid and His^{119} as a general base to promote hydrolysis.

Aspartate proteases

Besides serine proteases, other classes of proteolytic enzymes utilize cysteine (**cysteine proteases**) or aspartate (**aspartate proteases**) to perform their catalytic function. In *aspartate proteases*, it is actually two aspartic acids that make up the catalytic machinery of the enzyme. The carboxylate groups of these two aspartic acid residues assist in proton transfers from a water molecule that acts as the nucleophile to attack the peptide bond of the peptide or protein to be cleaved. Aspartate proteases are found in all forms of life. Members of this class include *renin*, an enzyme having a role in the regulation of blood pressure, and the digestive enzyme *pepsin*. **HIV protease** is also a member of the aspartate protease family of proteolytic enzymes. HIV protease plays a critical role in the life cycle of the virus and, for this reason, has become an important target for drug development in the battle against HIV infection.

Problem

The mechanism for lysozyme cleavage of its polysaccharide substrate requires Glu^{35} in its nonionized form, whereas the nearby Asp^{52} must be ionized. The pKs for the side chain carboxyl groups on the two amino acids in solution are virtually identical.

a. How can one carboxyl group be charged and the other uncharged in the active site of lysozyme?

b. The optimum pH for lysozyme is about 5. Why do you suppose that the activity decreases above and below this optimum?

Solution:

a. Amino acid side chains in proteins often have quite different p*K*s than they do in solution. Glu^{35} is uncharged because its local environment is non-polar, which makes ionization less favorable (raises its p*K*). The local environment of Asp^{52} is more polar, permitting ionization near its solution p*K*.

b. As the pH drops below 5, Asp^{52} picks up a proton and becomes nonionized, interfering with the mechanism. As the pH rises above 5, Glu^{35} begins to release its proton, also interfering with the mechanism.

Problem

The enzyme chymotrypsin is inactivated by DIPF. Which amino acid residue is likely to be present at the active site of chymotrypsin and what is the probable role of this residue in the catalytic mechanism?

Solution: Chymotrypsin is a serine protease. A highly reactive seryl residue, Ser^{195}, participates in a charge-relay network with His^{57} and Asp^{102}. As the serine oxygen attacks the carbonyl carbon of a peptide bond, the hydrogen-bonded His^{57} functions as a general base to abstract the serine proton, and the negatively charged Asp^{102} stabilizes the positive charge that forms on the His residue. DIPF reacts rapidly with active site serine residue, Ser^{195} and permanently inactivates the enzyme.

1.13 Chemistry in Biology

Biological processes in living organisms follow the laws of physics and chemistry, so in order to understand how biological systems work, it is important to understand the underlying physics and chemistry. Therefore, the fundamentals of chemistry are important to understand biological processes. In this section, we have described some important chemical concepts necessary to understand cellular chemistry.

Matter and Energy

Matter is anything that has mass and occupies space. All bodies consist of matter. Matter can exist in three physical states – solid, liquid and gas. **Solids** have definite volume and definite shape. **Liquids** have definite volume but not the definite shape. They take the shape of the container in which they are placed. **Gases** have neither definite volume nor definite shape. They completely occupy the container in which they are placed.

Law of conservation of matter or mass: *In a closed system, the total quantity of matter during a chemical reaction or during a physical change remains constant over time. In other words, matter cannot be created or destroyed in a chemical reaction or during a physical change; it can only be rearranged or transformed from one form to another.*

Energy is defined as the capacity to do work or produce heat. Energy can be classified into two principal types: kinetic energy and potential energy. A body in motion possesses energy because of its motion. Such energy is called **kinetic energy**. The energy a body possesses because of its position, condition, or composition is called **potential energy**.

Law of conservation of energy: *Energy cannot be created or destroyed in a chemical reaction or in a physical change. It can only be converted from one form to another.*

Atom and molecules

Matter is composed of one or more elements. The smallest particle of an element is called an **atom.** Atoms consist principally of three fundamental sub-atomic particles: *electrons*, *protons*, and *neutrons*. An atom comprises a *nucleus*, which is composed of protons and neutrons, and one or more electrons that surround the nucleus. The nucleus contains almost all of the atom's mass but occupies only a very small part of its volume. The electrons, which occupy most of the space within an atom, orbit around the nucleus.

A **molecule** is a definite group of atoms that are chemically bonded together. The types of atoms and their exact number in a molecule are represented by the **molecular formula**. For example, the hydrogen peroxide molecule contains two hydrogen atoms and two oxygen atoms chemically bonded together. Therefore, its molecular formula is H_2O_2.

Atomic number and mass number

The chemical identity of every element is determined by atomic number. The **atomic number** of an element is equal to the number of protons in the nucleus of any atom of that element. For example, hydrogen has an atomic number of 1, indicating that all atoms of hydrogen contain one proton. Uranium, on the other hand, has an atomic number of 92, meaning that all atoms of uranium have 92 protons. The atomic number is often represented by the letter Z.

Most atomic nuclei also contain neutrons. Neutrons do not affect the chemical identity of the atom, but they do contribute to the mass of the atom and help stabilize the nucleus. The **mass number** is an integer value equal to the sum of the number of protons and the number of neutrons in the nucleus of an atom of a particular isotope of an element. It varies for different isotopes of the same element. The mass number of the nucleus is represented by the letter A. If N represents the number of neutrons in the nucleus, then $A = Z + N$.

All atoms of a given element have the same number of protons. However, they may have different numbers of neutrons. Two atoms with the same number of protons but different numbers of neutrons are called **isotopes**. Isotopes of an element differ only in mass. Hydrogen, for example, has three isotopes, which contain 0, 1, and 2 neutrons, respectively. The isotope with a mass number of 1 is called **protium**, as its nucleus consists only of a single proton. The isotope with a mass number of 2 is called **deuterium** because its nucleus contains one proton and one neutron. The isotope with a mass number of 3, which is unstable, is called **tritium** because its nucleus contains one proton and two neutrons.

Water

Water (H_2O) is essential for life. The most abundant substance of the living cell is water. It accounts for up to 70% or more of a cell's weight. It provides the medium in which most substances remain dissolved. Water is colorless, odorless, and tasteless in nature. It is made up of two hydrogen atoms and one oxygen atom, with a total atomic mass of 18 daltons. The H—O—H **bond angle** is **104.5°**, which is smaller than the typical tetrahedral angle of 109°. Since oxygen is more electronegative than hydrogen, the oxygen nucleus attracts electrons more strongly than does the hydrogen nucleus. It means that the shared electrons are more shifted towards the oxygen atom than of the hydrogen. The result of this unequal electron sharing is the formation of two electric dipoles in the water molecule, one along each of the H—O bonds. Each hydrogen atom bears a partial positive charge (δ^+), and the oxygen atom carries a partial negative charge equal in magnitude to the sum of the two partial positives (δ^{2-}).

Water is a polar molecule. When atoms in a molecule share electrons unequally, they create what is called a **dipole moment**. The dipole moment is a measure of the polarity of the molecule. The shape of a molecule and the polarity of its bonds determine the *overall polarity* of that molecule. A molecule that contains polar bonds might not have any overall polarity, depending upon its shape. Although a polar bond is a prerequisite for a molecule to have a dipole moment, not all molecules with polar bonds exhibit dipoles. If a molecule is completely symmetric, then the dipole moment vectors on each molecule will cancel each other out, making the molecule non-polar. For example, CO_2 has a linear, symmetrical structure. The bonds in CO_2 are polar (or polarized), and therefore, each C=O bond has a bond dipole moment. However, the molecule itself is linear, and the two bond dipole moments are oriented at 180° with respect to each other and cancel each other out, so overall, the molecule does not have a dipole moment and is non-polar. Similarly, if water were linear, it would be a non-polar substance.

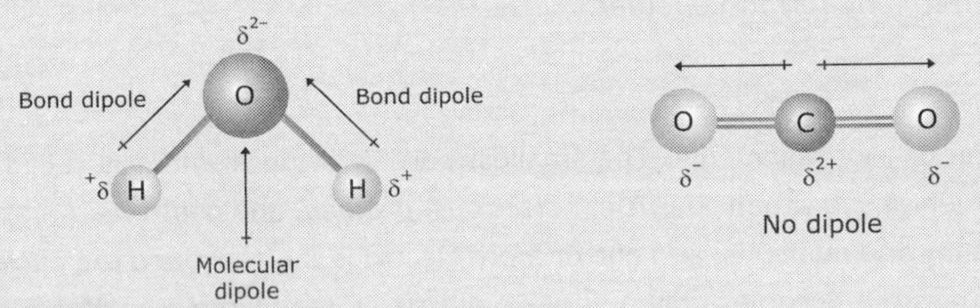

Figure 1.113 The H_2O molecule contains two polar O–H bonds in a bent (nonlinear) geometry. The bond dipole moments do not cancel so that the molecule forms a molecular dipole with its negative pole at the oxygen and its positive pole midway between the two hydrogen atoms. The arrow representing the dipole moment goes from positive to negative. CO_2 has two polar C=O bonds, but the geometry of CO_2 is linear so that the two bond dipole moments cancel out each other and there is no net molecular dipole moment; the molecule is non-polar.

The remarkable physical and chemical properties of water make it suitable for the living system. Water has a higher *melting point, boiling point, heat of vaporization* and *surface tension*. All of these physical properties are anomalously high for a substance of this molecular weight that is neither metallic nor ionic. These unusual properties are a consequence of *intermolecular* hydrogen bonding between water molecules. The oxygen atom of one water molecule and the hydrogen of another can form intermolecular hydrogen bond. Water can serve as both a hydrogen bond donor and hydrogen bond acceptor in hydrogen bond formation. Each water molecule can form four hydrogen bonds. Hydrogen bonding between water molecules provides the cohesive forces that make water a liquid at room temperature and a crystalline solid (ice) at low temperatures.

Water acts as an excellent solvent. It dissolves more substances than any other liquid. 'Solubility' of a solute depends on the ability of a solvent to interact with a solute more strongly than solute particles interact with each other. Water is loosely said to be the '**universal solvent.**' This statement cannot literally be true. Water cannot dissolve all solutes but certainly dissolves more types of solutes, and in higher amounts, than any other solvent. The polar character of water makes it an **excellent solvent** for polar and ionic compounds.

Polar or ionic compounds interact well with water molecules by forming hydrogen bonds or electrostatic interactions and are said to be **hydrophilic**. In contrast, non-polar compounds do not form hydrogen bonds with water molecules and are said to be **hydrophobic**. However, non-polar hydrophobic compounds are soluble in non-polar solvents.

Amphipathic (or **amphiphilic**) compounds contain both hydrophilic and hydrophobic regions. When an amphipathic compound is mixed with water, the polar, hydrophilic region interacts with the water, while the non-polar, hydrophobic region tends to avoid contact with the water.

Water has a very high value of **dielectric constant**, which is a measure of the capacity to neutralize the attraction between electrical charges. Because of this property, water acts as a powerful solvent for salts. Salts such as NaCl dissolve in water due to its high value of dielectric constant. Higher value weakens the attractive forces between oppositely charged ions (such as Na^+ and Cl^-) and therefore NaCl dissociates in Na^+ and Cl^- in water. Secondly, when an ion immersed in a polar solvent such as water, it attracts the oppositely charged ends of the solvent dipoles. Both positive and negative ions are thereby surrounded by one or more concentric shells (referred to as *solvation spheres*) of solvent molecules. Such ions are said to be **solvated** or, when water is the solvent, to be **hydrated**. As ions become hydrated, this thus counteracts their tendency to associate in a crystalline lattice.

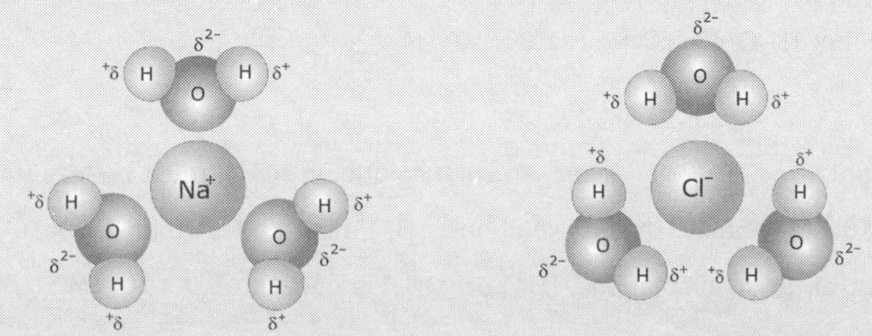

Figure 1.114 Hydration shells surrounding ions in solution. The partial negative charge of water is attracted to positively charged ions. Likewise, the partial positive charge on the other end of the water molecule is attracted to negatively charged ions.

Ionization of water

Water is **amphoteric** (a substance which can act as either an acid or a base) and **amphiprotic** (a substance which can either donate or accept a proton) molecule. Water molecules have a slight tendency to undergo ionization to yield a hydrogen ion (corresponds to a proton) and a hydroxide ion.

$$H_2O \rightleftharpoons H^+ + OH^-$$

Because water is *amphiprotic*, one water molecule can react with another to form a hydroxide ion (OH^-) and a hydronium ion (H_3O^+) in an autoionization process. The type of reaction, in which a substance ionizes when one molecule of the substance reacts with another molecule of the same substance, is referred to as **autoionization**. In pure water, a very small fraction of water molecules donates protons to other water molecules to form hydronium ions and hydroxide ions:

$$\underset{\text{Acid}}{H_2O} + \underset{\text{Base}}{H_2O} \rightleftharpoons \underset{\text{Conjugate base of } H_2O}{OH^-} + \underset{\text{Conjugate acid of } H_2O}{H_3O^+}$$

In pure water, the H^+ (or H_3O^+) concentration is equal to 10^{-7} M. In other words, in one litre of water, 0.0000001 M of H^+ ions will present. Likewise, OH^- concentration is also 10^{-7} M. The ionization of water can be measured by its electrical conductivity; pure water carries electrical current as H_3O^+ migrates toward the cathode and OH^- toward the anode. The ionization of water is expressed by an **equilibrium constant**. The degree of ionization of water at equilibrium is small. The equilibrium constant for the reversible ionization of water is,

$$K_{eq} = \frac{[H^+][OH^-]}{[H_2O]} \quad \text{or} \quad K_{eq} = \frac{[H_3O^+][OH^-]}{[H_2O]^2}$$

On rearranging the equation, this becomes

$$K_{eq} \times [H_2O] = [H^+]\,[OH^-]$$

Because the degree of autoionization of water is very small, we can treat the molar concentration of water, $[H_2O]$, in pure water is constant and equal to 55.5 moles/litre (M). The numerical value is 55.5 M can be obtained by dividing the number of grams of water in 1 L (1000 g), by the molecular weight of water, 18 g/mol. Thus,

$K_{eq} \times 55.5 = [H^+]\,[OH^-] = K_w$

K_w is the **ion product of water** and may be defined as *the product of concentration of H^+ and OH^- ions in pure water.* The numerical value of K_w can be determined experimentally by measuring the H^+ concentration of pure water. The value for K_{eq} is 1.8×10^{-16} M at 25°C.

$K_w = [H^+]\,[OH^-] = (55.5\ M)\,(1.8 \times 10^{-16}\ M) = 1.0 \times 10^{-14}\ M^2$

Thus, the product $[H^+][OH^-]$ in aqueous solutions at 25°C always equals $1 \times 10^{-14}\ M^2$. The H^+ concentration is also equal, by definition, to the OH^- concentration because water is a monoprotic acid. Thus, in case of pure water, the molar concentrations of $[H^+]$ or $[H_3O^+]$ and $[OH^-]$ are equal.
At 25°C, the value of K_w is $1.0 \times 10^{-14}\ M^2$.
In case of **pure water,** $[H^+]$ or $[H_3O^+] = [OH^-] = 1.0 \times 10^{-7}$ M.

Any solution in which,

$[H^+]$ or $[H_3O^+]$ greater than 1.0×10^{-7} M is **acidic**. In such solutions, $[OH^-]$ must be less than 1.0×10^{-7} M.

$[OH^-]$ greater than 1.0×10^{-7} M is **basic**. In such solutions, $[H^+]$ must be less than 1.0×10^{-7} M.

$[H^+]$ equal to $[OH^-]$ is **neutral**. In such solutions, $[H^+]$ or $[OH^-]$ is equal to 1.0×10^{-7} M.

The ion product of water, K_w, is the basis for the pH scale. It is a convenient means of designating the concentration of H^+ in any aqueous solution. The concentrations are more conveniently expressed as pH. In a neutral solution at 25°C, in which the concentration of $[H^+]$ is 1.0×10^{-7} M, the pH can be calculated as:

pH = –log [H⁺] $= -\log 1.0 \times 10^{-7} = 7$

The pH of a precisely neutral solution is 7. Solutions having a pH greater than 7 are alkaline or basic; the concentration of OH^- is greater than that of H^+. Conversely, solutions having a pH less than 7 are acidic. Keep in mind that the pH scale is logarithmic, not arithmetic. To say that two solutions differ in pH by 1 unit means that one solution has ten times the H^+ concentration of the other, but it does not tell us the absolute magnitude of the difference.

For example, pH 4 is ten times more acidic than pH 5 and 100 times (10 times 10) more acidic than pH 6. The same holds true for pH values above 7, each of which is ten times more alkaline (another way to say basic) than the next lower whole value. For example, pH 10 is ten times more alkaline than pH 9 and 100 times (10 times 10) more alkaline than pH 8. Just as pH is a convenient way to designate the concentration of $[H^+]$, pOH is a convenient way to designate the concentration of $[OH^-]$. The pH scale ranges from 0–14. At a pH of zero, the concentration of $[H^+]$ is one molar, while at pH 14, the concentration of $[OH^-]$ is one molar. However, the pH range does not have an upper or lower boundary. One can go somewhat below zero and above 14 in water because the concentrations of H^+ or OH^- can exceed one molar.

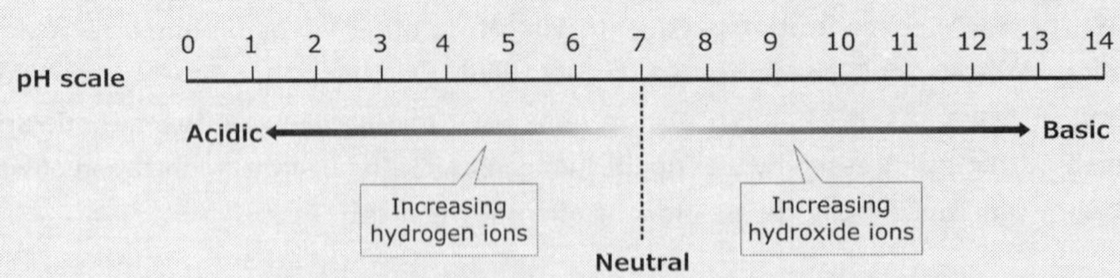

Problem

What is the pH of a solution that has an H^+ concentration of 6.50×10^{-10} mol/L?

Solution:

$$\begin{aligned} pH &= -\log [H^+] \\ &= -\log (6.50 \times 10^{-10}) \\ &= 10 - 0.81 = 9.19 \end{aligned}$$

Problem

Calculate the pH of a solution of 5×10^{-4} M HCl.

Solution: HCl is a strong acid and it will fully dissociates into H^+ and Cl^-. Thus, $[H^+] = [Cl^-] = [HCl]$.

$pH = -\log [H^+] = -\log (5 \times 10^{-4}) = 4 - 0.69 = 3.3$

Problem

Calculate the pH of a solution of 7.0×10^{-5} M NaOH.

Solution: NaOH is a strong base and it will fully dissociates into $[Na^+] = [OH^-] = [NaOH]$.

$pH + pOH = 14$

$pOH = -\log [OH^-]$

$pH = 14 + \log [OH^-] = 14 + \log (7.0 \times 10^{-5}) = 14 + 0.84 - 5 = 9.8.$

Problem

Calculate the pH of a solution prepared by diluting 3.0 mL of 2.5 M HCl to a final volume of 100 mL with H_2O.

Solution: HCl is a strong acid, hence, it dissociates completely to H^+ and Cl^-. There is 3 ml solution of 2.5 M HCl. The final molarity will be $(2.5 \times 3)/100 = 0.075$ M. In 100 mL of solution, there is 0.075 M H^+.

$pH = -\log [H^+] = -\log (0.075) = -(-1.1) = 1.1.$

Acids, Bases and pH

According to **Bronsted-Lowry concept** of acids and bases, an **acid** is defined as a substance that donates a proton (a hydrogen ion) and a **base** is a substance that accepts a proton. When a proton donor loses a proton, it becomes the corresponding proton acceptor. A proton donor and its corresponding proton acceptor make up a **conjugate acid-base pair**. When an acid transfers a proton to a base, the acid is converted to its *conjugate base*. When a base accepts a proton, it is converted to its *conjugate acid*.

Let us take an acid HCl in water. A proton transfer reaction between the acid HCl and the base H_2O to give the H_3O^+ and Cl^-. The Cl^- is the **conjugate base** of the acid HCl and the H_3O^+ is the **conjugate acid** of the base H_2O.

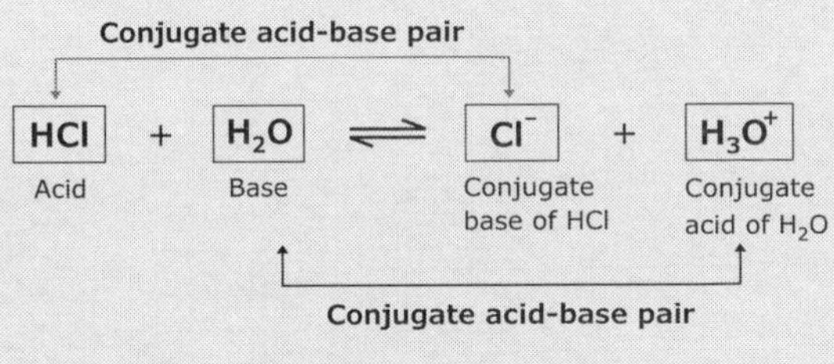

All acids are not equally strong. A strong acid ionizes almost completely in aqueous solution whereas a weak acid ionizes only partially in aqueous solution. Each acid has a characteristic tendency to lose its proton in an aqueous solution. The stronger the acid, the greater its tendency to lose its proton. It is important to understand that the strength of an acid or a base is not related to its concentration. HCl is a strong acid, whether it is concentrated or dilute, because it dissociates completely in water. The tendency of any acid to lose a proton and form its conjugate base is defined by the **equilibrium constant** (K_{eq}) for the reversible reaction. Imagine a generic acid, HA. The ionization of HA can be written as a simple dissociation, as follows:

$$HA \rightleftharpoons H^+ + A^-$$

The acid dissociates into its component ions, but the ions reassociate together again to form the original acid. When the rate of dissociation into ions is equal to the rate of ion reassociation, the system is said to be in *equilibrium*. An equilibrium does not always mean that half of the reactants have converted into products. Reactions don't stop when they come to equilibrium. But the rates of the forward and reverse reactions are the same when this system is at equilibrium, so there is no net change in the concentrations of the reactants or products. A strong acid dissociates completely whereas a weak acid does not dissociate completely i.e., have a lower percentage of molecules in a dissociated state.

$$K_{eq} = \frac{[H^+][A^-]}{[HA]} = K_a$$

The *equilibrium constant* for this reaction is expressed as an **acid ionization constant** or **acid dissociation constant** or **acidity constant**, often designated K_a. It is a quantitative measure of the strength of an acid in solution. Stronger acids have larger acid dissociation constant; weaker acids have smaller acid dissociation constant. If we take strong acid such as HCl, the value of K_a is very large. It dissociates completely in aqueous solution ($HCl = H^+ + Cl^-$). Hence, the concentration of HCl in aqueous solution will be very small. Because of this, the pH of HCl solutions is readily calculated from the amount of HCl used to make the solution: $[H^+]$ in solution = [HCl] added to solution. Thus, a 1 M solution of HCl has a pH of 0; a 1 mM HCl solution has a pH of 3.

But case is different in case of a weak acid which does not dissociate completely. Hence, a measure of K_a for a weak acid is given by its pK_a, which is equivalent to the negative logarithm of K_a. Acid strengths are therefore expressed as $-\log K_a$, which we call the pK_a.

$$pK_a = \log \frac{1}{K_a} = -\log K_a$$

The pK_a is a measure of the tendency of a group to give up a proton. The stronger the tendency to dissociate a proton (i.e., the stronger is the acid), the larger its K_a and the lower its pK_a.

Relation between pH and pK_a

pH is a measure of the concentration of hydrogen ions in a solution. As we have discussed before, it is the negative logarithm of the hydrogen ion concentration (the symbol 'p' denotes '*negative logarithm of*').

$$pH = \log \frac{1}{[H^+]} = -\log [H^+]$$

The relationship between the pH of a solution and the concentrations of a weak acid and its conjugate base can be easily derived. Let us take the ionization or dissociation of a weak acid, HA:

$$HA \rightleftharpoons H^+ + A^-$$

$$K_a = \frac{[H^+][A^-]}{[HA]}$$

$$[H^+] = K_a \frac{[HA]}{[A^-]}$$

Taking the negative log of each term,

$$-\log [H^+] = -\log K_a - \log \frac{[HA]}{[A^-]}$$

$$-\log [H^+] = -\log K_a + \log \frac{[A^-]}{[HA]}$$

As, $pH = -\log [H^+]$ and $pK_a = -\log K_a$

$$pH = pK_a + \log \frac{[A^-]}{[HA]}$$

This relationship is known as the **Henderson-Hasselbalch equation**. This equation relates the pH of a solution to the pK_a and concentrations of an acid and its conjugate base. When the molar concentrations of acid [HA] and its conjugate base $[A^-]$ are equal, then $\log ([A^-]/[HA]) = \log 1 = 0$, and the pH of the solution is numerically equivalent to the pK_a of the acid. That is, when the pH equals the pK_a, the concentration of the deprotonated form of the group or molecule is equal to the concentration of the protonated form; the deprotonation process is halfway to completion.

At pH = pK_a, [HA] = [A^-] = 50%

Titration curve of a weak acid and its pK_a

A **titration** is an analytical method of quantitative analysis. In this process, the stoichiometric volume of one reactant of known concentration, the **titrant**, that is required to react with another reactant of unknown concentration, the *analyte*, is measured. During an *acid-base titration*, an acid with a known concentration (a standard solution) is slowly added to a base with an unknown concentration (or *vice versa*). An acid-base titration can be used to determine the amount of acid in a solution. To plot a *titration curve* of a weak acid (such as acetic acid), a measured volume of the weak acid is titrated with a solution of a strong base, usually sodium hydroxide (NaOH), of known concentration. The NaOH is added in small increments until the acid is neutralized, as determined with an indicator dye or a pH meter. A plot of the pH of the solution versus the amount of OH^- added yields a **titration curve**. Titration curves reveal the pK_a of weak acids. Consider the titration of a 0.1 M solution of acetic acid with 0.1 M NaOH at 25°C.

After addition of each increment of NaOH to the acetic acid solution, the pH of the mixture is measured. At the starting point, the acid form (i.e., CH_3COOH) predominates. As NaOH is added, the acid is converted to its conjugate base (CH_3COO^-). At the midpoint of the titration, where pH = pK_a, the concentrations of the weak acid (CH_3COOH) and its conjugate base (CH_3COO^-) are equal. The pH at the **inflection point** is 4.76, which is the pK_a of acetic acid. At the end point (or **equivalence point**), the conjugate base predominates, and the total amount of OH^- that has been added is equivalent to the amount of acid that was present at the starting point.

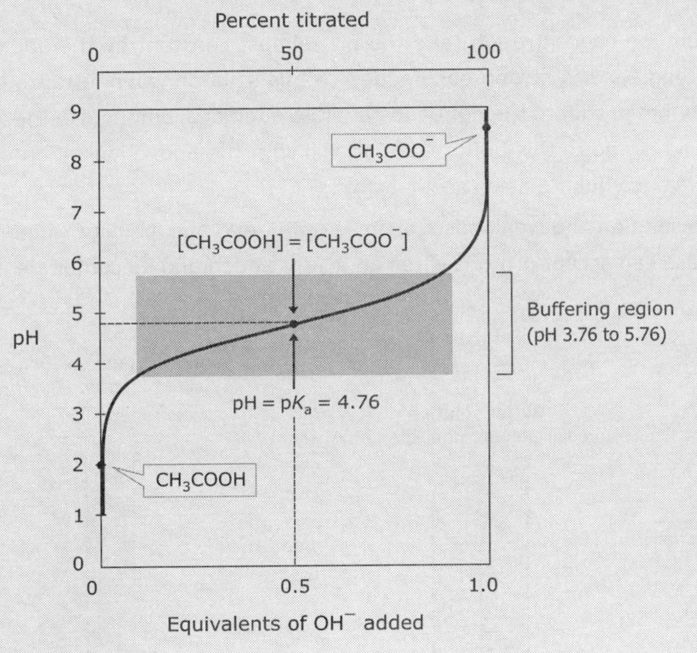

Figure 1.115
The titration curve of acetic acid. Shown in the boxes are the predominant ionic forms at the points designated. At the midpoint of the titration, the concentrations of the proton donor (CH_3COOH) and proton acceptor (CH_3COO^-) are equal, and the pH is numerically equal to the pK_a.

Buffer

Biological process is pH-dependent. Thus, maintenance of a constant pH is vital to all cells. Organisms have a variety of mechanisms to keep the pH of their intracellular and extracellular fluids essentially constant and this constancy of pH is achieved primarily by *buffers*. **Buffers** are aqueous solutions that tend to resist changes in their pH on addition of a small amount of acid or base and also on dilution. Although the pH of buffer changes on doing this but the change in pH values will be less (the pH remains relatively constant). There are two primary types of buffers: acidic and basic buffers. **Acidic buffer** has pH less than 7 whereas **basic buffer** has pH more than 7. A solution of weak acid and its conjugate base is an example of an *acidic buffer*. If a weak acid is HA (acts as the H^+ donor) then its conjugate base is A^- (acts as the H^+ acceptor). Similarly, a solution consists of a weak base and its conjugate acid is an example of a *basic buffer*. Two most common buffer systems in animals are—the phosphate buffer system and the bicarbonate buffer system. For phosphate buffer, the weak acid is $H_2PO_4^-$ and its conjugate base is HPO_4^{-2}. How much pH a buffer can maintain is determined by the nature of the conjugate pair and the concentrations of both components.

How do buffers work? In order for a buffer to resist changes in their pH on addition of a small amount of acid or base and also on dilution, it must have both an acidic and a basic component. However, you cannot mix any two acid and base together and get a buffer. If you mix HCl and NaOH, for example, you will simply neutralize the acid with the base and obtain a neutral salt, not a buffer. For a buffer to work, both the acid and the base components must be part of the same equilibrium system. Therefore, a buffer must consist of a mixture of a weak conjugate acid-base pair. The operation of a buffer solution depends on the **common ion effect.** To illustrate the function of a buffer solution, consider an acidic buffer solution. An **acidic buffer** solution is typically prepared by making a solution of a **weak acid** (such as *acetic acid*) and its salt (such as *sodium acetate*). For an acidic buffer to exist, it must satisfy two conditions: (1) the solution must contain a weak acid and its conjugate base, and (2) the concentrations of the weak acid and the conjugate base must be reasonably same. In aqueous solution, soluble ionic salt *sodium acetate* (CH_3COONa) dissociates (or ionizes) completely into its constituent ions, but *acetic acid,* as a weak acid, dissociates very less. Here, acetate ion (CH_3COO^-) is the conjugate base of a weak acid, acetic acid (CH_3COOH). Both *acetic acid* and *sodium acetate* are sources of *acetate ions*. The completely dissociated *sodium acetate* provides a high [acetate ions]. Hence, the concentration of nonionized weak acid, acetic acid, is approximately equal to the total acid concentration and the concentration of conjugate base, *acetate ions,* is equal to the concentration of the dissolved salt.

$$CH_3COONa \xrightarrow{H_2O} Na^+ + CH_3COO^- \quad \text{(to completion)}$$

$$CH_3COOH + H_2O \rightleftharpoons H_3O^+ + CH_3COO^- \quad \text{(reversible)}$$

This system acts to keep the hydronium ion concentration (and the pH) almost constant by the addition of either a small amount of a strong acid or a strong base. A strong base added to this solution will neutralize hydronium ion, causing the acetic acid ionization equilibrium to shift to the right and generate additional amounts of the weak conjugate base (acetate ion). Likewise, strong acid added to this buffer solution will shift the above ionization equilibrium left, producing additional amounts of the weak conjugate acid (acetic acid).

A **basic buffer** is prepared by making a solution of a weak base (such as ammonia) and its salt (ammonium chloride). Similarly, in a basic buffer, the weak base can accept protons when an acid is added and its conjugate acid can supply protons if a base is added.

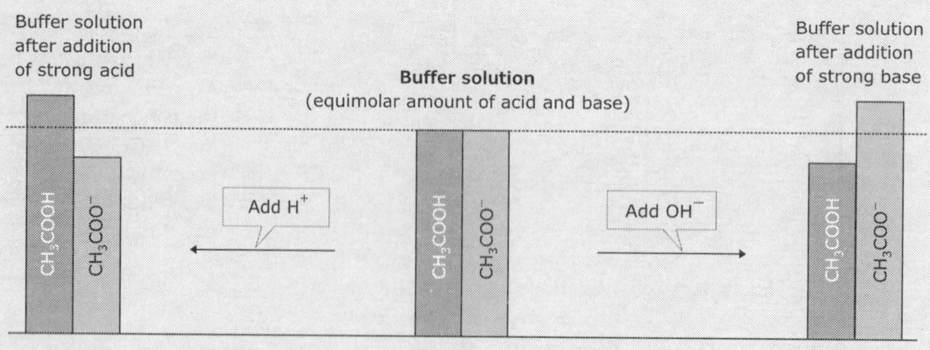

Figure 1.116 The acetic acid–acetate pair as a buffer system. The system is capable of absorbing either H^+ or OH^-.

Problem

Calculate the pH of 5×10^{-4} M HCl

Solution: HCl is a strong acid and fully dissociates into $[H^+]$ and $[Cl^-]$. Thus, $[H^+] = [Cl^-] = [HCl_{total}]$

$pH = -\log [H^+] = \log [HCl_{total}] = -\log [5 \times 10^{-4}] = 4 - 0.69 = 3.3$

Problem

Calculate the pH of a dilute solution that contains a molar ratio of potassium acetate to acetic acid of 2:1. pK_a of acetic acid is 4.76

Solution: Using the Henderson-Hasselbalch equation,

$pH = pK_a + \log [A^-]/[HA]$

pH = 4.76 + log ([acetate]/[acetic acid]), where ratio of [acetate]/[acetic acid] is 2/1.

$pH = 4.76 + \log (2/1)$

$pH = 4.76 + 0.30 = 5.06$

Problem

For a weak acid with a pK_a of 6.0, calculate the ratio of conjugate base to acid at a pH of 5.0.

Solution: Using the Henderson-Hasselbalch equation,

$pH = pK_a + \log ([A^-]/[HA])$

$5.0 = 6.0 + \log ([A^-]/[HA])$

$\log ([A^-]/[HA]) = -1.0$

$[A^-]/[HA] = 10^{-1.0} = 0.10$

Problem

What is the pH of a solution that contains 0.20 M sodium acetate and 0.60 M acetic acid (pK_a = 4.76)?

Solution: $pH = pK_a + \log ([base]/[acid])$

$= pK_a + \log ([acetate]/[acetic\ acid])$

$= 4.76 + \log (0.20/0.60)$

$= 4.76 + \log (0.33) = 4.76 + (-0.48) = 4.28$

Problem

The pH of a 1.0 L buffer solution containing 0.2 mol of acetic acid (CH_3COOH) and 0.3 mol of sodium acetate (CH_3COONa) is 5.0. The K_a of acetic acid is $P \times 10^{-5}$. What is the numerical value of P?

Solution: $pH = pK_a + \log \frac{[salt]}{[acid]}$

$5 = -\log K_a + \log \frac{0.3}{0.2}$

$\log K_a = \log 1.5 - 5 = -4.82$

$K_a = \text{antilog } (-4.82) = 0.000015 = 1.5 \times 10^{-5}$

Given that, $K_a = P \times 10^{-5}$

$P \times 10^{-5} = 1.5 \times 10^{-5}$

$P = 1.5$

Chemical interactions in living systems

Chemical interactions or bonds in the aqueous environment of living systems fall under two categories: **covalent** and **non-covalent.** Non-covalent interactions or bonds include *ionic bonds*, *hydrogen bonds*, *van der Waals forces*, and *hydrophobic forces*. In the aqueous environment of living organisms, covalent bonds are strong bonds, whereas non-covalent interactions are weak. When a bond is strong, it possesses higher bond energy because it requires more energy to break. The energy required to break non-covalent interactions is only 1-5 kcal/mol, which is significantly less than the bond energies of covalent bonds.

Covalent bonds

A *covalent bond* forms as a result of equal sharing of electron pairs between two atoms in order to achieve stable or inert gas configuration. Electron pairs that are shared between two atoms is called a **bonding pairs** (or *shared pairs*). Electron pairs not shared between two atoms are called *lone pairs*.

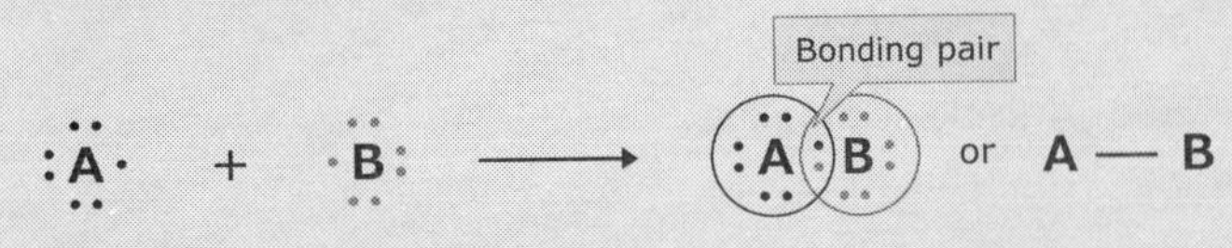

Covalent bonds may be either *polar* or *non-polar*. A **non-polar covalent bond** such as that in the hydrogen molecule, H_2, the electron pair is *shared equally* between the two hydrogen nuclei. Both hydrogen atoms have the same electronegativity (the electronegativity difference between the atoms is zero). Covalent bonds, such as the one in HF, in which the electron pairs are *shared unequally* due to difference in electronegativity are called **polar covalent bonds.** In HF, the shared electron pair between the two atoms gets displaced more towards fluorine since the electronegativity of fluorine is far greater than that of hydrogen. The atom towards which the electron pair shift gets partial negative charge while the other atom acquires a partial positive charge. The magnitude of electronegativity difference reflects the **degree of polarity**. The greater the difference in the electronegativities of the atoms forming the bond, the greater will be the charge separation and hence greater will be the polarity of the covalent bond.

A simple *covalent bond* is different from a *coordinate bond*. A covalent bond is formed between two atoms due to equal sharing of electrons (each atom supplies one electron to the bond). Whereas, a **coordinate bond** (also called a **dative bond**) is also form between two atoms due to sharing of electrons but both electrons come from the same atom. In simple diagrams, a co-ordinate bond is shown by an arrow. The arrow points from the atom donating the lone pair to the atom accepting it.

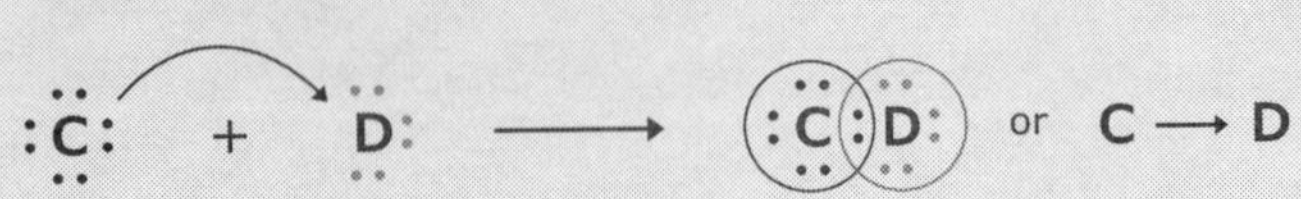

Covalent bond Vs coordinate bond

Definition	A bond formed by the equal sharing of electron pairs between two atoms	A bond in which both shared electrons come from one atom (donor)
Electron contribution	Each atom contributes one electron to the bond	Only one atom donates both electrons to the bond
Nature of bond	Strong and stable	Weaker than covalent bonds

Bond energy: Atoms bond together to form molecules because in doing so, they attain lower energies than they possess as individual atoms. In other words, the bonded atoms have lower energy than the individual atoms. When atoms combine to make a molecule, energy is always released, resulting in the compound having a lower overall energy. *Energy is required to break a bond, while energy is released when a bond is formed.* The energy of covalent bonds, which is the energy required to break a covalent bond in a molecule in the gas phase, depends on the number of covalent bonds (i.e., **bond order**) between two atoms and on the types of atoms involved. However, it is independent of the medium.

Types of atoms involved	*Bond energy* (kcal/mol)
O—H	110
C—H	99
C—N	73
N—H	93.5
C—O	85.5

Bond order	*Bond energy* (kcal/mol)
C—C	83
C=C	146
C≡C	200.5
C=N	147
C≡N	213

1 cal = 4.18 J

Non-covalent interactions

Ionic bonds: *Ionic bonds* are formed as a result of the transfer of electrons. Due to the transfer of electron(s), a positively charged ion (**cation**) and a negatively charged ion (**anion**) form. An *ionic bond* forms due to the electrostatic attraction between cation and anion. Ionic bonds form when the electronegativity difference between two atoms is large, as between a metal and a nonmetal.

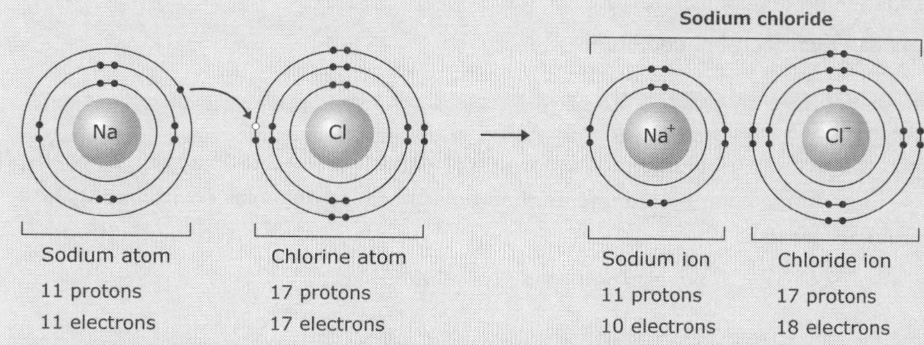

The electrostatic interactions can be either *attractive* or *repulsive*, depending on the signs of the charges and the force (F) of electrostatic interactions between ions in a solution depends on the magnitude of the charges (q), the distance between the charged groups (*r*) and the **dielectric constant** (ε) of the solvent in which the interactions occur:

$$F = \frac{1}{4\pi\varepsilon}\frac{q_1q_2}{r^2}$$

For water at 25°C, ε is 78.5, whereas, for acetone, it is 20.7. Thus, electrostatic interactions between dissolved ions are much stronger in acetone as compared to water. Similarly, the dependence on r^2 is such that ionic attractions or repulsions operate only over short distances.

Dielectric constant (or *relative permittivity*) **at 25°C**

Material	Dielectric constant	Material	Dielectric constant
Air	1.00	Acetone	20.7
Benzene	2.15	Methanol	33.5
Toluene	2.38	Water	78.5

Hydrogen bonds: Hydrogen bonding is a weak electrostatic attractive force that exists between a hydrogen atom covalently bonded to a very electronegative atom, **X** and an electronegative atom with a lone pair of electron, **Y.** Usually, hydrogen bonding is seen in the case where X and Y are the atoms F, O or N. A typical hydrogen bond may be depicted as X–H•••Y–, where the three dots denote the bond. X represents the **hydrogen bond donor** and Y is **hydrogen bond acceptor.** The atoms X and H are covalently bonded to one another and the X–H bond is polarized, the H•••Y bond strength increases with the increase in electronegativity of X.

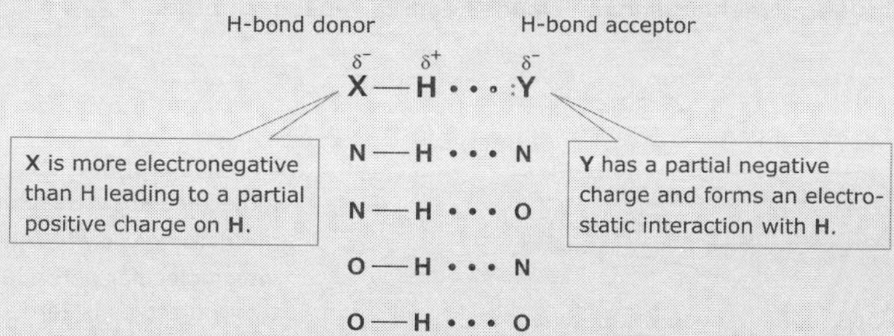

Figure 1.117 A typical hydrogen bond may be depicted as X–H•••Y, where the three dots denote the bond. X represents the hydrogen bond donor. The hydrogen atom participating in the hydrogen bond is covalently bonded to X which is usually a strongly electronegative atom such as N, O or F. The hydrogen bond acceptor, Y is an electronegative atom with a lone pair of electron. In some cases, X and Y are the same.

While hydrogen bonds are often thought to be primarily electrostatic in nature, studies on hydrogen-bonded complexes show many hydrogen bonds being shorter than the sum of van der Waals radii for the donor and acceptor atoms indicating orbital overlap and partially covalent character (about 10%). Hydrogen bonds can be **intermolecular** (between separate molecules) and **intramolecular** (within a single molecule) in nature. Although considerably weaker than ionic bonds, hydrogen bonds are stronger than most other non-covalent bonds. They have energies ranging from 1 to 5 kcal mol^{-1}. The strength of hydrogen bond depends on factors such as:

1. electronegativity difference between hydrogen-bonded atoms
2. nature of the solvent
3. alignment of the hydrogen-bonded atoms

Hydrogen bonds are strongest when the hydrogen-bonded atoms are in a straight line (i.e., 180° angle). Similarly, the strength of hydrogen bonds are more in nonpolar environments than polar because nonpolar environments lack competing hydrogen bond donors and acceptors.

Strength of H-bond : *High* 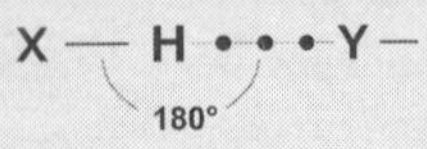

Strength of H-bond : *Low* 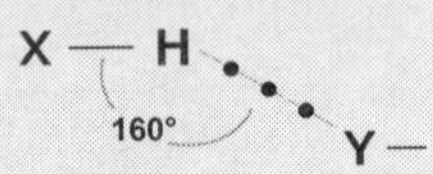

van der Waals force: van der Waals forces are weak **intermolecular** electrostatic interactions. These interactions involving either the permanent or induced dipoles, occur in all types of molecules, both polar and non-polar. These interactions may be attractive or repulsive in nature. There are three types of van der Waals forces:

Dipole-dipole interactions (Keesom interactions): These interactions occur between two permanent dipoles and interactions may be attractive or repulsive depending on the orientation of dipoles.

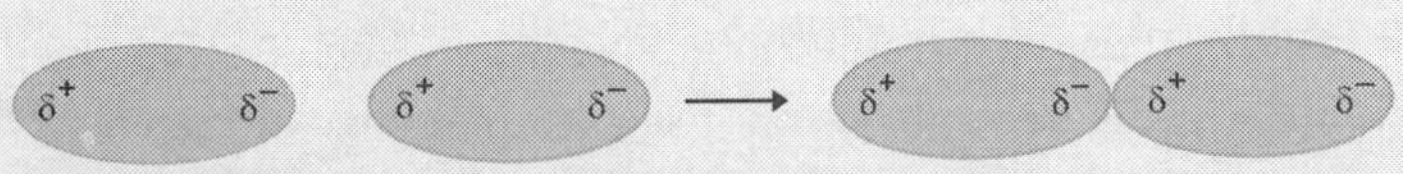

Dipole-dipole interactions

Dipole-induced dipole interactions (Debye interactions): These interactions occur between permanent dipole and induced dipole. It occurs because a permanent dipole induces a transient dipole in a nearby molecule by distorting its electron distribution. These interactions are attractive in nature.

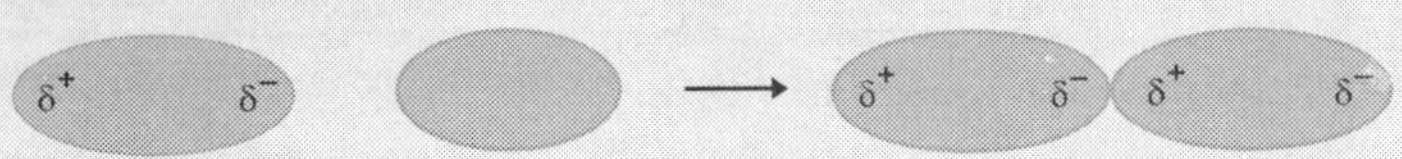

Dipole-induced dipole interactions

Induced dipole-induced dipole interactions (London dispersion force): These are extremely weak interactions occur between two induced dipoles and are attractive in nature.

Induced dipole-induced dipole interactions

The potential energy of van der Waals interactions based on their distance of separation can be approximated by the **Lennard-Jones expression.** The strength of attractive interactions increases as two molecules come closer to each other. The attractive interaction is greatest at a distance called the **van der Waals radius**. If distance further decreases, a repulsive force develops because their electron clouds begin to repel each other.

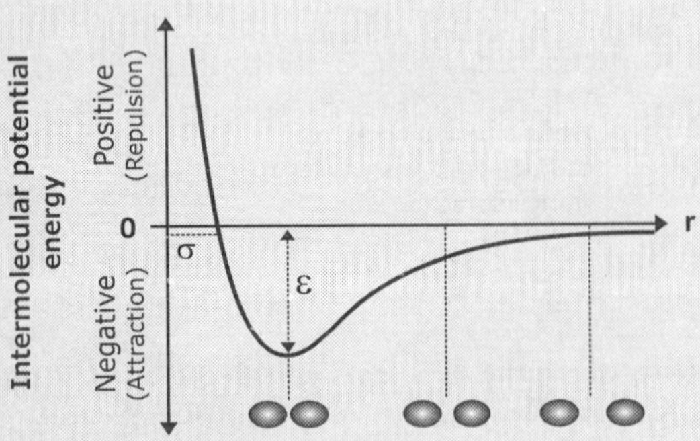

ε a measure of how strongly the two molecules attract each other.

σ the distance at which the intermolecular potential between the two molecules is zero.

r the distance of separation between both molecules.

Figure 1.118 The intermolecular potential energy (IMPE) of van der Waals interactions based on the distance of separation.

Estimation of the intermolecular potential energy of van der Waals interactions:

$E_{PE} = 4\varepsilon[(\sigma/r)^{12} - (\sigma/r)^{6}]$

$(\sigma/r)^{12}$ term represents a short-range repulsion (Pauli exclusion)

$(\sigma/r)^{6}$ term represents an attractive van der Waals interaction

Hydrophobic interaction: Hydrophobic interaction (also called **hydrophobic effect** or **hydrophobic bond**) describes the forces that cause non-polar substances to cluster together to minimize their contact with water. This self-association is driven neither by mutual attraction nor by what is sometimes incorrectly referred to as *hydrophobic bonds*. Hydrophobic interactions arise because water molecules prefer to interact with each other rather than with non-polar substances. Molecules in aqueous solution interact with water molecules through the formation of hydrogen bonds and other electrostatic interactions. However, non-polar molecules cannot participate in hydrogen bonding or other electrostatic interactions.

The interactions of non-polar molecules with water are not as favorable as are interactions between the water molecules themselves. When non-polar molecules enter an aqueous environment, hydrogen-bonded water molecules attempt to form a cage-like structure around them and becoming more ordered than water molecules free in solution. The number of ordered water molecules is proportional to the surface area of the non-polar molecules enclosed within the cage of water molecules. The ordering of water molecules reduces entropy. The free-energy change for dissolving a nonpolar solute in water is thus unfavorable ($\Delta G = \Delta H - T\Delta S$). However, when two such non-polar molecules come together, some of the water molecules are released, allowing them to interact freely with bulk water. The water molecules that initially 'caged' the non-polar molecules are released from the non-polar molecules' surfaces, creating an increase in entropy in the surrounding. The favorable release of water molecules from non-polar surfaces is responsible for phenomenon of the hydrophobic effect. Hydrophobic interactions have a profound effect on living cells. For example, they are primarily responsible for the structure of membranes and the stability of proteins.

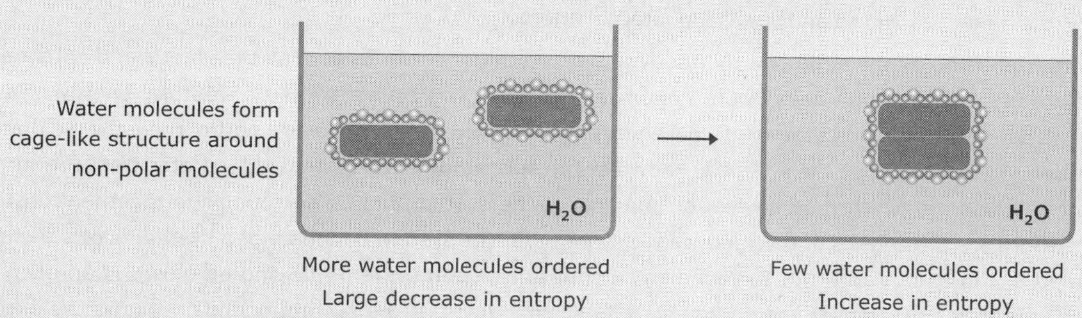

Figure 1.119 Thermodynamics of hydrophobic force.

The strength of hydrophobic interactions depends on temperature (decrease with decreasing temperatures), the number of carbons in non-polar molecules (increase with an increasing number of carbons) and the shape of molecules (aliphatic organic molecules have stronger interactions than aromatic molecules).

Problem

The electrostatic interaction energy between a positively charged atom A and negatively charged atom B separated by 3 Å in water is −6 kJ/mol. If the relative permittivity of water to be 80, what will be the electrostatic interaction energy in kJ/mol between atoms A and B in vacuum?

Solution: Coulomb's law in physics states that the electrostatic force between two charged particles is proportional to the product of the amount of charge of the particles divided by the square of the separation distance between them.

Electrostatic interaction energy, $E = \frac{1}{4\pi\varepsilon}\left[\frac{q_1 q_2}{r^2}\right]$ where, ε = permittivity of the medium.

The electrostatic force acting between nearby electrically charged bodies is inversely proportional to the permittivity of the medium. The relative permittivity (ε_r) of any medium is defined as the ratio of force acting between nearby electrically charged bodies in the vacuum to the force acting between the same bodies separated by the same distance in the medium. Hence, $\varepsilon_r = \varepsilon_w/\varepsilon_v$ where, ε_w = permittivity of the water and ε_v = permittivity of the vacuum.

$$\frac{E_v}{E_w} = \frac{\varepsilon_w}{\varepsilon_v} \qquad \text{Hence, } E_v = \frac{\varepsilon_w}{\varepsilon_v} \times E_w = (-6) \times 80 \text{ kJ/mol} = 480 \text{ kJ/mol}$$

Bioenergetics

A living cell is a dynamic chemical system. It requires energy to perform cellular work. Cells extract, transform, and use energy. The ability to harness the energy and channel it into biological work is a fundamental property of all living organisms. It is believed that an evolved and the adapted biological system converts energy in the most efficient manner. **Bioenergetics** is the study of energy flow in living systems, grounded in the principles of thermodynamics and redox chemistry. **Thermodynamics** explains how biological processes are energetically feasible and how energy is transformed and conserved, while **redox reactions** serve as mechanisms for energy transfer within cells.

Living cells function as biochemical factories. All reactions and processes occurring in living cells follow the laws of thermodynamics. The **first law of thermodynamics** is the principle of the conservation of energy: for any physical or chemical change, the total amount of energy in the universe remains constant; energy may change form or it may be transported from one region to another, but it cannot be created or destroyed i.e., the total energy of a system, including surroundings, remains constant. Mathematically, it can be expressed as:

$$\Delta \mathbf{U} = \Delta \mathbf{q} - \Delta \mathbf{w}$$

ΔU is the change in internal energy, Δq is the heat exchanged from the surroundings and Δw is the work done by the system. If Δq is positive, heat has been transferred to the system, giving an increase in internal energy. When Δq is negative, heat has been transferred to the surroundings, giving a decrease in internal energy. When Δw is positive, work has been done by the system, giving a decrease in internal energy. When Δw is negative, work has been done by the surroundings, leading to an increase in internal energy.

Internal energy is the total energy of a thermodynamic system (the sum total of all the kinetic and potential energy of all the atoms, ions and molecules in the system). In practice, we cannot measure the total energy of a system. However, we can determine a change in internal energy (ΔU). A **system** is defined as a part of the universe that is under consideration. All space outside the system is known as the **surroundings**. A system is separated from the surrounding by a system boundary, which may be real or imaginary. The system and its surroundings together constitute the **universe.** There are three kinds of thermodynamic systems. If the system boundary of a system allows the exchange of both matter and energy with the surrounding, then it is an **open system**. A living organism is an open system; it exchanges both matter (mass) and energy with its surroundings. If the system boundary allows the exchange of energy but does not matter with the surrounding, the system is considered as a **closed system** with constant mass. If the system boundary doesn't allow the exchange of both matter and energy with the surrounding, the system is considered an **isolated system.**

	Open system	Closed system	Isolated system
Exchange of mass with surroundings	Yes	No	No
Exchange of energy with surroundings	Yes	Yes	No

Concept of entropy

The universal tendency of the system to become disordered. The amount of disorder in a system can be quantified and expressed as the entropy of the system: the greater the disorder, the greater the entropy. The **second law of thermodynamics** introduces the concept of entropy. An organized or ordered state is a low-entropy state, whereas a disordered state is a high-entropy state. It is the quantity that increases in any spontaneous process. This law states that in any isolated system (a collection of matter that is completely isolated from the rest of the universe), the degree of disorder always increases.

A living cell represents complex organized system. If the cell generating order, it means it might appear to defy the second law of thermodynamics, a fundamental law of physics. How is this possible? The answer is that a cell is not an isolated system: it takes in energy from its environment in the form of food or light. It then uses this energy to generate order within itself. In the course of the chemical reactions that generate order, the cell converts part of the energy into heat. The heat is discharged into the cell's surrounding environment and disorders the surroundings. As a result, the total entropy—that of the cell plus its surroundings—increases, as demanded by the second law of thermodynamics. Mathematically, second law of thermodynamics can be expressed as:

$$\Delta S \geq \Delta q/T$$

where, ΔS is the any change in randomness of the system.

Entropy is unavailable form of energy and it is very difficult to determine it, so a new thermodynamic term called *free energy* is defined. **Free energy** (or **Gibbs free energy**) indicates the portion of the total energy of a system that is available for useful work. It is not possible to measure absolute values of free energy; only the changes in free energy that occur during a process can be measured. Under constant temperature and pressure, the relationship between free energy change (ΔG) of a reacting system and the change in entropy (ΔS) is expressed by following equation:

$$\Delta G = \Delta H - T\Delta S$$

where, ΔH is the change in enthalpy and T is the absolute temperature.

ΔH is the measure of change in **enthalpy** i.e., heat content of reactants and products (reflecting the kinds and numbers of covalent bonds and non-covalent interactions broken and formed). When chemical reaction releases heat, it is said to be **exothermic**; the heat content of the products is less than that of the reactants and ΔH has, by convention, a negative value. Chemical reactions that take up heat from their surroundings are **endothermic** and have positive values of ΔH.

Gibbs free energy and the spontaneity of chemical reactions

How can we predict the spontaneity of chemical reactions? A reaction is said to be **spontaneous** if it occurs without outside intervention. A spontaneous reaction proceed downhill and can be fast or slow. Spontaneous does not mean fast. With spontaneity, we are considering whether a process will occur, but can say nothing about the rate at which it will occur. Spontaneous process may also require energy to overcome an activation barrier. This means that some processes may be spontaneous, but do not occur at a noticeable rate. The most useful criterion for predicting the spontaneity of a process is the free energy. The change in free energy associated with a chemical reaction is a useful indicator of whether the reaction will proceed spontaneously. A *spontaneous reaction* is one that releases free energy. Hence, for a spontaneous reaction ΔG must be negative. Since ΔH and ΔS can be either positive or negative, depending on the characteristics of a particular reaction, there are four different outcomes for ΔG:

ΔH	ΔS	ΔG
Negative value (exothermic)	Positive value (increase disorder)	Always negative
Positive value (endothermic)	Positive value (increase disorder)	Negative at higher temperatures
Negative value (exothermic)	Negative value (decrease disorder)	Negative at lower temperatures
Positive value (endothermic)	Negative value (decrease disorder)	Always positive

Spontaneity is concerned only with whether the reaction is thermodynamically favorable (that is, ΔG is negative) or not. The free energy of a system decreases in a spontaneous (energy-releasing) process, so ΔG is negative ($\Delta G < 0$). Such a process is called **exergonic**, meaning that energy is released. Contrary to this, in a *non-spontaneous process,* the change in free energy is positive ($\Delta G > 0$); energy must be supplied for the process to occur. Non-spontaneous processes are **endergonic**, meaning that energy is absorbed. If ΔG is equal to 0, the process is at equilibrium, and there is no net flow either in the forward or reverse direction.

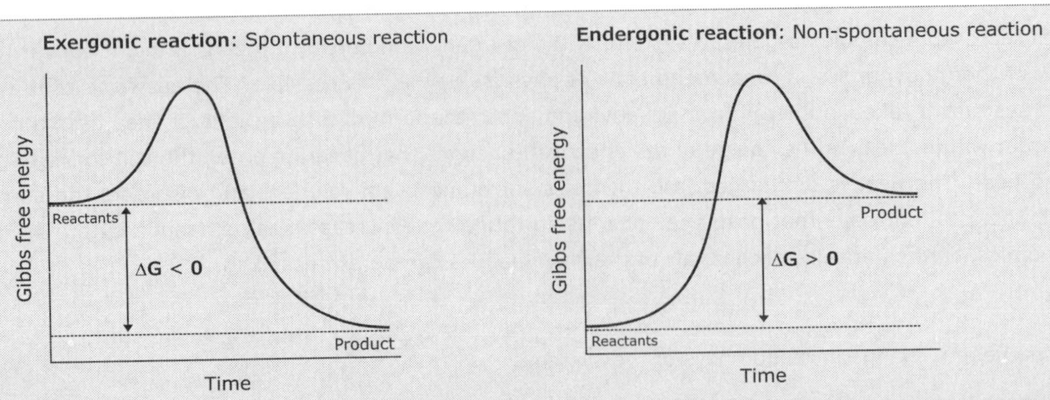

The change in the free energy, ΔG, can be used to predict the direction of a reaction at constant temp and pressure. If,

ΔG is *negative*, the reaction proceeds spontaneously with the loss of free energy (**exergonic**).

ΔG is *positive*, the reaction proceeds only when free energy can be gained (**endergonic**).

ΔG is 0, the system is at **equilibrium**; both forward and reverse reactions occur at equal rates.

The free energy change, ΔG, for any reaction depends upon the nature of the reactants and products, but it is also affected by the conditions of the reaction, including temperature, pressure, pH, and the concentrations of the reactants and products. The ΔG for a reaction can be expressed in terms of the equilibrium concentrations of the reactants and products. For a reaction A → B, ΔG at constant temperature and pressure can be expressed as:

$$\Delta G = \Delta G^0 + RT \ln \frac{[B]}{[A]}$$

where, ΔG^0 is the standard free energy change, R is the gas constant, T is the absolute temperature and [A] and [B] are the actual concentrations of reactant and product. ΔG^0 for any reaction is a fixed value. In contrast, ΔG is a variable and can be calculated for any set of product and reactant concentrations.

Relationship between standard free energy change and equilibrium constant

The tendency of a chemical reaction to go to completion can be expressed as an equilibrium constant. In a reaction $A \rightleftharpoons B$, a point of *equilibrium* is reached at which no further net chemical change takes place–that is, when A is being converted to B, B is also being converted to A, as fast as A into B. In this state, the ratio of [B] to [A] is constant, regardless of the actual concentrations of the two compounds:

$$K_{eq} = \frac{[B]_{eq}}{[A]_{eq}}$$

K_{eq} is the equilibrium constant and $[A]_{eq}$ and $[B]_{eq}$ are the concentrations of A and B at equilibrium.

The concentration of reactants and products at equilibrium defines the **equilibrium constant,** K_{eq}. The equilibrium constant K_{eq} depends on the nature of reactants and products, the temperature and the pressure. Under standard physical conditions (25°C and 1 atm pressure, for biological systems), the K_{eq} is always the same for a given reaction, whether or not a catalyst is present. Here we should note that *equilibrium does not always mean that half of the reactants have converted into products; rather, it is the point when no net conversion in any direction is taking place and therefore, the concentration of reactants or products remain unchanged.*

If the reaction $A \rightleftharpoons B$ is allowed to go to equilibrium at constant temperature and pressure, then at equilibrium the overall free energy change (ΔG) is zero. Therefore,

$$\Delta G = \Delta G^0 + RT \ln \frac{[B]_{eq}}{[A]_{eq}}$$

$$0 = \Delta G^0 + RT \ln \frac{[B]_{eq}}{[A]_{eq}}$$

$$\Delta G^0 = -RT \ln \frac{[B]_{eq}}{[A]_{eq}} = -RT \ln K_{eq}$$

Relationship between K_{eq}, ΔG^0 and the direction of chemical reactions under standard conditions

K_{eq}	ΔG^0	Direction of reaction
> 1.0	Negative	the reaction will proceed in forward direction (right)
= 1.0	Zero	the reaction is at equilibrium
< 1.0	Positive	the reaction will proceed in reverse direction (left)

As we know, the ionic composition of an acid or base varies with pH. So, the standard free energy calculated according to the biochemistry convention is valid only at pH=7. Hence, under biochemistry convention, ΔG^0 is symbolized by $\Delta G^{0\prime}$ and likewise, the biochemical equilibrium constant is represented by K'_{eq}.

So, $\Delta G^{0\prime} = -RT \ln K'_{eq}$

However, all reactions do not take place at standard conditions. A relationship has been worked out by which a distinction can be made between $\Delta G^{0\prime}$ and the actual free energy change, ΔG. ΔG is defined as $\Delta G^{0\prime}$ (standard conditions) plus whatever difference occurs in ΔG on moving to nonstandard conditions.

$$\Delta G = \Delta G^{0\prime} + RT \ln \frac{[\text{Product}]}{[\text{Reactant}]}$$

If concentration of products and reactants is unity, then $\Delta G = \Delta G^{0\prime}$. So, standard free energy change, $\Delta G^{0\prime}$, is the change in free energy when products and reactants are present in unit concentration. In all spontaneous biochemical reaction, the free energy of the reacting system ΔG is negative, but $\Delta G^{0\prime}$ may be *positive*, *negative* or *zero* depending upon the equilibrium constant of the reaction.

Problem

The equilibrium constant, K_{eq}, for the breakdown of ATP to ADP and P_i is 2.22×10^5 M. Calculate the standard free-energy change, for the synthesis of ATP from ADP and P_i at 25°C.

Solution: We should first calculate standard free-energy change (ΔG^0) for the breakdown of ATP to ADP and P_i.

$\Delta G^0 = -RT \ln K_{eq} = -(8.31 \text{ J/mol.K}) \times 298 \text{ K} \times (\ln 2.22 \times 10^5) = -30459.47 \text{ J/mol} = -30.5 \text{ kJ/mol}$

The standard free-energy change for the synthesis of ATP has the same value but the opposite sign. Hence, the standard free-energy change for the synthesis of 1 mol of ATP under standard conditions (25°C, 1 M concentrations of ATP, ADP, and P_i) is therefore 30.5 kJ/mol.

Standard free-energy changes of coupled reactions are additive

According to thermodynamics principles, the overall free-energy change for a chemically coupled series of reactions is equal to the sum of the free energy changes of the individual steps. For example, in the case of two sequential chemical reactions, $A \rightleftharpoons B$ and $B \rightleftharpoons C$, each reaction has its own equilibrium constant and characteristic standard free energy change, $\Delta G_1^{0\prime}$ and $\Delta G_2^{0\prime}$. As the two reactions are sequential, B cancels out to give the overall reaction $A \rightleftharpoons C$, which has its own equilibrium constant and thus its own standard free-energy change, $\Delta G^{0\prime}_{total}$. For the overall reaction $A \rightleftharpoons C$, $\Delta G^{0\prime}_{total}$ is the sum of individual standard free-energy changes, $\Delta G_1^{0\prime}$ and $\Delta G_2^{0\prime}$, of the two reactions: $\Delta G^{0\prime}_{total} = \Delta G_1^{0\prime} + \Delta G_2^{0\prime}$.

	$A \rightleftharpoons B$	Standard free energy change = $\Delta G_1{}^{0\prime}$
	$B \rightleftharpoons C$	Standard free energy change = $\Delta G_2{}^{0\prime}$
Overall reaction	$A \rightleftharpoons C$	Standard free energy change = $\Delta G^{0\prime}{}_{total} = \Delta G_1{}^{0\prime} + \Delta G_2{}^{0\prime}$

Free energy change for ATP hydrolysis

ATP is the chemical link between catabolism and anabolism. It is the energy currency of living cells. It acts as a donor of high-energy phosphate. Its central role in energy metabolism was first explained by Fritz Lipmann and Herman Kalckar. ATP consists of an adenosine (adenine + ribose) to which three phosphoryl groups are sequentially linked via a **phosphoester bond** followed by two **phosphoanhydride bonds**. In aqueous condition, the phosphoanhydride bonds of ATP cleave with the incorporation of water.

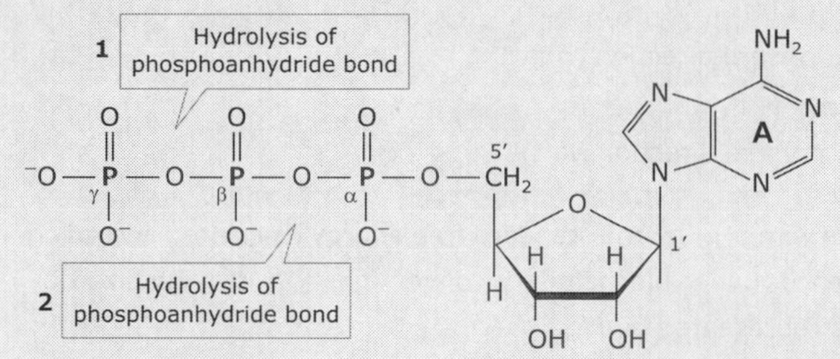

$$1 \quad ATP + H_2O \rightleftharpoons ADP + P_i \text{ (Orthophosphate, } PO_4^{3-}\text{)}$$

$$2 \quad ATP + H_2O \rightleftharpoons AMP + PP_i \text{ (Pyrophosphate, } P_2O_7^{4-}\text{)}$$

ATP contains two high energy phosphate groups and ADP contains one, whereas the phosphate in AMP is of the low energy type, since it is a normal ester link. A large amount of free energy is liberated when ATP is hydrolyzed to ADP and P_i or when ATP is hydrolyzed to AMP and PP_i. Bonds whose hydrolysis proceeds with large negative values of $\Delta G°'$ are often referred to as 'high-energy' bonds or 'energy-rich' bonds.

Compound	**Standard free energy change, $\Delta G^{0\prime}$**
$ATP + H_2O \rightleftharpoons ADP + P_i$	-30.5 kJ mol^{-1} (-7.3 kcal mol^{-1})
$ATP + H_2O \rightleftharpoons AMP + PP_i$	-45.6 kJ mol^{-1} (-10.9 kcal mol^{-1})

The standard free energy change of ATP hydrolysis is large and negative. These negative free energy values are often referred to as *phosphoryl transfer potentials*; they are a measure of the tendency of phosphorylated compounds to transfer their phosphoryl groups to water.

ATP has a stronger tendency to transfer its terminal phosphoryl group to water i.e., a higher phosphoryl transfer potential. The $\Delta G°'$ values for hydrolysis of several phosphorylated compounds of biochemical importance are tabulated in **table 1.25.** The negatives of these values are often referred to as **phosphoryl transfer potentials**; they are a measure of the tendency of phosphorylated compounds to transfer their phosphoryl groups to water.

Table 1.25 Standard free energies of hydrolysis of some phosphate compounds at pH 7

Phosphates	**Type of phosphate bond**	**$\Delta G^{0\prime}$ for hydrolysis** (kcal/mol)
Phosphoenolpyruvate	Enol phosphate bond	-14.8
1,3-bisphosphoglycerate	Anhydride bond to carbon	-11.7
Creatine phosphate	Phosphate bond	-10.3
Adenosine triphosphate	Phosphoanhydride bond	-7.3
Glucose-6-phosphate	Phosphoester bond	-3.3
Glycerol phosphate	Phosphoester bond	-2.2

The actual free energy change of hydrolysis of ATP in living cells is different because the cellular concentration of ATP, ADP and P_i are not only unequal, but also not 1.0 M concentration. For example, in human erythrocytes, the concentrations of ATP, ADP, and P_i are 2.25, 0.25, and 1.65 mM, respectively. The concentrations of ATP, ADP, and P_i also differ from one cell type to another. Thus, the *actual* free energy of hydrolysis of ATP under intracellular conditions differs from the standard free energy change. The actual free energy change (-52 kJ mol^{-1}) of hydrolysis of ATP is much larger than the standard free energy change (-30.5 kJ mol^{-1}).

Phosphagens also act as storage forms of high energy phosphate and include **creatine phosphate** (in vertebrate skeletal muscle, heart and brain) and **arginine phosphate** (in invertebrate muscle). When ATP is rapidly being utilized as a source of energy, phosphagens permit its concentration to be maintained. But, when the ATP/ADP ratio is high, their concentration can increase to act as a source of high energy phosphate. At pH 7, the standard free energy of hydrolysis of creatine phosphate is -10.3 kcal mol^{-1}, compared with -7.3 kcal mol^{-1} for ATP.

$$\text{Creatine phosphate} \underset{\text{ADP} \rightarrow \text{ATP}}{\overset{\textit{Creatine kinase}}{\rightleftharpoons}} \text{Creatine} \qquad \Delta G^{0'} = -10.3 \text{ kcal mol}^{-1}.$$

Redox reaction

A redox reaction (oxidation-reduction) is a chemical reaction involving both oxidation and reduction, resulting in changes in the oxidation numbers of participating chemical species, which can be atoms, ions, molecules, or radicals.

- **Oxidation** is the process where a chemical species loses electrons, resulting in an increase in its oxidation number.
- **Reduction** is the process where a chemical species gains electrons, leading to a decrease in its oxidation number.

If there is no change in oxidation number (or oxidation state), then there is no redox reaction. In a redox reaction, one species loses electrons while the other gains them. The species that gains the electrons is said to be reduced, while the species that loses the electrons is said to be oxidized. The electron-donating molecule in a redox reaction is called the **reducing agent** or **reductant**, and the electron-accepting molecule is called the **oxidizing agent** or **oxidant**. Although oxidation and reduction must occur together, it is convenient to divide redox reaction into two half-reactions. For example, the oxidation of ferrous ion by cupric ion,

$$Fe^{2+} + Cu^{2+} \rightleftharpoons Fe^{3+} + Cu^{+}$$

It can be described in terms of two half-reactions:

$$Fe^{2+} \rightleftharpoons Fe^{3+} + e^{-} \qquad \text{(Oxidation)}$$

$$Cu^{2+} + e^{-} \rightleftharpoons Cu^{+} \qquad \text{(Reduction)}$$

Reduction potential

It is a measure of the tendency of a chemical species to gain electrons and be reduced. It is also called the **redox potential** or **oxidation-reduction potential**. Reduction potentials are measured in volts (V). The value of reduction potential for a chemical species under standard conditions is its **standard reduction potential** (E°). The superscript '°' on the E denotes standard conditions (1 atm pressure, 1 M concentration of the reactants, and at 25°C temperature). The reduction potential varies with changes in concentration, temperature, and pressure. The reduction potential of a chemical species under non-standard conditions is called the **actual reduction potential** (E). Walther Nernst derived an equation (called **Nernst equation**) that relates standard reduction potential (E°) to the actual reduction potential (E) at any concentration of oxidized and reduced species in a living cell:

$$E = E^{0} + \frac{RT}{nF} \ln \frac{[\text{Electron acceptor}]}{[\text{Electron donor}]}$$

Where, n is the number of electrons transferred per molecule, and F is the Faraday constant.

Standard reduction potentials are measured relative to the **standard hydrogen electrode** (SHE), which serves as a reference electrode and is assigned a potential of zero volts (0 V) under standard conditions. A higher reduction potential means a greater tendency to gain electrons and undergo reduction. In a redox reaction, the substance with the higher reduction potential will be reduced (gain electrons), and the substance with the lower reduction potential will be oxidized (lose electrons). A strong reducing agent is poised to donate electrons and has a negative reduction potential, whereas a strong oxidizing agent is ready to accept electrons and has a positive reduction potential.

The **standard oxidation potential** is similar to the standard reduction potential. It is the tendency for a species to be oxidized under standard conditions. The standard oxidation potential and the standard reduction potential are opposite in sign for the same chemical species. For example, if the standard reduction potential of Fe^{3+} is +0.77 V, its oxidation potential is −0.77 V.

Free energy changes in redox reactions

Standard reduction potentials can be used to calculate the free-energy change of an oxidation–reduction reaction. Standard reduction potentials (E°) measure the tendency of a species to gain electrons and undergo reduction, while free energy change ($\Delta G°$) quantifies the spontaneity of a reaction, determining whether it will occur spontaneously or not. These two concepts are linked through the following equation.

$$\Delta G^0 = -nF\Delta E^0$$

where,

$\Delta G°$ is the standard free energy change (in Joules)

n is the number of moles of electrons transferred in the redox reaction

F is Faraday's constant (approximately 96485 C/mol)

E° is the standard cell potential (in volts), which is the potential difference between the two half-cells under standard conditions.

With this equation we can calculate the actual free-energy change for any redox reaction from the values of $\Delta E°$ in a table of reduction potentials and the concentrations of reacting species.

Table 1.26 The standard reduction potentials of some biologically important redox systems

Redox System	Half-Reaction	E° (V)
Oxygen molecule	$O_2 + 4H^+ + 4e^- \rightarrow 2H_2O$	+1.23
$NAD^+/NADH$	$NAD^+ + H^+ + 2e^- \rightarrow NADH$	−0.32
$FAD/FADH_2$	$FAD + 2H^+ + 2e^- \rightarrow FADH_2$	−0.22
Ubiquinone/Ubiquinol	$Q + 2H^+ + 2e^- \rightarrow QH_2$	+0.045
Ferricyanide/Ferrocyanide	$Fe(CN)_6^{3-} + e^- \rightarrow Fe(CN)_6^{4-}$	+0.36
Cytochrome b (Fe^{3+}/Fe^{2+})	Cyt b (Fe^{3+}) + e^- → Cyt b (Fe^{2+})	+0.03
Pyruvate/Lactate	Pyruvate + $2H^+ + 2e^-$ → Lactate	−0.19
Thioredoxin disulfide/Thioredoxin	$Trx\text{-}S_2 + 2H^+ + 2e^- \rightarrow 2\ Trx\text{-}SH$	−0.26
Glutathione reductase ($FAD/FADH_2$)	$FAD + 2H^+ + 2e^- \rightarrow FADH_2$	−0.22

The above table lists various redox couples and their corresponding standard reduction potentials (E°). A higher E° value indicates a stronger oxidizing agent, while a lower E° value indicates a stronger reducing agent.

Colligative properties

Colligative properties are special physical properties of solutions that depend entirely on the quantity (number) of dissolved solutes—whether molecules or ions—present in a given amount of solvent, and not on the nature of the solutes. This means that if two solutions have the same quantity of solutes per unit volume, they will show the same colligative effects, even if the solutes are chemically different. The addition of solutes changes the solution's vapor pressure, and its boiling point and freezing point are altered in predictable ways. The three main colligative properties are:

Relative lowering of vapor pressure – Adding solute lowers the solvent's vapor pressure.

Boiling point elevation – A solution boils at a higher temperature than the pure solvent.

Freezing point depression – A solution freezes at a lower temperature than the pure solvent.

Self Test

Q1. An amino acid has one proton donating group in the side chain (R). The pK_1, pK_2 and pK_R values for this amino acid are 2.19, 9.67 and 4.25, respectively. Which one of the following statements about this amino acid is *correct*?

a. Majority of the molecules will have a net charge of −1 at pH of 7.0.

b. Majority of the molecules will have a net charge of 0 at pH of 4.25.

c. All the molecules will have a deprotonated R group at pH of 3.22.

d. During titration with a strong base, deprotonation will start with the R group.

Q2. The isoelectric point of an enzyme is 6. It was observed that at this point there are 5 positively and 5 negatively charged side chains of amino acids. When the enzyme solution was titrated with HCl to pH 3, it was observed that two ionized aspartate chains got protonated. The net charge on the enzyme at pH 3 would therefore be

a. +3 b. +2

c. −3 d. −2

Q3. DNA polymerase contains a lysine residue that is important for binding to DNA. Mutations were found that converted this lysine to either glutamate, glycine, valine or arginine. Which mutations would be predicted to be the most and least harmful to the ability of the enzyme to bind DNA?

	Most	**Least**
a.	Glycine	Arginine
b.	Arginine	Glycine
c.	Glutamate	Valine
d.	Glutamate	Arginine

Q4. Match the entries in Column A against those in Column B

Column A	**Column B**
P. The amino acid with maximum number of codons.	1. Cys
Q. The characteristic amino acid in lysozyme active site.	2. Trp
R. The amino acid precursor in heme biosynthesis.	3. Ser
S. The amino acid contributing the most to protein absorbance at 280 nm.	4. Gly
	5. Glu

a. P-2, Q-3, R-1, S-4 b. P-3, Q-5, R-4, S-2

c. P-5, Q-3, R-2, S-1 d. P-4, Q-1, R-5, S-3

Q5. Myoglobin shows a hyperbolic response, while hemoglobin shows a sigmoidal response for oxygen binding. Which of the following statements are *true* with respect to this observation?

P. Hemoglobin binds 2,3-BPG while myoglobin does not.

Q. Hemoglobin exists in two different conformational states while myoglobin does not.

R. Hemoglobin is a tetramer while myoglobin is a monomer.

S. Hemoglobin is present in RBCs while myoglobin is present in the muscle.

a. R and S b. P and S

c. P and Q d. Q and R

Q6. Which of the following covalent bond types are found in the structure of ATP?

a. *N*-glycosidic, thioester, phosphodiester bond.

b. Phosphoanhydride, phosphomonoester, N-glycosidic bond.

c. Ester, ether, phosphoanhydride bond.

d. Ether, thioester, phosphomonoester bond.

Q7. In an individual, three distinct proteins bind oxygen depending on the location and developmental stage. While hemoglobin is the major oxygen binding protein in adults, myoglobin is present in skeletal muscles and fetal hemoglobin is present in fetal stage only. The following graph shows the oxygen dissociation curve of these proteins. The curves A, B and C represent oxygen dissociation curve of

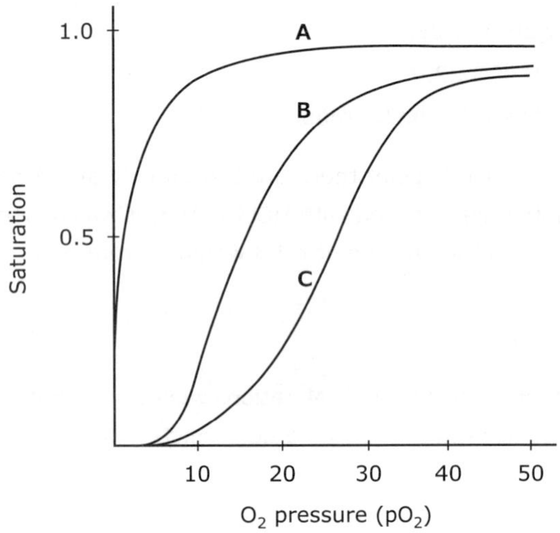

a. hemoglobin, fetal hemoglobin and myoglobin, respectively

b. fetal hemoglobin, hemoglobin and myoglobin, respectively

c. hemoglobin, myoglobin and fetal hemoglobin, respectively

d. myoglobin, fetal hemoglobin and hemoglobin, respectively

Q8. An amino acid has a non-ionizable R group. The pK_a for the NH_2 group is 9.4 and for the COOH group is 2.8. Consider the following statements:

P. At pH of 6.1, 50% of the amino acid residues migrate towards the cathode when placed between two electrodes.

Q. At a pH of 2.8, 50% of the amino acid residues in solution are zwitterions.

R. The pI of the amino acid is 6.1.

S. On titration of amino acids with NaOH, the amino group is deprotonated before the carboxylic group.

Which pair of the above statements is *correct*?

a. Q and R

b. P and S

c. P and R

d. Q and S

Q9. Purified duplex DNA molecules cannot exist in which one of the following forms?

a. Linear

b. Circular and supercoiled

c. Linear and supercoiled

d. Circular and relaxed

Q10. You have obtained a sample of DNA, and you transcribe mRNA from this DNA and purify it. You then separate the two strands of the DNA and analyze the base composition of each strand and of the mRNA. You obtain the data shown in the table below. Which strand of the DNA is serving as a template for mRNA synthesis?

	A	G	C	T	U
DNA strand 1	19.1	26.0	31.0	23.9	0
DNA strand 2	24.2	30.8	25.7	19.3	0
mRNA	19.0	25.9	30.8	0	24.3

a. Strand 1

b. Strand 2

c. Both strands 1 and 2

d. Neither strand 1 nor 2

Q11. NAD^+

P. is a flavin nucleotide.

Q. is the major electron acceptor used in metabolism.

R. contains a nicotinamide ring that accepts a hydride ion during reduction.

S. is a derivative of adenosine.

a. P and S

b. P, Q and R

c. Q, R and S

d. P, Q, R and S

Q12. Which of the following is *not* true? When RNA undergoes for alkali-catalyzed cleavage

a. transesterification reaction occurs.

b. cyclic 2′-3′-nucleoside monophosphate forms.

c. cyclic 5′-3′-nucleoside monophosphate forms.

d. 2′-OH is converted into 2′-alkoxide ion.

Q13. A student discovers and purifies an enzyme. From the table given below, find the *correct* statement/s.

Step	**Procedure**	**Total protein** (mg)	**Activity** (units)
1.	Crude extract	20,000	4000,000
2.	Precipitation (salting out)	5,000	3000,000
3.	Precipitation (isoelectric precipitation)	4,000	1000,000
4.	Ion exchange chromatography	200	800,000
5.	Affinity chromatography	50	750,000
6.	Size exclusion chromatography	45	675,000

a. Step 4 of the purification procedures is most effective step.

b. Step 4 gives the greatest increase in the specific activity.

c. The specific activity did not increase further after step 5.

d. All of the above statements are correct.

Q14. Which among the following statements are *correct*?

P. Linking number of nicked 2100 bp circular plasmid is 200.

Q. Linking number is sum of twist and writhe.

R. Twist and writhe always need to be integer values.

S. Linking number is a topological property.

a. P and R

b. Q and S

c. Q and R

d. P and S

Q15. Which of the following statements about allosteric enzymes are *correct*?

P. They are a class of regulatory enzymes.

Q. They function through reversible, noncovalent binding of modulators.

R. Most allosteric enzymes are oligomeric.

S. They don't obey Michaelis-Menten kinetics.

a. Q, R and S

b. P and S

c. P, R and S

d. P, Q, R and S

Q16. Which of the following fatty acids has the lowest melting point?

a. Fatty acids with sites of unsaturation with *cis* double bonds.

b. Fatty acids with sites of unsaturation with *trans* double bonds.

c. Fatty acids with no sites of unsaturation.

d. Fatty acids with longer hydrophobic tails.

Q17. Consider the following three groups

Group I : Vitamin

Group II : Coenzyme form

Group III : Reaction perform

Group I	Group II	Group III
P. B_2	1. TPP	A. Acyl group transfer
Q. B_6	2. FAD	B. Redox reaction
R. B_5	3. Pyridoxal phosphate	C. Aldehyde group transfer
S. B_1	4. Coenzyme A	D. Amino group transfer

a. P-1-B, Q-3-D, R-2-C, S-4-A
b. P-2-B, Q-3-D, R-4-A, S-1-C
c. P-3-D, Q-2-B, R-1-A, S-4-C
d. P-4-C, Q-3-A, R-2-D, S-1-B

Q18. Which of the following statements about a plot of V versus substrate concentration for an enzyme that follows Michaelis-Menten kinetics is *false*?

a. K_m is the substrate concentration at which V = 1/2 V_{max}.
b. The shape of the curve is a hyperbola.
c. As substrate concentration increases, the initial velocity of reaction, V, also increases.
d. At very high substrate concentration, velocity curve becomes a horizontal line that intersects the y-axis at K_m.

Q19. Which of the following statements about the reversible enzyme inhibition is *incorrect*?

a. Non-competitive inhibition occurs when a substrate and an inhibitor binding site is same.
b. Competitive inhibition occurs when a substrate and an inhibitor compete for the active site on the enzyme.
c. Non-competitive inhibition of an enzyme cannot be overcome by adding large amounts of substrate.
d. Competitive inhibitors are often similar in chemical structure to the substrate of the inhibited enzyme.

Q20. A nonapeptide was determined to have the following amino acid composition: 2 Lys, 2 Gly, 2 Phe, His, Leu and Met. The native peptide was incubated with 1-fluoro-2,4-dinitrobenzene (FDNB) and then hydrolyzed; 2,4-dinitrophenylhistidine was identified by HPLC. When the native peptide was exposed to cyanogen bromide (CNBr), an octapeptide and free glycine were recovered. Incubation of the native peptide with trypsin gave a pentapeptide, a tripeptide, and free Lys. 2,4-Dinitrophenyl-histidine was recovered from the pentapeptide, and 2,4-dinitrophenylphenylalanine was recovered from the tripeptide. Digestion with the enzyme pepsin produced a dipeptide, a tripeptide, and a tetrapeptide. The tetrapeptide was composed of 2 Lys, Phe and Gly. The native sequence was determined to be:

a. Gly–Phe–Lys–Lys–Gly–Leu–Met–Phe–His.
b. His–Leu–Gly–Lys–Lys–Phe–Phe–Gly–Met.
c. His–Leu–Phe–Gly–Lys–Lys–Phe–Met–Gly.
d. His–Phe–Leu–Gly–Lys–Lys–Phe–Met–Gly.

ANSWER KEY

01. a	02. b	03. d	04. b	05. d	06. b	07. d	08. a	09. c	10. b
11. c	12. c	13. d	14. b	15. d	16. a	17. b	18. d	19. a	20. c

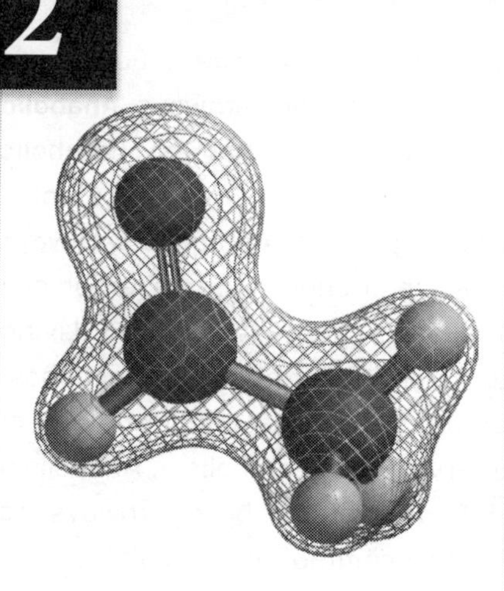

2 Metabolism

SUBJECT FOCUS

All cells function as biochemical factories. Within the living cell, biomolecules are constantly being synthesized and transformed into some other biomolecules. This synthesis and transformation constantly occur through enzyme-catalyzed chemical reactions. More than a thousand chemical reactions take place in a cell. Most of these chemical reactions do not occur in isolation but are always linked to some other reactions. All the interconnected chemical reactions occurring within a cell are called **metabolism** (derived from the Greek word for a *change*). Metabolism serves two fundamentally different purposes: 1. Generation of energy to drive vital functions and 2. Synthesis of biological molecules. The precursor is converted into a product during metabolic processes through a series of metabolic intermediates called **metabolites**. Cell metabolism is organized by enzymes. Enzyme-catalyzed reactions are connected in series so that the product of one reaction becomes the starting material, or substrate, for the next. The series of enzyme-catalyzed reactions transform substrates into end products through many specific chemical intermediates constitutes a **metabolic pathway**. Metabolism is sometimes referred to as **intermediary metabolism**. The term *intermediary metabolism* is often applied to the enzyme-catalyzed reactions that extract chemical energy from nutrient molecules and use it to synthesize and assemble cell components. The flow of metabolites through the metabolic pathway has a definite rate and direction. Metabolism is highly organized and regulated. Metabolic pathways are regulated through control of (1) the amounts of enzymes, (2) their catalytic activities, and (3) the availability of substrates. In multicellular organisms, the metabolic activities of different tissues are also regulated and integrated by growth factors and hormones that act from outside the cell.

Starting molecule A $\xrightarrow[\text{Reaction 1}]{\text{Enzyme 1}}$ B $\xrightarrow[\text{Reaction 2}]{\text{Enzyme 2}}$ C $\xrightarrow[\text{Reaction 3}]{\text{Enzyme 3}}$ D Product

Metabolism consists of energy-yielding and energy-requiring reactions. The oxidation of carbon compounds is an important source of cellular energy. An energy currency common to all life forms, ATP, links energy-releasing pathways with energy-requiring pathways. ATP serves as the principal immediate donor of free energy in biological systems rather than as a long-term storage form of free energy.

Metabolic pathways can be *linear* (such as glycolysis), *cyclic* (such as the citric acid cycle), or *spiral* (such as the biosynthesis of fatty acids). Metabolic pathways fall into two categories: Anabolic and catabolic pathways. **Anabolic pathways** are involved in synthesizing compounds and consuming energy (i.e., endergonic in nature). Catabolic pathways are characteristically energy-yielding, whereas anabolic pathways are energy-requiring. Synthesis of amino acids or synthesis of a polypeptide from amino acids is an example of an anabolic process. **Catabolic pathways** are involved in the oxidative breakdown of larger complex molecules and the release of energy (i.e., exergonic in nature). For example, when glucose is degraded to lactic acid in our skeletal muscle, energy is liberated. Living organisms have learned to trap this energy liberated during degradation and store it in the form of chemical bonds. As and when needed, this bond energy is utilized for biosynthetic and mechanical works. The most important form of energy currency in living systems is ATP. The generation of ATP is one of the primary roles of catabolism. Anabolism and catabolism occur simultaneously in the cell; they are not mutually exclusive. In general, catabolic pathways are convergent (catabolism of a large number of diverse substances converge on a few common intermediates) and anabolic pathways divergent (relatively few metabolites serve as starting materials for a host of varied products). Some pathways can be either anabolic or catabolic, depending on the energy conditions in the cell. They are referred to as **amphibolic pathways**. Amphibolic pathways occur at the 'crossroads' of metabolism, acting as links between the anabolic and catabolic pathways, e.g., the citric acid cycle.

Steady state system

A living system is not a closed system but an open system that can exchange both matter and energy with its surroundings. Because living organisms are **open systems**, they cannot be at equilibrium as long as they are alive. They can, however, achieve a *steady state*. A **steady state** system changes continually, but there is no net change in the system. In a metabolic pathway, steady state is maintained by balancing the rate of substrate provided by a previous step and the rate that the substrate is converted into a product, keeping substrate concentration relatively constant. The *steady state* and *equilibrium* are not same. In a reversible reaction, when the rate of forward and backward reactions are equal, then the reaction is said to be at **equilibrium**. It is important for you to understand that *equilibrium* means the *rates* of the forward and reverse reactions are equal; it does not mean that there are an equal amounts of reactants and products present at equilibrium. There can be a higher amount of reactants than the products or vice versa. Equilibrium is *dynamic* - both forward and reverse reactions continue, even though the reaction appears to have stopped.

An *equilibrium* can be considered as a special case of a steady state. If a system is in equilibrium, then it is definitely in a steady state, but the reverse is not necessarily true. That is if the system is in a steady state, it not necessarily in an equilibrium state. The living state is a non-equilibrium steady-state to be able to perform work. There is no net change over time in the concentrations of particular components such as ATP in a steady state, but they are being produced and degraded at constant rates. A constant supply of energy is required for maintaining steady state, as maintaining a constant concentration of a molecule preserves internal order and thus is entropically unfavorable. When a cell dies and no longer utilizes energy, its internal composition will proceed toward equilibrium with its surroundings.

2.1 Respiration

Living cells require an input of free energy. Energy is required for the maintenance of highly organized structures, synthesis of cellular components, movement, generation of electrical currents and many other processes. Cells acquire free energy from the **oxidation of organic compounds** that are rich in potential energy. Since all organisms use organic compounds for the source of energy, they must either make the organic compounds in a process like photosynthesis or they must obtain energy-containing organic compounds called *food* through diet. Only photosynthetic organisms can synthesize their own food (such as glucose) by the process of photosynthesis. Non-photosynthetic organisms such as animals cannot synthesize their own food. Hence, they obtain *food* from the diet.

Respiration is a metabolic process in which free energy released from the oxidation of organic compounds is used in the formation of ATP. The compounds that are oxidized during the process of respiration are known as **respiratory**

substrates, which may be carbohydrates, fats, proteins or organic acids. Carbohydrates are most commonly used as respiratory substrates. During cellular respiration, respiratory substrates such as glucose may undergo for complete or incomplete oxidation. In **complete oxidation**, respiratory substrates (usually carbohydrates) are oxidized completely to CO_2 and H_2O. In **incomplete** (or **partial**) **oxidation**, respiratory substrates are never totally oxidized. Hence, the energy generated through incomplete oxidation of respiratory substrates is lesser than that generated during complete oxidation.

2.1.1 Aerobic respiration

Respiration may be *oxygen-dependent* (aerobic respiration) and *oxygen-independent* (anaerobic respiration and fermentation). In aerobic respiration, molecular O_2 serves as the terminal (or final) acceptor of electrons. In this mode of respiration, complete oxidation of the respiratory substrate occurs, and the end products formed are primarily CO_2 and H_2O.

$$C_6H_{12}O_6 + 6 \times O_2 \longrightarrow 6 \times CO_2 + 6 \times H_2O + \text{Energy (ATP + Heat)}$$

Although carbohydrates, fats and proteins can all be oxidized as fuel, but here processes have been described by taking glucose as a respiratory substrate. Oxidation of glucose is an *exergonic process*. An **exergonic reaction** proceeds with a net release of free energy. During aerobic respiration, when one mole of glucose (180 g) is completely oxidized into CO_2 and water, approximately 2870 kJ or 686 kcal energy is liberated. Part of this energy is used for the synthesis of ATP. For each molecule of glucose degraded to carbon dioxide and water by respiration, the cell makes up to about 30 or 32 ATP molecules, each with 7.3 kcal/mol of free energy.

Not all organisms (or cells) require oxygen for oxidation of respiratory substrates. *Anaerobic respiration* and *fermentation* do not require oxygen for oxidation of respiratory substrates. In **anaerobic respiration**, compounds (such as sulfate, nitrate, sulphur, or fumarate) other than O_2 serves as a terminal electron acceptor. Both aerobic and anaerobic respiration involve electron transport system to establish an electrochemical proton gradient across a membrane and ATP synthesis occurs through both substrate-level phosphorylation and oxidative phosphorylation.

Fermentation, in contrast, does not involve electron transport system to establish an electrochemical proton gradient. Fermentation instead only uses substrate-level phosphorylation to produce ATP. The final electron acceptors are organic compounds often formed as a result of incomplete oxidation of organic substrates during the fermentation pathway itself.

Enzyme-catalyzed reactions during aerobic respiration can be grouped into three major processes: **glycolysis, citric acid cycle** and **oxidative phosphorylation**. Glycolysis takes place in the cytosol of cells in all living organisms. The citric acid cycle takes place within the mitochondrial matrix of eukaryotic cells and in the cytosol of prokaryotic cells. The oxidative phosphorylation takes place in the inner mitochondrial membrane. However, in prokaryotes, oxidative phosphorylation takes place in the plasma membrane.

Table 2.1 Intracellular location of major processes of aerobic respiration

In eukaryotes	
Glycolysis	Cytosol
Citric acid cycle	Mitochondrial matrix
Oxidative phosphorylation	Inner mitochondrial membrane
In prokaryotes	
Glycolysis	Cytosol
Citric acid cycle	Cytosol
Oxidative phosphorylation	Plasma membrane

2.1.2 Glycolysis

Glycolysis (from the Greek *glykys*, meaning *sweet*, and *lysis*, meaning *splitting*) also known as *Embden-Meyerhof pathway*, is a process in which one mole of glucose is partially oxidized into the two moles of pyruvate in a series of enzyme-catalyzed reactions. Glycolysis occurs in the cytosol of all cells. It is a unique pathway that occurs in both aerobic as well as anaerobic conditions and does not involve molecular oxygen i.e., *oxygen independent*.

Step 1 (**Phosphorylation**): Glucose is phosphorylated by ATP to form a glucose 6-phosphate (**G6P**). The negative charge of the phosphate prevents the passage of the glucose 6-phosphate through the plasma membrane, trapping glucose inside the cell. This *irreversible reaction* is catalyzed by *hexokinase*. In mammals, there are four hexokinases: I, II, III, and IV. Hexokinase I is present in all cells. Hepatocytes and pancreatic β-cells also contain **hexokinase IV**, commonly known as **glucokinase**. Hexokinase I can phosphorylate various hexose sugars (e.g., glucose and mannose), whereas glucokinase specifically uses glucose as its substrate. Glucokinase has a higher K_m and V_{max} compared to hexokinase I, indicating lower affinity but greater capacity at high glucose concentrations. The activity of hexokinase I is inhibited by G6P (negative allosteric modulator), whereas glucokinase is not.

Step 2 (**Isomerization**): A reversible rearrangement of the chemical structure (isomerization) moves the carbonyl oxygen from carbon 1 to carbon 2, forming a ketose from an aldose sugar. Thus, isomerization of glucose 6-phosphate to fructose 6-phosphate (**F6P**). is a conversion of an aldose into a ketose, catalyzed by enzyme *phosphoglucoisomerase*.

Step 3 (**Phosphorylation**): Fructose 6-phosphate is phosphorylated by ATP to fructose 1,6-bisphosphate (**FBP**). The prefix *bis-* in bisphosphate means that two separate monophosphate groups are present, whereas the prefix *di-* means that two phosphate groups are present and are connected by an anhydride bond. This *irreversible reaction* is catalyzed by an allosteric enzyme *phosphofructokinase-1* (PFK-1).

Step 4 (**Cleavage**): The fructose 1,6-bisphosphate is cleaved to produce two three-carbon molecules – *glyceraldehyde 3-phosphate* (**G3P**) and *dihydroxyacetone phosphate* (**DHAP**). This reaction is catalyzed by enzyme *aldolase*.

Step 5 (**Isomerization**): Only one of the two triose phosphates formed by aldolase—glyceraldehyde 3-phosphate – can be directly degraded in the subsequent reaction step of glycolysis. However, the other product, dihydroxyacetone phosphate, is rapidly and reversibly converted into glyceraldehyde 3-phosphate by the enzyme *triose phosphate isomerase*.

Step 6: The two molecules of glyceraldehyde 3-phosphate are oxidized. Enzyme *glyceraldehyde 3-phosphate dehydrogenase* catalyzes the conversion of glyceraldehyde 3-phosphate into 1,3-bisphosphoglycerate (**1,3-BPG**). The reaction occurs in two steps: first the **oxidation** of the aldehyde to a carboxylic acid by NAD^+ and second the **phosphorylation** of carboxylic acid by **inorganic phosphate** (HPO_4^{2-}). **Iodoacetate** is a potent inhibitor of *glyceraldehyde-3 phosphate dehydrogenase* because it forms a covalent derivative of the essential –SH group of the enzyme active site, rendering it inactive.

Step 7: In this step, high-energy phosphate group is transferred from 1,3-bisphosphoglycerate to ADP. This step is catalyzed by enzyme *phosphoglycerate kinase*. The formation of ATP is referred to as *substrate-level phosphorylation.* In **substrate-level phosphorylation**, ATP or GTP synthesis takes place through the direct transfer of a phosphoryl group from a 'high-energy' substrate to ADP or GDP. In red blood cells, a unique glycolytic bypass pathway occurs for the production of 2,3-bisphosphoglycerate (**2,3-BPG**), known as the **Rapoport-Luebering shunt**. This shunt bypasses the enzyme phosphoglycerate kinase catalyzed step and accounts for the synthesis of 2,3-BPG. This pathway involves two key enzymes – **mutase** (which converts 1,3-BPG into 2,3-BPG) and **phosphatase** (which dephosphorylates 2,3-BPG).

Step 8: The remaining phosphate ester linkage in 3-phosphoglycerate (**3PG**), which has a relatively low free energy of hydrolysis, is moved from carbon 3 to carbon 2 to form 2-phosphoglycerate (**2PG**).

Step 9: The removal of water from 2-phosphoglycerate results in the formation of phosphoenolpyruvate (**PEP**). The enzyme catalyzing this step is *enolase*, which is inhibited by *fluoride*.

Step 10: The transfer of the high-energy phosphate group that was generated in step 9 to ADP forms ATP (i.e., substrate-level phosphorylation). This step in glycolysis is the *irreversible* transfer of the phosphoryl group from phosphoenolpyruvate to ADP is catalyzed by *pyruvate kinase*. Pyruvate kinase requires K^+ and either Mg^{2+} or Mn^{2+}.

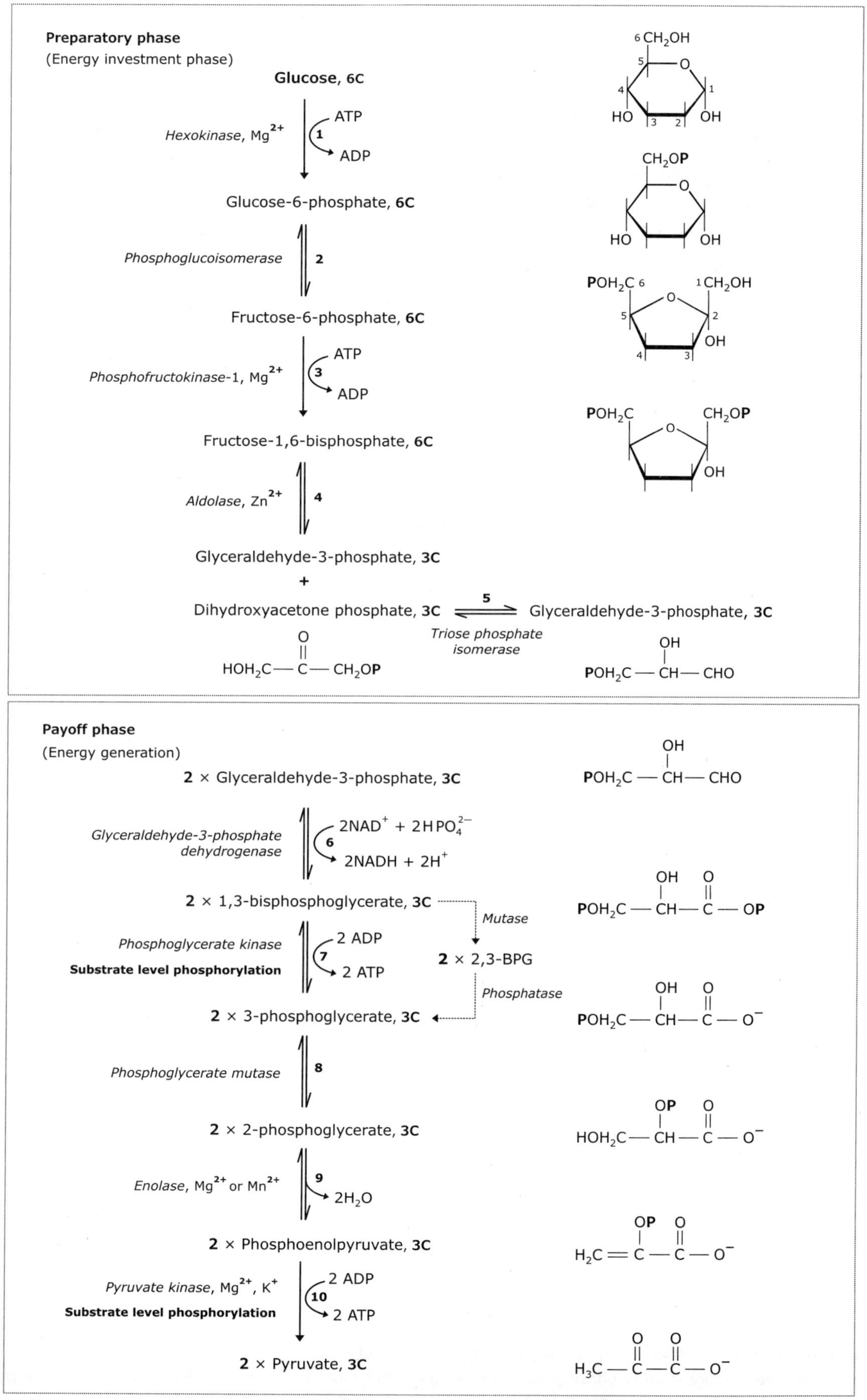

Net reaction: Glucose + $2\times NAD^+$ + $2\times ADP$ + $2\times HPO_4^{2-}$ $\longrightarrow$ $2\times$Pyruvate + $2\times NADH$ + $2\times ATP$ + $2\times H_2O$

Glycolysis: An overview

Glycolysis is the highly conserved ten-step metabolic pathway in which glucose is catabolized to pyruvate, leading to the formation of the ATP and NADH. All of the enzymes of glycolysis are found in the cytosol. Certain trypanosomes carry out the first seven reactions of glycolysis in an organized cytoplasmic organelles called **glycosome** (a peroxisome-related organelle). Three glycolytic reactions are irreversible. These reactions are catalyzed by hexokinase, phosphofructokinase-1 and pyruvate kinase. The breakdown of the six-carbon glucose into two molecules of the three-carbon pyruvate occurs in ten steps. The first five steps of this pathway constitute the **preparatory phase**. In this phase, energy is consumed as glucose is phosphorylated twice, and converted to fructose 1,6-bisphosphate (FBP). For both phosphorylations, ATP is the phosphoryl group donor. FBP is split to yield two three-carbon molecules. One of the products, dihydroxyacetone phosphate, is immediately converted to glyceraldehyde 3-phosphate (G3P). This yields two molecules of G3P, which are then converted to pyruvate in a five-step process of payoff phase.

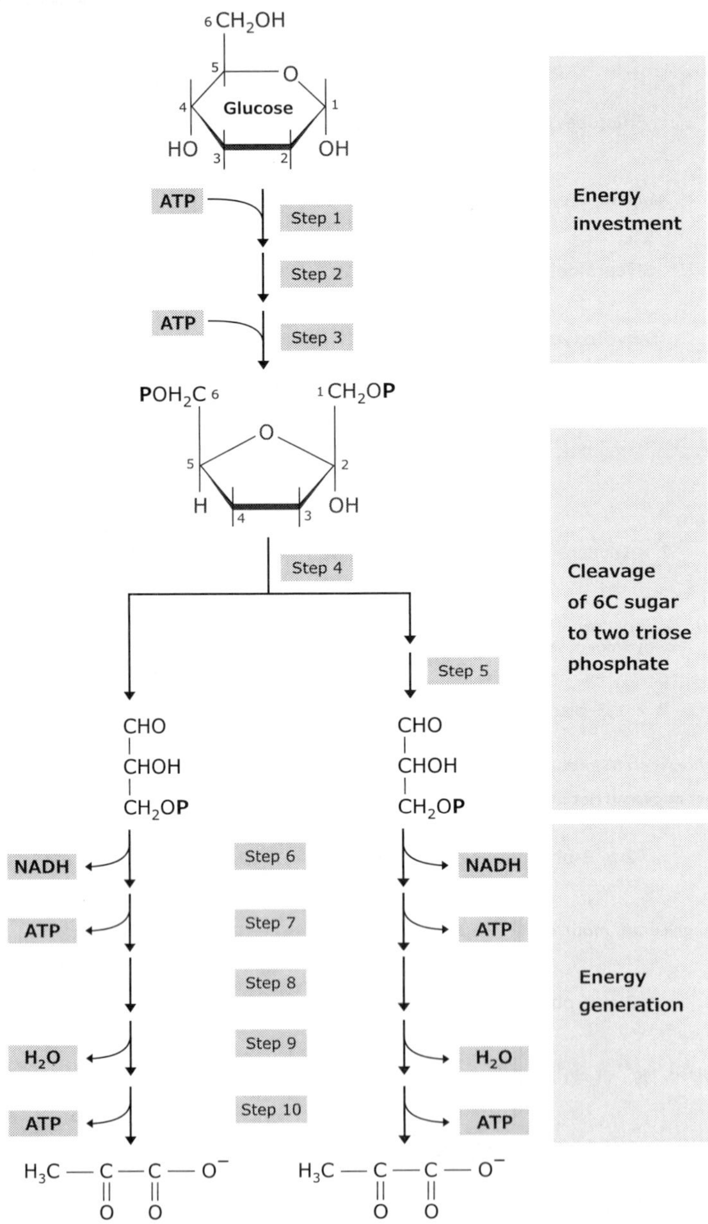

Figure 2.1 An overview of glycolysis. During glycolysis, a glucose molecule with six carbon atoms is converted into two molecules of pyruvate, each of which contains three carbon atoms. For each glucose molecule, two molecules of ATP are hydrolyzed to provide energy to drive the preparatory phase (energy investment), but four molecules of ATP are produced in the payoff phase (energy generation). At the end of glycolysis, there is a net gain of two molecules of ATP for each glucose molecule broken down. In addition, two molecules of the activated carrier NADH are also produced.

The energy gain comes in the **payoff phase** of glycolysis. First, G3P is oxidized with NAD^+ as the electron acceptor (to form NADH), and an inorganic phosphate (not by ATP) is simultaneously incorporated to give a high-energy molecule called 1,3-bisphosphoglycerate. The high-energy phosphate on carbon one is subsequently donated to ADP to produce ATP. This synthesis of ATP is called **substrate-level phosphorylation** because the production of ATP occurs by the transfer of a phosphate group from a high-energy substrate directly to ADP. Thus, the payoff phase of glycolysis yields ATP and NADH.

The energy yield from one molecule of glucose in glycolysis is 2 ATP and 2 NADH. In the *presence of oxygen*, one NADH is reoxidized to yield about 2.5 ATP through **oxidative phosphorylation**. Hence, glycolysis in the presence of oxygen yields 7 ATP (5 ATP from the oxidative phosphorylation of two molecules of NADH and 2 ATP from substrate-level phosphorylation). However, in the *absence of oxygen*, NADH does not enter into the process of ATP synthesis through oxidative phosphorylation. Hence, glycolysis in the absence of oxygen produces only 2 ATP as a result of substrate-level phosphorylation.

An interesting aspect of glycolysis is the utilization of 2 ATP in the preparatory phase (ATP investment), followed by the production of 4 ATP in the payoff phase. *Why expend 2 ATP initially*? There are two explanations. *First*, the phosphorylation of glucose using ATP converts glycolytic intermediates into phosphorylated metabolites, which are unable to diffuse out of the cell due to their negative charge. *Second*, these phosphorylated metabolites can serve for substrate-level phosphorylation, a process in which a phosphoryl group is transferred from a phosphorylated metabolite, such as 1,3-bisphosphoglycerate, to ADP, thereby generating ATP.

Problem

Iodoacetate is a potent inhibitor of enzyme glyceraldehyde 3-phosphate dehydrogenase. What chemical reaction does occur between iodoacetate and the enzyme?

Solution: Oxidation of glyceraldehyde 3-phosphate is catalyzed by glyceraldehyde 3-phosphate dehydrogenase. The aldehyde group of glyceraldehyde 3-phosphate first reacts with the –SH group of an essential *Cys* residue in the active site of the enzyme. Iodoacetate reacts with the –SH group of *Cys* residue in *glyceraldehyde 3-phosphate dehydrogenase*. Hence, iodoacetate is a potent inhibitor of *glyceraldehyde 3-phosphate dehydrogenase*.

Regulation of glycolysis

The rate of glycolysis is primarily controlled by allosteric regulation at three key regulatory steps catalyzed by the enzymes *hexokinase*, *phosphofructokinase-1*, and *pyruvate kinase*. These steps have large negative ΔG values and are essential for driving the overall flux toward pyruvate. They are essentially irreversible. There are two reasons for regulating glycolytic enzymes. First, when there is ample ATP, the cell should not needlessly devote resources to manufacturing more ATP. Second, glycolytic intermediates also serve as precursors for other biosynthetic pathways. Thus, regulating glycolytic enzymes can balance the energy-generating and biosynthetic capacities of these intermediates.

Hexokinase exhibits negative allosteric regulation in the presence of a high concentration of glucose 6-phosphate, acting as a negative modulator. **Phosphofructokinase-1** and **pyruvate kinase** show both negative and positive allosteric regulation. AMP acts as a positive modulator, while ATP acts as a negative modulator for both enzymes. A high concentration of AMP increases the catalytic activity of both enzymes, whereas a high concentration of ATP inhibits their activity. Additionally, for phosphofructokinase-1, citrate acts as a negative modulator, and fructose 2,6-bisphosphate acts as a positive modulator. In contrast, for pyruvate kinase, acetyl-CoA acts as a negative modulator, and fructose 1,6-bisphosphate acts as a positive modulator.

Enzyme	Allosteric activator (Positive modulator)	Allosteric inhibitor (Negative modulator)
Hexokinase	----------	Glucose 6-phosphate
Phosphofructokinase-1	Fructose 2,6-bisphosphate, AMP	Citrate, ATP
Pyruvate kinase	Fructose 1,6-bisphosphate, AMP	Acetyl-CoA, ATP

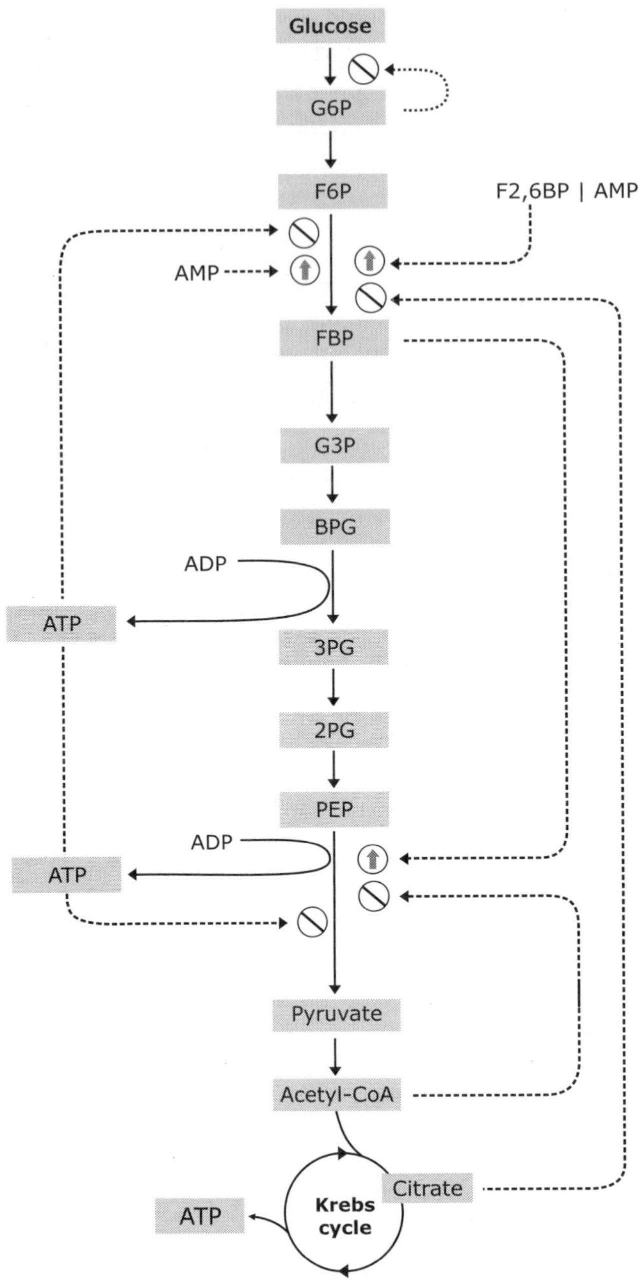

Figure 2.2 Overview of the regulation of glycolysis. The enzyme hexokinase, which catalyzes the first step of glycolysis, is allosterically inhibited by glucose 6-phosphate. The third step is catalyzed by the enzyme PFK-1. High levels of ATP and citrate allosterically inhibit the catalytic activity of PFK-1, whereas AMP and fructose 2,6-bisphosphate allosterically activate PFK-1. The tenth step is catalyzed by the enzyme pyruvate kinase. The product of PFK-1, fructose 1,6-bisphosphate, and AMP act as allosteric activators of pyruvate kinase, while ATP and acetyl-CoA allosterically inhibit the catalytic activity of pyruvate kinase. The circled upward arrows indicate activation and the circled downward slashes represent inhibition.

Fate of glucose carbons in the formation of pyruvate

During glycolysis, fructose 1,6-bisphosphate is cleaved to yield two triose phosphates: *glyceraldehyde 3-phosphate* and *dihydroxyacetone phosphate*. This reaction is catalyzed by the enzyme aldolase. Only one of the two triose phosphates formed by aldolase, glyceraldehyde 3-phosphate, can directly enter the subsequent steps of glycolysis. The other product, dihydroxyacetone phosphate, is rapidly and reversibly converted to glyceraldehyde 3-phosphate. Each carbon of glyceraldehyde 3-phosphate is derived from specific carbons of glucose. The first carbon of glyceraldehyde 3-phosphate derives from either the 3rd or 4th carbons of glucose, while the second carbon derives from either the 2nd or 5th carbons of glucose, and the third carbon from either the 1st or 6th carbons of glucose.

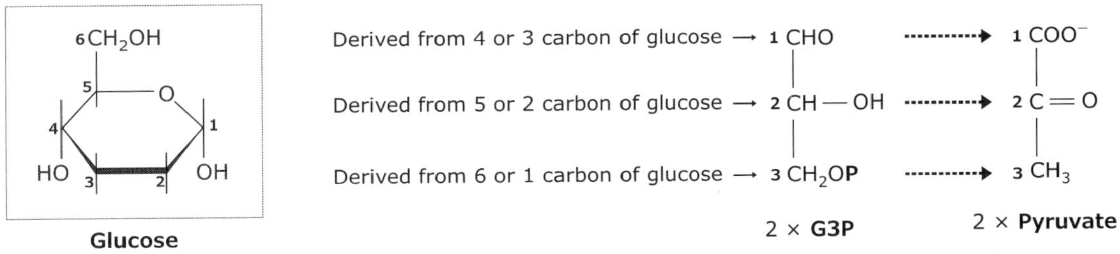

Figure 2.3 Fate of carbon atoms of glucose in the formation of glyceraldehyde-3-phosphate (G3P) and pyruvate. Each of the three carbon atoms of G3P is derived from either of two specific carbons of glucose. The numbering of the carbon atoms of G3P is not identical with the numbering of the carbon atoms of glucose.

2.1.3 Pyruvate oxidation

In the presence of oxygen, further oxidation of pyruvate occurs in the mitochondrial matrix (cytosol in case of prokaryotes). Pyruvate likely crosses the outer mitochondrial membrane through the large, relatively non-specific voltage-dependent anion channel (**porin**), while it crosses the inner mitochondrial membrane through the *pyruvate carrier*. In the mitochondrial matrix, pyruvate undergoes its first **oxidative decarboxylation** to yield acetyl-CoA.

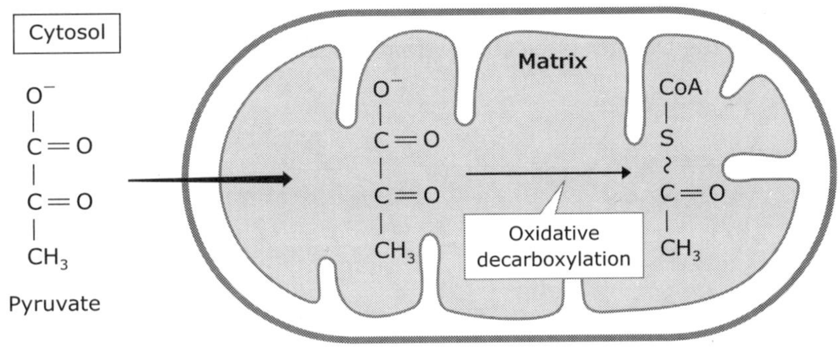

Figure 2.4 Conversion of pyruvate to acetyl-CoA. It is the junction between glycolysis and the citric acid cycle. Pyruvate is a charged molecule, so in eukaryotic cells, it must enter the mitochondrion with the help of a transport protein. Next, the pyruvate dehydrogenase complex catalyzes the process of oxidative decarboxylation.

The conversion of pyruvate to acetyl-CoA, catalyzed by highly organized multienzyme **pyruvate dehydrogenase complex** (PDC), is an oxidative decarboxylation process. In the overall reaction, the carboxyl group of pyruvate is lost as CO_2, while the remaining two carbons form the acetyl moiety of acetyl-CoA. The reaction is highly exergonic and essentially irreversible *in vivo*.

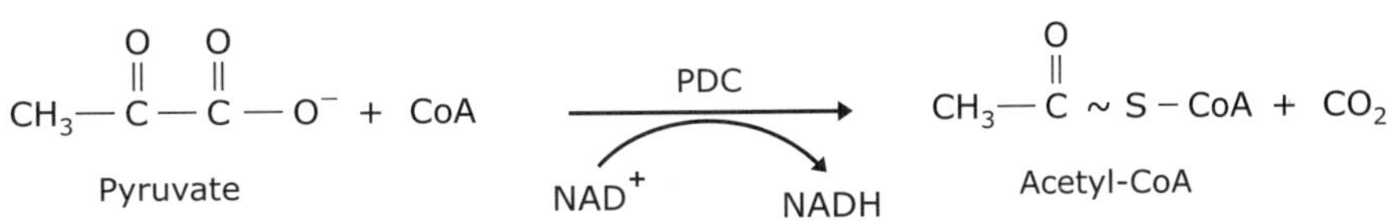

Pyruvate dehydrogenase complex is an assembly of three enzymes: *Pyruvate dehydrogenase* (**E_1**), *Dihydrolipoyl transacetylase* (**E_2**) and *Dihydrolipoyl dehydrogenase* (**E_3**). The oxidative decarboxylation of pyruvate to acetyl-CoA involves the coenzymes thiamine pyrophosphate (TPP), lipoic acid, FAD, NAD^+ and coenzyme A (CoA), acting in association with E_1, E_2 and E_3 of the pyruvate dehydrogenase complex. In eukaryotes, this enzyme complex also contains two regulatory enzymes as well–a **kinase** that phosphorylates serine residues and a **phosphatase** that removes those phosphates. Arsenite and mercuric ions inhibit the activity of pyruvate dehydrogenase.

Table 2.2 *E. coli* pyruvate dehydrogenase complex

Enzyme	Function	No. of polypeptide	Cofactors
Pyruvate dehydrogenase (E_1)	Oxidative decarboxylation	24	TPP
Dihydrolipoyl transacetylase (E_2)	Transfer of acetyl group to CoA	24	Lipoic acid, CoA
Dihydrolipoyl dehydrogenase (E_3)	Reoxidizes dihydrolipoamide	12	NAD^+, FAD

Mechanism of action of the pyruvate dehydrogenase complex: E_1 first catalyzes the *decarboxylation* of pyruvate, producing hydroxyethyl-TPP, and then the oxidation of the *hydroxyethyl group* to an *acetyl group*. The electrons from this oxidation reduce the disulfide bond of **lipoamide** (lipoate bound to E2) bound to E_2, and the acetyl group is transferred into thioester linkage with on –SH group of reduced lipoamide (termed **dihydrolipoamide**). E_2 catalyzes the transfer of the acetyl group to coenzyme A, forming acetyl-CoA. E_3 catalyzes the regeneration of the oxidized form of lipoamide; electrons pass first to FAD and then to NAD^+. Thus, the mechanism of action of the pyruvate dehydrogenase complex involves:

- Decarboxylation of pyruvate to form hydroxyethyl-TPP.
- Oxidation of hydroxyethyl-TPP to form an acetyl group and reduction of lipoamide to dihydrolipoamide.
- Transfer of the acetyl group to coenzyme A, resulting in the formation of acetyl-CoA.
- Regeneration of the oxidized form of lipoamide through the transfer of electrons to FAD.
- Formation of NADH through the transfer of electrons from reduced FAD to NAD^+.

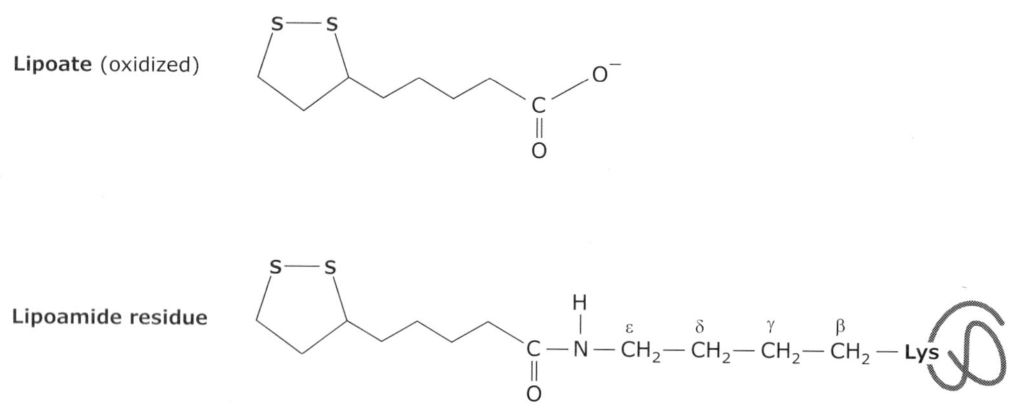

Figure 2.5 Structure of lipoate and lipoamide. Lipoate, also known as alpha-lipoic acid, is a coenzyme. Lipoamide, on the other hand, refers to the lipoic acid molecule when it is covalently bound to a lysine residue within a protein.

Regulation of catalytic activity of pyruvate dehydrogenase complex: The pyruvate dehydrogenase complex occupies a key position in the oxidation of glucose by linking the glycolytic pathway to the oxidative pathway of the citric acid cycle. Hence, its regulation is important for the maintenance of glucose homeostasis. The catalytic activity of enzymes in the pyruvate dehydrogenase complex is regulated by two processes – *allosteric regulation* and *covalent modification*.

Allosteric regulation is mediated by NADH and acetyl-CoA. E_2 is allosterically inhibited by the acetyl-CoA and activated by CoA while E_3 is allosterically inhibited by NADH and activated by NAD^+. Thus, the pyruvate dehydrogenase complex is allosterically inhibited when the [NADH]/[NAD^+] and [acetyl-CoA]/[CoA] ratios are high, and when these ratios decrease, allosteric activation occurs.

Regulation by reversible covalent modification, which occurs only in eukaryotes, is mediated by **phosphorylation-dephosphorylation** processes. Enzyme E_1 of pyruvate dehydrogenase complex undergoes reversible phosphorylation-dephosphorylation. E_1 is inactivated by the specific phosphorylation of one of its serine residues in a reaction catalyzed by serine specific *protein kinase*. This phosphoryl group is removed through the action of *phosphatase*, thereby reactivating E_1. The kinase is allosterically activated by ATP; when ATP concentration is high, the pyruvate dehydrogenase complex is inactivated by phosphorylation.

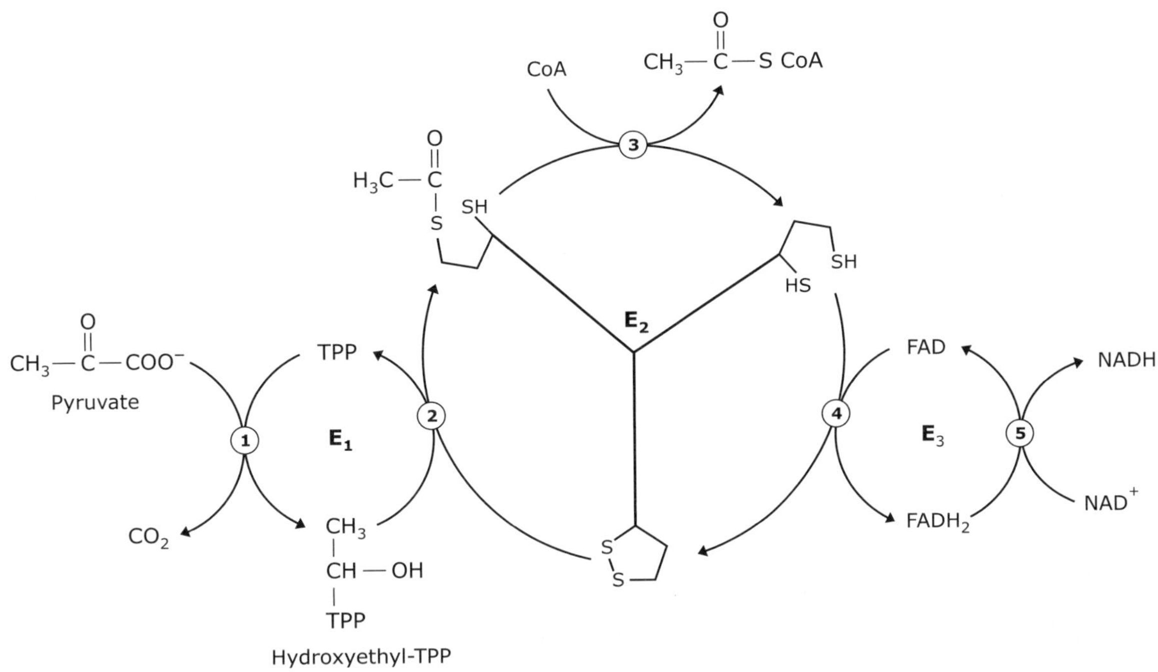

Figure 2.6 Structure of pyruvate dehydrogenase and its catalytic activities. Catalytic activities occur in four steps: *Step* 1. Decarboxylation of pyruvate occurs with formation of hydroxy ethyl–TPP. *Step* 2. Hydroxyethyl group is transferred to lipoate and oxidation of the hydroxyethyl group to an acetyl group. *Step* 3. Transfer of acetyl group to CoA. *Step* 4. Reoxidation of dihydrolipoamide.

2.1.4 Citric acid cycle

Citric acid cycle (also known as the **Krebs cycle** or **tricarboxylic acid cycle**) was discovered by H. A. Krebs, a German born British Biochemist, who received the Nobel prize in 1953. This cycle occurs in the matrix of mitochondria (cytosol in prokaryotes). The whole cycle is explained in the following **figure 2.7**. The net result of citric acid cycle is that for each acetyl group entering the cycle as acetyl-CoA, two molecules of CO_2 are produced.

Step 1: The citric acid cycle begins with the condensation of an oxaloacetate (four carbon unit) and the acetyl group of acetyl-CoA (two-carbon unit). Oxaloacetate reacts with acetyl-CoA and H_2O to yield citrate and coenzyme A. This reaction, which is an aldol condensation followed by a hydrolysis, is catalyzed by *citrate synthase*. Citrate is a **prochiral molecule** because it lacks a chiral center but can be converted into a chiral molecule by changing just one of its attached groups.

Step 2a and 2b: An isomerization reaction, in which water is first removed and then added back, moves the hydroxyl group from one carbon atom to its neighbour. The enzyme catalyzing this step, *aconitase* (nonheme iron protein), is the target site for the toxic compound **fluoroacetate** (used as a pesticide). Fluoroacetate blocks the citric acid cycle by its metabolic conversion of *fluorocitrate*, which is a potent inhibitor of aconitase.

Step 3: Isocitrate is oxidized and decarboxylated to α-ketoglutarate (also called oxoglutarate). In the first of four oxidation steps in the cycle, the carbon carrying the hydroxyl group is converted to a carbonyl group. The immediate product is unstable, losing CO_2 while still bound to the enzyme. The oxidative decarboxylation of isocitrate is catalyzed by *isocitrate dehydrogenase*.

Step 4: A second oxidative decarboxylation reaction results in the formation of succinyl-CoA from α-ketoglutarate. *α-ketoglutarate dehydrogenase* catalyzes this oxidative step and produces NADH, CO_2, and a high-energy thioester bond to coenzyme A.

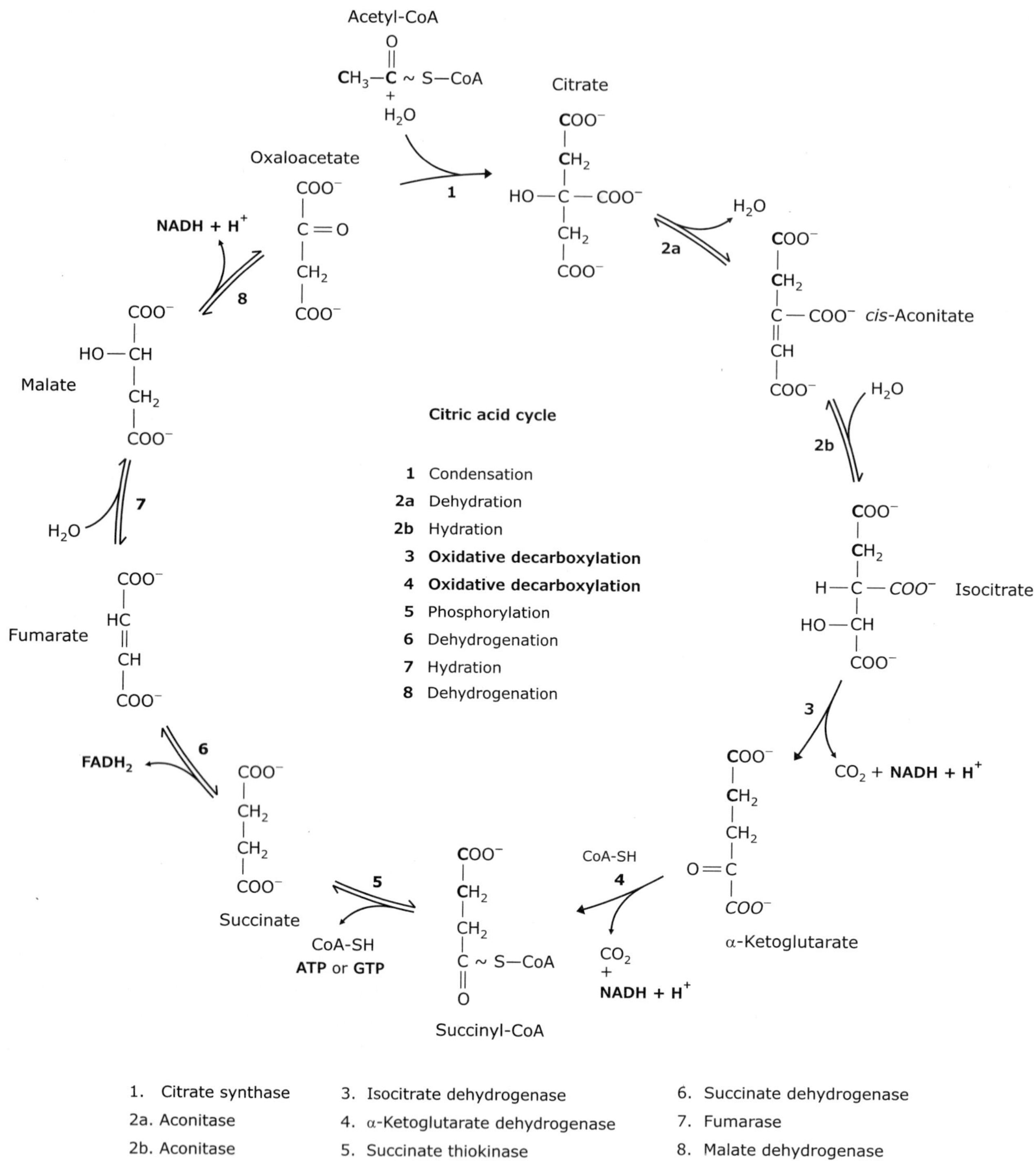

Figure 2.7 Citric acid cycle. Acetyl-CoA is the substrate for the citric acid cycle. A four-carbon compound (oxaloacetate) condenses with a two-carbon acetyl unit to yield a six-carbon tricarboxylic acid (citrate). An isomer of citrate is then oxidatively decarboxylated. The resulting five-carbon compound (α-ketoglutarate) also is oxidatively decarboxylated to yield a four carbon compound (succinate). Oxaloacetate is then regenerated from succinate. During oxidative decarboxylation, two carbon atoms come out as CO_2 from the oxidation of isocitrate and α-ketoglutarate. The energy released during this cycle is used in the reduction of three NAD^+ and one FAD and the production of one ATP or GTP. Note that the two carbon atoms appearing as CO_2 are not the same two carbons that entered in the form of the acetyl group; additional turns around the cycle are required to release these carbons as CO_2. In this figure, fate of carbon in the citric acid cycle has been shown. Acetyl-CoA entering the citric acid cycle is highlighted (in *bold*) to show the fate of its two carbons through reaction 4. After reaction 5, the carbon atoms most recently entered are no longer highlighted, because succinate is a symmetrical molecule. Carboxyl groups that leave the cycle as CO_2 in reactions 3 and 4 are shown in *italic* letter.

Step 5: The cleavage of the thioester bond of succinyl-CoA is coupled with the phosphorylation of an ADP or a GDP (**substrate-level phosphorylation**). This step is catalyzed by *succinyl-CoA synthetase* (also called *succinate thiokinase*). ATP and GTP are energetically equivalent. This is the only step in the citric acid cycle that directly yields ATP or GTP through a substrate-level phosphorylation. The reaction catalyzed by succinyl-CoA synthetase completes in three-steps. *First*, succinyl-CoA reacts with P_i to form succinyl-phosphate and CoA. In *second* step, the phosphoryl group is transferred from succinyl-phosphate to a His residue on the enzyme, releasing succinate. Finally, the phosphoryl group on the enzyme is transferred to GDP or ADP, forming GTP or ATP. Animal cells have two isozymes of succinyl-CoA synthetase, one specific for ADP and the other for GDP. The GTP formed by succinyl-CoA synthetase can donate its terminal phosphoryl group to ADP to form ATP, in a reversible reaction catalyzed by *nucleoside diphosphate kinase* (NDK). In the cells of plants, bacteria and some animal tissues, an ATP molecule forms directly by substrate-level phosphorylation.

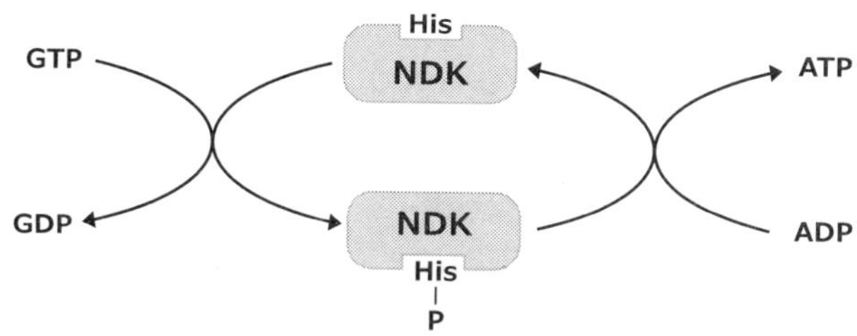

Step 6: In the third oxidation step in the cycle, FAD removes two hydrogen atoms from succinate. The enzyme catalyzing this step, succinate dehydrogenase, is strongly inhibited by **malonate**, a structural analog of succinate and a classic example of a competitive inhibitor.

Step 7: The addition of water to fumarate places a hydroxyl group next to a carbonyl carbon.

Step 8: In the last of four oxidation steps in the cycle, the carbon carrying the hydroxyl group is converted to a carbonyl group, regenerating the oxaloacetate needed for step 1. NAD^+ linked *malate dehydrogenase* catalyzes the reversible oxidation of malate to oxaloacetate.

Overall reaction: **Acetyl-CoA** + 3 × $\mathbf{NAD^+}$ + **FAD** + **ADP** (or **GDP**) ⟶ 2 × $\mathbf{CO_2}$ + 3 × **NADH** + $\mathbf{FADH_2}$ + **ATP** (or **GTP**)

Regulation of citric acid cycle

The citric acid cycle is regulated at its three strongly exergonic steps catalyzed by enzymes *citrate synthase*, *isocitrate dehydrogenase* and *α-ketoglutarate dehydrogenase*. The regulatory enzymes of the citric acid cycle seem to control flux primarily by three simple mechanisms: 1. **substrate availability** (limited by the availability of the citrate synthase substrates, acetyl-CoA and oxaloacetate) 2. **allosteric regulation** (enzyme *isocitrate dehydrogenase* is allosterically activated by ADP and NAD^+ and inhibited by ATP and NADH) and 3. **product inhibition** (enzyme *α-ketoglutarate dehydrogenase* catalyzes the rate-limiting step and it is allosterically inhibited by succinyl-CoA and NADH, the products of the reaction that it catalyzes).

Overall reaction: By taking one molecule of glucose

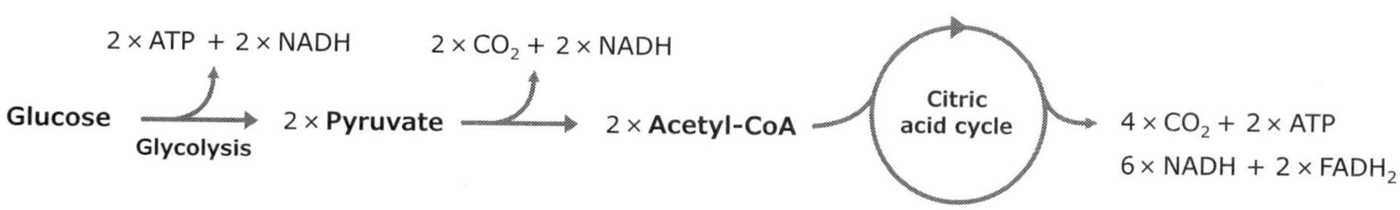

Figure 2.8 Glycolysis and the citric acid cycle produce only 4 ATP per glucose molecule, all by substrate-level phosphorylation: 2 net ATP from glycolysis and 2 ATP from the Krebs cycle. Up to this point, molecules of NADH and $FADH_2$ account for most of the energy extracted from the glucose. Oxidation of NADH and $FADH_2$ occurring during oxidative phosphorylation, powers most of ATP synthesis.

Problem

Using pyruvate, labeled with ^{14}C in its keto group, via the pyruvate dehydrogenase reaction and the citric acid cycle, where would the carbon label be at the end of one turn of the citric acid cycle? Where would the carbon label be at the end of the second turn of the cycle?

Solution: The labeled keto carbon of pyruvate becomes the labeled carboxyl carbon of acetyl–CoA. After condensation with oxaloacetate, the first carboxyl group of citrate is labeled. This label is retained through subsequent reactions to succinate. However, succinate is a symmetrical compound to the enzyme, so, in effect, both carboxyl group of succinate are labeled. This means that the oxaloacetate regenerated is labeled in both carboxyl groups at the end of one turn (actually, half the molecules are labeled in one carboxyl and half in the other) but this cannot be distinguished experimentally.

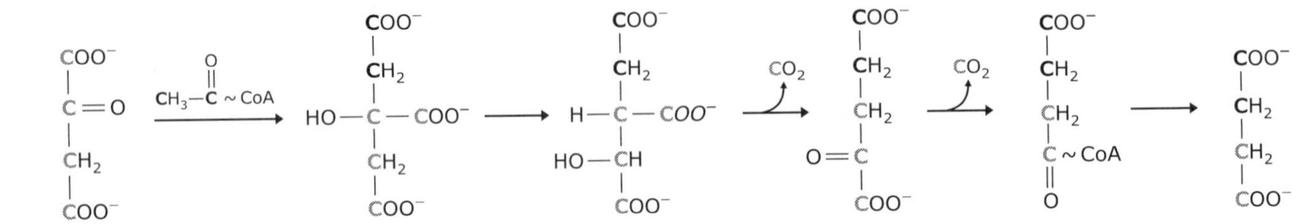

Oxaloacetate Citrate Isocitrate α-Ketoglutarate Succinyl-CoA Succinate

Problem

In the citric acid cycle, how many steps involve?

P. Oxidation-reduction, Q. Hydration-dehydration, R. Substrate-level phosphorylation and S. Decarboxylation

Solution:

P. Four steps involve in oxidation-reduction. The enzymes involved are *isocitrate dehydrogenase*, *2-oxoglutarate dehydrogenase*, *succinate dehydrogenase* and *malate dehydrogenase*.

Q. Two steps involve in hydration-dehydration reactions. The enzymes responsible are *aconitase* and *fumarase*.

R. One step involves in substrate-level phosphorylation, and the enzyme is *succinyl-CoA synthetase*.

S. Two steps involve in decarboxylation. The enzymes are *isocitrate dehydrogenase* and *2-oxoglutarate dehydrogenase*.

2.1.5 Anaplerotic reaction

Citric acid cycle intermediates are used in biosynthetic pathways as well. So, the anabolic nature of the citric acid cycle has raised the question of how the level of intermediates can be replenished when, certain intermediates are removed for anabolic purposes. Kornberg has proposed the term **anaplerotic** for these replenishing or *filling up* reactions. In animals, the most important anaplerotic reaction is catalyzed by *pyruvate carboxylase*, a mitochondrial enzyme, which converts pyruvate to oxaloacetic acid.

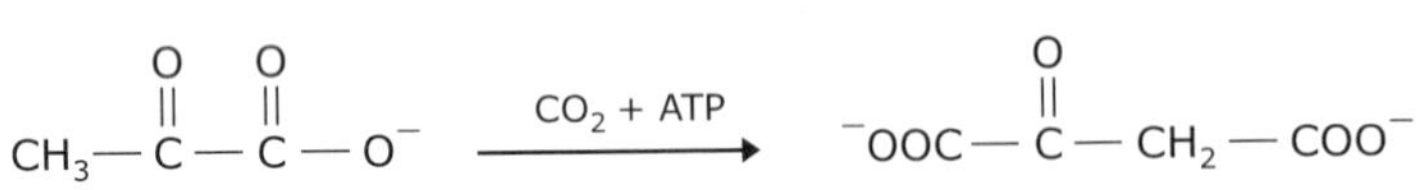

(Enzyme *pyruvate carboxylase*)

Pyruvate Oxaloacetate

In plants and bacteria, an alternative route leads directly from phosphoenolpyruvate (PEP) to oxaloacetate. This reaction is catalyzed by *phosphoenolpyruvate carboxylase*.

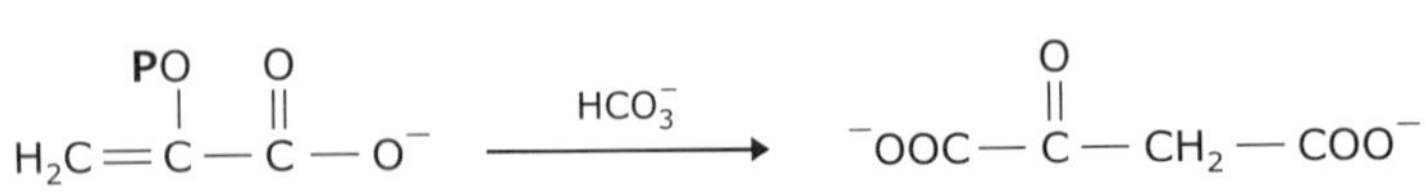

(Enzyme *PEP carboxylase*)

PEP Oxaloacetate

A related enzyme, phosphoenolpyruvate carboxykinase, also converts phosphoenolpyruvate to oxaloacetate.

In addition to pyruvate carboxylase and phosphoenolpyruvate carboxylase, a third anaplerotic process is provided by an enzyme commonly known as *malic enzyme*, but officially as *malate dehydrogenase*. The malic enzyme catalyzes the reductive carboxylation of pyruvate to give malate.

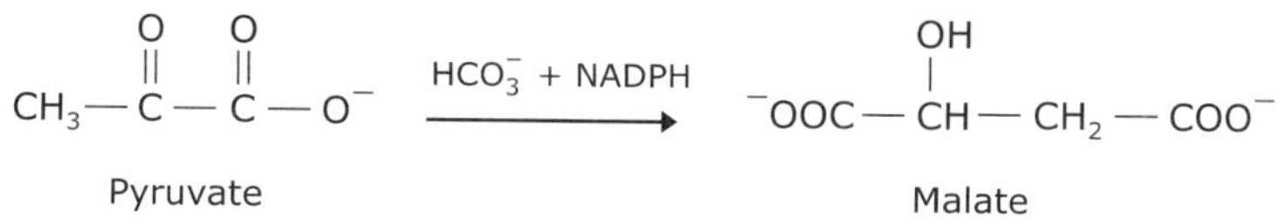

(Enzyme *malic enzyme*)

2.1.6 Oxidative phosphorylation

Most of the free energy released during the oxidation of glucose to CO_2 is retained in the reduced coenzymes NADH and $FADH_2$, generated during glycolysis and citric acid cycle. Electrons are released from NADH and $FADH_2$ and eventually transferred to O_2, forming H_2O.

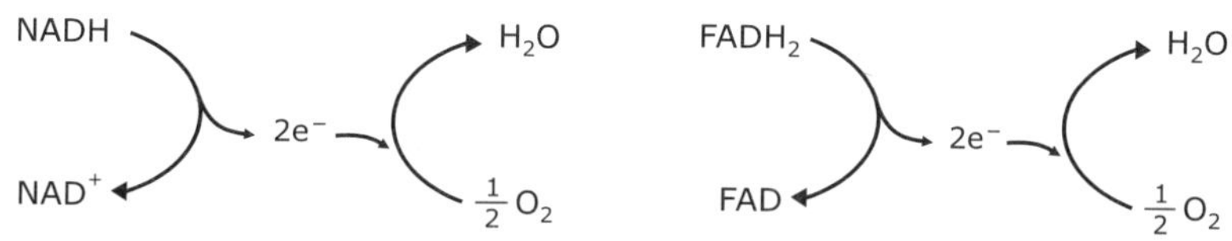

The standard free energy change for these exergonic reactions are –52.6 kcal/mol (for **NADH**) and –43.14 kcal/mol (for **$FADH_2$**). The large amount of free energy released during the oxidation of NADH and $FADH_2$ is used in the formation of ATP. For this reason, the term *oxidative phosphorylation* is used to describe this energy conversion process.

Electrons are transferred from NADH/$FADH_2$ to O_2 through a series of electron carriers present on the inner mitochondrial membrane (in case of prokaryotes, it is present in plasma membrane). The process of electron transport begins when the hydride ion is removed from NADH and is converted into a proton and two electrons. Most of the proteins (electron carriers) involved are grouped into four large *respiratory enzyme complexes*, each containing transmembrane proteins that hold the complex. The electrons start with very high energy and gradually lose it as they pass along the chain. Each complex in the chain has a greater affinity for electrons i.e., reduction potential than its predecessor and electrons pass sequentially from one complex to another until they are finally transferred to oxygen, which has the highest affinity for electrons. The four major respiratory enzyme complexes of electron transport chain in the inner mitochondrial membrane are:

- NADH–coenzyme Q reductase or NADH dehydrogenase (**Complex I**)
- Succinate–coenzyme Q reductase (**Complex II**)
- Coenzyme Q–cytochrome c reductase or cytochrome bc_1 complex (**Complex III**)
- Cytochrome c oxidase (**Complex IV**)

Complex I, II and III appear to be associated in a supramolecular complex termed the **respirasome.** All the four multiprotein enzyme complexes which act as electron carriers comprise prosthetic groups, such as flavins, heme, Fe–S clusters and copper. The table below lists the prosthetic group in each multiprotein enzyme complex.

Table 2.3 Name of enzyme complex and their prosthetic groups

Enzyme complex	**Prosthetic groups (cofactors)**
Complex I (46 subunits)	FMN, Fe-S cluster
Complex II (4 subunits)	FAD, Fe-S cluster
Complex III (11 subunits)	Heme, Fe-S cluster
Complex IV (13 subunits)	Heme, Cu^+

Electrons are transferred along the electron transport chain by the reversible reduction and oxidation of iron-sulfur clusters, coenzyme Q (abbreviated CoQ), heme and copper ions. Each carrier accepts an electron or an electron pair from a carrier with a less reduction potential and transfers the electron to a carrier with a more reduction potential. Thus, reduction potentials of electron carriers favour unidirectional electron flow from NADH and $FADH_2$ to O_2.

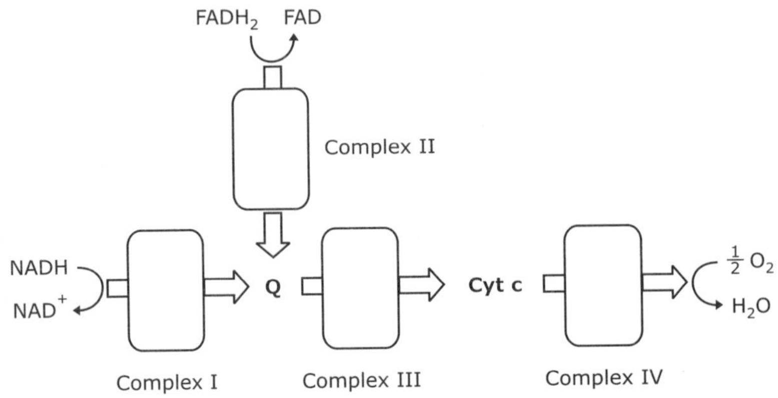

Figure 2.9 Overview of electron flow through the respiratory chain (Q, coenzyme Q; Cyt, cytochrome).

Complex I

Complex I is a large, multisubunit complex causes oxidation of NADH and passes electron from NADH to **coenzyme Q**. It contains one molecule of flavin mononucleotide (**FMN**) and six to seven iron-sulfur clusters that participate in the electron-transport process. During transport of each pair of electron from NADH to coenzyme Q, complex I pumps four protons across the inner mitochondrial membrane.

Box 2.1 Iron-Sulfur clusters

Iron-Sulfur (Fe-S) clusters are prosthetic group consist of inorganic sulfide-linked **nonheme iron**. They are required for the function of many **Fe-S proteins** involved in a wide range of functions ranging from electron transport to DNA repair. Fe-S clusters are best known for participation in oxidation-reduction reactions in photosynthetic electron transport in thylakoid membranes and respiratory electron transport in the inner mitochondrial membrane. Common types of Fe-S clusters include:

- Classic 2Fe-2S: coordinated by four cysteine residues of Fe-S proteins.
- NEET-type 2Fe-2S: coordinated by three cysteine and one histidine residues of Fe-S proteins.
- Rieske-type 2Fe-2S: coordinated by two cysteine and two histidine residues of Fe-S proteins.
- 4Fe-4S: coordinated by four cysteine residues of Fe-S proteins (or three Cys residues and the hydroxide group from water). 4Fe-4S clusters are **cubane-type** clusters (most common) whereas the three 2Fe-2S clusters are **rhombic-type** clusters, containing the same 2Fe-2S core.

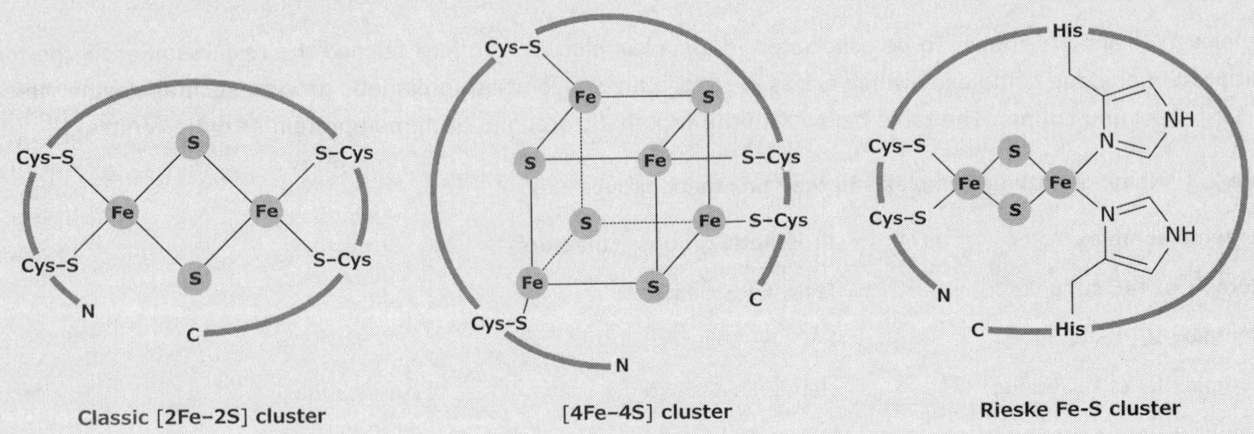

Figure 2.10 Iron-Sulfur proteins with common types of Fe-S clusters.

Coenzyme Q (also known as **ubiquinone**) is a lipid-soluble *benzoquinone* linked to a number of *isoprene units*. The name *ubiquinone* is for the ubiquitous nature of the quinone. **Q** refers to the quinone chemical group. There are three redox states of coenzyme Q - *fully oxidized* (**ubiquinone,** Q), *partially reduced* (**ubisemiquinone**) and *fully reduced* (**ubiquinol,** QH_2). *Coenzyme Q is the only electron carrier in the electron transport chain that is not a protein-bound prosthetic group*. It is a carrier of hydrogen atoms, that is protons plus electrons. Ubiquinone is both small and lipid-soluble, hence, it is freely diffusible within the lipid bilayer of the inner mitochondrial membrane.

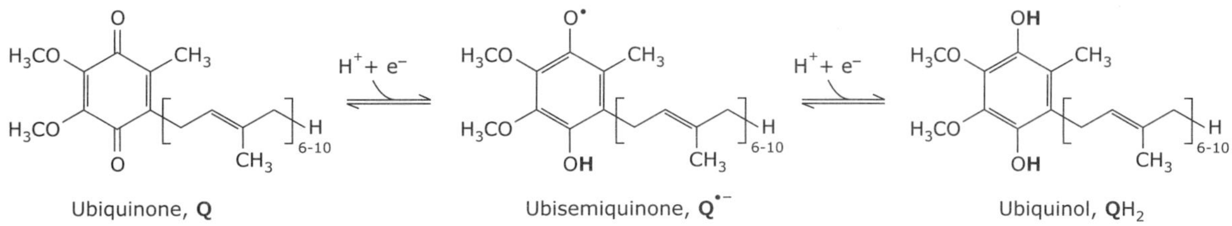

Complex II

Succinate dehydrogenase, an inner mitochondrial membrane-bound enzyme, is an integral component of the complex II. It converts succinate to fumarate during Krebs cycle. The two electrons released in the conversion of succinate to fumarate are transferred first to FAD, then to an iron-sulfur cluster and finally to coenzyme Q. Thus, coenzyme Q draws electrons into the respiratory chain, not only from NADH, but also from $FADH_2$. Complex II does not pump protons during transport of electrons across the inner mitochondrial membrane.

Complex III

Complex I and complex II transfer electrons to the complex III via coenzyme Q. Within complex III, the electrons released from coenzyme Q follow two paths. In one path, electrons are transported via **Rieske iron-sulfur cluster** and cytochrome c_1, directly to cytochrome c. In other path, electrons move through *b*-type cytochromes (b_{566} or b_L, L for low affinity and b_{562} or b_H, H for high affinity) and reduce oxidized coenzyme Q as shown in the figure. During transport of each pair of electron from coenzyme Q to cytochrome c, complex III pumps four protons across inner mitochondrial membrane. The mechanism involved in proton pumping is called the proton-motive **Q-cycle**.

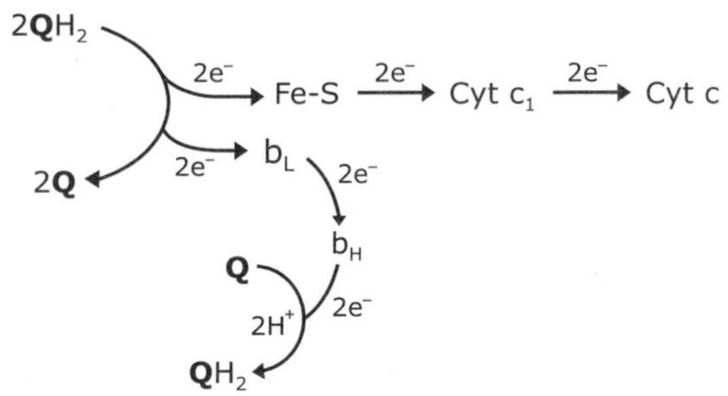

Figure 2.11
The path of electrons through complex III. Two molecules of QH_2 are oxidized to Q and release a total of four electrons. Two of the electrons are transported via iron-sulfur center protein and cytochrome c_1, directly to cytochrome c. The other two electrons move through cytochrome b_L and b_H and reduce an oxidized Q to QH_2.

Q-cycle: The mechanism of the participation of ubiquinone in the electron transport process was proposed by Peter Mitchell and termed as a proton motive *Q-cycle*. Ubiquinones are hydrophobic and uncharged, and hence can migrate along the hydrophobic core of the membrane. Diffusion of one ubiquinol takes place to the Q_P binding site adjacent to the iron-sulfur protein at the P-face of the mitochondrial membrane. One electron is transferred to Fe-S protein and the second electron is transferred to the heme b_L and two protons are released to the P-face. The Fe-S protein transfers the electron along the chain to Cyt c_1 and cytochrome oxidase. The electron moves from heme b_L to heme b_H. Ubiquinone then binds to b_H at the Q_n site and electron from the reduced b_H forms ubisemiquinone at this site. Now, a second ubiquinol molecule is oxidized at the Q_P site, the process follows as described above and the second electron formed completes the reduction of ubisemiquinone to ubiquinol. Two protons are taken from the matrix for this purpose and released to the P-face. The ubiquinol, then, goes back to the pool and the Q-cycle is completed.

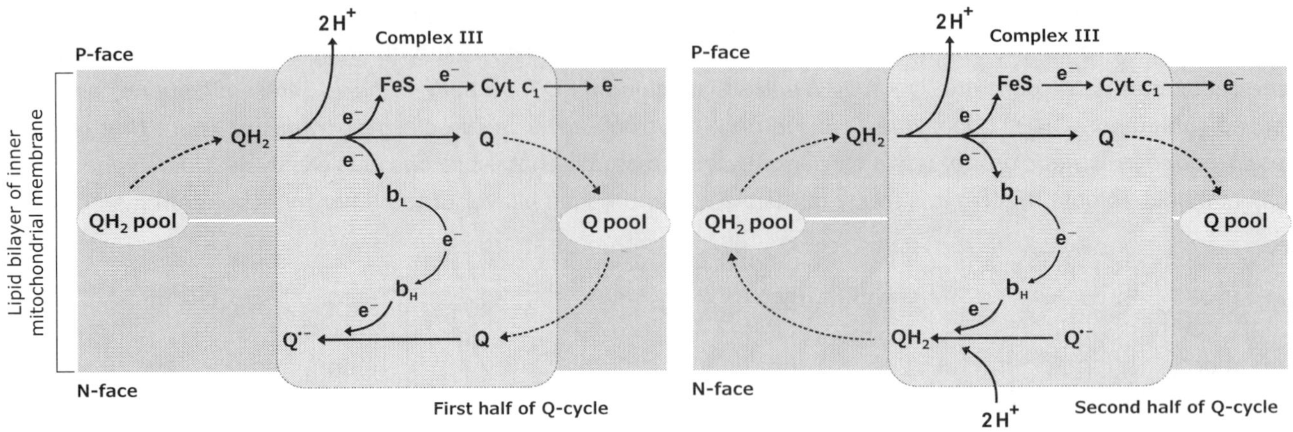

Figure 2.12 A simplified outline of Q-cycle in mitochondria. In the first half of the cycle, two electrons of a bound QH_2 are transferred, one to cytochrome c_1 and the other to a bound Q in a second binding site to form the ubisemiquinone. The newly formed Q dissociates and enters the Q pool. In the second half of the cycle, a second QH_2 also gives up its electrons to complex III, one to a molecule of cytochrome c_1 and the other to reduce $Q^{\bullet-}$ to QH_2. The second electron transfer results in the uptake of two protons from the matrix. Ubiquinol – QH_2, Ubisemiquinone – $Q^{\bullet-}$ and Ubiquinone – Q.

Complex IV

Complex IV (or **cytochrome c oxidase**) catalyzes the transfer of electrons from the reduced form of cytochrome c to molecular oxygen. It consists of 13 subunits and contains two **heme groups** and three **copper ions**, arranged as *two copper centers*. The two heme groups termed **heme a** and **heme** $\mathbf{a_3}$, have distinct properties because they are located in different environments within cytochrome *c* oxidase. The two copper centers are designated as *a* and *b*. One center, $\mathbf{Cu_a}$, contains two copper ions linked by two bridging cysteine residues. The second center, $\mathbf{Cu_b}$, is coordinated by three histidine residues.

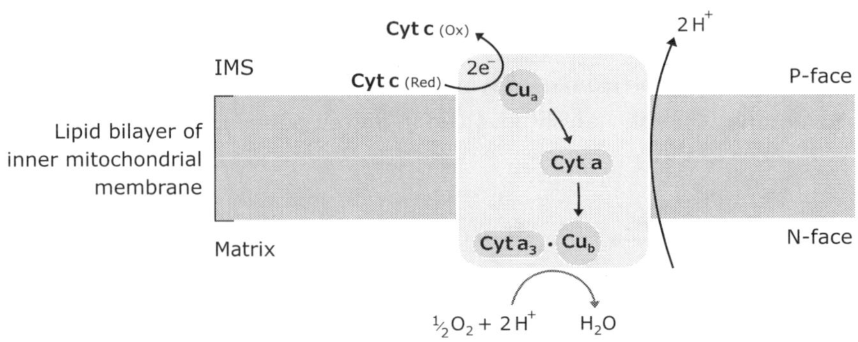

Figure 2.13 The electron transfer pathway for cytochrome oxidase (Cyt c $\longrightarrow$ Cu_a $\longrightarrow$ Cyt a $\longrightarrow$ Cu_b . Cyt a_3 $\longrightarrow$ O_2). Cytochrome c (a peripheral protein) binds on the P face of inner mitochondrial membrane, transferring electrons through the copper and heme centers to reduce O_2 on the matrix side of the membrane.

Box 2.2 Cytochromes

Cytochromes are **heme proteins** having distinctive visible-light spectra. Mitochondria contain three classes of cytochromes – classified as *b*, *c* or *a*, depending on the wavelengths of the spectral absorption peaks. Within each class, the cytochromes are distinguished by smaller spectral differences. In the respiratory electron carriers, there are two **b-type** cytochromes (b_{566} and b_{562}), two **c-type** cytochromes (c and c_1), and two **a-type** cytochromes (a and a_3).

The heme prosthetic groups of a and b-type cytochromes are tightly, but not covalently, bound to their associated proteins; whereas heme groups of c-type cytochromes are covalently (**thioether bond**) attached through Cys residues. Cytochrome c is present in all aerobic organisms. It is a peripheral protein of the inner mitochondrial membrane and binds via electrostatic interactions to acidic phospholipids in intermembrane space. It is composed of a single polypeptide chain of 104 amino acid residues covalently bound to the heme group. The degree of sequence homology in cytochrome c among species has been used as a measure of the evolutionary distances that separate species.

Cytochrome *c* transports electrons, one at a time, to the complex IV. Within this complex, electrons are transferred, first to a Cu_a center, then to Cyt a, next to Cu_b center and Cyt a_3, and finally to O_2, the ultimate electron acceptor, yielding H_2O. Together, heme a_3 and Cu_b form the active center at which O_2 is reduced to H_2O.

Two electrons, sequentially released from two molecules of reduced cytochrome c together with two protons from the matrix, combine with one O atom to form one water molecule. Additionally, for each electron transferred from cytochrome c to oxygen, one proton is transported from the matrix to the intermembrane space, or a total of four electrons are transferred for each O_2 molecule reduced to two H_2O molecules.

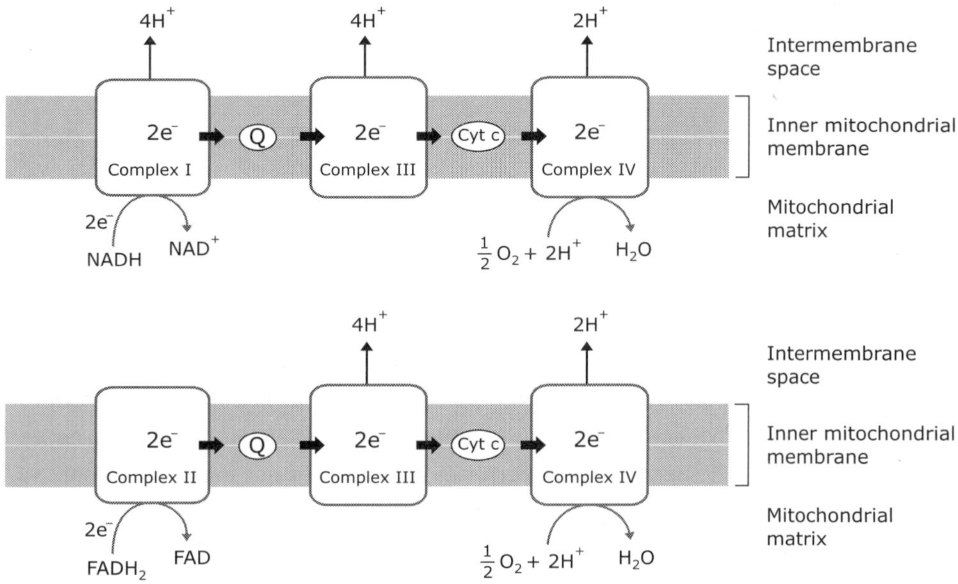

Figure 2.14 The journey of electrons through the respiratory chain begins with the transfer of electrons from NADH or $FADH_2$ to complex I or complex II, respectively. These complexes accept the electrons and transfer them to coenzyme Q, a mobile electron carrier. From coenzyme Q, the electrons move to complex III, where they are transferred to another mobile carrier, Cyt c. Subsequently, Cyt c transfers the electrons to complex IV, which facilitates their final transfer to O_2, forming water. As electrons flow through these complexes, they release energy, which is harnessed to pump protons across the inner mitochondrial membrane, creating an electrochemical gradient.

Problem

Each of the cytochromes in the mitochondria contains a heme prosthetic group, which permits these proteins to transport electrons in the electron transport system. **a**. Explain how heme prosthetic groups function as electron carriers? **b**. What property of the cytochromes assures unidirectional electron flow along the electron transport chain? **c**. As electrons flow through the electron transport chain, they lose energy. How much of this energy is utilized?

Solution:

a. Each of the heme prosthetic groups present in cytochromes contains an iron atom that accepts an electron as it is reduced and releases an electron as it is oxidized. Because the heme ring has numerous resonance forms, the second electron is delocalized to the heme carbon and nitrogen atoms.

b. Each cytochrome that participates in the electron transport has a different reduction potential, so that electrons can move only in a single direction through the electron carriers.

c. Much of the energy lost by electrons moving through the electron transport chain is used to pump protons from the matrix to the intermembrane space, thus generating the proton-motive force.

2.1.7 Inhibitors of electron transport

Many inhibitors have been identified that selectively target and inhibit specific electron transport complexes of the electron transport chain within mitochondria. By interfering with the flow of electrons, these inhibitors affect proton pumping and inhibit cellular energy production.

Rotenone is a naturally occurring compound found in several plant species, primarily from the Fabaceae family. It inhibits the transfer of electrons through **complex I** of the electron transport chain. It is commonly used as a fish poison and insecticide.

Amobarbital (Amytal) is a barbiturate that has been used as a sedative (to calm and relax patients) and hypnotic (to induce sleep) medication. It also inhibits electron transport through **complex I.**

Piericidin A is an antibiotic that blocks the transfer of electrons at **complex I** by competing with CoQ. The electrons from the complex are transferred to piericidin A instead of CoQ.

Antimycin A is an antibiotic that binds the **complex III,** blocking the electron transfer from ubiquinol to cytochrome *c.*

Cyanide, azide and **carbon monoxide** bind with **complex IV** and inhibit the terminal transfer of electrons to oxygen. Cyanide and azide bind with the ferric form (i.e., oxidized form) of the cytochrome a_3 and carbon monoxide binds with the ferrous form (i.e., reduced form) of the cytochrome a_3.

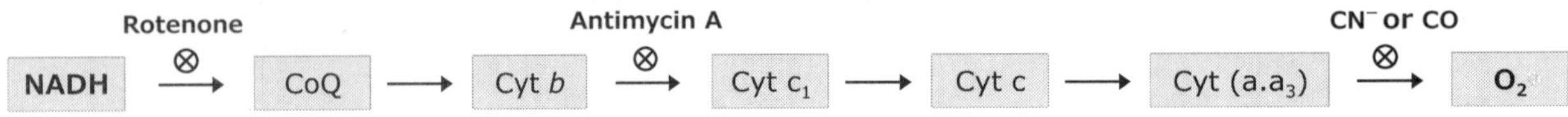

Cyanide-resistant respiration

Some organisms have alternative pathways for flow of electrons from NADH to oxygen. In this alternative pathway, complex I passes electrons from NADH to ubiquinone. Ubiquinone donates electrons directly to oxygen to form water with the help of **alternative oxidase,** bypassing complexes III and IV. Hence, this process does not involve H^+ pumping by complexes III and IV. Because transfer of electrons does not involve complex IV, NADH oxidation by this pathway is *cyanide resistant.* Since in this pathway most of the energy of electrons are not used for H^+ pumping and hence it is dissipated as heat.

Problem

Rotenone, a toxic natural product from plants, strongly inhibits NADH dehydrogenase of insect and fish mitochondria. Antimycin A, a toxic antibiotic, strongly inhibits the oxidation of ubiquinol. **a.** Why rotenone ingestion is lethal to some insects and fish species? **b.** Why antimycin A is a poison? **c.** Given that rotenone and antimycin A are equally effective in blocking their respective sites in the electron transport chain, which would be a more potent poison? Explain.

Solution:

a. Inhibition of NADH dehydrogenase by rotenone decreases the rate of electron flow through the respiratory chain, which in turn decreases the rate of ATP production. If this reduced rate is unable to meet the organism's ATP requirements, the organism dies.

b. Antimycin A strongly inhibits the oxidation of CoQ in the respiratory chain, reducing the rate of electron transfer and leading to the consequences described in (a).

c. Because antimycin A blocks all electron flow to oxygen, it is a more potent poison than rotenone, which blocks electron flow from NADH, but not from $FADH_2$.

2.1.8 Electrochemical proton gradient

The movement of electrons through the electron transport chain is accompanied by the pumping of protons across the inner mitochondrial membrane, from the matrix to the intermembrane space. This movement of protons against their gradient generates an electrochemical proton gradient, which has two components:

Chemical gradient: This is the difference in proton concentration across the inner mitochondrial membrane. The difference in proton concentration establishes a **pH gradient,** with the pH being higher in the matrix than in the intermembrane space.

Electrical gradient: This is the difference in charge across the inner mitochondrial membrane. It creates an **electric potential difference** (voltage) across the inner mitochondrial membrane, with the matrix side being negative and the intermembrane space side being positive. The electric potential difference across the membrane is termed as **membrane potential**.

The combination of the chemical gradient (pH gradient) and the electrical gradient (electric potential difference) across the inner mitochondrial membrane generates the **proton motive force** (**pmf**).

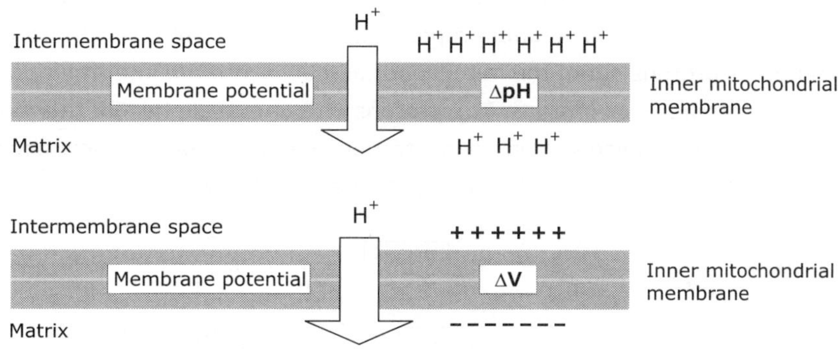

A mitochondrion actively involved in aerobic respiration typically has a membrane potential of about 160 mV (negative inside matrix) and a pH gradient of about 1.0 pH unit (higher on the matrix side). A difference of one pH unit represents a tenfold difference in proton concentration and a pH gradient of one unit across a membrane is equivalent to an electric potential of 59 mV (at 20°C). The total proton-motive force across the inner mitochondrial membrane is primarily due to the membrane potential, with a smaller contribution from the pH gradient. In a typical mitochondrion, the proton-motive force is approximately 220 mV. In contrast, in chloroplasts, the pH gradient contributes more significantly to the overall proton-motive force than the membrane potential.

Determination of membrane potential and pH gradient: Because mitochondria are very small, the membrane potential (electric potential difference) and pH gradient across the inner mitochondrial membrane cannot be determined by direct measurement. However, the inside pH can be measured by trapping fluorescent **pH-sensitive dyes** inside vesicles formed from the inner mitochondrial membrane.

Similarly, the membrane potential can be determined by adding radioactive K^+ ions and a trace amount of valinomycin to a suspension of respiring mitochondria. **Valinomycin** is an *ionophore*. Although the inner membrane is normally impermeable to K^+ ions, but valinomycin selectively binds K^+ ions in its hydrophilic interior and carries it across through the impermeable membranes. In the presence of valinomycin, K^+ ions equilibrates across the inner membrane of isolated mitochondria in accordance with the electric potential; the more negative the matrix side of the membrane, the more K^+ ions will accumulate in the matrix. At equilibrium, the value of membrane potential can be calculated from the Nernst equation.

Calculation of proton motive force

The **proton motive force** (pmf) is the potential energy stored in the form of an electrochemical gradient of protons across a biological membrane. It is the sum of the membrane potential and the pH gradient. The proton motive force can be expressed as:

$$\mathbf{pmf} = \Delta\psi - \mathbf{z}.\Delta\mathbf{pH}$$

where, $z = 2.303\ RT/F$, with values of 59 mV at 25°C

$\Delta\psi$ = the potential difference

Measurements on respiring mitochondria have shown that the electrical potential difference across the inner membrane is ~160 mV (negative inside matrix) and that ΔpH is ~1.0 (equivalent to ~60 mV). Thus, the total pmf is ~220 mV, with the membrane potential responsible for about 70 percent. In mitochondria, the electrical potential difference (~160 mV, inside negative) makes a larger contribution than the pH gradient (~1 pH unit, inside alkaline).

2.1.9 Chemiosmotic theory

What is the actual mechanism by which energy released from respiration is used to drive the synthesis of ATP? In 1961, Peter Mitchell, a British biochemist, proposed a mechanism of *chemiosmotic coupling* to answer this question. He explained how ATP synthase use the energy stored in a electrochemical gradient of protons across a biological membrane to synthesize ATP from ADP. This model proposes that energy from electron transport drives an active transport system, which pumps protons out of the mitochondrial matrix into the inter membrane space. This action generates an electrochemical gradient for protons. The protons on the outside have a thermodynamic tendency of flow back into the matrix so as to equalize proton concentration. When protons do flow back into the matrix, the energy is dissipated, some of it being used to drive the synthesis of ATP.

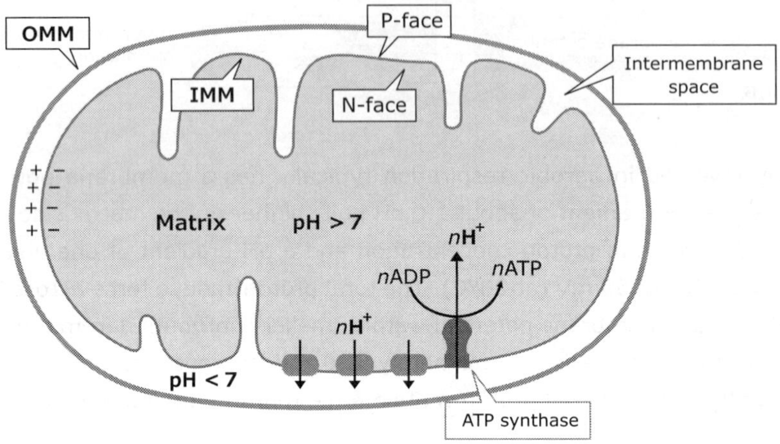

Figure 2.15 The general mechanism of oxidative phosphorylation. As a high-energy electron is passed along the electron transport chain, three respiratory enzyme complexes use some of the released energy to pump H^+ out of the matrix space. The resulting electrochemical proton gradient across the inner membrane drives H^+ back through the ATP synthase, a transmembrane protein complex that uses the energy of the H^+ flow to synthesize ATP from ADP and P_i in the matrix.

Experimental proof of chemiosmotic hypothesis

Experimental proof of chemiosmotic hypothesis was provided by Andre Jagendorf and Ernest Uribe in 1966. In an elegant experiment, isolated chloroplast thylakoid vesicles containing $CF_0\,CF_1$ particles were equilibrated in the dark with a buffered solution at pH 4. When the pH in the thylakoid lumen became 4, the vesicles were rapidly mixed with a solution at pH 8 containing ADP and P_i. A burst of ATP synthesis accompanied the transmembrane movement of protons driven by the electrochemical proton gradient. Because the formation of ATP occurred in the dark (with no input of energy from light), this experiment showed that a pH gradient across the membrane can mediate ATP synthesis. In similar experiments using *inside-out* preparations of submitochondrial vesicles, an artificially generated membrane electric potential also resulted in ATP synthesis.

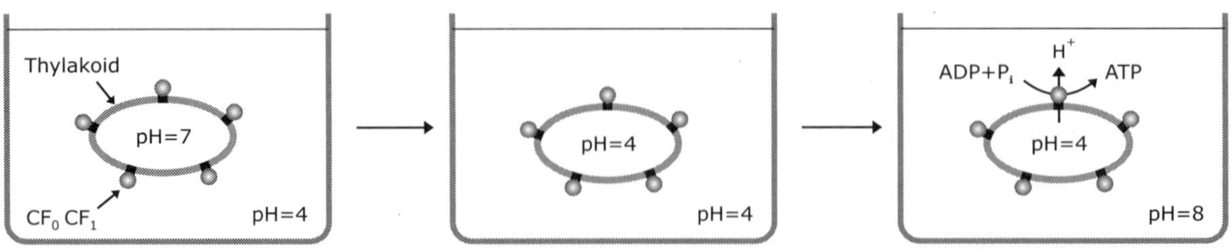

Figure 2.16 A proton gradient across the thylakoid membrane drives ATP synthesis. An artificial pH gradient was established across the thylakoid membrane. To create a transient pH gradient, thylakoids were soaked in a pH 4 buffer for several hours and then rapidly transferred them into a pH 8 buffer containing ADP and P_i. As protons moved out of the thylakoids into the medium, ATP was generated from ADP and P_i.

2.1.10 ATP synthase

The use of proton motive force for ATP synthesis is catalyzed by ATP synthase. The multiprotein ATP synthase (or **F_0F_1 complex** or **complex V**) catalyzes ATP synthesis as protons flow back through the inner membrane down the electrochemical proton gradient. It consists of two components – F_0 and F_1. The **F_0** component is embedded in the inner mitochondrial membrane. F_0 contains one **a subunit**, two **b subunits** and 9–12 **c subunits**. The c subunit consists of two α helices that span the membrane. An aspartic acid residue in the second helix lies at the center of the membrane. The structure of the 'a' subunit has not yet been directly observed, but it appears to include two *half-channels*. Protons can pass into either of these channels, but they cannot move completely across the membrane. The α-subunit is positioned such that each half-channel directly interacts with one c subunit. Each proton enters the cytoplasmic half-channel, follows a complete rotation of the c ring, and exits through the other half-channel into the matrix. The movement of protons through the half-channels from the high proton concentration of the cytoplasm to the low proton concentration of the matrix powers the rotation of the c ring. An antibiotic **oligomycin** completely blocks ATP synthesis by blocking the flow of protons through F_0 of ATP synthase (subscript 'O' denotes its inhibition by antibiotic oligomycin).

F_1 (made up of 3α, 3β, γ, δ and ε) is tightly bound to F_0 and protrudes into the matrix; it contains three β-subunits that are the sites of ATP synthesis. At the center of F_1 is the γ-subunit. The γ-subunit extends through F_1 and interacts with F_0. The $\gamma\varepsilon$ and C_{9-12} ring complex is the **rotor** (moving unit) and the a, b_2 and $\alpha_3\beta_3\delta$ complex is the **stator** (stationary unit). Rotational motion is imparted to the rotor by the passage of protons.

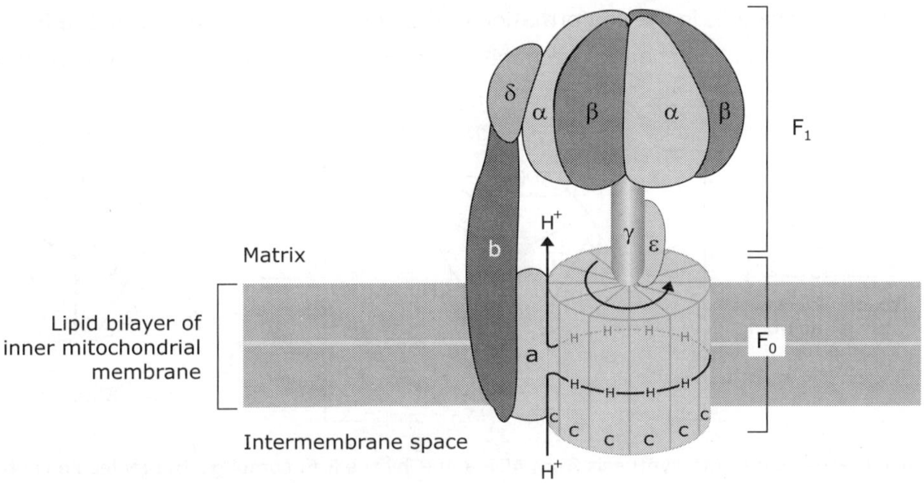

Figure 2.17 The enzyme complex consists of an F_0 and F_1 components. Proton passing through the disc of 'C' units cause it and the attached γ-subunit to rotate. The γ-subunit fits inside the F_1 of a three α and three β-subunits, which are fixed to the membrane and do not rotate.

ATP synthase synthesizes ATP by harnessing the proton motive force. ATP synthase can also function in reverse to hydrolyze ATP and pump H^+ across the inner mitochondrial membrane. It thus acts as a *reversible coupling device*, interconverting electrochemical proton gradient and chemical bond energies, or vice versa.

F_1 can be easily and reversibly dissociated from F_0 as a soluble enzyme that only hydrolyzes ATP and is often called **F_1-ATPase**. F_1 was first extracted from the mitochondrial inner membrane and purified by Efraim Racker and his colleagues. F_1 cannot synthesize ATP from ADP and P_i. It can catalyze the hydrolysis of ATP. Thus, the enzyme was originally called 'F_1 ATPase'. The complete F_0F_1 complex, like isolated F_1, can hydrolyze ATP to ADP and P_i, but its biological function is to catalyze the condensation of ADP and P_i to form ATP. The F_0F_1 complex is, therefore, more appropriately called **ATP synthase**.

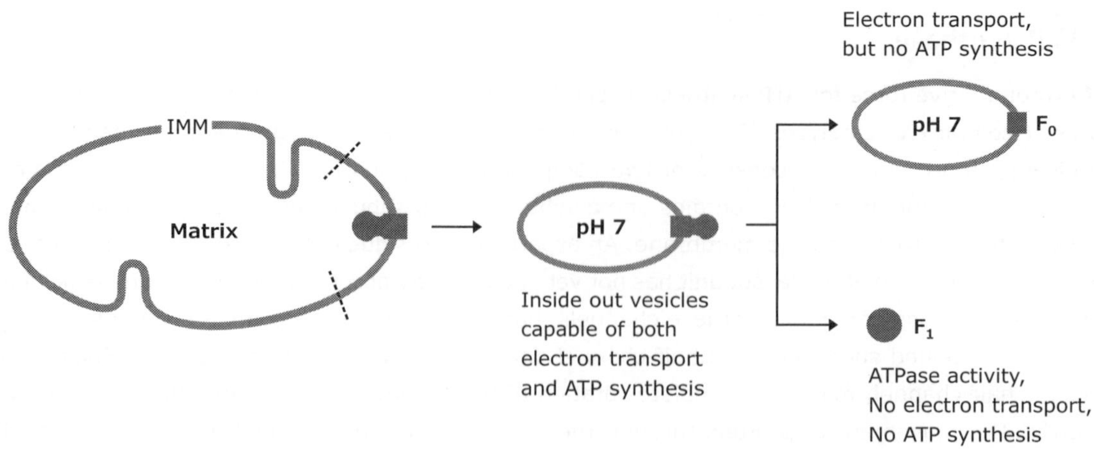

Figure 2.18 F_1 particles are required for ATP synthesis, but not for electron transport. Submitochondrial vesicles from which F_1 is removed by mechanical agitation cannot catalyze ATP synthesis. Because F_1 separated from membranes is capable of catalyzing ATP hydrolysis, it has been called the F_1 ATPase.

ATP synthesis

The **binding change mechanism** is a widely accepted model of ATP synthesis. Paul Boyer developed the binding change, or flip-flop mechanism, which postulated that ATP synthesis is coupled with a conformational change in the ATP synthase generated by rotation of the gamma subunit. Proton translocation through F_0 powers the rotation of the γ-subunit of F_1 ATPase, leading to changes in the conformation of the nucleotide-binding sites in the F_1 β-subunits (as described below). By means of this binding change mechanism, the F_0F_1 complex harnesses the proton-motive force to power ATP synthesis.

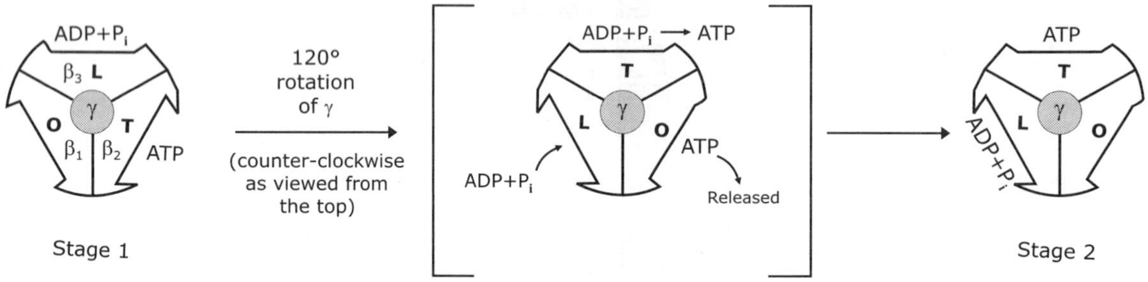

Figure 2.19 The binding-change mechanism of ATP synthesis from ADP and P_i by the F_0F_1 complex. The molecule contains three binding sites, which interconvert between three conformational states as the molecule rotates. The diagram shows one stage of the active cycle. The three $\alpha\beta$-dimers have three different states. In stage 1, the open state O is empty; the loose state L contains ADP + P_i ; and the tight state T contains ATP. In logical intermediate stage (bracketed), rotation of the γ within the $(\alpha\beta)_3$ hexamer converts the L state to a T state, the T state to an O, and the O state to an L. The L state can accept a new charge of substrate, the T state can form ATP. At stage 2, the ATP has fallen out of the O state, new ADP + P_i have bound to the L state, and ATP has been synthesized in the T state.

The three β-subunits alternate between three conformational states differing in their binding affinities for ATP, ADP and P_i:

O state (*open state*) binds ATP, ADP and P_i very weakly.

L state (*loose state*) binds ADP and P_i loosely.

T state (*tight state*) binds ADP and P_i very tightly and gives ATP.

The phosphoanhydride bond of ATP is synthesized only in the T state and ATP is released only in the O state. The free energy released on proton translocation is harnessed to interconvert three states. Change in conformations occurs due to rotation of γ-subunit. A 120° rotation of γ-subunit in counterclockwise direction changes one conformation state to another. Rotation of γ-subunit relative to fixed $\alpha_3\beta_3$ occurs in discrete 120° steps and conformation of each β-subunit changes in the order: O → L → T → O.

ATP synthase is the i.e., smallest rotary motor. Passage of H^+ ions through the membrane-embedded portion of ATP synthase (the F_0 component) causes rotation of the single, central axle-like γ-subunit inside the head group. The rotation of the γ-subunit induces conformational changes in the αβ dimers that allow ADP and P_i to be converted into ATP.

To demonstrate rotary motion, a modified form of the $\alpha_3\beta_3\gamma$ complex was used. The β-subunits were modified so they could be firmly anchored to a solid support. The γ-subunit was modified (the end that normally inserts into the F_0 component in the inner membrane) by attaching a fluorescently tagged, readily visible filament of actin. This arrangement allows rotations of the γ-subunit to be visualized as revolutions of the long actin filament. In these experiments, ATP synthase was studied in the reverse of its normal mechanism by allowing it to hydrolyze ATP. At low ATP concentrations, the actin filament was observed to revolve in steps of 120°. The hydrolysis of an individual ATP molecule provides the driving force for the 120° rotation of the γ-subunit, hence the corresponding revolution of the actin filament.

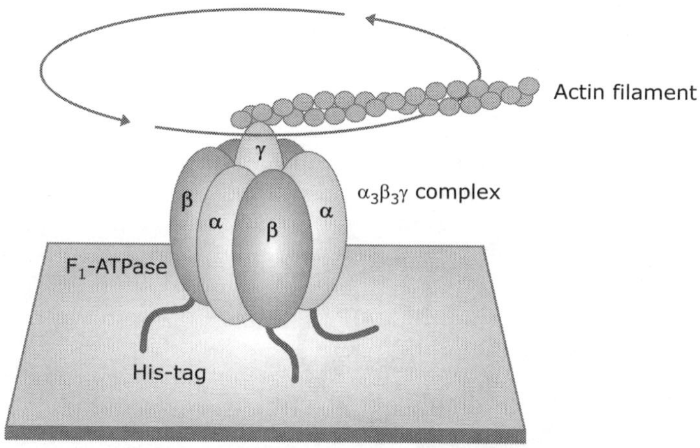

Figure 2.20
In this experiment, the F_1-ATPase was tethered to a glass surface by the β-subunit, using a His-tag at the N-terminus, and NTA-ligand on the glass. The motion was detected by attaching an actin filament to the γ-subunit, which was tagged with fluorescent dye to make it visible, and recorded using a video camera attached to a microscope. The motion was seen only under conditions of ATP-hydrolysis, and the direction of motion was always counter-clockwise when viewed from the F_0 portion, giving the sign of the catalytic mechanism.

Calculation of free energy change

The free energy change for the movement of protons along the gradient through ATP synthase can be calculated using the relationship between the membrane potential and free energy:

$$\Delta G = -nF\Delta E$$

where, n is the number of moles of protons being moved.
E is the membrane potential.
F is the Faraday constant (96,485 C/mol).

We can calculate the amount of free energy released by the passage of one mole of protons down an electrochemical gradient of 220 mV (0.22 V).

$$\Delta G = -1 \text{ mol} \times 96500 \text{ C/mol} \times 0.22 \text{ V} = -21230 \text{ J/mol} = -5.1 \text{ kcal/mol}$$

Thus, the free energy change is approximately -5.1 kcal/mol for the movement of one mole of protons down an electrochemical gradient of 220 mV.

ATP synthase probably requires *three* H^+ to synthesize one ATP. However, the most widely accepted experimental value for the number of protons required to drive the synthesis of one ATP molecule is *four* because it needs to be taken into account that the transport of ATP, ADP and P_i across the mitochondrial membrane are also driven by the proton gradient (discussed later). Hence, if 10 protons are pumped out per NADH, four must flow in to produce one ATP.

2.1.11 Uncoupling agents and ionophores

Uncoupling agents uncouple oxidation from phosphorylation. They allow the oxidation of NADH and $FADH_2$ and reduction of O_2 to continue at high levels but do not permit ATP synthesis. Thus, electron transport continues unabated, but ATP synthesis stops. Most common uncoupling agents are *2,4-dinitrophenol* (**DNP**), *dicoumarol* and carbonyl cyanide-p-(trifluoromethoxy) phenylhydrazone (**FCCP**). DNP is a weak acid that is soluble in lipid bilayer both in their protonated neutral forms and in their anionic states. DNP in an anionic state picks up protons in the inter-membrane space and diffuses readily across mitochondrial membranes. After entering the matrix in the protonated form, they can release a proton, thus dissipating the proton gradient and inhibiting ATP synthesis. The energy released by the oxidation of NADH in the presence of DNP is converted to heat. Dicoumarol and FCCP act in the same way. Similarly, **thermogenin** is a physiological uncoupler found in brown adipose tissue that functions to generate body heat, particularly for the newborn and during hibernation in animals.

Some ionophore such as **valinomycin** uncouples electron transport from oxidative phosphorylation by dissipating the electrochemical gradient across the mitochondrial membrane. **Ionophores** are lipophilic molecules that bind specific ions and facilitate their transport through the membrane. The addition of valinomycin makes inner mitochondrial membrane permeable for K^+. It causes the movement of K^+ along the concentration gradient from the cytosol into the matrix. This movement of K^+ reduces the value of membrane potential component of pmf i.e., $\Delta\psi$ (without a direct effect on the pH gradient) and uncouples electron transport from ATP synthesis.

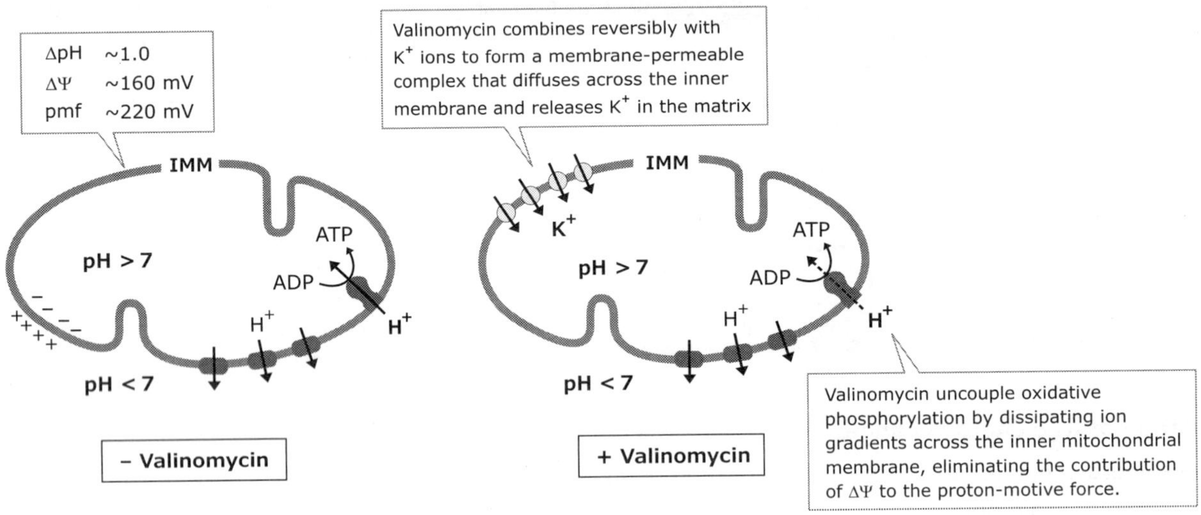

2.1.12 ATP synthasome

The major function of oxidative phosphorylation is to generate ATP from ADP and P_i. Most of the ATP generated by oxidative phosphorylation in mitochondria is exported to the cytoplasm. Thus, mitochondria must contain mechanisms to export ATP and import ADP and P_i. However, ATP and ADP do not diffuse freely across the inner mitochondrial membrane. A specific transport protein, **ATP-ADP translocase** (also called *adenine nucleotide translocase*), which acts as an antiporter, mediates the transport of ATP and ADP. ADP enters the mitochondrial matrix only if ATP exits, and vice versa. Because *ATP-ADP translocase* moves four negative charges out of every three moved in, its activity is favoured by the transmembrane electrochemical proton gradient, which gives the matrix a net negative charge. ATP-ADP translocase function is inhibited by a toxic glycoside **atractyloside**. ATP-ADP exchange is energetically expensive; transmembrane proton gradient across the inner mitochondrial membrane powers the exchange.

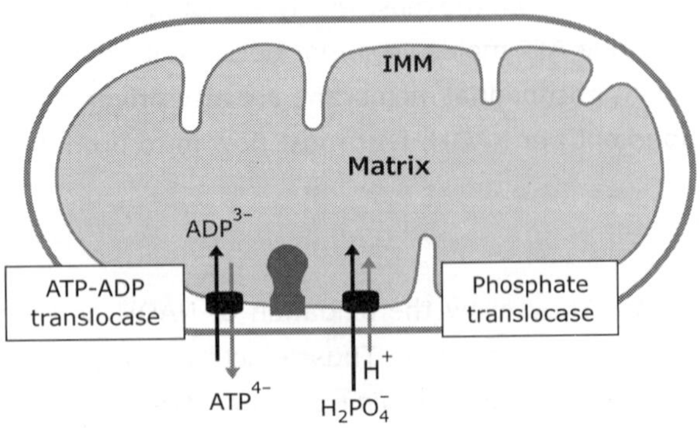

Figure 2.21
Transport systems of the mitochondrial inner membrane carry ADP and P_i into the matrix and allow the newly synthesized ATP to leave. The ATP-ADP translocase is an antiporter; the same protein moves ADP into the matrix and ATP out. The phosphate translocase is an symporter that carries P_i ($H_2PO_4^-$) along with H^+ into the matrix.

A second membrane transport system is the **phosphate translocase**, which promotes symport of one $H_2PO_4^-$ and one H^+ into the matrix. At pH 7, P_i is present as both HPO_4^{2-} and $H_2PO_4^-$; the phosphate translocase is specific for $H_2PO_4^-$. This transport process is also powered by the transmembrane proton gradient. Thus, the proton-motive force is responsible for both ATP synthesis and for transporting substrates (ADP and P_i) into and product (ATP) out of the mitochondria matrix. A complex of the ATP synthase and both translocases (ATP-ADP translocase and phosphate translocase) is called **ATP synthasome**.

2.1.13 Shuttle systems

The glycolytic pathway is a primary source of NADH formation. NADH synthesized during the glycolytic process finally transfers the electrons to electron transport chain. But, NADH cannot cross the inner mitochondrial membrane. So, two different shuttle systems help in the transfer of electrons from NADH to the electron transport chain.

The **malate-aspartate shuttle** is the principal mechanism for the movement of NADH from the cytoplasm into the mitochondrial matrix. The electrons are *carried* into the mitochondrial matrix in the form of malate. Cytoplasmic *malate dehydrogenase* reduces oxaloacetate to malate while oxidizing NADH to NAD^+. Malate then enters the mitochondrial matrix, where the reverse reaction is carried out by mitochondria malate dehydrogenase and the regeneration of NADH occurs.

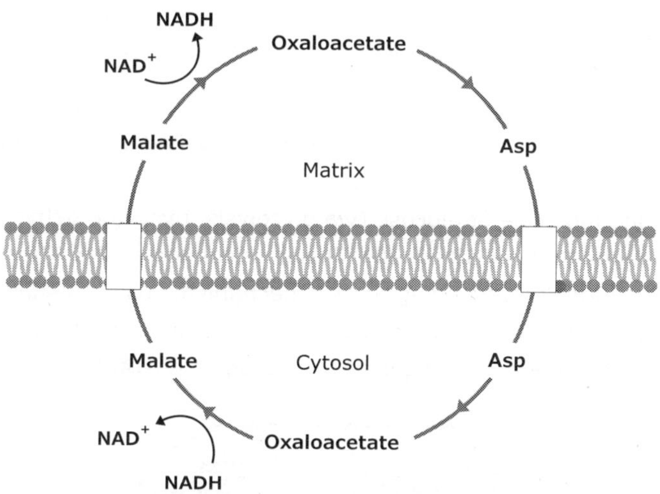

Figure 2.22
The malate-aspartate shuttle for transporting NADH from cytosol into the mitochondrial matrix. NADH in the cytosol transfers electrons to oxaloacetate, producing malate. Malate is transported across the inner membrane by the help of transporter. In the matrix, malate passes electrons to NAD^+; the resulting matrix NADH is finally oxidized by the mitochondrial respiratory chain.

In **glycerol 3-phosphate shuttle**, electrons from NADH can enter the mitochondrial electron transport chain by being used to reduce dihydroxyacetone phosphate to glycerol 3-phosphate. Glycerol 3-phosphate is reoxidized by electron transfer to an FAD prosthetic group in a membrane-bound glycerol 3-phosphate dehydrogenase. $FADH_2$ subsequently transfers electrons to Q to form QH_2, which allows these electrons to enter the electron-transport chain.

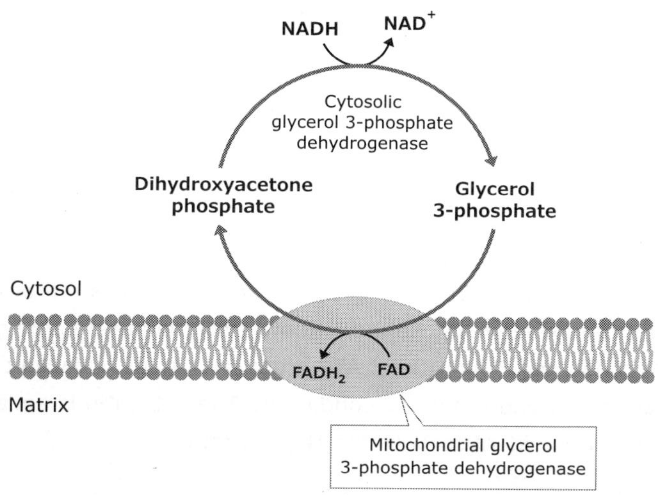

Figure 2.23
Glycerol 3-phosphate shuttle. Electrons from NADH can enter the mitochondrial electron transport chain by being used to reduce dihydroxyacetone phosphate to glycerol 3-phosphate. Glycerol 3-phosphate is reoxidized by electron transfer to a FAD prosthetic group in a membrane-bound glycerol 3-phosphate dehydrogenase.

Summary of ATP synthesis from the oxidation of one molecule of glucose

	NADH	$FADH_2$	ATP
Glycolysis (cytosol)			
Glucose ⟶ Glucose 6-phosphate			−1
Fructose 6-phosphate ⟶ Fructose 1,6-bisphosphate			−1
2 Glyceraldehyde 3-phosphate ⟶ 2 Glycerate 1,3-bisphosphate	+2		
2 Glycerate 1,3-bisphosphate ⟶ 2 Glycerate 3-phosphate			+2
2 Phosphoenolpyruvate ⟶ 2 Pyruvate			+2
Mitochondrial reactions			
2 Pyruvate ⟶ 2 Acetyl-CoA	+2		
Citric acid cycle			
2 Isocitrate ⟶ 2 α-ketoglutarate	+2		
2 α-ketoglutarate ⟶ 2 Succinyl-CoA	+2		
2 Succinyl-CoA ⟶ 2 Succinate			+2
2 Succinate ⟶ 2 Fumarate		+2	
2 Malate ⟶ 2 Oxaloacetate	+2		
	10 NADH	**2 $FADH_2$**	**4ATP**

Total yield of ATP from the complete oxidation of one molecule of glucose (*via* glycolysis, pyruvate dehydrogenase complex reaction, Krebs cycle and oxidative phosphorylation) = 32 (or 30). This is calculated as 2.5 ATP per NADH and 1.5 ATP per $FADH_2$. The total number is either 30 or 32 depending on the mechanisms used to shuttle NADH equivalents from the cytosol to the mitochondrial matrix. In prokaryotic organisms, complete oxidation of one molecule of glucose yields 32 ATP, because no shuttle systems are required for transport of NADH.

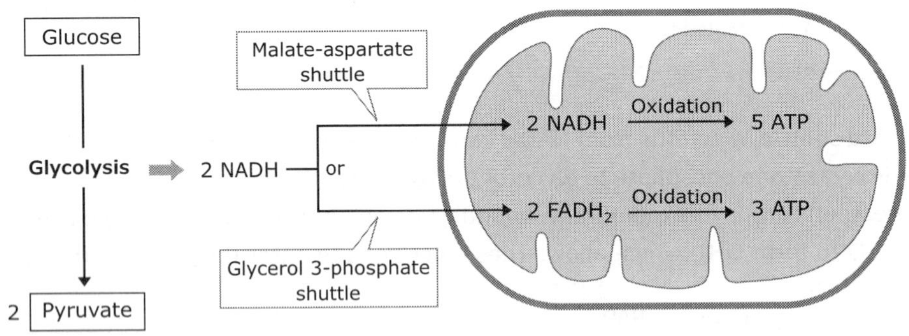

Figure 2.24 Cytosolic NADH transported by the malate-aspartate shuttle gives 2.5 ATP. But NADH can be brought into mitochondria by the malate-aspartate shuttle only if the $NADH/NAD^+$ ratio is higher in the cytosol than in the mitochondrial matrix. When cytosolic NADH transported by the glycerol 3-phosphate shuttle is oxidized by the respiratory chain, 1.5 rather than 2.5 ATP are formed.

2.1.14 P/O ratio

Under aerobic conditions, each mole of NADH or $FADH_2$ carries $2e^-$ and each $2e^-$ reduces one atom of oxygen. Therefore, under aerobic conditions ATP production from oxidative phosphorylation with O_2 as the electron acceptor can be equated to electron released or atoms of O consumed. The ratio of ATP production to e^- released or atoms of O consumed may be designated the P/O or $P/2e^-$ ratio, under aerobic conditions. The P:O ratio is equal to the product of $(H^+/2e^-)$ and $(\sim P/H^+)$. Note that the P:O ratio is identical with the $(P:2e^-)$ ratio.

Estimation of the number of ATP molecules formed during aerobic state can be calculated from the P/O ratio (the ratio of ATP synthesized to oxygen reduces to water molecules). During transport of two electrons from NADH to oxygen, about 10 protons are transported into the intermembrane space, while from $FADH_2$, the number is only six. ATP synthase probably requires *three* H^+ to synthesize one ATP, so that the maximum P/O ratio of around 3 (in case of NADH) or 2 (in case of $FADH_2$) is possible. However, the actual value is lower. It needs to be taken into account that the transport of ATP, ADP and P_i across the mitochondrial membrane are also driven by the proton gradient. The most widely accepted experimental value for number of protons required to drive the synthesis of an ATP molecule is 4, of which one is used in transporting ATP, ADP and P_i across the mitochondrial membrane. If 10 protons are pumped out per NADH and 4 must flow in to produce 1 ATP. The P/O ratio for the oxidation of NADH and $FADH_2$ are, therefore, 2.5 and 1.5, respectively.

Problem

When pure reduced cytochrome c is added to carefully prepared mitochondria along with ADP, P_i, antimycin A and oxygen, the cytochrome c becomes oxidized and ATP is formed with a P/O ratio (the ratio of ATP synthesized to O atoms reduced) approaching 1.0.

a. Indicate the probable flow of electrons in this system.
b. Why was antimycin A added?
c. What does this experiment tell you about the location of coupling sites for oxidative phosphorylation?

Solution:

a. Cyt c $\longrightarrow$ Cyt a $\longrightarrow$ Cyt a_3 $\longrightarrow$ O_2
b. To block oxidation of endogenous substrates.
c. One site associated with cytochrome oxidase.

2.1.15 Fermentation

Pyruvate, the end product of glycolysis has two fates. In the absence of oxygen, it undergoes *fermentation* and *anaerobic respiration* whereas in the presence of oxygen it enters the *aerobic respiration*. *Anaerobic respiration is different from fermentation*. In **anaerobic respiration**, final electron acceptor is a compound other than O_2 like nitrate, sulfate and fumarate whereas, in fermentation, the final electron acceptor is an endogenous organic molecule. Fermentation is a self-contained process and no outside electron acceptor is involved. It does not involve an electron transport system and ATP synthesis by oxidative phosphorylation. In this section, we have discussed only fermentation.

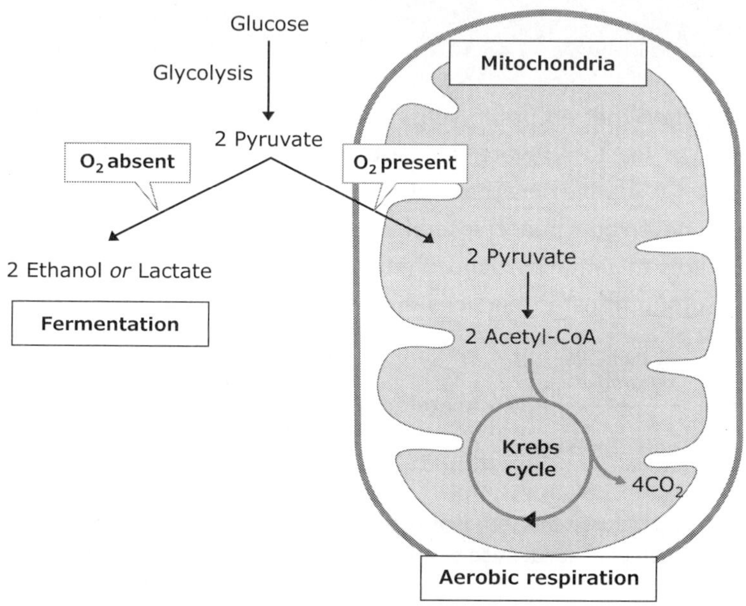

Figure 2.25
Glycolysis is common to fermentation and aerobic respiration. In a facultative anaerobe, which is capable of both aerobic respiration and fermentation, pyruvate is committed to one of those two pathways, usually depending on whether or not oxygen is present.

During fermentation, when O_2 is not present (or the cell cannot use it) NAD^+ is regenerated from NADH by transferring electrons to organic molecules. In this process, pyruvate is converted into organic molecules like lactate, ethanol. Fermentations are classified in terms of either the substrate fermented or the fermentation products formed. Some of the major types of fermentations on the basis of products formed are alcoholic, lactic acid, propionic acid and butyric acid fermentation.

Lactic acid fermentation: Muscle cells and certain bacterial species (e.g., *Lactobacillus*) oxidize NADH by transforming pyruvate into lactate and the process is known as *lactic acid fermentation*. Lactic acid fermentation is catalyzed by an enzyme, *lactate dehydrogenase* (LDH). In animals, lactate formed in the muscles is recycled to glucose in the liver.

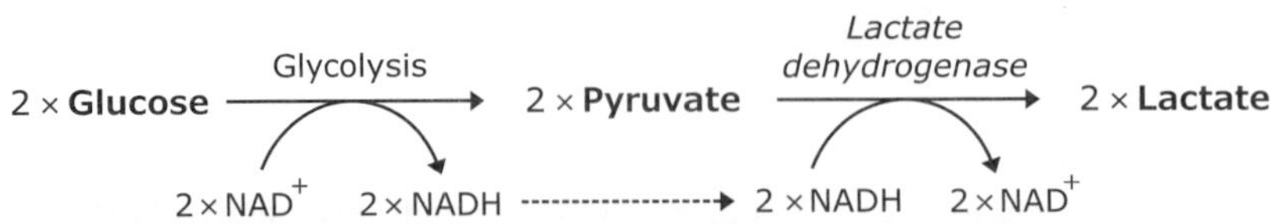

Figure 2.26 In lactic acid fermentation, the NADH formed in the oxidation of glyceraldehyde 3-phosphate is consumed in the reduction of pyruvate. The regeneration of NAD^+ in the reduction of pyruvate to lactate sustains the continued operation of glycolysis under anaerobic conditions.

Lactate produced in muscle is transported from the muscle to the liver, where it is reoxidized by liver LDH to pyruvate. By the process of gluconeogenesis, pyruvate is finally converted into glucose in the liver. Liver again exports glucose to muscle for glycolysis. This cycle is referred to as the **Cori cycle** (also known as **lactic acid cycle**). The Cori cycle is named for Carl and Gerty Cori, who received the Nobel Prize in physiology or medicine in 1947 for their studies of glycogen metabolism and blood glucose regulation.

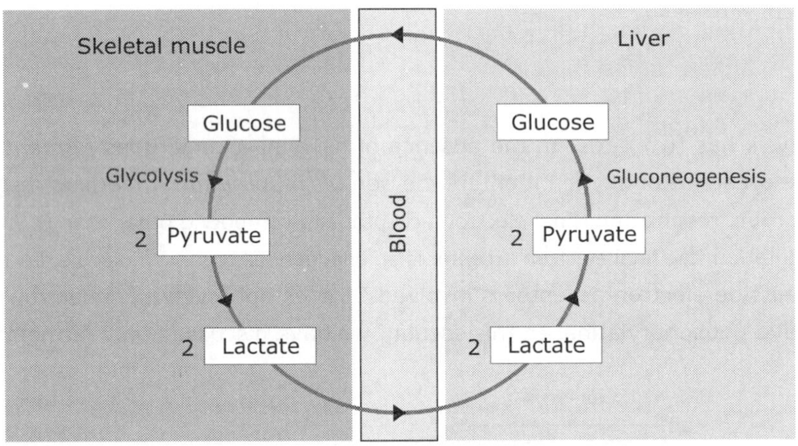

Figure 2.27
The Cori cycle refers to the metabolic pathway in which lactate produced by fermentation of glucose in the muscles moves to the liver and is converted to glucose, which then returns to the muscles and is converted back to lactate.

Alcoholic fermentation: In *alcoholic fermentation* that occurs in yeast and several bacterial species, pyruvate is converted into ethanol in a two-step pathway. In yeast, pyruvate is decarboxylated to form acetaldehyde, which is then reduced by NADH to form ethanol. The non-oxidative decarboxylation of pyruvate to acetaldehyde is catalyzed by *pyruvate decarboxylase* and NADH-dependent reduction of acetaldehyde to ethanol is catalyzed by *alcohol dehydrogenase*. Pyruvate decarboxylase requires thiamine pyrophosphate as a coenzyme. This coenzyme, derived from vitamin B_1, participates in a number of group transfer reactions involving an activated aldehyde moiety.

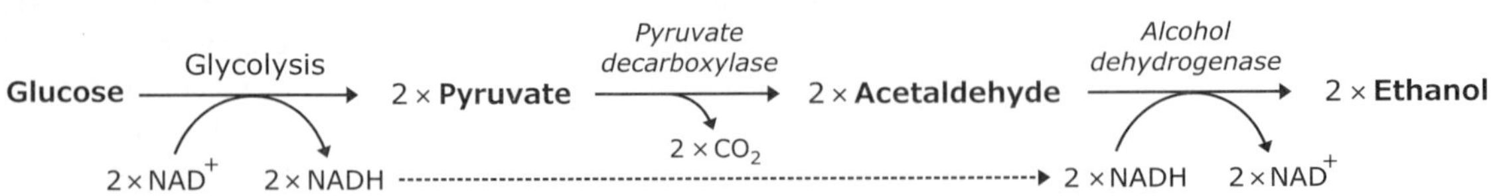

Figure 2.28 In alcoholic fermentation, conversion of glucose into ethanol occurs. The NADH generated by the oxidation of glyceraldehyde 3-phosphate is consumed in the reduction of acetaldehyde to ethanol. Thus, there is no net oxidation-reduction in the conversion of glucose into ethanol.

Problem

Using glucose, labelled with ^{14}C in its aldehyde group, via glycolysis and alcoholic fermentation, where would the labeled carbon be at the end of alcoholic fermentation?

Solution:

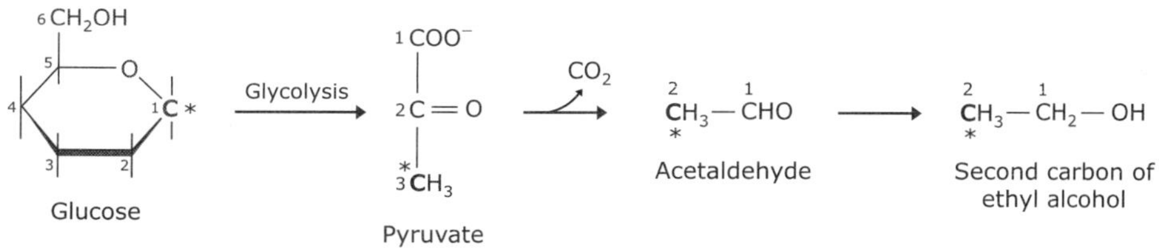

2.1.16 Pasteur effect

Louis Pasteur observed that when yeast is exposed to aerobic conditions (in the presence of oxygen), their glucose consumption and ethanol production drop. Whereas in the absence of oxygen, glucose consumption increases several fold. The reason for the decrease in consumption of glucose is that fermentation results in the production of 2 ATPs per glucose, whereas aerobic respiration yields 32 ATPs per glucose. Hence, for the generation of the same amount of ATP to perform essential metabolic activities, more consumption of glucose is needed in anaerobic conditions. This accounts for Pasteur's observation that yeast consumes more glucose when growing anaerobically than aerobically (called the *Pasteur effect*).

Box 2.3 Aerobic and anaerobic respiration

In **aerobic respiration**, the final electron acceptor is oxygen, whereas the exogenous terminal electron acceptor in **anaerobic respiration** is other than oxygen molecule. The most common terminal electron acceptors used during anaerobic respiration are nitrate, sulfate, and CO_2, but metals and a few organic molecules such as fumarate can also be used. Both aerobic and anaerobic respiration involves the activity of an electron transport chain. As electrons pass through the chain to the final electron acceptor, a type of potential energy called the proton motive force (PMF) is generated and used to synthesize ATP from ADP. Hence, during aerobic and anaerobic respiration, ATP is synthesized by substrate-level phosphorylation as well as oxidative phosphorylation. Anaerobic respiration does not produce as much ATP as aerobic respiration. Nevertheless, anaerobic respiration is useful because it allows ATP synthesis by oxidative phosphorylation in the absence of O_2.

In contrast, **fermentation** uses an electron acceptor that is endogenous (from within the cell) and does not involve an electron transport chain. The endogenous electron acceptor is usually an intermediate (e.g., pyruvate) of the catabolic pathway used to oxidize the organic energy source. During fermentation, ATP is synthesized almost exclusively by substrate-level phosphorylation.

Table 2.4 Comparison of aerobic respiration, fermentation and anaerobic respiration

Aerobic respiration	Oxygen-dependent Final electron acceptor: Oxygen molecule. Type of phosphorylation used to generate ATP: Substrate-level and oxidative.
Fermentation	Oxygen-independent Final electron acceptor: An organic substance. Type of phosphorylation used to generate ATP: Substrate-level.
Anaerobic respiration	Oxygen-independent Final electron acceptor: Substance such as nitrate, sulfate but not oxygen molecule. Type of phosphorylation used to generate ATP: Substrate-level and oxidative.

2.1.17 Warburg effect

Most cancer cells are characterized by increased glucose uptake and aerobic glycolysis. A very high rate of glycolysis followed by lactic acid fermentation, even in the presence of oxygen and fully functioning mitochondria is known as the **aerobic glycolysis** (or '**Warburg effect**'). Increased aerobic glycolysis is uniquely observed in cancer cells. It was Otto Warburg who demonstrated in 1924 that cancer cells show an increased dependence on glycolysis to meet their energy needs, regardless of whether they were well-oxygenated. Converting glucose to lactate, rather than metabolizing it through oxidative phosphorylation in the mitochondria, is far less efficient as less ATP is generated per unit of glucose metabolized. Nevertheless, cancer cells perform aerobic glycolysis. Therefore, a high rate of glucose uptake is required to meet increased energy needs to support rapid tumor progression.

Previously, it was thought the Warburg effect was a consequence of damage to the mitochondria or an adaptation to hypoxic conditions during the early avascular phase of tumor development. But this hypothesis has been shown to be incorrect. In the last 90 years, several hypotheses have been suggested, to this date, there is no clear explanation of this rather unusual effect.

2.1.18 Respiratory substrate and respiratory quotient

The organic substances, which are oxidized in the living cells to release energy, are called **respiratory substrates**. Carbohydrate, lipid or protein may act as a respiratory substrate. The most common and favoured respiratory substrate is glucose. The points of entry of different substrates in the respiratory pathway are different. For example, if lipid such as triacylglycerol is used as a respiratory substrate, it is first broken down into glycerol and fatty acids. Fatty acids are then oxidized to acetyl-CoA by the process of **β-oxidation**. Finally, acetyl-CoA enters the respiratory pathway. Glycerol enters the pathway after being converted to glyceraldehyde-3 phosphate. Similarly, the proteins would be degraded by *proteases* and the individual amino acids after deamination would enter the pathway at some stage within the Krebs cycle or even as pyruvate or acetyl-CoA, depending on their structure.

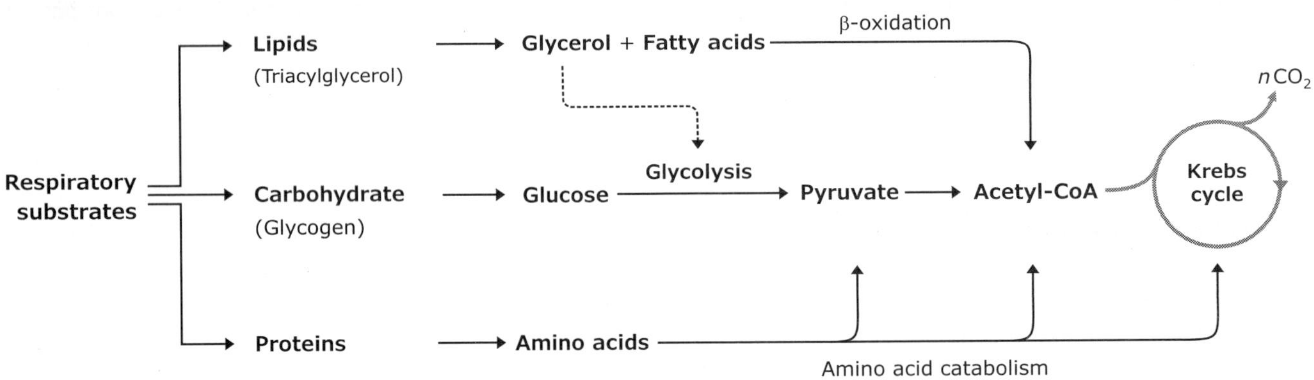

Respiratory quotient

Respiration is a metabolic process that involves the oxidation of respiratory substrates. As a result of oxidation, carbons are released in the form of carbon dioxide along with the release of energy. Though carbohydrate, fat or protein may act as a respiratory substrate, the common respiratory substrate is carbohydrate. **Respiratory quotient** (or **respiratory coefficient**) is defined as the ratio of moles of CO_2 produced to the moles of oxygen consumed during complete oxidation of a respiratory substrate to CO_2 and H_2O. It is a dimensionless value. It is calculated for a particular substrate i.e., carbohydrates, organic acid, fat and protein. The moles of oxygen required as well as the moles of carbon dioxide released depend on the nature of the respiratory substrate that is being oxidized. For carbohydrates, such as glucose, the respiratory quotient is 1.

$$\text{Respiratory quotient (RQ)} = \frac{6 \text{ mol of } CO_2 \text{ produced}}{6 \text{ mol of } O_2 \text{ consumed}} = 1 \qquad (C_6H_{12}O_6 + 6 \times O_2 \longrightarrow 6 \times CO_2 + 6 \times H_2O)$$

Here, 6 moles of CO_2 are produced to the 6 moles of oxygen consumed during complete oxidation of glucose. Thus, RQ is 1. RQ is less than one when respiration is aerobic, but the respiratory substrate is either fat or protein. *RQ is about 0.7 for lipids and about 0.9 in the case of proteins*. RQ is more than unity when organic acids such as malic acid, oxalic acid are broken down as a respiratory substrate under aerobic conditions. For malic acid, RQ value is 1.33.

Table 2.5 Name of the substance and their respiratory quotient

Glucose (carbohydrate)	1.00
Proteins	0.8 – 0.9
Oleic acid (lipid)	0.71
Malic acid (organic acid)	1.33
Oxalic acid (organic acid)	4.00

2.1.19 Entner–Doudoroff pathway

Entner-Doudoroff pathway is an alternative pathway that catabolizes glucose to pyruvate using a set of enzymes different from those used in either glycolysis or the pentose phosphate pathway. This pathway, first reported by Michael Doudoroff and Nathan Entner, occurs only in prokaryotes, mostly in gram-negative bacteria such as *Pseudomonas aeruginosa, Azotobacter, Rhizobium*. In this pathway, glucose phosphate is oxidized to 2-keto-3-deoxy-6-phosphogluconic acid (KDPG) which is cleaved by *2-keto-3-deoxyglucose-phosphate aldolase* to pyruvate and glyceraldehyde-3-phosphate. The latter is oxidized to pyruvate by glycolytic pathway wherein two ATPs are produced by substrate-level phosphorylations. This process yields one ATP as well as one NADH and one NADPH for every glucose molecule.

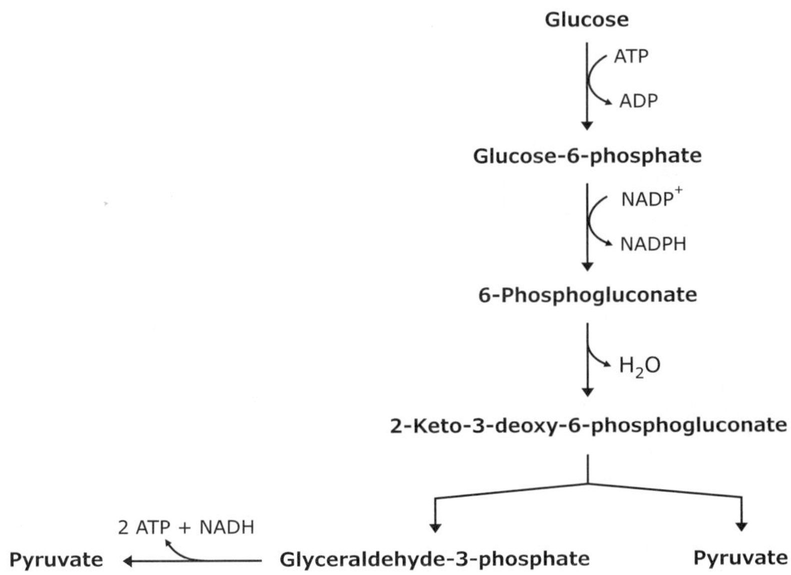

Figure 2.29
The Entner-Doudoroff pathway replaces the preparatory phase of the glycolysis and yields pyruvate and glyceraldehyde 3-phosphate. A key intermediate of the Entner-Doudoroff pathway is 2-keto-3-deoxy-6-phosphogluconate, which is formed from glucose by three reactions that consume one ATP and produce one NADPH.

Problem

When oxygen is added to an anaerobic suspension of cells consuming glucose at a high rate, the rate of glucose consumption declines greatly as the oxygen is used up, and accumulation of lactate ceases. This effect is characteristic of most cells capable of both aerobic and anaerobic glucose catabolism.

a. Why does the accumulation of lactate cease after oxygen is added?

b. Why does the presence of oxygen decrease the rate of glucose consumption?

Solution:

a. Because NADH is reoxidized via electron transfer instead of lactic acid fermentation.

b. Oxidative phosphorylation is more efficient and release more energy from one mole of glucose.

2.2 Glyoxylate cycle

The *glyoxylate cycle* is a cyclic pathway that converts two molecules of acetyl-CoA, to one molecule of succinate.

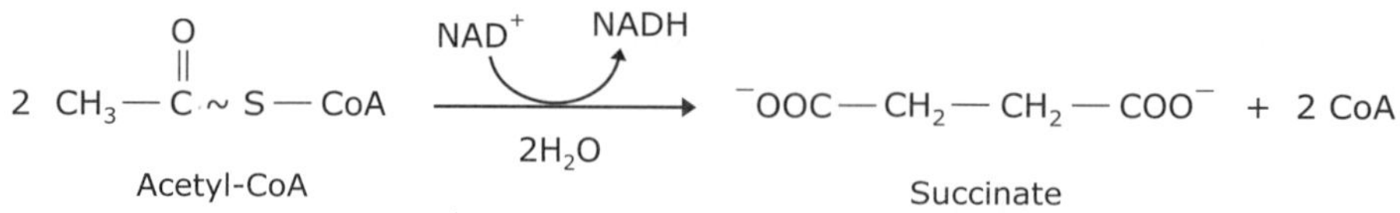

This process occurs in many bacteria, plants, protists, and fungi, *but absent in animals*. In plant cells, it occurs in the **glyoxysome** (present only in plant cells); a specialized peroxisome that carries out both β-oxidation of fatty acids to acetyl-CoA and utilization of that acetyl-CoA in the glyoxylate cycle. Most of the enzymes of the glyoxylate cycle are the same as those of the TCA cycle. Glyoxysomal oxaloacetate is condensed with acetyl-CoA to form citrate, which is isomerized to isocitrate as in the TCA cycle. Enzyme **isocitrate lyase** present within glyoxysome cleaves the isocitrate to succinate and glyoxylate. Another glyoxysomal enzyme **malate synthase** condenses glyoxylate with a second molecule of acetyl-CoA to form malate. Finally, malate dehydrogenase catalyzes the oxidation of malate to oxaloacetate. The succinate produced within glyoxysome is transported to the mitochondria, where it enters the TCA cycle and is converted to malate, which has two alternative fates:

1. It can be converted to oxaloacetate in mitochondria, continuing the TCA cycle.
2. It can be transported to the cytosol, where it is converted to oxaloacetate for entry into **gluconeogenesis**.

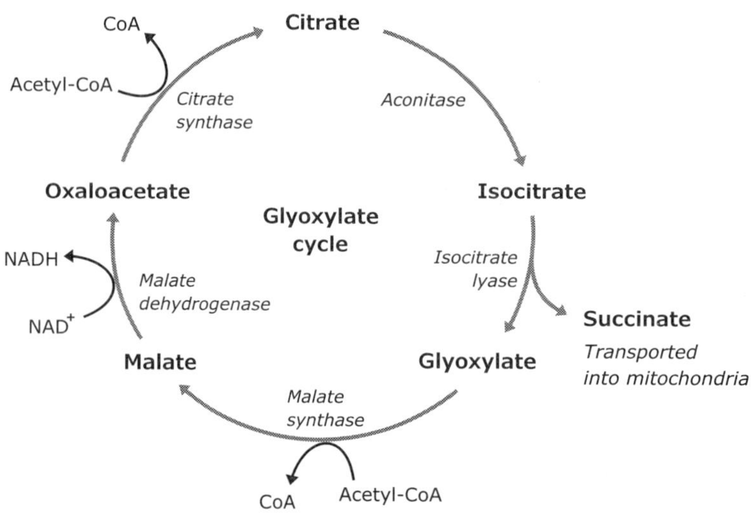

Figure 2.30 The glyoxylate cycle. The first two steps are identical to TCA cycle. The third step bypasses the CO_2-evolving steps of the TCA cycle to produce succinate and glyoxylate. The malate synthase catalyzes the synthesis of malate from glyoxylate and another acetyl-CoA. The succinate produced within glyoxysome is transported to the mitochondria, where it enters the TCA cycle.

Thus, the glyoxylate cycle, like the TCA cycle, begins with the condensation of acetyl-CoA and oxaloacetate to form citrate, which is then isomerized to isocitrate. Instead of being decarboxylated, isocitrate is cleaved by isocitrate lyase into succinate and glyoxylate. This bypasses the decarboxylation steps that take place in the TCA cycle. The subsequent steps regenerate oxaloacetate from glyoxylate. Organisms that lack the glyoxylate pathway cannot undertake the net synthesis of glucose from acetyl-CoA. This is the reason humans cannot convert fatty acids (which are catabolized to acetyl-CoA) to carbohydrates (that is, glucose). Some human pathogens such as *Mycobacterium tuberculosis* use the glyoxylate cycle to convert lipids into carbohydrates.

2.3 Pentose phosphate pathway

Pentose phosphate pathway (or **hexose monophosphate pathway** or **phosphogluconate pathway**) is an alternative pathway to glucose oxidation. The enzymes of pentose phosphate pathway shunt are located in the cytosol and in plastids. There are two distinct phases in the pentose phosphate pathway. The first phase is an **oxidative phase** in which there is an oxidation of glucose 6-phosphate and synthesis of NADPH and ribulose 5-phosphate. The second phase is a **non-oxidative phase** in which three molecules of five-carbon sugar ribulose 5-phosphate are rearranged to regenerate two molecules of glucose 6-phosphate and one molecule glyceraldehyde 3-phosphate.

Oxidative phase: The oxidative phase (an irreversible phase) of the pentose phosphate pathway starts with the oxidation of glucose 6-phosphate, a reaction catalyzed by enzyme *glucose 6-phosphate dehydrogenase* (**G6PD**). G6PD is an NADP-dependent enzyme that converts glucose 6-phosphate to 6-phosphogluconolactone. The latter is then hydrolyzed by the enzyme *gluconolactonase* to 6-phosphogluconate. 6-phosphogluconate is *oxidatively decarboxylated* to ribulose 5-phosphate with the generation of a second molecule of NADPH. This reaction is catalyzed by enzyme *6-phosphogluconate dehydrogenase*. The net result of the oxidative phase is the generation of 2 moles of NADPH, oxidation of one carbon to CO_2, and synthesis of one molecule of pentose phosphate, ribulose 5-phosphate. The activity of the enzyme G6PD, which catalyzes the pathway's first committed step, is regulated by the $NADP^+$ concentration. When the cell consumes NADPH, the $NADP^+$ concentration rises, increasing the activity of the G6PD and thereby stimulating NADPH regeneration.

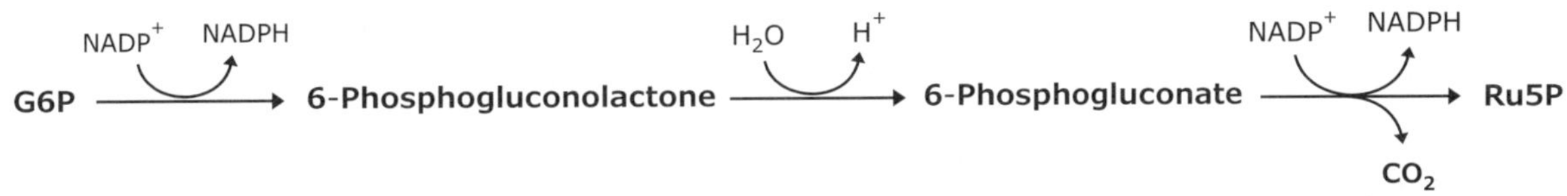

Figure 2.31 Oxidative phase of the pentose phosphate pathway. The first step of the pathway includes the oxidation of glucose 6-phosphate (G6P) to 6-phosphogluconolactone by an enzyme *glucose 6-phosphate dehydrogenase* (G6PD). The lactone is hydrolyzed to 6-phosphogluconate by an enzyme *gluconolactonase*. Finally, 6-phosphogluconate undergoes oxidative decarboxylation by an enzyme *6-phosphogluconate dehydrogenase* to form a ketopentose ribulose 5-phosphate (Ru5P).

The pentose phosphate pathway is fundamentally different from glycolytic pathway. In pentose phosphate pathway, oxidation of glucose 6-phosphate utilizes $NADP^+$ rather than NAD^+ and produces CO_2, whereas glycolytic process utilizes NAD^+ and does not produce CO_2. Similarly, no ATP is generated in the pentose phosphate pathway, whereas it is a major product of glycolysis.

Non-oxidative phase: The oxidative phase produces ribulose 5-phosphate and NADPH. The non-oxidative phase is concerned with the interconversion of three, four, five and seven carbon monosaccharides. In this phase, ribulose 5-phosphate is acted upon by an **epimerase** (ribulose 5-phosphate epimerase) to produce xylulose 5-phosphate while an **isomerase** (*phosphopentose isomerase*) converts ribulose 5-phosphate to ribose 5-phosphate. Then, in a series of rearrangements of the carbon skeletons, three five-carbon sugar phosphates are converted to two six-carbon sugar phosphates and one three-carbon sugar phosphates.

$$3 \times \text{Ribulose 5-phosphate} \longrightarrow 2 \times \text{Glucose 6-phosphate} + \text{Glyceraldehyde 3-phosphate}$$

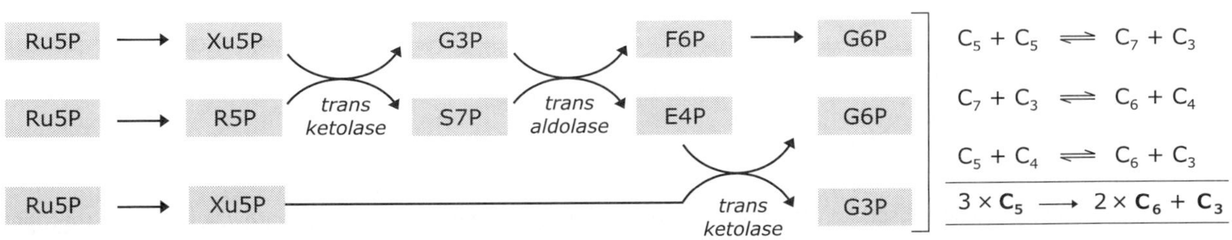

Figure 2.32 Flowchart of non-oxidative phase. Ru5P (Ribulose 5-phosphate), Xu5P (Xylulose 5-phosphate), R5P (Ribose 5-phosphate), G3P (Glyceraldehyde 3-phosphate), E4P (Erythrose 4-phosphate), S7P (Sedoheptulose 7-phosphate).

Two enzymes unique to the pentose phosphate pathway act in interconversions of three, four, five and seven carbon containing monosaccharides: **transketolase** and **transaldolase**. Transketolase and transaldolase catalyze the transfer of 2C and 3C units, respectively, in each case from a ketose donor to an aldose acceptor. However, the names of these enzymes should be changed since transketolase actually transfers an aldol moiety and transaldolase actually transfers a ketol moiety. However, the traditional enzyme names are used here. Transketolase catalytic activity requires **thiamine pyrophosphate** (**TPP**), as a coenzyme.

Function of pentose phosphate pathway

Synthesis of NADPH: The most crucial role of pentose phosphate pathway is the synthesis of NADPH, a reducing agent. NADPH is required for many *reductive biosynthetic processes*, *detoxification processes*, *oxidative defenses* and *ROS generation* (through the activity of NADPH oxidases). In biosynthetic processes such as synthesis of fatty acids, synthesis of steroids such as cholesterol, bile acids and steroid hormones, synthesis of sugars in the Calvin cycle, synthesis of carotenoids and conversion of ribonucleotide to deoxyribonucleotide, NADPH acts as an electron donor.

NADPH and **NADH** are not metabolically interchangeable. NADH uses the free energy of metabolite oxidation to synthesize ATP (*oxidative phosphorylation*), whereas NADPH uses the free energy of metabolite oxidation for reductive biosynthesis.

NADPH is also required in *detoxification* processes. For example, enzyme **cytochrome P450** mediated detoxification of xenobiotics requires NADPH for re-reduction. It is accomplished by NADPH-dependent cytochrome P450 reductases. They transfer electrons from NADPH to their FAD-FMN electron transport chain before eventually donating them to the heme moiety of cytochrome P450. Similarly, the maintenance and regeneration of *anti-oxidative defense systems* involving glutathione, thioredoxins and superoxide dismutase require NADPH as a reducing agent.

Synthesis of nucleotide and coenzyme's precursors: The five-carbon sugar ribose 5-phosphate serves as a precursor for nucleotides and coenzymes. Similarly, the four-carbon sugar erythrose 4-phosphate is used to synthesize aromatic amino acids and vitamin B6 (pyridoxal).

Synthesis of substrate for glycolysis: Intermediates in the pentose phosphate pathway may be used to produce ATP. Glyceraldehyde 3-phosphate from the pathway can enter the three-carbon stage of the glycolytic pathway and be converted to ATP and pyruvate.

Glucose 6-phosphate dehydrogenase (G6PD) deficiency and oxidative defense

G6PD deficiency is an X-linked recessive disease. G6PD deficiency impairs the ability to form NADPH, which is required for several reductive processes in addition to lipid biosynthesis. For example, RBC membrane integrity requires a plentiful supply of *reduced* **glutathione** (GSH), a *Cys*-containing tripeptide (γ-glutamyl-cysteinyl-glycine). A major function of reduced GSH in the RBC is to eliminate the reactive oxygen species H_2O_2. H_2O_2, a toxic byproduct of various oxidative processes, reacts with double bonds in the fatty acid residues of the RBC cell membrane to form organic hydroperoxides. These, in turn, result in premature cell lysis and **hemolytic anemia**. So, during the removal of H_2O_2 from the cell, the H_2O_2 is reduced into the water using electrons from the reduced glutathione by enzyme **glutathione peroxidase**. In this process, enzyme **glutathione reductase** recycles the oxidized glutathione to its reduced form, using electrons from the NADPH generated by the pentose phosphate pathway. Thus, G6PD deficiency results in hemolytic anemia caused by the inability to detoxify oxidizing agents.

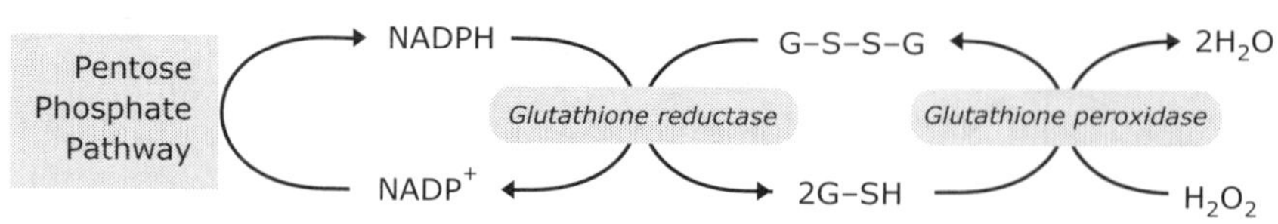

Figure 2.33 Role of the pentose phosphate pathway in the removal of hydrogen peroxide. This pathway indirectly contributes to hydrogen peroxide removal by providing the necessary reducing power, NADPH. NADPH is essential for maintaining the reduced form of glutathione. GSSG represents oxidized glutathione (two GSH molecules linked through a disulfide bond between their sulfhydryl groups).

2.4 Gluconeogenesis

Gluconeogenesis is a metabolic process that converts non-carbohydrate substances into glucose. It is a universal pathway found in all animals, plants, fungi, and microorganisms.

Site of gluconeogenesis: In higher animals, gluconeogenesis occurs in the liver and, to a smaller extent, in the kidney cortex. Under normal circumstances, the liver is responsible for 85% to 95% of the glucose that is made. During starvation or during metabolic acidosis, the kidney is capable of making glucose and then may contribute up to 50% of the glucose formed, since, in these conditions, the amount contributed by the liver decreases considerably.

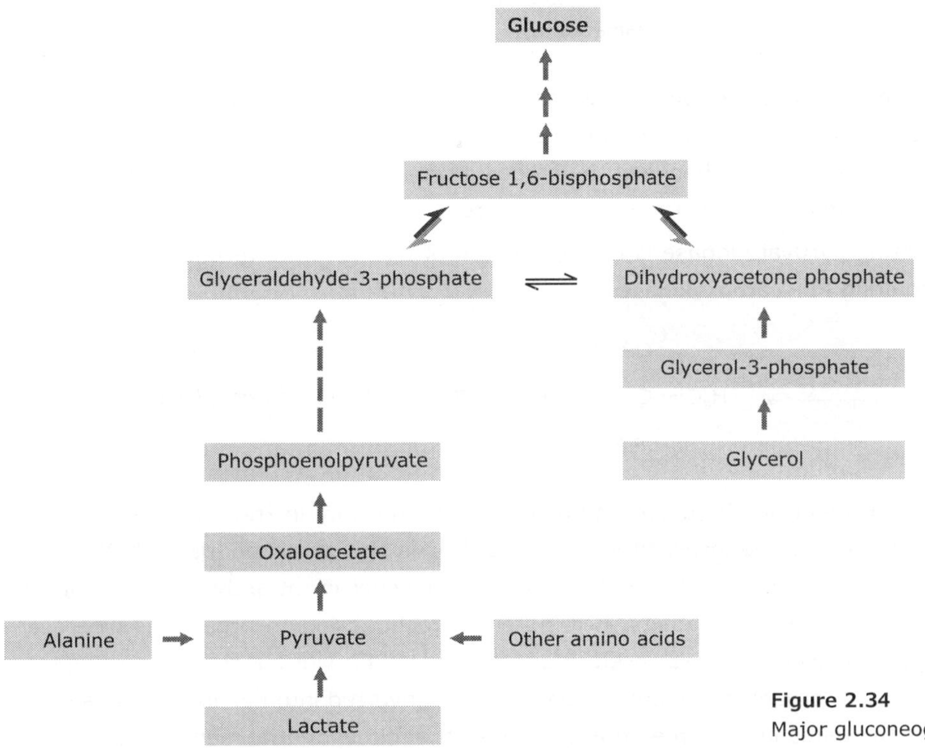

Figure 2.34
Major gluconeogenic precursors.

Precursors of gluconeogenesis: Gluconeogenetic precursors include:

Glycolytic products like lactate, pyruvate, glycerol

Citric acid cycle intermediates and

Carbon skeletons of glucogenic amino acids

The carbon skeletons of ketogenic amino acids are degraded to yield acetyl-CoA or acetoacetate, which are precursors for fatty acid or ketone body synthesis. Only leucine and lysine are exclusively ketogenic.

Animal cells can carry out gluconeogenesis from three- and four- carbon precursors, but not from the two acetyl carbons of acetyl-CoA. Animal cells have no way to convert acetyl-CoA to pyruvate or oxaloacetate. Thus, fatty acids are not substrates for gluconeogenesis in animals, because most fatty acids yield only acetyl-CoA upon degradation. Unlike animals, plants and some microorganisms can convert acetyl-CoA derived from fatty acid oxidation to glucose.

Gluconeogenetic pathway

Although glycolysis and gluconeogenesis share several steps but these pathways are not simply the reverse of each other. During gluconeogenesis seven steps are catalyzed by the same enzymes used in glycolysis, these are reversible. Three steps in glycolysis are irreversible. These irreversible steps are:

1. Conversion of glucose to glucose-6-phosphate catalyzed by *hexokinase*.
2. The conversion of fructose 6-phosphate to fructose 1,6-bisphosphate by *phosphofructokinase* (PFK-1).
3. The conversion of phosphoenolpyruvate to pyruvate by *pyruvate kinase*.

Conversion of pyruvate to phosphoenolpyruvate (PEP)

Pyruvate cannot be converted directly to PEP. The conversion requires two reactions that serve to bypass the irreversible pyruvate kinase step of glycolysis. The energy barrier involved in phosphorylating pyruvate to form the PEP requires the expenditure of two high energy phosphate bonds.

First reaction for bypassing pyruvate kinase is the conversion of pyruvate to oxaloacetate, catalyzed by **pyruvate carboxylase**. This reaction occurs in the mitochondrial matrix.

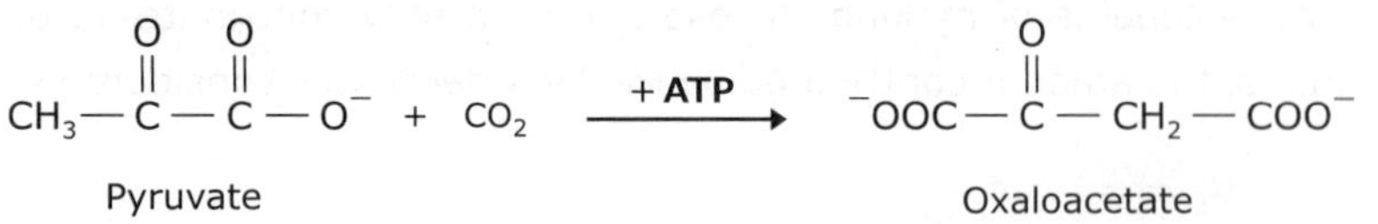

Enz: Pyruvate carboxylase

Pyruvate carboxylase is a mitochondrial allosteric enzyme. **Acetyl-CoA** acts as an allosteric activator of pyruvate carboxylase. The prosthetic group of the enzyme is **biotin**, which functions as a CO_2 carrier. Biotin is covalently bound to the enzyme by an amide linkage between the carboxyl group of its side chain and the ε-amino group of an enzyme lysine residue to form a **biocytin**. The enzyme also requires both Mg^{2+} and Mn^{2+} for activity.

Second reaction for bypassing pyruvate kinase is the conversion of oxaloacetate to phosphoenolpyruvate (PEP), catalyzed by the Mn^{2+}-requiring **PEP carboxykinase.**

Enz: PEP carboxykinase

Cellular location of PEP carboxykinase: Pyruvate carboxylase is found only in the matrix of the mitochondria. By contrast, PEP carboxykinase may be localized in the cytosol or in the mitochondria or both. In human, PEP carboxykinase is found in both the mitochondria and the cytosol, however in rat and mouse liver it only presents in the cytosol. In chickens, pigeons, and rabbits, it is purely mitochondrial. In organisms where enzyme *PEP carboxykinase* is found only in mitochondria, oxaloacetate is converted to PEP, which is then transported to the cytosol for gluconeogenesis. However, in organisms where oxaloacetate is converted into PEP in cytosol, a problem arises. Oxaloacetate cannot cross the mitochondrial membrane because the mitochondrial membrane has no transporter for oxaloacetate. So, oxaloacetate first reduces to malate by mitochondrial enzyme *malate dehydrogenase*, at the expense of NADH. Malate leaves the mitochondrion through a specific transporter in the inner mitochondrial membrane and in the cytosol it is reoxidized to oxaloacetate, with the production of cytosolic NADH.

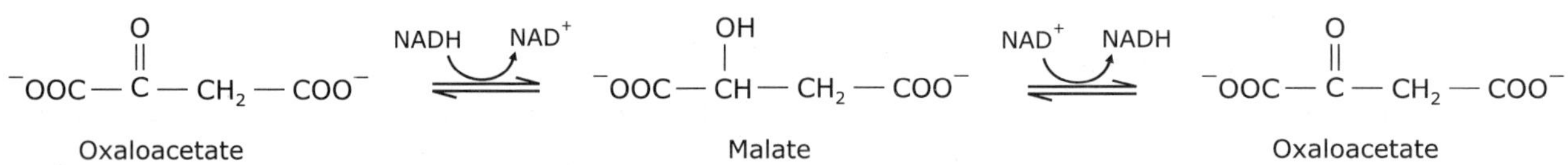

Conversion of PEP to glucose: This pathway is opposite of glycolysis. However, one step in glycolytic pathway where PFK-1 is involved is irreversible so during gluconeogenesis enzyme **fructose 1,6-bisphosphatase** acts without using ATP and converts fructose 1,6-bisphosphate to fructose 6-phosphate. Fructose 1,6-bisphosphatase is an allosteric enzyme. Citrate, acting as an allosteric activator, stimulates bisphosphatase activity, but fructose 2,6-bisphosphate is a potent allosteric inhibitor. AMP also acts as allosteric inhibitor and inhibits the bisphosphatase.

Another step where glucose converted into glucose 6-phosphate during glycolysis is catalyzed by hexokinase and requires ATP. This reaction is also irreversible. During gluconeogenesis, conversion of glucose 6-phosphate to glucose requires enzyme **glucose 6-phosphatase** and no ATP is required. This enzyme is present in the membranes of the endoplasmic reticulum of liver and kidney cells, but is absent in muscle and brain. For this reason, gluconeogenesis is not carried out in muscle and brain.

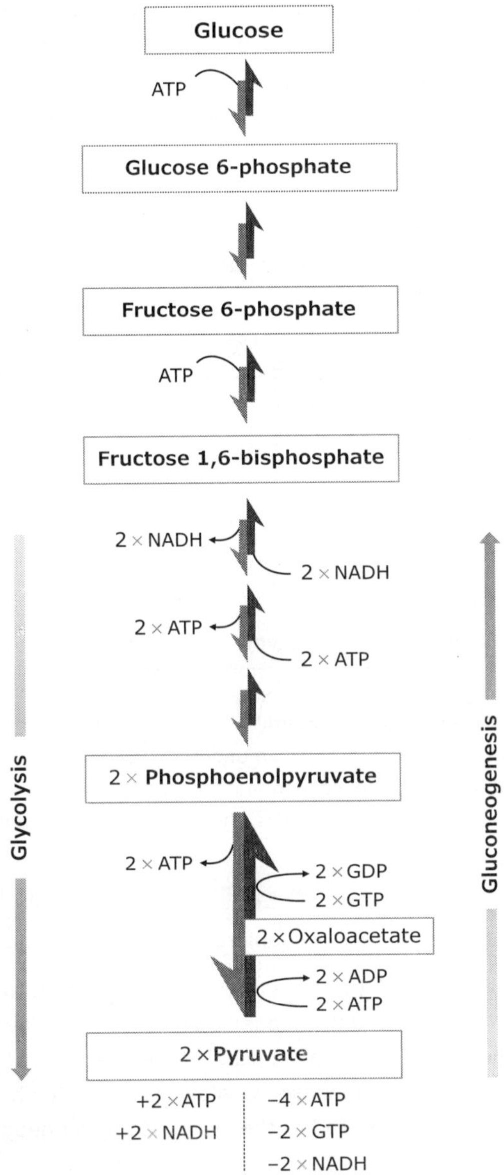

Figure 2.35
Comparison of the pathways of gluconeogenesis and glycolysis. Gluconeogenesis and glycolysis are not identical pathways running in opposite directions, although they do share several steps. Three steps of glycolysis are essentially irreversible and cannot be catalyzed by same enzymes during gluconeogenesis – the conversion of glucose to glucose 6-phosphate by hexokinase, the phosphorylation of fructose 6-phosphate to fructose 1,6-bisphosphate by PFK-1, and the conversion of phosphoenolpyruvate to pyruvate by pyruvate kinase. These three reactions are characterized by a large negative free energy change, hence irreversible. In gluconeogenesis, these three irreversible steps are bypassed by a separate set of enzymes. Thus, both glycolysis and gluconeogenesis are irreversible processes in cells. Pyruvate is converted to phosphoenolpyruvate in two steps – one catalyzed by pyruvate carboxylase catalyzes the ATP-driven formation of oxaloacetate from pyruvate and second is catalyzed by PEP carboxykinase converts oxaloacetate to phosphoenolpyruvate. The route from phosphoenolpyruvate to fructose 1,6-bisphosphate is catalyzed by the enzymes of glycolysis operating in reverse. However, the glycolytic reactions catalyzed by PFK-1 and hexokinase are bypassed by different gluconeogenic enzymes. Fructose 1,6-bisphosphate is hydrolyzed by fructose 1,6-bisphosphatase and glucose 6-phosphate is hydrolyzed by glucose 6-phosphatase.

Regulation of gluconeogenesis

Most of the reactions of gluconeogenesis take place in the cytosol, the same site where glycolysis occurs. Without proper metabolic control, simultaneous glycolytic degradation and gluconeogenic synthesis of glucose could occur, resulting in no net benefit to the cell and significant ATP consumption. Therefore, glycolysis and gluconeogenesis are regulated in a manner that when one pathway is active, the other is inhibited. The reciprocal regulation of these two pathways largely depends on the cell's energy status. In gluconeogenesis, the three key regulatory steps are catalyzed by enzymes glucose 6-phosphatase, fructose 1,6-bisphosphatase, and the pyruvate carboxylase–PEP carboxykinase pair. **Glucose 6-phosphatase** activity is dependent on substrate concentrations and is therefore under **substrate-level control** by glucose 6-phosphate. **Fructose 1,6-bisphosphatase** is an allosteric enzyme inhibited by AMP and fructose 2,6-bisphosphate, and activated by citrate. **Pyruvate carboxylase** is allosterically activated by acetyl-CoA. This intricate regulation ensures that glycolysis and gluconeogenesis do not occur simultaneously, allowing the cell to maintain energy efficiency and metabolic balance.

Glucose-alanine cycle

The glucose-alanine cycle involves the transfer of alanine from muscle to the liver. Similar to the Cori cycle, alanine, rather than lactate, is transported from muscle to the liver. Pyruvate, generated during glycolysis in muscle, undergoes **transamination** with glutamate to produce alanine. This amino acid is released into the bloodstream, transported to the liver, and converted back to pyruvate. This pyruvate serves as a substrate for **gluconeogenesis**, completing the **glucose-alanine cycle**. The amino group carried by alanine is ultimately converted to ammonia or participate in aspartate formation. Therefore, the glucose-alanine cycle is a mechanism for transporting nitrogen from muscle to liver.

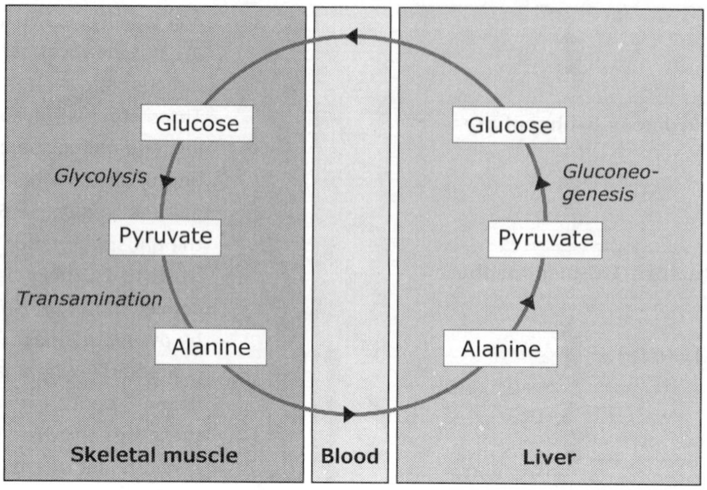

Figure 2.36 The glucose-alanine cycle transfers alanine to the liver in a manner similar to the Cori cycle, but with alanine instead of lactate traveling from muscle to liver. During glycolysis in muscle cells, pyruvate can undergo a transamination reaction with the amino acid glutamate to form alanine. This alanine is released into the bloodstream and transported to the liver, where it is converted back to pyruvate. The pyruvate then serves as a substrate for gluconeogenesis, thus completing the glucose-alanine cycle.

Problem

What factors determine whether pyruvate carboxylase acts primarily as an anaplerotic or a gluconeogenic enzyme?

Solution: The main factor is the intracellular location of pyruvate—if it accumulates in mitochondria, the anaplerotic role predominates, whereas pyruvate in the cytosol is used primarily as a gluconeogenic precursor. The levels of other intermediates are also important. For example, if intramitochondrial levels of oxaloacetate are adequate, then pyruvate can be either oxidized by pyruvate dehydrogenase or exported for gluconeogenesis. Oxaloacetate in mitochondria can also be converted by transamination to aspartate, however, which can be exported to the cytosol for gluconeogenesis.

2.5 Glycogen metabolism

Glycogen is a highly branched, very large polymer of glucose molecules linked along its main line by α-1,4-glycosidic linkages; branches arise by α-1,6-glycosidic bonds at about every tenth residue. Glycogen occurs in the cytosol as granules, which also contain the enzymes that catalyze its formation and use. Muscle and liver are the major sites for the storage of glycogen, and although its concentration in the liver is higher, the much greater mass of skeletal muscle stores a greater total amount of glycogen. Liver can mobilize its glycogen for the release of glucose to the rest of the body, but muscle can only use its glycogen for its own energy needs.

Glycogen synthesis (Glycogenesis)

Glycogen is synthesized from glucose 6-phosphate (G6P) mainly in the muscle and liver and stored within these tissues as **glycogen granules**. The first step in glycogen synthesis involves the isomerization of glucose 6-phosphate to glucose 1-phosphate (G1P) and this reaction is catalyzed by enzyme *phosphoglucomutase*.

Glucose 6-phosphate $\rightleftharpoons$ **Glucose 1-phosphate**

The glucose 1-phosphate is then activated to enable its incorporation into glycogen. The activated form is a **sugar nucleotide**, uridine diphosphate glucose (**UDP-glucose**). Hence, glucose 1-phosphate is then converted to UDP-glucose by the action of an enzyme *UDP-glucose pyrophosphorylase*. It is a condensation reaction which occurs between a nucleoside triphosphate (UTP) and a sugar phosphate (glucose 1-phosphate). UDP-glucose is the immediate donor of glucose residues in the reaction catalyzed by enzyme *glycogen synthase*.

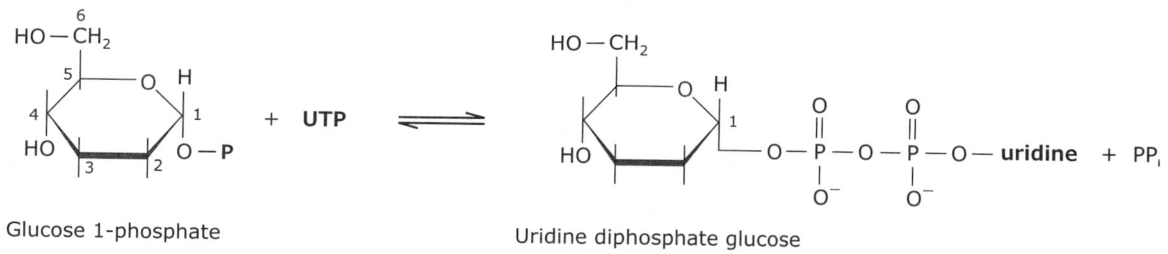

Action of glycogen synthase: New glucosyl units are added to the *non-reducing* terminal residues of glycogen. The activated glucosyl unit, UDP-glucose is transferred to the hydroxyl group at a C-4 terminus of glycogen to form an α-1,4-glycosidic linkage. In the process of elongation, UDP is displaced by the terminal hydroxyl group of the growing glycogen molecule. This reaction is catalyzed by **glycogen synthase**, the key regulatory enzyme in glycogen synthesis.

UDP-glucose + **Glycogen** (n glucose residues) ⟶ **UDP** + **Glycogen** ($n+1$ glucose residues)

Enzyme *glycogen synthase* cannot simply link two glucose residues; it can only extend an already existing α1→4 linked glucan chain containing more than four residues. Thus, glycogen synthesis requires a *primer*. This priming function is carried out by a homodimeric protein **glycogenin**, acting as a *glycosyltransferase*. Each subunit of glycogenin catalyzes the addition of a glucose residue donated by UDP-glucose to its partner in the glycogenin dimer. Glycogenin then extends the glucose chain to form a **glycogen primer**. Carbon 1 of the first glucose unit of this chain, the *reducing end*, is covalently attached to the specific tyrosine in each glycogenin subunit. After synthesizing oligosaccharide (a primer), *glycogen synthase* extends the glycogen molecule. *Glycogen synthase is a regulatory enzyme*. It has two enzymatically interconvertible forms; the phosphorylated form is *inactive* (**glycogen synthase b**), and the dephosphorylated form is *active* (**glycogen synthase a**). A regulatory kinase, **glycogen synthase kinase 3** (GSK3), catalyzes the phosphorylation of glycogen synthase.

Formation of branch chains

Glycogen synthase catalyzes only α1→4 glycosidic bond formation. Branching is accomplished by a separate enzyme called **branching enzyme**. Branching enzyme (also known as *amylo-1,4→1,6 transglycosylase*) moves a 6 or 7-unit segment of α1→4 residues from a glycogen main chain to a C-6 hydroxyl group of a glucosyl residue, that is at least four residues away from an existing branch. Branching increases the solubility of glycogen.

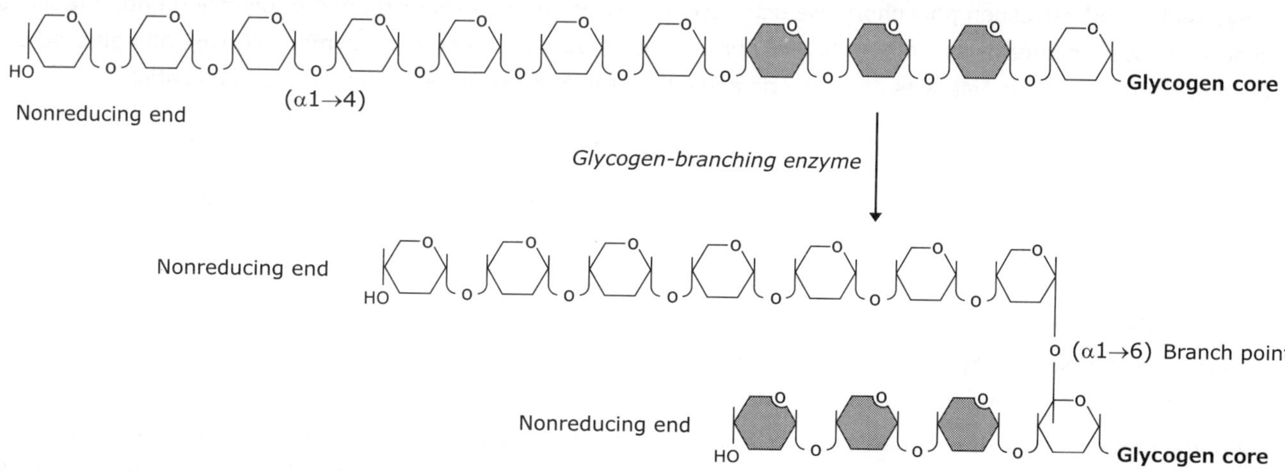

Figure 2.37 Branching of glycogen. Branches are formed by transferring a 6 or 7 residues terminal segment from an α1 → 4 linked glucan chain to the C6—OH group of a glucose residue on the same or another chain. Glycogen synthase cannot make the (α1→ 6) bonds found at the branch points of glycogen; these are formed by the glycogen-branching enzyme, also called amylo (1→ 4) to (1→ 6) transglycosylase.

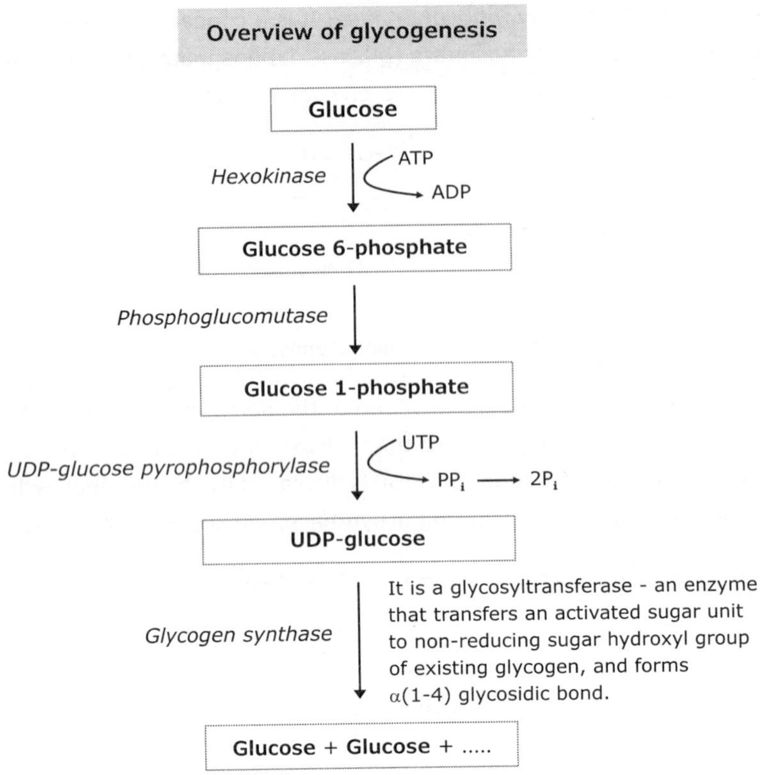

Figure 2.38 An overview of glycogenesis in which glucose is activated to UDP-glucose that acts as precursor for glycogen. A glycogen chain is elongated by glycogen synthase. The enzyme transfers the glucose residue of UDP-glucose to the nonreducing end of a glycogen branch to make a new ($\alpha1\rightarrow4$) linkage.

Glycogenolysis

During glycogenolysis, terminal glucose residue removes as α-D-glucose 1-phosphate (G1P) from the non-reducing end. This reaction, called **phosphorolysis**, is catalyzed by enzyme **glycogen phosphorylase**, a dimer of identical 842 amino acid residues subunits. Glycogen phosphorylase attacks exoglycosidic bonds. **Pyridoxal phosphate** *is an essential cofactor in the glycogen phosphorylase reaction*. Each catalytic site includes a pyridoxal-phosphate group, linked to lysine^{680} of the enzyme. Its phosphate group acts as a general acid catalyst, promoting attack by P_i on the glycosidic bond. Glycogen phosphorylase acts repetitively on the non-reducing end of glycogen until it reaches a point 4 glucose residues away from an ($\alpha1\rightarrow6$) branch point. It is an allosteric enzyme. ATP, G6P and glucose act as allosteric inhibitors and AMP acts as allosteric activator. It is also regulated by covalent modification.

Glycogen (n glucose residues) + $\mathbf{P}_i$ ⟶ **Glucose 1-phosphate** + **Glycogen** ($n-1$ glucose residues)

Glycogen phosphorylase is the key enzyme in glycogen breakdown but can carry out this process by itself only to a limited extent because α-1,6-glycosidic bonds at the branch points are not susceptible to cleavage by phosphorylase. Thus further degradation by glycogen phosphorylase occurs only after the action of a glycogen debranching enzyme **(α1,4→α1,4) glucantransferase**, which show two different activities: **transferase activity** and **α(1→6) glucosidase activity**.

First is the **transferase activity**, in which the enzyme removes terminal 3 of remaining glucose residues and transfers this trisaccharide moiety intact to the non-reducing end of another branch.

Second, the remaining glucose residue, which is still attached to the main chain is removed by an **α(1→6) glucosidase activity** of the same debranching enzyme. Thus, about 92% of glycogen's glucose residues are converted to G1P. The remaining about 8%, those at the branch points, are converted to glucose.

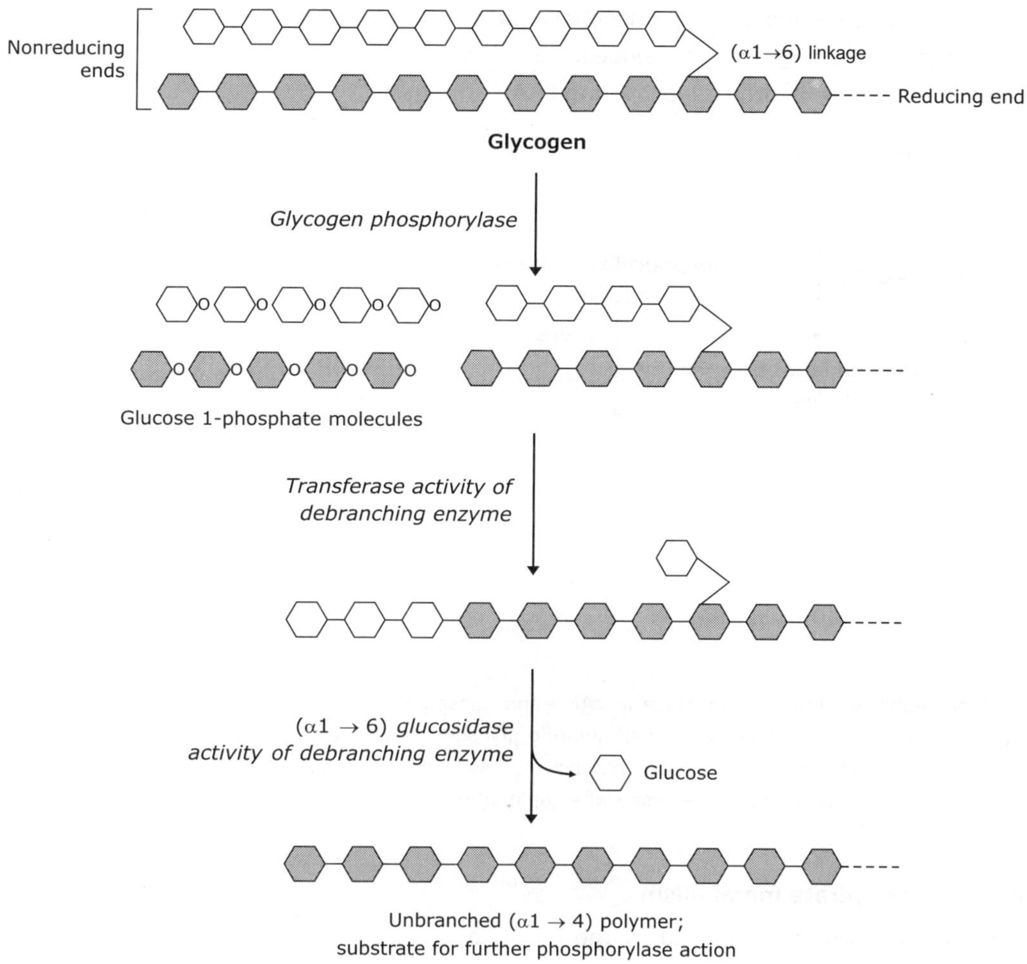

Figure 2.39 First, α-1,4-glycosidic bonds on each branch are cleaved by phosphorylase, leaving four residues along each branch. The transferase shifts a block of three glycosyl residues from one outer branch to the other. The glucose residue is then removed by α-1,6-glucosidase, leaving a linear chain with all α-1,4 linkages, suitable for further cleavage by phosphorylase.

Effect of glucagon and epinephrine on glycogenolysis

Glucagon and epinephrine markedly stimulate the breakdown of glycogen in muscle and liver. The liver is more responsive to glucagon whereas muscle is more to epinephrine. Glycogen phosphorylase, a key enzyme involved in glycogenolysis, is regulated by reversible phosphorylation, which is responsive to hormones such as epinephrine and glucagon.

Glucagon is a peptide hormone secreted by the α-cells of the **pancreatic islets**. Glucagon opposes many of the actions of insulin. Most importantly glucagon acts to maintain blood glucose levels by activation of hepatic **glycogenolysis** and **gluconeogenesis**. Glucagon is composed of 29 amino acids arranged in a single peptide chain. Unlike insulin, the amino acid sequence of glucagon is the same in all mammalian species examined to date. Glucagon is synthesized as a large precursor molecule that is converted to glucagons through a series of selective proteolytic cleavages.

Epinephrine (adrenaline) is synthesized from the amino acid tyrosine and secreted from the **adrenal medulla**. It is secreted on stimulation by a sympathetic nervous system for meeting an emergency or stress condition, like injury, pain, fear, accident, grief, fall in blood pressure etc. Hence called **emergency hormone.** It increases the sugar level in the blood by stimulating glycogenolysis in liver and skeletal muscles. In muscle, epinephrine causes activation of **protein kinase A** (PKA). PKA promotes glycogen degradation indirectly by phosphorylating and thus activating a kinase, *glycogen phosphorylase kinase*, that in turn phosphorylates and activates *glycogen phosphorylase*, the enzyme that degrades glycogen. The dimeric skeletal muscle *glycogen* phosphorylase exists in two interconvertible forms: *active* phosphorylase *a* and *inactive* phosphorylase *b*. Phosphorylase *b* is converted into phosphorylase *a* when it is phosphorylated at a single serine residue in each subunit. The entire process is reversed when epinephrine is removed and the level of cAMP drops, inactivating PKA.

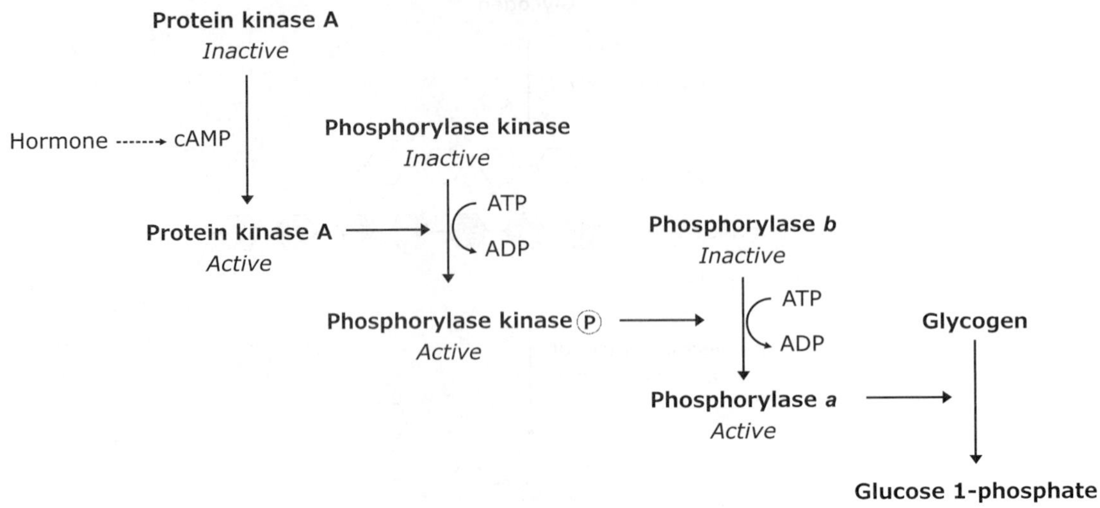

Figure 2.40 The epinephrine-stimulated increase in cAMP and subsequent activation of protein kinase A (PKA) enhance the conversion of glycogen to glucose 1-phosphate by stimulating glycogen degradation. PKA phosphorylates and thus activates an intermediate kinase, glycogen phosphorylase kinase, that in turn phosphorylates and activates glycogen phosphorylase, the enzyme that degrades glycogen. The entire process is reversed when epinephrine is removed and the level of cAMP drops, inactivating PKA.

Role of insulin in carbohydrate metabolism

Insulin is a polypeptide hormone produced by the β-cells of the islets of Langerhans. It favors the synthesis of glycogen, triacylglycerols, and protein. Insulin is composed of 51 amino acids arranged in two polypeptide chains, designated A and B, which are linked together by two disulfide bridges.

Insulin acts to *reduce* glucose concentrations in the blood and therefore stimulates the conversion of glucose to fats, proteins, ribulose 5-phosphate and glycogen. In the liver, insulin decreases the production of glucose by inhibiting gluconeogenesis and the breakdown of glycogen. In muscle and liver, insulin increases glycogen synthesis. In muscle, insulin increases glucose uptake by increasing the number of glucose transporters in the cell membrane. Epinephrine and glucagon have the opposite effects to insulin. It acts to *increase the glucose concentration* in the blood. They, therefore, stimulate the conversion of fats, glycogen and pyruvate to glucose.

Table 2.6 Comparisons of effect of insulin, glucagon and epinephrine on carbohydrate metabolism

Pathway	Effect of Insulin	Effect of Glucagon/Epinephrine
Glycogenesis	Stimulates	Inhibits
Glycogenolysis	Inhibits	Stimulates
Gluconeogenesis	Inhibits	Stimulates
Glycolysis	Stimulates	Inhibits

Glycogen storage diseases

Glycogen storage diseases are caused by a genetic deficiency of one or another of the enzymes of glycogen metabolism. Many diseases have been characterized that result from an inherited deficiency of the enzyme. These defects are listed in the table.

Table 2.7 Glycogen storage diseases

Name	Enzyme deficiency
Von Gierke's disease	Liver glucose-6-phosphatase
Pompe's disease	Lysosomal $\alpha 1 \rightarrow 4$ and $\alpha 1 \rightarrow 6$ glucosidase (acid maltase)
Hers' disease	Liver phosphorylase
Tarui's disease	Muscle and erythrocyte phosphofructokinase 1
McArdle's disease	Muscle glycogen phosphorylase
Andersen's disease	Amylo ($1,4 \rightarrow 1,6$) transglycosylase (branching enzyme)

2.6 Photosynthesis

Photosynthesis is a physiochemical process by which photosynthetic organisms use light energy to drive the synthesis of organic compounds (a process of **energy transformation**). In the process of photosynthesis, photosynthetic organisms, first convert light energy into chemical energy in the form of NADPH and ATP and later use these chemicals to reduce CO_2 into organic compounds (termed *carbon dioxide fixation*). Photosynthesis is the basis of life on earth because it is the primary source of food on earth. Photosynthetically produced carbohydrates, therefore, serve as an energy source for the organism that produces them as well as for non-photosynthetic organisms that directly or indirectly consume photosynthetic organisms.

Photosynthesis and respiration are complementary processes in photosynthetic organisms. All living cells are powered by energy stored in the chemical bonds of organic molecules such as carbohydrates, lipids. Energy is extracted from organic molecules (termed *food*) by a process of gradual oxidation (i.e., respiration). Photosynthetic organisms synthesize organic molecules by the act of photosynthesis. In this manner, photosynthesis converts the light energy into chemical energy. The organic molecules produced by photosynthesis in turn serve as food for respiration.

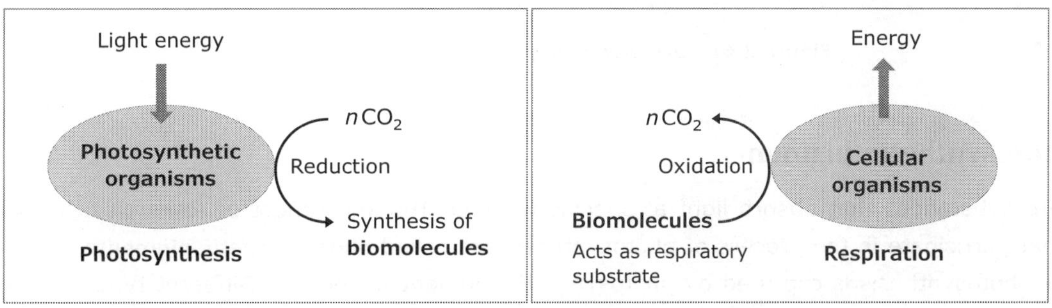

Photosynthesis is carried out by many different organisms (termed **photosynthetic organisms**), ranging from photosynthetic bacteria to green plants. These photosynthetic organisms may be **oxygenic** or **anoxygenic**, on the basis of generation of oxygen during photosynthesis. Oxygenic photosynthetic organisms release molecular oxygen via the light-dependent oxidation of water to molecular oxygen during photosynthesis whereas anoxygenic photosynthetic organisms do not produce oxygen. Oxygenic photosynthetic organisms include both eukaryotes as well as prokaryotes whereas anoxygenic photosynthetic organisms include only prokaryotes. In **oxygenic photosynthetic organisms**, overall photosynthetic process can be written as the following simplified chemical reaction:

$$nCO_2 + nH_2O \xrightarrow[\text{Chl}]{\text{Light}} (CH_2O)_n + nH_2O + nO_2$$

It is a two-stage processes. The first process is a light-dependent (involves *photochemical reaction* termed as **light reaction**) that requires the direct energy of light to make ATP and NADPH that are used in the second process.

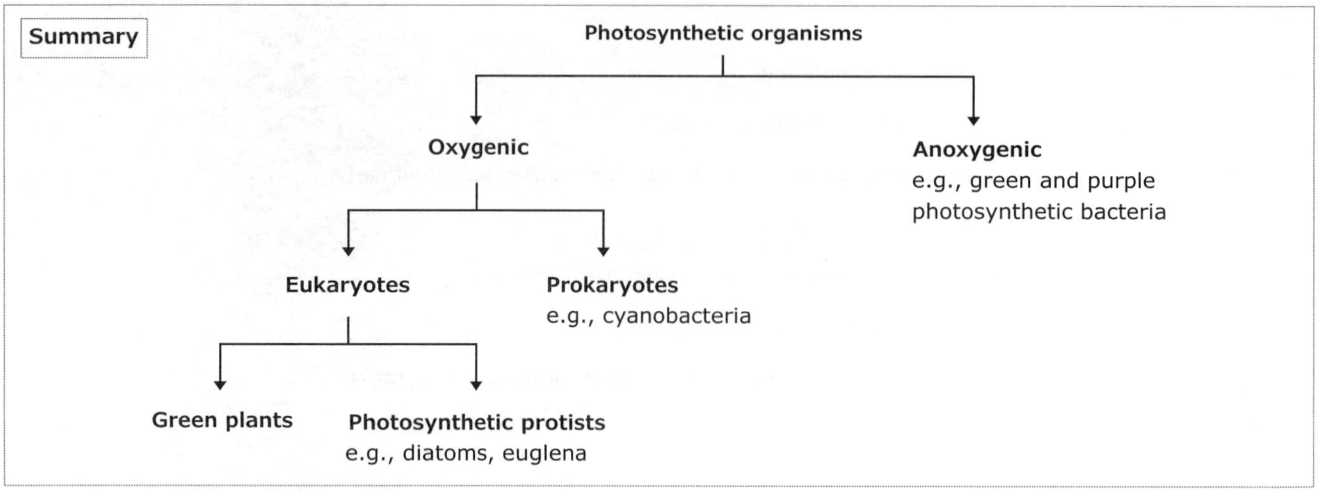

In the second process, *carbon-fixation cycle* (a **Calvin cycle**) occurs in which ATP and NADPH, the products of the light reaction, are used in the reduction or fixation of CO_2 into triose phosphate. However, the Calvin cycle does not occur in all photosynthetic organisms. Some anoxygenic photosynthetic organisms use other carbon-fixation pathways such as the 'reductive (reverse) tricarboxylic acid cycle' in green sulfur bacteria and the 'hydroxypropionate pathway' in green nonsulfur bacteria. Thus, although the Calvin cycle is quantitatively the most important carbon-fixation cycle in most photosynthetic organisms, other carbon-fixation pathways are also present.

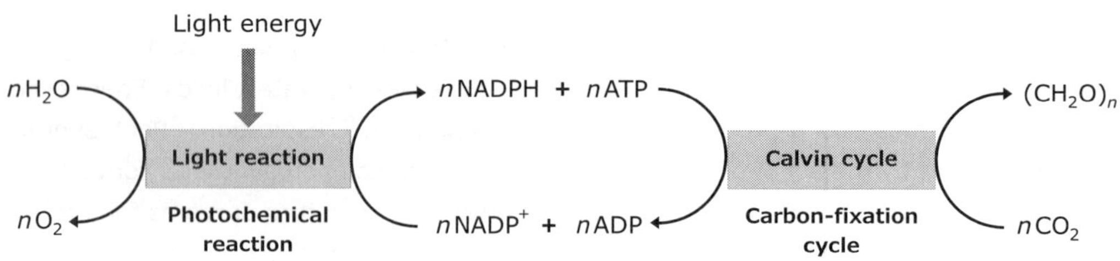

Figure 2.41 Overview of oxygenic photosynthetic process.

2.6.1 Photosynthetic pigments

Pigments are substances that absorb light at specific wavelengths and reflect or transmit other wavelengths. Pigments that participate in the process of photosynthesis are called **photosynthetic pigments**. The solar energy required for photosynthesis is captured by photosynthetic pigment molecules. Different types of photosynthetic pigments participate in this process. Three types of photosynthetic pigments are present in oxygenic photosynthetic organisms. These pigments are **chlorophylls, carotenoids** and **phycobilins.**

Chlorophylls

Chlorophylls are present in all oxygenic photosynthetic organisms. There are several types of chlorophyll molecules like Chl *a*, Chl *b*, Chl *c* and Chl *d*. These pigment molecules are *lipid-soluble* and absorb light most strongly in the blue and red but poorly in the green portions of the electromagnetic spectrum. A chlorophyll molecule consists of two major components:

- A five-ring cyclic structure
- A tetraisoprenoid alcohol

Five-ring cyclic structure: The five-ring cyclic structure in most chlorophylls (a, b, and d) is a derivative of **chlorin,** while chlorophyll c is a derivative of **porphyrin.** *Chlorin* consists of three **pyrrole rings** and one **pyrroline ring**, linked together by four methine (–CH=) bridges. A pyrrole is a five-membered ring containing four carbon atoms and one nitrogen atom. Reduction of one double bond in a pyrrole ring gives a *pyrroline structure*. **Porphyrin**, by contrast, is composed of four pyrrole rings. Both porphyrins and chlorins are aromatic compounds. Their highly conjugated systems are responsible for the strong absorption of light in the visible spectrum. Compounds containing four pyrrole or pyrrole-like rings are collectively called **tetrapyrroles**.

In chlorophylls, unlike in hemes, the central metal ion is **magnesium**. This magnesium ion is covalently bonded to two nitrogen atoms and coordinate-bonded to the other two nitrogens within the tetrapyrrole ring. Additionally, a **cyclopentanone ring** (ring V) is fused to pyrrole ring III, making the chlorophyll macrocycle slightly different from other tetrapyrroles.

Tetraisoprenoid alcohol: The second component of chlorophyll is a tetraisoprenoid alcohol, which consists of four **isoprene units** linked together. The specific tetraisoprenoid alcohol in chlorophyll is **phytol**. Phytol is a long, branched hydrocarbon chain containing one carbon-carbon double bond. In chlorophyll, the propionic acid group attached to pyrrole ring IV forms an **ester linkage** with phytol. This hydrophobic phytol tail anchors the chlorophyll molecule into the lipid bilayer of photosynthetic membranes.

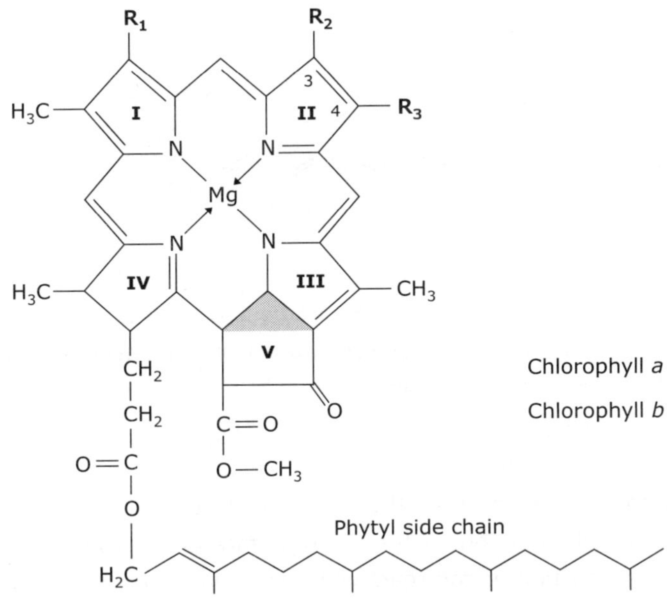

	R_1	R_2	R_3
Chlorophyll *a*	$-CH=CH_2$	$-CH_3$	$-CH_2CH_3$
Chlorophyll *b*	$-CH=CH_2$	$-CHO$	$-CH_2CH_3$

Figure 2.42 Structure of chlorophyll *a* and *b*.

Table 2.8 Differences between chlorophyll *a* and chlorophyll *b*

Chlorophyll *a*	**Chlorophyll *b***
1. It is $C_{55}H_{72}O_5N_4Mg$.	It is $C_{55}H_{70}O_6N_4Mg$.
2. In the pure state, chlorophyll *a* is blue-green.	In the pure state, chlorophyll *b* is olive-green.
3. It is an essential photosynthetic pigment.	It is accessory photosynthetic pigment.
4. Pyrrole ring II contains methyl ($-CH_3$) group.	Pyrrole ring II contains aldehyde ($-CHO$) group.
5. It absorbs more red wavelengths than violet-blue wavelength of light.	It absorbs more violet-blue wavelength than red wavelength of light.

Bacteriochlorophyll

Anoxygenic photosynthetic organisms contain **bacteriochlorophyll** molecules. They are related to chlorophyll molecules. Different groups of anoxygenic photosynthetic organisms contain different types of bacteriochlorophyll: BChl *a*, BChl *b*, BChl *c*, BChl *d* and BChl *e*. Bacteriochlorophyll molecules absorb light at longer wavelengths as compared to chlorophyll molecules.

Carotenoids

Besides the major light-absorbing chlorophyll molecules, there are two groups of *accessory pigments* which absorb light in the wavelength region, where chlorophylls do not absorb strongly. The two types of accessory pigments are *carotenoids* and *phycobilins*. **Carotenoids** are long-chain, conjugated hydrocarbons containing a string of isoprene residues and distinguished from one another by their end groups. They are generally C_{40} terpenoid compounds formed by the condensation of eight isoprene units. Carotenoids are *lipid-soluble pigments* and can be subdivided into two classes, **xanthophylls** (which contain oxygen) and **carotenes** (which are purely hydrocarbons, and contain no oxygen). The characteristic absorption spectrum (400 to 500 nm) of carotenoids is responsible for the yellow color of leaves in autumn and the orange color of carrots, for which this group of pigments is named. The upper wavelength limit of absorption by carotenoids depends on the number of conjugated double bonds, the isomeric configuration and the nature of the end groups.

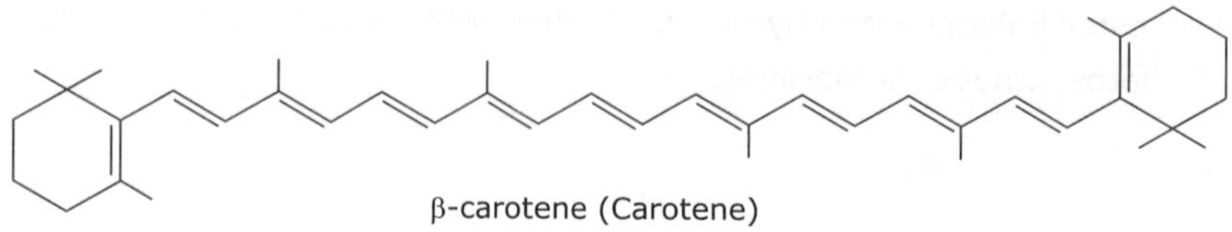

β-carotene (Carotene)

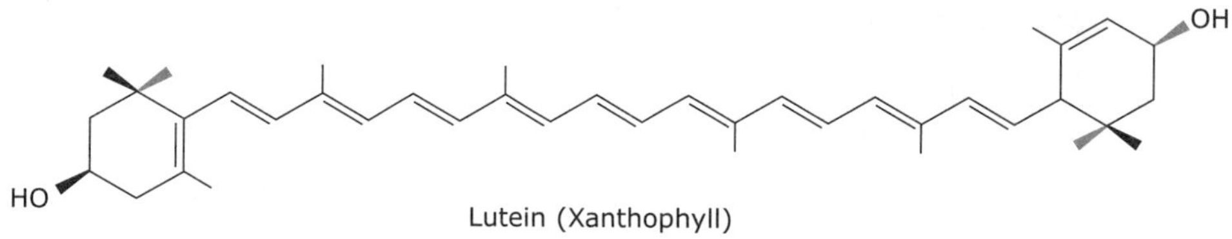

Lutein (Xanthophyll)

Carotenoid acts as an accessory light-harvesting pigment. It captures light energy and feeds it to the photochemical reaction center. The other role of carotenoids is to provide protection against photo-oxidative damage (**photoprotection**). In providing photoprotection, it acts as **quencher** as well as **scavenger**.

High light intensity may damage many cellular components, especially lipids. The photoprotection mechanism prevents the damage by removing excess energy. When the energy stored in chlorophylls in the excited state is rapidly dissipated by excitation transfer or photochemical reaction, the excited state is said to be **quenched**. This is called **photochemical quenching**. This is a normal condition. If the excited state of chlorophyll is not rapidly quenched by excitation transfer or photochemical reaction, it can react with molecular oxygen to form an excited state of oxygen known as **singlet oxygen** ($^1O_2^*$).

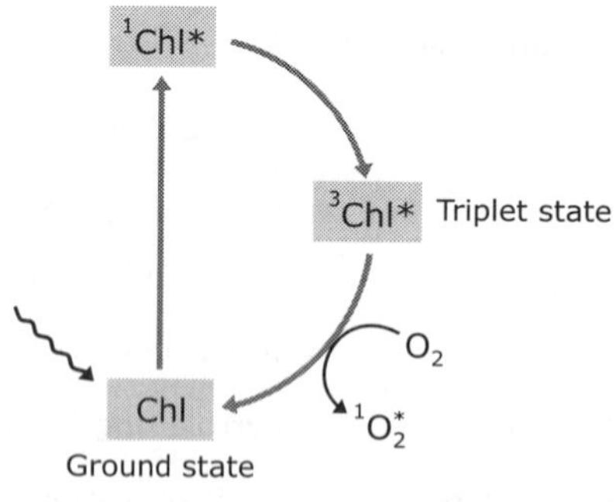

The extremely reactive singlet oxygen can damage the **D1 protein** of photosystem II. The damage leads to **photoinhibition**. Carotenoids exert their photoprotective action by rapidly quenching the excited state of chlorophyll. The excited state of carotenoids does not have sufficient energy to form singlet oxygen, so it decays back to its ground state while losing its energy as heat. It is called **non-photochemical quenching**. *Non-photochemical quenching* is the quenching of excitation energy by a process other than photochemistry. In this case, carotenoids accept the energy from an excited chlorophyll molecule and dissipate that energy as heat. This dissipation of excess light energy is achieved via the **violaxanthin cycle** (a type of **xanthophyll cycle**), where **violaxanthin** under high light intensity is converted to *zeaxanthin* via *antheraxanthin* as an intermediary. The stepwise conversion occurs through a process known as **de-epoxidation**. This action is reversed under low light levels. If this defense is not sufficient and toxic photoproducts form, carotenoids eliminate the reactive photoproducts by acting as a **scavenger**.

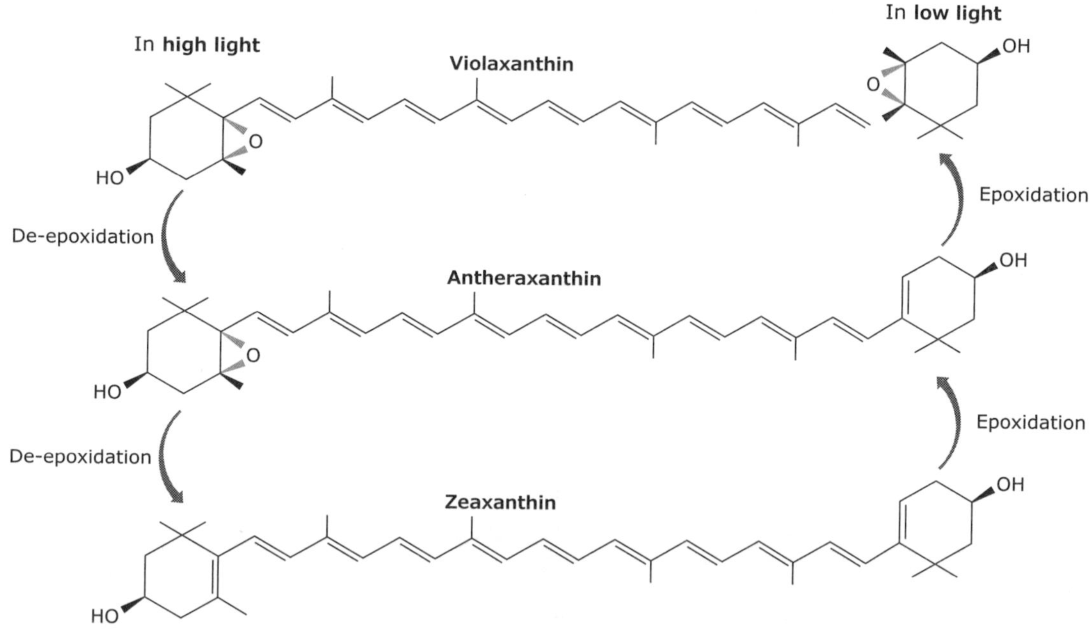

Figure 2.43 The violaxanthin cycle (a type of xanthophyll cycle) is a dynamic process that helps to protect plants from excess light. It involves the reversible conversion of specific xanthophyll pigments in response to changes in light intensity. Under high light intensity, the xanthophyll cycle facilitates the de-epoxidation of violaxanthin to form antheraxanthin and then zeaxanthin. This conversion helps dissipate excess light energy as heat protecting the plant's photosynthetic apparatus from damage. Under low light intensity or dark, the process reverses. Zeaxanthin is epoxidized back to antheraxanthin and then to violaxanthin.

Phycobilins

Phycobilins are noncyclic, linear **tetrapyrroles structures**, which are structurally similar to the bile pigment *bilirubin*. Chlorophylls are also composed of four pyrroles, but the pyrroles are arranged in a ring and contain a Mg^{2+} ion in the center. The three photosynthetic phycobilins are **phycoerythrobilin**, **phycocyanobilin** and **allophycocyanobilin**. They are unique among the photosynthetic pigments in that they are covalently bound (thioether bond) to certain water-soluble proteins to form **phycobiliproteins**. There are two major types of phycobiliproteins – *phycoerythrins* and *phycocyanins*. **Phycoerythrin** contains protein and *phycoerythrobilin* whereas **phycocyanin** contains protein and *phycocyanobilin*. All phycobiliproteins are water-soluble and therefore cannot exist within the membrane like carotenoids, but aggregate into clusters that adhere to the membrane called **phycobilisomes**. Phycobilins are present abundantly in red algae and cyanobacteria. They act as accessory light-harvesting pigments, which capture light energy and feed it to the chlorophyll molecules present at photochemical reaction center.

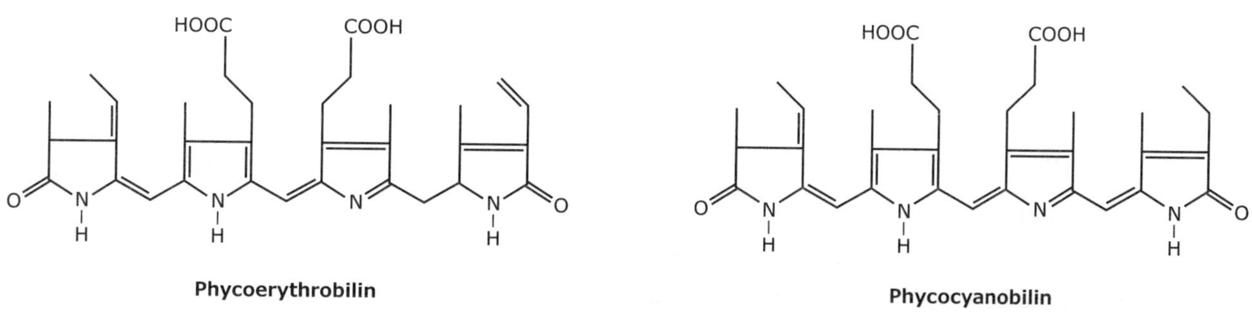

Figure 2.44 General structure of phycobilin: phycoerythrobilin and phycocyanobilin.

Table 2.9 Distribution of chlorophylls and other photosynthetic pigments in oxygenic photosynthetic organisms

	Chlorophylls				Carotenoids	Phycobilins
	a	b	c	d		
Eukaryotes						
Plants						
Angiosperm	+	+	–	–	+	–
Gymnosperm	+	+	–	–	+	–
Pteridophytes	+	+	–	–	+	–
Bryophytes	+	+	–	–	+	–
Algae: Green algae	+	+	–	–	+	–
Red algae	+	–	–	+	+	+
Brown algae	+	–	+	–	+	–
Photosynthetic protists						
Diatoms	+	–	+	–	+	–
Dinoflagellates	+	–	+	–	+	–
Euglena	+	+	–	–	+	–
Prokaryotes						
Cyanobacteria	+	–	–	–	+	+

+ Present, – Absent

Most cyanobacteria contain chlorophyll *a*, carotenoids, phycocyanin, and allophycocyanin as pigments for photosynthesis. Additionally, some cyanobacteria also contain phycoerythrin. A few specific cyanobacteria species contain chlorophyll *b*, such as *Prochlorococcus*, and chlorophyll *d*, such as *Acaryochloris* species.

Location of photosynthetic pigments

In oxygenic photosynthetic organisms, photosynthetic pigments are found in thylakoid membranes. In eukaryotic photosynthetic organisms, thylakoids present within the chloroplasts. In cyanobacteria, except *Gloeobacter violaceus*, there is an internal system of thylakoid membranes in cytosol in which the light reactions of photosynthesis and respiration occur. The thylakoid structure in cyanobacteria is organized differently compared to thylakoids present in chloroplasts. Chloroplasts contain two distinct types of thylakoid membrane structures, grana thylakoid and stroma thylakoid. Cyanobacterial thylakoids do not form grana. In anoxygenic photosynthetic organisms such as green sulfur bacteria, photosynthetic pigments are found in plasma membrane and vesicles called **chlorosomes** attached to the plasma membrane. In the purple sulfur bacteria, the bacteriochlorophylls are located in invaginations of the plasma membrane called **chromatophores**.

Table 2.10 Photosynthetic organisms and location of photosynthetic pigments

Oxygenic photosynthetic organisms		
Eukaryotic photosynthetic organisms	—	Thylakoid membrane of chloroplast
Prokaryotic photosynthetic organisms	—	Thylakoid membrane dispersed throughout in the cytosol
Anoxygenic photosynthetic organisms		
Green photosynthetic bacteria	—	Chlorosome and plasma membrane
Purple photosynthetic bacteria	—	Chromatophore of plasma membrane

2.6.2 Absorption and action spectra

Photosynthetic pigments absorb electromagnetic radiation in the visible and infrared region. A graph showing the degree of absorption of light by a pigment as a function of the wavelength is referred to as the **absorption spectrum** for that pigment. Different photosynthetic pigments have different values of absorption spectra. For example, chlorophylls absorb strongly in the blue and red regions of the spectrum, while carotenoids absorb in the blue and green regions.

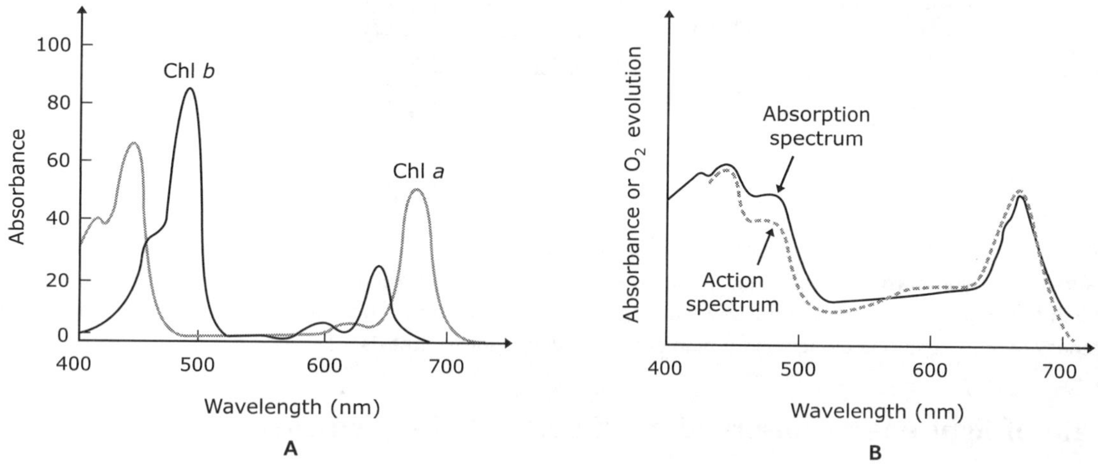

Figure 2.45 **A**. *Absorption spectra* of Chl *a* and Chl *b* in ether. **B**. An *action spectrum* compared to an absorption spectrum. An action spectrum is measured by plotting a response to light such as oxygen evolution, as a function of wavelength. If the pigments used to obtain the absorption spectrum are the same as those that cause the response, the absorption and action spectra will match. In the example shown here, the action spectrum for oxygen evolution matches the absorption spectrum of intact chloroplasts quite well, indicating that light absorption by the chlorophylls mediates oxygen evolution.

Pigment (dissolve in ether)	**Absorption maxima** (*nm*)
Chlorophyll *a*	430, 660
Chlorophyll *b*	463, 643
Bacteriochlorophyll *a*	364, 770
Bacteriochlorophyll *b*	373, 795
Bacteriochlorophyll *c*	434, 666

Similarly, a graph showing the degree to which different wavelengths affect photochemical reaction is called the **action spectrum** for photosynthesis. In oxygenic photosynthetic organisms, the photochemical reaction is performed by pigment chlorophyll *a* present at photochemical reaction center and this reaction produces oxygen due to photolysis of water. An action spectrum is measured by plotting photochemical reaction (measured by oxygen release in oxygenic photosynthetic organisms) as a function of wavelength. The wavelength most effectively absorbed by the chlorophyll *a* is also the most effective in driving the photochemical reaction.

Engelmann's experiment: Action spectra relate light absorption to photosynthetic activity. In 1883, Theodor W. Engelmann determined the first action spectra by measuring oxygen evolution at different wavelengths of light. He illuminated spirogyra, a filamentous green alga, with white light that had been passed through a prism, exposing different segments of the filamentous alga to different wavelengths. He used aerobic oxygen-seeking bacteria, which concentrate near an oxygen source, to determine which segments of the alga were releasing the most oxygen and thus photosynthesizing most. Bacteria congregated in great numbers around the parts of the alga illuminated with blue or red light.

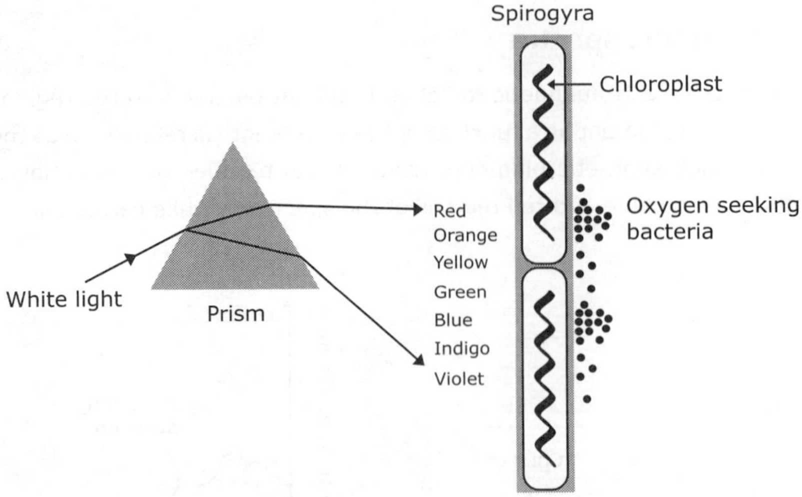

Figure 2.46 Schematic diagram of the action spectrum measurements by T. W. Engelmann. He projected a spectrum of light onto the filamentous chloroplast of green alga Spirogyra and observed that oxygen-seeking bacteria introduced into the system concentrated in the region of the spectrum where chlorophyll pigments absorb. This action spectrum gave the first indication of the effectiveness of light absorbed by accessory pigments in driving photosynthesis.

2.6.3 Fate of light energy absorbed by photosynthetic pigments

Each photon represents a quantum of light energy. A molecule of chlorophyll on the absorption of light becomes excited to a higher energy state. An excited chlorophyll molecule is not stable and it returns rapidly to their ground level (unexcited state), in three possible ways:

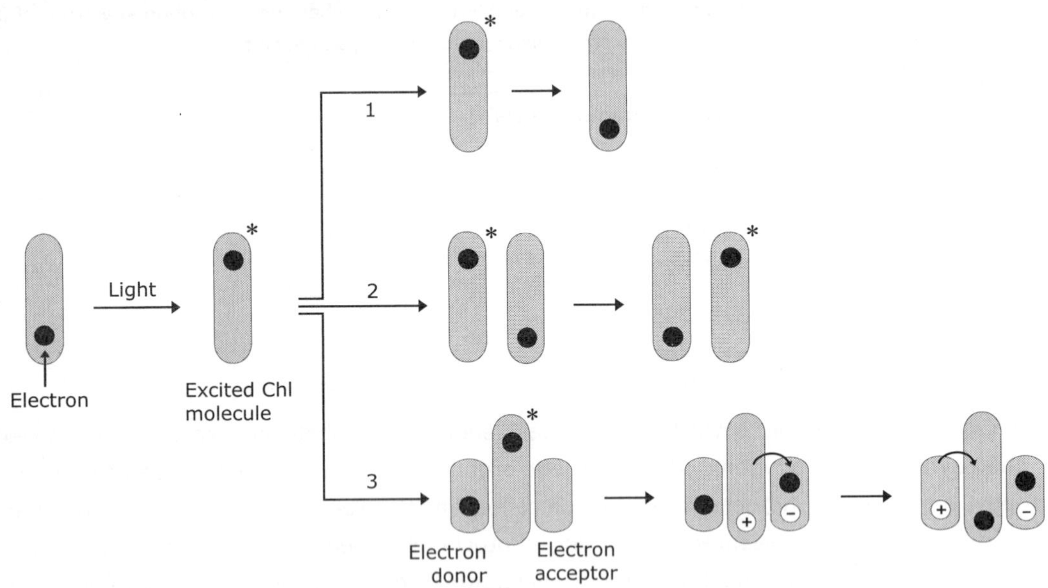

Figure 2.47 An excited molecule is unstable and will tend to return to its original, unexcited state in one of three ways: 1. by converting the extra energy into heat or to some combination of heat and light of a longer wavelength (*luminescence*) 2. by transferring the excitation energy directly to a neighboring chlorophyll molecule (*resonance energy transfer*) and 3. by transferring the high-energy electron to another nearby molecule (an electron acceptor) and then returning to its original state by taking up a low-energy electron from some other molecule (an electron donor). The last two mechanisms are exploited in the process of photosynthesis. *Adapted and modified from Molecular biology of the cell, Alberts et. al, Garland Science.*

Luminescence: By converting the extra energy into heat or to some combination of heat and light of a higher wavelength. Following light absorption, a chlorophyll molecule is usually excited to singlet excited electronic energy states (S_1 or S_2). The promotion of electrons to an excited electronic energy state is called *excitation*. Excited states may be classified as **singlet** or **triplet**. An excited molecule in a singlet or triplet excited energy state can undergo various modes of nonradiative as well as radiative decay. The radiative decay is called **luminescence**. If the luminescence arises because of the transition of electrons from a singlet excited energy state to a singlet ground energy state, then it is called **fluorescence**. If, however, luminescence arises due to the transition of electrons from a triplet excited state to singlet ground energy state, then the luminescence is called **phosphorescence**.

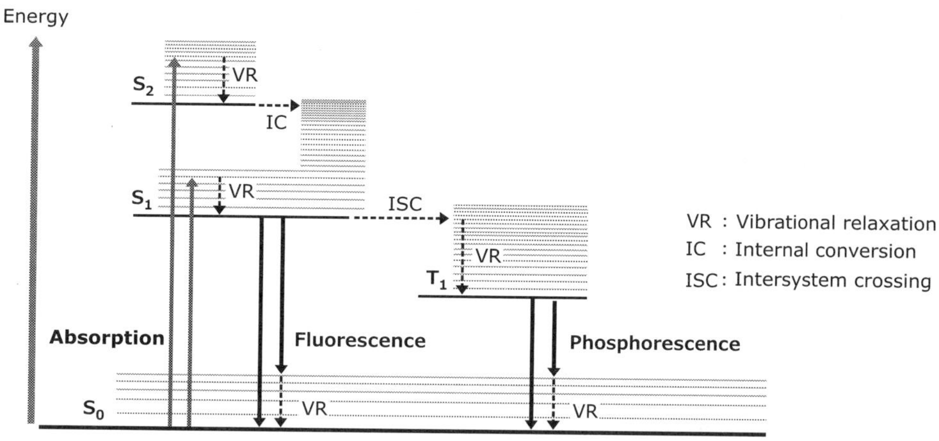

Figure 2.48 Excited states of Chl. The thick horizontal lines represent the singlet (S_n) and triplet (T_n) electronic energy states while the thin horizontal lines represent vibrational energy levels. S_0 represents the singlet ground energy state while S_1 and S_2 represent the first and second singlet excited energy states, respectively. T_1 represents the excited triplet energy state. An excited molecule in a singlet or triplet excited energy state can undergo various modes of nonradiative as well as radiative decay. The light emitted by the radiative, singlet excited-to-ground state transition is called fluorescence. The light emitted by the radiative, triplet-to-ground state transition is called phosphorescence.

Resonance energy transfer: By transferring the energy, but not the electron directly to a neighbouring chlorophyll molecule by a process called **resonance energy transfer** (also known as *Forster transfer*). The excitation energy is trapped by the reaction center because the excited state of its chlorophyll has lower energy than that of the antenna molecules.

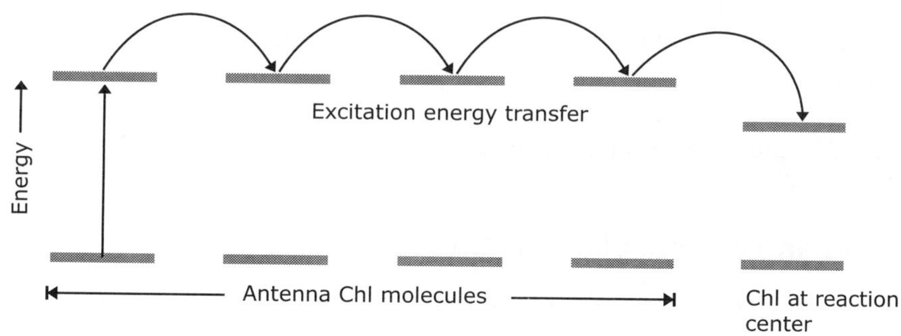

Figure 2.49 Energy level diagram illustrating excitation transfer. The excitation energy is trapped by the reaction center because the excited state of its Chl has a lower energy than that of the antenna molecules.

Photochemical reactions: By transferring the high energy electron to another nearby molecule (*electron acceptor*) and then returning to its original state by taking up a low energy electron from some other molecule (*an electron donor*) i.e., photochemical reaction. The photochemical reactions of photosynthesis are among the fastest known chemical reactions.

2.6.4 Concept of photosynthetic unit

In 1932, Robert Emerson and William Arnold provided the first evidence for the cooperation of many chlorophyll molecules in energy conversion during photosynthesis. They suggested that not all the chlorophyll molecules in a chloroplast were directly involved in the photochemical reaction. Using suspensions of the alga *Chlorella* and lights of saturating intensity for very short duration (~10 μsec), they determined the minimum amount of light needed to produce maximal oxygen production during photosynthesis. Based on the number of chlorophyll molecules present in the preparation, they calculated that one molecule of oxygen was being released after absorption of 8 photons of light for about 2400 chlorophyll molecules present. Emerson and Arnold explained that about 2400 chlorophyll molecules act as a unit (called **photosynthetic unit**) for producing one molecule of oxygen per 8 photons absorbed. In a photosynthetic unit, most chlorophyll molecules (constitute light harvesting antenna complex) absorb light and transfer the excitation energy to reaction center, where special pair of Chl *a* molecules performs photochemical reaction. The size of photosynthetic units varies among different species - between 300 and 5000 chlorophyll molecules.

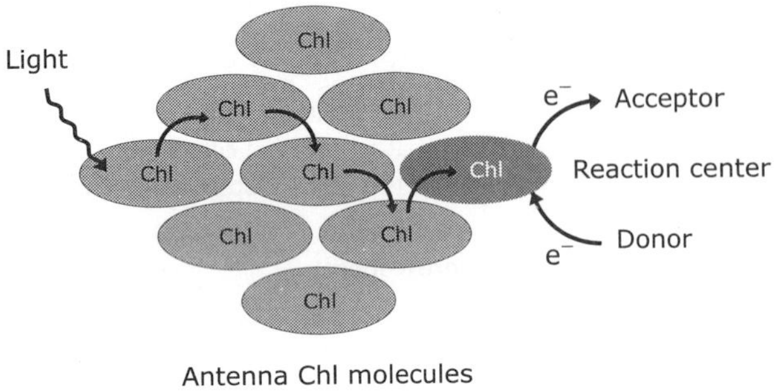

Figure 2.50
Simplified representation of the photosynthetic unit consisting of the light-harvesting antenna chlorophyll molecules and the reaction center, small arrows in the chlorophyll antenna represent transfer of excitation energy.

2.6.5 Hill reaction

The Hill reaction is the light-driven transfer of electrons from water to **Hill reagents** (non-physiological oxidants). The Hill reaction demonstrated that oxygen produced from the oxidation of water during photosynthesis occurs separately from the process that reduces (or fixes) carbon dioxide into sugars. In 1937, Robert Hill found that isolated chloroplasts from plants can release oxygen when they are illuminated by light in the presence of a suitable electron acceptor (oxidants) such as ferricyanide, ferric oxalate. The materials isolated by Hill actually consisted of thylakoid membranes which lacked the necessary enzymes for carbon dioxide fixation. One of the non-physiological oxidants used by Hill was the dye 2,6-dichlorophenolindophenol (**DCPIP**), now called a *Hill reagent*, which in its oxidized form is blue and in its reduced form is colorless. Later S. Ochoa showed that $NADP^+$ is the biological electron acceptor in the chloroplast. Light reduces $NADP^+$ which in turn serves as the reducing agent for carbon fixation in the Calvin cycle.

$$2 \times H_2O + 2 \times NADP^+ \xrightarrow{\text{Light}} 2 \times NADPH + 2 \times H^+ + O_2$$

2.6.6 Oxygenic and anoxygenic photosynthesis

In *anoxygenic photosynthesis*, light energy is captured and converted into ATP, without the production of oxygen. Water is, therefore, not used as an electron donor. In *oxygenic photosynthesis*, light energy is captured and converted into ATP, with the production of oxygen. Here, synthesis of oxygen occurs due to photooxidation or photolysis of water.

Before 1930, researchers considered carbon dioxide as source of oxygen in oxygenic photosynthetic organisms. This idea was challenged in the 1930s by C. B. van Niel of Stanford University. According to him, the O_2 produced by plants is derived from H_2O and not from CO_2. van Niel found that photosynthetic bacteria *Chromatium vinosum* assimilates CO_2 in light without evolving O_2. Such bacteria use H_2S, instead of water as an electron donor and forms sulphur instead of O_2.

$$CO_2 + 2H_2S \xrightarrow[\text{Bchl}]{\text{Light}} (CH_2O) + H_2O + 2S$$

The chemical similarity between H_2S and H_2O led van Niel to propose the general photosynthetic reaction:

$$CO_2 + 2H_2A \xrightarrow{\text{Light}} (CH_2O) + 2A + H_2O$$

where H_2A is H_2O in green plants and cyanobacteria and H_2S in photosynthetic sulfur bacteria. Thus, he hypothesized that in oxygenic photosynthetic organisms water acts as a source of oxygen.

The validity of van Niel's hypothesis was established in the year 1941 by Ruben and Kamen. They directly demonstrated by *isotopic study* using ^{18}O labeled water and CO_2 on green alga *chlorella* that the source of oxygen formed in photosynthesis is water. In the following equations, *bold* letter denotes labeled atom of oxygen (^{18}O).

Experiment 1: $CO_2 + 2H_2\mathbf{O} \longrightarrow [CH_2O] + H_2O + \mathbf{O}_2$

Experiment 2: $C\mathbf{O}_2 + 2H_2O \longrightarrow [CH_2\mathbf{O}] + H_2\mathbf{O} + O_2$

2.6.7 Concept of pigment system

In 1943, Robert Emerson and Charlton Lewis examined the action spectrum in the visible region for oxygen evolution in the green algae *Chlorella pyrenoidosa*. They found that the quantum yield remained fairly constant up to 680 nm, beyond which it declined sharply. This drop in quantum yield in the far–red region of the spectrum was called the **red drop phenomenon**. This suggests that light with a wavelength greater than 680 nm is much less efficient than light of shorter wavelengths. **Quantum yield** is the number of oxygen molecules produced per photon absorbed. The reciprocal of quantum yield is **quantum requirement** i.e., number of photons needed for each oxygen molecule produced.

In another experiment, Emerson and his colleagues set up two beams of light - one in the red region (wavelengths less than 680 nm) and the other in the far red region (wavelengths greater than 680 nm). Emerson found that when the two beams were applied simultaneously, the rate of photosynthesis was 2–3 times greater than the sum of the rates obtained with each beam separately. This phenomenon is known as an **Emerson enhancement effect**. The enhancement effect suggests that photosynthesis involves two photosystems - one driven by light of long wavelength (greater than 680 nm) and other driven by light of short wavelength (less than or equal to 680 nm).

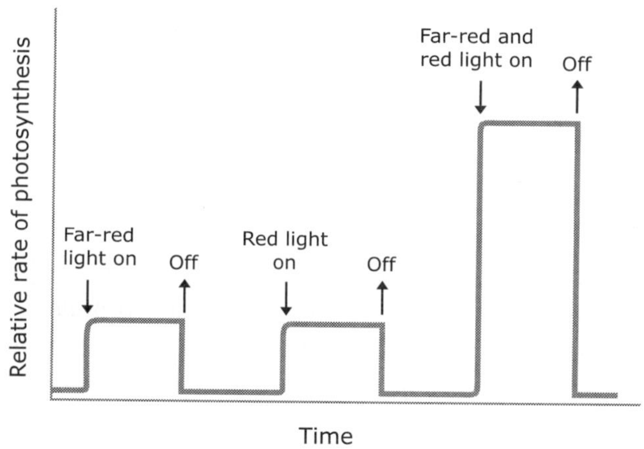

Figure 2.51
Emerson enhancement effect. The rate of photosynthesis when red and far-red light are given together is greater than the sum of the rates when they are given apart. The enhancement effect provided essential evidence in favor of the concept that photosynthesis is carried out by two different photosystems working in series but with slightly different wavelength optima.

Pigment systems

In all natural photosynthetic systems, pigment molecules are bound to proteins forming pigment–protein complexes called *pigment system* (or **photosystem**). The pigment systems have two components: *Photochemical reaction* center and *antenna complex*.

Photochemical reaction center is a protein-pigment complex that carries out photochemical reaction. There are two types of photochemical reaction centers - **Fe-S type reaction center** (or type I) and **Pheophytin-quinone type reaction center** (or type II).

Antenna complex (or **light-harvesting complex**) consists of a number of distinct pigment-protein complexes. It has two components - *core* or *inner antenna* and *peripheral* or *outer antenna*. The antenna complex captures light energy and feeds it to the reaction center by a process called resonance energy transfer. The size of the antenna complex varies considerably in different organisms, generally 200 to 300 chlorophylls per reaction center in higher plants. All photosynthetic organisms, with the exception of *Heliobacteria*, possess an antenna complex.

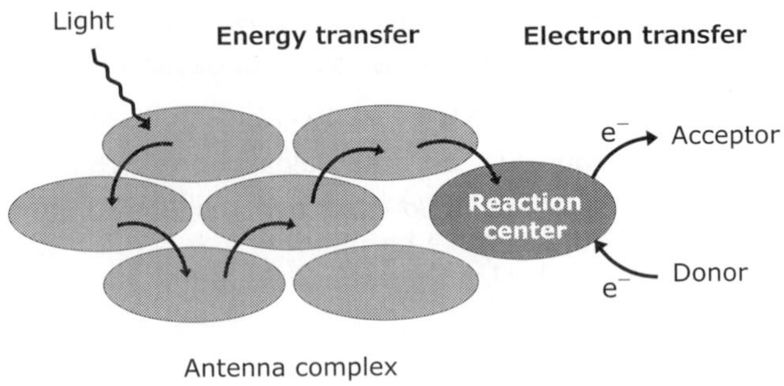

Figure 2.52 Organization of pigment system in the thylakoid membrane. Pigment systems are tightly packed in the thylakoid membrane, with several hundred antenna chlorophylls and accessory pigments surrounding a photoreaction center. Absorption of a photon by any of the antenna chlorophylls leads to excitation of the reaction center by exciton energy transfer (black arrow). Photochemical reaction here converts the energy of a photon into a separation of charge, initiating electron flow.

In oxygenic photosynthetic organisms (such as plants and cyanobacteria), two types of photosystems are present. Photosystem with Fe-S type reaction center is called photosystem I (**PSI**) and photosystem with pheophytin-quinone type reaction center is called photosystem II (**PSII**).

PSI and PSII in green plants

PSII

PSII (Photosystem II) is a pigment-protein complex consisting of a several proteins and cofactors. It has a *pheophytin-quinone type reaction center*. The photochemical reaction center Chl *a* of PSII is known as **P680** because it most effectively absorbs light of wavelength 680 nm. In higher plants, the reaction center contains membrane proteins **D1** and **D2** (about 39 kDa each), cytochrome b_{559} and other proteins along with Chl *a* molecules, pheophytin, plastoquinones and other cofactors. The reaction center is associated with light-harvesting antenna complexes - core antenna and peripheral antenna. The Chl *a* containing core antenna **CP47** and **CP43** remain closely associated with reaction center. The peripheral antenna includes Chl *a/b* binding proteins called **LHCII**. The LHCII protein is an integral membrane protein (~25 kDa) and readily forms trimers.

PSI

PSI (Photosystem I) is a protein-pigment complex that uses light energy to mediate electron transfer from plastocyanin to ferredoxin. It has a *Fe-S type reaction center*. It contains several proteins, Chl *a* molecules, carotenoids, phylloquinones, Fe-S centers and other cofactors. It is driven by light of wavelength 700 nm. The Chl *a* at the photochemical reaction center of PSI is called **P700** because it most effectively absorbs light of wavelength 700 nm (the P stands for *pigment*). *Two pigments, P680 and P700, are identical chlorophyll a molecules. However, their association with different proteins in the thylakoid membrane accounts for the slight differences in their light-absorbing properties*. PSI reaction center is composed of a number of polypeptides, of which the two major polypeptides that make up the heterodimer are **PsaA** and **PsaB**. In contrast to PSII, a core antenna is an integral part of the PSI reaction center. Hence, PSI consists of a *reaction center-core complex* and peripheral antenna, **LHCI**.

Distribution of PSI and PSII

The two photosystems are distributed differently in thylakoid membrane within chloroplast. PSI is found almost exclusively in *non-appressed* membranes of grana thylakoid (or grana lamellae) and stroma thylakoid (or stroma lamellae). PSII is located predominantly in the *appressed* membranes of grana thylakoid. Generally, there is an excess of PSII than PSI in chloroplasts. Most commonly the ratio of PSII to PSI is about 1.5:1, but it can change when plants are grown under different light conditions.

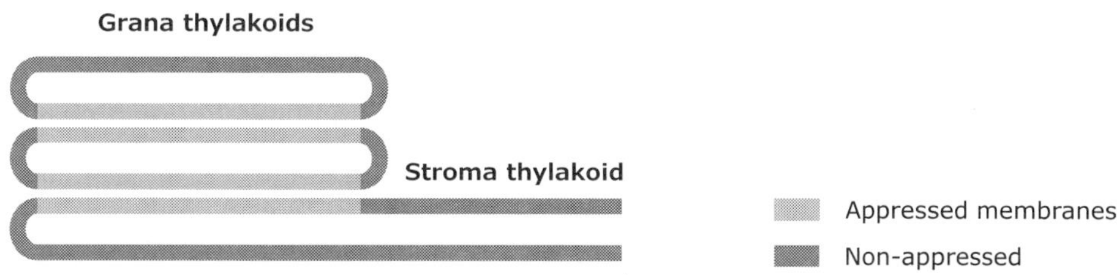

Figure 2.53 The outer membrane surface of the thylakoids can be divided into two structurally different regions: the appressed membranes of the grana thylakoids whose surface is in contact with other membranes, and the nonappressed membranes of the stroma thylakoids and the ends and margins of the grana thylakoids that are also exposed to the stroma.

2.6.8 Photosynthesis in green plants

Photosynthesis is a two-stage process: one stage involves *light reactions* which directly dependent on the light and other *carbon-fixation reactions*.

The **light reactions** (*light-dependent photochemical reactions*) occur in the thylakoid of chloroplast, and require the direct energy of light to make NADPH and ATP that are used in the carbon-fixation reactions. Light reactions are also known as the **thylakoid reactions** because almost all the reactions (i.e., oxidation of water, reduction of $NADP^+$ and ATP formation) take place within the thylakoids. A process of formation of ATP from ADP and inorganic phosphate during light reaction by utilizing light energy is called *photophosphorylation*.

The **carbon-fixation reactions** (sometimes misleadingly called the **dark reactions**), occur in the stroma of the chloroplasts and driven by the products of the light reactions, ATP and NADPH, to make glyceraldehyde 3-phosphate (a triose phosphate) from reduction of carbon dioxide. The carbon fixation and reduction reactions are also called the **stroma reactions** because the carbon reduction reactions take place in the aqueous region of the chloroplast, the stroma. By convention, carbon-fixation reactions are called as *dark reactions*. However, this should not be construed to mean that they occur in darkness or that they are not light-dependent.

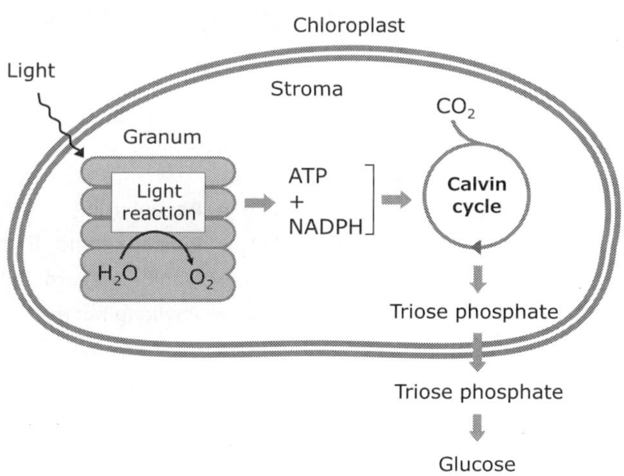

Figure 2.54
The chemical reactions in which water is oxidized to oxygen, $NADP^+$ is reduced, and ATP is formed are known as the thylakoid reactions because almost all the reactions up to $NADP^+$ reduction take place within the thylakoids. Since they are directly light driven, hence are also called light reactions. The carbon fixation and reduction reactions are called the stroma reactions because the carbon reduction reactions take place in the aqueous region of the chloroplast, the stroma. By convention, stroma reactions are called as dark reactions. However, this should not be construed to mean that they occur in darkness or that they are not light-dependent.

Table 2.11 Differences between light and carbon-fixation reactions in plants

Light reaction	Carbon-fixation reaction
Light-dependent reaction	Light-independent reaction
Occurs in the grana of chloroplast	Occurs in the stroma of the chloroplasts
Photochemical reaction occurs	Chemical reaction occurs
Formation of ATP and NADPH occurs	Utilization of ATP and NADPH occurs
Oxidation of H_2O occurs	Reduction of CO_2 occurs

2.6.9 Light reaction

Light reaction (photochemical reaction) in the photosystem starts electron flow. In green plants, flow of electron is of two types: *noncyclic* as well as *cyclic*.

Noncyclic electron flow

It is a light-induced electron transport from water to $NADP^+$ and a concomitant evolution of oxygen. It involves a collaboration of two photosystems: PSII and PSI. Electrons move from water through PSII to PSI and then to $NADP^+$. Electron transport leads to generation of a proton-motive force and synthesis of ATP. *Formation of ATP due to light-induced noncyclic electron flow is called* **noncyclic photophosphorylation.**

The diagram in **figure 2.55** often called the *Z scheme* because of its overall form, outlines the pathway of electron flow between the two photosystems and the energy relationship in the light reactions. Noncyclic electron flow begins with the absorption of a photon by PSII. Upon absorption of a photon, P680 is excited to P680*, which rapidly transfers an electron to a nearby pheophytin and changes into $P680^+$. **Pheophytin** is a chlorophyll in which the central magnesium atom has been replaced by two hydrogen atoms.

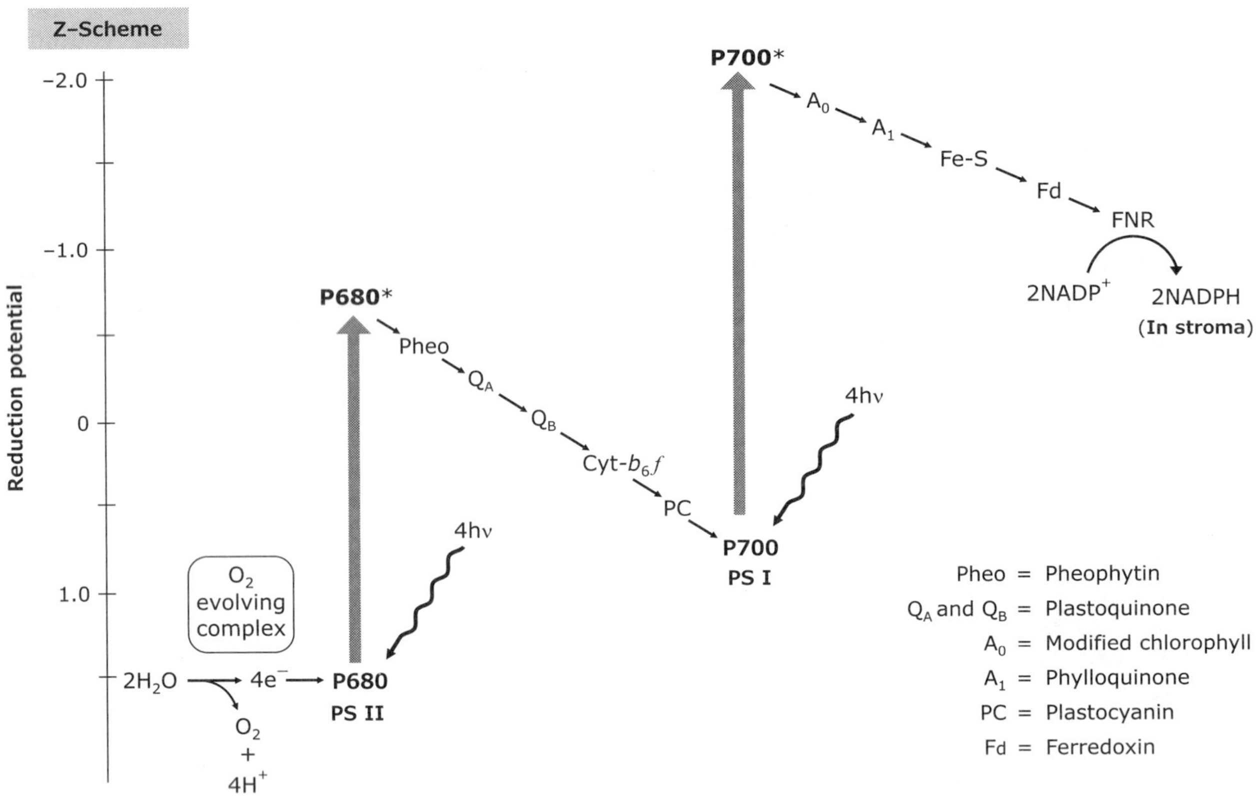

Figure 2.55 Z scheme. During noncyclic flow of electrons, PSII and PSI are linked in series. The excited PSII reaction center chlorophyll, P680*, transfers an electron to pheophytin. P680 oxidized by light is re-reduced by electrons from oxidation of water. Pheophytin transfers electrons to the plastoquinones Q_A and Q_B. The cytochrome b_6f complex transfers electrons to plastocyanin which in turn reduces $P700^+$ (oxidized P700). The acceptor of electrons from P700* is A_0. The next acceptor A_1 is a quinone. A series of membrane-bound iron-sulfur proteins (F_X, F_A and F_B) transfers electrons to soluble ferredoxin. The soluble flavoprotein ferredoxin-NADP reductase (FNR) reduces $NADP^+$ to NADPH.

The positively charged $P680^+$, *a* strong **oxidizing agent,** attracts an electron from an electron donor to regenerate the original P680. In oxygenic photosynthetic organisms, H_2O acts as an electron donor. Splitting of two water molecules yields four electrons, four protons and molecular oxygen.

$$2H_2O \xrightarrow{4\,h\nu} 4H^+ + 4e^- + O_2$$

The splitting of water is catalyzed by a protein complex, the **oxygen-evolving complex**, located on the luminal surface of the thylakoid membrane. The oxygen-evolving complex contains several proteins (**PsbO**, **PsbP** and **PsbQ**) as well as four *manganese ions* together with a *calcium ion*, *chloride ion* and *bicarbonate ion*. The four electrons abstracted from photolysis of two water molecules do not pass directly to P680$^+$, which can accept only one electron at a time. The oxygen-evolving complex oxidizes water and passes four electrons one at a time to P680$^+$. The oxygen-evolving complex cycles through a series of oxidation states while abstracting protons and electrons from the H_2O molecules and finally releases O_2 into the inner thylakoid space. Although calcium, chloride and bicarbonate ions are needed for water oxidation, their role is not clear.

Each photon absorbed by P680 transfers only a single electron, but four electrons must be removed from water to generate a molecule of O_2. *How do four photons cooperate in the production of O_2?* There is some sort of 'gear wheel' that collects the four electrons from two H_2O molecules and transfers them one at a time to a reaction center. Manganese ions in the oxygen-evolving complex cycles through five different states, S_0 through S_4. Each of the transitions between S_0 and S_4 is a photon-driven redox reaction; that from S_4 to S_0 results in the release of O_2. This model for the photooxidation of water is called the **S-state** mechanism.

The five reaction steps release a total of four water-derived protons into the thylakoid lumen in a stepwise manner. Oxygen-evolving complex does not transfer electrons directly to P680$^+$. One electron carrier, identified as Y_z, functions between the oxygen-evolving complex and P680$^+$. This is a radical formed from a **tyrosine residue** in the D1 protein of the PSII reaction center.

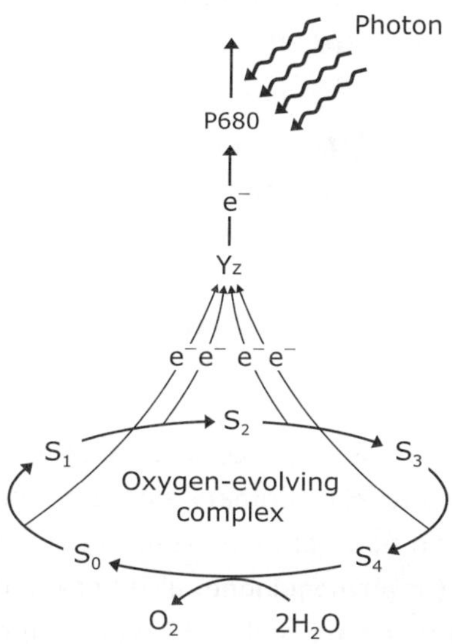

Figure 2.56
The sequential absorption of four photons, each causing the loss of one electron from the Mn center, produces an oxidizing agent that can take four electrons from two molecules of water, producing O_2. The electrons lost from the Mn center pass one at a time to a Tyr residue (Y_Z) in the D1 protein.

Reduced pheophytin transfers electron to **plastoquinone**. Plastoquinone is present in PSII both as a tightly-bound and a loosely-bound electron carrier, designated **Q_A** (primary quinone, bound to D2) and **Q_B** (secondary quinone, bound to D1), respectively. Plastoquinone is a photosynthetically active *quinone* present in PSII. Other photosynthetically active quinones are *ubiquinone* and *menaquinone* in green and purple photosynthetic bacteria, and *phylloquinone* in PSI. Q_A is photoreduced only to the *plastosemiquinone*, but Q_B can accept two electrons and two protons, forming a fully reduced plastoquinol (or plastohydroquinone).

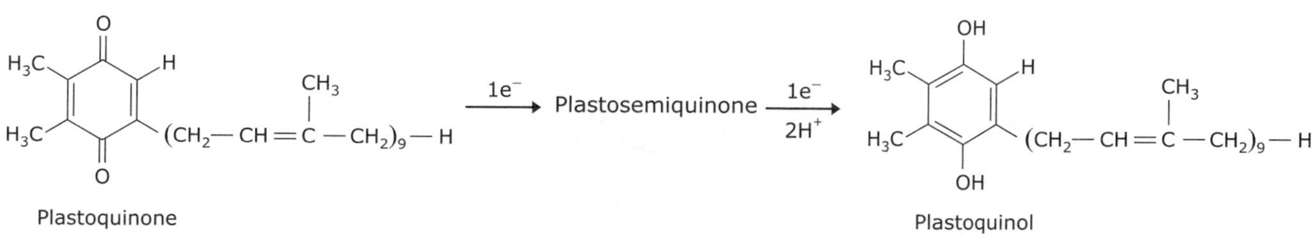

Figure 2.57 The acceptance of two electrons and two protons reduces plastoquinone to plastoquinol.

Plastoquinol diffuses in the membrane and binds with a Cyt b_6f complex. The Cyt b_6f complex lies between PS II and PS I in the electron-transport system. Its function is to oxidize the plastoquinol and pumps protons from the stroma into the thylakoid lumen. Cytochrome *f* then transfers an electron to the blue-colored protein plastocyanin (PC). **Plastocyanin** is a small, water-soluble and copper-containing protein that transfers electrons between the cytochrome b_6f complex and $P700^+$ of PSI. The protein is a monomer and resides in the on the lumenal side of thylakoid membrane.

Cytochromes are electron-transfer proteins containing a *heme*, as the prosthetic group. According to their characteristic absorption spectra and chemical composition, cytochromes may be divided into three groups, namely, cytochromes-*a*, –*b* and –*c*. In photosynthetic organisms, mainly *b*- and *c*-type *cytochromes* are found. It is present in the form of Cyt b_6f complex that resembles the Cyt bc_1 complex of mitochondria and anoxygenic photosynthetic bacteria. Cyt b_6f complex possesses one **Rieske iron-sulfur protein**, two **Cyt *b*** and **Cyt *c*** (Cyt *c*, historically called cytochrome *f*).

Cyt b_6f complex transfers electrons from a plastoquinol to a water-soluble protein plastocyanin. Similar to mitochondrial complex III, this complex mediates **Q-cycle** (*Quinone cycle*) in which electrons pass from plastoquinol to cytochrome b one at a time. Q-cycle results in the pumping of protons across the membrane. In chloroplasts, the direction of proton movement is from the stromal compartment to the thylakoid lumen.

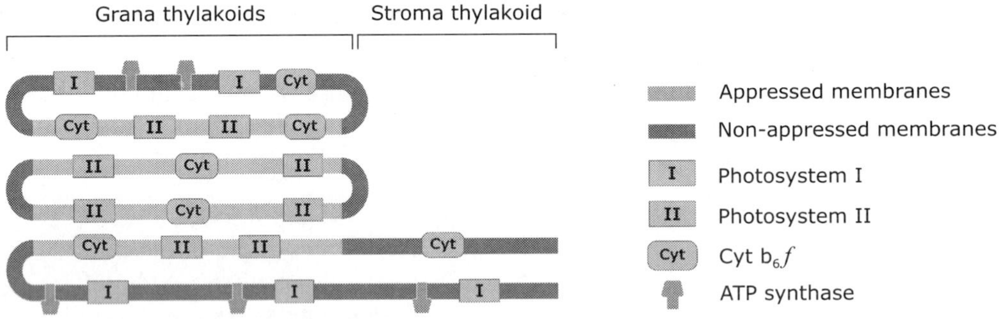

Figure 2.58 PSII units are located almost exclusively in the appressed regions while PSI and ATP synthase are located in non-appressed regions. The Cyt b_6f complex is uniformly distributed throughout the membrane system.

At the core of PSI is a special pair of *chlorophyll a* molecules known as P700. Upon absorption of a photon, P700 is excited to P700*. The photoexcited electron is then transferred to PSI's primary electron acceptor, $\mathbf{A_0}$, which is a modified chlorophyll molecule. The resulting oxidized $P700^+$ can now act as an electron acceptor, accepting an electron from plastocyanin. Reduced A_0 transfers electron to $\mathbf{A_1}$ (or **phylloquinone**, also known as vitamin K_1) to a series of Fe-S clusters, called F_X, F_A and F_B. These three Fe-S proteins are of 4Fe-4S type. The electrons are then transferred to the ferredoxin (Fd). **Ferredoxin** is a small, water-soluble iron-sulfur [2Fe-2S] protein located on the stromal side of thylakoid membrane. The soluble flavoprotein *ferredoxin–NADP⁺ reductase* (**FNR**) catalyzes the transfer of electrons from reduced ferredoxin to $NADP^+$. Two electrons are required for its reduction to NADPH.

For each electron transferred from H_2O to $NADP^+$, two photons are absorbed, one by each photosystem. To form one molecule of O_2, which requires transfer of four electrons from two H_2O to two $NADP^+$, a total of eight photons must be absorbed, four by each photosystem.

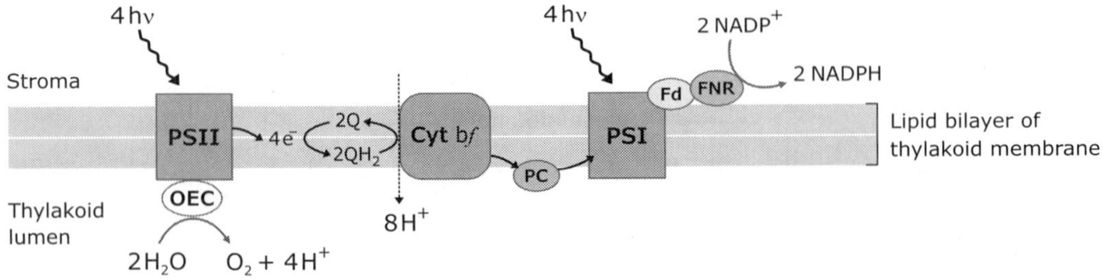

Role of DCMU and paraquat: DCMU (3-(3,4 dichlorophenyl)-1,1 dimethylurea) or diuron, a herbicide, abolishes photosynthetic oxygen production because it competes with plastoquinone for the Q_B binding site of PSII and blocks electron flow from PSII to Cyt b_6f complex. **Paraquat** acts as a herbicide, blocks photosynthetic electron flow by intercepting electrons between the ferredoxin acceptors and $NADP^+$ and then reduces oxygen to superoxide ($O_2^{\bullet -}$). Superoxide is a free radical that reacts non-specifically with a wide range of molecules in the chloroplast, leading to the rapid loss of chloroplast activity.

ATP synthesis

In oxygenic photosynthetic organisms, H_2O acts as an electron donor. Photooxidation of two water molecules yields four electrons, four protons and molecular oxygen. As the electrons are transported down the electron transport chain, some of the energy released is used to pump protons across the thylakoid membrane from the stroma of the chloroplast to the thylakoid lumen producing an electrochemical proton gradient. Electrochemical proton gradient generates proton motive force.

The absorption of 8 photons by PSII and PSI (4 photons each) and photooxidation of two water molecules yields four protons and one molecule of O_2 into the thylakoid lumen. It is also estimated that the transport of the four electrons through the Cyt b_6f complex results in the translocation of eight protons from the stroma to the thylakoid lumen. Hence, total 12 protons are released in the lumen. The accumulating protons in the thylakoid lumen pass back across the thylakoid membrane to the stroma through **ATP synthase** (CF_0-CF_1). ATP synthase catalyzes ATP synthesis as protons flow back along the electrochemical proton gradient. According to most estimates, chloroplast ATP synthase produces one ATP for every three protons it transports out of the thylakoid lumen. Noncyclic electrons transport, therefore, results in the production of ~4 molecules of ATP per molecule of O_2 evolved.

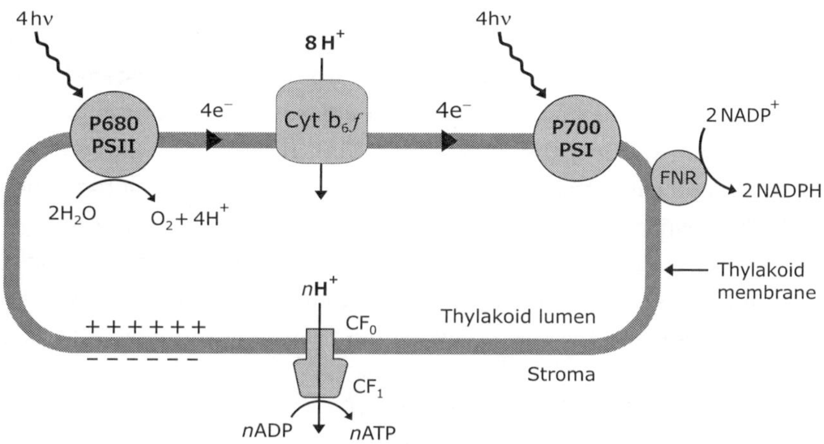

Figure 2.59 Electron and proton transport in chloroplast thylakoids. Electrons move from H_2O through photosystem II, Cyt b_6f complex, photosystem I, and finally to $NADP^+$. Protons are pumped into the thylakoid lumen by the flow of electrons through Cyt b_6f complex between photosystem II and photosystem I. Protons reenter into the stroma through proton channels formed by the F_0 portion of the ATP synthase, designated CF_0 in the chloroplast enzyme. The F_1 subunit (CF_1) catalyzes synthesis of ATP.

Cyclic electron flow

In certain cases, photoexcited electrons follow cyclic path, which involves PSI but not PSII. In cyclic electron flow, photoexcited electrons from P700 of PSI move through the b_6f complex and back to P700. This cyclic electron flow is coupled to proton pumping into the thylakoid lumen. When protons flow down their electrochemical gradient through ATP synthase complexes, ATP synthesis occurs. *The formation of ATP due to light-induced cyclic electron flow is called cyclic photophosphorylation*. There is no production of NADPH and no release of oxygen in cyclic electron flow. In plants, the cyclic flow of electrons is utilized only when the concentration of NADPH is sufficient, but still needs ATP to power other activities in the chloroplast. Cyclic photophosphorylation is somewhat more productive as compared to noncyclic photophosphorylation with regard to ATP synthesis. The absorption of 4 photons by PSI results in the release of 8 protons into the lumen by the Cyt b_6f complex. These protons flow through ATP synthase to yield ~3 molecules of ATP (assuming the same ratio of ATP molecules generated per proton).

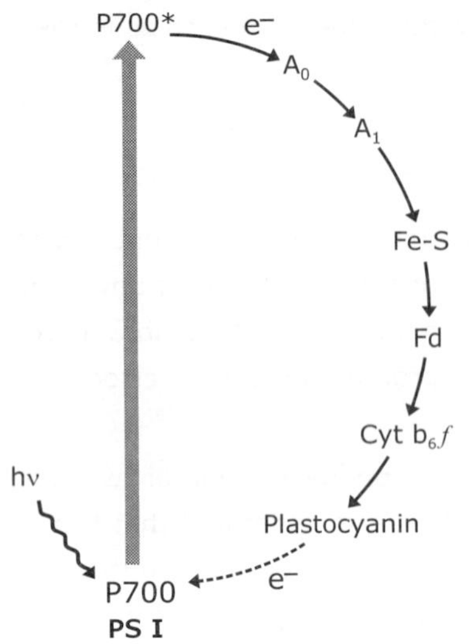

Figure 2.60
Cyclic electron flow.
The mechanism of cyclic electron flow remain a subject of controversy. Several pathways have been proposed. According to one pathway, electrons are passed from ferredoxin to the cyt b_6f. This electron flow generates electrochemical proton gradient and thus ATP but produces no NADPH. Photoexcited electrons from PSI are returned from ferredoxin to P700 via the cytochrome complex.

In noncyclic electron flow, the involvement of two photosystems with different light-absorbing properties possesses a special problem. If the light energy available to PSI and PSII is not precisely matched, the electron flow will be limited by the photosystem that is receiving less energy. In the most efficient situation, the input of energy would be the same to both photosystems. However, no single arrangement of pigments would satisfy this requirement because at different times of day the light intensity and spectral distribution tend to favour one photosystem or the other.

This problem can be solved by a mechanism that shifts energy from one photosystem to the other in response to different conditions. Thylakoid membranes contain a **protein kinase** that can phosphorylate a specific threonine residue of LHCII. Phosphorylation weakens the interaction of LHCII with PSII, and some LHCII dissociates and moves to the stroma thylakoid (i.e., out of the appressed regions of the membrane into the non-appressed regions); captures photons for PSI. Thus, when LHCII is not phosphorylated, it delivers more energy to PSII, and when it is phosphorylated, it delivers more energy to PSI. The protein kinase is activated when plastoquinone, one of the electron carriers between PSI and PSII, accumulates in the reduced state. Reduced plastoquinone accumulates when PSII is being activated more than PSI. This regulates the transition from noncyclic to cyclic electron flow.

Table 2.12 Differences between noncyclic and cyclic electron flow

Noncyclic electron flow	Cyclic electron flow
Both PSI and PSII	Only PSI
Photolysis of water	No photolysis of water
Formation of oxygen	No oxygen formation
ATP synthesis occurs	ATP synthesis occurs
NADPH synthesis occurs	No NADPH synthesis

Photophosphorylation versus oxidative phosphorylation

Oxidative phosphorylation is the process in which ATP synthesis is driven by oxidation of NADH or $FADH_2$ whereas in *photophosphorylation* ATP synthesis is driven by light. There are three fundamental similarities between oxidative phosphorylation and photophosphorylation:

- Both processes involve the flow of electrons through a chain of membrane-bound carriers.
- The free energy made available by 'downhill' (exergonic) electron flow is coupled to the 'uphill' transport of protons across membrane generating electrochemical proton gradient.
- The transmembrane flow of protons along concentration gradient through ATP synthase provides the free energy for synthesis of ATP.

Oxidative phosphorylation	**Photophosphorylation**
ATP synthesis driven by oxidation of NADH and $FADH_2$.	ATP synthesis driven by light.
Light-independent process.	Light-dependent process.
Occurs during aerobic respiration.	Occurs during photosynthesis.
In eukaryotes, occurs in mitochondria.	In eukaryotes, occurs in chloroplast.
Involves the reduction of O_2 to H_2O with electrons donated by NADH and $FADH_2$.	Involves the oxidation of H_2O to O_2, with $NADP^+$ as electron acceptor.

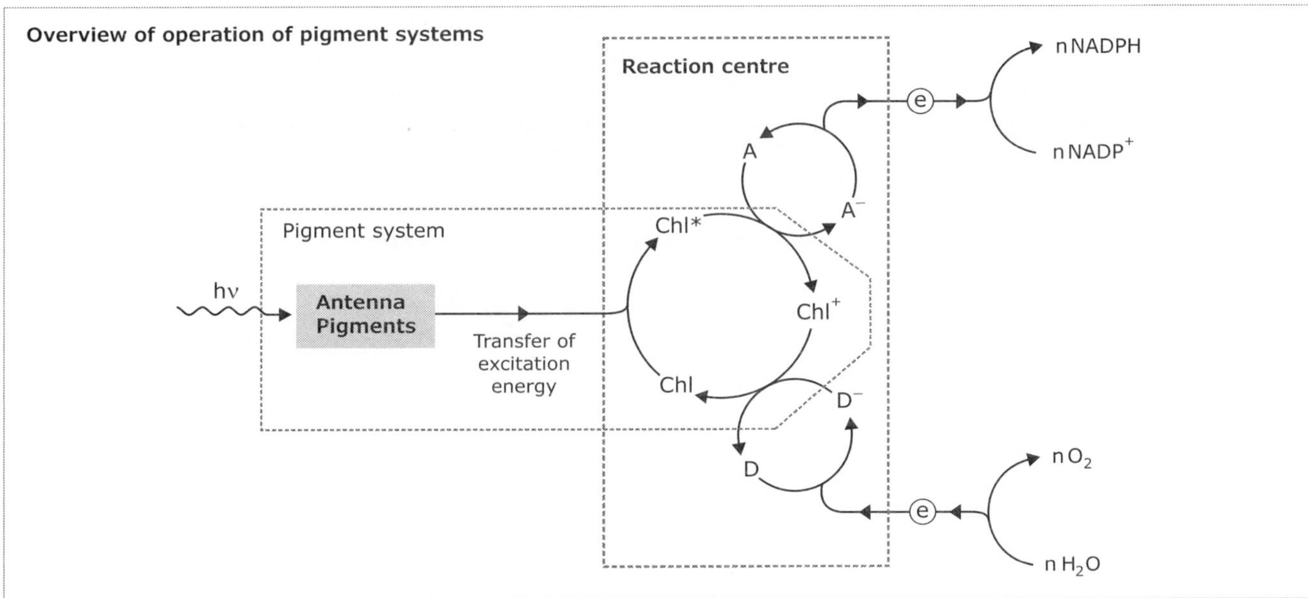

Box 2.4 Non-chlorophyll based photosynthesis

Non-chlorophyll-based photosynthesis refers to photosynthetic processes that do not rely on chlorophyll or bacteriochlorophyll pigments to capture light energy. Oxygenic and anoxygenic photosynthesis are chlorophyll-based photosynthesis. Pigment chlorophyll or bacteriochlorophyll is the major pigment used to absorb light and initiate the conversion of light energy to chemical energy. However, some archaea instead of using chlorophyll, use a membrane-bound purple pigment called **bacteriorhodopsin**. One such archaeon is the halophile *Halobacterium salinarum*. Bacteriorhodopsin is similar to the pigment *rhodopsin* found in the mammalian eye. It functions as a light-driven proton pump. It uses light energy to pump protons across the membrane, creating an electrochemical proton gradient for ATP synthesis. It has two distinct components – a chromophore that is a carotenoid derivative, **retinal** and multipass (seven pass) transmembrane protein. Retinal remains covalently attached via a Schiff base to the ε-amino group of a lysine residue of protein. When all-*trans*-retinal absorbs light, the double bond between carbons 13 and 14 changes from a *trans* to a *cis*-configuration and the Schiff base loses a proton. Protons move across the plasma membrane to the periplasmic space during these alternations. The light-driven proton pumping generates a electrochemical gradient that can be used to power the synthesis of ATP by a chemiosmotic mechanism.

Box 2.5 Prokaryotic photosynthesis

There are three groups of photosynthetic bacteria – the purple bacteria, the green bacteria and the cyanobacteria. The cyanobacteria differ most fundamentally from the green and purple photosynthetic bacteria in being able to carry out *oxygenic photosynthesis*. Similar to plants they have PSI and PSII, use water as an electron donor and generate oxygen during photosynthesis.

In contrast, purple and green bacteria have only one type of reaction center and perform anoxygenic photosynthesis (also called **bacterial photosynthesis**). In purple bacteria, the reaction center is similar to photosystem II and in green bacteria it is similar to photosystem I. However, neither of these two types of bacterial reaction center is capable of extracting electrons from water, so they do not evolve O_2. Because they are unable to use water as an electron source, they employ reduced molecules such as hydrogen sulfide, sulfur, hydrogen, and organic matter as their electron source for the generation of NADH and NADPH. Reaction center in anoxygenic photosynthetic bacteria:

- Pheophytin-Quinone type reaction center (similar to PSII).
- Fe-S type reaction center (similar to PSI).

Despite these differences, the general principles of energy transduction are the same in anoxygenic and oxygenic photosynthesis. Anoxygenic photosynthetic bacteria depend on bacteriochlorophyll, a family of molecules that are similar to the chlorophyll, that absorb strongly in the infrared between 700 and 1000 nm. The electron carriers include quinone (e.g., ubiquinone, menaquinone) and the cytochrome bc complex. As in oxygenic photosynthesis, electron transfer is coupled to the generation of an electrochemical proton gradient that drives ATP synthesis.

Table 2.13 Comparison of oxygenic and anoxygenic photosynthesis

Property	**Oxygenic photosynthesis**	**Anoxygenic photosynthesis**
Photosynthetic pigment	Chl *a*	BChl
Photosynthetic electron donors	H_2O	H_2, H_2S, S, organic matter
O_2 production	Present	Absent
Primary products of energy conversion	ATP + NADPH	ATP
Carbon source	CO_2	Organic compound and/or CO_2

Purple photosynthetic bacteria

There are two divisions of photosynthetic purple bacteria, the non-sulfur purple bacteria (e.g., *Rhodobacter sphaeroides* and *Rhodopseudomonas viridis*) and the sulfur purple bacteria (e.g., *Chromatium vinosum*). The determination of the three-dimensional structures of the reaction center of the *Rhodopseudomonas viridis* and *Rhodobacter sphaeroides* has provided an unprecedented opportunity to understand the structure and function of photosynthetic reaction centers. In 1984, Michel, Deisenhofer and Huber first described the three-dimensional structure of the Pheophytin-Quinone reaction center of *Rhodopseudomonas viridis*. Pheophytin-Quinone reaction center of *R. viridis* consists of three transmembrane proteins, H, L, M, four molecules of Bchl *b*, two molecules of bacteriopheophytin (BPh) and two quinones (one ubiquinone and other menaquinone). A C-type cytochrome containing four heme also forms an integral component of reaction center of *R. viridis*. The reaction center of other purple photosynthetic bacteria like *Rhodobacter sphaeroides* (formerly called *Rhodopseudomonas sphaeroides*), and *Rhodospirillum rubrum* also have similar organization except that the C-subunit is not present.

Photochemical reaction in *Rhodobacter sphaeroides*: Light drives the *cyclic* flow of electrons. The reaction begins with light absorption by a *special pair* of BChl *a* molecules. This *special pair* absorbs light maximally at 870 nm. For this reason, the special pair is often referred to as *P870* (P stands for pigment). Components of the reaction center include one L subunit, one M subunit, one H subunit, four bacteriochlorophyll *a*, two bacteriopheophytin, two ubiquinone (designated as Q_A and Q_B), one non-heme-Fe-protein and one carotenoid. Excitation of the special pair leads to the ejection of an electron, which is transferred to the bacteriopheophytin. From bacteriopheophytin electrons move through ubiquinone (Q_A and Q_B) and the cytochrome bc_1 complex, then through cytochrome c_2 back to the reaction center.

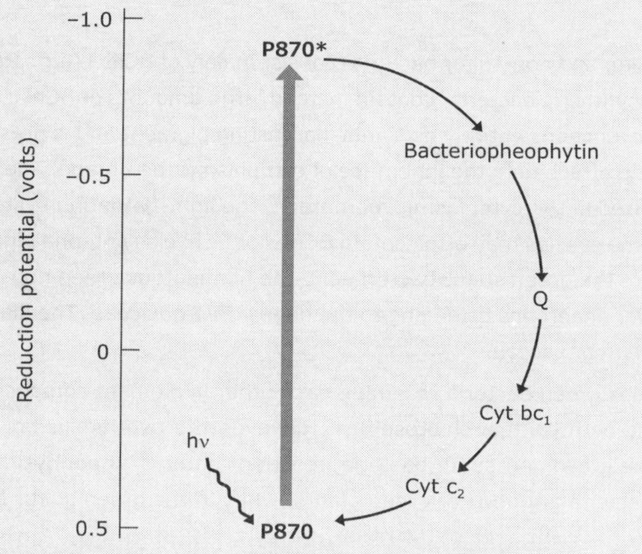

Figure 2.61 Cyclic electron flow in the single photosystem of purple bacteria, *R. sphaeroides*.

Table 2.14 Characteristics of anoxygenic photosynthetic bacteria

Purple sulfur	
Major photosynthetic pigments	Bacteriochlorophylls *a* or *b*
Location of photosynthetic pigments	Plasma membrane and chromatophore (lamellar membrane complexes that are continuous with the plasma membrane)
Photosynthetic electron donors	H_2, H_2S, S
Sulfur deposition	Inside the cell
Metabolic type	Photolithoautotrophs
Purple non-sulfur	
Major photosynthetic pigments	Bacteriochlorophylls *a* or *b*
Location of photosynthetic pigments	Plasma membrane and chromatophore
Photosynthetic electron donors	Usually organic molecules; sometimes reduced sulfur compounds or H_2
Sulfur deposition	Outside of the cell in few cases
Metabolic type	Mostly photoorganoheterotrophs
Green sulfur	
Major photosynthetic pigments	Bacteriochlorophylls *a* plus *c*, *d* or *e*
Location of photosynthetic pigments	Chlorosomes and plasma membrane
Photosynthetic electron donors	H_2, H_2S, S
Sulfur deposition	Outside of the cell
Metabolic type	Photolithoautotrophs
Green non-sulfur	
Major photosynthetic pigments	Bacteriochlorophylls *a* and *c*
Location of photosynthetic pigments	Chlorosomes and plasma membrane
Photosynthetic electron donors	Variety of sugars, amino acids and organic acids; H_2S, H_2
Metabolic type	Mostly photoheterotrophs

Green photosynthetic bacteria

The pigments of the purple bacteria (both sulfur and non-sulfur bacteria) consist mainly of BChl *a* (e.g., *Rb. sphaeroides*) or BChl *b* (e.g., *R. viridis*). The green photosynthetic bacteria, contain instead large amounts of BChl *c* and only minor amounts of BChl *a*. In these bacteria, BChl *c* functions entirely as a light-harvesting pigment and is present in separate structures called 'chlorosomes' that are found attached to the inner face of cytoplasmic membrane. The photosynthetic reaction centers of green bacteria are localized in the cytoplasmic membrane, the light-gathering systems are mainly localized in chlorosomes. Besides BChl *c*, some species may also contain BChl *d* or BChl *e* as antenna pigments. The two families of green photosynthetic bacteria are the green sulfur bacteria and the filamentous green non-sulfur bacteria. The green sulfur bacteria are small unicellular anaerobes belonging to the genus *Chlorobiaceae*. The filamentous green non-sulfur bacteria belong to the genus *Chloroflexaceae*.

The green sulfur bacteria and the filamentous green bacteria resemble each other in pigment composition and in one particular aspect of their morphology; they both contain chlorosomes. However, the two families of green bacteria contain quite different reaction center. In the green non-sulfur bacteria, reaction center is '**pheophytin-quinone type**,' resembling the reaction center of purple bacteria and PSII of green plants, while in the green sulfur bacteria, it is of the '**Fe-S type**'.

Problem

ATP synthesis in mitochondria and chloroplast depends on the electrochemical proton gradient, which is generated as a result of protons translocation across the membrane. However, the components that constitute electrochemical proton gradient differ in the mitochondria and chloroplast. *Explain*

Solution: The net effect of protons' translocation in the two organelles is similar. In chloroplasts, proton is pumped out of the stroma (pH 8) into the thylakoid space (pH about 5) creating a gradient of 3 to 3.5 pH units. This represents a proton-motive force of about 200 mV across the thylakoid membrane (nearly all of which is contributed by the pH gradient rather than by a membrane potential), which drives ATP synthesis by the ATP synthase embedded in this membrane. Like the stroma, the mitochondrial matrix has a pH of about 8, but this is created by pumping protons out of the mitochondrion into the cytosol (pH about 7) rather than into an interior space in the organelle. Thus, the pH gradient is relatively small, and most of the pmf across the mitochondrial inner membrane, which is about the same as that across the chloroplast thylakoid membrane, is caused by the resulting membrane potential.

Problem

The substance DCMU is a herbicide that inhibits photosynthesis by blocking electron transport from plastoquinone to cyt b_6f complex. Normally, DCMU blocks O_2 evolution, but the addition of ferricyanide to chloroplasts allows O_2 evolution in the presence of DCMU. *Explain*

Solution: The addition of ferricyanide as an electron acceptor allows the Hill reaction.

Problem

It is believed that the ratio of cyclic photophosphorylation to noncyclic photophosphorylation changes in response to metabolic demands. In each of the following situations, would you expect the ratio to increase, decrease or remain unchanged?

a. Chloroplasts carrying out both the Calvin cycle and the reduction of nitrite to ammonia (this process does not require ATP).
b. Chloroplasts carrying out not only the Calvin cycle but also extensive active transport.
c. Chloroplasts using both the Calvin cycle and the C4 pathway.

Solution:

a. Decrease
b. Increase
c. Increase

2.6.10 Carbon–fixation cycle

In all oxygenic photosynthetic organisms, CO_2 reduction and fixation occurs through the *carbon-fixation cycle* called **Calvin cycle**. The Calvin cycle (also known as **reductive pentose phosphate cycle** or **C_3 cycle**) is a series of biochemical reactions which reduce CO_2 to three-carbon sugar. The Calvin cycle takes place in the stroma of chloroplasts in eukaryotic photosynthetic organisms. In prokaryotic photosynthetic organisms, it occurs in the cytosol. The Calvin cycle was elucidated by Melvin Calvin and Andy Benson at the University of California, Berkeley in the 1950s. In recognition of their groundbreaking work, Melvin Calvin was awarded the Nobel Prize in Chemistry in 1961.

The carbohydrate produced directly from the Calvin cycle is actually not glucose but a three-carbon sugar: glyceraldehyde-3-phosphate (G3P). For the net synthesis of one molecule of glyceraldehyde-3-phosphate, three molecules of CO_2 are required. The reactions of the Calvin cycle can be divided into three phases: *carboxylation*, *reduction* and *regeneration of the ribulose-1,5-bisphosphate* (*RuBP*).

Carboxylation

In carboxylation phase, CO_2 is incorporated into a five-carbon compound *ribulose-1,5-bisphosphate* (**RuBP**). The enzyme which catalyzes this first step is ribulose-1,5-bisphosphate carboxylase/oxygenase (usually called **RuBisCo**). The product of the reaction is a six-carbon intermediate which immediately splits to form two molecules of 3-phosphoglycerate (also termed as glycerate-3-phosphate). Thus, for every three molecules of CO_2 that enter the cycle, there are six molecules of 3-phosphoglycerate formed.

$$\text{RuBP} + CO_2 \xrightarrow{\text{RuBisCo}} \text{3-phosphoglycerate}$$

$$3 \times \text{RuBP} + 3 \times CO_2 \xrightarrow{\text{RuBisCo}} 6 \times \text{3-phosphoglycerate}$$

RuBisCo is the pacemaker enzyme of the Calvin cycle. Plant RuBisCo is a multisubunit enzyme composed of eight large subunits and eight small subunits. Large subunits are encoded by the chloroplast genome whereas smaller subunits are encoded by nuclear genome. It makes up about 50% soluble protein in chloroplasts. RuBisCo is the most abundant protein in chloroplasts and is also said to be the most abundant protein on the Earth. Its activity is regulated by CO_2, O_2, Mg^{2+} and pH. The optimum pH for RuBisCo activity lies around pH 8.

This step in the Calvin cycle begins with the conversion of RuBP into a highly reactive **enediolate intermediate**. The CO_2 molecule combines with the enediolate intermediate to form an unstable six-carbon compound, which is rapidly hydrolyzed to two molecules of 3-phosphoglycerate. RuBisCo requires a bound divalent metal ion (Mg^{2+} ion) for activity. The Mg^{2+} ion serves to activate a bound substrate molecule by stabilizing a negative charge. Interestingly, a CO_2 molecule other than the substrate is required to complete the assembly of the Mg^{2+}-binding site in RuBisCo. This CO_2 molecule combines with the ε-amino group of lysine^{201} of large subunits of RuBisCo to form a **carbamate**. This negatively charged adduct then binds the Mg^{2+} ion. The metal center plays a key role in binding RuBP and activating it so that it reacts with CO_2.

$$\underset{\text{(Inactive)}}{\textbf{RuBisCo}} \xrightarrow{CO_2} \textbf{Carbamate} \xrightarrow{Mg^{2+}} \underset{\text{(Active)}}{\textbf{RuBisCo}}$$

Figure 2.62 The conversion of the inactive form of RuBisCo to an active state requires the *carbamylation* of a specific lysine residue (in spinach, Lys-201). As a consequence of the binding of the CO_2 molecule to the lysine residue, the enzyme acquires a binding site for the cofactor Mg^{2+}.

RuBP in active RuBisCO-RuBP complex causes conformational changes in RuBisCo that allows the enzyme to catalyze carboxylation reaction. RuBP is readily deprotonated to form an *enediolate* intermediate. This reactive species couples with CO_2 and forms 2-carboxy-3-keto-D-arabinitol 1,5–bisphosphate. A molecule of H_2O is then added to this β-ketoacid to form an intermediate that cleaves to form two molecules of 3-phosphoglycerate.

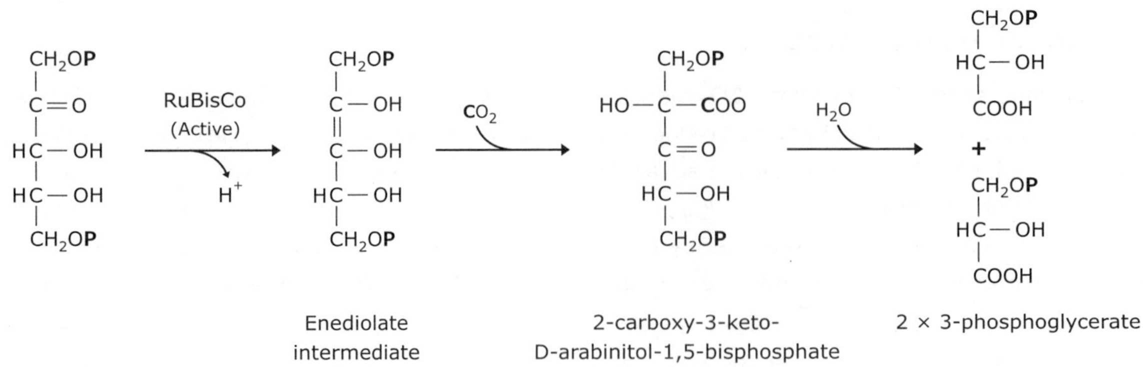

Figure 2.63 Rubisco catalyzes the incorporation of CO_2 to the C-2 of the enediolate form of RuBP and the subsequent cleavage of the unstable intermediate to yield two molecules of 3-phosphoglycerate.

Rubisco activase is essential for RuBisCo activity. The enzyme RuBisCo is inactive until carbamylated on ε-amino group of lysine[201]. RuBP inhibits carbamylation by binding tightly to the active site of RuBisCo. The enzyme *rubisco activase* uses ATP to induce structural changes in enzyme RuBisCo that allow release of the bound RuBP and formation of the required carbamate. The ATP requirement of rubisco activase coordinates RuBisCo activity with the light reactions.

Reduction

The next phase of the cycle involves reduction of *3-phosphoglycerate* into glyceraldehyde 3-phosphate. First, *3-phosphoglycerate* is phosphorylated at the expense of one ATP molecule to form 1,3-bisphosphoglycerate. This step is catalyzed by *phosphoglycerate kinase*. The latter molecule is then reduced by *NADP: glyceraldehyde 3-phosphate dehydrogenase* to form one molecule of glyceraldehyde 3-phosphate. Six molecules of ATP are utilized in phosphorylating six molecules of 3-phosphoglycerate to 1,3-bisphosphoglycerate, and six molecules of NADPH are consumed in reducing six molecules of 1,3-bisphosphoglycerate to glyceraldehyde 3-phosphate.

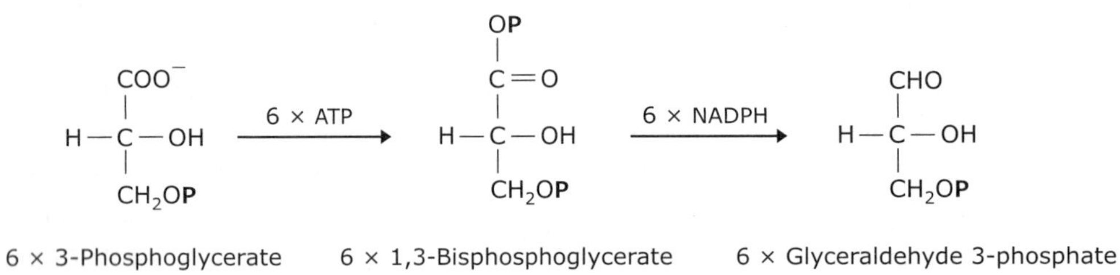

Regeneration of RuBP

As noted previously, the net production of fixed carbon in the Calvin cycle is one molecule of glyceraldehyde 3-phosphate. The other five glyceraldehyde 3-phosphate molecules are processed in the remainder of the Calvin cycle reactions to regenerate three molecules of RuBP as summarized below. This is accomplished in a series of reactions. The intermediates in this pathway include three–, four–, five–, six– and seven carbon sugars.

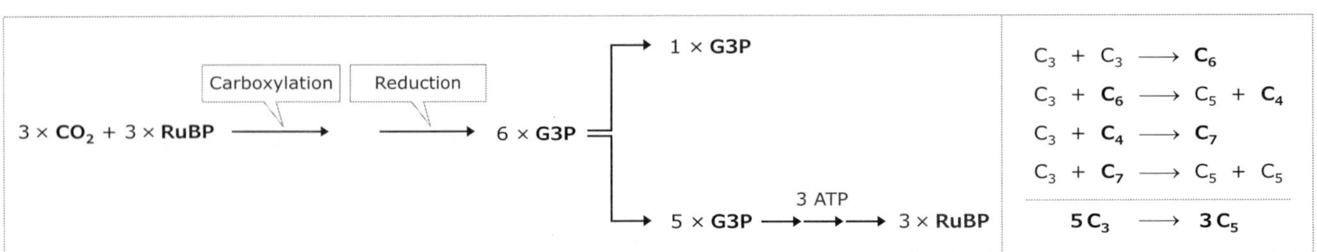

For three molecules of RuBP (total of 15 carbons) that are carboxylated, cleaved, phosphorylated, reduced and dephosphorylated, six molecules of glyceraldehyde 3-phosphate are produced (total of 18 carbons). Of these, one glyceraldehyde 3-phosphate (3-carbons) exits the pathway as a product and five of the 3-carbons molecules (total of 15 carbons) are recycled back into three 5-carbons molecules of RuBP. Regeneration of RuBP is an active process. For regeneration of one RuBP, one ATP is required. Thus, total of three ATP are required for regeneration of three RuBP. In summary, for the net synthesis of one glyceraldehyde-3-phosphate (G3P) molecule, the Calvin cycle consumes a total of nine molecules of ATP and six molecules of NADPH.

$$3 \times CO_2 + 6 \times \text{NADPH} + 9 \times \text{ATP} \longrightarrow \text{G3P} + 6 \times \text{NADP}^+ + 9 \times \text{ADP}$$

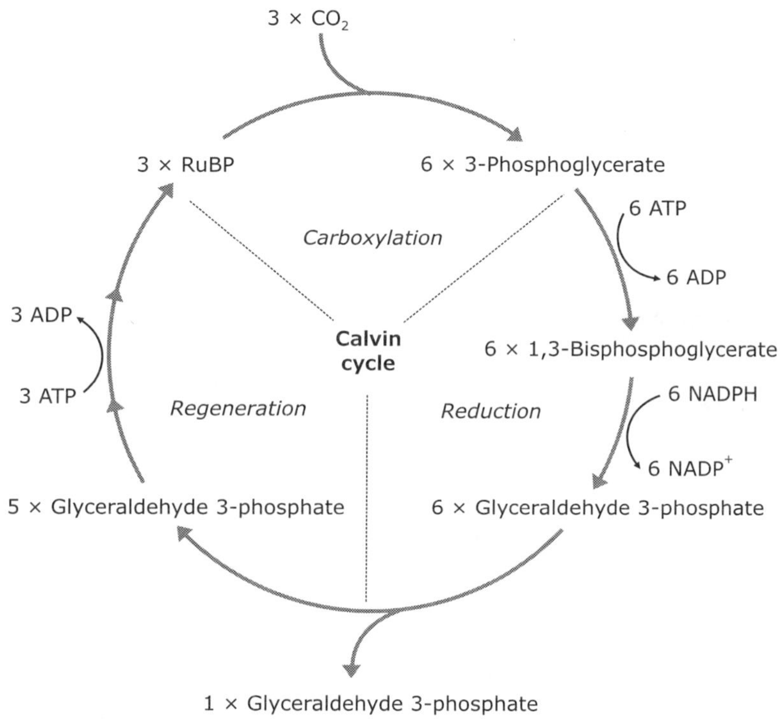

Figure 2.64 Calvin Cycle. The Calvin cycle consists of three phases. Carboxylation is the initial phase of the Calvin cycle, where carbon dioxide is added to a five-carbon compound called RuBP. The second phase of the Calvin cycle involves the reduction of the fixed carbon in 3-phosphoglycerate to produce triose phosphate molecules. This reduction process requires ATP and NADPH. The final phase of the Calvin cycle is regeneration, where the starting compound, RuBP, is regenerated to sustain the cycle for subsequent rounds of carbon fixation.

What is the energy expenditure for synthesizing a glucose? Six rounds of the Calvin cycle are required for synthesis of a glucose, because one carbon atom is reduced in each round. Twelve molecules of ATP are expended in phosphorylating 12 molecules of 3-phosphoglycerate to 1,3-bisphosphoglycerate, and 12 molecules of NADPH are consumed in reducing 12 molecules of 1,3-bisphosphoglycerate to glyceraldehyde 3-phosphate. An additional six molecules of ATP are spent in regenerating RuBP. Hence, total 18 ATP and 12 NADPH are required for synthesis of a glucose molecule.

$$3 \times CO_2 \xrightarrow{\text{9 ATP}} \xrightarrow{\text{6 NADPH}} \text{G3P}$$

$$6 \times CO_2 \xrightarrow{\text{18 ATP}} \xrightarrow{\text{12 NADPH}} 2 \times \text{G3P} \longrightarrow \text{Glucose}$$

Control of Calvin cycle

Calvin cycle occurs during the day time and is strictly dependent on the products of light reaction i.e., NADPH and ATP. Hence, it does not occur literally in the dark (at night). The metabolic activity at night is mainly shifted to carbohydrate oxidation, when plants consume oxygen rather than producing it. The control of the Calvin cycle, therefore, means the control of regulation between light and carbon-fixation cycle.

Regulation of enzymes involved in carboxylation

The enzymes of the Calvin cycle are sensitive to the pH. The optimum pH for RuBisCo activity lies around pH 8. In presence of light, protons are pumped from the stroma into the lumen of the thylakoids. The proton efflux is coupled to magnesium uptake into the stroma. These ion fluxes decrease the stromal concentration of proton (increasing the stromal pH from 7 to 8) and increase that of magnesium. Magnesium stabilizes carbamate formation. High pH and increased magnesium concentration activate RuBisCo and thus the Calvin cycle. RuBisCo is also regulated by a natural sugar phosphate, **2-carboxyarabinitol 1-phosphate**. This 'nocturnal inhibitor' has a structure similar to that of the β-keto acid intermediate of the RuBisCo catalyzed reaction. This compound, synthesized in the dark, is a potent inhibitor of carbamylated RuBisCo. It is either broken down when light returns or is removed by rubisco activase.

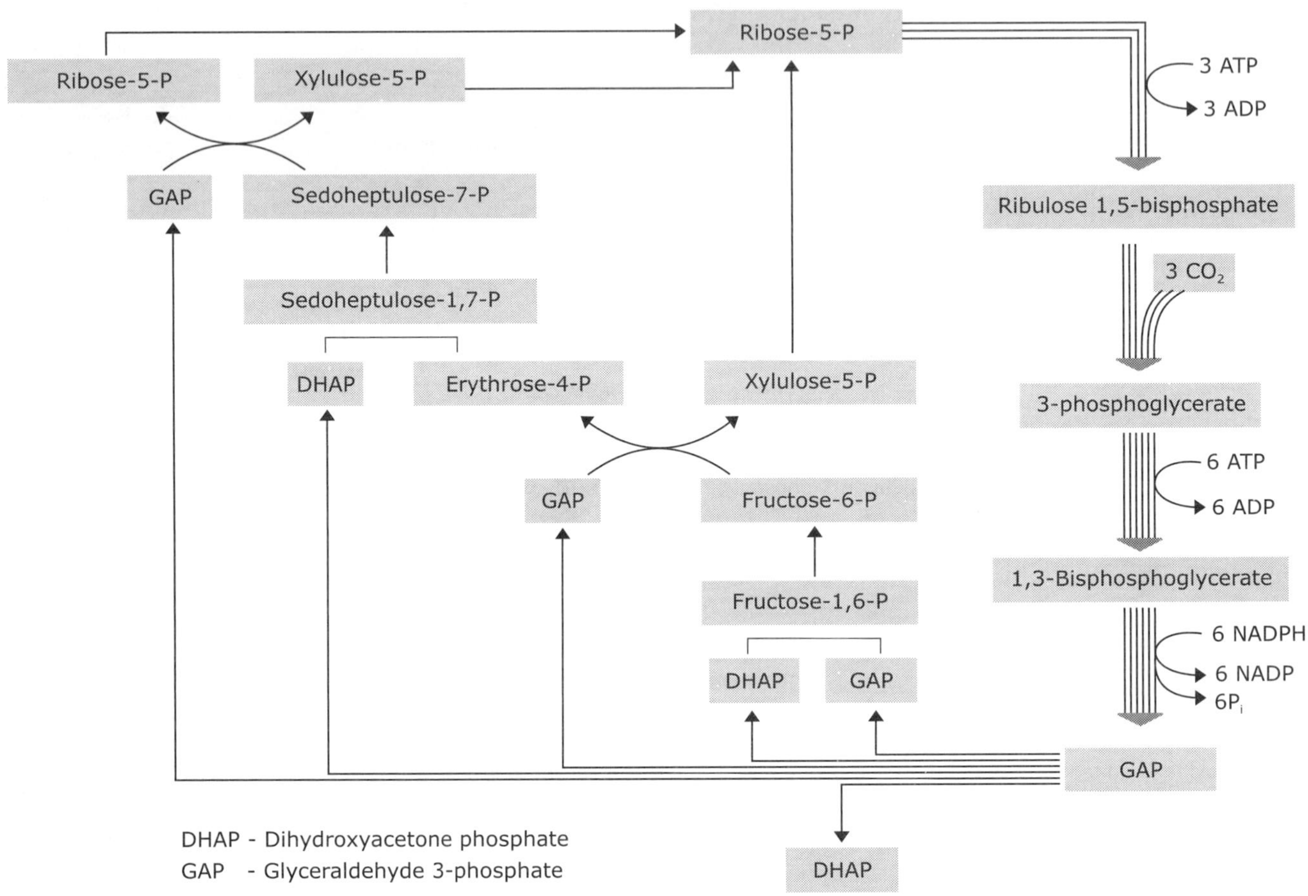

Figure 2.65 The cycle can be divided into three phases. The first phase is carboxylation and second is the reductive phase. The third phase is regeneration of the acceptor, ribulose 1,5-bisphosphate in the sugar phosphate shuffle, in which five C3 units are converted into three C5 units. One of the six molecules of triose-phosphate, deriving from three CO_2 molecules incorporated by Rubisco, is available for product synthesis or for regeneration. Aldolase converts both DHAP and GAP into fructose 1,6-bisphosphate, and DHAP and erythrose 4-phosphate to the seven carbon sugar, sedoheptulose 1,7-bisphosphate. Fructose and sedoheptulose bisphosphatases convert the bisphosphates into fructose 6-phosphate and sedoheptulose 7-phosphate, and transketolase catalyzes the reaction of these with GAP to generate pentose-phosphate and erythrose 4-phosphate. Interconversion of pentose-phosphate is then catalyzed by ribose-phosphate isomerase (ribose 5-phosphate to ribulose 5-phosphate) and ribulose 5-phosphate 3-epimerase (xylulose-phosphate to ribulose 5-phosphate). Finally, ribulose 5-phosphate kinase catalyzes the ATP-dependent conversion of ribulose 5-phosphate into ribulose 1,5-bisphosphate. Glyceraldehyde-phosphate dehydrogenase, the bisphosphatases and product synthesis recycle the phosphate required for continued ATP synthesis. *Adapted from Plant Biochemistry, Dey and Harborne, Eds. Academic Press, 1997.*

Regulation of enzymes involved in RuBP regeneration

The key enzymes involved in RuBP regeneration - *fructose bisphosphatase* and *sedoheptulose bisphosphatase* – are also more active at pH 8 than at pH 7 and require magnesium as a cofactor for catalysis. In addition, they are sensitive to the redox potential of the chloroplast stromal compartment. Bisphosphatases are active in their *reduced state* only sensing the oxidation state of PSI. The mediator molecule is the small protein **thioredoxin**. Thioredoxin is coupled to ferredoxin by ferredoxin-thioredoxin reductase. Thioredoxin also inhibits *phosphofructokinase*. In plant cells, light stimulates the Calvin cycle enzymes (PSI being the strong reductant) and inhibits glycolysis. The light activation is mediated by thioredoxin. In the light, thioredoxin is reduced by electrons moving from PSI through **ferredoxin** (Fd), then thioredoxin reduces critical disulfide bonds in enzymes such as sedoheptulose 1,7-bisphosphatase and fructose 1,6-bisphosphatase, activating these enzymes. In the dark, the –SH groups undergo reoxidation to disulfides, inactivating the enzymes.

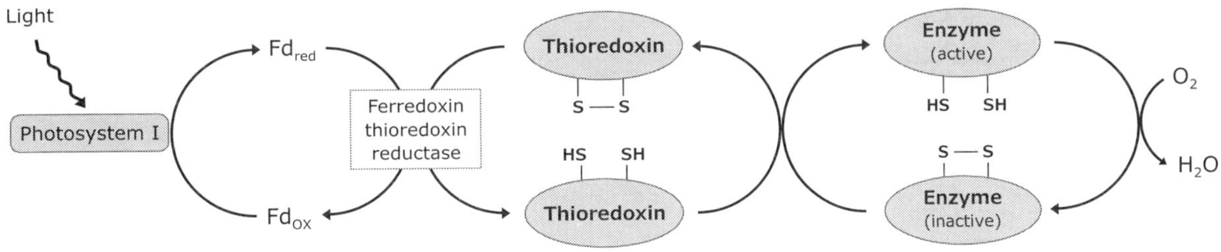

Figure 2.66 The *ferredoxin-thioredoxin system*. Light-driven reactions lead to electron transfer from water to ferredoxin. Reduced ferredoxin regulates enzymes from the Calvin cycle. One key protein in these regulatory processes is thioredoxin. In chloroplasts, oxidized thioredoxin is reduced by ferredoxin in a reaction catalyzed by *ferredoxin-thioredoxin reductase*. Reduced thioredoxin activates certain Calvin cycle enzymes by cleaving regulatory disulfide bonds.

2.6.11 Starch and sucrose synthesis

Triose phosphate generated by the Calvin cycle acts as precursor for the synthesis of both starch and sucrose. Sucrose is a transportable form of carbon whereas starch is a storage form of carbon in plants. The synthesis of starch and sucrose are competing processes that occur in the chloroplast and the cytosol, respectively. When the cytosolic P_i concentration is high, chloroplast triose phosphate is exported to the cytosol and sucrose is synthesized. The **phosphate translocator** catalyzes the movement of orthophosphate and triose phosphate in opposite directions between chloroplast and cytosol. An abundance of orthophosphate in the cytosol inhibits starch synthesis within the chloroplast and promotes the export of triose phosphate into the cytosol, where it is converted to sucrose. When the cytosolic P_i concentration is low, triose phosphate is retained within the chloroplast and starch is synthesized. During starch synthesis, triose phosphate is converted to ADP-glucose via fructose 1,6-bisphosphate. Finally, the glucose moiety of ADP-glucose is transferred to the non-reducing end of the terminal glucose of a growing starch chain. Sucrose synthesis from triose phosphates in the cytosol is similar to that of starch. As in starch synthesis, the glucose residue is activated as nucleoside sugar. But in sucrose synthesis, triose phosphate is converted to UDP-glucose. The conversion of the photoassimilates to either sucrose or starch is called **carbon allocation**.

Starch synthesis: It is synthesized from triose phosphate in chloroplasts. Triose phosphate is converted into glucose 1-phosphate. Glucose-1-phosphate is activated to **ADP-glucose**. This reaction is catalyzed by the enzyme ADP-glucose pyrophosphorylase. The glucose residue is finally transferred by *starch synthases* from ADP-glucose to the nonreducing end (carbon 4) of the terminal glucose of a growing starch chain. Branches are formed by a *branching enzyme*. At certain chain lengths, the polysaccharide chain is cleaved at the (α1→4) glycosidic bond and the chain fragment thus separated is connected via a newly formed (α1→6) bond to a neighboring chain.

Sucrose synthesis: The synthesis of sucrose, a disaccharide of glucose and fructose takes place in the cytosol of the plant cells. Sucrose is synthesized in the cytosol from triose phosphates. As in starch synthesis, triose phosphate is converted into glucose 1-phosphate. Glucose 1-phosphate is activated to **UDP-glucose**. This reaction is catalyzed by the enzyme UDP-glucose pyrophosphorylase. Enzyme sucrose phosphate synthase catalyzes the transfer of the glucose residue from UDP-glucose to fructose 6-phosphate forming sucrose 6-phosphate. Finally, the sucrose 6-phosphate phosphatase cleaves the phosphate from sucrose 6-phosphate, yielding sucrose.

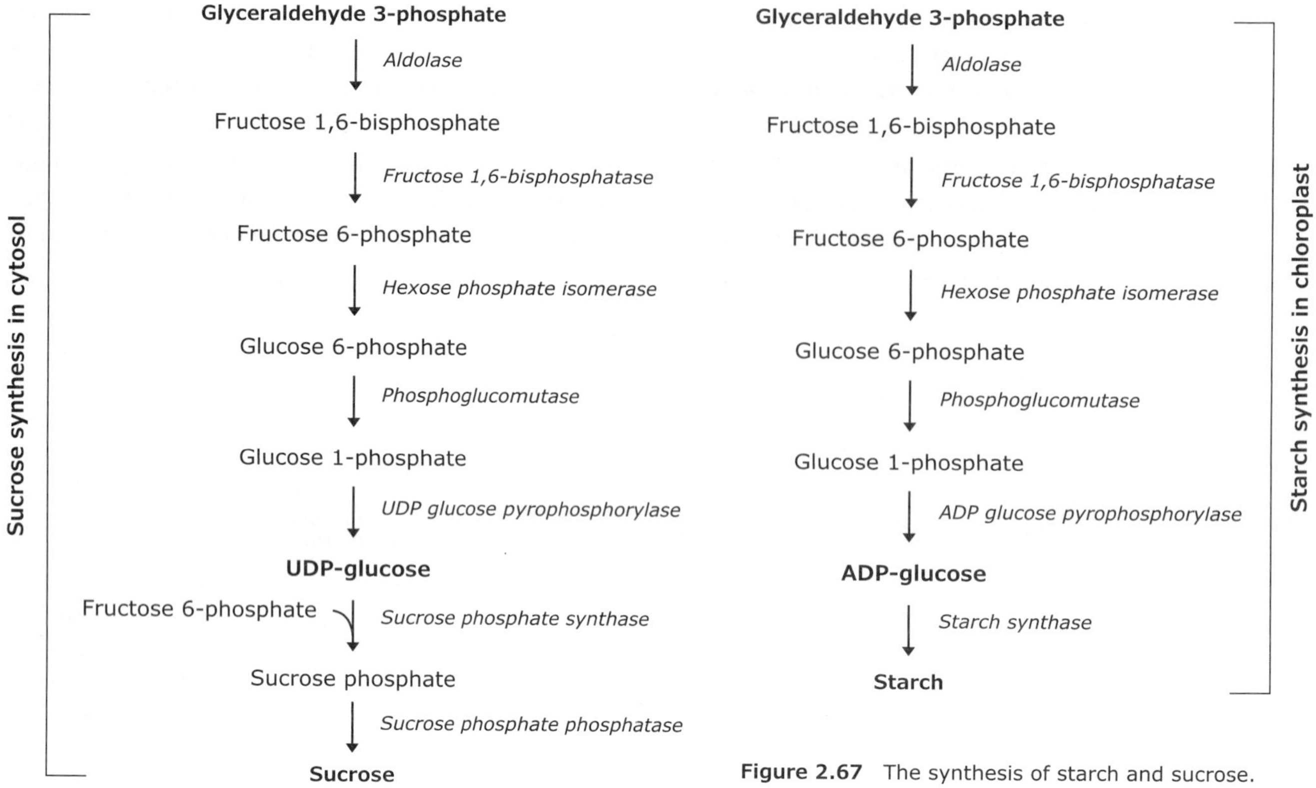

Figure 2.67 The synthesis of starch and sucrose.

2.6.12 Photorespiration

Photorespiration is the process of light-dependent uptake of O_2 and release of CO_2 from organic compounds. The gaseous exchange during photorespiration resembles aerobic respiration but photorespiration is a light-dependent process and catalyzed by RuBisCo. It was Otto Warburg who first made an observation that O_2 inhibits photosynthesis in C_3 plants. This phenomenon, originally known as the **Warburg effect**, was later recognized as the light-dependent release of CO_2 due to oxygenase activity of RuBisCo. RuBisCo is a bifunctional enzyme. It catalyzes both the carboxylation and the oxygenation of RuBP.

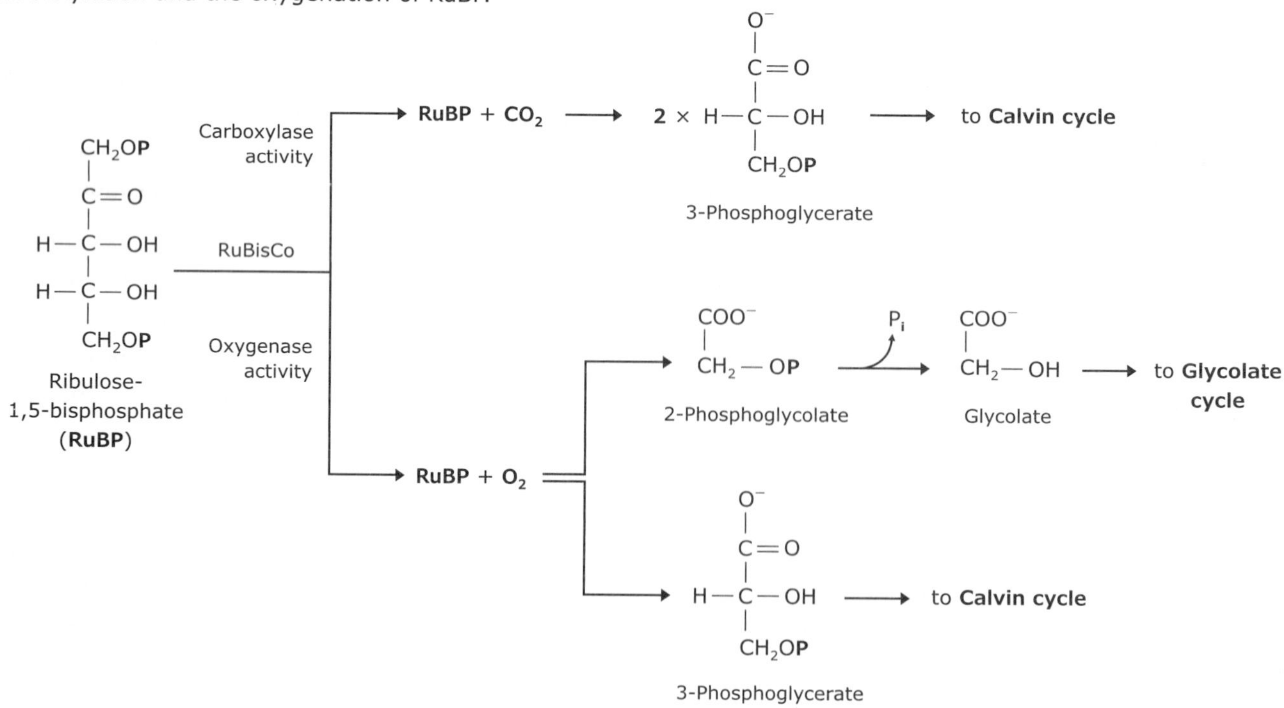

At low CO_2 and high O_2 concentration, RuBisCo performs oxygenase activity. Oxygenation of RuBP leads to the production of one molecule of 3-phosphoglycerate and one of 2-phosphoglycolate. 2-phosphoglycolate produced by oxygenase activity of RuBisCo cannot be utilized in the Calvin cycle. The pathway by which 2-phosphoglycolate is further metabolized is described as **glycolate cycle** (also termed as **C_2 oxidative photosynthetic carbon cycle**). The key feature of the pathway is the release of CO_2 from 2-phosphoglycolate. Release of CO_2 in this process decreases the photosynthetic output and limits the plant biomass production. In this pathway, there is no fixation of CO_2. Rather it results in the release of fixed carbon in form of CO_2 with the utilization of ATP. Therefore, photorespiration is a wasteful process.

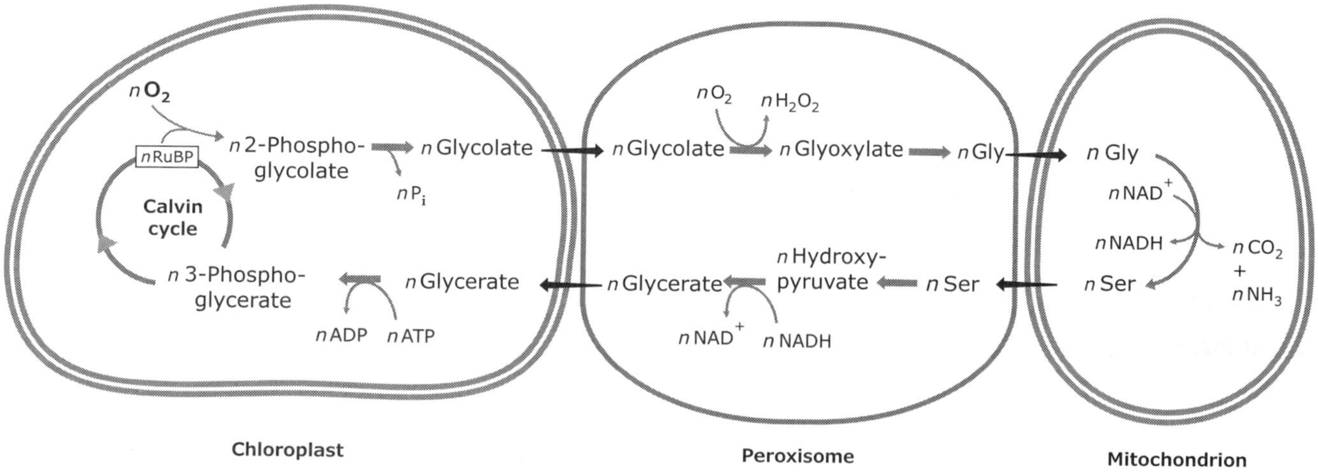

Figure 2.68 C_2 oxidative photosynthetic carbon cycle. Operation of this cycle involves the cooperative interaction among three organelles: chloroplasts, mitochondria and peroxisomes. Due to the oxygenase reaction of RuBisCo, the synthesis of 2-phosphoglycolate occurs in the chloroplast. Within the chloroplast, 2-phosphoglycolate is rapidly hydrolysed to glycolate. Glycolate leaves the chloroplast and diffuses into the peroxisome. There it is oxidized to glyoxylate and hydrogen peroxide (H_2O_2) by a flavin mononucleotide-dependent oxidase: glycolate oxidase. The glyoxylate undergoes a transamination reaction. The amino donor for this transamination is probably glutamate, and the product is the amino acid glycine. Glycine leaves the peroxisome and enters the mitochondrion. Enzyme glycine decarboxylase catalyzes the conversion of two glycine molecules to one serine molecule along with the release of CO_2, NH_3 and reduces NAD^+ to NADH. The newly formed serine leaves the mitochondria and enters the peroxisome, where it is converted first by transamination reaction to hydroxypyruvate and then by an NADH-dependent reduction to glycerate. Finally, glycerate enters the chloroplast, where it is phosphorylated to yield 3-phosphoglycerate. Thus overall, two molecules of phosphoglycolate (four carbon atoms), lost from the Calvin cycle by the oxygenation of RuBP, are converted into one molecule of 3-phosphoglycerate (three carbon atoms) and one CO_2. In other words, 75% of the carbon lost by the oxygenation of ribulose 1,5-bisphosphate is recovered by the C_2 oxidative photosynthetic carbon cycle and returned to the Calvin cycle.

The balance between the Calvin cycle and C_2 oxidative photosynthetic carbon cycle is determined by three factors: the kinetic properties of RuBisCo, the concentrations of the substrates CO_2 and O_2, and temperature. As the temperature increases, the concentration of CO_2 in a solution in equilibrium with air decreases more than the concentration of O_2 does. Because the solubility of CO_2 in water declines more rapidly than that of O_2 as the temperature increases, high temperatures promote oxygenase activity of RuBisCo, and hence the photorespiration. Second, the specificity factor of RuBisCo also decreases with increasing temperature. As a result of this property, photorespiration increases relative to photosynthesis as the temperature rises.

Many plants either do not photorespire at all, or they do so to only a limited extent. Lack of photorespiration in these plants is a consequence of mechanisms that concentrate CO_2 in the environment where RuBisCO present and thereby suppress the oxygenation reaction. In C3 plants, in the presence of light when O_2 level increases within chloroplast. This allows the RuBisCO to perform oxygenase reaction. Due to increased oxygenase activity of RuBisCO, photorespiration occurs in C3 plants. In C4 plants photorespiration does not occur. This is because they have a '**CO_2 enrichment pathway**' that increases the CO_2 concentration at the enzyme site. This ensures that the RuBisCO functions as a carboxylase minimizing the oxygenase activity.

2.6.13 C4 cycle

In some plant species, alternate modes of carbon fixation have evolved that minimize photorespiration and optimize the Calvin cycle. The most important of these photosynthetic adaptations are **C4 photosynthetic carbon cycle** (C4 cycle, named because initial CO_2 fixation product is four carbon acid). The C4 cycle was discovered by Hatch and Slack, in Australia in 1966, so it is sometimes called the **Hatch-Slack pathway**. The C4 cycle concentrates CO_2 at the site of carboxylation, keeping the CO_2 concentration high enough for RuBisCo to bind carbon dioxide rather than oxygen. In this way, C4 cycle has evolved to minimize photorespiration. Plants that have a C4 cycle are called **C4 plants**. These plants are adapted to arid climatic condition and able to give higher photosynthetic output even at high temperature and high light intensity. C4 plants include both monocots and dicots, and are particularly common in Gramineae (corn, sugarcane), Chenopodiaceae (*Atriplex*) and Cyperaceae (sedges) families. In C4 plants, there are two distinct types of photosynthetic cells: **bundle sheath cells** and **mesophyll cells**. In bundle sheath and mesophyll cells, the basic C4 cycle completes in five stages:

1. Fixation of CO_2 by the carboxylation of phosphoenolpyruvate in the mesophyll cell to form a C4 acid, oxaloacetic acid.
2. Oxaloacetate then converts into other C4 acids such as malate or aspartate.
3. Transport of the C4 acids to the bundle sheath cells.
4. Decarboxylation of the C4 acids within the bundle sheath cells and generation of CO_2, which enter in the C3 cycle.
5. Transport of the C3 acid that is formed by the decarboxylation step back to the mesophyll cell.

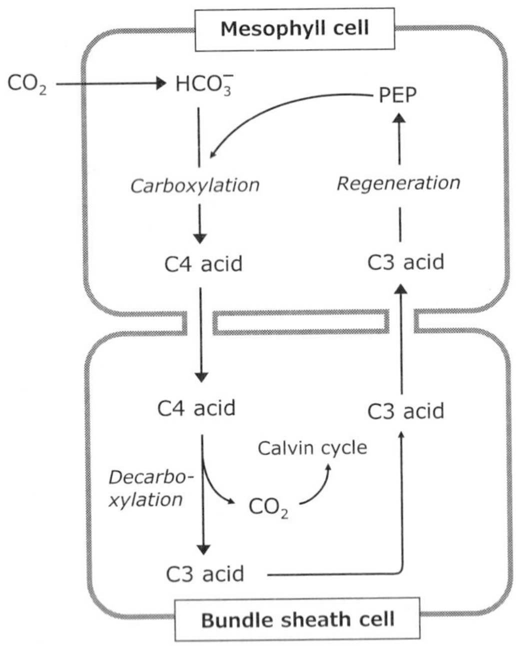

Figure 2.69
The basic C4 cycle involves five stages in two different cell types: 1. Fixation of CO_2 into a C4 acid in a mesophyll cell. 2. Conversion of oxaloacetate into other C4 acids. 3. Transport of the four-carbon acid from the mesophyll cell to a bundle sheath cell. 4. Decarboxylation of the four-carbon acid, and the generation of a high CO_2 concentration in the bundle sheath cell. The CO_2 released is fixed by RuBisCo and converted to triose phosphate by the Calvin cycle. 5. Transport of the residual three-carbon acid back to the mesophyll cell, where the first CO_2 acceptor, phosphoenolpyruvate (PEP), is regenerated.

The C4 cycle transports different C4 acids from mesophyll to bundle sheath cells, employs different enzymes to decarboxylate the C4 acids in the bundle sheath cells and transports different C3 acids from bundle sheath cells to mesophyll cells. Based on these differences, there are three different subtypes of C4 cycles – *NADP$^+$–malic enzyme type* (**NADP-ME**), *NAD$^+$–malic enzyme type* (**NAD-ME**) and *PEP carboxykinase type* (**PEPCK**).

Subtype	**Decarboxylating enzyme**	**C4 acid transported from mesophyll to bundle sheath cell**	**C3 acid transported from bundle sheath cell to mesophyll**
NADP-ME	NADP-malic enzyme	Malate	Pyruvate
NAD-ME	NAD-malic enzyme	Aspartate	Alanine
PEPCK	*PEP-carboxykinase*	Aspartate, malate	Phosphoenolpyruvate

NADP$^+$-malic enzyme type C4 cycle

In the first step of this cycle, phosphoenolpyruvate (**PEP**) is carboxylated to oxaloacetate (a **C4 acid**) in the cytosol of mesophyll cells and this is the first product of photosynthesis, in contrast to 3-phosphoglycerate in C3 cycle. This reaction is catalyzed by enzyme **PEP carboxylase**. Because initial CO_2 fixation product is a four carbon-containing organic acid, it is named as **C4 cycle**. Oxaloacetate is then reduced to malate in the chloroplast of mesophyll cells. Malate ions are then transferred through plasmodesmata to the bundle-sheath, where they are decarboxylated to give pyruvate. This generates a high concentration of CO_2 within the bundle-sheath cells. RuBisCo is confined to the bundle-sheath cells. High CO_2 concentration in the bundle-sheath suppresses the oxygenase activity of RuBisCo. The CO_2 is fixed by RuBisCo and converted to triose phosphate by the Calvin cycle. Pyruvate (a **C3 acid**) returns to the mesophyll cell from the bundle-sheath cell. In mesophyll cells, pyruvate is converted into phosphoenolpyruvate. This step is ATP dependent. C4 cycle is, therefore, an ATP-driven **CO_2 enrichment cycle**. The cost of concentrating CO_2 within the bundle sheath cell is 2 ATP per CO_2. Thus, the total energy requirement for fixing CO_2 by the combined C4 and Calvin cycles is five ATP (2 ATP for CO_2 enrichment and 3 ATP for CO_2 fixation) plus two NADPH per CO_2 fixed.

In fact, the C4 cycle concentrates CO_2 in the bundle sheath cells, keeping the CO_2 concentration in the bundle sheath cells high enough for RuBisCo to bind carbon dioxide rather than oxygen. In this way, C4 cycle minimizes photorespiration and enhances carbohydrate production.

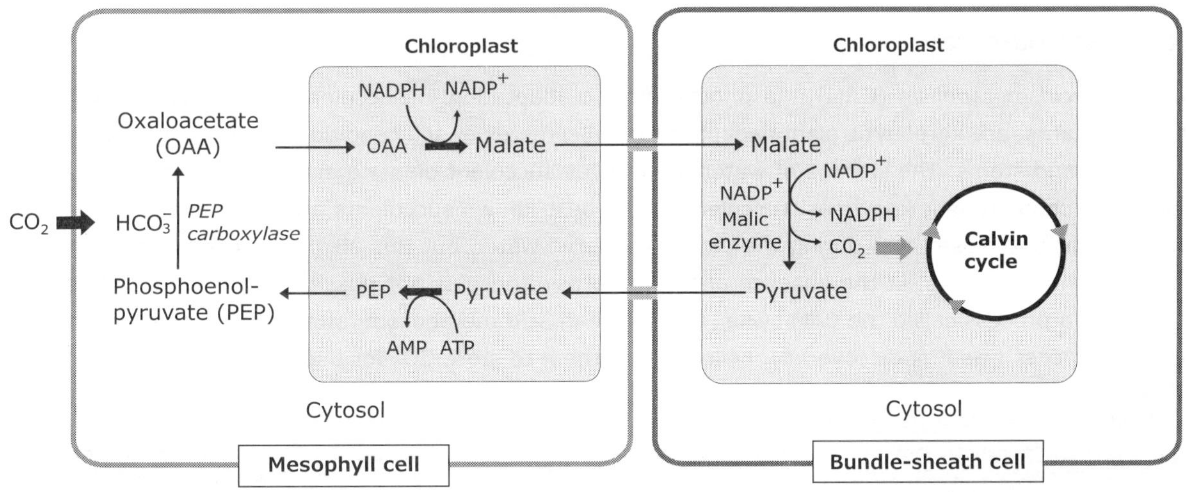

Figure 2.70 NADP$^+$-malic enzyme type C4 cycle. CO_2 is transported from mesophyll cells into the bundle sheath cells by coupling it to phosphoenolpyruvate, forming oxaloacetate (OAA). OAA is then reduced to malate, which is passed to bundle sheath cells and decarboxylated. The pyruvate product is returned to the mesophyll cells, where it is phosphorylated to regenerate phosphoenolpyruvate.

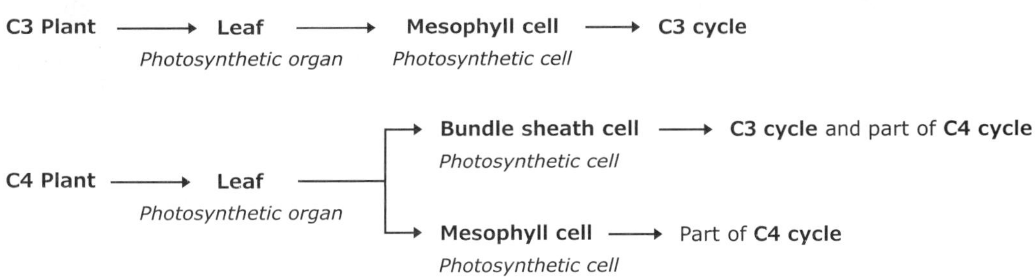

Regulation of PEP carboxylase: PEP Carboxylase (PEPCase) regulation is achieved through both allosteric control and reversible covalent modification. **Malate** acts as a **negative allosteric regulator**, while **glucose 6-phosphate** acts as a **positive regulator**. Covalent modification, catalyzed by PEPCase kinase, occurs through phosphorylation. Phosphorylation reduces sensitivity to inhibitors like malate, thereby increasing PEPCase activity.

Leaf anatomy of C4 plants: In the leaves of C4 plants, the mesophyll cells and bundle-sheath cells typically form two concentric layers around the vascular bundles. The compactly arranged bundle-sheath cells of the C4 plants contain chloroplasts. This concentric arrangement of the mesophyll and bundle-sheath layers in C4 plants is referred to as **Kranz**

(German for 'wreath') **anatomy**. In a typical of C3 plant, the mesophyll cells are not radially arranged around the bundle sheaths. Mesophyll cells are connected to the bundle-sheath cells by large numbers of plasmodesmata. Enzyme PEP carboxylase is present in the mesophyll cells whereas RuBisCo is located in the chloroplasts of bundle sheath cells. In addition, mesophyll cells contain chloroplasts with stacked thylakoids (i.e., well-developed grana) while chloroplasts in bundle sheath cells exhibit unstacked thylakoids (i.e., lacking grana). Hence, chloroplast dimorphism occurs in C4 plants. Kranz anatomy is not present in all photosynthetic organisms where C4 cycle present. In few land plants and diatoms complete C4 cycle occurs in a single photosynthetic cell.

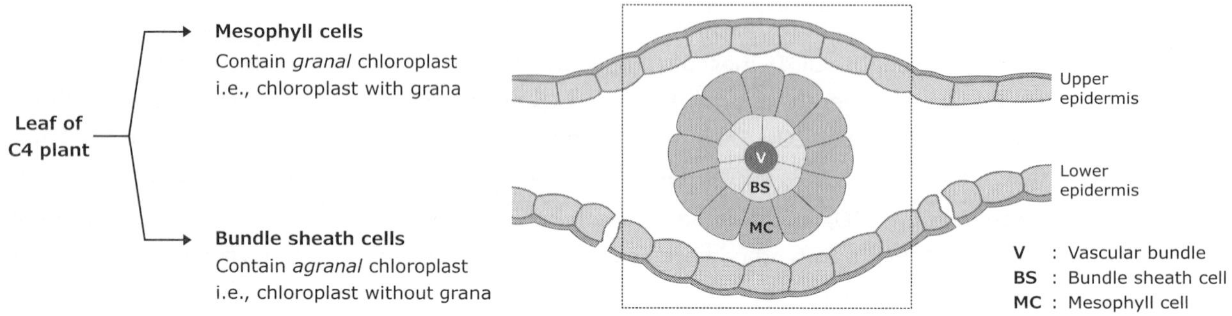

2.6.14 CAM pathway

Crassulacean acid metabolism (CAM) is a photosynthetic adaptation in succulent plants. **Succulent plants**, also known as **fat plants**, are xerophytic plants adapted to arid climates or soil conditions. Succulent plants store water in their leaves and stems. The storage of water often gives succulent plants a swollen or fleshy appearance than other plants, a characteristic known as '**succulence**'. The best-known succulents are cacti. These plants open their stomata at night and close them during the day to conserve water, but this also prevents CO_2 from entering the leaves during the day. Thus, in the absence of CO_2, photosynthesis is not possible. To overcome this, succulent plants perform a process called the **CAM cycle** (crassulacean acid metabolism, after the plant family *Crassulaceae*, in which the process was first discovered), which allows them to store CO_2 for use in photosynthesis in night.

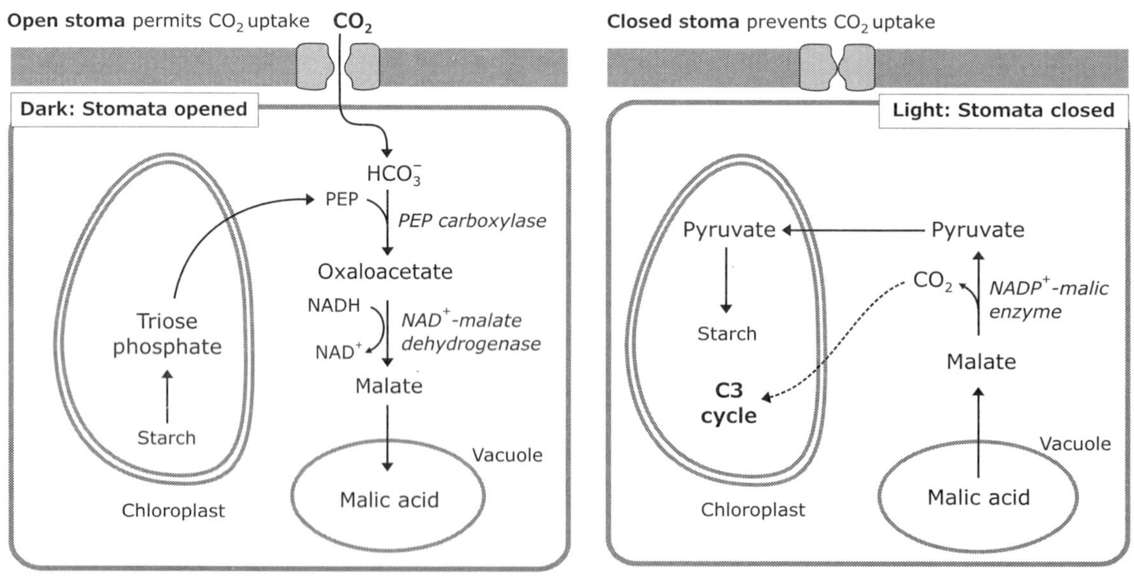

Figure 2.71 In CAM pathway, formation of the C4 acids is temporally separated. At night, CO_2 is captured by PEP carboxylase in the cytosol of mesophyll cell and PEP is carboxylated to oxaloacetate. The oxaloacetate is reduced to malate which is finally stored in the vacuole. Reduction of oxaloacetate is catalyzed by enzyme NAD^+-malate dehydrogenase. During the day, the stored malate is transported back into the cytosol, where it is decarboxylated by an $NADP^+$-malic enzyme. The CO_2 just released enters the chloroplast where it is fixed by the Calvin cycle. The adaptive advantage of CAM is the reduction of water loss by transpiration, achieved by the stomatal opening during the night.

Hence, CAM cycle is basically **CO_2 storage cycle**. night, when the stomata are open, the plants take in CO_2. In the cytosol of mesophyll cells, this CO_2 is converted into malate just like C4 cycle and stored in the vacuole as malic acid. During the day, when the stomata are closed, the stored malate is decarboxylated to release CO_2, which is then used in the Calvin cycle to produce triose phosphate using ATP and NADPH generated from the light reactions.

This CAM cycle differs from the C4 cycle. In C4 plants, the formation of malate and the Calvin cycle occur in different cells (mesophyll and bundle sheath cells, respectively), while in CAM plants, both processes occur at different times within the same mesophyll cells.

Table 2.15 Difference between C3, C4 and CAM plants

Characteristics	C3 Plant	C4 Plant	CAM Plant
1. Kranz Anatomy	Absent	Present	Absent
2. CO_2 : ATP	1 : 3	1 : 5	1 : 5
3. Initial CO_2 acceptor	RuBP	PEP	PEP
4. First stable product	3-PGA	Oxaloacetate	Oxaloacetate
5. Optimum temperature	15–25°C	30–40°C	>40°C
6. CO_2 compensation point (in ppm)	30–70	0–10	0–5 in dark
7. Photorespiration	Present	Not easily detectable	Detectable in afternoon
8. Calvin cycle operative	Alone	Along with the Hatch and Slack cycle	Along with the Hatch and Slack cycle
9. Carboxylating enzyme	RuBP carboxylase (RuBisCo)	*In mesophyll* - PEP carboxylase *In bundle sheath* - RuBP carboxylase	*In dark* - PEP carboxylase *In light* - RuBP carboxylase

2.6.15 Photosynthetic responses to environmental factors

Photosynthetic responses to environmental factors are complex and involve various physiological and biochemical processes. These factors can significantly impact the rate and efficiency of photosynthesis in plants. Key environmental factors affecting photosynthesis include light (intensity, wavelength and duration), temperature, carbon dioxide concentration, water availability, and nutrient availability.

Generally, we express photosynthetic efficiency in terms of **quantum yield** and overall productivity in terms of **photosynthetic yield**. *Quantum yield* refers to the efficiency with which absorbed photons of light are converted into chemical energy during photosynthesis. It is measured as the number of molecules of oxygen evolved or carbon dioxide fixed per photon of light absorbed. In contrast, *photosynthetic yield* refers to the overall productivity of photosynthesis, measured in terms of biomass produced by a plant over a given period.

Effect of light

Light is one of the most critical factors affecting the process of photosynthesis. Its impact can be described in terms of **light intensity**, **light quality** (wavelength), and **duration of light exposure** (photoperiod). At low light intensities, the rate of photosynthesis is limited by the amount of light available to drive the light-dependent reactions. On the other hand, very high light intensity can lead to **photoinhibition**, where excessive light damages the photosynthetic machinery. Similarly, different wavelengths of light (i.e., light quality) have varying effects on photosynthesis. Blue and red light are the most effective because they are absorbed by chlorophyll pigments. The duration of light exposure also influences overall photosynthetic activity. Longer day lengths can enhance the total amount of photosynthesis that occurs.

Light compensation point: In the absence of light, photosynthetic carbon dioxide fixation does not occur, and carbon dioxide is released by the plant due to aerobic respiration. When light is present, photosynthetic carbon fixation begins. As light intensity increases, the rate of photosynthetic carbon dioxide fixation also increases. At a certain light intensity, rate of carbon dioxide fixation by photosynthesis equals the carbon dioxide released through respiration. This light intensity, where rate of carbon dioxide uptake by photosynthesis matches rate of carbon dioxide release by respiration is known as the **light compensation point**. At this point, there is no net carbon dioxide fixation. The light compensation point varies among plant species and developmental stages. A lower compensation point indicates higher photosynthetic efficiency. Typically, **shade plants** have a lower light compensation point compared to **sun plants** due to their lower respiration rates.

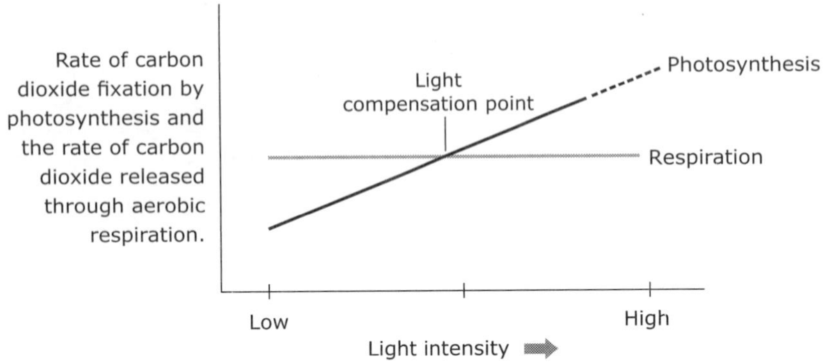

Figure 2.72
The light compensation point is the light intensity at which the rate of carbon dioxide fixation by photosynthesis equals the rate of carbon dioxide released through respiration.

Comparison between sun plants and shade plants

	Shade plants	Sun plants
Ratio of PS II to PS I	3:1	2:1
Ratio of chl b to chl a	High	Low
Rubisco	Low	High
Respiration rates	Low	High
Light compensation point	Low	High

Effect of carbon dioxide concentration

The concentration of carbon dioxide has a significant impact on the process of photosynthesis. At low concentrations of carbon dioxide, the rate of photosynthesis is limited because there is not enough carbon dioxide available for the fixation process in the Calvin cycle. Photosynthesis will proceed at a reduced rate, and the overall productivity of the plant will be lower.

C3 plants versus C4 plants: In the presence of adequate light, higher carbon dioxide concentrations support increased photosynthetic rates. For C3 plants, elevated atmospheric carbon dioxide concentrations enhances photosynthesis across a broad range of concentrations. Therefore, C3 plants may benefit significantly from rising atmospheric carbon dioxide levels. In contrast, C4 plants achieve carbon dioxide saturation at lower concentrations due to their efficient *carbon dioxide concentrating mechanisms*. As a result, these plants do not experience substantial benefits from increased atmospheric carbon dioxide concentrations.

Carbon dioxide compensation point: The concentration of carbon dioxide at which the rate of carbon dioxide uptake through photosynthesis exactly balances the rate of carbon dioxide release through respiration is called **carbon dioxide compensation point**. At this point, the net efflux of carbon dioxide from the plant is zero. This concept is analogous to the light compensation point. The carbon dioxide compensation point reflects the balance between photosynthesis and respiration as a function of carbon dioxide concentration, whereas the light compensation point reflects this balance as a function of light intensity. For **C3 plants**, the carbon dioxide compensation point is typically between 30 and 70 ppm at 25°C. **C4 plants**, on the other hand, have a much lower carbon dioxide compensation point, often less than 10 ppm. This lower compensation point in C4 plants is attributed to their *carbon dioxide concentrating mechanisms*, which ensure that carbon dioxide concentration at the carboxylation sites within C4 chloroplasts is often saturating for RuBisCO activity.

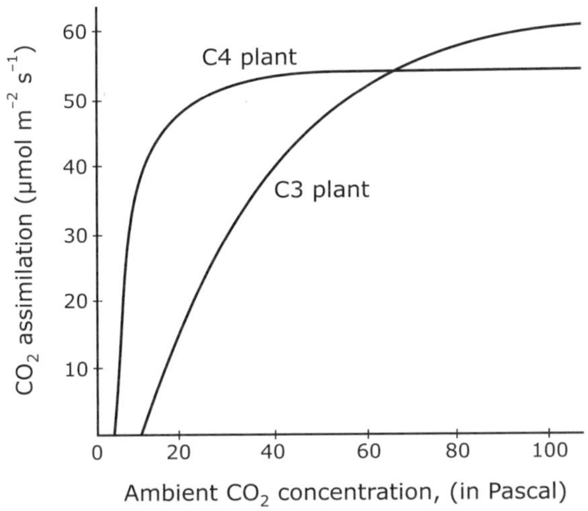

Figure 2.73
At CO_2 compensation point, the net efflux of CO_2 from the plant is zero. Because of the CO_2-concentrating mechanisms in C4 plants, CO_2 concentration at the carboxylation sites within C4 chloroplasts is often saturating for RuBisCo activity. Hence, the C4 plants are characterized by a much lower CO_2 compensation point.

Effect of temperature

Temperature has a significant impact on quantum yields. The process of photosynthesis involves several enzyme-mediated reactions, which are sensitive to changes in temperature. At low temperatures, the enzymes that facilitate photosynthetic reactions become less active, slowing down the overall rate of photosynthesis. At temperatures above the optimal range, the conformation of photosynthetic enzymes can become unstable, leading to denaturation and loss of function, which significantly reduces the rate of photosynthesis.

C3 plants versus C4 plants: The efficiency of photosynthetic carbon fixation in C3 and C4 plants is influenced by leaf temperature. As we know, photorespiration increases with temperature in C3 plants, which raises the energy cost of net CO_2 fixation and decreases quantum yields. Therefore, in C3 plants, the quantum yield decreases with increasing temperature. In contrast, C4 plants have CO_2 concentrating mechanisms that keep photorespiration low, so their quantum yield does not decline with increasing temperature. However, at lower temperatures (below 30°C), quantum yields of C3 plants are generally higher than those of C4 plants. Above 30°C, C4 plants typically have higher quantum yields than C3 plants. This indicates that photosynthesis in C3 plants is more efficient at lower temperatures, while C4 plants are more efficient at higher temperatures.

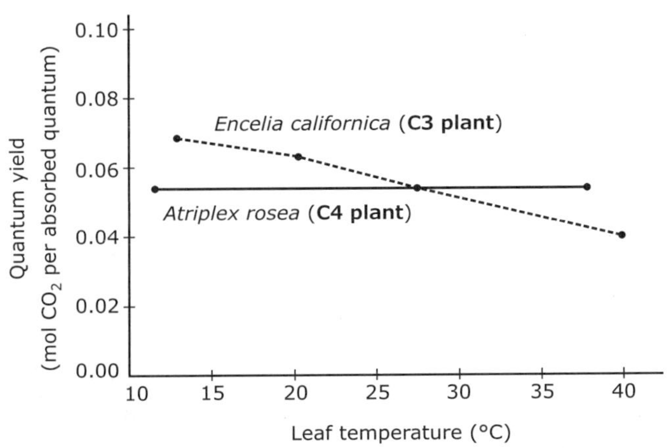

Figure 2.74
In the C4 plant the quantum yield remains constant with temperature, reflecting typical low rates of photorespiration. In the C3 plant, the quantum yield decreases with temperature, reflecting a stimulation of photorespiration by temperature and an ensuing higher energy demand per net CO_2 fixed.

2.7 Lipid metabolism

Lipid metabolism refers to the processes by which lipids are synthesized, transported, and degraded in the body to provide energy, build cell structures, and regulate bodily functions. Under lipid metabolism, we have discussed the synthesis, transport, and breakdown of triacylglycerols, fatty acid synthesis, fatty acid oxidation, ketone body formation, and cholesterol synthesis.

2.7.1 Synthesis of triacylglycerols

All animals and plants have the ability to synthesize triacylglycerol (TAG). In animals, many cell types and organs have the ability to synthesize triacylglycerols, but the liver and intestines are most active. Within all cell types, triacylglycerols are stored as cytoplasmic **lipid droplets**, also known as **fat globules**, **oil bodies**, **lipid particles**, **adiposomes**, and other names. These droplets are enclosed by a monolayer of phospholipids and are associated with hydrophobic proteins such as **perilipins** in adipose tissue and **oleosins** in seeds. Two main biosynthetic pathways are known, the **sn-glycerol-3-phosphate pathway** (or Kennedy pathway), which predominates in liver and adipose tissue, and a **monoacylglycerol pathway** in the intestines. The most important route to triacylglycerol biosynthesis is the *sn*-glycerol-3-phosphate. The 'sn' in sn-glycerol-3-phosphate stands for *stereospecific numbering*. This designation is used to specify the stereochemistry of glycerol-based molecules.

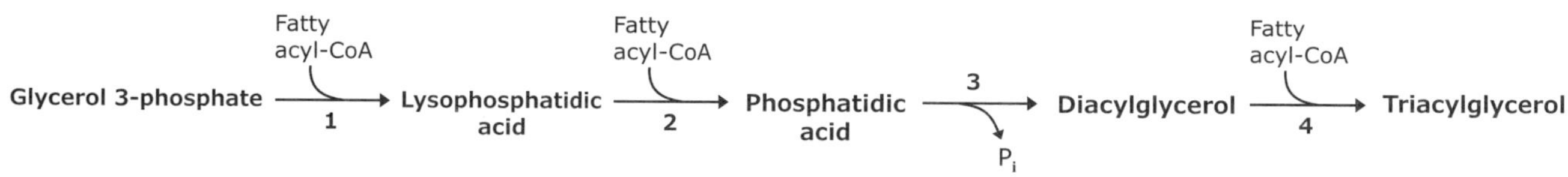

Enzymes

1 Glycerol 3-phosphate acyltransferase
2 Acylglycerophosphate acyltransferase
3 Phosphatidic acid phosphohydrolase
4 Diacylglycerol acyltransferase

Figure 2.75 The *sn*-glycerol-3-phosphate pathway. In this pathway, the glycerol backbone is *sn*-glycerol-3-phosphate. *First*, *sn*-glycerol-3-phosphate is esterified by a fatty acyl-CoA in a reaction catalyzed by the enzyme glycerol 3-phosphate acyltransferase at the 1st position to form lysophosphatidic acid. This is then esterified by a second fatty acyl-CoA in a reaction catalyzed by the enzyme acylglycerophosphate acyltransferase at the 2nd position to form phosphatidic acid. In the next step, phosphatidic acid phosphohydrolase removes the phosphate group to give diacylglycerol. Finally, the 3rd position of diacylglycerol is esterified by a fatty acyl-CoA in a reaction catalyzed by the enzyme diacylglycerol acyltransferase, resulting in the formation of triacylglycerol.

2.7.2 Digestion and transport of triacylglycerols

The **digestion** and **transport** of triacylglycerols present unique challenges due to the insolubility of lipids in water.

The *first* challenge pertains to digestion: the enzymes that act on lipids, whether soluble proteins or membrane-bound proteins, operate at the aqueous interface where lipids and water meet.

The *second* challenge concerns transport: lipids and their digestion products must be effectively transported through aqueous compartments within cells, as well as in the blood and tissue spaces.

Release of fatty acids from stored triacylglycerols of adipose cells: Triacylglycerols are important energy reserve in the organisms. In animals, they are mostly stored in insoluble form in the cells of adipose tissue—the **adipocytes**—where they are constantly being synthesized and broken down again. The hydrolysis of triacylglycerols by enzyme **lipases** is referred to as **lipolysis**. Triacylglycerols in adipose tissue are converted into free fatty acids and glycerol *under the influence of hormones like epinephrine, norepinephrine, glucagon*. A hormone-sensitive lipase (**TAG lipase**) initiates the process. The free fatty acids are released into the blood, where they bind to serum albumin. **Albumin** is a monomeric protein that comprises about half of the blood serum proteins.

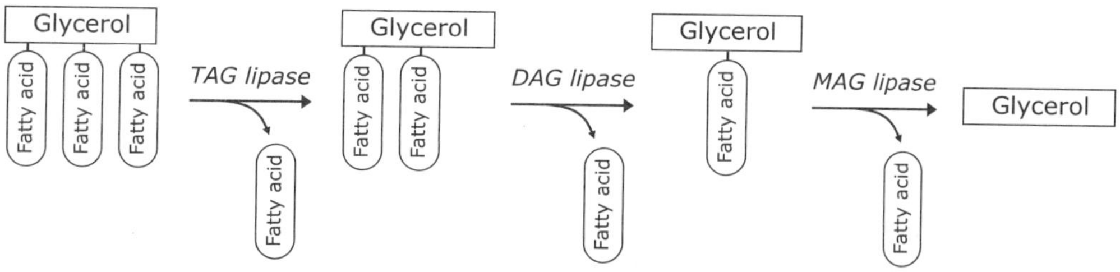

Figure 2.76 Liberation of fatty acids from triacylglycerols in adipose tissue.

Release of fatty acids from dietary triacylglycerols: Most dietary triacylglycerols are digested by **pancreatic lipases** in the intestinal lumen. Although the process actually begins in the stomach with **lingual lipase** released by the *serous gland* and **gastric lipase** produced by the *chief cells*. Pancreatic lipase cleaves fatty acids from C-1 and the C-3 position of triacylglycerol. Resulting monoacylglycerols with fatty acids at C-2 are hydrolyzed by **intestinal lipases**. Before hydrolytic activity of the lipases, **emulsification** of triacylglycerol occurs. *Emulsification* refers to the process of breaking down large fat globules into smaller droplets. In the intestinal lumen **bile salts** act on triacylglycerols. *Bile salts* are detergent substances synthesized in the liver and stored in the gallbladder. A *bile salt* molecule is made up of a **bile acid**, such as cholic acid, and an associated cation. The bile salt molecule has both hydrophobic and hydrophilic surfaces. It acts as the detergent and emulsifies triacylglycerols and yield *micelles*. Water-soluble digestive enzymes digest it and facilitates the absorption of lipid through intestinal mucosal cells. Bile salts not only facilitate the lipid digestion but are also essential for the absorption of lipid digestion products. The products of fat digestion comprise a mixture of glycerol, free fatty acids, monoacylglycerols, and diacylglycerols. Less than 10% of the original triacylglycerol also remains unhydrolyzed. During absorption through intestinal mucosal cells, resynthesis of triacylglycerols occurs from the hydrolyzed products. This resynthesis occurs in the endoplasmic reticulum and the Golgi complex of mucosal cells. Triacylglycerol packaged with *cholesterol* (dietary) and *apolipoproteins* into **lipoprotein** aggregates called **chylomicrons**. Lipoproteins are spherical particles composed of a central core of non-polar lipids (cholesterol esters and triacylglycerol) and a surface monolayer made up of phospholipids, free cholesterol and apolipoproteins.

Dietary triacylglycerols are thus packaged into chylomicrons and transported in the bloodstream as lipoproteins. Chylomicrons move through the **lymphatic vessels** (or *lymph vessels* or *lymphatics*) and blood vessels to the tissues. The extracellular enzyme **lipoprotein lipase** (LPL) in capillary converts triacylglycerols components of chylomicrons to fatty acids and glycerol. Finally, fatty acids enter cells where they are oxidized as fuel or reesterified for storage.

Most of its triacylglycerol content is released by the action of lipoprotein lipase to adipose and muscle tissues during transport through capillaries. The fatty acids are taken up by muscle cells for energy generation or by adipose cells for storage. The chylomicrons shrink as their triacylglycerols are progressively hydrolyzed. Finally, **chylomicron remnants** (containing mostly proteins and cholesterol) are taken up by the liver by receptor-mediated endocytosis. *Chylomicrons, therefore, deliver dietary triacylglycerols to muscle and adipose tissue and dietary cholesterol to the liver.*

Processing of dietary lipids

1. Emulsification of dietary triacylglycerol by bile salts in the small intestine.
2. Digestion of triacylglycerol with *intestinal lipases*.
3. Fatty acids and other breakdown products are absorbed by the intestinal mucosa and reconverted into triacylglycerol.
4. Triacylglycerols are incorporated into chylomicrons.
5. Chylomicrons move through the lymphatic and blood vascular system to the tissues.
6. *Lipoprotein lipase* in capillary converts triacylglycerols to fatty acids and glycerol.
7. Chylomicrons converted into *chylomicron remnants* due to removal of most of triacylglycerols.
8. Uptake of chylomicron remnants by hepatic cells of liver by receptor-mediated endocytosis.

Endogenous triacylglycerols and cholesterol synthesized by the liver are delivered to adipose and muscle tissue in the form of **VLDL** (very-low density lipoprotein). VLDLs are gradually degraded by **lipoprotein lipase** (LPL) in the capillaries. The depletion of triacylglycerol from VLDL (along with loss of some apolipoproteins) gradually converts it to **IDL** (intermediate density lipoprotein). IDL particles, which are either cleared by the liver through LDL receptor or further converted to **LDL** by **hepatic lipase** (HL), also called *hepatic triglyceride lipase* (HTGL). It is the main cholesterol-bearing lipoprotein in plasma. LDL is cleared from the circulation via the LDL receptors expressed in the liver (~70%) and other cells (~30%).

$$\textbf{VLDL} \xrightarrow{\textit{Lipoprotein lipase}} \textbf{IDL} \xrightarrow{\textit{Hepatic lipase}} \textbf{LDL}$$

Figure 2.77 VLDL is produced by the liver and released into the bloodstream. As it circulates, VLDL undergoes a series of modifications and is converted into IDL. IDL can either be taken up by the liver or further processed to mature into LDL.

2.7.3 Synthesis of fatty acids

Fatty acid synthesis in animal and yeast cells occurs in cytosol and in case of plant cells in chloroplast stroma. Biosynthesis of fatty acids involves stepwise addition of two carbon units. The two carbon units are supplied by the **acetyl-CoA**, which in turn is derived from the oxidation of glucose. Acetyl-CoA formed in the matrix of mitochondria cannot cross the inner mitochondrial membrane, and an **acetyl-CoA shuttle system** is required to transport the two-carbon units out of the mitochondria and into the cytosol. The acetyl group passes out of mitochondria as citrate. Within the mitochondria, acetyl-CoA reacts with oxaloacetate to form citrate in a reaction catalyzed by **citrate synthase**. Under conditions where acetyl-CoA and ATP are in high concentration, the citrate leaves the mitochondria and in the cytosol, reacts with cytosolic CoA and ATP to form acetyl-CoA and oxaloacetate in a reaction catalyzed by citrate cleavage enzyme, **citrate lyase**. Oxaloacetate cannot directly return to mitochondrial matrix by crossing the mitochondrial membrane so it is first reduced into malate by *malate dehydrogenase*. Malate is oxidatively decarboxylated to pyruvate by *malic enzyme* and returned in this form to the mitochondria. In mitochondria, pyruvate is carboxylated to oxaloacetate by enzyme *pyruvate carboxylase*.

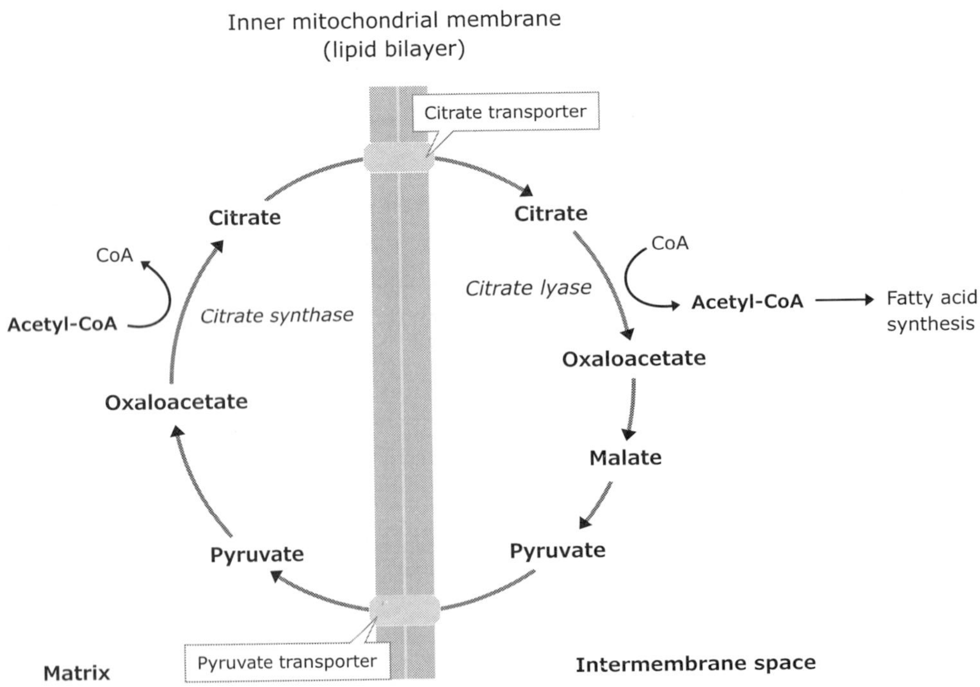

Figure 2.78 The acetyl-CoA shuttle system, also known as the citrate shuttle, is a biochemical pathway that facilitates the transport of acetyl-CoA from the mitochondria into the cytosol. This process is crucial because acetyl-CoA produced in the mitochondria cannot directly cross the mitochondrial membrane to participate in cytosolic processes like fatty acid synthesis.

Synthesis of palmitic acid

Palmitic acid is a 16-carbon containing saturated fatty acid. The pathway for the biosynthesis of saturated fatty acids is identical in all organisms. A sequence of seven enzyme-catalyzed reactions converts *two carbons unit* to *four carbons unit*.

The first committed and irreversible step in fatty acid synthesis is the ATP dependent carboxylation of **acetyl-CoA** to form **malonyl-CoA**. This reaction is catalyzed by **acetyl-CoA carboxylase** which has biotin as a prosthetic group. This enzyme is an allosteric enzyme. *Palmitoyl-CoA*, the final product of fatty acid synthesis acts as an allosteric inhibitor whereas *citrate* acts as an allosteric activator of this enzyme. Regulatory effects of citrate and palmitoyl CoA are dependent on the phosphorylation state of the enzyme. Phosphorylation of the regulatory sites decreases the affinity of the enzyme for citrate and in this case high levels of citrate are required for activation.

The next steps in the biosynthetic pathway are the formation of acetyl-ACP and malonyl-ACP by the enzymes *acetyl transacylase* (or acetyltransferase) and *malonyl transacylase* (or malonyl transferase) respectively.

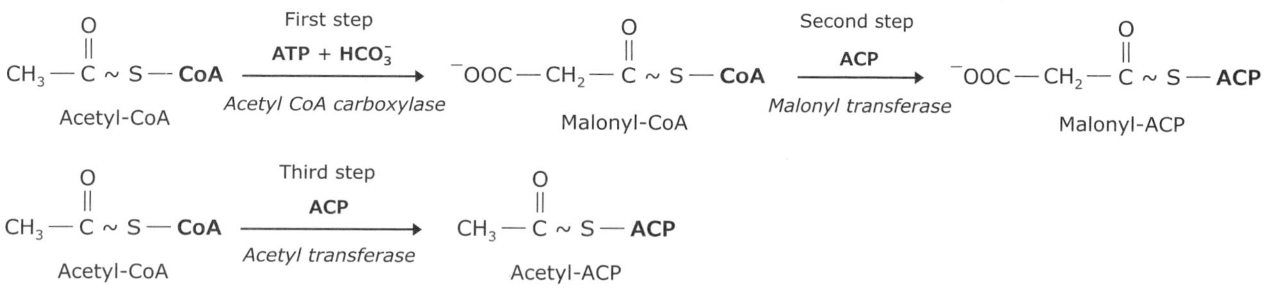

The activated intermediates of fatty acid biosynthesis are bound to a sulfhydryl group of a **phosphopantetheine** molecule. In prokaryotes, phosphopantetheine group is covalently bound to a small protein consists of a single polypeptide chain called **acyl carrier protein** (**ACP**). In eukaryotes, it is covalently bound to the ACP domain of multifunctional polypeptide termed *fatty acid synthase*.

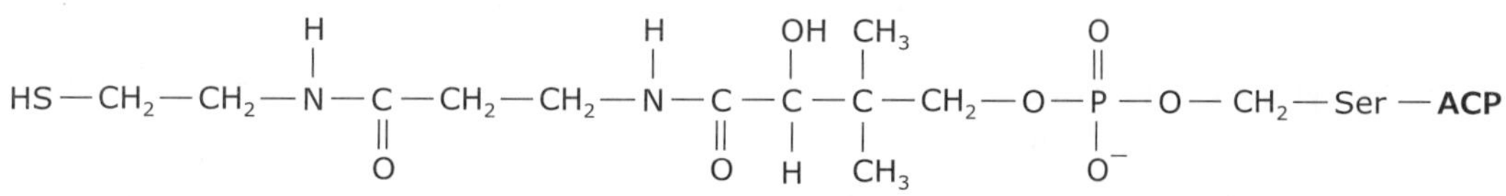

Figure 2.79 Phosphopantetheine prosthetic group of ACP.

The last four enzymatic reactions of fatty acid biosynthesis constitute the elongation step. It includes *condensation, reduction, dehydration* and *reduction*. Repetition of the elongation step, increases chain length by two carbon atoms. In this way, the seven elongation cycles produce palmitic acid. Finally, *palmitoyl thioesterase* catalyzes the hydrolysis of the thioester that binds the acyl chain to the pantothiene-enzyme, releasing free palmitate. In the synthesis of palmitic acid all the carbons have passed through malonyl-CoA except the two donated by original acetyl-CoA. Hence in palmitic acid carbon 16 and 15 are donated by acetyl-CoA and rest by malonyl-CoA.

The enzymes that catalyze reactions from 2 to 7 form a multienzyme complex known as *fatty acid synthase*. There are two major variants of fatty acid synthase– fatty acid synthase I (**FAS I**), found in vertebrates and fungi and fatty acid synthase II (**FAS II**), found in plants and bacteria. The FAS I found in vertebrates consists of a single large multifunctional polypeptide with seven domains. In mammals, fatty acid synthase consists of two identical polypeptides (homodimers).

In fungi, it consists of two different multifunctional polypeptides (α and β). Out of seven domains, three domains are present on the α-subunit and four on the β-subunit. The FAS II from bacteria and plants is a complex of seven different polypeptides and each catalyzing separate reaction.

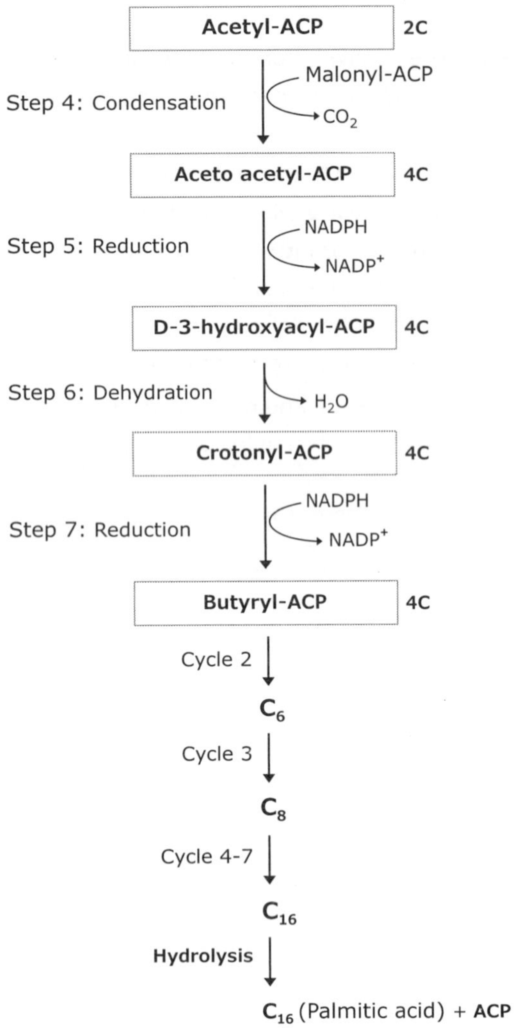

Steps 4, 5, 6 and 7 used to lengthen a growing fatty acyl chain by 2 carbons.

Figure 2.80
Reaction cycle for the biosynthesis of fatty acids. The biosynthesis of palmitate requires seven cycles of C2 elongation followed by a final hydrolysis step.

Stoichiometry of the synthesis of palmitate: Stoichiometry refers to the quantitative relationship between reactants and products in a chemical reaction. It involves calculating the amounts of each substance involved based on the balanced chemical equation, ensuring that mass is conserved throughout the reaction. For the synthesis of palmitate, 8 Acetyl-CoA molecules are required. Additionally, 7 ATP are required to convert acetyl-CoA into malonyl-CoA and drive the synthesis process. Furthermore, 14 NADPH provide the reducing power needed for the reduction steps in the synthesis. Byproducts of this reaction include 8 CoA molecules, 7 ADP resulting from the hydrolysis of ATP and 14 $NADP^+$ molecules, generated from the oxidation of NADPH.

$$\mathbf{7}\ \text{Acetyl-CoA} + \mathbf{7}\ CO_2 + \mathbf{7}\ \text{ATP} + \mathbf{7}\ H_2O \longrightarrow \mathbf{7}\ \text{Malonyl-CoA} + \mathbf{7}\ \text{ADP}$$

$$\text{Acetyl-CoA} + \mathbf{7}\ \text{malonyl-CoA} + \mathbf{14}\ \text{NADPH} \longrightarrow \text{Palmitate} + \mathbf{7}\ CO_2 + \mathbf{14}\ NADP^+ + \mathbf{6}\ H_2O$$

$$\textit{Sum}: \mathbf{8}\ \text{Acetyl-CoA} + \mathbf{7}\ \text{ATP} + \mathbf{14}\ \text{NADPH} + H_2O \longrightarrow \text{Palmitate} + \mathbf{7}\ \text{ADP} + \mathbf{14}\ NADP^+$$

Elongation of fatty acids

The normal product of the cytosolic fatty acid synthase complex is palmitic acid. Fatty acids longer than 16 carbons can be formed through the addition of two-carbon units by elongation reaction. In eukaryotes fatty acids elongation occurs in both *endoplasmic reticulum* and *mitochondria*. The most active elongation system is found in the endoplasmic reticulum. The **endoplasmic reticulum elongation system**, adds malonyl-CoA onto palmitate in a manner similar to the action of fatty acid synthase, except that CoA is involved rather than the ACP. Stearic acid (18 carbons) is a common product of this elongation system. A **mitochondrial elongation system** uses acetyl-CoA units, rather than malonyl-CoA units, to elongate fatty acids for the synthesis of structural lipids in this organelle.

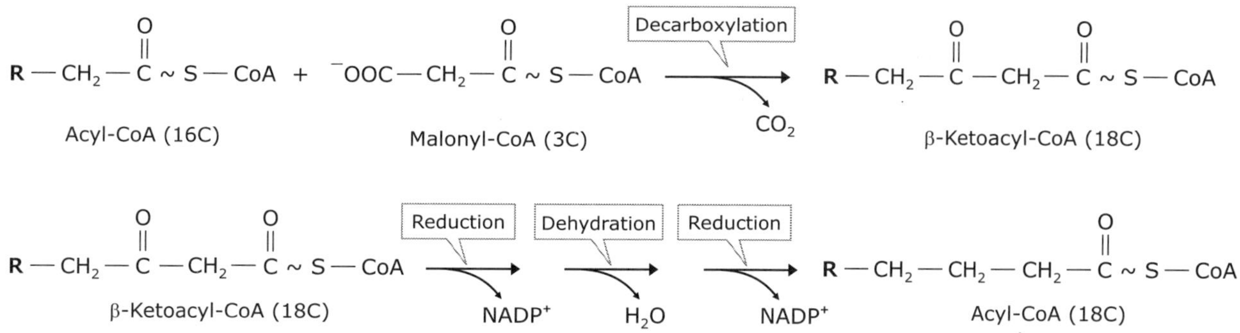

Unsaturation of fatty acids

Both prokaryotes and eukaryotes are capable of introducing double bond(s) in a newly synthesized fatty acid. In eukaryotes, a *microsomal system* that contains NADH-cyt b_5 reductase, Cyt b_5 and an oxygen-dependent **desaturase** (a *mixed-function oxidase*) containing a single *non-heme iron* atom cause desaturation. All components of the *desaturase system* are integral membrane proteins. Mammals are unable to introduce double bonds beyond Δ^9 in the fatty acid chain. Hence, they cannot synthesize either linoleic acid (18:2 : Δ^9, Δ^{12}) or linolenic acid (18:3 : Δ^9, Δ^{12}, Δ^{15}).

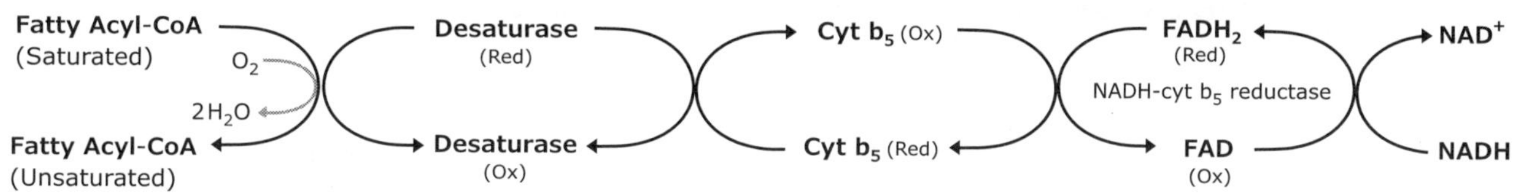

Figure 2.81 Electron transport reactions mediated by desaturase complex. This reaction is catalyzed by a complex of three membrane-bound proteins: NADH-cytochrome b_5 reductase, cytochrome b_5 and desaturase. First, electrons are transferred from NADH to the FAD moiety of NADH-cytochrome b_5 reductase. The heme iron atom of cytochrome b_5 is then reduced to the Fe^{2+} state. The nonheme iron atom of the desaturase is subsequently converted into the Fe^{2+} state, which enables it to interact with O_2 and the saturated fatty acyl-CoA substrate. A double bond is formed and two molecules of H_2O are released. Two electrons come from NADH and two from the single bond of the fatty acyl substrate.

2.7.4 Fatty acid oxidation

Oxidation of fatty acids includes α-oxidation, β-oxidation and ω-oxidation. These oxidations occur in different organelles in eukaryotic cells. **α-oxidation** occurs in the peroxisome, **β-oxidation** occurs in both mitochondria and peroxisome and **ω-oxidation** in the endoplasmic reticulum.

Mitochondrial β-oxidation

Most fatty acids are degraded by the sequential removal of two-carbon fragments from the carboxyl end of fatty acids. During this process, referred to as **β-oxidation**, acetyl-CoA is formed as the bond between the α- and β-carbon atoms are broken. β-oxidation is so named because the β-carbon of fatty acids is oxidized. β-oxidation occurs primarily within mitochondria.

Fatty acid activation and transport across the mitochondrial membrane: Before β-oxidation begins, each fatty acid is activated in a reaction with ATP and CoA. Fatty acids undergo for ATP dependent acylation reaction to form fatty acyl-CoA. This activation process is catalyzed by **acyl-CoA synthetase** (also called **acyl-CoA ligase** or **acyl-CoA thiokinase**) in the cytosol.

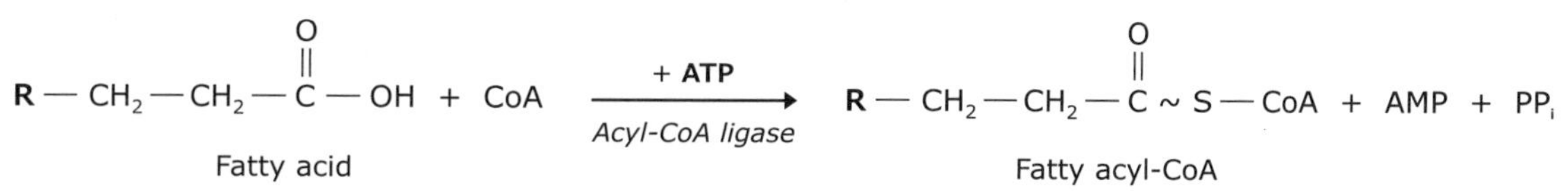

Although fatty acids are activated for oxidation in the cytosol, they are oxidized in the mitochondrion. A long chain fatty acyl-CoA cannot directly cross the inner mitochondrial membrane. Because the mitochondrial inner membrane is impermeable to most fatty acyl-CoA molecules, a special carrier called **carnitine** (β-hydroxy γ-trimethyl ammonium butyrate) is used to transport acyl groups into the mitochondrion (as shown in figure). However, the fatty acids with chain lengths of less than 12 carbons enter mitochondria without the help of carnitine. Carnitine-mediated transfer (**carnitine shuttle**) of fatty acyl-CoA into the mitochondrial matrix is accomplished through the following mechanism.

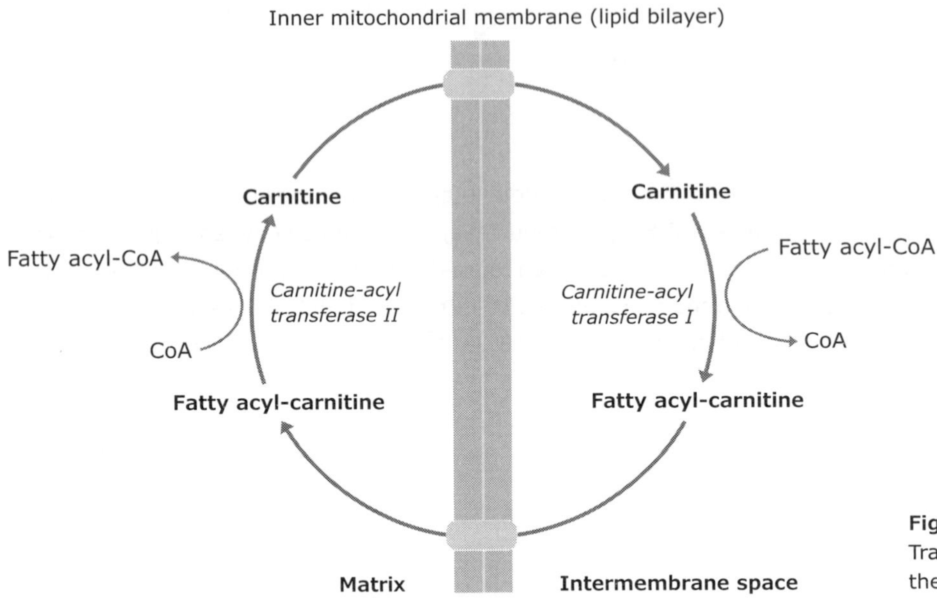

Figure 2.82
Transport of fatty acids into the mitochondrial matrix.

First, each molecule of fatty acyl-CoA is converted to a fatty acyl-carnitine derivative by the enzyme *carnitine-acyl transferase I*, located in the outer mitochondrial membrane. A carrier protein (*carnitine*: *acyl-carnitine translocase*) within the inner mitochondrial membrane transfers fatty acyl-carnitine into the mitochondrial matrix. Fatty acyl-CoA is regenerated by the enzyme *carnitine-acyl transferase II*, located on the matrix side of inner mitochondrial membrane. Finally, carnitine is transported back into the intermembrane space by the carrier protein.

β-oxidation of saturated fatty acids with an *even* number of carbon atoms

Once inside the mitochondrial matrix, fatty acyl-CoA is oxidized with oxidation of the β-carbon and long-chain fatty acyl-CoA are subjected to a repeated four-step process, which removes two carbons from the chain successively until the last two-carbon fragment is obtained. A summary of the reactions involved in the β-oxidation of palmitic acid (a saturated fatty acid) is shown.

Oxidation

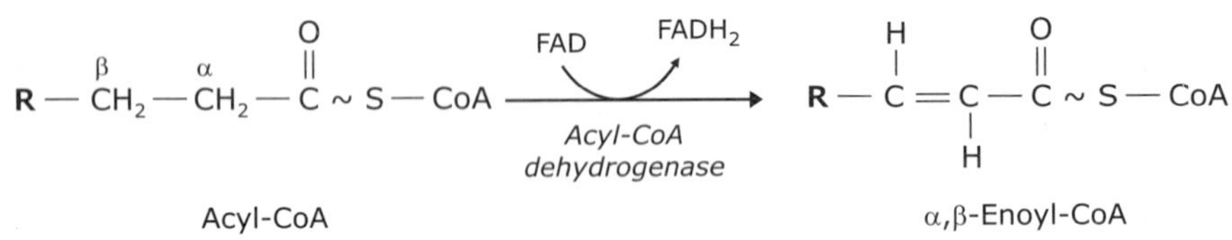

Hydrolysis

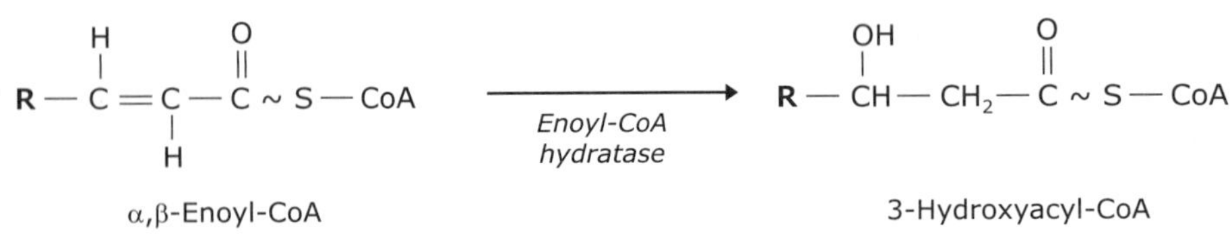

Oxidation

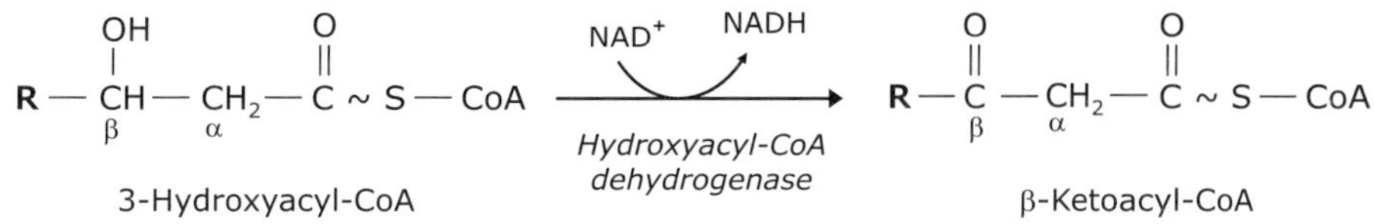

Thiolysis

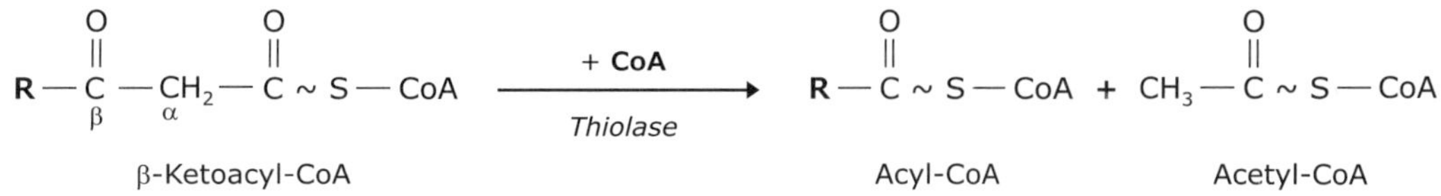

This series of four reactions has yielded a fatty acyl-CoA that has been shortened by two carbons and one molecule of acetyl-CoA. The shortened fatty acyl-CoA can now go through another β-oxidation cycle. Repetition of this cycle with palmitic acid with an even number of carbons eventually yields 8 molecules of acetyl-CoA.

Stoichiometry of β-oxidation

Fatty acid oxidation is highly exergonic. Each round of β-oxidation produces one NADH, one $FADH_2$, and one acetyl-CoA. Oxidation of acetyl-CoA via the citric acid cycle generates an additional $FADH_2$ and 3 NADH, which are reoxidized through oxidative phosphorylation to form ATP. Let's understand the stoichiometry of β-oxidation by considering **palmitate**, a 16-carbon saturated fatty acid. Oxidation of palmitoyl-CoA involves seven rounds of β-oxidation, yielding 7 $FADH_2$, 7 NADH, and 8 acetyl-CoA. Oxidation of the 8 acetyl-CoA via the TCA cycle, in turn, yields 8 ATP (from substrate-level phosphorylation), 24 NADH, and 8 $FADH_2$. Since oxidative phosphorylation of the 31 (7 from β-oxidation and 24 from TCA cycle) NADH molecules yields approximately 77.5 ATP, and that of the 15 (7 from β-oxidation and 8 from TCA cycle) $FADH_2$ yields approximately 22.5 ATP, subtracting the 2 ATP equivalents required for the activation of palmitate to palmitoyl-CoA, the oxidation of one palmitate molecule has a net yield of approximately 106 ATP.

Stoichiometry of β-oxidation : Summary

Activation of palmitate

Total number of ATP consumed for the activation of palmitate to palmitoyl-CoA : 2 ATP

Oxidation of palmitoyl-CoA involves

Total rounds of β-oxidation: 7

Products per round: 1 $FADH_2$, 1 NADH and 1 acetyl-CoA

Total products after 7 rounds: 7 $FADH_2$, 7 NADH and 8 acetyl-CoA

Oxidation of the 8 acetyl-CoA via the TCA cycle

Total number of ATP from substrate-level phosphorylation: 8

Total number of NADH: 24

Total number of $FADH_2$: 8

Oxidative phosphorylation

Total number of ATP from total 31 NADH: $31 \times 2.5 = 77.5$ ATP

Total number of ATP from total 15 $FADH_2$: $15 \times 1.5 = 22.5$ ATP

Net ATP synthesis from the complete oxidation of one palmitate molecule

Total ATP from NADH and $FADH_2$: $77.5 + 22.5 = 100$ ATP

Total ATP from substrate-level phosphorylation: 8 ATP

Total ATP synthesis = 108

Activation cost: 2 ATP

Net ATP from the oxidation = 104 ATP

β-oxidation of saturated fatty acids with *odd* number of carbon atoms

Fatty acids with odd numbered carbon chains are only a minor component of the diet. Oxidation of odd numbered fatty acids chains yields propionyl-CoA, a three carbon compound after the last cycle of β-oxidation. Propionyl-CoA finally gives a succinyl-CoA through *biotin dependent carboxylation* and a coenzyme *B_{12}-dependent rearrangement*. First, propionyl-CoA is carboxylated at the expense of the hydrolysis of an ATP to yield the D isomer of methylmalonyl-CoA. The D isomer of methylmalonyl-CoA is racemized to the L isomer. Finally, L-methylmalonyl-CoA converts into succinyl-CoA by an intramolecular rearrangement. Succinyl-CoA can enter the TCA cycle or be converted to acetyl-CoA.

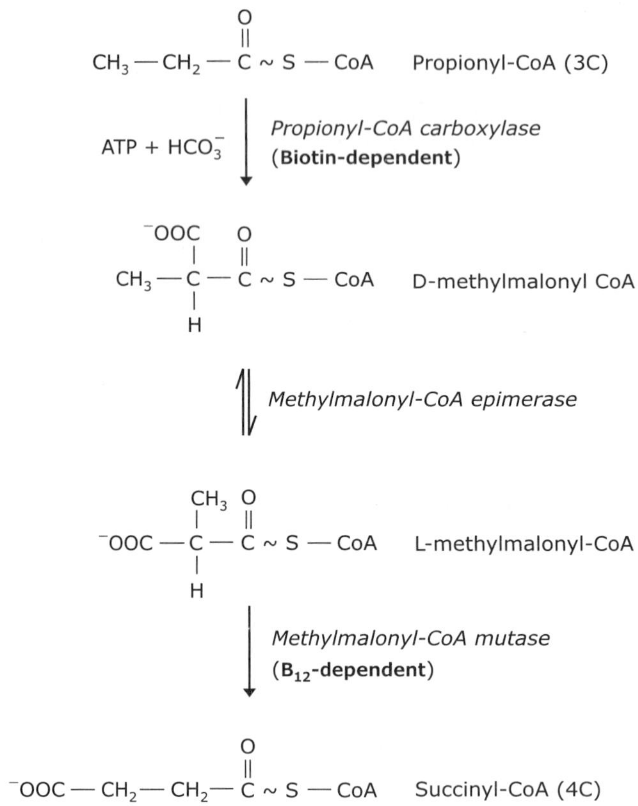

Figure 2.83 Propionyl-CoA is first carboxylated to form the D stereoisomer of methylmalonyl-CoA. The D-methylmalonyl-CoA thus formed is enzymatically epimerized to its L stereoisomer. The L-methylmalonyl-CoA then undergoes an intramolecular rearrangement to form succinyl-CoA.

β-oxidation of *monounsaturated* fatty acids with an even number of carbon atoms

The pathway of β-oxidation of unsaturated fatty acids is same as that for β-oxidation of saturated fatty acids until the double bond is reached. For example, consider the β-oxidation of monounsaturated fatty acids such as palmitoleic acid, a 16 carbon chain with a double bond at the 9, 10 position. Three cycles of β-oxidation of palmitoleoyl-CoA produce *cis* Δ^3-enoyl-CoA. But further oxidation requires additional mitochondrial enzymes.

Cis Δ^3-enoyl-CoA is not a substrate for acyl-CoA dehydrogenase. The presence of a double bond between C-3 and C-4 prevents the formation of another double bond between C-2 and C-3. This impasse is resolved by a new reaction that shifts the position and configuration of the *cis* Δ^3 double bond. Enzyme *enoyl-CoA isomerase* rearranges this *cis* Δ^3 double bond to a *trans* Δ^2 double bond, which then proceeds normally through the usual β-oxidation pathway. Thus, isomerase catalyzes *cis-trans* isomerization and transfer of double bond position. This enzyme is needed because unlike *trans* double bonds introduced during β-oxidation the double bonds of most naturally occurring unsaturated fatty acids have a *cis* configuration.

The energy yield from an unsaturated fatty acid is less as compared to saturated fatty acid. The energy yielding step that is bypassed during oxidation of unsaturated fatty acid is the first dehydrogenation reaction catalyzed by *Acyl-CoA dehydrogenase*. Since this is an FAD-linked dehydrogenation, oxidation of $FADH_2$ by electron transport, which produces 1.5 ATP molecules, is lost. Thus, palmitoleate yields 1.5 less ATP as compared to palmitic acid.

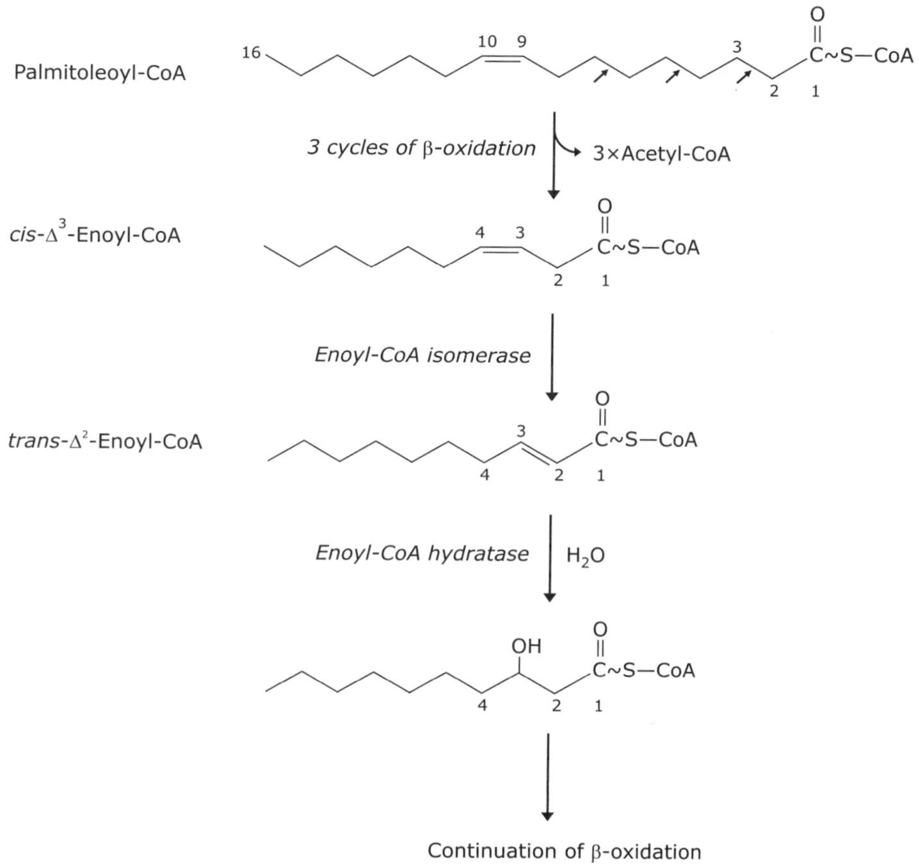

Figure 2.84 Oxidation of palmitoleate (16 carbon unsaturated fatty acid, which has one double bond between C-9 and C-10). Palmitoleoyl-CoA undergoes three cycles of degradation, which are carried out by the same enzymes as those in the oxidation of saturated fatty acids. However, the *cis* Δ^3- enoyl-CoA formed in the third round is not a substrate for acyl-CoA dehydrogenase. The presence of a double bond between C-3 and C-4 prevents the formation of another double bond between C-2 and C-3. This impasse is resolved by a new reaction that shifts the position and configuration of the *cis* Δ^3 double bond. Enoyl-CoA isomerase converts this double bond into a *trans* Δ^2 double bond. The double bond is now between C-2 and C-3. The subsequent reactions are those of the saturated fatty acid oxidation pathway, in which the *trans* Δ^2-enoyl-CoA is a regular substrate.

β-oxidation of *polyunsaturated* fatty acids with an even number of carbon atoms

The polyunsaturated fatty acids such as linoleic acid (18 carbon containing fatty acid with *cis*-Δ^9 and *cis*-Δ^{12} double bonds) pose two problems for the β-oxidation pathway that are solved through the actions of additional enzymes (**figure 2.85**). The first enzymatic difficulty occurs after the third round of β-oxidation. The resulting *cis*-β, γ double bond–containing enoyl-CoA is not a substrate for enzyme **enoyl-CoA hydratase**. This problem is solved by enzyme **enoyl-CoA isomerase**, which converts the *cis*-Δ^3 double bond to the *trans*-Δ^2 form. The resultant compound is the normal substrate of enoyl-CoA hydratase, so β-oxidation can continue. The second difficulty arises in the fifth round of β-oxidation: the presence of a double bond at an even-numbered carbon atom results in the formation of 2,4-dienoyl-CoA, which is a poor substrate for enoyl-CoA hydratase. This problem is solved by **2,4-dienoyl-CoA reductase**, the product of which depends on the organism. The mammalian form of this enzyme produces a *trans*-Δ^3 enoyl product, this enoyl product can be converted by an enoyl-CoA isomerase to the *trans*-Δ^2 enoyl-CoA, which can then proceed normally through the β-oxidation pathway.

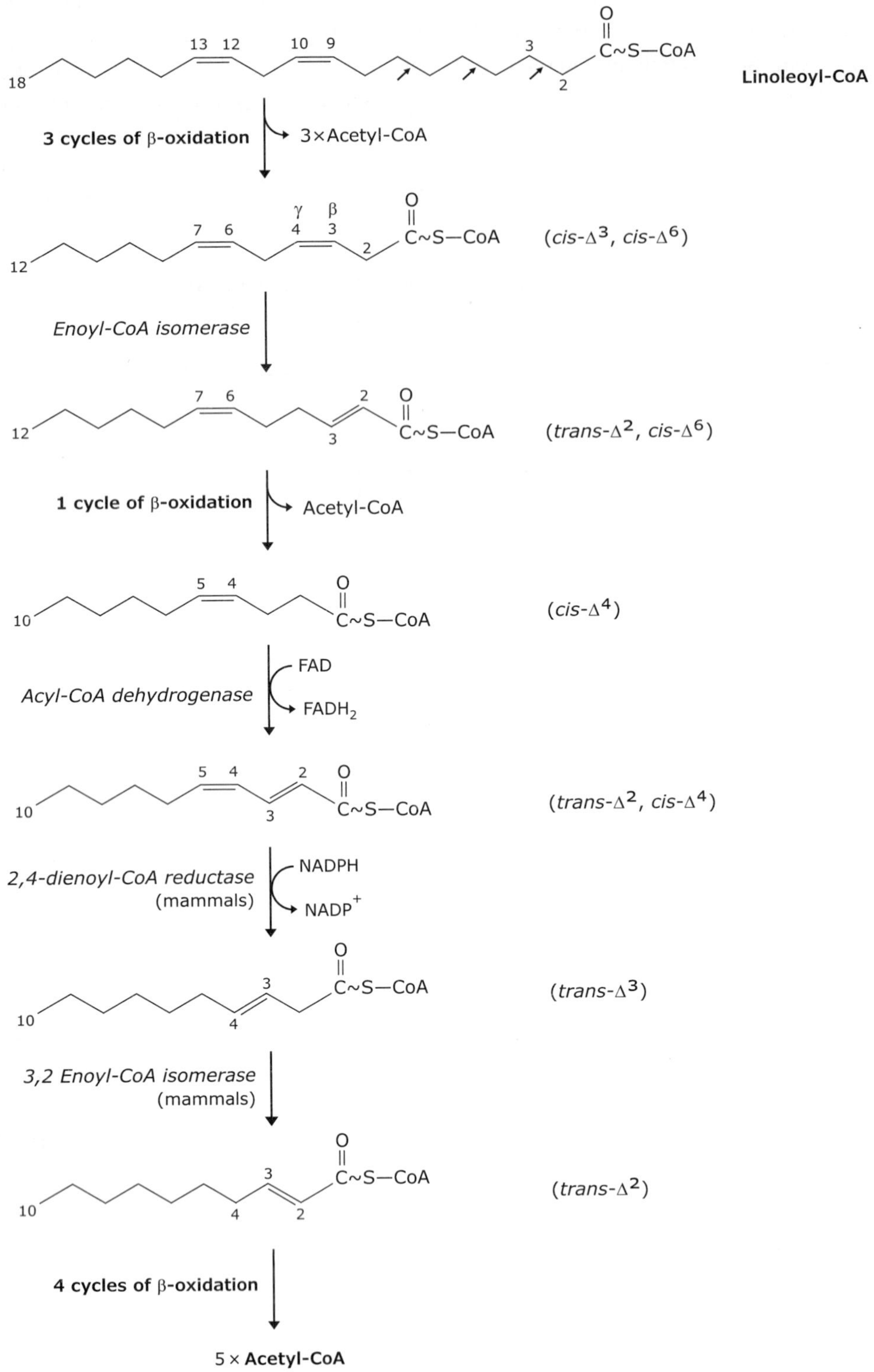

Figure 2.85 β-oxidation of an unsaturated fatty acid linoleic acid. In linoleic acid, one of the double bonds is at an odd-numbered carbon atom and the other is at an even-numbered carbon atom. The first enzymatic difficulty occurs after the third cycle of β-oxidation: The resulting *cis*-β,γ double bond–containing enoyl-CoA is not a substrate for enoyl-CoA hydratase. Enoyl-CoA isomerase, however, converts the *cis*-Δ^3 double bond to the trans-Δ^2 form. The Δ^2 compound is the normal substrate of enoyl-CoA hydratase, so β-oxidation can continue. The next difficulty arises in the fifth cycle of β-oxidation. The presence of a double bond at an even-numbered carbon atom results in the formation of 2,4-dienoyl-CoA, which is a poor substrate for enoyl-CoA hydratase. This problem is eliminated by the NADPH-dependent reduction of the Δ^4 bond by 2,4-dienoyl-CoA reductase. The product of which depends on the organism. The mammalian form of this enzyme produces a *trans*-Δ^3 enoyl product. This enoyl product can be converted by an 3,2 enoyl-CoA isomerase to the *trans*-Δ^2 enoyl-CoA, which can then proceed normally through the β-oxidation pathway.

Peroxisomal β−oxidation

In animals, β-oxidation occurs in both mitochondria and peroxisomes, whereas in plants and most fungi the β-oxidation occurs only in the peroxisomes. Peroxisomal β-oxidation is similar to but not identical with mitochondrial β-oxidation. The peroxisomal and mitochondrial β-oxidation enzymes are different but the chemical transformations of the fatty acids are the same in both. Peroxisomal β-oxidation does not degrade fatty acids completely but acts as a chain-shortening system, catalyzing only a limited number of β-oxidation cycles. Hence, the majority of long chain fatty acids (> C_{20} fatty acids) are metabolized by β-oxidation first in the peroxisome and then in mitochondria. $FADH_2$ and NADH produced during peroxisomal β-oxidation is not coupled to oxidative phosphorylation. In peroxisomal β-oxidation, electrons from $FADH_2$ directly transfer to oxygen which is reduced to H_2O_2. This reaction is catalyzed by **flavoprotein acyl-CoA oxidase**. Because it is not coupled to oxidative phosphorylation, hence no ATP synthesis occurs, but it does generate heat. However, in mitochondrial β-oxidation, electrons from $FADH_2$ is transferred to oxygen via electron transport chain which is coupled to ATP synthesis (oxidative phosphorylation). The NADH formed in the second oxidative step cannot be reoxidized in the peroxisome, so reducing equivalents are exported to the cytosol, eventually entering mitochondria. In mitochondria, oxidation of NADH is coupled to oxidative phosphorylation. Plant glyoxysomes (a special type of peroxisome) also carry out the β-oxidation of fatty acid to acetyl-CoA, which is used for succinate synthesis via the **glyoxylate pathway**.

Alternative pathways for fatty acid oxidation

α-oxidation of fatty acid: α-oxidation is a minor pathway of fatty acid oxidation. It occurs in both mitochondria as well as peroxisome (predominantly). In this case, the α-carbon undergoes for initial oxidation rather than the β-carbon. α-oxidation is a mechanism for degradation of branched chain fatty acid. α-oxidation of **phytanic acid** (a branched 20 carbon fatty acid) in an animal is the most common example.

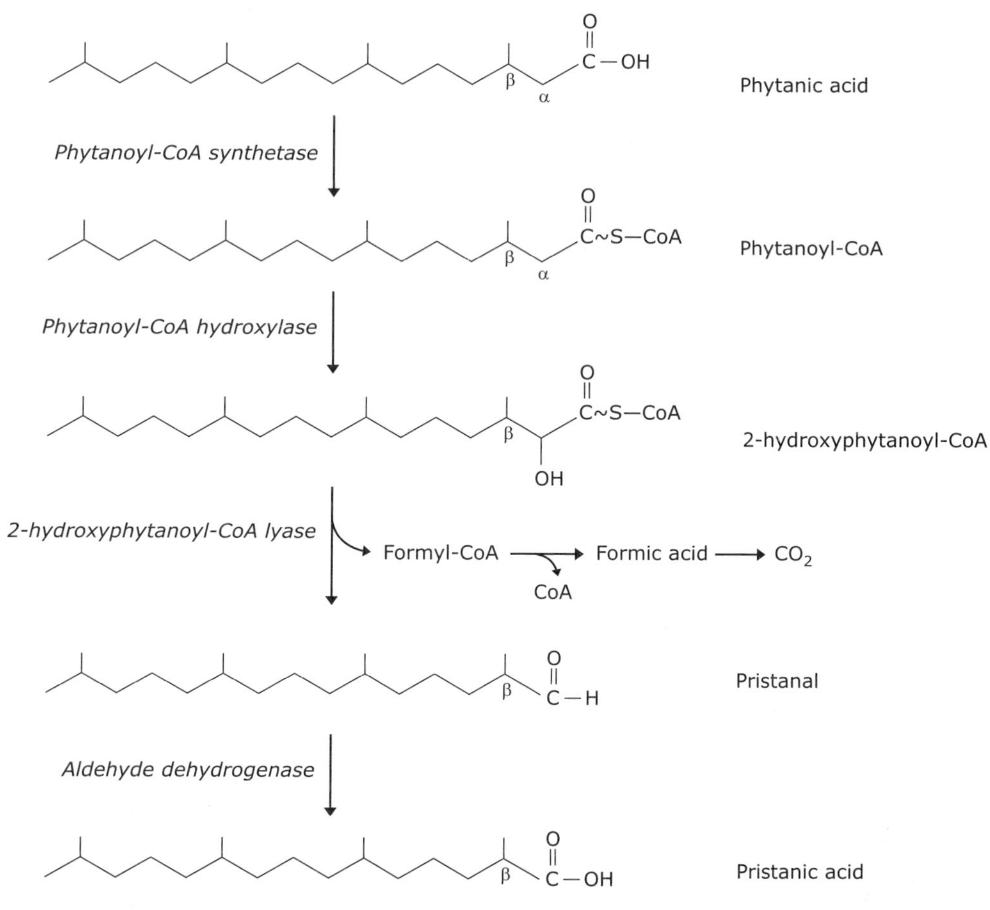

Figure 2.86 The phytanic acid α-oxidation pathway.

Phytanic acid is an oxidation product of phytol of chlorophyll. The presence of methyl group on the 3rd carbon of phytanic acid prevents β-oxidation from occurring. Instead, the terminal carboxyl group is first removed by α-oxidation (see **figure 2.86** for details). Pristanic acid forms as a result of α-oxidation is further degraded through β-oxidation pathway. The α-oxidation pathway is defective in **Refsum's disease** and thus phytanic acid is not converted to a compound that can be degraded. The symptoms of this metabolic disorder include defective night vision, tremors and other neurological abnormalities.

ω-oxidation of fatty acid: ω-oxidation of fatty acids is a minor pathway that involves the oxidation of terminal carbon of a normal fatty acids and leads to the synthesis of small amount of dicarboxylic acids. This process occurs in the endoplasmic reticulum of eukaryotic cells and catalyzed by cytochrome P450, a monooxygenase that utilizes NADPH and O_2. The steps of the process are as follow:

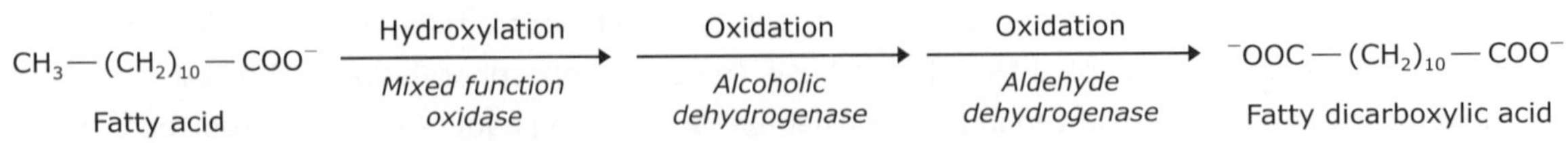

Table 2.16 Comparison of fatty acid synthesis and degradation

	Synthesis	**Degradation**
Major tissue site	Primarily liver	Muscle and liver
Subcellular site	Primarily cytosol	Primarily mitochondria
Oxidation/reduction cofactor	NADPH	NAD^+, FAD
Two carbon donor/product	Malonyl-CoA, donor of one acetyl group	Acetyl-CoA (product)
Hormonal state favouring pathway	High insulin/glucagon ratio	Low insulin/glucagon ratio

Ketone bodies

Most of the acetyl-CoA produced during fatty acid oxidation is used by the citric acid cycle or in fatty acid synthesis. Under normal conditions, fatty acid metabolism is so carefully regulated that only, small amounts of excess acetyl-CoA are produced. However, in mitochondria of liver when acetyl-CoA accumulates beyond its capacity to be oxidized or used for fatty acid synthesis it leads to the formation of **ketone bodies**. Formation of acetoacetate, β-hydroxybutyrate, and acetone, a group of molecules called the ketone bodies from acetyl-CoA molecules are known as **ketogenesis**.

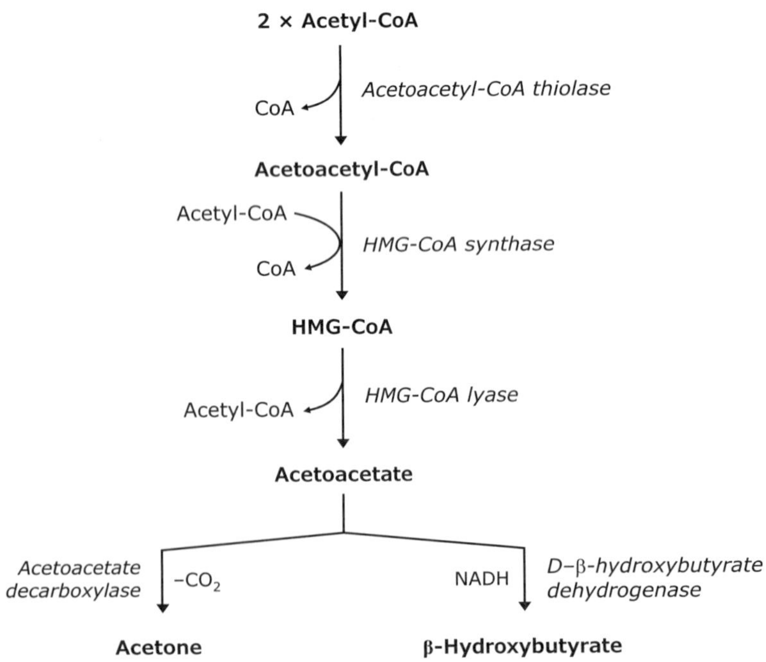

Figure 2.87
Ketone body formation. When acetyl-CoA accumulates, thiolase catalyzes the condensation of two acetyl-CoA molecules to acetoacetyl-CoA. Acetoacetyl-CoA gives six carbon compound HMG-CoA which in the presence of HMG-CoA lyase gives acetoacetate and acetyl-CoA. Acetoacetate is reversibly reduced into β-hydroxybutyrate and also decarboxylated into acetone.

Ketone body formation, which occurs within the matrix of liver mitochondria, begins with the condensation of two acetyl-CoAs to form acetoacetyl-CoA. Then acetoacetyl-CoA condenses with another acetyl-CoA to form β-hydroxy-β-methylglutaryl-CoA (HMG-CoA). In the next reaction, HMG-CoA is cleaved to form acetoacetate and acetyl-CoA. Acetoacetate is then reduced to form β-hydroxybutyrate. Acetone is formed by the spontaneous decarboxylation of acetoacetate when the latter's concentration is high. During starvation or uncontrolled diabetes, accumulation of acetyl-CoA accelerates the formation of ketone bodies. The increased blood levels of acetoacetate and β-hydroxybutyrate lower the blood pH, causing the condition known as **acidosis**. Very high concentration of ketone bodies in the blood, **ketonemia** (about 90 mg/100 ml as compared to normal level of <3 mg/100 ml) and urine, **ketonuria** (about 5000 mg/24 hr as compared to normal rate of less than or equal to 125 mg/24 hr) is known as **ketosis**.

Several tissues, most notably cardiac and skeletal muscle, use ketone bodies to generate energy. During prolonged starvation (i.e., in the absence of sufficient glucose) the brain uses ketone bodies as an energy source. The mechanism by which acetoacetate and β-hydroxybutyrate are converted to acetyl-CoA is illustrated in **figure 2.88**.

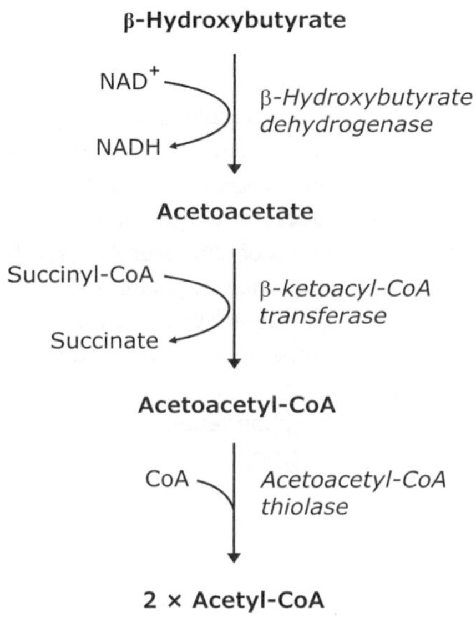

Figure 2.88
Conversion of ketone bodies to acetyl-CoA. Some organs (e.g., heart and skeletal muscle) can use ketone bodies as an energy source under normal conditions. During starvation the brain uses them as an important fuel source. Because liver does not have β-ketoacyl-CoA transferase, it cannot use ketone bodies as an energy source. These reactions are reversible.

2.7.5 Synthesis of cholesterol

Cholesterol is a major constituent of the plasma membranes of animal cells. Most of cholesterol derives from endogenous biosynthesis, which takes place mainly in the liver (about 50%). The rest is taken up from food. Most of the cholesterol is incorporated into the lipid layer of plasma membranes, or converted into bile acids. A very small amount of cholesterol is also used for the biosynthesis of the steroid hormones. All 27 carbon atoms in cholesterol are provided by acetate moiety (acetyl-CoA). Four basic steps are involved in cholesterol synthesis:

Formation of mevalonate from acetate: The first step in cholesterol biosynthesis leads to the intermediate mevalonate. The molecules of acetyl-CoA condense to form acetoacetyl-CoA, which condenses with a third molecule of acetyl-CoA to yield the six-carbon compound β-hydroxy-β-methylglutaryl-CoA (HMG-CoA). The third reaction is the committed and rate-limiting step: reduction of HMG-CoA to mevalonate. This step is catalyzed by an integral membrane protein of the smooth ER called *HMG-CoA reductase*. Drugs called **statins** (used for treatment of **hypercholesterolemia**), inhibit HMG-CoA reductase. Statins compete with HMG-CoA for binding with HMG-CoA reductase.

Conversion of mevalonate into isopentenyl pyrophosphate: After phosphorylation, mevalonate is decarboxylated to *isopentenyl pyrophosphate*, activated C5 isoprenoid compound, with consumption of ATP.

Polymerization of six isopentenyl pyrophosphate to form squalene: Isopentenyl pyrophosphate undergoes isomerization to form dimethylallyl diphosphate. The two C5 molecules condense to yield geranyl pyrophosphate, and the addition of another isopentenyl pyrophosphate produces farnesyl pyrophosphate. This can then undergo dimerization, in a *head-to-head reaction*, to yield **squalene**.

Cyclization of squalene forms steroid nucleus: Squalene, a linear isoprenoid, is cyclized, with O_2 being consumed, to form lanosterol, a C30 sterol. Three methyl groups are cleaved from this in the subsequent reaction steps, to yield the end product cholesterol.

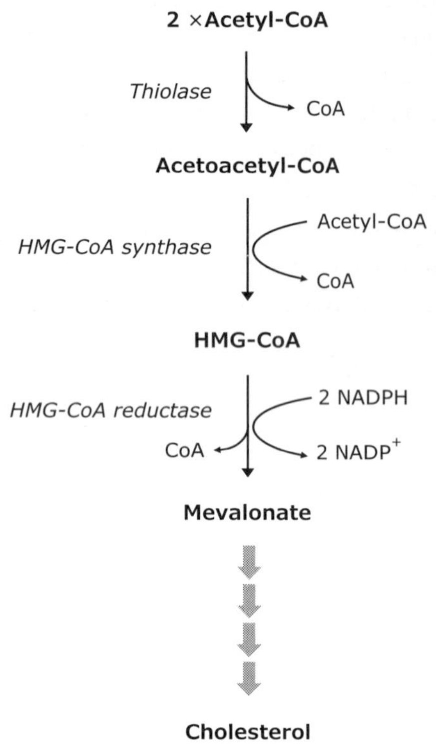

Figure 2.89
Cholesterol is synthesized from acetyl-CoA. The first stage in the synthesis of cholesterol is the formation of mevalonate from acetyl-CoA. The synthesis of mevalonate is the committed step in cholesterol formation. This set of reactions starts with the formation of HMG-CoA from acetyl-CoA. HMG-CoA synthesis requires thiolase and HMG-CoA synthase. In liver mitochondria, these two enzymes form HMG-CoA for ketone body synthesis. Cytosolic isozymes of the two enzymes generate the HMG-CoA that is used in cholesterol biosynthesis. HMG-CoA reductase, which catalyzes the rate-limiting step of cholesterol biosynthesis, is the pathway's main regulatory site. The enzyme is subject to short-term control by competitive inhibition, allosteric effects and covalent modification involving reversible phosphorylation.

2.7.6 Steroid hormones and Bile acids

Steroid hormones

Cholesterol is the biosynthetic source of all steroid hormones. Synthesis of steroid hormones involves shortening of the hydrocarbon chain of cholesterol and hydroxylation of the steroid nucleus. Biosynthetic pathway of steroid hormones begins with the synthesis of **pregnenolone**. Steroid hormones contain 21 or fewer carbon atoms, whereas cholesterol contains 27. Thus, the first stage in the synthesis of steroid hormones is the removal of a six-carbon unit from the side chain of cholesterol to form pregnenolone. The side chain of cholesterol is hydroxylated at C-20 and then at C-22, and the bond between these carbon atoms is subsequently cleaved by *desmolase*. Pregnenolone is converted to **progesterone**. Progesterone finally acts as a precursor for other steroid hormones like cortisol, corticosterone, aldosterone, testosterone and estradiol. There are five major classes of steroid hormones:

Progestins (progesterone)

Regulate events during pregnancy and are the precursors to all other steroid hormones.

Glucocorticoids (cortisol and corticosterone)

Promote gluconeogenesis and, in pharmacological doses, suppress inflammation reactions.

Mineralocorticoids (aldosterone)

Regulate ion balance by promoting reabsorption of potassium, sodium, chloride and bicarbonate ions in the kidney.

Androgens (androstenedione and testosterone)

Promote male sexual development and maintain male sex characteristics.

Estrogens (estrone and estradiol)

Support female sex characteristics.

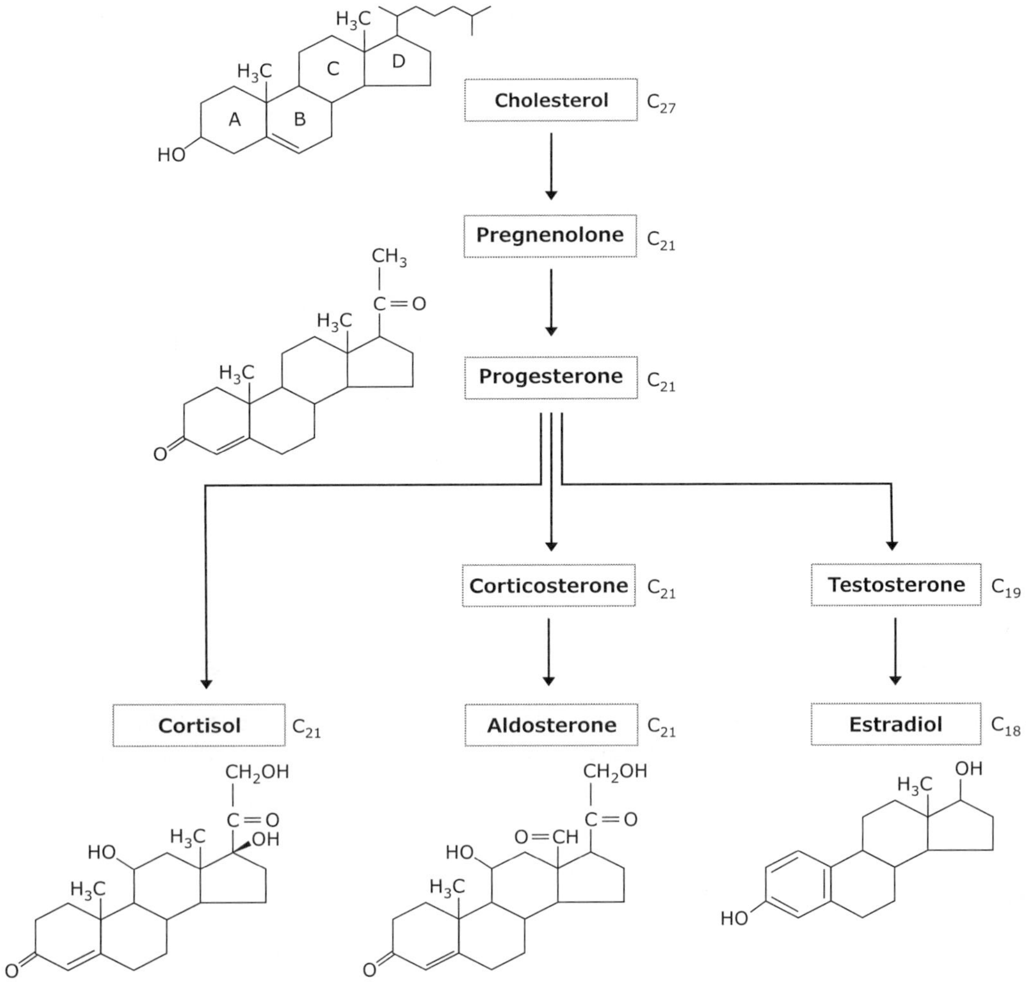

Figure 2.90 Biosynthetic routes from cholesterol to steroid hormones. Two classes of steroid hormones are synthesized in the cortex of the adrenal gland: mineralocorticoids and glucocorticoids. Sex hormones are produced in male and female gonads and the placenta. They include progesterone, androgens and estrogens. Synthesis of steroid hormones requires removal of the carbons present in the side chain on C-17 of the D ring of cholesterol. Formation of these hormones also requires the introduction of oxygen atoms. All the hydroxylation and oxygenation reactions in steroid biosynthesis are catalyzed by mixed-function oxygenases that use NADPH, O_2 and cytochrome P-450.

Bile acids

Bile acids are steroid derivatives. First, the cholesterol is oxidized to the trihydroxy derivative, and the end of the aliphatic chain is oxidized to the carboxylic acid. They are synthesized in the liver by the metabolism of cholesterol and stored in the gall bladder. Four bile acids – cholic acid, deoxycholic acid, chenodeoxycholic acid and lithocholic acid–are present in human bile. The most abundant bile acids in humans are *cholic acid* and *chenodeoxycholic acid*.

Cholic acid is usually conjugated with the amino acid glycine or taurine, giving compound called **glycocholate** and **taurocholate**, respectively. The sodium and potassium salts of these conjugated bile acids are called **bile salts**, cause emulsification of dietary lipids in the intestine and thereby promote fat digestion and absorption. Emulsification is possible because of the amphipathic nature of bile salts (one end of the molecule is strongly hydrophilic because of the negative charge, and the rest of the molecule is largely hydrophobic). An efficient recycling system allows the bile salts to re-enter the bloodstream and return to the liver for reuse several times each day. Very small amount of bile salts normally escapes this recycling system. This is the body's only route for cholesterol excretion.

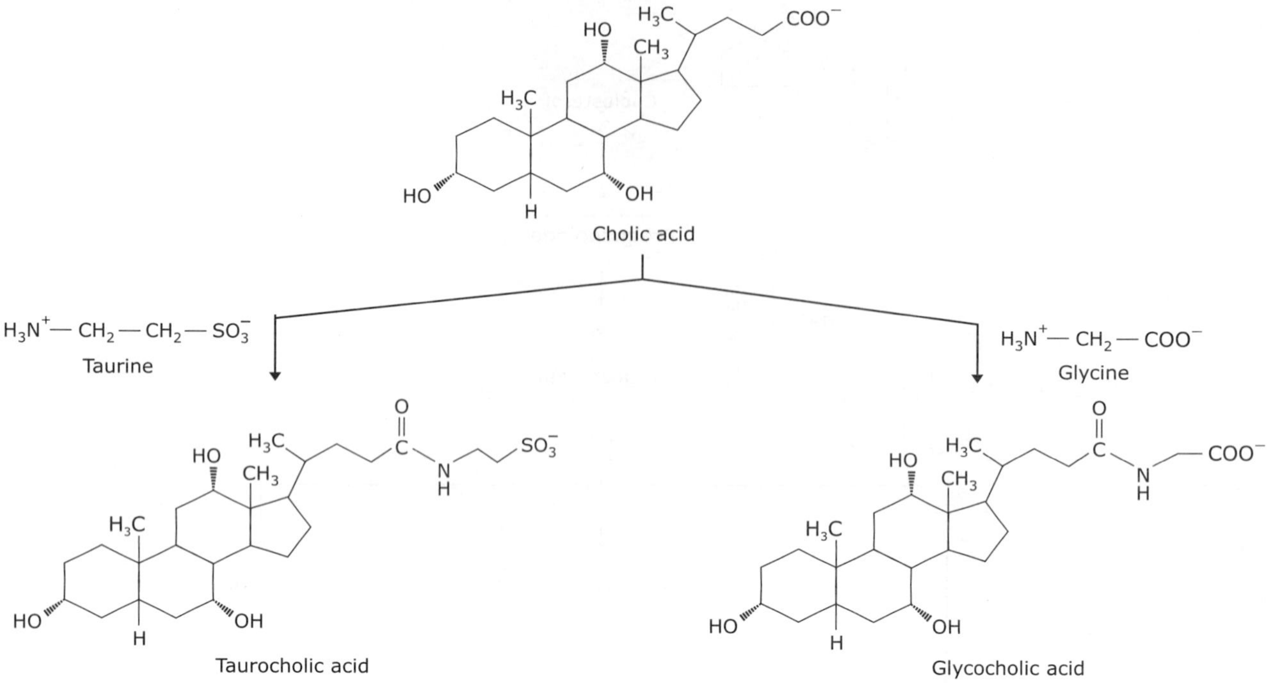

Figure 2.91 Bile acid biosynthesis pathway. Bile acids are oxidation products of cholesterol. First, the cholesterol is oxidized to the trihydroxy derivative, and the end of the aliphatic chain is oxidized to the carboxylic acid. The latter, in turn, forms an amide bond with an amino acid, either glycine or taurine.

2.8 Amino acid metabolism

Amino acids are not only the building blocks of proteins but also serve as precursors for various biologically important molecules, such as neurotransmitters, hormones, and nucleotides. Hence, amino acid metabolism is a complex and highly regulated process that involves the synthesis, degradation, and interconversion of amino acids. Amino acid metabolism can be divided into two main processes: the *synthesis* of amino acids and the *breakdown* of amino acids for energy or conversion into other molecules.

Living organisms differ in their capacity to synthesize the standard amino acids. Most bacteria and plants can synthesize all 20 standard amino acids. In contrast, animals have a limited capacity to synthesize all the standard amino acids they require. This leads to the classification of amino acids as essential and non-essential.

Essential amino acids: Amino acids required from diet as animals cannot synthesize them adequately (or not at all).

Non-essential amino acids: Amino acids that animals can synthesize from other metabolic precursors.

Classification of standard amino acids as essential and non-essential (with respect to humans)

Essential amino acids	**Non-essential amino acids**	
Histidine	**Core non-essential amino acids**	**Conditionally non-essential**
Isoleucine	(Synthesized in the body under normal conditions)	(In special conditions like illness, or metabolic stress)
Leucine	Alanine	Arginine
Lysine	Asparagine	Cysteine
Methionine	Aspartate	Glutamine
Phenylalanine	Glutamate	Tyrosine
Threonine	Serine	Glycine
Tryptophan		Proline
Valine		

2.8.1 Amino acid synthesis

All amino acids contain carbon and nitrogen atoms. Therefore, amino acid synthesis requires the availability of both carbon and nitrogen, which are obtained from various carbon and nitrogen sources.

Sources of nitrogen

Nitrogen is a key component of amino acids. **Ammonium ions** serve as the nitrogen source for all amino acids. In living systems, nitrogen from ammonium ions are first incorporated into amino acids and then into various other biomolecules, including nucleotides.

Direct incorporation of ammonium ions into amino acids: The amino acids glutamate and glutamine provide the critical entry points for nitrogen from ammonium ions. There are two principal ways in which ammonium ions are incorporated into amino acids:

- Reductive amination of α-keto acids
- Formation of the amides of glutamic acid

Reductive amination of α-keto acids: *Reductive amination* is a chemical reaction that converts a carbonyl group (typically a ketone or aldehyde) into an amine. Enzyme **glutamate dehydrogenase** catalyzes the reductive amination of α-ketoglutarate and forms glutamate. This pathway is present in all organisms. In eukaryotes, this is a minor pathway and occurs in the mitochondria. Glutamate dehydrogenase is an unusual enzyme because it does not discriminate between NADH and NADPH.

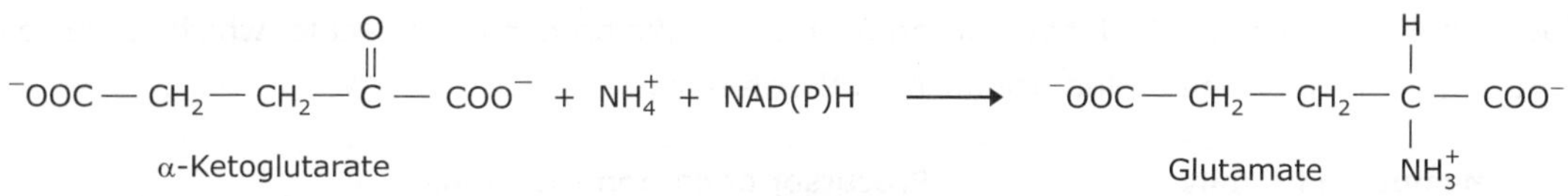

Formation of the amides of glutamic acids: Ammonium ions are also incorporated into cell metabolites by the formation of glutamine, the amide of glutamate. This **amidation reaction** is catalyzed by **glutamine synthetase** (present in all organisms) and is driven by the hydrolysis of ATP. ATP participates directly in the reaction by phosphorylating the side chain of glutamate to form an acyl-phosphate intermediate, which then reacts with ammonia to form glutamine.

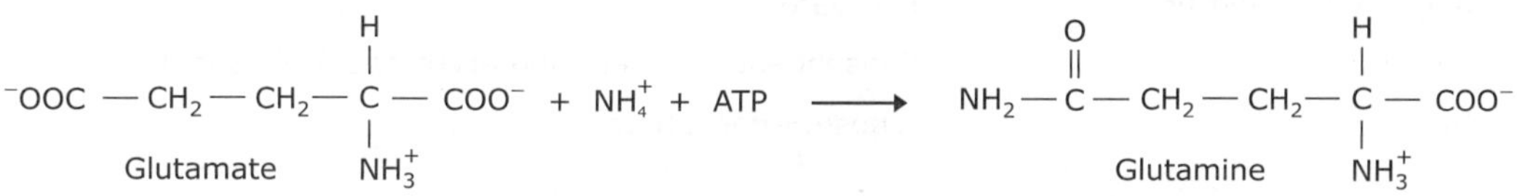

Indirect incorporation of ammonium ions through transamination reactions: Many amino acid biosynthetic pathways involve transamination reactions. The α-amino group from one amino acid is transferred to an α-keto acid to produce a new amino acid. This reaction is catalyzed by the enzyme called **aminotransferases** (formerly called **transaminases**). Aminotransferases require the participation of an aldehyde-containing coenzyme, **pyridoxal-5-phosphate**, a derivative of pyridoxine (vitamin B_6). Pyridoxal-5-phosphate is covalently attached to the enzyme via a Schiff base linkage formed by the condensation of its aldehyde group with the ε-amino group of lysine residue. Aminotransferases act by transferring the amino group of an amino acid to the pyridoxal part of the coenzyme to generate *pyridoxamine phosphate*. The pyridoxamine form of the coenzyme then reacts with an α-keto acid to form an amino acid and regenerates the original aldehyde form of the coenzyme. Eukaryotic cells possess a large variety of aminotransferase. Found within both the cytoplasm and mitochondria, these enzymes possess two types of specificities:

1. The type of α-amino acid that donates the α-amino group
2. The α-keto acid that accepts the α-amino group

Although the aminotransferases vary widely in the type of amino acids they use, most of them use *glutamate as the amino group donor*. The amino group from glutamate can be transferred to other α-keto acids by transamination reactions. Transamination reactions participate in the synthesis of most amino acids.

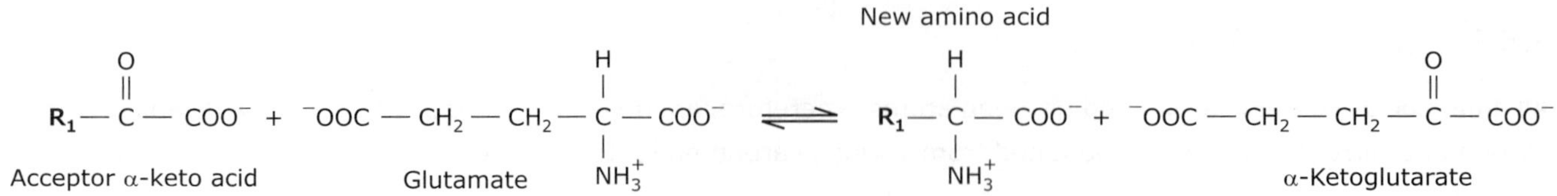

Sources of carbon

The standard amino acids differ from other classes of biomolecules in that each member of this class is synthesized by a unique pathway. Despite the tremendous diversity of amino acid synthetic pathways, they have one common feature. The key point to remember about amino acid biosynthesis is that an α-keto acid is first produced and then an amino group is introduced by transamination reaction. The carbon skeletons of each amino acid are derived from commonly available metabolic intermediates. All standard amino acids are synthesized from intermediates of central metabolic pathways such as glycolysis, TCA cycle, and HMP pathway. These intermediates serve as the primary carbon sources and include glycerate 3-phosphate, pyruvate, α-ketoglutarate, oxaloacetate, ribose 5-phosphate, phosphoenolpyruvate, and erythrose 4-phosphate.

Intermediates of glycolysis: Glycerate 3-phosphate, Phosphoenolpyruvate and Pyruvate

Intermediates of TCA cycle: α-ketoglutarate and Oxaloacetate

Intermediates of HMP pathway: Ribose 5-phosphate and Erythrose 4-phosphate

The 20 standard amino acids can be divided into six biosynthetic families on the basis of the primary carbon sources of each amino acid. Each family of amino acids derive carbon from a specific precursor molecule, which serves as the starting point for the synthesis of all the amino acids within that family.

Family	Members of family	Precursor of carbon skeletons
Glutamate family	Glu, Gln, Pro and Arg	α-ketoglutarate
Serine family	Ser, Gly and Cys	Glycerate 3-phosphate
Aspartate family	Asp, Asn, Lys, Met and Thr	Oxaloacetate
Pyruvate family	Ala, Val, Leu and Ile	Pyruvate
Aromatic family	Phe, Tyr and Trp	Phosphoenolpyruvate and erythrose 4-phosphate
Histidine family	His	Ribose 5-phosphate

2.8.2 Amino acid catabolism

The breakdown of proteins (from both dietary and cellular sources) in animals releases amino acids. Since amino acids cannot be stored, those not required for new protein synthesis or other metabolic processes are degraded. This degradation occurs within cells. The degradative catabolic pathway of amino acids involves two main steps:

- Removal of the α-amino group
- Breakdown of the amino acid's carbon skeleton

Removal of the amino group

In mammals, amino acid degradation typically begins with the removal of the α-amino group. This process occurs through two key types of biochemical reactions: *transamination* and *oxidative deamination*.

Transamination: The main reactions involved in the removal of nitrogen from amino acids are called transaminations. These reactions involve the transfer of an α-amino group from a donor α-amino acid to the keto group of an acceptor α-keto acid. As a result of this transfer, the original amino acid is converted into its corresponding α-keto acid, and the acceptor α-keto acid is converted into a new amino acid. All amino acids, except lysine, threonine, and proline, participate in transamination during their catabolism. It is a reversible reaction and is catalyzed by enzymes known as **aminotransferases** (or **transaminases**). Each aminotransferase is typically specific to one or a few amino group donors.

Importantly, *transamination* does not result in a net loss of amino groups. Instead, it only transfers amino group from one molecule to another molecule. The overall effect of transamination is the collection of amino groups from various amino acids into a common amino acid— glutamate. This glutamate then serves as a key amino group donor in subsequent reactions, including **oxidative deamination**.

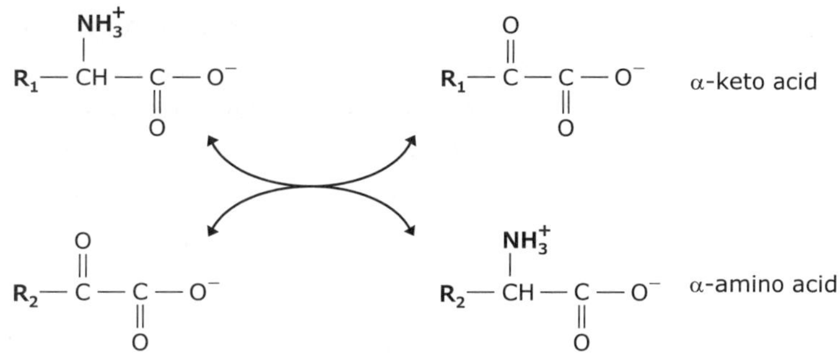

Figure 2.92 Transamination involves the transfer of amino group to an α-keto acid to yield the α-keto acid of the original amino acid and a new amino acid. These reactions are catalyzed by aminotransferases.

Oxidative deamination: Transamination does not result in a net loss of amino groups; it simply transfers an amino group from one molecule to another. The actual removal of amino groups from the body occurs through oxidative deamination, a process in which an amino acid is converted into its corresponding keto acid by the removal of the amino group as ammonia (NH_3). This reaction primarily involves the oxidative deamination of glutamate, catalyzed by the allosteric enzyme glutamate *dehydrogenase*, which is located in the mitochondrial matrix of mammalian cells. The reaction requires an oxidizing agent—either NAD^+ or $NADP^+$—as a cofactor. Glutamate dehydrogenase activity is allosterically inhibited by GTP and activated by ADP.

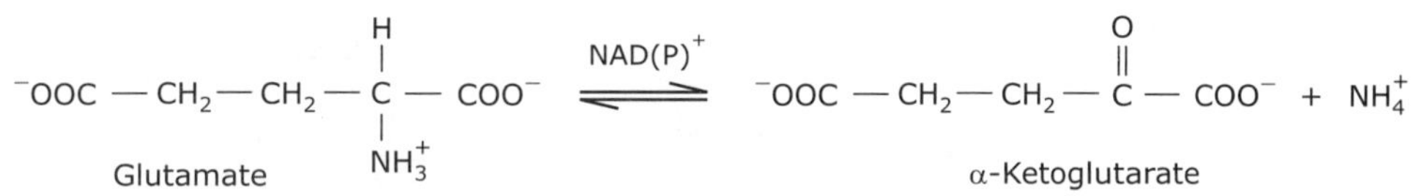

The combined action of an aminotransferase (which produces glutamate) and glutamate dehydrogenase (which removes the amino group from glutamate) is known as transdeamination.

Fate of the amino group

In mammals, the amino group released during amino acid catabolism does not accumulate freely in the body, as free ammonia is highly toxic. Instead, it follows two major fates. First, it can be recycled and used as a nitrogen source in various biosynthetic pathways, such as the synthesis of new amino acids, nucleotides, and other nitrogen-containing compounds. Second, excess amino groups are converted into a less toxic form for safe elimination. This occurs primarily in the liver, where nitrogen is incorporated into **urea** via the **urea cycle**. Urea is then transported through the bloodstream to the kidneys and excreted in urine. This process allows mammals to effectively manage nitrogen balance while preventing ammonia toxicity.

Urea cycle

Living organisms excrete ammonia resulting from the metabolic breakdown of amino acids in one of three ways. Many aquatic animals simply excrete ammonia. Where water is less plentiful, however, processes have evolved that convert ammonia to less toxic waste products that therefore require less water for excretion. One such product is urea and other is uric acid. Accordingly, living organisms are classified as being either **ammonotelic** (ammonia excreting), **ureotelic** (urea excreting) or **uricotelic** (uric acid excreting).

Fate of ammonia in different organisms

Organism type	Fate of ammonia	Main excretion product
Mammals (ureotelic)	Urea formation	Urea
Fish (ammonotelic)	Direct excretion	Ammonia
Birds (uricotelic)	Uric acid formation	Uric acid

In mammals, the primary fate of ammonia is conversion to **urea** via the **urea cycle** in the liver. Urea is formed from ammonia, CO_2 and aspartate in a cyclic pathway referred to as the urea cycle. Because the urea cycle was discovered by Krebs and Henseleit, it is often referred to as **Krebs-Henseleit cycle**. It is synthesized in the liver by the enzymes of the urea cycle. It is then secreted into the bloodstream and sequestered by the kidneys for excretion in the urine. Urea synthesis consists of five sequential enzymatic reactions. The first two reactions occur in the mitochondria and the remaining three reactions take place in the cytosol.

Mitochondrial reaction: Urea cycle begins with the formation of carbamoyl phosphate in the mitochondria. The substrates for this reaction are NH_4^+ and HCO_3^- and catalyzed by enzyme **carbamoyl phosphate synthetase I** (CPSI). Because two molecules of ATP are required in carbamoyl phosphate synthesis, this reaction is essentially irreversible (one is used to activate HCO_3^- and the second molecule is used to phosphorylate carbamate). Carbamoyl phosphate subsequently reacts with ornithine to form citrulline. Citrulline passes into the cytosol.

Cytosolic reaction: In the cytosol, the ATP-dependent reaction of citrulline with aspartate (aspartate provides second nitrogen that is ultimately incorporated into urea) occurs and results in the formation of argininosuccinate. The subsequent reaction involves the formation of arginine from argininosuccinate. This reaction releases fumarate, which enters the citric acid cycle. Finally, the formation of urea occurs along with the regeneration of ornithine.

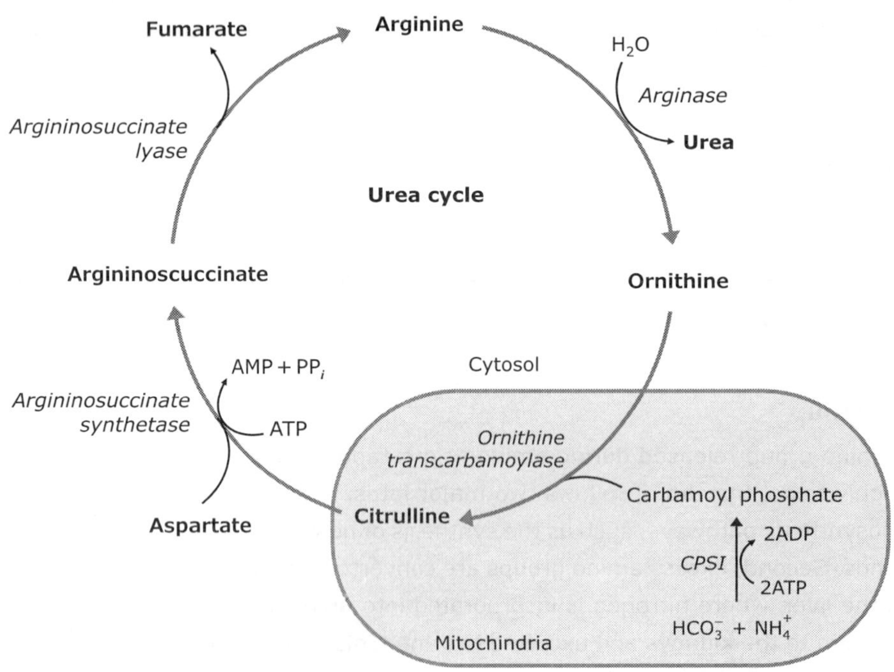

Figure 2.93 Urea cycle. Five enzymatic reactions are involved in the urea cycle, two of which are mitochondrial and three cytosolic. The first step involves the formation of carbamoyl phosphate within mitochondria. This step is catalyzed by an enzyme carbamoyl phosphate synthetase I (CPS I). Ammonia is the source of the first amine group of urea. In the second step, carbamoyl phosphate and ornithine combine to form citrulline by an enzyme ornithine transcarbamoylase. Citrulline is then transported from hepatocyte mitochondria into the cytosol. In the cytosol, citrulline reacts with aspartate to form argininosuccinate. Aspartate is the source of the second amine group of urea. In the fourth step, argininosuccinate is converted into arginine. This reaction also gives off fumarate. Finally, arginine undergoes hydrolysis to form urea and ornithine.

In the urea cycle, four equivalents of ATP are consumed per equivalent of urea synthesized: two ATPs in the synthesis of carbamoyl phosphate, and two more as one ATP is converted to AMP + PP_i in the synthesis of argininosuccinate from citrulline. Urea's two nitrogen atoms are contributed by ammonia and aspartate, whereas its carbon atom comes from HCO_3^-.

Regulation of the urea cycle

The urea cycle operates only to eliminate excess nitrogen. On high-protein diets the carbon skeletons of the amino acids are oxidized for energy or stored as fat and glycogen, but the amino nitrogen must be excreted. To facilitate this process, enzymes of the urea cycle are controlled at the gene level. With long-term changes in the quantity of dietary protein, changes of 20-fold or greater in the concentration of cycle enzymes are observed. When dietary proteins increase significantly, enzyme concentrations rise. On return to a balanced diet, enzyme levels decline. Under conditions of starvation, enzyme levels rise as proteins are degraded and amino acid carbon skeletons are used to provide energy, thus increasing the quantity of nitrogen that must be excreted.

Short-term regulation of the cycle occurs principally at CPS-I (carbamoyl phosphate synthetase-I), which is relatively inactive in the absence of its allosteric activator **N-acetylglutamate**. This metabolite is synthesized from glutamate and acetyl-CoA by *N*-acetylglutamate synthase.

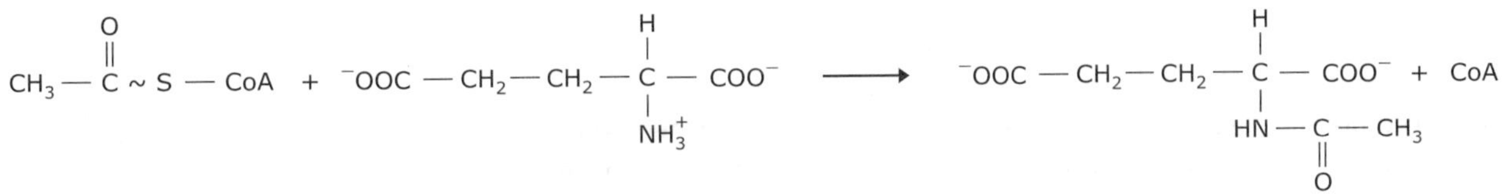

Acetyl-CoA Glutamate N-acetylglutamate

Increased urea synthesis is required when amino acid breakdown rates increase, generating excess nitrogen that must be excreted. Increases in these breakdown rates are signaled by an increase in glutamate concentration through transamination reactions. This situation, in turn, causes an increase in *N*-acetylglutamate synthesis, stimulating carbamoyl phosphate synthetase and thus the entire urea cycle.

Catabolism of amino acid's carbon skeletons

The carbon skeletons derived from the 20 standard amino acids are broken down into seven key metabolic intermediates: acetyl-CoA, acetoacetyl-CoA, pyruvate, α-ketoglutarate, succinyl-CoA, fumarate, and oxaloacetate. Based on the final catabolic products, amino acids are categorized into the following groups:

- Amino acids yielding acetyl-CoA: Leucine, isoleucine, threonine, and tryptophan.
- Amino acids yielding acetoacetyl-CoA: Leucine, lysine, phenylalanine, tryptophan, and tyrosine.
- Amino acids yielding pyruvate: Alanine, cysteine, glycine, serine, threonine, and tryptophan.
- Amino acids yielding α-ketoglutarate: Arginine, proline, histidine, glutamate, and glutamine.
- Amino acids yielding succinyl-CoA: Methionine, isoleucine, and valine.
- Amino acids yielding oxaloacetate: Aspartate and asparagine.
- Amino acids yielding fumarate: Phenylalanine and tyrosine.

Fate of the seven metabolic products derived from the carbon skeletons of standard amino acids

Depending on the metabolic needs of the organism, the seven key products derived from the catabolism of carbon skeletons of amino acids - pyruvate, α-ketoglutarate, succinyl-CoA, fumarate, oxaloacetate, acetyl-CoA, and acetoacetate—may serve as precursors for glucose, ketone bodies, or may be completely oxidized to CO_2 for energy production. Amino acids whose carbon skeletons are degraded into pyruvate, α-ketoglutarate, succinyl-CoA, fumarate, or oxaloacetate can enter the gluconeogenesis pathway and are termed **glucogenic amino acids**. *Exclusively glucogenic amino acids* are alanine, arginine, asparagine, aspartate, cysteine, glutamate, glutamine, glycine, histidine, methionine, proline, serine, valine.

Amino acids that are broken down into acetyl-CoA or acetoacetate (via acetoacetyl-CoA) are used for the synthesis of ketone bodies and are referred to as **ketogenic amino acids**. Leucine and lysine are the only amino acids that are exclusively ketogenic, yielding products that cannot contribute to net glucose synthesis. Some amino acids produce both glucogenic and ketogenic intermediates and are therefore classified as both glucogenic and ketogenic. Example of both **glucogenic** and **ketogenic** amino acids are isoleucine, phenylalanine, threonine, tryptophan and tyrosine.

Some human genetic disorders affecting amino acid catabolism

Many metabolic disorders, most are rare, have been described as a result of defects in amino acid metabolism especially in catabolic pathways. Some of the most commonly encountered diseases of amino acid catabolism given below:

Table 2.17 Name of some genetic disorder and associated enzyme symptoms

Medical condition	Defective process	Defective enzyme	Symptoms and effects
Albinism	Melanin synthesis from tyrosine	Tyrosine 3-mono-oxygenase (tyrosinase)	Lack of pigmentation; white hair, pink skin
Alkaptonuria	Tyrosine degradation 1,2-dioxygenase	Homogentisate	Dark pigment in urine
Homocystinuria	Methionine degradation	Cystathionine β-synthase	Faulty bone development; mental retardation
Maple syrup urine disease (branched-chain ketoaciduria)	Isoleucine, leucine, and valine degradation	Branched-chain α-keto acid dehydrogenase complex	Vomiting; convulsions; mental retardation; early death
Phenylketonuria	Conversion of phenylalanine to tyrosine	Phenylalanine hydroxylase	Neonatal vomiting; mental retardation

Although there are many hereditary errors of amino acid metabolism, *phenylketonuria* and *alkaptonuria* are the best known. **Phenylketonuria** is caused by an absence or deficiency of *phenylalanine hydroxylase*. Phenylalanine accumulates in all body fluids because it cannot be converted into tyrosine. By unknown mechanisms, this accumulation results in mental retardation. **Alkaptonuria** is an inherited metabolic disorder caused by the absence of *homogentisate oxidase*. It results in the accumulation of homogentisate. Homogentisate accumulates and is excreted in the urine, which turns dark on standing as homogentisate is oxidized and polymerized to a melanin-like substance.

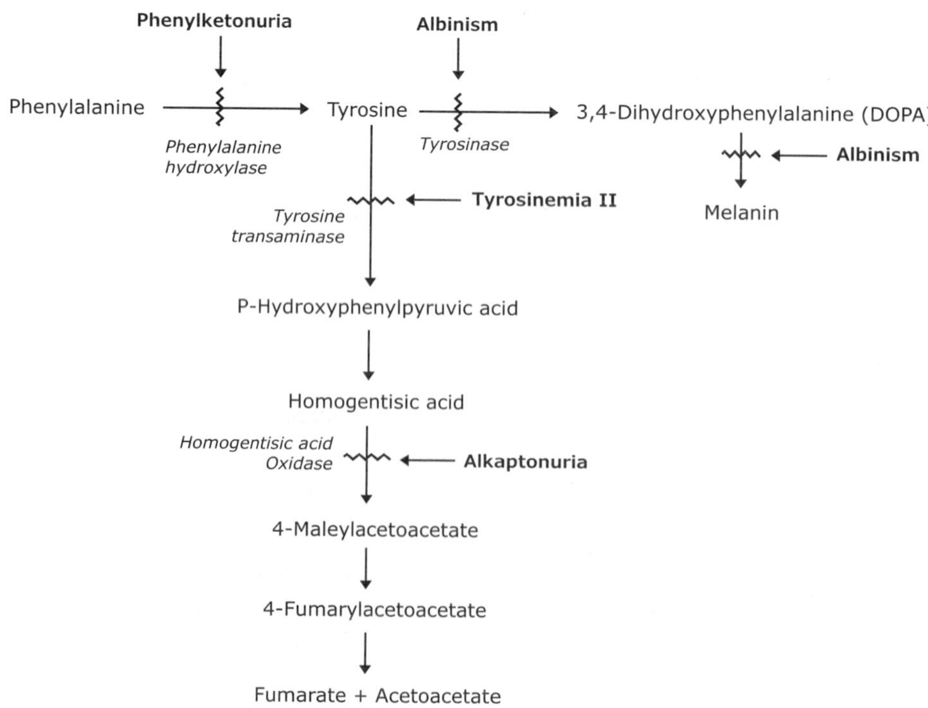

2.8.3 Molecules derived from amino acids

In addition to being the building blocks of proteins and peptides, amino acids serve as precursors of many kinds of small molecules that have important and diverse biological roles. Many important biomolecules including hormones, coenzymes, porphyrins, antibiotics, pigments, neurotransmitters are derived from amino acids.

Example of some common molecules derived from amino acids are given below:

Biomolecules	Precursor amino acid
Auxin (Indole 3-acetic acid)[1]	Tryptophan
Catecholamines (Dopamine, norepinephrine and epinephrine)[2]	Tyrosine
GABA (γ–amino butyrate)[3]	Glutamate
Serotonin[4]	Tryptophan
Histamine[5]	Histidine
Polyamines (like spermine and spermidine)	Methionine and Ornithine
Nitric oxide (Biological messenger)[6]	Arginine
Creatine (Energy buffer)	Glycine and Arginine
Lignin	Phenylalanine and Tyrosine
Porphyrin[7]	Glycine/Glutamate
Glutathione (Reducing agent)	Glycine, Glutamate and Cysteine

1. **Tryptophan** $\xrightleftharpoons[\text{Aminotransferase}]{}$ **Indole-3-pyruvate** $\xrightarrow[\text{Decarboxylase}]{}$ **Indole-3-acetate** (auxin) + $\mathbf{CO_2}$

2. **Tyrosine** $\xrightarrow[\text{Tyrosine hydroxylase}]{O_2}$ **Dopa** $\xrightarrow[\text{Decarboxylase}]{CO_2}$ **Dopamine** $\xrightarrow[\text{Dopamine }\beta\text{-hydroxylase}]{O_2}$ **Norepinephrine** $\xrightarrow[\text{Phenylethanolamine N-methyltransferase}]{O_2}$ **Epinephrine**

3. **Glutamate** $\xrightarrow[\text{Glutamate Decarboxylase}]{}$ **γ-Aminobutyrate** (GABA) + $\mathbf{CO_2}$

4. **Tryptophan** $\xrightarrow[\text{Tryptophan hydroxylase}]{O_2}$ **5-Hydroxytryptophan** $\xrightarrow[\text{Decarboxylase}]{}$ **Serotonin** + $\mathbf{CO_2}$

5. **Histidine** $\xrightarrow[\text{Histidine decarboxylase}]{}$ **Histamine** + $\mathbf{CO_2}$

6. **Arginine** $\xrightarrow[\text{Nitric oxide synthase}]{O_2}$ **Hydroxyarginine** $\xrightarrow[\text{Nitric oxide synthase}]{O_2}$ **Citrulline** + **NO**

7. **Porphyrins** are tetrapyrrole structures composed of four linked pyrrole rings. Several biologically important compounds are derived from porphyrins, including heme (a component of hemoglobin, myoglobin, and cytochromes), chlorophyll, and cobalamin (vitamin B12). In most organisms, porphyrin biosynthesis begins with the amino acid **glycine** and **succinyl-CoA**. In animals, all the nitrogen atoms in porphyrins are derived from glycine, while the carbon atoms originate from both glycine and succinate. Therefore, this pathway is commonly referred to as the succinate-glycine pathway. In contrast, plants utilize the amino acid glutamate as the precursor for porphyrin synthesis.

2.9 Nucleotide metabolism

2.9.1 Nucleotide synthesis

Nucleotides are phosphate esters of a pentose (ribose or deoxyribose) in which a purine or pyrimidine base is linked with the sugar. Nucleotides are primarily responsible for the formation of polynucleotides (nucleic acids) of the cell. However, they also act as precursors for many important compounds such as ATP, coenzyme-A that participate in a wide variety of metabolic processes. The pathways for the biosynthesis of nucleotides fall into two classes: ***de novo* pathways** and **salvage pathways**. In *de novo* (means *anew*) pathways, the nucleotide bases are synthesized from simpler compounds whereas, in *salvage pathways*, preformed bases are recovered and reconnected to a ribose unit. The salvage pathway recovers purine and pyrimidine bases released during nucleic acid turnover and degradation. The sugar of nucleotides are catabolized to generate energy, whereas the nitrogenous bases do not serve as energy sources.

***de novo* pathway:** 5-phosphoribosyl-1-pyrophosphate (PRPP) + Amino acids + ATP + CO_2 + ... ⟶ Nucleotide

Salvage pathway: PRPP + Base ⟶ Nucleotide

Both *de novo* and *salvage pathways* lead to the synthesis of *ribonucleotides*. All deoxyribonucleotides are synthesized from the corresponding ribonucleotides. The deoxyribose sugar is generated by the reduction of ribose within a fully formed nucleotide.

de novo synthesis of purine ribonucleotide

In *de novo* pathways, the framework for a pyrimidine base is assembled first and then attached to ribose. In contrast, the framework for a purine base is synthesized piece by piece directly onto a ribose ring. The purine ring is assembled from a variety of precursors: glutamine (N3 and N9), glycine (C4, C5 and N7), aspartate (N1), N^{10}-formyltetrahydrofolate (C2 and C8), and CO_2 (C6).

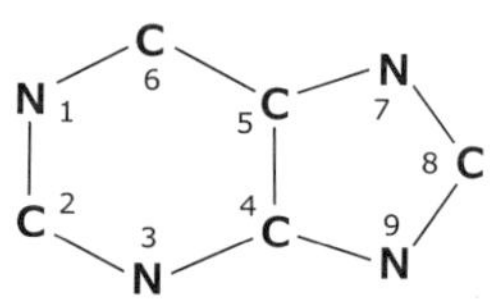

Purine ring

⟶

N1	From aspartate
C2 and C8	From N^{10}-formyl tetrahydrofolate
N3 and N9	From glutamine
N7	From glycine
C6	From CO_2

Figure 2.94 Sources of the individual atoms in the purine ring.

The purine bases are assembled onto a ribose ring. The pathway begins with 5-phosphoribosyl-1-pyrophosphate (**PRPP**), which is synthesized from ribose-5-phosphate after the addition of pyrophosphate from ATP. PRPP provides the foundation on which the bases are constructed step-by-step. The formation of the purine base is completed in ten steps.

Step 1: Acquisition of purine atom N9 — The initial committed step is the displacement of pyrophosphate by ammonia to produce *5-phosphoribosyl-1-amine*. Enzyme **amidophosphoribosyltransferase** catalyzes this reaction. This enzyme's activity is inhibited by glutamine analogs **azaserine** and **acivicin**, which are used as an antitumor agent.

Step 2: Acquisition of purine atoms C4, C5, and N7 — This step involves the addition of three atoms from glycine. The carboxylate group of a glycine residue is activated by phosphorylation and then coupled to the amino group of 5-phosphoribosyl-1-amine, yielding *glycinamide ribonucleotide* (or **GAR**). This step is catalyzed by *glycinamide ribonucleotide synthetase* (**GAR synthetase**) via its ATP-dependent condensation of the glycine carboxyl group.

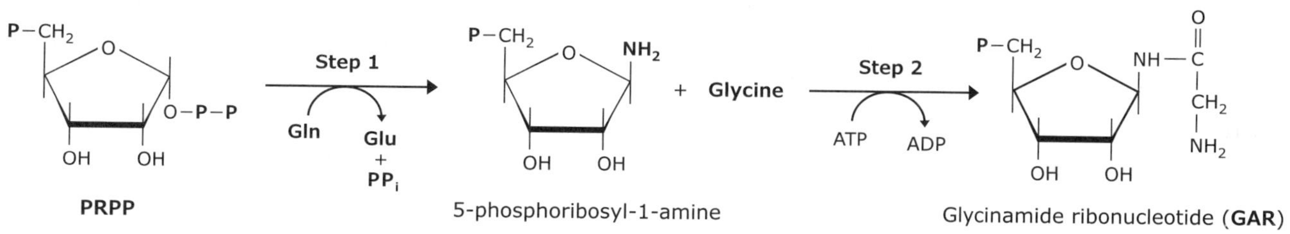

Step 3: Acquisition of purine atom C8 — Glycinamide ribonucleotide's free α-amino group is formylated to yield *formylglycinamide ribonucleotide* (**FGAR**). The formyl donor in the reaction is N^{10}-formyltetrahydrofolate and reaction is catalyzed by **GAR transformylase.**

Step 4: Acquisition of purine atom N3 — An ATP dependent reaction in which the amide amino group of glutamine is transferred to the growing purine ring to form *formylglycinamidine ribonucleotide* (**FGAM**). This step is catalyzed by *FGAR amidotransferase* (also known as **FGAM synthetase**).

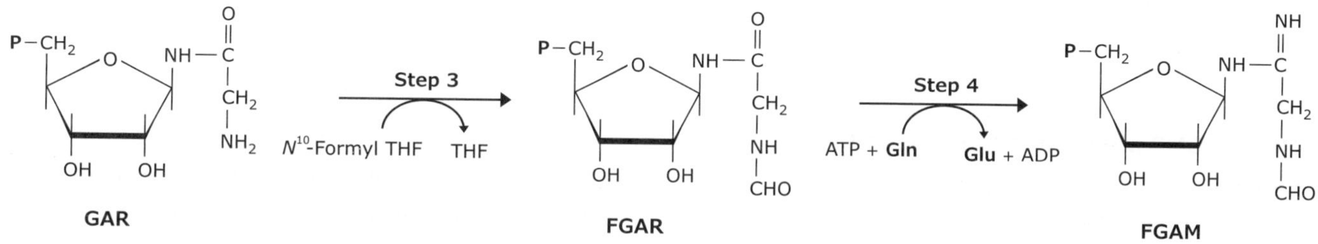

Step 5: Formation of the purine imidazole ring — Formylglycinamidine ribonucleotide (FGAM), cyclizes to form the five-membered *imidazole ring* found in purines. Although this cyclization is likely to be favorable thermodynamically, a molecule of ATP is consumed to ensure irreversibility. Because the product is *5-aminoimidazole ribonucleotide* (or **AIR**), this enzyme is called **AIR synthetase**.

Step 6: Acquisition of C6 — Carbon dioxide is added at the C4 position of the imidazole ring by **AIR carboxylase** in an ATP-dependent reaction; the carbon of CO_2 will become C6 of the purine ring. The product is *4-carboxy-5-aminoimidazole ribonucleotide* (**CAIR**).

Step 7: Acquisition of N1 — The imidazole carboxylate group is phosphorylated again and the phosphate group is displaced by the amino group of aspartate. ATP hydrolysis drives the condensation of aspartate with CAIR. The product is *N-succinyl-5-aminoimidazole-4-carboxamide ribonucleotide* (**SAICAR**). Enzyme **SAICAR synthetase** catalyzes this reaction.

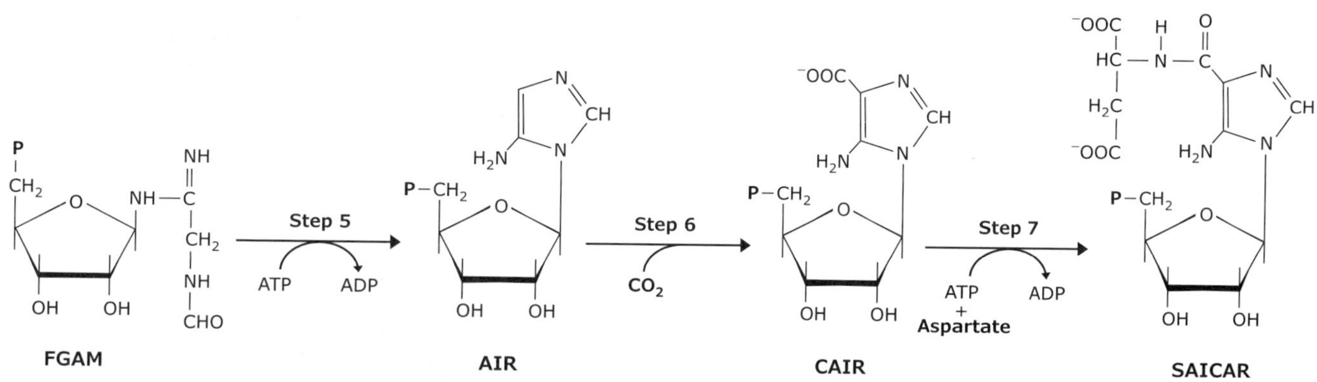

Step 8, 9 and **10**: Three more steps complete the ring construction.

Step 8 (elimination of fumarate): this step removes the four carbons of aspartate as fumarate in a nonhydrolytic cleavage. The product is *5-aminoimidazole-4-carboxamide ribonucleotide* (**AICAR**) and the enzyme is **adenylosuccinate lyase.**

Step 9 (acquisition of C2): There is a addition of the formyl carbon of N^{10}-formyl-THF as the ninth and last atom necessary for forming the purine nucleus. The enzyme is called **AICAR transformylase**; the products are THF and *N-formylaminoimidazole-4-carboxamide ribonucleotide* (**FAICAR**).

Step 10 (cyclization to form IMP): This step involves dehydration and ring closure to form the purine nucleotide IMP. The enzyme is **IMP cyclohydrolase** (also known as *IMP synthase* and *inosinicase*).

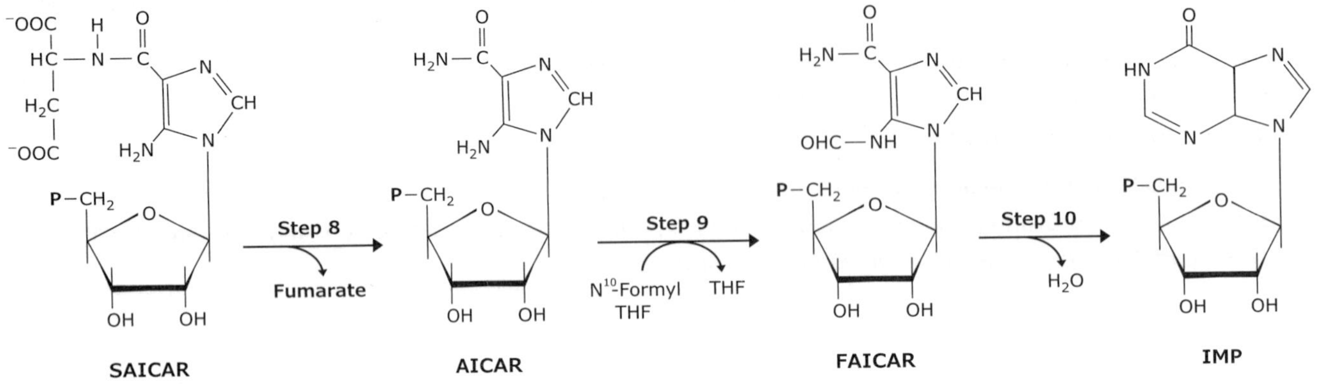

AMP and GMP are formed from the IMP

The conversion of inosine monophosphate (**IMP**) to either adenosine monophosphate (**AMP**) or guanosine monophosphate (**GMP**) utilizes a two-step, energy-requiring pathway. Conversion of IMP to AMP requires the insertion of an amino group derived from aspartate. GMP is formed by the oxidation of IMP at C2, followed by the addition of an amino group derived from glutamine. Note that the synthesis of AMP requires GTP as an energy source, whereas the synthesis of GMP requires ATP.

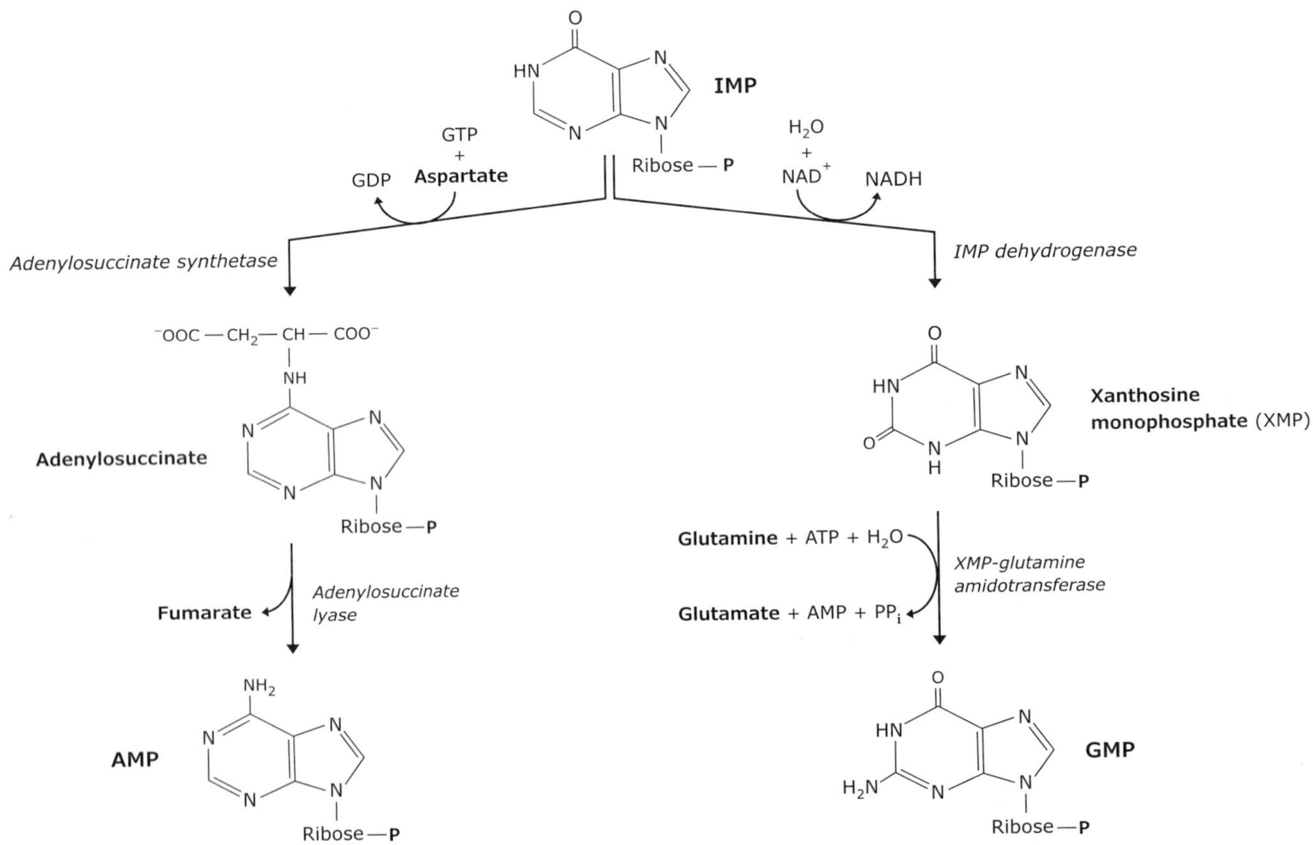

Figure 2.95 Conversion of IMP to AMP (adenylate) and GMP (guanylate).

Conversion of nucleoside monophosphates to nucleoside diphosphates and triphosphates

The products of *de novo* purine biosynthesis are the nucleoside monophosphates, AMP and GMP. These nucleotides are converted by successive phosphorylation reactions into their metabolically prominent triphosphate forms, ATP and GTP. The first phosphorylation, to give the nucleoside diphosphate forms, is carried out by two base-specific, ATP-dependent kinases, **adenylate kinase** and **guanylate kinase**. These nucleoside monophosphate kinases do not discriminate between ribose and deoxyribose in the substrate.

Enzyme **adenylate kinase**: AMP + ATP $\rightleftharpoons$ 2 ADP

Enzyme **guanylate kinase**: GMP + ATP $\rightleftharpoons$ GDP + ADP

Nucleoside diphosphates are converted to the corresponding triphosphates by enzyme **nucleoside diphosphate kinase**. This enzyme is not specific for base (purine or pyrimidine) or sugar (ribose or deoxyribose).

NDP + ATP $\rightleftharpoons$ NTP + ADP

de novo synthesis of pyrimidine ribonucleotide

In *de novo* synthesis of pyrimidines, the six-membered ring is synthesized first and then it is attached to ribose-5-phosphate to form a *pyrimidine nucleotide*. Pyrimidine rings are synthesized from *carbamoyl phosphate* and *aspartate*. Isotopic labeling experiments have shown that atoms N1, C4, C5 and C6 of the pyrimidine ring are derived from *aspartic acid*. The C2 and N3 is contributed by *carbamoyl phosphate*. UMP is synthesized first. CTP and UTP are derived from UMP.

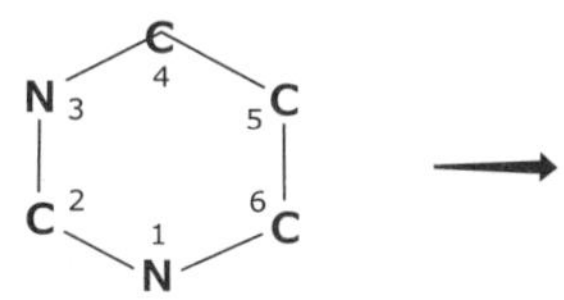

Pyrimidine ring

N3 and C2 — From carbamoyl phosphate

N1, C4, C5 and C6 — From aspartate

Figure 2.96 *de novo* synthesis of pyrimidine ring. The C2 and N3 atoms in the pyrimidine ring come from carbamoyl phosphate, whereas the other atoms of the ring come from aspartate.

The formation of the pyrimidine base is completed in following six steps.

Step 1: Synthesis of carbamoyl phosphate — The precursor of *carbamoyl phosphate* is bicarbonate and glutamine. This reaction is ATP dependent and catalyzed by cytosolic enzyme *carbamoyl phosphate synthetase* II. This reaction consumes two molecules of ATP: one provides a phosphate group and the other energizes the reaction. Carbamoyl phosphate is also synthesized in the urea cycle. In that reaction, catalyzed by the mitochondrial enzyme carbamoyl phosphate synthetase I, ammonia is the nitrogen source.

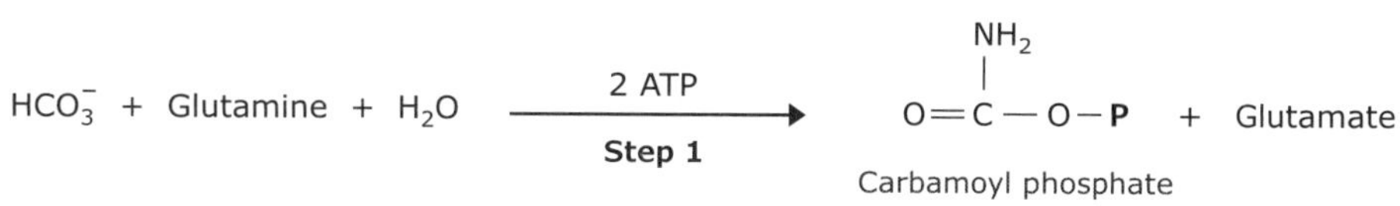

Step 2: Synthesis of carbamoyl aspartate — There is a formation of carbamoyl aspartate due to the condensation of carbamoyl phosphate with aspartate. This reaction is catalyzed by enzyme *aspartate transcarbamoylase* (ATCase).

Step 3: Ring closure to form dihydroorotate — Carbamoyl aspartate converted into dihydroorotate due to an intramolecular condensation. This step is catalyzed by enzyme *dihydroorotase*.

Step 4: Oxidation of dihydroorotate — Dihydroorotate is irreversibly oxidized to *orotate* by an enzyme *dihydroorotate dehydrogenase*. This enzyme is located on the outer surface of the inner mitochondrial membrane.

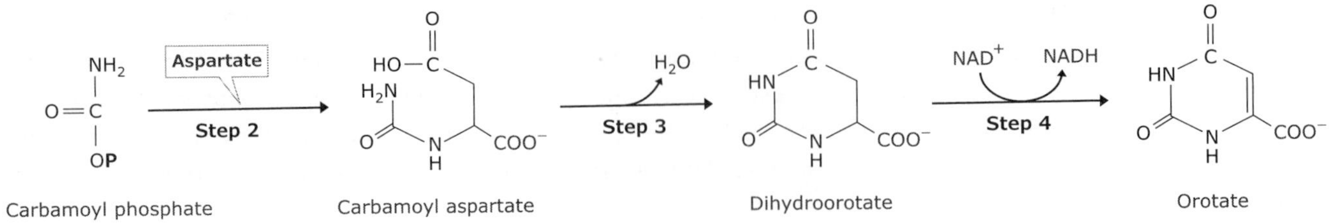

Step 5: Acquisition of ribose phosphate moiety — Orotate reacts with PRPP to yield *orotidylate or* orotidine-5′-monophosphate (**OMP**) in a reaction catalyzed by *orotate phosphoribosyl transferase*. The reaction, which is driven by the hydrolysis of the PP_i, fixes the anomeric form of pyrimidine nucleotides in the β configuration.

Step 6: Decarboxylation to form UMP — The final reaction of the pathway is the decarboxylation of OMP by enzyme *OMP decarboxylase* to form *uridylate* or *uridine monophosphate* (**UMP**).

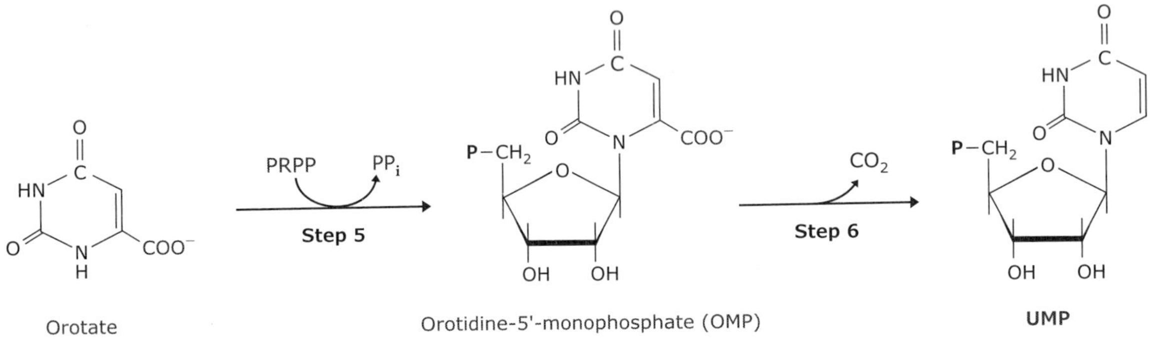

Synthesis of UTP

UMP synthesis leads to formation of the ribonucleotides—UTP. First, UDP is formed from UMP via an ATP dependent *nucleoside monophosphate kinase*. Then, UTP is formed by *nucleoside diphosphate kinase*.

Nucleoside monophosphate kinase: UMP + ATP $\rightleftharpoons$ UDP + ADP

Nucleoside diphosphate kinase: UDP + ATP $\rightleftharpoons$ UTP + ADP

Synthesis of CTP from UTP

Amination of UTP at the 6-position gives cytidylate or cytidine triphosphate (**CTP**). The enzyme **CTP synthetase** (or cytidylate synthetase) is a glutamine amidotransferase. ATP hydrolysis provides the energy to drive the reaction. Cytidine is synthesized from the uracil base of the UMP, but UMP is converted into UTP before the synthesis can take place. After uridine triphosphate has been formed, it can be transformed into CTP by the replacement of a carbonyl group by an amino group.

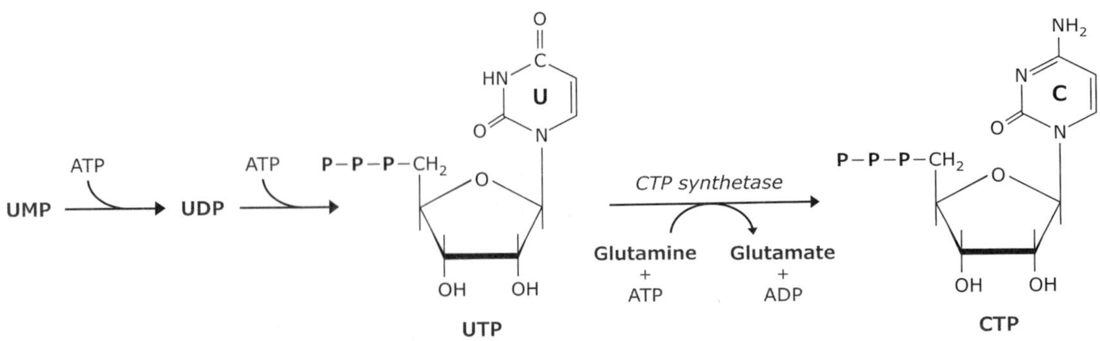

Figure 2.97 Synthesis of CTP from UMP.

Formation of deoxyribonucleotides

DNA differs chemically from RNA in two major respects: (1) Its nucleotides contain 2′-deoxyribose residues rather than ribose residues, and (2) it contains the base thymine (5-methyluracil) rather than uracil.

Deoxyribonucleotides are synthesized from their corresponding ribonucleotides by the reduction of their C2′ position. These conversions are catalyzed by enzyme **ribonucleotide reductase**. The reduction of the D-ribose of a ribonucleoside diphosphate to 2′-deoxy-D-ribose requires electrons. These electrons come from NADPH, but not directly. One carrier of reducing power linking NADPH with the reductase is **thioredoxin**.

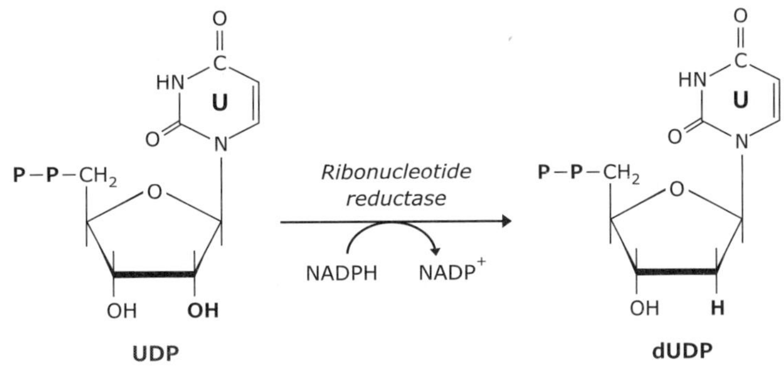

Thioredoxin has pairs of —SH groups that carry hydrogen atoms from NADPH to the ribonucleoside diphosphate. Its oxidized (disulfide) form is reduced by NADPH in a reaction catalyzed by **thioredoxin reductase**, and reduced thioredoxin is then used by ribonucleotide reductase to reduce the *nucleoside diphosphates* to *deoxyribonucleoside diphosphates*.

Synthesis of dTMP

DNA contains thymine rather than uracil. The immediate precursor of dTMP is dUMP. Conversion of dUMP to dTMP is catalyzed by **thymidylate synthase**. dTMP is formed by *methylation* of dUMP. Chemotherapeutic agent **fluorouracil** acts as inhibitor of thymidylate synthase. Fluorouracil itself is not the enzyme inhibitor. In the cell, salvage pathways convert it to the deoxynucleoside monophosphate FdUMP, which binds to and inactivates the enzyme. Inhibition by FdUMP is a classic example of mechanism-based enzyme inactivation.

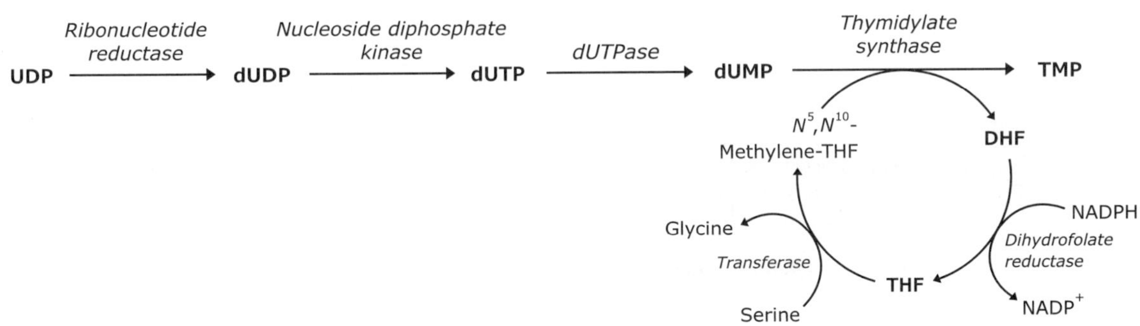

The donor of a methylene group in this reaction is N^5, N^{10}-methylenetetrahydrofolate, which is converted into dihydrofolate (**DHF**). Tetrahydrofolate (**THF**) is regenerated by the reduction of DHF by NADPH in the presence of the enzyme **dihydrofolate reductase**. Chemotherapeutic agents like **methotrexate** (*amethopterin*) and **aminopterin** inhibit the activity of dihydrofolate reductase. These folate analogs act as a competitive inhibitor and used as anticancer drugs.

Salvage pathways

Purines released from the normal turnover of cellular nucleic acids or that are obtained from the diet can be can be attached to PRPP to form purine nucleoside monophosphates. This is referred to as the *salvage pathway* for purines. This pathway involves two enzymes: **adenine phosphoribosyltransferase** (*APRT*) and **hypoxanthine-guanine phosphoribosyltransferase** (*HGPRT*). Both enzymes utilize PRPP as the source of the ribose 5-phosphate group.

Adenine phosphoribosyltransferase catalyzes the formation of adenylate

Adenine + PRPP ⟶ **Adenylate** + PP_i

whereas enzyme *hypoxanthine-guanine phosphoribosyltransferase* (*HGPRT*) catalyzes the formation of guanylate as well as *inosinate* (inosine monophosphate, IMP), a precursor of guanylate and adenylate.

Guanine + PRPP ⟶ **Guanylate** + PP_i

Hypoxanthine + PRPP ⟶ **Inosinate** + PP_i

Similar salvage pathways exist for *pyrimidines*. For example, thymine released from degraded DNA is salvaged in two steps. First, thymine is converted into the nucleoside thymidine by enzyme *thymidine phosphorylase*. Thymidine is then converted into a nucleotide by *thymidine kinase*.

$$\textbf{Thymine} + \textbf{Deoxyribose-1-phosphate} \xrightarrow{-P_i} \textbf{Thymidine} \xrightarrow{+\text{ATP}} \textbf{TMP} + \textbf{ADP}$$

2.9.2 Nucleotide catabolism

Degradation of purine nucleotides

Purine nucleotides are sequentially degraded by the removal or alteration of portions of the nucleotide. The end product of purine degradation in humans is **uric acid**, which is excreted in the urine. Below is a summary of the steps in the production of uric acid:

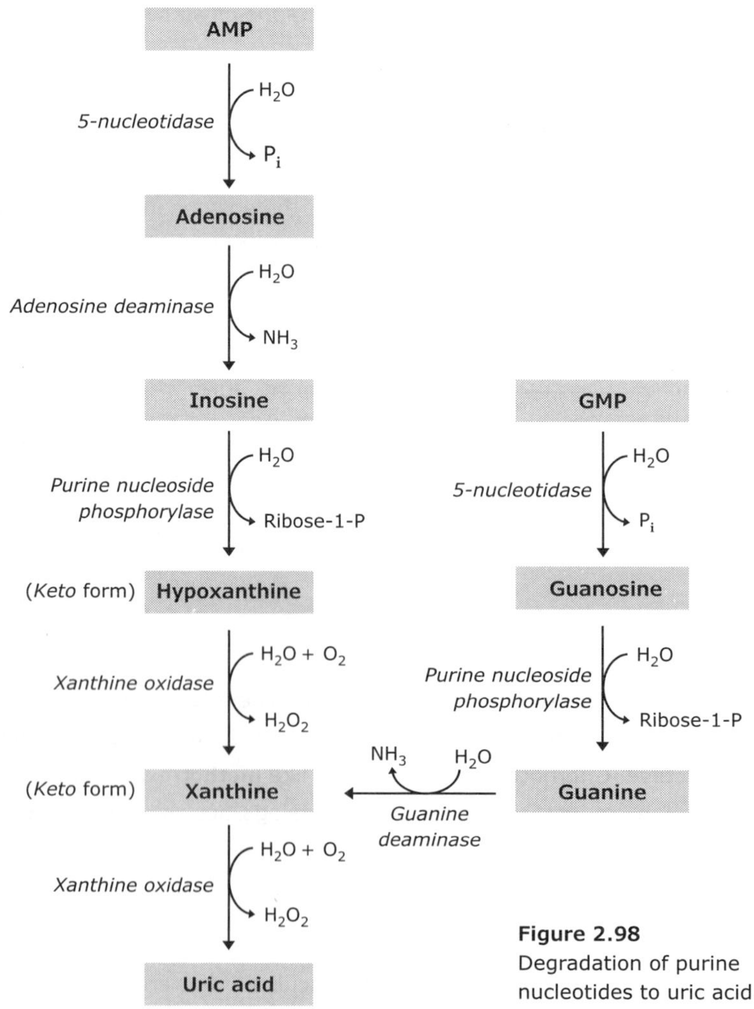

Figure 2.98
Degradation of purine nucleotides to uric acid.

1. An amino group is removed from AMP to produce IMP or from adenosine to produce inosine.
2. IMP and GMP are converted into their nucleoside forms – inosine and guanosine.

3. Inosine and guanosine converted into their respective purine bases, hypoxanthine and guanine.
4. Guanine is deaminated to form xanthine.
5. Hypoxanthine is oxidized to xanthine, which is further oxidized to uric acid, the final product of human purine degradation. Uric acid is then excreted in the urine.

Mammals other than primates oxidize uric acid further to **allantoin**, which, in teleost (bony) fish, may be further degraded to **allantoic acid**. Cartilaginous fish and amphibians further degrade allantoic acid to **urea** prior to excretion. Finally, marine invertebrates decompose urea to **ammonia**.

Uric acid ⟶ Allantoin ⟶ Allantoic acid ⟶ Urea ⟶ Ammonia

Degradation of pyrimidine nucleotides

The pathways for degradation of pyrimidines generally lead to ammonia production and thus to **urea** synthesis. Unlike the purine rings, which are not cleaved in human cells, the pyrimidine ring can be opened and degraded to highly water-soluble structures, such as β-aminoisobutyrate, β-alanine.

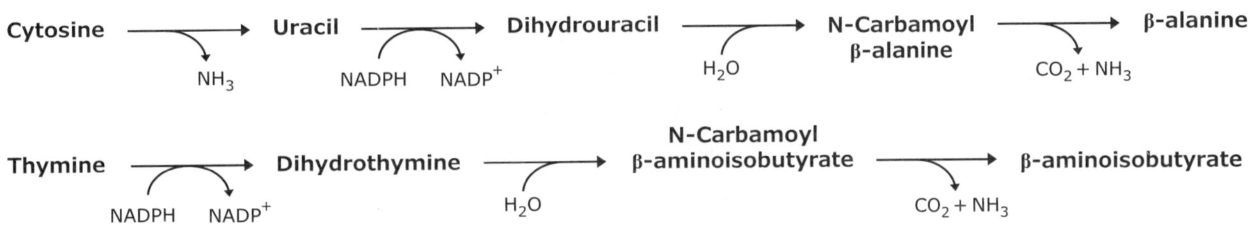

Figure 2.99 Catabolism of pyrimidine.

Box 2.6 Disease associated with nucleotide metabolism

Severe combined immunodeficiency (SCID): SCID is a group of rare genetic disorders characterized by a severe deficiency in the immune system, leaving affected individuals highly susceptible to infections. One type of SCID is caused by a deficiency in the enzyme **adenosine deaminase** (ADA), which plays a crucial role in the development and function of T and B-lymphocytes. Enzyme ADA deficiency leads to an increase in the cellular concentration of dATP, which acts as a strong inhibitor of *ribonucleotide reductase*. High levels of dATP produce a general deficiency of other dNTPs in T-lymphocytes. The basis of B-lymphocytes toxicity is less clear.

Gout: In human, urate is the final product of purine degradation and is excreted in the urine. High serum levels of urate induce *gout*. It causes inflammation of the joints by precipitation as sodium urate crystals. The treatment of gout includes the use of the drug **allopurinol**. This drug has a structure similar to *hypoxanthine* and acts by inhibiting the enzyme *xanthine oxidase*. Xanthine oxidase, a molybdenum- and iron-containing flavoprotein, oxidizes hypoxanthine to *xanthine* and then to *uric acid*. Hence inhibition of the activity of xanthine oxidase inhibits uric acid synthesis.

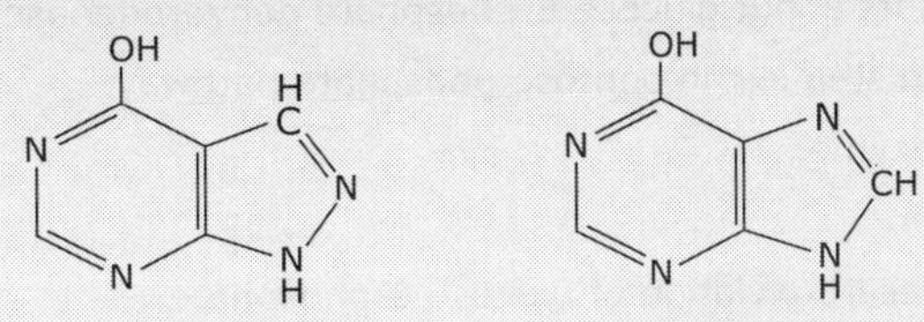

Allopurinol   Hypoxanthine (enol form)

Lesch-Nyhan syndrome: This genetic disorder is caused by a deficiency of the salvage enzyme hypoxanthine-guanine phosphoribosyl-transferase (**HGPRT**). The biochemical consequences of the virtual absence of HGPRT are an elevated concentration of PRPP, a marked increase in the rate of purine biosynthesis by the *de novo pathway*, and overproduction of urate. Children with deficiency display compulsive, self-destructive behavior. They also show signs of mental retardation. In addition, because there is less salvaging of bases, more uric acid is produced, causing gout.

Self Test

Q1. Incubation of a cell extract containing all enzymes of glycolysis with [γ^{32}P] ATP and unlabeled inorganic phosphate, results in the formation of which of the following labeled compounds (assume that pyruvate kinase is inactivated)?

P. Glucose-6-^{32}phosphate

Q. (3-^{32}P)-phosphoglycerate

R. (1-phospho-3-^{32}phospho)-bisphosphoglycerate

S. (1-phospho-6-^{32}phospho)-fructose bisphosphate

a. P and R
b. P, Q and R
c. Q and S
d. only S

Q2. One of the carbon atoms of a glucose molecule is [^{14}C]-labeled. If $^{14}CO_2$ is released during the conversion of pyruvate to acetyl-CoA, which carbon atom of glucose was radiolabeled?

a. C3 but not C4
b. C3 or C4
c. C1 or C6
d. C1 but not C6

Q3. 2,4-dinitrophenol uncouples electron transport from ATP synthesis in mitochondria by

a. causing dissipation of the proton gradient generated by the electron transport.
b. allowing the proton translocating function of ATP synthase while inhibiting its ATP synthesizing activity.
c. activating a second proton pump that sends back the protons into the mitochondrial matrix.
d. neutralizing the proton gradient by absorbing the protons generated during the electron transport.

Q4. Choose the mismatch

Inhibitor	Function
a. Malonate	Prevents oxidation of succinate in Krebs cycle
b. Cyanide	Inhibits cytochrome oxidase in ETC
c. Oligomycin	Inhibits ATP synthase
d. Rotenone	Blocks complex III in ETC

Q5. Under normal conditions, as electrons flow down the electron transport chain of the mitochondria

P. NADH and $FADH_2$ are oxidized

Q. the pH of the matrix increases

R. an electrochemical gradient is formed

S. protons are pumped against the gradient

a. P, Q and R
b. Q, R and S
c. P, R and S
d. P, Q, R and S

Q6. Which of the following statements about glucose 6-phosphate dehydrogenase are *correct*?

P. It catalyzes the rate limiting step in the pentose phosphate pathway.

Q. It is a $NADP^+$ dependent enzyme.

R. It contains TPP as a cofactor.

S. It catalyzes the oxidative decarboxylation of glucose 6-phosphate.

a. P and Q
b. R and S
c. P and R
d. Q and R

Q7. Which of the following *best* defines substrate-level phosphorylation?

a. Transfer of a phosphate group from ATP to a protein.
b. Generation of ATP by using the proton motive force.
c. Direct transfer of a phosphate group from a high-energy intermediate to ADP.
d. Addition of phosphate to ADP using light energy.

Q8. Which of the following statements about glycogen storage are *incorrect*?

P. Glycogen is stored in muscle and liver.

Q. Glycogen is a major source of stored energy in the brain.

R. Glycogen reserves are less rapidly depleted than fat reserves during starvation.

S. Glycogen storage occurs in the form of dense granules in the cytosol of cells.

a. P and Q
b. P and R
c. Q and R
d. Q and S

Q9. Which of the following statements *correctly* describe what happens when acetyl-CoA is abundant?

P. Pyruvate carboxylase is activated.

Q. Phosphoenolpyruvate carboxykinase is activated.

R. Phosphofructokinase is activated.

S. If ATP levels are high, oxaloacetate is diverted to gluconeogenesis.

a. P and Q
b. Q and R
c. Q and S
d. P and S

Q10. Which of the following statements about gluconeogenesis are *true*?

P. It occurs actively in the muscle during periods of exercise.

Q. It occurs actively in the liver during periods of exercise or fasting.

R. It occurs actively in adipose tissue during feeding.

S. It occurs actively in the kidney during periods of fasting.

a. P and Q
b. Q and R
c. Q and S
d. P and S

Q11. Which of the followings is *not correct* about fatty acid degradation and biosynthesis?

	Degradation	Biosynthesis
a. Location of pathway in the cell	Mitochondrion	Cytosol
b. Electron acceptor or donor used	FAD, NAD^+	NADPH
c. Participation of CO_2	No	Yes
d. Carrier of intermediate acyl groups	ACP-SH	CoA-SH

Q12. The physiological roles of bile salts include which of the following?

P. They aid in the digestion of lipid.

Q. They facilitate the absorption of sugars.

R. They facilitate the absorption of lipid.

S. They provide a means for cholesterol digestion.

a. P and Q
b. P and R
c. Q and S
d. P, Q and S

Q13. All of the following statements about acetyl-CoA carboxylase are correct *except*

a. it catalyzes the ATP dependent carboxylation.

b. its activity is biotin dependent.

c. its activity is inhibited by cAMP-mediated phosphorylation.

d. it is activated by both palmitoyl-CoA and citrate.

Q14. Which of the following statements are *correct*?

P. Hydroxyurea inhibits activity of ribonucleotide reductase.

Q. Methotrexate and aminopterin are analogs of dihydrofolate and inhibitors of dihydrofolate reductase.

R. The conversion of IMP to AMP requires GTP and aspartate.

S. The conversion of IMP to GMP requires GTP.

a. P and S
b. P and R
c. P, Q and R
d. P, Q, R and S

Q15. Which of the following are *correct* about C4 cycle and C4 plants?

P. Phosphoenolpyruvate carboxylase is located in cytosol.

Q. C3 cycle occurs in the chloroplasts of bundle sheath cells.

R. C4 cycle is a CO_2 enrichment cycle.

S. C3 cycle occurs in the chloroplasts of mesophyll cells.

a. P and Q
b. Q and R
c. P, Q and R
d. R and S

Q16. Which of the following statements are *correct* about photosynthesis and photosynthetic organisms?

P. In the presence of sunlight, pH is lowest in the spaces enclosed by the thylakoid membrane.

Q. DCMU inhibits photosynthesis by inhibiting electron flow from Q_B to Cyt $b_6 f$.

R. Cyanobacteria differ from purple photosynthetic bacteria because they produce oxygen during photosynthesis.

S. Plastocyanin is a mobile electron carrier between cytochrome $b_6 f$ complex and PSI.

a. P and S
b. Q and R
c. P, R and S
d. P, Q, R and S

Q17. Which of the following statements about noncyclic photophosphorylation in chloroplast are *correct*?

1. It can be uncoupled from electron flow by agents that dissipate the proton gradient.
2. Difference in pH between luminal and stromal side of the thylakoid membrane is about 3 units.
3. Luminal side of the thylakoid membrane has a higher pH than the stromal side.
4. Number of ATPs formed per oxygen molecule is about three.

a. 1, 3 and 4
b. 2, 3 and 4
c. 1, 2 and 4
d. 1, 2, 3 and 4

Q18. The difference between the PMF across the inner mitochondrial membrane and across the thylakoid membrane is that

a. the first is mainly due to potential difference, while the second is largely due to pH gradient.
b. the first is mainly due to pH gradient, while the second is largely due to potential difference.
c. it is due to an electron transport system in the first case, but not the second.
d. it drives the synthesis of ATP in the first case but not in the second.

Q19. Precursors of the atoms in the purine skeleton are

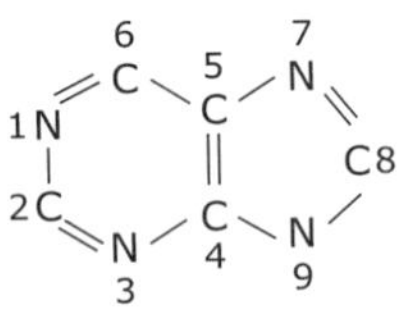

a. N1–Asp; C2 and C8–formate; N3 and N9–guanidine of Arg; C4, C5 and N7–Gly; C6–CO_2.
b. N1–Asp; C2 and C8–citrate; N3 and N9–amide nitrogen of Gln; C4, C5 and N7–Gly; C6–CO_2.
c. N1–Asp; C2 and C8–formate; N3 and N9–amide nitrogen of Gln; C4, C5 and N7–Gly; C6–CO_2.
d. N1–Glu; C and C8–acetate; N3 and N9–amide nitrogen of Asn; C4, C5 and N7–Gly; C6–CO_2.

Q20. Choose the *incorrect* statement.

a. Gluconeogenesis occurs in liver and to a smaller extent in kidney in animals.
b. Amino acids leucine and lysine does not participate in gluconeogenesis.
c. During glycogenolysis terminal glucose residue removes from non-reducing end.
d. Glycogen phosphorylase, an enzyme involved in glycogenolysis requires biotin as cofactor.

ANSWER KEY

01. b	02. b	03. a	04. d	05. d	06. a	07. c	08. c	09. d	10. c
11. d	12. b	13. d	14. c	15. c	16. d	17. c	18. a	19. c	20. d

3 Cell Structure and Functions

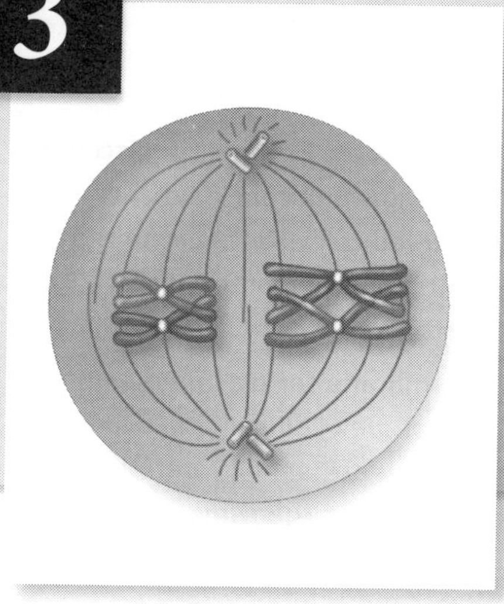

SUBJECT FOCUS

A great diversity of organisms exists on Earth, which can be classified into two broad categories: **cellular organisms** and **non-cellular organisms**. *Cellular organisms* are made up of one or many cells, whereas non-cellular organisms lack cells or cell-like structures. Cellular organisms are further subdivided into three distinct domains of life: **Bacteria** (or Eubacteria), **Archaea**, and **Eukarya**. Bacteria and Archaea are classified as **prokaryotes**, characterized by the absence of a nucleus within the cell. The domain Eukarya includes all **eukaryotes**, characterized by the presence of a nucleus within the cell. This domain encompasses *protists*, *fungi*, *plants*, and *animals*. Both prokaryotes and eukaryotes are cellular organisms. In contrast, **viruses** and **viroids** are non-cellular organisms because they lack cells or cell-like structures.

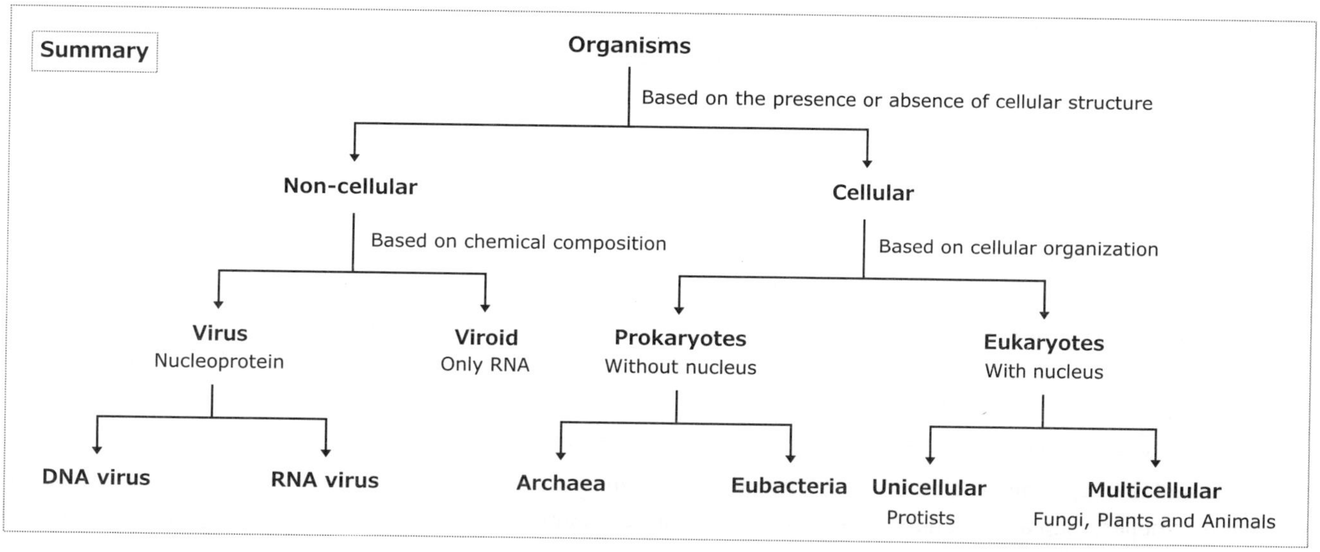

3.1 What is a cell?

The basic *structural* and *functional* unit of cellular organisms is the **cell**. In 1665, Robert Hooke first discovered cells in a piece of cork. The word 'cell' is derived from the Latin word 'cellula,' meaning small compartment. Hooke published his findings in his famous work, **Micrographia**. However, Hooke only observed cell walls because the cork cells were dead and lacked cytoplasmic contents. Antonie van Leeuwenhoek was the first person to observe living cells under a microscope, referring to them as '**animalcules**,' meaning little animals.

What is a cell? Broadly, a cell is an aqueous compartment surrounded by a cell membrane (or plasma membrane) that is capable of independent existence and performing the essential functions of life. Cellular organisms may consist of one cell (**unicellular**) or many cells (**multicellular**). Unicellular organisms are simple, performing all functions within that one cell. Most prokaryotes are unicellular. In contrast, multicellular organisms are complex, with specialized cells for specific functions. Most eukaryotic organisms are multicellular.

On the basis of the internal architecture, all cells can be subdivided into two major classes, *prokaryotic cells* and *eukaryotic cells*. Cells that have unit membrane-bound nuclei are called **eukaryotic cells**, whereas cells that lack a unit membrane-bound nucleus are **prokaryotic cells**. Eukaryotic cells have a much more complex intracellular organization with internal membranes as compared to prokaryotic cells. Besides the nucleus, the eukaryotic cells have sub cellular single or double unit membrane-bound **organelles** (*little organs*) like the endoplasmic reticulum, Golgi complex, lysosomes, mitochondria, microbodies and vacuoles. The region of the cell lying between the plasma membrane and the nucleus is the **cytoplasm**, comprising the **cytosol** (or *cytoplasmic matrix*) and the **organelles**. The prokaryotic cells lack such unit membrane-bound organelles.

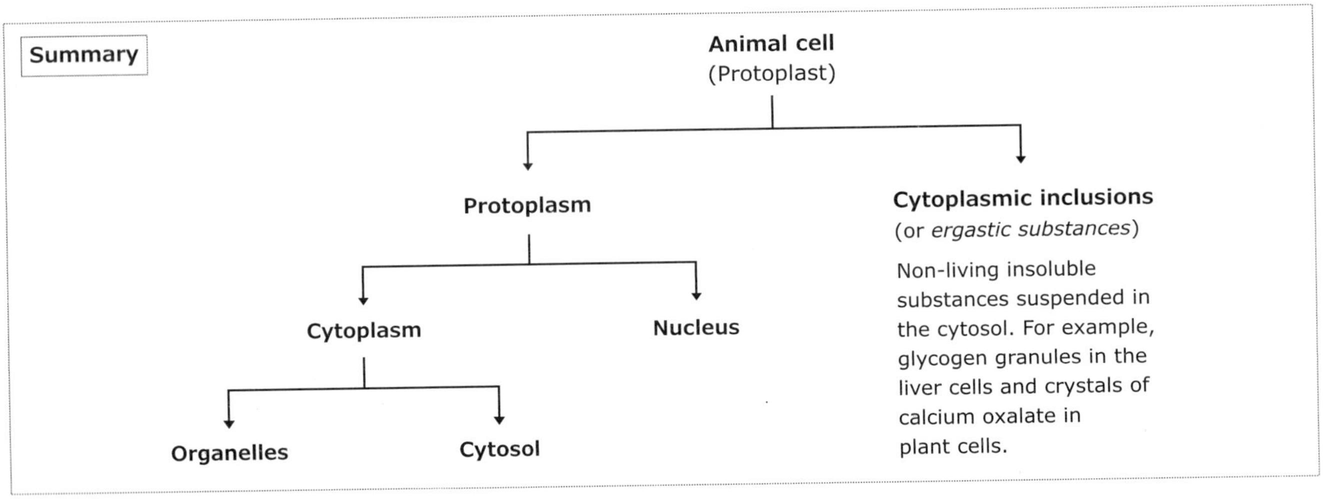

A living cell functions as a biochemical factory, importing, synthesizing, using, exporting, and degrading a variety of chemicals. Numerous chemical reactions occur within the cell, and the sum of these reactions represents the cell's **metabolism**. Cells or cellular organisms can be classified based on how they obtain energy and carbon. There are two broad categories based on *energy* sources: *phototrophs* and *chemotrophs*. **Phototrophs** use light as their energy source, whereas **chemotrophs** obtain energy from the oxidation of chemical compounds (either organic or inorganic). Similarly, cells or cellular organisms can be classified based on the nature of their *carbon* sources: *autotrophs* and *heterotrophs*. **Autotrophs** use inorganic carbon from carbon dioxide as their sole or principal carbon source, while **heterotrophs** use reduced, preformed organic molecules as their carbon source.

Chemical composition of cells: Cells are primarily composed of about 25-30 elements with relatively low atomic numbers. A few of these elements constitute the majority of the cellular mass. The most abundant elements are hydrogen, oxygen, nitrogen, and carbon, which together account for approximately 98% of the total cellular mass. These elements are crucial components of biomolecules and play essential roles in the overall functioning of the cell.

Cytosolic and non-cytosolic region of cells: The **cytosolic region** includes everything inside the cell membrane but outside organelles such as the endoplasmic reticulum and lysosomes, while the **non-cytosolic region** encompasses both the *extracellular* region outside the cell and *intracellular* regions within membrane-bound organelles such as the lumen of the endoplasmic reticulum and the mitochondrial matrix.

Oxidizing and reducing environments: A **reducing environment** is a chemical environment that promotes reduction reactions, where substances gain electrons. This type of environment generally has a high concentration of *reducing agents*. In contrast, an **oxidizing environment** is rich in *oxidizing agents* and favors oxidation reactions, where substances lose electrons. Typically, a cell's cytosolic region is characterized by a reducing environment.

Cell theory

In 1839, Schleiden, a German botanist, and Schwann, a British zoologist, led to the development of the *cell theory* or *cell doctrine*. According to this theory, *all living things are made up of cells* and *cell is the basic structural and functional unit of life*. In 1855, Rudolf Virchow proposed an important extension of cell theory that *all living cells arise from pre-existing cells* (*omnis cellula e cellula*). The cell theory holds true for all cellular organisms. Noncellular organisms such as virus do not obey cell theory. Over the time, the theory has continued to evolve. The modern cell theory includes the following components:

- All cellular organisms are made up of one or more cells.
- The cell is the structural and functional unit of life.
- All cells arise from pre-existing cells by division.
- Cells acquire and utilize energy.
- Cells evolve with time.
- Cells are able to respond to stimuli.
- Cells contain genetic materials (in the form of DNA) which is passed from cell to cell.
- All cells have basically the same chemical composition.
- Cells carry out a variety of chemical reactions.
- All cells are open thermodynamic systems that exchange both matter and energy with their surroundings.

Evolution of the cell

The origin of cells was the most important step in the evolution of life on earth. Evolution of cells refers to the evolutionary origin and subsequent evolutionary development of cells. The study of cell origins primarily includes the question of how cells became individual units, separate from the external environment and capable of performing metabolic process. The earliest cells probably arose about 3.5 billion years ago; they were almost certainly **chemoheterotrophs**. Primitive heterotrophs gradually acquired the capability to derive energy from certain compounds in their environment and to use that energy to synthesize more and more of their own precursor molecules, thereby becoming less dependent on outside sources. A very significant evolutionary event was the development of photosynthetic ability to fix CO_2 into more complex organic compounds.

One important landmark along this evolutionary road occurred when there was a transition from small cells with relatively simple internal structures - the so-called prokaryotic cells, which include various types of bacteria - to a flourishing of larger and radically more complex *eukaryotic* cells such as are found in higher animals and plants. The fossil record shows that the earliest eukaryotic cells evolved about 1.5 billion years ago. Details of the evolutionary path from prokaryotes to eukaryotes cannot be deduced from the fossil record alone, but morphological and biochemical comparison of modern organisms has suggested a reasonable sequence of events consistent with the fossil evidence.

Three major changes must have occurred as prokaryotes gave rise to eukaryotes. *First*, as cells acquired more DNA, mechanisms evolved to fold it compactly into discrete complexes with specific proteins and to divide it equally between daughter cells at cell division. These DNA-protein complexes called chromosomes become especially compact at the time of cell division. *Second*, as cells became larger and intracellular membrane organelles developed. Eukaryotic cells have a *nucleus* which contains most of the cell's DNA, enclosed by a double layer of membrane. The DNA is, thereby, kept in a compartment separate from the rest of the contents of the cell, the cytoplasm, where most of the cell's metabolic reactions occur.

Finally, primitive eukaryotic cells, which were incapable of photosynthesis or of aerobic metabolism, pooled their assets with those of aerobic bacteria or photosynthetic bacteria to form symbiotic associations that became permanent. Some aerobic bacteria evolved into the mitochondria of modern eukaryotes, and some photosynthetic cyanobacteria became the chloroplasts of modern plant cells.

3.2 Plasma membrane

All cells are bounded by a plasma membrane. Plasma membrane (also known as the *cell membrane*) is a dynamic, fluid structure and forms the external boundary of a cell. It acts as a **selectively permeable membrane** (that is, it allows some solutes to cross it more easily than others) and regulates the molecular traffic across the boundary. Plasma membrane behaves like a capacitor. A **capacitor** is simply a device that allows separation of electrical charge and establish an electric field (i.e., voltage) across the plates of the capacitor. Typical capacitors are made up of two metal plates closely apposed to one another but are separated by a non-conducting medium (such as air, vacuum). In the absence of integral membrane proteins, plasma membranes have similar electrical properties to those exhibited by parallel-plate capacitors. The non-conductive lipid bilayer of the membrane separates the conductive extracellular and intracellular electrolyte solutions. This results in the separation of charge across the lipid bilayer, and this charge separation brings about an *electrical potential* difference across the bilayer (referred to as the **membrane potential**).

Structure and composition of plasma membrane

Different models have been proposed to explain the structure of plasma membranes. Some landmark models include:

Overton model: Proposed by E. Overton, this model hypothesizes that the plasma membrane is composed of lipids.

Bimolecular lipid leaflet model: E. Gorter and F. Grendel experimentally demonstrated that the plasma membrane is made up of two layers of lipids with the polar head groups of lipid molecules pointing toward the aqueous environment.

Trilaminar model: Proposed by Davson and Danielli, this model hypothesizes that layers of proteins present on both sides of the lipid bilayer.

Unit membrane model: J. D. Robertson stated that layers of proteins present on both sides of the lipid bilayer and there is no space between two layers of lipids. He also mentioned that all membranes in the cell, i.e., plasma and organelle membranes, have the same structure.

Fluid-mosaic model: Proposed by Jonathan Singer and Garth Nicolson, is now the most accepted model. In this model, membranes are viewed as quasi-fluid structures in which proteins are inserted into lipid bilayers. It describes both the mosaic arrangement of proteins embedded throughout the lipid bilayer as well as the fluid nature of the lipid bilayer.

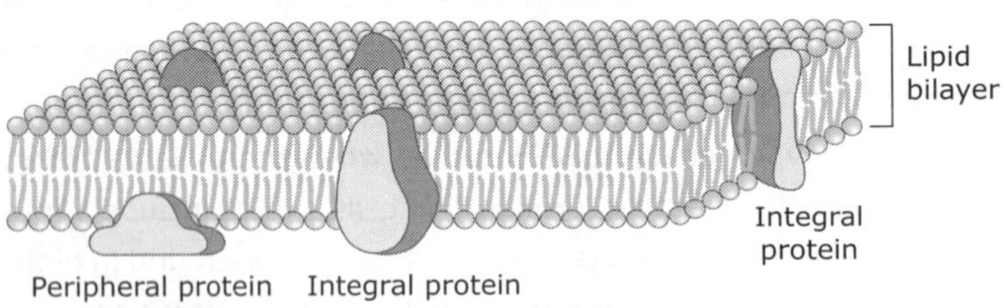

Figure 3.1 Fluid mosaic model for plasma membrane describes the structure of the membrane as a mosaic of lipids and proteins. According to this model, there is a lipid bilayer in which protein molecules are embedded, similar to icebergs floating in the ocean.

Chemical constituents of plasma membrane: All plasma membranes, regardless of source, contain proteins as well as lipids. The ratio of protein to lipid varies enormously depends on cell types. For example, the plasma membrane of human RBC contains 43% lipid and 49% protein by weight whereas plasma membrane of mouse liver cells contains 54% lipid and 46% protein by weight. Carbohydrates are also present in plasma membranes and comprise only 5 to 10% of membrane mass. Carbohydrates bound either to proteins as constituents of **glycoproteins** or to lipids as constituents of **glycolipids**. Carbohydrates are especially abundant in the plasma membranes of eukaryotic cells.

Lipid bilayer

The basic structure of the plasma membrane is the lipid bilayer. This bilayer is composed of two **leaflets** of **amphipathic** (*amphiphilic*) lipid molecules, whose *hydrophilic polar head* are in contact with the intra- or extracellular aqueous phase, whereas their *hydrophobic non-polar hydrocarbon tails* face each other, constituting the hydrophobic interior of the membrane. The primary physical forces for organizing lipid bilayer are *hydrophobic force of interactions*. Apart from the hydrophobic force, *van der Waals* forces of interaction between the hydrocarbon tails favor close packing of the tails. Finally, there are electrostatic interaction and hydrogen-bonding between the polar head groups and water molecules. All lipid molecules present in the lipid bilayer can be broadly classified into three classes– *phospholipids*, *glycolipids* and *sterol*.

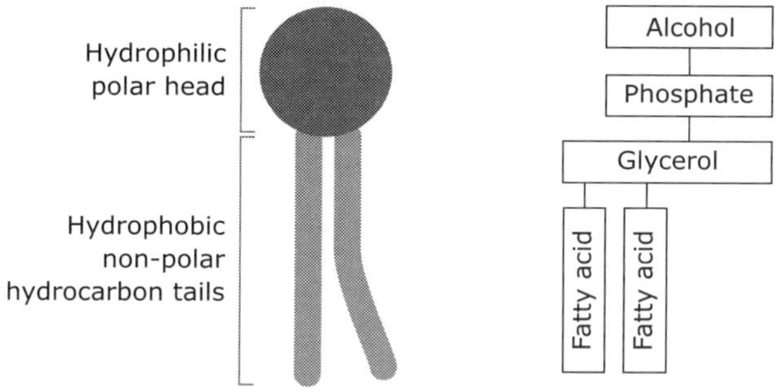

Figure 3.2
Glycerophospholipid structure. The hydrophilic unit, also called the polar head group, is represented by a circle, whereas the hydrocarbon tails are depicted by straight lines.

Phospholipids: Phospholipids are made up of four components: an alcohol (glycerol or sphingosine), fatty acids, phosphate, and an alcohol attached to the phosphate. The fatty acid components are hydrophobic, whereas the remainder of the molecule has hydrophilic. There are two types of phospholipids: *glycerophospholipids* and *sphingophospholipids*. Phospholipids derived from glycerol are called **glycerophospholipids**. Glycerophospholipids (or phosphoglycerides) contain glycerol, fatty acids, phosphate and an alcohol (e.g., choline). Phosphoglyceride molecules are classified according to the types of alcohol linked to the phosphate group. For example, if the alcohol is choline, the molecule is called phosphatidylcholine (also referred to as **lecithin**) and if serine, then it is called phosphatidylserine. Phosphoglycerides are the most numerous phospholipid molecules found in plasma membranes.

Sphingophospholipids contain an amino alcohol called **sphingosine** instead of glycerol, a fatty acid, phosphate and an alcohol attached to the phosphate. In sphingophospholipid, the amino group of the sphingosine backbone is linked to a fatty acid by an amide bond. *Sphingomyelin is the most abundant sphingophospholipid.*

The plasma membrane of animal cells contains four major phospholipids, such as *phosphatidylcholine* (the most abundant glycerophospholipids), *phosphatidylserine*, *phosphatidylethanolamine* and *sphingomyelin*. At neutral pH, the polar head group may have no net charge (phosphatidylcholine and phosphatidyl ethanolamine) or it may have net negative charges (phosphatidylinositol and phosphatidylserine). Rarer phospholipids have a net positive charge.

Glycolipids: Just like phospholipids, glycolipids are made up of four components: an alcohol (glycerol or sphingosine), fatty acid(s) and carbohydrate (either mono- or oligosaccharide). Among glycolipids, sphingoglycolipids are most common. The simple sphingoglycolipid, called a **cerebroside**, contains a single sugar residue such as glucose and galactose, whereas the complex sphingoglycolipid, called a **globoside**, contains oligosaccharide. **Gangliosides** are also globosides, containing an oligosaccharide with one or more **sialic acids** linked on the sugar chain. The glycolipids are found exclusively in the outer leaflet of the plasma membrane, with their carbohydrate portions exposed on the cell surface.

Table 3.1 Major lipid components of plasma membranes (composition in mol %)

Source	PC	PE + PS	SM	Cholesterol
Plasma membrane (human RBC)	21	29	21	26
Plasma membrane (*E. coli*)	0	85	0	0
Plasma membrane (human neuron)	16	37	13	34

PC – phosphatidylcholine; PE – phosphatidylethanolamine; PS – phosphatidylserine; SM – sphingomyelin.

Sterols: The basic structure of sterol is a *steroid nucleus*, consisting of four fused rings, three with six carbons and one with five. It is planar, and relatively a rigid structure. **Cholesterol** is the major sterol present in the plasma membrane of animal cells. The plasma membrane of plant cells lacks cholesterol, but they contain other sterols like stigmasterol, sitosterol. With rare exceptions like *Mycoplasma*, bacterial plasma membrane also lacks cholesterol.

Summary

- **Membrane lipid**
  - **Phospholipid**
    - **Glycerophospholipid** (major)
    - **Sphingophospholipid**
  - **Glycolipid**
    - **Sphingoglycolipid** (major)
    - **Glyceroglycolipid**
  - **Sterol**
    - **Cholesterol** (in animals)
    - **Ergosterol** (in fungi)
    - **Stigmasterol, sitosterol** (in plants)

Lipid rafts

Lipids are not randomly mixed in each leaflet of a bilayer. Certain lipids, particularly cholesterol and sphingolipids, in the lipid bilayer of the plasma membrane are aggregated to form stable (difficult to dissolve with non-ionic detergents), more ordered and slightly thicker microdomains called **lipid rafts** (or *membrane raft*). The term 'lipid raft' was originally used to denote a detergent-resistant liquid-ordered phase that is rich in cholesterol and glycosphingolipids. These microdomains also contain specific proteins (termed 'raftophilic' proteins). GPI-linked proteins are prominently present in the non-cytosolic leaflet of these rafts, and palmitoylated proteins are common in the cytosolic leaflet. While rafts have a distinctive protein and lipid composition, all rafts do not appear to be identical in terms of either the proteins or the lipids that they contain. Hence, *lipid rafts are heterogeneous, dynamic (in terms of both lateral mobility and association–dissociation), relatively ordered, detergent-resistant, cholesterol-and sphingolipid-enriched membrane microdomains whose formation is driven by lipid-lipid and lipid-protein interactions*.

There are two types of lipid rafts – **planar** and **caveolae**. Inwardly curved flask-shaped rafts called caveolae are especially enriched in the **caveolin protein**. Caveolin, an integral membrane protein, is a cholesterol-binding protein and is probably concentrated in caveolae because of its ability to bind this sterol. Planar rafts contain **flotillin proteins** and are found in neurons where caveolae are absent. Lipid rafts have been implicated in processes as diverse as signal transduction, endocytosis and cholesterol trafficking. For example, in the case of T-cells, rafts act as platforms for the assembly of the T-cell signaling machinery.

Micelle, bilayer and liposome

Amphipathic lipid molecules spontaneously form a variety of structures when added to an aqueous solution. Depending on the precise conditions and the nature of the lipids, three types of lipid aggregate can form – *micelle*, *bilayer* and *liposome*. All these structures form in ways that minimize contact between the hydrophobic lipid components with water. In the case of single-tailed phospholipids and glycolipids, the lipid molecules because of their tapered shapes form a small and spherical structure (diameter usually <20 nm) called **micelle** in which the hydrophobic fatty acid chains are hidden inside the sphere. A second type of lipid aggregate in water is the **bilayer**, in which two lipid monolayers combine to form a two-dimensional sheet. Because the hydrophobic regions at its edges are in contact with water, the bilayer sheet is relatively unstable and spontaneously folds back on itself to form a hollow vesicle called **liposome**. Liposomes are closed, self-sealing, solvent filled vesicles that are bound by only a single bilayer.

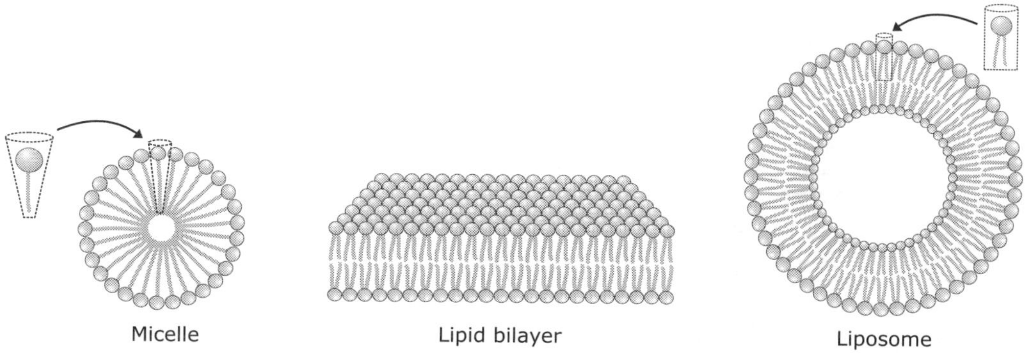

Figure 3.3 Micelle is a spherical structure formed by amphipathic lipid molecules such that their polar ends are in contact with water and nonpolar portions are inside the sphere. In the lipid bilayer, two lipid monolayers combine to form a sheet-like structure. A liposome is a closed solvent-filled, three-dimensional hollow vesicle made up of a lipid bilayer.

Asymmetry of lipid bilayer

Membrane lipids are asymmetrically distributed between the two leaflets of the bilayer. The two leaflets of the lipid bilayer have different lipid compositions. The phospholipids such as *phosphatidylserine*, *phosphatidylethanolamine*, *phosphatidylinositol* are mostly present in the cytosolic leaflet of the lipid bilayer, whereas *sphingomyelin* and *phosphatidylcholine* are found mainly in the non-cytosolic leaflet. This asymmetry is usually not absolute, except for glycolipids. The maintenance of chemical asymmetry is essential for normal membrane function. Changes in the distribution of lipids between two leaflets of lipid bilayer have different biological functions. For example, when the phosphatidylserine in the plasma membrane moves from cytosolic leaflet to the non-cytosolic leaflet, a platelet able to play its role in the formation of a blood clot. Similarly, in many cell types, phosphatidylserine movement to the non-cytosolic leaflet marks the apoptotic process.

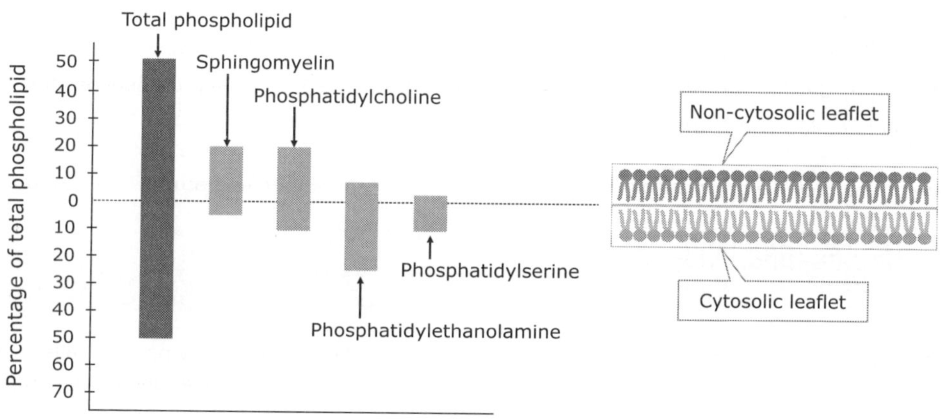

Figure 3.4 Distribution of phospholipids on the two monolayers (leaflets) of the RBC plasma membrane. Membrane lipids are asymmetrically distributed between the two leaflets of the bilayer. For example, phosphatidylcholine and sphingomyelin are mostly present in the extracellular non-cytosolic leaflet, whereas phosphatidylserine, phosphatidylethanolamine, and the phosphatidylinositols are almost exclusively in the cytosolic leaflet.

Motion of lipid molecules: Lipid bilayer is not rigid and static structure. In a lipid bilayer, lipid molecules can rotate freely around their long axis (**rotational motion**) and diffuse laterally (**lateral motion**) within each leaflet. The ability of lipids to diffuse laterally in a bilayer indicates that it can act as a fluid. The degree of bilayer fluidity depends on the lipid composition and temperature. The rapid lateral movement of membrane lipids has been visualized by means of fluorescence microscopy through the use of the technique of *fluorescence recovery after photobleaching* (FRAP).

The transition of a lipid molecule from one leaflet of the bilayer to the other is called **transverse diffusion**, or **flip-flop**. For this movement to occur, the lipid head group, which is polar and may be charged, must pass through the hydrophobic interior of the bilayer. As a result, rapid spontaneous transverse diffusion of phospholipids is a rare process and also depends on the characteristics of the lipid molecules, such as the acyl chain length and degree of unsaturation.

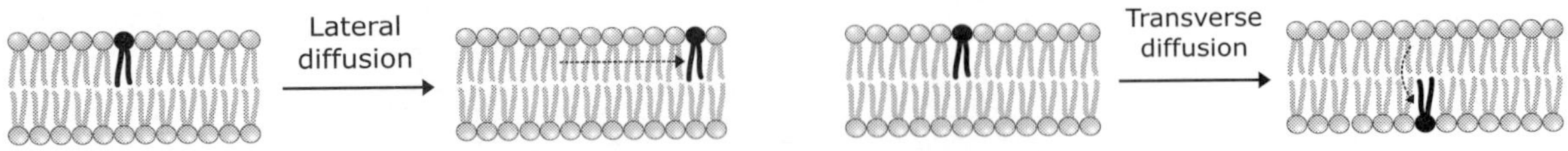

Figure 3.5 Different types of mobility of lipids molecules in a lipid bilayer.

Role of flippase and floppases: Although the barrier to rapid spontaneous flip-flop contributes to the maintenance of lipid asymmetry, other mechanisms must be responsible for the regeneration of lipid asymmetry. Perhaps, the most significant contributors to the maintenance and dissipation of transbilayer lipid asymmetry are proteins that catalyze the movement of lipid molecules across the membrane. These activities are classified according to substrate specificity, requirements for energy and direction of transport. Two classes of transport activities have been described that are responsible for the ATP-dependent transport of lipids. The most well-characterized activity, catalyzed by **flippase**, a **P-type ATPase**, transports phospholipids that contain free amino groups in their head groups (phosphatidylserine and phosphatidylethanolamine) from the extracellular non-cytosolic leaflet to the cytosolic leaflet of the lipid bilayer. A second *ATP-dependent* activity, catalyzed by **floppases**, ABC transport protein, transports phospholipids in the opposite direction. The plasma membrane also contains phospholipid translocator termed **scramblase**, which ensures that both monolayers remain equally populated with phospholipids. It moves phospholipid non-specifically in either direction, along the concentration gradient i.e., move any membrane phospholipid across the bilayer down its concentration gradient (from the leaflet where it has a higher concentration to the leaflet where it has a lower concentration). It does not require ATP but is activated by calcium. The activity rises sharply with an increase in cytosolic calcium concentration.

Fluidity of a lipid bilayer: The fluidity of the lipid bilayer, the optimal value of which is a prerequisite for normal cell growth and function, depends on **lipid composition** and **temperature**. In general, an increase in the temperature tends to elevate membrane fluidity. Lowering of temperature causes a freely-flowing, low-viscous, fluid-like membrane structure to a more rigid, gel-like organization. This change is described as **phase transition** and the temperature at which this happens is called the *transition* temperature.

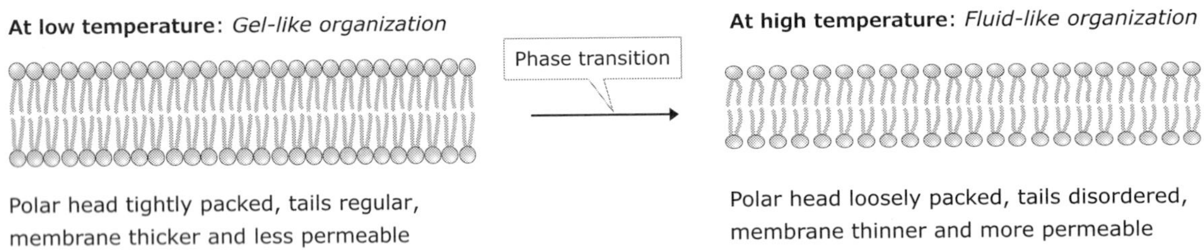

Figure 3.6 Phase transition. At low temperature, phospholipids with fatty acyl chains tend to assemble into a highly ordered, gel-like bilayer. Increased temperature disorders the nonpolar tails and induces a transition from a gel to a fluid within a temperature range of only a few degrees. As the chains become disordered, the bilayer also decreases in thickness.

The fluidity of the lipid bilayer also depends on lipid composition. The lipid composition includes a number of parameters. These parameters in the plasma membrane of an animal cell are:

- Types of phospho-and glycolipids
- Fatty acyl chain length in phospho- and glycolipids
- Saturated and unsaturated nature of fatty acyl chains
- Degree of unsaturation of fatty acyl chains
- Configuration of double bond (*cis* or *trans*) in fatty acyl chains
- Amount of cholesterol

For example, phospho- and glycolipids with short fatty acyl chains have less surface area to form van der Waals interactions with each other. Hence, a shorter chain length reduces the tendency of the hydrocarbon fatty acyl chains to interact with one another. This increases the fluidity of the lipid bilayer. Similarly, unsaturated fatty acyl chains have kinks due to the presence of double bonds, thus form less van der Waals interactions with other fatty acyl chains and tend to adopt a more random, fluid state. So, an increased proportion of unsaturated to saturated fatty acids in the membrane increases the fluidity of the bilayer at the reduced temperature. Cholesterol is also a major determinant of membrane fluidity. The presence of cholesterol increases order and rigidity. Its presence stabilizes the extended straight-chain arrangement of saturated fatty acids by van der Waals interactions. The presence of cholesterol is characteristic of the plasma membrane of animal cells rather than plant cells. As a result, animal cell plasma membranes are less fluid (more rigid) than plant cell plasma membranes.

Membrane proteins

Membrane proteins are responsible for most of the dynamic processes carried out by membranes. Most membrane proteins can be classified as being either *peripheral* or *integral*. Many of the proteins associated with the membrane can be released from the membrane by relatively gentle extraction procedures, such as by changing pH or ionic strength. These procedures interfere with weak noncovalent interactions between protein-protein or protein-membrane lipid but leave the lipid bilayer intact; these proteins are referred to as **peripheral proteins** (or *extrinsic proteins*). These proteins are bound to membranes primarily by electrostatic interactions and hydrogen bonds and do not interact with the hydrophobic core of the phospholipid bilayer. They are usually bound to the membrane indirectly by interactions with integral membrane proteins or directly by interactions with lipid polar head groups. Most peripheral proteins are soluble in an aqueous solution. **Spectrin** and **ankyrin** are very common examples of peripheral proteins present in the membrane of RBCs. Spectrin acts as a structural protein, determines the shape of the RBC. Some membrane proteins associate reversibly with the membrane and thus can be found in the cytosol, in the membrane, or in both places. Such proteins are termed as **amphitropic proteins**.

Proteins that are held in the lipid bilayer very tightly through hydrophobic interactions and can be separated from lipid bilayer only by treatment with **detergents** that disrupt bilayer are called **integral proteins** (or *intrinsic proteins*). Detergents are amphipathic molecules. Its nature may be ionic (anionic or cationic), zwitterionic or non-ionic. Integral proteins may be **monotopic** (interacting with just one leaflet of the bilayer) or **polytopic** (traverses the lipid bilayer once or several times). Integral membrane proteins are mostly polytopic transmembrane proteins that have one or more segments that are embedded in the phospholipid bilayer. Transmembrane proteins contain non-polar amino acid residues with hydrophobic side chains that interact with fatty acyl groups of the membrane phospholipids, thus anchoring the protein to the membrane. *All transmembrane proteins are amphipathic*. Transmembrane proteins may be *single-pass* or *multipass*. **Glycophorin** is a major single-pass transmembrane protein of RBC. It is a small glycoprotein of 131 amino acid residues. It was the first membrane protein for which the complete amino acid sequence was determined. Despite their abundance in the plasma membrane of RBC, their function remains unknown. Another prominent protein present on the plasma membrane of RBC is **band 3 protein** (or *chloride-bicarbonate exchanger*), a 95 kDa multipass transmembrane protein. It is responsible for mediating the electroneutral exchange of chloride for bicarbonate.

Transmembrane proteins are characterized by having transmembrane membrane-spanning segment. They contain a stretch of 21 to 26 nonpolar amino acid residues coiled into an α-helix that is believed to facilitate the spanning of a lipid bilayer. In a few membrane proteins, the transmembrane portion comprises β-barrel made up of antiparallel β-strands. The number of β-strands varies widely (8 to 22 strands).

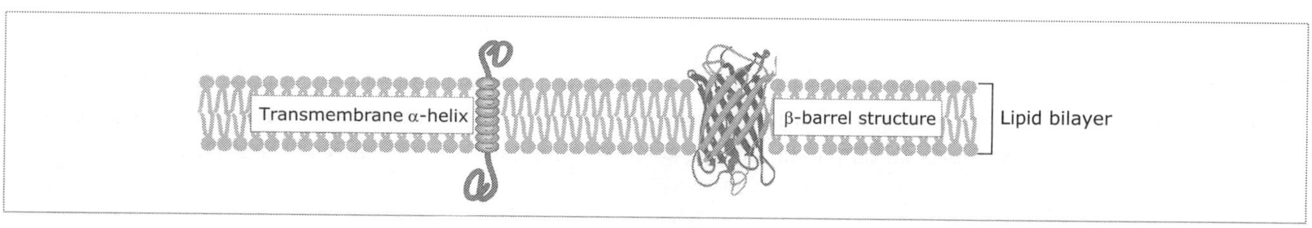

One common example is **porin**, a pore-forming protein, which allows hydrophilic solutes (up to 600 Da) to diffuse. The porin β-barrel is formed from 16 strands β-antiparallel and it is stabilized by extensive hydrogen bonding between the β-strands. The interior of the barrel is hydrophilic.

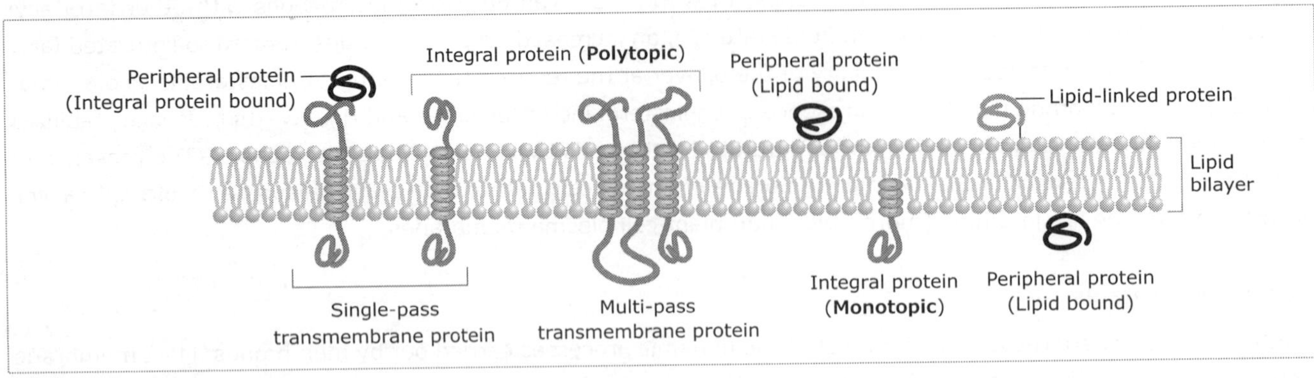

Figure 3.7 Schematic outline of integral protein, peripheral protein and lipid-linked protein.

Membrane proteins which are covalently bound to lipid molecules are called **lipid-linked** (or *lipid-anchored*) **proteins**. They form covalent attachments with three classes of lipids: compounds that are built from isoprene units such as farnesyl and geranylgeranyl residues; fatty acids such as myristic acid and palmitic acid; and glycosylated phospholipid (such as glycosylphosphatidylinositol, **GPI**). Proteins covalently attached with isoprenoid compounds such as farnesyl (15-carbon compound) and geranylgeranyl (20-carbon compound) are termed as **prenylated proteins**. In these proteins, isoprenoid compounds are covalently attached to a cysteine residue at the C-terminus via a *thioether linkage*.

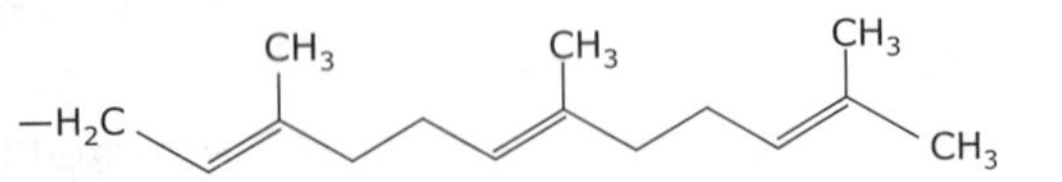

Farnesyl residue

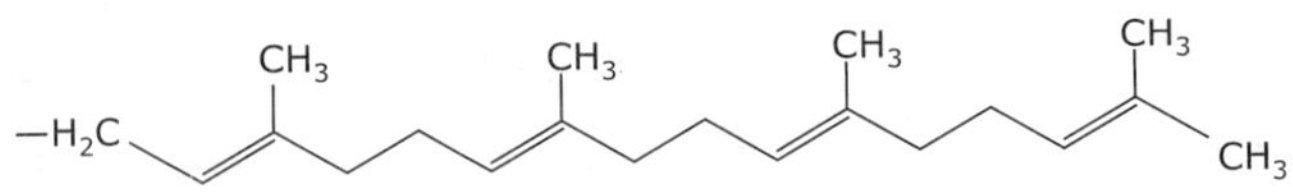

Geranylgeranyl residue

Why detergents are used to separate transmembrane proteins? If we separate the membrane-spanning segments of transmembrane proteins from the amphipathic membrane lipids that surround them, these hydrophobic sequences tend to interact tightly with one another rather than with water. The resulting large protein aggregates are generally insoluble and precipitate out of solution. If, however, we disrupt the lipid bilayer by adding detergent, the amphipathic detergent molecules interact with the hydrophobic membrane-spanning region of transmembrane proteins and form detergent-protein complex. This stops the formation of large protein aggregates.

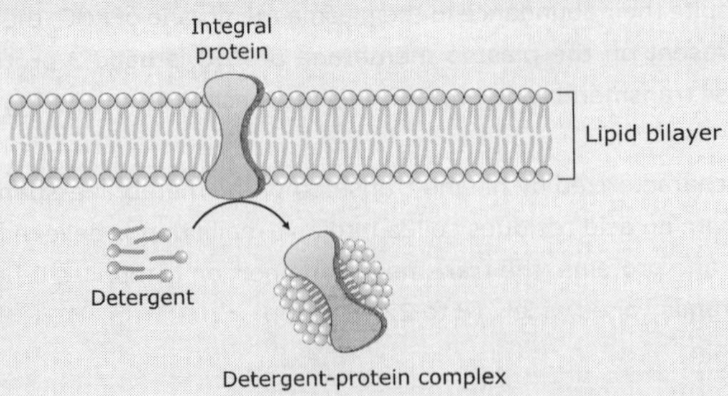

The hydrophobic membrane-spanning sequences remain insulated from interactions with the aqueous solvent, and the proteins remain soluble as components of detergent micelles. In this way, detergents remove transmembrane proteins from the lipid bilayer and at the same time maintain the solubility and native architectures of proteins.

Proteins covalently attached with fatty acids such as palmitic acid and myristic acid are termed as **fatty acylated proteins**. A myristic acid (14-carbon, saturated fatty acid) molecule attaches to a protein through an *amide linkage* to the α-amino group of an N-terminal *Gly* residue (**myristoylation**). A palmitic acid (16-carbon, saturated fatty acid) molecule attaches to a Cys residue close to the N- or C-terminus via a *thioester linkage* (**palmitoylation**). A glycosylphosphatidylinositol molecule (GPI) attaches to the C-terminal amino acid via an amide linkage. **GPI-linked proteins** occur on the exoplasmic face of the plasma membrane.

Table 3.2 Characteristics of lipid-linked proteins

Lipid anchor	Protein	Attachment site	Subcellular location
Lipids built from isoprene units	Prenylated protein	Cys residue at C-terminus	Intracellular
Myristic acid	Fatty acylated protein	Gly residue at N-terminus	Intracellular
Palmitic acid	Fatty acylated protein	Cys residue near N- or C-terminus	Intracellular
GPI	GPI-linked protein	Various residues at C-terminus	Cell surface

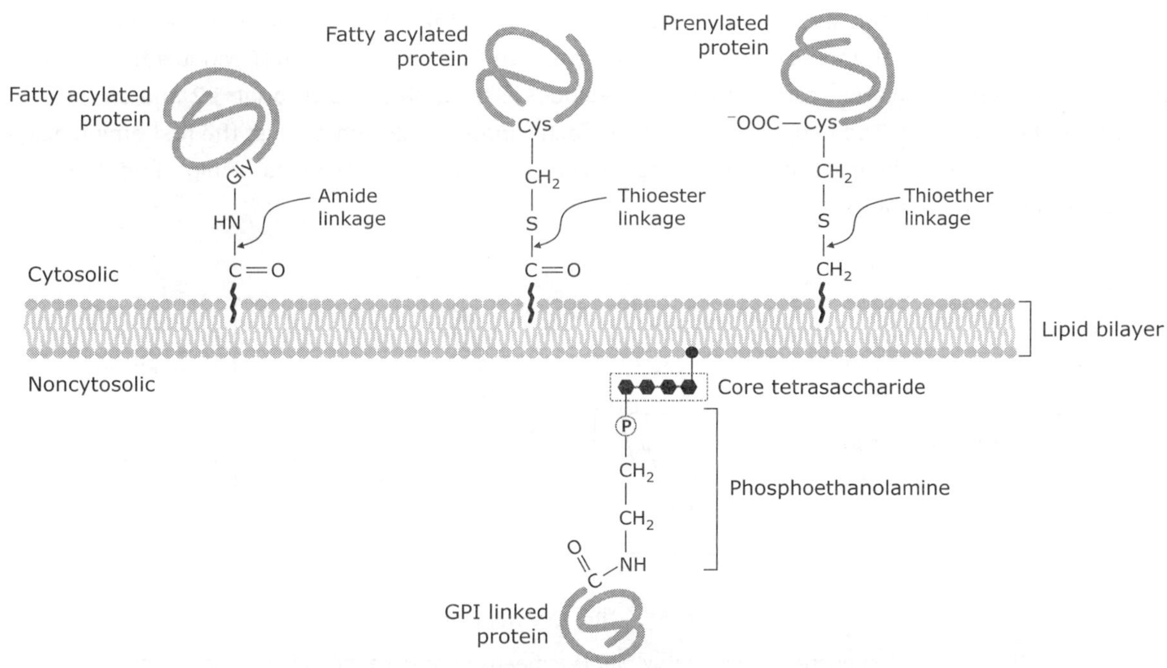

Figure 3.8 Lipid-linked membrane proteins are attached to the bilayer either through a fatty acid chain or lipids that are built from isoprene units in the cytoplasmic monolayer or, via glycosylphosphatidylinositol molecule (GPI), in the noncytoplasmic monolayer. A fatty acid chain, myristic acid, is attached via an amide linkage to an amino-terminal glycine. The palmitic acid is joined to a protein in thioester linkage to a specific cysteine residue. Lipids that are built from isoprene units (either farnesyl or geranylgeranyl group) is attached via a thioether linkage to a cysteine residue at carboxyl terminus. GPI anchors are derivatives of phosphatidylinositol in which the inositol bears a short oligosaccharide covalently joined to phosphoethanolamine.

Problem

Why animals that live in cold climates tend to have a higher proportion of unsaturated fatty acid residues in the lipids of the plasma membrane than animals that live in warmer climates?

Solution: The fluidity of a lipid bilayer depends on both its composition and its temperature. Unsaturated fatty acids in membrane lipids reduce the tendency of the hydrocarbon tails to interact with one another and make them more difficult to pack together. As a result, the membrane remains fluid even at lower temperatures. Hence, animals in cold climates tend to have a higher proportion of unsaturated fatty acids in the lipids of the plasma membrane to maintain the fluidity at a lower temperature.

Hydropathy plot

Transmembrane proteins, like glycophorin, contain membrane-spanning region(s). An α-helical sequence of 20 to 25 residues span the lipid bilayer. Typically, most of the residues in membrane-spanning region or transmembrane segment are nonpolar and almost none of them are charged. This information can be used to identify putative membrane-spanning regions in a transmembrane protein. Once the amino acid sequence of a transmembrane protein is known, the number and positions of membrane-spanning regions can be inferred from a **hydropathy** (or **hydrophobicity**) **plot**. It is a method to determine the hydrophobic and hydrophilic regions of a polypeptide. The relative polarity of each amino acid has been determined experimentally by measuring the free-energy change accompanying the movement of that amino acid side chain from a hydrophobic solvent into water. This free energy change is expressed as a **hydropathy index**. This value is negative ($\Delta G < 0$) for polar amino acid side chains, and positive ($\Delta G > 0$) for amino acids with nonpolar side chains.

With the help of hydropathy index of each amino acid, the overall hydrophobicity of a segment of a polypeptide chain can be estimated. The hydropathy index for any segment (window) is an average of the hydropathy values for its residues. To scan a polypeptide sequence for potential membrane-spanning segment, an investigator calculates the hydropathy index for successive segments of a given size, usually around 10-20 amino acids. The span of 10 to 20 residues chosen for this calculation is called a *window*. Let us take an example of a transmembrane protein glycophorin. We can take the amino acid sequence and estimate hydropathy index of window formed of residues 1 through 20. The same calculation can be made for residues 2 through 21, 3 through 22 and so forth, until we reach the end of the sequence. The hydropathy index for each window is plotted against the first amino acid residue of every window to create a hydropathy plot. A region with more than 20 residues of high hydropathy index is presumed to be a transmembrane segment.

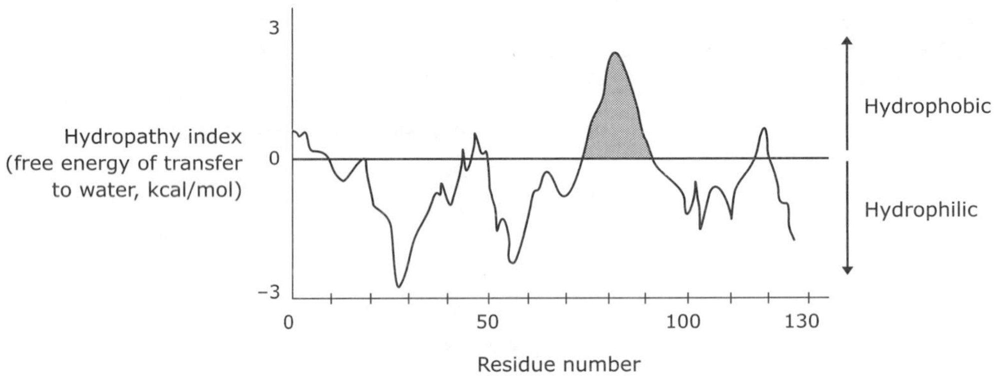

Figure 3.9 Hydropathy plot for glycophorin. A hydropathy plot is a means of representing hydrophobic regions (positive values) and hydrophilic regions (negative values) along the length of a protein. The plot has amino acid sequence of a protein on its x-axis, and hydropathy index on its y-axis. By convention, hydrophobic non-polar amino acids have positive hydropathy index values and hydrophilic polar residues have negative values. The hydropathy index for each amino acid residue in a segment of defined length, or window, is used to calculate the average hydropathy index for that window. The average of the hydropathy indices of the amino acid residues in a sliding window of 20 amino acids is plotted against the position of the first amino acid in the window.

Transport proteins

Membrane proteins can also be classified on the basis of functions like catalytic proteins, structural proteins and transport proteins. Transport proteins, responsible for selective transport of molecules may be **carrier** or **channel proteins**. All transport proteins are multi-pass transmembrane proteins.

Carrier proteins can be **uniporters** and **co-transporters**. *Uniporters* transport single solute from one side of membrane to the other. The single noncoupled transport by uniporter is called **uniport**. Co-transporters mediate coupled transport. Coupled transport involves either the simultaneous transfer of a second solute in the same direction, called **symport** or the transfer of second solute in the opposite direction, called **antiport**. Co-transporters that mediate symport and antiport are termed *symporters* and *antiporters*, respectively.

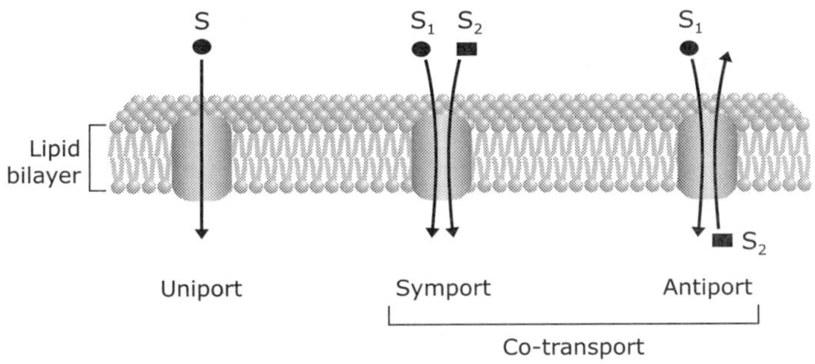

Figure 3.10
Three types of carrier mediated transport involving carrier proteins functioning as uniporters, symporters and antiporters.

Channel proteins transport solutes *down* their concentration gradients. Channels may be *gated* channels or *nongated* (leaky) channels. **Leaky channels**, which are open all the time, permit unregulated leakage of specific ion across the membrane. **Gated channels**, in contrast, have gates that can be open or closed, permitting ion passage through the channels when open and preventing ion passage through the channels when closed. Gated channels open only in response to specific signals. The main types of signals that cause ion channels to open are a change in the voltage across the membrane (**voltage-gated channels**), a mechanical stress (**mechanical-gated channels**), or the binding of a ligand (**ligand-gated channels**). The ligand can be either an extracellular mediator or an intracellular mediator, such as an ion (**ion-gated channels**) or a nucleotide (**nucleotide gated channels**).

Carrier mediated transport may be active or passive, but channel mediated transport is always passive and transport through channel proteins occurs at a much faster rate than mediated by carrier proteins.

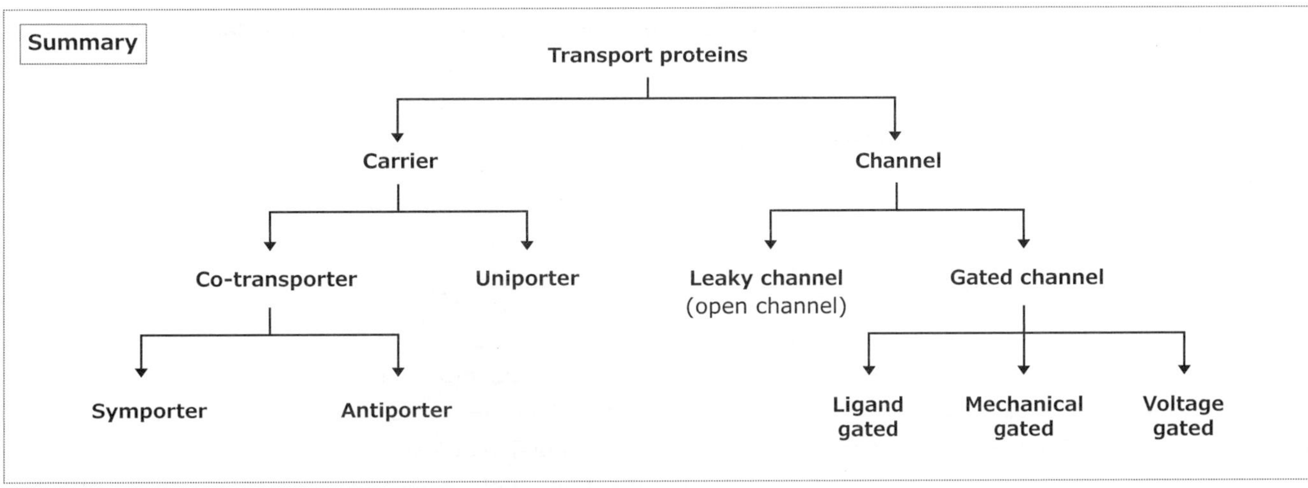

Cell coat or glycocalyx

Carbohydrates are present on the external side of the plasma membrane of all eukaryotic cells. These carbohydrates occur both as *glycoproteins* and *glycolipids*. Thick carbohydrate coat consists of mostly oligosaccharides attached to membrane proteins and lipids is termed as **cell coat** or **glycocalyx**. The biological roles of the glycocalyx are diverse. It helps to protect the cell surface from mechanical and chemical damage and also mediate specific, transient, cell-cell adhesion events. Specific functions are related to the carbohydrates structure and cell type.

3.2.1 ABO blood group

The plasma membrane of human RBCs contains many **antigens**. Based on the presence or absence of various antigens, blood is categorized into different **blood groups**. There are at least 24 blood groups. Blood group antigens are either carbohydrates (as in ABO blood group) or proteins (as in Rh blood group).

The **ABO blood group** system is based on the presence of **A**, **B** and **H antigens**. These antigens are complex oligosaccharides present in form of glycoproteins and glycolipids. Under ABO blood group, there are four **blood**

types – A, B, AB and O. The RBCs of people with A blood type contain A and H antigens, those with B blood type contain B and H antigens, those with AB blood type have A, B and H antigens and those with blood type O have only H antigen (do not have any A or B antigens). H antigen is found in every individual.

A and B antigens derive from H antigen. During the formation of A and B antigens, H antigen (encoded by *H* gene) acts as a precursor oligosaccharide. An enzyme *fucosyltransferase* is responsible for the synthesis of H antigen, that adds fucose to a precursor oligosaccharide. Gene encoding this enzyme is located on the 19th chromosome (**19q13.3**) in humans and has two alternative (allelic) forms—*H* and *h*. Individuals with genotypes *HH* or *Hh* produce H antigen whereas genotype *hh* do not produce H antigen. Because the H antigen is an essential precursor to the A and B antigens, individual with genotype *hh* cannot produce A and B antigens. In case of **A antigen**, H antigen contains an additional *N-acetylgalactosamine* (**GalNAc**). Similarly, in case of **B antigen** an additional galactose (**Gal**) is linked to H antigen. The addition of the terminal GalNAc to the H antigen is catalyzed by enzyme *GalNAc transferase*, a product of *A* gene. Similarly, the product of the *B* gene is the enzyme *Gal transferase* adding the Gal residue to the H antigen. Individuals of AB blood type possess both enzymes and thus have both A and B antigens and individuals of blood type O contain only H antigen.

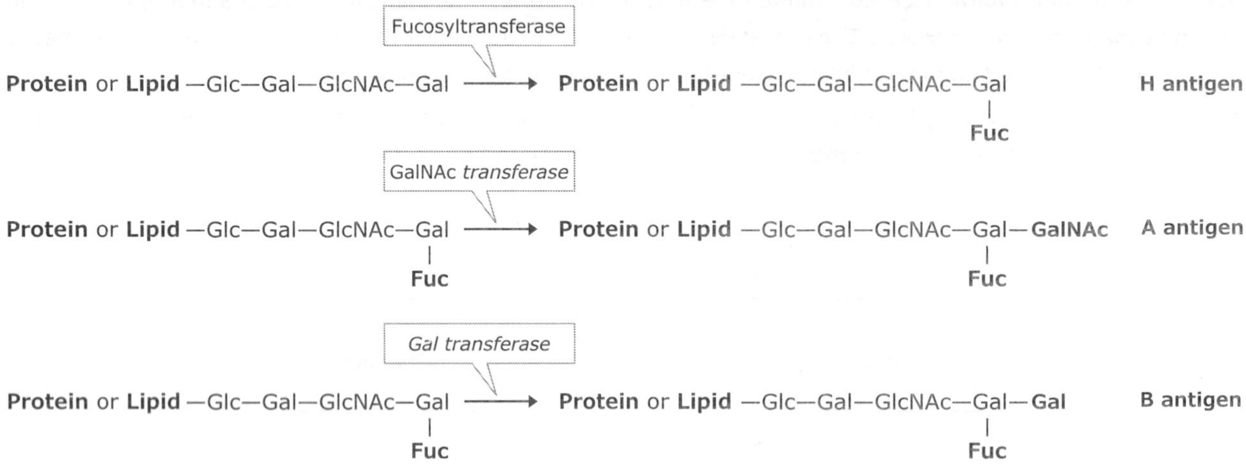

Abbreviation: Fuc = Fucose; Gal = Galactose; GalNAc = N-Acetylgalactosamine; GlcNAc = N-Acetylglucosamine; Glc = Glucose.

Enzyme for synthesis of A and B antigens are encoded by a genetic locus located on the 9th chromosome (**9q34**). It has three alternative (allelic) forms—A, B and O. These three alleles give rise to six possible genotypes—AA, AO, BB, BO, AB and OO. The *A* and *B* alleles are responsible for the production of A and B antigens. The allele *A* encoding the A antigen is *codominant* with the allele *B* encoding the B antigen. Both *A* and *B* are completely *dominant* to the allele *O*, which fails to specify A or B antigens. The hierarchy of dominance relationship is symbolized as (*A*=*B*) > *O*.

Antigens present on RBC	A and H	B and H	A, B and H	H
Genotype on 9th chromosome	AA or AO	BB or BO	AB	OO
Genotype on 19th chromosome	HH or Hh	HH or Hh	HH or Hh	HH or Hh
Blood type	**A**	**B**	**AB**	**O**

Blood plasma contains antibodies that react with the A or B antigens if the two are mixed. These are the **anti-A antibody**, which reacts with antigen A, and the **anti-B antibody**, which reacts with antigen B. The plasma of type A blood contains anti-B antibodies, type B blood contains anti-A antibodies, no anti-A and anti-B antibodies are present in type AB blood and both anti-A and anti-B antibodies are present in type O blood. During *blood transfusion*, any blood cannot be used; the blood of a donor has to be carefully matched with the blood of a recipient before any blood transfusion to avoid severe problems of clumping (destruction of RBC). Type 'O' blood can be donated to persons with any other blood group and hence 'O' group individuals are called '**universal donors**'. Persons with 'AB' blood type can accept blood from persons with AB as well as the other groups of blood. Therefore, such persons are called '**universal recipients**'. Consider what happens if a person with type A blood receives a transfusion of type B blood. The recipient's blood (type A) contains A antigens on the RBCs and anti-B antibodies in the plasma. The donor's blood (type B) contains B antigens on the RBCs and anti-A antibodies in the plasma. In this situation, two things can happen. First, the anti-B antibodies in the recipient's plasma can bind to the B antigens on the donor's RBCs, causing agglutination and hemolysis of the RBCs. Second, the anti-A antibodies in the donor's plasma can bind to the A antigens on the recipient's RBCs causing agglutination and hemolysis of the RBCs.

Rh blood group

The Rh blood group was discovered in 1940 by Landsteiner and Wiener. The Rh blood group system is based on the presence or absence of **Rh antigen** (or *Rh factor*) on the plasma membrane of RBC. The Rh factor was named after the rhesus monkey, *Macacus rhesus* in which it was discovered first. The Rh antigens are located on two *Rhesus proteins* – **RhD** and **RhCE** – encoded by two highly polymorphic genes, RHD and RHCE and are expressed *only* in RBCs. More than 170 alleles of RHD gene have been found. The RhD and RhCE proteins (encoded by RHD and RHCE genes, respectively) are both transmembrane, multipass proteins present on the plasma membrane of RBC. RhD protein carries the D antigen and the RhCE protein carries CE antigens in various combinations (ce, Ce, cE or CE).

The classification of Rh-positive and Rh-negative individuals is determined by the presence or absence of the **D antigen** on the surface of RBCs. If D antigen is present on a person's RBCs, the person is **Rh-positive**; if it is absent, the person is **Rh-negative**. Rh-negative condition arises either due to lack of the RhD protein or due to a series of changes in the RhD protein, which in turn change the phenotype of the D antigen. The Rh-positive condition is more common.

Just like the ABO alleles, each biological parent donates one of their two Rh alleles to their child. A person who is Rh-negative (genotype of Rh^-Rh^-) can only pass an Rh^- allele to son or daughter. A person who is Rh-positive (genotype could be either Rh^+Rh^+ or Rh^+Rh^-) can pass either an Rh^+ or Rh^- allele to son or daughter. *Rh-positive phenotype is dominant over Rh-negative phenotype*. If both of a child's parents are Rh negative, the child will definitely be Rh-negative. Otherwise the child may be Rh-positive or Rh-negative, depending on the parent's specific genotypes.

The Rh antigen is of particular significance when Rh-negative mothers give birth to Rh-positive babies. The fetal and maternal bloods are normally kept separate across the placenta and so the Rh-negative mother is not usually exposed to the Rh antigen of the fetus during the pregnancy. However, during the delivery of the first child, there is a possibility of exposure of the maternal blood to small amounts of the Rh-positive blood from the foetus. In such cases, the mother starts preparing antibodies against the Rh antigen in her blood. However, this does not occur always because the exposure may be minimal and because Rh-negative women vary in their sensitivity to the Rh antigen. If the woman does produce antibodies against the Rh antigen, these antibodies can cross the placenta in subsequent pregnancies and cause hemolysis of the Rh-positive red blood cells of the fetus. Therefore, the baby could be born anemic with a condition called **erythroblastosis fetalis** (or *hemolytic disease of the newborn*). Erythroblastosis fetalis can be prevented by injecting the Rh-negative mother with an antibody prepared against the Rh antigen (called **anti-Rh antibodies**) within 72 hours after the birth of each Rh-positive baby. This is a type of **passive immunization** in which the injected antibodies inactivate the Rh antigens and thus prevent the mother from becoming actively immunized to them.

Problem

The boundaries of cells are formed by plasma membranes, the barriers that define the inside and the outside boundary of a cell. These barriers prevent molecules generated inside the cell from leaking out and unwanted molecules to come inside. With respect to plasma membrane, answer the following questions:

P. Interaction between peripheral membrane proteins and lipid bilayer.

Q. Major force responsible for the formation of lipid bilayer.

R. Most abundant integral protein in plasma membrane of RBC.

S. Nature of sterol in the plasma membrane of RBC and mycoplasma.

T. Two major differences between RBC and archaeal plasma membranes.

U. Technique to measure lateral movements of specific plasma-membrane proteins and lipids.

V. Factors controlling fluidity of plasma membrane.

Solution:

P. Primarily by electrostatic and hydrogen-bond interactions

Q. Hydrophobic interaction

R. Glycophorin

S. Cholesterol

T. First, in archaeal membranes the nonpolar chains are joined to a glycerol backbone by ether rather than ester linkages. Second, the alkyl chains are branched rather than linear.

U. The lateral movements of specific plasma-membrane proteins and lipids can be quantified by a technique called Fluorescence Recovery After Photobleaching (FRAP).

V. Fluidity of plasma membrane depends on the length of the fatty acyl chains and on their degree of unsaturation. In animals, cholesterol is also a key regulator of membrane fluidity.

3.2.2 Transport across plasma membrane

The internal composition of the cell is maintained because the plasma membrane is a **selectively permeable** structure. The plasma membrane forms a barrier that blocks the free exchange of molecules between the cytoplasm and the external environment of the cell. Most biological molecules are unable to diffuse through the protein-free lipid bilayer (or synthetic lipid bilayer). Small non-polar molecules, such as O_2 and CO_2, readily dissolve in lipid bilayers and, therefore, diffuse rapidly across them. Small uncharged polar molecules, such as water or urea, also diffuse across a lipid bilayer. By contrast, lipid bilayers are highly impermeable for charged molecules (as shown in the **figure 3.11**). However, the plasma membrane unlike protein-free lipid bilayer allows the passage of ions and various charged or uncharged polar molecules such as sugars, amino acids and others. Special classes of transport proteins (carrier and channel) are responsible for transferring such solutes across plasma membrane. Thus, the transport across plasma membrane can occur either through the lipid bilayer or through the membrane transport proteins. The characteristics of lipid-phase diffusion and transport protein mediated transport are basically different. Transport across the plasma membrane is fundamentally of two types: **passive transport** and **active transport**.

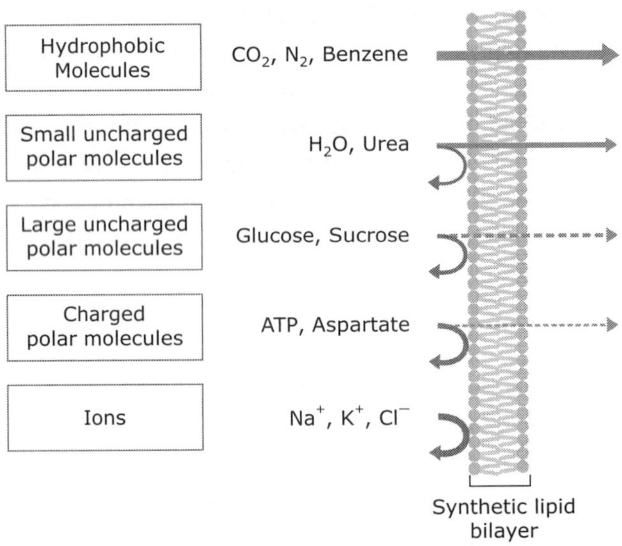

Figure 3.11 The relative permeability of different classes of molecules across synthetic lipid bilayer. Lipid bilayers are essentially impermeable to ions and virtually impermeable to most polar molecules. It is permeable to non-polar molecules such as benzene and small uncharged polar molecules such as water and urea.

1. Passive transport

Passive transport occurs along the gradient (*downhill*) and without the use of metabolic energy. If a solute is uncharged, its movement is influenced by its concentration gradient only whereas, if a transported solute carries a net charge, its movement is influenced by both its **chemical gradient** (the difference in solute concentration) and the *electrical gradient* across the membrane. The combination of these two forces, called the **electrochemical gradient**, determines the direction of transport of a charged molecule across a membrane. *Thus, an ion diffuses not simply down its concentration gradient but, more exactly, down its electrochemical gradient.* Passive transport across plasma membrane may be simple and facilitated diffusion.

Simple diffusion: During simple diffusion, a solute simply dissolves in the lipid bilayer, diffuses across it. No membrane proteins are involved and the direction of transport is determined simply by the relative concentrations of the solute inside and outside of the cell. The relative diffusion rate of any solute across a pure lipid bilayer is proportional to its *concentration gradient* across the layer and to its *hydrophobicity* and *size*. The hydrophobicity of a solute is measured by its **partition coefficient**. It is the equilibrium constant for partition of the solute between oil and water. The higher the molecules partition coefficient, the more lipid-soluble it is. Movement of solutes by simple diffusion is always from a higher to a lower concentration, and the rate is described by **Fick's law of diffusion**.

$$J = -D\frac{\Delta c}{\Delta x}$$

Where J is the flux per unit area, D is the **diffusion coefficient** (usually expressed as cm^2/sec), and Δc is the difference in concentration between two regions separated by a distance Δx (membrane thickness in case of membrane transport). The negative sign accounts for the fact that diffusion is towards the lower concentration. Simple diffusion across lipid bilayer is a *nonselective* in nature by which any non-polar solute able to dissolve in the lipid bilayer is able to cross the plasma membrane and equilibrate between inside and outside of the cell. Gases (such as O_2 and CO_2), non-polar molecules (such as benzene), and small polar but uncharged molecules (such as H_2O and ethanol) are able to diffuse across the lipid bilayer of the plasma membrane.

Diffusion and osmosis are different phenomena. **Osmosis** is a specialized case of diffusion that involves the passive transport of solvent (i.e., water). In this case, solvent (not solute) moves through a **semipermeable membrane** from a region of its higher concentration to a region of its lower concentration. Plasma membrane is a *selectively permeable membrane not a semipermeable membrane.*

Facilitated diffusion: Like simple diffusion, facilitated diffusion involves the movement of solutes along the concentration or electrochemical gradient. However, the passage is mediated by transport protein (**carriers** and **channels**) and is *selective* in nature. Facilitated diffusion may be *carrier proteins* or *channel proteins mediated*. Carrier proteins that mediate facilitated diffusion are called **transporters** or **permeases**. The rate of transport of the solute across the membrane is far greater in facilitated diffusion as compared to simple diffusion. Facilitated diffusion allows polar and charged molecules, such as monosaccharides, amino acids, nucleosides and ions to cross the plasma membrane.

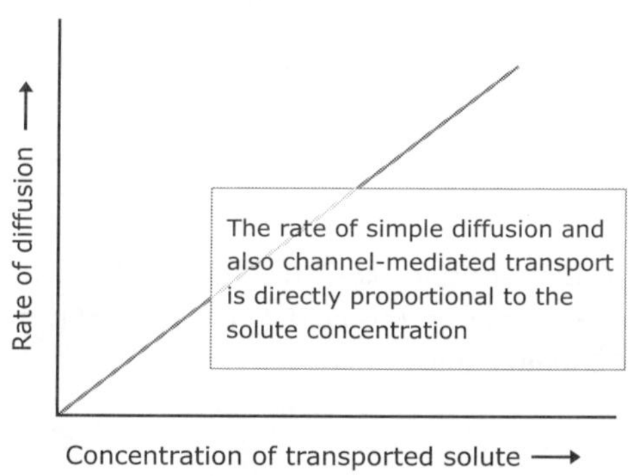

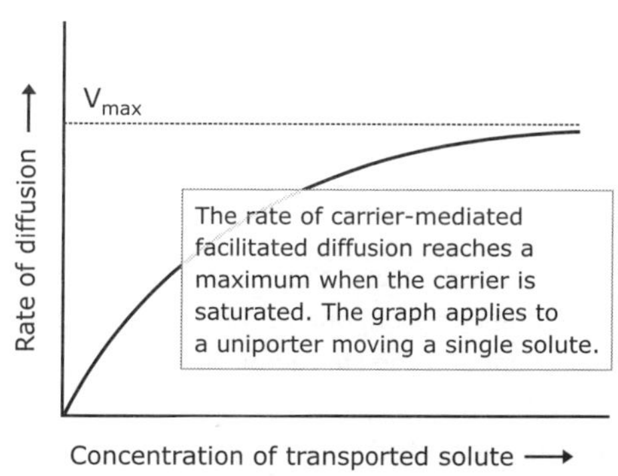

The kinetics of *simple diffusion* is different from *carrier-mediated facilitated diffusion*. In simple diffusion, the rate of diffusion is directly proportional to the solute concentration difference across membrane and non-saturable.

The rate of carrier-mediated facilitated diffusion reaches a maximum (V_{max}) when the transporter is saturated. Let us take the example of facilitated diffusion of glucose (a polar solute) through glucose transporter into the cell. The process of glucose transport can be described by its analogy with an enzymatic reaction in which the 'substrate' is glucose outside the cell (S_{out}), the 'product' is glucose inside the cell (S_{in}), and the 'enzyme' is the glucose transporter. When the facilitated diffusion of glucose is measured as a function of external (outside) glucose concentration, the resulting plot is **hyperbolic**: at high external glucose concentrations, the rate of uptake approaches V_{max}. The rate of facilitated diffusion (V) of glucose can be well described by the following equation that is analogous to Michaelis-Menten equation, which relates the velocity of enzyme-catalyzed reactions to the substrate concentration:

$$V = \frac{V_{max} \cdot [S]_{out}}{K_m + [S]_{out}}$$

Where V_{max} is the maximal rate of diffusion, K_m is the substrate (glucose) concentration at which the half-maximal transport rate is attained and S_{out} is the concentration of the substrate (glucose) outside the cell.

Classes of proteins that mediate facilitated diffusion:

Carrier proteins mediated

Carrier proteins (transporters) non-covalently bind specific molecules to be transported on one side of the membrane. They then undergo conformational changes that allow the molecule to pass through the membrane and be released on the other side. A classic example is the movement of glucose mediated by carrier protein, glucose transporter (GLUT). There are various isoforms of the **glucose transporter** (**GLUT**). In human, there are 14 GLUT isoforms which possess various substrate specificities and are involved in the transport of glucose and other hexoses such as galactose, fructose and mannose. These 14 GLUT isoforms are comprised of about 500 amino acid residues and can be categorized into 3 classes based on sequence similarity: **Class 1** (GLUTs 1–4, 14); **Class 2** (GLUTs 5, 7, 9, 11) and **Class 3** (GLUTs 6, 8, 10, 12). All GLUT isoforms possess 12 transmembrane segments with both their N and C termini positioned in the cytoplasm. GLUT isoforms differ in their kinetic properties, tissue distribution and regulation. Unlike most glucose transporters, **GLUT-5** is specialized for the transport of fructose, not glucose. Most isoforms of GLUTs such as GLUT-1 (erythrocyte), GLUT-2 (liver), GLUT-3 (brain) and GLUT-5 (small intestine) are constitutively expressed on the cell surface, whereas **GLUT-4**, an *insulin-responsive glucose transporter* that is found in the heart, skeletal muscle, adipose tissue and brain, is stored in intracellular vesicles, which upon insulin stimulation, fuses with the plasma membrane, thereby increasing the rate of sugar uptake by several-fold.

The **chloride-bicarbonate exchanger** (also called **anion exchange protein**) present on plasma membrane of RBC mediates the transport of two anions simultaneously. HCO_3^- ion moves in one direction and Cl^- moves in the opposite direction. This protein mediates the simultaneous movement of two anions: for each HCO^- ion that moves in one direction, one Cl^- ion moves in the opposite direction, with no net transfer of charge; the exchange is **electroneutral**. Electrical character of ion transport may be **electrogenic**, if it result in charge separation across the membrane.

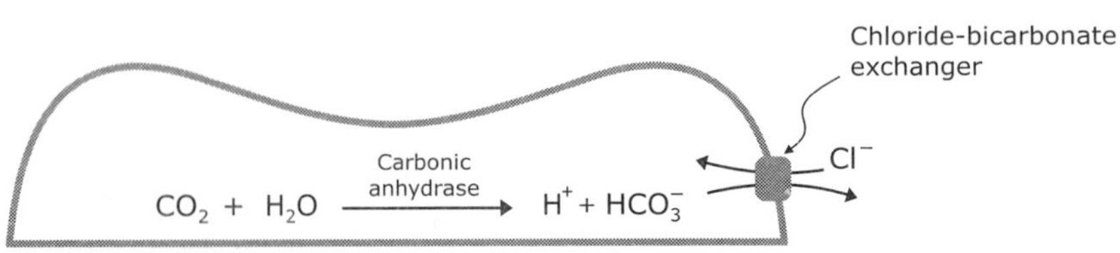

Figure 3.12 The chloride-bicarbonate exchanger (an antiporter) of the RBC membrane allows the exit of HCO_3^-. For each HCO_3^- ion that moves in one direction, one Cl^- ion moves in the opposite direction. The result of this paired movement of two monovalent anions is no net change in the charge or electrical potential across the RBC membrane.

Channel proteins mediated

Channel proteins form pores through the membrane, allowing the diffusion of specific solute of the appropriate size and charge. The rate of diffusion mediated by channel protein is higher than those mediated by carriers. Channels typically show less stereospecificity than carriers and are usually non-saturable. Channel proteins responsible for transport of inorganic ions are called **ion channels**. The properties of ion channels can be studied by means of the **patch clamp technique**. Ion channels are generally highly selective. Most of the ion channels are not permanently open. Some channels (called **voltage-gated channels**) open in response to change in membrane potential; others (called **ligand-gated channels**) open in response to the binding of ligands.

Many animal and plant cells contain specialized water channel in their plasma membrane to facilitate the water flow called **aquaporins**. These are a family of transport proteins that allow water and a few other small uncharged molecules, such as glycerol, ammonia to cross membrane. Aquaporins (AQPs) assemble as homotetramers in which each monomer consists of six membrane-spanning α-helical segments with cytoplasmically oriented amino and carboxyl termini. Two hydrophobic loops contain conserved **asparagine-proline-alanine** (**NPA**) **motif** for selectivity of the channel. Each monomer functions as an independent pore.

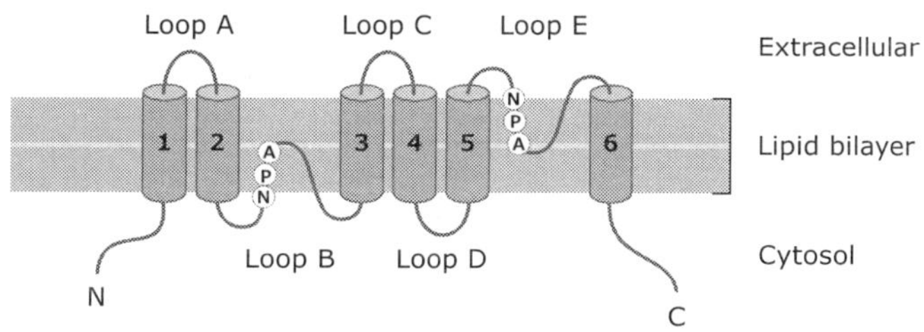

Figure 3.13 Topology of an aquaporin monomer within the membrane. It consists of six transmembrane α-helices (1-6) connected by five loops (A-E). Loops B and E, containing the conserved NPA motifs (in the single-letter amino-acid code), form short α-helices that fold back into the membrane from opposite sides.

In mammalian cells, more than 10 isoforms of aquaporins have been identified so far. They are differentially expressed in tissue-specific manner. Many mammalian AQPs, including AQP1, AQP2, AQP4, AQP5 and AQP8, function primarily as bidirectional water-selective transporters (called **orthodox AQPs**). A subset of the AQPs (such as AQP3, AQP7 and AQP9), called **aquaglyceroporins**, transport both water and glycerol. AQPs have also been proposed to transport other uncharged molecules, including ammonia and hydrogen peroxide. Water permeation through aquaporins is a passive process. Although many aquaporins function as always-open channels, a subgroup of aquaporins, particularly in plants, are gated channels. Most AQPs are constitutively expressed at the cell plasma membrane, whereas AQP2, found in the epithelial cells lining the renal collecting duct in the kidney, is stored in intracellular vesicle membranes, which after signal from **antidiuretic hormone** (**ADH**), fuses with the plasma membrane, thereby increasing the water permeability of epithelial cells. When the ADH level drops, AQP2 is resequestered within vesicles, reducing water uptake.

Ionophores

Ionophores are small, hydrophobic, lipid-soluble molecules that enter into lipid bilayers, increasing their permeability to specific inorganic ions. Ionophores shield the charge of the ion to be transported, enabling it to penetrate the hydrophobic interior of the lipid bilayer. There are two classes of ionophores – **mobile ion carriers** (which move within in the bilayer) and **channel formers** (which span the lipid bilayer). **Valinomycin** (isolated from *Streptomyces fulvissimus*) is an example of a mobile ion carrier. It transports K^+ down its electrochemical gradient. Similarly, ionophore **monensin** acts as a carrier for Na^+ ions. **Gramicidin A**, produced by the bacterium *Bacillus brevis*, is a 15-residue peptide composed of alternating D- and L-amino acids. In membranes, it forms a channel that allows the passage of water and monovalent cations but not anions.

2. Active transport

Active transport occurs against the concentration or electrochemical gradient (*uphill*) and is mediated by carrier proteins. Energy is required to move solutes against the gradient. The energy may come directly from ATP hydrolysis or may be supplied in the form of one solute moving down its electrochemical gradient, which provides energy to drive another solute against its gradient. Active transport results in the accumulation of solute on one side of membrane.

Active transport is different from carrier-mediated facilitated diffusion. Comparison of carrier-mediated facilitated and active transport is given in the following table.

Table 3.3 Comparison of carrier-mediated facilitated diffusion and active transport

Facilitated diffusion	**Active transport**
Passive (energy independent)	Active (energy dependent)
Selective	Selective
Occurs *along* the gradient	Occurs *against* the gradient
Saturable	Saturable
Entropy increases	Entropy decreases

Active transport can be classified into two types: *primary active transport* and *secondary active transport*, based on the nature of the energy source—either ATP or an electrochemical gradient.

Primary active transport

Primary (*direct*) active transport is coupled directly with a source of energy, such as ATP hydrolysis, or absorption of light. Transport of Na^+ and K^+ by carrier protein, Na^+-K^+ ATPase (or Na^+-K^+ pump), is the most common example of primary active transport. Virtually every animal cell maintains lower Na^+ concentration and high K^+ concentration in cytosol than they are found in its surrounding. This imbalance is established and maintained by an active transport system in the plasma membrane, involves the carrier protein Na^+-K^+ ATPase coupled with breakdown of ATP (discovered by Jens Skou in 1957).

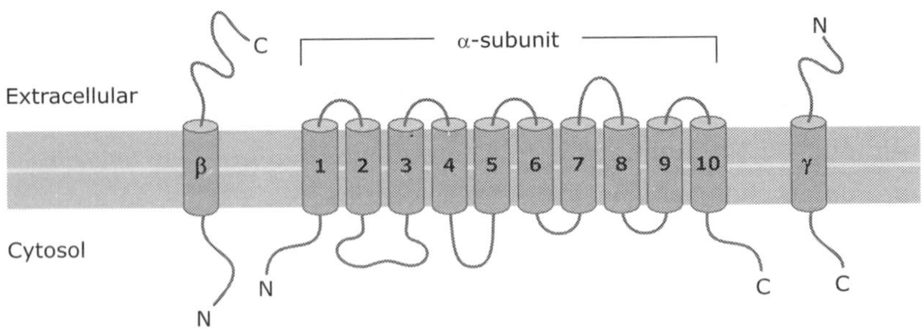

Figure 3.14 Schematic representation of the subunits of Na^+-K^+ ATPase, which is composed of a catalytic α-subunit, a glycosylated β-subunit and a γ-subunit (containing an extracellular invariant FXYD sequence).

Na^+-K^+ ATPase is composed of three different subunits, α-subunit, β-subunit and γ-subunit. The α-subunit is a multipass transmembrane protein, containing 10 transmembrane segments with a total molecular mass of about 110 kD. The α-subunit is responsible for ATP hydrolysis and ion transport. The β-subunit is a single-pass transmembrane protein with a molecular mass of about 55 kD. Its N-terminus is located in the cytosol, whereas the C-terminus (glycosylated) is located in the extracellular medium. A regulatory single-pass transmembrane γ-subunit also present which contains an extracellular invariant **FXYD** (Phe-X-Tyr-Asp) **sequence**. The Na^+-K^+ ATPase couples ATP hydrolysis with the active transport of 3 Na^+ ions out of the cell in exchange for 2 K^+ ions during each enzyme cycle. This cotransporter belongs to P-type transport ATPase. It couples phosphorylation- dephosphorylation of the critical Asp residue to the simultaneous movement of both Na^+ and K^+ against their electrochemical gradients. It is primarily responsible for setting and maintaining the intracellular concentrations of Na^+ and K^+ and for generating the transmembrane electrical potential. It is an example of the *electrogenic* pump because it contributes to the charge separation across the membrane.

Certain steroids like **digoxin** (from *Digitalis purpurea*) and **ouabain** (from *Strophanthus gratus*), which are known as **cardiotonic steroids** or *cardiac glycosides* are potent inhibitors of the Na^+-K^+ ATPase. These compounds inhibit the dephosphorylation of Na^+-K^+ ATPase when applied on the extracellular face of the membrane. These cardiotonic steroids are used in the treatment of congestive heart diseases because they increase the force of contraction of heart muscle by inhibiting the Na^+-K^+ ATPase. It happens as the level of Na^+ increases inside the cell, this slows the **Na^+-Ca^{2+} exchanger**, leading to increase in concentration of Ca^{2+} inside, which ultimately increases the force of contraction of the heart muscle. **Palytoxin** (toxic non-peptide substances) also inhibits the function of Na^+-K^+ ATPase. It converts Na^+-K^+ ATPase into a non-specific ion channel, which allows the passive transport of both Na^+ and K^+ ions, thereby destroying the ion gradient.

The active transport of calcium across the plasma membrane is driven by a Ca^{2+}-ATPase that is structurally related to the Na^+-K^+ ATPase and is similarly powered by ATP hydrolysis. The Ca^{2+}-ATPase transports calcium out of the cell, so intracellular calcium concentrations are extremely low.

Transport ATPase

Transport ATPases are the ATP powered carrier proteins, which transport various solutes against their gradients (i.e., perform primary active transport). Four major types of ATPases are associated with membranes that couple ATP hydrolysis with the translocation of various solutes across a membrane: P-, V-, F-ATPases and ABC transporter.

P-type ATPases are cation transporters that undergo reversible phosphorylation (thus the name P-type) of a key conserved aspartate residue during the transport of solutes. The primary structure of a P-type ATPase is generally identified by conserved cytosolic domains. These domains include a **nucleotide binding domain** (N), a **phosphorylation domain** (P) and an **actuator domain** (A). Examples of P-type ATPases are Na^+-K^+ ATPase (present in the plasma membrane of animal cells), H^+-ATPase (present in the plasma membranes of fungi and plants) and Ca^{2+}-ATPase (present in the membrane of sarcoplasmic reticulum).

V-type ATPases couple ATP hydrolysis to transport of protons against a electrochemical gradient. These transport ATPase are found on the vacuolar membranes (from which the 'V' is derived) in plant cells, endosomal and lysosomal membranes in animal cells and plasma membrane of osteoclasts. V-type ATPases generally function to maintain the low pH of plant vacuoles and of lysosomes and other vesicles in animal cells by pumping protons from the cytosolic to the non-cytosolic side of the membrane against a proton electrochemical gradient.

F-type ATPases have a complex polypeptide composition very similar to V-ATPases. All known V and F-ATPases transport only protons, in a process that does not involve phosphorylation during catalysis. In nonphotosynthetic eukaryotes, the F-ATPase is found exclusively on the inner mitochondrial membrane of mitochondria, whereas in green plants there are two distinct F-ATPases; one in mitochondria and the other on the thylakoid membrane of chloroplasts. In bacteria, F-ATPase is present in the plasma membrane. These ATPases couple the flow of protons with ATP hydrolysis and synthesis.

ABC (ATP binding cassette) **transporters** constitute a large family of ATP dependent transporters that pump a wide range of solutes, including ions, sugars, and amino acids. Most ABC transporters are present in the plasma membrane, but sometimes are also found in membrane of ER, mitochondria and lysosome. ABC transporters utilize energy derived from ATP hydrolysis to transport solutes. A functional ABC transporter has two *transmembrane domains* (**TMDs**) and two cytosolic *nucleotide binding domains* (**NBDs**, also called ATP-binding cassettes). Each TMD consists of six membrane-spanning segments (6 pass). ABC transporters are either *full-transporters* combining all required domains in one polypeptide (2 TMDs and 2 NBDs), or *half-transporters* consisting of 1 TMD and 1 NBD that need to form homo- or heterodimers to constitute a functional transporter. Eukaryotic ABC transporters are mostly full-transporters whereas prokaryotic ABC transporters are half-transporters. Most ABC transporters act as carriers, but some members of the superfamily act as ion channels that open and close by ATP hydrolysis.

An important member of ABC transporter family is **P-glycoprotein** (also called *multidrug resistance protein 1*, **MDR1**). It is a 170 kDa phosphorylated and glycosylated plasma membrane protein. MDR1 was initially identified because of its ability to confer multidrug resistance in lung cancer cells. It plays an important role in pumping of xenobiotics (such as toxins or drugs) against their concentration gradient from the cell and provides defense against harmful substances. However, transport exhibits very little substrate specificity. The only common characteristic of the substrates appears to be their high hydrophobicity, that is, works as a *hydrophobic vacuum cleaner*.

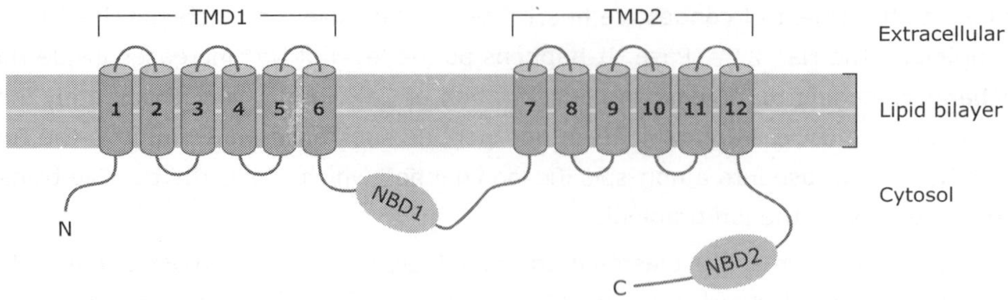

Figure 3.15 ABC full transporter structure. It contains two TMDs (TMD1 and TMD2) and two NBDs (NBD1 and NBD2). Each TMD contains 6 transmembrane segments. ABC half transporters have only one TMD and one NBD and need to homo or heterodimerize to form a functional transporter.

CFTR (*c*ystic *f*ibrosis *t*ransmembrane *c*onductance *r*egulator) also belongs to the ABC transporter family. It is a glycoprotein functions as a cAMP-activated ATP-gated chloride channel. The CFTR protein is widely expressed in the body including the lungs, gastrointestinal tract, liver, pancreas, sweat glands and the reproductive tract. The CFTR channel is unusual in that it requires both ATP hydrolysis and cAMP-dependent phosphorylation. Phosphorylation of the **R-domain** by the cAMP-dependent protein kinase A (**PKA**) and ATP binding with NBDs (NBD1 and NBD2) is a prerequisite for channel opening. The unphosphorylated R-domain inhibits channel opening. ATP hydrolysis is required for closing of channels. The CFTR protein acts as a channel that transports chloride ions out of cells. The transport of chloride ions helps control the movement of water across plasma membrane, which is necessary for the production of thin, freely flowing mucus. Mucus lubricates and protects the lining of the airways, digestive system, reproductive system and other organs and tissues. The CFTR protein also regulates the function of other channels, such as sodium ions channels. Defective CFTR protein is responsible for disease **cystic fibrosis**. It is an autosomal recessive disorder.

Secondary active transport

Secondary active (*indirect*) transport occurs when *endergonic* (uphill) transport of one solute is coupled with the *exergonic* (downhill) flow of a different solute that was originally pumped uphill by primary active transport. In this case, the energy for active transport comes from an **electrochemical gradient**. Secondary active transport is either symport or antiport, depending on whether the two solutes move in the same or opposite directions.

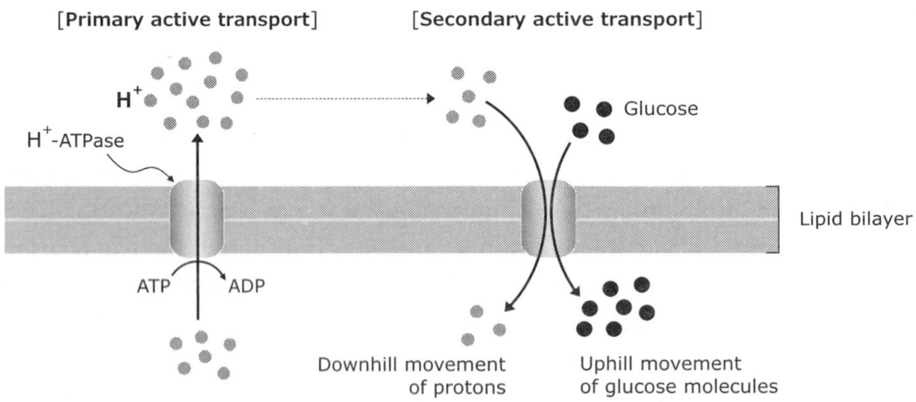

Figure 3.16 Comparison of primary and secondary active transport. In primary active transport, the energy released by ATP hydrolysis drives solute movement against the gradient. In secondary active transport, energy for against the gradient transport of a solute comes from electrochemical gradient. This electrochemical gradient of a solute has been established by primary active transport. Movement of this solutes down its electrochemical gradient now provides the energy to drive co-transport of a second solute, against its gradient.

A common example of secondary active transport is the symport of Na^+ and glucose in the epithelial cell of the small intestine. **Na^+-glucose symporters** (also known as **Na^+-glucose transporter**) are located on the apical surface (facing the lumen) of the epithelial cell and actively transport glucose molecules into the cell from the gut. The Na^+

flows down their electrochemical gradient while the glucose molecules are transported against their concentration gradient into the cell. Later, the Na^+ is pumped back out of the cell by the Na^+-K^+ ATPase, thus maintaining the inward Na^+ gradient. The GLUT confined to the basolateral (basal and lateral) surfaces of the cell allows the same molecules to leave the cell by facilitated diffusion into the extracellular fluid on the other side of the epithelium.

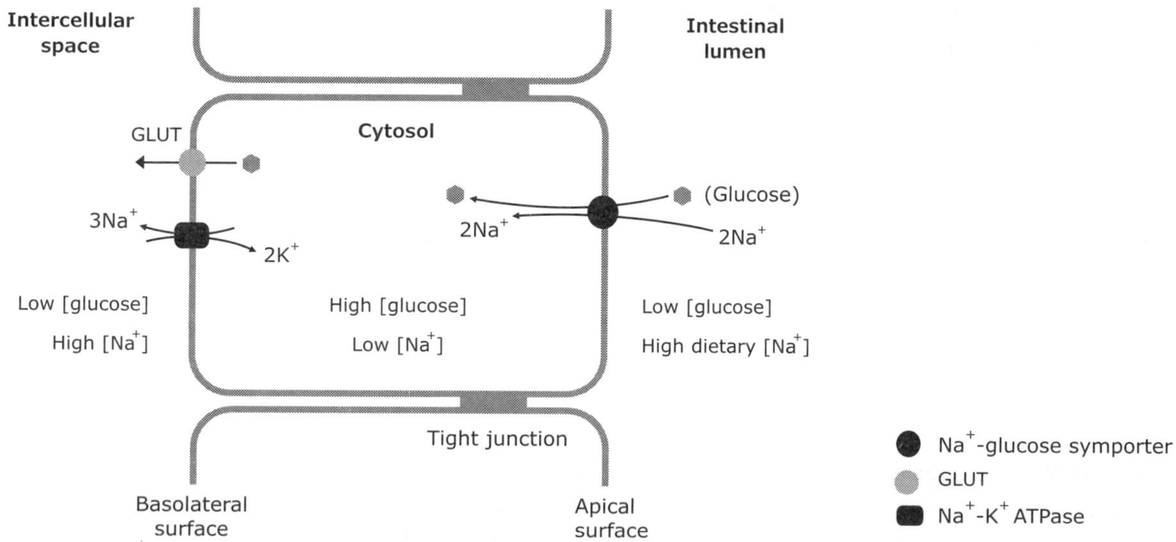

Figure 3.17 Glucose is actively transported into the cell by Na^+-driven glucose symporters at the apical surface, and it diffuses out of the cell by facilitated diffusion mediated by glucose transporter (GLUT) in the basolateral membrane. Tight junctions block the backflow of glucose from the basal side of the epithelium into the gut lumen.

Similarly, **lactose permease** (also known as **H^+-galactoside symporter**) present in the plasma membrane of bacteria such as *E. coli* utilizes the proton gradient across the membrane to co-transport proton and lactose. The primary transport of proton (H^+) out of the cell establishes both a proton gradient and an electrical potential (inside negative) across the membrane. Active transport of lactose into the cell involves symport of proton and lactose by the lactose transporter. The free energy released from the downhill movement of the proton is used for the uphill movement of lactose.

Thermodynamics of transport

Active transport is mediated by the transport protein coupled to an energy source. If the solute is uncharged, the difference in the concentration on the two sides of the membrane – its *concentration gradient* – influence its transport. The amount of energy needed for the transport of an uncharged solute against a concentration gradient can be calculated from the initial concentration gradient.

The free-energy change (ΔG) in transporting an uncharged solute from a compartment at concentration C_1 to one at C_2 is given by

$$\Delta G = RT \ln \frac{C_2}{C_1}$$

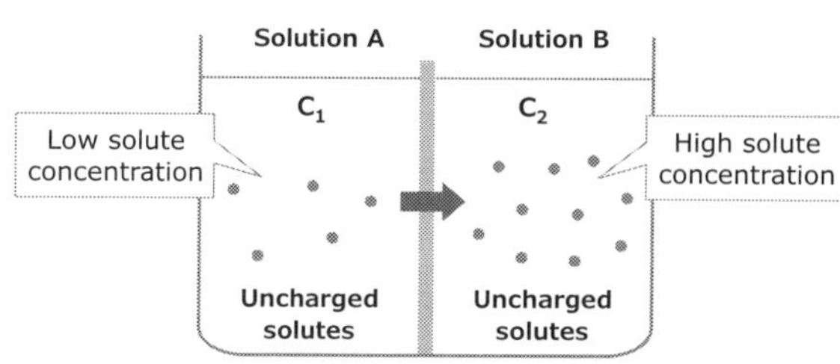

Chemical potential difference

In this equation, R is the *gas constant* and T is the *absolute temperature*. According to this equation, a transport process must be active when ΔG is *positive*, whereas it can be passive when ΔG is *negative*. However, if the solute carries a net charge, both its concentration gradient and the electrical potential difference across the membrane, the membrane potential, influence its transport. Thus, for the *charged* solute, the free energy change for transport across a membrane involves two contributors: the normal concentration term plus a second term describing the energy change involved in moving a charged solute across the potential difference. The sum of the concentration and electrical terms is called the **electrochemical potential**.

The free-energy change (ΔG) in transporting a charged solute from a compartment at concentration C_1 to one at C_2 is given by

$$\Delta G = RT \ln \frac{C_2}{C_1} + Z.F.\Delta\psi$$

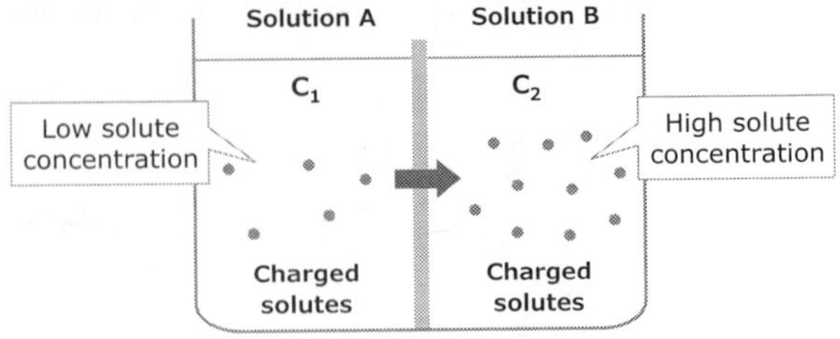

Chemical and electrical potential difference

In this equation, F is the *Faraday constant* (96.5 kJ $mole^{-1}$ V^{-1}) and $\Delta\psi$ is the *transmembrane electrical potential* (in volts). Eukaryotic cells typically have electrical potentials across their plasma membranes of about 0.05 to 0.1 V (with the inside negative relative to the outside).

Problem

For the Na^+-mediated active transport of a molecule of glutamate from a concentration of 0.1 mM outside the cell to 20 mM inside the cell, calculate the minimum number of Na^+ ions required to supply the necessary free energy. ΔG released for the transport of one Na^+ is 3.3 kcal/mol. Glutamate carries a net charge of −1 at pH 7.

(Use T = 37°C, pH = 7, $\Delta\Psi$ = −70 mV, R = 1.987 cal K^{-1} mol^{-1} and F = 23062 cal/mol.V).

Solution: According to the question, the solute carries a net charge. Hence, both its concentration gradient and the electrical potential difference across the membrane, the membrane potential, influence its transport. The concentration and electrical gradient combine to form a net driving force, the electrochemical gradient, for each charged solute. The free-energy change in transporting glutamate from outside the cell to inside the cell against an electrochemical gradient

$$\Delta G = RT\, ln \frac{[Glu^-]_{in}}{[Glu^-]_{out}} + z.F.\Delta\psi$$

$$= 1.987 \times 310 \times ln \frac{20}{0.1} + (-1) \times 23062 \times (-70 \times 10^{-3})$$

$$= 3286 + 1614 = 4900 \text{ or } 4.9 \text{ kcal/mole}$$

Because sodium ions release only 3.3 kcal/mole, at least 2 Na^+ are needed to co-transport one molecule of glutamate.

Summary

Overview of transport across plasma membrane

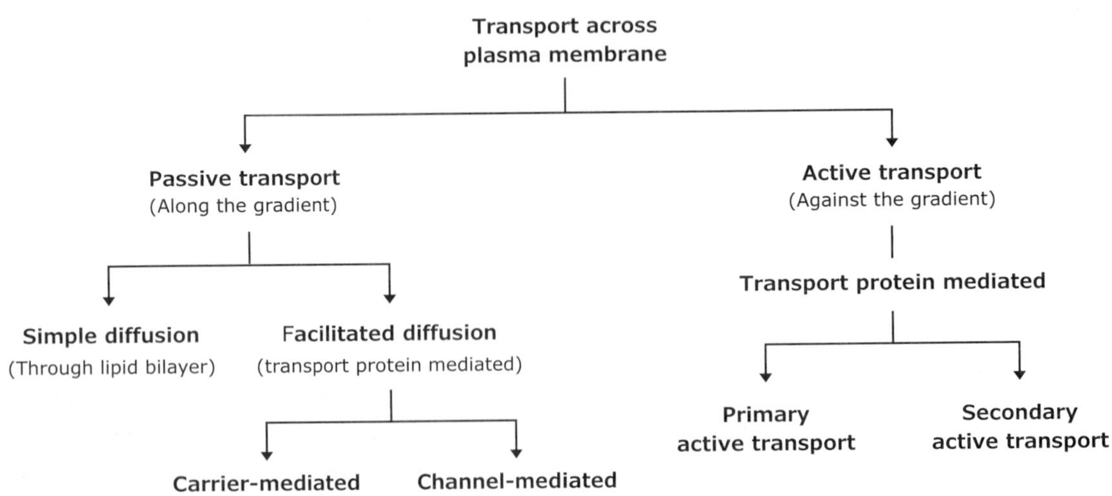

3.3 Membrane potential

All cells possess a difference in electrical potential across their plasma membrane, which is commonly referred to as **membrane potential**. In animal cells, the magnitude of this membrane potential ranges from 20 to 120 millivolts (mV), depending on the specific organism and cell type. According to convention, the polarity of the membrane potential is described based on the charge inside the cell. If the interior is negatively charged, the value is denoted with a negative sign, whereas if the interior is positively charged, the value is denoted with a positive sign.

How membrane potentials arise? Membrane potential is established due to the differences in ions concentrations across the membrane and the selective movement of the ions along the electrochemical gradient through ion specific channels present in the membrane. To help explain how an electric potential across the plasma membrane can arise, we first consider a set of simplified experimental systems. In system (A), the membrane is only permeable for K^+, which separates a 1 M KCl solution on the left from a 1 M KCl solution on the right. Because the concentrations of K^+ on both sides of the membrane are equal, there is no net flow of ions across the membrane and thus, no electric potential is generated. In system (B), the concentration of K^+ ions across the membrane is different and K^+ ions move down their electrochemical gradient from the left side to the right. It results in excess of negative Cl^- ions compared with K^+ ions on the left side and generates an excess of positive K^+ ions compared with Cl^- ions on the right side. The resulting separation of charge across the membrane constitutes an electric potential, with the left side of the membrane having excess negative charge with respect to the right. However, continued left-to-right movement of the K^+ ions is eventually inhibited by the mutual repulsion between the excess positive charges accumulated on the right side of the membrane and by the attraction of K^+ ions to the excess negative charges built up on the left side. The system soon reaches an *equilibrium point* at which the two opposing factors that determine the movement of K^+ ions—the membrane electric potential and the ion concentration gradient—balance each other out. When these two factors just balance each other, the electrochemical gradient for the ion is zero, and there is no net flow of the K^+ ions. The membrane potential at which this equilibrium is reached is called the **equilibrium potential** for the ion. In system (C), the membrane is impermeable for both ions. Even though the concentration of ions across the membrane is different, but no electric potential is generated. In system (D), the membrane is permeable for both ions. There is no selective permeability. Both K^+ and Cl^- ions move down their electrochemical gradient from the left side to the right. Thus, no electric potential is generated across the membrane.

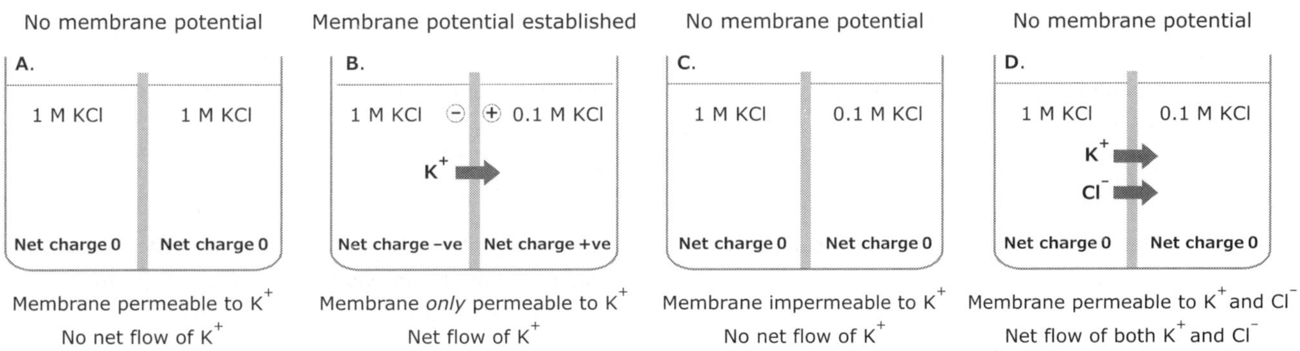

In case of system B at equilibrium, the electric potential across the membrane equals the potassium equilibrium potential in volts, E_K. The magnitude of E_K is given by the **Nernst equation**,

$$E_K = \frac{RT}{ZF} \ln \frac{[K_R]}{[K_L]}$$

Where, *R* (the gas constant) is 1.987 cal/(degree mol); *T* (the absolute temperature in degrees Kelvin) is 293 K at 20°C; *Z* (the charge, also called the valency) equals to 1; *F* (the Faraday constant) is 23,062 cal/(mol V), or 96,000 coulombs/(mol V); and $[K_R]$ and $[K_L]$ are the K^+ concentrations on the right and left sides, respectively, at equilibrium.

The Nernst equation enables us to calculate the membrane potential for only one ionic species at a time present in the system, and/or channels for only one ionic species are present; it is not applicable if two or more ions contribute to the membrane potential. In animal cells, the membrane potential is not governed by only one ion such as K^+, Na^+, Cl^-, etc. If this were the case, the membrane potential could be predicted by the equilibrium potential for that ion, and could be easily calculated by using the Nernst equation. Although, the membrane potential is established by several ions, in most animal cells, K^+, Na^+ and Cl^- are the main contributors to the membrane potential. Presence of selective ion channels allow these ions to move down its own electrochemical gradient. The movement of any ion down its own electrochemical gradient will tend to move the membrane potential toward the equilibrium potential for that ion. Therefore, the transmembrane movements of all three ions (K^+, Na^+ and Cl^-) collectively contribute to the membrane potential. To calculate membrane potential in such cases, we must employ the **Goldman–Hodgkin–Katz equation**, which relates the membrane potential to the concentration difference of different ions and their *permeability coefficient*. In this equation, the relative contribution of any given ion is determined not only by its concentration difference across the plasma membrane, but also by its relative membrane permeability. *Permeability* is directly proportional to the total number of open channels for a given ion in the membrane. Therefore, if many open K^+ channels are present, permeability coefficient for K^+ will be high. If only a few open K^+ channels are present, permeability coefficient for K^+ will be small. If all K^+ channels are closed or if no K^+ channels exist in the membrane, permeability coefficient for K^+ will be zero.

$$\Psi = \frac{RT}{F} \ln \frac{P_{K^+}[K^+]_{out} + P_{Na^+}[Na^+]_{out} + P_{Cl^-}[Cl^-]_{in}}{P_{K^+}[K^+]_{in} + P_{Na^+}[Na^+]_{in} + P_{Cl^-}[Cl^-]_{out}}$$

The equation provides a quantitative relation for predicting the membrane potential, where R is the universal gas constant, T is absolute temp, F is Faraday constant and, P is the permeability coefficient of the membrane to an ion.

Problem

KCl (100 mM) was entrapped inside large unilamellar vesicles. A diffusion potential across the bilayer can be generated by diluting with buffer containing

1. 100 mM KCl and a protonophore,
2. 100 mM NaCl and a protonophore,
3. 100 mM KCl and a K^+ specific ionophore and
4. 100 mM NaCl and a K^+ specific ionophore.

Solution: Ion concentration gradients across the membrane, and selective movements of ions along the gradient create a difference in potential across the bilayer. So, a diffusion potential across the bilayer can be generated by diluting with buffer containing 100 mM NaCl and a K^+ specific ionophore. In this case, only K^+ will move along the gradient from vesicles to buffer solution.

Problem

For a mammalian skeletal muscle, the extracellular potassium ion concentration, $[K^+]_{out}$ is 4 mM, and the intracellular potassium ion concentration, $[K^+]_{in}$ is 128 mM. Calculate the approximate potassium equilibrium potential (in mV). Assume: Faraday's constant = 9.65×10^4 C mol^{-1}; Gas constant = 8.31 J K^{-1} mol^{-1}; temperature = 37°C

Solution: $E_{K^+} = \frac{RT}{nF} \ln \frac{[K^+]_{out}}{[K^+]_{in}} = \frac{2.303 \times 8.31 \times 310}{1 \times 96500} \log \frac{4}{128} = -0.0925 \text{ V} = -92.5 \text{ mV}$

Resting potential and action potential

Animal cells can be divided into two categories – **non-excitable cells** (such as epithelial cells and adipose cells) and **excitable cells** (such as neurons, muscle cells, some endocrine cells). In case of non-excitable cells, membrane potential does not change whereas excitable cells have the ability to change their membrane potential when excited. The constant membrane potential in the non-excitable cells and those of excitable cells when they are at rest is known as the **resting membrane potential** (simply **resting potential**). In animal cells, the resting potential is dictated predominantly by the K^+ ions gradient. The predominant positive ion inside the cell is the K^+ ions. The high intracellular concentration of K^+ ions is, in part, generated by the Na^+-K^+ pump, which actively pumps K^+ ions into the cell. This leads to a large concentration difference for K^+ and Na^+ ions across the plasma membrane, with the concentration of K^+ ions being much higher inside the cell than outside and the concentration of Na^+ ions higher outside the cell.

The plasma membrane, however, also contains large number of **K^+-leaky channels**. These open channels allow potassium ions to move freely. Transfer of positive charge to the exterior leaves behind unbalanced negative charge within the cell, thereby creating *resting potential*. In the case of nerve cells, based on the concentration gradients that exist across the plasma membrane, K^+ tends to drive membrane potential to the equilibrium potential for K^+ (–90 mV), whereas Na^+ tends to drive membrane potential to the equilibrium potential for Na^+ (+60 mV). However, K^+ exerts the dominant effect on resting potential because the membrane is more permeable to K^+ due to the presence of a large number of K^+-leaky channels. These channels allow K^+ ions to move freely along the electrochemical gradient. Transfer of positive charge to cell's exterior leaves behind unbalanced negative charge within the cell, thereby creating *resting potential*. Its value is about –70 mV (much closer to E_{K^+} than to E_{Na^+}), with the inside of the cell is negative. A nerve cell that exhibits a resting membrane potential is said to be **polarized**.

Concentration (in millimoles per liter) and permeability of ions responsible for membrane potential in a resting nerve cell

Ion	Extracellular concentration	Intracellular concentration	Relative permeability
Na^+	150	15	1
K^+	5	150	25-30

Neurons or **nerve cells** are *excitable* (generate and propagate electrical signals when excited) and *secretory* (secrete neurotransmitters) cells. Its membrane potential changes in resting and excited state. Its membrane potential in resting state (when a cell not producing electrical signals) is referred to as **resting potential**. Changes in membrane potential are brought about by changes in ion movement across the membrane. For example, if the net inward flow of positively charged ions increases compared to the resting state, the membrane **depolarizes**. In this situation, the inside becomes less negative as compared to polarized resting state (for example, a change from –70 mV to –40 mV). This term is also used when the inside becoming positive (for example, a change from –70 mV to +30 mV as during an action potential). By contrast, if the net outward flow of positively charged ions increases compared to the resting state, the membrane **hyperpolarizes** (i.e., inside becomes more negative as compared to the resting state).

A rapid and large changes in membrane potential of nerve cells during which the potential actually reverses so that the inside of the cell transiently becomes more positive than the outside (i.e., depolarized) is termed as **action potential** (*nerve action potential* or *nerve impulse*). Action potentials allow communication over long distances within the body. Let us now consider how the changes in potential occurs during an action potential. Movement of potassium ions along the electrochemical gradient through potassium leaky channels is responsible for the establishment of the *resting potential*. By contrast, action potentials are the direct consequence of the voltage-gated Na^+ channels. During an action potential, movement of sodium ions occurs through voltage-gated Na^+ channels down their electrochemical gradients. This voltage-gated Na^+ channel can exist in three conformations:

1. Closed but capable of opening (activation gate closed, inactivation gate open)
2. Open (both activation and inactivation gates open)
3. Closed and not capable of opening or inactivated (activation gate open, inactivation gate closed)

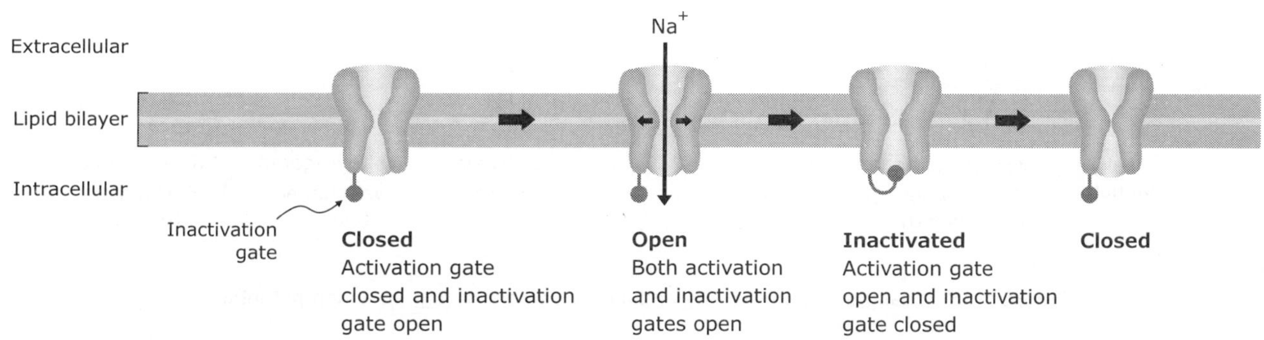

The channel undergoes through these various conformations as a result of voltage changes that take place during an action potential. At resting potential (about –70 mV), voltage-gated Na^+ channels are closed. Therefore, sodium ions cannot pass through these voltage-gated channels at resting potential. A stimulus that causes sufficient depolarization promptly causes voltage-gated Na^+ channels to open, allowing sodium ions to enter into the cell down its electrochemical gradient. The influx of positive charge *depolarizes* the membrane. This changes the membrane potential value of about –70 mV to about +30 mV within a fraction of a second.

The voltage-gated Na^+ channels have an automatic inactivating mechanism, which causes the channels to reclose rapidly even though the membrane is still depolarized. The voltage-gated Na^+ channels remain in this inactivated state, unable to reopen, until a few milliseconds after the membrane potential returns to its initial negative value.

In addition to the inactivation of voltage-gated Na^+ channels, another channels operate to help bring the depolarized plasma membrane more rapidly back toward its original polarized state. It is voltage-gated K^+ channels. The opening and consequent efflux of potassium ions quickly drives the membrane back toward the potassium ions equilibrium potential. This process is called **repolarization**.

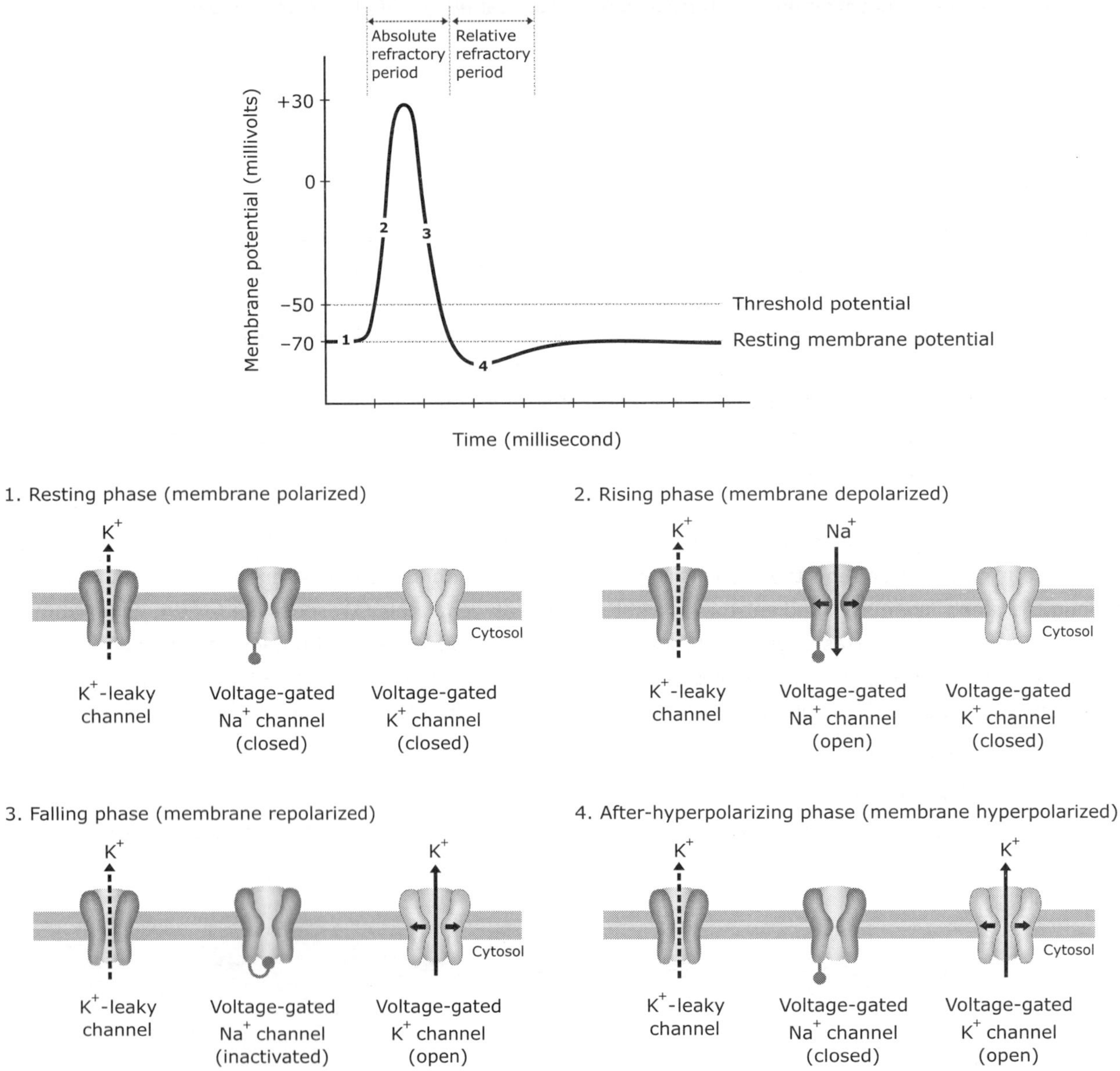

Figure 3.18 Changes in permeability and ion movement during an action potential.

Voltage-gated K^+ channels respond to changes in membrane potential in much the same way as the voltage-gated Na^+ channels do, but with slightly slower kinetics; for this reason, they are sometimes called **delayed K^+ channels**. Unlike voltage-gated Na^+ channels, most voltage-gated K^+ channels do not exhibit an inactivated state. Instead, they alternate between closed and open states. Hence, an action potential has two main phases: a depolarizing phase (i.e., rising phase) and a repolarizing phase (i.e., falling phase). During the **depolarizing phase**, the negative membrane potential becomes less negative, reaches zero, and then becomes positive. During the **repolarizing phase**, the membrane potential is restored to the resting state of –70 mV. Following the repolarizing phase, there may be an **after-hyperpolarizing phase**, during which the membrane potential temporarily becomes more negative (about –90 mV) than the resting state.

The period of time after an action potential begins during which an excitable cell cannot generate another action potential in response to a *normal* threshold stimulus is called the **refractory period**. It can be absolute or relative. During the **absolute refractory period**, even a very strong stimulus cannot initiate a second action potential. This period coincides with the period of voltage-gated Na^+ channel activation and inactivation. Inactivated Na^+ channels cannot reopen; they first must return to the closed state. The **relative refractory period** is the time period during which a second action potential can be initiated, but only by a larger-than normal stimulus. It coincides with the period when the voltage-gated K^+ channels are still open after inactivated voltage-gated Na^+ channels have returned to their closed state. The refractory period limit the number of action potentials that can be produced by an excitable membrane in a given period of time.

An action potential occurs in the membrane of the axon of a neuron when depolarization reaches a certain level termed the **threshold potential** (typically between –50 to –55 mV). The generation of an action potential depends on whether a particular stimulus is able to bring the depolarization to threshold. An action potential will not occur in response to a sub-threshold stimulus, a stimulus that causes weak depolarization. However, an action potential will occur in response to a threshold stimulus, a stimulus that is just strong enough to depolarize the membrane to threshold. It means that an action potential either occurs completely or it does not occur at all. This characteristic of an action potential is known as the **all-or-none principle**.

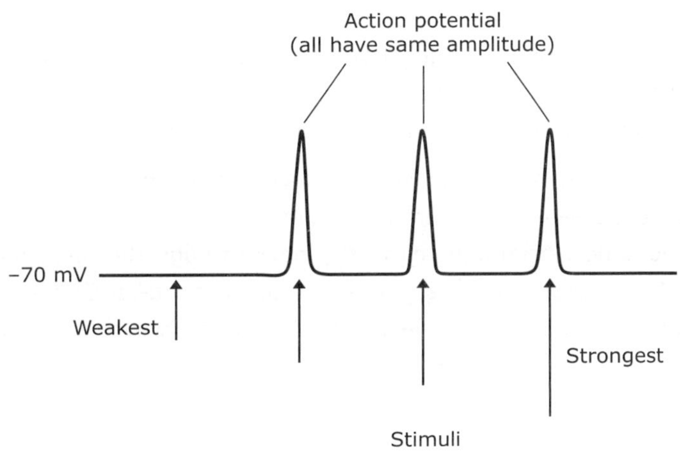

Figure 3.19 The all-or-none principle of action potentials. A single, quick shock delivered to an axon can serve as a depolarizing stimulus. If the stimulus is below threshold, no action potential is produced by the axon. Once the stimulus has reached threshold, a full action potential is produced. Any greater stimulus does not produce greater action potentials.

Apart from action potential, excitable cells — neurons and muscle fibers — also produce graded potentials. As compared to action potential, **graded potentials** are changes in membrane potential that are confined to a relatively small region of the plasma membrane and die out within 1 to 2 mm of their site of origin. They are usually produced by some specific change in the cell's environment acting on a specialized region of the membrane and they are called graded potentials simply because the magnitude of the potential change can vary (is graded). To say that these electrical signals are *graded* means that they vary in amplitude, depending on the strength of the stimulus.

They are larger or smaller depending on how many ligand-gated or mechanically gated channels have opened (or closed) and how long each remains open. The propagation of action potentials permits communication over long distances, but graded potentials can function only in short-distance communication because they are not propagated.

Transmission of nerve impulses

Neurons are the basic structural and functional units of the nervous system. Although neurons vary considerably in size and shape, they generally have three principal regions: a cell body, dendrites and an axon. The axon or nerve fiber, is a single, elongated, tubular extension that conducts action potentials *away from* the cell body and eventually terminates at other cells. The fundamental task of the neuron is to receive, conduct and transmit signals. These cells have the ability to respond to a stimulus by producing an electrical signal (i.e., *action potential* or nerve impulse). Nerve impulse propagates (travels) along the surface of the membrane of a neuron at speeds ranging from 0.5 to 130 meters per second. There are two types of propagation: *continuous conduction* and *saltatory conduction*. The **continuous conduction** involves step-by-step depolarization and repolarization of each adjacent segment of the plasma membrane. In this type of conduction, ions flow through their voltage-gated channels in each adjacent segment of the membrane. It occurs in unmyelinated axons. **Saltatory conduction** is a special type of nerve impulse propagation that occurs along myelinated axons. It occurs because of the uneven distribution of voltage-gated channels. Few voltage-gated channels are present in regions where a myelin sheath covers the axolemma (plasma membrane). By contrast, at the **nodes of Ranvier** (where there is no myelin sheath), the axolemma has many voltage-gated channels. Hence, flow of Na^+ and K^+ ions across the membrane mainly occurs at the nodes. Thus, action potentials literally jump from one node to the next as they propagate along a myelinated axon, and for this reason such propagation is called saltatory conduction. Propagation via saltatory conduction occurs faster than continuous conduction in nerve fibers of the same axon diameter.

How is the information transferred from one neuron to the next?

A neuron may terminate on one of three structures: a muscle, a gland, or another neuron. Therefore, depending on where a neuron terminates, it can cause a muscle cell to contract, a gland cell to secrete, another neuron to convey an electrical message along a nerve pathway, or some other function. The junction between two neurons is called a **synapse**. Typically, a synapse involves a junction between an axon terminal of one neuron, known as the **presynaptic neuron**, and the dendrites or cell body of a second neuron, known as the **postsynaptic neuron**. Synapses are not merely gaps, but are functional links between the two neurons. Synapses can be either *chemical* or *electrical*.

At **electrical synapse**, action potentials (nerve impulses) conduct directly between adjacent cells through structures called gap junctions. Gap junctions allow rapid communication between cells. No neurotransmitters are involved in an electrical synapse. As ions flow from one cell to the next through the gap junctions, the action potential propagates from cell to cell. At electrical synapses, the membranes of pre- and post-synaptic neurons are in very close proximity. Impulse transmission across an electrical synapse is always faster than that occurs at chemical synapse and also transmission occurs in *both* directions.

At a **chemical synapse**, the plasma membranes of the pre- and post-synaptic neurons are separated by a fluid-filled space called **synaptic cleft**. Chemicals called **neurotransmitters** are involved in the transmission of action potential at these synapses. Neurotransmitters are synthesized and packaged into the **synaptic vesicles** of the axon terminal of the presynaptic neuron. When an action potential arrives at the axon terminal, it stimulates the fusion of the synaptic vesicles with the plasma membrane and release their neurotransmitters in the synaptic cleft. The neurotransmitter binds to receptors present in the plasma membrane of the postsynaptic neuron and produces a **postsynaptic potential**. At a chemical synapse, a presynaptic neuron converts an electrical signal (nerve impulse) into a chemical signal (neurotransmitter release). The postsynaptic neuron then converts the chemical signal back into an electrical signal (postsynaptic potential). Most chemical synapses operate in one direction *only*. Only presynaptic neurons can release neurotransmitter, and only the postsynaptic neuron's plasma membrane has the receptor that can recognize and bind that neurotransmitter. As a result, action potentials move in one direction.

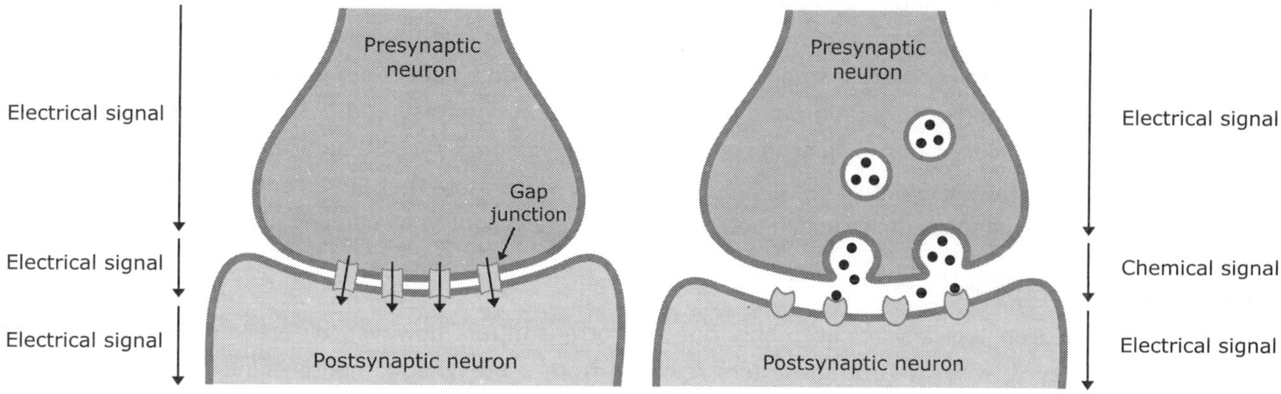

Electrical synapse	*Chemical synapse*
Uncommon in complex animals	Common in complex animals
Transmission fast	Transmission slow
Bi-directional transmission	Uni-directional transmission
Excitatory	Excitatory or inhibitory

Neurotransmitters are usually small molecular weight paracrine signal molecules, such as amino acids, amines, purines and neuropeptides. These molecules are synthesized in the presynaptic terminals of neurons and released on stimulation. Some neurotransmitters stimulate neurons to fire, while others inhibit firing. The effect of the neurotransmitter comes out by its binding with receptor proteins on the membrane of the postsynaptic neuron.

Table 3.4 The major known neurotransmitters

Neurotransmitter	Functional class
Ester	
Acetylcholine (Nicotinic)	Excitatory
Acetylcholine (Muscarinic)	Inhibitory
Biogenic amines	
Norepinephrine	Excitatory or inhibitory
Dopamine	Generally excitatory; may be inhibitory at some sites
Serotonin (5-hydroxytryptamine)	Generally inhibitory
Amino acids	
GABA (Gamma aminobutyric acid)	Inhibitory
Glycine	Inhibitory
Glutamate	Excitatory
Aspartate	Excitatory
Neuropeptides	
Substance P	Excitatory
Met-enkephalin	Generally inhibitory

Excitatory and inhibitory postsynaptic potential

At a chemical synapse, a presynaptic neuron converts an electrical signal (nerve impulse) into a chemical signal (neurotransmitter release). The postsynaptic neuron then converts the chemical signal back into an electrical signal (postsynaptic potential). Of the many synapses on a neuron, some tend to excite it (**excitatory synapses**), others to inhibit it (**inhibitory synapses**). Neurotransmitter released at an excitatory synapse causes a small *depolarization* in the postsynaptic membrane called an **excitatory postsynaptic potential** (EPSP), while neurotransmitter released at an inhibitory synapse generally causes a small *hyperpolarization* called an **inhibitory postsynaptic potential** (IPSP). EPSPs increase the likelihood of generation of a postsynaptic action potential, and IPSPs decrease this likelihood. During hyperpolarization, generation of an action potential becomes more difficult than usual because the membrane potential becomes inside more negative as compared to resting state. Note that EPSPs and IPSPs are produced by opening of ligand gated channels, unlike action potentials, which are produced by opening of voltage-gated channels.

Neurotransmitter receptors

Each presynaptic neuron typically releases only one neurotransmitter; however, different neurons vary in the neurotransmitter they release. Neurotransmitters released from a presynaptic neuron bind to *neurotransmitter receptors* in the plasma membrane of a postsynaptic neuron. When a neurotransmitter binds to the correct neurotransmitter receptor, a postsynaptic potential (either an EPSP or IPSP) forms in the plasma membrane of the postsynaptic neuron. Neurotransmitter receptors are classified as either *ionotropic receptors* or *metabotropic receptors* based on whether the neurotransmitter binding site and the ion channel are components of the same protein or are components of different proteins. An **ionotropic receptor** is a type of ligand-gated ion channel. In the absence of neurotransmitter (the ligand), the ion channel component of the ionotropic receptor remain closed. When the correct neurotransmitter binds to the ionotropic receptor, the ion channel opens, and an EPSP or IPSP occurs in the postsynaptic neuron. Most excitatory neurotransmitters bind to ionotropic receptors that act as cation channels. When cation channels open, they allow passage of the three most plentiful cations (Na^+, K^+ and Ca^{2+}) through the postsynaptic cell membrane, but sodium ions inflow is greater than either calcium ions inflow or potassium ions outflow and the inside of the postsynaptic cell becomes less negative (depolarized). In contrast, most inhibitory neurotransmitters bind to ionotropic receptors that act as chloride channels. When Cl^- channels open, a large number of chloride ions diffuse inward. The inward flow of chloride ions causes the inside of the postsynaptic cell to become more negative (hyperpolarized).

A **metabotropic receptor** is a type of neurotransmitter receptor that contains a neurotransmitter binding site, but an ion channel is not a part of its structure. This receptor is indirectly linked with ion channels present on the plasma membrane through signal transduction mechanisms. These receptors do not have ion channels as part of their structure; instead, they affect channels by the activation of intermediate molecules called G-proteins.

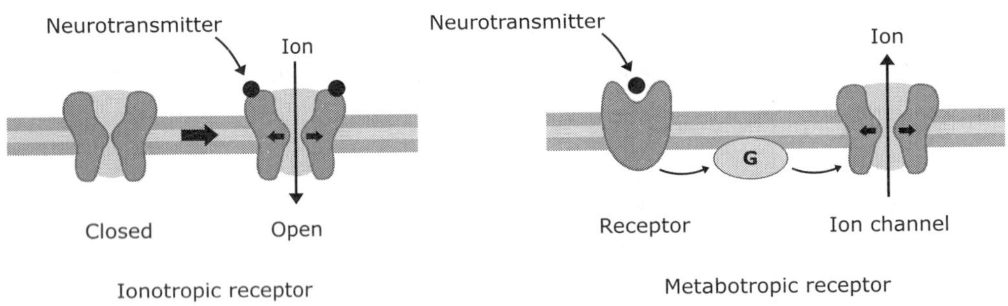

Figure 3.20 An ionotropic receptor is a type of neurotransmitter receptor that contains a neurotransmitter binding site and an ion channel whereas a metabotropic receptor is a type of neurotransmitter receptor that contains a neurotransmitter binding site and is coupled to a separate ion channel by a G-protein.

Transmission at chemical synapses

Transmission at chemical synapses occurs when a nerve impulse arrives at the terminal of the presynaptic neuron. A typical chemical synapse transmits a signal in following manner.

A nerve impulse arrives at axon terminal of a presynaptic axon. The change in membrane potential caused by the arrival of the action potential leads to the opening of voltage-gated Ca^{2+} channels in the presynaptic membrane.

Because concentrations of calcium ions are more in the extracellular fluid, calcium flows inward through the opened channels. An increase in the concentration of calcium inside the presynaptic neuron serves as a signal that triggers exocytosis of the synaptic vesicles. As vesicle membranes merge with the plasma membrane, neurotransmitter molecules within the vesicles are released into the synaptic cleft. Each synaptic vesicle contains several thousand molecules of neurotransmitter. The neurotransmitters diffuse across the synaptic cleft and bind to neurotransmitter receptors in the postsynaptic neuron's plasma membrane. Binding of neurotransmitter molecules to their receptors causes opening of channels and movement of ions across the membrane. As ions flow through the opened channels, the voltage across the membrane changes. This change in membrane voltage is a **postsynaptic potential.** Depending on which ions pass the channels, the postsynaptic potential may be a depolarization or a hyperpolarization.

A single postsynaptic neuron receives input from many presynaptic neurons, some of which release excitatory neurotransmitters and some of which release inhibitory neurotransmitters. The sum of all the excitatory and inhibitory effects at any given time determines the effect on the postsynaptic neuron. If the total excitatory effects are greater than the total inhibitory effects and threshold is reached, a nerve impulse (action potential) will be triggered. If the total inhibitory effects are greater than the excitatory effects, the membrane hyperpolarizes. The result is inhibition of the postsynaptic neuron and an inability to generate a nerve impulse.

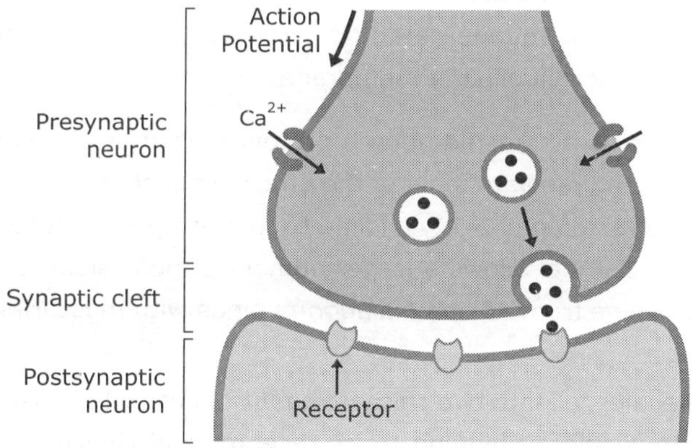

1. Action potentials arrive at axon terminal.
2. Voltage-gated Ca^{2+} channels open.
3. Ca^{2+} enters into the cell.
4. Ca^{2+}-dependent fusion of synaptic vesicles with the membrane.
5. Synaptic vesicles release neurotransmitter by exocytosis.
6. Neurotransmitter diffuses across the synaptic cleft and binds to receptors present at postsynaptic neurons.
7. Binding of neurotransmitter to receptor generates postsynaptic potential.

Figure 3.21 Transmission at chemical synapses.

Acetylcholine and acetylcholine receptor

Acetylcholine is a **cholinergic** neurotransmitter synthesized from choline and acetyl-CoA by enzyme **choline acetyl transferase.** It is synthesized in the axonal terminals. After synthesis, it is released by the process of exocytosis in the synaptic cleft. GPI linked enzyme **acetylcholinesterase** located on the postsynaptic membrane breaks acetylcholine into choline and acetyl-CoA. Acetylcholinesterase is a **serine esterase.** Insecticides like malathion, parathion, nerve gas like sarin and DIPF inhibit the activity of acetylcholinesterase. *Response of acetylcholine is both excitatory and inhibitory.* It can produce an excitatory response in some postsynaptic cells and an inhibitory response in others. Response is mediated by the binding of acetylcholine with **acetylcholine receptor** presents on postsynaptic cells. Acetylcholine receptors have been divided into two main types: *Nicotinic* and *muscarinic* acetylcholine receptor.

The **nicotinic acetylcholine receptor** (an **ionotropic receptor**) is a ligand-gated ion channel. It can be either neuronal type or muscle type. The muscle type nicotinic acetylcholine receptor is a pentamer of four kinds of membrane-spanning glycoprotein subunits 2α, β, γ and δ. Each α-subunit has a binding site for acetylcholine. It has a central pore and function as a ligand-gated channel for both Na^+ and K^+. Na^+ rushes in while K^+ streams out, but, because the Na^+ gradient across this membrane is steeper than that of K^+, the Na^+ influx greatly exceeds the K^+ efflux. The net influx of Na^+ ion depolarizes the postsynaptic membrane.

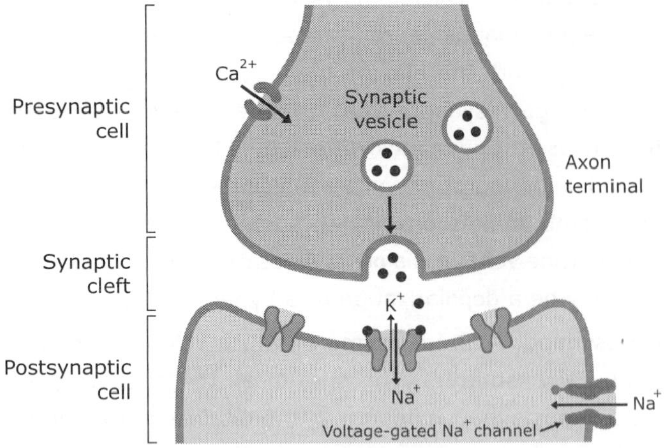

1. Acetylcholine is synthesized in the presynaptic cell.
2. Acetylcholine is packaged into synaptic vesicles.
3. Acetylcholine is released into the synaptic cleft.
4. Acetylcholine binds to its receptor on the postsynaptic cell.
5. Opening of nicotinic acetylcholine receptor.
6. Net influx of Na^+ into the postsynaptic cell.
7. Depolarization causes generation of EPSP in postsynaptic cell.
8. Opening of voltage-gated Na^+ channel.
9. Generation of action potential.

Figure 3.22 Nicotinic acetylcholine receptor and generation of action potential.

Opening of acetylcholine receptor channels following binding of acetylcholine produces a net depolarization in the postsynaptic cell. This localized depolarization triggers the opening of voltage-gated Na^+ channels, leading to the generation and conduction of an action potential in the postsynaptic cell plasma membrane.

The **muscarinic acetylcholine receptor** (a **metabotropic receptor**) is a transmembrane protein that interacts with G-proteins. Muscarinic acetylcholine receptors are metabotropic and mediate most of the effects of acetylcholine in brain. These receptors contain binding site for the acetylcholine. Binding of acetylcholine to this receptor activates a G-protein, which in turn opens a K^+ channel. Opening the K^+ channel allows a larger number of potassium ions to diffuse out of the cell and an IPSP forms. Antagonist like atropine from *Atropa belladonna* binds with muscarinic receptor and inhibits the function. It is used for pupil dilation.

Agonists and antagonists: Structural analogs of signaling molecules fall into two classes: *agonists* and *antagonists*. Structural analogs which mimic the function of a signaling molecule by binding to its receptor and causing the normal response are called *agonists*. Whereas *antagonists* are structural analogs which bind to the receptor but induces no response. Hence, an antagonist acts as an inhibitor of the natural signaling molecule (or agonist) by competing for binding sites on the receptor, thereby blocking the physiological activity of the signaling molecule.

Neurotoxins: Many plants and animals products act as neurotoxins. Some work by blocking the transmission of nerve impulse, other by blocking synaptic transmission. Example of some neurotoxins that inhibit the function of Na^+ and K^+ channels are given below:

Tetrodotoxin: Produced by puffer fish also called as swellfish, binds with Na^+-channel and blocks all ion movement.

Saxitoxin: Produced by dinoflagellates such as *G. catenella* and prevents the voltage gated Na^+ channel from opening.

Veratridine: Isolated from the sabadilla seeds and binds with Na^+ channel; and makes it permanently open.

Batrachotoxin: Produced by frog, *Phyllobates aurotaenia* and makes Na^+ channel permanently open.

Dendrotoxin: Produced by *Dendroaspis polylepis* and binds with K^+ channel; and blocks all ions movement.

3.4 Transport of macromolecules across plasma membrane

The plasma membrane is a dynamic structure that functions to segregate the chemically distinct intracellular milieu (the cytoplasm) from the extracellular environment by regulating and coordinating the entry and exit of small and large molecules. Essential small molecules, such as amino acids, sugars and ions, can traverse the plasma membrane through the action of transport proteins – carriers and channels. But transport of macromolecules is carried out by the process of *endocytosis* and *exocytosis*. In the case of **endocytosis**, materials are carried into the cell in membrane-bound endocytic vesicles derived by the invagination and pinching-off of pieces of the plasma membrane. As compared to endocytosis, in the case of **exocytosis**, materials are released from the cell and carried out by fusion of vesicular membrane to the plasma membrane.

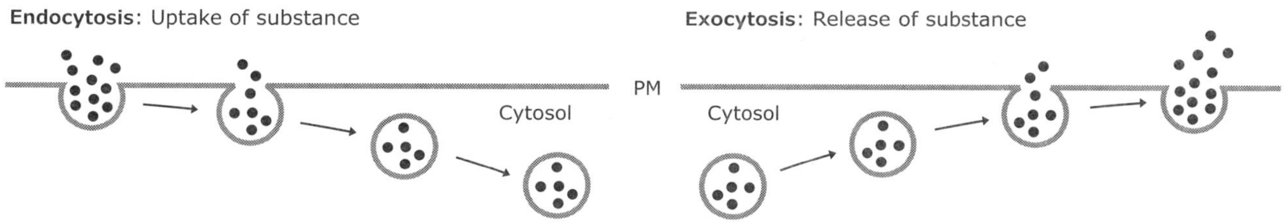

3.4.1 Endocytosis

The term *endocytosis* was coined by Christian de Duve in the year 1963. It is a process whereby cells internalize material from their surrounding environment. Internalization is achieved by the formation of membrane-bound vesicles at the cell surface that arise by progressive invagination of the plasma membrane, followed by pinching off and release of free vesicles into the cytoplasm. Classically, endocytosis has been divided into *phagocytosis* (cellular eating) and *pinocytosis* (cellular drinking).

Phagocytosis (first reported by Metchnikoff) describes the internalization of large particles following particle binding to specific cell-surface receptors and by the formation of large endocytic vesicles (generally >250 nm in diameter) called **phagosomes**. The phagosomes fuse with lysosomes to form **phagolysosomes**. The ingested material is then degraded in the phagolysosome. Indigestible substances remain in the phagolysosomes, forming residual bodies that can be excreted from cells by exocytosis. Phagocytosis is an active, actin-mediated and highly regulated process involving specific cell-surface receptors and signaling cascades mediated by **Rho protein**, a member of Rho-family GTPases. It regulates localized actin polymerization and formation of pseudopods. Rho family of GTPase is a family of monomeric small GTPase (such as Rho, Rac, Cdc42 and RhoD) that regulates many aspects of actin dynamics. In multicellular eukaryotes, phagocytosis is mediated by few specialized cells termed **phagocytes** (or **phagocytic cells**). These cells can be of two types - *professional phagocytes* (such as macrophages and neutrophils) and *non-professional phagocytes* (such as epithelial and endothelial cells).

Figure 3.23 Phagocytosis is a cargo-triggered process. Binding of cargo induce the phagocytic cell to extend pseudopods due to localized actin polymerization, which engulf the particle and fuse at their tips to form a phagosome.

Pinocytosis (also termed as **fluid-phase endocytosis**) involves the uptake of fluid by the formation of small endocytic vesicles (termed **pinocytic vesicles**) of about 100 nm in diameter. Virtually all eukaryotic cells perform pinocytosis. Uptake of soluble material dissolved in extracellular fluid during pinocytosis occurs both selectively as well as non-selectively. Selective uptake occurs when solutes are captured by specific high-affinity receptors (termed as **receptor-mediated endocytosis**). In receptor-mediated endocytosis, a specific receptor on the cell surface binds tightly to the extracellular macromolecule (the ligand) that it recognizes. The plasma membrane region containing the receptor-ligand complex then undergoes endocytosis. Pinocytosis occurs in all cells by at least four basic mechanisms: *macropinocytosis, clathrin-mediated endocytosis, caveolae-mediated endocytosis and clathrin- and caveolae independent endocytosis.*

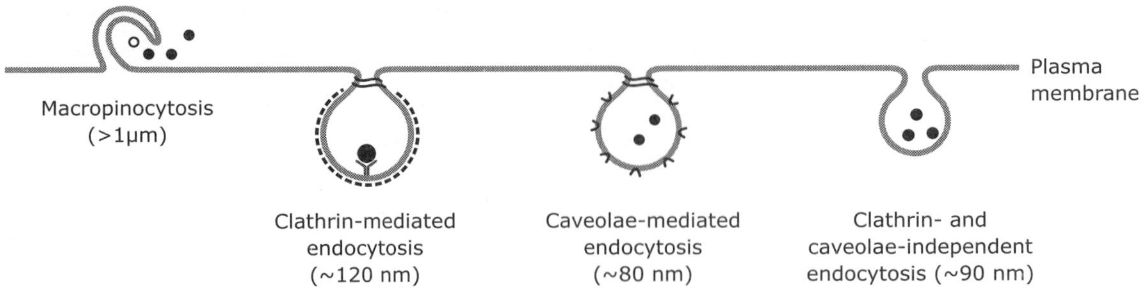

Figure 3.24 The pinocytic pathways differ with regard to the size of the endocytic vesicle, the nature of the cargo (the membrane components and soluble molecules carried by endocytic vesicles) and the mechanism of vesicle formation.

Macropinocytosis: This process of pinocytosis involves the membrane ruffling that is induced in many cell types upon stimulation by growth factors or other signals. Like phagocytosis, the signaling cascades that induce macropinocytosis involve Rho-family GTPases, which trigger the actin-driven formation of cell surface **ruffles**. As the ruffles collapse back onto the cell surface, they nonspecifically trap extracellular fluid and macromolecules contained in it, forming large endocytic vesicles, called **macropinosomes**. However, unlike phagocytosis, these protrusions do not 'zipper up' along a ligand coated particle.

Clathrin-mediated endocytosis: Clathrin-mediated endocytosis was previously referred to as *receptor mediated endocytosis*, but it is now clear that this is a misnomer, because most pinocytic pathways involve specific receptor and ligand interactions. In case of clathrin mediated endocytosis, macromolecules bind to cell-surface receptors, accumulate in clathrin-coated pits, and enter the cell as a receptor and ligand complexes in clathrin-coated vesicles. Each **clathrin** consists of three copies each of heavy chain and light chain, forming a three-legged structure called a **triskelion**. Clathrin triskelions are the assembly units of the polygonal lattice and assemble into a basket like convex framework of hexagons and pentagons to form coat. Clathrin assembles on the cytosolic side of the plasma membrane by interacting with its **adaptor proteins**. There are four structurally related adaptor protein complexes (**AP1**, **AP2**, **AP3** and **AP4**). Each of these four complexes is localized to different intracellular compartments and vary in their receptor specificity. AP2 participates in clathrin-mediated endocytosis from plasma membrane. It is heterotetramer consists of two large subunits α and β_2, one medium-sized subunit μ_2 and one small-sized subunit σ_2.

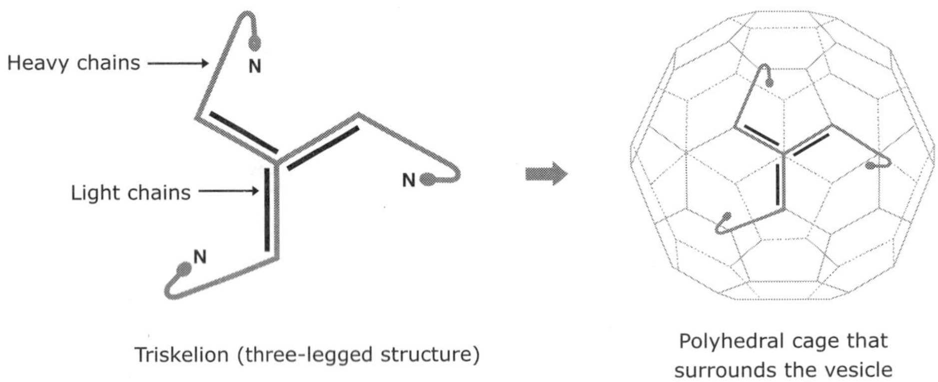

Figure 3.25 Structure of clathrin triskelion. Each triskelion consists of three clathrin heavy chains radiating from a central vertex, with a terminal globular domain at the tip of each triskelion leg and a clathrin light chain bound to the inner half of each leg.

After a clathrin-coated vesicle bud forms, **dynamin**, a ~100 kDa cytosolic protein, polymerizes around the neck. It is essential for release of complete clathrin-coated vesicles (i.e., *pinching off*). Dynamin polymerizes around the neck portion and then hydrolyzes GTP. The energy derived from GTP hydrolysis is essential for the final pinching off of a completed clathrin-coated vesicle. The clathrin coat is rapidly lost shortly after the vesicle forms. A **Hsc70 chaperone** in association with **auxilin** function as an uncoating ATPase to peel off the clathrin coat.

Uncoated endocytic vesicles are directed to fuse with and deliver their membrane and content to the intracellular organelles of the **endolysosomal pathway**, the endosomes and the lysosomes. Endosomes are single membrane-bound heterogeneous structure. It is of three types – **early endosome** (closer to plasma membrane), **late endosome** (closer to the nucleus) and **recycling endosome**. The endocytic vesicles deliver their contents and their membrane to early endosomes. Early endosomes mature into late endosomes that subsequently fuse with lysosomes. The fusion of an endosome with a lysosome generates a transient hybrid organelle, the **endolysosome**, in which active degradation takes place. *Recycling endosomes* are a sub-compartment of early or late endosomes that return material to the plasma membrane. Cargo (the membrane components and soluble molecules carried by endocytic vesicles) can be recycled from early and late endosomes. Late endosomes are more acidic than early endosomes. The interior of the endosomal compartment is kept acidic (pH ~6) by ATP driven H^+ pumps in the endosomal membrane that pump H^+ into the lumen from the cytosol.

Early endosomes mature into late endosomes called **endosome maturation**. As early endosomes mature, patches of their membrane invaginate into the endosome lumen and pinch off to form intralumenal vesicles. Late endosomes are typified by the appearance of numerous **intralumenal vesicles** and are often referred to as **multivesicular bodies** (or **multivesicular endosomes**). The multivesicular bodies carry endocytosed membrane proteins that are to be degraded. For the majority of late endosomes, their fate is to fuse with the lysosome, generating an **endolysosome** compartment that provides a controlled acidic environment for the degradation of the cargo-loaded intralumenal vesicles. At all events, the pathway is unidirectional, and a protein that has left the early endosome for the late endosome will end up in the lysosome. A number of **Rab proteins** typically associate with endosomes in their GTP-bound state. Rab-family of GTPases is a family of monomeric small GTPase that regulate biogenesis, transport, tethering and fusion and maturation of vesicles. Rab proteins are lipid-linked prenylated proteins. They alternate between GTP (active) and GDP (inactive) bound states.

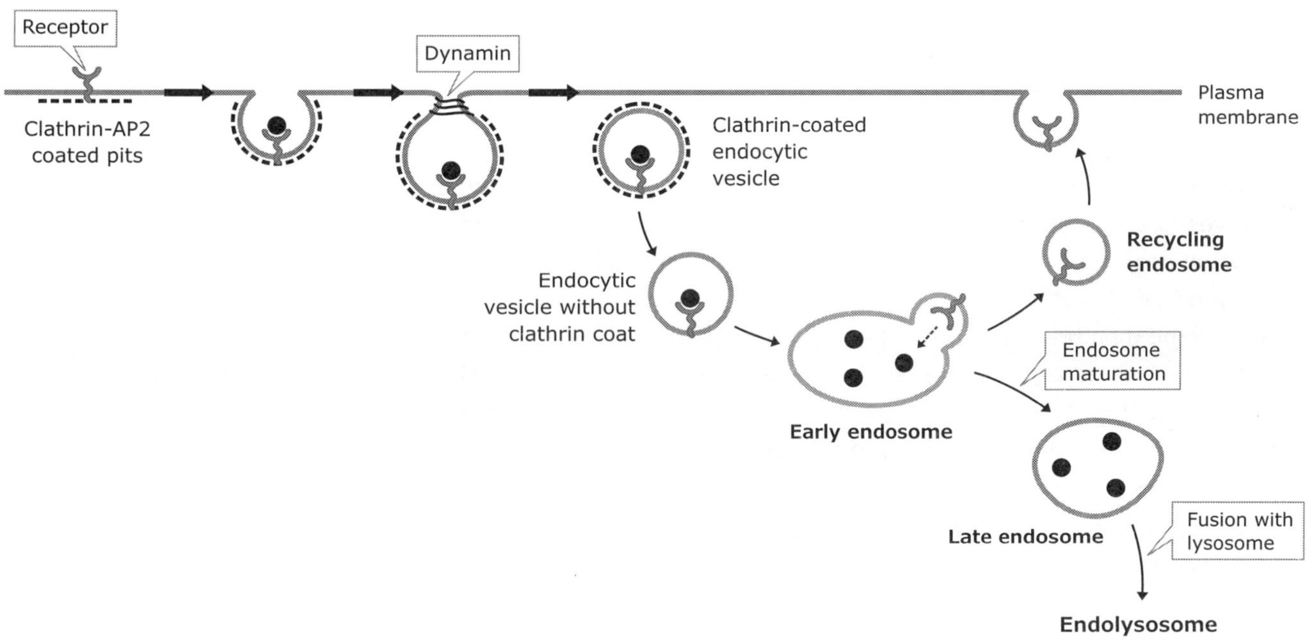

Figure 3.26 A generalized endolysosomal pathway in which ligands undergo for degradation and receptors are recycled.

A common example of clathrin-mediated endocytosis is the uptake of cholesterol-containing particles called **low-density lipoprotein** (LDL). Michael Brown and Joseph Goldstein demonstrated that the uptake of LDL by mammalian cells requires the binding of LDL to a specific cell-surface receptor that is concentrated in clathrin-coated pits and internalized by endocytosis. When a cell needs cholesterol for membrane synthesis, it makes transmembrane receptor proteins for LDL called **LDL receptor** and inserts them into its plasma membrane. They discovered that individuals with the genetic disease *familial hypercholesterolemia* (FH) have mutations in the LDL receptor that prevent the normal uptake of LDL by liver and peripheral tissues. LDL is a sphere of 20–25 nm in diameter. It has an outer phospholipid monolayer containing a large protein called **apo B100**. It contains free cholesterol, cholesterol ester and triacylglycerol. The LDL receptor, a monomeric protein made up of 839 amino acids, is a single-pass transmembrane glycoprotein. LDL receptors have four-residue sequence, *Asn–Pro–X–Tyr* (X = any amino acid) in the cytosolic domain that is crucial for their localization in clathrin-AP2 coated pits. This sequence binds to the AP2 complex.

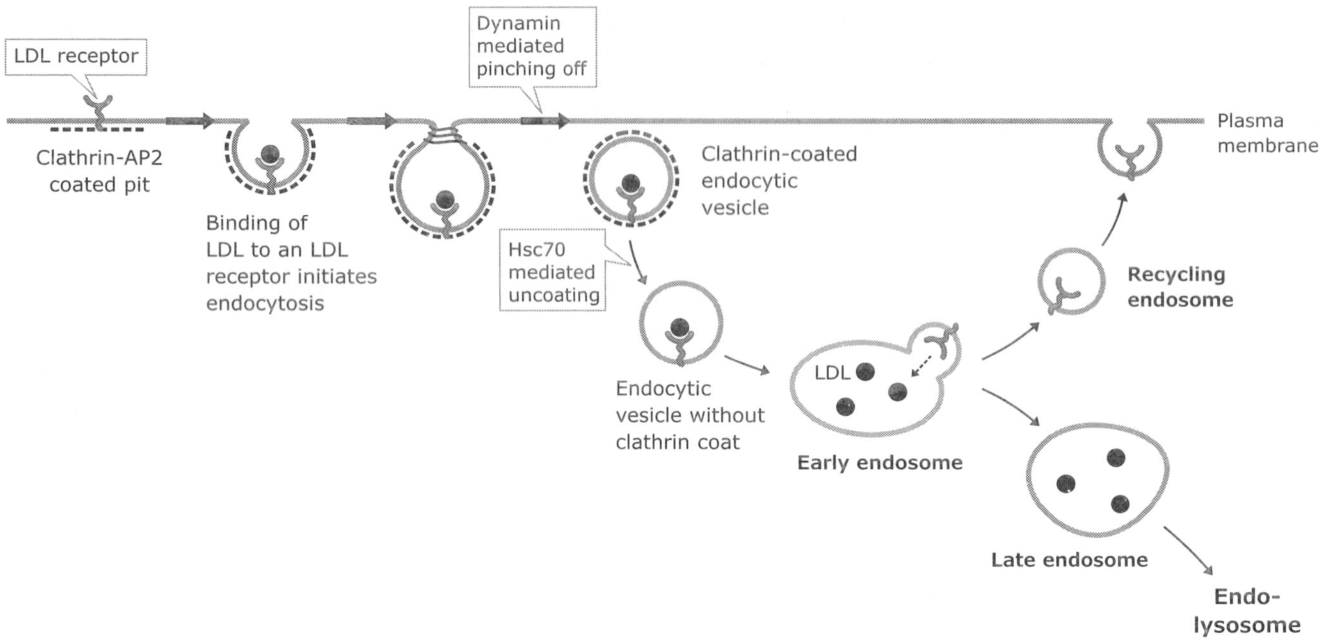

Figure 3.27 Cell-surface LDL-receptor mediated endocytosis of LDL. The LDL receptor functions to internalize LDL. The LDL is delivered to lysosomes, where it is degraded and its cholesterol is released for use in the synthesis of membranes, steroid hormones and bile acids.

Any LDL particles bound to LDL receptors in the clathrin-AP2 coated pits are rapidly internalized in clathrin-AP2 coated vesicles. After shedding their clathrin coats, the vesicles deliver their contents to early endosomes, which are located near the cell periphery. Once the LDL and LDL receptors encounter the low pH in the endosomes, LDL is released from its receptor and is delivered via late endosomes to lysosomes. The receptor-containing portions of the endosome membrane bud off and are returned to the cell surface, to function again in LDL uptake. Lysosomes are usually regarded as the graveyard of the cell. The endosome fuses with a lysosome, which contains enzymes that hydrolyze the cholesteryl esters, releasing cholesterol and fatty acids into the cytosol. The apoB-100 protein is also degraded to amino acids that are released to the cytosol.

Another example of clathrin-mediated endocytosis is the uptake of **transferrin**, an iron-binding monomeric (~80 kDa) glycoproteins. Most cells acquire iron from transferrin by a receptor mediated process, and the **transferrin receptor** controls iron uptake. The transferrin receptor is a glycosylated homodimer membrane protein linked by two disulfide bonds. Transferrin receptors have four-residue sequence motif, Tyr-X-X-ϕ (where X can be any amino acid and ϕ is a bulky hydrophobic amino acid), in the cytosolic domain for their localization in clathrin-AP2 coated pits.

At the pH of the extracellular space (~7.4), iron-bearing transferrin (termed **ferrotransferrin**) preferentially binds transferrin receptor. In the absence of bound Fe^{3+}, transferrin does not interact with receptor and circulates in the bloodstream until it catches an Fe^{3+} and becomes ferrotransferrin. Binding of ferrotransferrin to its receptor is rapidly followed by internalization of the ferrotransferrin-transferrin receptor complex to a *clathrin-coated vesicle*. After shedding their clathrin coats, the vesicles deliver their contents to early endosomes. The acidic environment of endosome causes ferrotransferrin to release the iron. The iron-free ligand, called **apotransferrin**, remains bound to the transferrin receptor, and recycles to the plasma membrane. In the neutral pH of the extracellular fluid, the apotransferrin dissociates from the receptor. This leaves transferrin free to bind another iron.

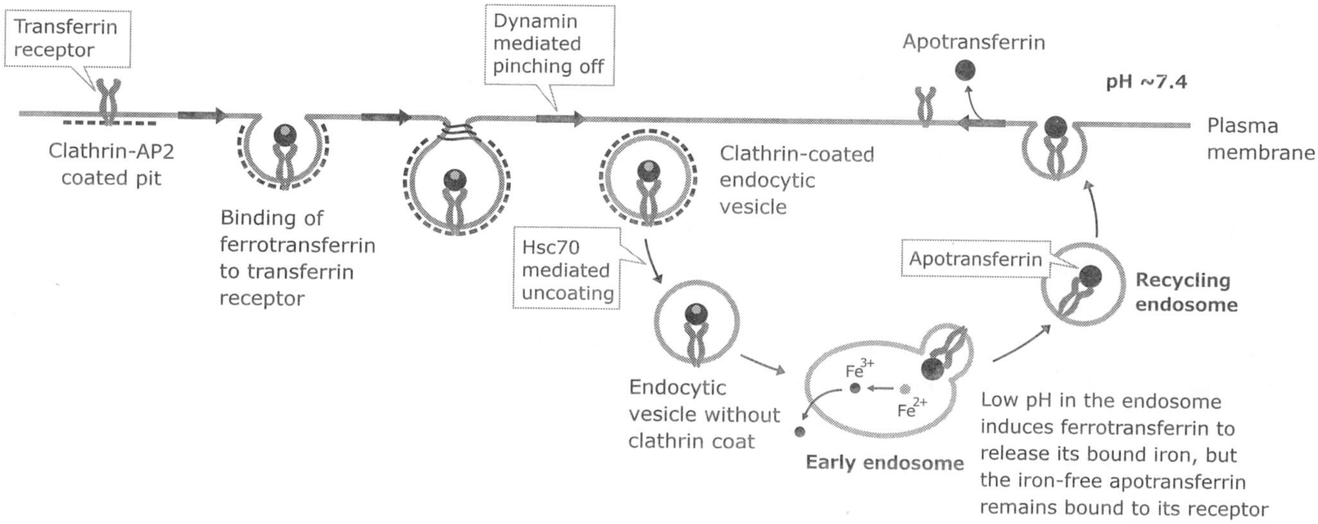

Figure 3.28 Cell-surface transferrin receptor-mediated endocytosis of ferrotransferrin.

Caveolae mediated endocytosis (clathrin-independent raft-dependent endocytosis): Caveolae (Latin for *little caves*) are flask shaped invaginations on the cell surface in many vertebrate cell types, especially in endothelial cells and adipocytes. These flask-shaped structures are rich in cholesterol and sphingolipids. Formation and maintenance of caveolae is primarily due to the protein caveolin. **Caveolins** are small proteins (18-24 kDa) and are found predominantly at the plasma membrane but also in the Golgi complex and the endoplasmic reticulum. This protein is a **monotopic** integral membrane protein with both C- and N-terminus at cytoplasmic side. There are palmitoylation sites at the carboxyl-terminal domain of the protein. **Palmitoylation** is the covalent attachment of fatty acids, such as palmitic acid, to cysteine residues of proteins. Three palmitoyl groups attached to the carboxyl-terminal domain of caveolin further anchor it to the membrane. It forms an oligomeric complex comprised of approximately 14-16 monomers. Caveolin binds cholesterol in the membrane, and the presence of caveolin forces the associated lipid bilayer to curve inward, forming *caveolae* in the surface of the cell. Caveolae pinch off from the plasma membrane using **dynamin**, and they deliver their contents either to an endosome like compartment with neutral pH (called a **caveosome**) or to the plasma membrane on the opposite side of a polarized cell (in a process called *transcytosis*). Caveolae contain some receptor proteins and are used for certain types of receptor-mediated endocytosis.

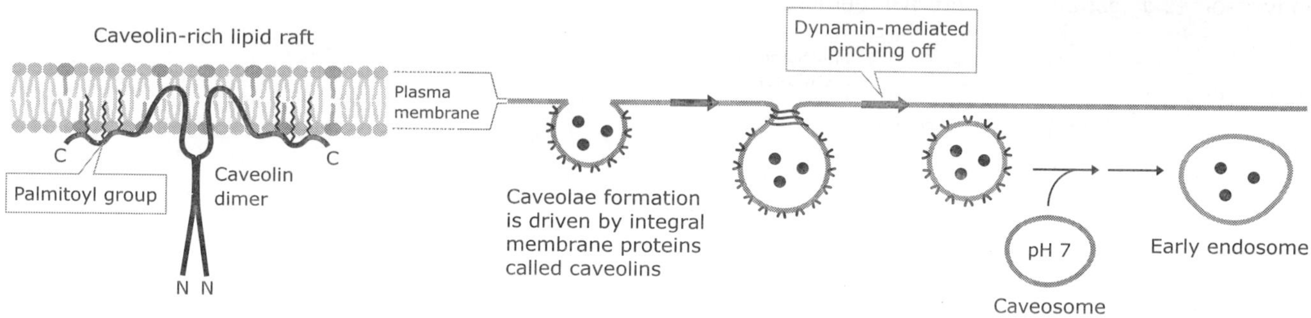

Figure 3.29 Caveolar endocytosis is a clathrin-independent endocytic process that involves flask-shaped invaginations called caveolae. The caveolae formation is driven by integral membrane proteins called caveolins. Caveolae bud off from the plasma membrane and budding is mediated by dynamin. The caveolar endocytic pathway involves the caveosome.

Clathrin- and **caveolae independent endocytosis**: Clathrin- and caveolae-independent endocytosis may constitute a specialized high capacity endocytic pathway for lipids and fluid. However, our understanding of the regulatory mechanisms and molecular components involved in this pathway are at a relatively primitive stage.

3.4.2 Fate of receptor

The fates of endocytosed receptors—and of any ligands remaining bound to them—vary according to the specific type of receptor. Most receptors are recycled and returned to the same plasma membrane the fate of a receptor-ligand complex depends on its response to the acidic environment of the endosome. In many cases, exposure to low pH changes the conformation of the external domain of the receptor, causing its ligand to be released. If the ligand that is endocytosed with its receptor stays bound to the receptor in the acidic environment of the endosome, it shares the same fate as the receptor; otherwise, it is delivered to lysosomes. Three possible fates of a receptor-ligand complex are described below:

Receptor recycled and ligand degraded: The classic example is the LDL receptor, whose ligands are the plasma low density lipoproteins (LDL). LDL binds with LDL receptor and the LDL is released from its receptor in the endosome. The receptor recycles to the surface to be used again and the LDL is sent on to the lysosome, where it is degraded.

Receptor and ligand both recycled: The *transferrin receptor* provides the classic example of this pathway. Transferrin receptor bound to transferrin (acts as ligand) carrying iron releases the iron in the endosome; the receptor now bound to apotransferrin (lacking iron) recycles to the surface, where receptor and ligand dissociate.

Receptor and ligand both are degraded: The classic example is the *epidermal growth factor receptor*, whose ligand is the epidermal growth factor (EGF). EGF is a small, extracellular signal protein that stimulates epidermal and various other cells to divide. Unlike LDL receptors, EGF receptors accumulate in clathrin-coated pits only after binding their ligand, and most do not recycle but are degraded in lysosomes, along with the EGF. EGF binding therefore first activates intracellular signaling pathways and then leads to a decrease in the concentration of EGF receptors on the cell surface, a process called receptor downregulation, that reduces the cell's subsequent sensitivity to EGF.

Internalized receptor protein as a cargo membrane protein has two potential destinies: either it is trafficked and delivered to the late endosomes and terminally, to lysosomes for degradation (via the **ESCRT system**); or, it is sorted and transported to the TGN or the plasma membrane for reuse (via the **retromer system**). Cargo receptor proteins (such as EGF receptor) destined for lysosomal degradation first undergoes ubiquitylation on lysine residues present within their cytosolic domain. This modification serves to direct the internalized receptor protein for degradation and is generally monoubiquitinated but may also multiubiquitinated. The presence of the ubiquitin is detected by a series of cytosolic multiprotein complexes belonging to the **ESCRT** (*endosomal sorting complexes required for transport*) family: **ESCRT-0**, **ESCRT-I**, **ESCRT-II** and **ESCRT-III**. Ubiquitylated membrane proteins are sorted into domains on the endosome membrane, which invaginate and pinch off to form intralumenal vesicles of multivesicular bodies. The ubiquitin marker is removed and returned to the cytosol for reuse. Eventually, proteases and lipases in lysosomes digest all of the internal membranes.

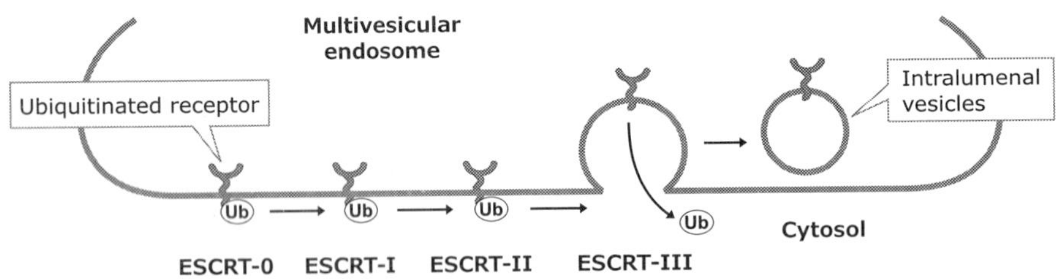

Figure 3.30 ESCRT-mediated degradation of receptor protein (considered as cargo membrane protein) sorting. Ubiquitylated receptor proteins are recognized by series of multiprotein complexes belonging to the endosomal sorting complexes required for transport (ESCRT) family: ESCRT-0, ESCRT-I, ESCRT-II and ESCRT-III.

Transcytosis

Transcytosis is a process of transcellular transport which combines both endocytosis and exocytosis. It is employed to import an extracellular ligand from one side of a cell, transport it across the cytoplasm, and secrete it from the plasma membrane at the opposite side. An example of transcytosis is the movement of maternal antibodies across the intestinal epithelial cells of the newborn rat. A newborn rat obtains antibodies from its mother's milk by transporting them across the epithelium of its gut. The lumen of the gut is acidic, and, at this low pH, the antibodies in the milk

The **hemifusome** is a newly discovered cellular organelle identified in 2025 using **cryo-electron tomography**. It appears in mammalian cells as a pair of vesicles joined by a **hemifusion diaphragm**, where the outer leaflets of their unit membranes are fused but the inner leaflets remain separate. Two forms exist – a **direct hemifusome**, where the smaller vesicle lies on the outer surface, and a **flipped hemifusome**, where smaller vesicle is inside. It is a dynamic structure-forms and disappears depending on the cell's activity. Functionally, the hemifusome serves as a platform for vesicle formation, recycling, and cargo exchange, helping in membrane turnover and **multivesicular body** formation through **ESCRT-independent pathways**. The discovery is important because it reveals a new organelle and a novel membrane fusion mechanism.

bind to specific receptors on the apical (absorptive) surface of the gut epithelial cells. The receptor-antibody complexes are internalized via clathrin-coated vesicles and are delivered to early endosomes. The complexes remain intact and are retrieved in transport vesicles that bud from the early endosome and subsequently fuse with the basolateral domain of the plasma membrane. On exposure to the neutral pH of the extracellular fluid that bathes the basolateral surface of the cells, the antibodies dissociate from their receptors and eventually enter the newborn's bloodstream.

3.4.3 Exocytosis

Exocytosis is a process in which cells release the substance in their surrounding environment. It may be **constitutive exocytosis** (carried out by all cells in a signal-independent manner) or **regulated exocytosis** (carried out by specialized cells in a signal-dependent manner). The constitutive exocytosis does not require a specific signal. Hence, it is also known as **default pathway**. The release of collagen by fibroblasts, serum proteins by hepatocytes, and antibodies by activated B-lymphocytes are examples of constitutive exocytosis. The regulated exocytosis is performed by some specialized cells (secreting products rapidly on demand such as hormones, neurotransmitters, or digestive enzymes). Four main types of specialized secretory cells preforming regulated exocytosis – *hematopoietic cells*, *neuronal cells*, *endocrine cells* and *exocrine cells*. In the regulated exocytosis, secretory vesicles form from the trans-Golgi network, and they release their contents to the cell exterior by exocytosis in response to specific signals. Proteins destined for secretion (called **secretory proteins**) are packaged into appropriate secretory vesicles in the trans-Golgi network. Specific signals direct secretory proteins into the secretory vesicles. However, the nature of signal that directs secretory proteins into such vesicles is not known.

Secretory cells employ three exocytosis modes— *kiss-and-run, full-collapse fusion* and *compound exocytosis*. In case of **kiss-and-run secretion**, fused secretory vesicles secrete their contents followed by closure of the fusion pore to reform the vesicle. If after fusion with the plasma membrane, release of substance involves the full collapse of the secretory vesicle, followed by integration of the vesicular membrane with the plasma membrane, it is termed as **full-collapse fusion**. In **compound exocytosis**, first giant vesicles form by vesicle-vesicle fusion and then fusion of giant vesicles occur with the plasma membrane.

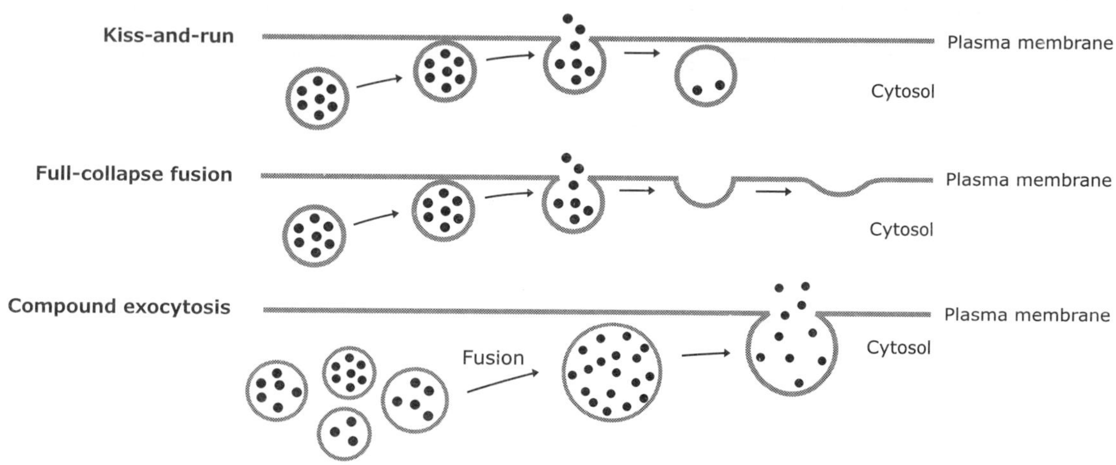

Figure 3.31 Exocytosis is a multistage process involving a merger between the vesicle and the plasma membranes. In kiss-and-run, a narrow fusion pore opens and then closes, giving a slow and/or partial release of contents; In full collapse, the fusion pore dilates while the vesicle flattens into the membrane, resulting in rapid and complete release. In compound exocytosis large vesicles are formed via vesicle-vesicle fusion, which thus fuse with the target plasma membrane and discharge the content from cells.

3.5 Ribosomes

The ribosomes are large **ribonucleoproteins** consisting of RNAs and proteins, ubiquitous in all cells, that translate genetic information stored in the mRNA into polypeptides. The ribosome is approximately spherical structure, its average diameter ranging from 2.5 nm (*Escherichia coli*) to 2.8 nm (mammalian cells). The functional ribosomes consist of two subunits of unequal size, known as the *large* and *small* subunits. Ribosomes consist of **rRNAs** and **r-proteins**. The r-proteins are termed as L or S depending on whether the protein is from the large or small subunit.

Table 3.5 Ribosome structure and chemical composition

Property	Prokaryote	Eukaryote
Overall size	70S	80S
Small subunit	30S	40S
Number of proteins	21	33
RNA size (number of nucleotides)	16S (1542)	18S (2300)
Large subunit	50S	60S
Number of proteins	31	46
RNA size (number of nucleotides)	23S (2904), 5S (120)	28S (4718), 5.8S (160), 5S (120)

'S' stands for the **sedimentation coefficient**. It is the ratio of a velocity to the centrifugal acceleration. The sedimentation coefficient has units of second. A sedimentation coefficient of 1×10^{-13} second is defined as one Svedberg, S.

rDNA organization: In eukaryotes, each 80S ribosome contains four different rRNAs - 18S, 28S, 5.8S and 5S. Genes for 18S, 28S, 5.8S rRNAs are organized as a single transcription unit and transcribed by **RNA polymerase I**. The primary transcript (**47S rRNA**) synthesized by this transcription unit is processed into the mature 18S, 5.8S and 28S rRNAs. In order to produce large amount of rRNAs, the transcription units encoding the rRNA are present in multiple copies and organized in tandem repeats. Each cluster in eukaryotes consists of tandem repeats, with each unit separated by a noncoding spacer DNA sequence. rRNA gene clusters are commonly called *ribosomal DNA* (**rDNA**). In humans, chromosome 13, 14, 15, 21 and 22 contain these gene clusters in a region called *nucleolar organizer region* (**NOR**). The 5S rRNA gene is a part of separate transcription unit and located separately. It is transcribed by **RNA polymerase III** rather than RNA polymerase I. It also occurs in tandem arrays. In humans, a gene cluster encoding 5S rRNA has been located on chromosome 1.

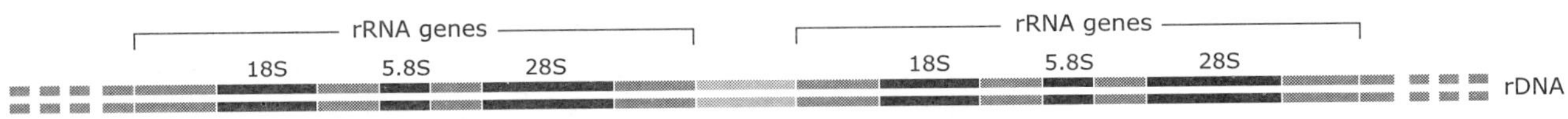

Figure 3.32 The rRNA gene clusters, known as rDNA, are part of the moderately repetitive and tandemly repeated DNA segments. These segments are found in multiple clusters across various chromosomes.

Table 3.6 Different types of ribosomes and their rRNAs

Ribosome source	Sedimentation coefficient	rRNA (*large subunit/small subunit*)
Bacterial	70S	5S, 23S/16S
Chloroplast	70S	5S, 23S/16S
Mitochondria (human)	55S	16S/12S
Archaebacteria	70S	5S, 23S/16S
Eukaryotes (cytosol)	80S	5S, 5.8S, 28S/18S

Most eukaryotes contain two distinct types of ribosomes: *cytosolic* and *organellar*. The **cytosolic ribosomes** of eukaryotic cells (other than mitochondrial and chloroplast ribosomes) are 80S types. **Organellar ribosomes** from mitochondria and chloroplast are smaller than cytosolic ribosomes and bear resemblance to the bacterial 70S ribosomes.

There are two spatially distinct populations of ribosomes in the cytosol: *membrane-bound ribosomes*, which are attached to the cytosolic side of the ER membrane, and *membrane-free ribosomes*, which are not attached to any membrane. Membrane-bound and free ribosomes are structurally and functionally identical; they differ only in the type of proteins they are synthesizing at any given time. In the cytosol, a single mRNA is typically translated by multiple ribosomes simultaneously, moving in the 5′ to 3′ direction, with each ribosome synthesizing a separate but identical polypeptide chain. This entire complex is known as a **polyribosome** or **polysomes**.

In eukaryotic cells, proteins are synthesized in cytosol and within organelles (mitochondria and chloroplasts). In the cytosol, proteins are synthesized on both *membrane-bound* as well as *membrane-free* 80S ribosomes. Proteins that are imported into organelles such as mitochondria, chloroplasts and peroxisome are synthesized on membrane-free ribosomes in the cytosol, whereas proteins that are imported into the ER-Golgi system are synthesized on ER membrane-bound ribosomes.

Table 3.7 Proteins synthesized by cytosolic 80S ribosomes

Location of ribosome	Classes of protein synthesized
Membrane free ribosomes	Soluble cytosolic proteins
	Extrinsic membrane proteins localized to the cytoplasmic surface (e.g., actin, spectrin)
	Mitochondrial and chloroplast proteins encoded by nuclear DNA
	Peroxisomal proteins
ER membrane-bound ribosomes	Secretory proteins
	Integral plasma membrane proteins
	Lysosomal proteins
	ER and Golgi complex proteins
	Extrinsic membrane proteins localized to the non-cytoplasmic surface (e.g., fibronectin)

3.6 Endoplasmic reticulum

Endoplasmic reticulum (ER) is the largest single membrane-bound intracellular compartment. It is an extensive network of closed and flattened membrane-bound structure. The enclosed compartment is called the *ER lumen*. ER membranes are physiologically active, interact with the cytoskeleton and contain differentiated domains specialized for distinct functions. ER membranes are differentiated into rough and smooth regions (**RER** and **SER**, respectively), depending on whether ribosomes are associated with their cytoplasmic surfaces. Regions of ER that lack bound ribosomes are called **SER** (sometimes also called **transitional ER**). The membranes and luminal spaces of the ER are normally continuous throughout the cell and that RER and SER form an interconnected membrane system. When cells are disrupted by homogenization, the ER breaks into fragments and reseals into small vesicles called **microsomes**. Microsomes derived from RER are studded with ribosomes on the outer surface and are called **rough microsomes**. Microsomes lacking attached ribosomes are called **smooth microsome**.

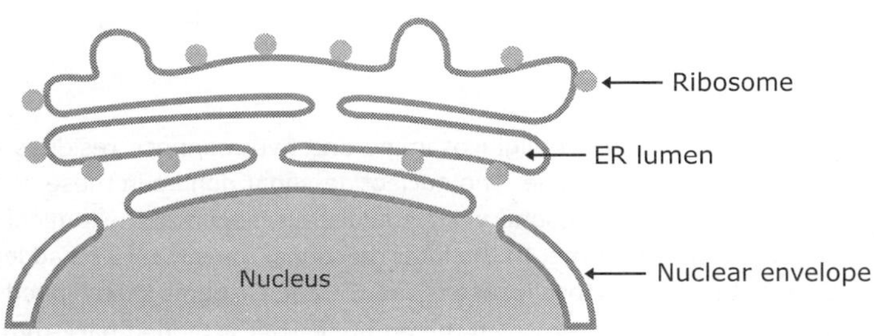

Figure 3.33
An endoplasmic reticulum is a membranous network of cisternae (sac-like structures). The cisternal space (or lumen) remains continuous with the perinuclear space.

Function of ER

Proteins synthesized by ribosomes associated with the membrane of RER enter into the lumen and membrane of RER by the process of co-translational translocation. In the lumen of the RER, five principal modifications of proteins occur before they reach their final destinations: addition and processing of carbohydrates (*N*-linked glycosylation), formation of disulfide bonds, proper folding, specific proteolytic cleavages and assembly into multimeric proteins. The SER acts as the site of lipid biosynthesis, detoxification and calcium regulation.

N-linked glycosylation of proteins

N-linked glycosylation is the attachment of a sugar molecule to a nitrogen atom in an amino acid residue in a protein. In the RER, this process involves the addition of a large preformed oligosaccharide precursor to a protein. This precursor oligosaccharide is linked by a pyrophosphoryl residue to **dolichol**, a long-chain (75–95 carbon atoms) polyisoprenoid lipid that is firmly embedded in the RER membrane and acts as a carrier for the oligosaccharide. The structure of *N*-linked oligosaccharide is the same in plants, animals and single-celled eukaryotes - a branched oligosaccharide, containing three glucose (Glc), nine mannose (Man) and two *N*-acetylglucosamine (GlcNAc) molecules which is written as **Glc_3–Man_9–$GlcNAc_2$**.

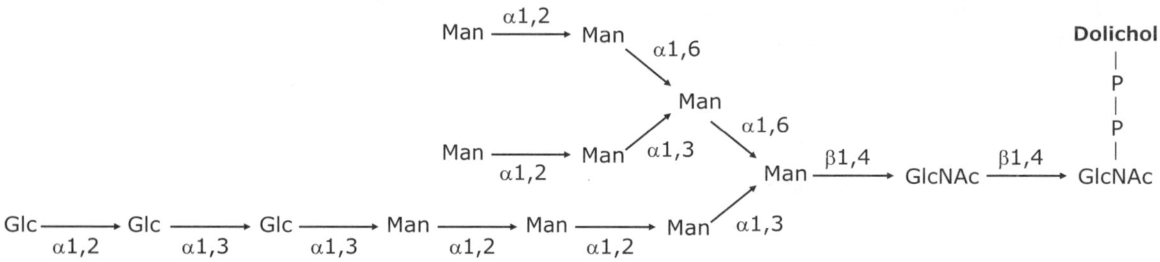

Figure 3.34 Structure of dolichol—P—P—oligosaccharide.

Biosynthesis of oligosaccharide begins on the cytosolic face of the ER membrane with the transfer of *N*-acetyl glucosamine to dolichol phosphate. Two *N*-acetylglucosamine (GlcNAc) and five mannose residues are added one at a time to a dolichol phosphate on the cytosolic face of the ER membrane. The first sugar, *N*-acetylglucosamine, is linked to dolichol by a pyrophosphate bridge. This high-energy bond activates the oligosaccharide for its transfer from the dolichol to an asparagine side chain of a nascent polypeptide on the luminal side of the RER.

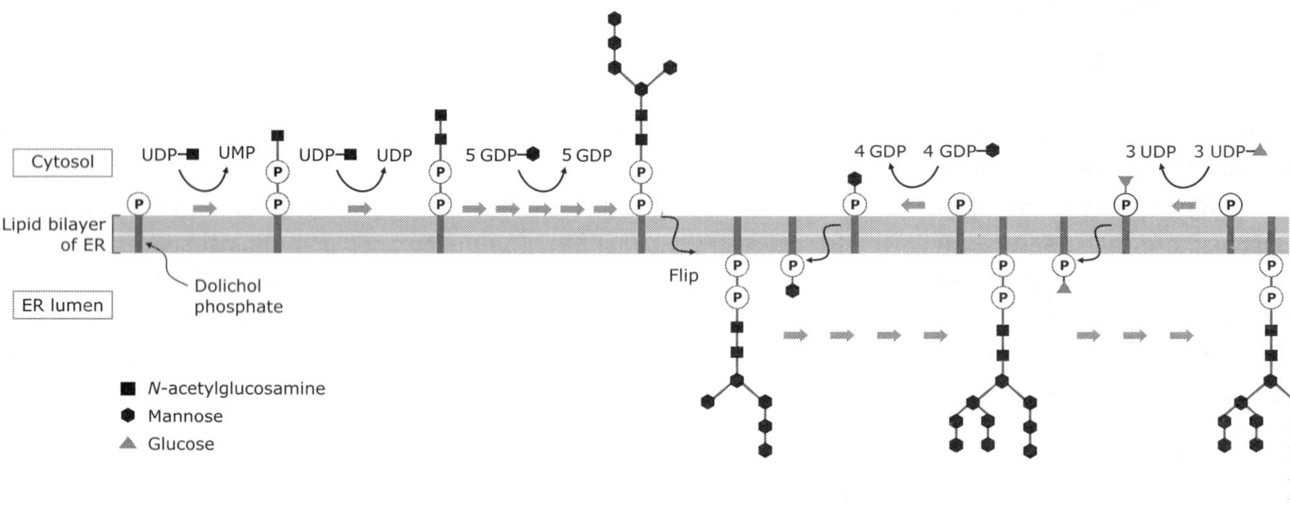

Figure 3.35 Biosynthesis of *N*-linked oligosaccharides. Two *N*-acetylglucosamine and five mannose residues are added one at a time to a dolichol phosphate on the cytosolic face of the ER membrane. The nucleotide-sugar donors in these and later reactions are synthesized in the cytosol. After the seven-residue dolichol pyrophosphoryl intermediate is flipped to the luminal face, the remaining four mannose and all three glucose residues are added one at a time. In the later reactions, the sugar to be added is first transferred from a nucleotide-sugar to a carrier dolichol phosphate on the cytosolic face of the ER; the carrier is then flipped to the luminal face, where the sugar is transferred to the growing oligosaccharide, after which the empty carrier is flipped back to the cytosolic face.

Tunicamycin, an antibiotic, blocks the first step in this pathway and thus inhibits the synthesis of oligosaccharide. After the seven-residue dolichol pyrophosphoryl intermediate is flipped to the luminal face. The remaining four mannose and all three glucose residues are added one at a time in the luminal side. The sugar molecules participate in oligosaccharide synthesis are first activated in the cytosol by the formation of **nucleotide-sugar**, which then donate their sugar (directly or indirectly) to the lipid in an orderly sequence. The entire Glc_3–Man_9–$GlcNAc_2$ oligosaccharide is transferred *en bloc* from the dolichol to an asparagine residue on a nascent polypeptide, a reaction catalyzed by enzyme *oligosaccharyl transferase*. Only asparagine residues in the sequences *Asn-X-Ser* and *Asn-X-Thr* (where X is any amino acid except proline) are substrates for this transferase.

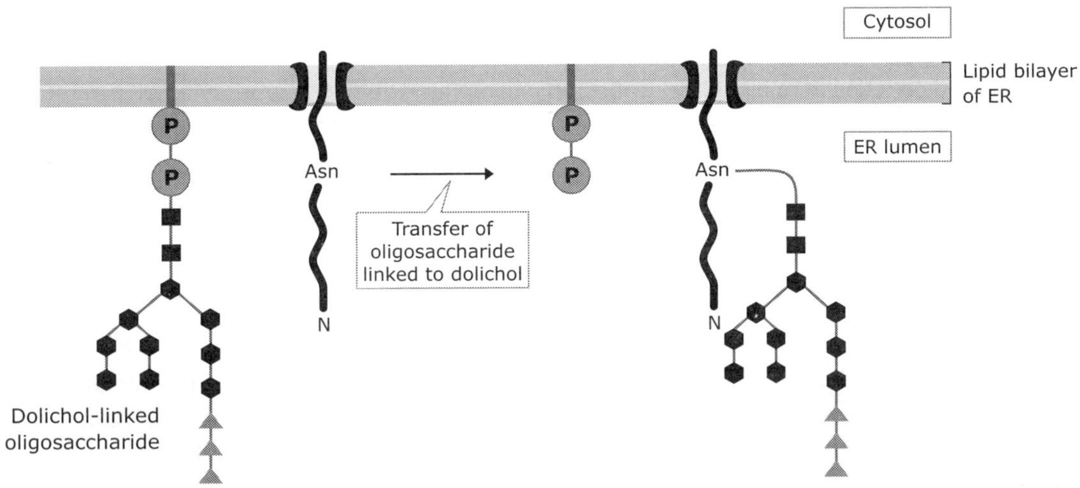

Figure 3.36 Transfer of an oligosaccharide from the dolichol to an asparagine residue on a protein.

Immediately after the oligosaccharide is transferred to a nascent polypeptide, all three glucose residues and one particular mannose residue are removed by different enzymes. The three glucose residues, which are the last residues added in the synthesis of Glc_3-Man_9-$GlcNAc_2$ on the dolichol carrier, appear to act as a signal that the oligosaccharide is complete and ready to be transferred to a protein. Five of its fourteen residues are conserved in the structures of all *N*-linked oligosaccharides on secretory and membrane proteins. Further modifications of *N*-linked oligosaccharides occur in the Golgi complex.

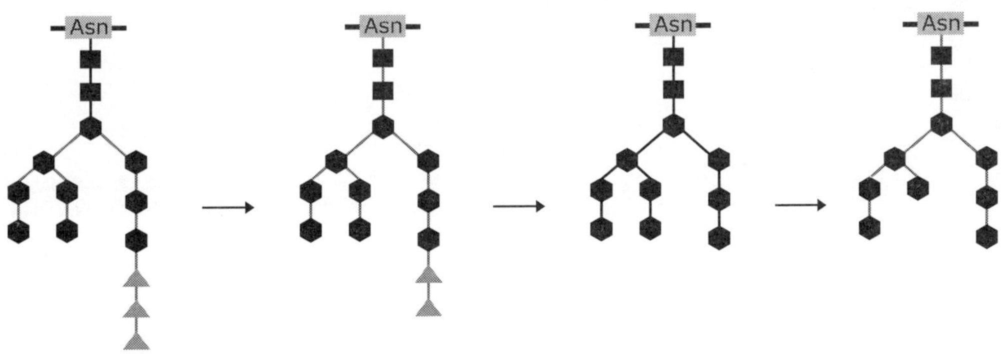

Figure 3.37 Oligosaccharide processing in the ER. In three separate reactions, at first one glucose residue, then two glucose residues, and finally one mannose residue are removed.

Function of glycosylation

The oligosaccharides attached to glycoproteins serve various functions:

1. Some proteins require *N*-linked oligosaccharides in order to fold properly in the ER.
2. *N*-linked oligosaccharides confer stability (proteases resistance) on many secreted glycoproteins.
3. Oligosaccharides on certain glycoproteins play a role in cell-cell adhesion.
4. Oligosaccharides present on glycoproteins also serve as antigens.

Protein folding

Protein folding is assisted by chaperone, which prevents segments of a nascent chain from misfolding. An important chaperone of Hsp70 family located in the lumen of the ER is BiP. **BiP** binds newly-synthesized proteins as they are translocated into the ER and maintains them in unfolded state. Two other chaperones in ER apart from BiP, **calnexin** and **calreticulin**, bind incompletely folded glycoproteins and prevents their exit from the ER. Calnexin and calreticulin are calcium binding **lectins** (carbohydrate-binding proteins) located in the ER membrane and ER lumen, respectively. Calnexin and calreticulin bind selectively to certain *N*-linked oligosaccharides on growing nascent chains. These two lectins recognize *N*-linked oligosaccharides that contain a single terminal glucose, and therefore bind protein only after two of the three glucoses that are initially attached have been removed by enzyme present in ER **glucosidases**. When the third glucose is removed, the protein dissociates from its chaperone and can leave the ER. Thus, the binding of calnexin and calreticulin to oligosaccharides on incompletely folded polypeptide helps in retaining it in the ER. A crucial enzyme **glucosyl transferase** (a soluble, ER protein that uses UDP-Glc as sugar donor) determines the completely and incompletely folded state of a protein. If the protein is incompletely folded, the enzyme transfers a new glucose to *N*-linked oligosaccharide, renewing the protein's affinity for calnexin/calreticulin and retaining it in the ER. The cycle repeats until the protein has folded completely.

Formation of disulfide bond

Disulfide bonds do not form in the cytosol due to reducing environment, which maintains cysteine residues in their reduced (–SH) state. Disulfide bond formation in ER lumen is facilitated by the enzyme **protein disulfide isomerase** (PDI). PDI also catalyzes rearrangement of disulfide bond. In bacterial cells, disulfide bonds are formed in the periplasmic space. Thus, disulfide bonds are found only in secretory proteins and in the exoplasmic domains of membrane proteins. Cytosolic proteins and organelle proteins synthesized on free ribosome lack disulfide bonds.

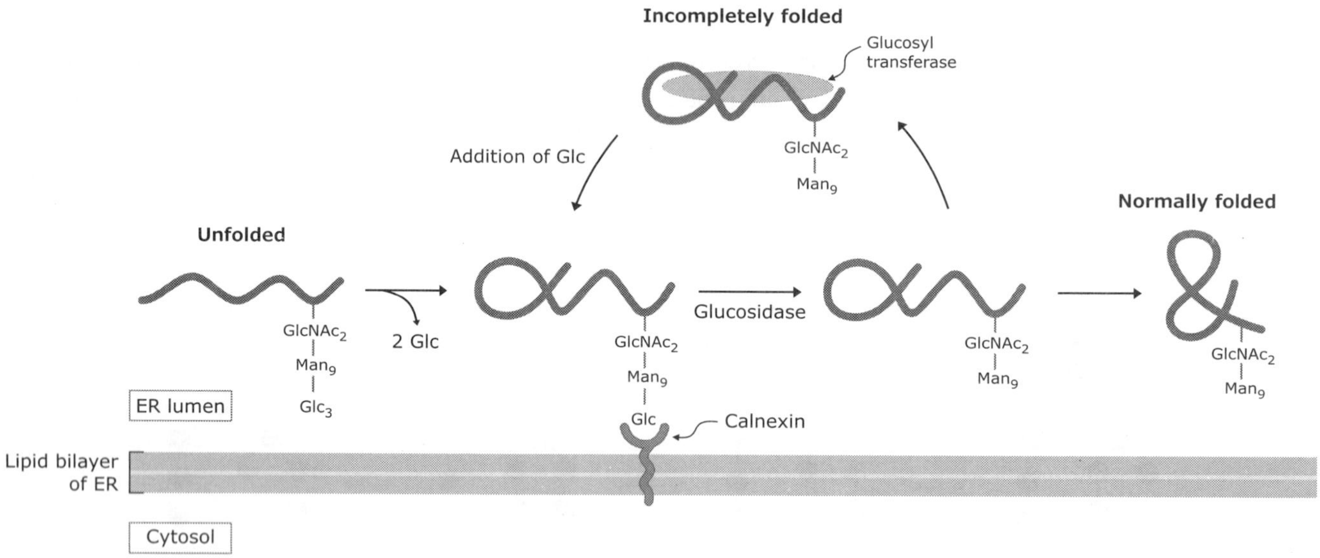

Figure 3.38 The role of *N*-linked glycosylation in ER protein folding. The ER-membrane-bound chaperone protein calnexin binds to incompletely folded proteins containing one terminal glucose on *N*-linked oligosaccharides, trapping the protein in the ER. Removal of the terminal glucose (Glc) by an enzyme *glucosidase* releases the protein from calnexin. An enzyme *glucosyl transferase* is the crucial enzyme that determines whether the protein is folded properly or not: if the protein is still incompletely folded, the enzyme transfers a new glucose from UDP-glucose to the *N*-linked oligosaccharide, renewing the protein's affinity for calnexin and retaining it in the ER. The cycle repeats until the protein has folded completely. Calreticulin functions similarly, except that it is a soluble ER resident protein.

Synthesis of membrane lipid

The SER produces most of the membrane lipids, including both phospholipids and cholesterol. Phospholipids are amphipathic molecules and their synthesis from fatty acyl-CoAs and glycerol 3-phosphate take place at the cytosolic leaflet of ER membrane and are catalyzed by membrane-associated enzymes. Fatty acids are not directly incorporated into phospholipids; rather, they are first converted into CoA esters. Fatty acids from fatty acyl-CoA are esterified to the phosphorylated glycerol backbone, forming phosphatidic acid, whose two long hydrocarbon chains anchor the molecule to the membrane.

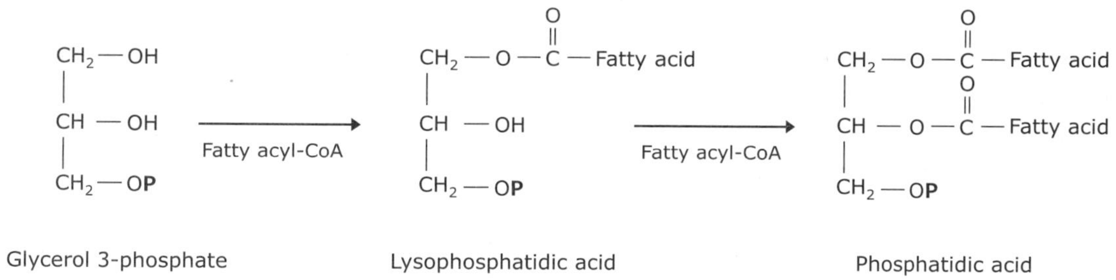

Figure 3.39 Synthesis of phosphatidic acid.

There are two strategies for attaching head-group. In the first strategy for head-group attachment, phosphatidic acid is activated by condensation of CTP to form CDP-diacylglycerol. The activated diacylglycerol unit then reacts with the hydroxyl group of an alcohol to form a phosphodiester linkage. If the alcohol is inositol, the products are **phosphatidylinositol** and CMP.

$$\textbf{Phosphatidic acid} \xrightarrow{\text{CTP} \curvearrowright \text{PP}_i} \textbf{CDP-diacylglycerol} \xrightarrow{\text{Inositol}} \textbf{Phosphatidylinositol} + \textbf{CMP}$$

In the second strategy for head-group attachment, an activated alcohol is used. Synthesis of phosphatidylethanolamine and phosphatidylcholine in mammals occurs by this strategy. It involves phosphorylation and activation of the head group, followed by condensation with diacylglycerol. For example, choline is phosphorylated by ATP to phosphocholine which is then converted to CDP-choline by condensation with CTP. A diacylglycerol displaces CMP from CDP-choline, producing **phosphatidylcholine**.

$$\textbf{Choline} \xrightarrow{\text{ATP} \curvearrowright \text{ADP}} \textbf{Phosphocholine} \xrightarrow{\text{CTP} \curvearrowright \text{PP}_i} \textbf{CDP-choline} \xrightarrow[\text{Diacylglycerol}]{} \textbf{Phosphatidylcholine + CMP}$$

(Phosphatidic acid $\rightarrow$ Diacylglycerol, releasing P_i)

As phospholipid synthesis takes place in the cytosolic leaflet of the ER bilayer, they need enzymes that transfer some of the newly formed phospholipid molecules to the other half of the bilayer. **Scramblase** mediates the transfer of lipid molecules from the cytosolic lipid layer to the non-cytosolic (luminal side) lipid layer to ensure that both monolayers remain equally populated with lipids.

After synthesis on the smooth ER, glycerophospholipids are inserted into specific cellular membranes. The process by which water-insoluble phospholipids move from the site of synthesis to the other locations is not fully understood. As we know, the plasma membrane and the membranes of the Golgi complex, lysosomes and endosomes all form part of an **endomembrane system** that communicates with the ER by means of transport vesicles, which transfer both proteins and lipids. Mitochondria and plastids, however, do not belong to this system, and they, therefore, require different mechanisms to import proteins and lipids for growth. Mitochondria import most of their lipids from the ER. The details of how lipid import occurs are not known. Water-soluble carrier proteins called **phospholipid exchange proteins** (or *phospholipid transfer proteins*) are thought to transfer individual phospholipid molecules between membranes. There are also sites in the ER where the outer membrane of the mitochondria is in close contact with the ER membrane, called **mitochondria-associated ER membranes** (**MAMs**). These contact sites can vary in size and are dynamic structures. MAMs are supposed to be involved in many functions. One important function is the exchange of lipids between the ER and mitochondria.

Detoxification

SERs in the hepatic cells are the major site for removal of **xenobiotics** (synthetic compounds not found in nature). In the SER, detoxification is catalyzed by microsomal P450-containing systems. Any enzyme system that includes cytochrome P450 can be termed as **P450-containing system**. P450-containing systems primarily fall into two major classes: bacterial/mitochondrial (type I) and microsomal (type II).

The **cytochrome P450** (or **P450**) is a *hemeprotein* that occurs in nearly all living organisms. The name '**P450**' was given because the reduced forms of cytochrome P450s bind carbon monoxide, generating a complex that absorbs light strongly at 450 nm. Cytochromes P450 are **monooxygenases** (*mixed-function oxygenases*) and catalyze the incorporation of a single atom of molecular oxygen into a substrate with the concomitant reduction of the other atom to water. Eukaryotic cytochromes P450 enzymes are generally membrane-bound proteins and mostly present in the ER membrane. However, several P450s enzymes that participate in the synthesis of cholesterol, steroid hormones and bile acids are located in the mitochondria. Microsomal P450-containing monooxygenase systems catalyze the hydroxylation reaction, which has the following overall stoichiometry:

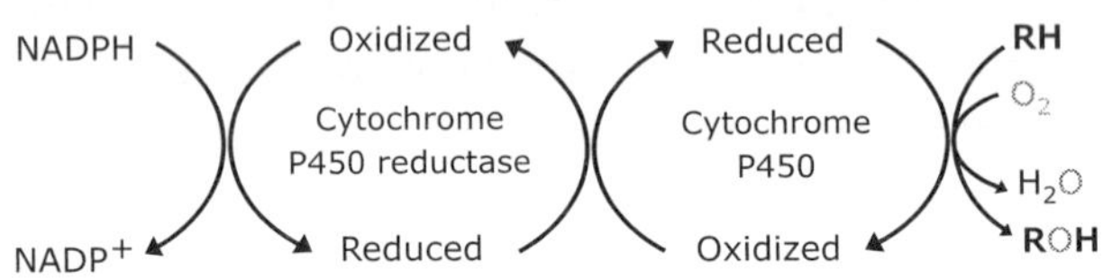

RH represents a wide variety of usually lipophilic compounds for which the different cytochromes P450 are specific and ROH is the product. Most cytochromes P450 enzymes have broad substrate specificity. A membrane-bound enzyme **cytochrome P450 reductase** which contains **FAD** and **FMN** as cofactors catalyzes the electron transfer from NADPH to cytochrome P450 (NADPH $\longrightarrow$ FAD $\longrightarrow$ FMN $\longrightarrow$ P450). The lipophilic xenobiotics are thereby converted to a more water-soluble form, which aids in their excretion by the kidneys. There are many types of cytochromes P450 in animals, which have different substrate specificities.

3.7 Golgi complex

The Golgi complex was first discovered in 1897 by Italian physician Camillo Golgi. The Golgi complex, also termed as **Golgi body** or **Golgi apparatus**, is a single membrane-bound organelle and part of endomembrane system. It consists of five to eight flattened membrane-bound sacs called the **cisternae**. Each stack of cisternae is termed as **Golgi stack** (or **dictyosome**). The cisternae in *Golgi stack* vary in number, shape and organization in different cell types. The typical diagrammatic representation of three major cisternae (*cis*, medial and *trans*) as shown in the **figure 3.40** is actually a simplification. In some unicellular flagellates, however, as many as 60 cisternae may combine to make up the Golgi stack. The number of Golgi complexes in a cell varies according to its function. A mammalian cell typically contains 40 to 100 stacks. In mammalian cells, multiple Golgi stacks are linked together at their edges.

Each Golgi stack has two distinct faces: a ***cis* face** (or entry face or forming face) and a ***trans* face** (or maturing face). Both *cis* and *trans* faces are closely associated with special compartments: the ***cis*-Golgi network** (CGN) and the ***trans*-Golgi network** (TGN), respectively. TGN was previously referred to as **GERL**, which stands for Golgi apparatus-endoplasmic reticulum-lysosome. This acronym was used to describe the region where these three cellular organelles seemed to interact. However, as our understanding of cellular biology has evolved, the term TGN has become more widely accepted to represent this specific subcompartment of the Golgi complex. Proteins and lipids enter the *cis*-Golgi network in vesicular tubular clusters arriving from the ER and exit from the *trans*-Golgi network. Both networks are thought to be important for protein sorting. As we have seen, proteins entering the CGN can either move onward in the Golgi complex or be returned to the ER. Similarly, proteins exiting from the TGN can either move onward and be sorted according to whether they are destined for lysosomes, secretory vesicles, or the cell surface, or be returned to an earlier compartment.

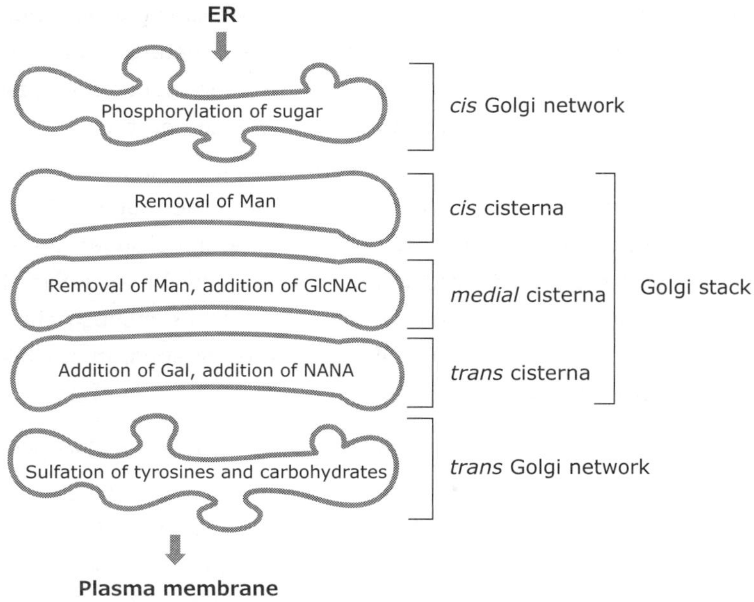

Figure 3.40
The functional compartmentalization of the Golgi complex.

The Golgi complex is especially prominent in cells that are specialized for secretion, such as the goblet cells of the intestinal epithelium, which secrete large amounts of polysaccharide-rich mucus into the gut. In such cells, unusually large secretory vesicles are found on the *trans* side of the Golgi complex. Secretory vesicles form from the *trans*-Golgi network, and they release their contents to the cell exterior by exocytosis. The membrane proteins and the lipids in these vesicles provide new components for the cell's plasma membrane, while the soluble protein and other compounds inside the vesicles are secreted to the extracellular space.

Function of Golgi complex

The Golgi complex is often considered the distribution and shipping department for the cell's chemical products. It modifies proteins and lipids that have been built in the endoplasmic reticulum and prepares them for export outside of the cell or for transport to other locations in the cell. Proteins and lipids from the smooth and rough endoplasmic reticulum bud off in tiny bubble-like vesicles that move through the cytoplasm until they reach the Golgi complex. The vesicles fuse with the Golgi membranes and release their internally stored molecules into the organelle. Once inside, the compounds are further processed by the Golgi complex. When completed, the product is extruded from the Golgi complex in a vesicle and directed to its final destination inside or outside the cell.

The modifications to molecules that take place in the Golgi complex occur in an orderly fashion. Substances from ER enter into the *cis* face of a Golgi stack for processing and exit from *trans* face. Consequently, the *cis* face is found near the endoplasmic reticulum and the *trans* face is positioned near the plasma membrane of the cell. The chemical make-up of each face is different and the enzymes contained in the cisternae between the faces are distinctive.

Glycosylation of proteins: *N*-linked oligosaccharides (or *N*-glycans) on proteins are altered as the proteins pass through the Golgi cisternae *en route* from the ER. Further modifications of *N*-glycans in the Golgi complex gives three broad classes of *N*-glycans: high-mannose *N*-glycans, hybrid *N*-glycans and complex *N*-glycans.

High-mannose *N*-glycans contain two *N*-acetylglucosamines and five mannose residues ($GlcNAc_2Man_5$). There is a removal of three mannose but no new sugars are added in the Golgi complex. If high-mannose *N*-glycans are elongated by the addition of sugar residues such as *N*-acetylgalactosamine or sialic acid in the Golgi complex, it gives **hybrid *N*-glycans**. For the formation of **complex *N*-glycans**, high-mannose *N*-glycans are subjected to removal of additional two mannose residues, which generates *N*-linked $GlcNAc_2Man_3$, the *core glycan* structure that are further elongated by the addition of sugar residues.

Some proteins undergo ***O*-glycosylation** in the cisternae. *O*-glycosylation involves an oxygen-carbon bond (*O*-glycosidic bond) between carbohydrate (termed ***O*-glycan**) and the hydroxyl group of a serine or threonine (to a lesser extent, hydroxyproline and hydroxylysine) amino acid residue of the protein. In contrast to *N*-glycosylation, a consensus amino acids sequence for carbohydrate addition to proteins is not required. The nature of proteins can be both intracellular and extracellular. Unlike *N*-glycan, *O*-glycans (or *O*-linked oligosaccharides) do not present a common structure. *O*-glycans are of different types based on the initial sugar attached to the protein.

In most common *O*-glycosylation pathway, the initial sugar linked to serine or threonine is *N*-acetylgalactosamine (GalNAc). The initial *O*-GalNAc structure is further modified by the addition of other sugars. Some proteins are *O*-glycosylated with *N*-acetylglucosamine, fucose, xylose, galactose or mannose as initial sugar. *O*-glycans synthesis occurs directly on proteins and sugars are added one at a time, and each sugar transfer is catalyzed by a different glycosyltransferase enzyme. As with *N*-glycosylation, sugar nucleotides are used as monosaccharide donors for *O*-glycosylation. Some of *O*-glycosylation start in the ER and continue in the Golgi apparatus, while others occur exclusively in the Golgi apparatus (also occur in the cytosol).

Lipid and polysaccharide metabolism: In addition to its activities in processing and sorting glycoproteins, the Golgi complex functions in lipid metabolism—in particular, in the synthesis of glycolipids and sphingomyelin. Ceramide, which is synthesized in the ER, is converted either to sphingomyelin or to glycolipids in the Golgi complex. The Golgi complex also acts as a major site of carbohydrate metabolism. In plant cells, it acts as the site where complex polysaccharides of the cell wall are synthesized. Complex cell wall polysaccharides such as hemicelluloses and pectins are synthesized in the Golgi complex and then transported in vesicles to the cell surface. In animals, most of the glycosaminoglycans of the extracellular matrix are synthesized in the Golgi complex.

Transport of proteins through cisternae

Several models have been proposed to explain the ordered transport of proteins through the cisternae. Two most accepted models are *cisternal maturation model* and *vesicular transport model*. According to **cisternal maturation model**, stacks of cisternae are dynamic. The *cis*-most cisterna is assembled by the fusion of transport vesicles from the ER, carrying newly synthesized cargo. Each Golgi cisterna matures as it migrates outward through a stack and at each stage, the Golgi resident proteins that are carried forward in a cisterna are moved backward to an earlier compartment. In this way, each cisterna progresses into the next one and COPI-coated vesicles function to transport resident Golgi components in the **retrograde** direction.

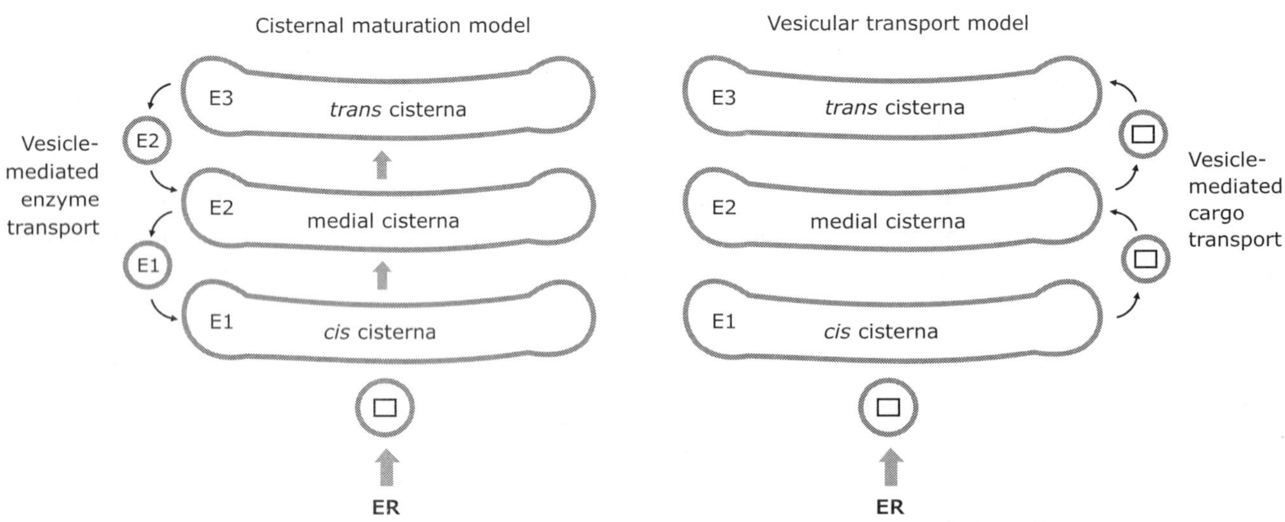

Figure 3.41 Models for transport through the Golgi stack. In the cisternal maturation model, the cisternae themselves are the carriers for cargo, and COPI-coated vesicles function to transport resident Golgi components in the retrograde direction to produce cisternal maturation. In the vesicular transport model, newly synthesized cargo proteins are transported in the forward or anterograde direction by vesicles coated with COPI.

Vesicular transport model postulates a stable stack of cisternae containing a fixed and ordered array of processing enzymes. The cargo is delivered to each cisterna in turn by vesicles that bud from one cisterna and fuse with the next in the stack. In this case, COPI coated vesicles carry cargo and move in an *anterograde* direction from one Golgi cisterna to the next. There is still controversy as to whether either model, or a hybrid one, is correct. Today most researchers agree that the most evidences favour the cisternal maturation model.

3.8 Lysosome

Lysosomes are single membrane-bound organelles present in animal cells. They are heterogeneous structure and greatly vary in size and shape. Lysosomes have *acidic* internal pH (about 5) and are filled with **hydrolytic enzymes**. They contain about 40 different types of hydrolytic enzymes (including proteases, nucleases, glycosidases, lipases, phospholipases, phosphatases and sulfatases) which are responsible for the controlled **intracellular digestion** of macromolecules. All are **acid hydrolases** because they require an acidic environment for optimal activity and the lysosome provides this by maintaining a pH of about 5.0. A v-type H^+ ATPase in the lysosomal membrane uses the energy of ATP hydrolysis to pump H^+ into the lysosome, thereby maintaining the internal acidic pH.

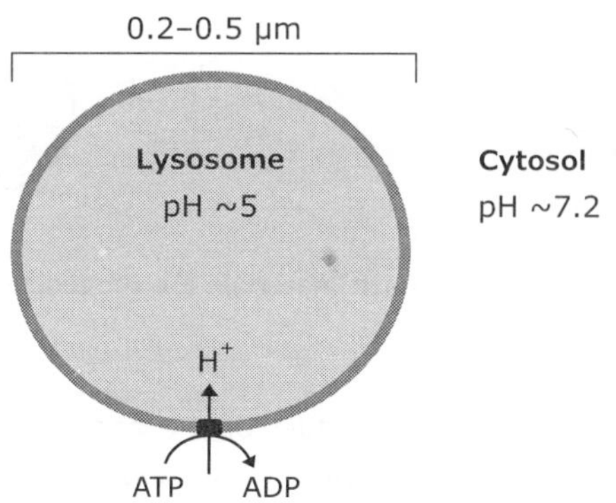

Figure 3.42
The interior of lysosomes has a pH of about 5.0. To create the low pH, V- type H^+ ATPase located in the lysosomal membrane pump protons into the lysosome using energy supplied from ATP. All the lysosomal enzymes work most efficiently at acidic pH and collectively are termed *acid hydrolases*.

There are two types of lysosomes: **primary lysosomes** (do not contain materials for intracellular digestion) and **secondary lysosomes** (contain materials that are undergoing digestion or that already have been digested). Lysosomes are responsible for the digestion of both *extracellular* as well as *intracellular* materials. Lysosomal digestion of materials can be classified into *autophagy* and *heterophagy*. The process by which substances are taken into the cell from external environment and broken down by lysosome is called **heterophagy**. In contrast, the degradation of cytoplasmic components within lysosomes is called **autophagy**.

In heterophagy, there are two different pathways that brings extracellular materials to lysosomes for degradation. Phagocytic cells, such as macrophages and neutrophils in vertebrates, engulf large particles by the process of **phagocytosis**. During phagocytosis, a single-membrane phagosome is generated, and this compartment fuses directly with a lysosome to form a **phagolysosome**.

Virtually all eukaryotic cells continually internalize fluid substances in small pinocytic (endocytic) vesicles by the process of **pinocytosis**. Most of endocytosed substances eventually end up in lysosomes, where they degraded. In this process, the endocytosed substances first move from the endocytic vesicles to the endosomes. At the end of this pathway, the late endosomes convert to **endolysosomes** and lysosomes as a result of both their fusion with preexisting lysosomes and progressive acidification.

Autophagy is an intracellular degradation process of cytoplasmic components within lysosomes. There are three main forms of autophagy pathways: *macroautophagy*, *microautophagy* and *chaperone-mediated autophagy*. During **macroautophagy**, sequestration begins with the formation of a **phagophore**. Phagophores form *de novo* in the cytosol from a cup-shaped membrane that expands into a double-membrane bound **autophagosome** surrounding a portion of the cytoplasm.

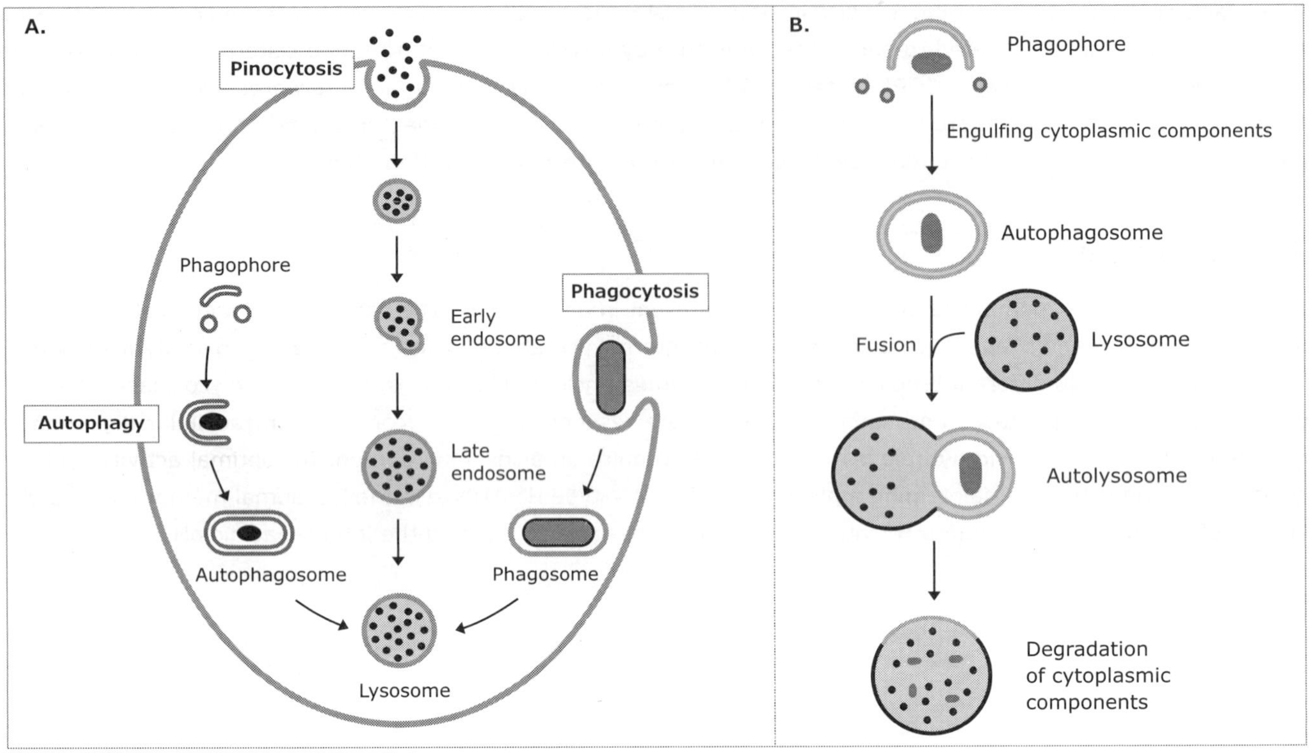

Figure 3.43 **A**. Schematic overview of three pathways by which materials are moved to lysosomes: phagocytosis, pinocytosis and autophagy. **B**. Process of autophagy.

The autophagosome may fuse with an endosome. The product of the endosome-autophagosome fusion is called an **amphisome**. The completed autophagosome or amphisome fuses with a lysosome. The resulting compartment (called **autolysosome**), with lysosomal acid hydrolases cause enzymatic breakdown of the inner membrane from the autophagosome and degrade the cytoplasmic components. Upon degradation of cytoplasmic components, autolysosomes undergo autophagic lysosome reformation.

Microautophagy is characterized by direct lysosomal engulfment of cytosolic materials into lysosomes, via the formation of characteristic invaginations of the lysosomal membrane. **Chaperone-mediated autophagy** is a selective autophagy pathway in which proteins that contain a KFERQ-like sequence are targeted by HSAP8/HSC70 chaperones and translocated into lysosomes. Products of lysosomal degradation has two fates. It can be trafficked to the Golgi apparatus for reuse or released from the cell through lysosomal exocytosis.

Many animal cells also have lysosome-related organelles. These organelles include **melanosomes** in the *melanocytes* (melanin producing cells), **dense granules** in platelets and **lytic granules** in cytotoxic T lymphocytes. Melanosomes produce and store melanin pigments. These pigment containing melanosomes release their pigment into the extracellular space of the epidermis by exocytosis.

Table 3.8 Example of some acid hydrolases present in lysosomes

Enzyme	Natural substrate
Phosphatases	
Acid phosphatase	Most phosphomonoesters
Acid phosphodiesterase	Oligonucleotides and other phosphodiesters
Nucleases	
Acid ribonuclease	RNA
Acid deoxyribonuclease	DNA

Polysaccharide/mucopolysaccharide hydrolyzing enzymes	
β-Galactosidase	Galactosides
α-Glucosidase	Glycogen
α-Mannosidase	Mannosides, glycoproteins
β-Glucuronidase	Polysaccharides and mucopolysaccharides
Hyaluronidase	Hyaluronic acids; chondroitin sulfates
Proteases	
Cathepsin(s)	Proteins
Collagenase	Collagen
Peptidases	Peptides
Lipid-degrading enzymes	
Esterase(s)	Fatty acyl esters
Phospholipase(s)	Phospholipids

3.9 Vacuoles

Most plants and fungal cells contain one or several very large, fluid-filled vesicles called **vacuoles**. They are surrounded by single membrane called **tonoplast** and related to the lysosomes of animal cells, containing a variety of hydrolytic enzymes, but their functions are remarkably diverse. Like a lysosome, the lumen of a vacuole has an acidic pH, which is maintained by similar transport proteins in the vacuolar membrane. In plant cells, the vacuoles can occupy up to 90 percent of the volume of the cell. Plant vacuoles are multifunctional compartments. Plant vacuole stores dissolved inorganic ions, organic acids, sugars, enzymes, pigments (such as anthocyanins) and a variety of secondary metabolites (such as nicotine and tannins). Solute accumulation causes osmotic water uptake by the vacuole, which is required for plant cell enlargement. This water uptake generates the *turgor pressure*.

The vacuole is different from contractile vacuole. A **contractile vacuole** is an organelle involved in osmoregulation. It pumps excess water out of the cell. It is found predominantly in protists (such as *Paramecium, Amoeba*) and in unicellular algae (*Chlamydomonas*). It was previously known as *pulsatile* or *pulsating vacuole*.

3.10 Mitochondria

Mitochondria (term coined by C. Benda) are *energy-transforming* organelles, which are present in virtually all eukaryotic cells. They are the sites of aerobic respiration. They produce cellular energy in the form of ATP, hence they are called 'powerhouses' of the cell. Apart from cell powerhouse, mitochondria have also been involved in the programmed cell death, the biosynthesis of heme complexes, calcium signalling, the oxidation of fatty acids and, more recently, as a platform for signal transduction in the innate immune response. Each mitochondrion is a double membrane-bound structure with outer and inner membranes. The space between the outer and inner membranes is called *intermembrane space* (**IMS**). The outer mitochondrial membrane (**OMM**) is fairly smooth. But the inner mitochondrial membrane (**IMM**) is highly convoluted; forming folds called **cristae**. Don't confuse between *cristae* and *cisternae*. Cristae are finger-like infoldings in inner mitochondrial membrane whereas, cisternae are a sac-like flattened structure of Golgi complex. The inner membrane is also very impermeable to many solutes due to very high content of a phospholipid called **cardiolipin**. The cristae greatly increase the inner membrane's surface area. The two faces of this membrane are referred to as the matrix side (**N-side**) and the cytosolic side (**P-side**). Inner membrane contains enzyme complex called **ATP synthase** (*or* F_0-F_1 particle *or* oxysome) that makes ATP. The outer membrane protects the organelle, and contains specialized transport proteins called **mitochondrial porin** which allows free passage for various molecules into the intermembrane space of the mitochondria. Mitochondrial porins (β-barrel structure) are *voltage-dependent anion-selective channels* (**VDAC**), adopt an open conformation at low or zero membrane potential and a closed conformation at potentials above 30-40 mV.

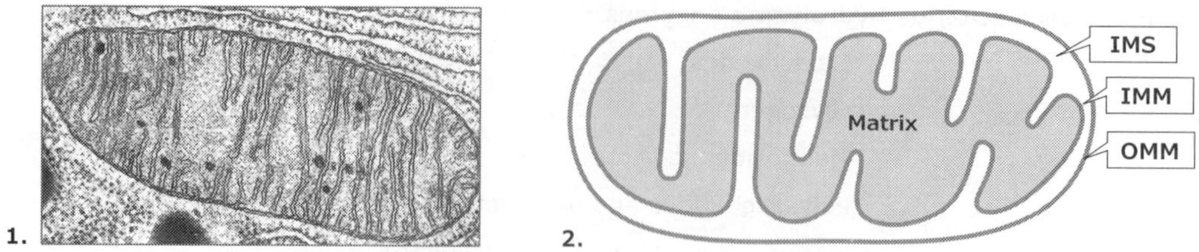

Figure 3.44 **1**. An electron micrograph of a mitochondrion. **2**. A mitochondrion has double-membraned organization and contains: the outer mitochondrial membrane (OMM), the inner mitochondrial membrane (IMM), the intermembrane space (IMS) and the matrix (space within the inner mitochondrial membrane).

The **matrix** (large internal space surround by inner mitochondrial membrane) contains multiple copies of the dsDNA (as genetic material), mitochondrial ribosomes (ranging from 55S-75S), tRNAs and various proteins. Mitochondrial dsDNA is mostly circular. The size of mitochondrial DNA also varies greatly among different species. Over time, much of the mitochondrial DNA was passed horizontally from the organelle to the host nucleus, allowing the eukaryotic cell to gain control over most aspects of mitochondrial function. Mitochondria are **semi-autonomous organelle** because they have their own genetic materials (DNA). The organelles also possess their own ribosomes and able to synthesize some of their own proteins. However, most of the mitochondrial proteins are encoded by nuclear genes and synthesized by cytosolic 80S ribosomes.

The mitochondria in living cells are dynamic with the ability to change size, shape, number and position. The number, size and shape of mitochondria vary in different cell types and can change in the same cell type under different physiological conditions. These changes are related to the ability of mitochondria to undergo *fission* or *fusion*. Mitochondrial fission is mediated by a cytosolic *dynamin family* member (Drp1 in mammals and Dnm1 in yeast).

Origin of mitochondria: In 1970, Lynn Margulis proposed **endosymbiotic hypothesis** about the origin of mitochondria. There are currently two alternative scenarios about the endosymbiotic origin of mitochondria. According to the **archezoan scenario**, the host of the proto-mitochondrial endosymbiont was a hypothetical primitive amitochondrial eukaryote, termed **archezoan**. The archezoan scenario most closely approximates the classical endosymbiont hypothesis of mitochondrial origin. In contrast, alternative **symbiogenesis scenario** consider a single endosymbiotic event involving the uptake of an α-proteobacterium by an archaeal cell led to the generation of the mitochondria, followed subsequently by the evolution of the nucleus and compartmentalization of the eukaryotic cell. The host cell for the mitochondrial endosymbiosis was a prokaryote—and specifically an archaeon, not a eukaryote.

Evidences to support endosymbiotic theory

- Mitochondria are self-replicating bodies like bacteria and divide in a manner resembling binary fission in bacteria.
- Mitochondria are surrounded by two membranes and the innermost of these membranes is very similar in composition to bacterial plasma membrane.
- Mitochondria have their own DNA, which is structurally similar to bacterial DNA.
- Mitochondrial ribosomes, enzymes and transport systems are all similar to those of bacteria.
- Mitochondria are of approximately the same size as bacteria.
- Protein synthesis in mitochondria is inhibited by a variety of antibiotics (e.g., chloramphenicol, tetracycline, erythromycin) that also inhibit protein synthesis by bacterial ribosomes, but have little effect on the cytosolic ribosome of eukaryotic cells.

Inheritance of mitochondria: Mitochondria are inherited cytoplasmically. Its inheritance in most eukaryotes is nearly **uniparental** (and more precisely **maternal inheritance** because female gametes mostly contribute mitochondria to the zygote). In some eukaryotes (such as budding yeasts), mitochondrial inheritance is **biparental** also. In such organisms, both parents contribute mitochondria to the zygote.

Mitochondrion-related organelles: *Hydrogenosomes* and *mitosomes* are two mitochondrion-related organelles which entirely lack mtDNA. Some protists (such as *Trichomonas vaginalis*) adapted to anoxic or microaerobic environments lack mitochondria. These protists contain a specialized double-membrane-bound organelle, involved in synthesis of ATP and hydrogen, called the **hydrogenosome**. Hydrogenosomes are the site of pyruvate fermentation, coupled with ATP production via substrate level phosphorylation. Pyruvate is broken down to acetate, CO_2 and molecular hydrogen. The organelle takes its name from the fact that it produces molecular hydrogen. In contrast to mitochondria, hydrogenosome has an incomplete TCA cycle and electron transport chain and no cytochromes. **Mitosomes**, organelles of mitochondrial origin, are double-membrane bound organelles found in some unicellular anaerobic parasitic eukaryotes that do not have mitochondria, including *Entamoeba histolytica*, *Giardia lamblia* and microsporidia. The name 'mitosome' was proposed to indicate that the organelles are highly reduced (cryptic) mitochondria. The mitosomes are unable to generate ATP and are even more reduced than hydrogenosomes.

3.11 Plastids

Plastids are double-membrane bound *semi-autonomous organelles* present in all living photosynthetic plant cells and photosynthetic protists. Plastids are believed to have arisen from an endosymbiotic event between a photosynthetic cyanobacterium and the ancestral eukaryotic cell. They possess their own genome and gene expression system. All plastids contain multiple copies of the dsDNA as genetic materials and 70S ribosomes for proteins synthesis. During evolution, many genes of endosymbiont were transferred to the nucleus. As a consequence, most plastid proteins are encoded by the nuclear genes and synthesized in the cytosol and are imported post-translationally. The size range of plastid DNA (or the plastome) vary between 120 to 160kbp in higher plants and they are mostly circular. Plastids differentiate from **proplastids**, which are small, undifferentiated organelles located in the meristematic regions of plants. Proplastids serve as the precursors for all types of plastids. These organelles have a simple structure, lacking the specialized features of mature plastids. Proplastids are typically small and colorless, with a minimal internal membrane system, distinguishing them from fully developed plastids. As immature plant cells differentiate, the proplastids develop according to the needs of the specialized cell: they can become chloroplast, leucoplasts or chromoplasts. A collective term used for different kinds of organelles, all derived from proplastids, is **plastid**. Plastid interconversions are tissue- and species-specific events. Plastids are classified into two main categories: *photosynthetic* and *non-photosynthetic* plastids. The **chloroplast** is the **photosynthetic plastid** and the most important member of plastid family. It contains the green pigment chlorophyll. It occurs in all photosynthetic eukaryotes and acts as site of photosynthesis. Transitions of proplastids to chloroplasts mainly occur in the shoot apical meristem and during embryogenesis. **Non-photosynthetic plastids** are types of plastids that do not participate in the process of photosynthesis. Based on pigmentation, the non-photosynthetic plastids can be broadly divided into leucoplasts, the 'white' or colourless plastids, and chromoplasts, the coloured plastids notable for their accumulation of carotenoids. **Chromoplasts** are plastids responsible for pigment synthesis and storage. They are mainly responsible for the yellow, orange, or red colors of many fruits and flowers, as well as of autumn leaves. **Leucoplasts** are colorless (non-pigmented) plastids and act as storage organelles. Based on the kind of substance they store, they are further classified into **amyloplasts** (for starch storage), **elaioplasts** (store lipids in lipid droplets) and **proteinoplasts** (also termed as *proteoplast, aleuroplast, aleuronaplast*; for storing and modifying proteins).

Chloroplast

Chloroplast is a photosynthetic plastid. It has a double membrane which encloses a fluid-filled region called the **stroma**. Embedded in the stroma is a complex network of stacked sacs. Each stack is called a **granum** and each of the flattened sacs which makes up the granum is called a **thylakoid**. The thylakoid membrane, which encloses a fluid-filled thylakoid lumen, contains photosynthetic pigments. There are many granum in each chloroplast (usually 10 to 100 granum) which are interconnected by unstacked *stroma thylakoids*. Thus, thylakoid has two distinct domains – **grana thylakoids** (or **grana lamellae**) and **stroma thylakoid** (or **stroma lamellae**).

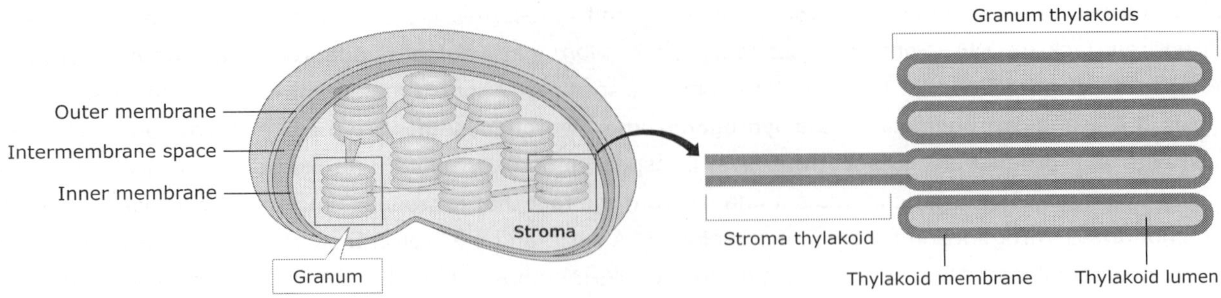

Figure 3.45 A detailed view of the internal structure of a chloroplast. Chloroplasts are oval-shaped structure and have two membranes: an outer membrane and an inner membrane. Between the outer and inner membrane is the intermembrane space. The space enclosed by the inner membrane is the stroma. Suspended within the stroma is the thylakoid system. Thylakoids consist of a thylakoid membrane surrounding a thylakoid lumen. A stack of thylakoids forms a granum (plural grana). Grana are connected by unstacked membranes called stroma thylakoids (or stroma lamellae).

The lipids of the thylakoid membrane have a distinctive composition. About 80% of lipids are uncharged mono- and digalactosyldiacylglycerol and only about 10% are phospholipids. Monogalactosyldiacylglycerol and digalactosyldiacylglycerol are **glycolipids** composed of a glycerol backbone attached to two fatty acid chains, forming diacylglycerol, and one or two galactose sugar molecules, respectively. The edges of the thylakoids also form unique hydrophobic pockets called **plastoglobuli**. They are enclosed by a lipid monolayer that is a continuation of the outer thylakoid monolayer. They perform different functions, which depend on the nature of the plastid. In chromoplasts, plastoglobuli are rich in carotenoid esters and enzymes involved in carotenoid metabolism, whereas in chloroplasts filled with lipophilic metabolites and function in lipid biosynthesis, storage and cleavage.

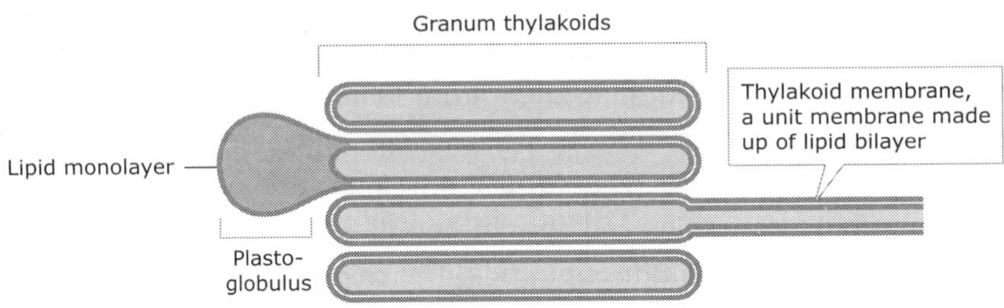

Figure 3.46 A plastoglobulus is a structure enclosed by a lipid monolayer that extends from outer leaflet of the thylakoid membrane.

Comparison of mitochondria and chloroplast

Chloroplasts are generally much larger than mitochondria and have a more complex internal structure. In addition to the outer and inner chloroplast membranes, chloroplasts possess a thylakoid membrane system that encloses the thylakoid lumen. In contrast, mitochondria have only outer and inner mitochondrial membranes, and the inner mitochondrial membrane is folded into structures known as **cristae**. These folds increase the surface area available for cellular respiration. The inner mitochondrial membrane is functionally analogous to the thylakoid membrane in chloroplasts.

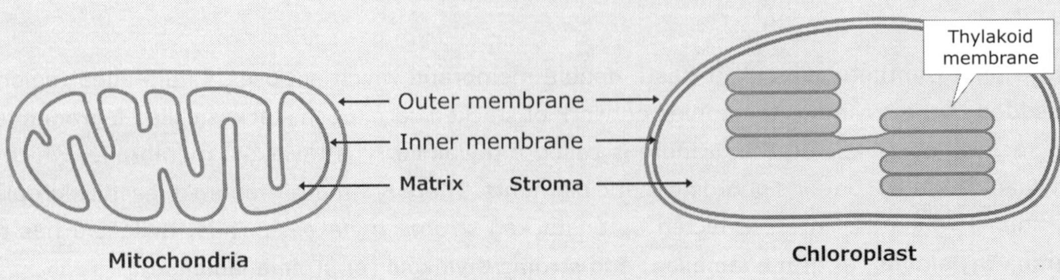

Chloroplasts can further differentiate depending on environmental stimuli and plant cell types into *chromoplasts*, *phenyloplasts* and *gerontoplast*. During senescence processes or under stress condition, chloroplasts undergo serial changes in their ultrastructures and change into **gerontoplasts**. They are characterized by the breakdown of chlorophyll and of the thylakoid membrane system. **Chromoplast** and **phenyloplast** accumulate phytochemicals such as carotenoids and phenylpropanoids, respectively.

In the dark-grown plants, proplastids develop into **etioplasts**. They are the transient state of development for chloroplasts. Etioplasts contain semicrystalline tubular arrays of a membrane known as **prolamellar bodies**, which contain a pale yellow-green precursor pigment, **protochlorophyllide**. When etioplasts are exposed to light, protochlorophyllide, the chlorophyll precursor of prolamellar bodies, is immediately converted to chlorophyllide by the light-dependent enzyme. Following this, chlorophyllide is finally converted to chlorophyll.

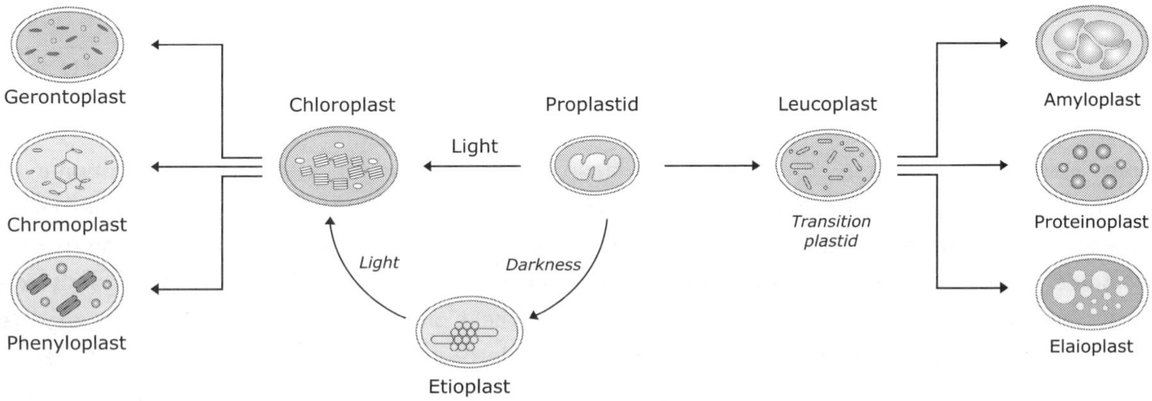

Figure 3.47 Diversity and differentiation of plastids depending on tissue type and developmental stages. Arrows indicate transitions between different plastid types. The proplastid is the progenitor plastid, point of differentiation, developing into either etioplast or chloroplast depending on exposure to darkness or light, respectively. Proplastids are also able to develop into the intermediate plastid, the leucoplasts that may further differentiate into either amylo-, proteino- or elaioplasts accumulating starch, proteins or oils, respectively. Chloroplasts can also further differentiate depending on environmental stimuli and plant cell types into chromoplasts, phenyloplasts and the dying gerontoplast, in which resources are recycled and redistributed. Chromoplast and phenyloplast accumulate phytochemicals such as carotenoids and phenylpropanoids, respectively.

3.12 Peroxisome

The peroxisome, discovered by Christian de Duve in 1965, is a small, single-membrane-bound organelle, approximately 0.5–1 μm in diameter, found in all eukaryotic cells. The term 'peroxisome' was proposed by de Duve because these organelles produce as well as consume hydrogen peroxide. Unlike mitochondria and plastids, peroxisomes are not semi-autonomous organelles; they do not contain their own DNA or ribosomes. All peroxisomal proteins, both matrix and membrane proteins, are encoded by nuclear genes and synthesized by 80S ribosomes in the cytosol.

It has long been debated whether new peroxisomes arise from pre-existing ones by organelle growth and division, like mitochondria and plastids (**growth and division model**) or whether they arise as specialized pre-peroxisomal vesicles from the endoplasmic reticulum (***de novo* biogenesis model**). Aspects of both views are true. During peroxisomal biogenesis, some peroxisomal membrane proteins are first inserted into the membrane of the ER, sorted to a region of the ER called the **pre-peroxisomal ER**, from where distinct **pre-peroxisomal vesicles** derived. New peroxisomal precursor vesicles may then fuse with one another and begin importing additional peroxisomal proteins from the cytosol to grow into mature peroxisomes, which can enter into a cycle of growth and division. The proteins required for peroxisome biogenesis are called **peroxins**. The importance of peroxisome biogenesis is dramatically demonstrated by the inherited human disease, **Zellweger syndrome**. It is a rare, congenital, autosomal recessive disorder.

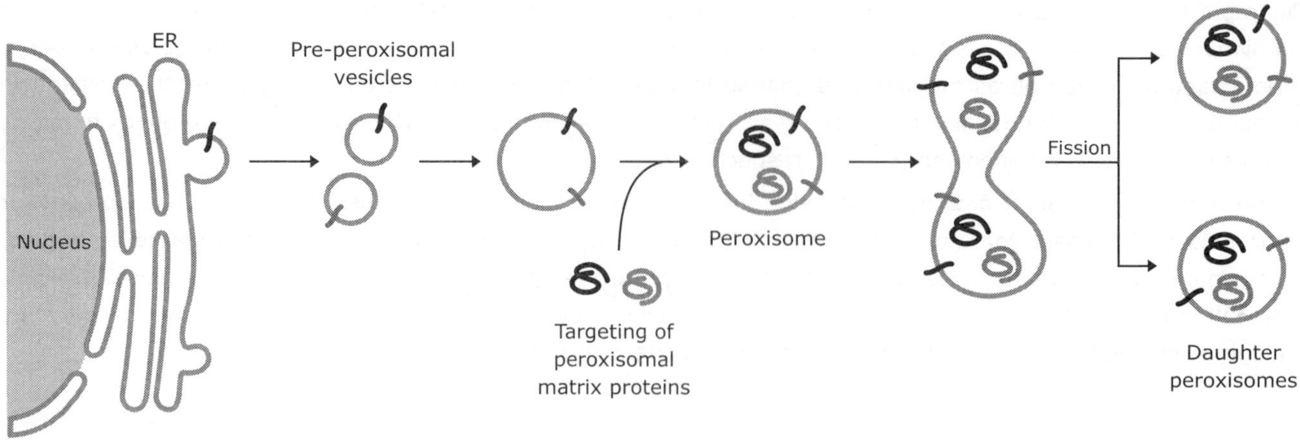

Figure 3.48 All of the peroxisomal proteins are encoded in the cell nucleus. Some of these proteins are conveyed to peroxisomes via pre-peroxisomal vesicles that bud from the ER, but most are directly imported from the cytosol.

Peroxisomes are unusually diverse organelles. A high degree of functional and metabolic specialization in different organisms has been reported. For example, in *trypanosomes*, the majority of glycolytic enzymes reside in specialized peroxisomes called **glycosomes**. Similarly, filamentous ascomycetes contain specialized peroxisomes in form of **Woronin bodies**. If peroxisomes contain enzymes of the **glyoxylate cycle**, they are referred to as **glyoxysomes**. Glyoxysomes are found in certain plant cells, particularly in the cells of germinating seeds. In the *glyoxylate cycle*, two molecules of acetyl-CoA, produced from the breakdown of fatty acids, are converted into succinate.

Like mitochondria, peroxisomes contain several oxidative enzymes, such as catalase, oxidases. Peroxisomal oxidases transfer hydrogen atoms to molecular oxygen and form hydrogen peroxide. Generally, hydrogen peroxide can be removed by two types of enzymes: *peroxidases* and *catalases*. **Peroxidases** eliminate hydrogen peroxide by using it to oxidize another substrate, following the reaction: $SH_2 + H_2O_2 \rightarrow S + 2H_2O$, where SH_2 represents the substrate. In contrast, **catalases** directly convert hydrogen peroxide into water and oxygen through the reaction: $2H_2O_2 \rightarrow 2H_2O + O_2$.

A major oxidative reaction carried out in peroxisomes is the **β-oxidation**. β-oxidation in mammalian cells occurs both in mitochondria and peroxisomes; in plant cells, however, this is exclusively occurred in peroxisomes. Peroxisomes also play an important role in photorespiration. **Photorespiration** is a metabolic process in plants that occurs when the enzyme RuBisCO oxygenates RuBP instead of carboxylating it, leading to the consumption of oxygen and the release of carbon dioxide. When RuBisCO reacts with oxygen rather than carbon dioxide, it produces one molecule of 3-phosphoglycerate (which continues in the Calvin cycle) and one molecule of 2-phosphoglycolate. The 2-phosphoglycolate, a two-carbon compound, undergoes a series of reactions involving the chloroplast, peroxisome, and mitochondrion, in a pathway known as the **glycolate cycle**. Within the peroxisome some steps of glycolate cycle occurs. Here, glycolate is oxidized to form glyoxylate and hydrogen peroxide, and the glyoxylate is then converted into glycine.

3.13 Nucleus

The nucleus is the **controlling center** of a eukaryotic cell. It contains most of the genetic materials of a cell. Most eukaryotic cells have one nucleus (**uninucleate**) each, but some have many nuclei (**multinucleate**) and certain cells, such as mature mammalian red blood cells, do not have it. *Paramecia* (unicellular ciliate protozoa) have two nuclei – a **macronucleus** and a **micronucleus**. Genes in the macronucleus control the vegetative functions of the cell, such as feeding, waste removal, and maintenance of water balance, whereas the micronucleus controls the sexual reproduction.

Nuclei also differ in size depending on the cell type. Most nuclei are spherical, but multilobed nuclei are also common, such as those found in polymorphonuclear leukocytes or mammalian epididymal cells. A nucleus in G0 phase has four components: *Nuclear envelope, nucleolus, nuclear matrix* and *chromatins*.

Nuclear envelope and nuclear matrix

The nuclear envelope consists of two concentric membranes called the *inner* and *outer* nuclear membranes. The outer nuclear membrane is continuous with the endoplasmic reticulum, so the space between the inner and outer nuclear membranes, the **perinuclear space**, is directly connected with the lumen of the endoplasmic reticulum. In addition, the outer nuclear membrane is functionally similar to the membranes of the endoplasmic reticulum and has ribosomes bound to its cytoplasmic surface. In contrast, the inner nuclear membrane carries unique proteins that are specific to the nucleus. The critical function of the nuclear membrane is to act as a barrier that separates the contents of the nucleus from the cytoplasm. The nuclear envelope contains **nuclear pores** for transport of macromolecules between the cytoplasm and nucleus. Each nuclear pore consists of large multiprotein complex and termed as **nuclear pore complex**. Each nuclear pore complex is a cylindrical structure with octagonal symmetry. The inner and outer membranes fuse at the nuclear pore complexes. Each nuclear pore complex consists of multiple copies of roughly 30 different proteins. The proteins that make up the nuclear pore complex are known as **nucleoporins**. The nucleus of a typical mammalian cell contains about 3000 to 4000 pores.

The **nuclear matrix** (or nuclear-scaffold) is a network of protein filaments in the nucleus which provides a structural framework for organizing chromatin, while facilitating transcription and replication. The term 'nuclear matrix' is defined as the biochemical entity that can be isolated from cell's nuclei after sequential extraction with non-ionic detergents, nucleases and high-salt buffers. The ultrastructure of the nuclear matrix consists of a **nuclear lamina** and a network-like **internal nuclear matrix**. The structural proteins of the nuclear lamina have been well characterized, but the structural biochemistry of the internal nuclear matrix is less known. The *nuclear lamina* is network of intermediate filaments present on the nuclear side of the inner membrane. It is made up of **lamin proteins**. The nuclear lamina gives shape and stability to the nuclear envelope. It links the internal nuclear matrix to the nuclear membranes.

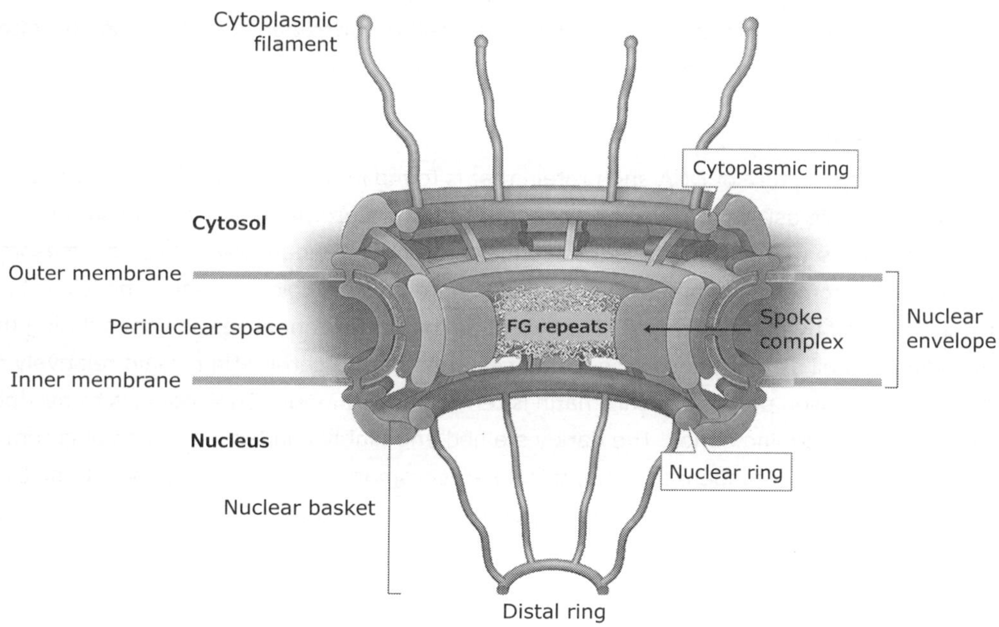

Figure 3.49 The nuclear pore complex is a cylindrical structure and displays an octagonal symmetry. At the center of the pore is a spoke assembly of 8 annular units anchored to the membrane by the luminal ring. There are two rings, one facing the nucleus (*nuclear ring*) and the other the cytoplasm (*cytoplasmic ring*). The cytoplasmic side of the nuclear pore complex is associated with cytoplasmic filaments. On the nucleoplasmic side, a nuclear basket is attached.

Nucleolus

Nucleolus (first described by F. Fontana) is a non-membrane bound *dynamic body* which disappears in the late prophase and reappears in the telophase stage of cell division. Each nucleolus is produced by a **Nucleolus-Organizing Region** (NOR) of a chromosome which is termed as **nucleolus-organizing chromosome**. All eukaryotic cells contain at least one such chromosome. Its number may be one or more (several hundred per nucleus), but 1 to 4 being the most common. The number of nucleoli per nucleus also differs. The yeast cell contains one relatively large nucleolus with respect to its nuclear volume. At the other extreme, *Xenopus oocytes* contain over 1000 nucleoli per nucleus.

It is a site of transcription of ribosomal RNA and assembly of ribosome. rRNA genes present in the NOR of chromosome is responsible for synthesizing a large nascent pre-rRNA that is 45S in mammals and the processing (cleavage and base modification) of this RNA yield mature ribosomal RNA of 18S, 5.8S and 28S. The concomitant assembly of these RNAs with incoming ribosomal proteins generates small and large ribosomal subunits that then pass into the cytoplasm.

Nucleolus structure: It consists of three major regions.

Fibrillar centers: Containing rRNA genes in the form of partly condensed chromatin.

Fibrillar component: Surrounds the fibrillar centers, which contains RNA molecules in the process of transcription.

Granular regions: Outermost regions having mature ribosomal precursor particles.

Nucleolus-organizing regions: The nucleolus-organizing region (NOR) is a region of chromosome around which the nucleolus forms. In human, five chromosomes contain NORs, which can be identified as *secondary constriction* on metaphase chromosomes. However, not all secondary constrictions are NORs. The position of secondary constriction in a chromosome is specific and species specific. As compared to secondary constrictions, the *primary constriction*, also referred to as **centromere**, attaches sister chromatids together. The difference between these two constrictions can be noticed during anaphase, as chromosome can bend only at the site of primary constriction. The area of a chromosome distal to a nucleolus-organizing region is called **satellite** (or *trabant*). A chromosome with a secondary constriction usually associated with a nucleolus is called *SAT-chromosome*.

Chromatin and chromosome

A **chromatin** is an organized structure of DNA and protein that is found in the nucleus of eukaryotic cells. In G_0 stage, one chromatin contains a single dsDNA in coiled and condensed form. Chromatin and chromosomes are basically the same things. The difference is that chromatin is less condensed and extended DNA while chromosomes are highly condensed DNA. The word '**chromosome**' comes from the Greek word *chroma*, color and *soma*, body due to their property of being very strongly stained by particular dyes. The extent of chromatin condensation varies during the life cycle of the cell. In non-dividing as well as interphase stages of a cell, most of the chromatin remain relatively decondensed. The light-staining, less condensed portions of chromatin is termed **euchromatin**. This region is transcriptionally active and contains most of the transcribing genes. The darkly stained and highly condensed region of chromatin is termed as **heterochromatin**. Because of its condensed state, this heterochromatin is generally believed to be transcriptionally silent. Subnuclear positioning of chromatin and transcriptional activity are related. Transcriptionally active chromatin is often found at the periphery whereas active chromatin tends to be located more centrally.

Centromere: The constricted region of linear chromosomes is known as the *centromere*. Although this constriction is called the centromere, it is usually not located exactly in the center of the chromosome and, in some cases, is located almost at the chromosome's end. The regions on either side of the centromere are referred to as the *chromosome's arms*. The centromeres serve both as the sites of association of sister chromatids and as the attachment sites for microtubules of the mitotic spindle.

Telomere: Telomeres are specialized structures, which cap the ends of eukaryotic chromosomes. It consists of a long array of short, tandemly repeated sequences. Sequencing of telomeres from different organisms has shown that most are repetitive sequences with a high G content in the strand with its 3′ end.

Origin of replication: The origin of replication (also called the *replication origin*) is a *cis*-acting sequence in a chromosome at which replication is initiated. One chromosome contains multiple origin of replication.

Chromosome number

All eukaryotic cells have multiple linear chromosomes. *Chromosomes number in eukaryotes are species specific.* Every species maintains a characteristic number of chromosomes. Depending on the eukaryotic organism, the number of chromosomes varies from 2 to several hundreds. Eukaryotes can be monoploid (having one set of chromosomes), diploid (having two sets of chromosomes) and polyploid (having more than two sets of chromosomes). The majority of eukaryotes are diploid.

Table 3.9 Chromosome number in different eukaryotic organisms

Species	Haploid number of chromosome
Saccharomyces cerevisiae (budding yeast)	16
Schizosaccharomyces pombe (fission yeast)	03
Caenorhabditis elegans	06
Arabidopsis thaliana	05
Drosophila melanogaster	04
Tetrahymena thermophila	05 (in micronucleus)
Homo sapiens (human)	23

Tetrahymena thermophila is a ciliated protozoan. It has two nuclei – somatic *macronucleus* (responsible for vegetative function) and germline *micronucleus* (responsible for sexual reproduction). The micronucleus is diploid and contains five pairs of chromosomes. Macronuclear chromosomes are derived from site-specific fragmentation of the five original micronuclear chromosomes.

3.14 Cytoskeleton

Cytoskeleton is an intracellular network of protein filaments present in the cytoplasm. There are three types of cytoskeletal filaments— *actin filaments*, *intermediate filaments* and *microtubules*. All these fibers are polymers built from small protein subunits held together by noncovalent interactions. Each type of filament has distinct structural properties, dynamics and biological roles.

3.14.1 Microtubules

Microtubules are hollow, cylindrical (approximately 25 nm in diameter), polymerized, polarized and dynamic structure. They are present in all eukaryotic cells. The basic building block of the microtubule is an 'αβ-tubulin heterodimer', composed of two 50 kDa subunits known as **α-tubulin** and **β-tubulin**. Tubulins are highly conserved globular proteins found in all eukaryotes. A linear array of αβ-tubulin heterodimers through longitudinal non-covalent interactions forms a linear filamentous structure called **protofilament**. A *microtubule* comprises 13 laterally associated protofilaments and forms a hollow cylindrical structure whose external diameter is about 25 nm. However, many examples exist in which microtubules have a different number of protofilaments (from 11 to as many as 15). The 13 protofilaments are aligned in parallel with the same polarity. α-tubulin subunits of all protofilaments face one end of the microtubule, and the β-subunits face the opposite end. The ends are designated either plus or minus, based upon their different dynamic and structural properties. β-subunits are exposed at the *plus ends* (fast-growing) while the α-subunits are exposed at the *minus ends* (slow-growing). In a typical microtubule, α-subunits of one protofilament are next to α-subunits of laterally associated next protofilament (α–α) and β next to β (β–β). However, at the seam, the α-subunits associate laterally with β-subunits in the adjacent protofilaments (α–β). The α- and β-tubulin heterodimer undergoes multiple post-translational modifications. These include common modifications such as phosphorylation, acetylation and sumoylation, as well as tubulin-specific modifications such as polyglutamylation (addition of free glutamates to the side-chain of glutamate in the polypeptide).

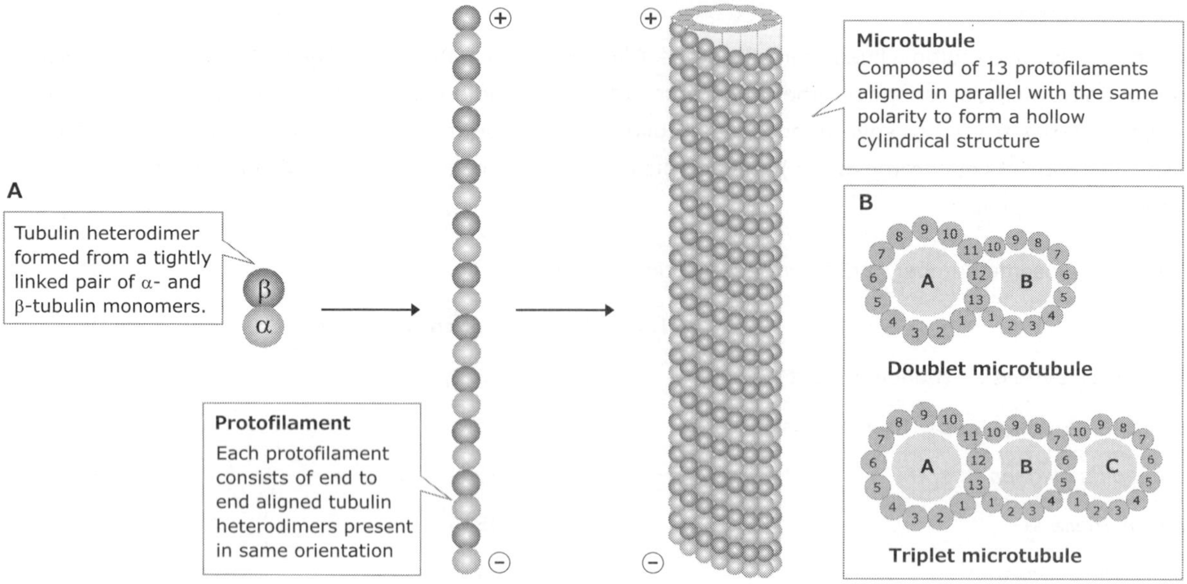

Figure 3.50 Structure of tubulin heterodimers and their organization in a microtubule.

Singlet microtubule (made up of 13 protofilaments) in the cytosol is very common, but many specialized microtubules arrays also exist in which microtubules are fused along their lengths into doublet or triplet microtubule structures. **Doublet microtubules** consist of 10 or 11 protofilaments containing incomplete second microtubule (B-tubule) fused to an entire 13 protofilament containing the first microtubule (A-tubule), and **triplet microtubules** have an additional 10 or 11 protofilaments containing incomplete third microtubule (C-tubule) fused to the second microtubule (B-tubule). Doublet microtubules occur in the *filament* of motile cell appendages called *cilia* and *flagella*. Triplet microtubules occur in the *basal body* structures, situated at the base of cilia and flagella and in *centrioles*, which are situated within the centrosomes.

Microtubule organizing center (**MTOC**): Microtubules in cells are usually organized at the MTOC. In interphase, it is typically located on one side of the nucleus, close to the outer surface of the nuclear envelope. In animal cells, MTOC contains a pair of centrioles and known as **centrosome**. The *minus ends* of microtubules are embedded at the MTOC and the *plus ends* are away from it. One of the known proteins of the MTOC is a form of tubulin called **γ-tubulin,** which does not form microtubules itself and does not become incorporated into microtubules, but does appear to function in the *nucleation* of microtubule formation. **γ-tubulin ring complex** (γ-TuRC), a protein complex containing γ-tubulin and several accessory proteins, nucleates microtubule polymerization. γ-TuRC is not the sole microtubule nucleator. In *Xenopus* egg, **XMAP215** acts as a microtubule nucleator. In the case of yeast, the **spindle pole bodies** (or **duplication plaques**) serve as MTOCs. In contrast to centrosomes, spindle pole bodies do not contain centrioles. Instead, they are large proteinaceous structures that are either continuously embedded in the nuclear envelope (budding yeast) or inserted into the nuclear envelope before mitosis (fission yeast). Therefore, the spindle pole body is able to organize two types of microtubules, the *nuclear* and the *cytoplasmic microtubules,* with functions in chromosome segregation and nuclear positioning, respectively. Similarly, the MTOCs in most plant cells do not contain centrioles, but they still function as MTOCs.

Microtubule polymerization and dynamics

Microtubules are dynamic structures that are constantly being polymerized and depolymerized. Its polymerization occurs by a nucleation-elongation mechanism, in which the formation of a short microtubule *nucleus* is followed by the growth of the microtubule at both ends by the reversible noncovalent addition of tubulin heterodimers. The whole course of polymerization is divided into three phases:

Nucleation phase: This phase corresponds to the formation of a short microtubule *nucleus*. Microtubule nucleation is unfavourable under normal conditions found in most living cells. It is mediated by γ-tubulin ring complex (γ-TuRC), which nucleates and caps the *minus end* of new filaments.

Elongation phase: After the slow nucleation phase, microtubules elongate rapidly. The fast elongation phase is marked by addition of tubulin heterodimers to the exposed *plus end* of the growing filament, causing net filament elongation.

Steady state: The steady state is reached when the growth of the filament due to the tubulin heterodimers addition (polymerization) is exactly balanced by depolymerization from the ends.

The rate of polymerization and depolymerization is greater at the *plus end* than the *minus end*. The number of tubulin heterodimers that add to the polymer per second (i.e., polymerization rate) depends on the concentration of the free tubulin heterodimers and it is directly proportional to the free tubulin heterodimer concentration. Hence, with increase in free tubulin heterodimers concentration, polymerization rate at both ends increases. Contrary to polymerization, the rate of depolymerization is independent of the free tubulin heterodimers concentration.

What implications do these polymerization and depolymerization rates have for microtubule dynamics? First, let's consider just one end, the *plus end*. As we noted above, the polymerization rate depends on the free tubulin heterodimers concentration, whereas the depolymerization rate does not. The concentration of free tubulin heterodimers at which the polymerization rate at plus end equals the depolymerization rate, is called the **critical concentration** for the plus end. At free tubulin heterodimers concentrations above the critical concentration, the tubulin heterodimers polymerize into microtubules, whereas at concentration below the critical concentration, microtubules depolymerize.

The critical concentrations for the two ends are different and this value for the *minus end* is higher than *plus end*. Because the critical concentrations for the two ends are different, at steady state the free tubulin heterodimer will be intermediate between critical concentration for the plus end and the minus end so the plus end will grow and the minus end will lose tubulin heterodimers. Thus, when the concentration of free tubulin heterodimers is higher than the critical concentration at the plus end but lower than the critical concentration at the minus-end, microtubules can treadmill by a net polymerization at the plus end and a net depolymerization at the minus end at an identical rate. This special state in polymer dynamics, known as **treadmilling**, keeps the polymer length unchanged.

GTP hydrolysis: Each α and β-tubulin has a binding site for one molecule of GTP. The GTP that is bound to the α-tubulin is never hydrolyzed or exchanged. By contrast, the β-tubulin has a GTP-binding site in the tubulin heterodimer that is exchangeable with free GTP, and this bound GTP can be hydrolyzed. Thus, two different types of αβ-tubulin heterodimer can exist, one is the '**T-form**' (β-tubulin is GTP bound) and other is the '**D-form**' (β-tubulin is GDP bound). In free αβ-tubulin heterodimer, hydrolysis of GTP bound to β-tubulin proceeds very slowly. In living cells, most of the free tubulin heterodimers are in the GTP bound form i.e., T-form. However, it is accelerated when the tubulin heterodimers are incorporated into filaments. The longer the time that tubulin heterodimers have been in the filament, the more likely they are in D-form.

Hydrolysis of the bound GTP reduces the binding affinity of the tubulin heterodimer for neighbouring heterodimer and makes it more likely to dissociate from each end of the filament. Thus, the normal role of GTP hydrolysis is apparently to allow microtubules to depolymerize by weakening the bonds between tubulin heterodimers in the microtubule. Thus, under physiological conditions, GTP-bound tubulin heterodimer tends to polymerize and GDP-bound tubulin heterodimer to depolymerize. Whether the tubulin heterodimer at each end of a filament is in the T- or the D-form, depends on the rate of GTP hydrolysis compared with the rate of tubulin heterodimer addition. At high concentrations of free tubulin heterodimers, when a microtubule grows rapidly, tubulin heterodimers add to a polymer end faster than the GTP they carry can be hydrolyzed. This results in the presence of many GTP-bound tubulin heterodimers at the end of the microtubule. This is termed as a **GTP cap**. The presence of a GTP cap at the end of the microtubule, depends on the relative rates of GTP hydrolysis and tubulin heterodimers addition. Since GTP-bound tubulin heterodimers bind to one another with higher affinity than GDP-bound tubulin heterodimers, the GTP cap will encourage a growing microtubule to continue growing. Only microtubules whose ends are associated with GTP-bound tubulin heterodimers (those with a GTP cap) are stable and can serve as primers for the polymerization of additional tubulin heterodimers. Microtubules with GDP-bound tubulin heterodimer (D-form) at the end are rapidly depolymerized. As a consequence, critical concentration for a T-form end is lower than critical concentration for a D-form end.

Microtubules in most cell types display a behavior known as **dynamic instability**, in which, a single microtubule end may undergo transitions between a growing state and a shrinking state. This occurs primarily at the plus ends. The change from growth to shrinkage is called a *catastrophe*, while the change to growth is called a *rescue*.

What is the 'mechanism' of dynamic instability? A growing microtubule has a GTP cap at its end and this allows continued polymerization. However, if the cap is lost due to more rapid nucleotide hydrolysis than tubulin heterodimers addition, the microtubule begins to shrink rapidly, an event called a **catastrophe**. But GTP containing tubulin heterodimers may still add to the shrinking end, and if enough add to form a new cap, then microtubule growth resumes, an event called **rescue**.

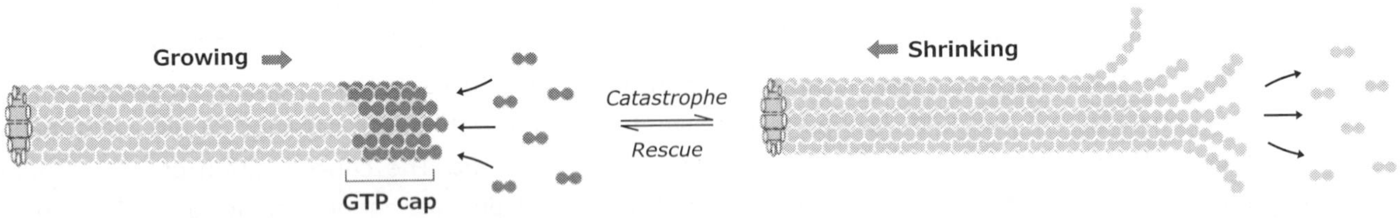

Figure 3.51 A growing microtubule has GTP containing tubulin heterodimers at its end, forming a GTP cap. If the cap is lost, the microtubule begins to shrink, an event called a *catastrophe*. But GTP containing heterodimers may still add to the shrinking end, and if enough add to form a new cap, then microtubule growth resumes, an event called *rescue*.

Microtubule-associated proteins: Proteins that bind to microtubules are collectively called *microtubule-associated proteins* (MAPs). A large number of MAPs bind to the surface of the microtubule and play crucial roles in nucleation, dynamics and stability. MAPs can be categorized functionally as *stabilizers* (such as tau, MAP4), *destabilizers* (such as katanin), *capping proteins* (e.g., patronin), *bundlers/cross-linkers* (such as tau, CLIP170) and *microtubule motors* (e.g., kinesin and dynein). Destabilizers include *sequestering proteins* (e.g., protein stathmin), *tip destabilizers* (e.g., depolymerizing kinesin-13) and *microtubule severing proteins* (e.g., katanin).

Function of microtubules

Microtubules present in all eukaryotic cells and perform diverse functions. They determine the positions of cell organelles within the cell, direct intracellular transport of transport vesicles and organelles, segregation of chromosomes during cell division by forming mitotic spindle. They form the structural framework of flagella and cilia, which function as motile structures. Non-motile cilia function as sensory and signaling devices on the surface of the cell. In plant cells, organized arrays of microtubules help to direct the pattern of cell wall synthesis and also determine the plane of formation of the cell wall during cytokinesis.

3.14.2 Microtubule–based motor proteins: Kinesins and Dyneins

Kinesin is a microtubule-based motor protein. It was first identified in the neuron extract as the motor protein responsible for *anterograde* transport in neurons. The genomes of mammals encode more than 40 kinesin proteins, organized into at least 14 families named kinesin-1 through kinesin-14. Members of the kinesin superfamily are characterized by a common ATP-binding domain. Since most members of the kinesin superfamily are involved in active transport and movement, this domain is usually called *motor domain*. According to the position of the motor domain, the kinesin family can be classified into **N-type kinesins** (with the motor domain at or near to the N-terminus, as in Kinesin-1 to 12), **M-type kinesins** (with the motor domain internally located, as in kinesin-13) and **C-type kinesins** (with the motor domain close to the C-terminus, as in kinesin-14). Most of kinesins are microtubule based plus end-directed motor proteins. Kinesin-14, by contrast, are minus end directed motors.

The conventional kinesin, **kinesin-1**, consists of two heavy chains and two light chains. The heavy chain has three functional domains: the *motor head domain*, the *α-helical stalk domain* and the *globular tail domain*. The kinesin-1 molecule comprises a pair of large globular *motor head domains* connected by an elongated *coiled-coil stalk domain* to a pair of small globular *tail domains*, which contain the light chains. Each head has two separate binding sites: one for the microtubule and the other for ATP. The tail domain is responsible for binding to receptors on the membrane of cargoes. It is a plus end-directed motor protein involved in organelle transport.

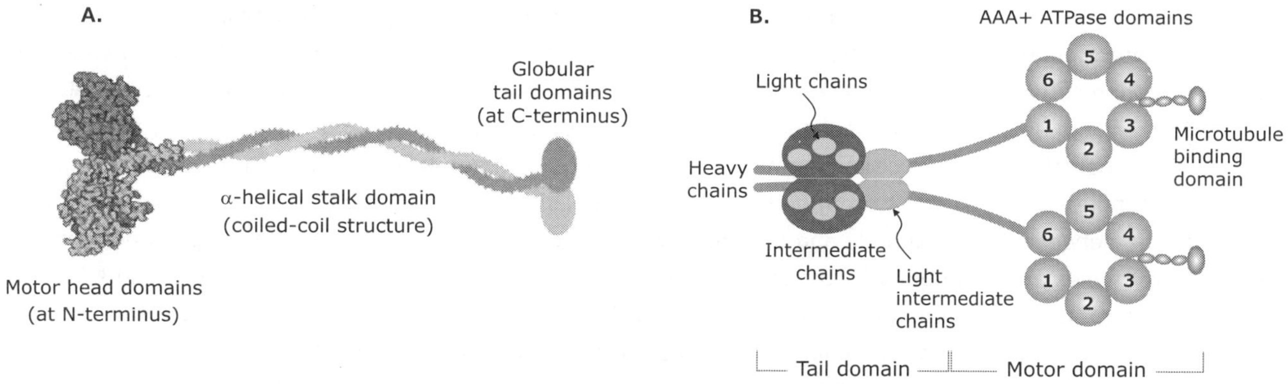

Figure 3.52 **A**. Structure of kinesin-1. It consists of two heavy chains and two light chains. **B**. Structure of cytoplasmic dynein 1. It consists of two heavy chains, light intermediate chains, intermediate chains and light chains.

Although most kinesins have two heavy chains (e.g., kinesin-1), others may have a single heavy chain or four heavy chains. The kinesin-5 family members have four heavy chains and act as *bipolar* motor proteins. Kinesin-5 protein contains two motor domains that interact with two antiparallel microtubules and move towards the plus end.

Dyneins are a family of minus-end directed microtubule-based motor proteins. They are the largest of the known molecular motors and they are also among the fastest. The dynein family can be classified into two major groups: *cytoplasmic dyneins* and *axonemal dyneins*.

Cytoplasmic dyneins are of two different types – cytoplasmic dynein 1 and cytoplasmic dynein 2. **Cytoplasmic dynein 1** is present in most eukaryotic cells and has role in vesicles trafficking. They mediate transport of vesicles toward the *minus end* of microtubules. It drives *retrograde* axonal transport in neurons. **Cytoplasmic dynein 2** found only in eukaryotic organisms that have cilia or flagella and has a role in intraflagellar transport and is required for cilia and flagella assembly. Cytoplasmic dynein 1 is a large, multisubunit complex that is composed of heavy chains, light intermediate chains, intermediate chains and light chains. It has two identical heavy chains (homodimer). Each heavy chain can be divided into two functional regions – a C-terminal *motor domain* and an N-terminal *tail domain*. The C-terminus motor domain comprises of six AAA+ ATPase domains and a microtubule binding domain. The N-terminal tail domain is responsible for dimerization of the heavy chains and also binds additional subunits known as the dynein 'tail' subunits, which include the light intermediate chain, the intermediate chain and the light chains. Unlike kinesin, cytoplasmic dynein, cannot mediate cargo transport by itself. Rather, it requires **dynactin**, a large multi subunit protein complex that links vesicles to the dynein tail domain and mediates dynein-cargo interaction. The complex consists of 23 individual subunits that are assembled around a filament consisting of **Arp1** (actin-related protein 1). A critical component of the dynactin complex is the homodimeric **p150^{Glued}** which contains an N-terminal microtubule binding domain, dynein intermediate chain binding site and a C-terminal scaffold for the vesicle binding.

Axonemal dyneins are responsible for the movement of cilia and flagella. They are highly specialized for the rapid and efficient sliding movements of microtubules that drive the beating of cilia and flagella. Heavy chains in axonemal dyneins may present as heterodimers or heterotrimers.

3.14.3 Cilia and Flagella

Flagella is a locomotory organ present in many prokaryotes and eukaryotes. Eukaryotic flagella are different from prokaryotic flagella. Eukaryotic flagella (singular, *flagellum*) have a specialized arrangement of microtubules. A flagellum has two components–a **filament** and a **basal body** (or *kinetosome*). A *filament* possesses a bundle of microtubules, called the **axoneme**, in which nine outer doublet microtubules surround a central pair of singlet microtubules. This is termed as 9 + 2 arrangement. All the microtubules have the same polarity: the plus ends are located at the distal tip. Each doublet microtubule consists of A- and B-tubules. The A-tubule is a complete microtubule with 13 protofilaments, while the B tubule contains 10 protofilaments. The junction between A and B tubules of one doublet is probably strengthened by the protein **tektin**, a highly α-helical protein that is similar in structure to intermediate-filament proteins. The axoneme is surrounded by the plasma membrane. The axoneme of filament connects with the *basal body*. The basal body consists of both mother and daughter centrioles, but only the former acts as a site for the subsequent nucleation of microtubules during the formation of a filament. It consists of a barrel-shaped structure of nine triplet microtubules, each triplet built from A-, B- and C-tubules. The A and B tubules of basal bodies continue into the axonemal shaft, whereas the C tubule terminates within the transition zone between the basal body and the shaft. Within the axoneme, the two central singlet and nine outer doublet microtubules are continuous for the entire length of the structure. Permanently attached to the A tubule of each doublet microtubule is an inner and an outer row of **dynein arms**. These axonemal dyneins reach out to the B tubule of the neighboring doublet. A linker made up of protein **nexin**, joins adjacent outer doublet microtubules. A second linker **radial spokes**, which radiate from the central singlets to each A tubule of the outer doublets, form the third linkage system. The radial spoke and central pair complex are involved in beat regulation.

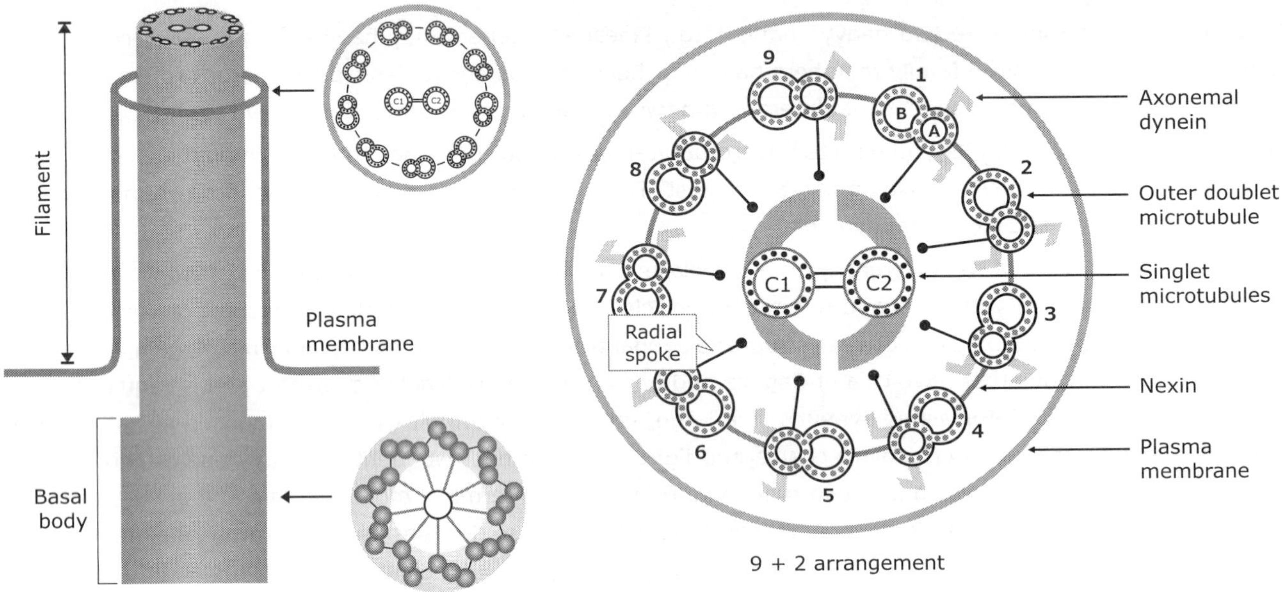

Figure 3.53 Arrangement of microtubules in a flagellum. A cross-section of the filament of a sperm flagellum. It has a bundle of microtubules called the axoneme which is surrounded by the plasma membrane. In axoneme, nine outer doublet microtubules surround a central pair of singlet microtubules. The outer doublets are joined to each other by *nexin* protein and to the central pair of singlet microtubules by *radial spokes*.

Eukaryotic flagella and cilia share a common structural organization. They differ in length, number per cell and beating pattern. There are two types of cilia: *motile cilia* and *non-motile cilia*. **Motile cilia** are usually present in large numbers per cell (multiciliated), for example, on the surface of epithelial cells of the oviduct and the respiratory tract *or* on surface of protists such as *Paramecium* and *Tetrahymena*. In multicellular organisms, cilia move fluid through various tracts. **Multiciliated motile cilia** consist of an axoneme of nine doublet microtubules and central pair of singlet microtubules (9+2 arrangement). Uncommon **monociliated motile cilia** lack the central pair of singlet microtubules (i.e., have 9 +0 arrangement). In (9+0) motile cilia, motor proteins dynein generate a rotational movement. **Non-motile cilia** are classified as **primary** or **sensory cilia**, fulfilling mainly sensory and signaling functions. In contrast to those of motile 9+2 cilia, axonemes of non-motile primary cilia lack the central pair of singlet microtubules (9+0) and also the dynein arms. Beating pattern of flagella and motile cilia differs. A flagellum has a *wave-like motion* that drives a cell in the same direction as the axis of the flagellum. In contrast, motile cilia generate alternating *power* and *recovery strokes*. The rapid power stroke moves the cell in a direction perpendicular to the axis of the cilium.

	Cilia (motile)	**Flagella**
Number	Many, occurring all over the surface of cell.	Very less, usually 1–4 per cell.
Size	Very small, 5–10 μ long.	Longer, about 150 μ long.
Beating pattern	Power and recovery strokes	Wave-like motion, propagates along the length.
Function	Propel single cells through a fluid or simply move liquid over their surface.	Help in locomotion of cells or organisms.

Mechanism of ciliary and flagellar locomotion: The basis for axonemal bending is the sliding of doublet microtubules relative to one another. The doublet microtubules are arranged with their plus end at the outer tip of the axoneme. The dynein arms on the A-tubule of one doublet slide along the adjacent doublet's B-tubule toward its base, the minus end. The force producing active sliding requires ATP and is caused by successive formation and breakage of cross-bridges between the dynein arm and the B-tubule. Successive binding and hydrolysis of ATP causes the dynein arms to successively release from and attach to the adjacent doublet.

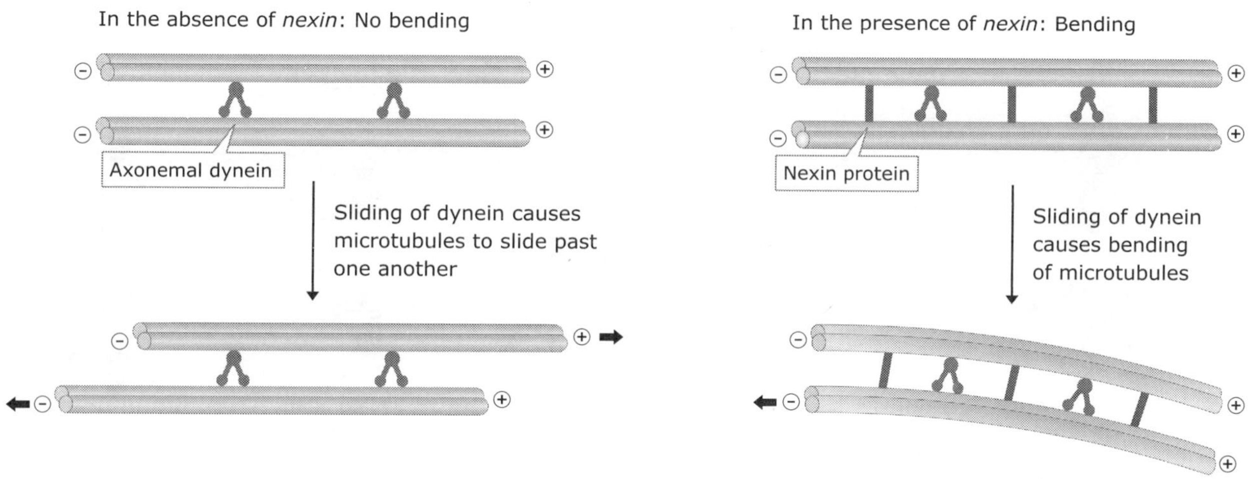

Figure 3.54 Axonemal dynein attached to an A-tubule of an outer doublet slides on the B-tubule of the adjacent doublet trying to move toward the minus end. Because the adjacent tubules are joined by nexin, the force generated by dynein bends the flagellum.

3.14.4 Centriole

A centriole is a barrel-shaped polarized structure made up of microtubules. Centrioles are present in most animal cells, cells of fungi and algae but not commonly in plant cells. The walls of each centriole are composed of nine triplet microtubules (9 + 0) arrangement or, in the case of *Drosophila*, nine doublet microtubules. There is a presence of **cartwheel** structures at the proximal end. A single cartwheel is composed of a central ring (*hub*) from which nine filaments (*spokes*) emanate. It is made up of **SAS-6 protein**. SAS-6 forms a coiled-coil dimer. Nine SAS-6 dimers can self-associate to form a ring. This SAS-6 ring is thought to generate the ninefold symmetry of the centriole. In animal cells, a pair of centrioles present in MTOC (microtubule-organizing center). MTOC with a pair of centrioles is known as **centrosome**. Two centrioles (one centriole is termed as *mother centriole* and the other termed as *daughter centriole*) are arranged perpendicular to each other in the center of the centrosome. The cloud of amorphous material that surrounds a pair of centrioles is called **centrosome matrix** (or *pericentriolar material*). Although the localization of centrioles within the centrosome together with their precise duplication prior to mitosis has suggested a role in bipolar spindle assembly or function, the actual role of centrioles in cell division remains unclear and controversial. Cells from which centrioles and centrosomes are ablated can still form bipolar spindles via a centrosome-independent self-organization process.

Centrosome cycle: Most animal cells contain a single centrosome that nucleates most of the cell's cytoplasmic microtubules. The duplication of the centrosome occurs during the interphase stage of the cell cycle. The process of centrosome duplication and separation is known as the *centrosome cycle*. During the interphase of each cell cycle, the centrioles and other components of the centrosome are duplicated. At a certain point in G1 phase, the two centrioles separate.

During S phase, a daughter centriole begins to grow near the base of each mother centriole and at a right angle to it. The G1/S-CDK that triggers cell cycle entry also initiates centrosome duplication. The elongation of the daughter centriole is usually completed by G2. The two centriole pairs remain close together in a single centrosomal complex till the late G2 phase. Finally, this complex splits into two and each centriole pair becomes part of a separate MTOC that nucleates a radial array of microtubules called an **aster**. One centrosome moves to opposite side of the nucleus to form the two poles of the mitotic spindle. As mitosis ends and the nuclear envelope re-forms around the separated chromosomes, each daughter cell receives a centrosome. There are interesting parallels between centrosome duplication and chromosome duplication. Both use a semiconservative mechanism of duplication, in which the two halves separate and serve as templates for construction of a new half. Centrosomes, like chromosomes, must replicate once and only once per cell cycle, to ensure that the cell enters mitosis with only two copies.

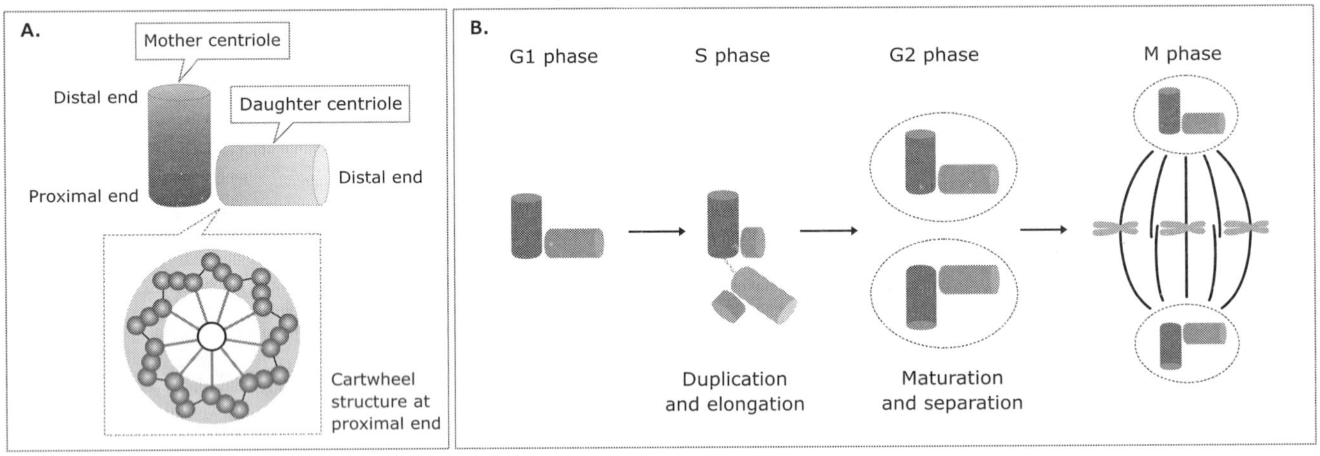

Figure 3.55 **A**. Structure and arrangement of centrioles. **B**. The centrosome duplication cycle in animal cells. At the beginning of the G1 phase of the cell cycle, cells contain a single centrosome that is composed of two centrioles -one is the mother centriole and other is the daughter centriole. The mother centriole serves as a template to assemble the daughter centriole. In late G1 phase, the tight juxtaposition of the mother and daughter centrioles is resolved but they remain connected by a fibrous structure called the tether. At the S-phase, each centriole acts as mother centriole and initiates the nucleation of new daughter centriole. The new daughter centrioles elongate fully by late G2 phase and finally the centrosome splits, and one centrosome with centriole pair migrates to opposite end of the cell.

3.14.5 Actin filament

Actin filament (also termed as *microfilament*) is made up of **G-actins** (globular actins). The G-actin is a 43 kDa ATPase and like tubulin, it has a binding site for a nucleotide, but the nucleotide is ATP (or ADP) rather than GTP (or GDP). Each G-actin contains a Mg^{2+} ion complexed with either ATP or ADP. It is a highly conserved cytoskeletal protein that is present at high concentrations in nearly all eukaryotic cells. It is the most abundant intracellular protein in most eukaryotic cells. As for tubulin, the G-actin subunits assemble head-to-tail to generate **F-actin** (filamentous actin) with a distinct structural polarity. Two parallel F-actins twist around each other in a *right-handed helix* to form an actin filament. The structural polarity of actin filament is created by the regular, parallel orientation of all of their subunits.

Actin filaments are thinner (diameter ~7 nm) and more flexible, and usually much shorter, than microtubules. Like a microtubule, an actin filament is a polar structure, with two structurally different ends – a slow-growing *minus end* and a faster-growing *plus end*. The minus end of an actin filament is also referred to as the '**pointed end**' and the plus end as the '**barbed end**.' The plus end polymerizes at up to 10 times the rate of the minus end. Since G-actin is an ATPase, it can hydrolyze the ATP to ADP. Hence, just like tubulin heterodimer, there are two forms of G-actins – one is ATP bound form and the other is the ADP-bound form. Most of the free G-actins are found in ATP-bound form. The role of ATP hydrolysis in actin polymerization is similar to the role of GTP hydrolysis in tubulin polymerization. In neither case is hydrolysis required to form the filament; instead, it serves to weaken the bonds in the polymer and thereby promotes depolymerization.

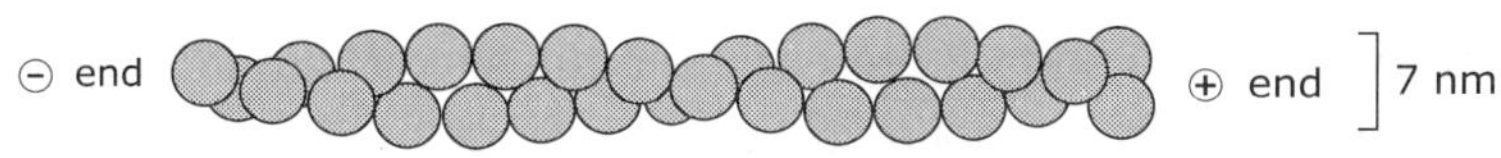

Figure 3.56 G-actins (monomers) assemble to form polarized filaments (F-actins) that have a fast-growing *plus end* and a slower-growing *minus end*. Two F-actins coiled about each other in a right-handed helix termed actin filament.

Actin polymerization and dynamics

The *in vitro* polymerization of G-actin occurs in three sequential phases. The first phase, termed **nucleation phase,** is a lag phase in which G-actin aggregates into a short actin nucleus. In the second phase, called **elongation phase,** actin filaments elongate rapidly. The fast elongation phase is marked by the addition of G-actins, causing net filament elongation. In the third phase, **steady-state phase**, equilibrium is reached between filaments and monomers. The growth of the filament due to the G-actins addition (polymerization) is exactly balanced by depolymerization from the ends.

Nucleation and nucleating proteins: The initiation of actin filament assembly requires the formation of a trimeric nucleus in a process that is called *nucleation*. Spontaneous nucleation is kinetically unfavourable. Two classes of protein have been identified that bypass the need for spontaneous nucleation and nucleate actin assembly. These proteins, commonly referred to as **actin nucleating proteins**, are the **Arp2/3** (actin-related protein-2/3) and **formins**. The Arp2 and Arp3 and five other proteins (ArpC1, ArpC2, ArpC3, ArpC4, and ArpC5) form a complex of ~220 kDa called **Arp2/3 complex**. This complex has been found in all eukaryotes and is highly conserved across species. The complex binds to the sides of existing filaments and initiates polymerization of a new filament at a distinctive 70° angle from the existing filaments. The activation of Arp2/3 complex requires nucleation promoting factors (NPFs). Mammalian cells express several NPFs, including the well-characterized **WASP** and **WAVEs**.

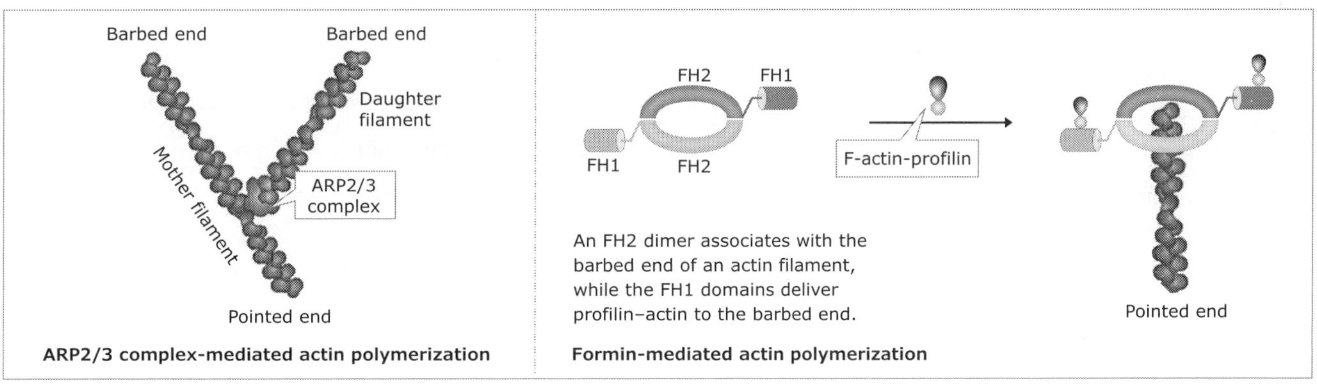

Formins are multi-domain proteins. They are characterized by the presence of **FH** (formin homology) **domains** - FH1 and FH2 domains. The FH1 domain interacts with the G-actin binding protein **profilin**, providing G-actin for filament assembly, while the adjacent FH2 domain nucleates F-actin. FH2 domain remains persistently associated with the fast growing plus end. Formin function is regulated by binding with **Rho GTP** to its Rho binding domain. In addition to nucleation, formins also accelerate elongation of the plus ends of actin filaments.

Dynamic instability and treadmilling: Just like microtubules, the actin filaments are highly dynamic structure. Actin filaments also display the properties like dynamic instability and treadmilling. However, dynamic instability is believed to predominate in microtubules, whereas treadmilling may predominate in actin filaments.

Function of actin filaments

Actin filaments perform diverse functions in eukaryotes. Actin filaments determine the shape of animal cells and support cell-surface structures such as microvilli and membrane ruffles. Besides forming stable, specialized cell-surface structures, the actin filaments are also responsible for cell-cell junctions, cytoplasmic streaming, muscle contraction and cellular endocytosis. In animal cells, organized arrays of actin filaments form *contractile ring* responsible for cytokinesis. They also form many types of dynamic structures, such as the *lamellipodia* and *filopodia* for cellular crawling movement.

The crawling movements of cells across a surface represent a basic form of cell locomotion, employed by different kinds of cells. Examples include the movements of amoebas, the migration of embryonic cells during development, the invasion of tissues by white blood cells to fight infection and the migration of cells involved in wound healing. All of these movements are based on the dynamic properties of the actin cytoskeleton. The crawling movements of cells across a surface can be viewed as three stages of coordinated movements: **extension** (or *protrusion*) of the leading edge, **attachment** of the leading edge to the substratum and **retraction** of the rear of the cell into the cell body. Extension of the leading edge involves the polymerization and cross-linking of actin filaments.

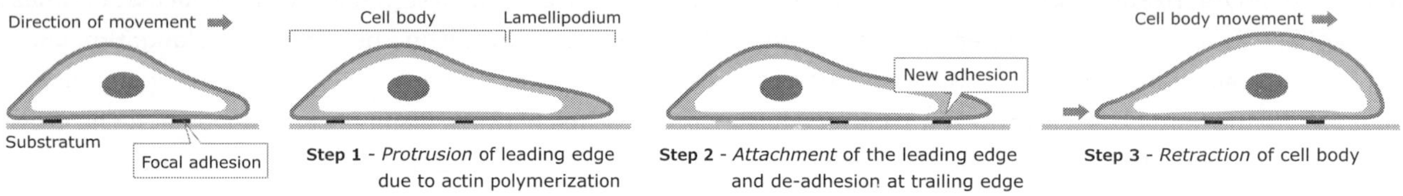

Different cell types generate different types of protrusive structures, including **filopodia**, **lamellipodia** and **pseudopodia**. The three structures differ primarily in the way in which the actin is organized—in one, two, or three dimensions, respectively. *Pseudopodia*, formed by amoebae and neutrophils, are three-dimensional projections. Following their extension, protrusive structures must attach to the substratum in order to function in cell locomotion. For slow-moving cells, such as fibroblasts, attachment involves the formation of *focal adhesions*. Cells moving more rapidly, such as amoebas or white blood cells, form more diffuse contacts with the substratum. In the third *retraction stage* of cell crawling, the attachments of the trailing edge to the substratum are broken, and the rear of the cell recoils into the cell body.

Table 3.10 Properties of microtubules and actin filaments

	Actin filaments	Microtubules
Structure	Two intertwined chains of F-actin	Hollow, cylindrical, consists of 13 protofilaments
Diameter	~7 nm	Outer : ~25 nm, Inner : ~15 nm
Monomeric unit	G-actin	α-tubulin, β-tubulin
Polarity	*Plus* and *minus* ends	*Plus* and *minus* ends
Nucleotide bound	ATP	GTP

Drugs that affect microtubules and actin filaments

Microtubule and actin filaments are the targets of a variety of *drugs* that act by interfering with the polymerization and depolymerization of subunits. Example of some common drugs that affect microtubules and actin filaments:

Actin filament

Cytochalasin D : Binds plus ends of actin filaments and prevents elongation.

Latrunculin : Binds G-actin monomers and prevents them from polymerizing into filaments.

Phalloidin : Binds tightly all along the sides of actin filaments and stabilize them against depolymerization.

Jasplakinolide : Induces actin polymerization by stimulating actin filament nucleation; stabilizes F-actin.

Swinholide : Severs filaments.

Microtubule

Nocodazole	:	Causes microtubules to depolymerize to tubulin subunits.
Colchicine	:	Binds tubulin subunits and prevents their polymerization.
Colcemid	:	Binds tubulin subunits and prevents their polymerization.
Taxol	:	Binds to and stabilizes microtubules, preventing their depolymerization.
Vinblastine	:	Binds β-tubulin to prevent polymerization.
Vincristine	:	Binds free tubulin to prevent polymerization.

3.14.6 Myosin

Myosin is an actin filament-based motor protein. The form of myosin found in muscle and first identified was myosin-II. Each myosin-II molecule is an oligomer composed of one pair of identical heavy chains and two pairs of non-identical light chains. Each of the heavy chains has a globular head domain at its N-terminus that contains an actin-binding site and a catalytic site that hydrolyzes ATP. Each myosin head binds and hydrolyses ATP, using the energy of ATP hydrolysis to walk towards the *plus end* of an actin filament. Globular head domain is followed by a very long amino acid sequence that forms an extended left-handed coiled-coil tail that mediates heavy chain dimerization. The two light chains bind close to the N-terminal head domain. A major role of the rodlike tail of myosin-II is to allow the molecules to polymerize into **bipolar filaments**. The long coiled-coil tail bundles itself with the tails of other myosin molecules. These tail-tail interactions result in the formation of large bipolar **thick filaments** that have several hundred myosin heads, oriented in opposite directions at the two ends of the thick filament.

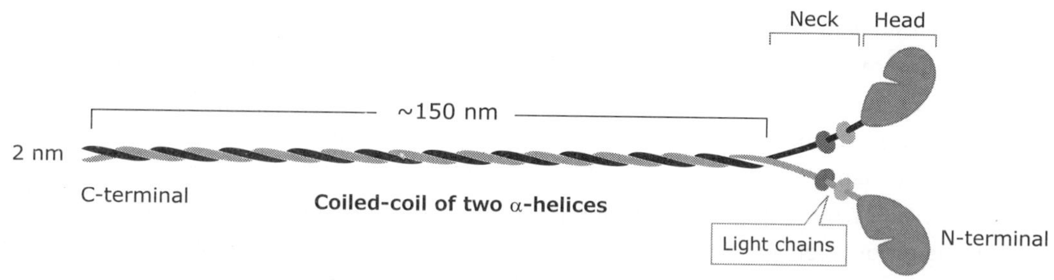

Figure 3.57 A myosin-II molecule is composed of six subunits– two heavy chains (each about 2000 amino acids long and four light chains. The light chains are of two distinct types, and one copy of each type is present on each myosin head. Dimerization occurs when the two α-helices of the heavy chains wrap around each other to form a coiled-coil structure. This part of the molecule is called the tail. At its N terminus, each heavy chain has a large globular domain containing an actin-binding site and a catalytic site that hydrolyzes ATP.

When myosin-II is treated with the proteases trypsin, it is cleaved into two fragments called **light meromyosin** and **heavy meromyosin**. Light meromyosin consists of most of the α-helical rod of the myosin molecule. Heavy meromyosin consists of the globular heads with the light chains and the remaining rod section. Subsequent treatment of heavy meromyosin with papain releases two globular protein heads called **subfragment 1** (S_1) and a rod-like section called an **subfragment 2** (S_2).

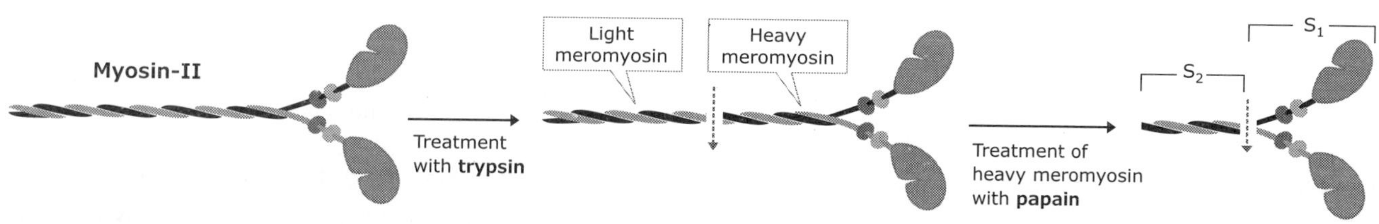

Figure 3.58 Cleavage of myosin by the proteases trypsin and papain. The globular domain–called myosin subfragment 1 or S_1 is liberated from heavy meromyosin by cleavage with papain, leaving myosin subfragment 2 or S_2.

In addition to myosin-II (conventional two-headed myosin), several other types of myosin (I, III, IV.... XIV) are found in eukaryotic cells. Most of myosins are two-headed like myosin-II (with two motor domains per molecule), whereas others are one-headed (with just one motor domain). In contrast to myosin-II, these unconventional myosins do not form bipolar thick filaments and therefore are not involved in muscle contraction. They may, however, be involved in a variety of other kinds of cell movements, such as the transport of membrane vesicles and organelles along actin filaments, phagocytosis and extension of pseudopods in amoebae. The functions of most of the myosins remain to be determined. The common feature of all myosins is a conserved motor domain (motor head); the other domains vary from myosin to myosin and determine the specific role of the molecule in the cell. All myosins move towards the *plus end* of an actin filament – with one exception, **myosin VI**.

3.14.7 Muscle contraction

Molecular structure of skeletal muscle and sarcomere

Skeletal muscles are usually attached to bone by tendons composed of connective tissue. This connective tissue also ensheaths the entire muscle and is called **epimysium**. Skeletal muscles consist of numerous bundles called *fascicles*. Each fasciculus is surrounded by a layer of connective tissue called the **perimysium**. Each fasciculus is composed of numerous **muscle fibers** (or muscle cells) and each individual muscle cell is surrounded by connective tissue called the **endomysium**. Muscle fibers are long, cylindrical and striated fibers with many peripherally located nuclei. The cell membrane of a muscle fiber is called the **sarcolemma**. The sarcoplasm is the specialized cytoplasm of a muscle fiber that contains a modified ER known as the sarcoplasmic reticulum. Transverse (T)-tubules invaginate the sarcolemma, allowing impulses to penetrate the cell and activate the sarcoplasmic reticulum. Sarcoplasm contains fine thread like contractile structure called *myofibrils*.

In each myofibril, actin thin filaments and myosin thick filaments are organized into a linear chain of highly ordered structures, called **sarcomeres**, the basic functional units of a myofibril. One end of the thin filaments is attached at their plus ends to the Z-disc, the demarcation between adjacent sarcomeres. α-actinin anchors the actin to Z-disc and stabilizes actin filaments. The capped minus ends of the actin filaments extend towards the middle of the sarcomere, where they overlap with thick filaments. Thin filaments contain the proteins *actin*, *nebulin*, *tropomodulin*, *tropomyosin* and *troponin*. **Tropomyosin** is a fibrous molecule that consists of two chains, alpha and beta, that attach to F-actin in the groove between its filaments. **Troponin**, a complex of three polypeptides, troponins T, I and C (named for their tropomyosin-binding, inhibitory, and calcium-binding activities, respectively). **Troponins T** binds to tropomyosin as well as to the other two troponin components. **Troponin I** binds to actin as well as to troponin T and inhibits the F-actin-myosin interaction. **Troponin C** is a calcium-binding polypeptide that is structurally and functionally analogous to *calmodulin*. Four molecules of calcium ion bind per molecule of troponin C. **Nebulin**, a repeating 35-amino-acid actin-binding motif stretches from the Z-disc to the minus end of each thin filament and acts as a *molecular ruler* to dictate the length of the filament. The minus ends of the thin filaments are capped and stabilized by **tropomodulin**. Thus, the actin filaments in sarcomeres are remarkably stable.

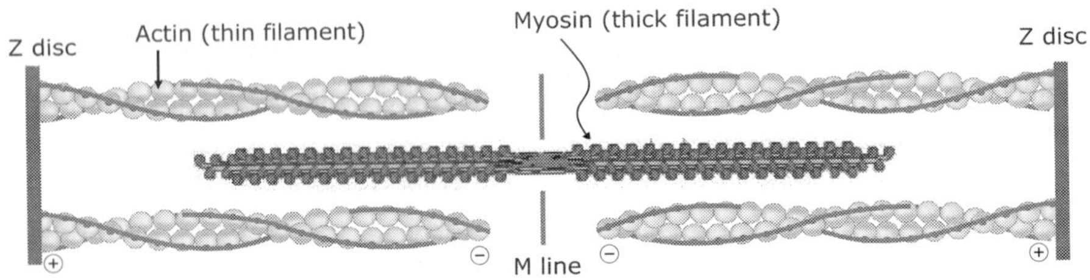

Figure 3.59 The arrangement of thick myosin and thin actin filaments in the relaxed state.

Thick filaments are composed of several hundred myosin molecules which associate by ordered tail-to-tail interactions to form thick filaments up to 1.5 μm long. The thick filaments positioned midway between the Z-discs by opposing pairs of an even longer template protein, called **titin**, act as a molecular spring. Titin, the largest protein in the body, may have a role in the relaxation of the muscle.

Table 3.11 Major proteins associated with sarcomere

Protein	Function
Actin	Component of thin filaments.
Myosin	Component of thick filaments.
Tropomyosin	Binds along the length of thin filaments.
Troponin	Binds along the thin filaments.
Titin	Acts as molecular spring.
Nebulin	A structural protein that wraps around the entire length of each thin filament; it helps anchor the thin filaments to the Z-discs and regulates the length of the thin filaments during development.
Myomesin	Myosin-binding protein present at the M-line.
α-actinin	A structural protein of the Z-discs that attaches to actin molecules of thin filaments and to titin molecules.
CapZ	Attaches actin filaments to Z-disc.
Tropomodulin	Maintains thin filament length and stability.
Dystrophin	A structural protein that links the thin filaments of the sarcomere to integral membrane proteins in the sarcolemma, which are attached in turn to proteins in the connective tissue matrix that surrounds muscle fibers.

Bipolar thick filaments walk toward the plus ends of two sets of thin filaments of opposite orientations, driven by dozens of independent myosin heads that are positioned to interact with each thin filament. Sarcomere shortening is caused by the myosin filaments sliding past the actin thin filaments, with no change in the length of either type of filament. The thick and thin filaments of sarcomeres form a pattern of alternating light and dark bands. The light bands, called **I bands** (*isotropic*) contain only thin filaments. The dark bands of sarcomeres are called **A-bands** (*anisotropic*). A-band contains both thin and thick filaments. A narrow **H-zone** in the center of each A-band contains thick but not thin filaments. Supporting proteins that hold the thick filaments together at the center of the H-zone form the **M-line**, so named because it is at the middle of the sarcomere.

When muscle contracts, the I-band shortens. The length of each sarcomere of a myofibril decreases when the muscle contracts. However, thick and thin filaments do not shorten during muscle contraction. On the basis of this observation, two different groups, Andrew Huxley and Ralph Niedergerke, and Hugh Huxley and Jean Hanson, concluded that thick filaments slide along the thin filaments during muscle contraction, which is described as a **sliding filament model**.

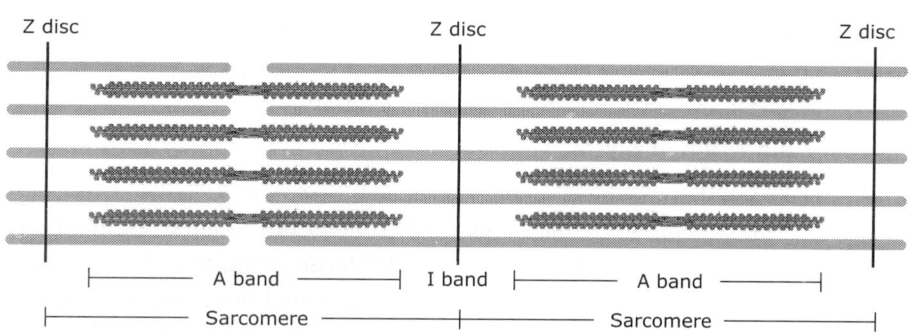

Figure 3.60 Diagram of a sarcomere. The (+) ends of actin filaments are attached to the Z discs.

Table 3.12 Components of the sarcomere

Component	Description
Z-discs	Narrow, plate-shaped regions that separate one sarcomere from the next.
A-band	The dark, middle part of the sarcomere that extends the entire length of the thick filaments and also includes those parts of the thin filaments that overlap with the thick filaments.
I-band	The lighter region of the sarcomere that contains the thin filaments but no thick filaments. A Z-disc passes through the center of each I-band.
H-zone	A narrow region in the center of the sarcomere that contains thick filaments but no thin filaments.
M-line	A region in the center of the H-zone that contains protein, *myomesin*, that holds the thick filaments together at the center of the sarcomere.

Biochemical events occurring during one cycle of muscle contraction

The signal from the nerve triggers an action potential in the sarcolemma. The action potential propagates through the **T-tubules** (transverse tubules). T-tubules extend inward from the sarcolemma around each myofibril. T-tubule membrane contains voltage-sensitive proteins, which are activated by the incoming action potential. Activated voltage-sensitive proteins trigger the opening of calcium release channels in the sarcoplasmic reticulum. Increase in cytosolic calcium initiates the contraction of each myofibril. Because the signal from the sarcolemma is passed within millisecond to every sarcomere in the cell, all of the myofibrils in the cell contract at the same time. The increase in calcium concentration is transient because calcium is rapidly pumped back into the sarcoplasmic reticulum by an abundant, calcium ATPase, in its membrane. Typically, the cytoplasmic calcium concentration is restored to resting levels within 30 milliseconds, allowing the myofibrils to relax. The calcium dependence of skeletal muscle contraction is due to the presence of tropomyosin and troponin. Each tropomyosin presents along the groove of thin filaments. In resting muscle, troponin I and troponin T interact with tropomyosin to keep tropomyosin away from the groove of thin filament. This prevents the binding of myosin heads with thin actin filaments, thereby preventing any force generating interaction. When the level of calcium is raised, troponin C which binds up to four molecules of calcium causes troponin I to release its hold on the actin. This allows the tropomyosin molecules to slip back into their normal position so that the myosin heads can walk along the actin filaments.

Steps in contraction

1. Release of neurotransmitter at motor end-plate.
2. Generation of action potential in muscle fibers.
3. Inward propagation of depolarization along T-tubules.
4. Release of calcium from sarcoplasmic reticulum.
5. Binding of calcium to troponin C, uncovering myosin binding sites on actin.
6. Formation of linkages between actin and myosin and sliding of thin on thick filaments.

Coupling of actin-myosin and ATP hydrolysis

Myosin head without ATP locks tightly on to an actin filament. Binding of ATP to myosin head causes a slight change in the conformation of the actin binding site. This reduces the affinity of the head for actin and allows it to move along the filament. Hydrolysis of ATP causes the head to be displaced along the filament by a distance of about 5 nm. However, product of ATP hydrolysis, ADP and P_i remain tightly bound to the myosin head. Release of P_i causes binding of the myosin head to a new site on the actin filament. This release triggers the *power stroke* (the force generating change in shape during which the head regains its original conformation). In the course of the power stroke, the head loses its bound ADP and returns to the start of a new cycle.

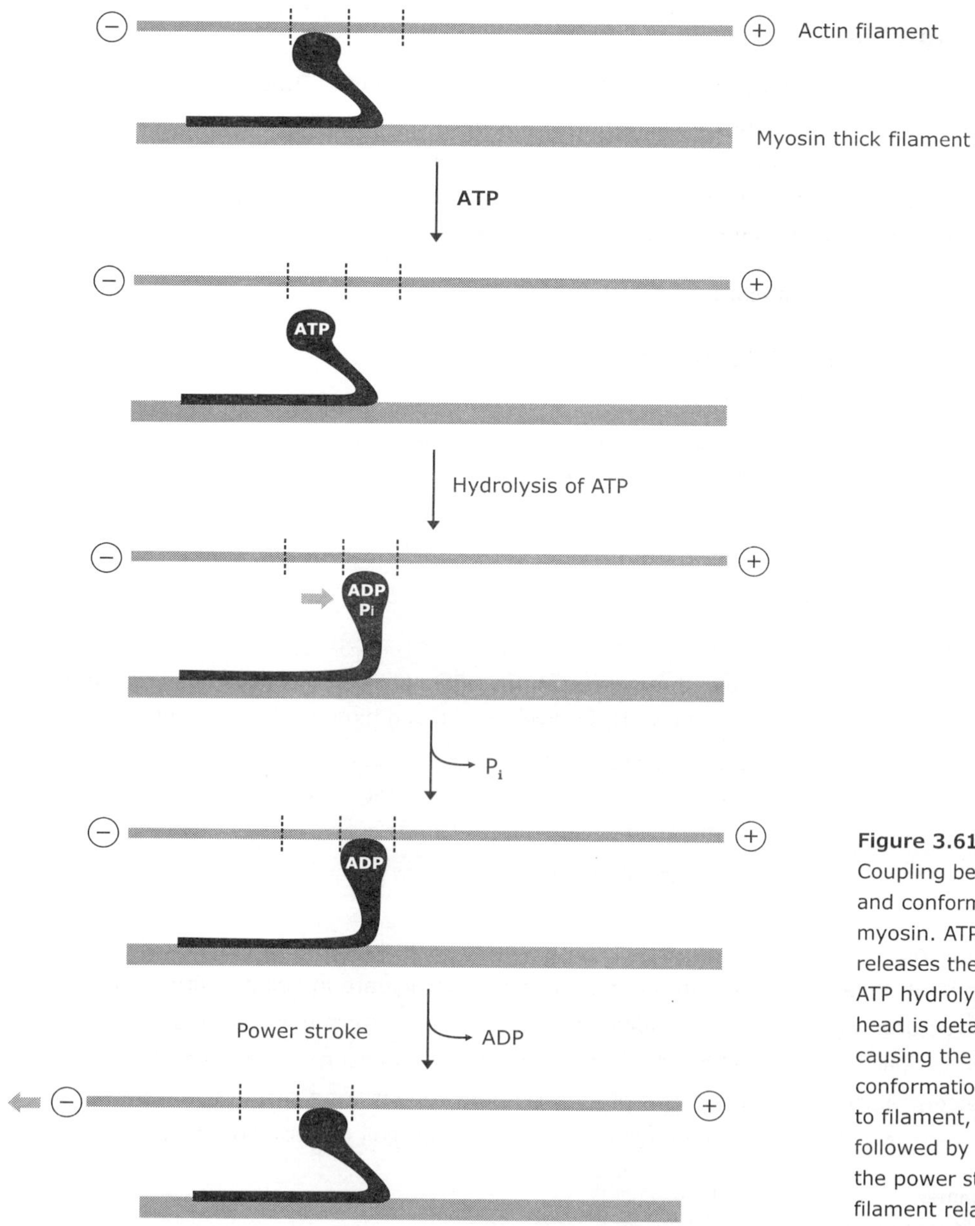

Figure 3.61
Coupling between ATP hydrolysis and conformational changes for myosin. ATP binding with myosin releases the head from the filament. ATP hydrolysis occurs while the myosin head is detached from the filament, causing the head to assume different conformation. When the head rebinds to filament, the release of phosphate, followed by the release of ADP, triggers the power stroke that moves the filament relative to the motor protein.

Smooth muscle contraction

The skeletal muscle contraction is regulated by the tropomyosin-troponin complex bound to the thin actin filament switching between the contraction-inducing state in the presence of calcium and the relaxed state in its absence.

In contrast, contraction of vertebrate smooth muscle is regulated primarily by a pathway in which the *myosin regulatory light chain* associated with the myosin II undergoes phosphorylation and dephosphorylation. The smooth muscle contracts when the regulatory light chain is phosphorylated by the enzyme **myosin light chain kinase**. Because this enzyme is activated by calcium, the cytosolic calcium level indirectly regulates the extent of light chain phosphorylation and hence contraction. The calcium-dependent regulation of myosin light chain kinase activity is mediated through the calcium-binding protein calmodulin. Calcium first binds to calmodulin, and the calcium calmodulin complex then binds to myosin light chain kinase and activates it. Because this regulation involves myosin, it is known as *thick filament regulation*. Smooth muscle contraction also occurs in a calcium-independent manner. In this situation, **Rho kinase** activates the regulatory light chain by phosphorylation.

3.14.8 Intermediate filaments

Intermediate filaments are ropelike cytoplasmic filaments of about 10 nm diameter. These filaments are found in many metazoans, including vertebrates, nematodes and molluscs but not in plants and fungi. Unlike the actin and tubulin proteins, the intermediate filament proteins are chemically heterogenous and show tissue as well as species-specific variations in molecular weight. More than 50 different intermediate filament proteins have been identified and classified into six groups based on their sequences and tissue distribution:

Type	Protein	Site of expression
I	*Acidic keratins*	*Epithelial cells*
II	*Neutral or basic keratins*	*Epithelial cells*
III	*Vimentin*	Most widely distributed of all intermediate filament proteins is vimentin, which is typically expressed in leukocytes, blood vessel endothelial cells, some epithelial cells, and mesenchymal cells such as fibroblasts.
	Desmin	*Muscle cells*
	Glial fibrillary acidic protein	*Glial cells*
IV	*Neurofilament proteins*	*Neurons* In mammals, three different neurofilament proteins have been recognized: NF-L, NF-M and NF-H, for low, middle and high molecular weight, respectively.
V	*Nuclear lamins*	Most ubiquitous group of intermediate filaments are found exclusively in the nucleus. Lamins form a network structure that lines the inside surface of the inner nuclear membrane termed *nuclear lamina*.
VI	*Nestin*	Stem cells of central nervous system.

The principal functions of intermediate filaments are structural to reinforce cells and to organize cells into tissues. Unlike microfilaments and microtubules, intermediate filaments do not participate in cell motility. All intermediate filaments share a common structural organization. The individual polypeptide of intermediate filament is an elongated molecule consisting of a non-α-helical N-terminal head domain, a central α-helical *rod domain* and a non-α-helical C-terminal tail domain. The central rod domain consists of long tandem repeats of a distinctive seven amino acid sequence called the *heptad repeat*. Polypeptide chain forms a parallel coiled coil dimeric structure with another.

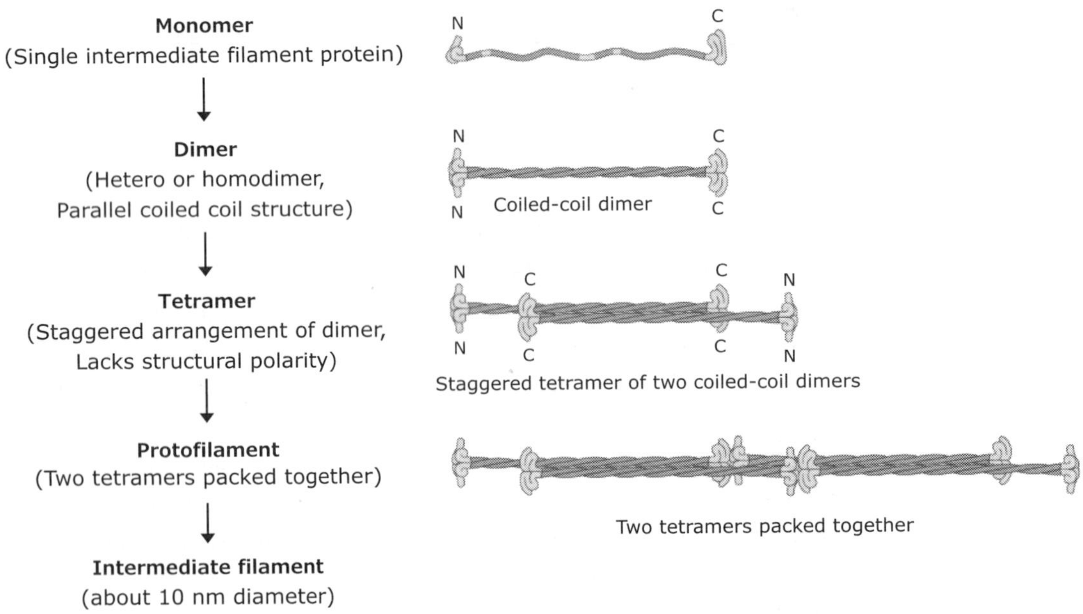

Figure 3.62 A model of intermediate filament construction.

Two dimers then line up side by side to form an *antiparallel* tetramer of four polypeptide chains. Tetramer, the soluble subunit of intermediate filament, further organizes to form higher level organization. Tetramer is analogous to the $\alpha\beta$-tubulin heterodimer or G-actin. Unlike the actin or tubulin subunits, the intermediate filament subunits do not contain a binding site for a nucleoside triphosphate. The antiparallel arrangement of dimers implies that the tetramer, and hence the intermediate filament that it forms, is a non-polarized structure.

3.15 Protein targeting and sorting

Protein targeting is the process by which a protein is transported from its site of synthesis, typically on 80S ribosomes in the cytosol, to its final destination within or outside the cell. This ensures that proteins reach the correct organelles where they can perform their specific functions. Although the terms 'protein targeting' and 'protein sorting' are often used interchangeably, they refer to distinct processes. **Protein sorting** is a process that ensures resident proteins remain within their specific organelles, while non-resident proteins are directed to their appropriate destinations. For example, when proteins are imported into the ER from the cytosol, the ER sorts these proteins by retaining those that are intended to stay within the ER and directing non-resident proteins to the Golgi complex for further processing and transport.

In a eukaryotic cell, the synthesis of most proteins occurs on 80S ribosomes in the cytosol, except for a few that are synthesized by 70S ribosomes in semi-autonomous organelles such as mitochondria and plastids. The fate of proteins synthesized by cytosolic ribosomes depends on the presence or absence of specific **targeting** or **sorting signals** that direct their transport from the cytosol to specific organelles such as the nucleus, ER, mitochondria, plastids, or peroxisomes. Proteins without targeting signals remain in the cytosol as permanent residents. For example, proteins destined for the ER contain a specific signal at their N-terminus. If this signal is removed, these proteins remain in the cytosol. Therefore, targeting signals are essential for proper protein targeting.

Protein targeting can occur either **co-translationally** or **post-translationally**. Proteins synthesized by membrane-bound ribosomes are typically targeted co-translationally, while proteins synthesized by membrane-free ribosomes are targeted post-translationally.

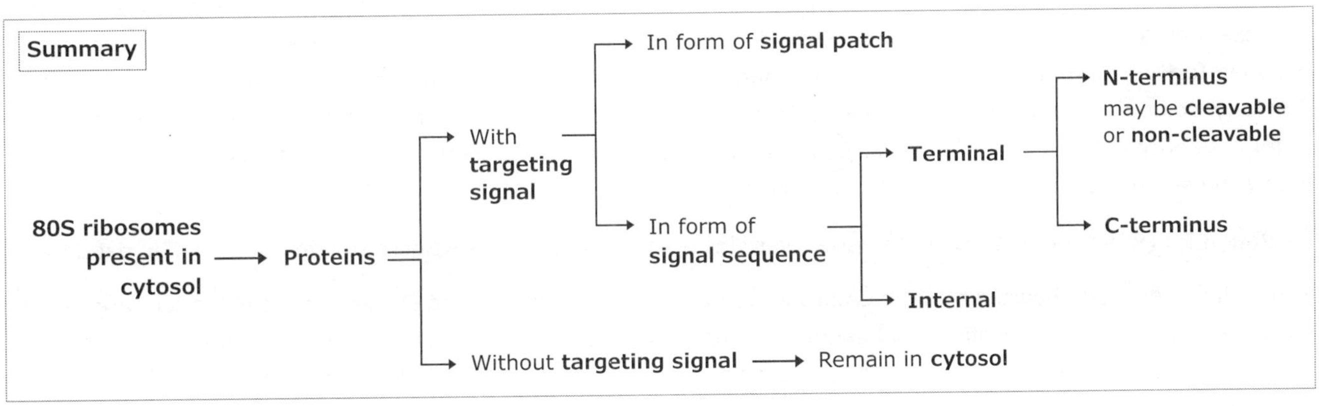

Targeting or sorting signals in proteins can be either a *signal sequence* or a *signal patch*. A **signal sequence** refers to a specific, continuous stretch of amino acids, typically 15 to 60 residues long, that directs the protein to its destination. Signal sequences often occur at the end of the polypeptide chain (as *terminal signal sequences*), but they can also be located internally (as *internal signal sequences*). Most terminal signal sequences are present at the N-terminus. The signal sequence is often (but not always) removed from the protein once the sorting or targeting process has been completed. A **signal patch** can be formed by the juxtaposition of amino acids from regions that are physically separated before the protein folds. It represents a specific three-dimensional arrangement of atoms on the protein's surface that forms when the protein folds up.

Each newly synthesized organelle protein must find its way from a ribosome in the cytosol, where the protein is made, to the organelle where it functions. It does so by following a specific pathway, guided by targeting or sorting signals.

The movement of a protein within the cell is described as **protein transport**. Transport of proteins from the cytosol to a specific organelle, from an organelle to the cytosol, or from one organelle to another occurs in three different ways:

Gated transport: Protein transport between the cytosol and the nucleus occurs through nuclear pore complexes. This process is called gated transport because the nuclear pore complexes function as selective gates that actively transport specific proteins.

Transmembrane transport: In transmembrane transport, membrane-bound transport proteins directly transport specific proteins across a membrane from the cytosol into an organelle or organelle into the cytosol. Examples of transmembrane transport include the movement of selected proteins:

- From the cytosol to the ER or from the ER to the cytosol.
- From the cytosol to mitochondria and plastids.
- From the cytosol to peroxisomes.

Vesicular transport: In vesicular transport, proteins move from one organelle to another via transport vesicles. For example, the transfer of proteins from the ER to the Golgi complex, or from the Golgi complex to the ER, occurs in this way. Transport vesicles continually bud off from one membrane and fuse with another, transporting both membrane components and the soluble contents inside, collectively referred to as **cargo**. Examples of vesicular transport include the movement of selected proteins:

- From the ER to the Golgi complex or from the Golgi complex back to the ER.
- From one cisterna to another within the Golgi complex.
- From the Golgi complex to the lysosomes or from lysosomes back to the Golgi complex.
- From the Golgi complex to the plasma membrane or the cell exterior.

3.15.1 Targeting of proteins from cytosol to ER

Proteins synthesized by the membrane-bound ribosomes of the ER include both soluble and membrane-bound proteins. Soluble proteins are fully translocated across the ER membrane and released into the ER lumen, while membrane-bound integral proteins are only partially translocated and remain embedded in the ER membrane. Some of these membrane-bound proteins are ER-resident proteins and are retained in the ER membrane, but many are destined for the plasma membrane or the membranes of other organelles such as Golgi complex and lysosomes. Similarly, soluble proteins that are not ER-resident proteins are destined either for secretion (released outside cell) or for residence in the lumen of other organelles. Proteins destined for secretion (referred to as **secretory proteins**) follow the **secretory pathway** in the following order:

Rough ER (RER) ⟶ ER-to-Golgi transport vesicles ⟶ Golgi complex ⟶ Secretory vesicles ⟶ Cell exterior

Thus, all proteins synthesized by ER membrane-bound ribosomes, regardless of their final destination, are initially directed to the ER by a specific signal sequence that initiates their translocation through a common mechanism. This concept of signal sequence-mediated protein transport was proposed by Blobel and Sabatini in 1971. According to this **signal hypothesis**, secretory proteins are synthesized with an N-terminal signal sequence that is recognized by a cytosolic factor. This signal sequence is crucial for directing the proteins to the endoplasmic reticulum, where their further processing and transport can occur.

Targeting of *soluble proteins* to ER lumen

Proteins synthesized by membrane-bound ribosomes translocate the ER membrane *co-translationally*. Some proteins, however, are translocated into the ER after their synthesis has been completed (*post-translational translocation*). Synthesis of these proteins begins on an unattached ribosome in the cytosol. Ribosomes engaged in the synthesis of proteins are then targeted to the ER by a **signal sequence** (a short sequence of 15 to 35 amino acid residues that contain a sequence of at least six non-polar amino acid residues) at the *N*-terminus of the growing polypeptide chain. *N*-terminal signal sequences are cleaved from the polypeptide chain during its transfer into the ER lumen. A **signal-recognition particle** (SRP), a cytosolic particle binds to the signal sequence of a nascent polypeptide chain.

ER signal sequences vary greatly in amino acid sequence, but each has six or more nonpolar amino acids at its center. How can the SRP bind specifically to so many different sequences? It occurs because the signal-sequence-binding site is a large hydrophobic pocket lined by amino acid methionines. The complex of SRP, nascent polypeptide, and ribosome then binds to the α-subunit of the **SRP receptor** in the ER membrane. SRP receptor contains two polypeptide subunits: a transmembrane β-subunit and a peripheral α-subunit.

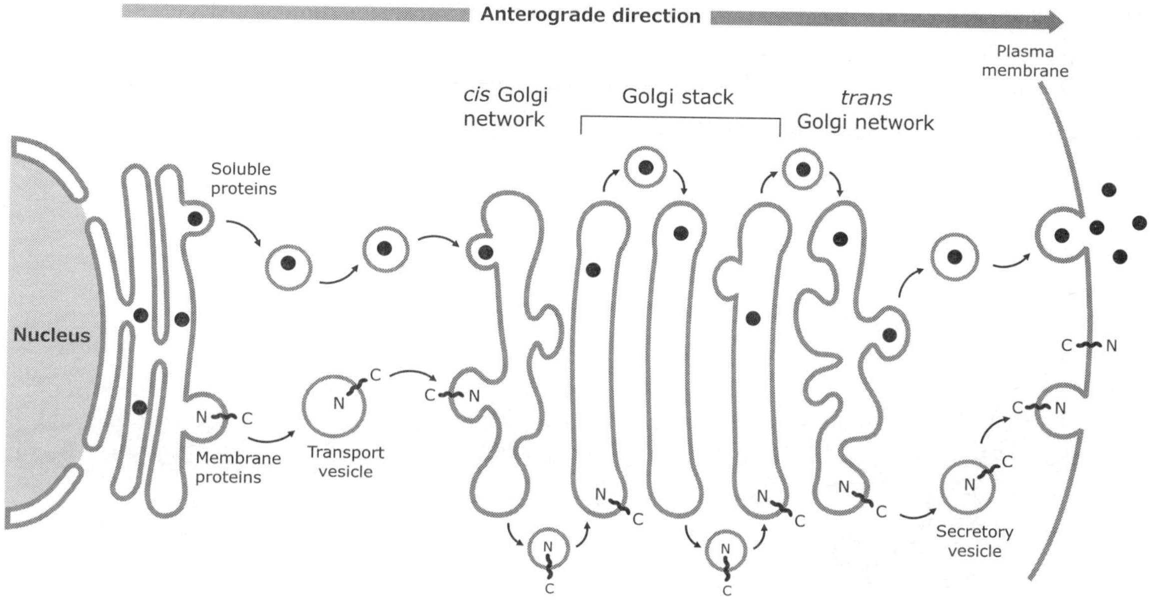

Figure 3.63 Diagrammatic representation of secretory pathway. Newly synthesized proteins are inserted into the lumen and membrane of the ER. Those proteins that are transported out of the ER may then pass through various sub-compartments of the Golgi until they reach the *trans*-Golgi network. In the *trans*-Golgi network, proteins are segregated and sorted. Proteins destined for the plasma membrane or those that are secreted are carried out to the cell surface in secretory vesicles.

Mammalian SRPs are composed of **7SL scRNA** of ~300 nucleotides in length, which is complexed with six different polypeptides having molecular masses of 9, 14, 19, 54, 68 and 72 kDa, to form an 11S RNP particle. The 7SL scRNA is a transcript of RNA polymerase III and has a remarkable sequence homology with the *Alu element* (SINE) in primates and rodents. SRP has two binding sites - one end of the SRP binds to a signal sequence on a growing polypeptide chain, while the other end binds to the ribosome itself. The 7SL scRNA in the particle may mediate an interaction with ribosomal RNA. The SRP directs both the binding of the ribosome to the ER membrane and the insertion of the nascent polypeptide into the transmembrane channel. Both the SRP and the SRP receptor have a GTP binding domain and GTPase activity. The P54 subunit of the SRP proteins and both subunits of the SRP receptor contain GTP-binding domains. The interaction of the SRP with the SRP receptor is promoted when GTP is bound to both the P54 subunit of SRP and the α-subunit of the SRP receptor. SRP and SRP receptor dissociate after the hydrolysis of bound GTP.

SRP binding to the signal sequence slows translation, a phenomenon termed **elongation arrest**. This ensures that the protein will not release into the cytosol and it also ensures that large portions of a protein could not fold before reaching the translocon. The interaction of SRP and the SRP receptor directs the SRP-ribosome complex to the **translocon**. The translocon is a multiprotein complex contains a gated translocation channel. In mammals, translocation channel is made up of three polypeptides called the **Sec61 complex** (Sec61α, Sec61β, Sec61γ). The binding with the Sec61 complex is facilitated by the additional factor called **TRAM** (translocating chain-associating membrane protein). *N*-terminal of polypeptide chain enters into the ER lumen through the translocon. Hydrolysis of GTP of SRP and the SRP receptor is essential to drive the insertion of the nascent polypeptide into the translocon. The polypeptide chain elongates; then the signal sequence is cleaved by a **signal peptidase** (transmembrane ER protein associated with the translocon is a protease, recognizes a sequence on the C-terminal side of the hydrophobic core of the signal sequence and cleaves the chain) and is rapidly degraded. The driving force for unidirectional translocation across the ER membrane is provided by a protein called **Sec63** and a member of the Hsp70 family of molecular chaperones known as **BiP** (BiP for *bi*nding *p*rotein). The Sec63 protein is a polytopic ER membrane protein. BiP, like other Hsp70s, is a soluble ATPase that binds hydrophobic patches in unfolded proteins in an ATP-dependent manner. It binds and stabilizes unfolded proteins. The ATP driven cycle of BiP binding and release pulls the protein into the lumen. Transport from the ER back into the cytosol occurs by a reversal of the usual process of import. This is called **reverse translocation** (also sometimes called **retrotranslocation** or **dislocation**). By this process, misfolded soluble proteins in the ER lumen are translocated back into the cytosol. Once the misfolded protein has reached the cytosol, its oligosaccharides are removed. Deglycosylation is catalyzed by an enzyme ***N*-glycanase**. The deglycosylated polypeptide is rapidly ubiquitylated and then fed into proteasome, where it is degraded.

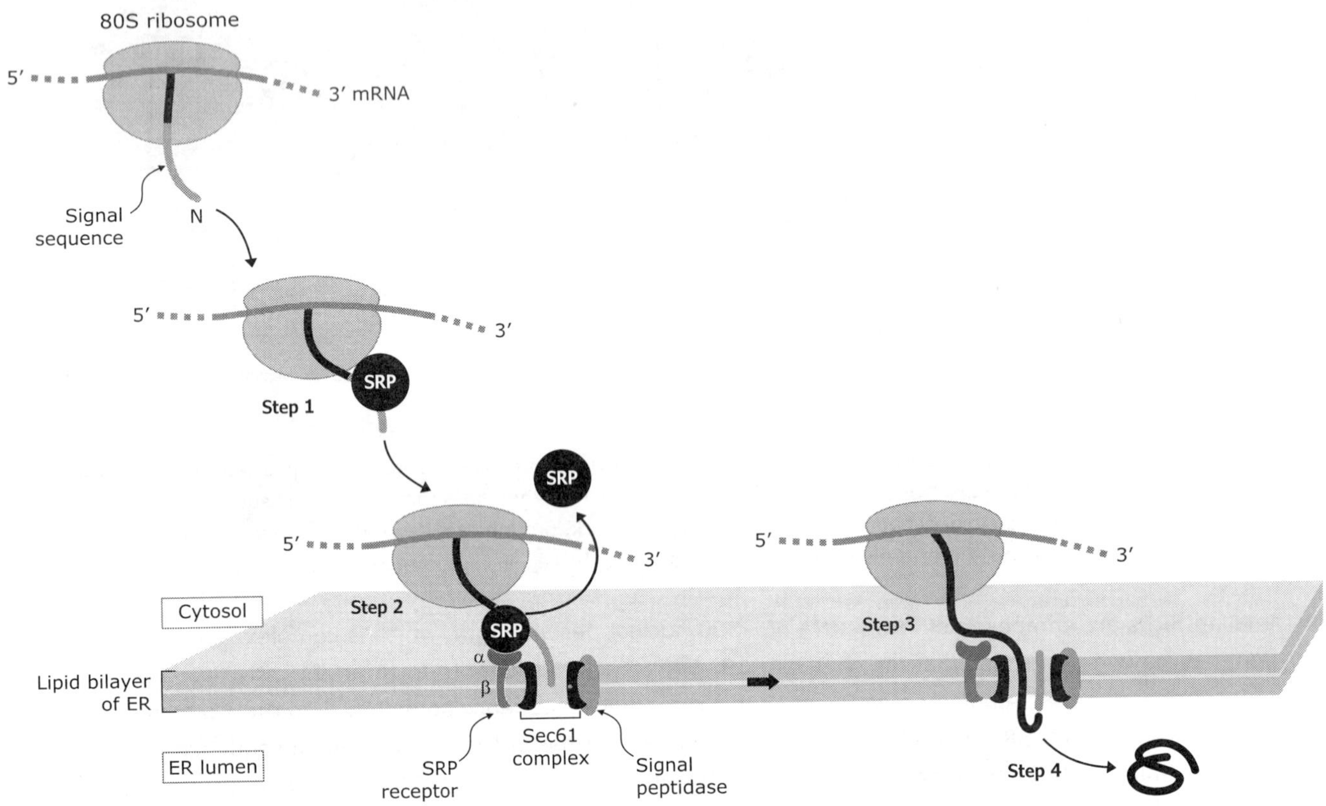

Figure 3.64 Synthesis of secretory proteins and their co-translational translocation across the ER membrane.

Sequence of events during co-translational targeting of secretory proteins to the ER:

Step 1: Signal sequence emerges from the ribosome, it is recognized and bound by the SRP.

Step 2: The SRP directs both the binding of the ribosome to the SRP receptor and the insertion of the nascent polypeptide into the transmembrane channel.

Step 3: Translation resumes, and the growing polypeptide chain is translocated across the membrane.

Step 4: Cleavage of the signal sequence by signal peptidase releases the polypeptide into the ER lumen.

Targeting of *membrane proteins* into the ER membrane

Integral membrane proteins located in the ER, Golgi, lysosomal membranes and in the plasma membrane are synthesized on the RER. These proteins remain as integral proteins of the ER membrane rather than being released into the ER lumen. From the ER membrane, they proceed to their final destination along the same pathway as that of secretory proteins: ER → Golgi → lysosome or plasma membrane. During this transport, the orientation of a membrane protein also remains unchanged.

Transmembrane *integral* membrane proteins

Transmembrane integral membrane proteins are embedded in the membrane by hydrophobic region that spans the lipid bilayer. These membrane proteins have four topological classes: Type I, Type II, Type III and Type IV.

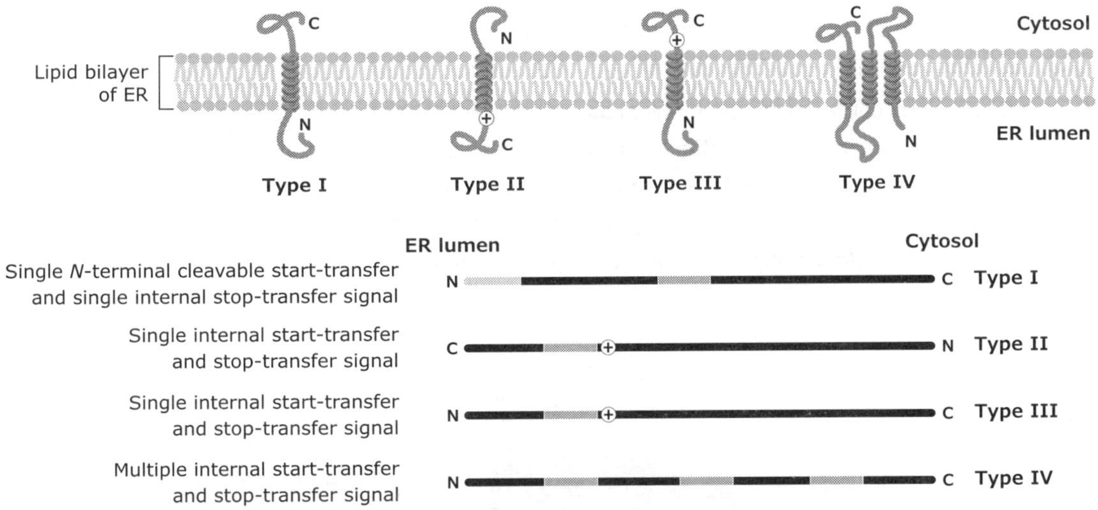

Figure 3.65 Major topological classes of transmembrane proteins synthesized on the RER. These proteins contain internal stop-transfer signal sequence (one or many) and terminal or internal start-transfer signal sequence.

Type I protein: Single-pass transmembrane proteins have their hydrophilic *N*-terminal segment in the ER lumen (non-cytosolic) and hydrophilic *C*-terminal segment in the cytosol. It contains internal **stop-transfer signal sequence** (also acts as **membrane-anchor sequence**) and cleavable *N-terminal signal sequence* (functions as **start-transfer signal sequence**). The *N*-terminal signal sequence on a nascent type I protein initiates cotranslational translocation of the protein. Once the *N*-terminus of the growing polypeptide enters the lumen of the ER, the signal sequence is cleaved. A sequence of nonpolar amino acids (termed *stop-transfer signal sequence*) in these proteins stops transfer of the growing polypeptide.

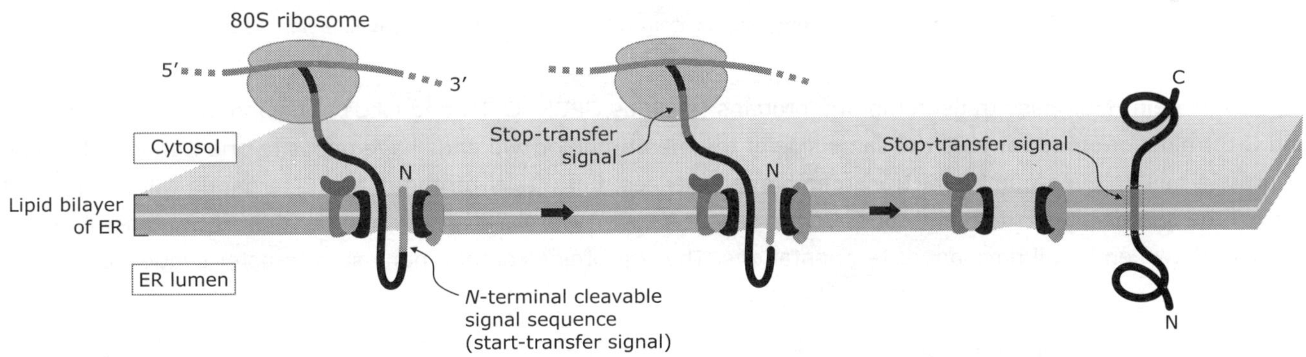

Figure 3.66 Insertion of a type I transmembrane protein with a cleavable *N*-terminal signal sequence (acts as start-transfer signal sequence) and a single internal stop-transfer signal sequence.

This internal sequence moves laterally and becomes anchored in the lipid bilayer of the membrane. Although translocation is stopped, translation continues at the ribosome. As the C-terminus of the protein chain is synthesized, it loops out on the cytosolic side of the membrane. Common examples of the type I proteins are LDL receptor, insulin receptor and growth hormone receptor.

Type II protein: Single-pass transmembrane proteins have their N-terminus on the cytosolic face and the C-terminus on the non-cytosolic (*luminal* in case of ER) side. Proteins with this orientation have a single *noncleavable* internal signal sequence, which acts as both *start-transfer signal sequence* and *stop-transfer signal sequence*. Examples of type II proteins are transferrin receptor and Golgi galactosyl transferase.

Type III protein: Single-pass transmembrane proteins similar to type I, but do not contain a *N*-terminal cleavable signal sequence. These proteins (such as Cyt P450) have *N*-terminus in the ER lumen and C-terminus in the cytosol. Like type II proteins, these proteins have a single *noncleavable* internal signal sequence, which acts as both start-transfer signal sequence and stop-transfer signal sequence.

Type II and type III proteins contain a single internal start-transfer signal sequence which also acts as a stop-transfer signal sequence. The difference in the orientation of these proteins depends primarily on whether there is a high density of positively charged amino acids on the N-terminal side of the internal stop-transfer signal sequence (type II) or the C-terminal side of the internal stop-transfer signal sequence (type III). *Positively charged residues in membrane proteins are found predominantly on the cytosolic side of the membrane*. This is known as the **positive–inside rule.**

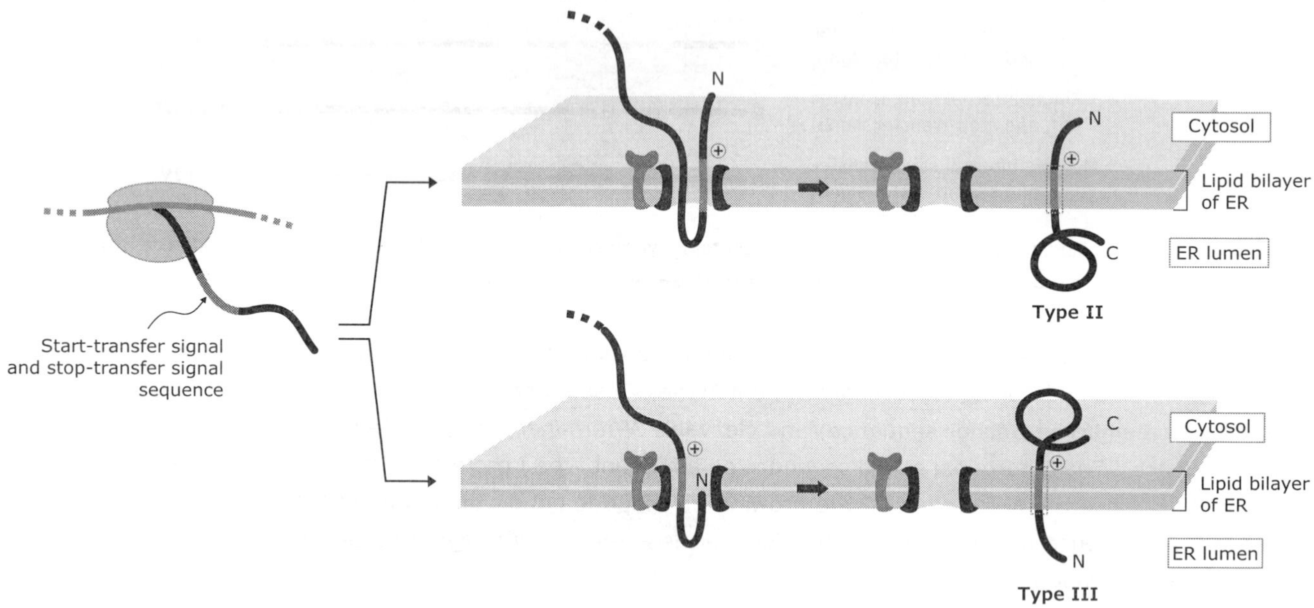

Figure 3.67 Insertion of a transmembrane protein with an internal non-cleavable signal sequence.

Type IV protein: Multipass transmembrane proteins (such as GPCR, CFTR and GLUT1) having both its N-terminal and C-terminal oriented towards the same side of the membrane or two ends have opposite orientations. If a type IV protein has an even number of transmembrane a helices, both its *N*-terminus and C-terminus will be oriented toward the same side of the membrane. Conversely, if a type IV protein has an odd number of transmembrane a helices, its two ends will have opposite orientations. These proteins contain many stop transfer sequences.

Box 3.1 Endomembrane system

The endomembrane system is composed of membrane-bound structures that are suspended in the cytosol of a eukaryotic cell. These membranes divide the cell into functional and structural compartments. The membrane-bound structures of the endomembrane system include: the nuclear envelope, the endoplasmic reticulum, the Golgi complex, lysosomes, vacuoles and transport vesicles. The system is defined more accurately as the set of membranes that form a single functional and developmental unit, either being connected together directly, or exchanging material through vesicular transport. The endomembrane system does not include the membranes of mitochondria and chloroplasts. Peroxisome is not considered as part of endomembrane system by many authors. However, growing evidence supports the view that peroxisome is actually a part of endomembrane system that originates from the endoplasmic reticulum.

Lipid-linked membrane proteins

GPI-linked proteins are **lipid-linked** (or **anchored**) membrane proteins. These proteins are exactly like type I transmembrane proteins, with a cleavable *N*-terminal signal sequence and internal stop-transfer sequence. These proteins are synthesized and initially inserted into the ER membrane. After insertion in the ER membrane, these proteins are transferred to a **glycosylphosphatidylinositol** (**GPI**) anchor. The enzyme **transamidase**, located in the ER membrane, cleaves the protein from its membrane-bound C-terminus and simultaneously attaches the new C-terminus to an amino group on a GPI anchor. The GPI anchor helps direct these proteins to the cell membrane.

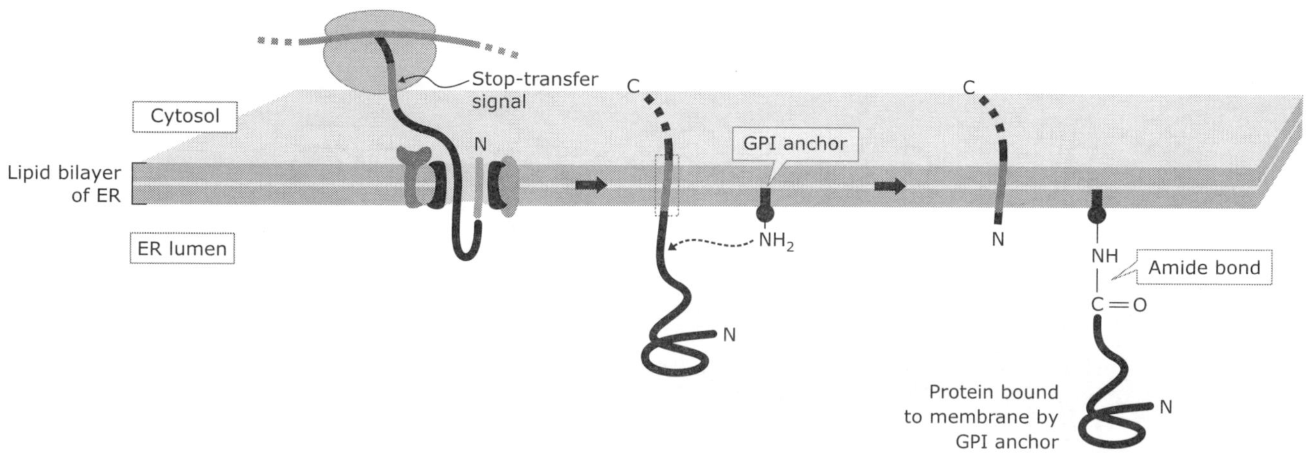

Figure 3.68 GPIs are added to polypeptides anchored in the membrane by a carboxy-terminal membrane spanning region. The membrane-spanning region is cleaved, and the new carboxy terminus is joined to the NH_2 group after translocation is completed leaving the protein attached to the membrane by the GPI anchor.

3.15.2 Transport of proteins from ER to *cis*-Golgi

Proteins entering into the lumen of the ER are of two types – **resident proteins** such as BiP and non-resident **export proteins** such as secretory proteins and lysosomal proteins. Following the ER-specific folding, oligomerization and processing, export proteins are exported from the ER to the *cis*-Golgi network, the first compartment of the Golgi complex. This transport occurs through the formation of **transport vesicles** followed by the targeting and fusion of these vesicles.

Transport vesicles: To be transported from one compartment to another, protein products must be packaged into transport vesicles. Most of the protein components in transport vesicle are highly specific in order to maintain organelle distinction. These vesicles arise from specialized protein-coated regions of membranes, which are surrounded by a coat of proteins covering the cytosolic face so that these membranes eventually bud off as **coated transport vesicles.** Prior to fusing with the target membrane, this protein coat is discarded to allow the membranes to fuse directly.

Mainly three types of coated transport vesicles are known, each with a different type of protein coat and formed by reversible polymerization of a distinct set of protein subunits. In addition to coat proteins, various adaptor proteins and small GTP-binding proteins are required for formation of coated vesicles. Each type of vesicle transports proteins from particular parent organelles to particular destination organelles.

Clathrin coated transport vesicles: Clathrin forms multiple complexes based on its association with different **adaptor proteins** (APs). Clathrin that is associated with AP1 and AP3 forms vesicles for transport from the *trans*-Golgi network to the lysosome. Clathrin associated with AP2 forms vesicles from the plasma membrane during endocytosis that transport to the early endosomes.

COPI coated: COPI (Coat protein I) forms vesicles for both intra-Golgi transport and retrograde transport from the Golgi to the ER. The COPI coat assembles upon activation of a small GTPase **Arf1**, which is driven by either of the redundant GEFs, **Gea1** or **Gea2**. Activated Arf1 in turn recruits the 'inner coat' complex of **Sec21/Sec26/Ret2/Ret3**.

COPI 'outer coat' is formed by **Sec27/Ret1/Sec28**, which assembles in a triskelion structure. A lactone antibiotic, **Brefeldin A**, prevents COPI coated vesicles formation. It targets the activity of GEF which catalyzes the activation of Arf1.

COPII coated: COPII forms vesicles for anterograde transport from the ER to the Golgi. In the COPII coat, a small GTPase **Sar1** is activated by ER membrane-bound guanine nucleotide exchange factor (GEF) termed **Sec12**. Activated Sar1–GTP recruits the **Sec23/Sec24** dimer, which corresponds to the 'inner coat' layer. A heterotetramer of **Sec13/ Sec31** is subsequently recruited, forming the 'outer coat' and polymerizing into a lattice-like structure that drives membrane curvature.

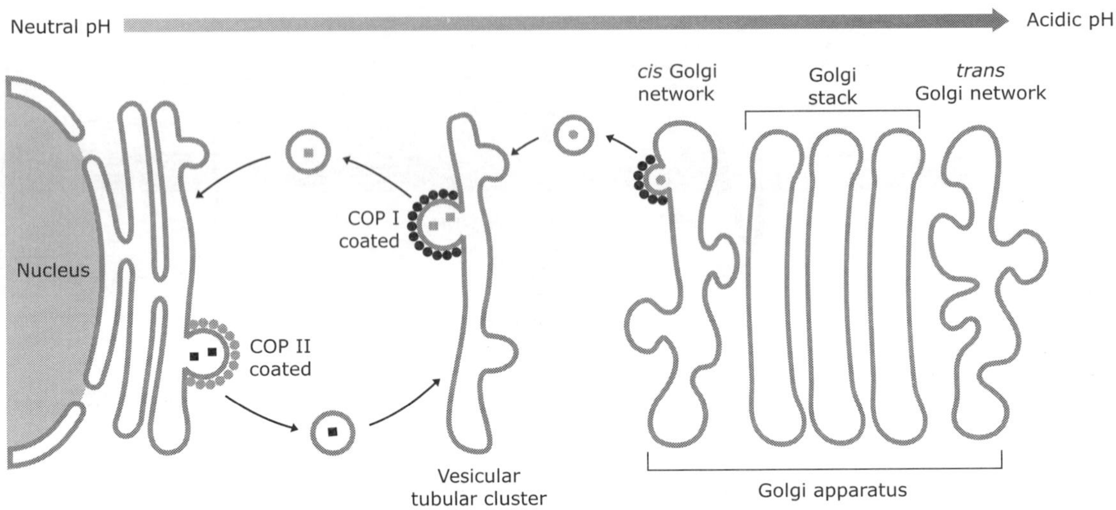

Figure 3.69 Coated transport vesicle-mediated protein trafficking between ER and *cis*-Golgi.

Table 3.13 Coated vesicles found within eukaryotic cells

Coated vesicle	Coat proteins	Transport
Clathrin	Clathrin, AP1	Golgi complex to endosome
Clathrin	Clathrin, AP2	Plasma membrane to endosome
COPI	COPI	Golgi complex to the ER or intra Golgi complex
COPII	COPII	ER to Golgi complex

The coat proteins surrounding transport vesicles that move from the late endosome to lysosomes and to the plasma membrane have not yet been identified.

ER-resident proteins often are retrieved from the *cis*-Golgi

As we have mentioned in the previous section that proteins entering into the lumen of the ER are of two types- *resident proteins* and non-resident *export proteins*. How, then, are resident proteins retained in the ER lumen to carry out their work? The answer lies in a specific C-terminal sequence present in resident ER proteins. Most ER-resident proteins have a **Lys-Asp-Glu-Leu** (KDEL in the one-letter code) **sequence** at their C-terminus. Several experiments demonstrated that the **KDEL sequence**, which acts as **sorting signal** is both necessary and sufficient for retention in the ER. If this *ER retention signal* is removed from BiP, for example, the protein is secreted from the cell; and if the signal is transferred to a protein that is normally secreted, the protein is now retained in the ER. The KDEL sorting signal sequence is recognized and bound by the **KDEL receptor** found on the ER and the *cis*-Golgi. The KDEL receptor acts mainly to retrieve soluble proteins with the KDEL sorting signal that has escaped to the *cis*-Golgi network and returns them to the ER. The finding that most KDEL receptors are localized to the membranes of small transport vesicles shuttling between the ER and the *cis*-Golgi also supports this concept. The retention of transmembrane proteins in the ER is carried out by short C-terminal sequences that contain two lysine residues (**KKXX** sequences).

The affinity of the KDEL receptor for proteins with KDEL sorting signal changes in different compartments. How can the affinity of the KDEL receptor change depending on the compartment in which it resides? The answer may be related to the differences in pH. In the low-pH environment of *cis*-Golgi and transport vesicles, the KDEL receptor has greater binding affinity with the KDEL sorting signal whereas in the neutral-pH environment of the ER, the ER proteins dissociate from the KDEL receptor due to lesser affinity.

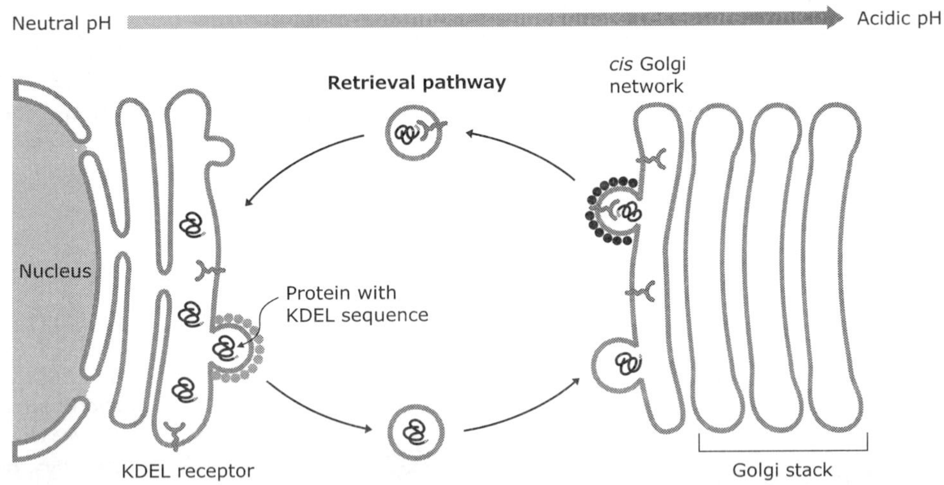

Figure 3.70 ER resident proteins with the KDEL sorting signal that escape from the ER are returned by transport vesicles. KDEL receptor serves to retrieve KDEL tagged proteins from *cis*-Golgi and return them to the ER. KDEL receptors localized primarily to membranes of *cis*-Golgi itself and to small vesicles that shuttle between ER and *cis*-Golgi. KDEL-receptors bind to KDEL tagged proteins in the low pH environment of the Golgi and release those proteins in the neutral pH of the ER. In the environment of the ER, the ER resident proteins dissociate from the KDEL receptor, which is then returned to the Golgi complex for reuse.

Clearly, the transport of newly synthesized proteins from the RER to the Golgi cisternae is a highly selective and regulated process. The selective entry of proteins into membrane-bound transport vesicles is an important feature of protein targeting as we will encounter them several times in our study of the subsequent stages in the maturation of secretory and membrane proteins.

3.15.3 Transport of proteins from the TGN to lysosomes

All of the proteins that pass through the Golgi complex, except those that are retained there as permanent residents, are sorted in the *trans*-Golgi network (**TGN**) according to their final destination. The mechanism of sorting is especially well understood for those proteins destined for the lumen of lysosomes. Some *N*-linked oligosaccharides help in targeting lysosomal proteins to lysosomes and prevent their secretion. In the ***cis*-Golgi**, one or more mannose residues present in the *N*-linked oligosaccharide ($Man_8\ GlcNAc_2$) of lysosomal proteins become phosphorylated. This process occurs in two steps. First, the enzyme *phosphotransferase* transfers a phosphorylated *N*-acetylglucosamine to carbon 6 of one or more mannose residues. Subsequently, the enzyme *phosphodiesterase* removes the *N*-acetylglucosamine (GlcNAc), leaving a phosphorylated mannose residue on the lysosomal proteins.

$$\textbf{Mannose} \xrightarrow[\textit{Phosphotransferase}]{\text{UDP-GlcNAc} \quad \text{UMP}} \textbf{Mannose—P—GlcNAc} \xrightarrow[\textit{Phosphodiesterase}]{H_2O \quad \text{GlcNAc}} \textbf{Mannose 6-phosphate}$$

Mannose 6-phosphate (**M6P**) acts as a targeting signal patch for lysosomal proteins from the TGN to the lysosome. The M6P residues that are formed then bind to **mannose 6-phosphate receptors**, which are found primarily in the TGN. The luminal domain of this transmembrane protein contains a region that binds M6P very tightly and specifically. Clathrin-API coated transport vesicles containing the M6P receptor and bound lysosomal protein bud from the TGN and then fuse with a sorting vesicle, **late endosome**, which has an internal pH of ~5.5. Because M6P receptors can bind M6P at the slightly acidic pH (~6.5) of the TGN but not at a pH less than ~6, the bound lysosomal proteins are released within late endosomes. Furthermore, a phosphatase within late endosomes generally removes the phosphate from lysosomal proteins, preventing their rebinding to the M6P receptor. Two types of vesicles bud from late endosomes. One type contains lysosomal proteins but not the M6P receptor. After these vesicles bud from late endosomes, they fuse with lysosomes, delivering the lysosomal protein to their final destination. The other type of vesicle (coated with **retromer complex**) recycles the M6P receptor back to the *trans*-Golgi network.

Retromer was first discovered in yeasts in 1998 and was aptly named due to its function in transporting protein cargo in the retrograde direction from the endosome to the TGN. Retromer is a heteropentameric protein complex. It has two components – one is **cargo-selective complex** (made up of VPS26, VPS35 and VPS29), which sorts cargo for delivery to the TGN and second is **retromer-associated sorting nexin** (made up of Vps5 and Vps17).

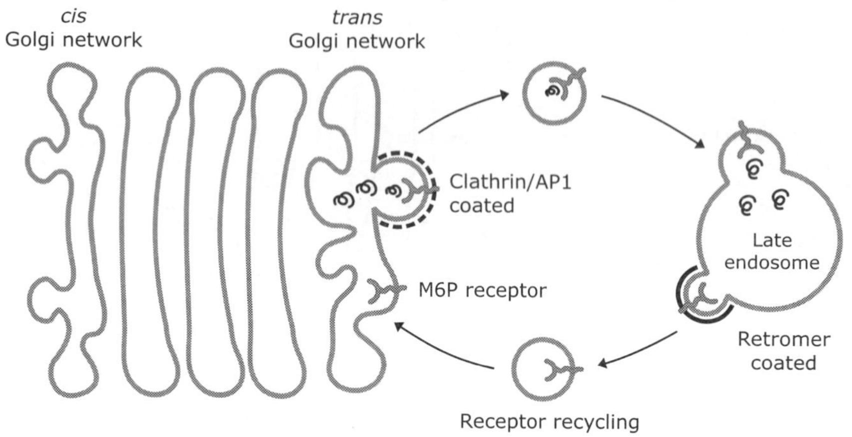

Figure 3.71
Vesicles coated with clathrin bud from the *trans*-Golgi network; after uncoating, these vesicles fuse with late endosomes. An endosomal coat protein complex named 'retromer' is required for retrieval of the M6P receptor back to the *trans*-Golgi network.

Table 3.14 Examples of sorting signals that direct soluble and membrane proteins to specific transport vesicles

Signal sequence	Type of protein	Transport step	Vesicle type
Lys-Asp-Glu-Leu (KDEL)	Soluble	Golgi to ER	COP I coated
Lys-Lys-X-X (KKXX)	Membrane	Golgi to ER	COP I coated
Di-acidic (e.g., Asp-X-Glu)	Membrane	ER to Golgi	COP II coated
Mannose 6-phosphate (M6P)	Soluble	*Trans*-Golgi to late endosome	Clathrin coated

X = any amino acids. *Adapted from Molecular Cell Biology, fifth edition, Lodish et. al., W. H. Freeman and Company.*

3.15.4 Membrane fusion

Vesicle-mediated trafficking includes *vesicle formation*, *vesicle translocation*, *membrane tethering*, *membrane docking* and *vesicle fusion* with the target compartment. Membrane fusion is a process by which two initially separated lipid bilayers merge to form a single unity. It is a universal biological process in life that is involved in many cellular events such as in viral infection, fertilization and intracellular trafficking.

The fusion of the membrane of a transport vesicle with its target involves two types of events. First, the transport vesicle must specifically recognize the correct target membrane and second, the fusion of the vesicle and target membranes. Membrane fusion also does not occurs spontaneously. The spontaneous membrane fusion is opposed by electrostatic repulsive forces between equally charged membrane surfaces. Rothman and his colleagues proposed a general model, called the **SNARE hypothesis**, to explain the selective and non-spontaneous process of vesicle fusion. According to this model, vesicle fusion with the target is mediated by interactions between specific pairs of proteins, called **SNAREs** (soluble *N*-ethylmaleimide sensitive factor attachment protein receptors), on the vesicle and target membranes (**v-SNAREs** and **t-SNAREs**, respectively). v-SNAREs pair with cognate t-SNAREs in the target membrane in a highly specific manner. SNAREs are a family of 20 to 30 kDa proteins that harbor a conserved coiled-coil SNARE motif of about 60 to 70 residues. Each SNARE has 1 or 2 SNARE motifs.

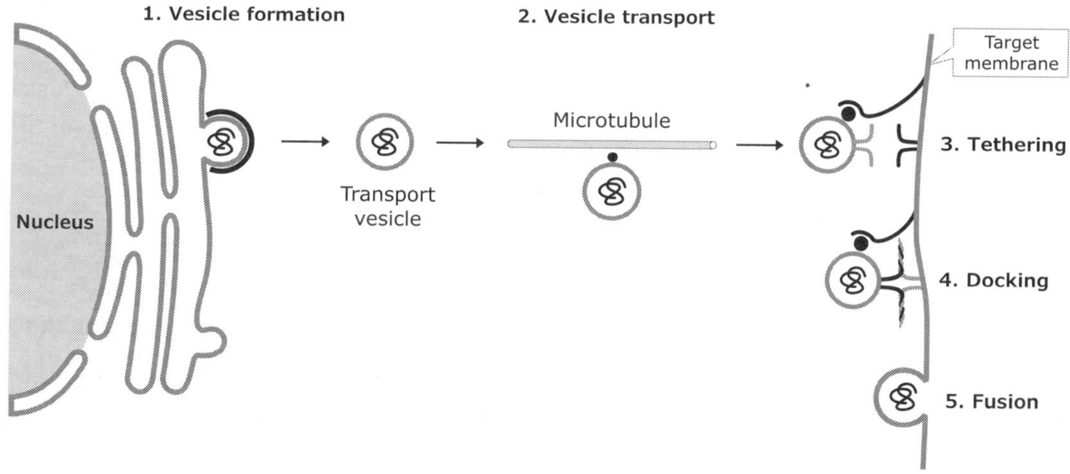

In neurons, v-SNARE present on synaptic vesicles is designated **synaptobrevin** (also called *vesicle-associated membrane protein*, VAMP) and SNARE **syntaxin** and **SNAP-25** (25 kDa synaptosome-associated protein) acting as t-SNAREs. SNAREs syntaxin and synaptobrevin consist of a cytoplasmic domain (SNARE motifs), a short linker domain, and a carboxy-terminal transmembrane domain (TMD). SNAP-25 is a lipid-linked protein (attached to the membrane by palmitoylation of four cysteine residues) anchored to the cytosolic face of the membrane and does not contain a trans-membrane domain. The SNARE proteins are the target for botulinum and tetanus neurotoxins and blocks neurotransmitters release. SNAREs were initially classified according to their preferential localization as vesicle-localized (v)- or target-membrane-bound (t)-SNAREs. This nomenclature turned out to be somewhat ambiguous since t-SNAREs are also found on vesicles and v-SNAREs can be found on target membranes. A systematic sequence analysis revealed that most v-SNAREs have an *arginine residue* in the SNARE motif (**R-SNAREs**), whereas a *glutamine residue* is found in the SNARE motif of syntaxins and SNAP-25 (**Q-SNAREs**). Mammalian cells contain between 35 to 40 different SNAREs, and SNAREs involved in different intracellular fusions differ in their composition.

A vesicle is likely to encounter many potential target membranes before it finds the correct one. Thus, transport vesicles must be highly accurate in recognizing the correct target membrane with which to fuse. This crucial process occurs in two steps: the *first* is vesicle tethering and *second* is the docking and fusion of the membranes. **Tethering**, a reversible step, is mediated by **tethering factors**. So far, ~20 different tethering factors are known that fall into two major groups: multi-subunit tethering complexes (e.g., exocyst, HOPs) and homodimeric coiled-coil tethering proteins (e.g., p115, EEA1).

The membrane tethering processes before membrane docking and fusion work in association with the **Rab family** of small monomeric GTPases. Cells contain many types of **Rab proteins**, each associated with the membrane of a particular organelle and transport vesicle. There are over 60 Rab proteins. Their highly selective distribution on membrane systems makes Rab proteins ideal molecular markers for identifying each membrane type. Rab proteins can function on transport vesicles, on target membranes, or both. Rab proteins cycle between a membrane and the cytosol.

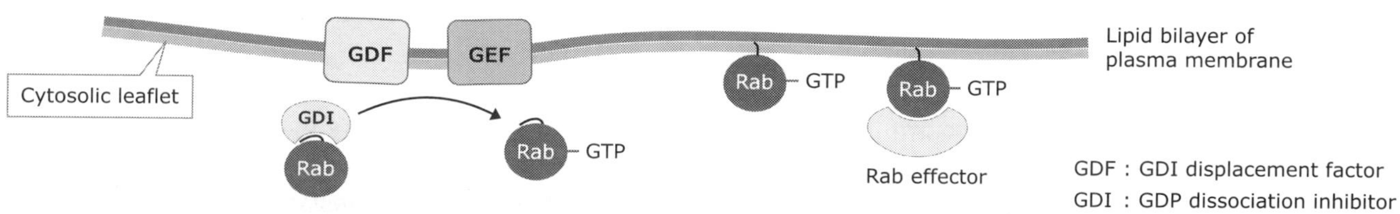

In their GDP-bound state, they are inactive and bound to another protein (Rab-GDP dissociation inhibitor or **GDI**) that keeps them soluble in the cytosol. Membrane-bound Rab-GEFs activate Rab proteins on the cytosolic surface of the membrane. Once in GTP-bound and membrane-bound state, Rab proteins interact with Rab-interacting proteins termed **Rab effectors**. Rab effectors include tethering factors. It establishes the first connection between the two membranes that are going to fuse. After tethering, SNAREs mediate *docking* and *fusion*. t-SNAREs in target membranes are often present in inactive conformations that must be released before the t-SNARE can function.

The activation step appears to be regulated by the SM and tethering proteins. The binding of v-SNARE to t-SNARE causes the vesicle to remain bound for long enough to allow the Rab protein to hydrolyze its bound GTP, which locks the vesicle onto the target membrane. The pairing of v-SNARE with t-SNARE before membrane fusion is termed as ***trans*-SNARE complex**. After fusion, the *trans*-SNARE complex becomes a ***cis*-SNARE complex** (or **SNAREpin**) on the target membrane.

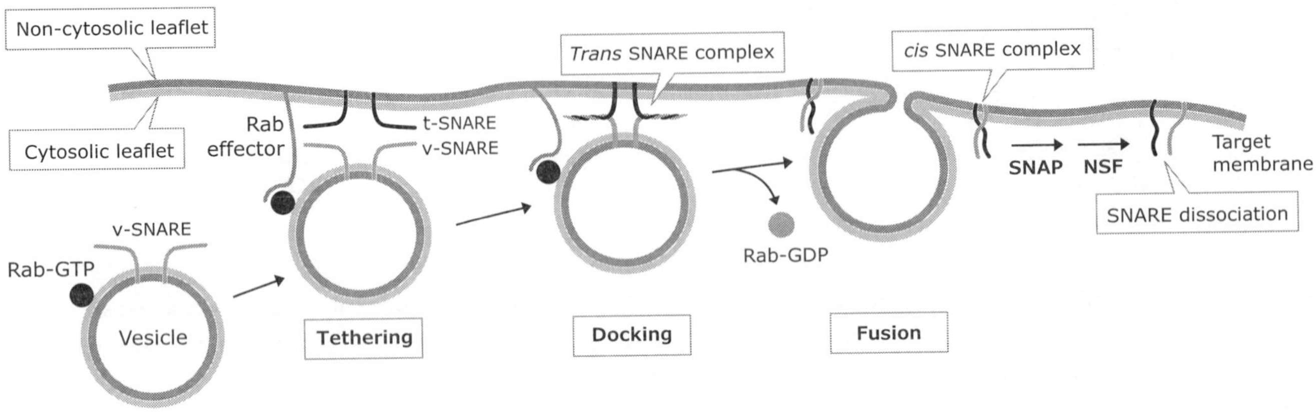

Figure 3.72 The membrane fusion event includes reversible membrane tethering, irreversible membrane docking, and, finally, membrane fusion. In the irreversible membrane docking stage, complementary sets of v-SNAREs and t-SNAREs determine the selectivity of docking and form trans SNARE complex. The v- and t-SNARE proteins are in trans (on opposing membranes) state before fusion and *cis* state (on the same membrane) after fusion. The Rab protein hydrolyzes its bound GTP, locking the vesicle onto the target membrane and releasing Rab-GDP into the cytosol, from where it can be reused in a new round of transport. The vesicle then fuses with the target membrane. NSF is an ATPase that hydrolyzes ATP to release the complex once it has done its job.

The interacting SNAREs need to separate apart before they can function again. Most SNARE proteins in cells participate in multiple rounds of vesicular transport. A crucial protein called **NSF** (NEM sensitive factor, a member of type II AAA+ ATPases) cycles between membranes and the cytosol and catalyzes the disassembly process. The NSF binds to the SNARE complex via adaptor proteins, **SNAPs** (soluble NSF attachment proteins). NSF and SNAPs are not necessary for actual membrane fusion but rather are required for the regeneration of free SNARE proteins. NSF (a hexamer of identical subunits) is a soluble ATPase and hydrolyzes ATP to dissociate the SNAREs apart. However, it is not known how the activity of NSF is controlled. It is also not known how v-SNAREs are selectively retrieved and returned to their compartment of origin so that they can be reused in newly formed transport vesicles.

Note: The SNARE proteins are the target for *botulinum* and *tetanus neurotoxins* and blocks neurotransmitters release. *Botulinum neurotoxins* and *tetanus neurotoxin* are both classified as *clostridial neurotoxins*. **Tetanus neurotoxin**, also referred to as **tetanospasmin**, is a potent exotoxin produced by the bacterium *Clostridium tetani*. It falls into the category of **A-B toxins**. Operating as a protease, tetanus neurotoxin targets v-SNARE, inhibiting the release of inhibitory neurotransmitters like gamma-aminobutyric acid (*GABA*) and *glycine*. On the other hand, **botulinum neurotoxin**, produced by *Clostridium botulinum*, is responsible for **botulism**. Similarly, it belongs to the A-B toxin class. Acting as a protease, botulinum neurotoxin cleaves v- and t-SNAREs, effectively blocks the release of the neurotransmitter *acetylcholine*.

3.15.5 Targeting of mitochondrial proteins

Mitochondrial proteins are synthesized by 80S cytosolic as well as 70S matrix ribosomes. About 99% of mitochondrial proteins are encoded by nuclear genes and are synthesized by cytosolic membrane-free ribosomes. Proteins synthesized by cytosolic ribosomes are translocated into the mitochondria *post-translationally* and in *unfolded state*. Proteins imported into the mitochondria have several destinations. These proteins may enter into the OMM, the IMS, the IMM or the mitochondrial matrix. Mitochondrial protein import requires mitochondrial targeting signal sequences, membrane receptors and translocons. Mitochondrial targeting signal sequences present in imported proteins are categorized in two major classes:

- *N*-terminal cleavable matrix targeting sequences (termed **presequences**)
- Internal non-cleavable targeting sequences.

Presequences are rich in positively charged basic amino acids (arginine and lysine) and hydroxyl group containing amino acids (serine and threonine), but lack negatively charged acidic residues. A typical presequence has a length of about 10-30 amino acid residues. About 60% of all imported mitochondrial proteins contain presequence. Many mitochondrial proteins are not synthesized with cleavable presequences but contain *internal non-cleavable targeting sequences* that contain hydrophobic elements but have not been fully characterized.

Mitochondrial import pathway: There are five major import pathways of precursor proteins into mitochondria. Based on the nature of mitochondrial targeting signal sequences, these pathways can be divided into two broad categories:

Precursor proteins with presequence

- Imported by the **TOM** and **TIM23** complex: Many IMM and matrix proteins.

Precursor proteins with internal non-cleavable targeting sequences

- Imported by **TOM** and **TIM22** complex: Several multipass TMP of IMM.
- Imported by **TOM** and **SAM** (sorting and assembly machinery): β-barrel proteins of OMM.
- Imported by **TOM** and **MIA** (mitochondrial import and assembly): Many IMS proteins with cysteine motifs.
- Imported by **TOM** and **MIM** (mitochondrial import complex): OMM proteins with α-helical transmembrane segments.

1. Import of precursor proteins with presequence

Import of matrix proteins (TOM and TIM23 complex mediated): Two distinct translocation complexes that mediate translocation are situated in the outer and inner mitochondrial membranes, referred to as **TOM** (*translocase of the outer membrane*) complex and **TIM** (*translocase of the inner membrane*) complex. The TOM complex consists of *receptor proteins* (Tom20, Tom22 and Tom70), the *channel-forming protein* (Tom40) and three small Tom proteins (Tom5, Tom6 and Tom7). **Tom40** (a β-barrel protein) belongs to the voltage-dependent anion channel-porin superfamily. It is characterized by 19 β-strands. There are two TIM complexes – **TIM23 complex** and **TIM22 complex** – in the inner membrane that transport different classes of proteins. The TIM23 complex consists of Tim50 (functions as presequence receptor), Tim23 (channel-forming protein) and Tim17 (involved in motor recruitment). In the absence of translocation, Tim50 also helps to keep the Tim23 channel in a closed state.

Matrix targeting precursor proteins enter into mitochondrial matrix are synthesized by cytosolic 80S ribosomes and are maintained in an unfolded or loosely folded conformation. This is carried out by cytosolic chaperone such as **Hsc70** (a member of Hsp70 family). During translocation, precursor proteins first interact with TOM complex. Tom20 receptor of TOM complex recognizes the presequences and transfers the precursor proteins to the central receptor Tom22. This matrix targeting sequence directs proteins through the TOM complex to the TIM23 complex. The membrane potential across the inner membrane plays an important role in protein translocation. First, membrane potential (negative on the matrix side) drives the positively charged presequences towards the matrix. Second, membrane potential directly activates the Tim23 channel. TIM23 complex remains associated with *presequence translocase-associated motor* (**PAM**). The motor consists of the mitochondrial Hsp70 (**mtHsp70**) and several co-chaperones. mtHsp70 binds to a translocating polypeptide chain and responsible for ATP-driven unidirectional movement. Soon after the presequence of a protein enters the matrix, it is removed by *mitochondrial processing peptidase* (**MPP**), a heterodimeric peptidase located in the matrix. After the initial interaction with mtHsp70, many imported matrix proteins are passed on to another chaperone protein, mitochondrial Hsp60. Hsp60 helps the unfolded polypeptide chain to fold.

Import of membrane proteins to IMM (TOM and TIM23 complex mediated): These precursor proteins have an internal hydrophobic *stop-transfer signal* behind the presequences. Due to presence of stop transfer signal, translocation of these proteins are arrested in the TIM23 complex and are then released by the lateral gatekeeper Mgr2 into the IMM.

Import of membrane proteins to IMM (OXA translocase mediated): There are some presequence-carrying multipass transmembrane proteins of IMM which are first transported into the matrix from cytosol and are then incorporated into the membrane by the **OXA** (oxidase assembly) **translocase**. Proteins synthesized by mitochondrial 70S ribosomes in the matrix are also targeted into the IMM co-translationally by the OXA translocase.

2. Import of precursor proteins with internal non-cleavable targeting sequences

Import of multi-pass transmembrane proteins to IMM (TOM and TIM22 complex mediated): These proteins do not have *N*-terminal presequences; they have internal targeting signals. Cytosolic chaperones of the Hsp90 and Hsp70 classes deliver these inner membrane precursor proteins to the receptor **Tom70**. After their release from the cytosolic chaperones, the precursors pass through the Tom40 and enter the intermembrane space. Here, they are bound by small **TIM chaperones** (the main form is the soluble Tim9-Tim10 heterohexameric complex), which prevent their aggregation and guide them to the TIM22 complex. The **TIM22 complex** contains Tim18, Tim22 (the channel-forming protein) and Tim54. The TIM22 complex operates in a membrane potential dependent manner to insert these multi-pass proteins in the inner membrane.

Import of β-barrel proteins to OMM (TOM and SAM complex mediated): The OMM contains different classes of membrane protein: single- pass and multi-pass proteins with α-helical transmembrane segments and β-barrel proteins. The precursors of β-barrel proteins are initially translocated by the TOM complex to the intermembrane space and finally, insertion of β-barrel precursors into the OMM is mediated by the *sorting and assembly machinery* (**SAM**).

Import of proteins with characteristic cysteine motifs to IMS (TOM and MIA complex mediated): Many proteins of the mitochondrial intermembrane space contain characteristic cysteine motifs. The *mitochondrial intermembrane space import and assembly* (**MIA**) *system*, which mediates the import and oxidative folding of IMS proteins. Upon passage through the Tom40 channel, MIA system recognizes the precursor proteins that contain an **intermembrane space sorting signal**, typically consisting of a hydrophobic element flanked by a cysteine residue.

Import of OMM proteins with α-helical transmembrane segments (TOM and MIM complex mediated): Many OMM proteins with α-helical transmembrane segments enter into OMM is mediated by **MIM** (mitochondria import) **complex**. α-helical OM proteins typically do not use the Tom40 channel, but Tom70 can be involved in their recognition.

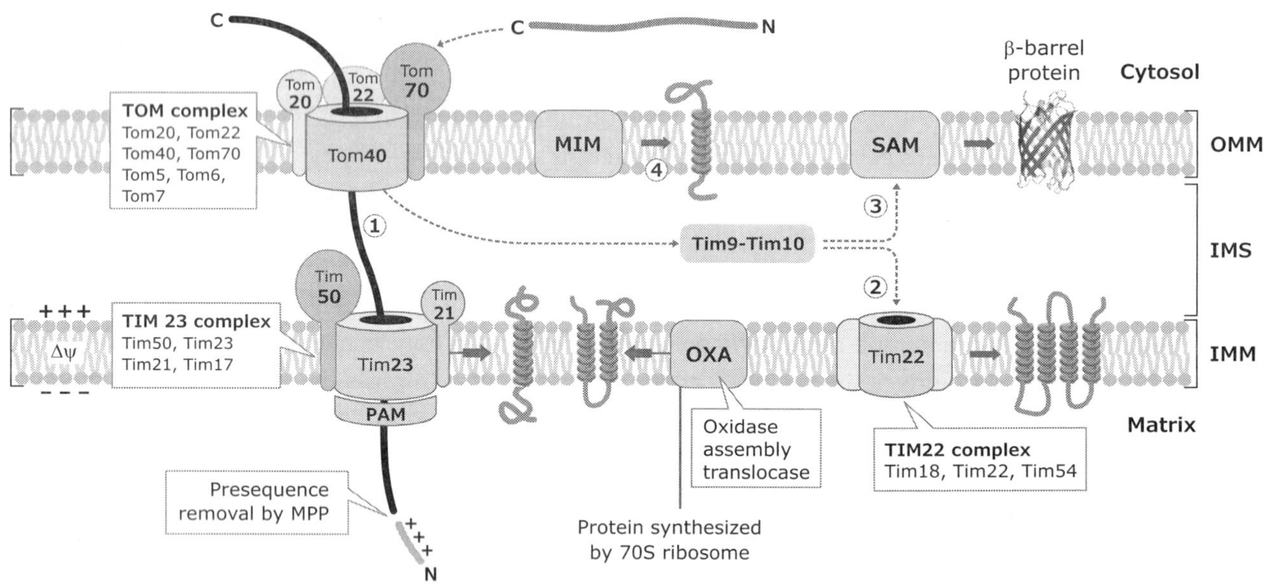

Figure 3.73 Protein import pathways into mitochondria. Five major pathways of mitochondrial protein import have been identified. *First*, TOM and TIM23 complex mediated pathway transports presequence- carrying precursor proteins through the TOM and TIM23 complexes. The presequences are removed by the MPP in the matrix. IMM proteins are either laterally released from the TIM23 complex or are transported via the matrix and inserted into the IMM by the OXA translocase. IMM proteins synthesized on mitochondrial ribosomes are also inserted by OXA. *Second*, TOM and TIM22 complex mediated pathway transports internal non-cleavable targeting sequences carrying precursor proteins into the IMM. *Third*, the precursors of OMM β-barrel proteins use the TOM complex and small TIM chaperones and are inserted into the OMM by the SAM. *Fourth*, many OMM proteins with α-helical transmembrane segments are inserted into the membrane by the MIM complex. *Fifth*, TOM and MIA complex mediated pathway transports proteins with characteristic cysteine motifs destined for the IMS (not shown in the figure).

3.15.6 Targeting of peroxisomal proteins

Peroxisomes are unique among single-membrane organelles because they can import both their matrix and membrane proteins directly from the cytosol. Peroxisomal protein targeting involves the import of both *peroxisomal matrix proteins* and *membrane proteins*. The mechanism of targeting of peroxisomal membrane proteins is less understood.

Peroxisomal matrix proteins are encoded by nuclear genes and synthesized on membrane-free ribosomes. These proteins are imported into the peroxisome post-translationally, in their fully folded state. The targeting of peroxisomal matrix proteins involves several steps: recognition of the proteins in the cytosol by specific receptors, docking of the receptor-protein complex at the peroxisomal membrane, translocation of the matrix proteins into the peroxisome, and recycling of the receptors for further use.

Peroxisomal matrix proteins have peroxisomal targeting signals – PTS1 and PTS2. The **PTS1** is a tri- or tetrapeptide sequence at the C-terminus. The consensus sequence of PTS1 is (S/A/C)–(K/R/H)–(L/M). It was first characterized in enzyme catalase as a *Ser-Lys-Leu* sequence (**SKL** in one-letter code) at the C-terminus. PTS1 containing proteins are recognized by the cytoplasmic receptor **Pex5** and are imported into peroxisomes in their fully folded form. The **PTS2** signal is a sequence of nine amino acids and located at the N-terminus and recognized by the soluble receptor **Pex7**. PTS2 exhibits the consensus sequence (R/K)–(L/V/I)–X_5–(H/Q)–(L/A). Proteins are translocated into the matrix through **translocons** present in the membrane of the peroxisome. Translocons are made up of **docking** and **RING complex**. In yeast, a docking complex is typically comprised of Pex13, Pex14 and Pex17 and RING complex is comprised of Pex2, Pex10 and Pex12.

The peroxisomal membrane proteins bear membrane peroxisomal targeting signals and their targeting are either a **Pex19-dependent** (*direct pathway*) or **Pex19-independent** (*indirect pathway*) manner. In the indirect pathway, peroxisomal membrane proteins have been shown to traffic to the peroxisomes via the ER.

3.15.7 Transport of nuclear proteins

Protein transport between the cytosol and the nucleus occurs bidirectionally through the nuclear pores. Transport of proteins from the cytosol to the nucleus is referred to as **import**, while transport from the nucleus to the cytosol is called **export**. Proteins imported into the nucleus are encoded by nuclear genes and synthesized on membrane-free ribosomes in the cytosol. These proteins are imported post-translationally in their fully folded state.

Molecules up to 50 kDa can enter the nucleus by passive diffusion, though they can also be actively transported. Proteins larger than 50 kDa do not enter the nucleus by passive diffusion; instead, they are actively transported into and out of the nucleus. Proteins destined for import into or export from the nucleus contain specific amino acid sequences known as **nuclear localization signals** (**NLS**) or **nuclear export signals** (**NES**), respectively.

An **NLS** selectively directs nuclear proteins from the cytosol to the nucleus (import). NLSs consist of short, non-cleavable sequences that are generally rich in the positively charged basic amino acids lysine and arginine, with the precise sequence varying between different proteins. The NLS was first identified in the SV40-encoded viral protein called **large T-antigen** (PKKKRKV). NLSs can be classified into classical and non-classical types. Classical NLSs are further divided into two categories:

Monopartite classical NLSs: A single cluster composed of 4–8 positively charged amino acids, arginine and lysine.

Bipartite classical NLSs: Two clusters of 2–3 positively charged amino acids separated by a 9–12 amino-acid linker region, often containing several proline residues. Unlike classical NLSs, many proteins contain unusual NLSs that are neither similar to classical signals nor rich in arginine or lysine residues. These are known as **non-classical NLSs**.

A nuclear protein containing an NLS is transported through the nuclear pores post-translationally and in a fully folded conformation. A **NES** directs nuclear proteins from the nucleus to the cytosol (*export*). It is a *leucine-rich* short internal sequence in a protein.

Several types of nuclear-localization and export signals have been identified. Each type of nuclear-transport signal interacts with a specific receptor protein described as **exportin** (nuclear-export receptor) or **importin** (nuclear-import receptor). *Importins* interact with NLS of the cargo proteins in the cytosol and release it in the nucleus. Recognition of the NLS of a cargo protein is the first step in assembling an import-complex. Classical nuclear import involves the recognition of the NLS by the adaptor protein **importin-α**, followed by binding of the **importin-β**, thereby forming a trimeric import complex. Importin-β acts as the transport factor and carries the cargo protein through the nuclear pore complex. In other cases, such as when the cargo protein contains an atypical NLS, importin-β binds to the cargo protein directly. In a similar fashion, *exportins* bind with NES of proteins in the nucleus and release it in the cytosol. These two types of receptor proteins are highly homologous in sequence and belong to the *nuclear transport receptors family* called **karyopherin-β**. During translocation through the pore, exportin and importin interact with Phe-Gly repeats (**FG repeats**) on nucleoporins that line the central pore.

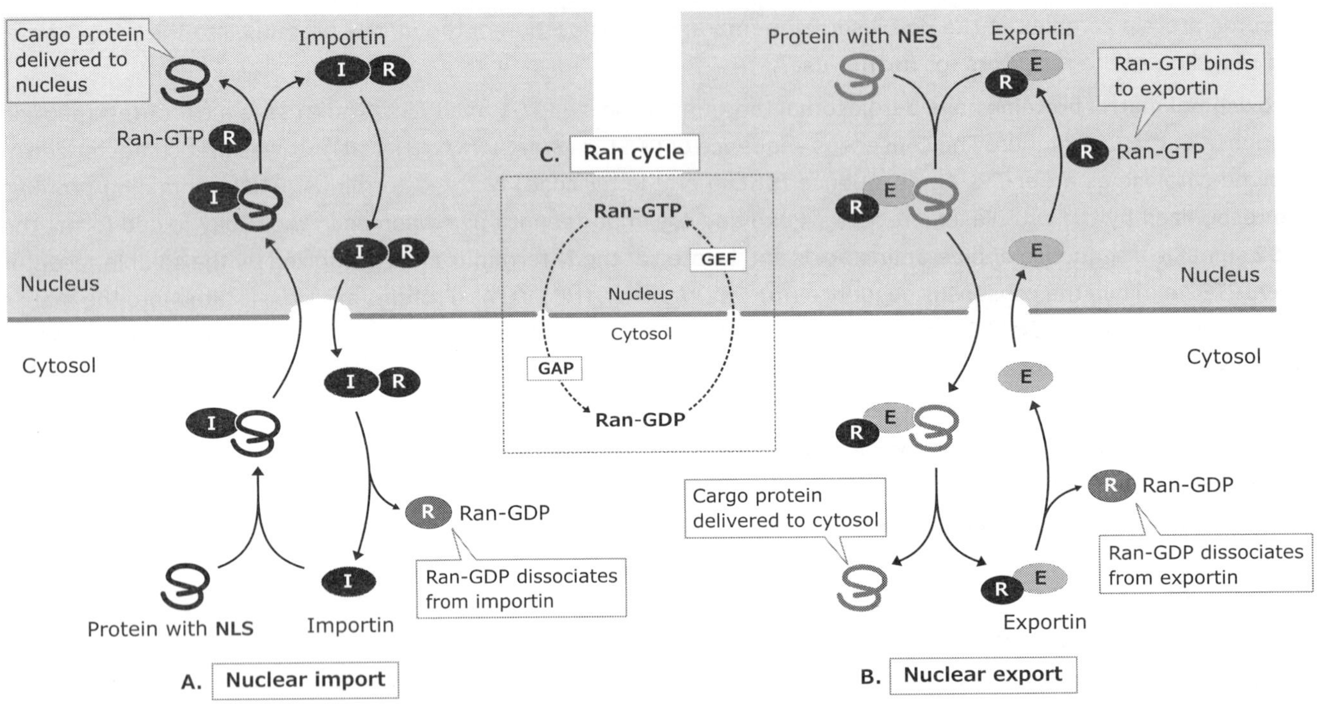

Figure 3.74 Transport through the nuclear pore complex. A. In nuclear import, importin binds with cargo protein with NLS in the cytosol and carries the cargo protein through the nuclear pore complex. Within the nucleus, Ran-GTP binds with importin and causes dissociation of cargo protein-importin complex. Finally, the importin and Ran-GTP complex are transported back to the cytosol. In the cytosol, Ran-GTP converted into Ran-GDP due to the presence of Ran-specific GAP and dissociated from importin. B. In nuclear export, exportin binds with cargo with NES in the nucleus. This complex formation is promoted by Ran-GTP. Once the export complex enters the cytosol, Ran-GTP bound with the exportin converted into Ran-GDP due to the activity of cytosolic Ran-specific GAP. Ran-GDP finally dissociates from exportin. C. Ran shuttles across the nuclear envelope through nuclear pores. In the nucleus, a high concentration of Ran-GTP is generated by Ran-specific GEF. In the cytosol, Ran-GTP meets Ran-specific GAP, which stimulates GTP hydrolysis.

Another important protein called **Ran**, small monomeric GTPases, plays a critical regulatory role in active transport and directionality. Ran can exist in two states, depending on whether GDP or GTP is bound. Ran-GTP occurs in the nucleus and Ran-GDP in the cytosol. Localization of Ran-GDP in the cytosol and Ran-GTP in the nucleus results from the localization of two Ran regulatory proteins: **Ran-specific GAP** (*RanGAP*) is located in the cytosol, and **Ran-specific GEF** (**RCC1**) located in the nucleus. In the nucleus, Ran-specific GEF stimulates replacement of GDP by GTP, thus converting Ran-GDP to Ran-GTP. In the cytosol, Ran-specific GAP causes the GTP to be hydrolyzed to GDP. The directionality of import is determined by a gradient of nuclear Ran-GTP. Once an import complex (cargo protein with NLS and importin) enters the nucleus, Ran-GTP binds importin, which releases the cargo protein. The importin Ran-GTP complex itself is transported back to the cytosol. In cytosol, Ran-specific GAP triggers Ran-GTP to hydrolyze its bound GTP, thereby converting it to Ran-GDP, which dissociates from the importin. The importin is then ready for another cycle of nuclear import. This directional flow is dependent on a Ran-GTP gradient, whereby the concentration of Ran-GTP is greater in the nucleus than in the cytosol. This Ran-GTP gradient is maintained by a Ran-specific GEF that is preferentially located in the nucleus and by Ran-specific GAPs in the cytosol.

Nuclear export occurs by a similar mechanism, except that Ran-GTP in the nucleus promotes cargo binding to the exportin, rather than promoting cargo dissociation. Once the export complex forms inside the nucleus moves through the pore to the cytosol, it encounters Ran-specific GAP, which induces the conversion of Ran-GTP to Ran-GDP. As a result, the exportin releases both its cargo and Ran-GDP in the cytosol. Free exportins are then returned to the nucleus to complete the cycle. *Nuclear transport factor 2* (**NTF2**) mediates the import of GDP-bound RAN (RAN-GDP) from the cytosol into the nucleus. Thus, the state of the Ran controls directionality of nuclear import and export. It provides both the free energy and the directionality for nuclear transport. Interestingly, the general nuclear export pathway for mRNAs does not rely directly on RanGTP-binding exportins. Instead, the process is driven by the ATP-dependent RNA helicase.

3.16 Cell junctions

Many cells in tissues are linked to one another and to the extracellular matrix at specialized contact sites called cell junctions. The cell junctions are critical to the development and functions of multicellular organisms. Cell junctions can be classified into three functional groups: occluding junctions, anchoring junctions and communicating junctions.

Occluding junctions

Occluding junctions seal cells together in epithelium in a way that prevents even small molecules from leaking from one side of the sheet to the other (i.e., forms permeability barrier across epithelial cell sheets). These junctions are of two types– *tight junction* and *septate junction*.

Tight junctions (or zonula occludens) are cell-cell occluding junctions mediated by two major transmembrane proteins – **claudins** and **occludin**. Claudins and occludins associate with intracellular peripheral membrane proteins called **ZO proteins**. Tight junctions make the closest contact between adjacent cells and prevent the free passage of molecules (including ions) across an epithelial sheet in the spaces between cells. They also maintain the polarity of epithelial cells by preventing the diffusion of molecules between the apical and the basolateral regions of the plasma membrane. **Septate junctions** are the main occluding junctions in invertebrates.

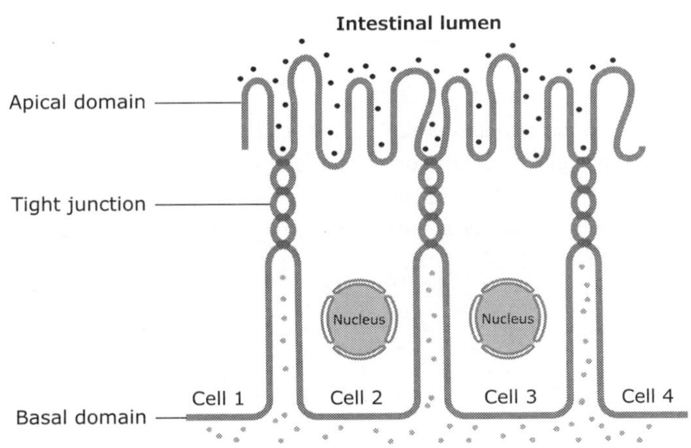

Figure 3.75
Tight junctions enable intestinal epithelial cells to function as barriers, preventing solute diffusion. This schematic illustration demonstrates how a small extracellular molecule on one side of the epithelial cells is unable to cross the tight junctions that seal adjacent cells together.

Anchoring junctions

Anchoring junctions mechanically attach cells (and their cytoskeletons) to their neighbours or to the extracellular matrix and perform the key task of holding cells together into tissues. It includes two main types of junctions - *adherens junction* and *desmosome*.

Adherens junctions

Adherens junctions connect bundles of actin filaments from cell to cell or from cell to the extracellular matrix.

Adhesion belt (or *zonula adherens*): It is a cell to cell junction, mediated by actin filaments and proteins belonging to the *cadherin family*. Adhesion belts are usually located near the apical surface, just below the tight junctions.

Focal contact (or *adhesion plaque*): It is a cell-matrix junction which is mediated by transmembrane adhesion proteins of the *integrin family* and by actin filament.

Desmosomes (or **macula adherens**)

Desmosomes are buttonlike points of intercellular contacts which bond neighbouring cells together. It has a dense cytoplasmic plaque which is composed of a mixture of intracellular attachment proteins, including **plakoglobin** and **desmoplakins**. The cytoplasmic plaque is responsible for connecting the cytoskeleton to the transmembrane linker proteins of the *cadherin family* of cell-cell adhesion molecules. Desmosomes contain two specialized cadherin proteins, **desmoglein** and **desmocollin**. Through extracellular domains, cadherins are responsible for holding the adjacent membranes together. Each plaque is associated with a thick network of *keratin intermediate filaments* (in most epithelial cells) and *desmin intermediate filaments* (in heart muscle cells), which are attached to the surface of the plaque.

Hemidesmosomes (or *half-desmosomes*), resemble desmosomes, but instead of joining adjacent epithelial cell membranes, they connect the basal surface of epithelial cells to the underlying **basal lamina**- a specialized mat of extracellular matrix at the interface between the epithelium and connective tissue. The transmembrane linker proteins in hemidesmosomes belong to the *integrin family* of extracellular matrix receptors, rather than to the cadherin family of cell-cell adhesion proteins used in desmosomes.

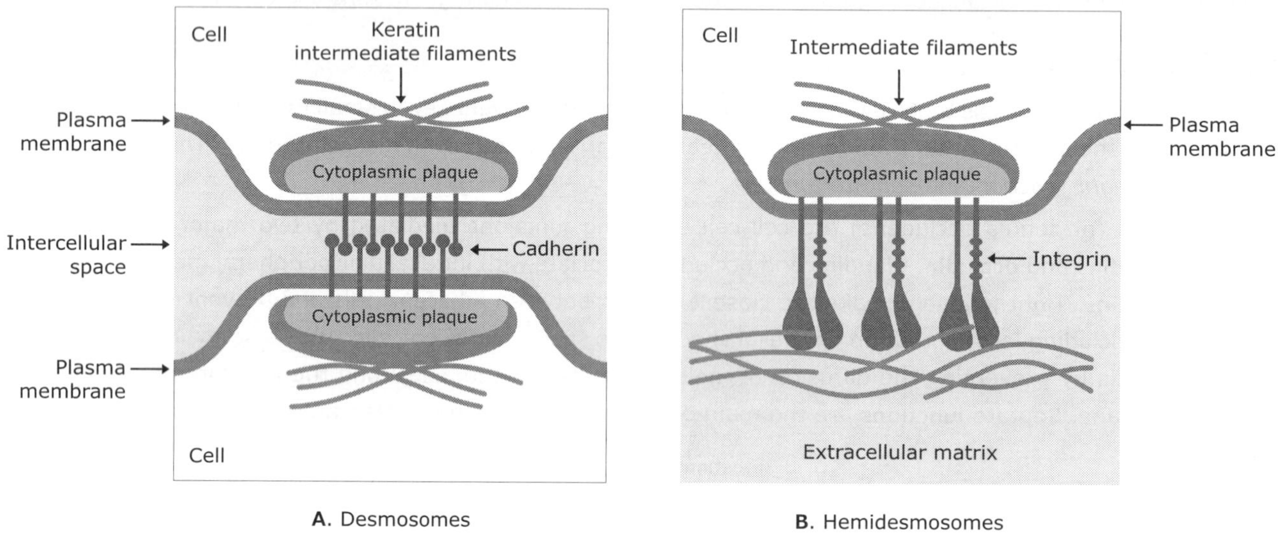

Figure 3.76 **A.** Schematic drawing of a desmosome. On the cytoplasmic surface of each interacting plasma membrane is a cytoplasmic plaque. Each plaque is associated with a network of keratin intermediate filaments. Transmembrane adhesion proteins, which belong to the cadherin family of cell-cell adhesion molecules, bind to the plaques and interact through their extracellular domains to hold the adjacent membranes together. **B.** Schematic drawing of a hemidesmosome, joining adjacent epithelial cell membranes to the underlying basal lamina.

Table 3.15 Characteristics of anchoring junctions

Junction type	Transmembrane protein	Intracellular linkage
Zonula adherens	Cadherin	Actin filaments
Focal contact	Integrin	Actin filaments
Desmosome	Cadherin	Intermediate filaments
Hemi-desmosome	Integrin	Intermediate filaments

Communicating junctions

Communicating junctions mediate the passage of chemical or electrical signals from one interacting cell to its partner.

Gap junction: Gap junctions serve as direct connections between the cytoplasms of adjacent cells. They act as channels, which allow inorganic ions and other small water-soluble molecules up to 1000 Da to pass directly from the cytoplasm of one cell to the cytoplasm of the other, thereby coupling the cells both electrically and metabolically.

In nervous tissue, some neurons are connected by gap junctions through which ions pass rapidly, thereby allowing very rapid transmission of electric signals. Gap junctions also allow the passage of some intracellular signaling molecules, such as cAMP and calcium, between adjacent cells, potentially coordinating the responses of cells in tissues. Gap junction channels are unusual in that they typically remain open at rest, and only close under specific conditions. They close in response to low pH, high intracellular Ca^{2+} concentration and voltage differences between cells. Gap junctions consist of transmembrane proteins called **connexins**. All connexins have four transmembrane helices. Six connexins assemble to form a cylinder with an open aqueous pore in its center called **connexon**. When the connexons in the plasma membranes of two cells in contact are aligned, they form a continuous aqueous channel called gap junction. A completely different family of proteins, the *innexins* form the gap junction in invertebrates.

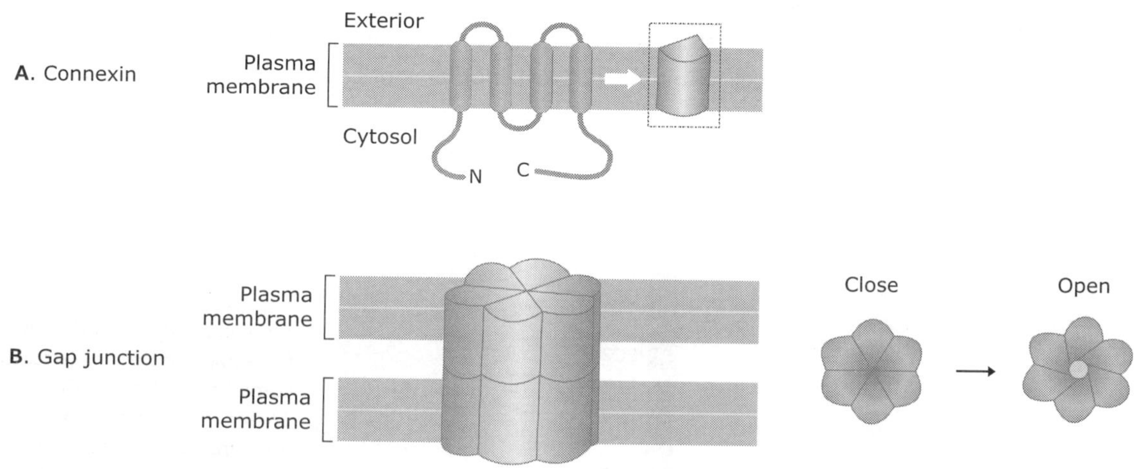

Figure 3.77 A. Structure of one connexin, which has four transmembrane domains (TM1-4). B. Gap junctional channels are comprised of connexins. Six connexins oligomerize and form connexons. Connexons from two cells form a gap junction.

Plasmodesmata: Adjacent plant cells communicate with each other through cytoplasmic connections called *plasmodesmata* (singular, plasmodesma), which function analogously to animal cell gap junctions. Plasmodesmata are intercellular channels that establish a symplastic communication pathway between neighbouring cells in plants. At each plasmodesma, the plasma membrane of one cell is continuous with that of its neighbour, creating an open channel between the two cytosols. An extension of the smooth endoplasmic reticulum called **desmotubule** passes through the pore, leaving a ring of surrounding cytoplasm through which ions and small molecules are able to pass freely between the cells. Plasmodesmata can be classified on the basis of their genesis: primary plasmodesmata and secondary plasmodesmata. The **primary plasmodesmata** are formed during cell division when the new cell wall is being established, whereas **secondary plasmodesmata** are inserted into an existing cell wall. The structure of plasmodesmata ranges from simple, characterized by a single sheath of cytoplasm, to complex, characterized by branched, H-shaped, and twinned structures.

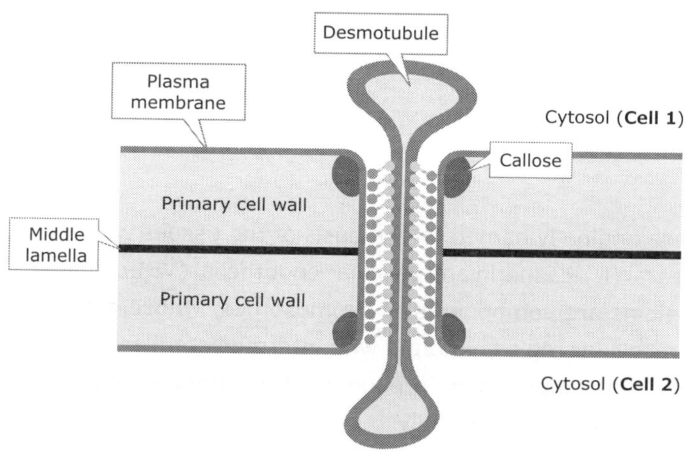

Figure 3.78 A schematic diagram of a plasmodesma - a dynamic plasma membrane and ER-based intercellular open channel.

3.17 Cell adhesion molecules

Cells adhere to each other and to the extracellular matrix through cell membrane proteins called **cell adhesion molecules (CAMs)**. CAMs consist of a group of chemically heterogeneous transmembrane proteins that fall into two categories: cell-cell adhesion molecules and cell-matrix adhesion molecules. These proteins perform a variety of functions, including involvement in cell differentiation, cell cycle regulation, cell migration, cell survival, and cell communication.

Cadherins (Calcium adhering) are cell-cell adhesion molecules. Most cadherins are single-pass transmembrane glycoprotein composed of about 700–750 amino acid residues. They are present in the plasma membrane in the form of dimers or oligomers. The large extracellular part of the polypeptide chain is usually folded into five *extracellular cadherin domains* (**EC domains**), each containing about 100 amino acid residues. The cadherins are calcium-binding proteins which hold cells together by *homophilic interactions* (molecules on one cell bind to other molecules of the same kind on adjacent cell). The extracellular domains of cadherins mediate homophilic cell-cell adhesion and the cytoplasmic tails of typical cadherins, including all classical and some non-classical ones interact with the cytoskeleton (actin or intermediate filaments) via a number of intracellular *anchor* or *adaptor proteins* (such as β-catenin, α-catenin, vinculin and plakoglobin).

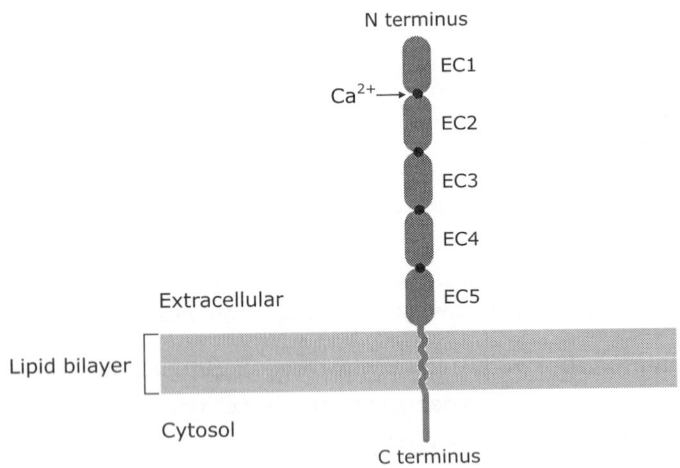

Figure 3.79
A typical classical cadherin molecule. The principle feature common to all cadherins is the presence of extracellular cadherin domains (EC domains) in the extracellular region of a membrane protein. There are Ca^{2+}-binding sites between each pair of EC domains. To generate cell-cell adhesion, the cadherin domain at the N-terminal tip of one cadherin molecule binds the N-terminal domain from a cadherin molecule on another cell.

Cadherins comprise a large superfamily with over 350 members. The most salient feature of this superfamily is the presence of a variable number of extracellular cadherin repeat domains, that are rigidified by binding Ca^{2+} ions at linker regions between these domains. Based on sequence similarity, members of cadherin superfamily can be classified into classical and non-classical cadherins.

Classical cadherins

Type I cadherins: E-cadherin, N-cadherin, R-cadherin

Type II cadherins: VE-cadherin

Non-classical cadherins

Desmosomal cadherins: Desmocollin and Desmoglein

Atypical cadherins: T-cadherin, LI-cadherin

Protocadherins: Pcdhα, Pcdhβ, and Pcdhγ

The type I and type II classical cadherins were originally named on the basis of the tissues within which they were first identified e.g., epithelial (E)-cadherin, neural (N)-cadherin and vascular endothelial (VE)-cadherin. Desmosomal cadherins such as desmocollins and desmogleins are components of desmosomes, whose extracellular cadherin repeats are responsible for adhesion and intracellular regions interact with intermediate filaments via desmosomal plaque proteins plakoglobin and desmoplakin. Protocadherins are predominantly expressed in the nervous system, and constitute the largest subgroup within the cadherin superfamily.

Two other families of transmembrane *cell-cell adhesion* molecules are *selectins* and *immunoglobulin superfamily*. **Selectins** mediate cell-cell adhesion by heterophilic binding (the molecule on one cell binds to the molecule of a different kind on adjacent cells). Each selectin is a transmembrane protein with a conserved **lectin domain** that binds to a specific oligosaccharide on another cell. It also depends on extracellular calcium to function in cell adhesion. There are at least three types of selectin: **L-selectin** on white blood cells, **P-selectin** on blood platelets and on endothelial cells and **E-selectin** on activated endothelial cells.

Immunoglobulin superfamily members mediate calcium-independent cell-cell adhesion. The members undergo both homophilic and heterophilic adhesion. Members of this family are defined by the presence of one or more copies of the immunoglobulin domains in their extracellular regions. **ICAM** (intercellular cell adhesion molecule), **VCAM** (vascular cell adhesion molecule) and **NCAM** (neural cell adhesion molecule) are important members of this *superfamily*. ICAM and VCAM on endothelial cells mediate heterophilic binding to integrins on WBCs whereas NCAM, which is expressed by various cell types, mediates homophilic binding.

Integrins are transmembrane glycoproteins and act as principal cell-matrix adhesion molecules. They are composed of two non-covalently associated transmembrane glycoprotein subunits – α and β. Integrins link the actin cytoskeleton of a cell to various external structures.

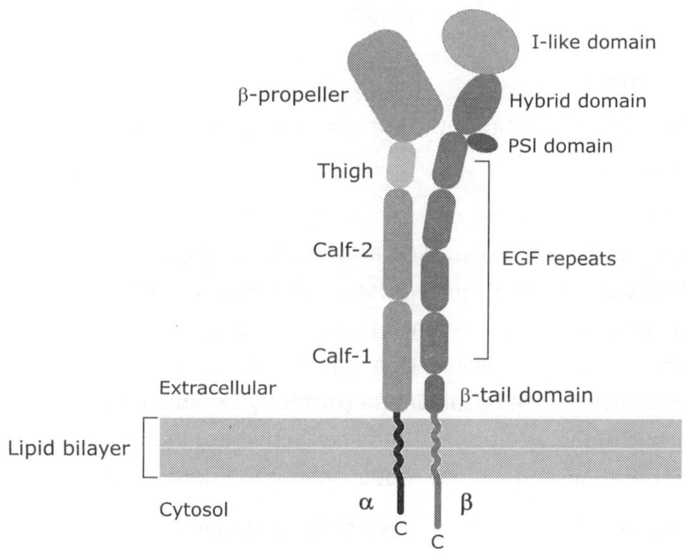

Figure 3.80
The structure of an integrin. Integrins are heterodimers of non-covalently associated a and β-subunits. The size varies, but typically the α- and β-subunits contain around 1000 and 750 amino acids, respectively. The α-chain consists of four or five extracellular domains: a β-propeller, a thigh and two calf domains. The β-subunit comprises of 4 epidermal growth factor (EGF) repeats, a hybrid domain, a I-like domain and a plexin-semaphorin-integrin (PSI) domain.

The cytoplasmic portion of each integrin molecule binds to adaptor proteins (such as talin, α-actinin, vinculin) that interacts with the actin filaments inside the cell. The extracellular portion of the integrin then binds to molecules (such as fibronectin, fibrinogen, collagen) in the extracellular matrix. The binding of integrins to their ligands depends on extracellular divalent cations (such as Ca^{2+} or Mg^{2+}). Some integrins can also bind cells together through heterophilic interactions with other cell-surface proteins, although most integrins mediate the attachment of cells to the extracellular matrix.

3.18 Extracellular matrix of animals

The cells of multicellular organisms are embedded in an extracellular matrix consisting of secreted proteins and polysaccharides. The extracellular matrix fills the spaces between cells, and binds cells and tissues together. One type of extracellular matrix is a sheet-like **basal laminae**, upon which layers of epithelial cells rest. The extracellular matrix is most abundant in connective tissues. Extracellular matrices are composed of tough fibrous proteins embedded in a gel-like polysaccharide ground substance. The components of the extracellular matrix can be divided into several groups:

Structural proteins (such as collagens and elastins)

The major structural protein of the extracellular matrix is **collagen**, which is the single most abundant protein in animal tissues. Connective tissues also contain *elastic fibers*, composed principally of a protein called **elastin** (collagens and elastins are discussed in chapter 1).

Proteoglycan (such as heparan sulfate, chondroitin sulfate)

Proteoglycans are a subclass of *glycoproteins* in which the carbohydrates are **glycosaminoglycans**. All of the glycosaminoglycans except hyaluronic acid are found covalently attached to protein forming *proteoglycan*.

The fibrous structural proteins of the extracellular matrix are embedded in gels formed from polysaccharides called **glycosaminoglycans** (GAGs), which consist of repeating units of disaccharides, $[\text{Acidic sugar} — \text{Amino sugar}]_n$. Amino sugar of the disaccharide is either *N*-acetylglucosamine or *N*-acetylgalactosamine, which in most cases is sulfated and the second is usually acidic (either glucuronic acid or iduronic acid) sugar. GAGs are highly negatively charged. There are four main groups of GAGs: *hyaluronan, chondroitin sulfate* and *dermatan sulfate, heparan sulfate* and *heparin* and *keratan sulfate*. Hyaluronan is the simplest of the GAGs. Except hyaluronan, all of the other GAGs are linked to proteins in the form of proteoglycans. The polysaccharide chains are mainly assembled on the core protein in the Golgi complex before delivery to the exterior of the cell by exocytosis.

Adhesion proteins (such as laminins and fibronectins)

Adhesion proteins, the third class of extracellular matrix constituents, are responsible for linking the components of the matrix both to one another and to the surface of cells.

Laminins are extracellular heterotrimeric glycoproteins composed of three polypeptide chains (α, β and γ) that are disulfide-bonded. Each of the polypeptide chains is more than 1500 amino acid residues long. Five types of α-chains, four types of β-chains, and three types of γ-chains are known, and various combinations of these subunits can assemble to form a large variety of different laminins. Each isoform tends to have a specific tissue distribution. The α-chain of laminin contains globular **LG domain** which mediates calcium-dependent binding to specific carbohydrates. Laminins play the central role in organizing and establishing the **basal lamina** (formerly called **basement membrane**). Their primary role is in cell-matrix attachment, but many additional biological activities, including promoting cell growth and migration, tumor growth, nerve regeneration and wound repair have been demonstrated.

Fibronectin is an extracellular glycoprotein, present in all vertebrates. It exists as a dimer, consisting of two nearly identical monomers linked by a pair of disulfide bonds at their C-terminal ends. Both are encoded by a single gene but differences appear due to alternative splicing. Each chain is about 2500 amino acids long and is folded into multiple domains. Each domain is specialized for binding to a particular molecule or to a cell. Each chain consists of three types of fibronectin repeats (termed **FN repeats**): 12 fibronectin type I repeats (FN I), 2 fibronectin type II repeats (FN II) and 15-17 fibronectin type III repeats (FN III). FN I repeating unit is about 40 amino-acid residues in length and contain two disulfide bonds; FN II repeating unit is approximately 60 amino acid residues long and with two intrachain disulfide bonds; and FN III repeating unit is about 90 amino acid residues long and without any disulfide bonds.

Fibronectins help attach cells to the extracellular matrix by binding to ECM components (particularly collagens), proteoglycans and to cell surface adhesion molecules such as integrins. A specific Arg-Gly-Asp tripeptide sequence (termed as **RGD sequence**) present on type III fibronectin repeat is required for integrin binding and mediates cell adhesion. Fibronectin plays a major role in cell adhesion, growth, migration and differentiation. Fibronectins are of two types– soluble plasma fibronectin and insoluble cellular fibronectin. **Soluble plasma fibronectin** is a major protein component of blood plasma and is produced in the liver by hepatocytes. **Insoluble cellular fibronectin** is secreted by various cells, particularly fibroblast, as soluble protein dimer and then assembled into an insoluble matrix.

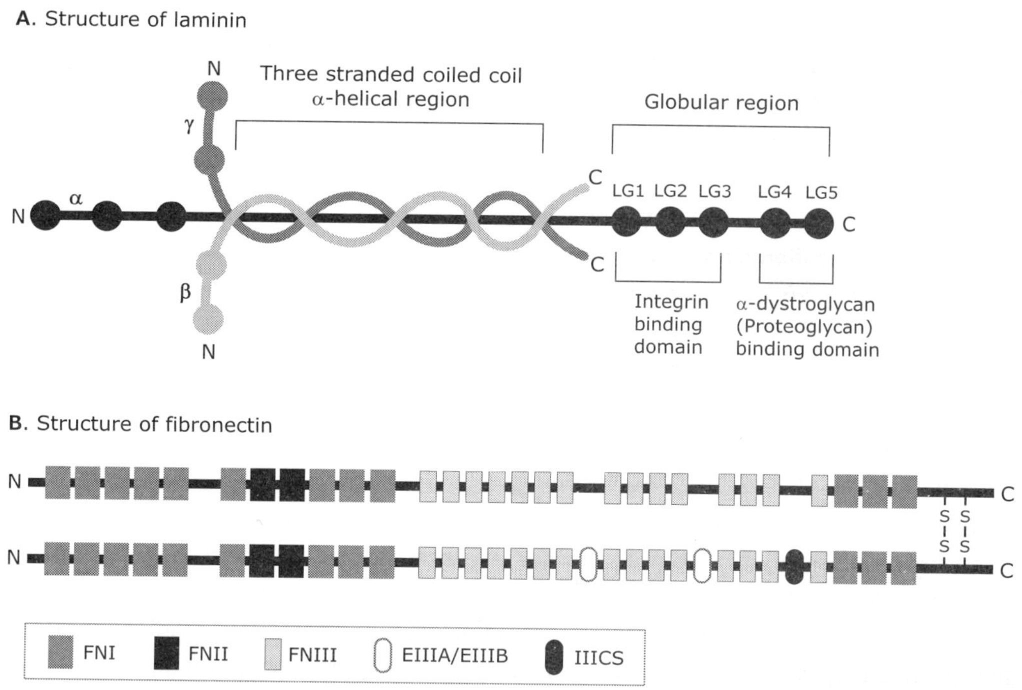

Figure 3.81 **A**. Structure of laminin – a heterotrimeric glycoprotein. **B**. A fibronectin molecule consists of two nearly identical polypeptide chains joined by two disulfide bonds near their carboxyl ends. Each polypeptide of a cellular fibronectin heterodimer, consisting of 12 FN type I repeats (FNI), 2 FN type II repeats (FNII), and 15 FN type III repeats (FNIII). The lower subunit is splice variant, which can include two alternatively spliced FNIII domains (EIIIA/EIIIB) and one FNIII connecting segment (IIICS). Though both subunits of fibronectin are encoded by a single gene, they contain different arrangements of domains due to alternative splicing.

Table 3.16 Comparison of extracellular matrix of animals and plants

	Animals	**Plants**
Chemical nature	Protein rich	Carbohydrate rich
Structural fiber	Collagens and elastins	Cellulose
Components of hydrated matrix	Proteoglycans	Pectins
Adhesive molecules	Fibronectins and laminins	Hemicelluloses

3.19 Plant cell wall

Plant cells are surrounded by rigid cell walls, made up of insoluble secreted macromolecules. These macromolecules in a typical plant cell wall include carbohydrates (major component), proteins and phenolic compounds. The composition of cell walls varies among species and tissues. The plant cell wall plays many important roles - determining size and shape, providing mechanical support for the plant body, conducting water and nutrients, defending against biotic and abiotic stresses, and others.

Structural components of plant cell walls

Structural polysaccharides

The cell wall contains several types of carbohydrates. These carbohydrates occur in the form of polysaccharides and can be classified into two major categories: *microfibrillar* and *matrix polysaccharides*.

Microfibrillar polysaccharide is made up of cellulose, a linear unbranched polymer of D-glucose residues. Several cellulose chains (18 to 24) then associate in parallel with one another to form cord-like structures of various diameters (from 20 nm to as high as 60 nm in diameter) called **cellulose microfibrils**. The extensive noncovalent bonding (such as

Van der Waals forces and hydrogen bonding) between adjacent chains within a cellulose microfibril gives this structure a high tensile strength. Cellulose is also water insoluble, chemically stable and relatively resistant to chemical and enzymatic attack. Cellulose microfibrils are synthesized by plasma membrane-bound enzyme **cellulose synthase** (CESA), which are oligomerize into six-lobed rosette structures termed **cellulose synthase complex**. Different isoforms of cellulose synthase are responsible for cellulose synthesis during primary and secondary cell wall synthesis. In *Arabidopsis*, CESA1, CESA3 and CESA6 are involved in primary wall cellulose synthesis, and CESA4, CESA7 and CESA8 in secondary wall synthesis.

In growing cells, cellulose microfibrils are mostly arranged in a transverse orientation that is perpendicular to the axis of elongation. As a consequence of transversely oriented cellulose microfibrils, radial cell expansion is restricted while longitudinal cell expansion is promoted. There is a relationship between cortical microtubules and cellulose microfibril deposition. The *microtubule–microfibril alignment hypothesis* proposes that cortical microtubules, which lie beneath the plasma membrane, provide tracks for cellulose synthase complexes that convert glucose molecules into cellulose microfibrils. As a result, the orientation of extracellular microfibrils synthesized by cellulose synthase complexes remain parallel with cortical microtubules.

Matrix polysaccharides: Cellulose microfibrils are embedded in a matrix consisting of proteins and non-cellulosic polysaccharides. Non-cellulosic matrix polysaccharides are synthesized by membrane-bound enzymes in the Golgi complex and are delivered to the cell wall via exocytosis. Two major types of matrix polysaccharides are **hemicelluloses** (cellulose-binding glycans) and **pectins** (acid polysaccharides). Hemicelluloses are a heterogeneous group of highly branched polysaccharides include xylans, xyloglucans, mannans, and glucomannans. Pectins, gel-forming components of the matrix, are heterogeneous group of polysaccharides, characteristically containing acidic sugars such as galacturonic acid. It has roles in forming connections between plant cells, adjusting pH and ion balance, recognizing foreign molecules to alert the cell to the presence of microbes and establishing cell wall porosity.

Lignin

Lignin is an amorphous, irregular and highly branched phenolic polymer, consisting of **p-hydroxyphenyl** (H), **guaiacyl** (G) and **syringyl** (S) units, derived from the three lignin monomer precursors (called **monolignols**) p-coumaryl, coniferyl and sinapyl alcohols, respectively. These monolignols are derived from phenylalanine (or tyrosine) through complex *phenylpropanoid pathways*. Although lignin is amorphous, it reinforces cell wall structure and often functions as a physical barrier against pathogen attack.

Structural proteins

The cell wall also contains several classes of structural proteins. These proteins usually are classified according to their predominant amino acid composition— for example, **hydroxyproline-rich glycoprotein**, **glycine-rich protein** and **proline-rich protein**. With the exception of glycine-rich proteins, all are glycosylated and contain hydroxyproline. **Extensin**, a major structural protein in the cell walls of higher plants, is a hydroxyproline-rich glycoprotein. It seems to contribute to plant defense, helping to protect against pathogen attack, elicitation, or mechanical wounding. Cell walls also contain **expansin** proteins, a group of non-enzymatic pH-dependent wall-loosening proteins. They cause pH-dependent cell wall extension.

Primary and secondary cell walls: Plant cell walls are commonly classified into two major types: *primary* and *secondary* cell walls. Plant cell first secretes a relatively thin and flexible wall called the **primary cell wall**. When the cell matures and stops growing, it strengthens its wall. Some plant cells do this simply by secreting hardening substances into the primary wall. Other cells add a secondary cell wall between the plasma membrane and the primary wall. The **secondary wall** is deposited after cells cease enlargement. It is more specialized in structure and composition as compared to the primary cell wall. They are often quite thick and layered. It is comprised of three layers: **S1**, **S2** and **S3**; each of these layers has cellulose laid down at a different angle (referred to as the microfibril angle) as well as different thicknesses with the S2 layer being much thicker than S1 and S3.

Middle lamella: A thin layer of material, the middle lamella, is present at the junction, where the walls of neighboring cells come into contact. It acts as cementing material. The composition of the middle lamella differs from the rest of the wall. It is high in **pectin** (as calcium pectate) and may be complexed with hydroxyproline-rich glycoproteins.

3.20 Cell signaling

All cells receive and respond to signals from their surroundings. This is accomplished by a variety of extracellular signal molecules that are either secreted by the signaling cells or expressed on the surface of signaling cells. These signal molecules bind to receptors expressed by other cells, thereby integrating and coordinating the functions of the many individual cells that make up multicellular organisms. Each cell in a multicellular organism is programmed to respond to specific extracellular signal molecules. Signaling by a signal molecule may be **cell-cell contact-dependent** or **cell-cell contact independent**. Extracellular secretory signal molecules perform *cell-cell contact-independent signaling.* This mode of signaling and usually involves the following steps:

1. Synthesis and release of the signal molecule by the signaling cell;
2. Transport of the signal molecule to the target cell;
3. Binding of the signal by a specific receptor leading to its activation;
4. Initiation of signal-transduction pathways.

Some extracellular secretory signal molecules operate over long distances (signaling to cells far away); others work only with immediate neighbors. In animals, extracellular signaling by secretory signal molecules can be classified into—*endocrine*, *paracrine* and *autocrine* signaling.

In **endocrine signaling**, the signaling molecules, called *hormones*, act on target cells distantly located from their site of synthesis. It is long-range signaling in which a signal molecule is transported by the bloodstream. The blood carries the signal molecules far and wide, allowing them to act on target cells that may lie anywhere in the body.

In **paracrine signaling**, the signal molecules released by a cell affect target cells only in close proximity. Usually, the signaling and target cells in paracrine signaling are of different cell types.

In **autocrine signaling**, the signal molecules produce an effect on the same cell that produces it. One important example of autocrine signaling is the response of certain types of T-cells to an antigenic stimulus by synthesizing a growth factor that drives their own proliferation, thereby increasing the number of responsive T-cells and amplifying the immune response.

Some signal molecules are not secreted by the signaling cells but are expressed on the cell surface. These signal molecules participate in **cell-cell contact-dependent** signaling (also termed **juxtacrine signaling)**. In this type of **signaling**, signal molecules do not diffuse from the cell producing it, and cell-bearing signal molecules interact with receptor proteins of adjacent responding cells. Unlike other modes of cell signaling, juxtacrine signaling requires physical contact between the cells involved. *Notch signaling* and *classical cadherin signaling* are examples of juxtacrine signaling.

3.20.1 Signal molecules

Signal molecules, act as chemical messengers, are low molecular weight chemically heterogeneous compounds. These molecules can be classified based on the following parameters:

Based on the location: Signal molecules can be divided into *membrane-bound* and *secretory* signal molecules. Membrane-bound signal molecules present on the surface of the cells and mediate *cell-cell contact-dependent signaling*, whereas secretory signal molecules perform *cell-cell contact-independent signaling*. Most of the signal molecules are secretory in nature.

Based on the distance over which signals are transmitted: The extracellular secretory signal molecules can be – *endocrine* (act on distantly located target cells), *paracrine* (act on neighboring target cells), and *autocrine* (act on the same cell producing a signal molecule) – based on the distance signal molecules are transported.

Based on solubility: Extracellular signal molecules fall into two broad categories based on solubility–**lipophilic** molecules (soluble in lipid) and **hydrophilic** molecules (soluble in water). These signal molecules are released by signaling cells and produce a specific response only in target cells that have either **cell-surface receptors** or **intracellular receptors**

for these signal molecules. Small *lipophilic* signal molecules can diffuse across the plasma membrane and interact with intracellular receptors, whereas *hydrophilic* signal molecules bind to cell-surface receptors. Few lipophilic signal molecules bind to cell-surface receptors also. Most of these molecules are members of eicosanoids, which include prostaglandins, prostacyclin, thromboxanes and leukotrienes.

When a signal molecule binds to a cell-surface receptor that is embedded in the plasma membrane of the target cell, the receptor activates one or more intracellular signaling pathways involving **second messengers**. Finally, the intracellular signaling pathways alter the activity of effector proteins and, thereby, the behavior of the cell. Depending on the signal molecule's nature and the receiving cell's type, these effectors can be metabolic enzymes, transcription regulatory proteins, or cytoskeletal proteins.

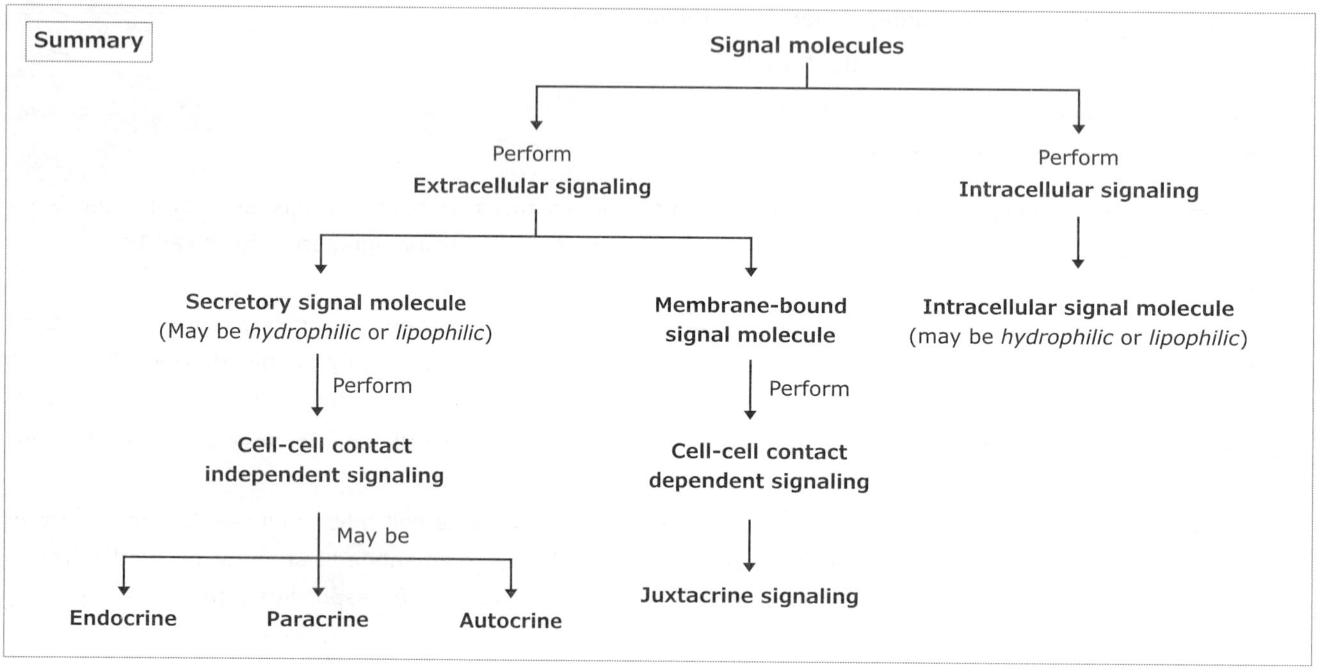

3.20.2 Receptors

Regardless of the nature of the signal, the target cell responds by means of a *receptor*, which reversibly binds the signal molecule and then initiates a response in the target cell. The cellular response to a particular extracellular signal molecule depends on its binding to a specific receptor located on the surface of a target cell or within the cell (nucleus or cytosol). Receptors are chemically *protein* or *glycoprotein* molecules that bind to signal molecules (termed *ligands*). The binding of a ligand to its receptor causes a conformational change in the receptor that initiates a sequence of reactions leading to a specific cellular response. Based on location, receptors are classified into two broad categories - **intracellular receptors** and **cell-surface receptors**.

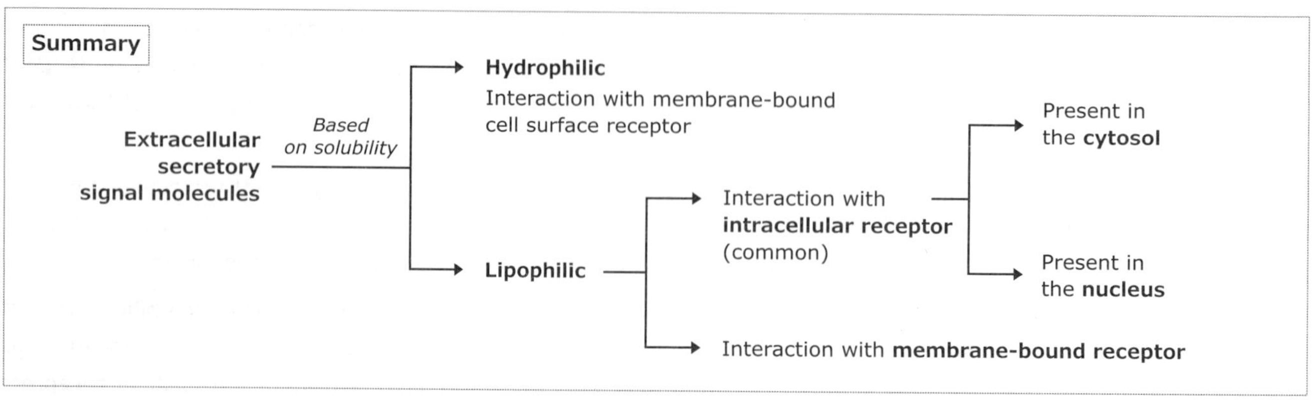

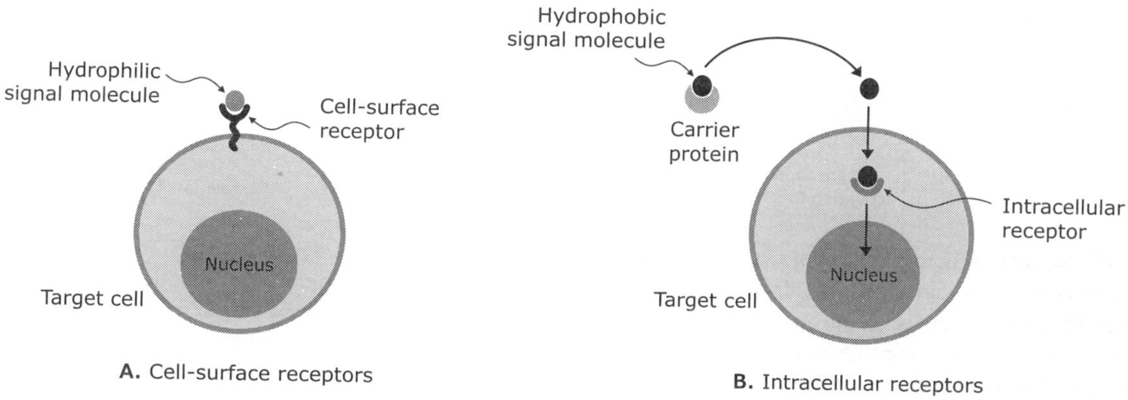

Figure 3.82 The binding of extracellular signal molecules to either cell-surface or intracellular receptors. **A.** Most signal molecules are hydrophilic and are therefore unable to cross the target cell's plasma membrane directly; instead, they bind to cell-surface receptors, which in turn generate signals inside the target cell. **B.** Some small signal molecules, by contrast, diffuse across the plasma membrane and bind to receptor proteins inside the target cell—either in the cytosol or in the nucleus. Many of these small signal molecules are hydrophobic and poorly soluble in aqueous solutions; they are therefore transported in the bloodstream and other extracellular fluids bound to *carrier proteins*, from which they dissociate before entering the target cell. In target cells, these signal molecules pass through the plasma membrane by simple diffusion.

Intracellular receptors

Intracellular receptors are located in the *cytosol* or the *nucleus*. These include receptors for *steroid hormones* (such as corticosteroids, sex steroids and vitamin D), *non-steroid hormones* (such as thyroid hormone and retinoic acid) as well as different 'orphan' receptors. All intracellular receptors are structurally related and belong to the **nuclear receptor superfamily**. Within the cell, the intracellular receptor-ligand complex controls the activities of responsive genes. A large number of nuclear receptors have been identified through sequence similarity to known receptors but have no identified natural ligand and are referred to as **nuclear orphan receptor**. Nuclear receptors (NRs) are a family of highly conserved *transcription factors* that regulate transcription in response to small lipophilic signal molecules. They are ubiquitous and unique to the animal kingdom.

Nuclear receptors act as regulatory transcription factors and bind with regulatory DNA sequences termed **response elements**. They can bind with response elements as monomers (for example, steroidogenic factor-1 receptor), homodimers (for example, steroid receptors) or heterodimers (for example, retinoic acid receptor, thyroid hormone receptor and vitamin D receptor). Nuclear receptors positively regulate gene expression by binding to response elements in target genes and recruiting (in a ligand-dependent manner) diverse co-activator complexes that modify chromatin and recruit core transcription factors.

Structure of nuclear receptors: Nuclear receptors share a common structural organization. Most members of the nuclear receptor superfamily consist of an N-terminal **activation domain** (also known as the A/B region), a central **DNA binding domain** (DBD) and a C-terminal **ligand-binding domain** (LBD). N-terminal domain contains an AF-1 (activation function-1) sequence which functions as a ligand-independent transcriptional activator. AF-1 is recognized by co-activators and/or other transcription factors. The DBD is comprised of two zinc-binding motifs that each coordinate a zinc ion through four precisely positioned cysteines. The LBD is responsible for ligand binding. This domain also contains a ligand-regulated AF-2 (activation function-2) sequence which is necessary for recruiting transcriptional co-activators. The LBD also contributes to homodimerization and heterodimerization of many nuclear receptors.

The receptors for **steroid hormones** are located in the cytosol. In the cytosol, it remains inactive after making a complex with *heat-shock protein* (HSP). Ligand binding with it (receptor) in the cytosol results in the dissociation of HSPs and translocation from the cytosol into the nucleus. Once the ligand-receptor complex is in the nucleus, the DNA-binding domain of receptor binds to the specific *hormone-response element* of the DNA. Steroid receptors bind as *homodimers* to inverted repeats spaced by three nucleotides spacer sequence. A **hormone response element** (HRE) is a *cis*-acting regulatory DNA sequence that a regulatory transcription factor recognizes with high affinity. HRE typically contains two consensus hexameric half-sites.

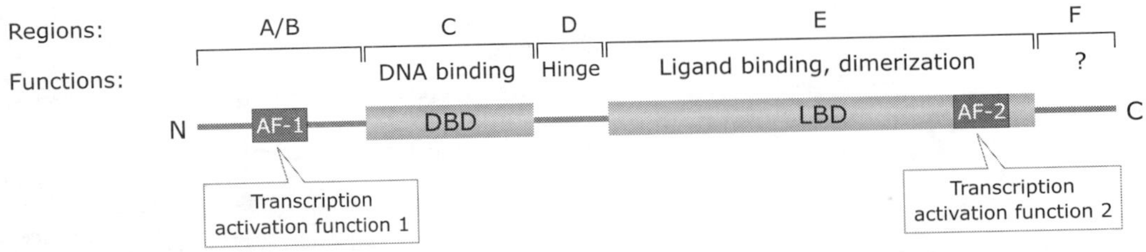

Figure 3.83 Nuclear receptors consist of five to six structural and functional domains denoted A to F. The DNA binding domain (DBD) is composed of two zinc-finger motifs and mediates sequence-specific DNA recognition. Transcriptional regulation is mainly mediated by the multifunctional ligand-binding domain (LBD), which contains a ligand-binding pocket and a dimerization site. This domain also has the ligand-induced activation function (known as AF2). The N-terminal A/B region contains a ligand-independent AF-1 sequence. The short D region corresponds to a linker between DBDs and LBDs and finally the C-terminal F domain, for which no clear function has been assigned.

The identity of a response element resides in three features: the sequence of the base pairs in the half-site, the number of base pairs between the half-sites and the relative orientation of the two half-sites. Thus, each receptor protein dimer that binds the DNA has to recognize the sequence, spacing and orientation of the half-sites within their response element.

Unlike the steroid hormone receptor proteins, the thyroid hormone receptors are located in the nucleus bound to DNA even in the absence of their ligand (thyroid hormone). Its response element has two half-sites, but unlike the case with the steroid receptors, the thyroid hormone receptor binds to only one of the half-sites. The other DNA half-site binds to the **retinoid X receptor** (RXR). When the thyroid hormone receptor (abbreviated TR) and RXR bind to the two DNA half-sites of the hormone response element, the two receptors form a *heterodimer*. In the absence of their thyroid hormone ligand, the thyroid receptors recruit corepressor proteins that inhibit gene transcription. Thus, although the TR and RXR are bound to DNA, the hormone response element is inhibited. When the thyroid receptor binds to its ligand, the corepressor proteins are removed and degraded by proteasomes, while coactivator proteins are recruited. Thus, the nuclear receptor proteins for thyroid hormone cannot stimulate gene transcription until they bind to their hormone ligands.

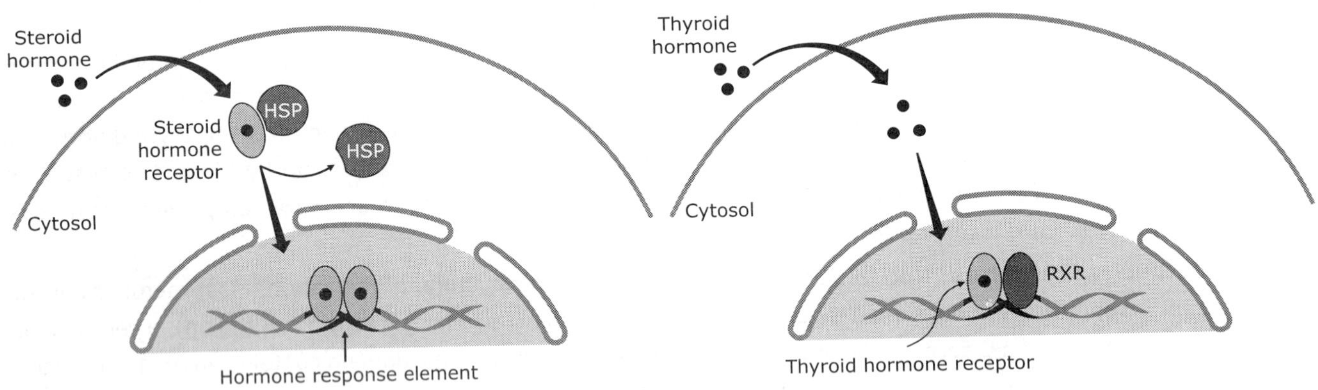

Figure 3.84 Classical steroid hormone receptors remain associated with heat-shock protein (HSP) in the cytosol. Hormone binding causes dissociation of steroid receptors from HSP complexes and allows binding to hormone response element as homodimer. The thyroid-hormone receptors are heterodimeric nuclear receptors bind constitutively to DNA with RXRs (retinoid X receptors) as obligate partners. In the absence of ligand, receptors are often complexed with corepressor proteins. Ligand binding to the nuclear receptor causes dissociation of corepressor and recruitment of coactivator proteins.

Cell-surface receptors

All hydrophilic signal molecules, as well as some lipophilic signal molecules, bind to the cell-surface receptors. These cell-surface receptors act as signal transducers by converting an extracellular ligand-binding event into intracellular signals. Numerous intracellular signal molecules, which are often called **second messengers** (the 'first messengers' being the extracellular signals), relay signals received by cell-surface receptors into the cell interior.

Second messengers are generated in large amounts in response to receptor activation and diffuse away from their source, spreading the signal to other parts of the cell. Some, such as cAMP and Ca^{2+}, are water-soluble and diffuse in the cytosol, while others, such as diacylglycerol (DAG), are lipid-soluble and diffuse in the plane of the plasma membrane. In either case, they pass the signal on by binding to and altering the behavior of selected signaling or effector proteins. Most cell-surface receptor proteins belong to one of three classes:

1. G protein-coupled receptors (GPCRs)
2. Ion-channel-coupled receptors, also known as *transmitter-gated ion channels* or *ionotropic receptors*
3. Enzyme-linked receptors

3.20.3 GPCR and G-proteins

GPCRs are the largest family of cell-surface receptors that transmit signals to intracellular targets via the intermediary action of trimeric GTP-binding proteins called **G-proteins**. GPCRs are present in all eukaryotes. They include the receptors for many neurotransmitters and hormones. In addition, the GPCR family includes a large number of receptors that are responsible for smell, light and taste. Despite the chemical and functional diversity of the signal molecules that bind to them, all GPCRs have a common structure. GPCRs consist of a single transmembrane polypeptide of multipass nature. They cross the lipid bilayer *seven times* and are therefore called **serpentine receptors** as well.

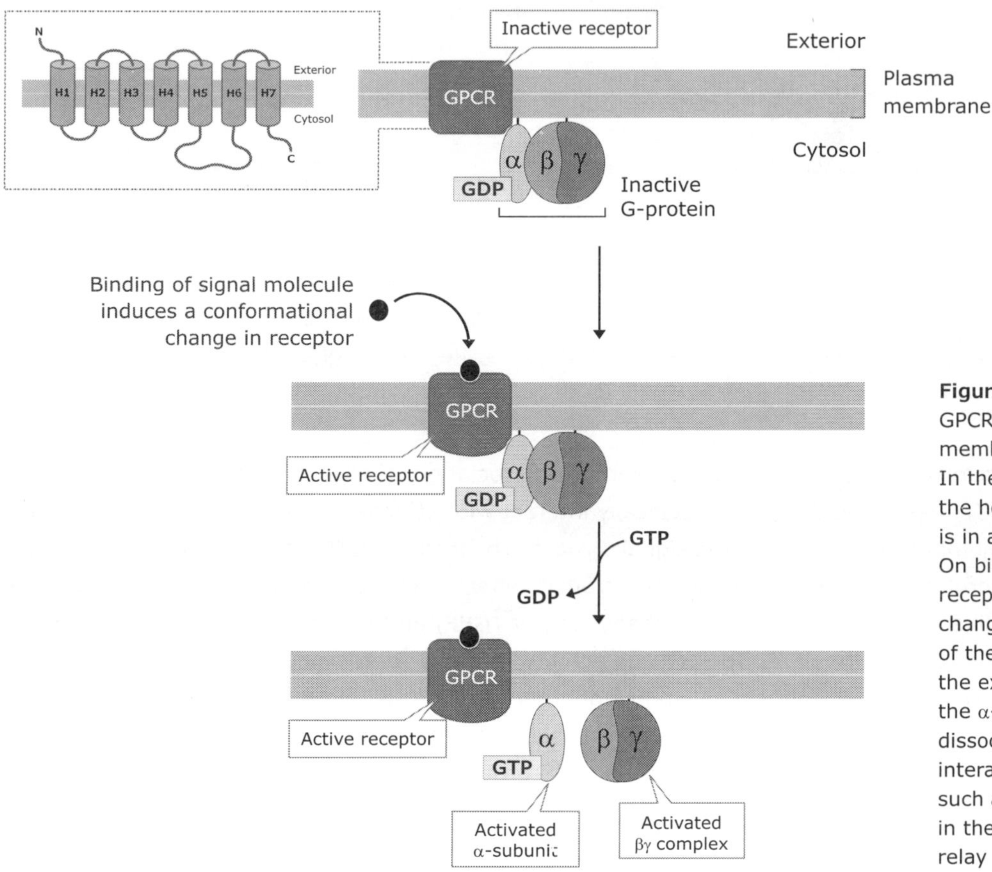

Figure 3.85
GPCRs typically have seven membrane-spanning domains. In the absence of signal molecule, the heterotrimeric G-protein complex is in an inactive GDP-bound form. On binding of signal molecule to the receptor, there is a conformational change of the receptor and activation of the G-protein. This results from the exchange of GDP with GTP on the α-subunit, after which α and βγ dissociate—both of which then interact with various targets, such as enzymes and ion channels in the plasma membrane, which relay the signal onward.

GPCRs are linked to **trimeric G-proteins** (simply **G-proteins**). G-proteins are **GTPase switch proteins**. These proteins are turned *on* when bound to GTP and turned *off* when bound to GDP. G-proteins are attached to the cytosolic face of the plasma membrane. Ligand binding to GPCR leads to activation of a trimeric G-protein. All trimeric G-proteins contain three subunits: α, β and γ. The α and γ-subunits of G-proteins are anchored to the membrane lipids covalently. The β-subunit is always complexed with the γ-subunit, forming the heterodimeric structure $G_{\beta\gamma}$. The α-subunit is a GTPase switch protein that alternates between an active state with bound GTP and an inactive state with bound GDP.

Box 3.2 GTP-binding proteins

GTP-binding proteins act as molecular switches. A GTP-binding protein switches between an 'on' state when GTP is bound and an 'off' state when GDP is bound. In the 'on' state, they have intrinsic GTPase activity and hydrolyze their bound GTP to GDP. There are two major types of GTP-binding proteins:

Small **monomeric GTP-binding proteins** (also called **monomeric GTPases**).

Large, **heterotrimeric GTP-binding proteins** (also called **G-proteins**).

Monomeric GTP-binding proteins are monomeric proteins with molecular masses of 20–40 kDa and constitute a superfamily consisting of more than 100 members. This superfamily is classified into at least five families: the Ras, Rho, Rab, Sar1-Arf, and Ran families. Most monomeric GTP-binding proteins are localized either in the cytosol or on membranes. These small proteins have two interconvertible forms: GDP-bound inactive and GTP-bound active forms. Specific regulatory proteins control interconversion. *GTPase-activating proteins* (**GAPs**) drive the proteins into an 'off' state by stimulating them to hydrolyze their bound GTP to GDP. Conversely, *guanine nucleotide exchange factors* (**GEFs**) activate GTP-binding proteins by promoting the release of bound GDP, which allows a new GTP to bind.

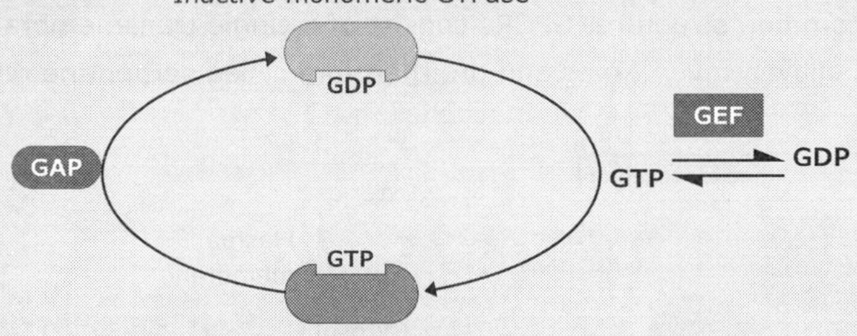

Figure 3.86
The regulation of a monomeric GTPase.

Heterotrimeric G proteins are cytosolic, membrane-associated proteins made up of three subunits: α, β and γ. It is activated when GTP binds to the G_α subunit. G_α subunit also has intrinsic GTPase activity. GTP hydrolysis to GDP inactivates the G-protein. The activated GPCR promotes its activation by allowing GDP dissociation and GTP association i.e., serves as the GEF. Hydrolysis of bound GTP is accelerated by GAPs. Regulators of *G protein-signaling* (**RGS**) proteins act as GAPs for G-proteins.

Binding of a trimeric G-protein to an activated receptor leads to dissociation of GDP, binding of GTP to G_α, and dissociation of G_α-GTP from $G_{\beta\gamma}$. G_α-GTP and $G_{\beta\gamma}$ can specifically interact with effector proteins such as enzymes and ion channels in the plasma membrane, which relay the signal onward. The intrinsic GTPase activity of G_α inactivates G_α-GTP by catalyzing GTP hydrolysis. G_α-GDP then dissociates from its effector and reassociates with $G_{\beta\gamma}$. Thus, when a GPCR is activated, it acts like a *guanine nucleotide exchange factor* (**GEF**) and induces the α-subunit to release its bound GDP, allowing GTP to bind in its place. The GTPase activity of the G_α determines the length of time that the signal remains on. It possesses a built-in mechanism of signal termination; within a short time the G_α-subunit undergoes auto-inactivation due to its GTPase activity. In many cases, a protein termed **RGS** (regulator of G-protein signaling) accelerates GTP hydrolysis by the G_α subunit. Thus, RGS proteins act as α-subunit-specific **GAPs**.

The α-subunit defines the basic properties of a heterotrimeric G-protein. About 20 distinct types of α-subunit have been identified in mammals. These fall into four main classes on the basis of both sequence similarities and functions. The activation of a specific G-protein may cause activation or inhibition of a particular effector. All effector proteins in GPCR signal transduction pathways are either ion channels or membrane-bound enzymes that catalyze the formation of one or more of the *second messengers*.

Problem

Suppose a patient is suffering from a disorder in which adenylyl cyclase is non-functional. As a result, cAMP levels are not readily increased by hormones. Explain why the infusion of cAMP probably will not remedy of the problem.

Solution: cAMP is a polar molecule that does not readily traverse the plasma membrane. If a more hydrophobic derivative were used to overcome the permeability problem, there would be no tissue specificity, and all cells would have increased cAMP levels, leading to a massive, non-specific response.

Table 3.17 Classes of trimeric G-proteins based on amino acid sequence relatedness of the α-subunits

G_α class	Some members	Action mediated by	Associated effector(s)
G_S	$G\alpha_s$	α	activates adenylyl cyclase
	$G\alpha_{olf}$	α	activates adenylyl cyclase
$G_{i/o}$	$G\alpha_i$	α	inhibits adenylyl cyclase
		βγ	activates K^+ channels
	$G\alpha_t$	α	activates cGMP phosphodiesterase
	$G\alpha_o$	βγ	activates K^+ channels; inactivates Ca^{2+} channels
		α and βγ	activates phospholipase C-β
	$G\alpha_{gust}$	α	activates phosphodiesterase
$G_{q/11}$	$G\alpha_q$	α	activates phospholipase C-β
	$G\alpha_{11}$	α	activates phospholipase C-β
$G_{12/13}$	$G\alpha_{12}$, $G\alpha_{13}$	α	activation of the RhoGEF

G_s mediated signal transduction

Many GPCRs exert their effects *via* G-protein called G_s. In the case of G_s, the $G_{s\alpha}$ subunit activates effector, **adenylyl cyclase** (or **adenylate cyclase**). Because this G-protein is involved in enzyme *activation*, it is called **stimulatory G-protein** (G_s). The $G_{s\alpha}$ subunit binds and hydrolyzes GTP and activates plasma membrane-bound enzyme *adenylyl cyclase*. It is a large multipass transmembrane protein with its catalytic domain on the cytosolic side of the plasma membrane. Activated adenylyl cyclase catalyzes the synthesis of cAMP from ATP. cAMP acts as a *second messenger*.

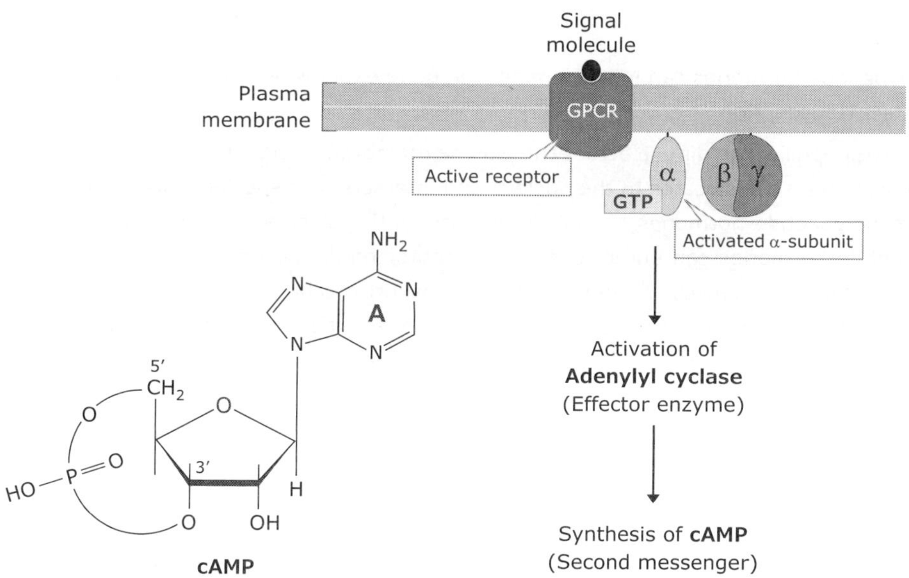

Figure 3.87
The binding of an extracellular signal molecule to its GPCR activates adenylyl cyclase via Gs and thereby increases cAMP concentration in the cytosol. cAMP is synthesized from ATP through a cyclization reaction that removes two phosphate groups as pyrophosphate. cAMP is a unstable molecule in the cell because it is hydrolyzed by specific phosphodiesterases to form 5'-AMP.

cAMP and protein kinase A

The second messenger cAMP, synthesized by adenylyl cyclase, transduces a wide variety of physiological signals in different cell types in multicellular animals. Most of the diverse effects of cAMP are mediated through activation of **protein kinase A (PKA)**, also called *cAMP-dependent protein kinase*. cAMP also induces the opening of certain types of ion channels in the plasma membrane of some highly specialized cells. PKA catalyzes the transfer of the terminal phosphate group from ATP to specific serines or threonines of selected target proteins, thereby regulating their activity. In the inactive state, PKA consists of a complex of two *catalytic* subunits and two *regulatory* subunits. The binding of cAMP to the regulatory subunits alters their conformation, causing them to dissociate from the complex. The released catalytic subunits are, thereby, activated to phosphorylate specific substrate protein molecules. The active catalytic subunits phosphorylate a number of target proteins on serine and threonine residues. Mammalian cells have at least two types of PKAs: type I is mainly in the cytosol, whereas type II is bound via its regulatory subunits to the plasma membrane, nuclear membrane, outer mitochondrial membrane and microtubules. In both types, once the catalytic subunits are freed and active, they can migrate into the nucleus (where they can phosphorylate transcription regulatory proteins), while the regulatory subunits remain in the cytosol. One of the major nuclear targets for PKA is the transcription factor **CREB** (cAMP response element binding protein), which is activated by phosphorylation. Once phosphorylated, CREB recruits the transcriptional coactivator **CBP** (CREB-binding protein), which stimulates gene transcription. Phosphorylation at a single *serine* residue greatly increases the activity of CREB bound to the **CRE** (cAMP response element), which is found in genes whose transcription is induced by cAMP.

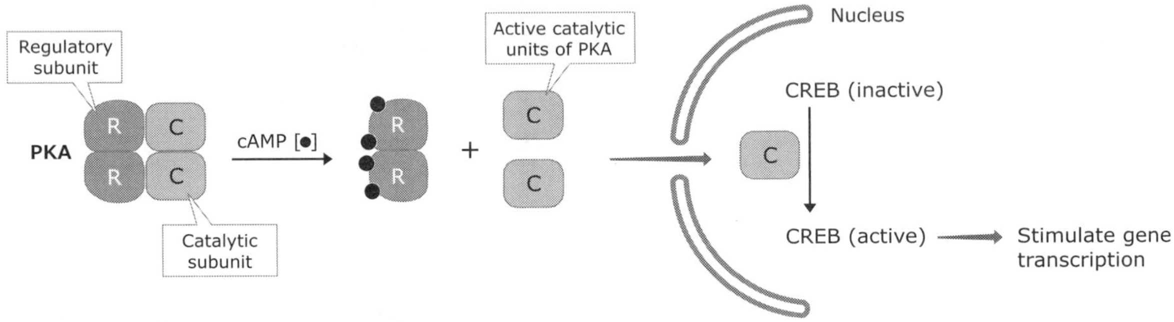

Figure 3.88 The activation of PKA. Enzyme PKA has two regulatory and two catalytic subunits. The binding of cAMP to the regulatory subunits induces a conformational change, causing these subunits to dissociate from the complex, thereby activating the catalytic subunits. Each regulatory subunit has two cAMP-binding sites. Once the catalytic subunits are freed and active, they can migrate into the nucleus (where they can phosphorylate transcription factors), while the regulatory subunits remain in the cytosol.

Problem

Both steroid hormones and some polypeptide hormones can induce changes in gene expression. Explain the difference in how these two types of hormones affect transcription.

Solution: Steroid hormones, which are lipophilic, can diffuse across the plasma membrane, and interact with intracellular receptors. The receptor-hormone complex then translocates to the nucleus and interacts with specific response elements, stimulating transcription. In contrast, polypeptide hormones cannot diffuse across the plasma membrane because they are hydrophilic. The only way polypeptide hormones can enter cells is by receptor-mediated endocytosis. Endocytosed hormones are encapsulated within a phospholipid bilayer; without a specific transport mechanism, they cannot enter the nucleus because of solubility problems. In fact, most polypeptide hormones do not exert their effect in this way. Rather, they bind to cell-surface receptors, triggering an intracellular signal-transduction pathway that ultimately leads to the activation of nuclear transcription factors.

Problem

Compare the properties of water-soluble signal molecules (e.g., adrenaline) and lipid-soluble signal molecules (e.g., estrogen).

Solution: Comparison of water-soluble signal molecules (adrenaline) and lipid-soluble signal molecules (estrogen)

Property	*Adrenaline*	*Estrogen*
Solubility	Water-soluble	Lipid-soluble
Receptor	Membrane-bound	Cytosolic
Primary effect	Enzyme activation	Gene expression
Duration of effect	Short (seconds to minutes)	Long (hours to days)

Phosphatase, phosphodiesterase, kinase and phosphorylases

A **phosphatase** is an enzyme that removes a phosphate group from its substrate by hydrolyzing phosphoric acid monoesters into a phosphate ion and a molecule with a free hydroxyl group.

A **phosphodiesterase** is an enzyme that breaks a phosphodiester bond.

A **kinase** is an enzyme that transfers phosphate groups from high-energy donor molecules, such as ATP, to substrates.

A **phosphorylase** is an enzyme that catalyzes the addition of an inorganic phosphate to an acceptor.

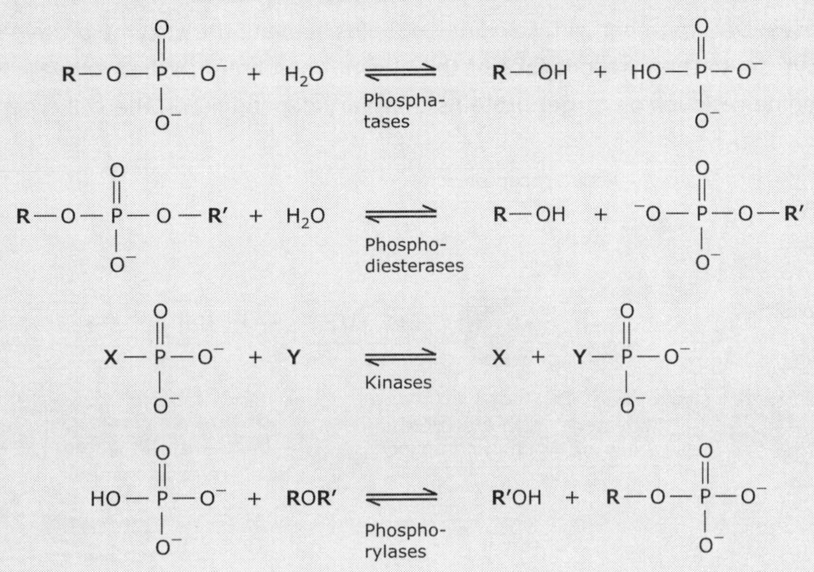

G_i mediated signal transduction

Many GPCRs exert their effects via inhibitory G-protein (G_i). Once activated, the α-subunit of G_i ($G_{i\alpha}$) inhibits adenylyl cyclase, while the $\beta\gamma$-subunits bind to K^+-channels in the plasma membrane and open them. GPCRs bind with signal molecules like prostaglandin and adenosine activate G_i. After the active $G_{i\alpha}$ dissociates from $G_{\beta\gamma}$, it binds to and inhibits (rather than stimulates) adenylyl cyclase. It results in the lowering of the cAMP levels. Ligand binding to $G_{s\alpha}$-coupled receptors causes activation of adenylyl cyclase, whereas ligand binding to $G_{i\alpha}$-coupled receptors causes inhibition of the enzyme.

G_q mediated signal transduction

Many GPCRs exert their effects via G-proteins like G_q that activate the plasma-membrane-bound enzyme *phospholipase C-β* (**PLC-β**). Mammals express four classes of phosphoinositide specific PLCs – PLC-β, PLC-γ, PLC-δ and PLC-ε. All of these PLCs require the presence of Ca^{2+} for enzymatic activity.

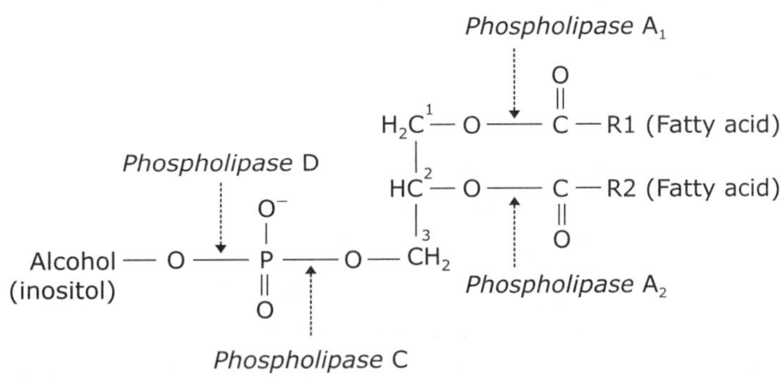

Figure 3.89 A phospholipase is named (as A, C and D) according to the bond that it cleaves on a glycerophospholipid.

The activated PLC-β cleaves phosphatidylinositol 4,5-bisphosphate (**PIP_2**) to generate two second messengers: *inositol 1,4,5-trisphosphate* (**IP_3**) and *diacylglycerol* (**DAG**). The membrane phospholipid PIP_2 is a minor component of the plasma membrane, localized to the inner leaflet of the phospholipid bilayer. One second messenger DAG remains associated with the plasma membrane, the other second messenger produced by PIP_2 cleavage, IP_3, is a small polar molecule that is released into the cytosol, where it acts to signal the release of calcium ion from the endoplasmic reticulum. IP_3 acts to release calcium ion from the endoplasmic reticulum by binding to receptors that are ligand-gated calcium ion channels (IP_3-gated calcium-release channels, also called IP_3 receptors). As a result, cytosolic calcium ion levels increase, which affects the activities of a variety of target proteins, including protein kinases and phosphatases. DAG together with calcium ion, helps activate the enzyme *protein kinase C* (**PKC**), which is recruited from the cytosol to the cytosolic face of the plasma membrane. When activated, PKC phosphorylates specific serine or threonine residues on target proteins that vary depending on the cell type.

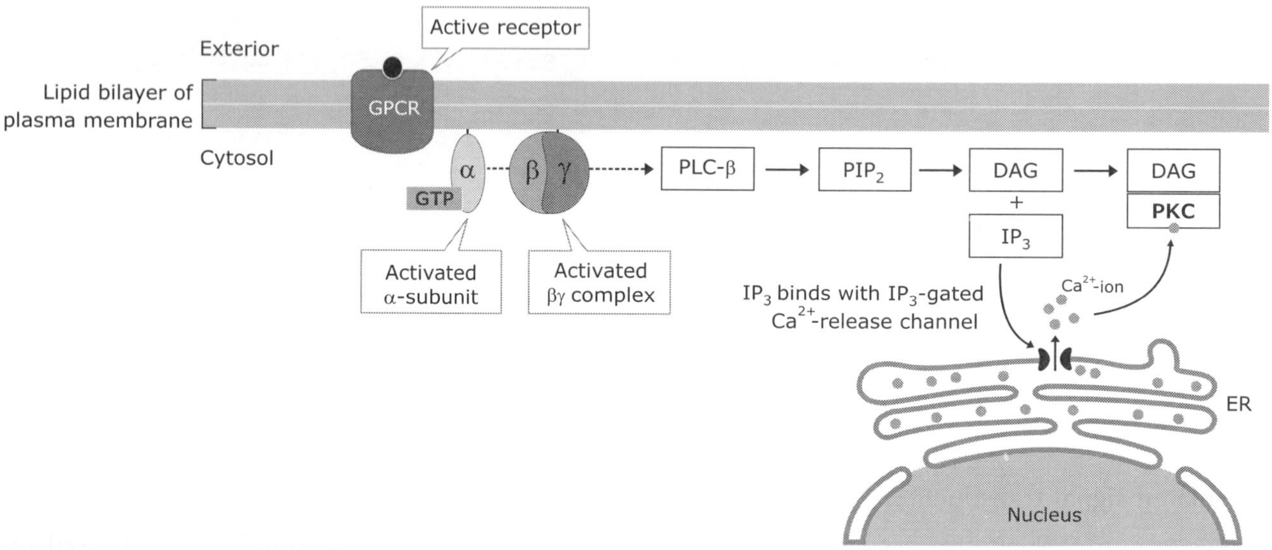

Figure 3.90 The activated receptor binds to a specific trimeric G-protein (G_q), causing the α-subunit to dissociate and activate PLC-β. Two intracellular second messengers are produced when PIP_2 is hydrolyzed by PLC-β: IP_3, which diffuses through the cytosol and releases Ca^{2+} from the ER, and DAG, which remains in the membrane and helps activate the enzyme PKC.

Calcium-Calmodulin complex

Various Ca^{2+}-binding proteins help to relay the cytosolic Ca^{2+} signal. The most important is calmodulin, which is found in all eukaryotic cells. Many of the effects of calcium ion are mediated by the protein **calmodulin,** which is activated by calcium ion binding when the concentration of cytosolic calcium ion increases. Calmodulin (17 kDa protein) is a small, highly conserved calcium-binding cytosolic acidic monomeric protein found in all eukaryotic cells. It binds up to four calcium ions and acts as an important intracellular receptor for regulatory calcium signals. Calcium ion binds to calmodulin in a cooperative fashion. Thus, a small change in the level of cytosolic calcium ion leads to a large change in the level of active calmodulin. As it binds calcium, calmodulin undergoes conformational changes which can increase its affinity for target proteins. It acts both *directly*, through interaction with key target enzymes, and *indirectly*, via specific kinases. Many effects of calcium, however, are more indirect and are mediated by protein phosphorylations catalyzed by a family of serine-threonine protein kinases called *calcium-calmodulin-dependent kinases* (**CaM-kinases**). Some CaM-kinases phosphorylate gene regulatory proteins, such as the CREB protein and in this way, activate or inhibit the transcription of specific genes. One of the best-studied CaM-kinases is CaM-kinase II, which is found in most animal cells but is especially enriched in the nervous system. Calmodulin participates in the regulation of several biological processes including energy and biosynthetic metabolism, cell motility, exocytosis, cytoskeletal assembly and intracellular modulation of both cAMP and calcium concentrations.

Mode of action of cholera and pertussis toxins

Cholera toxin is an enterotoxin secreted by the bacterium *Vibrio cholerae*. Genes for cholera toxin are present on the integrated phage genome, CTXϕ. The cholera toxin is an oligomeric complex made up of six protein subunits: a single copy of the **A-subunit** and five copies of the **B-subunit**. The A-subunit has catalytic property that causes ADP-ribosylation of G-proteins. The pentameric protein binds to the ganglioside GM1 present on the surface of the intestinal epithelium. The A-subunit ribosylates the *Arg* residue of the α-subunit of G_s protein. ADP ribose is provided by the intracellular NAD^+. This ADP ribosylation alters the α-subunit so that it can no longer hydrolyze its bound GTP, causing it to remain in an active state that stimulates adenylyl cyclase indefinitely. The resulting prolonged elevation in cAMP levels within intestinal epithelial cells causes activation of PKA. PKA phosphorylates the CFTR and Na^+-H^+ exchanger present in the intestinal epithelial cells. This causes a large efflux of chloride and sodium ion and water into the gut, thereby causing the severe diarrhea that characterizes cholera.

Pertussis toxin, an exotoxin that causes pertussis (whooping cough), is secreted by *Bordetella pertussis*. *B. pertussis* colonizes the respiratory tract, where it destroys the ciliated epithelial cells that normally sweep away mucus. Without this ciliary action, vigorous coughing is needed to clear the tract. Pertussis toxin catalyzes the ADP ribosylation of the *Cys* residue of an α-subunit of the G_i ($G_{i\alpha}$). G_i is an inhibitory G-protein. In activated state, $G_{i\alpha}$ binds GTP and dissociates from the $\beta\gamma$ complex. The released $G_{i\alpha}$ inhibits the adenylyl cyclase. The ADP ribosylation of $G_{i\alpha}$ prevents the G_i complex from interacting with receptors. So the complex remains bound to GDP and is unable to inhibit adenylyl cyclase. The resulting increase in cAMP in epithelial cells of the airways promotes loss of fluids and electrolytes and mucus secretion.

G_t mediated signal transduction

Vision depends on GPCR that regulates cyclic-nucleotide dependent gated ion channels. The first step in vision is the absorption of light energy by **rhodopsin**. The rhodopsin molecule is a protein, **opsin** (an integral protein with seven membrane-spanning α-helices), that is covalently associated with the molecule **retinal**, a polyene pigment closely related to vitamin A. Retinal (chromophore) is connected at the chain end by a Schiff's base linkage to a lysine amino acid side chain of the opsin protein. When a photon is absorbed by the retinal component of rhodopsin, the energy causes a photochemical change; **11-*cis*-retinal** is converted to **all-*trans*-retinal**. This change in the structure of the chromophore causes conformational changes in the rhodopsin molecule.

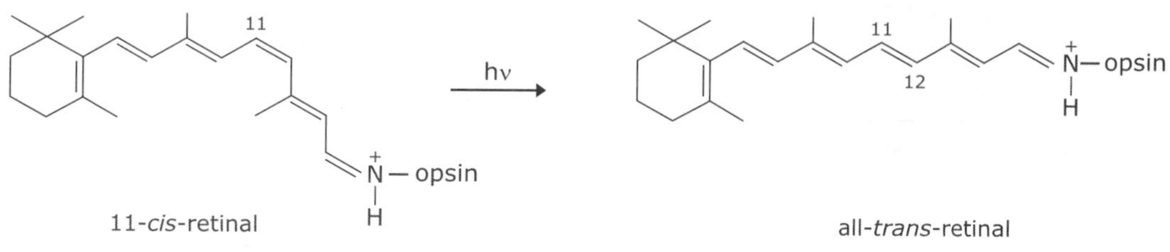

In its excited conformation, rhodopsin interacts with a second protein, **transducin**. Transducin (Gt) is a heterotrimeric G-protein. It can bind either GDP or GTP. In the dark, GDP is bound, all three subunits of the G-protein (α, β and γ) remain together, and no signal is sent. When rhodopsin is excited by light, it interacts with transducin, catalyzing the replacement of bound GDP by GTP from the cytosol. Transducin then dissociates into $G_{t\alpha}$ and $G_{t\beta\gamma}$ and the $G_{t\alpha}$-GTP carries the signal from the excited receptor to the effector molecule *cGMP phosphodiesterase* (**PDE**). Enzyme PDE converts cyclic GMP (cGMP) to 5′-GMP. The cGMP levels in the cytosol fall. This drop in cGMP concentration leads to a decrease in the amount of cGMP bound to the plasma membrane Na^+ channels, allowing more of these highly cGMP-sensitive channels to close. Closure of these channels inhibits the influx of Na^+. These channels are kept open in the dark by cyclic GMP that has bound to them. In this way, light causes a hyperpolarization rather than a depolarization of the plasma membrane. So, the activation of rhodopsin molecules by light results in hyperpolarization.

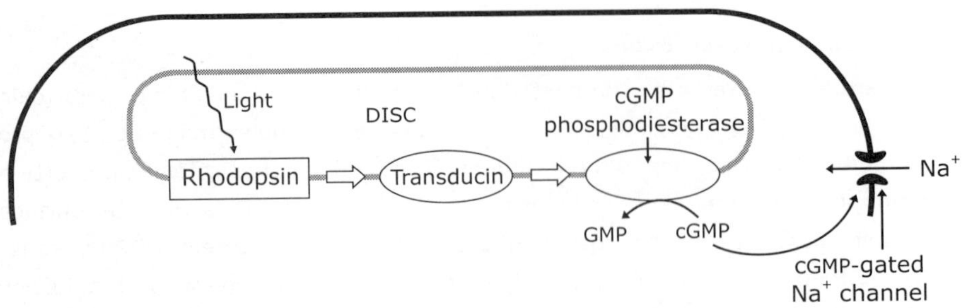

Figure 3.91 Light activates rhodopsin, which activates transducin. Activated transducin activates cGMP phosphodiesterase which catalyzes the conversion of cGMP to GMP. The resulting decrease in the cytosolic cGMP concentration causes cGMP-gated Na^+ channels to close.

A number of mechanisms operate in rods to allow the cells to revert quickly to a resting, dark state. First, the Na^+ channels that close in response to light are also permeable to calcium ion, so that when they close, the normal influx of calcium ion is inhibited, causing the calcium ion concentration in the cytosol to fall. The decrease in calcium ion concentration stimulates guanylyl cyclase to replenish the cGMP, rapidly returning its level to where it was before the light was switched on. A specific calcium ion-sensitive protein mediates the activation of guanylyl cyclase in response to a fall in calcium ion levels. In contrast to calmodulin, this protein is inactive when calcium ion is bound to it and active when it is calcium ion-free.

Second, a **rhodopsin-specific kinase**, a member of a GPCR kinase, phosphorylates the cytosolic tail of activated rhodopsin and partially inhibits the ability of the rhodopsin to activate transducin. An inhibitory protein called **arrestin** then binds to the phosphorylated rhodopsin, further inhibiting rhodopsin's activity. At the same time as rhodopsin is being shut off, a *regulator of G-protein signaling* (**RGS**) protein, which acts like GTPase activating protein, binds to activated transducin, stimulating the transducin to hydrolyze its bound GTP to GDP, which returns transducin to its inactive state.

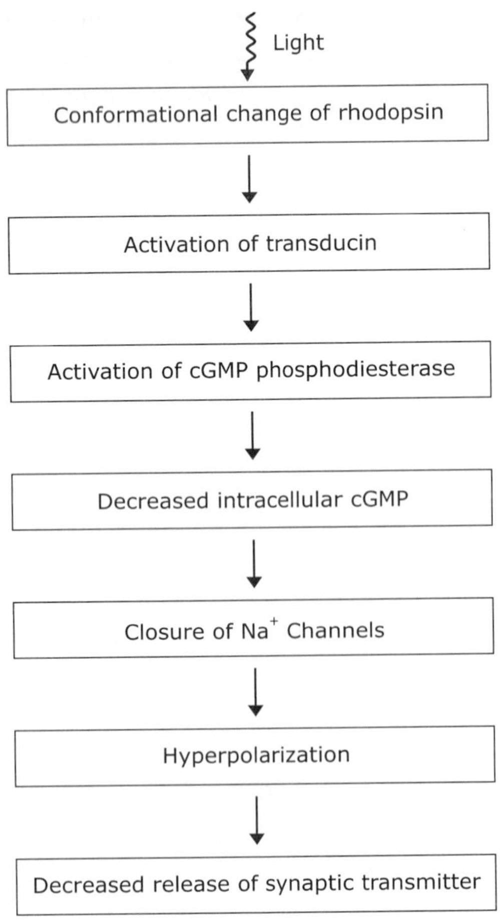

Figure 3.92
Sequence of events involved in phototransduction in rods. Rhodopsin is activated by light. The activated rhodopsin molecule then alters the conformation of the G protein transducin. Activated transducin subsequently activate enzyme cGMP phosphodiesterase. The phosphodiesterase then hydrolyzes cGMP, so that cGMP levels in the cytosol fall. This drop in cGMP concentration decreases the amount of cGMP bound to the plasma membrane cation (Na^+) channels, allowing more of these cGMP-sensitive channels to close. It results hyperpolarization of the rod cell plasma membrane.

Regulation of ion channels by G-proteins

G-proteins do not act exclusively by regulating the activity of membrane-bound enzymes that alter the concentration of second messengers in the cytosol. In some other cases, G-proteins directly activate or inactivate ion channels in the plasma membrane of the target cell, thereby altering the ion permeability. As an example, acetylcholine released by the vagus nerve reduces both the rate and strength of heart muscle cell contraction. This effect is mediated by a special class of acetylcholine receptors called **muscarinic acetylcholine receptors** that activate the G_i-protein. Once activated, the α-subunit of Gi (Giα) inhibits adenylyl cyclase, while the $\beta\gamma$-subunits bind to K^+-channels in the heart muscle cell plasma membrane and open them. The opening of these K^+-channels makes it difficult to depolarize the cell and thereby contributes to the inhibitory effect of acetylcholine on the heart. Other G-proteins regulate the activity of ion channels less directly, either by stimulating channel phosphorylation (by PKA, PKC or CaM-kinase, for example) or by causing the production or destruction of cyclic nucleotides that directly activate or inactivate ion channels.

GPCR adaptation

Target cells can adjust their sensitivity to a signal. A prolonged exposure to a stimulus decreases the cells' response to that level of stimulus. The target cells accomplish this through a reversible process of **adaptation**. Adaptation is defined as the diminution of receptor signaling in the presence of continued or repeated stimulation. Target cells usually use two processes to adapt, when they are exposed to a high concentration of signal molecules for prolonged periods: *desensitization* and *internalization*.

Desensitization

The desensitization of a GPCR response can be described as the loss of response to prolonged or repeated stimulation. It starts with a phosphorylation of several Ser and Thr residues in the cytoplasmic domains of the receptor. Receptor phosphorylation is catalyzed by a family of kinases called the *G protein-coupled receptor kinases* (**GRKs**). The GRK-phosphorylated receptor then acts as a substrate for the binding of a family of proteins called **arrestins**, which uncouple the receptor and G-protein. Other kinases, principally the second messenger-dependent protein kinases, are also known to play a role in the desensitization of many GPCR responses.

Traditionally, GPCR desensitization has been characterized by events that contribute to the uncoupling of receptors from their heterotrimeric G-proteins. However, GPCR signaling can also be terminated at the level of the heterotrimeric G-protein. For example, a family of proteins, termed *regulators of G-protein signaling* (RGS) acts to increase the rate of hydrolysis of GTP bound to G_α thereby dampening signaling *via* G-protein regulated signaling pathways.

Internalization

The process of internalization involves removal of receptors from the cell surface. The internalized receptors may be either re-exposed through exocytosis or degraded in lysosomes. The internalization of cell surface receptors to intracellular membranous compartments is termed **receptor sequestration** whereas destruction of receptors in lysosomes after internalization is termed **receptor down-regulation**.

The time frames over which these processes occur range from seconds (phosphorylation) to minutes (endocytosis) and hours (down-regulation). The extent of receptor desensitization is regulated by a number of factors that include receptor structure and cellular environment.

Box 3.3 Nitric oxide

Nitric oxide (NO) is a paracrine signaling molecule. Like the steroid hormones, NO is able to diffuse directly across the plasma membrane of its target cells. Nitric oxide is synthesized from the amino acid *arginine* by the enzyme *nitric oxide synthase*. Once synthesized, NO diffuses out of the cell and can act locally to affect nearby cells. In mammals, one well-characterized example of NO action is to relax smooth muscle. This causes the dilation of blood vessels.

The neurotransmitter acetylcholine stimulates NO synthesis by activating a GPCR on the membranes of the endothelial cells that line the interior of the vessel. The activated receptor triggers IP_3 synthesis and Ca^{2+} release, leading to stimulation of enzyme nitric oxide synthase that synthesizes NO. NO then diffuses to neighboring smooth muscle cells in the walls of blood vessels where it interacts with iron bound to the active site of the enzyme *guanylyl cyclase*. This increases enzymatic activity, resulting in the synthesis of the second messenger cGMP, which in turn activates cGMP-dependent **PKG** and/or other effector proteins. PKG (protein kinase G) is a serine/threonine-specific protein kinase. In this signaling process, guanylyl cyclase acts both as an intracellular receptor for NO and as an intracellular signaling protein.

$$\textbf{NO} \longrightarrow \textbf{Guanylyl cyclases} \longrightarrow \textbf{cGMP} \longrightarrow \textbf{PKG}$$

NO acts only locally because it has a short half-life—about 5-10 seconds—in the extracellular space before oxygen and water convert it to nitrates and nitrites. Many types of nerve cells directly produce NO to signal to their neighbors. For example, NO released by autonomic nerves in the penis causes the local blood vessel dilation that is responsible for penile erection. NO is also produced by activated macrophages and neutrophils to help them to kill invading microorganisms.

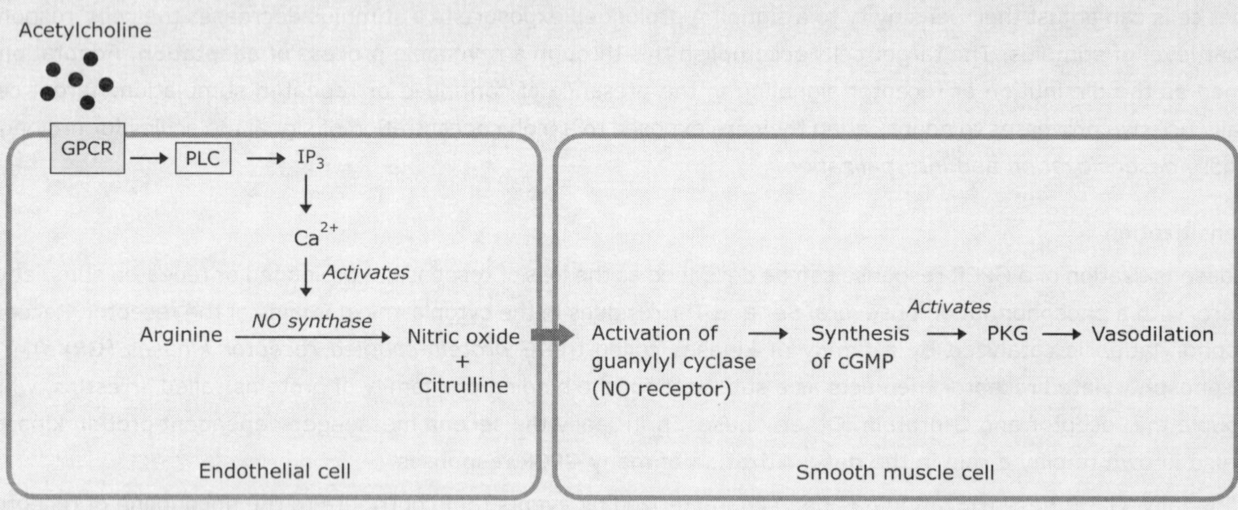

Figure 3.93 Action of nitric oxide (NO). The neurotransmitter acetylcholine activates GPCR—the *muscarinic acetylcholine receptor*—on the surface of endothelial cells. This receptor activates a G-protein, Gq, thereby stimulating IP_3 synthesis and Ca^{2+} is released from ER. Ca^{2+} activates nitric oxide synthase, causing the cells to produce NO from arginine. The NO diffuses out of the endothelial cells and into the neighboring smooth muscle cells, where it activates enzyme guanylyl cyclase to produce cGMP, which in turn activates cGMP-dependent PKG and/or other effector proteins. The effector proteins trigger a response that causes the smooth muscle cells to relax, increasing blood flow through the vessel.

Effect of Viagra: Nitric oxide can increase cGMP in the cytosol. But, the concentration of cGMP decreases because a specific phosphodiesterase converts cGMP to the inactive 5′-GMP. Sildenafil (Viagra) causes cGMP levels to remain high by inhibiting the activity of phosphodiesterase in the penis. Hence, increases the time that cGMP levels remain elevated in the smooth muscle cells of penile blood vessels after NO production is induced by local nerve terminals. The cGMP, in turn, keeps the blood vessels relaxed and thereby the penis erect.

3.20.4 Ion channel-linked receptors

Ion channel-linked receptors, also known as *transmitter-gated ion channels* or *ionotropic receptors*, are involved in rapid synaptic signaling between electrically excitable cells. This type of signaling is mediated by a small number of neurotransmitters that transiently open or close an ion channel formed by the protein to which they bind, briefly changing the ion permeability of the plasma membrane and thereby the excitability of the postsynaptic cell. The ion-channel-linked receptors belong to a large family of homologous, multipass transmembrane proteins.

3.20.5 Enzyme–linked receptors

Enzyme-linked receptors are a second major type of cell-surface receptor. Like GPCRs, enzyme-linked receptors are transmembrane proteins with their ligand-binding domain on the non-cytosolic side of the plasma membrane. Instead of having a cytosolic domain that associates with a trimeric G-protein in GPCR, their cytosolic domain either has an intrinsic enzyme activity or associates directly with an enzyme. Several classes of enzyme-linked receptors have been identified. We focus our discussion on the three major classes:

- Receptor tyrosine kinases (the most numerous of the enzyme-linked receptors)
- Tyrosine kinase associated receptors
- Receptor serine/threonine kinase receptors

A. Receptor tyrosine kinases

The *receptor tyrosine kinases* (**RTKs**) are the second major type of cell-surface receptors. The ligands for RTKs may be insulin, epidermal growth factor (EGF), transforming growth factor-α (TGFα), platelet-derived growth factor (PDGF), fibroblast growth factor (FGF) and colony stimulating factor-1 (CSF-1). The receptors are generally activated by ligands whose normal physiologic functions are to promote growth, proliferation, development, or maintenance of differentiated properties. All RTKs comprise an extracellular domain containing a ligand-binding site, a single hydrophobic transmembrane α-helix, and a cytosolic domain that includes a region with protein tyrosine kinase activity. In all cases, the binding of the signal molecules to the ligand-binding domain on the extracellular side of the receptor activates the tyrosine kinase domain on the cytosolic side. This leads to phosphorylation of tyrosine side chains on the cytosolic part of the receptor, creating phosphotyrosine docking sites for various intracellular signaling proteins that relay the signal.

In the absence of extracellular signals, most RTKs exist as monomers in which the intrinsic tyrosine kinase domain is inactive. Binding of ligand brings two monomers together to form a dimer. In most cases, the close proximity in the dimer leads the two kinase domains to phosphorylate each other. Mechanisms of dimerization vary widely among different RTK family members. In some cases, the ligand itself is a dimer and brings two receptors together by binding them simultaneously. In other cases, a monomeric ligand can interact with two receptors simultaneously to bring them together, or two ligands can bind independently on two receptors to promote dimerization. In some RTKs—as in the insulin receptor family—the receptor is always a dimer.

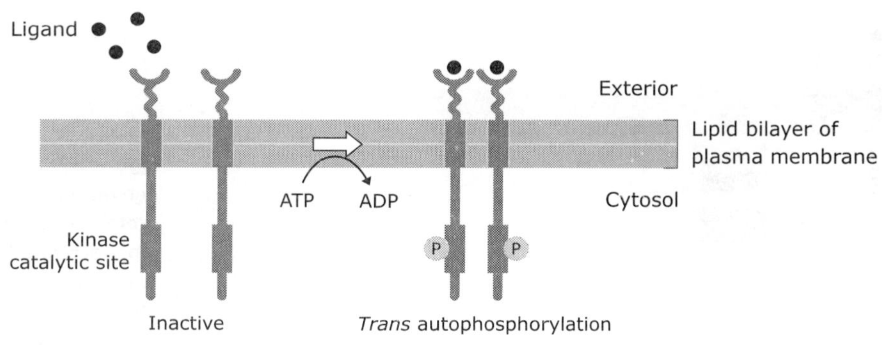

Figure 3.94 General structure and ligand-induced activation of receptor tyrosine kinases (RTKs). The cytosolic domain of RTKs contains a protein tyrosine kinase catalytic site. Ligand binding leads to activation of the intrinsic protein-tyrosine kinase activity of the receptor and autophosphorylation of tyrosine residues in its cytosolic domain. Once the kinase domains of an RTK dimer are activated, they phosphorylate multiple additional sites in the cytosolic parts of the receptors. This phosphorylation creates high-affinity docking sites for intracellular signaling proteins.

The intracellular signaling proteins that bind to phosphorylated tyrosines have varied structures and functions. However, they usually share highly conserved phosphotyrosine-binding domains. These can be either **SH2 domains** (for *Src homology region*) or, less commonly, **PTB domains** (for *phosphotyrosine-binding*). Presence of SH2 or PTB domains enables the signal proteins that contain them to bind to specific phosphorylated tyrosine of activated RTK.

Three major pathways can transduce a signal from the activated RTK:

- Ras–MAP kinase pathway
- IP_3-DAG pathway and
- PI-3 kinase pathway

Ras–MAP kinase pathway

Ligand-induced activation of an RTK stimulates its tyrosine kinase activity, which subsequently stimulates several signal-transduction pathways including the *Ras–MAP kinase pathway*. Ras is an intracellular monomeric GTPase switch protein and functions in transducing signals from many different RTKs. There are three major, closely related Ras proteins in humans (H-, K- and N-Ras). These are lipid-linked (covalently attached lipid groups) proteins present at the cytoplasmic face of the membrane. Ras cycles between an inactive GDP-bound form and active GTP-bound form. Ras cycling requires the assistance of two proteins, GEF and GAP. Ras activation is accelerated by a protein called GEF, which binds to the Ras–GDP complex, causing dissociation of the bound GDP. Because GTP is present in cells at a higher concentration than GDP, GTP binds spontaneously to *empty* Ras molecules, with the release of GEF. The average lifetime of a GTP bound to Ras is about 1 minute. GAP, which binds to Ras–GTP, accelerates its intrinsic GTPase activity. Binding of a ligand to an RTK leads to activation of Ras. Two cytosolic proteins - Grb2 (acts as adaptor protein) and Sos (acts as GEF) provide the key links between RTK and Ras.

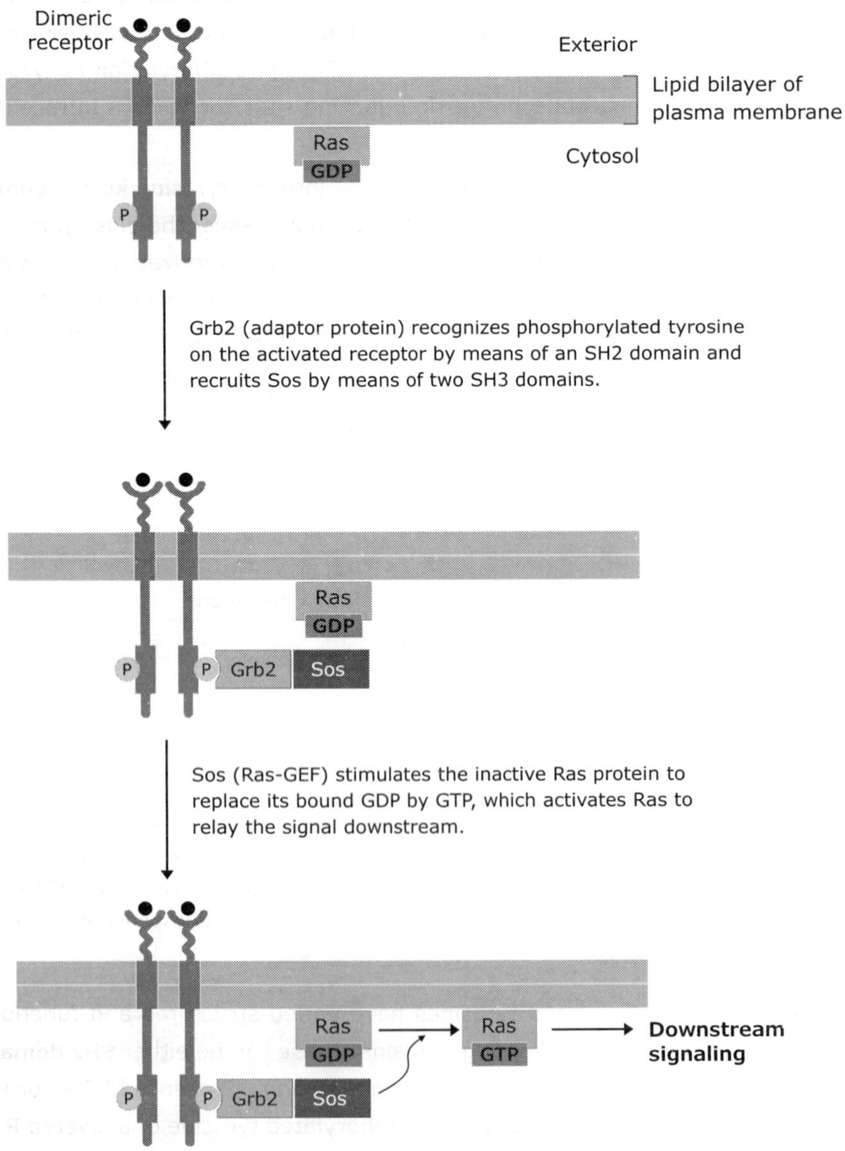

Figure 3.95
Activation of Ras. An adaptor protein, Grb2 and GEF, Sos link most activated receptor to Ras. The SH2 domain in Grb2 binds to a phosphotyrosine in activated RTKs, while its two SH3 domains bind Sos, thereby bringing Sos close to membrane-bound Ras-GDP and activating its nucleotide exchange activity. Binding of Sos to inactive Ras causes a large conformational change that permits release of GDP and binding of GTP, forming active Ras. GAP, which accelerates GTP hydrolysis, is localized near Ras-GTP by binding to activated RTKs.

Some signaling proteins function as **adaptor proteins** to couple tyrosine-phosphorylated proteins to other proteins that do not have their own SH2 domains. Adaptor proteins, which lack enzymatic activity, link signaling molecules via their protein–protein interaction domains. Grb2 is a prototypical adaptor protein. It helps to couple activated RTKs to the important signaling protein Ras. It binds to a specific phosphotyrosine on an activated, ligand-bound RTK and to the cytosolic GEF, Sos protein. Sos then promotes formation of active Ras-GTP. Grb2 has one SH2 and two SH3 domains. Its *SH2 domain* binds to specific phosphotyrosine residues in the activated receptor whereas *SH3 domains* bind to proline-rich motifs in Sos.

Examples of monomeric GTPase

Family	**Function**
Ras (H-Ras, K-Ras, N-Ras)	Relay signals from RTKs
Rab	Vesicle targeting and fusion
Ran	Functions in the transport of RNA and protein into and out of the nucleus
Arf	Regulate assembly of protein coats on intracellular vesicles
Rho (Rho, Rac, Cdc42)	Reorganizes cytoskeleton through serine-threonine protein kinases, controlling cell shape, polarity, motility and adhesion

MAP Kinase pathways

Activation of an RKT may itself trigger multiple pathways: for example, activation of EGF receptor activates the Ras-dependent pathway as well as Ras-independent pathways involving second messengers. The activation of Ras triggered by activated RTKs is short-lived. Ras activates a downstream serine/threonine phosphorylation cascade that includes a **MAP-kinase** (*mitogen-activated protein kinase*). Activated Ras induces a *kinase cascade* that culminates in activation of MAP kinase. This serine/threonine kinase, which can translocate into the nucleus, phosphorylates many different proteins including transcription factors that regulate expression of important cell-cycle and differentiation-specific proteins. Activation of MAP kinase in two different cells can lead to similar or different cellular responses, as can activation in the same cell by stimulation of different RTKs.

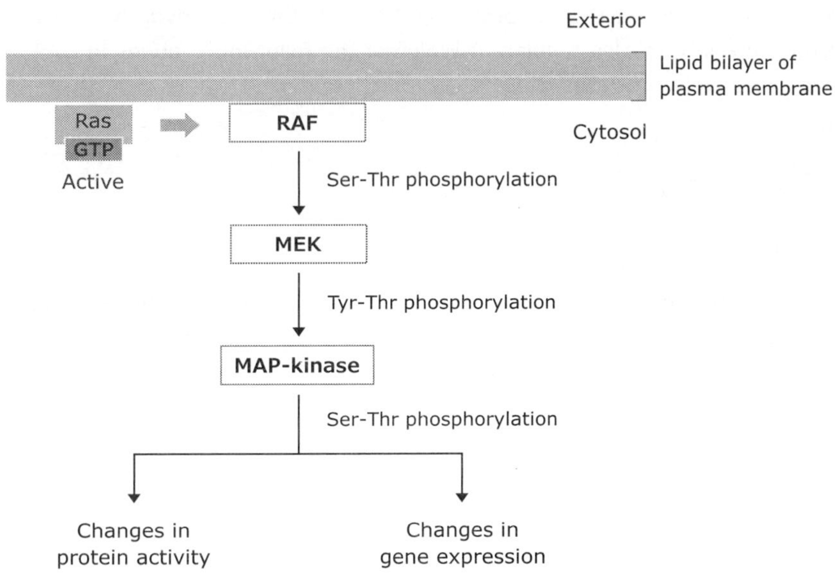

Figure 3.96 MAP kinase pathway. Activated Ras triggers the downstream kinase cascade, culminating in activation of MAP kinase. Interaction of the RAF N-terminal regulatory domain with Ras-GTP leads to activation of RAF kinase activity. Note that in contrast to many other protein kinases, activation of RAF does not depend on phosphorylation. Hydrolysis of Ras-GTP to Ras-GDP releases active RAF, which phosphorylates and thereby activates MEK. Active MEK then phosphorylates and activates MAP kinase, another serine/threonine kinase. MAP kinase phosphorylates many different proteins, including nuclear transcription factors, that mediate cellular responses.

Many serine/threonine kinases participate in this phosphorylation cascade, but three of them constitute the core module of the cascade. The last of the three is called MAP-kinase. Downstream serine/threonine phosphorylation cascade follows the following pattern:

1. Activated Ras binds to the N-terminal domain of **RAF** (**MAP-kinase-kinase-kinase**), a ser/thr kinase.
2. RAF activity leads to the activation of **MEK** (**MAP-kinase-kinase**). RAF directly phosphorylates MEK, which is activated by phosphorylation on two serine residues. MEK is an unusual enzyme with dual specificity, which can phosphorylate both threonine and tyrosine. Its target is the **ERK** (**MAP kinase**).
3. MEK phosphorylates and activates MAP kinase. The MAP kinases are serine/threonine kinases. After this point in the pathway, all the activating events take the form of serine/threonine phosphorylations. MAP kinase phosphorylates many different proteins, including nuclear transcription factors, that mediate cellular responses.

The ultimate effect of the MAP kinase pathway is a change in the pattern of transcription. In the classic MAP kinase pathway, MAP kinase moves into the nucleus, where it phosphorylates target transcription factors. In alternative pathway, it phosphorylates a cytoplasmic factor; this may be a transcription factor that then moves to the nucleus or a protein that regulates a transcription factor (for example, by releasing it to go to the nucleus).

Three-component MAP kinase signaling pathways operate in all eukaryotic cells, that are activated by different extracellular signals and that activate different MAP kinase proteins mediating different responses in the same cell. Hence, there is a chance of cross-talk. One way in which cells avoid cross-talk between the different parallel MAP kinase signaling pathways and ensure that each response is specific is to use **scaffold proteins**. Such scaffolds bind all or some of the kinases in each MAP kinase module to form a complex and thereby help to ensure response specificity and prevent cross-talk between different MAP kinase pathways. Pathway-specific scaffold proteins enable the signal transducing kinases in a particular pathway to interact with one another, but not with kinases in other pathways. This ensures that activation of one MAP kinase pathway by a particular extracellular signal does not lead to activation of other pathways containing shared components.

Problem

The activity of Ras is carefully regulated by two other proteins, a guanine nucleotide-exchange factor (GEF) that stimulates the uptake of GTP by Ras, and a GTPase-activating protein (GAP) that stimulates hydrolysis of GTP by Ras. The activities of these regulatory proteins are in turn also regulated. Which of the following changes in GAP and GEF proteins might cause a cell to proliferate excessively?

a. a nonfunctional GAP

b. a permanently active GAP

c. a nonfunctional GEF

d. a permanently active GEF

Solution: A nonfunctional GAP (choice a) or a permanently active GEF (choice d) would allow Ras to remain in the active state (with GTP bound) longer than normal, and thus might cause excessive cell proliferation.

IP_3–DAG pathway

Many RTKs can initiate the IP_3-DAG pathway by activating isoform of phospholipase C, the **phospholipase C-γ** (PLC-β in the case of GPCRs). The SH2 domains of PLC-γ bind to specific phosphotyrosines of the activated receptors, thus positioning the enzyme close to its membrane-bound substrate PIP2. Membrane-bound PLC-γ after activation cleaves PIP2 to generate two second messengers, DAG and IP_3. Signaling via the IP_3-DAG pathway leads to an increase in cytosolic calcium and to activation of protein kinase C (**PKC**).

PI-3 kinase pathway

Some activated RTKs initiate phosphoinositide pathway, the *PI-3 kinase pathway*. PI-3 kinase (phosphoinositide 3-kinase) binds to phosphotyrosine residues in the cytosolic domain of activated RTKs. PI-3 kinase principally phosphorylates inositol phospholipids rather than proteins, and both RTKs and GPCRs can activate it. *Phosphatidylinositol* is unique among membrane lipids because it can undergo reversible phosphorylation at multiple sites on its inositol head group to generate a variety of phosphorylated phosphatidylinositol lipids called *phosphoinositides*. Activated PI-3 kinase catalyzes the formation of PI 3,4-bisphosphate or PI 3,4,5-trisphosphate which act as docking sites for various signal-transducing proteins. There are various types of PI-3 kinase. Some PI-3 kinases are activated by the $\beta\gamma$-complex of a trimeric G-protein when GPCRs are activated by their signals.

A primary binding target of PI 3,4,5-trisphosphate is **PKB** (protein kinase B, also called **Akt**), a serine/threonine kinase. Besides its kinase domain, PKB contains a PH (**Pleckstrin Homology**) domain that tightly binds the 3-phosphate in PI 3,4,5-trisphosphate. In an inactive form, PKB is present in the cytosol. In case of a rise in PI 3,4,5-trisphosphate, PKB binds to them and is localized at the cell surface. PI 3,4,5-trisphosphates also recruit protein kinase, **PDK1** (phosphoinositide-dependent protein kinase 1), to the plasma membrane via binding of its PH domain. Active PDK1 and **mTORC2** (mammalian target of rapamycin complex 2) cause phosphorylation of PKB. Fully activated PKB then dissociates from the plasma membrane and phosphorylate its many target proteins at the plasma membrane, as well as in the cytosol and nucleus. The effect on most of the known targets is to inactivate them.

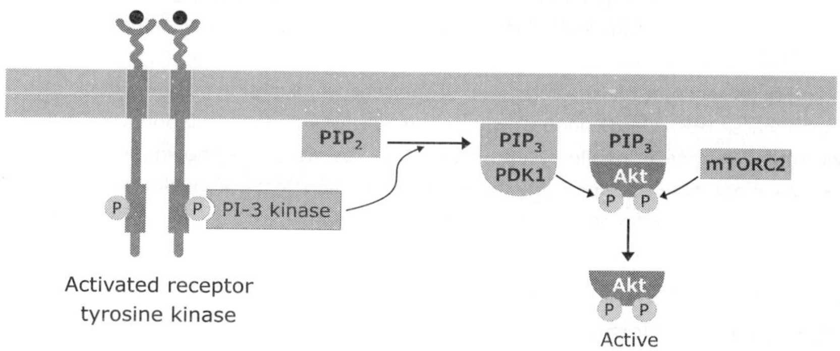

Figure 3.97 An extracellular signal activates an RTK, which recruits and activates PI 3-kinase. The PI 3-kinase produces PI 3,4,5-trisphosphate, which serves as a docking site for two serine/threonine kinases with PH domains—Akt (PKB) and PDK1—and brings them into proximity at the plasma membrane. The Akt is phosphorylated on a serine by a third kinase (usually mTORC2), which alters the conformation of the Akt so that it can be phosphorylated on a threonine by PDK1, which activates the Akt. The fully activated Akt dissociates from the plasma membrane and phosphorylates various target proteins.

Insulin signaling pathways

The insulin receptor (INS-R) is an RTK. It consists of two α-subunits on the outer face of the plasma membrane and two transmembrane β-subunits (an $\alpha_2\beta_2$ heterotetrameric complex). The two α-subunits are linked by disulfide bonds. There is a single disulfide bond between the α- and β-subunits also. Binding of insulin to the α-subunits triggers a conformational change that allows the autophosphorylation of *tyrosine* residues in the carboxyl-terminal domain of the β-subunits. The phosphorylated insulin receptor next phosphorylates members of the **insulin receptor substrate** (IRS) family, which act as *adaptor proteins* with many potential phosphorylation sites. Phosphorylated IRS binds to the SH2 domains of a variety of proteins that are directly involved in mediating different effects of insulin. Among them, PI-3 kinase has a major role in insulin function. Phosphorylated IRS protein acts as docking site for enzyme PI-3 kinase. The PI-3 kinase then phosphorylates PI 3,4-bisphosphate (PIP2) leading to the formation of PI 3,4,5-trisphosphate (PIP3). Akt (PKB) and PDK1 bind to PIP3 produced by activated PI-3 kinase so that PDK1 can phosphorylate and activate Akt.

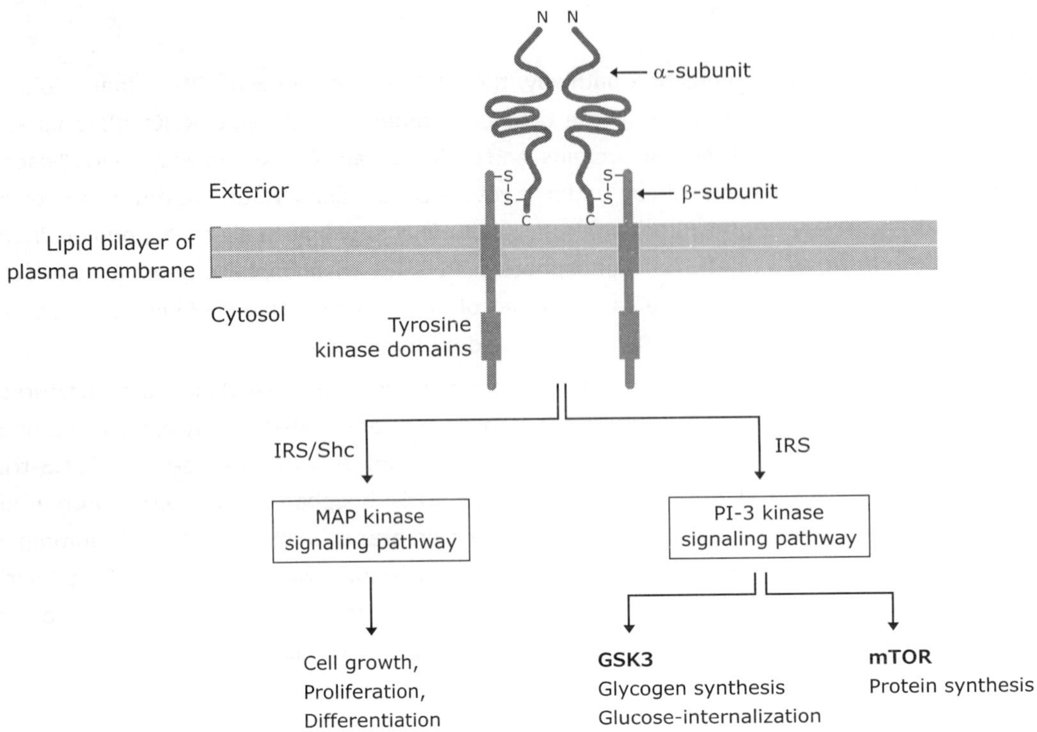

Figure 3.98 Insulin binding to its receptor causes activation of the receptor tyrosine protein kinase and autophosphorylation. The receptor kinase also phosphorylates IRS, a large adaptor with many potential phosphorylation sites. IRS is an essential intermediate in insulin action. The two major canonical insulin receptor signaling cascades are shown — PI-3 kinase pathway and Ras-MAP kinase pathway. The PI-3 kinase pathway is responsible for most metabolic effects of insulin, and is connected exclusively through IRS, while the Ras-MAP kinase pathway is involved in the mitogenic responses.

The activated Akt phosphorylates glycogen synthase kinase 3 (**GSK3**) and inactivates it. Inactivation of GSK3 makes *glycogen synthase* active which accelerates the synthesis of glycogen from glucose, therefore the inactivation of GSK3 by Akt promotes glucose storage as glycogen. In addition to promoting glucose storage, insulin inhibits the production and release of glucose by the liver by blocking gluconeogenesis and glycogenolysis. In muscle and fat tissue, Akt also triggers the movement of glucose transporters (**GLUT4**) from internal vesicles to the plasma membrane, stimulating glucose uptake from the blood.

Activated Akt induces protein synthesis via mTOR and downstream elements; and cell survival through inhibition of several pro-apoptotic agents. Insulin signaling also has mitogenic effect, which is mediated by the activation of the Ras-MAP kinase pathway. The PI-3 kinase pathway is connected exclusively through IRS, while the MAP kinase pathway emanates from both IRS and Shc. In this pathway, signal transduction proteins interact with IRS (or Shc) including Grb2, an adaptor protein that contains SH3 domains, which in turn associates with the GEF Sos and elicits activation of the MAP kinase cascade leading to mitogenic responses.

PI-3 kinase–Akt–mTOR pathway

For a multicellular organism to grow, its cells must grow (accumulate mass and enlarge). If the cells simply divided without growing, they would get progressively smaller. Extracellular signals are usually required for animal cells to grow and divide, as well as to survive. The PI-3 kinase–Akt pathway that signals cells to grow depends on a large *protein kinase* called **TOR** (named as the *target of rapamycin*). In mammalian cells, it is called **mTOR**. mTOR is an atypical serine/threonine protein kinase that belongs to the phosphoinositide 3-kinase (PI3K)-related kinase family. mTOR exists in cells in two functionally distinct multiprotein complexes–mTOR complex 1 (**mTORC1**) and 2 (**mTORC2**). mTORC1 contains the protein *raptor*; this complex is sensitive to rapamycin, and it stimulates cell growth by promoting protein synthesis and by inhibiting protein degradation. mTORC1 promotes protein synthesis by phosphorylating the eIF4E-binding protein 1 (4E-BP1). The phosphorylation of 4E-BP1 prevents its binding to eIF4E, enabling eIF4E to promote cap-dependent translation. mTORC2 contains the protein *rictor* and is insensitive to rapamycin; it helps to activate Akt.

In the presence of extracellular growth factors, activation of mTORC1 occurs via the PI-3 kinase–Akt pathway. Akt activates mTORC1 indirectly by phosphorylating, and thereby inhibiting, a GAP called **Tsc2**. Tsc2 acts on a monomeric Ras-related GTPase called **Rheb**. Rheb in its active form (Rheb-GTP) activates mTORC1. The net result is that Akt activates mTORC1 and thereby promotes cell growth.

In the absence of growth factor

Tsc2 (Active) ⟶ **Rheb** (Inactive) ⟶ **mTORC1** (Inactive)

In the presence of growth factor

Growth factor receptor (Active) ⟶ **PI-3 kinase** (Active) ⟶ **Akt** (Active) ⟶ **Tsc2** (Inactive) ⟶ **Rheb** (Active) ⟶ **mTORC1** (Active) ⟶ **Cell growth**

Figure 3.99 In the presence of growth factors, activated Akt phosphorylates and inhibits Tsc2 (GAP), thereby promoting the activation of Rheb. Activated Rheb (Rheb-GTP) helps activate mTORC1, which in turn stimulates cell growth.

B. Tyrosine kinase associated receptors

Rather than possessing intrinsic enzymatic activity, **tyrosine kinase associated receptors** act by recruiting and activating intracellular protein tyrosine kinases. Like RTK, these receptors contain the N-terminal extracellular ligand-binding domains, single transmembrane α-helices and C-terminal cytosolic domains. However, the cytosolic domains of the tyrosine kinase associated receptors are devoid of any known *catalytic activity*. Instead, these receptors function in association with non-receptor **cytosolic tyrosine kinases**, which are activated as a result of ligand binding. A variety of receptor classes belong to this category, including the receptors for interleukins, integrins, various cytokines and some hormones. The largest and most diverse class of tyrosine kinase associated receptors is the **cytokine receptors**. These receptors depend on various cytoplasmic tyrosine kinases for their action. These classes of receptors include the receptors for most cytokines (e.g., interleukin-2 and erythropoietin) and for some polypeptide hormones (e.g., growth hormone and prolactin) whose cytosolic domains are closely associated with a member of a family of *cytosolic tyrosine kinases*, the **Janus kinases** (JAKs). JAKs phosphorylate and activate regulatory transcription factors called **STATs** (*signal transducers and activators of transcription*). STAT proteins are located in the cytosol and after activation migrate into the nucleus and regulate gene transcription.

JAK-STAT pathway

The JAKs take their name (originally Janus kinases) from the characteristic presence of two kinase domains in each molecule. Several members of the family are known (JAK1, JAK2, JAK3 and Tyk2); each associated with a specific set of cytokine receptors. The JAKs are tyrosine kinases whose major substrates are transcription factors called STATs. There are several types of STATs; each STAT is phosphorylated by a particular set of JAKs. All STAT proteins contain an N-terminal **SH2 domain** that binds to a phosphotyrosine in the receptor's cytosolic domain, a central DNA-binding domain, and a C-terminal domain with a critical tyrosine residue.

The binding of cytokines with cytokine receptors activate the stably associated JAKs. Once the JAKs become activated, they phosphorylate each other on tyrosines and also phosphorylate several tyrosine residues on the cytosolic domain of the cytokine receptors. Phosphorylation of receptors generates the binding sites for the STATs.

Once a STAT is bound to the receptor, the C-terminal tyrosine is phosphorylated by an associated JAK. STATs dissociate from the receptors and form either homodimers or heterodimers. The basis for dimerization is a reciprocal interaction between an SH2 domain in one subunit and a phosphorylated Tyr in the other subunit. The STAT dimers move into the nucleus, where they bind to specific enhancer sequences controlling target genes.

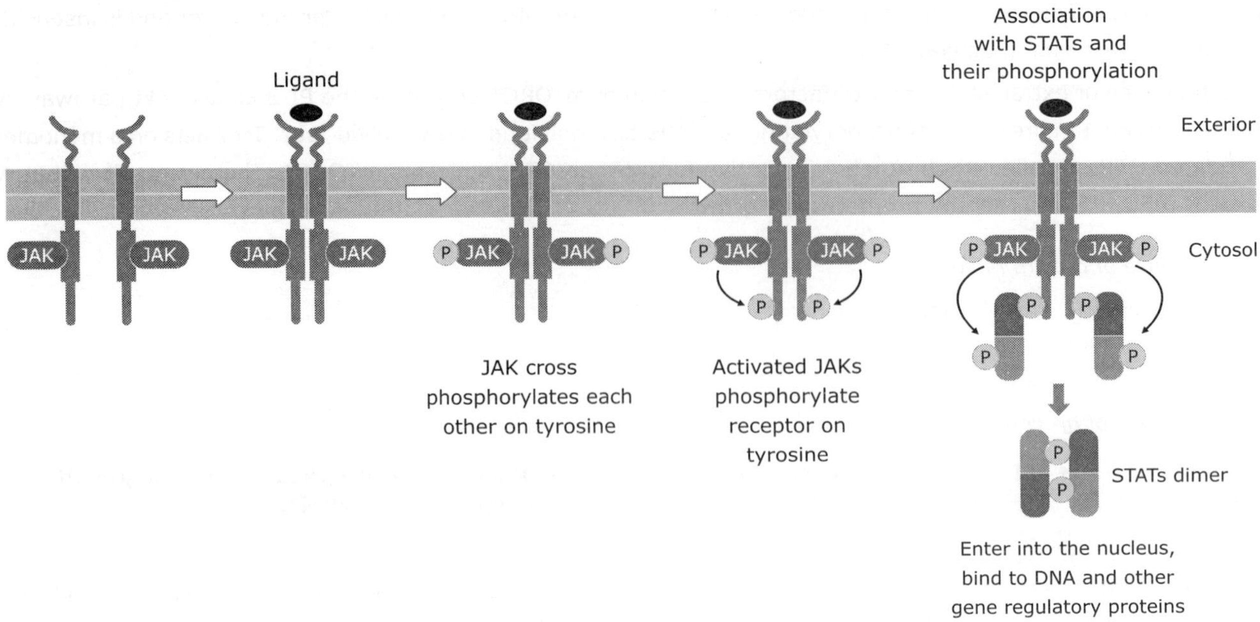

Figure 3.100 The JAK-STAT signaling pathway. The binding of the cytokine either causes two separate receptor polypeptide chains to dimerize (as shown) or re-orients the receptor chains in a preformed dimer. Receptor binds to JAK. JAKs phosphorylate each other and then phosphorylate tyrosines on the cytosolic domains of cytokine receptors, creating phosphotyrosine docking sites for STATs. JAKs phosphorylate and activate transcription regulators called STATs. They dimerize and translocate to the nucleus. The complex binds to DNA and activates transcription.

C. Serine/threonine kinase receptors

Serine/threonine kinase receptors are enzyme-linked single-pass transmembrane proteins with a serine/threonine kinase domain on the cytosolic end. These receptors bind with TGF-β (Transforming growth factor-β) family of signaling molecules. There are two classes of these serine/threonine kinase receptors– *type I* and *type II*. Both receptors are present in the form of homodimers.

The TGF-β superfamily consists of a large number of structurally related, secretory, dimeric proteins. The superfamily includes the TGF-βs themselves, the **activins**, and the **bone morphogenetic proteins** (BMPs). The BMPs constitute the largest family. Each member of the TGF-β superfamily binds to a characteristic combination of type-I and type-II receptors, both of which are required for signaling. Typically, the ligand first binds to and activates a type-II receptor homodimer, which recruits, phosphorylates, and activates a type-I receptor homodimer, forming an active tetrameric receptor complex. Once activated, the receptor complex uses a strategy for rapidly relaying the signal to the nucleus that is very similar to the JAK-STAT strategy. The type-I receptor directly binds and phosphorylates a latent gene regulatory protein of the **Smad** family. In unstimulated cells, Smads are located in the cytosol, but when activated, they move into the nucleus to regulate transcription of genes.

Activated TGFβ/activin receptors phosphorylate Smad2 or Smad3, while activated BMP receptors phosphorylate Smad1, Smad5 or Smad8. Once one of these *receptor-activated Smads* (**R-Smads**) has been phosphorylated, it dissociates from the receptor and binds to Smad4 (called a **co-Smad**), which can form a complex with any of the five R-Smads. The Smad complex then translocates into the nucleus, where it associates with other transcription regulators and controls the transcription of specific target genes. Because the partner proteins in the nucleus vary depending on the cell type and state of the cell, the genes affected vary.

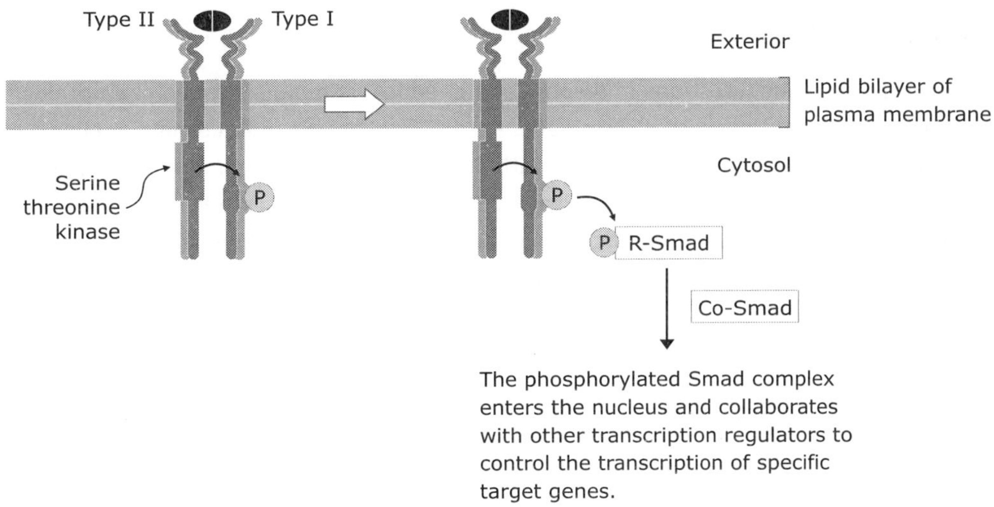

Figure 3.101 The Smad-dependent signaling pathway activated by ligand TGFβ. The TGFβ dimer promotes the assembly of a tetrameric receptor complex containing two copies each of the type-I and type-II receptors. The type-II receptors phosphorylate specific sites on the type-I receptors, thereby activating their kinase domains and leading to phosphorylation of R-Smads (generally Smad2 and Smad3 in the case of TGF-β /activin receptors; Smad1, Smad5 and Smad8 in the case of BMP receptors). Smads open up to expose a dimerization surface when they are phosphorylated, leading to the formation of a trimeric Smad complex containing two R-Smads and the co-Smad, Smad4. The phosphorylated Smad complex enters the nucleus and collaborates with other transcription regulators to control the transcription of specific target genes.

Protein kinases and phosphatases

Protein kinases catalyze the phosphorylation of proteins. There are many types of protein kinases involved in signal transduction. They all have the same basic catalytic activity: they add a phosphate group to an amino acid in a target protein and the phosphate is provided by ATP. Protein kinases can be classified by the types of amino acids that they phosphorylate in the protein target. Five groups of protein kinases are distinguished by the types of amino acid targets:

- Protein serine/threonine kinases (phosphorylate either serine or threonine in the target protein).
- Protein tyrosine kinases (phosphorylate tyrosine in the target protein).
- Dual specificity kinases (phosphorylate target proteins on either tyrosine or serine/threonine).
- Histidine kinases (phosphorylate target proteins on histidine).
- Aspartate kinases (phosphorylate target proteins on aspartate).

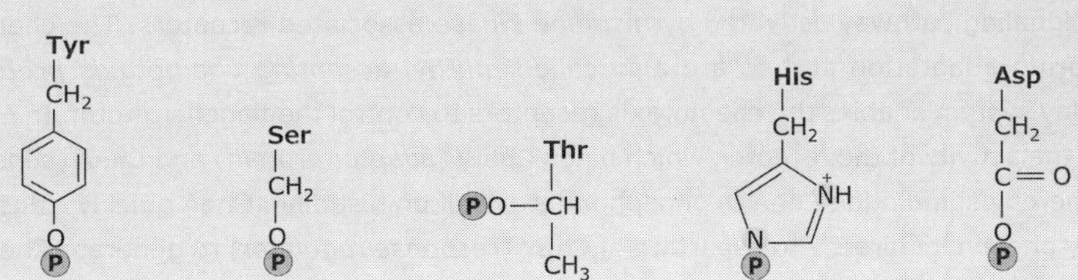

Protein kinases may be membrane-bound or cytosolic on the basis of their location in the cell. *Cytosolic protein kinases* are most often ser/thr protein kinases. The activity of protein kinases is opposed by the activity of protein **phosphatases**, which remove phosphate groups from specific substrate proteins. Depending on structural parameters, the protein phosphatase family is classified into subfamilies:

- Ser/Thr-specific phosphatases
- Phosphotyrosine phosphatases
- Thr/Tyr-specific phosphatases
- Prokaryotic phosphohistidine and phosphoaspartate phosphatases.

3.20.6 Chemotaxis in bacteria

Movement of organisms in specific directions in response to chemical stimulus is called **chemotaxis**. Chemotaxis in bacteria depends on a signaling pathway that terminates at the flagellar motor. Bacterial flagellar motion is rotatory in nature. Membrane proteins MotA and MotB along with FliG create a proton channel that drives the rotation of the flagellum. The rotation of flagella can be *clockwise* or *counterclockwise*. When the flagella rotate clockwise, forward motion ceases and the cells **tumble**. But counterclockwise rotations of flagella impart forward motion (**run**).

In the absence of a chemical gradient, bacteria such as *E. coli* move in a random fashion that includes runs, where the cell is swimming forward and tumbles when the cell stops. Following a tumble, the direction of the next run is random. However, if a gradient of a chemical attractant is present, these random movements become biased. As the bacterium senses that it is moving toward higher concentrations of the attractant, runs become longer and tumbles less frequent. If the bacterium is sensing a repellent, the same general mechanism applies, although in this case, it is the decrease in the concentration of the repellent that promotes runs.

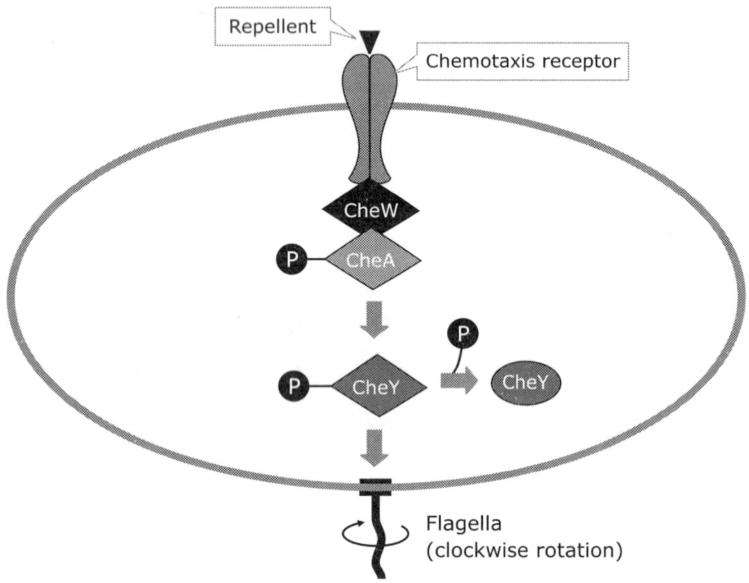

Figure 3.102
The two-component signaling pathway that enables chemotaxis receptors to control the flagellar motor during bacterial chemotaxis.

Bacterial chemotaxis is mediated by transmembrane receptors and a phosphorylation relay system. It depends on a two component signaling pathway activated by *histidine kinase* associated receptors. The chemotaxis receptors are methylated during adaptation and so are also called *methyl-accepting chemotaxis proteins* (MCPs). The phosphorylation relay system enables the chemotaxis receptors to control the flagellar motor. In *E. coli*, binding of a *repellent* increases the activity of the receptor, which binds **CheW** (*adaptor protein*) and **CheA** (*sensor protein* acts as histidine kinase), thereby stimulating CheA to phosphorylate itself on histidine. CheA quickly transfers its covalently bound, high-energy phosphate directly to aspartate of **CheY** (*response regulator*) to generate CheY-phosphate. The phosphorylated CheY dissociates from the receptor, diffuses through the cytosol and binds to the flagellar motor and causes it to rotate clockwise, resulting in **tumbling**. Phosphorylated state of CheY remains only for a few seconds. Protein CheZ accelerates the dephosphorylation of CheY-phosphate, thereby inactivating it. The binding of an attractant has the opposite effect. It inactivates the receptor and, therefore, decreases the phosphorylation of CheA and CheY, which results in counterclockwise flagellar rotation and **run**. Each of the phosphorylated intermediates decays in about 10 seconds, enabling the bacterium to respond very quickly to changes in its environment. The response to an increase in the concentration of an attractant or repellent is only transient, even if the higher level of ligand is maintained, as the bacteria *desensitize*, or *adapt*, to the increased stimulus. The adaptation is mediated by the covalent methylation. A methyltransferase, CheR, catalyzes methylation of the MCP. [In other species of bacteria such as *B. subtilis*, attractants may stimulate and repellents inhibit CheA activity].

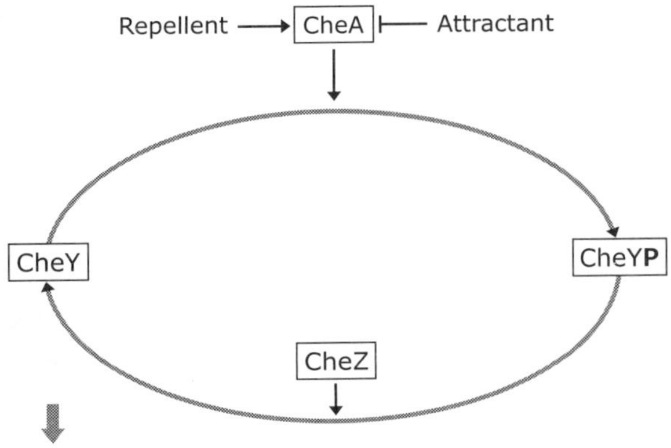

Flagellum	Counterclockwise rotation	Clockwise rotation
Sensor	Degree of methylation increases	Degree of methylation decreases
Behavior	Run	Tumbling

Chemotaxis proteins

1. **CheA**, a cytoplasmic *sensor kinase*.
2. **CheW**, an adaptor protein linking the sensor protein with CheA.
3. **CheY**, the *response regulator* controlling the flageller motor.
4. **CheZ**, an Asp–specific protein phosphatase for signal termination.
5. **CheR**, a methyltransferase catalyzing methylation of the MCP.

Box 3.4 Two-component signaling systems

Two-component signaling system is the most common form of signaling pathway that responds to extracellular signals in bacteria and plants. The canonical two-component system in bacteria consists of a **sensor** that is an autophosphorylating *histidine kinase* and a **response regulator**, which transfers the phosphate from sensor histidine kinase to a conserved aspartate within itself.

The sensor histidine kinase is located in the membrane. It can be activated by binding a ligand that is in the extracellular medium. Activation causes the sensor histidine kinase to autophosphorylate. The reaction transfers the phosphate from ATP on to a histidine residue in the kinase domain. The sensor histidine kinase interacts with an effector protein i.e., *response regulator*. The response regulator has two domains – conserved **receiver domain** and **effector domain**. The receiver domain catalyzes transfer of the phosphate group from the histidine on the sensor histidine kinase to an aspartic acid residue in its own domain. This activates the effector domain. The usual end target of a two-component pathway is the regulation of gene transcription.

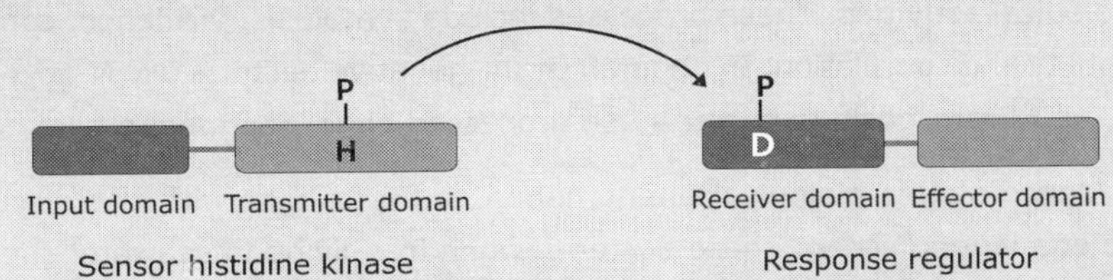

Figure 3.103 The canonical two-component signaling system is composed of a transmembrane sensor histidine kinase which regulates the activity of response regulator. In the transmembrane sensor histidine kinase, a conserved carboxy-terminal histidine-kinase domain, catalyzing auto-phosphorylation, with a phosphoryl residue being transferred from ATP to a conserved histidine residue. This phosphoryl is then transferred to an aspartate residue in the conserved receiver domain of the response regulator. Once phosphorylated the associated effector domain of the response regulator is activated.

3.20.7 Quorum sensing

The term *quorum sensing* describes a bacterial communication phenomenon that allows bacteria to communicate using secreted signal molecules to assess their population density. This process enables a population of bacteria to collectively regulate gene expression and, therefore, behaviour. In quorum sensing, bacteria assess their population density by detecting the concentration of a particular signal molecule termed autoinducer, which is correlated with cell density.

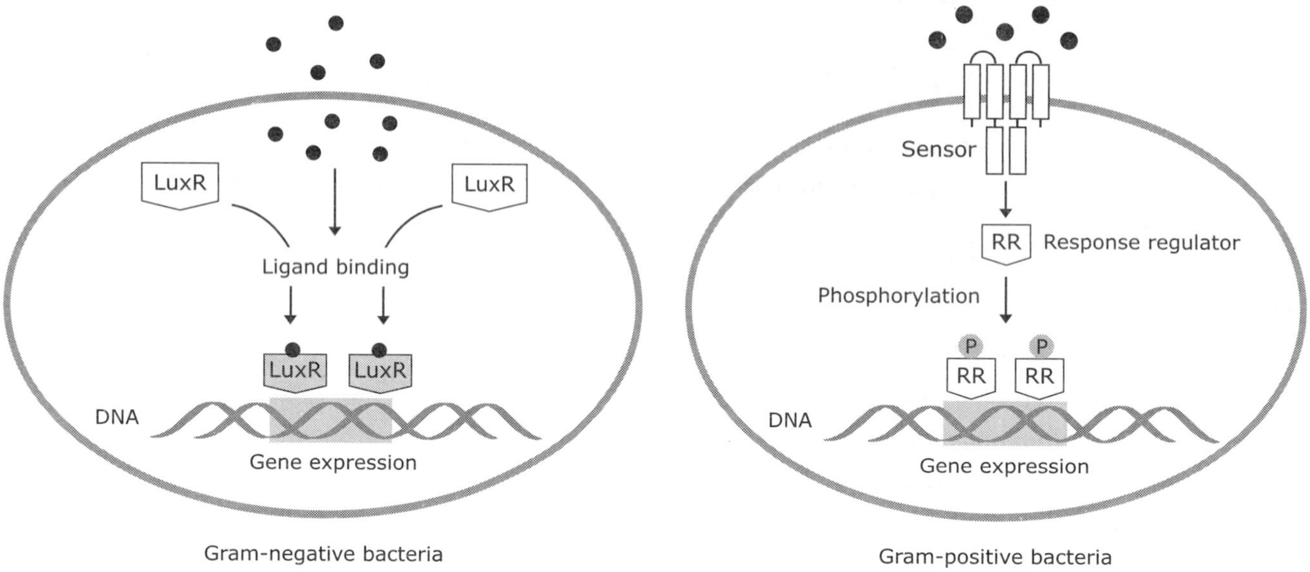

Figure 3.104 Mechanisms of action of auto-inducers: two major pathways along which extracellular signals control gene transcription. Depending on the chemical structure, auto-inducers (black dots) activate transcription factors either by direct interaction or via a receptor-mediated cascade. In contrast to AHL as auto-inducer in Gram-negative bacteria, the auto-inducers of Gram-positive species are unable to penetrate cellular membranes. Instead their effects are mediated by two component system controlling the transcription of corresponding genes.

Quorum sensing is the regulation of gene expression in response to fluctuations in cell-population density. Bacteria that use quorum sensing constantly produce and secrete certain signaling molecules (called **autoinducers**). These bacteria also have a receptor for the autoinducer. When the inducer binds to the receptor, it activates the transcription of a set of genes, including those responsible for the synthesis of the autoinducer itself. The concentration of the autoinducer in the surrounding medium depends on cell-population density. As the bacterial population grows, the concentration of the autoinducer in the surroundings increases, causing more autoinducer molecules to be synthesized. The detection of a minimal threshold stimulatory concentration of an autoinducer leads to an alteration in gene expression. Both gram-positive and gram-negative bacteria use quorum sensing communication circuits to regulate a diverse array of physiological activities. These processes include symbiosis, virulence, competence, conjugation, antibiotic production, motility and sporulation. In general, Gram-negative bacteria use **N-acyl-L-homoserine lactones (AHLs)** as autoinducers, and Gram-positive bacteria use processed **oligo-peptides** to communicate.

Examples: The first incidence of this biological phenomenon came to light with the discovery of luminescence produced by marine bacteria *Vibrio fischeri*. These bacteria, when free-living in seawater (i.e., at a low cell density) are non-luminescent. However, when grown to high cell densities, they bioluminescence with a blue-green light. This bacterium commonly forms symbiotic relationships with some fishes and squid species. These marine organisms carry a specialized organ called the light organ, in which bacteria luminescent appearance in dark environments is due to the maintenance of a high-density *V. fischeri* population in the light organ. In the marine environment, the bacteria only luminesce when colonizing the light organs and do not emit light when in the free-living state. Research on how *V. fischeri* regulates bioluminescence led to the discovery of bacterial quorum sensing via AHLs.

Synthesis of lipophilic AHL is catalyzed by an enzyme called *ALH synthase*, the product of the *luxI* gene. The *luxI* gene is subject to positive autoregulation i.e., transcription of *luxI* increases as AHL accumulates in the cell. This is accomplished through a transcriptional activator, LuxR, which is active only when it binds AHL. Thus, without AHL-activated LuxR, the *luxI* gene will be transcribed only at basal level. AHL freely diffuses out of the cell and accumulates in the environment. When cell density increases, the concentration of AHL also increases. Greater concentration of AHL flows back into the cell and activates high-level transcription of *luxI* and other genes whose products are needed for bioluminescence.

Box 3.5 Analysis of receptor–ligand interactions

Ligand binds specifically and non-covalently with the receptor. A receptor may possess one binding site per molecule or more than one independent binding sites. A receptor has a limited number of binding sites, and is therefore saturated at high ligand concentrations. Receptor-ligand binding is described by the **binding constant**. It is analogous to the equilibrium constant in a chemical reaction.

$$\text{R (Receptor)} + \text{L (Ligand)} \rightleftharpoons \text{R} - \text{L (Receptor} - \text{Ligand complex)}$$

At equilibrium, the ratio of the concentration of receptor-ligand complex [R-L] to the product of the concentrations of free ligand [L] and free receptor [R] is the *equilibrium constant*. The equilibrium constant for association reaction (also called *equilibrium association constant* or *affinity constant*), is K_a.

$$K_a = \frac{[RL]}{[R][L]}$$

In biological chemistry, the equilibrium constant for dissociation reaction (also called *equilibrium dissociation constant*), K_d is used more frequently. The equilibrium dissociation constant refers to the reciprocal of the equilibrium association constant.

$$K_d = \frac{1}{K_a} = \frac{[R][L]}{[RL]} \qquad ...(1)$$

The *equilibrium dissociation constant* is a measure of the *affinity* (or tightness of binding) of the receptor for its ligand. The smaller the equilibrium dissociation constant, the more stronger the binding between receptor and ligand.

Now, the **fractional saturation** of sites is

$$Y = \frac{\text{Concentration of L bound to R}}{\text{Total concentration of R}} = \frac{[RL]}{[R]+[RL]} \qquad ...(2)$$

The value of Y ranges from zero, when [RL] = 0, to 1, when [R] = 0. To determine the value of K_d, we can rearrange the equation (1),

$$[RL] = \frac{[R][L]}{K_d}$$

Substituting the expression for [RL] in the equation (2), we obtain

$$Y = \frac{[R][L]/K_d}{[R]+[R][L]/K_d}$$

$$Y = \frac{[L]}{[L]+K_d} \qquad ...(3)$$

This is an equation for **rectangular hyperbola**. It can be rearranged to give a linear form. By taking the reciprocal of the equation (3), we get

$$\frac{1}{Y} = 1 + \frac{K_d}{[L]}$$

Alternatively, it can be rearranged to $\frac{Y}{[L]} = \frac{1}{K_d} - \frac{Y}{K_d}$

A plot of Y/[L] versus Y (known as a **Scatchard plot**) gives a straight line of slope $-1/K_d$.

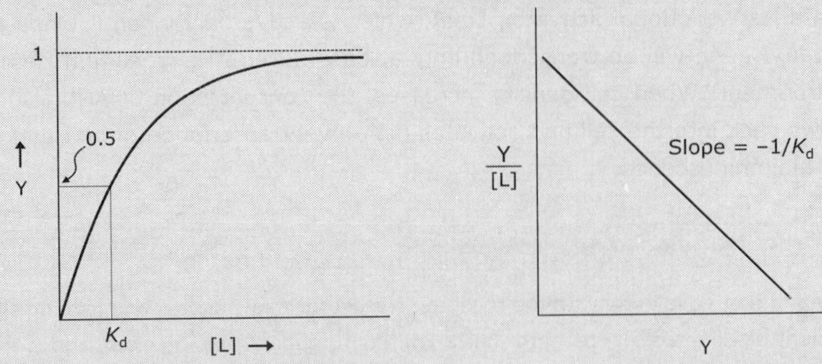

A. Hyperbolic plot B. Scatchard plot

If receptor has *n* equivalent binding sites for ligand

Now, consider the case in which a macromolecule has *n* equivalent sites; that is, each binding site has the same K_d value, regardless of whether other sites on the same molecule are occupied. In this case, the equation will be,

$$Y = \frac{n[L]}{[L]+K} \quad ...(4)$$

For *n* equivalent sites, we have $K = (K_1\, K_2\, K_3\, ...\, K_n)^{1/n}$

From equation (4),

$$Y[L] + KY = n[L]$$

$$\frac{Y[L]}{K} + Y = \frac{n[L]}{K}$$

$$Y = \frac{n[L]}{K} - \frac{Y[L]}{K}$$

$$\frac{Y}{[L]} = \frac{n}{K} - \frac{Y}{K}$$

Nonlinear Scatchard plots

The *Scatchard plot* in some cases is nonlinear, rather than linear. Following situations lead to such nonlinear Scatchard plots. The binding sites for the ligand may be heterogeneous; the ligand might be binding to one site with a dissociation constant of K_{d1} and a second site with a dissociation constant of K_{d2}. The binding of one molecule of ligand may change the affinity or the receptor for the next molecule of ligand (i.e., cooperative binding).

3.21 Cell Cycle

All organisms begin their life from a single cell. According to the cell theory, cells arise from pre-existing cells. The process by which this occurs is called *cell division*. By the process of division single cell divides and gives rise to two daughter cells. These newly formed daughter cells can themselves grow and divide, giving rise to a new cell population. An ordered series of events by which a cell duplicates its genome and eventually divides into two daughter cells is called **cell cycle**. The cell cycle has two main phases – *interphase* and *M-phase*. The **M-phase** is the period of actual division of the cell. It involves **karyokinesis** (division of the nucleus) and **cytokinesis** (division of the cytoplasm). The **interphase** is the time during which the cell is preparing for division by undergoing both cell growth and DNA replication in an orderly manner. The interphase is further subdivided into;

G1 phase (Gap 1, the period between the end of M phase and the start of DNA replication);

S phase (Synthesis, the period during which DNA synthesis occurs); and

G2 phase (Gap 2, the gap period following DNA replication and preceding the initiation of the M phase).

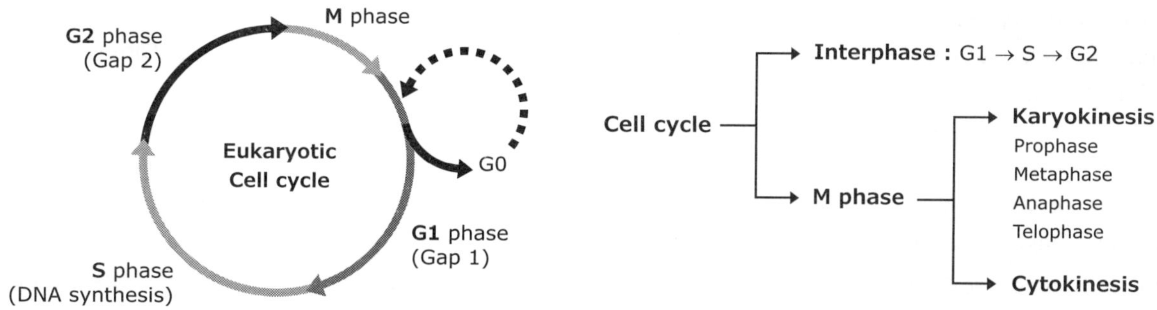

Figure 3.105 The four successive phases of a standard eukaryotic cell cycle. During interphase the cell grows continuously; during M phase it divides. DNA replication is confined to the part of interphase known as S phase. G1 phase is the gap between M phase and S phase; G2 is the gap between S phase and M phase. Cells in G1, if they have not yet committed themselves to DNA replication, can pause in their progress around the cycle and enter a specialized resting state, often called G0.

Approximately 95% of the cell cycle is spent in **interphase**. The duration of the three stages (G1, S and G2) varies from species to species, and also from cell to cell within a species. Although the length of all phases of the cycle is variable to some extent, by far, the greatest variation occurs in the duration of G1. Its length is adjusted in response to growth conditions. In most cells, the whole of M phase takes only about an hour, which is only a small fraction of the total cycle time. For a typical rapidly proliferating human cell in culture with a total cycle time of approximately 24 hours, the G1 phase might last about 11 hours, S phase about 8 hours, G2 about 4 hours and M about 1 hour.

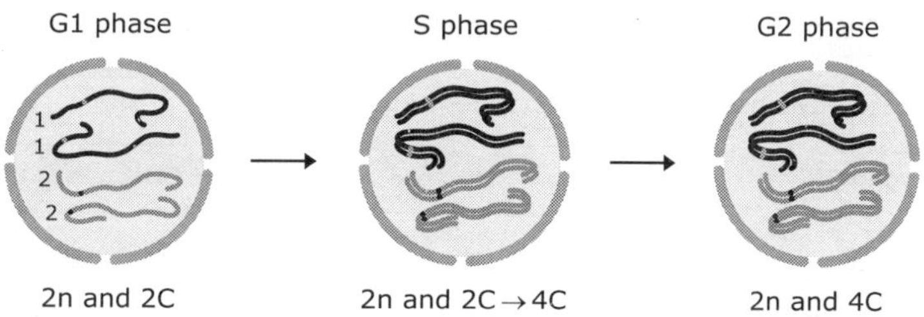

Figure 3.106 Change in number of chromosomes (n) and amount of DNA (C) during interphase nucleus of a diploid cell.

Thus, the interphase, though called the **resting phase**, is very active phase during which the cell is preparing for division by undergoing both cell growth and DNA replication in an orderly manner. During S phase, DNA replication takes place. Thus, the amount of DNA per cell doubles. If the initial amount of DNA is denoted as 2C, then it increases to 4C. However, there is no increase in the chromosome number; if the cell had diploid (2n) number of chromosomes at G1, even after S phase the number of chromosomes remains the same, i.e., 2n. The M phase starts with the nuclear division, corresponding to the formation of daughter nuclei (**karyokinesis**) and usually ends with division of cytoplasm (**cytokinesis**).

Cells that do not divide enter into G0 state. Most cells in our body remain in G0 state. Cells may enter into G0 state reversibly or irreversibly. If a cell enters into G0 state reversibly, it is termed as **quiescent state**. Cells in the quiescent state remain metabolically active but no longer proliferate unless called on to do so, depending on the requirement of the organism. This state can remain for days, weeks, or even years before resuming proliferation. If a cell enters into G0 state irreversibly, it may be **senescence** or **terminally differentiated** states. *Senescence* is the irreversible loss of proliferative potential. *Senescent cells* are dysfunctional cells that have ceased proliferation and are permanently withdrawn from the cell cycle. *Terminally differentiated cells* (e.g., mammalian skeletal muscle cells and nerve cells) are those cells that have irreversibly lost their ability to proliferate in the course of acquiring specialized functions.

Cell cycle control system

Cell cycle is a highly regulated and ordered series of events (G0 ↔ G1 → S → G2 → M). The engines that drive the progression from one step of the cell cycle to the next are **cyclin-CDK** complexes. These complexes are composed of two subunits: **cyclin** and **cyclin dependent protein kinase** (abbreviated **CDK**).

Cyclin is a regulatory protein, whereas **CDK** is catalytic protein and acts as serine/threonine protein kinase. Cyclins are so named because they undergo a cycle of synthesis and degradation in each cell cycle. Different cyclins are required at different phases of the cell cycle, each defined by the stage of the cell cycle at which they associate with CDKs and function. Cyclins bind to CDK molecules and control their ability to phosphorylate appropriate target proteins. Each cyclin is rapidly synthesized during a specific phase of the cell cycle and is again promptly broken down after it serves its purpose. They are broken down not only because they are no longer needed, but also because the breakdown is required for transition from one phase of cell cycle to next phase.

CDKs are so named because their activities are regulated by cyclins. They catalyze the phosphorylation of specific serine and threonine residues of specific target proteins. In human, there are about 20 different CDKs. Some CDKs such as CDK1, CDK2, CDK4 and CDK6 directly regulate cell-cycle and cell division, whereas CDKs such as CDK7–11 regulate gene transcription. The associated cyclin determines the target proteins for CDK phosphorylation. CDKs unbound to cyclins are usually inactive. CDKs are constitutively expressed in the cell, while cyclin expression is highly dependent on the cell cycle stage. Because different cyclins are present at different phases of the cell cycle, different phases of the cell cycle are characterized by the phosphorylation of different target proteins. The phosphorylation events are transient and reversible. When the cyclin CDK complex disappears, the phosphorylated substrate proteins are rapidly dephosphorylated by enzyme *phosphatases*.

In fission yeast, *Schizosaccharomyces pombe*, a single cyclin and single CDK drive all cell-cycle events, whereas, in budding yeast, *Saccharomyces cerevisiae*, a single CDK protein binds more than one classes of cyclins and drives all cell-cycle events by changing cyclin partners at different stages of the cycle. In vertebrate cells, by contrast, there are more than one CDKs to interact with different cyclins. Accordingly, the different cyclin-CDK complexes form. Each of the different cyclin-CDK complexes serves as a molecular switch that triggers a specific cell cycle event.

Table 3.18 Examples of selected cyclins and cyclin-dependent kinases (CDKs)

Organism	Cyclin	CDK
S. pombe	Cdc13	Cdc2 (CDK1)
S. cerevisiae	G1 phase: Cln3	Cdc28 (CDK1)
	G1/S phase: Cln1, Cln2	Cdc28 (CDK1)
	S phase: Clb5, Clb6	Cdc28 (CDK1)
	M phase: Clb1, Clb2, Clb3, Clb4	Cdc28 (CDK1)
Vertebrates	G1 phase: Cyclins D (cyclin D1, D2 and D3)	CDK4, CDK6
	G1/S phase transition: Cyclin E	CDK2
	S phase: Cyclin A	CDK2
	G2/M phase transition: Cyclin A	CDK1
	M phase: Cyclin B	CDK1

Note: The original name of CDK1 was Cdc2 in both vertebrates and fission yeast and Cdc28 in budding yeast.

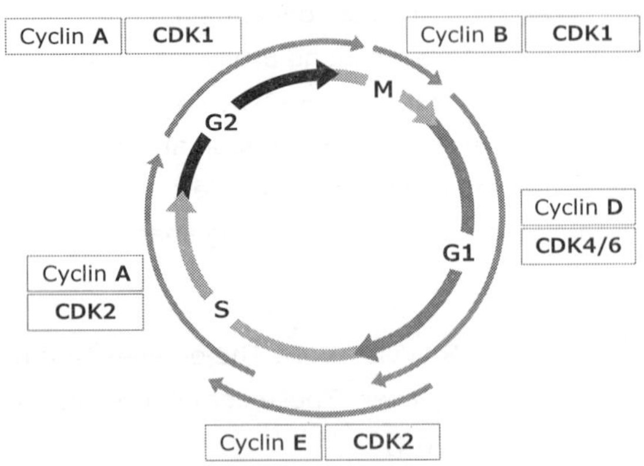

Figure 3.107
The cell cycle control system.
Where and when do cyclins act on the cell cycle? Cyclin-CDKs complexes trigger the transition from G1 to S phase and from G2 to M phase by phosphorylating distinct sets of substrates. According to the classical model of cell cycle control, D cyclins and CDK4 /CDK6 regulate events in the early G1 phase, E-CDK2 triggers S phase, A-CDK2 regulate the completion of S phase. The transition from G2 to M is driven by the sequential activity of cyclin A–CDK1 and cyclin B–CDK1 complexes.

Box 3.6 Estimating duration of cell-cycle phases (G1, S, G2 and M)

Duration of cell-cycle phases and the whole cycle can vary considerably among different cell types. Measurement of cell-cycle phase duration is desirable for kinetic studies of the cell. One method for measuring cell-cycle phase duration is based on pulse/chase labeling with [^{3}H] thymidine or the thymidine analog **5′-bromo-2′-deoxyuridine** (BrdU). Cell nuclei that have incorporated [^{3}H]-thymidine are visualized by *autoradiography*, whereas those that have incorporated BrdU are visualized by staining with anti-BrdU antibodies.

To estimate duration of different phases of cell cycle, asynchronous cell culture is pulsed for short period (e.g., 15 minutes) with [^{3}H] thymidine and then incubated (chased) for various times in unlabeled medium. **Asynchronous culture** is one in which cells are randomly distributed with respect to the phase of cell division whereas in **synchronized culture** all cells are in the same phase of cell division.

At regular intervals thereafter, a sample of cell population is fixed, dried onto a microscope slide and autoradiographed. After autoradiography, the frequency of [^{3}H] thymidine-labeled mitotic cells is scored. Initially, no labeled mitotic cells are observed because they are not engaged in DNA synthesis during the labeling period; they are in G2 phase. After 1 or 2 hours, the frequency of labeled mitotic cells begins to increase. The time it takes for the mitotic labeling index to reach 50% of maximal levels corresponds to the length of the G2 phase.

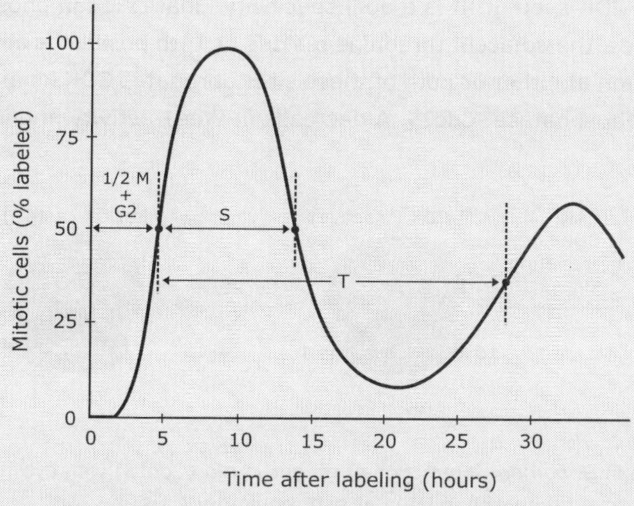

Figure 3.108
Determination of cell cycle phase durations by the fraction of labeled mitoses method.

After some time, the frequency of labeled mitotic cells begins to decrease. The time between 50% labeling on the ascending curve and 50% labeling on the descending curve corresponds to the length of S phase. The time between half-maximal labeling on the first and second ascending curve corresponds to the length of the entire division cycle (T). The length of G1 can be calculated by subtracting the length of G2 and S phase from the length of the entire division cycle (T).

Regulation of activity of cyclin-CDK complexes

Cyclins undergo a cycle of synthesis and degradation in each cell cycle. CDKs levels, by contrast, remain constant during the cell cycle. Cyclic changes in the cyclin levels result in the cyclic assembly and activation of the cyclin-CDK complexes. Cyclin-CDK complexes are inactivated by regulated proteolysis of cyclins at specific cell cycle stages. Cyclin levels in cells are controlled by changes in cyclin destruction and cyclin synthesis.

Cyclin destruction occurs by ubiquitin-mediated proteasomal degradation. Ubiquitin-mediated proteolysis of cyclin is catalyzed by enzyme **E3 ubiquitin ligase**. Two major classes of E3 ubiquitin ligases, **SCF** (SKP1–CULLIN1–F-box) and **APC/C** (anaphase-promoting complex/cyclosome) have a central role in cyclin degradation. SCF is named for three of its central components – **SKP1** (adaptor protein), **CULLIN1** (Scaffold protein) and the **F-box** protein (substrate recognition protein). The complex also contains a RING domain protein, **RBX1** (RING-finger catalytic protein). Enzyme **SCF** is active from late G1 to early M phase. Another E3 ubiquitin ligase, **APC/C** remains active from anaphase to the end of G1 phase. The APC/Cs are composed of 15-17 subunits depending on the organism. But unlike SCF, the APC/C does not have an F-box protein. APC/Cs have CDC20 and CDH1, which confer substrate specificity in the same way that F-box proteins do in the SCF complex.

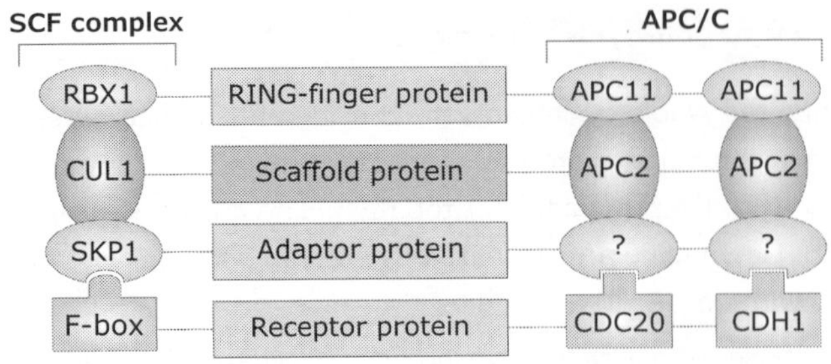

The rise and fall of cyclin levels (i.e., cyclin synthesis and degradation) is the primary determinant of CDK activity during the cell cycle. Several additional mechanisms also control the CDK activities at specific stages in the cell cycle. These mechanisms are:

- Phosphorylation and dephosphorylation reaction,
- Binding of CDK inhibitor proteins (**CKIs**).

The protein kinase activity of the cyclin-CDK complex also depends on the phosphorylation state of the catalytic CDK subunit. In the fission yeast, the M-CDK activity is inhibited by protein kinase, **Wee1**, which phosphorylates an inhibitory tyrosine residue at 15th position in the CDK subunit. It is a dual specificity kinase: it can phosphorylate serine/threonine and tyrosine. In higher vertebrates, the adjacent threonine residue at 14th position is also a site of inhibitory phosphorylation, and that phosphorylation at either or both of these sites abrogates CDK kinase activity. This inhibitory phosphate is removed by protein phosphatase, **Cdc25**. A decrease in Wee1 activity and increase in Cdc25 activity, resulting in activation of the CDK.

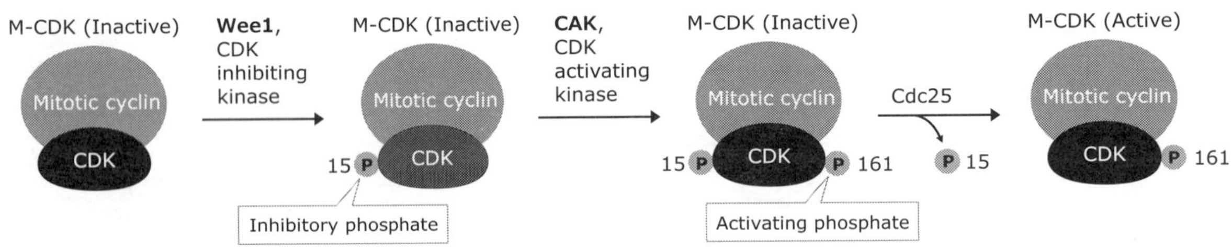

Figure 3.109 Regulation of activity of M-CDK complex in *S. pombe*. Interaction of mitotic cyclin (Cdc13) with cyclin-dependent kinase (CDK1) forms M-CDK complex. The CDK subunit can be phosphorylated at two regulatory sites: by Wee1 at tyrosine-15 and by CAK at threonine-161. When both residues are phosphorylated, M-CDK is inactive. Finally, removal of the phosphate from tyrosine-15 by Cdc25 phosphatase yields active M-CDK complex.

Full activation of the cyclin-CDK complex occurs when a separate kinase, the **CDK-activating kinase** (CAK), phosphorylates an activating *threonine* residue at 161 positions near the CDK active site. This causes a small conformational change that further increases the activity of the CDK, allowing the kinase to phosphorylate its target proteins effectively.

Cyclin-CDK complexes can also be regulated by the binding of **CDK inhibitor proteins** (CKIs). CKIs binding makes the cyclin-CDK complex inactive. Two types of CKIs contribute to cell-cycle control in mammals — **CIP/KIP family** and **INK4 family**. Members of CIP/KIP family (Cdk Interacting Protein/Kinase Inhibitory Protein) are **p21, p27** and **p57**. The members of INK4 (INhibitors of CDK4) family are p16 (INK4a), p15 (INK4b), p18 (INK4c) and p19 (INK4d). INK4 CKIs target specifically to the CDK4 and CDK6 and inhibit their kinase activities by interfering with their association with D-type cyclins. Conversely, the CIP/KIP CKIs bind to D-, E-, A- and B- cyclin-CDK complexes and inhibit their kinase activities.

Mutant analysis: The **Wee1** and **Cdc25** play antagonistic roles. Wee1 usually inhibits cells from initiating mitosis until their size is adequate. Hence, loss-of-function mutations in the wee1 gene cause premature entry into mitosis resulting in small cells, whereas overproduction of Wee1 protein increases the length of G2, resulting in elongated cells. Inhibitory phosphate is removed by protein phosphatase, Cdc25. Hence, due to loss-of-function mutations, the cell does not divide but continues to grow.

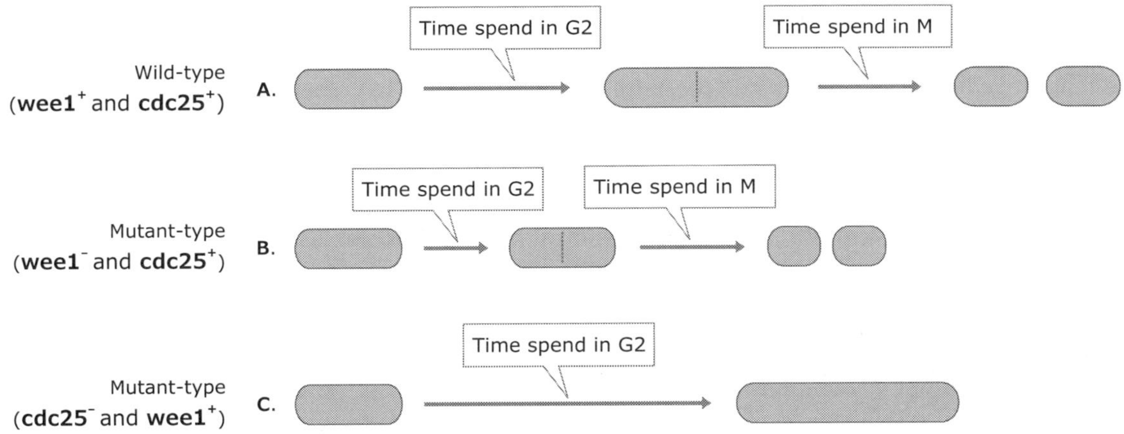

Figure 3.110 Comparison of the effects of wee1⁻ and cdc25⁻ mutants in fission yeast. Figure 'A' shows the G2 and M stages of a wild-type cell, figure 'B' shows the effect of a loss-of-function mutation of wee1 gene, the cell divides prematurely, forming small (wee) cells. Figure 'C' shows the effect of a mutant cdc25 gene; the cell does not divide but continues to grow.

Control of DNA duplication in S phase

Preparations for DNA replication begin in G1 with the assembly of *prereplicative complexes* at replication origins. S-CDK activation leads to the formation of multiprotein *preinitiation complexes* that unwind the DNA at origins and begin the process of DNA replication. A key player involved in this process is a large, multiprotein complex called the *origin recognition complex* (**ORC**). It binds to origins of replication. In early G1, Cdc6 and Cdt1 associate with the ORC. The APC/C triggers the destruction of a Cdt1 inhibitor called **geminin**, thereby allowing Cdt1 to be active. The resulting protein complex then assembles **MCM proteins** (MCM for mini-chromosome maintenance). MCM (acts as helicase) is a hexamer of six related polypeptides (Mcm2–7) that form a ring structure. The resulting complex is called **prereplicative complex (pre-RC)**.

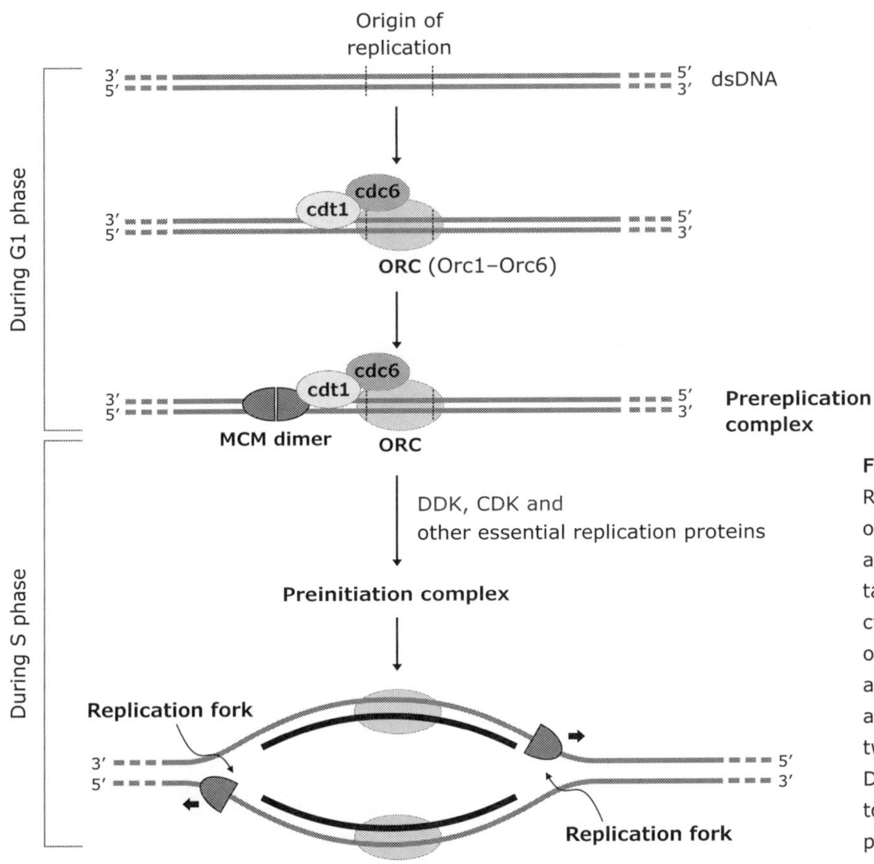

Figure 3.111
Replication is initiated by the formation of the pre-replication complex (pre-RC) at the origins of replication. This process takes place in the G1 stage of the cell cycle. The pre-RC formation involves the ordered assembly of ORC, Cdc6, Cdt1 and MCMs. Once the pre-RC is formed, activation of the complex is triggered by two kinases, S phase–specific CDK and DDK that cause transition of the pre-RC to the pre-initiation complex (pre-IC) prior to the initiation of replication.

The MCM proteins act as *licensing factors* that allows replication to initiate. However, the loaded Mcm2–7 complex is inactive at this point. In the second step, which is called initiation, or firing, the Mcm2–7 complex is activated, and active replicative helicase is formed i.e., **pre-initiation complex (pre-IC)**. The active form of replicative helicase consists of **Cdc45** and **GINS** complex (Sld5, Psf1, Psf2, and Psf3) in addition to the Mcm2–7 complex and is called the **CMG complex** (Cdc45–Mcm2–7–GINS). The formation of pre-IC is regulated by two protein kinases, Dbf4/Drf1-dependent kinase (**DDK**) and cyclin-dependent kinase (**CDK**). DDK and S-CDK enhance the recruitment of Cdc45 and GINS, respectively, onto Mcm2–7 in the pre-RC to form the CMG complex. Once replication has initiated, Cdc6 proteins undergo degradation. The degradation of Cdc6 prevents reinitiation. It ensures that each origin is activated only once in each cell cycle.

Box 3.7 Cell fusion experiments

The cell cycle is a dependent phase of events. It is divided into four distinct phases. Control mechanisms operate to regulate the onset of each phase and avoid improper transitions between phases. Initial insights about the nature of cell-cycle regulation came from cell fusion experiments of Rao and Johnson in 1970. They also demonstrated that the cytoplasm of cells contains regulatory factors that affect cell cycle activities. These investigators used an inactivated **Sendai virus** to fuse together mammalian cells that had reached different stages of the cell cycle. The resulting heterokaryons possessed two different nuclei — one from each parent cell—and share the same cytoplasm. The behaviour of the two nuclei was then monitored.

In the first set of experiments, when **G1 cells** were fused with **S phase cells**, the G1 cells abruptly resumed DNA synthesis and entered into S phase. Thus, the cytoplasm of S phase cells contained the factors that initiated DNA synthesis in the G1 nucleus.

In the second set of experiments, **S-phase cells** were fused with **G2-phase cells.** Although chromosome replication continued in the S nucleus of the heterokaryon, the G2 nucleus was unable to synthesize DNA, indicating that the G2 nucleus is prevented from entering further rounds of DNA replication.

Finally, when **G1 cells** were fused with **G2 cells**, the rate of initiation of DNA synthesis and of mitosis was similar to that of G1/G1 cells rather than G2/G2 cells. Although the G2 nucleus had no effect on the G1 nucleus, entry of the G2 nucleus into M phase was delayed by factors associated with the G1 component. This elegant series of experiments was the first indication in mammalian cells that the sequential and unidirectional phases of the cell cycle are controlled by a series of chemical signals that can diffuse freely between the nucleus and cytoplasm.

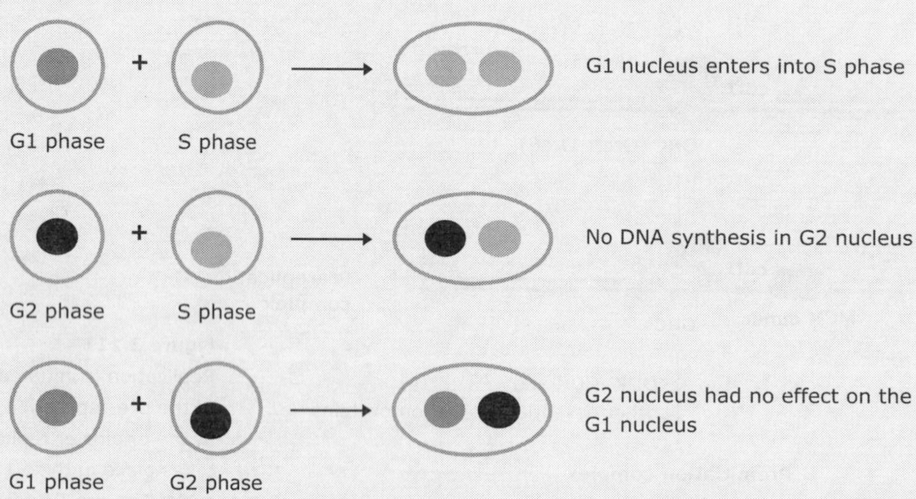

Figure 3.112 Cell fusion experiments. Cells in S phase were fused either to cells in G1 or to cells in G2. When G1 cells were fused with S phase cells, the G1 nucleus immediately began to replicate DNA. In contrast, when G2 cells were fused with S phase cells, only the S phase nucleus continued DNA replication. It, therefore, appeared that the G2 nucleus had to pass through M and enter G1 before another round of DNA replication could be initiated. This elegant series of experiments was the first indication in mammalian cells that the sequential and unidirectional phases of the cell cycle are controlled by a series of chemical signals that can diffuse freely between the nucleus and cytoplasm.

Role of M phase cyclin-CDK complex (M-CDK)

M-CDK is commonly referred to as a **mitosis promoting factor** (or *maturation promoting factor*, MPF). It is synthesized during the S and G2-phase. M-CDK complexes induce chromosome condensation, breakdown of the nuclear envelope, assembly of the mitotic spindle apparatus and alignment of condensed chromosomes at the metaphase plate.

To perform these activities, M-CDKs phosphorylate a wide range of proteins. These include **condensin** proteins, which are essential for the extensive condensation of mitotic chromosomes and **lamin** proteins, which form a stabilizing network under the nuclear membrane that dissembles during mitosis. *Condensin* proteins are made up of SMC (structural maintenance of chromosome) and non-SMC proteins. It is a key driver of mitotic chromosome condensation. During mitosis, condensin is phosphorylated by the cyclin-CDK.

M-CDKs also influence the assembly of the mitotic spindle by phosphorylating proteins that regulate microtubule behavior. The net effect of these coordinated phosphorylation reactions is the accurate separation of chromosomes during mitosis. M-CDK initiates these changes in microtubule behavior by phosphorylating two classes of proteins that control microtubule dynamics. These include **microtubule-dependent motor proteins** and **microtubule-associated proteins** (MAPs). Two additional families of protein kinases, the **polo-like kinases** and the **aurora kinases**, also make important contributions to the control of early mitotic events. The polo-like kinase, for example, is required for the normal assembly of a bipolar mitotic spindle. Aurora kinases (aurora kinase A and aurora kinase B) regulate mitotic spindle assembly and chromosome segregation.

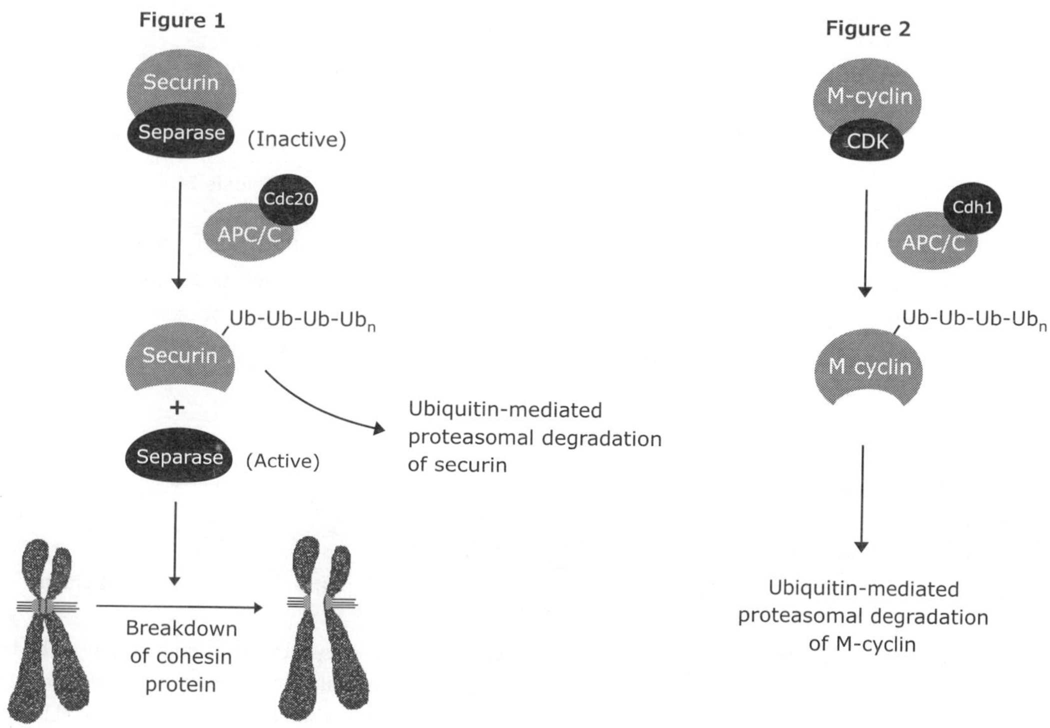

Figure 3.113 APC/C is activated in late M-phase by the association of Cdc20 (or Cdh1). The activation of APC/C by Cdc20 (or Cdh1) leads to the ubiquitylation and destruction of securin and M-cyclin. The destruction of securin allows separase to cleave a subunit of the cohesin complex. The pulling forces of the mitotic spindle then pull the sister chromatids apart.

After the proper association of all chromosomes with spindle microtubules has occurred, the M-CDK complexes activate the APC/C. Thus, M-CDK not only triggers the early mitotic events leading up to metaphase, but it also sets the stage for progression into anaphase. APC/C acts on different substrates at different times. APC/C functions in coordination with two homologous mitotic coactivators, **Cdc20** and **Cdh1** (Cdc20 homologue 1). APC/C initiates the metaphase-anaphase transition through mediating the ubiquitination and degradation of *M-cyclin* and *securin*. **Securin** holds enzyme **separase**, a ubiquitous **cysteine protease**, in an inactive state. The destruction of securin allows separase to cleave **Scc1**, a subunit of the cohesin which holds the sister chromatids together.

To prevent premature separation of sister chromatids and exit from mitosis, APC/C^{Cdc20} is inhibited by Mad2 and BubR1 through the spindle assembly checkpoint mechanism. The inhibition of APC/C^{Cdc20} is released only when the sister chromatids are aligned at the metaphase plate and have established bivalent spindle attachment. In contrast to APC/C^{Cdc20}, APC^{Cdh1} is inactive during early M-phase and only becomes active from late M-phase to G1 phase. The destruction of cyclin is as important for exit from mitosis as its synthesis is for entry. The resulting decrease in M-CDK activity permits the separated chromosomes to decondense, the nuclear envelope to re-form around daughter-cell nuclei during telophase, and the cytoplasm to divide at cytokinesis, yielding the two daughter cells.

Cdh1 activity is regulated by cell-cycle-dependent phosphorylation and dephosphorylation. The phosphorylation of Cdh1 by cyclin–CDK during S, G2 and early M phases inhibits APC/C activation by preventing Cdh1 from binding to the core APC/C subunits, whereas dephosphorylation of Cdh1 during G1 and late M phases by **CDC14** phosphatase induces APC/C activation by allowing Cdh1 to access the core APC/C subunits.

Box 3.8 Discovery of maturation promoting factor (MPF)

The identification of the factor that induces mitosis came from studies of oocyte maturation in the frog *Xenopus laevis*. During oocytes development in the ovary, oocytes in the *Xenopus laevis* arrest in the G2 stage of the cell cycle for up to 8 months, and are then induced by the steroid hormone **progesterone** to enter meiosis I. The oocytes then undergo a second arrest at the metaphase of meiosis II, where they remain until fertilization.

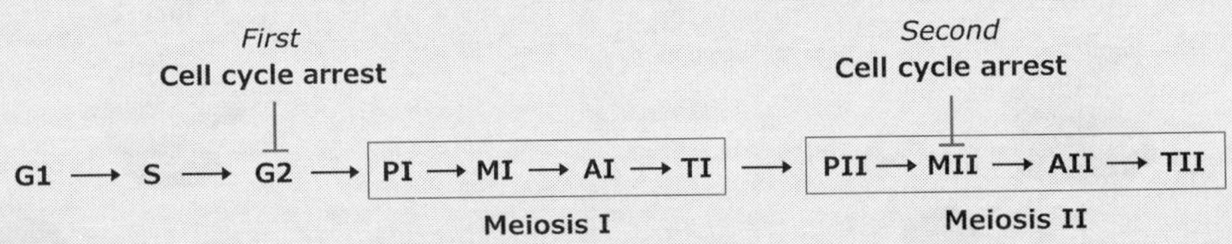

In 1971, Yoshio Masui and Clement Markert found that oocytes in the frog *Xenopus laevis* arrested in G2 phase could be induced to enter meiosis I by microinjection of cytoplasm from oocytes that had been stimulated with hormone progesterone. It thus appeared that a cytoplasmic factor present in hormone-treated oocytes was sufficient to trigger the transition from G2 to meiosis I in oocytes that had not been exposed to hormone.

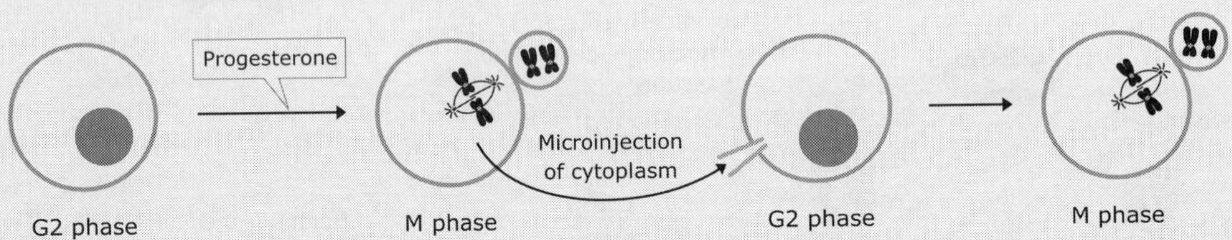

Figure 3.114 Frog oocytes are arrested in the G2 phase of the cell cycle, and entry into meiosis I is triggered by the hormone progesterone. In the experiment diagrammed here, G2-arrested oocytes were microinjected with cytoplasm extracted from oocytes that had undergone the transition from G2 to M phase. Such cytoplasmic transfer induced the G2 to M phase transition in the absence of hormonal stimulation, demonstrating that a maturation cytoplasmic factor (MPF) is sufficient to induce entry into the M phase of meiosis.

Because the entry of oocytes into meiosis is frequently referred to as **oocyte maturation**, this cytoplasmic factor was called **maturation promoting factor** (MPF). Further studies showed, however, that the activity of MPF is not restricted to the entry of oocytes into meiosis. Following its discovery in frog oocytes, MPF was also found to be present in somatic cells, where it induces the G2 to M transition of mitosis. Thus, MPF appeared to be a general regulator of entry into the M phase of both mitotic and meiotic cell cycles. The eventual purification of MPF from frog oocytes was found to be a dimer of cyclin and CDK. The discovery of MPF in frog oocytes thus paved the way to understanding a cell cycle regulatory apparatus that is conserved throughout all eukaryotes.

Cell cycle checkpoints

The cell cycle is a highly regulated and a dependent series of events. Cell cycle checkpoints are surveillance mechanisms that monitor the order and fidelity of events during the cell cycle. These points ensure that incomplete or damaged chromosomes are not replicated and passed on to daughter cells. Hartwell and Weinert hypothesized the existence of 'checkpoint pathways' by which an uncompleted cell cycle event sends an inhibitory signal to later events. In most cells, there are several checkpoints in the cell cycle which can be classified into: Cell cycle checkpoint, DNA damage checkpoint and spindle-assembly checkpoint. Each checkpoint arrest utilizes different mechanisms that sense the stress or damage and impose the cell cycle arrest.

Cell cycle checkpoint ensures the fidelity of cell division. These checkpoints verify whether the processes at each phase of the cell cycle have been accurately completed before progression into the next phase. An important checkpoint in G1 has been identified in both yeast and mammalian cells. Referred to as a **start** in yeast and the **restriction point** in mammalian cells, this is the point at which the cell becomes committed to DNA replication and completes a cell cycle. It is during the G1 phase that the cell integrates mitogenic and growth inhibitory signals, and makes the decision to proceed, pause or exit the cell cycle. It controls the cell's commitment to division. The restriction checkpoint is largely controlled by the Rb/E2F signaling pathway: release of E2F transcription factors from Rb allows E2F to transcriptionally activate genes that promote the initiation of DNA replication and S phase entry.

Spindle assembly checkpoint (or *mitotic checkpoint*) guarantees that anaphase onset is initiated only when all chromosomes are properly attached to microtubules and aligned at the metaphase plate. It monitors the correct attachment of chromosomes to the mitotic spindles; it prevents segregation of sister chromatids until they are properly aligned on the metaphase plate. During mitosis, chromosome segregation is carefully monitored to prevent aneuploidy. When microtubules from two opposite spindle poles attach to the kinetochores of a metaphasic chromosome, tension develops across the paired kinetochores owing to the mitotic force that tends to pull the sister chromatids toward two opposite poles.

Configuration	Amphitelic	Monotelic	Syntelic	Merotelic
Spindle checkpoint	Inactive	Active	Active	Inactive

Kinetochores harbour an error correction mechanism that is regulated by **aurora B kinase**, which eliminates incorrect microtubule attachments by sensing whether or not the centromere is under tension. By this method, the kinetochore can distinguish between the correct **amphitelic** (sister kinetochores are anchored to microtubules from opposite poles) versus the erroneous **monotelic** (only one kinetochore is anchored to microtubules) and **syntelic** (both kinetochores are anchored to microtubules emanating from the same pole) attachments. Thus, kinetochores have a crucial role in cell cycle progression. The mechanism that monitors and responds to kinetochore-microtubule attachment is the **spindle assembly checkpoint** (SAC). The SAC is composed of several proteins that are conserved from yeast to mammals; the core components include **Mad1** (Mitotic Arrest Deficient), **Mad2**, **Mad3** (BubR1 in mammals), **Bub1** and **Bub3** (Budding Uninhibited by Benzimidazole). During metaphase, Mad1 and Bub1 monitor proper spindle microtubule-kinetochore attachment/tension. Until proper attachments are formed, the SAC inhibits the APC/C. When problems are sensed and SAC is activated, Mad2 interacts with Mad1 at the kinetochore, facilitating conformational changes in Mad2 to promote the formation of the **mitotic checkpoint complex** (MCC) with Mad3, Bub3 and Cdc20. The MCC is a complex of mitotic spindle assembly checkpoint proteins Mad2, Mad3, Bub3 and APC/C co-activator protein Cdc20. Mad2 in the MCC prevents Cdc20 from binding and activating the APC/C. Once kinetochores have established stable amphitelic attachments to the spindle, the SAC is silenced and inhibition of Cdc20 is alleviated. The anaphase-promoting complex (APC/C) is activated. However, **merotelic** attachments (a single kinetochore is attached to microtubules from both poles) can go uncorrected, as they do not activate the SAC, which leads to segregation errors. SAC failure results in aneuploidy in the daughter cells.

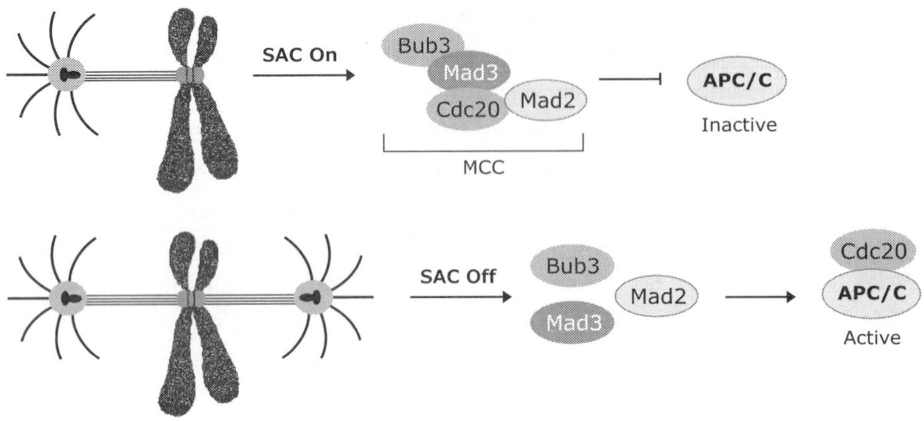

Figure 3.115 Molecular basis of spindle assembly checkpoint (SAC) signaling. The SAC is activated by the presence of unattached kinetochores. Unattached kinetochore recruits SAC proteins to generate the Mitotic Checkpoint Complex (MCC), the diffusible inhibitory signal composed of Mad2, Mad3, Bub3 and Cdc20. By sequestering Cdc20, the MCC keeps the APC/C inactive, preventing it from targeting securin.

DNA damage checkpoint involves a signal transduction pathway induced by DNA damage that blocks cell cycle progression until DNA is properly repaired. Its function to ensure that incomplete or damaged chromosomes are not replicated and passed on to daughter cells. According to the cell cycle stages, DNA damage checkpoints are classified into at least 3 checkpoints: **G1/S checkpoint**, **intra-S phase checkpoint** and **G2/M checkpoint**. The G1/S checkpoint inhibits G1/S phase transition in cells that have not yet committed to DNA replication. At the G1/S checkpoint, cell cycle arrest induced by DNA damage is p53-dependent. The intra-S checkpoint prevents initiation of DNA replication at origins that have not yet been activated. The G2/M checkpoint inhibits entry into mitosis. The *replication checkpoint*, a specialized branch of the DNA damage checkpoint, monitors fork problems, and triggers a cellular response aimed at preserving genome integrity.

DNA damage response signaling pathway

ATM (Ataxia Telangiectasia Mutated) and **ATR** (Ataxia Telangiectasia and Rad3 related) are closely related kinases that are activated by DNA damage. These serine-threonine protein kinases are members of the *phosphatidylinositol 3′-kinase-like kinase* (**PIKK**) family. Both ATM and ATR are activated by DNA damage. The DNA damage may be caused by the action of exogenous (e.g., ionizing radiation and chemical mutagens) and endogenous (e.g., metabolic byproducts, stalled replication forks) sources. In response to DNA damage, eukaryotic cells activate elaborate cellular networks, collectively termed the **DNA damage response** (DDR). These signaling pathways lead to DNA repair, cell-cycle arrest and, eventually, apoptosis. ATM responds to DNA double-strand breaks (**ATM pathway**), while ATR responds to a wide range of DNA lesions, especially those associated with DNA replication (**ATR pathway**). At the molecular level, the DDR pathway contains several key components: DNA damage sensors, signal transducers and effectors.

Various types of DNA damage can be detected by distinct sensor proteins. In mammals, the **MRN** (Mre11/Rad50/Nbs1) complex has been proposed as double-strand breaks sensors in the ATM pathway. The MRN complex recruits ATM at the double-strand break sites, and the interaction with MRN complex activates ATM kinase, resulting in the phosphorylation of the kinase **Chk2** (checkpoint kinase 2). Replication protein A (**RPA**), a single-stranded DNA-binding protein, functions as a sensor in the ATR pathway. RPA binds to single-stranded DNA generated at the site of stalled replication forks. *ATR-interacting protein* (**ATRIP**) binds to the RPA-ssDNA complex in order to recruit ATR to ssDNA, which is followed by the activation of the downstream kinase **Chk1** (checkpoint kinase 1).

Eventually, DDR signaling spreads away from the damaged locus owing to the engagement of diffusible kinases Chk2 (which is mainly phosphorylated by ATM) and Chk1 (which is mainly phosphorylated by ATR) with signaling converging on downstream effectors such as p53 and Cdc25. DDR-mediated cellular outcomes may be cell death by apoptosis; transient cell cycle arrest followed by repair of DNA damage and resumption of proliferation; or cellular senescence caused by the persistence of unrepaired DNA damage. An additional layer of control of the DDR that is based on small RNAs called **DDRNAs** have also recently been reported.

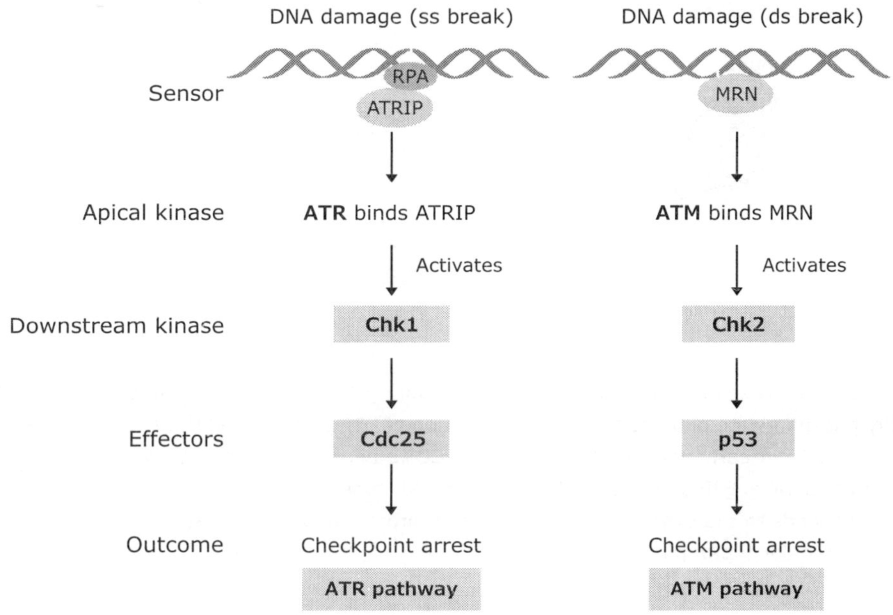

Figure 3.116 Upon recruitment by the DNA damage binding proteins/complexes (ATRIP for ATR; MRN for ATM), ATM/ATR initiate the DNA damage checkpoint by phosphorylating a number of key proteins. Once activated, the checkpoint leads to cell cycle arrest and either DNA repair or apoptosis. ATM is activated by double stranded breaks and phosphorylates Chk2, while ATR is activated by single strand breaks and phosphorylates Chk1.

3.21.1 Role of Rb protein in cell cycle regulation

The ***RB1*** (retinoblastoma 1) **gene** codes protein called **pRb**. It is a **tumor suppressor gene** (genes whose inactivation contribute to the development of a tumor are called *tumor-suppressor genes*). The protein encoded by this gene is a negative regulator of the cell cycle and was the first tumor suppressor gene discovered. Loss-of-function mutations in *RB1* genes are associated with the *retinoblastoma* and many other tumors. In human, the *RB1* gene is located on chromosome 13q14.2. The **pRb** protein encoded by the *RB1* gene is a nuclear protein of 110 kDa. Based on sequence similarity, two other members of the RB family were identified, ***RBL1*** and ***RBL2*** that code for the **p107** and **p130** proteins, respectively. All three RB family members contain a conserved domain referred to as the '*pocket'* that interacts with the LXCXE motif found in some viral proteins. For this reason, the RB family is also frequently called the **pocket protein** family.

How the product of the RB1 gene regulates cell division? The active, un or hypophosphorylated form of the pRb protein binds transcription factor **E2F** and represses gene transcription which is required for transition from G1 to S phase. E2F acts as a *transcription factor* and induces many genes to transcribe. The products of these genes are required for S-phase of the cycle. Five main E2F family members have been identified and these molecules show preferential binding to different Rb family members. E2F activity is controlled by pRb protein. When pRb protein binds to E2F, its activity is suppressed. Phosphorylation of pRb protein, reduces its affinity for E2F and allows E2F to heterodimerize with factor **DP** (DNA-binding Proteins). E2F-DP complex induces the expression of critical late G1 genes, the products of which are required to prepare the cell for entrance into S-phase. pRb protein is a substrate for cyclin-CDK complexes. Phosphorylation of pRb protein is initiated by cyclin D-CDK4/6 and cyclin E-CDK2 in G1. Un or hypo-phosphorylated pRb proteins block cell cycle progression. The levels of the D-type cyclins (D1, D2 and D3) are controlled primarily through extracellular signals. The D-type cyclins convey information about extracellular mitogenic signals to the core cell cycle machinery.

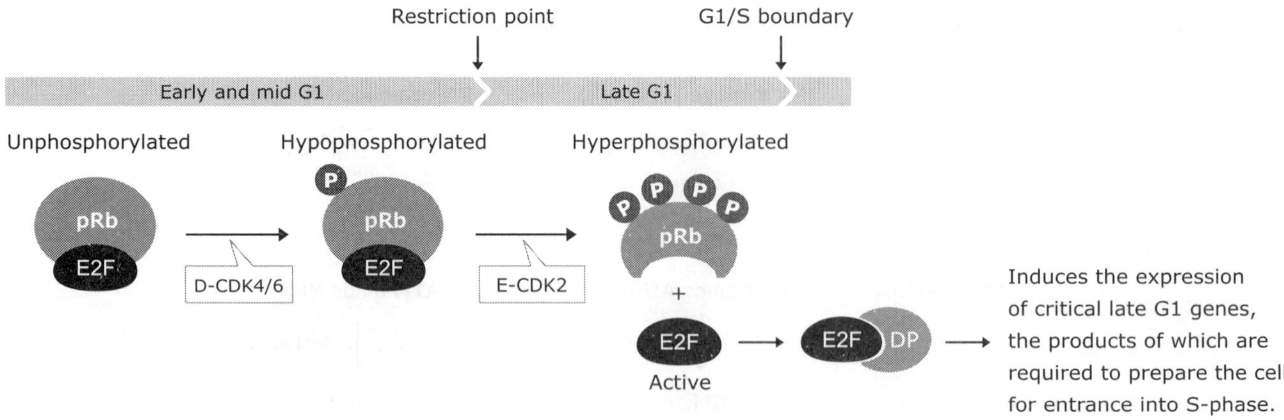

Figure 3.117 Cyclin-CDK complexes regulate pRb/E2F activity. During the G1 phase of the cell cycle, D-CDK4/6 and E-CDK2 complexes sequentially phosphorylate pRb, leading to the activation of E2F proteins and the expression of E2F responsive genes. D-CDK4/6 phosphorylates pRb in early and mid G1 whereas E-CDK2 near the end of G1. When E-CDK2 complexes drive pRb hyperphosphorylation, this liberates E2F transcription factors from pRb control, enabling the E2Fs to trigger increased transcription of the cyclin E genes; this leads to the synthesis of more cyclin E protein and the formation of more E-CDK2 complexes, which function, in turn, to drive additional pRb phosphorylation.

The ability of mitogenic factors to increase the levels of cyclin D depends on several distinct signaling pathways. One of the best studied of these signals flow via the Ras → Raf → MAPK pathway. The cyclin D and cyclin E control the degree to which pRb is phosphorylated. Cyclin D-CDK4/6 drive pRb *hypophosphorylation* in early and mid G1. It is prerequisite to the **restriction point** (R-point) transition in late G1 phase. This ensures that this transition is responsive to extracellular signals. Later, cyclin E levels increase dramatically. The cyclin E then associates with CDK2, and this complex drives pRb phosphorylation to completion, leaving pRb in its *hyperphosphorylated*, functionally inactive state. The R-point represents a point at which the cell commits itself, to complete the remainder of the cell cycle or, alternatively, to remain in G1 and possibly retreat from the active cell cycle into the G0, quiescent state.

Two families of CKIs have been identified that can block the kinase activity of D-CDK4/6 and E-CDK2. The **INK CKIs** (p15, p16, p18 and p19) is believed to bind preferentially to CDK4/6 and **CIP/KIP CKIs** (p21, p27 and p57) bind with either D-CDK or E-CDK complexes.

This scheme reveals why pRb is such a critical player in the regulation of cell proliferation. If its services are lost from the cell, then this protein can no longer stand as the guardian of the G1 to S phase transition. Hence, loss of pRb protein functions may induce cell cycle deregulation and lead to a malignant phenotype. pRb protein can also be functionally inactivated by mutations or viral oncoprotein binding. pRb function can be lost through mutation of the *RB1* gene, as is seen in retinoblastomas, osteosarcomas and small-cell lung carcinomas. A functionally similar outcome can be observed in cells that have been infected and transformed by human papillomavirus (HPV); pRb binding by the viral **E7 oncoprotein** plays a key role in the development of the great majority of *cervical carcinomas*.

3.21.2 Role of p53 protein in cell cycle regulation

The ***TP53*** gene codes for p53 protein (also known as TP53) of an apparent molecular mass of 53 kDa. The *TP53* gene like the *RB1* gene, is a tumor suppressor gene, i.e., its activity stops the formation of tumors. It is located on human chromosome **17p13.1** and encodes a polypeptide chain of 393 amino acid residues.

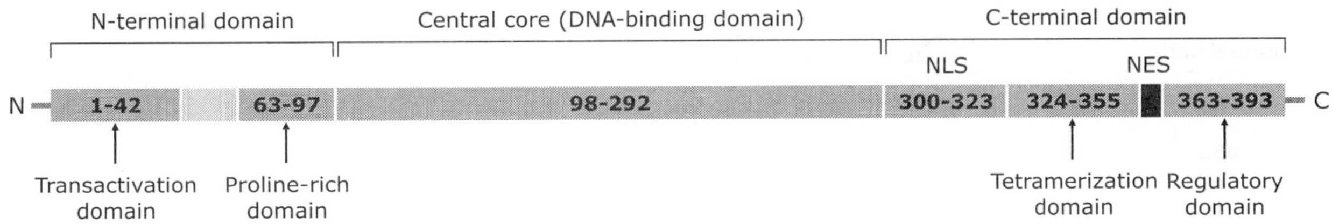

p53 protein is a *transcription factor* that regulates the expression of several genes (~500 genes) involved in DNA repair, cell growth, apoptosis, antioxidant defence and senescence. Because mutations in *TP53* gene are found in most tumor types and are involved in the complex network of cellular events, it is described as the **guardian of the genome** and the **cellular gatekeeper**. In a normal unstressed cell, p53 is present at very low concentrations. This occurs due to interaction with E3 ubiquitin ligase **Mdm2** (mouse double minute 2), which causes polyubiquitination of p53 and targets it for proteasomal destruction. Under cellular stresses such as mitotic apparatus dysfunction, DNA replication stress, telomere erosion, oxidative stress, DNA damage, various pathways lead to the reduced interactions of the p53 and Mdm2. Once p53 concentration increases due to reduced proteasomal destruction, it induces a cell cycle arrest to allow either repair and survival of the cell or apoptosis to discard the damaged cell.

For example, DNA damage induces an increase in the p53 concentration. DNA damage, such as double-strand breaks in DNA, causes the activation of protein kinase ATM, which in turn activates Chk2 kinase. ATM and Chk2 then both phosphorylate p53 at distinct sites. Phosphorylation of p53 alters the domain of p53 that is normally recognized and bound by Mdm2 and, in this way, prevents the association of Mdm2 with p53. The ATM kinase also phosphorylates Mdm2, which causes its functional inactivation.

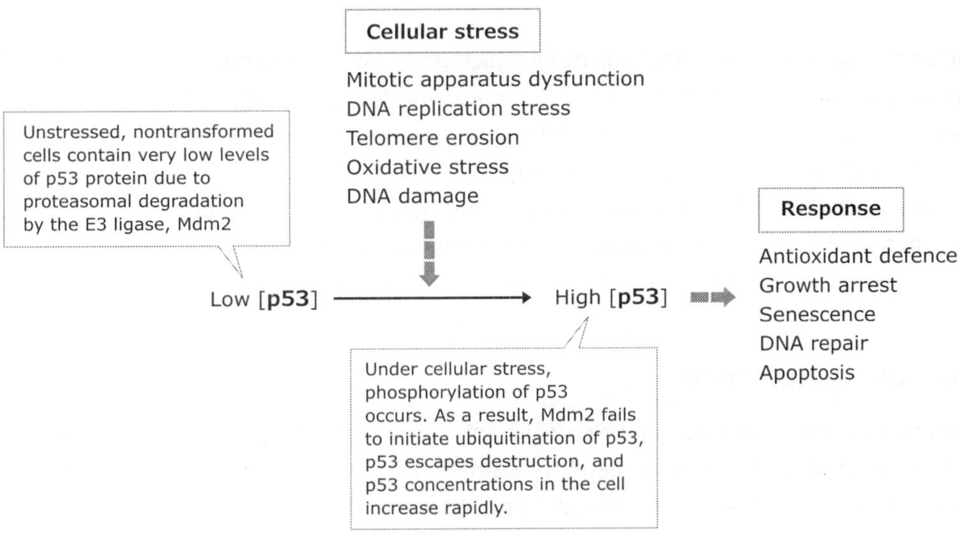

Figure 3.118 Role of p53 protein.

As a consequence of this phosphorylation of p53, Mdm2 fails to initiate ubiquitination of p53, p53 escapes destruction, and p53 concentrations in the cell increase rapidly. Once present in substantial amounts, p53 is then poised to evoke a series of downstream responses. Protein p53 stimulates transcription of the gene encoding a CKI protein called **p21**; this protein binds to G1/S-CDK and S-CDK complexes and inhibits their activities, thereby helping to block entry into the cell cycle. Hence, in response to DNA damage, p53 levels increase and arrest the cell at the G1-phase of the cell cycle. If all of the repairs have been made to the DNA, the cell divides normally and completes the cycle. However, if the cell still contains mutated or duplicated DNA sequences, it dies by a suicidal *apoptotic* mechanism to prevent its proliferation. In cells with *loss-of-function* mutations in the *TP53* gene, the G1 arrest does not occur, allowing cells with mutated genomes to proliferate and become cancerous.

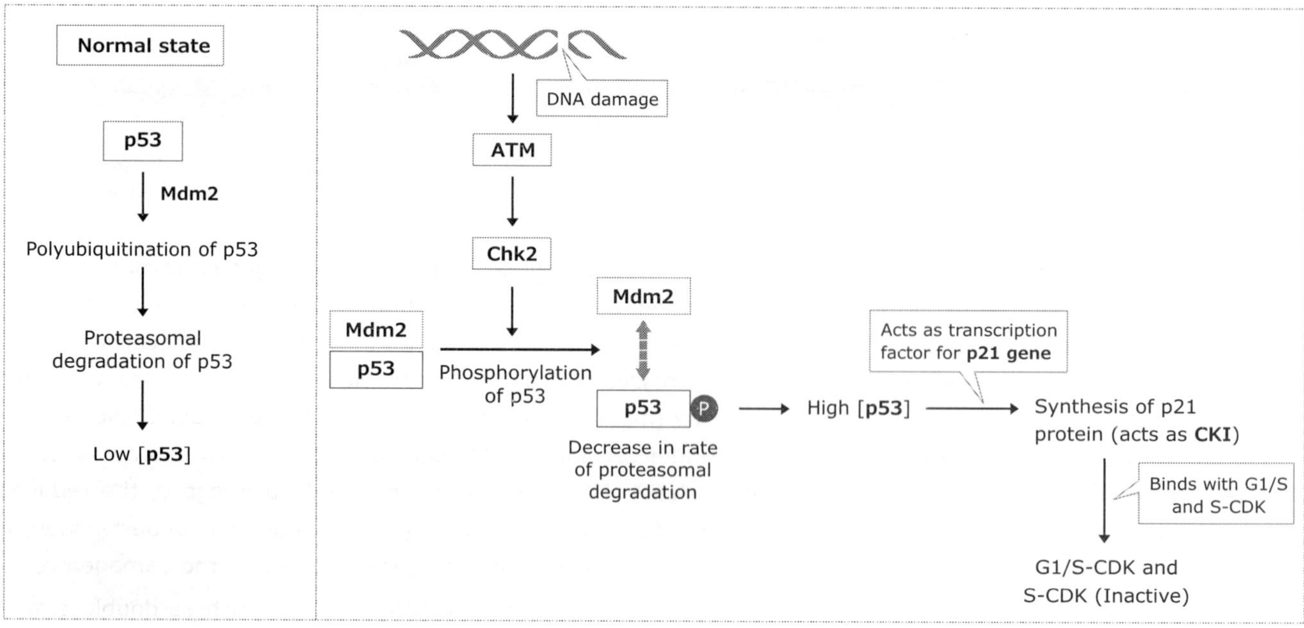

Figure 3.119 DNA damage and role of p53 protein. When DNA is damaged, various protein kinases are recruited to the site of damage and initiates a signaling pathway that causes cell-cycle arrest. The protein kinases cause phosphorylation of the protein p53. Mdm2 normally binds to p53 and promotes its ubiquitination and destruction by proteasomes. Phosphorylation of p53 blocks its binding to Mdm2; as a result, p53 accumulates to high levels and stimulates transcription of the gene that encodes the CKI protein p21. The p21 binds and inactivates G1/S-CDK and S-CDK complexes, arresting the cell in G1.

Numerous reports have described the mechanism by which p53 induces apoptosis. p53 induces apoptosis through the **Bcl-2-regulated pathway** (also called *intrinsic* or *mitochondrial pathway*). In the Bcl-2-regulated apoptotic pathway, cell death is initiated by pro-apoptotic **BH3-only** members of the Bcl-2 protein family (Bim, Puma, Bid, Bad, Bik, Noxa). The BH3-only proteins bind and inhibit the pro-survival Bcl-2 proteins (Bcl-2, Bcl-XL, Mcl-1 and Bcl-W), thereby unleashing the cell death effectors Bax and Bak (the pro-apoptotic multi-BH domain members of the Bcl-2 family). Activation of Bax/Bak causes *mitochondrial outer membrane permeabilization* (**MOMP**) and the release of cytochrome c from the mitochondria, the point of no return in apoptosis signaling.

3.21.3 Replicative senescence

Senescence is defined as a phenomenon in which cells enter in a state of permanent irreversible cell cycle arrest. A variety of stresses such as oxidative damage, DNA damage can induce senescence. The first observation of cell senescence was reported by Hayflick and Moorhead. They observed that primary human fibroblast cells stop dividing after a certain number of division and described it as **replicative senescence**. It appears to be a fundamental feature of somatic cells, with the exception of most tumor cells and possibly certain stem cells. Normal eukaryotic cells have only a limited capacity for cell division. The number of mitotic divisions a cell is capable of undergoing in tissue culture before it stops dividing is described as the **Hayflick limit**. Telomere shortening is considered as the main causal mechanism of replicative senescence. The telomeres are short tandemly repetitive DNA sequences that cap the ends of eukaryotic chromosomes. It serves a dual role in protecting the chromosome ends and in intracellular signaling for regulating cell proliferation. A complex of six telomere-associated proteins has been identified – the **telosome** (or **shelterin complex**) – that is crucial for both the maintenance of telomere structure and its signaling functions. The length of telomeric DNA is maintained by the enzyme **telomerase**. It is a reverse transcriptase that maintains the length of telomeres by overcoming '**end replication problem**'. Most human somatic cells are telomerase negative and thereby experience progressive telomere shortening, at each cell division, due to the end replication problem. As human cells proliferate in culture, their telomeres get progressively shorter and shorten down to a point when they elicit a DNA-damage response. It activates a p53-dependent cell-cycle arrest that resembles the arrest caused by other types of DNA damage. It leads to an irreversible growth arrest, a phenomenon called cellular senescence. Telomerase therefore constitutes a telomere maintenance mechanism conferring infinite replicative potential. However, telomerase is normally expressed in stem cells, tumor cells and germ-line cells, but is nearly absent in most somatic cells. Induction of telomerase synthesis bypasses normal cellular senesce in cancer cells and endows them with unlimited replicative potential. Rodent cells, by contrast, maintain telomerase activity when they proliferate in culture and therefore do not have such a telomere-dependent mechanism for limiting proliferation.

About 90% of human tumors have been found to be telomerase positive. The remaining about 10% lack detectable enzyme activity, but these cells have learned to maintain their telomeric DNA using a mechanism that does not depend on the actions of telomerase. This non-telomerase-based mechanism termed as **Alternative Lengthening of Telomeres** (ALT) was first discovered in the yeast *Saccharomyces cerevisiae*. This ALT mechanism is also used by the minority of human tumor cells that lack significant telomerase activity. The available data indicate that ALT involves homologous recombination-mediated DNA replication.

3.22 Cell division

Cell division is a part of the cell cycle that occurs during the **M-phase**, which consists of **karyokinesis** (nuclear division) and **cytokinesis** (cytoplasm division). In eukaryotes, two types of cell divisions partition the genetic material into progeny, or daughter cells. In one process called **mitosis**, a parent cell divides into two daughter cells and each receives an exact copy of the chromosomes (genetic material) in the parent cell. Since the number of chromosomes in the parent and progeny cells is the same, it is also called as equational division. In the other partitioning process, the genetic material must precisely halve so that fertilization will restore the diploid complement. This cellular process is termed **meiosis**.

3.22.1 Mitosis

Mitosis is the process that partitions newly replicated chromosomes equally into two daughter cells. The term mitosis (derived from the Greek word, meaning *thread*) was introduced by Walther Flemming in 1882. During mitosis, one round of DNA replication is followed by a single round of chromosome segregation and generating two genetically identical daughter cells.

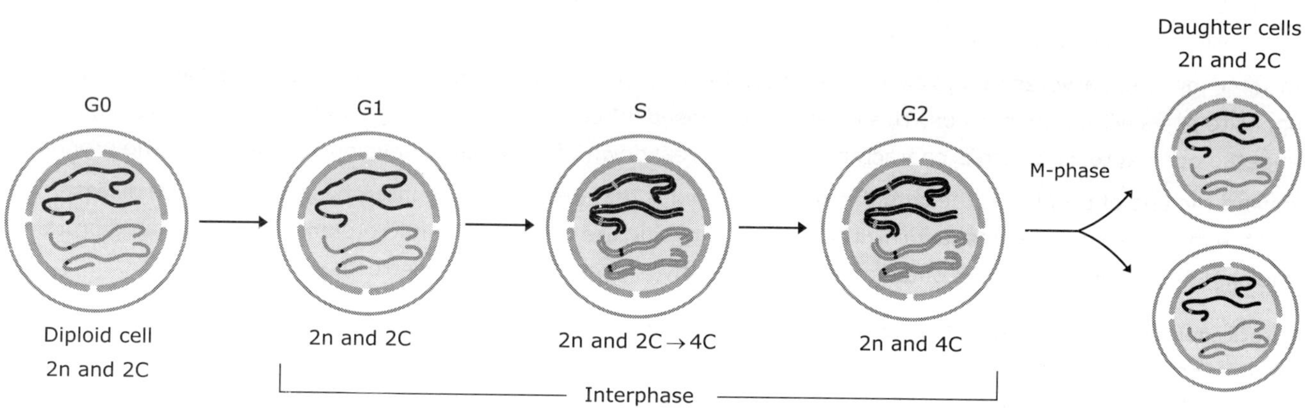

Figure 3.120 Change in chromosome number (n) and amount of DNA (C) during mitosis.

Stages of M-phase: The M-phase starts with the nuclear division (**karyokinesis**), corresponding to the formation of daughter nuclei and usually ends with division of cytoplasm (**cytokinesis**). Mitosis is a continuous process. They are conventionally divided into four substages: **prophase**, **metaphase**, **anaphase**, and **telophase** (Greek: *pro-*, before; *meta-*, mid; *ana-*, back; *telo-*, end).

Prophase

The chromatin, which is diffuse in interphase, slowly condenses into well-defined chromosomes. Each chromosome has duplicated during the preceding S phase and consists of two sister chromatids; each of these sister chromatids is held together at a constricted region, the centromere. Each chromatid contains one of the two new daughter DNA molecules. At centromere, the sister chromatids are kept together by a member of the **SMC** (Structural Maintenance of Chromosomes), family of proteins, called **cohesin**. Cohesin is a protein complex made up of four subunits. Two subunits are Smc1 and Smc3 with two ATPase domains. Two additional subunits Scc1 and Scc3, connect the ATPase domains forming a ring structure.

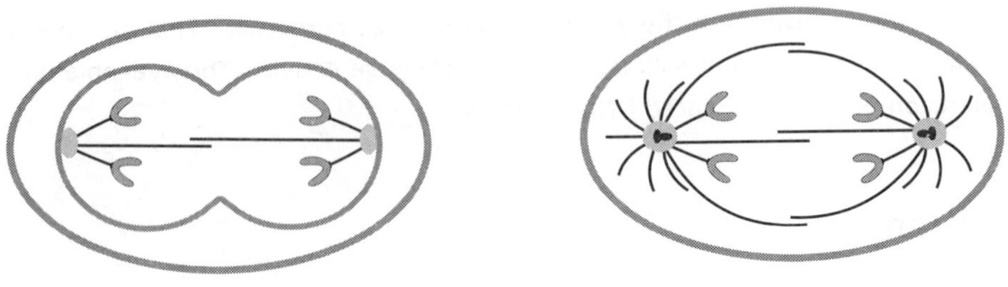

(A) (B)

Figure 3.121 (**A**) In yeasts, the nuclear envelope remains intact during cell division. The spindle fibers form within the nucleus. Spindle fibers separate the chromosomes, and the nucleus splits into two daughter nuclei. (**B**) In most of eukaryotes, the spindle fibers form outside the nucleus and the nuclear membrane breaks down during late prophase. Spindle fibers separate the chromosomes, and the nuclear envelope then re-forms.

Prophase ends with the disappearance of **nucleolus** and disruption of the nuclear envelope. The nuclear envelope breaks into membrane vesicles that are indistinguishable from bits of endoplasmic reticulum. Nuclear envelope breakdown is a complex, multi-step processes that begin when M-CDK phosphorylates several subunits of the nuclear pore complexes present in the nuclear envelope. This initiates the disassembly of nuclear pore complexes. M-CDK also phosphorylates components of the nuclear lamina, the structural framework that lies beneath the envelope. The phosphorylation of these lamina components and other proteins leads to disassembly of the **nuclear lamina** and the breakdown of the envelope membranes into small vesicles. In most cells, the disruption of the nuclear envelope marks the end of the prophase of mitosis. However, this disruption of the nuclear envelope is not a universal feature of mitosis and does not occur in all cells.

In some lower eukaryotes (e.g., yeasts, diatoms), the nuclear envelope remains intact and chromosomes migrate to opposite poles within the nucleus. This is termed as **closed mitosis**. The cells of higher eukaryotes, however, usually undergo **open mitosis**, which is characterized by the breakdown of the nuclear envelope at the end of the prophase.

Toward the end of prophase, the cytoplasmic microtubules that are part of the interphase cytoskeleton disassemble and the mitotic spindle begins to form. This is a bipolar structure composed of microtubules and associated proteins. The spindle initially assembles outside the nucleus between separating the centrosomes.

Mitotic spindle: The nuclear division is mediated by a microtubule based mitotic spindle, which separates the chromosomes. Spindles are microtubules, each of which is a polarized tubulin polymer with one end, the so-called minus end, embedded in a spindle pole and the other end, the plus end, pointing outward from the pole. The mitotic spindle is of three types: kinetochore microtubules, polar microtubules and astral microtubules.

Kinetochore microtubules, which attach with specialized protein complexes called **kinetochores** mature on centromere of each chromosome. The plus ends of kinetochore microtubules remain attached with the kinetochore. The number of kinetochore microtubules bound to a kinetochore varies from one in budding yeast to over 40 in some mammalian cells. At anaphase it pulls the two sister chromatids toward opposite poles.

Polar microtubules do not interact with chromosomes but overlap with polar microtubules (also termed as **interpolar microtubules**) from the opposite pole.

Astral microtubules, which form the aster and radiate outward from the centrosome (the *centrosome matrix* associated with a pair of *centrioles*) toward the cortex of the cell. The centrioles which are associated with the centrosome matrix, are not required for the nucleation of spindle fibers. Plant cells lack centrioles altogether, but the nucleation of spindle fibers occur. It is, therefore, thought that the centrosome matrix, which contains a set of proteins, is very important for nucleation of spindle fibers.

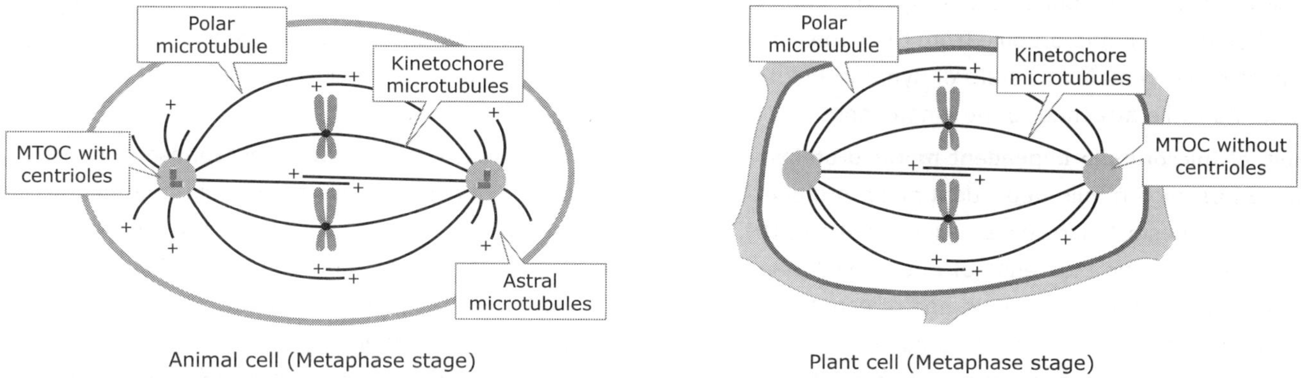

Figure 3.122 Basic features of the mitotic spindle of animal and plant cells in metaphase. In animal cell, the spindle fibers have one end (the minus end) embedded in the centrosome and the other (plus end) pointing outward. The mitotic spindle in plant cells is similar to that of animal cells except that there are no centrosomes at the spindle poles and no astral microtubules.

Metaphase

Metaphase is an extremely dynamic part of the cell cycle. Spindle fibers rapidly assemble and disassemble as they grow out of the MTOC, seeking out attachment sites at chromosome. To attach to spindle fibers, each chromosome has a specialized structure called a **kinetochore**. It is located at the centromere. There are two kinetochores on each chromosome (one on each sister chromatid) facing in opposite directions. The plus ends of kinetochore microtubules are embedded head-on in specialized microtubule attachment sites within the outer region of the kinetochore. The kinetochore of an animal cell can bind 10-40 microtubules, whereas a budding yeast kinetochore can bind only one.

Box 3.9 Kinetochore

The *kinetochore* assembles at centromeric region of the chromosome. It is a giant, multilayered protein structure. It has three layers: the inner kinetochore, which forms the interface with chromatin; the outer kinetochore that forms the interaction surface for spindle microtubules and the central kinetochore, the region between the inner and outer kinetochore. The mature kinetochore is an amazing complex consisting of 80 or more proteins. In recent years, biochemical and genetic analyses have allowed scientists to identify subcomplexes of proteins within the kinetochores that are required for the kinetochore's numerous functions. Many of these functions involve microtubules (e.g., microtubule attachment, polymerization and motor-directed movements). Other kinetochore proteins are part of the spindle checkpoint that allows only cells with correctly assembled spindles to pass into anaphase.

The primary function of the *centromere* is to provide the foundation for assembly of the kinetochore. The centromeres of human chromosomes are heterochromatic regions that consist largely of a repeated sequence known as *alpha satellite DNA*. A single repeat unit of alpha satellite DNA is 171 base pairs in length. But, most organisms lack a precise DNA sequence that determines the site of kinetochore assembly. Therefore, in most eukaryotes, the site of kinetochore assembly is thought to be controlled primarily by epigenetic, rather than sequence based mechanisms. The primary candidate for an epigenetic mark of kinetochore specification is the presence of **CENP-A** (a variant of histone H3 that replaces H3 in nucleosomes). CENP-A is found exclusively at the centromere. Other CENP proteins play a variety of different roles. Today, the number of known CENP proteins is about 20, and that number may increase as our understanding of the kinetochore grows. Most eukaryotic chromosomes are **monocentric**, having a single kinetochore assembly site, but some are **holocentric** (or **polycentric**) and have multiple kinetochores present all along the length of chromosome. Thus, in holocentric chromosomes spindle microtubules bind to chromosomes along their entire length.

Attachment of each microtubule depends on multiple copies of a rod-shaped protein complex called the **Ndc80 complex**, which is anchored in the kinetochore.

How does a kinetochore become attached to spindle fibers? Chromosomes make attachment with the spindle fibers by a process known as **search and capture**, in which the *plus ends* of some of the microtubules radiating out from the MTOC attach to kinetochores. Some microtubules randomly hit kinetochore and are subsequently stabilized to form kinetochore microtubules. Eventually, the opposite kinetochore, on the other sister chromatid, will be captured by the free end of a microtubule from the opposite pole. This leads to bipolar orientation of chromosome. Kinetochore microtubules remain in a state of dynamic flux. The plus ends of kinetochore microtubules can add and lose tubulin subunits while attached to the kinetochore.

Role of microtubule-dependent motor proteins: The movement of chromosomes during metaphase depends on numerous microtubule-dependent motor proteins. These proteins belong to two families—the kinesin-related proteins (such as kinesin-5, kinesin-14, kinesins-4 and 10) and dyneins. **Kinesin-5** protein (plus-end directed motor protein) interacts with the plus ends of antiparallel polar microtubules in the spindle midzone and *push* the poles apart. **Kinesin-14** proteins are minus-end directed motor proteins. In addition to their motor domain, they contain other domains that can interact with another microtubule, enabling them to cross-link antiparallel polar microtubules at the spindle midzone and slide them past each other and tend to pull the poles together. **Kinesin-4** and **kinesin-10** proteins (also called **chromokinesins**), are plus-end directed motors that associate with chromosome arms and push the attached chromosome away from the pole. Finally, dyneins, the minus-end directed motors, link the plus ends of astral microtubules to components of the actin cytoskeleton at the cell cortex. The dynein motors pull the spindle poles toward the cell cortex and away from each other.

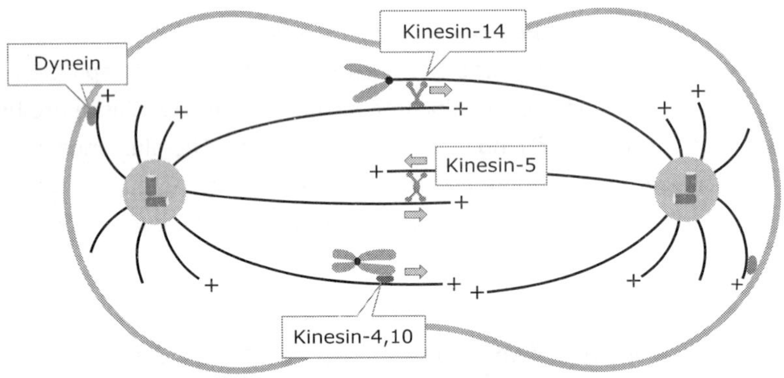

Figure 3.123 Four major classes of microtubule-dependent motor proteins chromosomal movements. The arrow indicates the direction of motor movement along a microtubule.

How different forces move chromosomes during metaphase? At metaphase stage, chromosomes aligned at the midpoint (equator) between the two spindle poles. During this process, chromosomes often oscillate backward and forward before arriving at the midpoint. Multiple forces move chromosome at the equator. One major force pulls the kinetochore and its associated chromosome along the kinetochore-microtubule toward the spindle pole. It is produced by proteins at the kinetochore itself. Depolymerization at the plus end of the microtubule somehow generates such force that pulls the kinetochore poleward. Kinetochore localized **kinesin-13** (a class of microtubule depolymerizing protein) and **CENP-E** (a member of kinesin-7 family) play an important role.

Apart from poleward forces, each chromosome is simultaneously subjected to anti-poleward forces. The force acts on chromosomes is the **polar ejection force**. Plus end directed motor proteins kinesin-4 and 10 located on the chromosome arms are believed to interact with the polar or astral microtubules to produce the anti-poleward polar ejection forces. This force pushes the chromosomes toward the equator. The combination of these forces results in the movement of the chromosomes and leads to their alignment on the **metaphase plate**. The alignment of chromosomes at the metaphase plate, midpoint between the two spindle poles, is called **congression**.

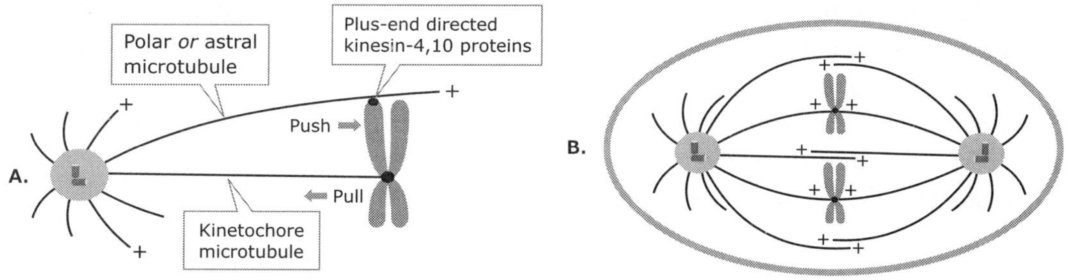

Figure 3.124 **A.** A model of how two opposing forces may cooperate to move chromosomes to the metaphase plate. Plus-end-directed motor proteins (kinesin-4 and kinesin-10) on the chromosome arms are thought to interact with microtubules to generate the polar ejection force, which pushes chromosomes toward the spindle equator. Kinetochore located kinesin-7 and kinesin-13 generate pulling forces. **B.** At metaphase, the chromosomes are aligned at the equator. The plane of alignment of the chromosomes at metaphase is referred to as the metaphase plate.

Anaphase

As mentioned, each sister chromatid of a metaphase chromosome is attached to kinetochore microtubules via its kinetochore. The opposite ends of these kinetochore microtubules associate with one of the spindle poles. At anaphase, the kinetochore microtubules pull the two kinetochores toward the opposite poles. During metaphase, sister chromatids do not separate because they are held together at their centromeres by multiprotein complexes called **cohesins**. However, during anaphase, **separase** degrades cohesins. Before anaphase, **securin** protein keeps separase in an inactive state. APC/C mediates the destruction of the securin. APC/C functions in coordination with two homologous mitotic coactivators, Cdc20 and Cdh1. APC/C^{Cdc20} initiates the ubiquitination and degradation of securin. The destruction of securin releases separase, which is then free to cleave the cohesin complex.

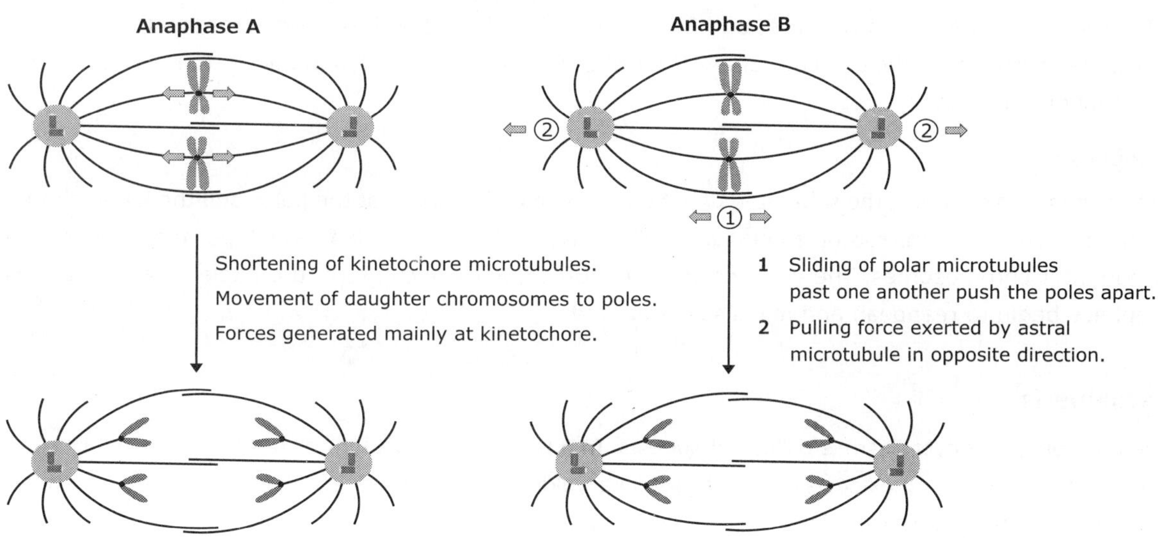

Figure 3.125 Separation of daughter chromosomes at anaphase A and B in animal cells.

After separation, each chromatid (now called a daughter chromosome) is pulled slowly towards the pole it faces. All of the newly separated chromosomes move at the same speed, typically about 1 µm per minute. The chromosomes move by two independent and overlapping processes. Hence anaphase can be divided into two distinct stages, *anaphase A* and *anaphase B* (or early and late anaphase). The first, referred to as **anaphase A**, is the initial poleward movement of the chromosomes, which is accompanied by the shortening of the kinetochore microtubules. In this case, the force is generated by microtubule depolymerization at the kinetochore, which results in the loss of tubulin subunits at the plus end as the kinetochore moves toward the pole. The movement towards the spindle poles are facilitated by the kinesin-7 and kinesin-13 proteins that are localized at the kinetochore. Kinesin-13 proteins (KinI) do not have motor activity.

Anaphase B depends on motor proteins at the poles that pull the poles apart, as well as on motor proteins at the central spindle that pushes the poles apart. During anaphase B, the two poles move farther apart. It happens due to the sliding of polar microtubules past one another and pulling forces exerted by astral microtubules. A plus-end-directed **kinesin-5** motor proteins cross-link adjacent, overlapping, antiparallel polar microtubules and slide the microtubules past each other, thereby *pushing* the spindle poles apart. In addition, **dynein** motor proteins that anchor astral microtubule plus end to the cell cortex pull the poles apart.

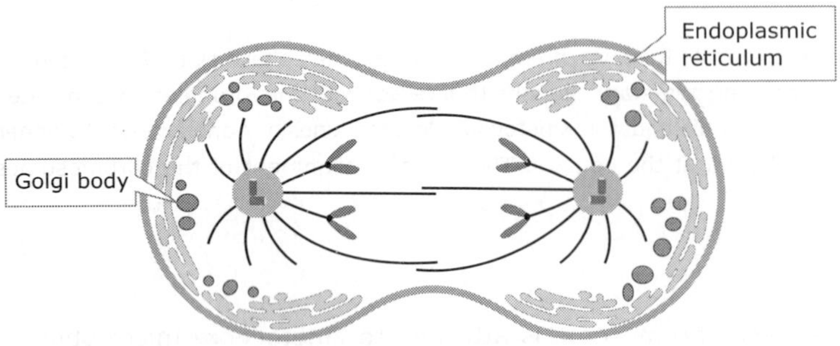

Figure 3.126
At anaphase the sister chromatids split apart and are drawn to opposite poles. Kinetochore microtubules pull the two sister chromatids toward opposite poles. During end of anaphase, pre-existing organelles, such as ER and Golgi apparatus, mitochondria are remodelled, distributed and reformed. The ER is partitioned into future daughter cells. The Golgi apparatus which was disassembled during prometaphase into vesicles are again reformed

Organelle dynamics during division: During cell division, the partitioning of organelles also occurs. Organelles can be large or small, exist in single or high copy numbers and can be dynamic in shape and location. During prophase, the nuclear pore complex disassembles and the nuclear envelope merges with the endoplasmic reticulum. This organelle is then partitioned and inherited by daughter cells. The Golgi complex is disassembled during early metaphase into vesicles, segregated in late metaphase, and then reformed during telophase. Recycling endosomes cluster at the spindle pole. The distribution mitochondria also occurs between daughter cells. Mitochondria fuse during the G1-phase, elongate during S-phase, and fragment during the G2–M transition. Fragmented mitochondria remain distributed throughout the dividing cell. As the cell exits mitosis, mitochondria begin to re-fuse. During cytokinesis, mitochondria are mostly fused.

Telophase

In telophase (*telos*- end), the separated daughter chromosomes arrive at the poles and the kinetochore microtubules disappear. The polar microtubules elongate still more, and a new nuclear envelope re-forms around each group of daughter chromosomes. The condensed chromatin expands once more, the nucleoli which had disappeared at prophase begin to reappear, and mitosis is at an end.

Cytokinesis

The division of the cytoplasm is called *cytokinesis*. In a typical cell, cytokinesis accompanies every karyokinesis. But in certain organisms, cytokinesis does not follow karyokinesis, and repeated nuclear divisions lead to multinucleated cells. The mechanism of cytokinesis in animal and plant cells varies; in the former case, it is achieved by *cleavage* and in the latter, cytokinesis occurs by *cell plate* formation.

Cytokinesis in animal cell

Cytokinesis initiates during anaphase when the two sets of sister chromatids segregate toward opposite poles. The whole process of cytokinesis can be subdivided into *central spindle assembly*, *contractile ring assembly* and *abscission*.

Central spindle assembly: It involves the reorganization of the spindle microtubules into microtubule bundles called **central spindle**. This bundling is promoted by **Aurora B kinase** and **centralspindlin complex** (CSC).

Contractile ring assembly: During cytokinesis, the cytoplasm divides by **cleavage furrow**. Cleavage is accomplished by contraction of the circumferentially oriented **actomyosin** contractile ring made up of **actin filaments** and **myosin II** bound to the cytoplasmic face of the plasma membrane. The muscle-like sliding of actin and myosin II filaments in the contractile ring generates the force required for cleavage. Actomyosin contractile ring assembly is initiated in response to a signaling pathway where **Polo-like kinase 1** and **Aurora B kinase** phosphorylate the **centralspindlin complex**, leading to activation of the Rho-GEF, **Ect2**. It activates the **RhoA**, a small GTPase of the Ras superfamily. RhoA regulates the assembly and constriction of the contractile ring during cytokinesis by activating two parallel signaling pathways. First, RhoA activates **Rho-associated kinase** (ROCK), which phosphorylates the myosin regulatory light chain to enhance myosin II activity. Second, RhoA stimulates actin filament formation by activating **diaphanous-related formin proteins** (a member of the formin protein family) and also regulates the scaffold protein **anillin.**

Abscission: The contractile ring tightens to reduce the cell's circumference, forming a **cortical midbody ring**. The central spindle compacts into a microtubule-based midbody positioned in the center of the thin bridge connecting the daughter cells. As the contractile ring transitions into the cortical midbody ring, abscission occurs through disassembly of nearby microtubules and membrane fission, physically separating the two daughter cells.

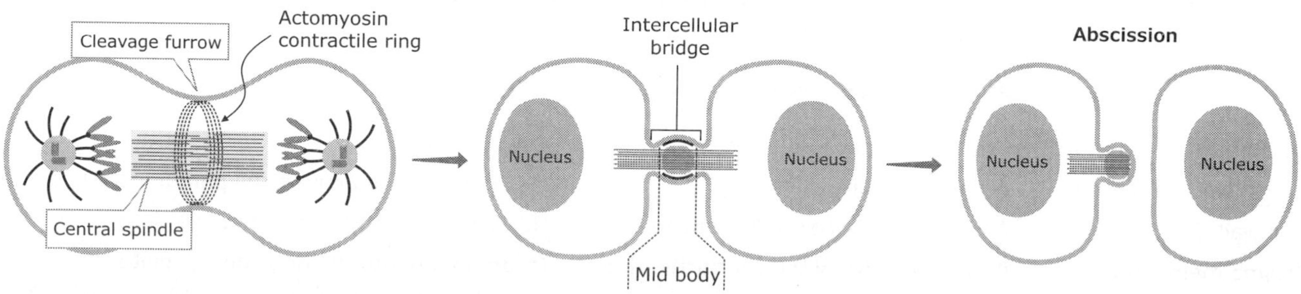

Figure 3.127 Cytokinesis in animal cells begins in anaphase with the formation of a cleavage furrow, which ingresses to divide the mother cell. The mitotic spindle reorganizes into the central spindle, derived mainly from interpolar microtubules. An actomyosin contractile ring forms and constricts to separate the daughter cells. The central spindle develops into a midbody at the intercellular bridge, while the contractile ring transitions into a midbody ring. The final step is abscission where the intercellular bridge is physically severed to complete their separation.

Role of chromosome passenger complex: The chromosome passenger complex (CPC) is a group of proteins that 'travel' along chromosomes during mitosis, changing their location at different stages to coordinate chromosome alignment, segregation, and final cell division. The CPC consists of four core proteins:

Aurora B kinase: Responsible for phosphorylating key substrates to regulate mitotic processes.

INCENP (Inner Centromere Protein): Acts as a scaffold that recruits and activates Aurora B.

Survivin: Enhances the stability and activity of the CPC and is involved in inhibiting apoptosis.

Borealin: Stabilizes the complex and helps localize it to specific regions during mitosis.

Cytokinesis in plant cell

Plant cell cytokinesis differs from the animal cell because of a rigid cell wall. Hence, instead of forming a *cleavage furrow*, the cytoplasm is partitioned by constructing the **cell plate** inside the cell. A cytoskeleton framework determines the plane of plant cell division. An array of cortical microtubules appears in the G2 phase and forms a ring around the entire cell just beneath the plasma membrane, i.e., in the cell cortex. It is called the **preprophase band.** It also contains actin filaments in addition to microtubules. The microtubules disappear during prophase when the nuclear envelope breaks down, but the actin filaments remain and provide a memory of the predetermined division plane. In the late anaphase stage, an array of microtubules together with actin filaments assemble in this plane and form a cylinder-like structure called **phragmoplast**.

The phragmoplast assembles at the center of the cell and grows centrifugally toward the parental cell wall. Compared with microtubules, the role of actin in the phragmoplast is less clear. Small membrane-bound vesicles filled with cell wall precursors derived from the Golgi complex fuse with the phragmoplast and form the **cell plate**. The membranes of the vesicles become the plasma membranes of the daughter cells. The polysaccharide molecule delivered by these vesicles forms the matrix polysaccharide. Later during the process of maturation, cellulose microfibrils are laid down within the cell plate to complete the new cell wall.

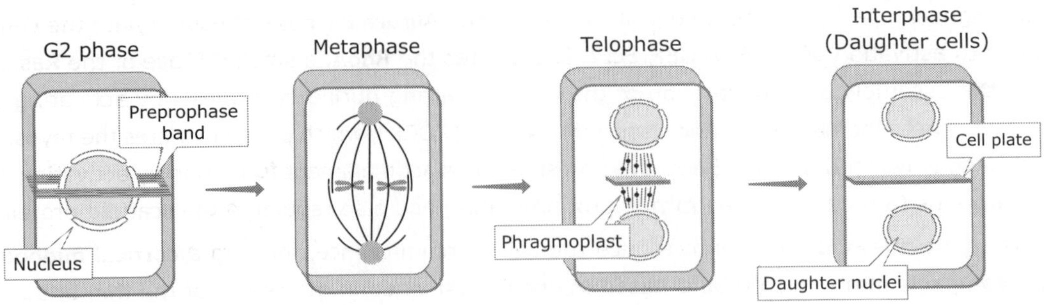

Figure 3.128 Cytokinesis in a plant cell. The preprophase band forms during G2 at the future division plane and disappears during prophase. In the late anaphase stage, an array of microtubules and actin filaments assemble at the center of the cell and form a cylinder-like structure called phragmoplast. Small membrane-bound vesicles filled with cell wall precursors derived from the Golgi complex fuse with the phragmoplast and form the cell plate.

Feature	Animal cell cytokinesis	Plant cell cytokinesis
Mechanism	Cleavage furrow formation	Cell plate formation
Cytoskeletal elements	Actin forms contractile ring	Microtubules and actin in the phragmoplast
Cell wall	Absent; no new cell wall formed	New cell wall formed from the cell plate
Plasma membrane	Pinched inward by the contractile ring	Incorporated into the growing cell plate
Structure involved	Cleavage furrow	Phragmoplast and preprophase band

Syncytium and **coenocyte**: In some organisms, karyokinesis is not followed by cytokinesis, resulting in a multinucleate condition that leads to the formation of a **coenocyte**. In contrast to a coenocyte, a **syncytium** is a multinucleate cell that forms due to fusions of multiple uninuclear cells (i.e., cells with a single nucleus). A classic example of a syncytium is the formation of skeletal muscle. In animals, well-studied examples of the coenocytic state are found in the blastoderm of *Drosophila*. However, the word 'syncytium' is used incorrectly to describe it.

3.22.2 Meiosis

Meiosis (term coined by Farmer and Moore) is a specialized cell division in which the number of chromosomes is reduced to half. The reduction in chromosome number is achieved by one round of DNA replication, followed by two rounds of chromosome segregation with no intervening round of DNA replication. Meiosis is divided into two parts– **meiosis I** and **meiosis II**. At the end of the meiotic process, there are four daughter cells rather than the two produced at the end of the mitosis. Each resulting daughter cell has one-half of the number of chromosomes as the parent cell. *Meiosis occurs in sexually reproducing eukaryotic organisms*. Most eukaryotic organisms reproduce sexually. The cells of these organisms are generally diploid: they contain two sets of chromosomes. During sexual reproduction, these cells undergo meiosis to produce haploid cells carrying one set of chromosomes, i.e., only a single copy of each chromosome.

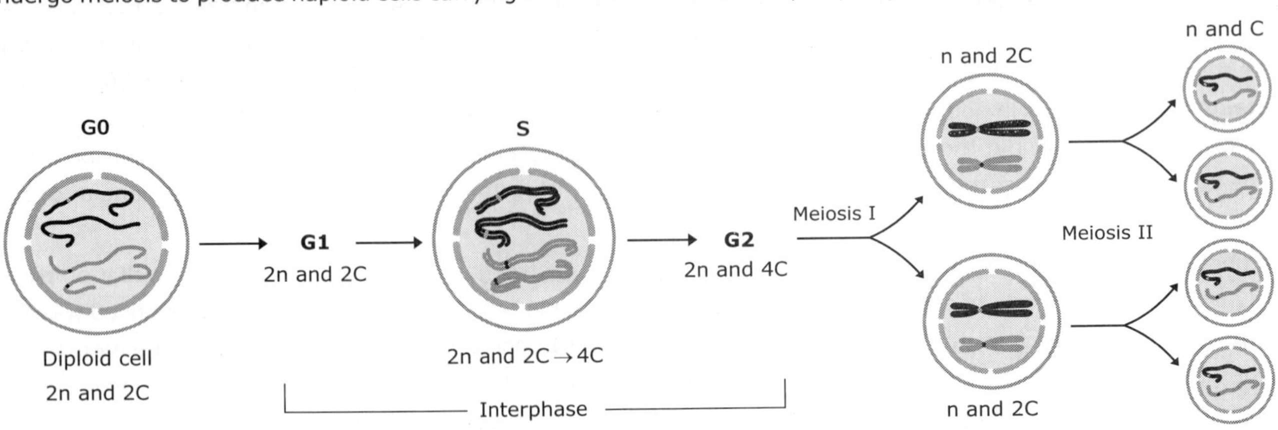

Figure 3.129 Change in chromosome number and amount of DNA during meiosis I and meiosis II.

Meiosis I

Meiosis I, the first meiotic division, begins with prophase I. It is referred to as a *reductional division* because the number of chromosomes is reduced to half after the completion of meiosis I.

Prophase I

Prophase I of meiosis I is divided into five sub-stages: Leptotene, Zygotene, Pachytene, Diplotene and Diakinesis.

Leptotene: Prophase I begins at the leptotene stage. Although each chromosome has replicated and consists of two sister chromatids, these chromatids are unusually closely apposed, and each chromosome, therefore, appears to be single (separate chromatids will not become visible until late in prophase, at either the diplotene stage or in diakinesis). At this stage, chromosome ends are attached to the inner nuclear envelope. In the leptotene to zygotene transition, the tips of the chromosomes move until most end up in a limited region near each other. This form of arrangement is called a **bouquet stage**. Bouquet formation directly facilitates homologous chromosome pairing and synapsis.

Zygotene: Leptotene is considered to end and the zygotene stage of prophase to begin as soon as **synapsis**, or *intimate pairing*, between the two homologs is initiated. *How the maternal and the paternal copy of each chromosome recognizes each other is still unknown*? Synapsis often starts when the homologous ends of the two chromosomes are brought together on the nuclear envelope and proceeds inward in a zipper like manner from both ends. In other cases, synapsis may begin in internal regions of the chromosomes and proceed toward the ends. The pairing of the sex chromosomes occurs in similar fashion as homologous autosomes. Mammalian females have two X chromosomes, which pair and segregate like autosomes. But the males have one X and one Y chromosome. Although these chromosomes are not homologous, they too must pair and undergo crossing-over. Pairing and crossing-over are possible because of a small region of homology between the X and the Y chromosomes. The two chromosomes pair and crossover in this region ensuring that each sperm receives either one Y or one X chromosome and not both or neither. Each pair of homologous chromosomes forms as a result of synapsis is called a **bivalent** (sometimes referred to as a **tetrad**).

Synaptonemal complex: The synaptonemal complex is a protein structure that forms between homologous chromosomes during meiosis and is thought to mediate chromosome pairing. It is a *tripartite proteinaceous structure* consisting of two parallel **lateral elements** and a **central element**. Each lateral element is associated with a pair of sister chromatids. The central region between the two lateral elements is composed of numerous *transverse filaments* and a *central element*. In vertebrates, the lateral elements are made up of proteins SYCP2 and SYCP3 whereas the *central element* is made up of SYCE1, SYCE2 and SYCE3. Transverse filaments are composed of SYCP1 proteins. The synaptonemal complex has been demonstrated to function both in stabilization of homolog pairing and in promoting the formation of crossovers. How the synaptonemal complex provides these functions and whether it also plays a role in inhibiting crossover formation has been a matter of debate.

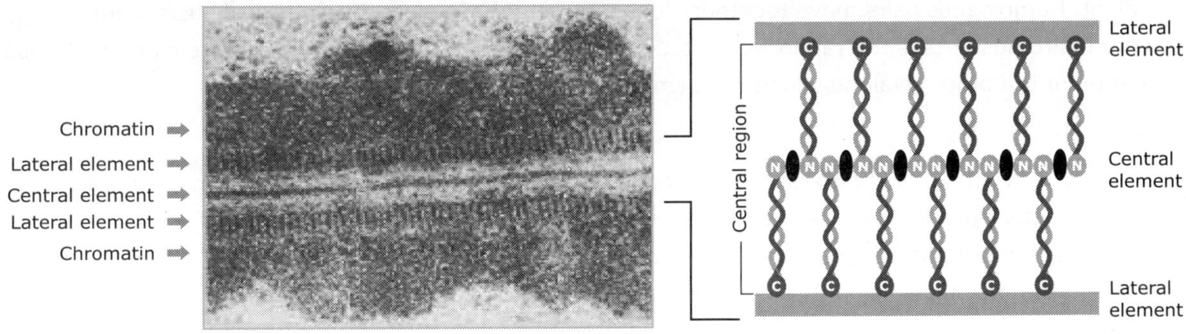

Figure 3.130 During prophase I a meiosis-specific proteinaceous tripartite structure, the synaptonemal complex, forms a scaffold to connect homologous chromosomes along their lengths. This process is required to promote recombination between homologs.

Pachytene: As soon as synapsis is complete all along the chromosomes, the cells are said to have entered the pachytene stage of prophase, where they may remain for days. At this stage, large **recombination nodules** (large protein complexes contain Rad51; eukaryotic version of RecA protein) appear at intervals on the synaptonemal complexes and are thought to mediate crossing over. The **crossing over** is a reciprocal exchange of equal and corresponding segments between non-sister chromatids in a pair of homologous chromosomes. It leads to the recombination of genes present on two homologous chromosomes. Meiotic recombination begins with a programmed double-strand break. A specialized protein (called **Spo11** in budding yeast) breaks both strands of the DNA double helix in one of the recombining chromosomes. A double Holliday junction is formed and is cleaved by specialized enzymes to create a crossover. There are some examples (such as male *Drosophila* and female silkworm, *Bombyx mori*) where crossing over does not occur during meiosis. The crossing over can also occur in mitotically proliferating somatic cells (termed **mitotic recombination**). It was first described by Stern in *Drosophila*. Meiotic recombination occurs during prophase I of meiosis I, whereas most mitotic recombination probably does not occur during M phase of mitosis. Although the crossing over can occur almost anywhere along the length of a chromosome pair, they are not occurring uniformly. There are many regions along the length of a chromosome pair where crossing over frequencies are higher or lower than would be expected on the basis of the genome's average crossing over frequencies.

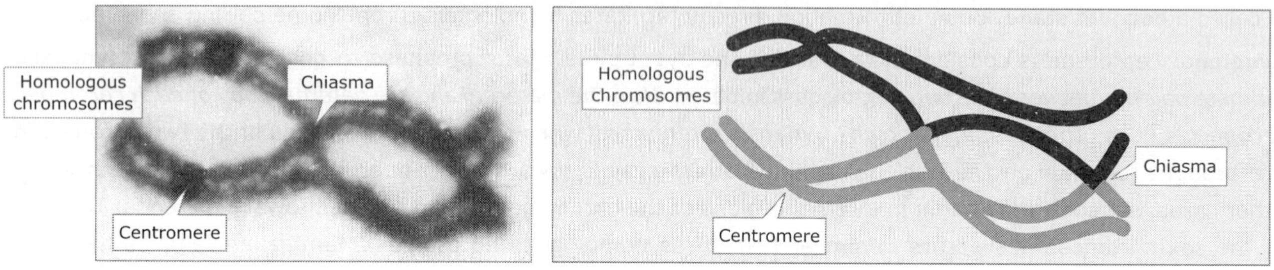

Figure 3.131 Crossing over and chiasmata.

Diplotene: Desynapsis begins in the diplotene stage of meiotic prophase I. The synaptonemal complex dissolves, allowing the two homologous chromosomes in a bivalent to pull away from each other to some extent. However, each bivalent remains joined by one or more **chiasmata** representing the sites where crossing over has occurred. In oocytes (developing eggs), diplotene can last for months or years, since it is at this stage that the chromosomes decondense and engage in RNA synthesis to provide storage materials for the egg. In the extreme, the diplotene chromosomes can become highly active in RNA synthesis and expand to an enormous extent, producing the **lampbrush chromosomes** found in amphibians and some other organisms.

Diakinesis: Diplotene merges imperceptibly into diakinesis, the stage of transition to metaphase, as RNA synthesis ceases and the chromosomes condense, thicken and become detached from the nuclear envelope. Each bivalent contains four separate chromatids, with each pair of sister chromatids linked at their centromeres.

Metaphase I

Metaphase I is marked by the breakdown of the nuclear membrane and the attachment of kinetochore microtubules to the bivalent. Homologous pairs move together along the metaphase plate. The physical basis of the independent assortment of chromosomes is the random orientation of each bivalent along the metaphase plate, with respect to the orientation of the other bivalents along the same equatorial line.

Anaphase I

Unlike in mitosis, in which sister chromatids are pulled apart; in anaphase I homologous chromosomes are separated. In anaphase I, sister chromatids stay together. A special meiosis specific **cohesin** termed **Rec8** (expressed only during meiosis I) inhibits the separation of sister chromatids. Homologous chromosomes separate and move to opposite poles. The meiotic division is, therefore, called a **reductional division**, because it reduces the number of chromosomes to half the diploid number in each daughter cell.

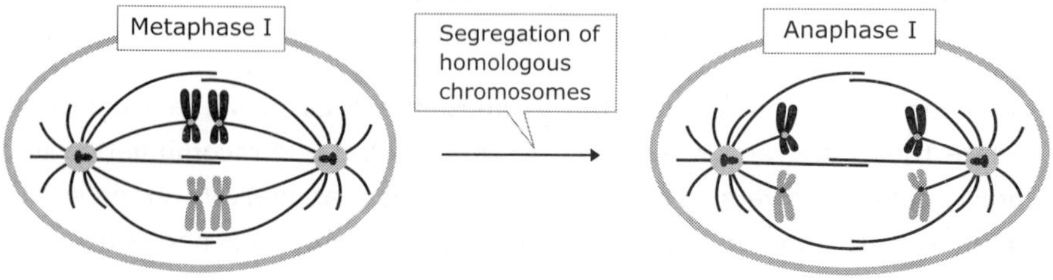

Telophase I

The meiosis I effectively ends when the chromosomes arrive at the poles. Each daughter cell now has half the number of chromosomes but each chromosome consists of a pair of chromatids. A new nuclear membrane surrounds each haploid set. The chromosomes uncoil back into chromatin. Cytokinesis occurs, completing the creation of two daughter cells.

Meiosis II

The time gap between meiosis I and meiosis II is called **interkinesis**. Generally, it is short or may not occur at all. No DNA replication occurs during this stage. Meiosis II is similar to mitosis. However, there is no S phase. The chromatids of each chromosome are no longer identical because of recombination during prophase I of meiosis I. Meiosis II separates the sister chromatids producing two daughter cells each with a haploid chromosome number.

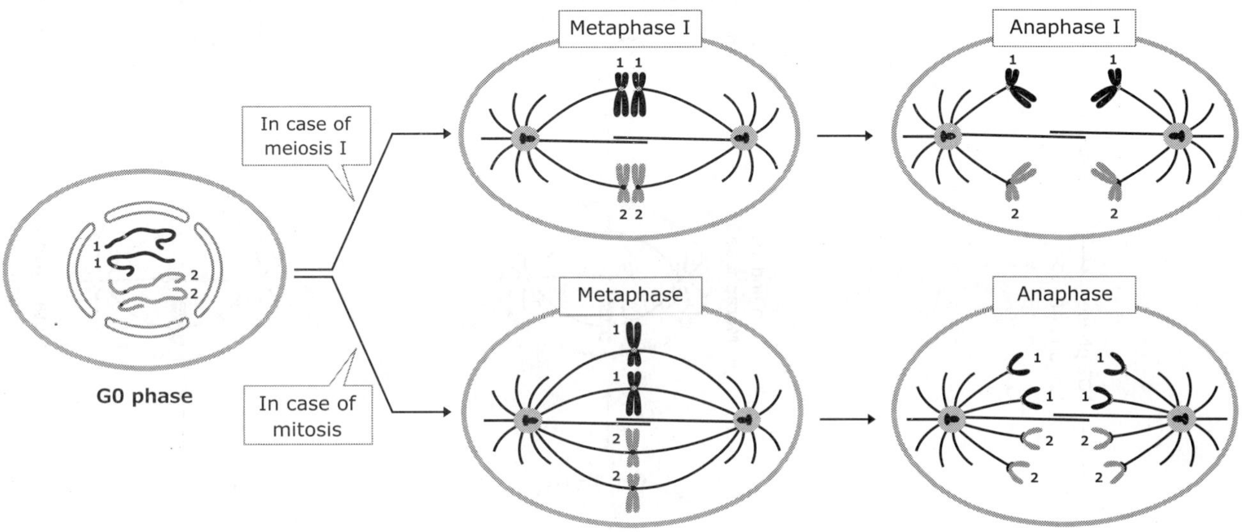

Figure 3.132 Comparison of chromosome alignment and separation in meiotic division I and mitosis (or meiosis II).

Table 3.19 Comparison between mitosis and meiosis

Mitosis	Occurs in all eukaryotic organisms.
	Fundamental type of cell division.
	Cell undergoing mitosis may be: monoploid, diploid and polyploid.
	One round of DNA replication is followed by one round of segregation of sister chromatids.
	Equational division: No change in number of chromatin and amount of DNA between parent cell and daughter cells.
	Recombination (crossing over) occurs rarely.
	No genetic variation between parent cell and daughter cells.
Meiosis	Only in sexually reproducing eukaryotes.
	Cells undergo meiosis (meiocytes) may be diploid or polyploid (4n, 6n, ...).
	Results in meiospore formation or gamete formation.
	Meiosis refers to one round of replication is followed by two rounds of segregation. First round of segregation – homologous chromosomes at anaphase I. Second round of segregation – sister chromatids at anaphase II.
	Reductional division: Reduction in number of chromatin and amount of DNA between parent cell and daughter cells.
	Recombination (crossing over) occurs commonly.
	Genetic variation between parent cell and daughter cells.

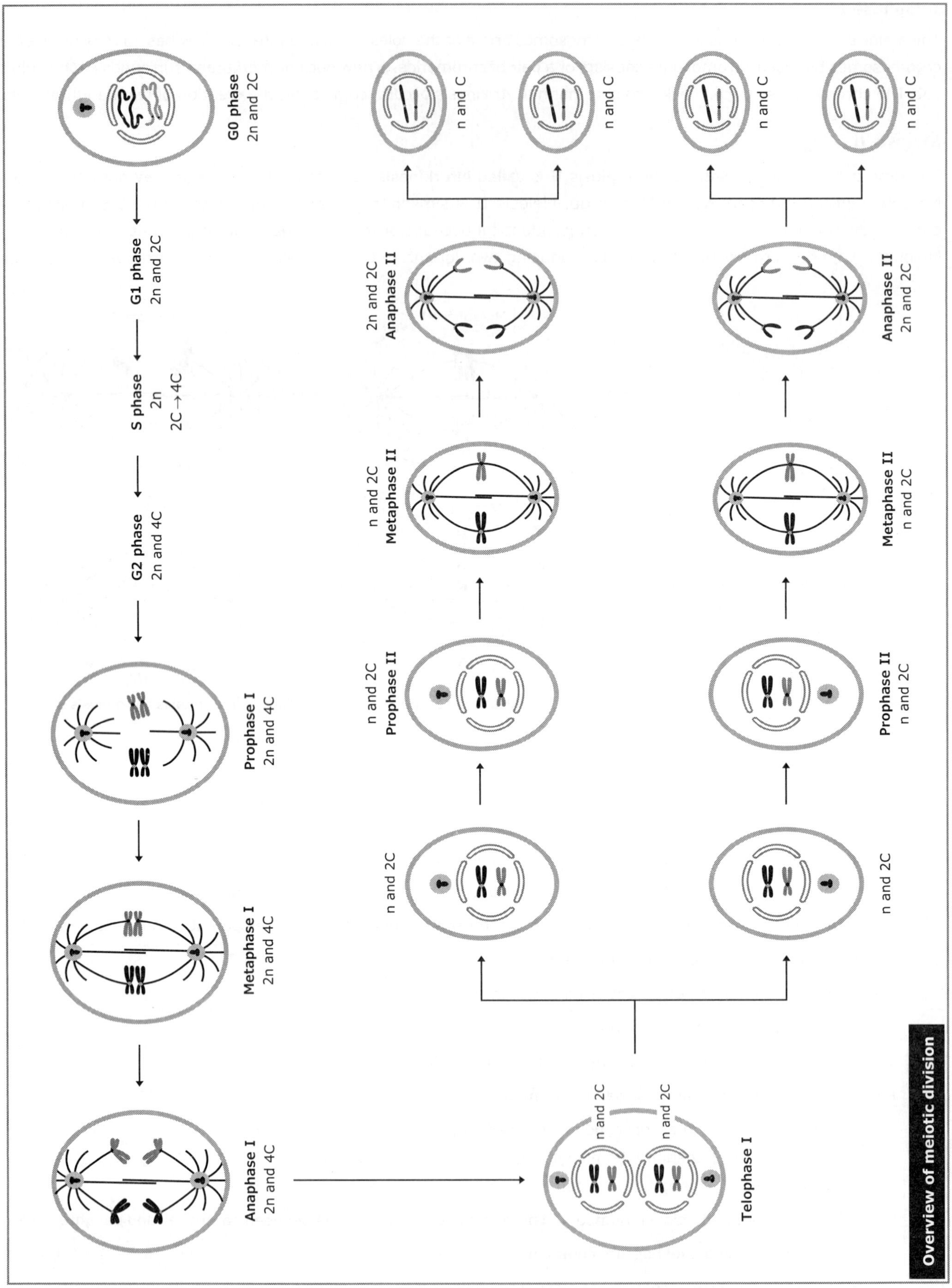

Overview of meiotic division

3.22.3 Nondisjunction and aneuploidy

During mitosis, each chromosome replicates and the two sister chromatids separate, with one going to each daughter cell. Similarly, during meiosis, the two homologous chromosomes separate during the first division, and then the two sister chromatids move to separate cells during the second division. The result of a normal mitosis or meiosis is that all the progeny cells receive complete sets of chromosomes. Occasionally, however, homologous chromosomes and sister chromatids fail to separate or disjoin properly during mitosis or meiosis. The failure of chromosomes to separate properly during mitosis or meiosis is called **nondisjunction**. Nondisjunction produces cells or gametes with extra or missing chromosomes; it is the primary cause of the **aneuploidy**.

During meiosis, non-disjunction can occur during meiosis I or meiosis II. In meiosis I, when non-disjunction of homologous chromosome occurs, both homologs move towards the same pole. In meiosis II, non-disjunction of sister chromatids occurs with both chromatids going to the same pole. Depending on where in meiosis this non-disjunction occurs, some gametes will end up with one or more extra chromosomes and the other will end up with fewer chromosomes than a complete set.

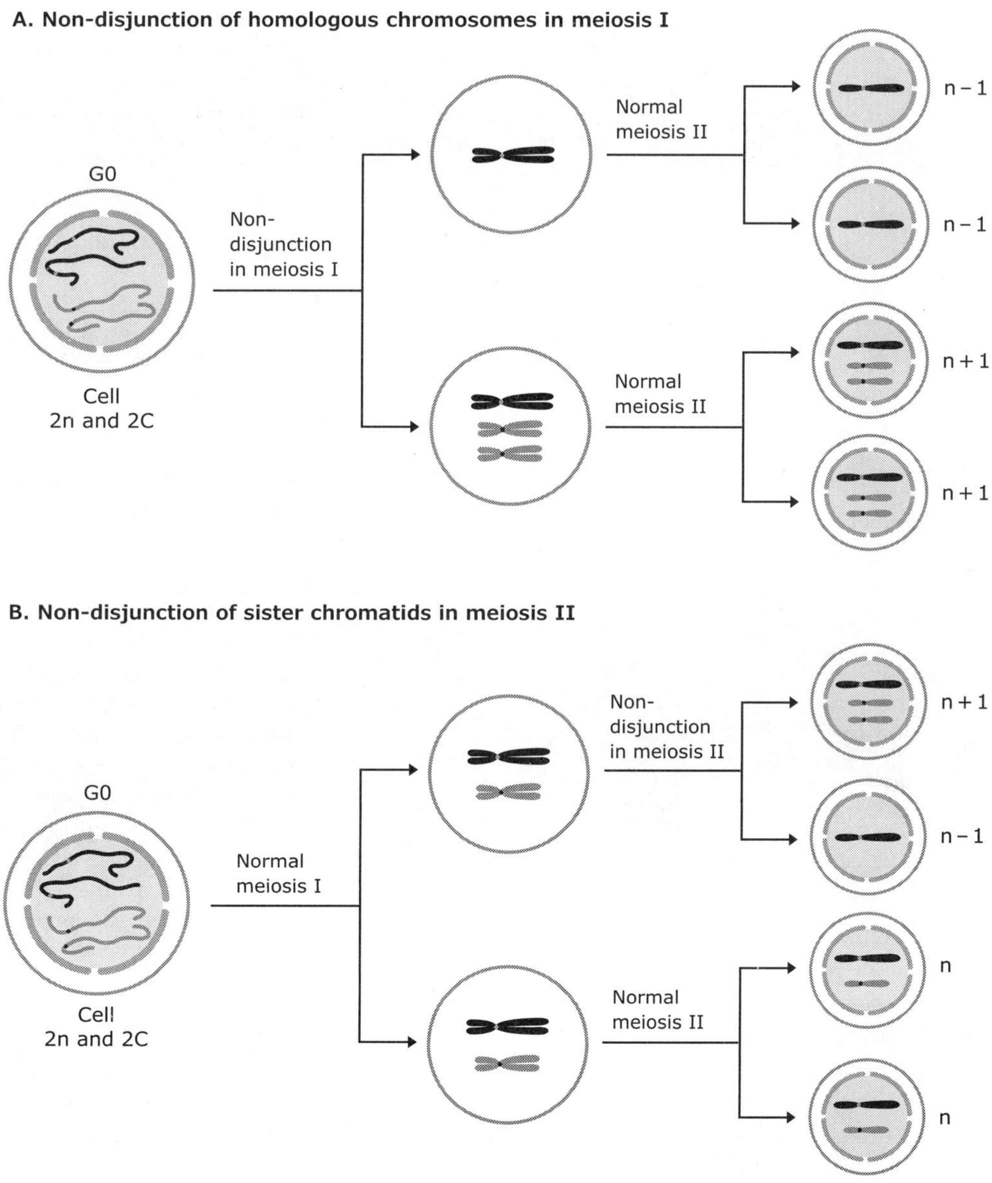

Figure 3.133 Mechanisms of formation of aneuploid gametes during meiosis. A. Non-disjunction of homologous chromosomes in meiosis I and B. Non-disjunction of sister chromatids in meiosis II.

Box 3.10 Types of meiosis

Meiosis occurs during sexual life cycle of all eukaryotes. Fertilization and meiosis alternate in sexual life cycles, maintaining a constant number of chromosomes in each species from one generation to the next. Although the alternation of meiosis and fertilization is common to all organisms that reproduce sexually, the timing of these two events in the life cycle varies, depending on the species. Meiosis is of three types – *gametic, zygotic* and *sporogenic* – depending on the stage, where it occurs during sexual cycle.

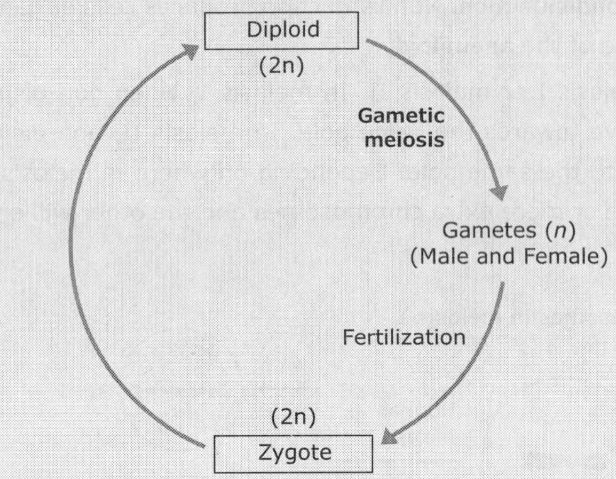

In the *gametic meiosis*, meiosis occurs at the time of gametes formation. Gametes are the only haploid cells. Gametes fertilize to form the zygote. The diploid zygote undergoes repeated mitotic division to give organism. This type of meiosis occurs in most animals including human.

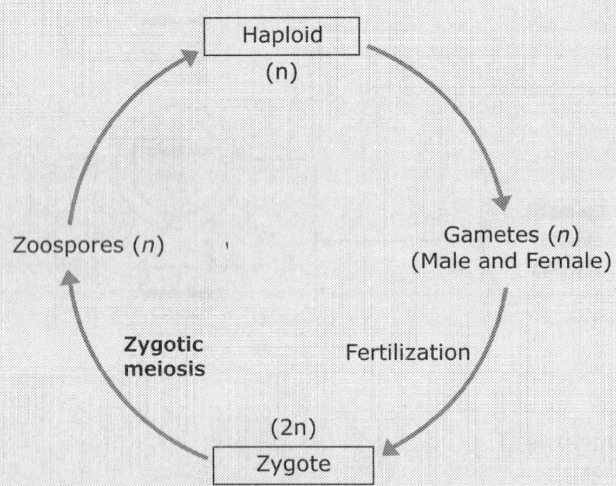

Zygotic meiosis occurs in most fungi and algae. In this case after gametic fusion and formation of diploid zygote, meiosis occurs. Meiosis does not produce gametes but haploid cells that then divide by mitosis.

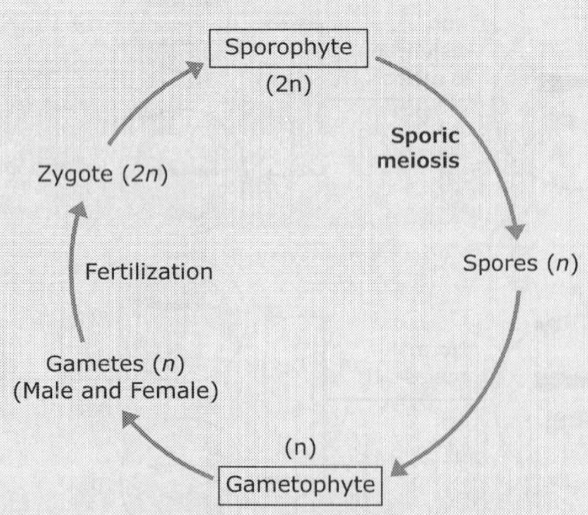

Plants and some species of algae exhibit *sporogenic meiosis*. In this case multicellular diploid body (called the sporophyte) produces haploid spores by meiotic division. Unlike a gamete, a haploid spore doesn't fuse with another cell but divides mitotically, generating a multicellular haploid body called the gametophyte. Cells of the gametophyte give rise to gametes by mitosis. Fusion of two haploid gametes at fertilization results in a diploid zygote, which develops into the next sporophyte generation.

Figure 3.134 Gametic, zygotic and sporogenic meiosis.

Box 3.11 Stem cells

Stem cells are unspecialized (undifferentiated) cells that can differentiate into other cells and self-regenerate. When a stem cell divides, each new cell has the potential either to remain a stem cell or become differentiated cell with a more specialized function. Because the division of stem cells produces new stem cells as well as differentiated daughter cells, stem cells are self-renewing populations of cells that can serve as a source for the production of differentiated cells throughout life. Cell division in stem cells may be *symmetric* or *asymmetric*. In **symmetric division**, both daughter cells are identical as parent stem cells, and both of the daughters are stem cells whereas in **asymmetric division** one of two cells is identical to parent stem cell and the second differentiate into a more specialized cell.

All stem cells—regardless of their source—have three general properties: **1**. they are capable of dividing and renewing themselves for long periods; **2**. they are unspecialized i.e., cells do not have any tissue-specific structures that allow them to perform specialized functions and **3**. they can give rise to specialized cell types including heart muscle cells or nerous.

Stem cell classification

Stem cells can be classified on the basis of their *potency* as well as their *origin*.

Based on potency: Stem cells could be classified according to their potency (i.e. ability to differentiate into other cell types).

Totipotent Ability to produce all the differentiated cells in an organism, including extraembryonic tissues (i.e., ability to give rise to all embryonic and extraembryonic tissues).

Pluripotent Ability to form all the derivatives of three germ layers (ectoderm, endoderm and mesoderm), but not the extraembryonic tissue, the placenta and the umbilical cord.

Multipotent Ability to differentiate into a limited types of cells from one germ layer.

Oligopotent Ability to differentiate into a few types of cells.

Unipotent Ability to differentiate into one cell type.

Based on origin: Stem cells could be classified according to their origin. There are two broad types of stem cells: *embryonic stem cells* and non-embryonic *adult stem cells*. **Embryonic stem cells** are obtained from the inner cell mass of the blastocyst. Embryonic stem cells are *pluripotent*, because they can give rise to all embryonic but not all extraembryonic tissues. **Adult stem cells** (also called *tissue-specific stem cells* or *somatic stem cells*) are located among differentiated cells in a tissue or organ. They are found in a specific microenvironment called *stem cell niche*. Unlike embryonic stem cells, which are defined by their origin (the inner cell mass of the blastocyst), the origin of adult stem cells in mature tissues is mostly unknown. Adult stem cells typically generate the cell types of the tissue in which they reside. For example, the bone marrow contains at least two kinds of stem cells. One population, called **hematopoietic stem cells**, forms all the types of blood cells in the body. It is generally accepted that a blood-forming hematopoietic stem cell—cannot give rise to the cells of very different tissue, such as nerve cells in the brain. A second population of non-hematopoietic stem cells, called **bone marrow stromal stem cells** (also called **mesenchymal stem cells**) can give rise to a variety of cell types: bone cells (osteoblasts and osteocytes), cartilage cells (chondrocytes), fat cells (adipocytes) and stromal cells that support blood formation. The adult brain also contains stem cells (**neural stem cells**) that are able to generate the brain's three major cell types—*astrocytes* and *oligodendrocytes*, which are non-neuronal cells and neurons or nerve cells.

In 2006, Kazutoshi Takahashi and Shinya Yamanaka made a breakthrough by identifying conditions that would allow some specialized adult cells to be 'reprogrammed' genetically to a pluripotent state, called an **induced pluripotent stem cell**, similar to that of an embryonic stem cell. They used the transcription factors Oct3/4, Sox2, c-Myc, and Klf4 to reprogram mouse fibroblast cells into pluripotent cells.

Problem

An animal cell enters in the process of cell division. Name the drugs affecting the following steps.

a. a drug that inhibits microtubule formation.

b. a drug that allows microtubules to form but prevents them from shortening.

c. a drug that inhibits cytokinesis.

Solution: a. Colchicine; b. Taxol; c. Cytochalasin

Problem

An organism has 56 chromosomes in its diploid stage. Indicate how many chromosomes are present in the following:

P. Somatic cells in G0 stage; Q. Metaphase (mitosis); R. Anaphase (mitosis); S. Metaphase II (meiosis); T. Gametes

Solution: P. 56 chromosomes; Q. 56 chromosomes; R. 112 chromosomes; S. 28 chromosomes; T. 28 chromosomes

3.23 Apoptosis

Apoptosis (from the Greek words apo = from and ptosis = falling) is a process of **programmed cell death**. Cell death can be fundamentally divided into accidental cell death and programmed cell death. Programmed cell death is a genetically controlled cell-intrinsic suicide process that eliminates specific cells. It is essential for controlling cell number, removing unwanted diseased or damaged cells and maintaining the cellular homeostasis. 'Apoptosis' and 'programmed cell death' are often used synonymously. Although apoptosis is the most common form of programmed cell death, there are also non-apoptotic programmed cell deaths such as **autophagy** and **regulated necrosis**.

Not all cell death is apoptotic. Cell death also occurs due to injury. When a cell is damaged to such an extent that it simply cannot survive, it is called **unregulated necrosis**. Term **necrosis** was earlier regarded as an unregulated mode of cell death. However, many recent studies reported the existence of **regulated necrosis** (termed **necroptosis**). Necroptosis is a regulated necrosis mediated by death receptors. Unregulated necrosis or simply necrosis is considered as an accidental and uncontrolled cell death. It is characterized by loss of cell membrane integrity and an uncontrolled release of cellular components into the extracellular space. This release initiates an inflammatory response attracting leukocytes and nearby phagocytes to eliminate the dead cells and its products by phagocytosis. In contrast, necroptosis shows morphological features similar to necrosis, but, as apoptosis, is strictly regulated. However, while apoptosis depends on caspase activation, necroptosis is negatively regulated by caspases and needs the intervention of the *receptor-interacting protein* (RIP) that is thought to be a necroptosis key mediator. It is conceivable that when the apoptotic caspases fail to be activated, then cells undergo necroptosis as an alternative death pathway.

Autophagy is an intracellular degradation process of cytoplasmic components through the formation of **autophagosomes**. The autophagosomes fuse with lysosomes. The resulting compartment, called **autolysosome**, causes enzymatic breakdown of the cytoplasmic components.

The demise of cells by **apoptosis** is marked by a well-defined sequence of morphological changes. Apoptosis exhibits cell shrinkage, chromatin condensation (**pyknosis**), nuclear fragmentation (**karyorrhexis**), and plasma membrane *blebbing*, culminating with the formation of apparently intact small vesicles (commonly known as **apoptotic bodies**) that are efficiently taken up by neighboring cells with phagocytic activity and degraded within lysosomes. Importantly, the intracellular constituents are not released into the extracellular milieu, where they would probably have deleterious effects on neighboring cells, but instead are phagocytosed by neighboring cells.

Chemical changes in the surface of apoptotic cells or bodies allow the surrounding cells or macrophages to recognize and engulf them. An especially important change occurs in the plasma membrane of apoptotic cells. The negatively charged phospholipid phosphatidylserine is normally exclusively located in the inner leaflet of the lipid bilayer of the plasma membrane, but it flips to the outer leaflet in apoptotic cells, where it can serve as a marker of these cells. There is essentially no inflammatory reaction associated with the process of apoptosis nor with the removal of apoptotic cells because:

1. apoptotic cells do not release their cellular constituents into the surrounding interstitial tissue;
2. they are quickly phagocytosed by surrounding cells and,
3. the engulfing cells do not produce anti-inflammatory cytokines.

Mechanisms of apoptosis

Apoptosis can be initiated by a wide variety of stimuli including DNA damage, nutrient deficiency, endoplasmic reticulum stress, growth factor withdrawal, heat shock, developmental cues, and ligation of death-receptors on the cell surface through the activation of apoptotic caspases. The mechanisms of apoptosis are highly complex and regulated, involving an energy-dependent cascade of molecular events. There are multiple apoptotic pathways. These pathways are both *caspase-dependent* as well as *caspase-independent*.

Caspases (*cysteine aspartate specific proteases*) have proteolytic activity (**endoproteases**) and are so named because they contain a key cysteine residue in the catalytic site and selectively cleave proteins at C-terminal of aspartate residues. Caspases are involved in both *apoptotic* and *non-apoptotic* cell death. But caspase function is not limited to cell death. A caspase can mediate both cell death and non-cell death functions including proliferation, tumor suppression and differentiation. Caspases have been broadly classified by their known roles in *apoptosis* and in *inflammation*. In mammal, caspase-2, -3, -7, -8, -9 and -10 are **apoptotic caspases**, whereas caspase-1, -4, -5, -11 and -12 are **inflammatory caspases**. Caspases involved in apoptosis have been subclassified by their mechanism of action into **initiator caspases** (caspases-2, -8, -9, -10) and **executioner caspases** (caspases-3, -6 and -7). Inflammatory caspases function as critical mediators of innate immune responses rather than proapoptotic factors. Caspase-1, -4, -5, and -12 comprise the inflammatory subset in humans, whereas caspase-1, -11 and -12 serve the same function in mice.

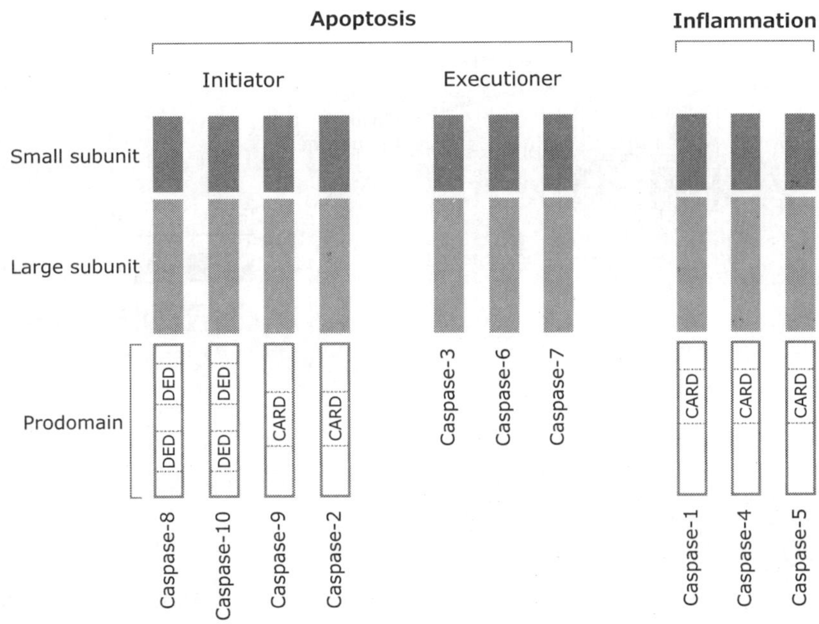

Figure 3.135 Domain structure of human caspases.

Caspases are initially produced as inactive monomeric **procaspases**. Executioner caspases are activated by cleavage, whereas initiator caspases are activated by dimerization. Assembly into dimers is facilitated by various adaptor proteins that bind to specific regions in the *prodomain* of the procaspase. The exact mechanism of assembly depends on the specific adaptor involved. Different caspases have different protein-protein interaction domains in their prodomains, allowing them to complex with different adaptors. For example, caspase-1, -2, -4, -5, and -9 contain a *caspase recruitment domain* (**CARD**), whereas caspase-8 and -10 have a *death effector domain* (**DED**).

Apoptotic pathways

There are two well-characterized caspase-dependent apoptotic pathways initiated either by extrinsic or intrinsic factors: **Extrinsic** or **death receptor pathway** and **intrinsic** or **mitochondrial pathway**.

Extrinsic apoptotic pathway

A number of extracellular signal molecules is specialized to induce apoptosis. These extracellular signal molecules bind with cell surface receptors (termed **death receptors**). One typical example is a **Fas** (also called **CD95** or **APO-1**), a member of the *TNF receptor* family. Its ligand is **FasL** (Fatty acid synthetase ligand), a homotrimeric transmembrane protein, expressed in cytotoxic T-lymphocytes and natural killer cells. The interaction of FasL and Fas on the target cell triggers apoptosis. When Fas binds its ligand, FasL, an adaptor protein called *Fas-associated protein with death domain* (**FADD**) is recruited. FADD contains two domains– a **death domain** (**DD**) and a **death-effector domain** (**DED**). Death receptor Fas also shares a death domain. Interaction between Fas and FADD occurs through interaction between the death domains of FADD and Fas. The death-effector domain of FADD in turn recruits procaspase-8 (via DED interactions) to generate active caspase-8. The complex of death receptor, FADD, and procaspase-8 is called a *death-inducing signaling complex* (**DISC**). Once caspase-8 is activated, the execution phase of apoptosis is triggered. Caspase-8 activates executioner caspases (such as caspases-3 and -7), which cleave substrates within the cell and the cell dies by apoptosis. Death receptor-mediated apoptosis can be inhibited by a protein called c-FLIP which will bind to FADD and caspase-8, rendering them ineffective.

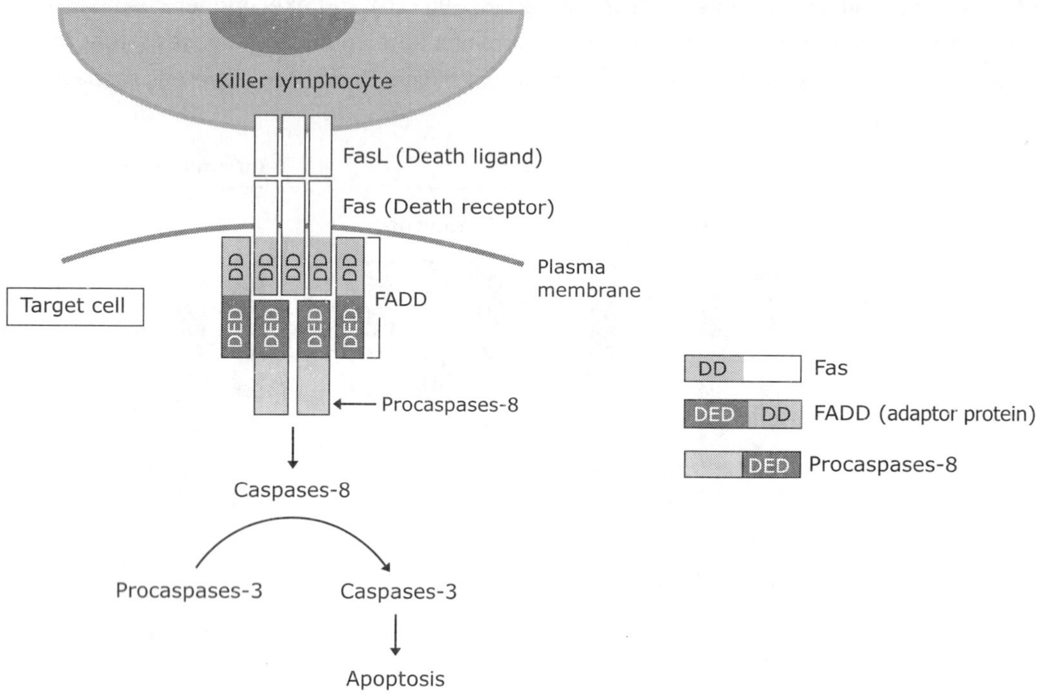

Figure 3.136 FasL bound Fas on the surface of a cell recruits the adaptor protein, FADD (Fas-associated death domain). This occurs through interaction between the death domains (DD) of FADD and Fas. The death-effector domain (DED) of FADD in turn recruits procaspase-8 via DED–DED interactions to generate active caspase-8. This complex is called the DISC (death-inducing signal complex). Active caspase-8 then initiates apoptosis directly by cleaving and thereby activating executioner caspase.

Intrinsic or mitochondrial apoptotic pathway

Apoptosis is induced not only by exogenous signals reacting with death receptors but also by intracellular death signal released from the mitochondria. Various cellular stresses such as DNA damage, hypoxia and growth factor deprivation lead to release of cytochrome *c* from the mitochondria and activation of *intrinsic apoptotic pathway*. This type of induced cell death has, therefore, been called **apoptosis by neglect** as counterpart to the receptor-mediated **apoptosis by instruction**.

The defining event during intrinsic apoptotic pathway is *mitochondrial outer membrane permeabilization* (**MOMP**). Following MOMP, cytochrome c, is released into the cytosol. Once in the cytosol, cytochrome c binds to adaptor protein **APAF-1** (apoptotic proteases activating factor), a mammalian homologue of *C. elegans* CED-4 protein. APAF-1 exists in a resting cell as cytosolic, inactive monomers. The binding of cytochrome *c* to the APAF-1 monomer leads to a conformational change that exposes a nucleotide-binding site. The nucleotide deoxy-ATP (dATP) binding and its hydrolysis induces a second conformational change in APAF-1 that exposes both its oligomerization and **CARD** domains. Seven such activated APAF-1 monomers then assemble into a heptameric complex, the **apoptosome**. The center of this complex contains the CARDs that recruit and activate **caspase-9**. Caspase-9, in turn, cleaves procaspase-3 to generate caspase-3, which cleaves targets that cause apoptosis of the cell.

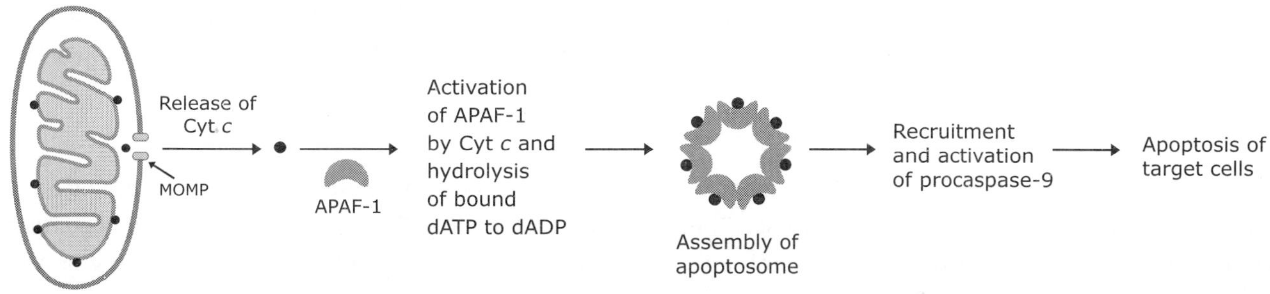

Figure 3.137 Schematic representation of the role of mitochondria in apoptosis. Cytochrome c activates APAF-1 to form an apoptosome, a complex of seven APAF-1 molecules. It recruits and activates initiator caspase, caspase-9. It is activated by dimerization when the CARD domain binds to the adaptor protein APAF-1. Once activated, caspase-9 cleaves and activates the executioner caspases-3 and apoptosis proceeds. The caspase-8 activated in the extrinsic pathway and caspase-9 in the intrinsic pathway cleave procaspase-3 to mature caspase-3.

The **inhibitors of apoptosis proteins** (**IAPs**) comprise a family of proteins with different functions; some of these proteins bind to and inhibit caspases. IAP was first identified in an insect virus (*baculovirus*), which encode IAP proteins to prevent a host cell that is infected by the virus from killing itself by apoptosis. Subsequently, IAPs were identified by sequence homology. A common feature of all IAPs is the presence of *Baculovirus IAP Repeat* (**BIR**) domain. Some IAPs—including *X-linked IAP* (**XIAP**), which is found in mammals—act as potent inhibitors of caspases, especially the initiator caspase-9 and the executioner caspases -3 and -7.

The intrinsic apoptotic pathway is regulated by the **Bcl-2 family** (Bcl-2 stands for B-cell lymphoma/leukemia-2 gene) of proteins. All members of the Bcl-2 family share *Bcl-2 homology* (**BH**) domains. At least one BH domain is contained in each of the Bcl-2 family members. This family of proteins comprises both **anti-apoptotic** members and **pro-apoptotic** members. Anti-apoptotic members inhibit apoptosis whereas pro-apoptotic members promote apoptosis. The pro-apoptotic Bcl-2 proteins consist of two subfamilies – the **BH123 proteins** (pro-apoptotic *effectors*) and the **BH3-*only*** proteins (pro-apoptotic *activators*). The main BH123 proteins are **Bax** and **Bak**. Important members of the BH3-*only* proteins are Bid, Bim, Bik, Bad, Puma and Noxa.

When an apoptotic stimulus triggers the intrinsic pathway, the pro-apoptotic BH123 proteins - Bax and Bak - promote **MOMP** (mitochondrial outer membrane permeabilization) and the release of cytochrome *c* and other intermembrane proteins by an unknown mechanism. Bax and Bak, in general, do not function to cause MOMP unless activated by the BH3-*only* proteins, Bid and Bim. The activation and function of Bax and Bak are inhibited by the anti-apoptotic members of the Bcl-2 family, including Bcl-2, Bcl-x and others. In this way, the anti-apoptotic Bcl-2 family members prevent MOMP and prevent apoptosis.

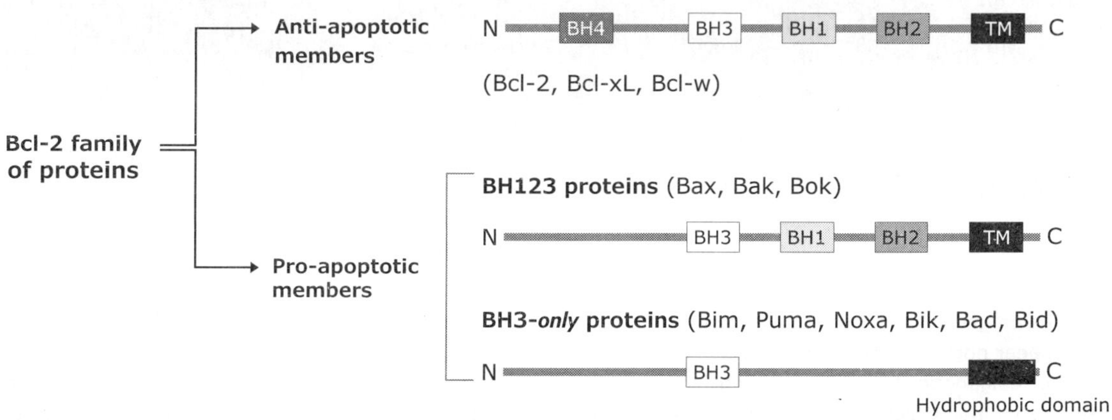

Figure 3.138 Structures of members of the Bcl-2 family of proteins. Bcl-2 homology (BH) domains are found in all proteins belonging to the Bcl-2 family. There are four distinct BH domains – BH1, BH2, BH3 and BH4. Anti-apoptotic Bcl-2 family proteins contain four BH domains. The pro-apoptotic Bcl-2 members are divided into pro-apoptotic effectors BH123 proteins (which also contain BH1-4) and pro-apoptotic activators BH3-*only* proteins.

BH3-*only* proteins provide the crucial link between apoptotic stimuli and the intrinsic pathway of apoptosis, with different stimuli activating different BH3-*only* proteins. These proteins carry out their pro-apoptotic function by two mechanisms:

- Neutralization of the anti-apoptotic Bcl-2 family proteins and
- Direct activation of the pro-apoptotic effectors Bax and Bak.

In the absence of an apoptotic stimulus, anti-apoptotic Bcl-2 proteins bind to and inhibit the BH123 proteins on the mitochondrial outer membrane and in the cytosol. They block the ability of BH123 proteins Bak or Bax to oligomerize and form pores in the outer mitochondrial membrane. In the presence of an apoptotic stimulus, BH3-only proteins are activated and bind to the anti-apoptotic Bcl-2 proteins so that they can no longer inhibit the BH123 proteins. Some activated BH3-*only* proteins may stimulate mitochondrial protein release directly by binding to and activating the BH123 proteins.

3.24 Cancer

A normal cell undergoes regulated division, differentiation and apoptosis (programmed cell death). Cell growth is a highly controlled and regulated process. When normal cells lose their usual control over division, they become **neoplastic** or **tumor cells**. Abnormal growth of cells in the body is referred to as **neoplasia**. Since neoplastic cells undergo continuous division, they give rise to masses of cells called **tumor** or **neoplasm**. The proliferation of neoplastic cells and the progressive increase in tumor size eventually leads to a breach in the barriers between tissues, leading to **tumor invasion** into surrounding normal tissues. After acquiring the ability to invade surrounding tissue, tumor cells breaking away from the **primary tumor**, migrating to a new location and establishing a **secondary tumor**. This is referred to as **metastasis**, the ability of tumor cells to migrate to a new location and proliferate to produce the secondary tumor.

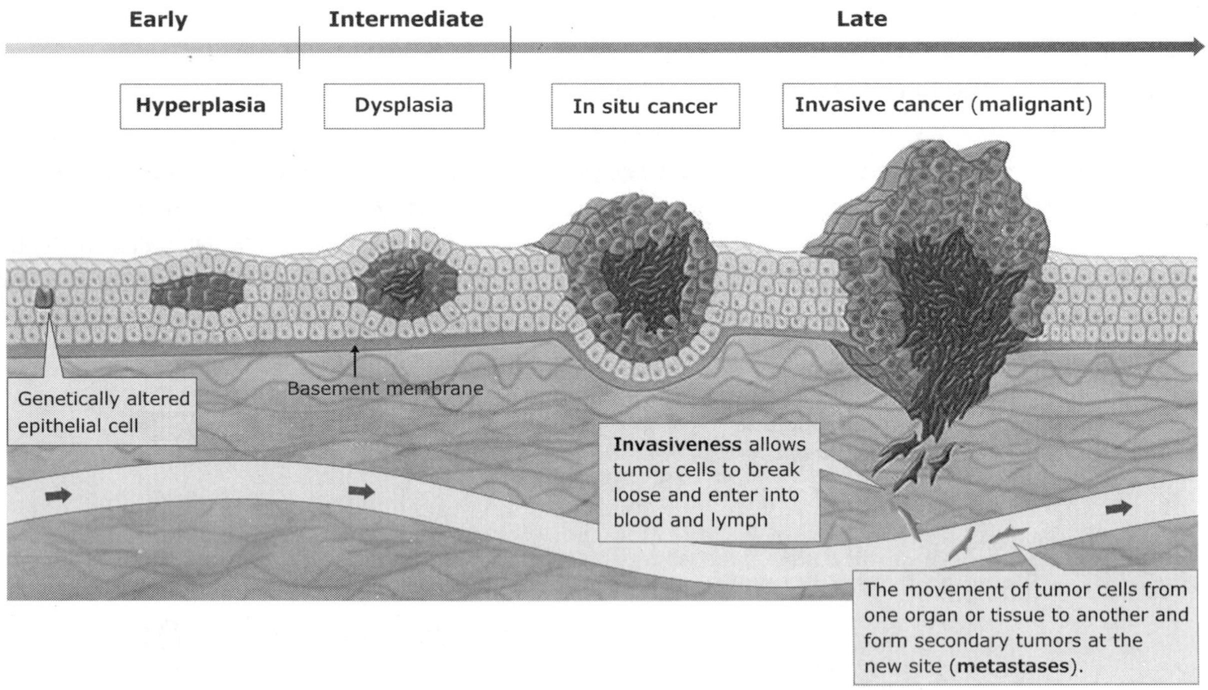

Figure 3.139 The progression begins with a mutation that makes the cell more likely to divide. The altered cell divides and increase in number but appear normal under a microscope (a condition called *hyperplasia*). At some point, one of these cells experiences another genetic *or* epigenetic change that further increases its tendency to divide; this cell's descendants divide excessively and look abnormal (a condition called *dysplasia*). As time passes, cells experience another genetic *or* epigenetic change, causing very abnormal structure, loss of differentiation and loss of contact between the cells; however, it is still confined to one location where it arose, so it is called a *in situ* cancer. The *in situ* cancer may remain contained indefinitely, but additional changes may occur that enable it to invade neighboring tissues and enter the bloodstream by crossing the wall of a blood vessel or through lymphatic system. The tumor is said to be an invasive cancer (malignant). The escaped cells may establish new tumors at other locations in the body (*metastases*).

Benign and malignant tumor

A tumor can be either benign or malignant. In a **benign tumor** (non-cancerous), the tumor cells remain clustered together in a single mass at their original location and do not spread to other sites. Benign tumors typically consist of well-differentiated cells that closely resemble normal cells and may function like normal cells. In contrast, **malignant tumors** (cancerous) are characterized by tumor cells that do not remain localized. They become progressively *invasive*, meaning they have the ability to invade surrounding tissues, and metastatic, meaning they can migrate to new locations and proliferate to form **secondary tumors**. As these cells actively divide and grow, they also starve normal cells by competing for vital nutrients. The term 'cancer' specifically refers to *malignant tumors*. Malignant tumor cells tend to be **anaplastic** (lack of cellular differentiation is termed as *anaplasia*) or less well differentiated than normal cells of the tissue in which they arise, whereas benign tumor cells are well differentiated and appear normal.

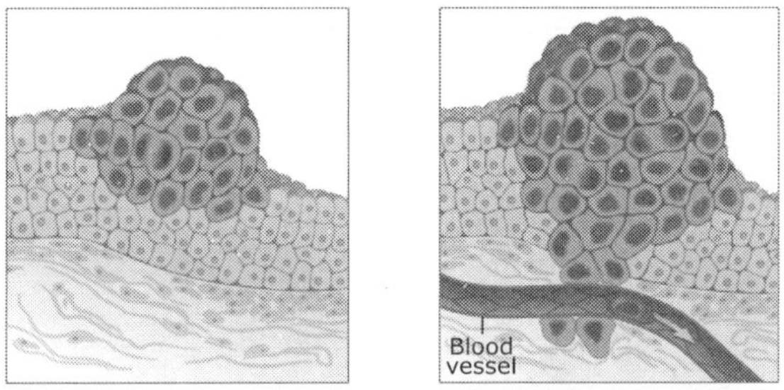

Benign tumor **Malignant tumor**

Both benign and malignant tumors are classified according to the type of cell from which they arise. Tumors are classified into four major groups according to their origin (*epithelial*, *mesenchymal*, *hematopoietic* and *neuroectodermal*). Each broad category has many subdivisions according to the specific cell type, the location in the body, and the microscopic appearance of the tumor. All cell types in the body can give rise to cancer, but the most common human cancers are of epithelial origin - the **carcinomas**. Most carcinomas fall into two categories: *squamous cell carcinomas* arise from epithelia that form protective cell layers, while adenocarcinomas arise from secretory epithelia. **Sarcomas** are cancers of mesenchymal (*mesenchyme* is a type of embryonic connective tissue) origin. **Hematopoietic** cancers arise from the blood. There are three major types of hematopoietic cancers- **leukemias** (cancer of blood-forming tissues, including bone marrow), **myelomas** (cancer of the plasma cells) and **lymphomas** (cancers of the lymphatic organs, especially the lymph nodes). **Neuroectodermal** tumors originate from components of the nervous system. Some tumors do not fit this classification scheme. *Leukemias differ from most other types of cancers*. They arise from blood cells or their precursors and proliferate as individual cells in the bloodstream, rather than forming solid tumors. Since leukemias are already present in circulation, they do not need to promote angiogenesis, nor do they need to invade surrounding tissues or metastasize, although some types of leukemia may still exhibit metastatic tendencies.

Clonal evolution in cancer

How many normal cells act as ancestors to form a tumor? Do the tumor cells descend from a single ancestral cell (i.e., **monoclonal origin**) or did a large number of normal cells undergo change, each becoming the ancestor of a distinct subpopulation of cells within a tumor mass (i.e., **polyclonal origin**)? Most cancers originate from single abnormal cell i.e., monoclonal origin. Cancers are probably initiated by changes in the cell's DNA sequence (**genetic changes**). Cancers are also driven by change in pattern of gene expression without a change in DNA sequences (**epigenetic changes**). Most cancers are initiated by genetic changes and majority of them are caused by changes in somatic cells and therefore are not transmitted to the next generation. About 1% of all cancers is due to genetic changes in germinal cells and is therefore inherited. About 80% of these inherited cancers are dominant in nature.

The transition of a normal cell into a tumor cell is referred to as transformation. At the cellular level, the development of cancer is viewed as a multistep process involving genetic and epigenetic changes and selection for cells with progressively increasing capacity for *proliferation, survival, invasion* and *metastasis*.

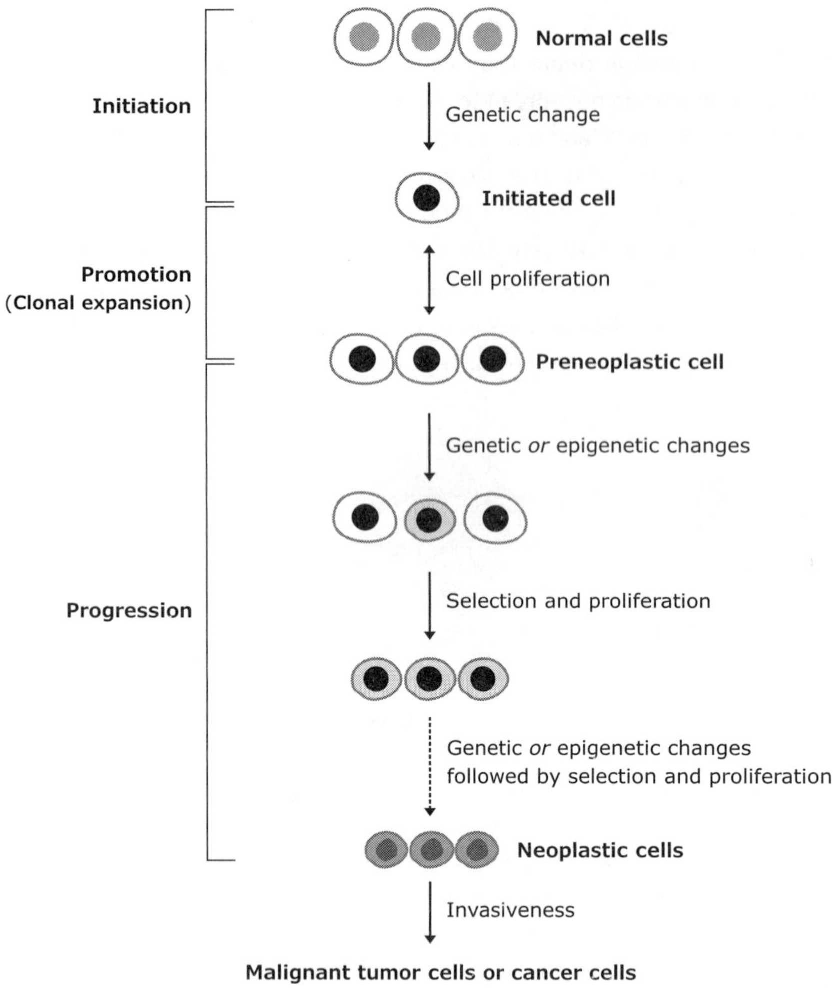

Figure 3.140
Clonal evolution.
In this schematic diagram, a tumor develops through repeated rounds of genetic or epigenetic changes and proliferation, giving rise eventually to a clone of fully malignant tumor cells. The development of cancer requires a gradual accumulation of genetic and epigenetic changes in a number of different genes. These changes either enhances cell proliferation or decreases cell death.

- **Initiation** involves genetic changes in cancer-related genes. Although the genetic changes are the most common change in a cell that can produce a cancer-initiating event, epigenetic changes can also cause a cancer-initiating event. It may arise spontaneously or induced by the exposure to a carcinogenic agent. Change in the gene affects the processes associated with cellular proliferation, survival and differentiation.
- **Promotion** is generally associated with increased proliferation of the initiated cell. The promotion stage is considered to be a relatively lengthy and reversible process in which actively proliferating preneoplastic cells accumulate.
- **Progression** is the final stage of neoplastic transformation. The development of cancer usually requires a gradual accumulation of genetic and epigenetic changes in a number of different genes. The process of acquiring additional genetic and epigenetic changes within cells of the tumor population is referred to progression. Some of these genetic and epigenetic changes confer a selective advantage to the cell, such as more rapid growth and survival. The descendants of a cell bearing such genetic and epigenetic changes will consequently become dominant within the tumor population. The process is called **clonal selection** since a new clone of tumor cells has evolved on the basis of its increased growth rate or other properties (such as invasiveness and metastatic potential) that confer a selective advantage. The clonal selection continues throughout tumor development, so tumors continuously become more rapid-growing and increasingly malignant.
- **Metastasis** involves the spread of cancer cells from the primary site to other parts of the body. It itself is a multistep process. The process includes **intravasation** (movement of cancer cells through the wall of a blood or lymph vessel), spread through the circulation and **extravasation** (movement of cells out of a blood vessel into tissue), leading to growth at a secondary distant sites.

Properties of cancer cells

Cancer cells typically display several abnormal properties as compared to normal cells that provide a description of malignancy at the cellular level. Understanding these distinct properties is crucial for developing effective strategies in the diagnosis and treatment of cancer. Some of these abnormal properties include

Immortalization: Normal cells have a limited capacity to grow and divide both *in vivo* and *in vitro*. Even when provided with optimal growth conditions, normal cells will cease dividing after a certain number of cell divisions and then undergo senescence and die. The exact mechanism that limits the life expectancy of normal cells in culture is not fully understood, but it may be related to the continual shortening of telomeres with each cell division. In contrast, cancer cells are immortal and can grow indefinitely.

Loss of anchorage-dependent growth: Most normal cells must be attached to a rigid substratum (i.e., they must be anchored) to grow. They do not proliferate well when suspended in fluid or a semisolid agar gel. However, when these cells make contact with a suitable surface, they proliferate, a type of growth known as **anchorage-dependent growth**. In contrast, cancer cells can proliferate even when they are suspended in culture media without attachment to a substratum. This is called **anchorage-independent growth**.

Loss of density-dependent inhibition of proliferation: Normal cells in culture display *density-dependent inhibition* of cell proliferation and proliferate until they reach a finite cell density, which is determined partly by availability of growth factors in culture medium. But the proliferation of cancer cells is not sensitive to density-dependent inhibition.

Loss of contact inhibition: Normal cells migrate across the surface of a culture dish until they make contact with a neighboring cell. Further cell migration is then inhibited and normal cells adhere to each other forming an orderly array of cells on the culture dish surface. This inhibition of growth after contact is called *contact inhibition*. Cancer cells in contrast continue moving after contact with their neighbouring cells migrating over adjacent cells and growing in disordered multilayered patterns.

Invasiveness and metastasis: One of the most important characteristics of cancer cells is their *invasiveness* and *metastasis*. *Invasiveness* refers to the ability of tumor cells to invade neighboring tissues. In contrast, *metastasis* describes the ability of cancer cells to migrate to a new location and proliferate to produce the secondary tumor. Metastasis causes the spread of cancer cells to tissues and organs beyond where the tumor originated and the formation of new tumors. There are two properties of cancer cells that play important roles in invasion and metastasis. *First*, malignant cells generally secrete proteases that digest extracellular matrix components, allowing the cancer cells to invade adjacent normal tissues. *Second*, cancer cells also secrete growth factors that promote the formation of new blood vessels (**angiogenesis**). Angiogenesis is needed to support the growth of a tumor by supplying oxygen and nutrients to the proliferating tumor cells.

Lower growth factors requirements: Normal cells grown in culture require various growth factors to continue proliferating. In normal human tissues, growth factors are generally produced at distant sites and then either carried through the bloodstream or diffuse to their nearby target cells. However, tumor cells often produce their own growth factors that bind to and stimulate the activity of receptors that are also present on the same tumor cells that are producing the growth factor. This results in a continuous self-generated proliferative signal known as autocrine stimulation that drives proliferation of the tumor cell continuously even in the absence of any exogenous proliferative signal. Autocrine stimulation is manifested as a reduced requirement for serum because serum is the source of many of the growth factors in the media used to propagate cells *in vitro*.

Fail to undergo apoptosis: Another general characteristic of most cancer cells is that they fail to undergo apoptosis and, therefore, exhibit increased life spans compared to their normal counterparts.

Molecular basis of cancer

All genes whose genetic and epigenetic changes contribute to the causation of cancer are described as **cancer-critical genes** (or **cancer-related genes**). These genes contribute to the transformation process by driving cell proliferation or reducing sensitivity to cell death and differentiation. These genes may be involved in the processes such as *cell cycle progression*, *differentiation process*, *DNA repair*, *dell death*.

Cancer-critical genes are grouped into two broad classes, according to whether the cancer risk arises from a *gain -of-function* mutation of a gene, or *loss-of-function* mutation. Genes for which a gain-of-function mutation drives a cell toward cancer, are called **proto-oncogenes.** Whereas genes for which a loss-of-function mutation creates the cancer are called **tumor suppressor genes**. Proto-oncogenes encode proteins that generally stimulate cell growth, division and survival whereas tumor suppressor genes involved in DNA damage repair, cell cycle checkpoint activation, induction of apoptosis and prevent unregulated cellular growth. Therefore, gain of proto-oncogenes function and loss of tumor suppressor genes function would result in the onset and progression of cancer.

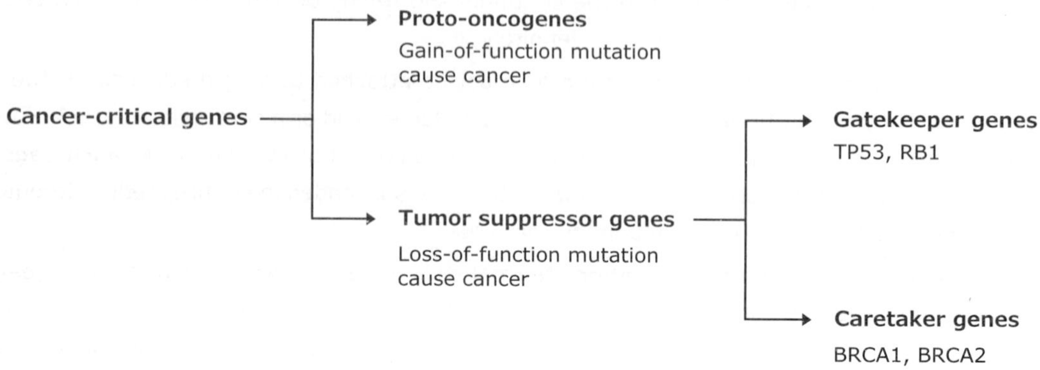

Mutation of a cancer-critical gene can be either *dominant* or *recessive*. A *gain-of-function mutation* in a single copy of a proto-oncogene can drive a cell toward the cancer. That is, gain-of-function mutations in proto-oncogenes are typically *dominant* in nature, and the mutated versions of these genes are known as **oncogenes**. On the other hand, the cancer-causing mutations of tumor suppressor genes are generally *recessive*. It means both copies of the normal gene must be removed or inactivated in the diploid somatic cell before an effect is seen.

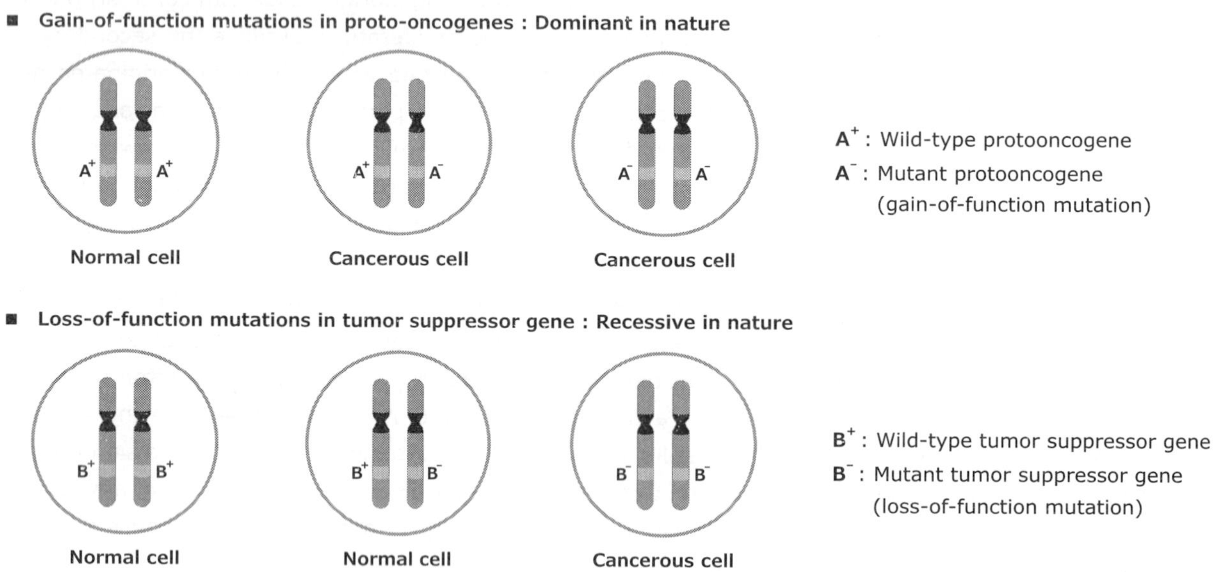

Figure 3.141 The gain-of-function mutation of a single copy of a proto-oncogene can drive a cell toward cancer. The loss-of-function mutations in tumor suppressor genes, on the other hand, generally act in a recessive manner: the function of both alleles must be lost to drive a cell toward cancer.

Proto-oncogenes

Proto-oncogenes control the growth and division of cells. The proteins encoded by proto-oncogenes include growth factors, growth factor receptors, transcription factors and signal transducers. They contribute to the transformation process by driving cell proliferation or reducing sensitivity to cell death.

Table 3.20 Examples of proto-oncogenes and their products

Proto-oncogenes	Protein function
	Growth factor receptors
ERB-B1	Receptor tyrosine-protein kinase
ERB-B2	Receptor tyrosine-protein kinase
EGFR	Receptor of the epidermal growth factor (EGF)
	Growth factor
SIS	Platelet-derived growth factor
INT-2	Fibroblast growth factor
	Protein kinase
ABL	Tyrosine kinase
SRC	Tyrosine kinase
RAF	Serine-threonine kinase
	G-protein signal transducers
H-RAS	GTPase
K-RAS	GTPase
N-RAS	GTPase
	Transcription factor (nuclear protein)
JUN	Transcription factor
FOS	Transcription factor
MYC	Transcription factor

Today, about 40 different human proto-oncogenes are known. Several types of genetic and epigenetic changes convert these proto-oncogenes into oncogenes. Oncogenes arise as a result of genetic or epigenetic changes that increase the expression level or activity of a proto-oncogene. Underlying mechanisms associated with proto-oncogene activation include the following:

Point mutation

A proto-oncogene may be converted into an oncogene through a single alteration of a nucleotide. This alteration may be the deletion of a base, the insertion of an extra base or the substitution of one base for another. However, regardless of the type or cause of such a mutation, it usually changes the amino acid sequence of the encoded protein and thus alters protein function. A point mutation can increase gene function or it can interrupt gene function. One example in which point mutation converts proto-oncogene to oncogene is reported in the *RAS* proto-oncogenes. In human cells, three closely related *RAS* genes are *HRAS*, *KRAS* and *NRAS*.

Chromosomal translocation

Chromosomal translocation may result in the activation of proto-oncogene. Translocation induced overexpression of a proto-oncogene is best exemplified by **Burkitt's lymphoma**. It is a childhood tumor particularly affecting the jaw and found mainly in Africa. In Burkitt's lymphoma, the *MYC* containing segments of chromosome 8 (**8q24**) translocate to chromosome 14 (**14q32**). This translocation places *MYC* gene close to the Ig heavy chain gene. The translocated *MYC* gene here regulated by the Ig gene enhancer, is continually expressed, causing cell to become cancerous. The product of *MYC* gene (Myc proto-oncogene protein) acts as a transcription factor that affects diverse cellular processes involved in cell growth, proliferation, apoptosis and cellular metabolism. Hence, altered expression of *MYC* gene leads to deregulation of a large number of target gene. MYC is a family of proto-oncogenes that code for transcription factors. The MYC family consists of three related human genes: *c-myc* (*MYC*), *l-myc* (*MYCL*) and *n-myc* (*MYCN*).

Similarly, patients with **chronic myelogenous leukemia** (also called *chronic granulocytic leukemia*) contain an abnormal Philadelphia chromosome (Ph[1]) which forms as a result of balanced reciprocal 9;22 translocation. This translocation creates a novel chimeric *BCR-ABL* gene. *ABL* gene present on chromosome 9 and exchange transfers the *ABL* gene to chromosome 22 (known as **Philadelphia chromosome**). *ABL* is a proto-oncogene encodes a tyrosine kinase (*abl* stands for *abelson*, the name of leukemia virus which carries similar protein). The *BCR gene* codes for BCR protein whose function is not clear. Chimeric *BCR-ABL* gene codes fusion protein of 185 to 230 kDa depending on the breakpoint in the *BCR* and *ABL* genes. In contrast to normal ABL protein, **BCR-ABL fusion protein** exhibits high tyrosine kinase activity.

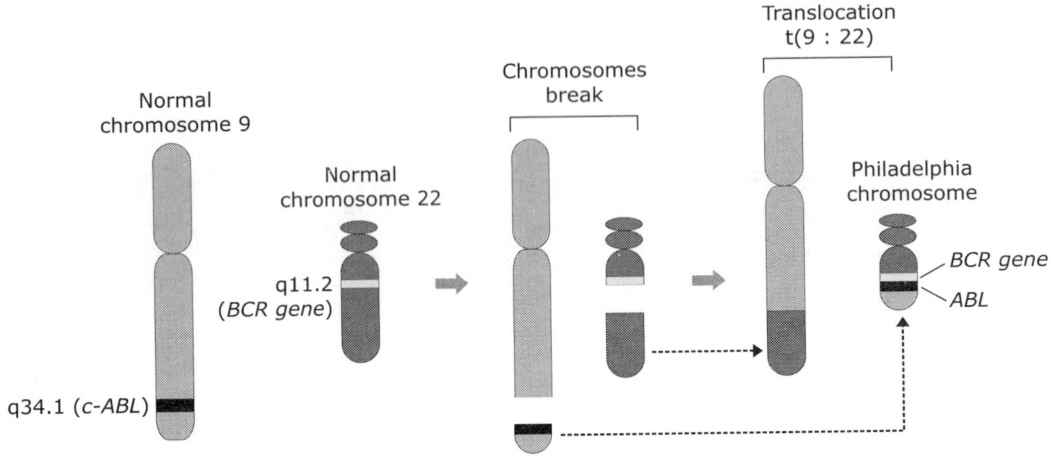

Figure 3.142 Generation of the chimeric *BCR-ABL* gene by chromosomal translocation. The *c-ABL* gene in a normal cell, is located on chromosome 9 and encodes a tyrosine kinase. During malignant transformation of myeloid cells, a portion of chromosome 9 that contains the *ABL* locus translocates to chromosome 22 at the breakpoint cluster region (*BCR*) gene and generates the chimeric *BCR-ABL* gene.

Table 3.21 Examples of specific chromosome aberration and associated cancer

Cancer	Chromosome alteration
Chronic myelogenous leukemia	Translocation (9;22)
Acute myelogenous leukemia	Translocation (8;21)
Retinoblastoma	Deletion (13q)
Wilms tumor	Deletion (11p)

Gene amplification

Activation of proto-oncogenes is also associated with their amplification i.e., increase in copy numbers. It results in overexpression of the amplified gene(s). The most interesting example is the amplification of proto-oncogene **MYCN** (codes N-myc proto-oncogene protein) in neuroblastoma, one of the most common extracranial tumor occurring in children. Gene amplification is usually an unstable genetic condition that can only be maintained under strong selective pressure.

Insertional activation

Insertion of mobile genetic element such as retrovirus changes the expression of genes, but leave their coding sequence unaltered. The best characterized is *MYC* gene, whose expression is elevated after the insertion of a non-defective retrovirus in the vicinity of the gene. **Avian leukosis virus** (ALV) is a retrovirus that does not carry any viral oncogenes, yet is able to transform B cells into lymphomas. This particular retrovirus has been shown to integrate within the *MYC* proto-oncogene, which contains three exons. Exon 1 of *MYC* gene has an unknown function; exons 2 and 3 encode the MYC protein. Insertion of ALV between exon 1 and exon 2 has been shown in some cases to allow the provirus promoter to increase transcription of exons 2 and 3, resulting in increased synthesis of MYC protein.

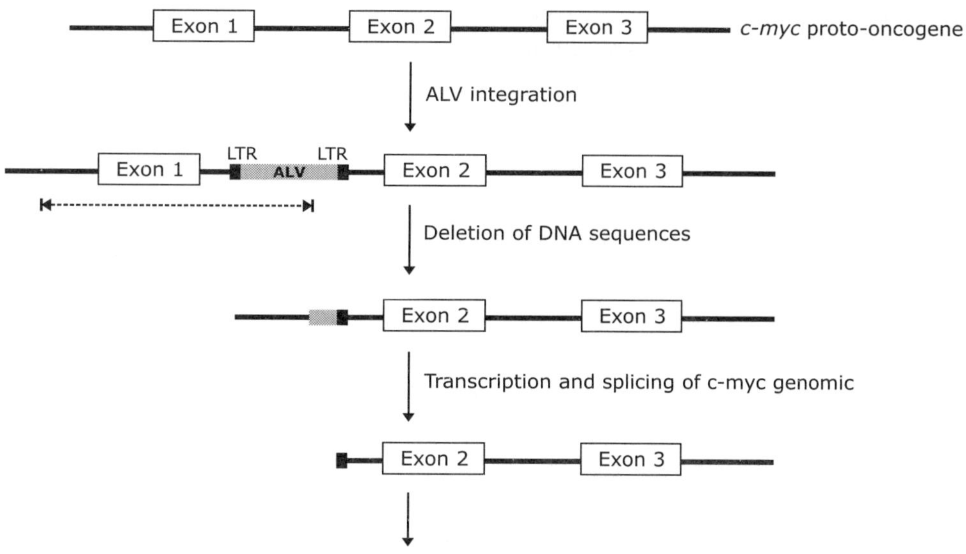

Figure 3.143 Activation of the *MYC* oncogene as a consequence of ALV integration. In a normal cell, the three exons of the *MYC* gene are normally spliced into an mRNA that can be translated into the MYC protein (only exons 2 and 3 actually code for the protein). When ALV integrates into the *MYC* locus (usually between exons 1 and 2), the presence of the LTR sequences in the transcript results in increased expression of the MYC protein, which is harmful to the cell. The integration of ALV is often followed by deletion of portions of viral sequences, leaving one of the LTRs intact.

Tumor suppressor genes

Tumor suppressor genes involved in cell cycle checkpoint activation, DNA damage repair, induction of apoptosis and prevent unregulated cellular growth. Those that directly inhibit cell growth or promote cell death are known as **gatekeepers** and their activity is rate limiting for tumor cell proliferation. Those tumor suppressor genes that do not directly suppress proliferation, but function to promote genetic stability are known as **caretakers**. Caretakers function in DNA repair pathways and elimination of caretakers results in increased mutation rates. Five broad classes of genes are generally grouped into tumor-suppressor genes:

- Genes that regulate or inhibit cell cycle progression (e.g., *RB1*).
- Genes that encode receptors or developmental signals that inhibit cell proliferation (e.g., the hedgehog receptor).
- Genes encoding checkpoint-control proteins that arrest the cell cycle, if DNA is damaged (e.g., *TP53*).
- Genes that promote apoptosis.
- Genes that encode enzymes that participate in DNA repair.

Example of tumor suppressor genes and their functions

Tumor suppressor genes	Gene location	Function
TP53	17p13.1	Transcription factor
RB1	13q14	Cell cycle control
NF1	17q11.2	Signal transduction
DCC	18q21.3	Cell-cell adhesion
APC	5q21	Cell-matrix adhesion
MTS1	9p21	Cell cycle control
MSH2	2p22	DNA repair
MLH1	3p21.3	DNA repair
BRCA1	17q21	DNA repair
BRCA2	13q12.3	DNA repair

TP53 is well-studied **tumor suppressor gene** that encodes a polypeptide which acts as a transcription factor (*TP53* refers to the gene and p53 refers to the protein). **p53 protein** induces cell cycle checkpoint activation, cellular senescence, apoptosis or autophagy. Mutations in the *TP53* gene are associated with more than 50 percent of human cancers. **p53 protein** (also known as **TP53**) plays an important role in the maintenance of genomic stability and negatively regulates the cell cycle. Loss of p53 abolishes the DNA-damage checkpoint. Cells with functional p53 become arrested in G1 when exposed to DNA-damaging irradiation, whereas cells lacking functional p53 do not. This permits the cells to repair the DNA damage, prior to stages of its fixation and propagation, which may lead to tumor formation. Moreover, p53 was shown to facilitate general genomic repair of DNA damage and to bind proteins involved in DNA repair. On the other hand, in many cellular systems, p53 promotes *apoptosis* of cells harboring irreparable damaged DNA. The active form of p53 is a tetramer of four identical subunits.

A **loss-of-function** mutation in *TP53* gene is described as a **dominant-negative mutation**. Thus, this mutation in one of the two normal *TP53* copies in a cell can abrogate almost all p53 activity. The mutation in *TP53* gene is considered *dominant* because the active protein forms a tetramer of identical subunits, and the presence of even one defective subunit in the tetramer disrupts its function. It is termed a *negative mutation* because it leads to the loss of the protein's normal function. Dominant-negative mutations typically occur in proteins that form multimers or those whose function depends on interactions with other proteins.

In contrast, loss-of-function mutations in other tumor-suppressor genes (such as *RB1*) are recessive because the encoded proteins function as monomers and mutation of a single allele has little functional consequence effect. The product of ***RB1* gene** regulates the G1-S phase transition by repressing E2F transcription factors that stimulate the expression of genes required for cell cycle progression. Cyclin D1-CDK4 complex phosphorylates RB, leading to its dissociation from the RB-E2F complex, which frees E2F for activation of cyclin D1 and S-phase genes transcription. E2F targets include cell cycle regulatory genes such as cyclin D1 and S-phase genes. The positive feedback loop among RB, E2F, and cyclin D1 allows for cell cycle progression through G1/S and S phases. Deregulation of RB pathways occurs in most cancer and is mediated either by loss-of-function mutation of negative players including RB and CDK inhibitors (CKIs, p15, p16, p21, etc.) or by amplification or overexpression of cyclin D1.

BRCA1 (BReast-CAncer susceptibility gene 1) and **BRCA2** are tumour-suppressor genes encoding proteins involved in the maintenance of genome stability through repair of DNA double-strand breaks by homologous recombination (HR), cell growth regulation and control of cell division. Cells that lack either BRCA1 or BRCA2 repair these lesions by alternative, more error-prone mechanisms. Individuals carrying germline pathogenic mutations in BRCA1 or BRCA2 are at highly elevated risk of developing breast and/or ovarian cancer.

Apoptotic genes can function as proto-oncogenes or tumor suppressor genes. Anti-apoptotic genes (such as BCL-2) behave as proto-oncogenes because overproduction of their encoded proteins prevent normal apoptosis. Conversely, apoptotic genes whose protein products stimulate apoptosis behave as tumor suppressors.

Cancer cells and cancer stem cells: Cells that have undergone genetic and epigenetic changes, allowing uncontrolled growth, evasion of apoptosis, and potential to invade and metastasize are called cancer cells. Cancer stem cells are a small subpopulation of cancer cells with stem cell–like properties, capable of self-renewal and differentiation into the various cell types that make up the tumor.

Table 3.22 Key differences between cancer cells and cancer stem cells

Feature	Cancer cells	Cancer stem cells (CSCs)
Self-renewal	Limited or absent	High capacity for self-renewal
Differentiation	Differentiated, limited plasticity	Multipotent; can differentiate into various tumor cell types
Therapy tesistance	Generally sensitive to therapy	Highly resistant to therapy
Role in tumor	Form bulk of the tumor	Drive initiation, progression, recurrence
Metastasis	Some cells can metastasize	Key drivers of metastasis
Biomarkers	No specific markers	Markers like CD44, CD133, ALDH1

Box 3.12 Retinoblastoma

Retinoblastoma is a childhood tumor of the retina. The gene, whose loss is critical for development of the cancer is the *RB1* gene. Retinoblastoma arises when both copies of the *RB1* genes are inactivated. There are two forms of the disease, one hereditary, the other sporadic. In the **hereditary retinoblastoma** (*familial form*), individuals inherit a single defective copy of the *RB1* gene, and tumors occur where the remaining normal copy is lost or inactivated by a somatic mutation. In this instance, there are usually multiple foci of tumors arising in both eyes (and is therefore called *bilateral* retinoblastoma). In the **non-hereditary retinoblastoma** (*sporadic form*), all cells initially contain two functional copies of the *RB1* gene, and the tumor arises because both copies are lost or inactivated through the coincidence of two somatic mutations in one cell. Because this is an unlikely occurrence, sporadic retinoblastoma is rare, develops late in life, and usually affects only one eye.

Carcinogen

Agents that *initiate* or *promote* tumor formation are called *carcinogens*. Three classes of carcinogenic agents are known: *physical* (radiations such as UV-ray and γ-ray), *chemicals* (like benzopyrene and benzene) and *biological* (oncovirus) agents. The ability of chemical and physical carcinogens to induce cancer can be accounted for by the DNA damage that they cause and by the errors introduced into DNA during the cells' efforts to repair the damage.

Chemical carcinogens have a very broad range of structures that have little or no obvious structural or biochemical similarity to each other. There are two types of chemical carcinogens, one called **direct-acting** carcinogens that act directly without any metabolic activation and the other, called **indirect-acting** carcinogens, which require metabolic activation for them to act as carcinogens. **Aflatoxin** (a mycotoxin) is an example of indirect-acting carcinogen. It is activated into aflatoxin-2,3, epoxide by the action of intracellular enzymes which is associated with characteristic mutations of the p53 gene. Aflatoxins, produced by the fungi *Aspergillus flavus* and *Aspergillus parasiticus* are among the most potent liver carcinogens known. Chemically, the aflatoxins consist of a difurofuran ring system fused to a substituted coumarin moiety, with a methoxy group attached at the corresponding benzene ring. After chemical modification by liver enzymes, aflatoxin becomes linked to G-residues in DNA and induces G-to-T transversions. Other common examples of chemical carcinogens which are associated with a number of human cancers are benzene (leukemia), arsenic (lung and skin), cadmium (prostate), radon (lung), asbestos (lung and gastrointestinal tract) and vinyl chloride (angiosarcoma, liver).

Most of chemical carcinogens are **tumor initiators**, which cause cancer by inducing mutations. Some carcinogens contribute to cancer development by stimulating cell proliferation, rather than by inducing mutations. Such compounds are referred to as **tumor promoters**. **Phorbol esters** that stimulate cell proliferation by activating protein kinase C are classic examples which stimulate proliferation of the mutated cells.

Oncovirus or tumor virus

In 1964, the first human oncovirus was discovered, when **Epstein-Barr virus** (EBV) was detected in Burkitt lymphoma cells. The transforming activity of a tumor virus depends on the presence of *oncogene* or *oncogenes* in the viral genome. In general, cancer development is a complex multistep process, and this is also true for cancers arising from the oncoviruses, which exert effects on different stages of tumor formation depending on the virus. Viruses can exert their effects on the early stage of oncogenesis involving genetic events that are involved in **tumor initiation** or, alternatively, act at later stages by modulating signaling pathways involved in the regulation of cell proliferation, apoptosis, replicative immortality, and others, such as **tumor promotion**. Oncovirus containing viral oncogene may be:

DNA-containing oncovirus like hepatitis B viruses and SV40 virus carry oncogenes without cellular counterparts. These oncogenes may work by inhibiting the activities of the cellular tumor suppressor. DNA containing oncovirus act mainly by interfering with cell cycle controls. For example, papillomavirus (which causes human warts and carcinomas of the uterine cervix) uses two viral proteins, **E6** and **E7**, to sequester the host cell's p53 and Rb tumor suppressor proteins, respectively. Similarly, **E1A** and **E1B** proteins of adenoviruses inactivate the Rb and p53 tumor suppressor proteins, with E1A binding to Rb and E1B binding to p53. Some examples of *DNA-containing oncovirus* that cause cancer are **Hepatitis B virus** (*liver cancer*), **Papillomavirus** (*cervical and other anogenital cancers*), **Epstein-Barr virus** (*Burkitt's lymphoma*) and **Kaposi's sarcoma-associated herpesvirus** (*Kaposi's sarcoma*).

RNA-containing oncovirus, such as transforming retrovirus contain oncogenes. Viral oncogenes were first reported in Rous Sarcoma virus by Peyton Rous in 1911, which transforms chicken embryo fibroblasts in culture and induces sarcoma. The first oncogene, originally found in the Rous sarcoma virus, was designated as the *src* oncogene. Some examples of *RNA-containing oncoviruses* that cause human cancer are Human T-cell lymphotropic virus-1, HTLV-1 (*Adult T-cell leukemia/lymphoma*), and HTLV-2 (*Hairy cell leukemia*).

Retroviral oncogenes

American microbiologist H. Varmus and M. Bishop in 1976 demonstrated that normal chicken cells contain genes that are closely related to the retroviral *src* oncogenes (codes for *Src* protein tyrosine kinase) of Rous Sarcoma Virus. They published the remarkable conclusion that the oncogene in the virus did not represent a true viral gene but was a normal cellular gene, which the virus had acquired during replication in the host cell and thereafter carried along. *src*-related sequences were also found in the normal DNA of a wide range of other vertebrates (including human). Until now, more than 40 different oncogenes have been demonstrated. The normal cell genes from which the retroviral oncogenes originate are called **proto-oncogenes**. In 1972, R.J. Huebner and G.J. Todaro suggested that mutations or genetic rearrangements of proto-oncogenes by carcinogens or viruses might alter the normally regulated function of these genes, converting them into potent cancer-causing oncogenes. The viral oncogenes and their cellular counterparts are described by using prefixes *v* for viral and *c* for cellular. So, the oncogene carried by Rous sarcoma virus is called *v-src*, and the proto-oncogene related to it in cellular genomes is called *c-src*.

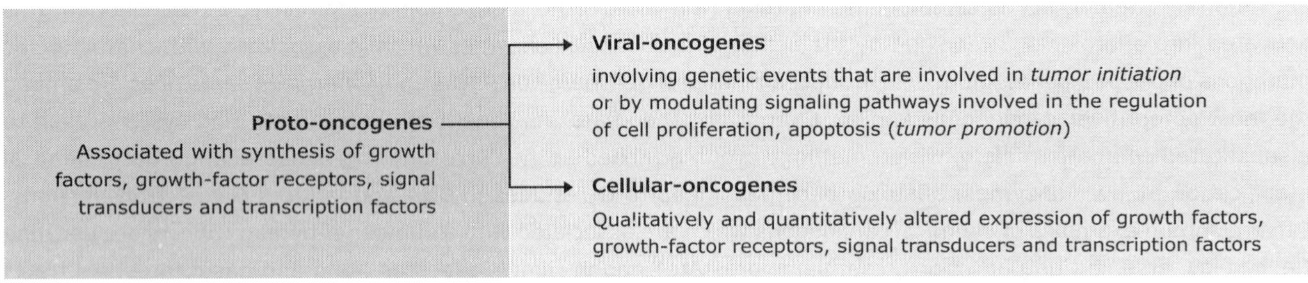

Cancer treatment

Cancer treatment is a complex and evolving field. Various treatment modalities are used depending on the type and stage of cancer, as well as the tissues involved. Cancer treatment includes:

Surgery – The physical removal of tumors along with surrounding tissue to prevent recurrence.

Radiation therapy – Uses high-energy X-rays or protons to kill cancer cells.

Chemotherapy – Involves cytotoxic drugs that kill rapidly dividing cells, including cancer cells.

Targeted therapy – Uses drugs that specifically block molecules involved in cancer growth and survival.

Immunotherapy – Stimulates the body's immune system to attack cancer cells.

Hormone therapy – Used for cancers that are sensitive to hormones (e.g., breast, prostate cancer).

Stem cell transplantation – Used for certain blood cancers, replacing damaged bone marrow with healthy stem cells.

Anti-cancer drugs

Anticancer drugs are used in **chemotherapy** to selectively kill rapidly dividing cancer cells. Different drugs target specific aspects of cancer cell growth and division. Listed below are some commonly used anticancer drugs:

Aphidicolin – Inhibits DNA polymerase, blocking DNA replication.

Cyclophosphamide – An alkylating agent that damages DNA by adding alkyl groups and interfering with DNA replication.

Methotrexate and **Fluorouracil** – Antimetabolites that interfere with DNA and RNA synthesis.

Bleomycin and **Mitomycin C** – DNA-damaging agents that cause strand breaks and cross-links, interfering with replication.

Vincristine, **Vinblastine**, and **Taxol** (Paclitaxel) – Interfere with spindle microtubule.

Self Test

Q1. Which of the following statements are *true* with respect to membrane fluidity of a phospholipid bilayer?

P. Increasing proportion of long chain fatty acids decreases membrane fluidity.

Q. Increase in cholesterol content increases membrane fluidity.

R. Increasing proportion of *cis* unsaturated fatty acids increases membrane fluidity.

S. Increasing proportion of *trans* unsaturated fatty acids increases membrane fluidity.

a. P and Q
b. P and R
c. R and S
d. Q and S

Q2. Which of the following statements are *correct*?

P. Plasma membrane is highly impermeable to all charged molecules.

Q. All membrane transport proteins so far known are transmembrane multipass proteins.

R. Ionophores shield the charge of the transported ion so that it can penetrate the lipid bilayer.

S. Na^+-K^+ ATPase exchanges equal numbers of Na^+ and K^+ ions in each pumping cycle.

a. P and Q
b. Q and R
c. R and S
d. P and S

Q3. Which of the following statements are *true* regarding the dolichol phosphate pathway?

P. A 14-residues precursor oligosaccharide chain is synthesized in the ER.

Q. A 14-residues precursor oligosaccharide chain is synthesized in the Golgi complex.

R. It helps in *N*-linked glycosylation of proteins.

S. It helps in *O*-linked glycosylation of proteins.

a. P and R
b. Q and R
c. Q and S
d. P and S

Q4. A protein that has not been synthesized by membrane free ribosomes in cytosol

P. most likely synthesized in smooth endoplasmic reticulum.

Q. most likely synthesized by ribosomes attached with rough endoplasmic reticulum.

R. enters through the *trans* face of endoplasmic reticulum.

S. enter into the Golgi complex from *cis* face.

a. P only
b. P and R
c. Q and S
d. Q and R

Q5. Why do glycolipids exist almost exclusively on the exterior side, but not the cytoplasmic side of the cell membrane?

a. The inner layer of the membrane is not thick enough to accommodate carbohydrates.
b. Carbohydrates are added only to lipids on the lumen side of the ER and Golgi membranes.
c. Flippases move the glycolipids to this side of the membrane.
d. Carbohydrates are removed from the cytoplasmic side by glycosylase enzymes.

Q6. Evidence indicating the chloroplasts were originally free-living prokaryotes that subsequently evolved a symbiotic relationship with a eukaryotic host includes all of the following *except* the

a. similarities of rRNA sequences between chloroplasts and free-living prokaryotes.
b. similarities of structures between chloroplasts and some contemporary free-living prokaryotes.
c. presence of circular DNA in chloroplasts and in free-living prokaryotes.
d. ability of chloroplasts to synthesize all their own proteins.

Q7. Which of the following are *true* about plant cell?

P. Plant cell wall is composed of the same monomer as the yeast cell wall.

Q. Plant cells divide faster than the yeast cells.

R. During division of plant cells, Golgi complex plays vital role in cell plate formation.

S. Cellulose present in plant cell wall is an unbranched polymer.

a. P and R
b. P and S
c. Q and R
d. R and S

Q8. Membrane carrier proteins differ from membrane channel proteins by which of the following characteristics?

a. Carrier proteins are glycoproteins, while channel proteins are lipoproteins.

b. Carrier proteins transport molecules down their electrochemical gradient, while channel proteins transport molecules against their electrochemical gradient.

c. Carrier proteins can mediate active transport, while channel proteins cannot.

d. Carrier proteins are synthesized on free cytoplasmic ribosomes, while channel proteins are synthesized on ribosomes bound to the endoplasmic reticulum.

Q9. Which of the following statements are *correct*?

P. A typical value for the resting membrane potential of a neuron is –70 mV and a cell that exhibits a membrane potential is polarized.

Q. The resting membrane potential is determined by two major factors – unequal distribution of ions in the extra-cellular fluid and cytosol and inability of most cytosolic anions to leave the cell.

R. According to the all-or-none principle, if a stimulus is strong enough to generate an action potential, the impulse generated is of a constant size. A stronger stimulus does not generate a larger action potential.

S. An excitatory neurotransmitter is one that can depolarize the postsynaptic neuron's membrane, bringing the membrane potential closer to threshold.

a. P and Q
b. P, Q and R
c. Q, R and S
d. P, Q, R and S

Q10. In a tissue, cells are bound together by physical attachment between cell to cell or between cell to extracellular matrix (ECM). Following are some of the characteristics of cell junctions:

1. adherens junctions are cell-cell anchoring junctions connecting actin filament in one cell with other cell.
2. spot desmosomes are cell-matrix anchoring junctions connecting actin filament in cell to ECM.
3. gap junctions are channel forming junctions allowing passage of small water-soluble molecules between cells.
4. tight junctions are occluding junctions, which seal gap between two cells.
5. hemidesmosomes are cell-matrix anchoring junctions connecting intermediate filament in cell to ECM.

Which of the following combination of statements is *not* correct?

a. 1 and 2
b. 1 and 3
c. 2 and 3
d. 4 and 5

Q11. The cell cycle is an ordered series of events. It is the sequence of events by which a cell duplicates its genome and eventually divides into two daughter cells. It is controlled by

P. cyclin synthesis and degradation

Q. phosphorylation of cyclin-dependent kinases

R. binding of CDK inhibitor proteins (CKIs)

S. dephosphorylation of cyclin-dependent kinases

a. P and Q
b. R and S
c. P and R
d. P, Q, R and S

Q12. A diploid somatic cell from a rat has a total of 42 chromosomes (2n=42)

P. rat has 21 different chromosomes.

Q. rat has 42 DNA molecules in the nucleus during G1.

R. rat has 21 bivalents in metaphase I of meiosis.

S. rat has 42 DNA molecules in metaphase II of meiosis.

a. P and Q
b. Q and S
c. P, Q and R
d. P, Q, R and S

Q13. Aneuploidy arises as a random error during the production of gametes. Aneuploidy arises if, during one of the divisions of meiosis, one of the homologous chromosomes in meiosis I (or chromatids in meiosis II) does not migrate to the opposite pole. This result in an uneven distribution of that particular chromosome. Depending upon where in meiosis this nondisjunction occurs, some gametes will end up with one or more extra chromosomes and other will end up with fewer chromosomes than a complete set. Which of the following genetic event can produce an XYY man?

a. Non-disjunction in first meiotic division.
b. Non-disjunction in the second meiotic division in the cell with two Y chromatids.
c. Non-disjunction in the first meiotic division in the cell with two Y chromatids.
d. Non-disjunction in the second meiotic division in the cell with two X chromatids.

Q14. Properties of chemical and electrical synapses make them suitable for different functions. Which of the following properties are *true* for cells with chemical synapses, but not true for cells with electrical synapses?

1. Can stimulate an action potential in postsynaptic cells.
2. Can amplify signals.
3. Can integrate excitatory or inhibitory signals from multiple sources.
4. Do not require membrane-fusion events for synaptic transmission to occur.
5. Often utilize ligand-gated ion channels.

a. 1, 2 and 3
b. 2, 3 and 5
c. 2, 4 and 5
d. 1, 2, 3, 4 and 5

Q15. Which of the following statements are *true*?

1. When signal molecules first bind to receptor tyrosine kinases, the receptors undergo for autophosphorylation.
2. In response to some G protein mediated signals, a special type of lipid molecule associated with the plasma membrane is cleaved to form IP_3 and calcium.
3. In most cases, signal molecules interact with the cell at the plasma membrane and then enter the cell and eventually the nucleus.
4. Toxins that cause botulism and cholera interfere with the ability of activated G proteins to hydrolyze GTP to GDP, resulting in phosphodiesterase activity in the absence of an appropriate signal molecule.
5. Protein kinase A activation is one possible result of signal molecules binding to G protein linked receptors.

a. 1 and 2
b. 3 and 4
c. 1 and 5
d. 2 and 4

Q16. A recently discovered membrane-associated protein exhibits the following properties: molecular weight = 130,000; three separate stretches of nonpolar amino acids that form α helices; long hydrophilic extracellular domain that contains sugar residues; and a short hydrophilic intracellular domain. This protein would be most *accurately* described by which of the following?

a. Tripartite, single-pass integral membrane glycoprotein.
b. Multipass integral membrane glycoprotein with one extracellular loop.
c. Multipass integral membrane glycoprotein with two intracellular loops.
d. Large transmembrane protein with an extracellular ligand-binding domain large integral membrane protein with two extracellular loops.

Q17. A patient with an advanced colon carcinoma is admitted for surgery. Pathological analysis of the tumor is done. Remembering that Rb is important in tumor biology, you ask for a full characterization of Rb in the tumor from the lab. Assume that the lab can distinguish phosphorylated from dephosphorylated Rb and can measure Rb binding to transcription factors. Comparison of Rb in actively growing tumor cells with Rb in normal, non-proliferating cells would then reveal which of the following?

a. Tumor: dephosphorylated Rb in the nucleus, bound to transcription factors;
   Normal: phosphorylated Rb in the cytoplasm
b. Tumor: phosphorylated Rb in the nucleus, bound to transcription factors;
   Normal: dephosphorylated Rb in the nucleus, not bound to transcription factors
c. Tumor: dephosphorylated Rb in the nucleus, not bound to transcription factors;
   Normal: dephosphorylated Rb in the cytoplasm
d. Tumor: phosphorylated Rb in the nucleus, not bound to transcription factors;
   Normal: dephosphorylated Rb in the nucleus, bound to transcription factors

Q18. How do steroid hormone estrogen modulate genome expression in responsive cells?

a. By binding to enhancer sequences.
b. By binding to receptors in the cytoplasm which then migrate to the nucleus where they bind to DNA to regulate genome expression.
c. By binding to receptors in the nucleus that are activated and then bind to DNA to regulate genome expression.
d. By binding to the cell membrane receptors, the signal is then transduced to the nucleus through secondary messenger.

Q19. ATP-driven pumps hydrolyze ATP to ADP and phosphate and use the energy released to pump ions or solutes across a membrane. There are many classes of these pumps and representatives of each are found in all prokaryotic and eukaryotic cells. Which of the following statements about these pumps is *not* correct?

a. P-type pumps are multipass transmembrane proteins which phosphorylate themselves during pumping and involve in ion transport.
b. F-type pumps normally use the H^+ gradient across the membrane to drive the synthesis of ATP.
c. V-type pumps normally use voltage gradient for transport of small molecules.
d. ABC transporters primarily act as carrier for transport of small molecules across cell membrane.

Q20. The discovery that cyt *c* promotes apoptosis focused attention on how cytochrome c (cyt *c*) is released into the cytosol. It was initially unclear whether the cyt *c* that causes apoptosis comes from mitochondria, or instead was expressed from a nuclear gene and synthesized in the cytosol. Which one of the following observations would have provided the best evidence that it is the cyt *c* released from mitochondria that causes apoptosis?

a. Active Fas death receptors trigger release of cyt *c* from mitochondria.
b. ḄCL-2 blocks release of cyt *c* from mitochondria and also inhibits apoptosis.
c. Caspase inhibitors block release of cyt *c* from mitochondria.
d. Intracellular signals that block apoptosis do not produce cytosolic cyt *c*..

ANSWER KEY

01. b	02. b	03. a	04. c	05. b	06. d	07. d	08. c	09. d	10. a
11. d	12. d	13. b	14. b	15. c	16. b	17. d	18. b	19. c	20. b

4

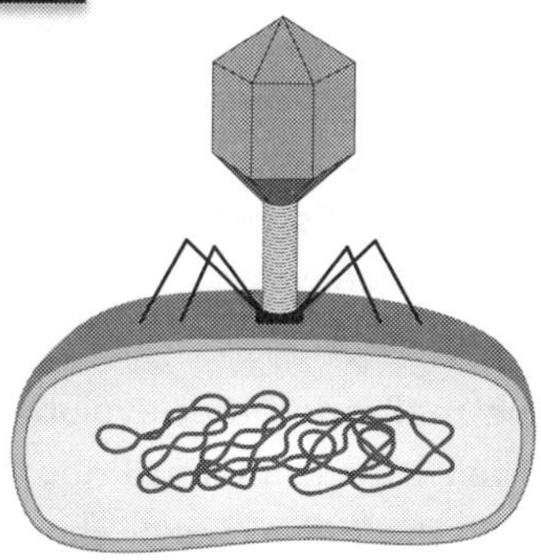

Prokaryotes and Viruses

SUBJECT FOCUS

- **4.1 Phylogenetic overview**
- **4.2 Structure of bacterial cell**
- **4.3 Bacterial genome**
- **4.4 Bacterial nutrition**
- **4.5 Horizontal gene transfer and recombination**
- **4.6 Mapping of chromosomal genes**
- **4.7 Bacterial taxonomy**
- **4.8 General features of important bacterial groups**
- **4.9 Archaebacteria**
- **4.10 Bacterial toxins**
- **4.11 Control of microbial growth**
- **4.12 Viruses**
- **4.13 Prions and Viroids**
- **4.14 Host-parasite interactions**

Prokaryotes (*pro* means before and *karyon* means kernel or nucleus) are cellular organisms that include two domains– **Bacteria** (sometimes referred to as **true bacteria** or **eubacteria**) and **archaea** (previously known as **archaebacteria** or **archaeobacteria**). The term *true bacteria* or *eubacteria* refers to those that belong to the domain Bacteria, and the term *archaea* is used to refer to those that belong to domain Archaea. *The informal name 'bacteria' is occasionally used loosely in the literature to refer to all the prokaryotes, and care should be taken to interpret its meaning in any particular context.* In recent years, the use of the term 'prokaryote' has declined because bacteria and archaea represent evolutionarily distinct domains of life. However, in this book we have used 'prokaryote' to collectively refer to both bacteria and archaea. Prokaryotic organisms are usually microscopic, single-celled organisms that have a relatively simple structure – neither nucleus nor unit membrane-bound organelles. Prokaryotes can be distinguished from eukaryotes based on differences in cellular organization and cellular processes. The major distinguishing characteristics of prokaryotic and eukaryotic cells are as follows:

Feature	Prokaryotic cells	Eukaryotic cells
Membrane-bound nucleus	Absent	Present
DNA complexed with histone	Absent	Present
Number of chromosomes	One (mostly)	More than one
Mitosis and meiosis	Absent	Present
Sterol (in plasma membrane)	Absent, except *Mycoplasma*	Present
Ribosome	70S (cytosol)	80S (cytosol)
Unit-mem. bound organelle	Absent	Present
Cell wall	Present in *most* of prokaryotic cells. In eubacteria, it is made up of *peptidoglycan*.	Made up of *cellulose* in plant and *chitin* in fungi. Absent in animal cells.

4.1 Phylogenetic overview

Historically, prokaryotes were classified on the basis of their phenotypic characteristics. Prokaryotic taxonomy, therefore, involved measuring a large number of morphological and biochemical characteristics (e.g., ability to grow on different substrates, cell wall structure, antibiotic sensitivities, and many others). This contrasts with the classification of eukaryotic organisms, for which phylogenetic (evolution-based) classification was possible through the availability of fossil evidence.

A major revolution in the classification of prokaryotic organisms occurred with the realization that evolutionary relationships could be deduced on the basis of differences in the gene sequence. The rRNAs from small ribosomal subunits (16S from eubacteria and archaea and 18S from eukaryotes) have become the molecules of choice for inferring prokaryotic phylogenies. The small subunit rRNAs (**SSU rRNAs**) are an integral part of the ribosome. The genes encoding these rRNAs change very slowly with time and do not appear to be subject to horizontal gene transfer. The SSU rRNAs contain certain sequences that are variable among organisms and other regions that are quite similar. The variable regions enable comparison between closely related organisms, whereas the stable sequences allow the comparison of distantly related microorganisms. Comparative analysis of SSU rRNA sequences from thousands of organisms has demonstrated the presence of **oligonucleotide signature sequences**. These are short, conserved nucleotide sequences that are present in one taxonomic group but not in other groups. Thus, the signature sequences found in eubacterial rRNAs are rarely or never found in archaeal rRNAs and vice versa. Likewise, the 18S rRNA of eukaryotes bears signature sequences that are specific to the domain *eukarya*.

Based on ribosomal RNA signature sequences, Carl Woese proposed a radical reorganization of the five-kingdoms into three-domains. In his classification system, Woese placed all four eukaryotic kingdoms (protista, fungi, plantae, animalia) into a single domain called **eukarya**, also known as the *eukaryotes*. He then split the former kingdom of Monera into the **eubacteria** and the **archaea** domains. Unlike Whittaker's five kingdom system, Woese's three domain system organizes biodiversity by evolutionary relationships.

Carl Woese's comparative studies of rRNA sequences proved the universal relatedness of all life. Life was seen to fall into one of three phylogenetic domains: Archaea, Bacteria (eubacteria) and Eukarya (eukaryotes). The **universal phylogenetic tree** based on rRNA sequence comparisons presents a picture in which all life, regardless of the eventual domain, arose from a single common ancestor. However, the evolutionary relationship of archaea and eukarya is still a matter of considerable debate.

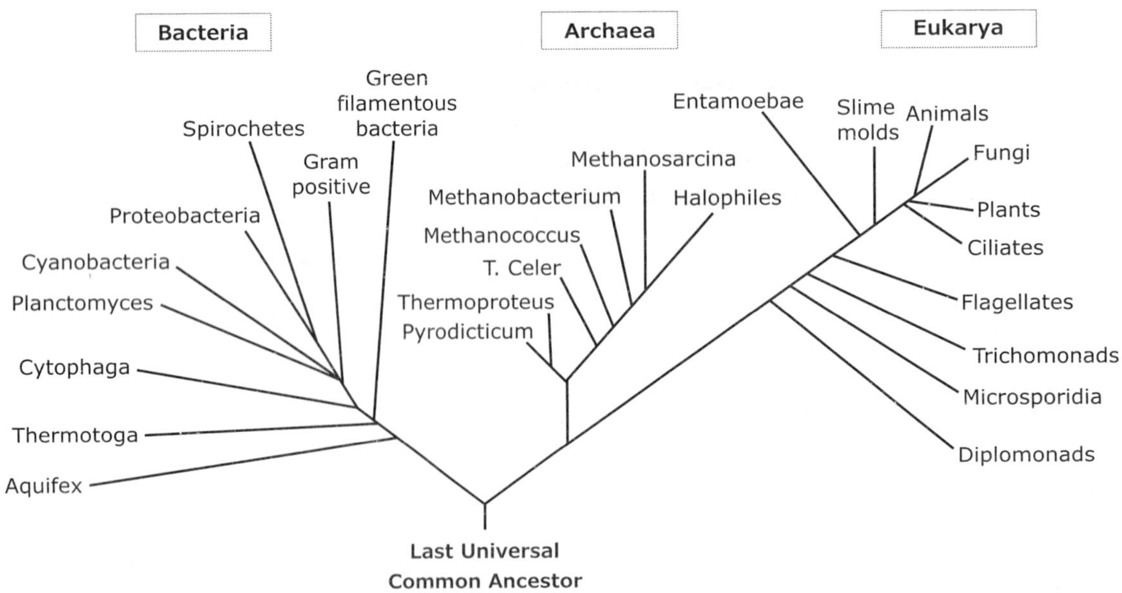

Figure 4.1 Universal phylogenetic tree (rooted) based on comparison of SSU rRNA sequences. All cellular organisms fall into one of three phylogenetic domains: Archaea, Bacteria and Eukarya. The root is considered the *last universal common ancestor* (**LUCA**).

According to the universal phylogenetic tree, archaea and eukarya shared common ancestry but diverged and became separate domains. It indicates that although bacteria and archaea share similar cellular organization, they are not phylogenetically linked. Archaea and eukarya descended from the same ancestor but diverged to become separate domains.

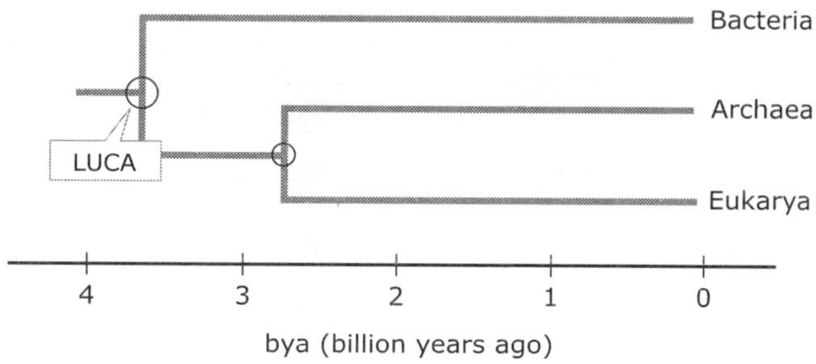

Origin of eukaryotic semi-autonomous organelles

In 1970, Lynn Margulis published *'Origin of Eukaryotic Cells'* in which she proposed that eukaryotic semi-autonomous organelles – mitochondria and chloroplasts – evolved from free-living bacteria *via* symbiosis within a eukaryotic host cell (**endosymbiotic hypothesis**). Over the past several decades, various endosymbiotic models have been proposed as a result of detailed biochemical and molecular data bearing on the endosymbiont hypothesis of organelle origins. Endosymbiotic models for the origin of mitochondria are basically variations of two fundamentally different themes that have been referred to, respectively, as the *'archezoan scenario'* and the *'symbiogenesis scenario'*.

In the **archezoan scenario**, the host that acquired the mitochondrion was an anaerobic nucleus-bearing eukaryotic cell, termed 'archezoan'. In contrast, in the **symbiogenesis scenario**, an endosymbiotic event involving the uptake of an α-Proteobacterium (*Rickettsia prowazekii*) by an archaeal cell led to the generation of the mitochondria, followed subsequently by the evolution of the nucleus and compartmentalization of the eukaryotic cell. The archezoan scenario most closely approximates the classical endosymbiont hypothesis of mitochondrial origin, whereas the hydrogen hypothesis is an example of the symbiogenesis scenario. However, it would seem that a symbiogenesis scenario (bacterial endosymbiont in an archaeal host) better accommodates the accumulated data relevant to the question of mitochondrion origin than does an archezoan scenario (bacterial endosymbiont in an amitochondriate but essentially eukaryotic host).

The meaning of **endosymbionts** and **organelles** are different. The usual way to distinguish organelles from endosymbionts is by their reduced genome sizes. As an endosymbiont evolves into an organelle, most of its genes are transferred to the host cell genome.

4.2 Structure of bacterial cell

Members of domain bacteria are microscopic, relatively simple, prokaryotic organisms whose cells lack a nucleus. Bacteria are usually single-celled organisms, and most have cell walls made up of peptidoglycan. Although most bacteria exhibit a typical prokaryotic cell structure (i.e., they lack a membrane-bound nucleus), a few members of the unusual phylum Planctomycetes have their genetic material surrounded by a membrane.

Size, shape and arrangement of bacterial cells

Bacteria usually range in size from 0.3-2.0 micrometers in diameter and 0.5-5.0 micrometers in length. However, a few species — for example, *Thiomargarita namibiensis* and *Epulopiscium fishelsoni* — are very large and visible to the unaided eye. The rod-shaped *E. fishelsoni* is about 600 micrometers in length and 75 micrometers in diameter. The smallest known bacteria are members of the genus *Mycoplasma* (about 0.3 micrometers in diameter).

Most bacteria are very small in size. Because of their small size, bacteria have a large surface area-to-volume ratio. The large surface area-to-volume ratio of bacteria also means that no internal part of the cell is very far from the surface, and the nutrients can easily and quickly reach all parts of the cell. It also allows rapid uptake and intracellular distribution of nutrients and excretion of wastes. Conversely, at a low surface area-to-volume ratio, the diffusion of nutrients and waste products across the cell membrane limits the rate at which microbial metabolism occurs, making the cell less evolutionarily fit.

	1 mm cube	2 mm cube	4 mm cube
Surface area	6 mm^2	24 mm^2	96 mm^2
Volume	1 mm^3	8 mm^3	64 mm^3
Surface to volume ratio	6/1	3/1	1.5/1

Cell shape is generally characteristic of a given bacterial species. The four basic shapes of bacteria are **bacillus** (rod-like), **coccus** (spherical or ovoid), **vibrio** (comma-shaped), and **spirilla** (spiral or helical shaped). The term 'Bacillus' has two meanings. Bacillus refers to a bacterial shape as well as genus. When capitalized and italicized, it refers to a specific genus. For example, *Bacillus anthracis*, the causative agent of anthrax.

When cocci divide, cells can remain attached to one another. Cocci that remain in pairs after dividing are called *diplococci*; those that divide and remain attached in chain-like patterns are called *streptococci*. Some cocci divide in two planes and remain in groups of four, forming squares are known as *tetrads*. Those that divide in three planes and remain attached in cubelike groups of eight are called *sarcinae*. Those that divide in multiple planes and form grapelike clusters are called *staphylococci*. Most bacilli appear as single rods. *Diplobacilli* appear in pairs after division, and *streptobacilli* occur in chains. Bacteria that look like curved rods are called *vibrios*. Spirilla have a helical shape and fairly rigid bodies. Another group of spirals are helical and flexible; they are called *spirochetes*. Most bacteria maintain a single shape (**monomorphic**). However, some bacteria like *Corynebacterium*, have many shapes, and lack a single, characteristic shape. These bacteria are called **pleomorphic**. *The modern definition of pleomorphism in the context of bacteriology is based on the variation of the shape of the cell rather than a change of shape.*

Staining

Staining is a biochemical technique of coloring specimens. Dyes are used to stain specimens. Generally, dyes are organic compounds consisting of two functional chemical groups – one group gives dyes its characteristic color, while another group contains an ionizable chemical structure, which helps to solubilize the dye and facilitates its binding to different structures. Previously, dyes were classified as acidic or basic, depending upon whether the dye was negatively or positively charged at neutral pH. More accurately, dyes can be referred to as anionic or cationic. **Cationic** or **basic dyes** (such as crystal violet, methylene blue, safranin, malachite green) will react with groups that have a negative charge. **Anionic** or **acidic dyes** (such as eosin, acid fuchsin) will react with groups that have a positive charge.

Bacterial staining protocols can be divided into three basic types – simple, differential, and specialized. **Simple stains** react uniformly with all cell types and only distinguish the organisms from their surroundings. **Differential stains** do not stain all types of cells with the same color. It discriminates different cell types depending upon the chemical or physical composition of the cells. The differential stains most frequently used for bacteria are the Gram stain and the acid-fast stain. **Specialized stains** detect specific structures of cells such as flagella and endospores. These stains are used to color and isolate specific parts of organisms.

Gram staining: It is a *differential staining method* for differentiating bacterial species into two groups based on the physical properties of their cell walls. The method is named after the Danish scientist Hans Christian Gram, who developed the technique in 1884. The Gram staining procedure involves four basic steps:

1. The bacteria are first stained with the basic dye **crystal violet**. Crystal violet (it is referred to as a **primary stain**) imparts purple color to all cells.

2. The bacteria are then treated with Gram's iodine solution. This allows the stain to be retained better by forming an insoluble crystal violet-iodine complex. Iodine is used as a **mordant**. A mordant is used to increase the affinity of a stain for a biological specimen.
3. Gram's decolorizer, usually a mixture of ethyl alcohol and acetone, is then added. A **decolorizer** (or *decoloring agent*) removes the stain from the specimen. This is the differential step. After this step, some bacteria retain the purple color while some others lose purple color. Bacteria that retain color are classified as **Gram-positive,** and bacteria that lose the color after decolorization are classified as **Gram-negative**.
4. Because Gram-negative bacteria are colorless after the treatment with decolorizer, they are no longer visible. Thus, the counterstain **safranin** (also a *basic dye*) is applied. Since the Gram-positive bacteria are already stained purple, they are not affected by the counterstain. Gram-negative bacteria that are now colorless become directly stained by the safranin. Thus, Gram-positive appear purple, while Gram-negative appear red or pink.

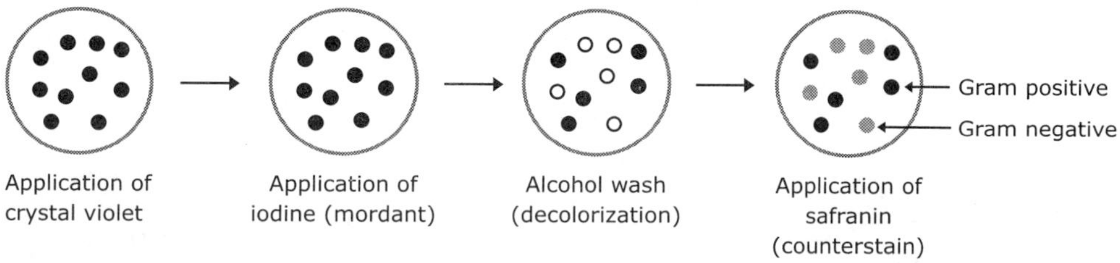

Figure 4.2 The Gram-staining procedure. In the first step of the Gram-staining procedure, the smear is stained with the basic dye crystal violet, the primary stain. It is followed by treatment with an iodine solution functioning as a mordant. The decolorization with ethanol or acetone removes crystal violet from Gram-negative cells but not from Gram-positive cells. The Gram-negative cells then turn pink to red when counterstained with safranin.

Acid-fast staining: The acid-fast stain is a differential stain used to identify acid-fast organisms such as members of the genus *Mycobacterium*. The acid-fast staining procedure involves the heating of bacteria with a mixture of basic fuchsin and phenol (also known as **Ziehl-Neelsen stain**). The presence of phenol and heat treatment helps the stain penetrate the cell wall. Once basic fuchsin has penetrated the cell wall, acid-fast cells are not easily decolorized by an acid-alcohol treatment and hence remain red. It occurs due to the presence of large amounts of **mycolic acid,** a branched-chain hydroxy fatty acid. Non-acid-fast bacteria are decolorized by acid-alcohol. Because non-acid-fast bacteria are colorless after the treatment with decolorizer, they are no longer visible. Finally, the counterstain **methylene blue** is applied. Methylene blue colors non-acid-fast bacteria blue.

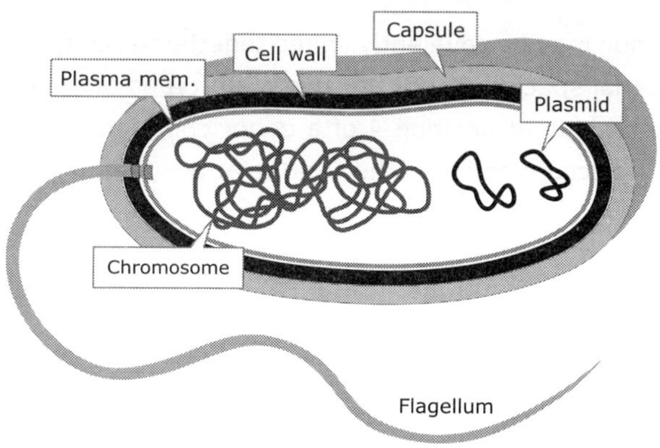

Figure 4.3 Structure of a bacterium. Bacterial cells almost always are bounded by a chemically complex cell wall. Inside this wall, and separated from it by a periplasmic space, lies the plasma membrane. A bacterial cell does not contain internal unit membrane-bound organelles; hence, its interior appears morphologically simple. The chromosomal DNA is localized in a discrete region, the nucleoid, and is not separated from the surrounding cytoplasm by nuclear membrane. Ribosomes and inclusion bodies are scattered in the cytoplasmic matrix. Both Gram-positive and Gram-negative cells can use flagella for locomotion. In addition, many cells are surrounded by a capsule or slime layer external to the cell wall.

Cell Wall

Bacterial cells almost always are bounded by a chemically complex cell wall. It protects bacteria against osmotic lysis. The cell wall is chemically composed of **peptidoglycans** (also termed **murein**). The peptidoglycan cell wall is unique to a bacterial cell. It presents in both Gram-positive and Gram-negative bacteria. In Gram-positive bacteria, peptidoglycan cell walls consist of a single 20 to 80 nm thick homogeneous layer lying outside the plasma membrane. In contrast, the Gram-negative bacterial cell wall consists of 2 to 7 nm thick peptidoglycan layer. Peptidoglycan consists of carbohydrates and peptides. The nature of carbohydrate is *heteropolysaccharide*- consisting of two sugar derivatives ***N*-acetylmuramic acid** (NAM) and ***N*-acetylglucosamine** (NAG) joined through β-1,4 glycosidic bond. NAM is NAG with lactic acid attached by an *ether* linkage. A peptide chain (termed **stem peptide**) is connected to the carboxyl group of the NAM by an **amide linkage**. Typically, the peptide chains consist of two to five amino acids. The most common composition of the peptide chain is L-Ala–D-Glu–*meso*-diaminopimelic acid (or L-Lys)–D-Ala–D-Ala in the nascent peptide chain, the last D-Ala residue being lost in the mature peptide chain. The amino acid at the third position is generally a **diamino acid**, either *meso*-diaminopimelic acid (in most Gram-negative bacteria) or L-Lys (in most Gram-positive bacteria).

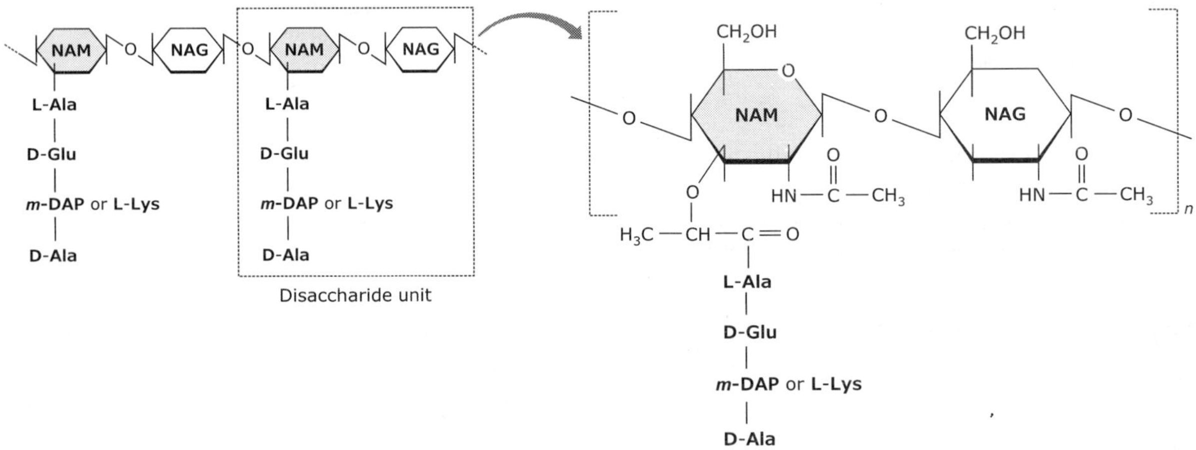

Figure 4.4 Structure of peptidoglycan. Heteropolysaccharide chains are made up of repeating disaccharide units, composed of amino sugars *N*-acetylglucosamine (NAG) and *N*-acetylmuramic acid (NAM) linked via a β-1,4 glycosidic bond. The stem peptide is composed of alternating D- and L-amino acids. Amino acids present in stem peptide include L-alanine, D-glutamic acid, L-lysine or *meso*-diaminopimelic acid (*m*-DAP) and D-alanine.

Two peptide chains lying side-by-side may be covalently linked together directly or indirectly. The degree and types of cross-linking vary among bacterial species. There are two main types of cross-linkage: **4–3 cross-linkage** (the cross-linking occurs between the residue at position 4 of a *donor* chain and position 3 of an *acceptor* chain) and **3–3 cross-linkage** (the cross-linking occurs between the residue at position 3 of a *donor* chain and position 3 of an *acceptor* chain).

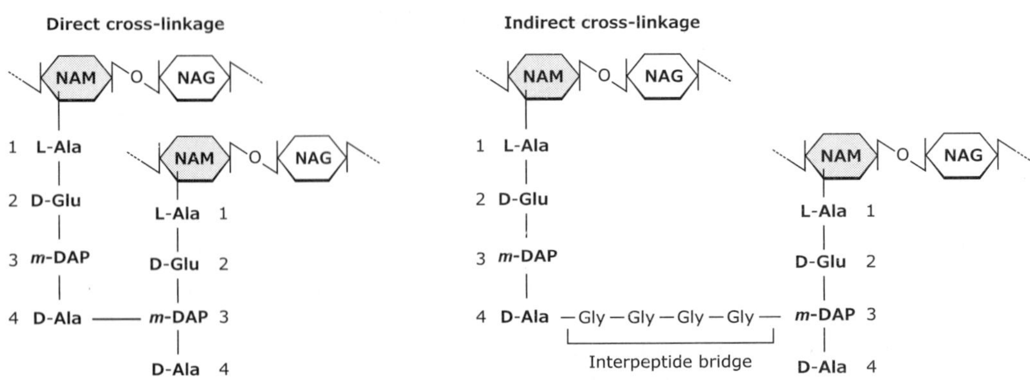

The 4–3 cross-linkage is the most common kind of cross-linkage. It can be either *direct* (as in most Gram-negative bacteria) or *indirect* by an **interpeptide bridge**, consisting of a short chain of amino acids (as in most Gram-positive bacteria). The size of the interpeptide bridge ranges from one to seven amino acid residues.

Biosynthesis of peptidoglycan: Synthesis of peptidoglycan is a complex process that occurs in two distinct locations: the cytosol and the periplasm. The biosynthesis of peptidoglycan can be divided into the following stages:

The *first* stage occurs in the cytoplasm and leads to the synthesis of the nucleotide sugar-linked precursors **UDP-NAM** and **UDP-NAG**. In the *second* stage, sequential addition of amino acids to UDP-NAM occurs, which results into the formation of NAM-pentapeptide. In the *third* stage, which takes place at the plasma membrane, the NAM-pentapeptide from UDP-NAM-pentapeptide is transfered to the **C55P** (a dolichol phosphate with a 55-carbon hydrocarbon chain) and generates **lipid I**. Then, NAG from UDP-NAG is added to lipid I, yielding **lipid II**. Lipid II is subsequently transported by a *flippase* from the innerside of the membrane to the outer side. The *last* stage of peptidoglycan biosynthesis, which takes place in the periplasmic space, involves the polymerization of the newly synthesized disaccharide-peptide units and incorporation into the growing peptidoglycan.

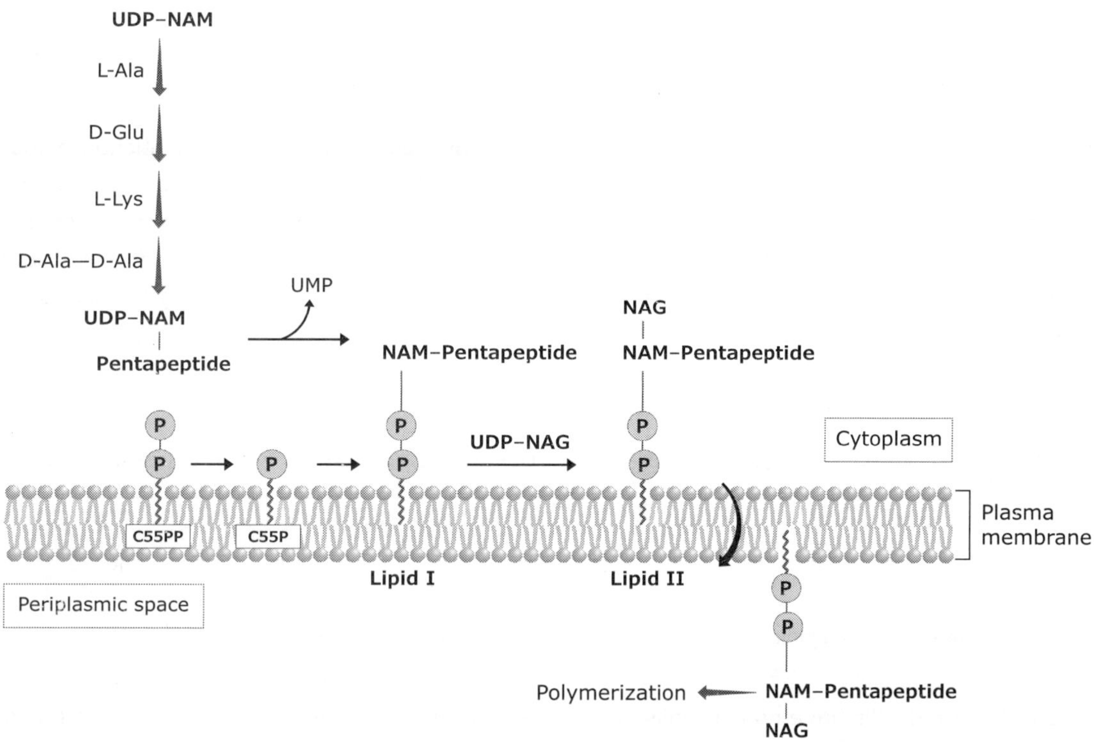

Figure 4.5 Peptidoglycan synthesis pathway. Undecaprenyl-pyrophosphate (C55PP) present at the cytoplasmic side of the inner membrane is dephosphorylated to form undecaprenyl-phosphate (C55P), a glycan subunit carrier. Transfer of the NAM-pentapeptide and NAG to the C55P carrier, generating lipid I and lipid II, respectively. Lipid II is translocated by a dedicated flippase to the periplasmic side of the membrane where polymerization occurs.

Transpeptidation: The cross-linking reactions during peptidoglycan synthesis are called *transpeptidation*. There are several types of cross-linking among bacterial species. The most common type of cross-linkage is **4–3 cross-linkage** (the cross-linking occurs between the residue at position 4 of a donor chain and position 3 of an acceptor chain). Cross-linking reactions are catalyzed by **transpeptidases**. The 4–3 cross-linkage (also termed as **DD type**) is catalyzed by the *DD-transpeptidase*. D,D-Transpeptidases are also called *penicillin-binding proteins* as they are inhibited irreversibly by beta-lactam antibiotics. During DD-transpeptidation, the terminal D-Ala from a pentapeptide is cleaved and a new peptide bond (cross-link) is formed between the fourth D-Ala of the donor stem and the meso-diaminopimelic acid (mDAP) in the third position of the neighboring, acceptor stem.

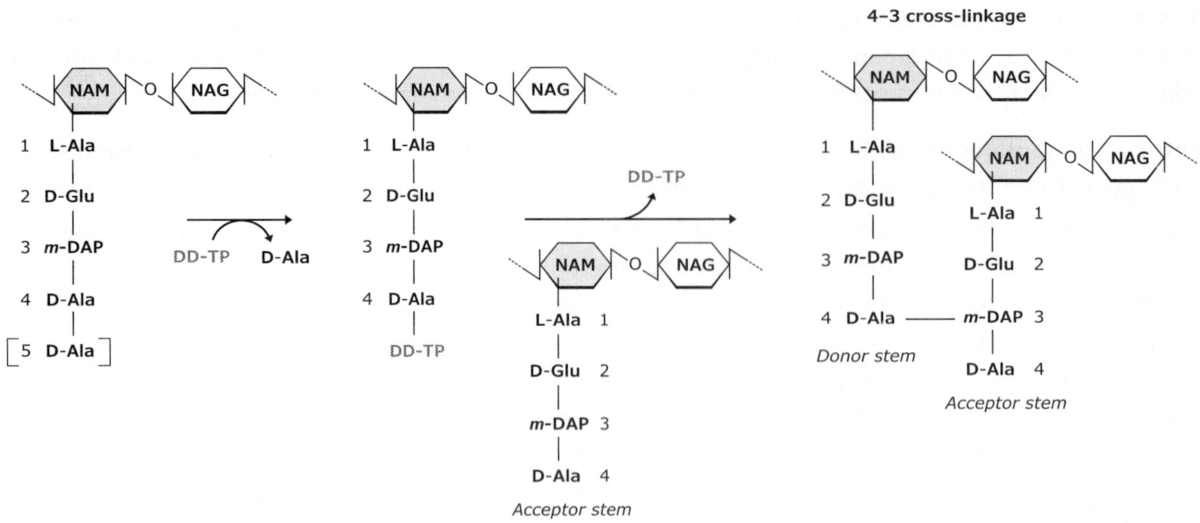

Figure 4.6 The 4–3 cross-linkage (DD type) is catalyzed by the DD-transpeptidase (DD-TP). During DD-transpeptidation, the terminal D-Ala from a pentapeptide is cleaved and a new peptide bond (cross-link) is formed between the fourth D-Ala of the donor stem and the *meso*-diaminopimelic acid (mDAP) in the third position of the acceptor stem.

Many Gram-positive bacteria have acidic substances called **teichoic acids** in their cell wall. Teichoic acids are polyol phosphate polymers (a polymer of glycerol or ribitol joined by phosphate) bearing a strong negative charge. They can be covalently linked to *N*-acetylmuramic acid of the peptidoglycan layer or to the lipids of the plasma membrane. The combination of teichoic acids and lipids are referred to as **lipoteichoic acids**. *Teichoic acids are absent in Gram-negative bacteria*. The main function of teichoic acids is to provide rigidity to the cell wall by attracting cations such as magnesium and sodium.

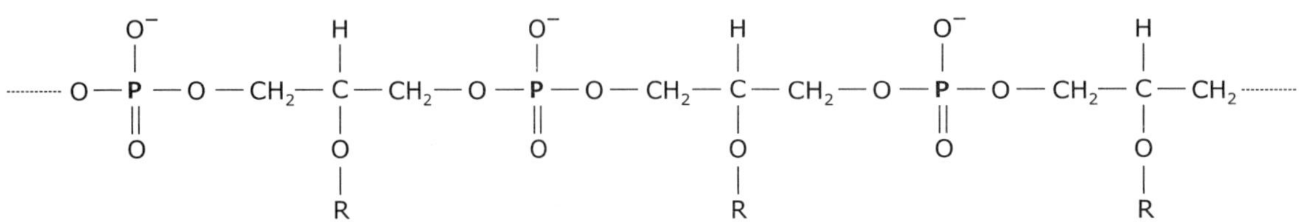

Figure 4.7 Teichoic acids (polymer of glycerol or ribitol joined by phosphate group).

Certain types of bacterial cells have no cell walls or have very little wall material. A common example is members of the genus *Mycoplasma*. Members of this genus of bacteria lack a cell wall. *Mycoplasmas* are the smallest known bacteria that can grow and reproduce outside living host cells. **L-form** bacteria, also known as *L-phase bacteria* and *cell wall deficient bacteria*, also lack cell walls. L-forms can be generated from many bacterial species that usually have cell walls, such as *Bacillus subtilis* or *Escherichia coli*. This is done by inhibiting peptidoglycan synthesis with antibiotics or treating the cells with *lysozyme*, an enzyme that digests cell walls. As L-form has no cell wall, its morphology is different from that of the strain of bacteria from which it is derived. Typical L-form cells are spheres or spheroids. *Mycoplasmas* also lack a cell wall, but these are not considered L-forms since they are not derived from bacteria that normally have cell walls.

Protoplast and spheroplasts: The plasma membrane and everything within is called the **protoplast**. Protoplast lacks a cell wall. If Gram-positive bacteria are incubated with antibiotic penicillin in an isotonic solution, protoplast formation occurs. Penicillin inhibits peptidoglycan synthesis. Gram-negative cells retain their outer membrane after penicillin treatment and are classified as **spheroplasts** because some of their cell walls remains.

Outer membrane

In addition to peptidoglycan cell wall, the Gram-negative bacterium contains an additional membrane, the *outer membrane*. The constituents of this layer are not completely similar to the plasma membrane. It contains lipopolysaccharides, lipoproteins, proteins and phospholipids. The lipid and polysaccharide are linked in the outer membrane to form a *lipopolysaccharide*. Because of this, the outer membrane is often called the **lipopolysaccharide (LPS) layer**. LPS consists of three components, the **core polysaccharide**, the **O-side chain** (also termed as O-antigen) and lipid portion referred to as **lipid A**. Lipid A is not a glycerol lipid. It contains two glucosamine sugar derivatives, each with fatty acids and phosphate or pyrophosphate attached. Lipid A often is toxic; as a result the LPS can act as an endotoxin. The O-polysaccharide functions as an antigen and is useful for distinguishing species of Gram-negative bacteria.

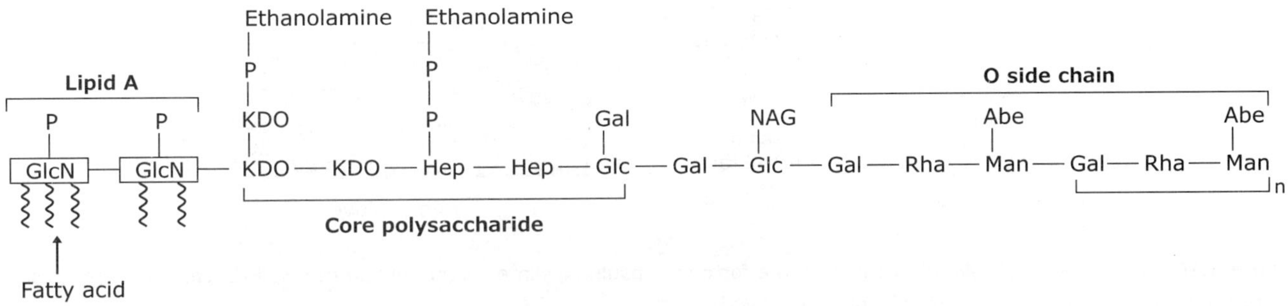

Figure 4.8 The structure of lipopolysaccharide from *Salmonella* (Abe-abequose, Gal-galactose, Glc-glucose, GlcN-glucosamine, Hep-heptulose, KDO-keto deoxyoctonate, Man-mannose, NaG-N-acetylglucosamine, P-phosphate, Rha-L-rhamnose).

The outer membrane of Gram-negative bacteria is relatively more permeable as compared to the plasma membrane. This is due to the presence of proteins called **porins** in the outer membrane. Porins are transmembrane pore-forming proteins with a β-barrel structure, which forms a water-filled open channel and allows the passive transport of hydrophilic low-molecular-weight compounds.

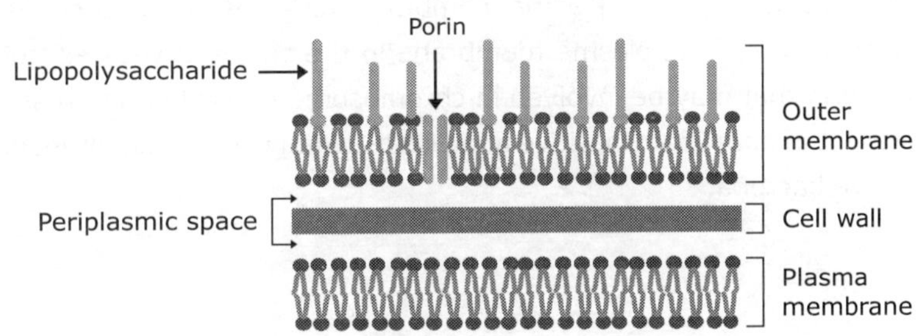

Outer membrane of Gram-negative bacteria

Figure 4.9 The outer membrane lies outside the thin peptidoglycan layer. The most abundant membrane protein is Braun's lipoprotein, a small lipoprotein covalently joined to the underlying peptidoglycan and embedded in the outer membrane. The most unusual constituents of the outer membrane are its lipopolysaccharides (LPSs).

Periplasmic space

A space between the plasma membrane and the outer membrane in Gram-negative bacteria is called the **periplasmic space**. The substance present in the periplasmic space is the **periplasm**. A similar but thinner periplasmic space is found between the plasma membrane and cell wall in Gram-positive bacteria. The periplasmic space is a highly metabolically active compartment in bacteria. It functions as a central hub for nutrient processing and transport, cell wall synthesis, detoxification, and environmental signal sensing. Through these activities, the periplasmic space plays a critical role in bacterial growth, survival, and virulence.

Glycocalyx

Glycocalyx is a thick, high-molecular-weight secretory substance and is present in many bacteria external to the cell wall. It is composed of polysaccharide, polypeptide, or both. The glycocalyx may be thick or thin, rigid or flexible, depending on their chemical nature. The terms **capsule** and **slime layer** are frequently used to describe glycocalyx layers. The rigid layers are organized in a tight matrix called a *capsule*. If the layer is more easily deformed and loosely attached to the cell wall, is called a *slime layer*. Most capsules consist of polysaccharides. However, the capsules of some bacilli (*Bacillus anthracis*) consist of polypeptides, mainly poly-D-glutamic acid. The possession of capsules makes some pathogenic bacteria resistant to phagocytosis and enhance their virulence.

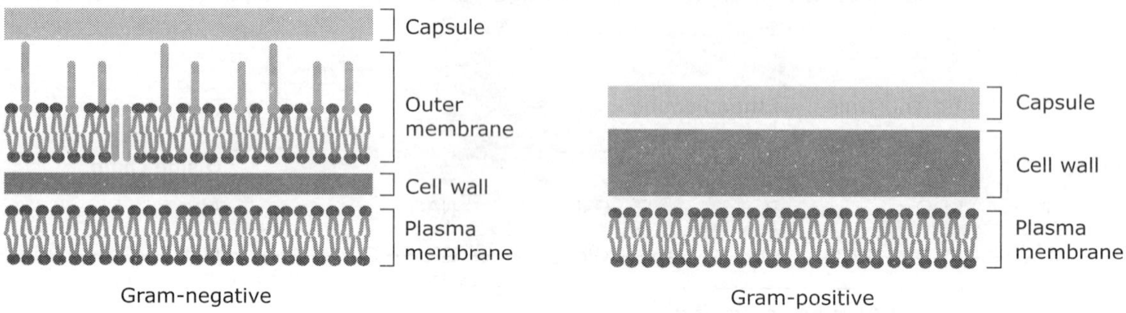

Figure 4.10 Many bacteria have glycocalyx (in the form of capsule or slime layer) outside cell wall (in case of Gram-positive bacteria) or outer membrane (in case of Gram-negative bacteria).

Plasma membrane

The bacterial plasma membrane is a unit membrane composed primarily of protein and phospholipid. Its structural and chemical features are similar to eukaryotic plasma membrane. One major difference in chemical composition of plasma membranes between eukaryotic and prokaryotic cells is that eukaryotes have sterols in their membranes. Sterols are absent from the plasma membranes of all bacteria except *Mycoplasma*. Molecules similar to sterols called **hopanoids** (a group of pentacyclic triterpenoids), are present in the membranes of many bacteria, and are likely to play a role similar to that of sterol in eukaryotic cells. Plasma membrane performs many functions, including transport, and energy transduction. An invagination of the plasma membrane in the shape of vesicles, tubules, or lamellae (called **mesosome**) is present in bacteria that may be involved in chromosome replication or cross wall formation in dividing bacteria. Mesosomes are present in both Gram-positive and Gram-negative bacteria, although they are generally more prominent in the Gram-positive bacteria.

Cytoplasm

For a prokaryotic cell, the term *cytoplasm* refers to the substance of the cell inside the plasma membrane. Cytoplasm is about 80% water and contains primarily proteins, carbohydrates, lipids, inorganic ions, and many low molecular-weight compounds. It lacks unit membrane-bound organelles. The major structures present in the cytoplasm are ribosomes and reserve deposits called **inclusion bodies**.

The bacterial cytoplasm contains **70S ribosomes**. Bacterial 70S ribosomes differ from eukaryotic 80S ribosomes present in cytosol in the number of proteins and rRNA molecules they contain. The subunits of a 70S ribosome are a small 30S subunit containing one molecule of rRNA (16S rRNA) and a larger 50S subunit containing two molecules of rRNA (23S and 5S rRNA).

Bacterial cytoplasm also contains many organic and inorganic reserve deposits (granules) known as **inclusion bodies**, that may be membrane-bound or membrane less. Membranes surrounding inclusion bodies are not a typical unit membrane (*exception* **magnetosome**). These membranes vary in composition. Some are proteinaceous in nature, whereas others contain lipid. Examples of inclusion bodies present in bacterial cytoplasm are glycogen, cyanophycin granules, carboxysomes, polyphosphate granules and others.

Glycogen is a polymer of glucose and present in the form of granules in the cytosol. In the presence of iodine, glycogen granules appear reddish brown. **Cyanophycin granules** are composed of large polypeptides containing approximately equal amount of amino acids, arginine and aspartic acid. It is non-ribosomally produced amino acid polymer and present in cyanobacteria and a few heterotrophic bacteria.

Carboxysomes are polyhedral inclusion bodies that contain the CO_2 fixation enzymes ribulose-1,5-bisphosphate carboxylase (RuBisCO). These structures are found in all cyanobacteria and in many chemotrophic bacteria that fix carbon dioxide.

Polyphosphate granules (or **volutin granules**) are reserve form of inorganic phosphate (polyphosphate) present in the cytoplasm of some bacteria. Volutin granules show red or a different shade of blue when stained with blue basic dyes, methylene blue or toluidine blue. This is known as **metachromatic effect**. Hence these granules are sometimes called **metachromatic granules**.

Magnetosomes are membrane-bound structure sharing many features of eukaryotic organelles. It consists of magnetic mineral crystal surrounded by a lipid bilayer and present in magnetotactic bacteria. Magnetotactic bacteria are motile and mostly aquatic. Magnetosomes usually contain crystals of **magnetite** (Fe_3O_4), or crystals of **greigite** (Fe_3S_4). It acts like a compass needle to orient magnetotactic bacteria in geomagnetic fields.

Gas vesicle is a hollow spindle-shaped structure made of protein. It is impermeable to liquid water, but it is highly permeable to gases and is normally filled with air. It is a rigid structure of low compressibility. It provides buoyancy to planktonic cells by decreasing their overall cell density.

Surface appendages

Bacteria may or may not possess surface appendages. Three types of surface appendage can be recognized on different bacterial species: the **flagella**, which are organs of locomotion, **pili** (*Latin* hairs), meant for conjugation and **fimbriae**, meant for attachment.

Flagella

Flagella occur in both Gram-positive and Gram-negative bacteria. Structurally, bacterial flagella are long, filamentous surface appendages. In most bacteria, flagella are located on the surface and are exposed to the cell exterior. On the other hand, the flagella of spirochetes reside within the periplasmic space, and so they are called **periplasmic flagella**. A flagellum of a Gram-negative bacterium such as *E. coli* consists of three parts:

- The long **filament**, which lies external to the cell surface;
- The **hook** structure at the end of the filament; and
- The **basal body**, to which the hook is anchored and which imparts motion to the flagellum.

Some bacteria have sheaths surrounding their flagella. For example, *Vibrio cholerae* flagella have lipopolysaccharide sheaths. The flagellar **filament** is made up of **flagellin** protein. In filament, the flagellin proteins are assembled to form a cylindrical structure with a hollow core. The filament is rigid. The **hook**, on the other hand, is flexible. The **basal bodies** of typical Gram-negative bacteria have four rings: L, P, MS and C, which are connected to a central *rod*. Earlier, it was thought that the basal body comprises four rings M (for Membrane), S (for Supramembranous), P (for Peptidoglycan) and L (for Lipopolysaccharide). Later it was found that both the M- and S-rings (now called the MS-ring) comprise different domains of the same protein. Therefore, they function as a unit. A fourth ring, C-ring (for Cytoplasmic) is present inside the cell. Typical Gram-positive bacteria have only two rings: an *inner ring* connected to the plasma membrane and an *outer ring* probably attached to the peptidoglycan.

The **motor complex** is composed of two components: the *rotor* and the *stator*. In typical Gram-negative bacteria, the *rotor* is composed of the MS-ring and the C-ring. The *stator* is composed of the proteins **MotA** and **MotB**, which form a channel through the plasma membrane. As with all motors, the flagellar motor must have a power source that allows it to generate torque and cause flagellar rotation. The power is provided by the electrochemical proton gradient.

The channels created by the MotA and MotB proteins allow protons to move across the plasma membrane from the periplasmic space into the cytosol. This movement releases energy that is used to rotate the flagellum. The C-ring consists of three proteins, **FliG**, **FliM**, and **FliN**. The C-ring is also called the **switch complex** as it can switch the direction of flagellar motor.

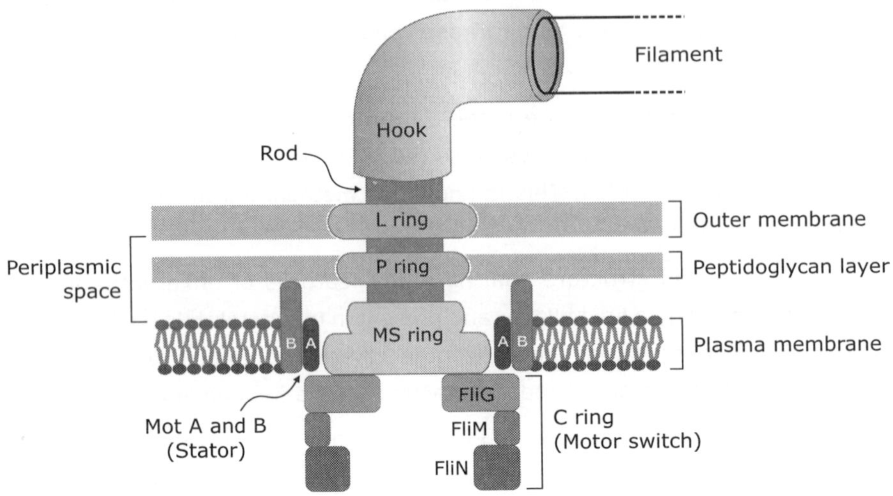

Figure 4.11 Structure of a flagella in Gram-negative bacteria. A typical flagella consist of three main parts: a basal body, a hook and a filament. The basal body consists of four rings (L, P, MS and C-ring) and rod which is located just above the MS-ring and connected to the proximal region of the hook. The C-ring consists of three proteins, FliG, FliM, and FliN. FliG is the most directly involved in the rotation of the flagella among the C-ring proteins, as it interacts with the motor complex (MotA and B). The C-ring is also called the *switch complex* as it can switch the direction of flagellar motor.

Bacterial flagellar motion is **rotatory** in nature. The maximum motor speed reaches up to 300 revolutions per second in *E. coli*. The exact mechanism that drives basal body rotation is still not clear. The necessary free energy is derived from the proton gradient that exists across the plasma membrane. ATP is *not* directly required for flagellar motion. Membrane proteins MotA and MotB create a proton channel that drives the rotation of the flagellum. The rotation of flagella can be *clockwise* or *counterclockwise*. When the flagella rotate clockwise, the forward motion ceases, and the cells **tumble**. In contrast, counterclockwise rotations of flagella impart forward motion (**run**). During run mode, the flagellar motor rotates counterclockwise, and the left-handed helical filaments bundle together and produce a force on the cell body. An intracellular signal transduction system transmits the signals to the flagellar motor to switch the direction of motor rotation from counterclockwise to clockwise.

Number and distribution of flagella: The number and distribution of flagella on the bacterial surface (**flagellation pattern**) are characteristic for a given species and hence are useful in identifying and classifying bacteria. Based on number and patterns of distribution of flagella, bacteria may be:

- **Monotrichous** (*trichous* means hair)
  Have one flagellum.
- **Amphitrichous** (*amphi* means on both sides)
  One flagellum attached at each end.
- **Lophotrichous** (*lopho* means tuft)
  Cluster of flagella at one end or both ends.
- **Peritrichous** (*peri* means around)
  Flagella are spread fairly evenly over the whole surface.

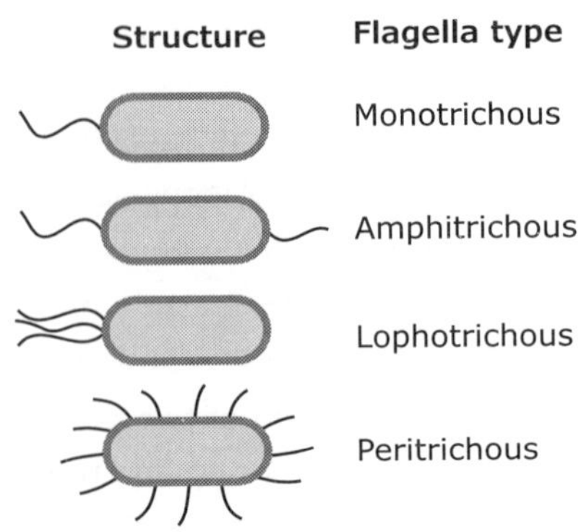

Table 4.1 Difference between bacterial (prokaryotic) and eukaryotic flagella

Bacterial flagella	Eukaryotic flagella
Filament is rigid.	Filament is flexible.
Filament made up of flagellin protein.	Filament made up of tubulin protein.
Perform rotatory movement.	Perform whiplash movement.
Not surrounded with plasma membrane.	Surrounded with plasma membrane.

Pili and fimbriae

The term **pili** (singular: pilus) is used to describe the thin, hairlike appendages on the surface of bacteria. Pili occurs almost exclusively on Gram-negative bacteria. Only a few Gram-positive bacteria such as *Corynebacterium renale* bear pili. Proteins that form pili are referred to as **pilins**. Pili are more rigid in appearance than flagella. It plays an important role in the process of conjugation (hence sometimes called **sex pili**). It also functions as a receptor for donor-specific (male-specific) phages.

Fimbriae are filamentous cell appendages, present in both Gram-negative and Gram-positive bacteria. They are composed of helically arranged protein subunits. Fimbriae mediate cell attachment to surface. It can occur at the poles of the bacterial cell or can be evenly distributed over the entire surface of the cell. They can number anywhere from a few to several hundreds per cell.

Table 4.2 Differences between pili and fimbriae

Pili	Fimbriae
Present in Gram-negative bacteria.	Present in both Gram-negative and Gram-positive bacteria.
Required for bacterial conjugation.	Used for cell attachment to surface.
Number about 1 to 10 per cell.	Number up to several hundreds per cell.
Long filamentous structure.	Short filamentous structure.

Endospores

Bacteria in the genera *Bacillus* and *Clostridium* form an exceptionally heat resistant and dehydrated structure capable of surviving for long periods in an unfavorable environment. This dormant structure is called an *endospore* since it develops within the cell. These structures are extraordinarily resistant to environmental stresses such as heat, ultraviolet radiation, gamma radiation, chemical disinfectants and desiccation.

Table 4.3 Differences between endospores and vegetative cells

Characteristic	Vegetative cell	Endospore
Dipicolinic acid	Absent	Present
Enzymatic activity	High	Low
mRNA	Present	Low or absent
Heat resistance	Low	High
Radiation resistance	Low	High
Water content	High, 80–90%	Low, 10–25% in core
Cytoplasmic pH	About pH 7	About pH 5.5–6.0 (in core)
Calcium content	Low	High

Endospore structure

The endospore structure is very complex and has many layers that are absent from the vegetative cell.

Exosporium: It is a thin delicate protein covering.

Spore coat: It lies beneath the exosporium composed of several protein layers.

Cortex: It is present beneath the spore coat, made up of a peptidoglycan.

Core wall (or *spore cell wall*): It is present beneath the cortex and surrounds the protoplast or spore core. The spore core has the normal cell structures such as ribosomes and a nucleoid, but is metabolically inactive.

The endospore contains large amount of **dipicolinic acid** complexed with calcium ions. It is thought to contribute to the endospore's heat resistance. Endospore morphology and location vary with species. Hence staining is used to determine the morphology and location. The most commonly used endospore stain is the **Schaeffer-Fulton endospore stain**. Staining of endospore through *Schaeffer-Fulton* procedure first involves heating of bacteria with malachite green that penetrates endospores. It gives the endospore green color. After the malachite treatment cell is washed with water and is counterstained with safranin.

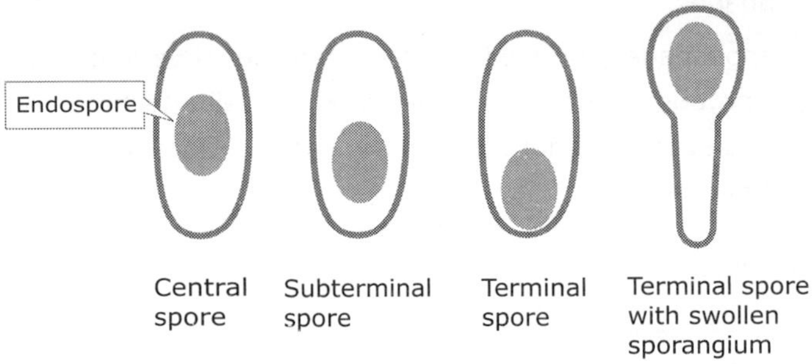

Figure 4.12 Endospore location and size.

Endospore formation: When a growing bacterium (the vegetative cell) is faced with starvation, the process of sporulation begins. The first morphological change is the transformation of the two identical chromosomes (the parent chromosome and the newly replicated daughter chromosome) into an axial filament of DNA. A septum then divides the cell, and the smaller prespore cell is engulfed by the spore mother cell. In this cell-within-a-cell, the plasma membranes separate the cytoplasm of one cell from the cytoplasm of the other and leave a space in between. In this space the spore wall material is deposited.

Table 4.4 Difference between Gram-negative and Gram-positive bacteria

Property	Gram-negative bacteria	Gram-positive bacteria
Cell wall	2 to 7 nm thick	20 to 80 nm thick
Teichoic acids	Absent	Present
Periplasmic space	Prominent	Negligible
Outer membrane	Present	Absent
Motility	Motile or non-motile.	Mostly non-motile
Appendages	Usually bears appendages like pili, fimbriae	Usually lack appendages
Flagellar structure	4 rings in basal body	2 rings in basal body
Toxin produced	Endotoxins and exotoxins	Exotoxins
Endospores	Cannot form endospores	Some genera form endospores
Gram reaction	Stained with dye crystal violet but does not retain purple color when washed with decolorizer alcohol and acetone.	Stained with dye crystal violet and does retain purple color when washed with decolorizer alcohol and acetone.

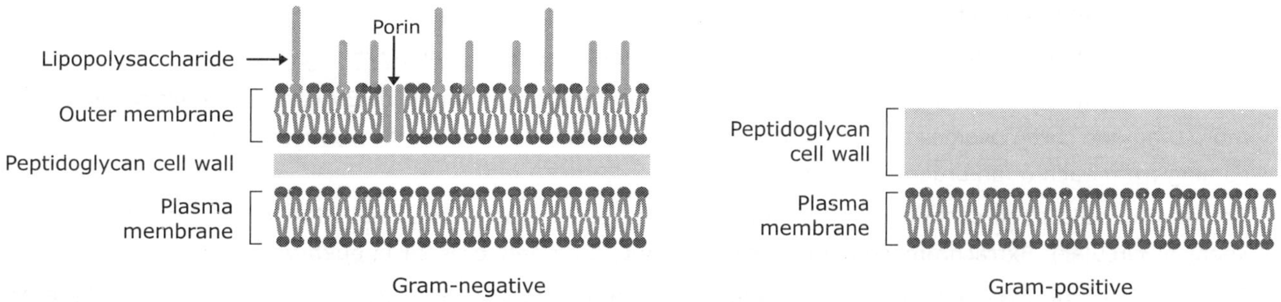

Figure 4.13 A comparison of bacterial cell wall. In Gram-positive bacteria, the cell wall is made mostly of peptidoglycan, interspersed with teichoic acid. The amount of crosslinking is higher and the wall is thicker than in Gram-negative cell walls. The cell wall in Gram-negative bacteria contains much less peptidoglycan and is surrounded by an outer membrane. There is much less cross-linking between the peptidoglycan.

4.3 Bacterial genome

Bacterial chromosome

The bacterial chromosome is mostly a circular, double-stranded DNA molecule. The region of a bacterial cell containing the bacterial chromosome is called the **nucleoid**, which lacks a surrounding nuclear membrane. Unlike eukaryotic chromosomes, it does not make complex with basic histone proteins but is associated with low-molecular-weight polyamines. The bacterial chromosome is organized into independently supercoiled loops known as domains. Nucleoid-associated proteins, such as **HU** (heat-unstable nucleoid protein), **H-NS** (histone-like nucleoid structuring protein), **IHF** (integration host factor), and **SMC** (structural maintenance of chromosomes), are crucial for condensation of chromosomal DNA. These proteins also participate in chromosome segregation, DNA bending, and recombination events.

Most bacteria, like *E. coli*, contain a single circular DNA molecule as a chromosome. The recent studies have indicated that some bacteria contain more than one chromosomes of linear or circular nature. For example, *Vibrio cholerae*, the bacterium that causes cholera, contains two circular chromosomes. One of these chromosomes contains the genes involved in metabolism and virulence, while the other contains the remaining essential genes. An even more extreme example is provided by *Borrelia burgdorferi*, the bacterium that causes **Lyme disease**. It contains up to 11 copies of a single linear chromosome. Unlike *E. coli*, *Borrelia* cannot supercoil its linear chromosomes into a tight ball within the nucleoid; rather, these strands are diffused throughout the cell. The DNA molecules of Archaea share many similarities with eukaryotes. Archaeans are the only group of prokaryotes that use eukaryote-like histones to condense their DNA molecules. DNA molecules of Archaea can also be negatively supercoiled, positively supercoiled or not supercoiled at all.

Table 4.5 Some examples of bacterial chromosome

Bacteria	**Chromosome** (Number, shape and size)
Agrobacterium tumefaciens	One linear (~2.1 Mb) + One circular (~3.0 Mb)
Bacillus subtilis	One circular (~4.2 Mb)
Brucella melitensis	Two circular (~2.1 + ~1.2 Mb)
Vibrio cholerae	Two circular (~2.9 + ~1.1 Mb)
Rhodobacter sphaeroides	Two circular (~3.0 + ~0.3 Mb)
E. coli K-12	One circular (~4.6 Mb)

Prokaryotic versus Eukaryotic genome

The prokaryotic genome differs from that of eukaryotes in several important ways:

- Most prokaryotes contain a single circular chromosome and are monoploid. By contrast, eukaryotes contain more than one chromosomes and are mostly diploid (i.e., two copies of each chromosome exist—with one copy coming from each of an organism's parents).
- Prokaryotic cells often contain one or more plasmids (i.e., extrachromosomal DNA molecules that are either linear or circular). Extrachromosomal plasmids are not commonly present in eukaryotes.
- Since prokaryotic DNA does not remain separated from cytoplasm through nuclear membrane, therefore, transcription and translation take place simultaneously. In eukaryotes, transcription and translation are separated in space and time. The transcription occurs in the nucleus whereas translation occurs in the cytoplasm.
- Prokaryotic chromosome(s) is/are present in the condense form in the nucleoid (not surrounded by nuclear membrane) and DNA is not complexed with histone proteins. Eukaryotic chromosomes are present in a membrane-bound nucleus where DNA is complexed with histones.
- Prokaryotic genomes are much smaller as compared to eukaryotes. For example, the *E. coli* K12 genome is just ~4.6 Mb, two-fifths the size of the budding yeast genome (~12 Mb). Most prokaryotes contain only one copy of each gene. Gene density is also higher in prokaryotic genome as compared to eukaryotic genome.
- Prokaryotic genomes contain very small amounts of noncoding and repetitive DNA as compared to eukaryotic genomes. Most eukaryotic genes are interrupted i.e., contains introns. Introns are rarely present in the prokaryotic genes.

Bacterial plasmid

Plasmids, a term introduced by J. Lederberg, are autonomous, self-replicating DNA molecules that exist as extrachromosomal DNA within bacterial and archaeal cells. As **replicons**—units of nucleic acid capable of independent replication—plasmids multiply independently from the host chromosomal DNA and often occur in multiple copies within a single cell. Structurally, most bacterial plasmids are circular, negatively supercoiled, double-stranded DNA molecules, although linear plasmids also occur in a few genera, such as *Borrelia* and *Streptomyces*. Bacterial plasmids are typically much smaller than the chromosome, with sizes ranging from less than 5 kbp to several hundred kbp, though exceptionally large plasmids up to 2 Mbp have been reported. While not essential for basic survival, plasmids often carry genes that confer selective advantages, such as antibiotic resistance or metabolic functions.

Plasmids are widespread in bacteria and archaea, but they are also found in eukaryotes, particularly in fungi. Most plasmids are DNA molecules; however, rare **RNA plasmids**, present in both single-stranded and double-stranded forms, have been identified in some fungi and plants.

Types of plasmid

Conjugative and mobilizable plasmid

Based on mobility, plasmids can be *conjugative* (self-transmissible), *mobilizable* and *non-mobilizable*. A **conjugative plasmid** is a *self-transmissible* plasmid in that it possesses all the necessary genes to transmit itself to another bacterium by conjugation. It contains both **Mpf genes** (involved in mating pair formation) and **Dtr genes** (involved in DNA transfer and replication). Mpf genes encode proteins responsible for pilus-mediated cell-to-cell contact and formation of *Type IV secretion system* (**T4SS**) which act as a channel through which proteins or protein–DNA complexes can be translocated. Dtr genes encode proteins that bind to the DNA at the origin of transfer, *ori*T, forming a complex called **relaxosome.** The key catalytic component of the relaxosome is the **relaxase.** The relaxase produces a nick within *ori*T and becomes transiently attached to the 5′ end of the DNA single strand.

A **mobilizable plasmid** possesses a functional *ori*T and Dtr genes for DNA transfer and replication. It carries the genes necessary for relaxosome formation and DNA transfer, but lack the genes required for mating pair formation. Mobilizable plasmids are not able to promote their own transfer unless an appropriate conjugation system is provided by a conjugative plasmid. Plasmids are called **nonmobilizable** if they are neither conjugative nor mobilizable. Most naturally occurring plasmids are either conjugative or mobilizable.

F-plasmid

The *F-plasmid* is an example of **self-transmissible plasmid**. Bacteria that possess a copy of F-plasmid are called F-positive or F-plus (denoted F^+). Cells that lack F-plasmids are called F-negative or F-minus (F^-). The F-plasmid is also an **episome**. A plasmid that can exist autonomously in a cell or can integrate itself into the bacterial chromosome is termed as an episome. A bacterial cell that contains an F-plasmid integrated with the bacterial chromosome is referred to as an **Hfr** (High frequency recombination) cell. Integration involves homologous recombination between two covalently closed circular DNA molecules forming one circular molecule containing both of the original DNA structures. It is thought that the IS element present in the F-plasmid and those in the host chromosome serve as regions of homology for the insertional event.

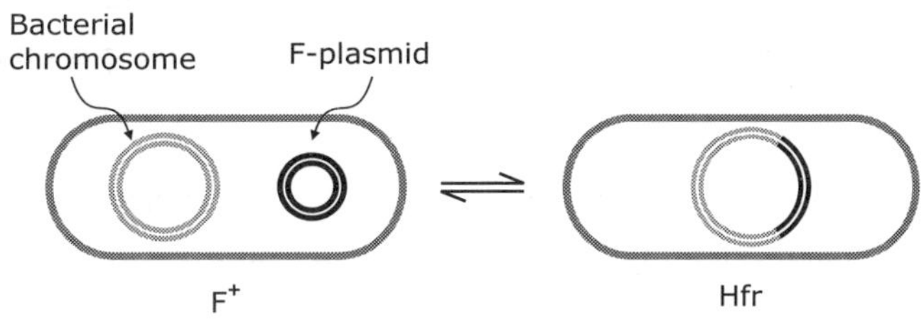

Figure 4.14 The F-plasmid is an episome and can integrate into the bacterial chromosome at several different locations by recombination between homologous insertion sequences present on both the plasmid and host chromosomes. Such a donor bacterial cell is called an Hfr strain (for high frequency of recombination) because it exhibits a very high efficiency of chromosomal gene transfer in comparison with F-cells.

R (*resistance*) plasmid

R-plasmids make the host cell resistant to one or more antibiotics. They typically have genes that code for enzymes capable of destroying or modifying antibiotics. Some R-plasmids have only a single antibiotic resistance gene, whereas others have many. Most R-plasmids are mobilizable plasmids.

Col (*colicinogenic*) plasmids

Col plasmids synthesize proteins termed as **bacteriocin** that prevent the growth of susceptible bacterial strains that do not contain a Col plasmid. Bacteriocins are bactericidal proteins that inhibit the growth of other strains of the same species as well as other closely related species. Bacteriocins are peptides that may give their producers, which are naturally immune to their bacteriocins, an adaptive advantage against other bacteria. A bacterium that makes a particular bacteriocin isn't killed by that bacteriocin but may be killed by other ones. Bacteriocins produced by *E. coli* are termed **colicins**. There are many types of colicins, each designated by a letter (for example, colicin B) and each having a particular mode of inhibition of sensitive cells.

Table 4.6 List of some common plasmids and their functions

Type of plasmid	Gene functions
Resistance	Antibiotic resistance
Fertility	Conjugation and DNA transfer between bacteria
Killer	Synthesis of toxins that kill other bacteria
Degradative	Enzymes for metabolism of unusual molecules
Virulence	Pathogenicity

Properties of plasmids

Plasmid replication

Typical plasmids made up of circular dsDNA use two alternative mechanisms for replicating their DNA. Most plasmids replicate like bacterial chromosomes. They have an origin of replication where the DNA opens and bidirectional replication begins. The two replication forks move around the circular plasmid in opposite directions until they meet.

The other replication mechanism is **rolling circle replication**. It starts by nicking at the origin of replication and unrolling one strand and using the other, still circular, strand as a template for DNA synthesis. Some plasmid, such as F-plasmid of *E. coli*, can transfer themselves from one bacterium to another. Such plasmids have two separate origins of replication. Bidirectional replication (also known as **vegetative replication**) starts at *ori*V, and transfer starts from *ori*T. All plasmids must have a vegetative origin since they all replicate to survive. But only those plasmids that can transfer themselves have the origin of transfer.

Host range

Most plasmids can exist in only a limited number of closely related bacteria; these are called **narrow host range** plasmids. Some plasmid like IncP of *E. coli* can be transferred to and maintained in bacteria of a large number of species. These are called **broad host range** plasmids. Why some plasmids have a broad host range is still unknown?

Copy number

The average number of molecules of a given plasmid per bacterial cell is called its *copy number*. More precisely it is the number of copies of plasmid in a cell immediately after cell division. Plasmids may be classified as a **low copy number** or **stringent plasmid** (with 1 to 2 copies per cell) or **high copy number** or **relaxed plasmid** (with 10 to 100 copies per cell). Each type of plasmid possesses its own genes for regulation of replication initiation and hence the number of plasmid copy per cell. Bacterial plasmids maintain their number of copies by negative regulatory systems that adjust the rate of replication of plasmid. The initiation of plasmid replication may be controlled by regulating the amount of available primer for the initiation of DNA replication, regulating the amount of essential replication proteins, or regulating the function of essential replication proteins. Three major mechanisms are used to control the initiation of plasmid replication:

1. Regulation by antisense RNA.
2. Regulation by binding of replication proteins to repeated 18-22 bp sites called iterons.
3. Regulation by ctRNA (counter-transcribed RNA, a plasmid-encoded noncoding RNA) and a protein.

Plasmid incompatibility

Incompatibility is defined as the inability of two closely related plasmids to stably coexist in the same cell. Thus, a cell containing *incompatible plasmids* A and B will give rise eventually to descendants containing either A or B but not both. Two plasmids that cannot coexist in the same bacterial cell are members of the same *incompatibility group* i.e., *two plasmids are incompatible if they belong to the same incompatibility group*. Incompatible plasmids share the same replication control mechanism. Thus, the replication control system will not recognize the two incompatible plasmids as different, and so either may be randomly selected for replication.

Partitioning

Partitioning is an active process which assures that after cell division each daughter cell gets a copy of plasmid. For plasmids present in high copy numbers (50 to 100 copies per cell), random diffusion may be enough to get at least one copy of the plasmid to each daughter cell. However, random segregation of low-copy-number plasmids (only 1 to 2 copies per cell) would most likely mean that, following cell division, one of the daughter cells would not receive a plasmid. The plasmid would eventually be diluted from the population. Consequently, regulated partitioning mechanisms are essential for these plasmids. The mechanism used for partitioning differs depending on the plasmid. Partitioning, especially of low-copy-number plasmids, is regulated by *par* genes present on plasmids. The **par systems** consist of a *cis-acting* centromere-like site, often called *parS* and two genes termed *parA* and *parB*, which encode *trans-acting proteins*, ParA and ParB.

Functions of plasmids

Depending on their size, plasmids can encode a few or hundreds of different proteins. However, plasmids rarely encode gene products that are essential for growth, such as RNA polymerase, ribosomal subunits, or enzymes of the tricarboxylic acid cycle. Instead, plasmid genes usually give bacteria a selective advantage under only some conditions. Gene products encoded by plasmids include enzymes for the utilization of unusual carbon sources such as toluene, resistance to substances such as heavy metals and antibiotics, synthesis of antibiotics, and synthesis of toxins and proteins that allow the successful infection of higher organisms. A plasmid that confers no identified functions or phenotypic properties is termed as **cryptic plasmid**.

Table 4.7 List of some plasmid-coded traits

Trait	Organisms in which trait is found
Antibiotic resistance	*E. coli, Salmonella sp., Staphylococcus sp.*
Pilus synthesis	*E. coli, Pseudomonas sp.*
Tumor formation in plants	*Agrobacterium tumefaciens*
Nitrogen fixation (in plants)	*Rhizobium sp.*
Oil degradation	*Pseudomonas sp.*
Gas vacuole production	*Halobacterium sp.*
Insect toxin synthesis	*Bacillus thuringiensis*
Plant hormone synthesis	*Pseudomonas sp.*
Antibiotic synthesis	*Streptomyces sp.*
Increased virulence	*Yersinia enterocolitica*

Plasmids in eukaryotic organisms

Plasmids are not limited to prokaryotes only. Plasmids are also found in eukaryotic organisms like yeast. One yeast plasmid is called the **2μ circle**. The 2μ circle is a 6.3 kb circular, extrachromosomal element found in the nucleus of most *Saccharomyces cerevisiae* strains. It is stably maintained at about 50 to 100 copies per haploid genome of the yeast cell. Like the nuclear chromosomes, the 2μ circle is coated with nucleosomes and replication is initiated by host replication enzymes once per cell cycle.

4.4 Bacterial nutrition

Nutrients are substances used in biosynthesis and energy production and therefore are required for bacterial growth. All bacteria require several macro- and micronutrients. **Macronutrients** (e.g., C, O, H, N, S, P, K, Ca, Mg and Fe) are needed in relatively large quantities; **micronutrients** (e.g., Mn, Zn, Co, Mo, Ni and Cu) are used in very small amounts. In addition to the need for carbon, hydrogen and oxygen, all organisms require sources of energy and electrons for growth to take place. On the basis of sources of carbon, energy and hydrogen/electrons bacteria can be categorized into following types:

Based on carbon sources

The carbon requirements of bacteria must be met by CO_2 or organic carbon. Bacteria that primarily use carbon dioxide as their source of carbon to synthesize organic compounds necessary for growth are called **autotrophs**. Bacteria that use organic carbon are **heterotrophs**.

Based on energy sources

All living organisms require a source of energy. Bacteria that use light as their energy source are called **phototrophs**. Bacteria obtain energy from the oxidation of chemical compounds (either organic or inorganic) are **chemotrophs**.

Based on hydrogen/electron sources

Bacteria use reduced inorganic substances as their electron source are called **lithotrophs**, whereas bacteria extract electrons from organic compounds are **organotrophs**.

Major nutritional types of bacteria

Based on the primary source of carbon, energy and electrons, bacteria are placed in four major nutritional classes.

Photolithotrophic autotrophy (**Photolithoautotrophy**)

Source of carbon : Carbon dioxide
Source of energy : Light energy
Source of electrons : Inorganic hydrogen/electron donor
Representative bacteria : Purple and green sulfur bacteria, Blue-green bacteria

Photoorganotrophic heterotrophy (**Photoorganoheterotrophy**)

Source of carbon : Organic carbon source (CO_2 may also be used)
Source of energy : Light energy
Source of electrons : Organic hydrogen/electron donor
Representative bacteria : Purple nonsulfur bacteria, Green nonsulfur bacteria

Chemolithotrophic autotrophy (**Chemolithoautotrophy**)

Source of carbon : Carbon dioxide
Source of energy : Chemical energy source (inorganic)
Source of electrons : Inorganic hydrogen/electron donor
Representative bacteria : Sulfur-oxidizing bacteria, Hydrogen bacteria, Nitrifying bacteria

Inorganic electron-donor	Groups	Representatives species
$NH_3 \xrightarrow{O_2} NO_2^-$	Ammonia oxidizers	*Nitrosomonas europaea*
$NO_2^- \xrightarrow{O_2} NO_3^-$	Nitrite oxidizers	*Nitrobacter winogradskyi*
$S^0, S_2O_3^{2-} \xrightarrow{O_2} SO_4^{2-}$	Sulphur oxidizers	*Thiobacillus thiooxidans*
$Fe^{2+} \xrightarrow{O_2} Fe^{3+}$	Iron bacteria	*Thiobacillus ferrooxidans*
$H_2 \xrightarrow{O_2} H_2O$	H_2 producers	*Alcaligenes eutrophus*
$CO \xrightarrow{O_2} CO_2$	Carboxidobacteria	*Pseudomonas carboxidovorans*

Chemoorganotrophic heterotrophy (**Chemoorganoheterotrophy**)

Source of carbon : Organic carbon source
Source of energy : Chemical energy source (organic)
Source of electrons : Organic hydrogen/electron donor
Representative bacteria : Most nonphotosynthetic bacteria

4.4.1 Culture media

For any bacterium to be propagated for any purpose it is necessary to provide the appropriate biochemical and biophysical environment. A culture media is a solid or liquid medium that contain all the nutrients the microorganism requires for growth. It is used to grow, transport and store microorganisms. Depending upon the special needs of particular bacteria (as well as particular investigators) a large variety and types of culture media have been developed with different purposes and uses. Culture media are employed in the isolation and maintenance of pure cultures of bacteria and are also used for identification of bacteria according to their biochemical and physiological properties. Culture media can be classified on the basis of physical nature (liquid, semi-solid and solid), chemical composition (synthetic and complex) and functional type (supportive, enriched, selective and differential).

Minimal and supplementary media

Minimal media are those that contain the minimum nutrients possible for the growth of wild-type organisms. Minimal medium typically contains: a carbon source, which may be a sugar such as glucose, various inorganic salts and water. **Supplementary media** are a type of minimal media that also contains a single selected agent, usually an amino acid or a sugar, for the culturing of specific auxotroph.

A strain bearing a mutation which eliminates the capacity of the mutant to make an essential molecule such as an amino acid or nucleotide and make strain unable to grow on medium that lacking that molecule but grows when the molecule is provided. Such mutants are called **auxotrophs**, and they are said to be *auxotrophic* for the molecule they cannot synthesize. Auxotrophs unable to grow on a minimal medium. The wild-type strains from which such mutants arose are able to grow on a minimal medium and are called **prototrophs**.

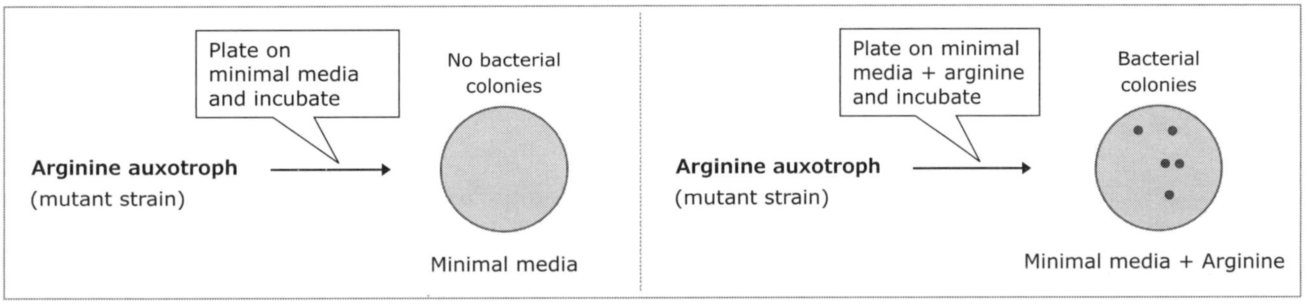

Synthetic and complex media

A *synthetic medium* is chemically-defined medium in which the exact chemical composition is known. A *complex medium* is undefined medium in which the exact chemical constitution of the medium is not known. Examples of some common complex media are nutrient broth, tryptic soy broth and MacConkey agar.

Enriched media

An enriched medium contains some component that permits the growth of specific types or species of bacteria, usually because they alone can utilize the component from their environment. However, an enriched media may have selective features. Blood agar is an example of enriched media because it encourages the growth of many fastidious microbes.

Selective media

A *selective medium* is prepared by the addition of specific substances to a culture medium that will permit growth of one group of bacteria while inhibiting growth of some other groups. For example, *Salmonella Shigella agar* and *mannitol salt agar* are commonly used as selective media. Mannitol salt agar is used for the isolation of *staphylococci*. The mannitol helps differentiate pathogenic from nonpathogenic *staphylococci*. Thus, this medium is also differential.

Differential media

A culture medium is described as a differential medium if it allows the investigator to distinguish between different types of bacteria based on some observable trait in their pattern of growth on the medium. Blood agar is an example of differential media and is used to distinguish between hemolytic and non-hemolytic bacteria. Eosin methylene blue agar, MacConkey agar and Mannitol salt agar are also used as differential media.

Pure culture

A *pure culture* is one that contains only a single kind of microbial population grown from a single cell. A pure culture is usually derived from a mixed culture (containing many species) by methods that separate the individual cells so that, when they multiply, each will form an individually distinct colony, which may then be used to establish new cultures with the assurance that only one type of organism will be present. Pure cultures may be more easily isolated if the growth medium of the original mixed culture favours the growth of one organism to the exclusion of others.

4.4.2 Bacterial growth

Bacterial growth is an orderly increase in the quantity of cellular constituents (i.e., cell mass) and number. It depends upon the ability of the cell to form new protoplasm from nutrients available in the environment. The increase in bacterial cell number occurs by cell division which is known as **binary fission**. Binary fission begins when the DNA of the cell is replicated. Each circular strand of DNA then attaches to the plasma membrane. The cell elongates, causing the two replicated DNA to separate. The plasma membrane then invaginates (grows inward) and splits the cell into two daughter cells through a process called cytokinesis. The principles that underlie chromosome segregation in bacteria and eukaryotes share similarities, although bacteria segregate DNA as it replicates and lack a eukaryote-like mitotic apparatus for segregating chromosomes. A few bacterial species reproduce by budding; they form a small bud that enlarges until its size approaches that of the parent cell, and then it separates.

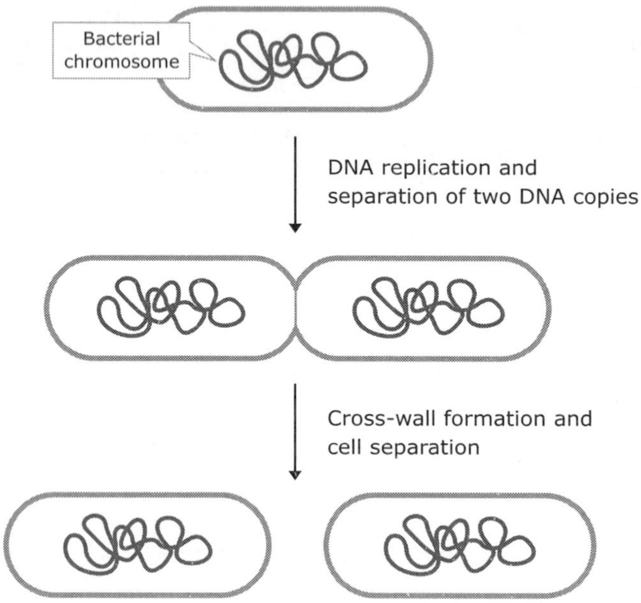

Figure 4.15 Binary fission. A method of asexual reproduction in which the cell divides into two nearly equal sized daughter cells. The genetic material is also equally partitioned, therefore, the daughter cells are genetically identical.

FtsZ protein plays an important role in cell division. FtsZ is homologous to tubulin, the building block of the microtubule in eukaryotes. The cellular concentration of FtsZ regulates the frequency of division. At the time of onset of septal invagination, the FtsZ protein is recruited from the cytoplasm to the division site, where it assembles into a ring that remains associated with the leading edge of the invaginating septum until the separation is completed.

When a bacterial cell is inoculated into a flask containing fresh culture medium and incubated, it enters into a rapid growth phase during which the bacterial cell divides and increases its population in the flask medium. Since the bacteria are not transferred to a new medium or no fresh nutrients are added to the medium, the increasing population of bacterial cells, after some time, enters into a stationary-phase with the exhaustion of the required nutrients and the accumulation of inhibitory end products in the medium. Eventually, the stationary phase of bacterial population culminates into death-phase when the viable bacterial cells begin to die. A **batch culture** can be considered to be a *closed system*. Growth in batch culture can be divided into four distinct phases – these are *lag phase*, *log phase*, *stationary phase* and *death phase*.

Lag phase

During the lag phase, there is no increase in cell number. It is a period of adaptation of cells to a new environment. There is no change in number, but an increase in mass. Thus, in this phase, the bacterial cells are not dormant. The length of the lag phase is determined in part by the characteristics of the bacterial species and in part by conditions in the media.

Log or **growth phase**

In this phase, cell number increases *exponentially* with time. The *log phase* is also known as the **exponential phase**. During exponential growth, the rate of increase of cells in the culture is proportional to the number of cells present at any particular time. During exponential growth, the number of cells increases in the *geometric progression* 2^1, 2^2, 2^3 until, after *n* divisions, the number of cells is 2^n. In reality, exponential growth is only part of the bacterial life cycle and not representative of the normal pattern of growth of bacteria in nature. The cells divide at a constant rate depending upon the composition of the growth medium and the conditions of incubation. The rate of exponential growth of a bacterial culture is expressed as **generation time**, also the **doubling time** of the bacterial population. The time interval required for the cells (or population) to divide is called the *generation time* or the doubling time.

Stationary phase

Exponential growth cannot be continued forever in a *batch culture* (e.g., a closed system). In this phase, the cell growth rate has leveled off and become constant. The number of cells multiplying equals the number of cells dying. Population growth is limited by one of three factors:

- Exhaustion of available nutrients;
- Accumulation of inhibitory metabolites or end products;
- Exhaustion of space, in this case called a lack of *biological space*.

Death phase

If incubation continues after the population reaches stationary phase, a death phase follows, in which the viable cell population declines. During the death phase, the number of viable cells declines exponentially, much like the exponential increase seen in the log phase, but in reverse. The rate of decline varies depending on the species, environmental conditions, and the degree of nutrient depletion or toxic accumulation.

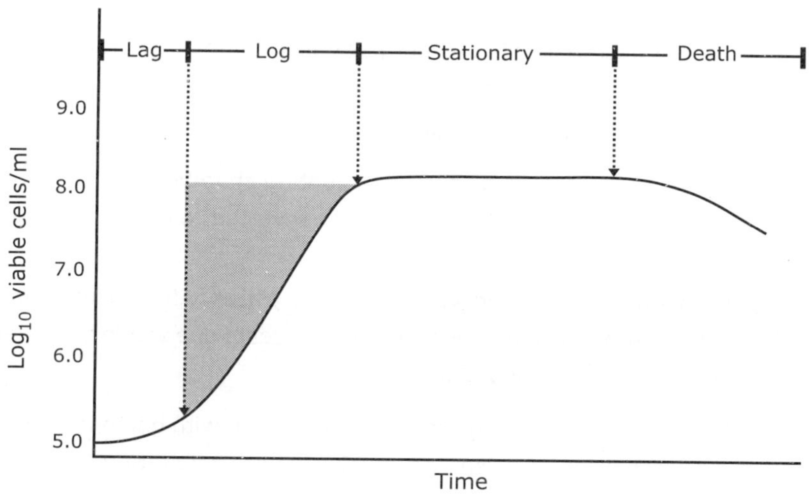

Figure 4.16 Bacterial growth curve in a closed system. When bacteria are introduced into a fresh culture medium, usually no immediate increase in cell number occurs, and therefore this period is called the lag phase. This phase varies considerably in length with the condition of the bacteria and the nature of the medium. During log phase, bacteria divide exponentially. In a closed system, population growth remains exponential for only a few generations and then enters a stationary phase due to factors such as nutrient limitation and waste accumulation. The final phase of the growth curve is the death phase, which is characterized by a net loss of cells.

Calculation of number of generation

When growing exponentially by binary fission, the increase in a bacterial population is by geometric progression. If we start with one cell, when it divides, there are 2 cells in the first generation, 4 cells in the second generation, 8 cells in the third generation, and so on. The time interval required for the bacterial cells (or population) to divide during the log phase is called the **generation time** or the **doubling time**. Alternatively, we can say it is the time needed for the bacterial cells to complete one generation. Generation times for bacteria are species-specific.

Generation time = t (duration of the log phase, in minutes or hours) / n (number of generations)

If N_0 = number of bacteria at the beginning of a time interval;

N = number of bacteria at the end of the time interval and

n = number of generations (number of times the cell population doubles during the time interval) then

$\mathbf{N = N_0 \times 2^n}$ (this equation is an expression of bacterial growth by binary fission during log phase).

Applying logarithms, $\log N = \log N_0 + n \log 2$

The number of generations, $n = \dfrac{\log N - \log N_0}{\log 2} = \dfrac{\log N - \log N_0}{0.301} = 3.3 \log N/N_0$

Problem

A bacterial culture contains 500 cells/mL in the exponential growth phase at 8 AM. If you consider a generation time of 20 minutes, what will be the total number of cells/mL after three hours (i.e., at 11 AM)?

Solution:

$N = N_0 \times 2^n$

N_0 = initial number of cells = 500 cells/mL

n = number of generations = 3 hours/20 minutes = 180/20 = 9

N = number of cells after n generations = $500 \times 2^9 = 500 \times 512$ = 2,56,000.

Calculation of bacterial cell density

Cell density refers to the number of bacterial cells present per unit volume of a culture (usually expressed as cells per milliliter). The estimation of bacterial cell density can be carried out by *direct* and *indirect methods*.

Direct methods provide an actual count of bacterial cells.

Microscopic count: A known volume of culture is placed in a counting chamber and observed under a microscope. The number of cells within the defined grid area is counted and converted to cells/mL. However, this method does not distinguish between living and dead cells.

Viable plate count: A sample is serially diluted and spread on agar plates. After incubation, colonies are counted, and results are expressed as colony-forming units. Each colony represents one viable bacterial cell or colony-forming unit. This method measures only the number of viable cells.

Indirect methods estimate cell density by measuring properties correlated with bacterial mass, turbidity or metabolic activity. These methods are quicker but less precise and usually require calibration.

Turbidity measurement: The culture's turbidity is measured using a spectrophotometer at 600 nm (OD_{600}). Optical density is proportional to cell number, and standard curves are used to convert OD values to cells/mL.

Biochemical or **metabolic activity**: Cell number is estimated based on metabolic indicators such as oxygen consumption or carbon dioxide production.

Influence of environmental factors on growth

The growth of bacteria is profoundly influenced by the chemical and physical conditions of their surrounding environment. Because bacteria are unable to regulate these external factors, they must adapt to or tolerate changes in their surroundings. Many environmental factors like temperature, pH, water availability and oxygen play major roles in controlling the growth of bacteria. On the basis of their response to major environmental factors bacteria can be divided into various classes as given in the **table 4.8**.

Table 4.8 Bacterial classes based on responses to environmental factors

Bacterial class	Definition	Example
Halophile	Requires high levels of salt concentration	*Halobacterium*
Acidophile	Growth optimum between pH 0 and 5.5	*Sulfolobus*
Alkalophile	Growth optimum between pH 8.0 and 11.5	*Bacillus alcalophilus*
Psychrophile	Grows well at 0°C and has an optimum growth temperature of 15°C or lower	*Chlamydomonas nivalis*
Psychrotroph	Can grow at 0–7°C; has an optimum growth between 20 and 30°C	*Pseudomonas fluorescens*
Thermophile	Can grow at 55°C or higher; optimum growth often between 55 and 65°C	*Thermus aquaticus*
Hyperthermophile	Has an optimum often between 80 and ~110°C	*Pyrococcus, Pyrodictium*
Obligate aerobe	Completely dependent on O_2 for growth	*Pseudomonas*
Facultative anaerobe	Does not require O_2 for growth, but grows better in its presence	*Escherichia, Enterococcus*
Aerotolerant anaerobe	Grows equally well in presence or absence of O_2	*Streptococcus pyogenes*
Obligate anaerobe	Does not tolerate O_2 and dies in its presence	*Clostridium*
Microaerophile	Requires O_2 levels below up to 10% for optimum growth	*Treponema pallidum*

4.5 Horizontal gene transfer and recombination

Gene transfer refers to the movement of genetic information between organisms. Gene transfer can be *horizontal* or *vertical*. Transfer of genes from parents to offsprings is termed as **vertical gene transfer** whereas transfer of genes between two independent organisms is called **horizontal** or **lateral gene transfer**. Sexual reproduction in eukaryotes is an example of vertical gene transfer. Prokaryotes do a vertical gene transfer when they reproduce by binary fission. Prokaryotes can also do horizontal gene transfer when they pass the gene to other prokaryotic cells. Three mechanisms of horizontal gene transfer in prokaryotes have been discovered. These are **transformation, transduction** and **conjugation**.

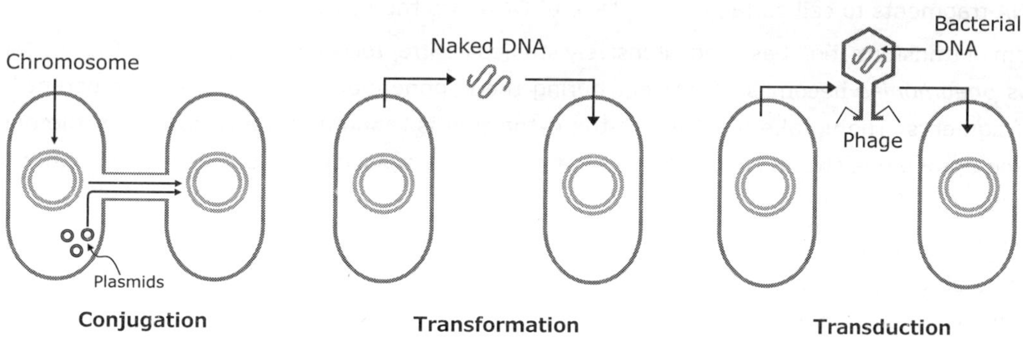

Figure 4.17 Conjugation is the transfer of genes between bacteria that depends upon direct cell-cell contact. Transformation is the uptake of a naked DNA molecule by a competent cell and its incorporation into the genome. Transduction is the transfer of bacterial genes by viruses.

The fragment of DNA that has been transferred during horizontal gene transfer from a donor cell to a recipient cell is referred to as an **exogenote**. The recipient bacterial cell's own genetic material into which the donor DNA can integrate is called **endogenote**. A bacterial cell that has received an exogenote is initially diploid for part of its genome, and is said to be a **merozygote** (*partial diploid* or *merodiploid*).

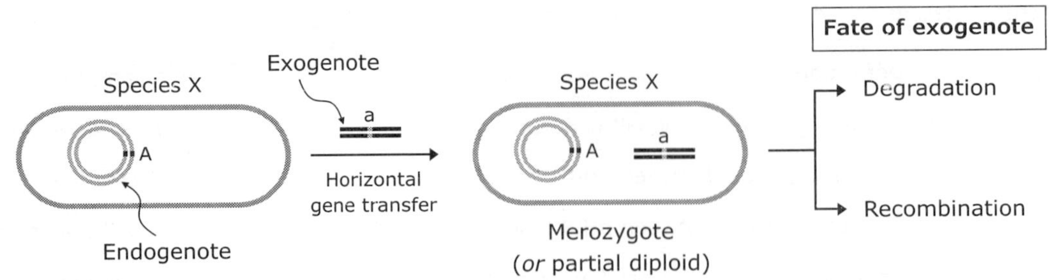

Figure 4.18 Formation of merozygote. During horizontal gene transfer, a piece of donor DNA, sometimes called the *exogenote*, enters a recipient cell. The transfer can occur in three ways: conjugation, transformation and transduction.

In merozygote, genes (alleles) of exogenote may or may not substitute alleles of endogenote. In molecular biology, the process of replacement of one allele by different alleles from the same genes by preserving the structure of genes is termed as **genetic recombination**. Such recombination generally requires that the two molecules be homologous-that they have very similar, although not necessarily identical DNA sequences. If they are non homologous (with no sequence homology), due to originating from different species, then recombination is very unlikely. Exogenote are normally degraded rapidly so that there is essentially a race between the processes of degradation of the exogenote and recombination.

4.5.1 Transformation

Transformation was the first horizontal gene transfer mechanism discovered in bacteria. It was first described in 1928 by Fred Griffith, who demonstrated that non-virulent strains of *Streptococcus pneumoniae* could be converted into virulent forms when exposed to heat-killed virulent bacteria. Transformation is the uptake of a naked DNA molecule or fragment from the surrounding environment by a cell and the incorporation of this molecule into the chromosome of the recipient.

Transformation may be natural or artificial. Natural transformation is a very rare event and has been observed in both Gram-positive (e.g., *Streptococcus pneumoniae*, *Bacillus subtilis*) as well as Gram-negative bacteria (e.g., *Haemophilus influenzae*). The ability of a recipient bacterium to take up DNA molecules from the surrounding environment and become transformed is known as **competence**. Competence is an inheritable characteristic. Competent bacteria that can take up DNA encode proteins called **competence factors**. These proteins facilitate the binding of DNA fragments to cell surface and uptake of DNA into the cytoplasm.

The mechanism of transformation has been intensively studied in *Streptococcus pneumonia*, a Gram-positive bacteria. *Streptococcus pneumoniae* becomes competent during the exponential growth phase. Competent bacterial cells bind dsDNA fragments. The uptake of DNA into the cytoplasm is random and any portion of the donor's may be entered. During uptake one strand is hydrolyzed by a membrane-associated exonuclease; the other strand moves into the cytoplasm.

Transformation in *Haemophilus influenzae* (the first Gram-negative bacterium in which natural competence was found) and some other Gram-negative bacteria are different from that in Gram-positive bacteria like *Streptococcus pneumoniae*. In *Haemophilus influenzae*, DNA uptake is associated with the formation of small membranous structures, called **transformasomes**, which protrude outside the cell. The transforming DNA is taken into these vesicles where it is then internalized into the cell. Second, unlike *Streptococcus pneumoniae*, DNA uptake in *Haemophilus influenzae* is not random i.e., DNA from only closely related species can enter into the cytoplasm. DNA uptake requires the presence of specific sequence termed **uptake sequence**, an 11 base pair sequence repeated many times In the *Haemophilus influenzae* genome. DNA must have this sequence to be bound by a competent cell. Thus, *Haemophilus influenzae* take up preferentially DNA of their own species by recognizing uptake sequences, whereas *Streptococcus pneumoniae* and *Bacillus subtilis* do not discriminate between their own and foreign DNA.

Process of transformation

In the process of transformation, naturally competent bacteria actively pull DNA fragments from their environment into their cells. DNA can be naturally released into the environment when bacterial cells die and subsequent lysis. Once the free DNA comes in the contact with competent bacteria, linear, dsDNA enters into the cell. One strand is translocated across the membrane into the cytoplasm, with its 3′ end leading. The strand not translocated, is degraded at membrane surface by exonuclease. The translocated strand integrates with chromosome by homologous recombination. Recipient cells that undergo this process and acquire a new phenotype as a result are said to be **transformed**.

Single-stranded exogenotes are unstable and will usually be degraded unless they are integrated into the endogenote. By the process of homologous recombination the transforming DNA integrates into the bacterial chromosome. If the exogenote contains an allele of the endogenote, the resulting recombinant double helix would contain one or more mismatched base pairs, and is referred to as a **heteroduplex** (heteroduplex is a dsDNA in which the two strands have different origins). These mismatches are repaired by DNA repair enzymes that scan the DNA and repair. The enzyme systems preferentially replace the base in the new strand, thus restoring the genotype of the recipient. If the region is replicated before it is repaired, however, one of the two daughter chromosomes will be recombinant and other will be identical to the recipient.

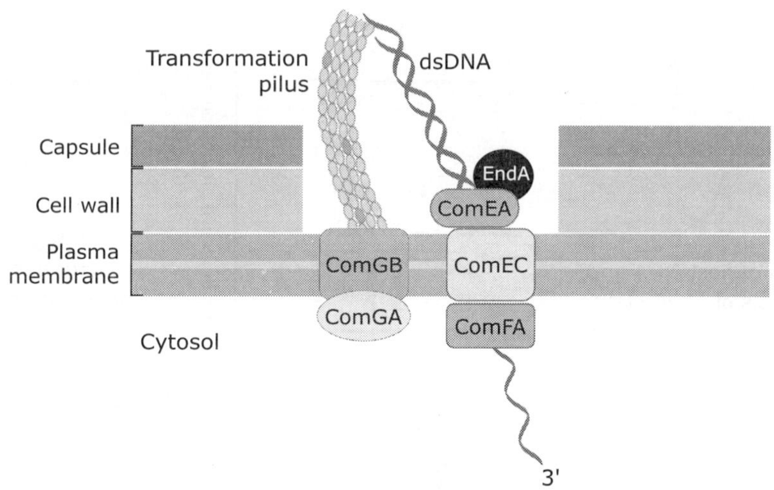

Figure 4.19 Mechanism of pneumococcal natural transformation. Environmental signals can trigger the onset of natural competence in a pneumococcal cell. Once competent, cells can capture foreign dsDNA via a long transformation pilus. After capture, dsDNA is passed to the DNA receptor ComEA, before transfer to the EndA nuclease. EndA degrades one strand of the captured dsDNA, and the resulting ssDNA is transferred across the membrane via the ComEC pore. After internalization, ssDNA is coated with SsbB (not shown in the figure), which protects it from nucleases.

4.5.2 Transduction

In transduction, bacteriophages (or simply phage) function as vectors to transfer DNA from donor bacteria into recipient bacteria. The transfer of bacterial genes by phage was discovered by Lederberg and Zinder in 1951 in *Salmonella typhimurium*. There are two kinds of transduction: *generalized* and *specialized*. In **generalized transduction**, transducing phages produced during lytic growth are aberrant and contain a random fragment of the bacterial genome instead of phage DNA. Each individual transducing phage carries a different set of closely linked genes, representing a small segment of the bacterial genome.

So in generalized transduction, each part of the bacterial genome has approximately the same probability of being transferred from donor to recipient bacteria. When a generalized transducing phage infects a recipient cell, expression of the transferred donor genes occurs. Typical phage that can mediate generalized transduction include P1 (*E. coli*) and P22 (*Salmonella*).

Not all phages are capable of transduction. This process occurs when

1. the phage degrades the bacterial chromosome.
2. the process of packaging DNA into the phage capsid not be specific for phage DNA.
3. the bacterial genes transferred by the bacteriophage recombine with the chromosome in the recipient cell.

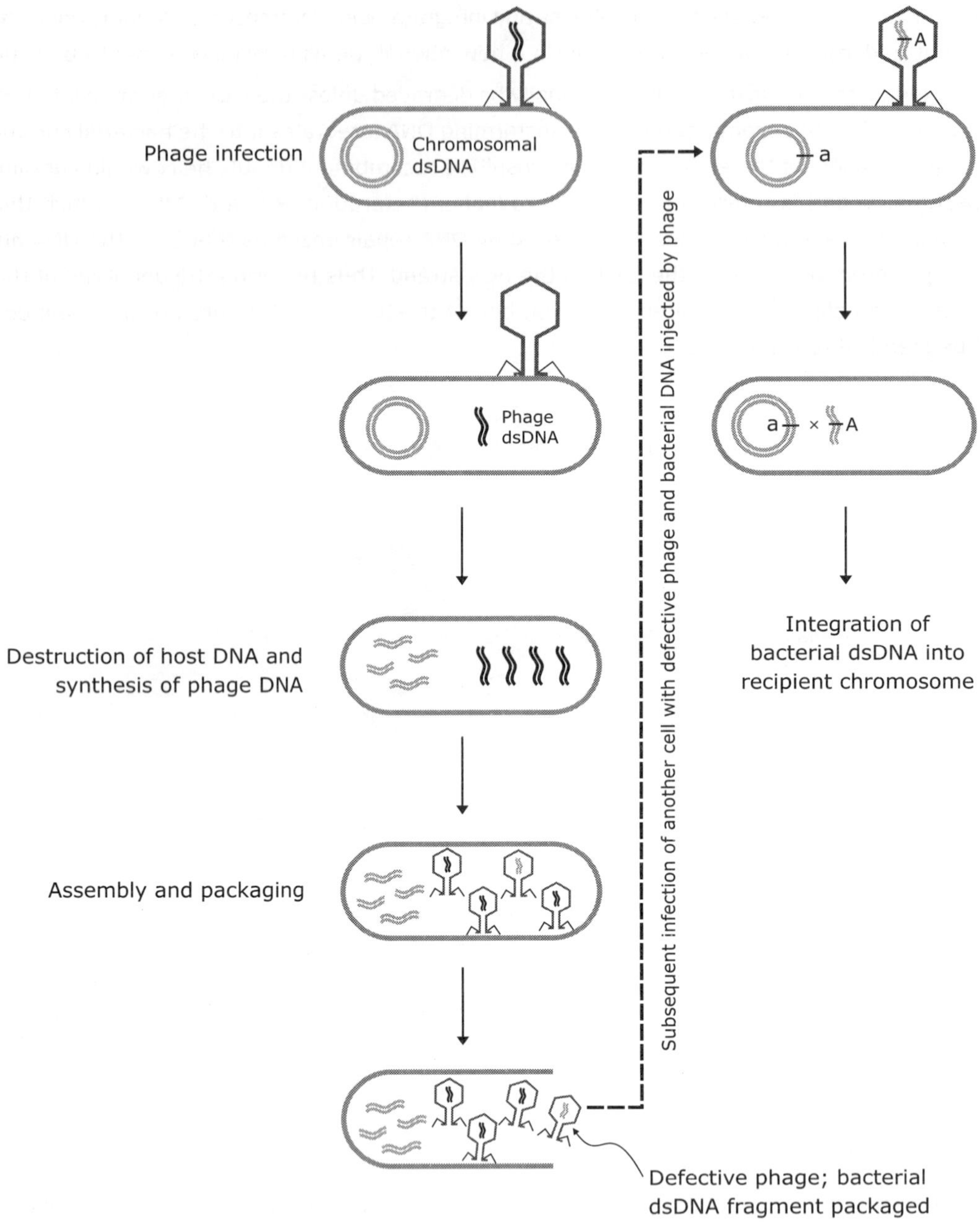

Figure 4.20 Generalized transduction. Bacteria are infected with phage. The bacterial chromosome is fragmented and some of the bacterial genes become incorporated into a few phages. Cell lysis releases transducing phages. If the phage transfers bacterial genes to another bacterium, recombination may take place and produce a transduced bacterial cell.

The generalized transduction may be **abortive** or **complete**. *Abortive transduction* refers to the transient expression of one or more donor genes without formation of recombinant progeny, whereas *complete transduction* is characterized by production of stable recombinants that inherit donor genes and retain the ability to express them. The DNA remains double-stranded during transfer and both strands are integrated into the endogenote. In abortive transduction, the donor DNA fragment does not integrate with endogenote and also not replicate, and among the progeny of the original transductant only one bacterium contains the donor DNA fragment. The frequency of abortive transduction is typically one to two orders of magnitude greater than the frequency of complete transduction, indicating that most cells infected by generalized transducing phages do not produce recombinant progeny.

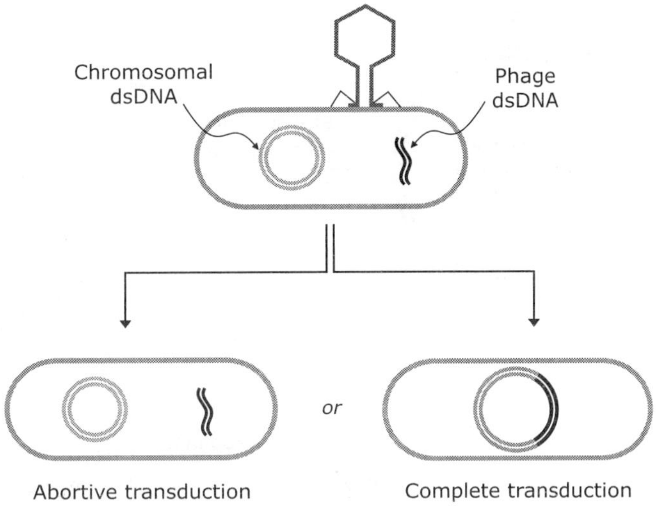

Figure 4.21 Complete and abortive transduction.

Specialized transduction differs from generalized transduction in several ways. It is mediated only by specific temperate phages, and only a few specific donor genes can be transferred to recipient bacteria. Specialized transducing phages are formed only when lysogenic donor bacteria enter the lytic cycle and release phage progeny. There are two distinguishing characteristics of specialized (*restricted*) transduction.

1. The only bacterial genes that can be transduced are those very near the site at which the prophage is integrated. For example, the only site at which lambda phage integrates into the host chromosome is between the genes for galactose fermentation (*gal*) and biotin synthesis (*bio*). So, if the prophage disintegrates abnormally from the host chromosome, only the *gal* or *bio* genes could be transduced.
2. It results from defective excision of the prophage from the host chromosome.

The specialized transducing phages contain both host and phage DNA linked in one single DNA molecule. They are rare recombinants which lack part of the normal phage genome and contain part of the bacterial chromosome located adjacent to the prophage attachment site.

Formation of the **λgal** and **λbio** transducing particles causes loss of some λ genes. λ*gal* particles lack the tail genes and sometimes head genes, both of which are located at the right end of the prophage; the λ*bio* particle lacks genes from the left end of the prophage (*int*, *xis*). The number of missing phage genes depends on the position of the cuts that generated the particle. The head and the tail genes are essential, so λ*gal* transducing particles are unable to perform lytic cycles and thus plaques. They are defective, and this is denoted **λdgal**. The genes missing in λ*bio* transducing particles are not essential for lytic growth, so λ*bio* phages are usually plaque forming and are called **λpbio**, in which the 'p' stands for plaque forming.

If λd*gal* transducing particles lack phage genes required to grow lytically, then how are they formed? The transducing particle is produced by aberrant excision from a normal prophage. The prophage contains all of the essential genes, and hence the necessary gene products (head and tail proteins) are still present in the chromosome. Initially producing the defective transducing particles is not a problem, but there is a deficiency of essential gene products when the transducing particle infects a new cell. If a bacterial cell is double infected with a wild type lambda phage and a λd*gal* phage, the wild-type phage can supply the functions missing in the defective phage and the progeny will contain about equal numbers of both types.

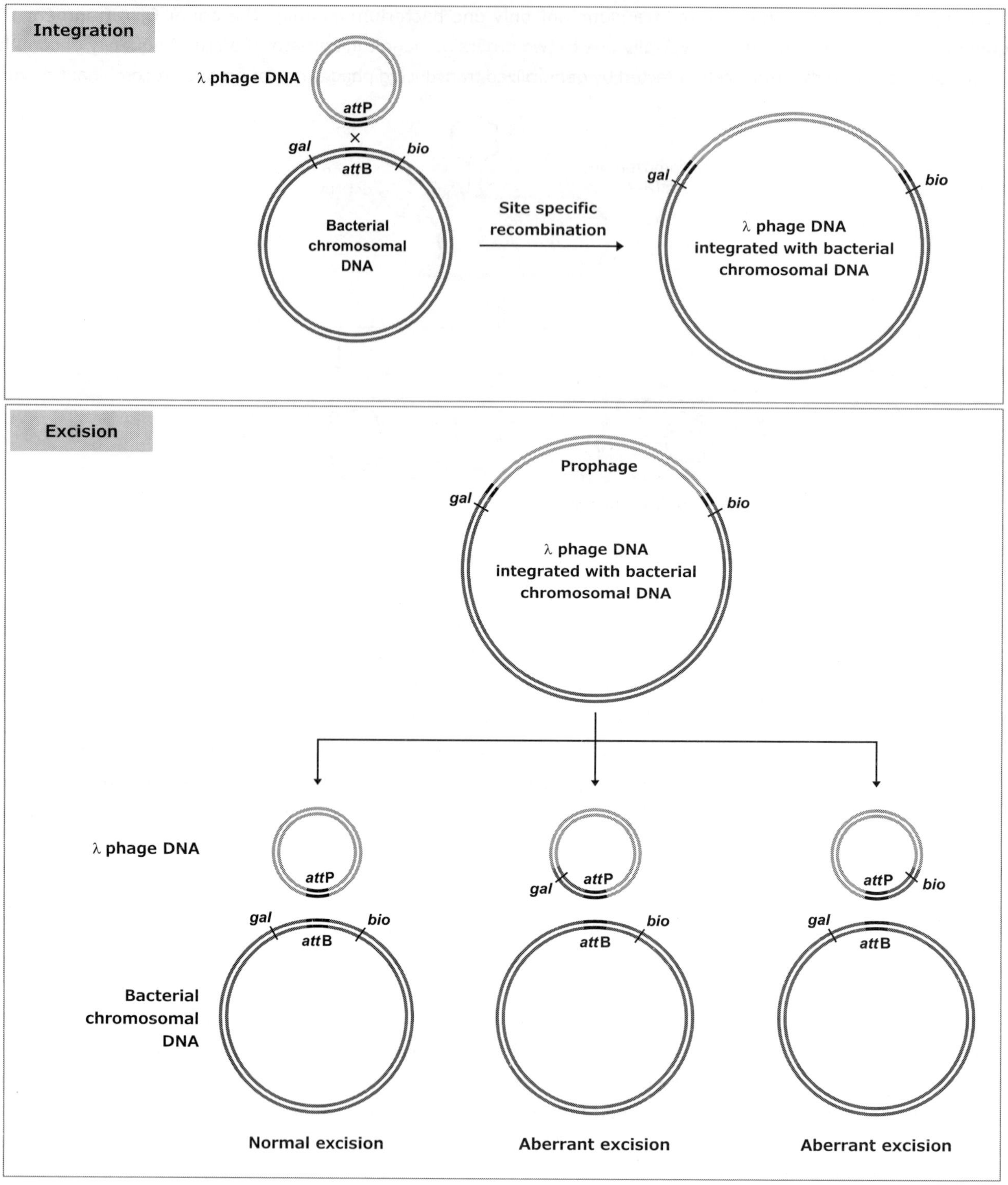

Figure 4.22 The production of defective lambda phage.

Specialized transducing phages are formed by aberrant excision of a lambda lysogen. This is a very rare event compared to the normal excision via recombination between *att*L and *att*R. When the aberrant excision initially occurs, it will yield less than one specialized transducing phage per 1,000,000 wild-type phage. Thus, this lysate is called a *low frequency transducing* (**LFT**) *lysate*. If this specialized transducing phage co-infects a new host together with a wild-type phage, a dilysogen can result. Induction of the dilysogen yields a lysate containing 50% specialized transducing phage and 50% wild-type phage. Thus, this lysate is called a *high frequency transducing* (**HFT**) *lysate*.

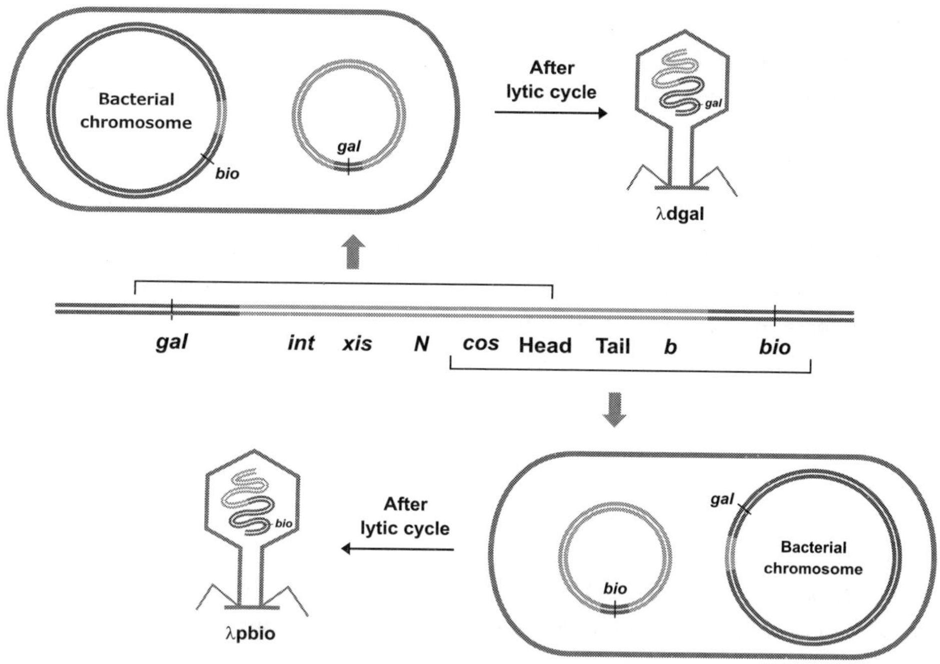

Figure 4.23 Aberrant excision leading to production of λdgal and λpbio phages.

Table 4.9 Comparison between generalized and specialized transduction

	Generalized transduction	Specialized transduction
1.	Occurs during the lytic cycle of virulent and temperate phage.	Occurs during the lysogenic cycle of temperate phage.
2.	Phages enter into lytic cycle.	Phages enter into lysogenic cycle.
3.	Viral DNA begins to replicate immediately the bacterial cytoplasm.	Viral DNA integrates into the DNA of the bacterium in and replicates later.
4.	Any bacterial genes are randomly packaged into new phage particles.	Bacterial genes adjacent to previously incorporated virus are packaged into new phage particles.
5.	Some new phages have no viral DNA.	Some new phages have both viral and bacterial DNA.
6.	Donor bacterial genes are incorporated into chromosome of new bacterium.	Donor bacterial genes are incorporated into chromosome of new bacterium together with genome of transducing phages.

4.5.3 Conjugation

In 1946, Joshua Lederberg and Edward Tatum showed that bacteria undergo conjugation, a process in which the genetic information from one bacteria is transferred to, and recombined with, that of other bacteria. In conjugation, direct contact between the donor and recipient bacteria leads to the establishment of a cytoplasmic bridge between them and transfer of a part or all of the donor genome to the recipient takes place. Donor ability is determined by the presence of **conjugative plasmids**. The best-studied conjugative plasmid is **F-plasmid**. Conjugative plasmids exist in both Gram-positive and Gram-negative bacteria. Although most research on conjugation has been done using *E. coli* and other Gram-negative bacteria, conjugation also occurs in Gram-positive bacteria. However, much less is known about conjugation in Gram-positive bacteria. A recipient cell that has received DNA as a result of conjugation is called **transconjugant**. Transfer of plasmids is generally *intraspecific*; however, many plasmids have a transfer system that enables them to transfer DNA between unrelated species. These are known as **promiscuous plasmids**.

F^+ – F^- conjugation

The F-plasmid (also called **F-factor**) of *E. coli* is the prototype for conjugative plasmids in Gram-negative bacteria. Strains of *E. coli* with an extrachromosomal F-plasmid are called F^+ and function as **donors**, whereas strains that lack the F-plasmid are F^- and behave as **recipients**. The conjugative functions of the F-plasmid are specified by a cluster of at least 25 *transfer* (*tra*) *genes* which determine the expression of sex pili, synthesis and transfer of DNA during mating, interference with the ability of F^+ bacteria to serve as recipients, and other functions.

The *tra* genes can be divided into two groups: Mpf genes (involved in mating-pair formation) and Dtr genes (involved in DNA transfer and replication). Mpf genes encode proteins responsible for the formation of **sex pilus** for cell-to-cell contact and type IV secretion system (**T4SS**) which act as a channel through which proteins or protein–DNA complexes can be translocated.

The sex pilus is used to establish contact between the F^+ and F^- cells. The F^+ cell prepares for DNA transfer by assembling a T4SS. *Dtr* genes encode proteins that bind to the plasmid DNA at the origin of transfer, *ori*T, forming a complex called **relaxosome**. The key catalytic component of the relaxosome is the enzyme **relaxase**. This enzyme produces a nick within *ori*T and becomes transiently attached to the 5′ end of the DNA single strand. One strand of the plasmid DNA is transferred in the 5′ to 3′ direction from donor to recipient. The transferred strand is converted to circular ds plasmid DNA in the recipient bacterium. Both of the exconjugant bacteria are F^+, and the F-plasmid can, therefore, spread by infection among genetically compatible populations of bacteria.

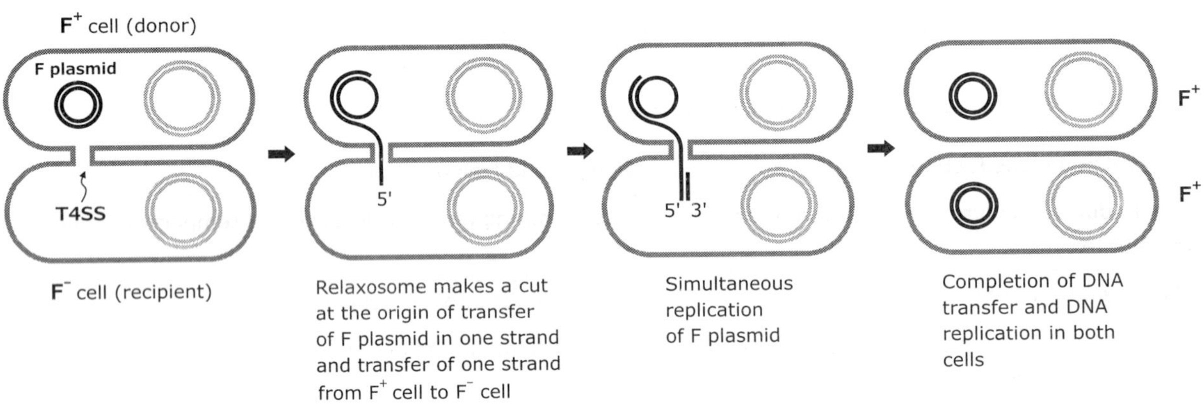

Figure 4.24 F^+–F^- conjugation. The F-plasmid encodes proteins for building the sex pilus and the type IV secretion system (T4SS). The sex pilus is used to establish contact between the F^+ and F^- cells. Once contact is made, the F^+ cell prepares for DNA transfer by assembling a T4SS. The F-plasmid replicates by rolling-circle replication. During conjugation, rolling-circle replication is initiated by a complex of proteins called the relaxosome, which are encoded by the F-plasmid. The relaxase nicks one strand of the F-plasmid at a site called *ori*T (for origin of transfer). During plasmid transfer, the entering strand is copied to produce dsDNA. When this is completed, the F^- recipient cell becomes F^+. During F^+–F^- conjugation, only the F-plasmid is transferred.

Hfr – F^- conjugation

The F-plasmid in *E. coli* can exist as an extrachromosomal genetic element or be integrated into the bacterial chromosome. An *E. coli* strain with an integrated F-plasmid retains its ability to function as a donor in conjugal matings. Because donor strains with integrated F-plasmids can transfer chromosomal genes to recipients with high efficiency, they are called **Hfr** (*high-frequency recombination*) strains. Transfer of single-stranded DNA from an Hfr donor to a recipient begins from the origin of transfer (*ori*T) within the F-plasmid and proceeds as described in the F^+-F^- conjugation, except that the transferred DNA is the hybrid replicon consisting of F-plasmid integrated into the bacterial chromosome.

In matings between F^+ and F^- bacteria, only the F-plasmid is transferred to recipients. In case of matings between Hfr and F^- strains, part of the F-plasmid is transferred last after the entire bacterial chromosome has been transferred. Because only a part of the F-plasmid is transferred at the start, the F^- does not become F^+ unless the whole chromosome is transferred. A complete transfer takes about 100 minutes in *E. coli*, and the conjugation usually breaks before this process is finished. Thus, a complete F-plasmid usually is not transferred, and the recipient remains F⁻. After the replicated donor chromosome enters the recipient cell, it may be degraded or incorporated into the F⁻ genome by recombination.

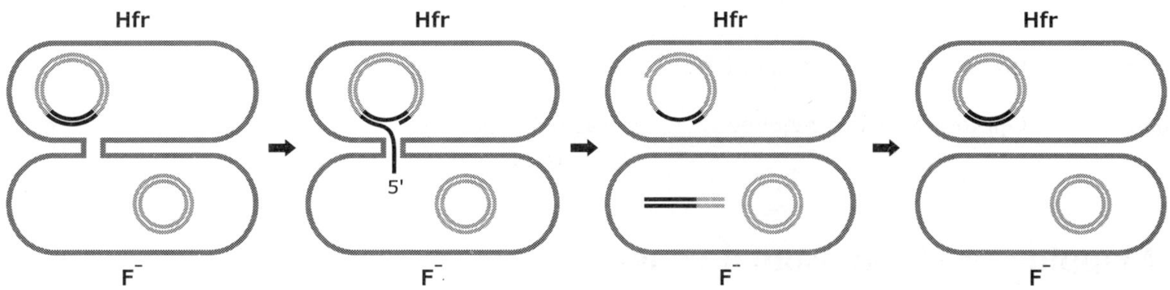

Figure 4.25 During conjugation between an Hfr cell and a F⁻ cell, only a part of the F-plasmid is transferred. Random breakage interrupts the transfer before the entire chromosome is transferred. The chromosomal fragment may be degraded or incorporated into the recipient genome by recombination.

F′ – F⁻ conjugation

Integrated F-plasmids in Hfr strains can sometimes be excised from the bacterial chromosome. If excision precisely reverses the integration process, F⁺ cells are produced. On rare occasions, however, excision occurs by recombinations involving insertion sequences or other genes on the bacterial chromosome that are located at some distance from the original integration site. In such cases, a segment of the bacterial chromosome becomes part of the F-plasmid. Because this erroneously excised plasmid is genotypically distinct from the original F-plasmid, it is called **F′-plasmid**. A cell containing F′-plasmid retains all of its chromosomal genes, although some of them are on the plasmid.

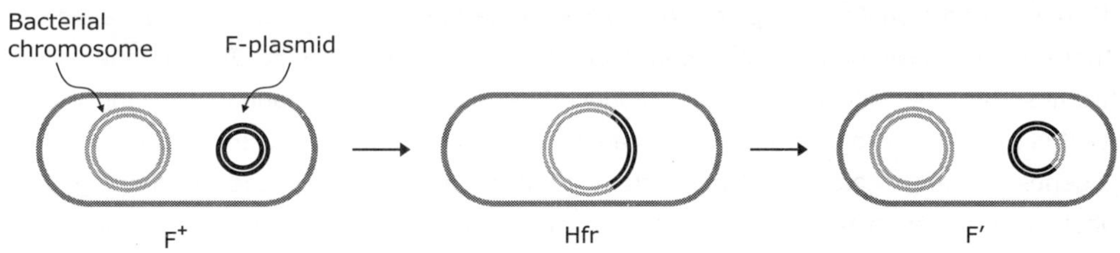

Figure 4.26 The F-plasmid is an episome and can integrate into the bacterial chromosome. However, this integration is reversible. It can leave the bacterial chromosome. When the F-plasmid leaves an Hfr chromosome, it occasionally picks up some bacterial genes to become an F′-plasmid.

F′– F⁻ conjugation is virtually identical with F⁺ – F⁻ conjugation. Bacterial genes on the F′-plasmid are transferred with it and need not be incorporated into the recipient chromosome to be expressed. The recipient becomes F′ and is a partially diploid merozygote since it has two sets of the genes carried by the plasmid. Such transfer of bacterial genes is often called **sex-duction.**

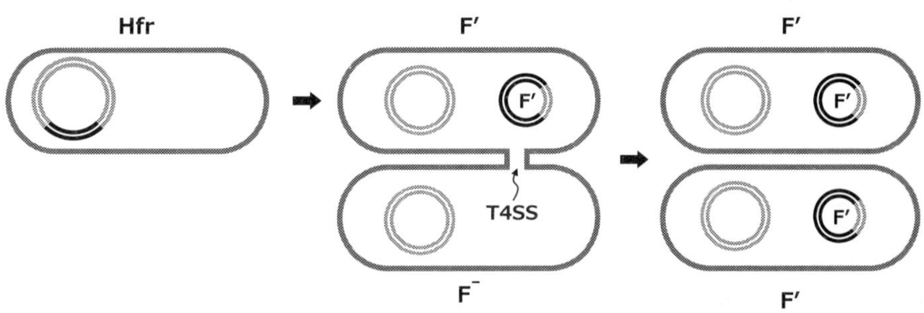

Figure 4.27 F′ conjugation occurs when an imprecise excision of the F factor from the chromosome of an Hfr cell results in the incorporation of a segment of chromosomal DNA into the F plasmid. The resulting F′ plasmid carries both fertility genes and host chromosomal genes. During conjugation, this F′ plasmid is transferred to an F⁻ recipient cell, thereby introducing the chromosomal segment along with the F factor.

Table 4.10 Comparison of mechanism of horizontal gene transfer

Mechanism	Main feature	Size of DNA transferred	Polarity	Sensitivity to DNase
Transformation	Naked DNA transferred	Part of the chromosome	No	Yes
Transduction	DNA enclosed in a phage capsid	Part of the chromosome	No	No
Conjugation	Cell-to-cell contact required	F-plasmid or part of chromosome and F-plasmid	Yes	No

4.6 Mapping of chromosomal genes

Genetic mapping is a method used to determine locations of genetic markers, order of genetic makers and distances between genetic markers. The strategy used for genetic mapping in bacteria differs from sexually reproducing eukaryotes because bacteria do not perform meiosis. In bacteria, during genetic mapping, we measure a double crossover between the homologous segment of DNA horizontally transferred from the donor bacterial cells and the DNA of recipient bacterial cells. The horizontal gene transfer is usually set up between a donor strain that possesses the wild-type alleles and a recipient with the recessive alleles, so that the transfer of genes into the recipient strain can be monitored by looking the acquisition of the biochemical function(s) specified by the genes being studied.

Mapping by transduction

During transduction, there is a maximum size of the DNA segment that can be packaged by bacteriophages. If two genes are close enough along the chromosome, a bacteriophage may package a single piece of the chromosome that carries both genes and transfer that piece to another bacterium. This phenomenon is called **co-transduction**. The likelihood that two genes will be co-transduced depends on how close they lie. If two genes are far apart along the bacterial chromosome, they will never be co-transduced because the bacteriophage cannot physically package a DNA fragment that is too large. The co-transduction can be used to map genes present in the bacterial chromosome. The mapping of genes by the process of co-transduction is based on the fact that the closer the genes to each other, greater the probability of their co-transduction. That is, the frequency of co-transduction is inversely proportional to the distance between two genes. A mathematical formula (proposed by Wu) is used to relate co-transduction frequencies to map distance:

$$C = \left[\frac{1-d}{L}\right]^3$$

Where, C is the co-transduction frequency,

d is the distance in minutes between two genes,

L is the size of the transducing fragment in minutes.

Closer the two genes →	Greater chance that both will be present on same DNA fragment →	Packaged in a single transducing particle →	Higher frequency of co-transduction

Conclusion: Transduction mapping is similar to transformation mapping. Small fragments of DNA are carried by the phage from donor to recipient bacteria, and the frequencies of co-transduction, like the frequencies of co-transformation, provide information about the relative distances between the genes. Genes located close to one another are more likely to be co-transduced; so the frequency of co-transduction is inversely proportional to the distances between genes.

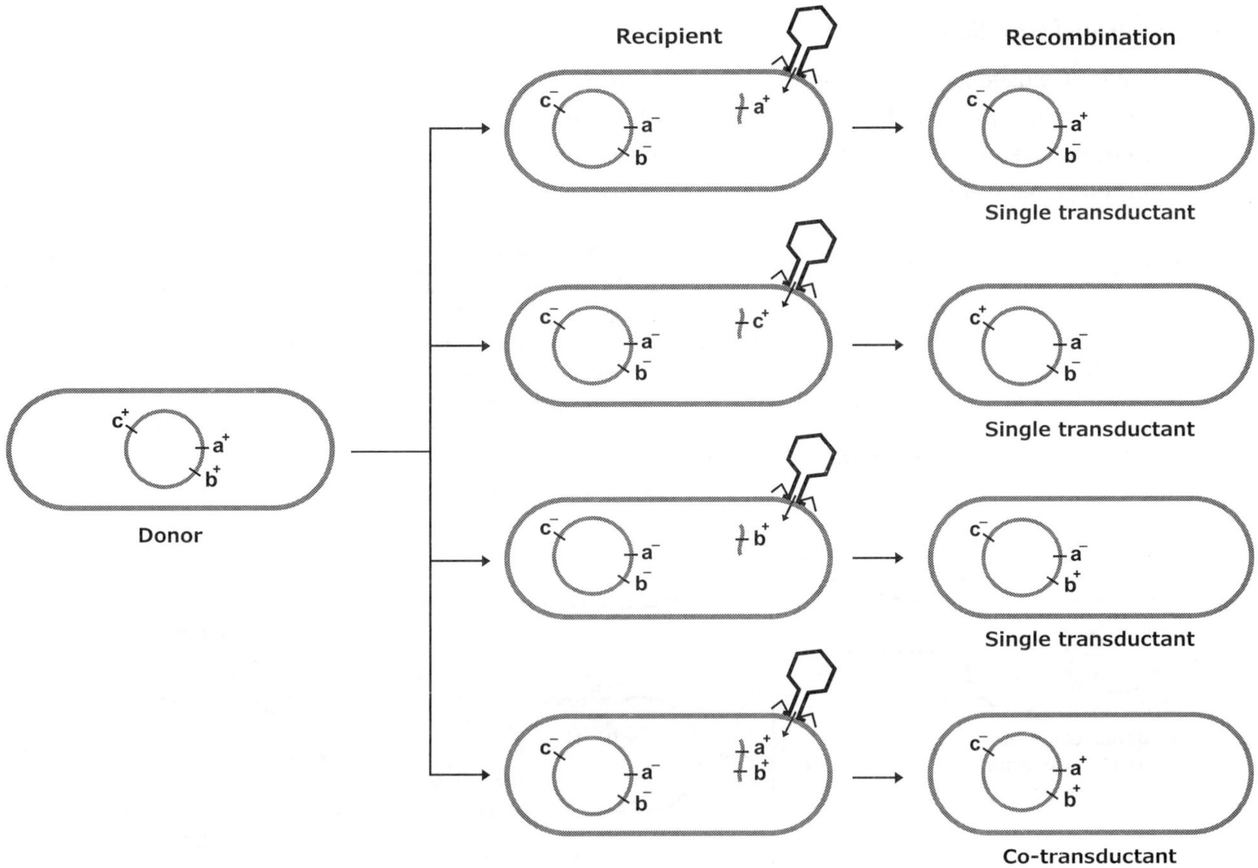

Figure 4.28 If two genes are close to one another along the bacterial chromosome, they can be transduced simultaneously (co-transduction). As shown in the figure, gene a and b are very close, so there is a high chance to be present in the same fragment and thus have high co-transduction frequency. The frequency of co-transduction is inversely proportional to the map distance between the two genes.

Problem

A co-transduction experiment was performed to decipher the linear order of four genes: a, b, c and d. Three sets of experiments were done where transductants were selected for a (set-1) or b (set-2) or c (set-3) and screened for co-transduction of the other markers.

Set-1			Set-2			Set-3		
Selected for	Co-transduction	Frequency	Selected for	Co-transduction	Frequency	Selected for	Co-transduction	Frequency
a	b	31	b	a	22	c	a	0
a	c	3	b	c	78	c	b	69
a	d	89	b	d	68	c	d	43

Based on the frequencies shown above, what will be the most likely order of genes in the genome.

Solution: The correct order of genes is a – d – b – c. This is based on the principle that the closer two genes are on a chromosome, the higher the probability that they will be cotransduced together during generalized transduction. Conversely, as the distance between genes increases, the likelihood of cotransduction decreases, since larger fragments of DNA are less likely to be packaged into a single transducing phage particle.

Mapping by transformation

Transformation is also used for gene mapping. Mapping by transformation experiments is based on the principle that two genes co-transform together if they are near enough to be carried on the same DNA fragment. The closer the genes to each other, greater the probability of their **co-transformation**. That is, the frequency of co-transformation is inversely proportional to the distance between two genes.

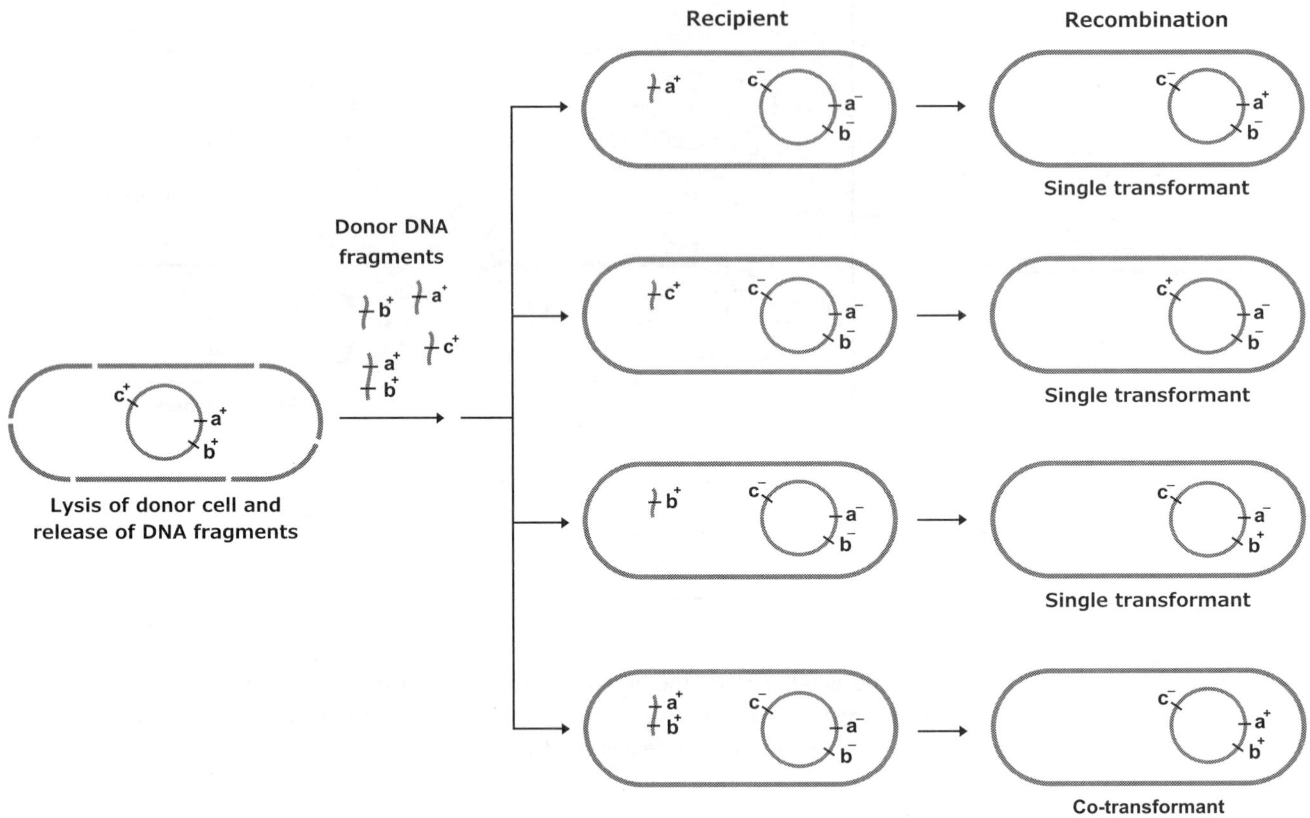

Figure 4.29 Co-transformation is the probability of simultaneous transformation of two genes. It can occur for two genes near each other. The frequency of co-transformation is inversely proportional to the distance between two genes.

Mapping by conjugation: Interrupted mating experiment

Mapping of chromosomal genes by conjugation is performed by *interrupted mating experiment* introduced by E. Wollman and F. Jacob. Conjugation between different Hfr and F^- strains can be used to map the relative positions of genes in the bacterial chromosome. The mapping procedure is based on the fact that genes closer to the origin of transfer will be transferred at a higher frequency than genes farther away from the origin of transfer.

In an **interrupted mating experiment**, Hfr and F^- strains with suitable marker genes are mixed and assessed the recombination of specific genes at different times. To accomplish this, a culture containing a mixture of Hfr and F^- strain are incubated, samples are removed at various intervals and each is placed in an agitating kitchen blender. Agitation in blender separates the conjugating bacteria and thus transfer of DNA. To assay the cells for genetic recombination following the blender treatment, they are grown on medium containing antibiotic in order to ensure the recovery of only recipient cells.

The rationale behind interrupted mating mapping strategy is that the time it takes for genes to enter a recipient cell is directly related to their order along the bacterial chromosome. In this mapping strategy, it was hypothesized that the chromosome of the donor strain in an Hfr mating is transferred in a *linear manner* to the recipient strain. The order of genes along the chromosome can be deduced by determining the time it takes various genes to enter the recipient strain. Thus, the interruptions of mating between Hfr and F^- at different times would lead to various lengths of the Hfr chromosome being transferred to the F^- recipient cell. If two bacterial cells had mated for a short period of time, only a small segment of the Hfr chromosome would be transferred to the recipient bacterium. However, if the bacterial cells are allowed to mate for a longer period of time before being interrupted, a longer segment of the Hfr chromosome could be transferred. Hence by determining which genes were transferred during the short mating and which required longer mating times, the order of genes can be deduced. The transfer begins from oriT of the integrated F-plasmid. The F-plasmid may be inserted in either orientation. Consequently, gene transfer may be either *clockwise* or *anticlockwise* for any particular Hfr strain.

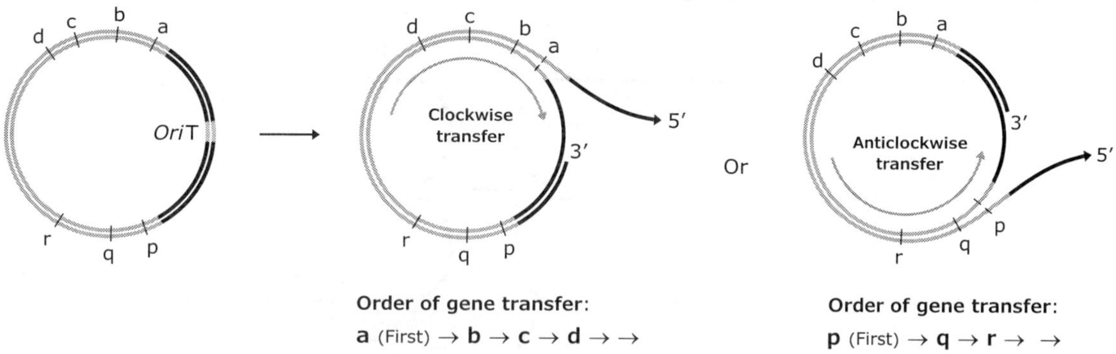

Figure 4.30 Genes closest to the site of plasmid integration are transferred first. First, a single-stranded nick is made at the *ori*T of the integrated plasmid. The free 5′ end enters the recipient cell through the conjugation bridge. The transfer of the ssDNA does not end with the F-plasmid DNA and continues into the chromosomal DNA. Genes closest to the site of plasmid integration are transferred first and transfer may be clockwise or anticlockwise.

When Hfr chromosome is transferred to the F^- cell, the transfer begins from a specific point at the integrated F-plasmid, called the *ori*T. The farther a gene is from the origin of transfer, the later it is transferred to the F^-. Since different Hfr-strains have their F-plasmids inserted at different sites on the bacterial chromosome, transfer of chromosomal genes begins at different points.

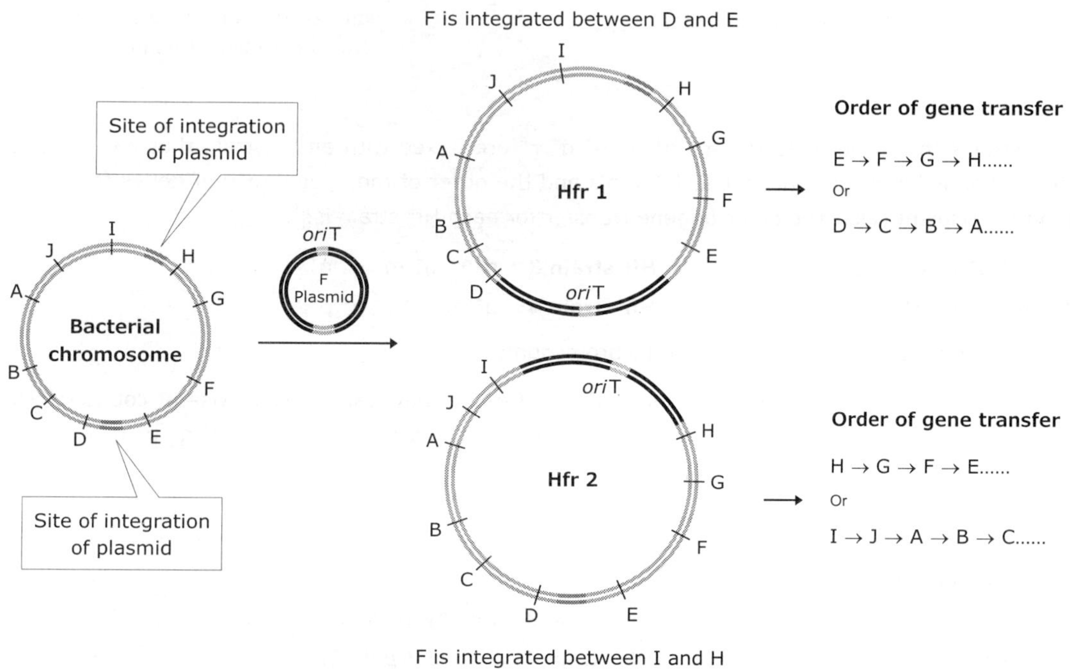

Figure 4.31 Manner of formation of different Hfr strains, which donate genes in different orders and from different origins.

The following example can illustrate how three genes (*leu*, *lac* and *gal*) can be mapped by Hfr interrupted mating. The Hfr donor is wild type for each (leu^+, lac^+ and gal^+), whereas the recipient is leu^-, lac^- and gal^- meaning it requires external supply of leucine, lactose and galactose to grow. In addition, the Hfr is streptomycin sensitive (str^S) while the recipient is resistant to this antibiotic (str^R). After mixing donor and recipient cells (t=0), aliquots of the mating mixture are removed at different time intervals and mating pairs disrupted in a Waring blender. To kill all the Hfr cells, the cell suspension is plated on a medium containing streptomycin. The remaining cells are then plated on medium without leucine. The only colonies that have received the *leu* allele from the Hfr will grow on a medium lacking leucine. In a similar way, different types of media are used to select colonies that have received the *lac* allele or *gal* allele. The order and timing of gene transfer can be determined because they are a direct reflection of the order of genes on the bacterial chromosome.

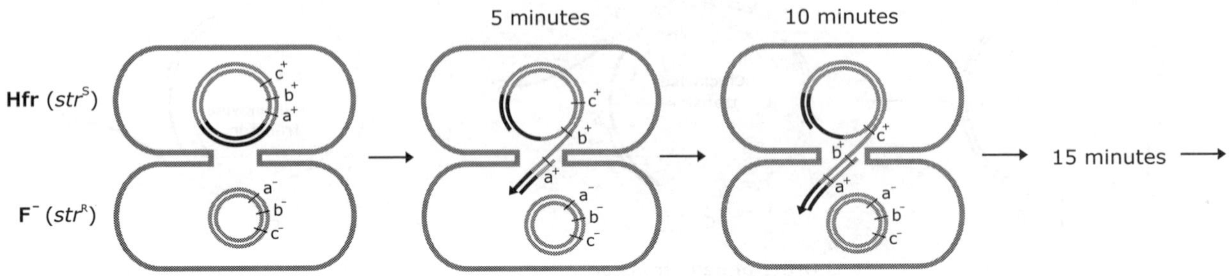

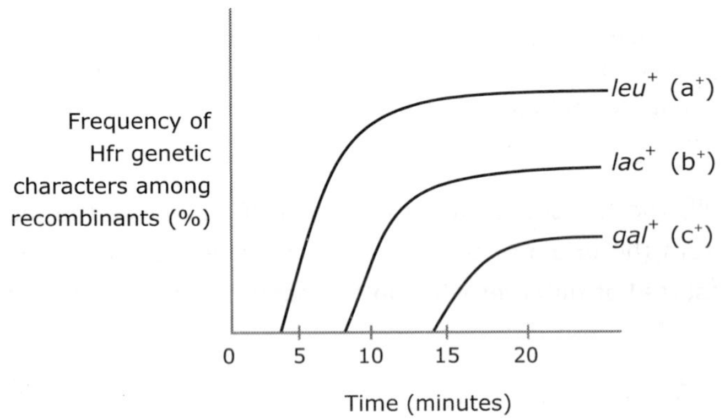

Figure 4.32
Mapping by interrupted mating. The linear transfer of genes is stopped by breaking the conjugation bridge to study the sequence of gene entry into the recipient cell. The entering strand recombines with the resident chromosome, replacing the mutant alleles (leu^-, lac^-, gal^-) with wild-type counter-parts, and recombinants are selected by plating on medium with streptomycin (to stop growth of donors).

Problem

A series of Hfr strains that have genotype m^+ n^+ o^+ p^+ q^+ r^+ are mixed with an F^- strain that has genotype m^- n^- o^- p^- q^- r^-. Conjugation is interrupted at regular intervals and the order of the appearance of genes from the Hfr strain is determined in the recipient cells. The order of gene transfer for each Hfr strain is:

Hfr strain 1 m^+ q^+ p^+ n^+ r^+ o^+

Hfr strain 2 o^+ m^+ q^+ p^+ n^+ r^+

Hfr strain 3 n^+ r^+ o^+ m^+ q^+ p^+

Hfr strain 4 q^+ m^+ o^+ r^+ n^+ p^+

What is the order of genes on the circular bacterial chromosome?

Solution: Each Hfr strain starts at a different origin of transfer and may transfer clockwise or counterclockwise around the circular chromosome. The overlaps help reveal the true order. The order of genes is m^+ q^+ p^+ n^+ r^+ o^+.

Problem

Several Hfr strains are mated with an auxotrophic F⁻ strain by the interrupted mating technique. The order of transfer for the loci are given in the table.

Hfr strain 1 *thr lip trp his thy*

Hfr strain 2 *str thy his trp lip*

Hfr strain 3 *his thy str ilv thr*

Hfr strain 4 *thy his trp lip thr*

What is the order of the loci on the chromosome?

Solution: Each Hfr strain begins transferring from a different origin of transfer and can move in either clockwise or counter-clockwise orientation. By overlapping the sequences, we can reconstruct the circular chromosomal gene order:
thr-lip-trp-his-thy-str-ilv

4.7 Bacterial taxonomy

Taxonomy is the science of classification, identification and nomenclature. In the process of classification (orderly arrangement of organisms into groups), organisms are usually organized into species, genera, families, order, class, phylum and domain. The highest taxonomic rank is called a *domain*. All prokaryotic organisms are placed within two domains, *archaea* and *bacteria*.

Taxonomic ranks	Example
Domain	Bacteria
Phylum	Proteobacteria
Class	Alphaproteobacteria
Order	Legionellales
Family	Legionellaceae
Genus	*Legionella*
Species	*pneumophila*

Note: According to the first edition of Bergey's Manual of Systematic Bacteriology, *a strain is made up of the descendants of a single isolation in pure culture and usually is made up of a succession of cultures ultimately derived from an initial single colony*. This is a rather standard definition of the strain as the basic operational unit in bacteriology. However, we can also define '*strain as an isolate or group of isolates that can be distinguished from other isolates of the same genus and species by phenotypic characteristics or genotypic characteristics or both'*.

Concept of species

The basic taxonomic unit is the *species*. Each species is assigned to a *genus*, the next rank in the taxonomic hierarchy. For eukaryotes, the definition of 'a species typically considers the ability of members of the same species to interbreed (reproduce sexually with the formation of a zygote) and produce fertile offspring'. However, since bacteria do not undergo **sexual reproduction** in the same way as eukaryotic organisms, other criteria or approaches are used to define a bacterial species.

Approximately 4000 bacterial species have been described till now. Classifying bacteria requires knowledge of their morphological, biochemical, physiological, and genetic characteristics. Due to the absence of sexual reproduction, the limited range of extensive morphological features, and the lack of a fossil record in bacteria, classification based on the phenetic system has always been considered limited. The **phenetic system** of classification relies on measuring overall similarity based on all available characteristics without assigning any weighting to specific traits.

It has long been recognized that the most accurate basis for classification is phylogenetic. **Phylogenetic classification systems** are based on evolutionary relationships. One major constraint in the development of the phylogenetic system in bacteria is the lack of fossil record. But the comparison of genetic materials and gene products have overcome these problems. The total DNA of one bacterium can be compared with that of any other bacterium. Five factors can be used to determine DNA relatedness:

- Genome size
- G+C content
- DNA relatedness under conditions optimal for DNA-DNA hybridization,
- Thermal stability of related DNA sequences and
- DNA relatedness under conditions supraoptimal for DNA-DNA hybridization

Bacteriologists define a bacterial species based on genomic similarities between strains. According to this definition, two strains belong to the same species if they have a similar G+C content. The G+C content in bacterial DNA ranges from approximately 25 to 75 percent. While this percentage is specific to a species, it is not exclusive; two strains with similar G+C content may or may not be the same species. However, if the G+C contents are significantly different, the strains cannot be members of the same species. Although G+C content provides important information, it does not reveal the linear arrangement of the bases in the DNA. The linear arrangement of the bases can be compared using the method of DNA-DNA hybridization.

DNA relatedness by the method of DNA-DNA hybridization is determined by allowing single-stranded DNA from one strain to reassociate with complementary single-stranded DNA from a second strain, to form a double-stranded DNA molecule. This is a specific, temperature-dependent reaction. A number of different DNA–DNA hybridization methods have been used to determine relatedness among bacteria. Experience with thousands of strains from several hundred well-established and new species led taxonomists to formulate a phylogenetic definition of a species (**genomospecies**) as 'strains with approximately 70% or greater DNA–DNA relatedness and with 5°C or less ΔT_m. Both values must be considered'. According to Stackebrandt and Goebel (1994), the genetic definition of 70% relatedness with 5% or less divergence within related sequences continues to be the best means of creating species. They also concluded that 16S rRNA sequence similarity of less than 97% between strains indicates that they represent different species, but at 97% or higher 16S rRNA sequence similarity, DNA relatedness by using DNA-DNA hybridization must be used to determine whether strains belong to different species.

4.8 General features of important bacterial groups

Rickettsias and Chlamydiae

Rickettsias are Gram-negative bacteria. They are non-motile, obligate intracellular parasites (grow and reproduce within host cells). Rickettsias are named after their discoverer, the American pathologist Harold Taylor Ricketts. *Rickettsia* species live in vertebrates and are transmitted by blood-sucking arthropods such as fleas, ticks, lice, and mites. Rickettsias are causative agents of several human diseases including typhus fever (*R. typhi*), Rocky Mountain spotted fever, and Q fever (*Coxiella burnetii*).

Chlamydiae, like the *Rickettsias*, are obligate intracellular non-motile Gram-negative bacteria. Phylum *Chlamydiae* has one class, one order, four families and six genera. Among six genera, genus *Chlamydia* is best studied. Chlamydial cells are unable to carry out energy metabolism and lack many biosynthetic pathways; therefore, they are entirely dependent on the host cell to supply them with ATP and other intermediates. Because of their dependence on host biosynthetic machinery, the chlamydiae were originally thought to be viruses; however, they have a cell wall and contain DNA, RNA, and ribosomes and therefore are now classified as bacteria. Chlamydial cells reproduce within the cytoplasmic vacuoles of host cells by a life cycle involving two stages:

1. Infectious particles called *elementary bodies* and
2. Intracytoplasmic, reproductive forms called *reticulate bodies*.

Difference between elementary body and reticulate body

Characteristic	Elementary body	Reticulate body
Size	0.2–0.3 microns	0.5–1 micron
Morphology	Electron dense core; rigid	Fragile, pleomorphic
Infectivity to host	Infectious	Non-infectious
Metabolic activity	Relatively inactive	Active
Adaptation	For extracellular survival	For intracellular survival
Trypsin digestion	Resistant	Sensitive

Table 4.11 Comparison of typical bacterial, rickettsias/chlamydias and virus

	Typical bacteria	Virus	Rickettsias/Chlamydias
Intracellular parasite	No	Yes	Yes
Binary fission	Yes	No	Yes
DNA and RNA	Both	DNA or RNA	Both
Ribosomes	Yes	No	Yes
Sensitive to antibiotics	Yes	No	Yes
Sensitive to interferon	No	Yes	No

Actinomycetes

Actinomycetes are aerobic, Gram-positive, mold-like bacteria that form branched, septate hyphae and asexual spores. The thin walled asexual spores are *conidiospores* or conidia (located at the tip of hyphae) and *sporangiospores* (located in a sporangium). Classification of actinomycetes is primarily based on the properties like conidia arrangement, the presence or absence of the sporangium, cell wall type. Most actinomycetes are nonmotile. When motility is present, it is confined to flagellated spores only.

Streptomyces is the largest genus of actinomycetes. Members of the genus are strict aerobes, mostly non-pathogenic saprophytes and bear the chains of nonmotile conidia. The natural habitat of most streptomycetes is the soil. In fact, the odor of moist soil is largely due to the production of volatile substances such as **geosmin** from streptomycetes. Streptomycetes are best known for their synthesis of a vast array of antibiotics like amphotericin B, chloramphenicol, erythromycin, neomycin, nystatin, streptomycin and tetracycline.

Spirochetes

Spirochetes are a group of Gram-negative, chemoheterotrophic bacteria. They are slender, long organisms with a flexible, helical shaped. Spirochetes lack external rotating flagella. They exhibit creeping or crawling movements. Their unique pattern of motility is due to an unusual morphological structure called the **axial filament** (or **periplasmic flagella**). The central *protoplasmic cylinder*, which contains cytoplasm and the nucleoid, is bounded by a plasma membrane and Gram-negative type cell wall. Two or more than a hundred prokaryotic flagella, called *axial filaments*, extend from both ends of the cylinder often overlap. The whole complex of periplasmic flagella lies inside a flexible outer membrane. The outer membrane contains lipid, protein and carbohydrate. *Treponema pallidum* (causes **syphilis**) and *Borrelia burgdorferi* (responsible for **Lyme disease**) are examples of spirochetes.

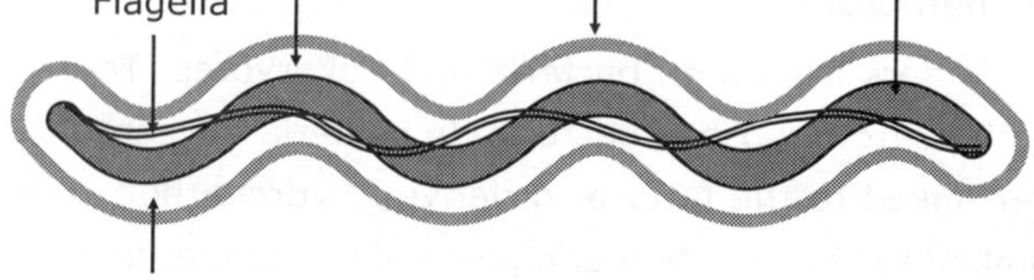

Figure 4.33 The most peculiar feature of spirochetes may be the location of their flagella. Flagella present in the periplasmic space between the plasma membrane and outer membranes. *Spirochete Borrelia burgdorferi* has 7-11 flagella attached near each end of the 'protoplasmic' or cell cylinder, with each flagellum extending through the periplasm towards the center of the spirochete.

Mycoplasmas

Mycoplasmas are the smallest and simplest self-reproducing Gram-negative bacteria. Mycoplasmas lack cell walls and thus placed in a separate class *Mollicutes* (*mollis, soft*; *cutis, skin*). Formerly, Mycoplasmas were called *pleuropneumonia-like organisms* (PPLO) because it was first isolated from cattle suffering from pleuropneumonia. The trivial term *mollicutes* is frequently used as a general term to describe any member of the class, replacing in this respect the older term mycoplasmas. Mycoplasmas are pleomorphic (vary in shape) and mostly non-motile. General metabolic nature is chemoorganoheterotrophic and require cholesterol for growth. They can be saprophytes or parasites and usually facultative anaerobes. Characteristically, mycoplasmas growing on solid media produce *fried egg* colonies with a central dense region surrounded by a lighter peripheral zone.

Cyanobacteria

Cyanobacteria are ubiquitous Gram-negative bacteria. They are oxygenic photosynthetic and obligate photolitho-autotrophs. Photosynthetic pigments present in cyanobacteria are Chl *a* (in very few cases Chl *b* and Chl *d*), carotenoids and phycobilins (phycocyanin and phycoerythrin). Cyanobacteria vary greatly in shape and appearance.

Both unicellular and filamentous (termed **trichome**) forms of cyanobacteria occur in nature. Filamentous forms may be unbranched or branched. All cyanobacteria known to date, except *Gloeobacter violaceus*, have an internal system of thylakoid membranes in which the light reactions of photosynthesis and respiration occur. Besides the thylakoid membranes, the cyanobacterial cytosol contains components such as carboxysomes, glycogen granules, cyanophycin granules, polyphosphate bodies, lipid bodies and polyhydroxybutyrate granules.

Cyanobacteria reproduce by binary fission, budding and multiple fission. Among the filamentous cyanobacteria fragmentation of filaments form motile **hormogonia**. In some species, resting spores or **akinetes** are formed, which protect the organism during unfavourable periods. Cyanobacteria lack the enzyme *α-ketoglutarate dehydrogenase*, thus, they do not have a fully functional citric acid cycle. Many nitrogen-fixing cyanobacteria form **heterocysts**, which are specialized cells in which nitrogen fixation occurs.

4.9 Archaebacteria

Members of domain archaea are distinguished from bacteria by many features, most notably their distinctive oligonucleotide signature sequences present in small subunit rRNAs (**16S rRNA**). Archaea are highly diverse with respect to morphology, physiology and ecology. Archaeal species may be Gram-positive or Gram-negative based on their response to Gram staining. They can be spherical, rod shaped, spiral and other. They can be aerobic or anaerobic and facultative or obligate. Archaea are very similar to bacteria (or eubacteria) with respect to cellular organization and metabolic processes. The similarity in cellular organization includes cell size, absence of nucleus, absence of unit membrane-bound organelles, circular organization of their genomes, presence of 70S ribosomes, etc. Apart from structural similarities most of the metabolic pathways are common between archaea and bacteria. However, archaea are very different from bacteria with respect to features associated with information transfer such as DNA replication, transcription and translation.

Archaeal cell wall and plasma membrane

The archaeal plasma membrane differs from both bacteria and eukaryotes. There are several important features where the archaeal membrane differs from those of bacteria. In bacteria, glycerophospholipid is consists of **glycerol-3-phosphate** (G3P) that is **ester linked** to the fatty acid derived hydrocarbon chains. In archaea, the isoprenoid hydrocarbon chains are **ether linked** to the enantiomeric glycerol backbone, **glycerol-1-phosphate** (G1P).

Archaeal plasma membrane may consist of either **diphytanyl glycerol diethers** (also known as *archaeol*), which have 20-carbon isoprenoid structure (called **phytanyl**) or **dibiphytanyl diglycerol tetraether** (also known as *glycerol dibiphytanyl glycerol tetraether*), which have 40-carbon isoprenoid structure (called **biphytanyl**). Membrane structure may be bilayer or monolayer. When glycerol diethers are used, a typical bilayer membrane is formed. The diglycerol tetraethers forms a lipid monolayer instead of a lipid bilayer. In contrast to lipid bilayers, lipid monolayer membranes are extremely resistant to heat and are therefore widely distributed among hyperthermophilic archaea, organisms that grow best at temperatures above 80°C.

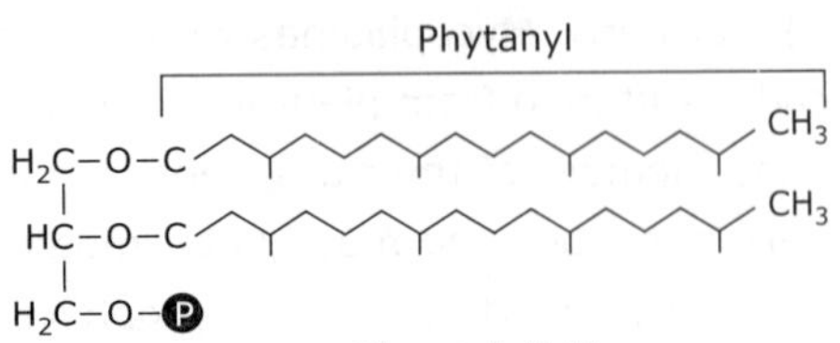

Glycerol diether

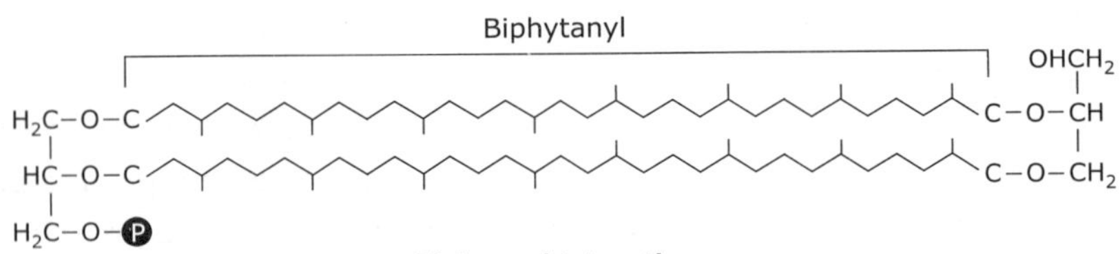

Diglycerol tetraether

Archaeal **cell walls** display chemical diversity. Chemically cell wall may be polysaccharides, proteins, glycoproteins and others but not peptidoglycan. Some archaea lack a cell wall altogether. The most common type of archaeal cell wall is an **S-layer** composed of either glycoprotein or protein. In some archaea, the S-layer is the outermost layer and is separated from the plasma membrane by a peptidoglycan-like molecule called **pseudomurein** (also known as **pseudopeptidoglycan**). Archaea lack peptidoglycan whereas the cell wall of bacteria is chemically peptidoglycan.

Pseudomurein is a heteropolysaccharide consists of repeating disaccharide units. The disaccharide unit is made up of *N*-acetyltalosaminuronic acid and *N*-acetylglucosamine linked with a β-1,3 glycosidic bond. Bacterial peptidoglycan (or murein) is also a heteropolysaccharide but made up of repeating disaccharide consisting of *N*-acetylmuramic acid and *N*-acetylglucosamine linked with a β-1,4 glycosidic bond. Bacterial peptidoglycan cell wall has both L- and D-amino acids in its cross-links but archaeal pseudomurein has L-amino acids only in cross-links. As a result of these differences, lysozyme, penicillin, and other chemicals that affect bacterial cell wall structure and synthesis have no effect on archaeal cell walls.

Table 4.12 Comparison between bacteria and archaea

Property	**Bacteria** (*Eubacteria*)	**Archaea** (*Archaebacteria*)
Nucleus	Absent	Absent
Unit membrane-bound organelles	Absent	Absent
Cell Wall	Peptidoglycan	Variety of types, no peptidoglycan
Membrane lipid	Have ester-linked, straight-chained fatty acid	Have ether-linked, branched aliphatic chains
tRNA	Thymine present, *N*-formylmethionine carried by initiator tRNA	No thymine in TψC arm, Methionine carried by initiator tRNA
Ribosomes		
Elongation factor 2	Does not react with diphtheria toxin	React with diphtheria toxin
Sensitivity to chloramphenicol	Sensitive	Insensitive
Sensitivity to anisomycin	Insensitive	Sensitive
DNA-dependent RNA polymerase		
Number of enzymes	One	Several
Rifampicin sensitivity	Sensitive	Insensitive
Polymerase II type promoters	Absent	Present
Metabolism		
Methanogenesis	Absent	Present
Chlorophyll-based photosynthesis	Present	Absent

Major groups of archaea

There are three major known groups of archaea based on the nature of habitats occupy and metabolic patterns– methanogens, extreme halophiles and thermophiles. Since most archaeal groups are found under extreme environmental conditions, they are known as **extremophiles**.

Methanogens: Methanogens are obligate anaerobes and produce methane as an end-product by combining hydrogen with carbon. There are no known bacterial methanogens. Methanogens comprise the largest group of archaea.

Extreme halophiles: Extreme halophiles are aerobic chemoorganoheterotrophs. The most distinguishing trait is its absolute dependence on a high salt concentration (require at least 1.5 M NaCl for growth). Thus they only grow in high-salinity habitats. The best-studied member of this group is *Halobacterium salinarum*. *H. salinarum* can carry out photosynthesis without chlorophyll or bacteriochlorophyll by using *bacteriorhodopsin* (now termed *archaerhodopsin*).

Thermophiles: Thermophiles are heat-loving archaea found near hydrothermal vents and hot springs. The optimum growth temperature is between 70–110°C. They are Gram-negative and usually strict anaerobes. Most of the members are sulphate metabolizers and may be autotrophic or heterotrophic.

4.10 Bacterial toxins

A **toxin** (Latin *toxicum, poison*) is a specific substance, often a metabolic product of the organism that damages the host. Toxins can even induce disease in the absence of the organism that produced them. Diseases that result from the entrance of a specific toxin into the body of a host is called **intoxication**. The term 'toxemia' refers to the condition caused by toxins that have entered the host's body. Toxins produced by bacteria can be divided into two main categories: **exotoxins** and **endotoxins.**

Table 4.13 Main features of exotoxins and endotoxins

Property	Exotoxin	Endotoxin
Source	Some species of Gram-positive and Gram-negative bacteria	Lipopolysaccharide of most Gram-negative bacteria
Secreted from cell	Yes	No
Chemical nature	Polypeptide	Lipopolysaccharide
Location of genes	Plasmid or prophage or chromosome	Bacterial chromosome
Toxicity	High	Low
Immunogenicity	High	Low
Vaccines	Toxoids used as vaccines	No toxoids formed
Heat stability	Heat labile, inactivated rapidly at 60 to 80°C	Heat stable

Types of exotoxin

Exotoxins can be divided into different categories based on their structure and physiological activities. The exotoxin can also be categorized on the basis of the site affected: **neurotoxins** (nerve tissue), **enterotoxins** (intestinal mucosa), and **cytotoxins** (general tissues). Based on the mode of action on target cells exotoxins can further divided into following three categories:

Toxins that act from the cell surface

Toxins that act from the cell surface bind to a receptor on the cell surface and stimulate intracellular signaling pathways. One common example is superantigen. Superantigens are produced by several bacteria. The best characterized superantigens are those produced by the strains of *Staphylococcus aureus* and *Streptococcus pyogenes* that cause toxic shock syndrome. Superantigens bridge the class II MHC protein on antigen presenting cells with the T cell receptor on the surface of T cells. Consequently, up to 30% of all T cells are activated, leading to the massive secretion of cytokines, which produce the symptoms of toxic shock.

Membrane damaging toxins

Membrane damaging toxins disrupt the integrity of the plasma membrane. There are two subtypes of membrane damaging toxins - the channel-forming toxins and toxins that function as enzymes that act on the membrane.

Channel-forming toxins: Channel-forming toxins insert itself into the host cell membrane and make an open channel (pore). Alpha toxin of *Staphylococcus aureus* is an example of channel-forming toxins.

Toxins that enzymatically damage the membrane: One common example is an *alpha toxin* of *Clostridium perfringens*, which causes gas gangrene. Alpha toxin has *phospholipase* activity which enzymatically damage the membrane by removing the charged polar head groups from the phospholipids.

AB toxins

AB toxins are intracellular toxins. The *B-subunit* attaches to target regions on cell membranes and the *A-subunit* enters through the membrane and possesses enzymatic activity that affects internal cellular bio-mechanisms. Isolated A-subunits are enzymatically active but lack binding and cell entry capability, whereas isolated B-subunits bind to target cells but are nontoxic and biologically inactive. Toxins of this type include cholera toxin, pertussis toxin, Shiga toxin, tetanus toxin, botulinum toxin, anthrax toxin and heat-labile enterotoxin from *E. coli*.

Table 4.14 Important bacterial exotoxins and their mode of action

Bacterium	Disease	Mode of action
Corynebacterium diphtheriae	Diphtheria	Inactivates EF-2 by ADP-ribosylation
Clostridium tetani	Tetanus	Blocks release of the inhibitory neurotransmitter glycine
Clostridium botulinum	Botulism	Blocks release of acetylcholine
Clostridium perfringens	Gas gangrene	Alpha toxin is a lecithinase
Bacillus anthracis	Anthrax	One of the toxins is an adenylate cyclase
Staphylococcus aureus	Toxic shock	Binds to class II MHC protein; induces IL-1 and IL-2
Vibrio cholerae	Cholera	Stimulates adenylate cyclase by ADP-ribosylation of Gsα
Bordetella pertussis	Whooping cough	Stimulates adenylate cyclase by ADP-ribosylation of Giα

4.11 Control of microbial growth

Control of microbial growth means to inhibit or prevent growth of microorganisms. This control is affected in two basic ways:

1. By killing microorganisms or
2. By inhibiting the growth of microorganisms.

Control of growth usually involves the use of physical or chemical agents which either kill or prevent the growth of microorganisms. Agents which kill cells are called **cidal agents** and agents which inhibit the growth of cells are referred to as **static agents**. Thus, the term **bactericidal** refers to killing bacteria and **bacteriostatic** refers to inhibiting the growth of bacterial cells. Terms commonly used to describe antimicrobial agents and processes:

Disinfectants

Disinfectants are chemical agents used to kill or inactivate microorganisms on **inanimate objects**, thereby reducing the risk of infection. Examples include:

Hypochlorites – oxidize and destroy microbial cell components.

Copper sulfate – toxic to microbial enzymes and membranes.

Formaldehyde – reacts with amino, sulfhydryl and carboxyl groups, cross-linking proteins and nucleic acids.

Phenolic compounds – denature proteins and disrupt cell membranes.

Mercuric chloride – inactivates proteins by reacting with sulfhydryl groups.

Antiseptics

Antiseptics are chemical agents that kill or inhibit the growth of microorganisms and are sufficiently non-toxic to be safely applied to living tissues such as skin or mucous membranes. Examples include:

Alcohols (e.g., ethanol, isopropanol) – denature proteins and dissolve lipids, disrupting cell membranes.

Silver nitrate – precipitates and inactivates proteins.

Iodine solutions – oxidize and inactivate proteins and enzymes.

Detergents (e.g., quaternary ammonium compounds) – disrupt cell membranes and cause leakage of cellular contents.

Sterilization

Sterilization refers to the complete and total destruction or elimination of all viable organisms, including microbial endospore, in or on a substance being sterilized. Sterilization procedures involve the use of heat, radiation or chemicals, or physical removal of cells. The common processes used for sterilization are flaming, autoclaving (steam under pressure), tyndallization (steam not under pressure) and filtration.

Tyndallization is a process used to sterilize culture media that might be spoiled by exposure at higher temperatures. These heat sensitive media are steamed for 30-45 minutes each time for 3 successive days. On the first occasion, vegetative bacteria are killed; any spores that survive will germinate in the nutrient medium overnight, producing vegetative forms that are killed by the second or third steaming.

Pasteurization

Pasteurization is a brief heat treatment used to reduce the number of spoilage organisms and to kill disease-causing microbes. It uses precisely controlled heat to reduce the microbial populations in milk and other heat-sensitive liquids. The process is named after Louis Pasteur, who first used heat for controlling the spoilage of the wine. Pasteurization does not kill all organisms and is therefore not synonymous with sterilization. Milk is usually pasteurized by heating, typically at 63°C for 30 minutes (**batch method**) or at 71°C for 15 seconds (**flash method**), to kill bacteria and extend the milk's usable life.

Microbial control methods

Physical agents

Heat, radiation and filtration are most common physical agents normally used to control microbial growth. **Heat** is the most rapid and efficient physical agent used to control a population of microbes. Both *dry* and *moist heat* is used to kill microbes. Moist heat generally coagulates and causes denaturation in microorganisms. In dry heat, by contrast, the primary effect on microbes is due to oxidation of large molecules.

Similarly, there are many different kinds of **radiations** having antimicrobial effects. Ionizing radiations which include X-rays and gamma rays, form free radicals in the cytoplasm and the free radicals damage microbial protein and DNA. Another important form of radiation is ultraviolet radiations. These radiations damage nucleic acids.

Filtration involves the physical removal of all cells in a liquid or gas. It is especially important for sterilization of solutions which would be denatured by heat (e.g., antibiotics, amino acids, vitamins, etc.). In this process solutions or gases are passed through a filter of sufficient pore diameter (generally 0.22 micron) to remove the smallest known bacterial cells. Filtration is carried out commonly by using membrane filters. Membrane filters are made from cellulose esters (cellulose acetate, cellulose nitrate, collodion, etc.). A range of pore sizes is available. Bacterial filters have a pore size of less than 0.75 micron.

Chemical agents

A large number of chemicals such as alcohol, aldehyde, heavy metals, halogens and dyes are commonly used as **antimicrobial agents**. *Alcohols* like ethyl alcohol and isopropyl alcohol cause denaturation of proteins and are used as an antiseptic. Two *heavy metals*, mercury and silver, are used as an antimicrobial agents. Mercury is used as mercuric chloride and as a component of mercurochrome. Silver is commonly used as silver nitrate. Two important halogens, *chlorine* and *iodine*, act as oxidizing agents that react with the amino acids in proteins and change the nature of the protein. Similarly, gases like ethylene oxide, formaldehyde, and beta propiolactone are used to achieve sterilization.

Antibiotics

Antibiotics are low molecular-weight antimicrobial agents produced as secondary metabolites by microorganisms that kill or inhibit other microorganisms. The term, coined by Waksman, originally described only those formulations derived from living organisms. A more broadened definition of an antibiotic includes any chemical of natural origin which can kill or inhibit the growth of other types of cells. Since most clinically-useful antibiotics are produced by microorganisms and are used to kill or inhibit infectious bacteria, we will follow the classic definition.

Antibiotics may have a **cidal effect** or a **static effect** on a range of microbes. The range of bacteria or other microorganisms that are affected by a certain antibiotic is expressed as its *spectrum of action*. Antibiotics effective against a wide range of microorganisms such as both Gram-positive and Gram-negative bacteria are said to be **broad spectrum** antibiotics. If effective mainly against Gram-positive or Gram-negative bacteria but not both, they are **narrow spectrum**. If effective against a single microorganism, they are referred to as **limited spectrum**. Antibiotic molecules produced by a microbe that are subsequently modified by an organic chemist to enhance their antimicrobial properties or to render them unique for a pharmaceutical patent are described as *semi-synthetic antibiotics*.

Table 4.15 Microbial sources of some antibiotics

Microorganism	**Antibiotics**
Bacteria	
Streptomyces sp.	Amphotericin B, Chloramphenicol (also synthetic), Erythromycin, Kanamycin, Neomycin, Nystatin, Rifampin, Streptomycin, Tetracycline
Micromonospora sp.	Gentamicin
Bacillus sp.	Bacitracin, Polymyxin
Fungi	
Penicillium sp.	Griseofulvin, Penicillin
Cephalosporium sp.	Cephalosporins

Mode of action of antibiotics

Antibiotics inhibit microbial populations by any of five major methods. They disrupt the cell wall synthesis; they interfere with cell membrane function; they inhibit protein synthesis or interfere with its completion; they disrupt the functioning of nucleic acids; and they interrupt selected metabolic pathways.

Table 4.16 Mechanism of action/target of some antibiotics

Antibiotics	**Mechanism of action**
Cell wall synthesis inhibition	
Penicillin	Inhibit transpeptidation enzymes involved in the cross-linking
Vancomycin	Binds directly to the D–Ala-terminus and inhibits transpeptidation
Bacitracin	Inhibits cell wall synthesis
Protein synthesis inhibition	
Puromycin	A site of ribosome
Kanamycin	16S rRNA
Neomycin	16S rRNA
Streptomycin	30S ribosome
Thiostrepton	23S rRNA
Gentamicin	16S rRNA
Tetracycline	A site of ribosome
Chloramphenicol	Peptidyltransferase
Erythromycin	23S rRNA
Fusidic acid	Translation elongation factor G
Kirromycin	Translation elongation factor Tu

Replication inhibition	
Antibiotic	*Target*
Ciprofloxacin	Inhibit bacterial DNA gyrase
Hydroxyurea	Ribonucleotide reductase
Nalidixic acid	*gyr*A subunits of gyrase
Novobiocin	*gyr*B subunits of gyrase
Mitomycin C	Cross-links DNA
Transcription inhibition	
Streptolydigin	β-subunit of RNA polymerase
Actinomycin D	Binds DNA
Rifampin	β-subunit of RNA polymerase
Bleomycin	Cuts DNA
Cell membrane disruption	
Polymyxin B	Disrupts the structure and permeability of the plasma membrane
Metabolic antagonism	
Sulfonamides	Inhibits folic acid synthesis by competition with p-aminobenzoic acid
Trimethoprim	Blocks tetrahydrofolate synthesis
Dapsone	Interferes with folic acid synthesis
Isoniazid	May disrupt pyridoxal or NAD metabolism and functioning

Example of some commonly used antibiotics

Sulfonamides or Sulfa drugs: Sulfonamides or sulfa drugs are structurally related to sulfanilamide, an analogue of **p-aminobenzoic acid**. The latter substance is used in the synthesis of the cofactor folic acid. When sulfanilamide or another sulfonamide enters a bacterial cell, it competes with p-aminobenzoic acid for the active site. It results in a decrease in folate concentration. The decline in folic acid is detrimental to the bacterium because folic acid is essential for the synthesis of purines and pyrimidines.

Penicillins: Penicillin was first discovered by Alexander Fleming as a metabolic by-product of the fungus *Penicillium notatum*. All penicillins share a common bicyclic nucleus that is composed of fused β-lactam and thiazolidine rings. The most crucial feature of the molecule is the **β-lactam ring**, which appears to be essential for activity. The mechanism of action of penicillins is still not completely known. It has been proposed that penicillins inhibit the enzyme catalyzing the transpeptidation reaction because of their structural similarity, which would block the synthesis of a complete, fully cross-linked peptidoglycan and lead to osmotic lysis.

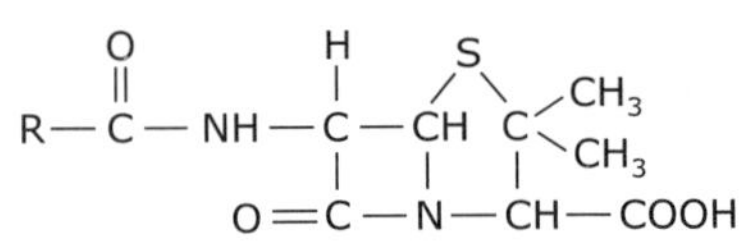

Figure 4.34 Structure of penicillin nucleus.

Cephalosporins: Cephalosporins originally isolated from the fungus *Cephalosporium*, and their β-lactam structure is very similar to that of the penicillin. Members of the cephalosporin family of antibiotics are effective in preventing the synthesis of bacterial cell walls and mostly useful against Gram-positive bacteria.

Tetracyclines: The tetracyclines are a family of antibiotics with a common four-ring structure to which a variety of side chains are attached. Tetracyclines are broad-spectrum antibiotics effective against Gram-negative bacteria, Gram-positive bacteria, rickettsias, chlamydiae, and mycoplasmas.

Aminoglycoside antibiotics: The aminoglycoside antibiotics are inhibitors of protein synthesis in bacteria. All members of this family of antibiotics have amino groups and carbohydrate molecules associated with the main molecules. The members include gentamicin, kanamycin, tobramycin, and streptomycin. The aminoglycosides are most active against Gram-negative pathogens.

Erythromycin: Erythromycin, a macrolide antibiotic, is synthesized by *Streptomyces erythraeus*. The macrolides contain a 12- to 22-carbon lactone ring linked to one or more sugars. Erythromycin is useful against Gram-positive bacteria and acts as an inhibitor of protein synthesis.

Chloramphenicol: Chloramphenicol was first produced from cultures of *Streptomyces venezuelae*, it is now made through chemical synthesis. Antibiotic has a very broad spectrum of activity.

4.12 Viruses

Viruses are simple, noncellular entities consisting of one or more molecules of either DNA or RNA enclosed in a coat of protein. They can reproduce only within living cells and are **obligate intracellular parasites**. Viruses are smaller than prokaryotic cells ranging in size from 0.01 to 0.4 µm. A fully assembled infectious virus is called a **virion**. The main function of the virion is to deliver its DNA or RNA genome into the host cell so that the genome can be expressed (transcribed and translated) by the host cell. Each viral species has a very limited **host range**; i.e., it can reproduce in only a small group of closely related species.

Discovery of viruses: The discovery of viruses began in 1892, when Dmitri Ivanovsky showed that sap from tobacco plants infected with mosaic disease could still cause infection even after being filtered to remove bacteria. In 1898, Martinus Beijerinck confirmed that these infectious agents could only reproduce inside living cells, coining the term 'virus.' Shortly after, Friedrich Loeffler and Paul Frosch identified the first animal virus, responsible for **foot-and-mouth disease**. In 1935, Wendell Stanley isolated and crystallized the tobacco mosaic virus, which opened the door to detailed study of viral structures.

Viral structure

The structure of virions is highly diverse, varying widely in size, shape, and chemical composition. All viruses are chemically **nucleoproteins**, composed of **nucleic acid** surrounded by a **protein capsid**. The nucleic acid together with the capsid constitutes the **nucleocapsid**. The capsid serves as a protective shell for the viral genome, shielding it from nucleases and enabling the virion to attach to specific receptors on the host cell during infection. The protein subunits that make up the capsid are called **capsomeres**.

Some viruses possess a membranous envelope outside the nucleocapsid. Virions with such an envelope are termed **enveloped viruses**, whereas those lacking it are called **naked viruses** (or *non-enveloped viruses*). In enveloped viruses, the nucleocapsid is surrounded by a lipid bilayer and often displays glycoprotein spikes, known as **peplomers**. Viruses acquire their envelope from the host cell's plasma membrane or other intracellular membranes.

Viral genomes are smaller in size. The largest known viral genome, that of **bacteriophage G**, is 670 kbs. The genome of a virus may consist of DNA or RNA, which may be single-stranded (ss) or double-stranded (ds), linear or circular. Single-stranded RNA genomes can be either *plus* (+) *sense* or *minus* (−) *sense*. **Plus sense RNA** serves as mRNA and translated into the host cell. **Minus sense RNA** acts as a template for synthesis of mRNA. An RNA molecule that is plus-sense in some regions and minus-sense in other regions is referred to as **ambisense**.

Based on the organization and packaging of viral genome, viruses can be divided into three categories: *monopartite, segmented* and *multipartite viruses*. **Monopartite viruses** have a single non-segmented nucleic acid molecule present in a single virus particle. Most viruses are the monopartite viruses. The genome of **segmented viruses** is divided into two or more nucleic acid segments that are all present together in a single virus particle. There may be as many as 10 to 12 segments in a single viral particle. **Multipartite viruses** (also called *multicomponent, multiparticle* or *multicompartment viruses*) have their genome divided into two or more nucleic acid segments, just as the segmented type, but these segments are each packaged into separate virus particles. dsDNA viruses are exclusively monopartite; their genome is never segmented or multipartite. ssDNA viruses are either mono- or multipartite; there are no segmented ssDNA viruses. (+) ssRNA viruses are mostly mono- or multipartite and (−) ssRNA viruses are mostly monopartite or segmented.

Table 4.17 Features of viral nucleic acids

Type of nucleic acid	Number of strand	Shape
DNA		
Single-stranded	Single-stranded DNA	Linear
	Single-stranded DNA	Circular
Double-stranded	Double-stranded DNA	Linear
	Double-strand DNA with single chain breaks	Linear
	Double-strand DNA	Circular
RNA		
Single-stranded	Single-stranded, positive-strand RNA	Linear
	Single-stranded, negative-strand RNA	Linear
	Single-stranded, segmented RNA	Linear
Double-stranded	Double-stranded, segmented RNA	Linear

Shape and symmetry

All viruses possess a nucleoprotein structure, where proteins form the protective capsid surrounding the nucleic acid. The capsid is composed of repeating subunits called *capsomeres*. The *symmetry of the capsid*—referring to the arrangement of capsomeres—can be either *icosahedral* (spherical) or *helical* (rod-shaped).

Helical symmetry is characteristic of the nucleocapsids of many filamentous viruses. In these viruses, capsomeres are arranged in a helical fashion around a helical strand of nucleic acid. TMV is a classic example of a virus with helical symmetry. **Icosahedral symmetry**, on the other hand, is characteristic of many spherical viruses. An icosahedron is a regular polyhedron with 20 equilateral triangular faces and 12 vertices.

Some viruses, such as **phage T4**, exhibit **complex symmetry**, which is neither purely icosahedral nor purely helical. These viruses possess a combination of structural features, often including an icosahedral head and a helical tail.

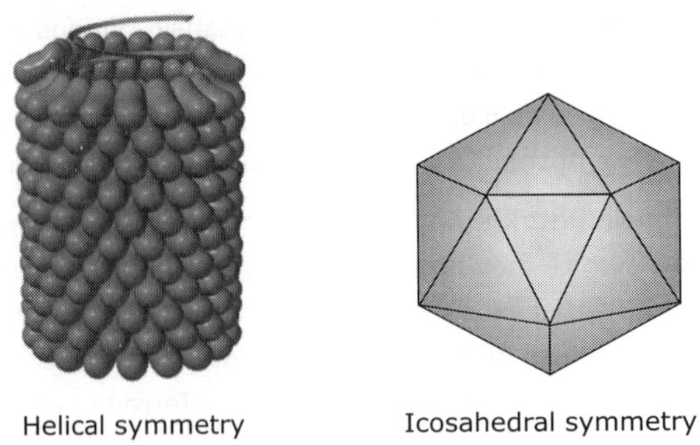

Figure 4.35 Diagrammatic representation of helical and icosahedral symmetry. In helical viruses, the protein subunits (capsomers) are arranged around the viral genome in a spiral or helical fashion, forming a rod-like or filamentous structure. In icosahedral viruses, the capsid is arranged in the form of a regular polyhedron with 20 triangular faces, 12 vertices, and 30 edges.

Classification of viruses

Viruses are classified into distinct taxonomic groups based on various parameters, including host range, virion structure, life cycle strategy, and the type of nucleic acid. For instance, based on the nature of their host, viruses are categorized as animal viruses, plant viruses, bacterial viruses (bacteriophages or phages), insect viruses, and others.

Table 4.18 Some common animal virus groups and their characteristics

	Picornaviridae	**Orthomyxoviridae**	**Parvoviridae**	**Adenoviridae**	**Poxviridae**
Nucleic acid	RNA	RNA	DNA	DNA	DNA
Strandedness	Single	Single	Single	Double	Double
Capsid symmetry	Icosahedral	Helical	Icosahedral	Icosahedral	Complex
Envelope	–	+	–	–	+

4.12.1 Animal viruses

Animal viruses are viruses that infect animals. Animal viruses have a variety of shapes, sizes, and nature of the genome. The genome of animal viruses may be DNA or RNA, ss or ds, linear or circular, segmented or non-segmented. Animal viruses can be classified on the basis of

1. the type and structure of the viral nucleic acid and the strategy used in its replication
2. the type of symmetry of the virus capsid (helical vs. icosahedral)
3. the presence or absence of a lipid envelope

According to the **Baltimore system** of virus classification, which is based on characteristics such as genome type and its replication strategy, animal viruses are classified into seven classes. The central theme in this system is that all viruses must generate positive-strand mRNAs from their genomes in order to produce proteins and replicate themselves. The precise mechanisms whereby this is achieved differ for each virus family.

CLASS I (**Genome: dsDNA**)
It is the most common type of animal virus. Viral DNA enters the cell nucleus, where cellular enzymes transcribe the DNA and process the resulting RNA into viral mRNA.

Class Ia DNA replicates in host-cell nucleus; use host enzymes for DNA replication.
Example: Adenoviruses, Herpesviruses (Herpes simplex, Varicella zoster and Epstein Barr virus) and Papovaviruses (Papilloma and Polyoma).

Class Ib DNA replicates in host-cell cytoplasm using viral enzymes.
Example: Pox virus (Smallpox, Vaccinia and Cow pox)

CLASS II (**Genome: ssDNA**)
Example: *Parvoviruses* (from Latin *parvo*, poor), are simple viruses that contain one molecule of single-stranded DNA (ssDNA). Some parvoviruses encapsidate (enclose) both plus and minus strands of DNA, but in separate virions; others encapsidate only the minus strand. In both cases, the ssDNA is copied inside the cell into dsDNA, which is then itself copied into mRNA.

CLASS III (**Genome: dsRNA**)
Example: *Reoviruses*

CLASS IV (**Genome: Plus sense ssRNA**)
Example: Picornaviruses (Poliovirus and Rhinovirus) and Togavirus (Rubella virus).

CLASS V (**Genome: Minus sense ssRNA**)
Contain a single negative strand of genomic RNA, whose sequence is complementary to that of the

viral mRNA. The genomic RNA in the virion acts as a template for synthesis of mRNA but does not itself encode proteins.

Example: Rhabdovirus (Rabies), Paramyxovirus (Measles and Mumps) and Orthomyxovirus (Influenza).

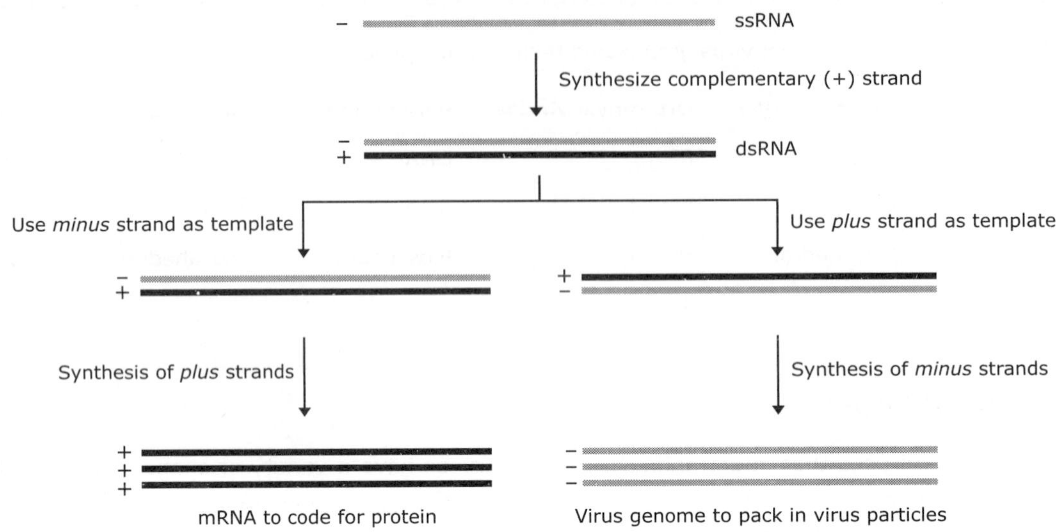

Figure 4.36 Strategy of negative-strand RNA virus. The negative strand of RNA has a sequence complementary to the coding strand. Therefore, viruses that use this type of genome must synthesize the complementary plus-strand upon entry into the host cell. The plus RNA strand can then be used as a template to manufacture more viral genomes. The negative RNA strand is then free to manufacture more copies of the plus-strand. These act as mRNA and then direct viral protein synthesis.

CLASS VI (**Genome: Plus sense ssRNA that replicates with DNA intermediate**)

Example: *Retroviruses*

CLASS VII (**Genome: dsDNA that replicates with RNA intermediate**)

Example: *Hepadnavirus* such as human hepatitis B virus.

Like the retroviruses, hepadnaviruses use reverse transcriptase in their replication cycle. However, unlike retroviruses, the DNA genome of hepadnaviruses is replicated through an RNA intermediate, the opposite of what occurs in retroviruses.

The subclasses within each class differ mainly in capsid structure and in the presence or absence of a membranous envelope.

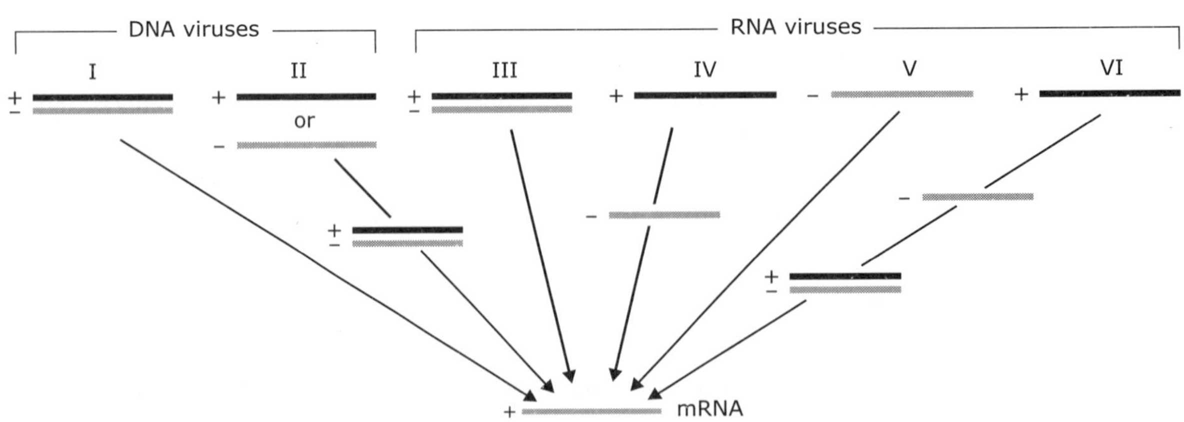

Figure 4.37 Baltimore's simplified classification of viruses. This classification is based on the type of nucleic acid in the genome and the mode of production of mRNA.

Table 4.19 Examples of animal virus and their nature of nucleic acid

Herpesvirus	dsDNA	Togavirus	(+) ssRNA
Pox virus	dsDNA	Coronavirus	(+) ssRNA
Papovavirus	dsDNA	Picornavirus	(+) ssRNA
Adenovirus	dsDNA	Retrovirus	(+) ssRNA
Parvovirus	ssDNA	Orthomyxovirus	(−) ssRNA
Reovirus	dsRNA	Paramyxovirus	(−) ssRNA

Effects of animal viruses on animal cells

Animal viruses can exert a range of effects on host cells, depending on the nature of the virus and the host response:

Lytic infection: This type of infection leads to the destruction of the host cell through lysis, releasing newly formed virions into the surrounding environment.

Persistent infection: In persistent infections, the virus continuously multiplies without killing the host cell. The infected cell remains alive and continues to produce new viruses over an extended period.

Latent infection: A latent infection is characterized by a delay between the initial viral entry and the onset of productive infection. During this period, the viral genome remains dormant within the host cell. An example is **herpes simplex virus**, which can remain inactive and later reactivate to cause **cold sores**.

Transformation: Some animal viruses have the ability to alter normal cellular regulation, converting a healthy cell into a tumor cell. This process is known as *transformation* and is associated with certain oncogenic (cancer-causing) viruses.

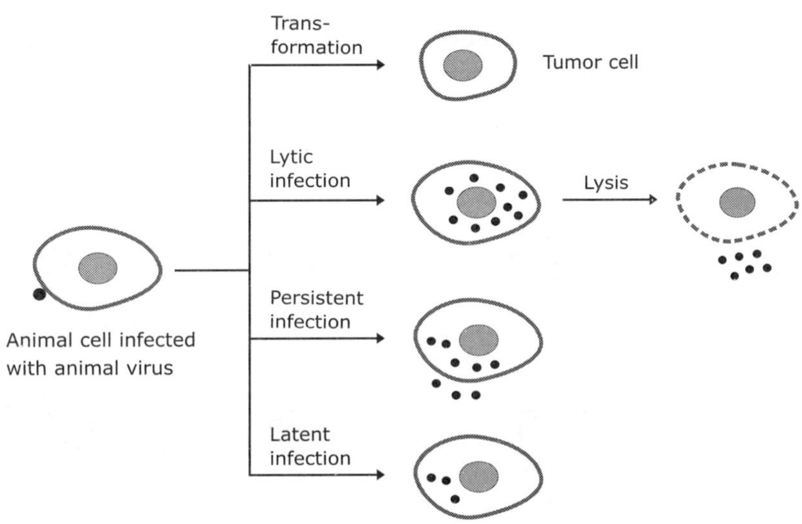

Figure 4.38 Possible effects that animal viruses may have on cells they infect.

Lytic cycle of animal viruses

The generalized productive lytic cycle of animal viruses consists of five main stages: attachment (adsorption), entry, synthesis, assembly, and release (lysis or budding).

Attachment: The cycle begins when the virus binds to specific receptor molecules on the surface of the host cell.

Entry: The virus enters the host cell, usually through membrane fusion or endocytosis.

Synthesis: Once inside, the viral genome is replicated and viral proteins are synthesized using the host cell's machinery.

Assembly: Newly synthesized viral components are assembled into complete viral particles.

Release: Mature viruses exit the host cell—either by causing its rupture (lysis) or by budding through the cell membrane—to infect new cells and repeat the cycle.

Viral adsorption or attachment to the host cell: Viruses typically attach to cells via specific cell surface receptors. Animal viruses have specialized attachment sites distributed over the surface of the virion. Adsorption involves the binding of these attachment sites on the viral surface to receptor sites on the host cell's cytoplasmic membrane. Table 4.20 lists some examples of viruses and their receptors.

Table 4.20 Examples of some viruses and their receptors

Virus	Receptor
HIV-1	CD4
Influenza virus	Sialic acid
SARS-CoV-2	ACE2 (Angiotensin-Converting Enzyme 2)
Epstein-Barr virus	CD21 (also known as CR2)
Rabies virus	Nicotinic acetylcholine receptor (for neuronal entry)
Human papillomavirus	Heparan sulfate proteoglycans (for initial attachment)
Rhinovirus (common cold virus)	ICAM-1 (major receptor)
Dengue virus	Heparan sulfate proteoglycans (for initial attachment)
Poliovirus	CD155
Herpes simplex virus (HSV)	Heparan sulfate (for initial attachment)
Ebola virus	NPC1 (Niemann-Pick C1)

Viral entry into the host cell: After recognition and attachment to the host cell surface, the virus must enter the cell to replicate. This requires that the virus must traverse the lipid bilayer surrounding the cell, without killing the cell. For some viruses, detailed mechanisms of penetration are unclear. Most viruses enter host cells by direct fusion with plasma membrane or by receptor-mediated endocytosis.

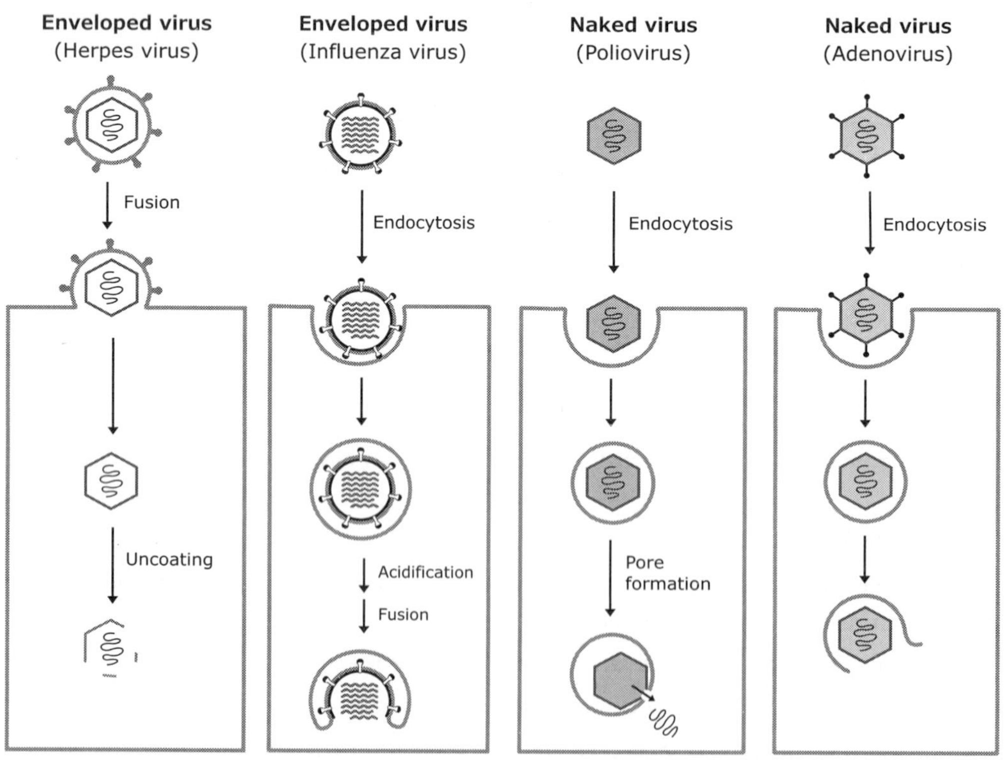

Figure 4.39 Mechanisms of animal virus attachment and entry into host cells. Many enveloped viruses fuse directly with the host cell plasma membrane and release nucleocapsid into the cytoplasm. Most naked viruses and some enveloped viruses enter cells by receptor-mediated endocytosis.

Direct fusion with plasma membrane: Some enveloped viruses (such as HIV) enter the host cell by fusing their envelope with the plasma membrane. The viral envelope fuses with the host cell plasma membrane and the nucleocapsid is released into the cytoplasm.

Receptor-mediated endocytosis: Most naked (non-enveloped) viruses and some enveloped viruses enter by receptor-mediated endocytosis whereby the host cell plasma membrane invaginates and pinches off, placing the virus in an endocytic vesicle. **Adenovirus**, a non-enveloped virus, induces receptor-mediated endocytosis and then disrupts the endosomal membrane, releasing capsid into the cytosol. **Poliovirus**, which causes poliomyelitis, is a non-enveloped virus. It induces receptor-mediated endocytosis, and after entry one of the capsid proteins inserts into the endosomal membrane to form a pore. The viral RNA genome then enters the cytosol through the pore, leaving the nucleocapsid in the endosome. Some enveloped viruses also enter into the host cell by receptor-mediated endocytosis. For example, **influenza virus**, an enveloped virus, first binds to the cell surface receptors and induces receptor-mediated endocytosis. Influenza viruses have segmented genomes consisting of seven to eight different RNA molecules. Each is coated by capsid proteins to create seven to eight flexible nucleocapsids. When the endosome acidifies, the virus envelope fuses with the endosomal membrane, releasing the nucleocapsid into the cytosol.

Synthesis of the viral genome: **DNA viruses** soon after penetration, the viral nucleic acid is prepared for expression and replication. Genome replication and transcription in DNA viruses follow a similar pattern. In DNA viruses, early viral mRNA and proteins are involved in taking over the host cell and the synthesis of viral DNA and RNA. DNA replication usually occurs in the host cell nucleus; **poxviruses** are exceptions since their genomes are replicated in the cytoplasm. **Hepadnaviruses** (hepatitis B virus) are unique since they contain a partially dsDNA genome that must be converted into an RNA form by the virion enzyme reverse transcriptase during the virus life cycle. After infecting the cell, the virus DNA is released into the nucleus. Transcription of viral genes occurs in the nucleus using host RNA polymerase and yields mRNAs. The RNA moves to the cytoplasm where it is reverse transcribed into minus-strand DNA. After RNA has been degraded by RNaseH, the remaining RNA fragment serves as a primer for synthesis of the gapped dsDNA genome, using the minus-strand DNA as template.

The **RNA viruses** are much more diverse in their reproductive strategies than are the DNA viruses. Most RNA viruses can be placed in one of four general groups based on their modes of genome replication and transcription, and their relationship to the host cell genome.

1. Viral RNA genome can act as mRNA (plus sense) or the complementary strand can be the mRNA (minus sense).
2. All RNA viruses except *retroviruses* encode an *RNA-dependent RNA polymerase*. In the negative strand RNA viruses, this polymerase is part of the virion, and it must enter the cytosol along with the viral genome. This is necessary in order for the virus to generate mRNAs from its genome.
3. All RNA viruses replicate in the cytoplasm except *orthomyxoviruses*, *hepatitis delta virus* and *retroviruses*.
4. Retroviruses are unique. These viruses have a positive sense RNA genome which must be converted into a dsDNA form by the virion enzyme *reverse transcriptase* (an RNA-dependent DNA polymerase). This dsDNA is then integrated (at random sites) into the host cell chromosome by the viral integrase enzyme. Upon integration into the host chromosome, the viral DNA can then be transcribed by cellular RNA polymerase II, to produce new genomic RNA molecules.

Viral assembly: Some *viral genes* direct the synthesis of capsid proteins, and these spontaneously self-assemble to form the capsid. The nucleic acid is then inserted into the capsid. The assembly of enveloped virus capsids is generally similar to that of naked virions.

Viral release: Mechanisms of virion release differ between naked and enveloped viruses. Naked viruses are predominantly released by *host cell lysis*. *Enveloped viruses* released from the host cell by *budding*. All viral envelopes are derived from host cell membranes by a multi-step process. Most envelopes arise from the plasma membrane. However, in herpes viruses, envelope formation usually involves the nuclear membrane. Prior to budding, viral proteins and glycoproteins are incorporated into the host cell's membranes. During budding the host cell membrane with incorporated viral proteins and glycoproteins pinches off to form the viral envelope.

Differences between bacterial viruses and eukaryotic viruses

The differences between prokaryotic and eukaryotic cells also determine the features of the viruses that infect them. For example, in prokaryotes, transcription and translation are coupled processes. In eukaryotes, by contrast, transcription and DNA replication occur in the nucleus while translation occurs in the cytoplasm. In addition, mRNAs in eukaryotes are capped and contain poly-A-tails. Some of the major differences between bacteriophages and eukaryotic viruses are mentioned in the table below.

Table 4.21 Some differences between bacteriophages (virulent) and eukaryotic viruses

Bacterial viruses	Eukaryotic viruses
Generally, the viral genome is injected into host cells along without the capsid.	Generally, the viral genome is injected into host cells along with the capsid.
No segmented genomes	Some ssRNA viruses have segmented genomes
No 5′ capping	5′ end of ssRNA (+) strand or viral mRNA is capped
No poly-A tails	3′ end of ssRNA viruses have poly-A tail
Phage proteins rarely penetrate the host cell (phage M13 is an exception)	Viral proteins commonly enter the cell

Retroviruses

Retroviruses are ssRNA containing enveloped animal viruses that replicate through a DNA intermediates. The genomic RNA is 7 to 12 kb long, and it is linear, single-stranded, plus sense and non-segmented. There are two copies of identical ssRNA molecules. All retroviral genomic RNA contain *gag*, *pol* and *env* genes. Some complex retroviruses, such as HIV-I contains additional regulatory genes.

The retroviral life cycle proceeds by reverse transcribing the RNA genome into dsDNA, which is inserted into the host genome. In the cytosol, ssRNA genome is reverse transcribed into dsDNA. It is catalyzed by reverse transcriptase. It has two enzymatic activities, a DNA polymerase that can use a DNA or an RNA strand as template and an RNase H. The RNase H degrades the RNA part of the RNA-DNA hybrid. Like other DNA polymerases, reverse transcriptase requires a primer. The native primer is tRNA. The two enzymatic functions of reverse transcriptase, polymerase and RNase H, convert the RNA into a linear dsDNA (**figure 4.40**). After DNA synthesis has been completed, the resulting linear dsDNA is translocated to the nucleus where the viral DNA is integrated into the host genome by enzyme integrase. Integrated retroviral DNA remains in the cellular genome as an endogenous **provirus**. The provirus is transcribed by the host RNA polymerase II to produce viral mRNAs as well as genomic RNA. Retroviral mRNA has a conventional structure; it is capped at the 5′ end and polyadenylated at the 3′ end.

Overall process of multiplication of a retrovirus

- Entrance into the cell via fusion with cell membrane.
- Uncoating of the virion.
- Reverse transcription of RNA genomes into a ssDNA that is subsequently converted to a linear dsDNA by DNA polymerase activity, which then enters the nucleus.
- Integration of retroviral DNA into the host genome.
- Transcription of retroviral DNA, leading to the formation of viral mRNAs and viral genomic RNA.
- Assembly and encapsidation of the genomic RNA into nucleocapsids in the cytoplasm.
- Budding of enveloped virions at the cytoplasmic membrane and release from the cell.

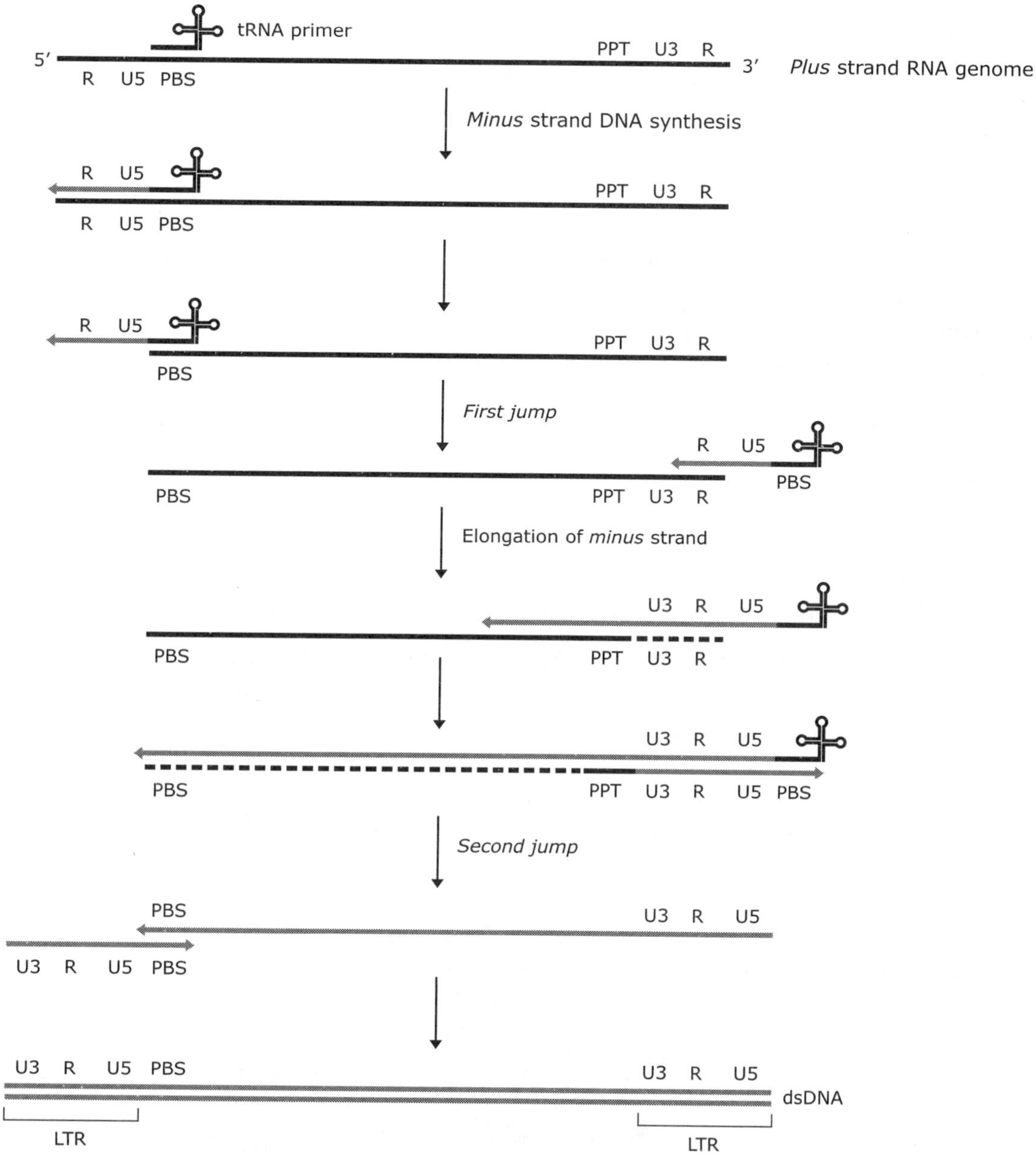

Figure 4.40 *Reverse transcription of the HIV-1 genome.* Reverse transcription initiates from an RNA primer provided by a specific cellular tRNA (tRNA^{Lys3}). The primer hybridizes to the Primer Binding Site (PBS) of the genomic RNA. Reverse transcriptase catalyzes RNA-dependent DNA synthesis. Synthesis of the minus-strand DNA generates an RNA-DNA hybrid. RNase H activity of reverse transcriptase degrades the RNA strand, leaving the nascent minus-strand DNA single-stranded. The newly synthesized minus-strand DNA hybridizes with the terminal R-region of the 3′-end of the viral RNA (called the *first jump* or minus-strand transfer). After the nascent DNA hybridizes to R, minus-strand DNA synthesis can continue along the viral RNA. As DNA synthesis proceeds, RNase H degrades the RNA strand. There is a purine-rich sequence (called the polypurine tract or PPT) near the 3′ end of the viral RNA which is relatively resistant to RNase H cleavage, and it serves as the primer for plus-strand DNA synthesis. Plus-strand DNA synthesis proceeds until reverse transcriptase starts to copy the tRNA primer. Once the 3′ end of the tRNA has been reverse transcribed, an RNA/DNA hybrid that is a substrate for RNase H is created. The tRNA associated with the nascent viral DNA is then removed by the RNase H activity. This may facilitate annealing to the PBS complement on the minus-strand DNA, providing the complementarity for the *second jump* or plus-strand transfer. Once this second transfer happens, both the minus- and plus-DNA strands are extended until the entire DNA is double-stranded and creating a DNA that has the same sequences at both ends (these repeats are called the Long Terminal Repeats or LTRs).

HIV and AIDS

The **acquired immunodeficiency syndrome** (AIDS) was first recognized in the United States in 1981 in the Los Angeles, New York, and San Francisco when a group of patients displayed *Pneumocystis carinii pneumonia* (PCP), caused by opportunistic fungal pathogen *Pneumocystis carinii* and *Kaposi sarcoma*, an extremely rare skin tumor. A more complete evaluation of the patients showed that they had in common a marked deficiency in *cellular immune* responses and a significant decrease in the sub-population of T cells that carry the CD4 marker.

Etiologic agent of AIDS is **Human Immunodeficiency Virus** (**HIV**). It was discovered and characterized by *Luc Montagnier* (in Paris) and *Robert Gallo* (in Bethesda) in the year 1983 from a patient suffering from **lymphadenopathy**. HIV belongs to the family of human retrovirus and the subfamily of lentiviruses. AIDS is caused primarily by the HIV-1 virus (some cases result from an HIV-2 infection). This virus is closely related to HTLV-I, the cause of adult T-cell leukemia, or disabling progressive neurologic disorder called HTLV-I-associated myelopathy and HTLV-II, which has been isolated from individuals with hairy-cell leukemia.

Recently, a virus **simian immunodeficiency virus** (**SIV**) related to HIV-1 and HIV-2 has been isolated from African green monkey and is believed to be the ancestor of the HIV. Somehow, this virus entered in humans and mutated to the two current African human viruses SBL and IAV-2, which are intermediate viruses; these intermediate viruses may have evolved into the highly virulent HIV-1. HIV was formerly called lymphadenopathy associated virus (**LAV**), human T-lymphotropic viruses (**HTLV-III**) and AIDS associated retrovirus (**ARV**).

Structure: HIV-1 has an icosahedral structure. It is an enveloped **lentivirus** within the family **retroviridae**. The envelope is derived from the host cell. The envelope contains spikes, made up of glycoproteins gp 120 (external) and gp 41 (transmembrane). Gp stands for glycoprotein and the number refers to the mass of protein, in thousands of Daltons. These glycoproteins serve as the viral receptor for CD4 on the host cells. Within the envelope is a cone-shaped nucleocapsid, which consists of approximately 2000 copies of the p24 protein. Between the capsid and envelope is a matrix protein, p17 (**figure 4.41**).

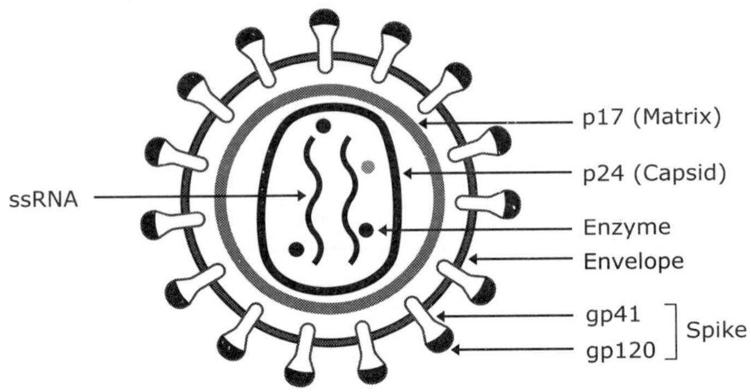

Figure 4.41 Human Immunodeficiency Virus (HIV).

Genome: It contains two copies of *plus* single-stranded RNA genome. Genome of most retroviruses contains only three genes namely *gag*, *pol* and *env*. HIV-I contains nine different genes in its ~9kb (9749 nucleotides) RNA genome (*gag*, *pol*, *env*, *vif*, *vpu*, *vpr*, *tat*, *rev* and *nef*). The reverse-transcribed dsDNA within host is marked by the presence of **long terminal repeats** (LTR), which contain regulatory elements involved in gene expression. The major difference between the genome of HIV-1 and HIV-2 is that HIV-2 lacks the *vpu* gene and has a *vpx* gene not contained in HIV-1.

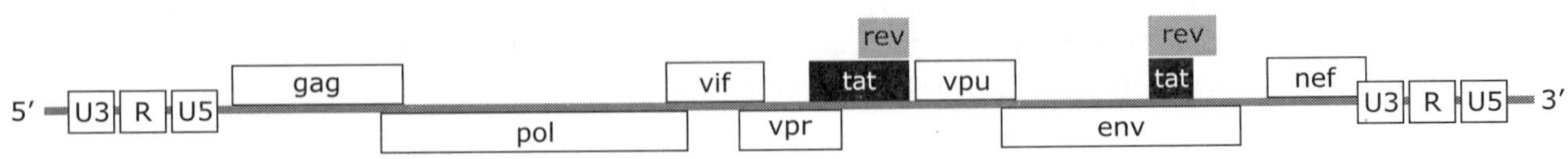

Gene	Function of encoded protein
gag	Nucleocapsid proteins
pol	Enzymes like reverse transcriptase, protease and integrase
env	Envelope glycoprotein
vif	Promotes infectivity of viral particle
vpu	Required for efficient viral assembly and budding
vpr	Weakly activates transcription of proviral DNA
tat	Strongly activates transcription of proviral DNA
rev	Allows export of unspliced and singly spliced mRNAs from nucleus
nef	Increases viral replication down-regulates host-cell CD4

Infection

HIV-1 primarily infects T_H cells and macrophages. An initial interaction occurs between **gp120** and the surface receptor **CD4**. CD4 (cluster of differentiation 4) is a glycoprotein found on the surface of immune cells such as helper T cells (T_H), monocytes, macrophages and dendritic cells. Fusion and viral entry also requires interaction with chemokine receptors - **CCR5** (present on macrophages and monocytes) and **CXCR4,** also known as **fusin** (present on T_H cells). Chemokine receptors are GPCR that are found in the plasma membrane of leukocytes.

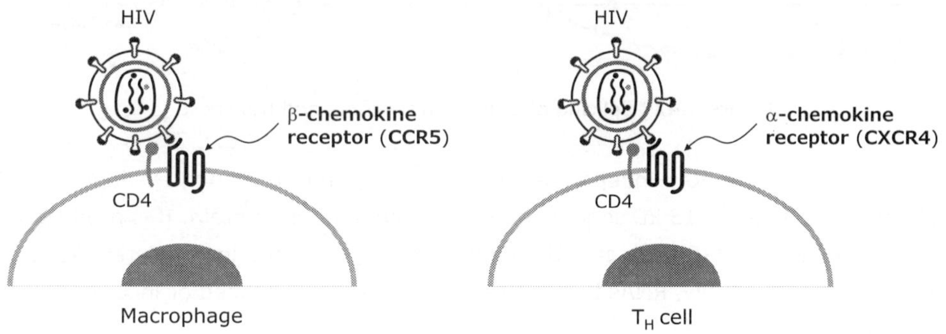

After fusion with the host cell membrane, nucleocapsid containing viral genome and enzymes (reverse transcriptase, protease and integrase) released into the cell cytoplasm. Viral genome and enzymes are released following removal (uncoating) of the viral capsid. In the cytosol, ssRNA genome is reverse transcribed into RNA-DNA hybrid by reverse transcriptase (RNA-dependent DNA polymerase). The two other enzymatic functions of RT, DNA-dependent DNA polymerase and RNase H, cooperate to convert the genomic RNA into a double-stranded linear DNA. DNA synthesis is initiated from a host tRNA primer. Near the 5′ end of the viral genome, there is a sequence called the **primer binding site** (PBS). The tRNA primer is hybridized to the PBS. The viral RNA genome, which serves as the template, is plus-strand. First (minus) strand DNA synthesis is initiated from the tRNA primer. Synthesis of the minus-strand DNA generates an RNA-DNA hybrid that is a substrate for RNase H. RNase H degrades the RNA strand, leaving the nascent minus-strand DNA single-stranded. Finally, ssDNA is converted into dsDNA. After DNA synthesis has been completed, the resulting linear dsDNA is translocated to the nucleus where the viral DNA is integrated into the host genome by enzyme *integrase*. This inserted DNA copy, called a provirus, transcribes into mRNAs.

Viral mRNA biogenesis and transport

HIV transcription is mediated by a single promoter in the 5′ LTR. Transcription from the 5′ LTR generates a ~9 kb primary transcript, which is alternatively spliced to >30 mRNAs. HIV gene expression is regulated at both the transcriptional and post-transcriptional levels. HIV transcription is mediated by a single promoter in the 5′ LTR. Expression from the 5′ LTR generates a ~9 kb primary transcript. The primary transcripts are synthesized by cellular RNA polymerase II. Some primary transcripts are spliced into more than 30 mRNA species. Thus, infected cells contain three different classes of RNAs – the unspliced primary transcript (~9 kb), a class of singly spliced RNAs (<~4 kb) and a class of completely spliced RNAs (<~2 kb). The unspliced viral mRNA codes for Gag and Gag-Pol fusion proteins, whereas singly spliced mRNAs code for Vif, Vpr, Vpu and Env proteins. The completely spliced mRNAs code for Tat, Rev and Nef proteins.

For HIV-1 gene expression, both unspliced and spliced RNAs must be transported to the cytoplasm. In general, unspliced and incompletely spliced RNAs are not exported from the nucleus to cytosol. But in case of retrovirus even unspliced and incompletely spliced RNAs exported from nucleus. In the early phase of HIV-1 gene expression, only completely spliced mRNAs are exported to the cytoplasm, these RNAs give the Tat, Rev and Nef proteins. Subsequently, Rev binds to its target sequence called *rev response element* (RRE), on unspliced or incompletely spliced HIV-1 RNAs and mediates their nuclear export.

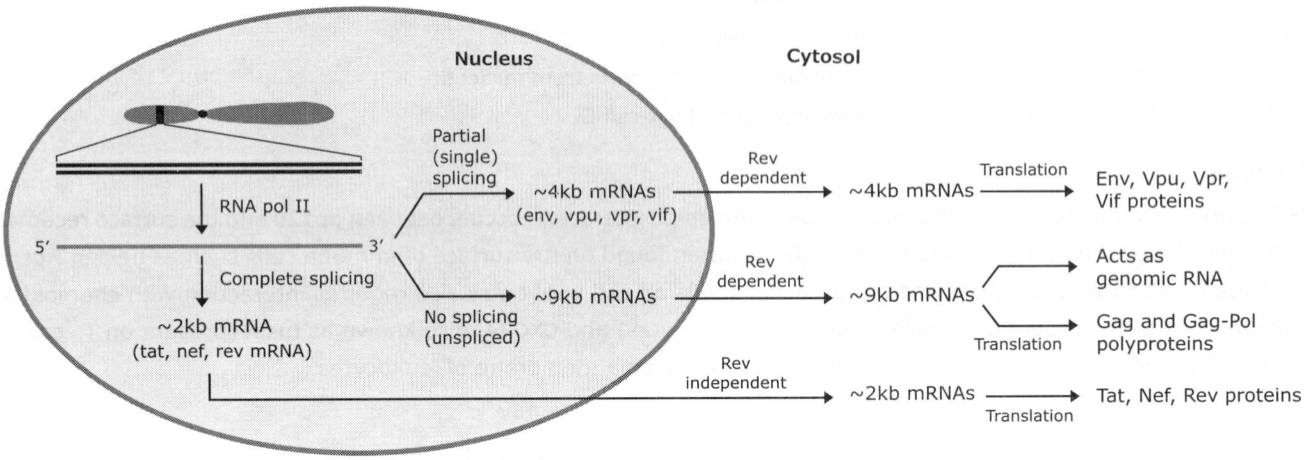

Figure 4.42 Splicing of primary transcripts and transport.

HIV-1 RNAs can thus be divided into Rev-independent RNAs lacking an intron and Rev-dependent RNAs containing at least one functional intron. Rev is a 13 kD sequence-specific RNA binding protein. It is produced from fully spliced mRNAs. The binding of Rev to the RRE facilitates the export of unspliced and incompletely spliced viral RNAs from the nucleus to the cytoplasm. Normally, RNAs that contain introns (i.e., unspliced or incompletely spliced RNA) are retained in the nucleus.

Proteins and their functions

The provirus contains nine different genes. Among nine genes, three genes — gag, pol and env - encode structural proteins. The gag gene gives rise to the 55 kDa Gag polyprotein, also called p55, which is expressed from the unspliced viral mRNA. p55 is cleaved by the virally encoded protease (a product of the *pol* gene) into matrix (MA), capsid (CA) and nucleocapsid (NC) proteins.

Gag polyprotein ⟶ CA (p24), MA (p17) and NC (p6, p9)

Pol polyprotein ⟶ RT, PR and IN

Env polyprotein ⟶ TM (gp41) and SU (gp120)

The pol gene encodes the viral enzymes protease (PR), reverse transcriptase (RT) and integrase (IN). Initially Pol polyprotein synthesizes as a Gag-Pol fusion protein from unspliced RNA. The Gag-Pol fusion protein (p160) is generated by a ribosomal frameshifting event. During viral maturation, the virally encoded protease cleaves the Pol polyprotein away from Gag polyprotein and further digests it to separate the protease, reverse transcriptase and integrase proteins. Reverse transcriptase has both RNA-dependent and DNA-dependent polymerase activities. The HIV-1 protease is an **aspartyl protease.** It is required for cleavage of the Gag polyprotein and Gag-Pol fusion protein during virion maturation. The integrase protein mediates the insertion of the HIV proviral DNA into the genomic DNA of an infected cell. This process is mediated by three distinct functions of integrase. First, an exo-nuclease activity trims two nucleotides from each 3′ end of the linear viral DNA duplex. Then, a double-stranded endonuclease activity cleaves the host DNA at the integration site. Finally, a ligase activity forms a covalent linkage at each end of the proviral DNA.

The 160 kD Env protein (gp160) is expressed from singly spliced mRNA. A cellular protease cleaves gp160 to generate gp41 and gp120. The gp41 moiety contains the transmembrane domain of Env. Interactions between HIV and the virion receptor, CD4, are mediated through specific domains of gp120.

Hepatitis virus

Hepatitis is a liver inflammation commonly caused by an infectious agent. Hepatitis sometimes results in destruction of functional liver anatomy and cells, a condition known as **cirrhosis**. Some forms of hepatitis may lead to liver cancer. Although many viruses and a few bacteria can cause hepatitis, a restricted group of viruses is often associated with liver disease termed hepatitis viruses. Hepatitis viruses are diverse, and none of these viruses are genetically related, but all infect cells in the liver, causing hepatitis.

Characteristics of hepatitis viruses

	Features	Incubation period
Hepatitis A	ssRNA; No envelope	2–6 weeks
Hepatitis B	dsDNA; enveloped	4–26 weeks
Hepatitis C	ssRNA; enveloped	2–22 weeks
Hepatitis D	ssRNA; enveloped	6–26 weeks
Hepatitis E	ssRNA; No envelope	2–6 weeks

The genome of **hepatitis B virus** (hepadnavirus) is among the smallest known of any viruses, 3-4 kb. Like retroviruses, hepatitis B virus uses reverse transcriptase during replication cycle. However, unlike retroviruses the DNA genome of hepatitis B virus is replicated through an RNA intermediate. **Hepatitis D virus**, classified as a *hepatitis delta virus*, is considered to be a subviral satellite because it can propagate only in the presence of the hepatitis B virus. Transmission of hepatitis D virus can occur either via simultaneous infection with hepatitis B virus (coinfection) or via infection of an individual previously infected with hepatitis B virus (*superinfection*). The hepatitis D virus genome consists of a single-stranded, negative sense, circular RNA.

4.12.2 Plant viruses

Plant viruses typically occur in two main shapes: **rod-shaped** and **polyhedral**. Most plant viruses possess single-stranded RNA (ssRNA) genomes, usually of the positive-sense type, meaning their RNA can directly function as mRNA for protein synthesis. The most well-known example is the **tobacco mosaic virus** (**TMV**), which is rod-shaped and contains a positive-sense ssRNA genome.

In contrast, DNA-containing plant viruses are relatively rare and fall into two main categories:

Caulimoviruses (e.g., Cauliflower mosaic virus): These viruses possess a double-stranded DNA (dsDNA) genome enclosed in a polyhedral capsid. They replicate via reverse transcription, similar to retroviruses. However, unlike true retroviruses, they do not integrate into the host genome and are therefore classified as **pararetroviruses**.

Geminiviruses (e.g., Tomato yellow leaf curl virus): These are characterized by their distinctive **geminate** (twin) capsid, with each half containing a circular single-stranded DNA (ssDNA) molecule of about 2,500–3,000 nucleotides. They replicate in the nucleus via rolling circle replication, and do not involve an RNA intermediate.

Virus name	Type of genetic material genome type
Tobacco Mosaic Virus (TMV)	RNA Single-stranded RNA (+ssRNA)
Cucumber Mosaic Virus (CMV)	RNA Single-stranded RNA (+ssRNA, segmented)
Tomato Spotted Wilt Virus (TSWV)	RNA Single-stranded RNA (-ssRNA, segmented)
Cauliflower Mosaic Virus (CaMV)	DNA Double-stranded DNA (dsDNA, circular)
Banana Bunchy Top Virus (BBTV)	DNA Single-stranded DNA (ssDNA, multipartite)

Tobacco Mosaic Virus (TMV) causes leaf mottling and discoloration in tobacco and many other plants. It was the first virus to be discovered (by Dmitri Ivanovsky) and first virus to be crystallized (by W. Stanley). TMV is a rod shaped virus with ~2130 capsomeres arranged in a hollow right-handed helix. It contains a single genetic RNA (ss, plus sense) of ~6400 nucleotides.

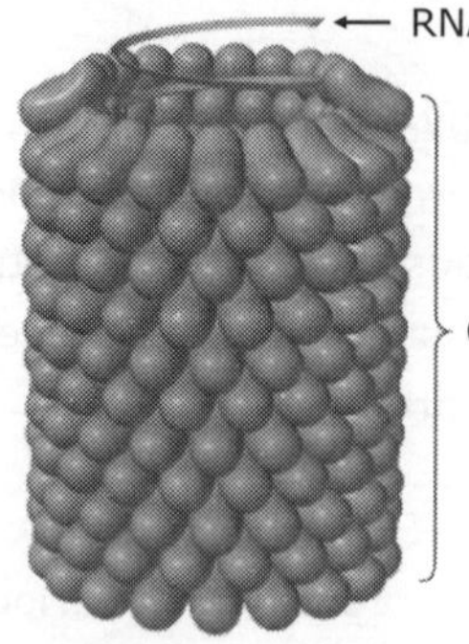

Figure 4.43
Tobacco mosaic virus has a rod-like appearance. Its capsid is made up of ~2130 capsomeres. One molecule of genomic ssRNA, 6400 nucleotides long, present in the center of the capsid. The capsomere self-assembles into the rod-like helical structure (16.3 capsomeres per helical turn) around the RNA.

4.12.3 Bacteriophages (or Phage)

Bacteriophages were first observed in 1915 by *F. Twort* in England and in 1917 by *F. d'Herelle* in France. D' Herelle used the term **bacteriophage** (*eaters* of *bacteria*). Several morphologically distinct types of phage have been described, including polyhedral, filamentous, and complex. Complex phages have polyhedral heads to which tails and sometimes other appendages (tail plates, tail fibers, etc.) are attached.

Phage T4 is an example of a complex phage. It contains a linear double-stranded DNA genome (172 kb) enclosed in a capsid and attached to a tail. The T4 capsid is an elongated *icosahedron*. It has a very elaborate tail structure including a **collar** at the base of the head and a rigid **tail core** surrounded by a contractile *sheath*. The core and sheath are attached to a hexagonal **base plate**. Attached to the tail plate are **tail pins** and six kinked **tail fibers**.

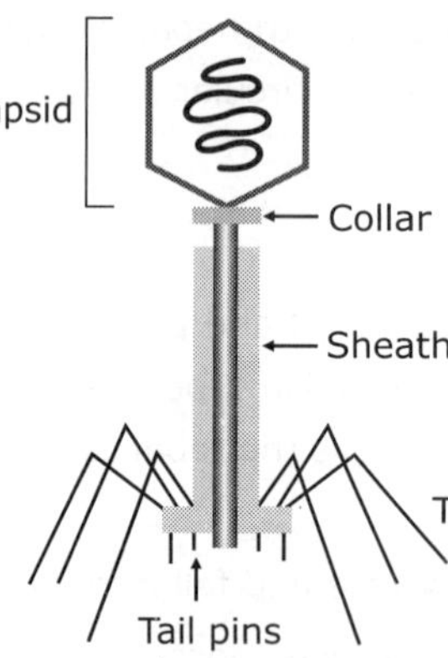

Figure 4.44
Schematic diagram of T-even phage.

Phage genome: Most of the phages are double-stranded DNA viruses. However, some phages contain single-stranded DNA and single and double-stranded RNA genome. Few examples of phages and their nature of the genome are given below:

Nature of genome	Example
Single-stranded DNA	ϕX174, fd
Double-stranded DNA	T-phages, λ-phages
Single-stranded RNA genome of plus sense	MS2
Double-stranded RNA	ϕ6

T-phages are classified into T-even (T2, T4 and T6) and T-odd phages (T1, T3, T5 and T7), in which 'T' stands for type. The T-even and T-odd phages differ in several parameters such as tail structure and chemical composition.

Virulent and temperate phages: Based on their life cycles, phages are classified into two types: virulent and temperate phages. A **virulent phage** (also called a **lytic phage**) exclusively follows the *lytic cycle*. It infects the host, rapidly replicates, and causes host cell lysis to release new phage particles. One common example is T4 phage (infects *E. coli*). During the lytic cycle, the phage attaches to the bacterial surface, injects its DNA, replicates, assembles new virions, and lyses the host cell.

A **temperate phage** can undergo both *lytic* and *lysogenic cycles*. In the *lysogenic cycle*, the phage genome integrates into the host DNA as a **prophage** and replicates passively with the host genome until triggered to enter the lytic cycle. λ **phage** and **P1 phage** (infects *E. coli*) are examples of temperate phages. like lambda phage, P1 phage also contains linear double-stranded DNA (~90 kb). Unlike lambda phage, P1 phage DNA does not integrate into the host genome. Instead, it exists as a low-copy-number plasmid, replicating independently using the host's plasmid replication machinery.

4.12.4 Life cycle of phage

All phages must undergo a specific sequence of steps to replicate themselves. First, the phage must recognize and attach to a suitable bacterial host by binding to receptors on the bacterial cell surface. Next, it injects its genome into the host cell. The phage genome is then replicated, transcribed, and translated to produce viral components. These components are assembled into complete virions, which are eventually released from the host cell to infect new targets. Phages can follow one of two main life cycles: the **lytic cycle**, in which the host cell is lysed to release new virions, and the **lysogenic cycle**, in which the phage genome integrates into the host genome and remains dormant until induced to enter the lytic phase.

Lytic pathway

The **lytic** (or **vegetative**) cycle of phages culminates in the lysis (rupture) of the host cell, leading to the release of numerous viral progeny. Phages that exclusively follow this cycle are called **virulent phages** (or **lytic phages**), as they invariably cause the lysis of the host bacterium. Classic examples include the T-even phages. The lytic cycle comprises five main stages: attachment, penetration, synthesis, assembly, and release.

Attachment (or **adsorption**): The phage binds to specific receptor molecules on the bacterial cell wall.

Penetration (or **injection**): The phage genome is injected into the host cell, leaving the capsid outside.

Synthesis: Once inside, the phage genome hijacks the host's machinery to produce viral components.

Assembly: Newly synthesized viral components self-assemble into complete phage particles.

Release (or **lysis**): Phage-encoded enzymes lyse the host cell, releasing the newly formed viruses into the environment. the average number of phage particles produced per infected cell (called **burst size**) varies by virus type, typically ranging from 50 to several hundred.

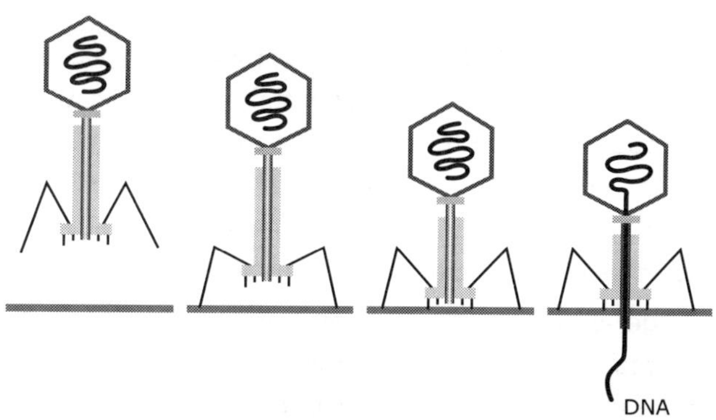

Figure 4.45 Injection of T4 DNA into the cell. The tail fibers recognize the membrane first. The tail spikes interact with the membrane. The tail sheath contacts, driving the internal tail tube through the outer membrane, peptidoglycan and to the plasma membrane where the DNA is released.

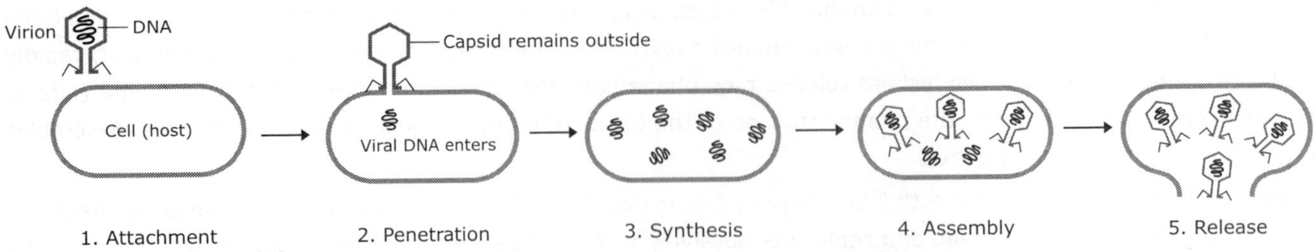

Figure 4.46 The lytic pathway of a bacteriophage.

One-step growth curve: Since phages are released more or less simultaneously, their multiplication follows what is known as a *one-step growth curve*. This curve represents the change in the quantity of infectious virus over time in a single host cell infected by a single viral particle. The one-step growth curve of virus multiplication illustrates a single cycle of viral infection in a host cell. After infection, the **latent period** begins, during which no infectious particles are detected as the virus undergoes genome replication and protein synthesis. Within this, the **eclipse period** represents the time when even intracellular infectious particles are absent, since only viral components exist. Once assembly is complete, the **rise period** follows, during which mature virions are released, causing a sharp increase in extracellular virus count. Finally, the curve reaches a **plateau**, where all susceptible cells have released their progeny.

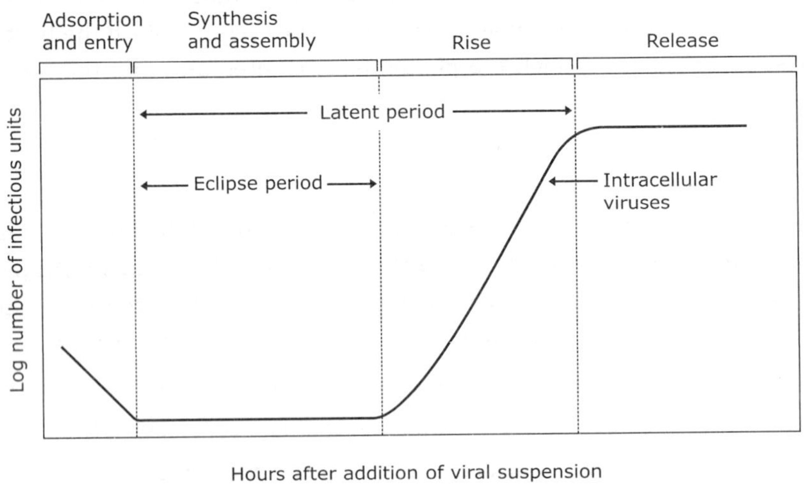

Figure 4.47 The one-step growth curve shows that virus multiplication occurs in distinct phases: an initial latent period (including the eclipse phase) when no infectious particles are detected, followed by the rise period when progeny virions are suddenly released, and finally a plateau when maximum virus output is reached.

Lysogenic pathway

In the *lysogenic pathway*, the viral DNA is inserted into the host's DNA and replicates as the host's DNA replicates. A lysogenic phage (*temperate phage*) can remain in this state for numerous replications of host cell DNA until it excises itself from the host DNA and undergoes a lytic pathway. When the genetic material of these phages is inserted into the DNA of host cells, it is said to be in the **prophage** state. A cell that contains a prophage is known as a **lysogen**. When a cell becomes lysogenized, occasionally extra genes carried by the phage genome get expressed in the cell. These genes can change the properties of the bacterial cell. This process is called **lysogenic** or **phage conversion**.

The physical state of the prophage is not identical for all temperate viruses. For example, the prophage of bacteriophage λ in *E. coli* is integrated into the bacterial chromosome at a specific site and replicates as part of the bacterial chromosome, whereas the prophage of phage P1 in *E. coli* replicates as an extrachromosomal plasmid. Most common example of a temperate phage is the lambda (λ) phage. The lysogenic phage λ, like phage T4, also uses its tail to inject the viral DNA into the host *E. coli*. Once the viral DNA is inside the host, it can either undergo a lytic pathway similar to that of T4 or integrate itself into the host DNA (lysogenic pathway).

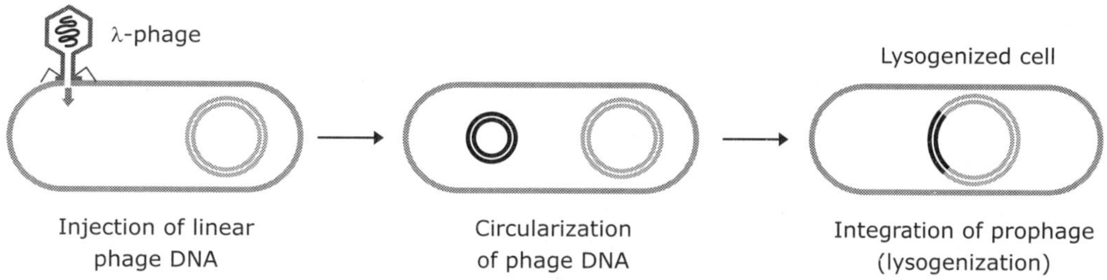

Figure 4.48 In the lysogenic pathway, the phage DNA first integrates into the bacterial chromosome to produce the prophage. When the bacterium reproduces, the prophage is also copied and is present in each of the daughter cells.

The integration of the phage lambda genome into *E. coli* chromosomal DNA is a classic example of site-specific recombination. After infection, the linear lambda DNA enters the *E. coli* cell and circularizes using cohesive ends. Recombination occurs at a unique site in the *E. coli* chromosome (called **attB**) and a corresponding site on the phage DNA (**attP**). This process establishes a lysogenic state, where the phage DNA (now called a **prophage**) is stably maintained and replicated along with the host genome.

Lysogeny is maintained by the **CI repressor protein** (also known as the **lambda repressor**), which is encoded by the *cI* gene of the lambda prophage. The CI protein binds to specific DNA sequences and blocks the expression of lytic genes, thereby keeping the phage genome dormant within the *E. coli* chromosome. Under certain stress conditions, the prophage can switch from the lysogenic to the lytic cycle, resulting in the production of new phages and the eventual death of the host cell. This process is called *induction*. Two important types of induction are UV induction and zygotic induction:

UV induction: When *E. coli* DNA is damaged by ultraviolet light, the **RecA protein** becomes activated. Activated RecA acts as a **co-protease**, promoting the self-cleavage of the CI repressor. Once CI is degraded, repression of the lytic promoters is lost, allowing lytic genes to be expressed and the phage to exit lysogeny.

Zygotic induction: If a lysogenic Hfr cell (which carries a λ prophage) conjugates with a non-lysogenic F^- recipient, the λ prophage DNA transferred into the new host is not repressed by CI, since the recipient cell does not have the repressor. As a result, the prophage genes are expressed, the lytic cycle is initiated, and the recipient cell is lysed.

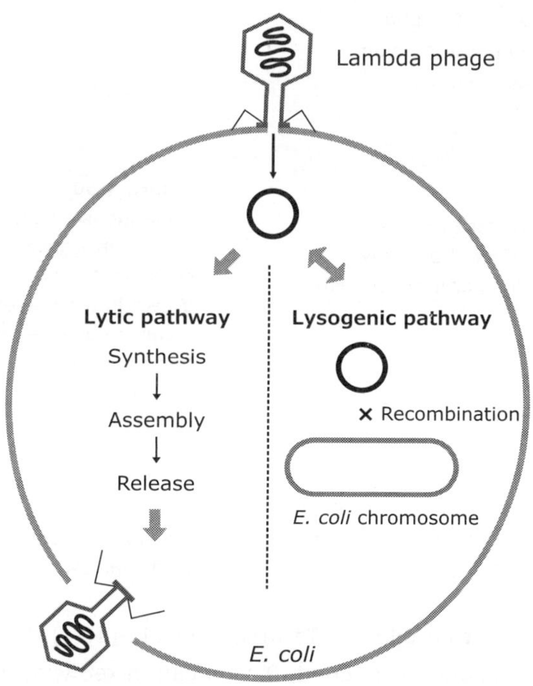

Figure 4.49
Temperate λ phage can follow lytic cycle (phage multiplication and host lysis) or lysogenic cycle (integration as a prophage).
The choice depends on regulatory proteins and host cell conditions.

4.12.5 Plaque assay

It is often necessary to determine the number of phage particles in a sample. There are two approaches to determine the number – a direct approach (such as counting phage particles with the help of a microscope or measuring the amount of a viral protein or genome in a sample) or an indirect approach (such as plaque assay). **Plaque assay** is a type of infectivity assay. An infectivity assay measures virus particles capable of replicating in a particular cell type. Before quantification of infectious phage particles by plaque assay, first, understand what a **plaque** is? It is a clear area in a lawn of host cells that results from their lysis by phages. Depending on the bacteriophage, a plaque may be clear or can be an area containing slow-growing cells. A plaque assay is performed by culturing a dilute sample of phage particles on a plate covered with host cells and then counting the number of plaques that develop. A plaque develops on the plate wherever a single phage particle initially infects a single host cell. The phage particle replicates in this initial host cell and then lyses the cell, releasing many progeny phage particles that infect the neighbouring cells on the plate. After a few such cycles of infection, enough cells are lysed to produce a visible plaque in the layer of remaining uninfected host cells. A bacteriophage capable of productively infecting a cell is called a **plaque-forming unit** (PFU).

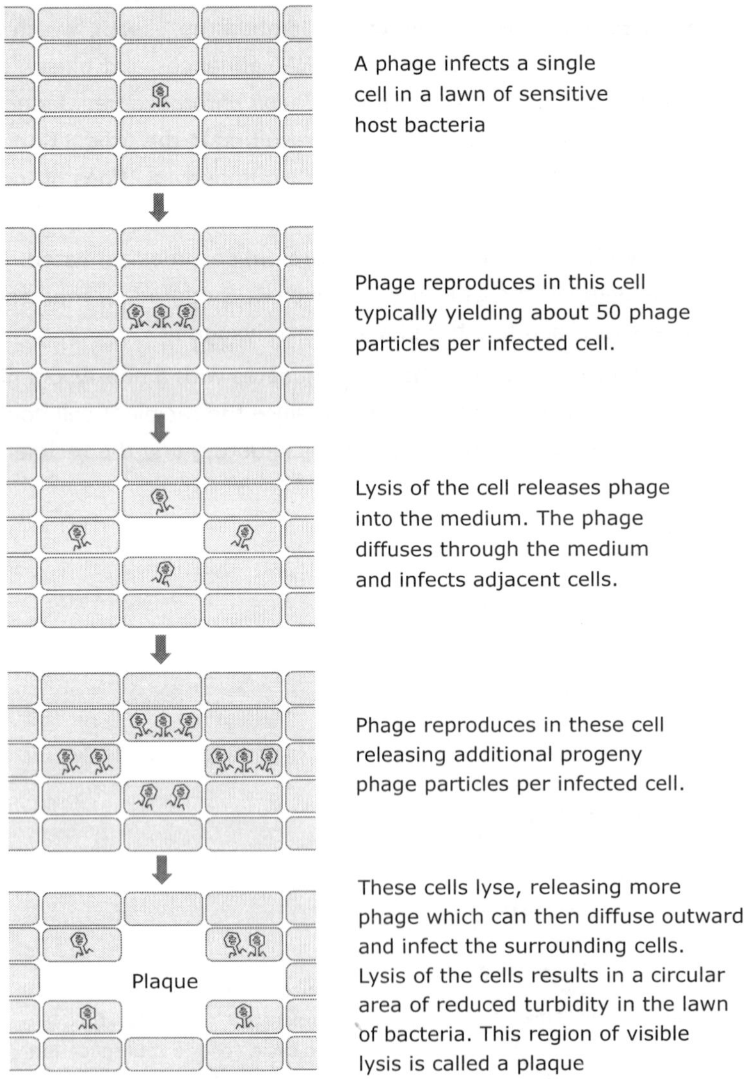

Figure 4.50
A plaque is a visible structure formed in a lawn of susceptible cells due to cell lysis. Phages are grown in the presence of a dense layer of bacteria (also called a bacterial lawn). Lysis of the bacterial hosts by virulent phage can then be readily observed when a clear zone called a plaque is detected. As the phage kills the bacteria, many plaques are observed among the cloudy bacterial lawn.

To obtain the PFUs in a particular sample, the sample must be diluted. To make 10-fold (10^{-1}) dilution, one can mix 1.0 ml sample with 9.0 ml diluent. If 100 fold (10^{-2}) dilution is needed, 0.1 ml can mixed with 9.9 ml diluent. In the **figure 4.51**, dilutions (10^{-2}, 10^{-3}, 10^{-5},...) are analyzed using the plaque assay technique. In each case 1 ml of diluted culture is used. Each dilution can now be analyzed by number of plaques. Each plaque represents the initial infection of one bacterial cell by one bacteriophage. In the 10^{-3} dilution, too many plaques are present to count as shown in the figure. Whereas in the 10^{-4} dilution, countable numbers of plaques (25) are produced. In the 10^{-5} dilution, the dilution factor is so great that no phages are present in the 1 ml sample, and thus no plaques form. A count of the plaques produced at a particular dilution can be used to calculate the PFUs in the original sample. Therefore, we can estimate number of PFUs per ml in the undiluted sample by taking 1 ml aliquot of the 10^{-4} dilution. From the 1 ml sample of the 10^{-4} dilution, PFUs in the undiluted original sample can be calculated by using the following formula:

PFUs per ml in the undiluted sample = (**Plaque number/ml**) × **1/ml** × **Dilution factor**

$$= 25 \times 1 \times 10^4 = 25 \times 10^4/\text{ml}$$

Here, we should understand that the number of plaques are equal to the number of plaque-forming units (PFUs), not equal to the number of phage particles. It is not possible to be certain that each plaque arose from an individual phage particle because not all phage particles may be infective. Secondly, it is also possible for more than one phage particle to infect the same cell. However, the number of PFU is proportional to the number of phage particles, a preparation with twice as many phage particles will have twice the PFUs.

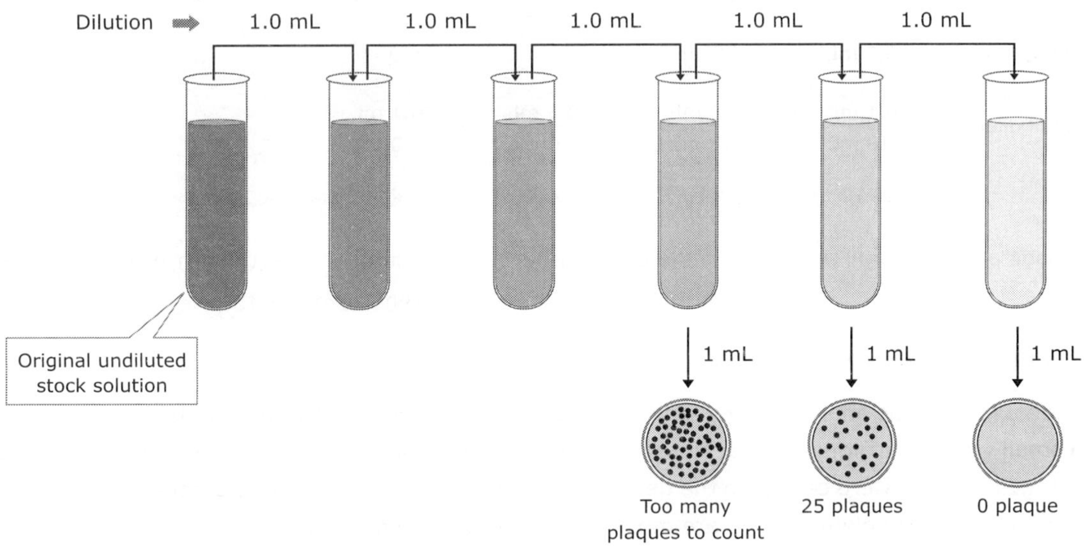

Total volume	10 mL	10 mL	10 mL	10 mL	10 mL
Dilution	10^{-1}	10^{-2}	10^{-3}	10^{-4}	10^{-5}
Dilution factor	10	10^2	10^3	10^4	10^5

Figure 4.51 The plaque assay for bacteriophage analysis. This assay is used to count infectious particles.

Multiplicity of infection

When phages and their bacterial hosts are mixed together, the phage particles and bacteria collide randomly, resulting in phage infection of the bacteria. The proportion of bacterial cells that become infected depends on the concentrations of both phages and bacteria in the mixture. Generally, higher concentrations lead to a greater likelihood of infection. The efficiency of infection is influenced not only by the absolute concentrations, but also by the ratio of phages to bacteria, known as the **multiplicity of infection** (MOI). The MOI represents the average number of phage particles available per bacterial cell. For example, if 1,000 phages are mixed with 100 bacteria, the MOI is 1,000 ÷ 100 = 10, meaning each bacterium will encounter, on average, 10 phage particles. If only 500 phages are added to 100 bacteria, the MOI is 5. The MOI can be either high or low. When there are significantly more phages than bacteria (high MOI), most bacterial cells will be infected by multiple phage particles. Conversely, at a low MOI, fewer bacteria may be infected, and most infections will be due to a single phage particle.

Problem

A phage stock is diluted in the following manner: 0.1 mL of the phage stock is diluted into 9.9 mL of dilution buffer (making a total volume in this first dilution tube of 10.0 mL). From this first dilution tube, 0.1 mL is withdrawn and diluted into a second tube containing 9.9 mL of dilution buffer. From the second dilution tube, 0.1 mL is taken and diluted into a third tube containing 9.9 mL of dilution buffer. From this third tube, 1.0 mL is withdrawn and added to 9.0 mL in a fourth tube. Finally, 0.1 mL is withdrawn from the fourth dilution tube and plated on lawn of susceptible bacterial cells. After incubating the plate overnight, 180 plaques are counted. What is the titer of the phage stock?

Solution:

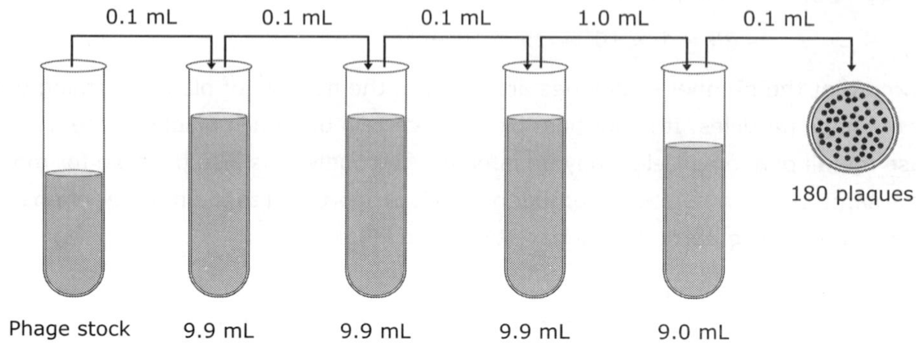

Overall dilution $\dfrac{0.1\text{ mL}}{10\text{ mL}} \times \dfrac{0.1\text{ mL}}{10\text{ mL}} \times \dfrac{0.1\text{ mL}}{10\text{ mL}} \times \dfrac{0.1\text{ mL}}{10\text{ mL}}$

$$(1\times10^{-2}) \times (1\times10^{-2}) \times (1\times10^{-2}) \times (1\times10^{-1}) = 1 \times 10^{-7}$$

Number of phage particles (or PFUs) per ml in the stock suspension = Number of plaque × 1/ml × Dilution factor

$= 180 \times 1/0.1 \times 10^{7} = 1.8 \times 10^{10}$ phage/mL

4.12.6 Genetic analysis of phage

Phages are ideal for genetic analysis. They have a short generation time and large number can be propagated on plates or in small volumes of liquid media. Mutant strains of phages can be stored for long periods also. Because of these advantages, phages were central to the development of molecular genetics, and important genetic principles such as recombination, complementation are most easily analyzed by phages.

rII locus of T4 phage: T4 is a virulent phage. The wild-type T4 phage gives small plaques (1.0-1.5 mm in diameter) and have a clear center surrounded by diffuse *halo*. The plaques have fuzzy edges because of the phenomenon called **lysis inhibition**, which delays lysis of the infected cells. One type of mutant T4 phage produced larger (2.0-2.5 mm in diameter) plaque with a sharp periphery due to rapid lysis of host: these are *r* (*rapid lysis*) *mutants*. Rapid lysis mutants are linked to three loci named *r*I, *r*II and *r*III. *r*-mutants do not show lysis inhibition, which causes them to form sharp edged, clear plaque (*r* plaque). Among the *r* mutants, the *r*II class of mutants are very informative. *r*II locus actually consists of two neighboring genes *r*IIA and *r*IIB.

Wild-type T4 phage ⟶ Lysis inhibition ⟶ Small plaque

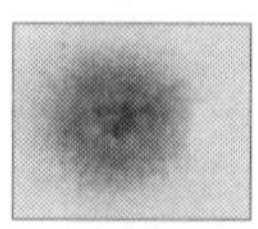

rII mutant T4 phage ⟶ Rapid lysis ⟶ Large clear plaque
(Rapid lysis mutants) (*r* plaque)

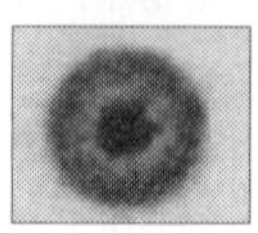

The host range of *r*II mutants and wild-types phages is different. One type of bacterial strains, *E. coli* B allows both to grow, but plaques of different size result: wild-type phages produce small plaques, and *r*II mutants produce large plaques. Another *E. coli* strain that carries the λ-prophage, designated *E. coli* K12λ or K(λ), does not permit the growth of *r*II mutants, but it does allow wild-type phage to grow. The *r*II mutants are then *conditional mutants*—namely, mutants that can grow under one set of conditions but not under another. *E. coli* B is said to *be permissive* for *r*II mutants because it allows phage growth, whereas *E. coli* K12(λ) is said to be *nonpermissive* for *r*II mutants because it does not allow phage growth.

T4 phage strain	***E. coli*** **B**	***E. coli*** **K-12**
Wild-type (rII^+)	Small plaques	Small plaques
*r*II mutant (rII^-)	Large plaques	No plaques

Complementation

A complementation test can reveal if mutations are in the same gene or in different genes. Benzer studied the concept of *complementation*. He had isolated many *r*II mutant strains that could form large plaques in *E. coli* B but could not produce plaques in *E. coli* K12(λ). To attempt gene mapping, he needed to know if the various *r*II mutations were in the same gene or in different genes. To accomplish this, he conducted a '**complementation test**'. The goal of this type of approach is to determine if two different mutations that affect the same trait are in the same gene or in two different genes. To do so, he carried out a **mixed infection experiment** with different *r*II mutants.

In the example described in the **figure 4.52**, two different mutant strains of a phage infect the same host cell, *E. coli* K12(λ). This host cell is normally a permissive host for the wild-type phage but cannot propagate either of the mutant phages by itself because they cannot make a gene product required for multiplication on that host. The outcome of the infection depends upon whether the mutations are in the same or different genes.

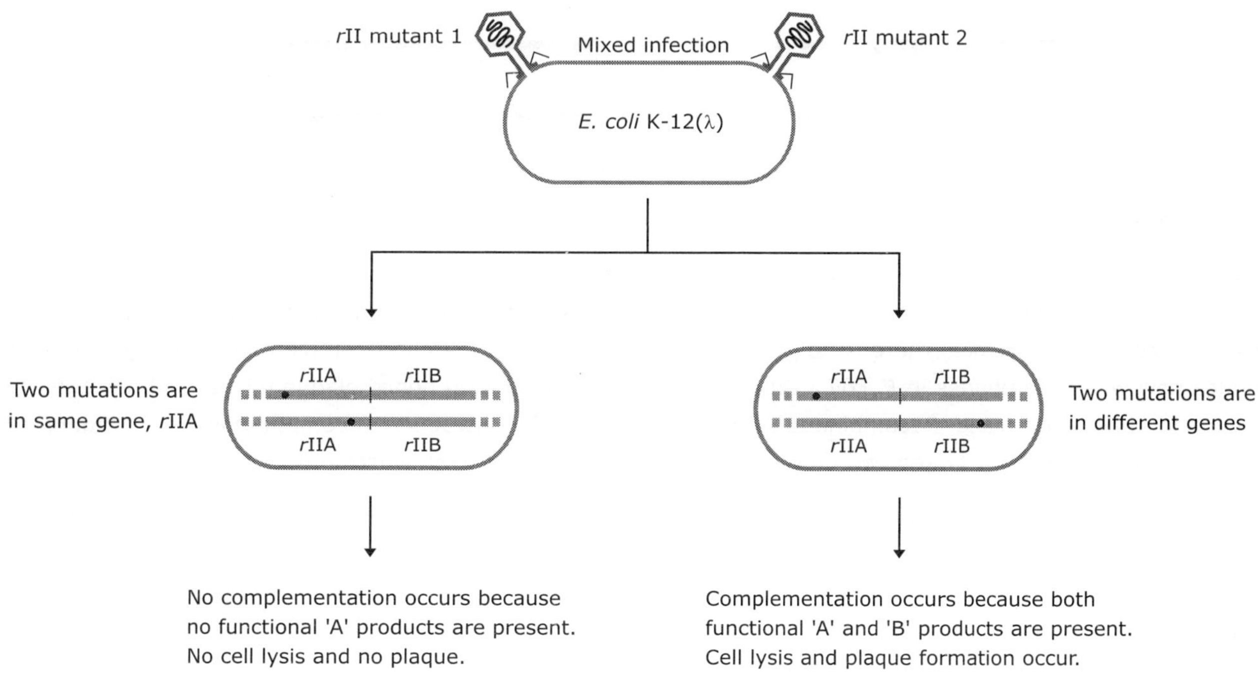

Figure 4.52 Complementation test: a schematic view of *r*II complementation. Two different *r*II mutants are used to simultaneously infect *E. coli* K12(λ) (mixed infection). Normally, an *r*II mutant cannot lyse *E. coli* K12(λ). However, if the two different mutants can complement each other, then lysis and phage growth will result. If the two *r*II mutants cannot complement each other, then no lysis or phage growth will result.

If the mutations are present in different genes, each viral genome is able to provide the functional product that the other lacks. In such a case, the defective gene product of one mutant is compensated for by the corresponding normal gene product of the other. As a result, both genomes together supply a complete set of functional proteins, enabling the viruses to undergo normal replication within the host cell. Consequently, both mutant strains are able to multiply. If the two mutations occur in the same gene, then neither viral genome is capable of producing a functional version of that gene product.

By carefully considering the pattern of complementation and noncomplementation, Benzer found that the *r*II mutations occurred in two different genes, which were termed ***r*IIA** and ***r*IIB**. Benzer coined the term **cistron** to refer to the smallest genetic unit that gives a negative complementation test. In other words, if two mutations occur within the same cistron, they cannot complement each other. In recent decades, the term **gene** has become widely popular, whereas the term **cistron** is seldom used. It is important to realize that a gene is not a point on a chromosome, but a segment of a chromosome. Mutations within a single gene may occupy different sites (that is, different nucleotides) within the gene. Any two mutations within a single gene are said to be 'alleles' in the sense that they affect the same genetic function.

Intragenic mapping

In the early 1950s, S. Benzer carried out detailed genetic studies on the rII locus, introducing the concept of **intragenic** or **fine-structure mapping**. *Intragenic mapping* is used to determine the relative distances between two or more mutant sites within the same gene, whereas **intergenic mapping** is employed to establish the distance between two different genes.

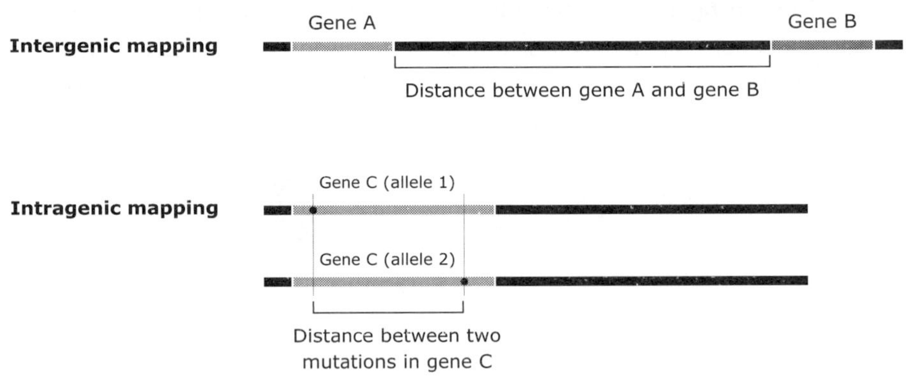

General strategy for intragenic mapping of mutations in ***r*II locus**. As we have seen that complementation does not occur when two different *r*II mutant phages have mutations in the same gene. The *r*II mutant phages cannot grow in *E. coli* K12(λ). Hence, there is no plaque formation. However, two non-complementing phage strains can produce new wild-type phages in *E. coli* K12(λ) after mixed infection and hence plaque formation if intragenic recombination has taken place. Recombination within a gene is called **intragenic recombination**. In the **figure 4.53**, intragenic recombination between two mutations in the *r*IIA gene has been illustrated.

However, these intragenic recombinants were produced at a very low rate. The frequency of recombinant phages can be determined by comparing the number of wild-type phages, produced by intragenic recombination, and the total number of phages. The total number of phages can be deduced from the number of plaques obtained from the infection of *E. coli* B. The frequency of recombinants provides a measure of map distance. Like intergenic mapping, the frequency of intragenic recombinants is correlated with the distance between the two mutations; the farther apart they are, the higher the frequency of recombinants. Genetic mapping distance is computed by dividing the number of recombinants by the total population (non-recombinants and recombinants) times 100. In this experiment, intragenic recombination produced an equal number of two types of recombinants: wild-type phages and double-mutant phages. Only the wild-type phages are detected in the infection of *E. coli* K12(λ). Therefore, to obtain the total number of recombinants, the number of wild-type phages must be multiplied by 2.

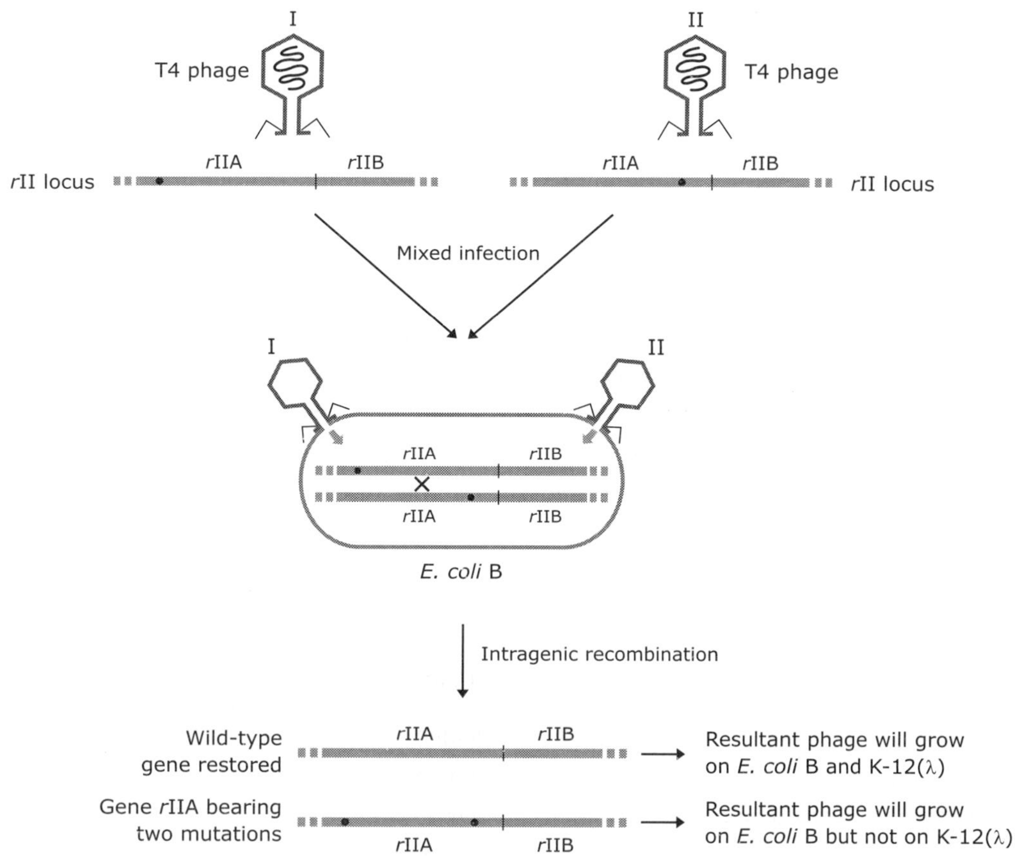

Figure 4.53 Illustration of intragenic recombination between two mutations in the *r*IIA gene. Two phage strains are used for mixed infection and both contain mutations in the *r*IIA gene. These mutations are located at different places within the same gene. First, these two different non-complementing *r*II phage mutants were mixed together in equal numbers and then infected into *E. coli* B. On rare occasions, a crossover may occur in the very short region between each mutation. This crossover produces a double mutant gene *r*IIA and a wild-type gene *r*IIA. Because this event has produced a wild-type gene *r*IIA, the function of the protein encoded by gene *r*IIA is restored. Therefore, new phages can be made in *E. coli* K12(λ), resulting in the formation of a viral plaque.

4.13 Prions and Viroids

Prions are proteins. Prion proteins are designated as **PrP**. The word *prion*, coined in 1982 by Stanley B. Prusiner, is derived from the words *protein* and *infection*. In 1997, Prusiner won the Nobel Prize for pioneering work with the prion proteins. The endogenous, normal cellular form is denoted $\mathbf{PrP^C}$ (for Cellular) while the disease-causing, infectious and misfolded form is denoted $\mathbf{PrP^{Sc}}$ (for Scrapie, after one of the diseases first linked to prions). Surprisingly, PrP^{Sc} is derived from the PrP^C by a conformational misfolding event characterized by the transition of α-helixes into β-sheet structures. PrP^C (made up of 253-amino acid residues) are glycoproteins and linked to the membrane by a GPI-linkage. It is expressed mainly in the CNS but can also be found in other non-CNS tissues. Its physiological functions remain to be defined; however, several studies have revealed that PrP^C may play a role in oxidative stress reduction, signal transduction, apoptosis regulation, cellular uptake or binding of copper ions, adhesion of the extracellular matrix, and the formation and maintenance of synapses.

The PrP^{Sc} is responsible for neurodegenerative diseases in animals including human. The normal cellular PrP^C form is converted into PrP^{Sc} through a process whereby a portion of its α-helical structure is refolded into a β-sheet. This structural transition is accompanied by profound changes in the physicochemical properties of the PrP. PrP^C is sensitive to proteases whereas PrP^{Sc} is protease resistant. High content of β-sheet in PrP^{Sc} results in the formation of amyloid fibrillous structure that is absent from the PrP^C form. The PrP^{Sc} form can perpetuate itself by causing the newly synthesized PrP protein to take up the PrP^{Sc} form instead of the PrP^C form.

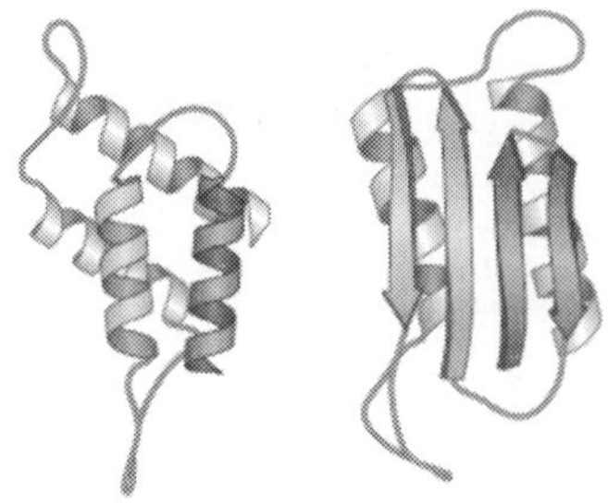

Figure 4.54
The normal prions (PrP^{C}) have a large percentage of α-helix, but the abnormal forms (PrP^{Sc}) have more β-pleated sheets.

Prions are novel transmissible agents causing a group of neurodegenerative diseases that can be perpetuated by inoculating animal with tissue extracts from infected one. Collectively, prion diseases are described as **spongiform encephalopathies**. No prion diseases of plants are known. **Kuru** was the first naturally occurring spongiform encephalopathy of humans shown to be caused by prions. It was first described by *Gajdusek* and *Zigas* in 1957. Kuru is characterized by cerebellar ataxia and a shivering-like tremor that produces complete motor incoordination. Currently, Kuru is virtually extinct due to a ban on ritualistic cannibalism in the area of Papua New Guinea where it was endemic.

Table 4.22 Prion disease of human/animals

Disease	Organism
Creutzfeldt-Jakob	Human
Kuru	Human
Bovine spongiform encephalopathy (*Mad cow disease*)	Cow
Scrapie	Sheep
Chronic wasting disease	Mule deer

Viroid

Viroids (discovered and named by Otto Diener) are the smallest infectious agents of plants that are single-stranded, covalently closed circular RNA molecule (about 250 to 400 nucleotides long) not associated with any protein. Viroid RNA does not code for any proteins. They do not need a helper virus for replication even though they do not encode any proteins. Although viroids are nonprotein-coding RNAs, some viroids display catalytic activity via **hammerhead ribozymes.** Viroid replication takes place in the nucleus or in plastids, mostly chloroplasts, through a rolling-circle mechanism with RNA intermediates. The infecting circular (+) RNA is repeatedly transcribed into (−) strands. These replicative intermediates serve as templates for synthesis of (+) strands. Despite the existence of several RNA-dependent RNA polymerases in plants, transcription of viroid RNA is catalyzed by nuclear or plastid DNA-dependent RNA polymerases. However, despite this simplicity, when viroid RNAs enter appropriate host cells they manage to replicate, move through the plant, and avoid the host defensive response, causing plant diseases. Viroids have so far been shown to infect plants only. No viroid diseases of animals are known, and the precise mechanisms by which viroids cause plant diseases remain unclear. A few well-studied viroids include coconut cadang-cadang viroid and Potato Spindle-Tuber Viroid (**PSTV**).

Table 4.23 Comparison of viruses and viroids

Features	Virus	Viroid
Nucleic acid	DNA or RNA (ss or ds)	RNA (ss)
Protein	Present	Absent
Capsid	Present	Absent
Host	Bacteria, animal and plants	Plants

Satellite viruses and Satellite nucleic acids

Satellites are subviral agents which comprise nucleic acids that depend for their replication on helper virus. Satellites include both *satellite viruses* as well as *satellite nucleic acids*. **Satellite nucleic acids** may be single-stranded satellite RNA, single-stranded satellite DNA or double-stranded satellite RNA. Most of the characterized satellite nucleic acids are associated with plant viruses, and mostly are single-stranded RNA. Satellite nucleic acids do not have capsids, rely on helper virus to enclose their genome. Satellite nucleic acids are always functionally dependent on specific helper viruses and are encapsidated by the protein coat of these helper viruses.

Single-stranded satellite RNAs are short RNA molecules, usually <1,500 nucleotides, that depend on helper viruses for replication, movement, and transmission. Certain single-stranded satellite RNAs code for nonstructural proteins, but most single-stranded satellite RNAs do not encode any functional proteins. Because satellite RNAs do not encode a capsid protein and therefore require helper virus proteins for both genome encapsidation and replication. They depend on the co-infection of a host cell with a helper virus for its replication. Single-stranded satellite RNA genomes range in length from 220-1500 nucleotides, and have been placed into one of three classes.

Class 1 Large *linear single-stranded satellite RNAs* (800-1500 nts long) with open reading frame encoding.

Class 2 Small *linear single-stranded satellite RNAs* (less than 700 nts long) without an open reading frame.

Class 3 Small *circular single-stranded satellite RNAs* (350-400 nts long) without an open reading frame (*virusoids*).

Virusoids are single-stranded satellite RNAs. They replicate via rolling circle mechanism. The strand of RNA that is packaged into the helper virus is called the plus strand. RNA replication of virusoids is similar to that of *viroids* but, unlike viroids, virusoids require that the cell also be infected with a specific 'helper' virus.

Satellite viruses are satellites which are chemically nucleoproteins and encode a structural protein to encapsidate their genomes, but rely on a helper virus to replicate. Satellite viruses are completely dependent on a helper virus for replication while the replication of the helper virus does not depend on the satellite virus. Satellite viruses are classified into single-stranded RNA satellite viruses and double-stranded DNA satellite viruses.

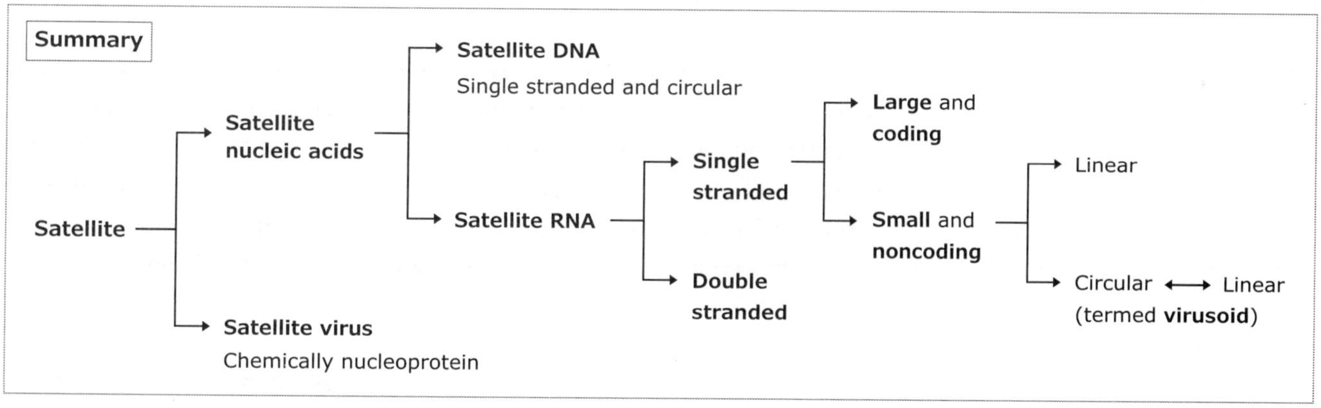

4.14 Host-parasite interactions

Host–parasite interactions describe an ecological relationship between two species in which one organism—the **parasite**—benefits at the expense of the other—the **host**. These interactions may be temporary or permanent, depending on the parasite's life cycle. Host–parasite relationships range from highly specific (infecting only one or a few host species) to generalist (infecting a broad range of species). Parasites typically live on the host (**ectoparasites**) or within the host (**endoparasites**), deriving nutrients or shelter. This relationship often causes harm to the host, which may range from mild effects to severe disease, and in some cases, can result in death. Parasites enter the host through defined routes of infection (oral, vector-borne, skin penetration, respiratory tract, etc.). Successful establishment depends on the parasite's ability to overcome host barriers such as skin, mucosa, and immune defenses.

Features of host-parasite interaction

Specificity of interaction: Parasites often have a specific host range (narrow or broad), which is determined by compatibility with host receptors and the ability to evade host immune defenses.

Entry and establishment: During the early stages of infection, a complex and dynamic interaction occurs between pathogens and animal host cells. This process involves entry of the pathogen into the host cell. Once a pathogen contacts a host cell and is recognized, it must enter the cell to establish infection. Different pathogens have evolved various strategies to cross the host cell's physical barrier—the plasma membrane.

Bacterial entry mechanisms

Bacteria use several mechanisms to invade host cells:

Zipper mechanism: Bacterial surface proteins (adhesins) bind to specific receptors on the host cell, triggering actin rearrangement and leading to engulfment of the bacteria. Bacteria such as Listeria monocytogenes and Yersinia spp. utilize this mechanism to gain entry into the cell.

Trigger mechanism: Bacteria such as *Salmonella spp*. inject effector proteins into the host cell using secretion systems. These effectors manipulate the host cytoskeleton, causing membrane ruffling and bacterial entry.

Phagocytosis: Some bacteria can be passively taken up by professional phagocytes (such as macrophages and neutrophils) as part of the host's immune surveillance. However, some bacteria manipulate this process to gain entry into the phagocyte.

Lipid raft-mediated entry: Lipid rafts are specialized areas of the host cell membrane rich in cholesterol and signaling proteins. Some bacteria use these regions for attachment and entry, as lipid rafts can cluster receptors and facilitate internalization.

Viral entry mechanisms

Viruses must enter host cells to replicate. This involves precise recognition of host receptors and mechanisms to cross the membrane barrier:

Receptor-mediated endocytosis: Most naked viruses and some enveloped viruses enter cells via receptor-mediated endocytosis. In this process, viruses bind to specific receptors on the host cell surface, triggering the formation of an endocytic vesicle. The virus is internalized and eventually escapes from the endosome to reach the cytosol.

Direct fusion with plasma membrane: Enveloped viruses, such as HIV, enter host cells by directly fusing their lipid envelope with the host cell membrane. This process is mediated by specialized viral fusion proteins. As the membranes fuse, the viral capsid and genetic material are released into the cytosol, initiating infection

Host responses

When a host is attacked by a pathogen (such as bacteria, viruses, fungi, or other parasites), it activates a complex defense system called the immune response. This response works to detect, neutralize, and eliminate the pathogen, and to establish long-term protection.

Parasite strategies for survival and growth – A pathogen's ability to propagate depends on its capacity to grow within the host while avoiding detection or destruction by the host defence system.

Immune evasion (evading host immune response): Successful pathogens can persist by either avoiding the immune response altogether or by evading it once triggered. Several immune evasion strategies have evolved. Some pathogens evade this response by altering their surface antigens during infection. These antigenic variations can occur in the following ways:

Multiple antigenic types: Many pathogens exist in multiple antigenic forms. For example, Streptococcus pneumoniae has numerous serotypes, each differing in its polysaccharide capsule. Immunity to one serotype does not confer protection against others.

Antigenic drift and antigenic shift: **Antigenic drift** results from point mutations in genes encoding surface antigens. For example, the influenza virus frequently generates mutated versions of its **hemagglutinin** and **neuraminidase** proteins, leading to new variants that can evade immunity developed against earlier strains.

Antigenic shift involves genomic reassortment. For example, when two different strains of influenza viruses infect the same host cell, segments of their RNA genomes can exchange, producing a new viral strain that carries genetic material from both parent viruses. The resulting virus has substantially altered surface proteins compared to previously circulating strains. Since these new antigens are unfamiliar to the human immune system, the population has little or no pre-existing immunity.

Gene rearrangement: Antigenic variation can also occur through programmed DNA rearrangements in the pathogen. A striking example is seen in *Trypanosoma brucei*, the protozoan parasite that causes **African sleeping sickness** and is transmitted by **tsetse flies**. This parasite is coated with a single type of surface protein called **variant-specific glycoprotein** (**VSG**), which triggers an antibody response. The *T. brucei* genome contains about 1,000 VSG genes, each encoding a protein with distinct antigenic properties. However, only one VSG gene is expressed at a time.

To express a new VSG, an inactive gene is copied and moved into an expression site via DNA recombination. Each VSG gene encodes a different antigen on the parasite surface. When the host mounts an immune response against the current VSG, most parasites expressing that antigen are cleared. However, a few parasites switch to a different VSG through gene rearrangement and escape detection. These new variants multiply until the immune system produces antibodies against them. By then, some parasites will have switched to yet another VSG, allowing the cycle to continue.

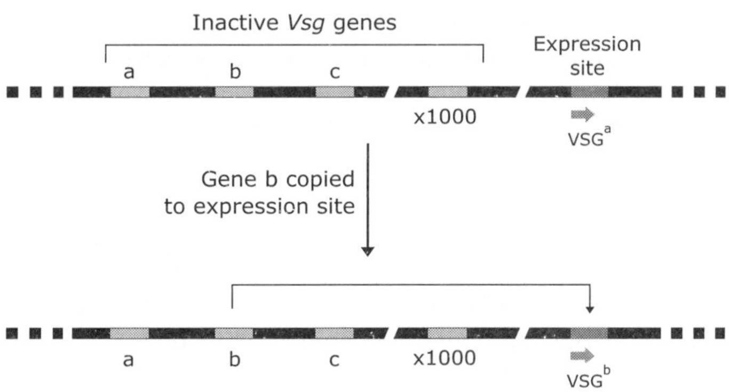

Figure 4.55 Antigenic variation in trypanosomes. There are about 1000 distinct *Vsg* genes in *Trypanosoma brucei*, and they are expressed one at a time from approximately 20 expression sites in the genome. To be expressed, an inactive gene is copied and the copy is moved into an expression site through DNA recombination. Each *Vsg* gene encodes a different surface protein (antigen). These switching events allow the trypanosome to repeatedly change the surface antigen it expresses.

Cellular invasions (evading host defenses within cells): Certain pathogens have evolved specialized mechanisms to resist destruction by the host's defense systems following phagocytosis. Once endocytosed by a host cell—typically a phagocyte—these intracellular pathogens are enclosed within a **phagosome**. Normally, the phagosome fuses with lysosomes to form a **phagolysosome**, where pathogens are exposed to degradative enzymes and an acidic environment, leading to their destruction. However, some pathogens evade destruction by manipulating this intracellular process. Key strategies employed by these pathogens include:

- *Inhibition of phagosome-lysosome fusion*: Bacteria such as *Mycobacterium tuberculosis* have developed ways to prevent the phagosome from maturing and fusing with lysosomes. By disrupting host cell signaling, *M. tuberculosis* survives and multiplies inside the arrested phagosome, protected from lysosomal enzymes.
- *Escape from the phagosome*: Bacteria such as *Listeria monocytogenes* produce **listeriolysin O** and **phospholipases**, which break down the phagosomal membrane. This allows the bacteria to escape into the host cell's cytosol, where they can use host resources and avoid many immune defenses.

- *Survival within the phagolysosome*: bacteria *Coxiella burnetii* (cause **Q fever**) can survive and grow in the harsh, acidic, and enzyme-rich environment of the phagolysosome. *C. burnetii* uses protective factors and special adaptations to replicate in these tough conditions.

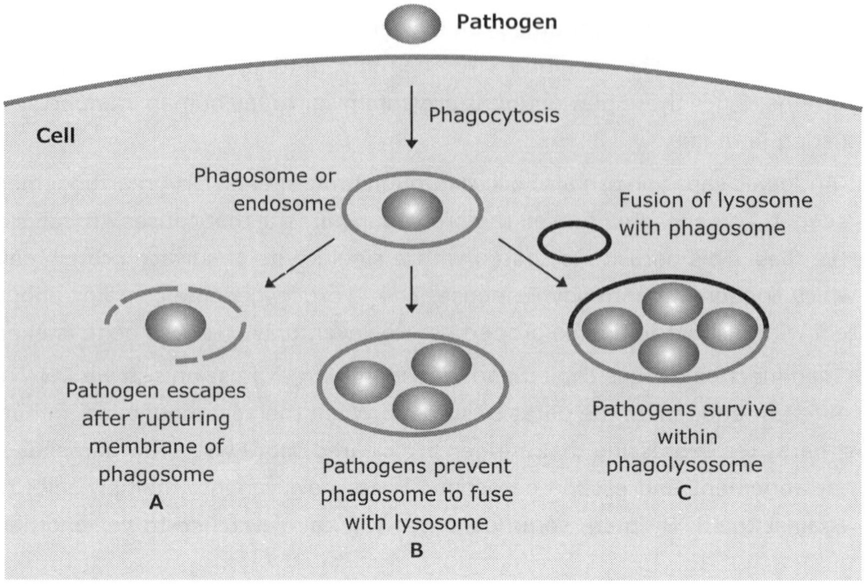

Figure 4.56 Pathogens may follow one of the three strategies to survive and multiply after phagocytosis. A. Pathogens (such as *Trypanosoma cruzi*, *Listeria monocytogenes*) escape after rupturing membrane of phagosome. B. Pathogens (such as *Plasmodium falciparum*, *Mycobacterium tuberculosis*, *Salmonella enterica*, *Legionella pneumophila*) prevent phagosome to fuse with lysosome. C. Pathogens (such as *Coxiella burnetii* and *Leishmania*) survive within phagolysosome.

Host damage and pathogenesis

Pathogenesis refers to the process by which a disease develops, progresses, and causes damage to the host following infection by a pathogen. The harmful effects on the host result from a combination of direct actions by the pathogen and the host's own immune response. How pathogens cause host damage?

Direct effects of pathogens

Toxin production: Many bacteria and fungi produce toxins that directly injure host cells. For example, diphtheria toxin and cholera toxin disrupt normal cellular functions.

Enzymatic destruction: Pathogens can release enzymes that degrade tissue barriers or cellular components, helping them invade and cause local damage.

Nutrient stealing: Some pathogens consume host nutrients, depriving host cells and contributing to tissue damage.

Cytopathic effects: Viruses as pathogens can kill host cells during their growth, leading to cell death.

Apoptosis or **necrosis**: Certain pathogens induce apoptosis or necrosis in host tissues.

Indirect damage via the immune response

Inflammation: The host's immune reaction to pathogens often includes inflammation. While meant to control infection, excessive or uncontrolled inflammation can cause tissue injury—for example, pneumonia or meningitis.

Chronic inflammation: Ongoing immune activation can lead to scarring (fibrosis) and organ dysfunction, as seen in chronic infections like tuberculosis.

Immune complex edposition: The formation and deposition of antigen-antibody complexes can trigger local immune responses, causing conditions such as glomerulonephritis or vasculitis.

Molecular mimicry and autoimmunity: When immune responses against pathogens target molecules similar to those in the host, autoimmune diseases or tissue destruction can occur (e.g., *rheumatic* fever after *Streptococcus infection*).

The severity and type of damage depend on both pathogen virulence factors and the host's immune status. Pathogenicity is not absolute—a microbe might be harmless in one host or context but cause significant damage in another, depending on immune competence, underlying conditions, or genetic susceptibility. Sometimes, host response itself is the main cause of disease symptoms, rather than the direct action of the microorganism.

Bacterial and viral diseases

The term **disease** broadly refers to any condition that impairs normal function of an organism. Any organism or agent that causes a disease is a **pathogen**. Its ability to cause disease is called **pathogenicity**. When a pathogen is growing and multiplying within or on a host, the host is said to have an **infection**. Although the terms *infection* and *disease* are sometimes used interchangeably, they differ somewhat in meaning. Disease occurs when an infection results in any change from a state of health. A disease resulting from an infection is called **infectious diseases**. Any infectious disease that spreads from one host to another, either directly or indirectly, is said to be a **communicable disease** (not all infectious diseases are communicable). Some infectious diseases are *contagious*, a disease that spreads from person to person by direct contact with the infected person or their secretions.

Table 4.24 Some important human diseases and their causative agents

	Diseases	*Causative agents*
Bacterial diseases	Anthrax	*Bacillus anthracis*
	Botulism	*Clostridium botulinum*
	Cholera	*Vibrio cholerae*
	Legionnaire's disease	*Legionella pneumophila*
	Typhoid fever	*Salmonella typhi*
	Diphtheria	*Corynebacterium diphtheriae*
	Meningococcal meningitis	*Neisseria meningitidis*
	Pneumococcal pneumonia	*Streptococcus pneumoniae*
	Tuberculosis	*Mycobacterium tuberculosis*
	Whooping cough	*Bordetella pertussis*
	Gonorrhea	*Neisseria gonorrhoeae*
	Syphilis	*Treponema pallidum*
	Tetanus	*Clostridium tetani*
Viral diseases	*Disease*	*Causative agent*
	Hepatitis	Hepatitis A, B, C, D, E
	Influenza	Influenza virus
	Measles	Measles virus
	AIDS	Human immunodeficiency (HIV) virus
	Rabies	Rabies virus

Self Test

Q1. Which statement is *true* of both prokaryotic and eukaryotic cells?

a. Prokaryotic cells are generally much larger than eukaryotic cells.

b. Eukaryotic cells have ribosomes and prokaryotic cells do not.

c. Both have DNA as their primary genetic material.

d. Eukaryotic cells have plasma membranes and prokaryotic cells do not.

Q2. Which of the following is a fact that argues against a symbiotic origin of eukaryotic flagella from bacterial flagella?

a. Bacterial flagella typically contain flagellin; eukaryotic flagella contain tubulin.

b. Bacterial flagella rotate; eukaryotic flagella do not rotate.

c. Bacterial flagella derive energy from proton gradient; eukaryotic are not.

d. More than one of the above argue against the symbiotic theory.

Q3. A bacterial culture contained 32×10^6 cells after 2.5 hours of exponential growth. If the doubling time was 30 min, what was the initial population size in this culture?

a. 20×10^4 cells

b. 10×10^5 cells

c. 40×10^5 cells

d. 16×10^6 cells

Q4. In the exponential phase of growth of a bacterial culture, 100 cfu/ml cells increased to 3200 cfu/ml cells in 2 hours. What is the generation time for this bacterium?

a. 12 minutes

b. 15 minutes

c. 24 minutes

d. 30 minutes

Q5. Interrupted mating process is used to determine the order in which genes are present on the bacterial chromosome. It is based on the kinetics of transfer of individual mating. In case of interrupted mating, conjugation is mediated between

P. Hfr donor and F^- recipient

Q. antibiotic resistant strain of Hfr and F^-

R. F^+ and F^-

S. prototropic Hfr donor and auxotropic F^- recipient

a. P and S

b. P and Q

c. R and S

d. Q and S

Q6. Match the following

Column A	Column B
P. Retroviridae	1. linear double-stranded DNA
Q. Herpesviridae	2. minus strand RNA
R. Rhabdoviridae	3. circular double-stranded DNA
S. Baculoviridae	4. plus strand RNA

a. P-1, Q-2, R-3, S-4

b. P-2, Q-3, R-4, S-1

c. P-3, Q-4, R-1, S-2

d. P-4, Q-1, R-2, S-3

Q7. Which of the following are the functions of reverse transcriptase in retroviruses?

1. It hydrolyzes the host cell's DNA.
2. It uses viral RNA as a template for DNA synthesis.
3. It converts host cell RNA into viral DNA.
4. It translates viral RNA into proteins.
5. It uses viral RNA as a template for making complementary RNA strand.
6. It degrades RNA from DNA-RNA hybrid.

a. 2 and 6

b. 2 and 3

c. 1, 4 and 5

d. 2, 4, 5 and 6

Q8. The life cycles of eukaryotic viruses and bacteriophages have many similarities, including the establishment of new replication and transcription systems, regulation of gene action (e.g., early versus late transcription) and synthesis of large quantities of structural proteins. There are certain aspects of eukaryotic viral life cycles, however, that are not (or only rarely) found in the life cycles of phage. These unique aspects are

P. eukaryotic virus usually enter the infected cell along with the capsid.

Q. the RNA of some eukaryotic viruses are converted to DNA.

R. the mRNAs of eukaryotic viruses are processed just like the cellular mRNA of their eukaryotic hosts.

S. some single-stranded RNA viruses have segmented genomes.

a. P and Q
b. R and S
c. P, Q and R
d. P, Q, R and S

Q9. *Correctly* match the microorganisms with their respective source of carbon and energy.

Microorganism types	Source of carbon and energy
P. Photoautotrophs	1. Energy from chemical oxidation & use organic compounds as a carbon source.
Q. Chemoheterotrophs	2. Light as an energy source and CO_2 as a carbon source.
R. Chemoautotrophs	3. Energy from light and use organic compounds as a carbon source.
S. Photoheterotrophs	4. Energy from chemical oxidation and use CO_2 as their carbon source.

a. P-2, Q-1, R-4, S-3
b. P-2, Q-1, R-3, S-4
b. P-1, Q-2, R-4, S-3
d. P-4, Q-1, R-2, S-3

Q10. In *E. coli* four Hfr strains donate the following genetic markers in the order shown below:

Strain 1:	L	Q	W	X	Y
Strain 2:	M	T	A	D	Y
Strain 3:	E	C	M	T	A
Strain 4:	W	Q	L	E	C

Which of the following depicts the *correct* order of the markers and the site of integration (→) of the F-plasmid in the four Hfr strains?

a. 

b. 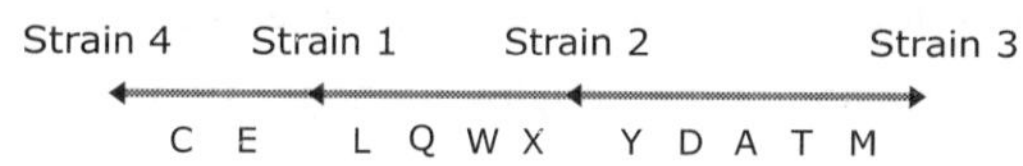

c. 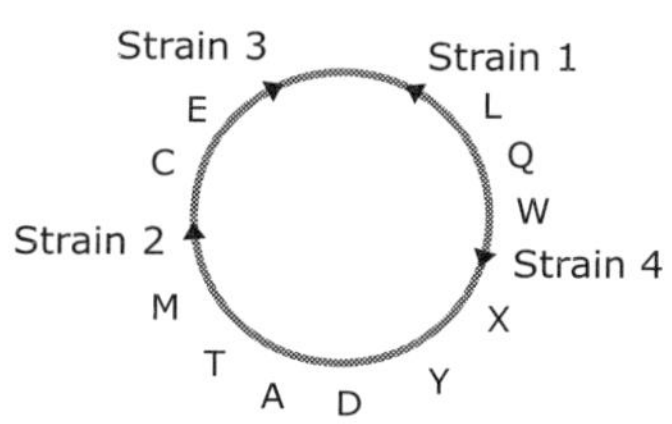

d. 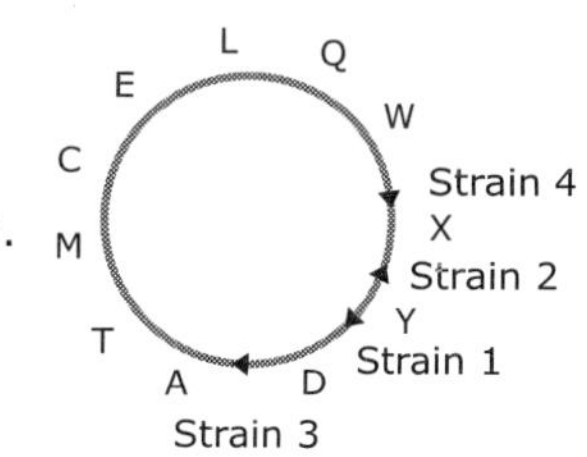

Q11. Which of the following is *not* correct about of mycoplasma, rickettsias and virus?

	Mycoplasma	Rickettsias	Virus
a. Obligate intracellular parasite	No	Yes	Yes
b. Binary fission	Yes	Yes	No
c. DNA and RNA	Both present	Either DNA or RNA	Either DNA or RNA
d. Ribosomes	Present	Present	Absent

Q12. Which of the following statement is *correct* about bacterial chromosome?

a. Bacterial chromosome has many origin of replication.

b. Bacterial chromosome is present mostly in positively supercoiled structure.

c. The bacterial chromosome is typically present as a circular dsDNA.

d. Bacterial chromosome has no centromeric and telomeric sequences.

Q13. Match the *correct* combination of *toxin* and the mode of action

Toxin	Mode of action
P. Pertussis toxin	1. Prevents release of glycine by nerve end
Q. Diphtheria toxin	2. Blocks G-protein signal transduction
R. Botulinum toxin	3. Induces fluid loss from intestinal cells
S. Tetanus toxin	4. Inhibits protein synthesis in eukaryotes
	5. Causes haemolysis
	6. Blocks release of acetylcholine by nerve end

a. P-3, Q-2, R-5, S-4
b. P-2, Q-4, R-6, S-1
c. P-5, Q-6, R-3,S-2
d. P-1, Q-3, R-2, S-5

Q14. Phages λ and P1 are both temperate phages. Which of the following statements about the P1 phage are *correct*?

P. Its genome is double-stranded linear DNA.

Q. It can undergo both lytic and lysogenic cycles.

R. It does not integrate into the host genome (unlike the lambda phage).

S. It replicates independently using plasmid replication machinery.

a. P and Q
b. Q and R
c. P, Q and R
d. P, Q, R and S

Q15. Which of the following statements are *correct*?

P. Diseases caused by pathogens; may or may not be transmissible are infectious diseases.

Q. Infectious diseases that can spread between hosts are communicable diseases.

R. Invasion of the body by pathogens; may or may not cause disease is called infection.

S. Any organism that causes disease is a pathogen, and its ability to cause disease is referred to as pathogenicity.

a. P and Q
b. Q and R
c. P, Q and R
d. P, Q, R and S

ANSWER KEY

01. c	02. d	03. b	04. c	05. a	06. d	07. a	08. d	09. a	10. c
11. c	12. d	13. b	14. d	15. d					

5

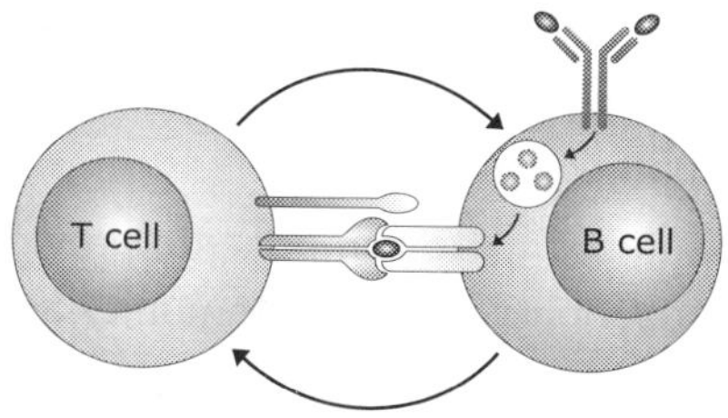

Immunology

SUBJECT FOCUS

Immunology is the science that is concerned with immune response to foreign challenges or simply, study of the body's defense against infection. It addresses the questions such as how does the body defend itself against infection, when an infection does occur, how does the body eliminate the pathogens and how does long-lasting immunity to many infectious diseases develop? The ability of an organism to resist infections by pathogens or state of protection against foreign organisms or substances is called **immunity** (derived from Latin term *immunis*, meaning 'exempt'). The array of cells, tissues and organs which carry out this activity constitute the **immune system**. The immune response is a complex process and is divided into two categories — **innate** (or **native**) and **adaptive** (or **acquired**) immunity. *Innate immunity* is a general, non-specific immune response which presents in all individuals at all times. In contrast to innate immunity, *adaptive immunity* is highly specific to the particular pathogen that induced it. It develops during the lifetime of an individual as a response to infection and adaptation to the infection. Thus, when a given pathogen is new to the host, it is initially recognized by the innate immune system and then the adaptive immune response is activated. Innate immunity is the most ancient form of defense, found in most multicellular organisms, while adaptive immunity is a recent evolutionary phenomenon, having arisen in vertebrates. Thus, vertebrates are protected by both innate immunity and adaptive immunity.

5.1 Innate immunity

Innate immunity is present since birth, evolutionarily primitive and is relatively nonspecific. It provides the *early defense* against pathogens, before adaptive immune responses can develop. It is not specific to any one pathogen but rather acts against all foreign molecules and pathogens. It also does not rely on previous exposure to a pathogen and response is functional since birth and has no memory.

Components of the innate immune system

An organism can adopt three strategies to deal with the threat posed by pathogens (the agents that are capable of causing infectious diseases): *avoidance*, *resistance* and *tolerance*. **Avoidance** mechanisms prevent exposure to pathogens. If an infection is established, **resistance** is aimed at reducing or eliminating pathogens. Finally, **tolerance** involves responses that enhance a host's capacity to resist damage induced by pathogens.

Innate immunity is the host's first line of defense and is intended to prevent infection. Its components provide defenses against infection that are ready for immediate action. The principal components of innate immunity are:

- physical and chemical barriers such as skin and antimicrobial chemicals produced at epithelial surfaces.
- soluble effector proteins, including components of the complement system and other mediators of inflammation.
- cellular components such as phagocytic cells (neutrophils, macrophages), NK cells and other innate lymphoid cells.
- cell-associated pattern recognition receptors and sensors.

Physical and chemical barriers

The physical and chemical barriers are provided by the skin and mucous membranes (or mucosa). These barriers are the **first line of defense** against pathogens and provide the initial defenses against infection. This represents a kind of avoidance strategy that prevents exposure of internal tissues to pathogens. Skin and mucous membrane prevent infection by blocking pathogens from entering the body. Most microbes and foreign substances cannot penetrate intact skin and mucous membrane but can enter the body if these membrane is damaged. Skin and mucous membrane act as not only a physical barrier but also a chemical shield. Chemical barriers at these surfaces include specialized antimicrobial proteins and peptides (generally less than 100 amino acids long) as well as acidic pH. Some human antimicrobial proteins and peptides at epithelial surfaces are *lysozyme*, *lactoferrin* and *defensins*. **Lysozyme** is an enzyme found in saliva, tears, and fluids of the respiratory tract that cleaves the peptidoglycan components of bacterial cell walls. **Lactoferrin** binds and sequesters metal ions needed by bacteria and fungi, limiting their growth. **Defensins** are cysteine-rich cationic peptides (29-35 amino acid residues) help in killing phagocytosed microbes.

The acidic pH of sweat and sebaceous secretions and the presence of various fatty acids and hydrolytic enzymes like lysozyme inhibit the growth of most microorganisms. Similarly, respiratory and gastrointestinal tracts are lined by mucous membranes. Mucous membranes entrap foreign microorganisms. Mucosal surfaces produce a variety of antimicrobial proteins that act as natural antibiotics to prevent pathogens from entering the body.

Soluble effector molecules

Pathogens do occasionally breach the *first line of defense*. If it is breached or evaded, other components of the innate immune system can immediately come into play. These consist of many types of cells and soluble proteins in tissues and blood that constantly prevent pathogens from establishing infections. A variety of chemicals mediate protection against pathogens during the period before adaptive immunity develops. The blood and other extracellular fluids contain numerous proteins with antimicrobial activity, some of which are produced in response to an infection, while others are produced constitutively. The most important of these are proteins of the **complement system**.

The *complement proteins* are over 30 serum proteins that are mainly synthesized by the liver and circulate in the blood and extracellular fluid. They were originally identified by their ability to amplify and complement the action of antibodies; hence, the name 'complement'. It also bridges innate and adaptive immunity and removes immune complexes. Activation of complement proteins in response to certain microorganisms results in a controlled enzymatic cascade, which targets the membrane of pathogenic organisms and leads to their destruction.

A group of serum proteins also increase in concentration in response to infection are termed as **acute-phase proteins**. These proteins are a heterogeneous group of plasma proteins mainly produced in the liver as the result of a microbial stimulus. They include C-reactive protein (**CRP**), serum amyloid protein A (**SAA**) and mannose-binding protein (**MBP**). These proteins maximize activation of the complement system and opsonization of invading pathogens.

Cellular components

Many specialized cell types like *neutrophils*, *macrophages*, *monocytes*, *natural killer cells* participate in innate host defense mechanisms. Once a pathogen evades the physical and chemical barriers, these specialized cells play an important role in protection. Cellular defenses constitute the innate immune system's second line of defense.

Phagocytosis is a fundamental protective mechanism against pathogens that have penetrated the epithelial cell barriers. *Monocytes* in the blood and *macrophages*, *neutrophils* and *dendritic cells* in tissues are the main cell types that carry out phagocytosis. Macrophages are long lived cells, which patrol the tissues of the body. The second major type of phagocytic cells in vertebrates, the neutrophils, are short lived cells which are abundant in blood but are not present in normal healthy tissues. *Phagocytosis* is the ingestion of invading foreign particles, such as bacteria by individual cell. Phagocytosis may be enhanced by a variety of factors collectively referred to as **opsonins** (Greek word meaning 'prepared food for'), which consist of antibodies and various serum components of complement. The process by which particulate antigens are rendered more susceptible to phagocytosis is called **opsonization**. How does a phagocytic cell recognize microbes, triggering their phagocytosis? Phagocytes express on their surfaces a variety of receptors that directly recognize specific features on the surfaces of microbes, such as cell wall components of bacteria and fungi.

After uptake, the foreign particle is entrapped in a phagocytic vacuole (**phagosome**), which fuses with lysosomes forming the **phagolysosome**. The antimicrobial agents present within the lysosome destroy the phagocytosed microorganisms. These agents include antimicrobial proteins and peptides (such as *defensins*), low pH, hydrolytic enzymes including lysozyme and proteases and specialized molecules that mediate oxidative attack. Oxidative attack on the phagocytosed microbes, which occurs in neutrophils, macrophages, and dendritic cells, employs highly toxic **reactive oxygen species** (such as hydroxyl radicals, superoxide radicals, hydrogen peroxide) and **reactive nitrogen species** (nitric oxide, peroxynitrite), which damage microbial membranes and intracellular components.

Cell-associated pattern recognition receptors and sensors

Cells and many soluble proteins of the innate immune system have the ability to recognize **pathogen-associated molecular pattern** (**PAMP**) for the initial detection of pathogens. PAMPs are pathogen-specific molecular signatures. Different types of pathogens (e.g., viruses, Gram-negative and Gram-positive bacteria, fungi) express different PAMPs. These structures or patterns (such as dsRNA found in many viruses, unmethylated CpG DNA sequences in bacterial genome, pilin and flagellin proteins in bacteria, lipopolysaccharide in outer membrane of Gram-negative bacteria, lipoteichoic acid in the cell wall of Gram-positive bacteria) are unique to or more abundant in pathogens than in host cells. The innate immune system also recognizes endogenous molecules that are produced by or released from damaged and dying cells. These substances are called **damage-associated molecular patterns** (**DAMPs**).

The innate immune system uses several types of cellular receptors, present in different locations in cells, and soluble proteins in the blood and mucosal secretions, to recognize PAMPs and DAMPs. PAMPs are recognized by **pattern-recognition receptors** (**PRRs**). Most cell types express pattern recognition receptors and therefore are capable of participating in innate immune responses. Macrophages, neutrophils and dendritic cells express the widest variety and greatest number of these receptors. Pattern recognition receptors are linked to intracellular signal transduction pathways that activate various cellular responses, including the production of molecules that promote inflammation and molecules that destroy pathogens.

Mammals have several distinct classes of cell-associated and soluble PRRs including Toll-like receptors (**TLRs**), RIG-I-like receptors (**RLRs**), Nod-like receptors (**NLRs**), AIM2-like receptors (**ALRs**) and C-type lectin receptors (**CLRs**). Among these, TLRs were the first to be identified, and are the best characterized.

Toll-Like Receptors (TLRs) are a class of pattern-recognition receptors that function exclusively as signaling receptors. It was originally identified as a protein involved in the establishment of dorso-ventral polarity in developing *Drosophila melanogaster* embryos. It is also involved, however, in the adult fly's resistance to fungal infections. TLRs are type I integral trans-membrane glycoproteins. Each TLR is composed of an extracellular N-terminal domain and an intracellular C-terminal region (human TLRs are 700-1100 amino acids long). The N-terminal domain is constituted by about 16-28 **leucine rich repeats** (LRRs) and has the function to recognize PAMPs, whereas the second, also called Toll/IL-1 receptor (TIR) domain that initiates downstream signaling.

The TLR family comprises 10 members (TLR1–TLR10) in human and 12 (TLR1–TLR9 and TLR11-TLR13) in mice. TLRs localize to the plasma membrane (i.e., cell surface) or to membrane of intracellular compartments such as the endoplasmic reticulum (ER), endosome, lysosome or endolysosome and they recognize distinct or overlapping PAMPs such as lipid, lipoprotein, protein and nucleic acid. TLRs are expressed in innate immune cells such as dendritic cells and macrophages as well as non-immune cells such as fibroblast cells and epithelial cells. TLRs are largely classified into two subfamilies based on their localization, **cell surface TLRs** and **intracellular TLRs**. In human, cell surface TLRs include TLR1, TLR2, TLR4, TLR5, TLR6 and TLR10, whereas intracellular TLRs are localized in the intracellular compartments such as endosome include TLR3, TLR7, TLR8 and TLR9. Different TLRs recognize different ligands. Cell surface TLRs mainly recognize microbial membrane components such as lipids, lipoproteins and proteins.

TLRs and their ligands

TLR	Ligand
TLR2/TLR1	Bacterial triacyl lipopeptides
TLR2	Fungal phospholipomannan, Bacterial peptidoglycans
TLR2/TLR6	Fungal zymosan, Bacterial diacyl lipopeptides and lipoteichoic acid, GPI anchor (*Trypanosoma cruzi*)
TLR3	Viral dsRNA
TLR4	Bacterial lipopolysaccharide, Fungal mannan
TLR5	Bacterial flagellin
TLR7	Viral ssRNA
TLR8	Viral ssRNA
TLR9	Bacterial CpG DNA, Viral CpG DNA, Hemozoin (*P. falciparum*)
TLR10	Unknown
TLR11	Unknown
TLR12	Profilin (*Toxoplasma gondii*)
TLR13	Bacterial 23S rRNA

*All function as homodimers except TLR1, TLR2 and TLR6, which form TLR2/1 and TLR2/6 heterodimers. TLR10 is present in humans but not in mice; TLR11, TLR12 and TLR13 are found in mice but not in humans.

Toll-like receptor signaling pathways

TLRs function exclusively as signaling receptors. When TLRs bind their PAMP ligands via their extracellular LRR domains, they are induced to dimerize, either as a homodimer or as a heterodimer. TLRs signal through the recruitment of specific adaptor molecules, leading to activation of the transcription factors NF-κB and IRFs (interferon regulatory factors), which dictate the outcome of innate immune responses by producing inflammatory cytokines, type I interferon and other mediators. The two key adaptors that are recruited to TLR dimers are **MyD88** (myeloid differentiation factor 88) and **TRIF** (TIR domain–containing adaptor-inducing IFN-β factor). MyD88 is the adaptor used by most TLRs—all of the plasma membrane TLRs and most of those in endosomes. TRIF uniquely associates with TLR3 and also with TLR4 when it localizes to endosomes. On the basis of nature of adaptor protein, TLR signaling are of two different types: a **MyD88-dependent pathway** that leads to the production of inflammatory cytokines, and a **TRIF-dependent signaling pathways** associated with the stimulation of IFN-β and the maturation of dendritic cells.

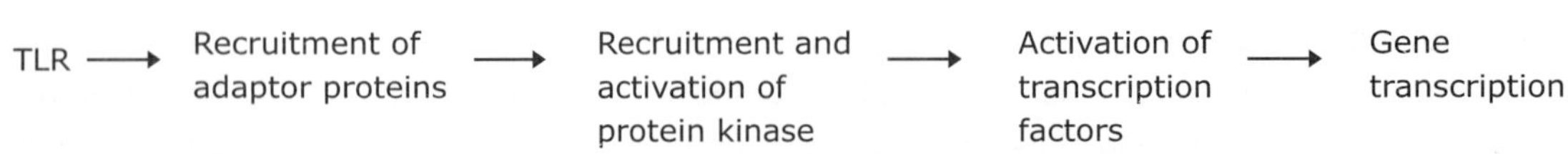

Figure 5.1 TLR and basic signaling mechanisms.

Inflammatory response

Macrophages, neutrophils and dendritic cells act as sensor cells that detect infection and initiate immune responses by producing inflammatory mediators. Activation of PRRs on sensor cells can directly induce effector functions in these cells, such as the phagocytosis and degradation of bacteria they encounter. But sensor cells serve to amplify the immune response by the production of *inflammatory mediators*. Inflammatory mediators are the secreted proteins called **cytokines**.

Leukocytes and plasma proteins, which are critical for innate defense against microbes, normally circulate in the blood and are recruited to sites of infection and injury, where they perform the effector functions that kill pathogens. The cytokines released by activated sensor cells act to recruit leukocytes and plasma proteins from the blood into infected tissues, a process, known as **inflammation**, that helps to destroy the pathogen. The inflammatory response delivers the cells and molecules of host defense to the sites where infecting agents need to be combated. Inflammation is described clinically by the Latin words *calor*, *dolor*, *rubor* and *tumor*, meaning heat, pain, redness (**erythema**) and swelling (**edema**), respectively. Each of these is the result of specific changes in the local blood vessels. Erythema is caused by increased vascular diameter, which leads to increased blood flow, thereby causing heat and redness in the area. Heat, redness and swelling result from the dilation and increased permeability of blood vessels during inflammation, leading to increased local blood flow and leakage of fluid and blood proteins into the tissues. Leukocytes migration from blood into tissues depend on adhesion molecules expressed on the leukocytes and vascular endothelial cells as well as chemokines. **Chemokines** are small chemoattractant proteins that stimulate leukocyte movement and regulate the migration of leukocytes from the blood to tissues.

The main cell types seen in the initial phase of an inflammatory response are macrophages and neutrophils. Macrophages and neutrophils are thus also known as **inflammatory cells**. Typically, the leukocyte that is recruited first from the blood into sites of inflammation is the neutrophil because it is the most abundant leukocyte in the blood and respond most rapidly to the chemotactic signals. Blood monocytes, which become macrophages in the tissue, become increasingly prominent over time. The migration of cells into the tissue and their local actions account for the pain. Later, if the inflammation continues, eosinophils also migrate into inflamed tissues and contribute to the destruction of the invading microorganisms.

Box 5.1 Cytokines

Cytokines (not to be confused with *cytokinin*, a plant hormone) are low molecular weight (generally less than 30 kDa) soluble proteins, non-immunoglobulin in nature, secreted by cells of the immune system and perform cellular communication. Cells of the immune system communicate through the exchange of secreted cytokines. Depending on the spatial location of the cytokine-responding cell, such communication can be **autocrine** (signaling to same cell responsible for their production), **paracrine** (signaling to neighbouring cells) or **endocrine** (signaling distantly located target cells through the circulation). They are highly potent hormone-like substances, active even at femto molar concentration. However, they differ from hormones and growth factors. All three are secretory proteins that elicit their biological effects at very low concentrations by binding to receptors on target cells. Growth factors tend to be produced constitutively, whereas cytokines and hormones are secreted in response to discrete stimuli. Unlike hormones, which generally act long range in an endocrine fashion, most cytokines act over a short distance in an autocrine or paracrine fashion. Besides, most hormones are produced by specialized glands and tend to have a unique action on one or a few types of the target cell. In contrast, cytokines are often produced by, and bind to, a variety of widely distributed cells.

Cytokines produce biological actions only when they bind to specific, high-affinity receptors on the surface of target cells. These receptors then convert an external signal (binding of the cytokine to the receptor) to an intracellular biochemical signal, usually resulting in gene transcription. **Cytokine receptors** are transmembrane proteins where the binding of the cytokine occurs in the extracellular region and interaction with signaling proteins occurs in the cytoplasm.

There are over 100 different cytokines. The generic name of cytokines includes all proteins with a small molecular weight, released by cells of the immune system. But they are also secreted by many cells in addition to those of the immune system, such as endothelial cells and fibroblasts. They used to have different names depending either on their origin, such as **lymphokines** (produced by lymphocytes), **monokines** (substances produced by monocytes or macrophages), or on their activity: **chemokines, interleukins, interferons**. Cytokines may be broadly grouped into the following categories: hematopoietins, interleukins, interferons, chemokines and members of the tumor necrosis factor (TNF) family.

Interleukins: Interleukins (ILs) are a group of cytokines secreted by a variety of leukocytes that have effects on other leukocytes. However, this term is imperfect because many cytokines that are synthesized only by leukocytes and that act only on leukocytes are not called interleukins, whereas many cytokines called interleukins are made by or act on cells other than leukocytes. The function of the immune system depends largely on interleukins. The majority of interleukins are synthesized by T_H cells, as well as through monocytes, macrophages, and endothelial cells. They promote the development and differentiation of T cells, B cells and hematopoietic cells.

Chemokines: Chemokines are a family of small proteins that are defined by four conserved cysteine residues. Their name (derived from chemoattractant cytokines) is due to their ability to induce directed chemotaxis in nearby responsive cells. These proteins activate GPCRs and induce cells to migrate through a concentration gradient. The role of chemokines is to promote the accumulation of these cells at the source of chemokine production.

Interferons: The interferons (IFNs) are a large family of cytokines involved in antiviral defense, cell growth regulation and immune activation. Interferon was the first cytokine to be described in 1957. Based on the type of receptor through which they signal, human interferons have been classified into three major types— Type I IFN, Type II IFN and Type III IFN.

Tumor necrosis factor family: The tumor necrosis factor (TNF) family of cytokines activate signaling pathways for cell survival, death and differentiation. It constitutes 19 members that mediate diverse biological functions in a variety of cellular systems.

Hematopoietins: This is a generic name given to hematopoietic growth factors or hematopoietic cytokines. These factors include the various colony-stimulating factors (**CSF**, including G-CSF, GM-CSF, M-CSF), **Epo** (erythropoietin), **SCF** (stem cell factor), **SCPF** (stem cell proliferation factor), and various interleukins (IL-1, IL-3, IL-4, IL-5, IL-6, IL-11, IL-12).

Role of cytokines

Cytokines are the critical regulator of cell growth, migration, development and differentiation. They are immunomodulating agents and required for immunoregulation of both innate as well as adaptive immune responses. They have important roles in the regulation of immune responses, induction of the inflammatory response, regulation of hematopoiesis, leukocytes movement, control of cellular proliferation and differentiation.

The biological activities of cytokines exhibit **pleiotropy** (a given cytokine has different biological effect on different target cells), **redundancy** (two or more cytokines that mediates similar functions), **synergy** (combined effect of two cytokines on cellular activity is greater than the additive effect of the individual cytokines) and **antagonism** (effect of one cytokines inhibit the effect of another cytokines).

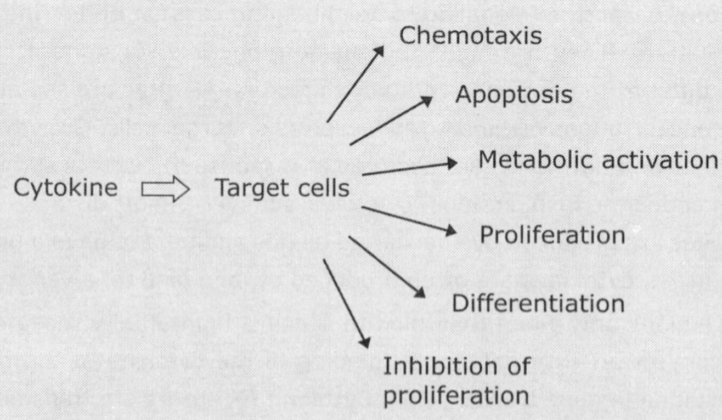

Role of cytokines in innate immune responses: Several cytokines facilitate innate immune responses because they induce macrophage and NK cell activation, generating inflammatory and chemotaxis processes. The main cytokines that have a role in the innate response are: IL-1, IL-6, IL-12, TNF-α, IFN-α and β. The IL-1, IL-6, IL-12 activate the monocytes-macrophages and NK cells. Tumor necrosis factor is the main trigger of the inflammatory response.

Examples of some cytokines of innate immunity

IL-1	Synthesized by: monocytes, macrophages, endothelial cells and epithelial cells. Effects: inflammation, fever, induction of acute phase proteins.
IL-12	Synthesized by: macrophages, dendritic cells. Effects: NK cells, influences adaptive immunity.
IL-6	Synthesized by: macrophages, endothelial cells and T_H2 cells. Effects: influences adaptive immunity, induction of acute phase proteins.
TNF-α	Synthesized by: macrophages, monocytes, neutrophils, activated T cells and NK cells. Effects: inflammation, induction of acute phase proteins, neutrophil activation.
IFN-α	Synthesized by: macrophages, dendritic cells, virus-infected cells. Effects: activates NK cells, increases class I MHC expression.
IFN-β	Synthesized by: macrophages, dendritic cells, virus-infected cells. Effects: activates NK cells, increases class I MHC expression.

Role of cytokines in adaptive immune responses: Cytokines are involved in the development and regulation of both cellular and humoral adaptive immune responses. T_H cells exert most of their helper functions through secreted cytokines. Although CTLs also secrete cytokines, their array of cytokines generally is more restricted than that of T_H cells. Antigen stimulation of naive T_H cells in the presence of certain polarizing cytokines can lead to the generation of subpopulations of T_H cells – T_H1, T_H2, T_H9, T_H22, T_H17, T_{REG} and T_{FH}. Each subset displays characteristic and different profiles of cytokine secretion.

5.2 Adaptive immunity

Adaptive immunity, also known as **acquired immunity**, is capable of recognizing and selectively eliminating specific foreign antigens. It does not come into play until there is an antigenic challenge to the organism. It is adapted to recognize, eliminate, and remember the foreign antigens. Adaptive immunity displays following four characteristics:

Antigenic specificity: It is the ability to discriminate among different antigens.

Immunologic memory: It is the ability to recall the previous contact with a foreign antigen and respond to it in a learned manner-that is, with a more rapid and larger response.

Diversity: The ability to respond to different antigens.

Self and non-self recognition: It is the ability to recognize and respond to molecules that are foreign and to avoid making a response to those molecules that are self (**self-tolerance**).

Table 5.1 Difference between the innate and adaptive immune response

Attribute	Innate immune response	Adaptive immune response
Specificity	Antigen non-specific	Antigen specific
Response time	Rapid response (minutes to hours)	Slow response (days to weeks)
Diversity	Limited	Very high
Memory	Absent or low	Present
Major cell types	Phagocytes, NK cells and others	T and B cells, antigen presenting cells
Distribution	Found in vertebrates and invertebrates	Found only in jawed vertebrates

Adaptive immunity may be *natural* or *artificial*. In **natural immunity**, an organism acquires immunity naturally. It can be **active** (developing his or her own immunity after exposure to pathogen) or **passive** (acquired by receiving preformed immunity made by another, for example, transfer of maternal antibodies from mother to fetus through the placenta). In **artificial immunity**, an organism acquires immunity through medical procedure. It can be **active** (developing his or her own immunity as a result of vaccination) or **passive** (acquired by receiving preformed antibodies or immune cells made by another).

Table 5.2 Difference between active and passive immunity

Active immunity	Passive immunity
Exposure to antigen	No exposure to antigen
Immunity achieved by injecting antigens	Immunity achieved by injecting antibody or immune cells
Activation of immune system	No immune system activation
Immune state develops over a period of weeks	Immunity develops immediately
Immunological memory develops	No immunological memory develops

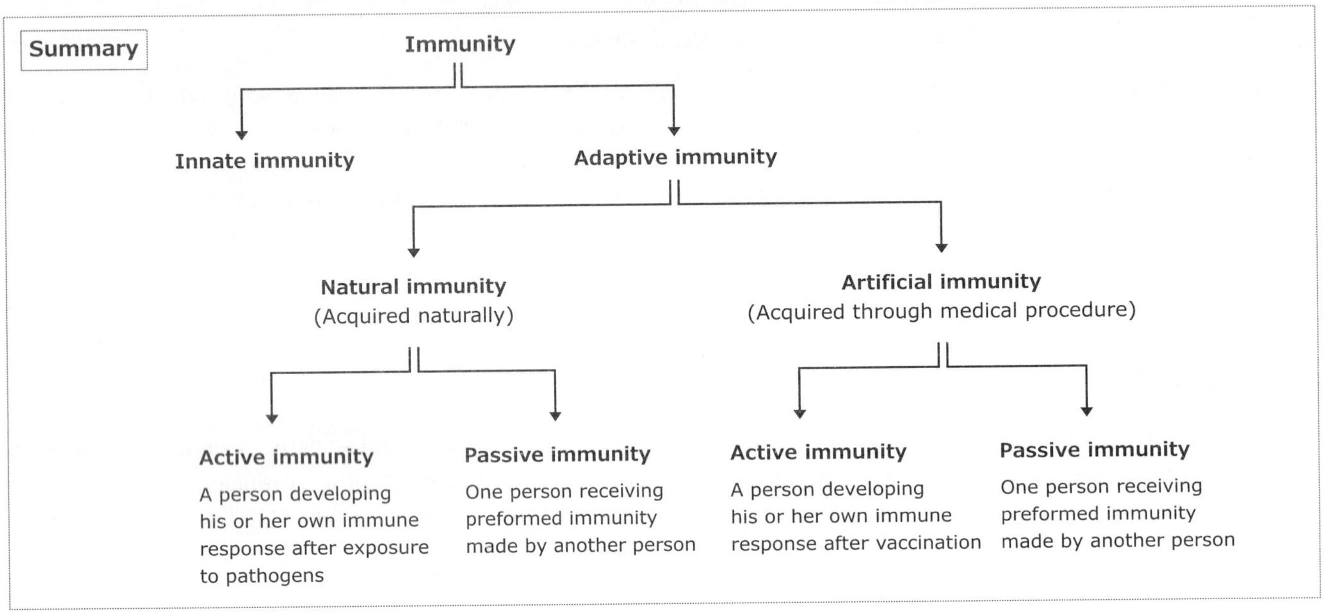

Immune response of adaptive immunity

There are two arms of adaptive immunity, which have different mediators and effectors and different purposes but one common aim: to eliminate the antigen. These two arms interact with each other and collaborate to achieve the final goal of eliminating the antigen. Of these two arms of the adaptive immune response, one is mediated mainly by **B cells** and circulating **antibodies**, a form of immunity which is referred to as **humoral immunity** (the word *humors* was formerly used to define *body fluids*). The other is mediated by **T cells**, which, do not synthesize antibodies but instead synthesize and release various cytokines that affect other cells and also directly kill target cells. Hence, this arm of the acquired immune response is termed **cellular** or **cell-mediated immunity**.

In humoral immunity, **B cells** (or **B-lymphocytes**) synthesize and secrete antibodies with specificity against the foreign substance, whereas the **T cells** (or **T-lymphocytes**) do not make antibodies but perform various effector functions when *antigen-presenting cells* (**APCs**) bring antigens into the secondary lymphoid organs. T cells also interact with B cells and help the latter make antibodies and have a central role in the development and regulation of adaptive immunity.

Innate and adaptive immunity are not independent

The innate and adaptive immunity operate in cooperative and interdependent ways. The activation of innate immune responses produces signals that stimulate and direct subsequent adaptive immune responses. They cooperate in many ways. The encounter between macrophages and microbes can generate 'danger' signals that stimulate and direct adaptive responses. It may increase the ability of macrophages to display antigen for recognition by antigen specific T cells. Macrophage stimulated by encounters with microbes also secretes immunoregulatory molecules called **cytokines**. These cytokines guide adaptive immune response. Vice-versa, adaptive immune system also produces signals and components which stimulate and increase the efficacy of innate response. The cells of adaptive system (e.g., T cells) secrete cytokines and increase the ability of macrophage to kill the ingested microbes. By binding to the pathogens, antibodies mark it as a target for attack by complement.

5.3 Cells of the immune system

The immune system is a defense system in a host consisting of widely distributed cells, tissues and organs that recognize foreign substances and microorganisms and act to neutralize or destroy them. The cells responsible for both nonspecific and specific immunity are the *leukocytes* (or white blood cells). Leukocytes include neutrophils, eosinophils, basophils, mast cells, monocytes and lymphocytes. All leukocytes arise from **hematopoietic stem cell** (HSC). During hematopoiesis, hematopoietic stem cell differentiates along one of two pathways, giving rise to either a **common lymphoid progenitor cell** or a **common myeloid progenitor cell**.

Summary

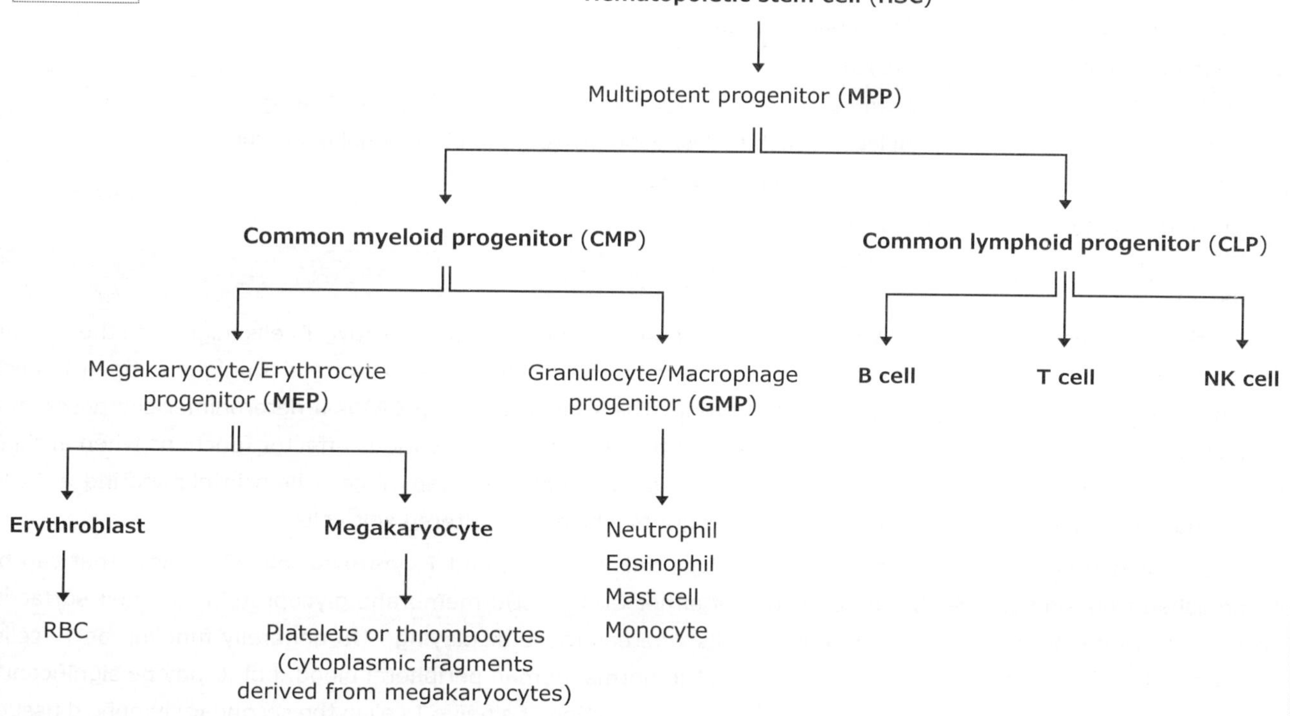

5.3.1 Common lymphoid progenitor

Common lymphoid progenitor cells give rise to B cells, T cells and natural killer cells. Lymphocytes (responsible for adaptive immune response) are mononuclear leukocytes which constitute 20 to 40% of total white blood cells (or leukocytes). They occur in large numbers in the blood and lymph and in lymphoid organs such as the thymus, lymph nodes, spleen and appendix. Up to 99% of lymphocytic cells are found in lymph. Lymphocytes are of three main types:

1. **B cells** (or B-lymphocytes)
2. **T cells** (or T-lymphocytes)
3. **NK cells** (or Natural killer cells)

B cells

The **B cells** mature in the bone marrow in many mammalian species, including humans (in birds it is *Bursa of Fabricius*) and express membrane-bound antibodies. Contact with antigen induces **naïve B cells** (cells that have not been exposed to an antigen) to proliferate and differentiate into *effector cells* known as **plasma cells** and **memory cells**. Effector cells carry out specific functions to combat the pathogen, while memory cells persist in the host, and when re-challenged with the same antigen, respond faster and more efficiently. B cells also serve as **antigen presenting cells** (APCs). Defense against microbes that is mediated by B cells is called *humoral immunity*. This form of immunity neutralizes and eliminates extracellular pathogens and toxins that are accessible to antibodies, and antibodies enhance phagocytosis of extracellular pathogens, which can then be killed inside phagocytes. However, antibodies cannot attack pathogens that survive inside phagocytes and other cells. T cell–mediated immunity evolved to provide defense against such pathogens.

Properties of B cells	
Origin	Bone marrow
Maturation	Bone marrow (Bursa of Fabricius in bird)
Expression of Ag receptor	Bone marrow
Differentiation	In lymphoid tissue
Surface immunoglobulin	Present
Immunity	Humoral
Distribution	Spleen, Lymph nodes, Bone marrow and other lymphoid tissue
Secretory product	Antibodies and cytokines
Complement receptors	Present

T cells

T cells arise in the bone marrow. Unlike B cells, which mature within the bone marrow, T cells migrate to the *thymus gland* to mature. During its maturation within the thymus, the T cell comes to express a unique antigen-binding molecule, called the *T cell receptor*, on the membrane. The T cell receptor (**TCR**) is a heterodimer composed of α and β chains or γ and δ chains. T cells do not make antibodies but perform various effector functions when antigen presenting cells (**APCs**) bring antigens into the secondary lymphoid organ. T cells help in eliminating antigen presenting cells, cancer cells, virus-infected cells or grafts which have altered self-cells.

T cells are divided into two major cell types—**T helper cells** (T_H cells) and **T cytotoxic cells** (T_C cells)—that can be distinguished from one another by the presence of either CD4 or CD8 membrane glycoproteins on their surfaces. T cells displaying CD4 generally function as T_H cells whereas those displaying CD8 generally function as T_C cells. The ratio of T_H cells and T_C cells is approximately 2:1 in normal human peripheral blood, but it may be significantly altered by immunodeficiency and autoimmune diseases. Activation of a naïve T cell in the secondary lymphoid tissues results in the generation of *effector* and *memory* T cells. When naïve T_C cells become activated, they proliferate and differentiate into a type of effector cell called a **cytotoxic T lymphocyte** (CTL). T_H cells can be activated and differentiate into a variety of effector T cell subsets such as T_H1, T_H2, T_H17, T_{REG} (regulatory T cells) and T_{FH} (follicular helper T cells). The defining characteristics of differentiated subsets of effector cells are the cytokines they produce.

Defense against pathogens that is mediated by T cells is called **cell-mediated immunity.** T cells can provide protection against intracellular and extracellular pathogens and also assist in the elimination of tumor cells. T_C cells provide protection against intracellular pathogens such as viruses and some bacteria and parasites that multiply in the host-cell cytoplasm, where they are sheltered from attack by antibodies. They provide this protection by killing the infected cell before the microbes can proliferate and escape from the infected cell to infect neighbouring cells. T_H cells are crucial for defense against both extracellular and intracellular pathogens. They produce cytokines that activate B cells to make antibodies that inactivate or eliminate extracellular pathogens and their toxic products. They also activate macrophages to destroy any intracellular pathogen multiplying within the macrophage's phagosomes, and they help activate T_C cells to kill infected target cells.

Properties of T cells

Origin	Bone marrow
Maturation	Thymus
Expression of Ag receptor	Thymus
Differentiation	Lymphoid tissue
Surface Ig	Absent
Immunity	Cell mediated as well as humoral
Secretory product	Cytokines
Receptor	TCR on membrane

B and T cells express many different CD proteins on their surface, depending on their stage of development and state of activation. In addition, each B or T cell also expresses an antigen-specific receptor (the B-cell receptor or the T-cell receptor, respectively) on its surface. Surface proteins expressed by cells of the immune system (as well as some other cells) are often referred to by the cluster of differentiation (CD) nomenclature.

NKT cells (*natural killer T cells*) are a subset of T cells that share surface markers and functional characteristics with both conventional T cells and natural killer cells. They express markers associated with both T cells and NK cells. Most NKT cells express a semi-invariant T-cell receptor (TCR) and some express CD4. Unlike most T cells, TCR of NKT cells recognize glycolipid antigens presented by the class I MHC-related protein CD1 on the surface of antigen-presenting cells.

NK cells

NK cells are a class of large, granular, cytotoxic lymphocytes belong to the **innate lymphoid cell** (ILC) family. Innate lymphoid cells are derived from common lymphoid progenitors, but do not express antigen-specific receptors. Currently, they are subdivided into three groups (ILC1, ILC2 and ILC3), distinguished by the cytokines they secrete. ILCs are largely tissue-resident cells.

Like B cells and T cells, NK cells are also derived from the common lymphoid progenitor in the bone marrow. Although some NK cells develop in the thymus, this organ is not required for NK cell maturation. NK cells are distinct from cytotoxic T cells. However, NK cells also play a role in destroying cells infected with intracellular pathogens. NK cells are neither T cells nor B cells. They constitute 5-10% of lymphocyte population. Their numbers are not enhanced, nor do they exhibit memory after stimulation. NK cells destroy the target cell not by phagocytosis but by releasing biologically potent molecules. They resemble T_C cells in their ability to destroy infected cells. For example, NK cells also use perforin and granzymes to kill their targets. However, NK cells differ from T_C cells in that they kill targets in antigen non-specific manner. The most distinctive phenotypic characteristic of NK cells is their expression of a set of unique activating and inhibiting **NK receptors** (NKRs). These receptors are responsible for determining the target of NK cells. NK cells are capable of destroying malignant and virus-infected cells without previous exposure or contact with the foreign antigen. **Chediak-Higashi syndrome** – an autosomal recessive disorder- is associated with a lack of NK cells.

5.3.2 Common myeloid progenitor

The common myeloid progenitor cells give rise to granulocytes (neutrophils, basophils, eosinophils and mast cells), monocytes, macrophages, erythrocytes and megakaryocytes (platelets).

Granulocytes

Granulocytes have irregular-shaped nuclei with two to five lobes (multilobed), and are often called **polymorphonuclear leukocytes** (due to irregular-shaped nuclei). Granulocytes are *white blood cells* (leukocytes) that are classified as *neutrophils*, *eosinophils*, *basophils* and *mast cells* on the basis of differences in cellular morphology and the staining of their characteristic cytoplasmic granules.

Neutrophils (also called *polymorphonuclear neutrophils* or PMNs): The neutrophils have a multilobed nucleus and a granulated cytoplasm that stain with both acidic and basic dyes. Neutrophils (constitute 50-70% of the circulating white blood cells) are produced by hematopoiesis in the bone marrow. They are released into the peripheral blood and circulate for 7-10 hours before migrating into the tissues, where they have a life span of only a few days. Movement of circulating neutrophils into tissues, called extravasation, takes several steps: the cell first adheres to the vascular endothelium, then penetrates the gap between adjacent endothelial cells lining the vessel walls, and finally penetrates the vascular basement membrane, moving out into the tissue spaces. Like macrophages, neutrophils are active phagocytic cells.

Eosinophils have bilobed nucleus and stain with acidic dye **eosin**. They comprise 2-5% of WBCs and are motile phagocytic cells that can migrate from the blood into the tissue space. Their role is important in the defense against protozoan and helminth parasites, mainly by releasing cationic peptides and reactive oxygen intermediates into the extracellular fluid.

Basophils have lobed nucleus and stain with basic dye **methylene blue**. It comprises less than 1% of total WBCs. They are non-phagocytic, release substances that cause an *allergic responses*. These molecules include histamine, prostaglandins, serotonin, and leukotrienes. Basophils (and mast cells) possess high-affinity receptors for one type of antibody, known as IgE.

Mast cells are originated from pluripotent progenitor cells of the bone marrow, and mature under the influence of the c-kit ligand and stem cell factor in the presence of other distinct growth factors. Like circulating basophils, these cells have large numbers of cytoplasmic granules that contain *histamine* and other pharmacologically active substances. Mast cells also play an important role in the development of allergies.

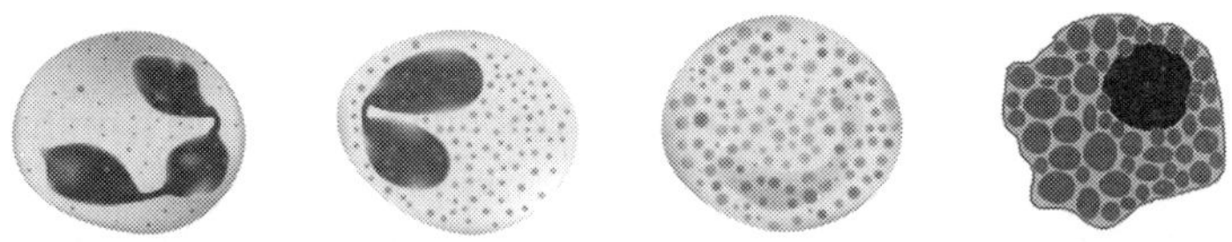

Neutrophil Eosinophil Basophil Mast cell

Monocytes

Monocytes are *mononuclear phagocytic leukocytes* that circulate briefly in the bloodstream before migrating into the tissues where it becomes macrophages or into dendritic cells. Monocytes circulate in the bloodstream for about 8 hours, during which they enlarge; then they migrate into the tissues and differentiate into specific tissue macrophages or into dendritic cells.

Macrophages

Macrophages are phagocytes and can be found in most tissues. They have two major origins. Some differentiate from circulating monocytes that migrate into tissues in response to an infection and differentiate into specific tissue macrophages. These **inflammatory macrophages** are expert phagocytes and typically participate in the innate immune response. They have a dual role in the immune response: (1) they contribute directly to the clearance of pathogens from a tissue, and (2) they act as antigen-presenting cells. Others, known as **tissue-resident macrophages**, originate from embryonic cells rather than from circulating, activated monocytes and do not circulate. These resident macrophages, which include Kupffer cells in the liver, microglia in the brain, and alveolar macrophages in the lungs. They adopt a variety of tissue-specific functions in addition to their role as antigen-presenting cells.

List of tissue-resident macrophages

Brain	Microglia	**Spleen**	Red pulp macrophage
Lung	Alveolar macrophage	**Bone marrow**	Bone marrow macrophage
Liver	Kupffer cell	**Lymph node**	Subcapsular sinus macrophage
Skin	Langerhans cell		

Dendritic cells

Dendritic cells are bone marrow-derived cells that arise from both the myeloid and lymphoid lineages. The myeloid pathway that gives rise to the monocyte also gives rise to dendritic cells. Some dendritic cells also arise from the lymphoid lineage. Dendritic cells perform the distinct functions of antigen capture in one location and antigen presentation in another. They constitutively express high levels of class II MHC molecules and act as professional antigen-presenting cells. Dendritic cells acquire antigen by phagocytosis; the antigen is processed, and mature dendritic cells present it to T_H cells. Dendritic cells are classified into four types: *langerhans cells*, *interstitial dendritic cells*, *myeloid dendritic cells* and *lymphoid dendritic cells.*

Follicular dendritic cell: It is a type of dendritic cell but does not arise in the bone marrow and has a different function from the antigen presenting dendritic cells. Follicular dendritic cells do not express class II MHC molecules and therefore do not function as antigen presenting cells. Although they do not express class II MHC molecules, they are richly endowed with receptors for antibody which allow the binding of Ag-Ab complexes. They are of a lineage that is distinct from class II MHC bearing dendritic cells.

5.4 Organs involved in the adaptive immune response

The maturation, differentiation and proliferation of B and T cells take place in the lymphatic organs. These organs are divided into two categories – *primary* and *secondary lymphoid organs*.

5.4.1 Primary lymphoid organs

The **primary** (or **central**) **lymphoid organs** are those in which the maturation of T and B cells into antigen-recognizing lymphocytes occur. *Bone marrow* and *thymus* are examples of primary lymphoid organs.

Bone marrow

In most mammals including humans and mice, bone marrow is the site of B cell synthesis and maturation. Before birth, fetal liver and fetal bone marrow are the major sites of B cell maturation; after birth, the generation of mature B cells occurs in the bone marrow. After maturation, the mature B cells are transported by the circulating blood to the secondary lymphoid organs, where they encounter and respond to foreign antigens. Bone marrow is not the site of B cell maturation in all species. In birds, B cells undergo maturation in the **bursa of Fabricius**. *Mammals do not have a bursa of Fabricius*.

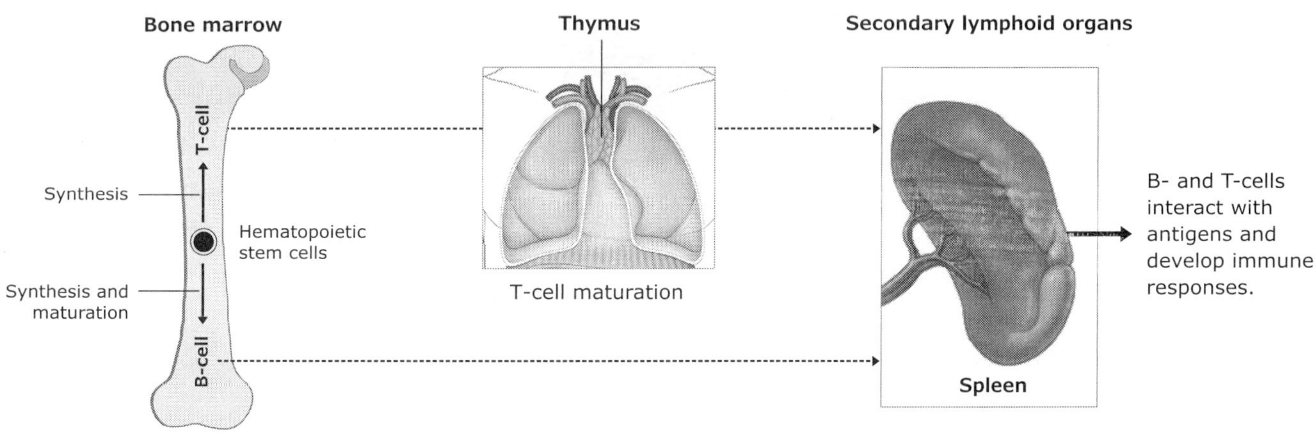

Figure 5.2 In humans, the bone marrow is the site for the synthesis of both B- and T-lymphocytes (or cells). Maturation of B-lymphocytes occurs in the bone marrow itself, whereas maturation of T-lymphocytes occurs in the thymus. After synthesis and maturation in primary lymphoid organs, lymphocytes migrate to secondary lymphoid organs such as the spleen. In secondary lymphoid organs, they encounter antigens and initiate an immune response.

Thymus

Thymus is the site where T cells mature. T cell precursors from the bone marrow migrate into the thymus gland, where they differentiate into mature T cells. It is a flat, bilobed organ situated above the heart. Each lobe is surrounded by a capsule and is further divided into lobules, which are separated from each other by strands of connective tissue called **trabeculae**. Each lobule is organized into two compartments: the outer compartment, or **cortex**, and the inner compartment, or **medulla**. T cells mature in the cortex and migrate to the medulla, where they encounter macrophages and dendritic cells. Here, they undergo thymic selection, which results in the development of mature, functional T cells, which then leave to enter the peripheral blood circulation, through which they are transported to the secondary lymphoid organs. It is in these secondary lymphoid organs where the T cells encounter and respond to foreign antigens.

5.4.2 Secondary lymphoid organs/tissues

Mature B and T cells migrate from bone marrow and thymus, respectively, through the bloodstream to the **secondary** (or **peripheral**) **lymphoid organs**. These secondary lymphoid organs are those organs where the mature antigen-specific lymphocytes first encounter antigen and begin their differentiation into effector and memory cells. The major secondary lymphoid organs are **spleen, lymph nodes** and **mucosa associated lymphoid tissue** (MALT). Spleen and lymph nodes are the highly organized secondary lymphoid organs. The secondary lymphoid organs have two major functions: They are highly efficient in trapping and concentrating foreign substances, and they are the main sites of production of antibodies and the induction of antigen-specific T cells.

Spleen

The spleen is the *largest* of the secondary lymphoid organs. It is highly efficient in trapping and concentrating foreign substances carried in the blood. It is the major organ in the body in which antibodies are synthesized and from which they are released into the circulation. The parenchyma of the spleen consists of two different kinds of tissue called white pulp and red pulp. **White pulp** is lymphatic tissue, consisting mostly of lymphocytes and macrophages. The **red pulp** consists of blood-filled **venous sinuses** and cords of splenic tissue called **splenic** (**Billroth's**) **cords**. Splenic cords consist of red blood cells, macrophages, lymphocytes, plasma cells, and granulocytes. Blood flowing into the spleen through the splenic artery enters the central arteries of the white pulp. Within the white pulp, B cells and T cells carry out immune functions, similar to lymph nodes, while spleen macrophages destroy blood-borne pathogens by phagocytosis. Within the red pulp, the spleen performs three functions related to blood cells: (1) removal of ruptured, worn out, or defective blood cells and platelets; (2) storage of platelets, up to one-third of the body's supply; and (3) production of blood cells (hemopoiesis) during fetal life.

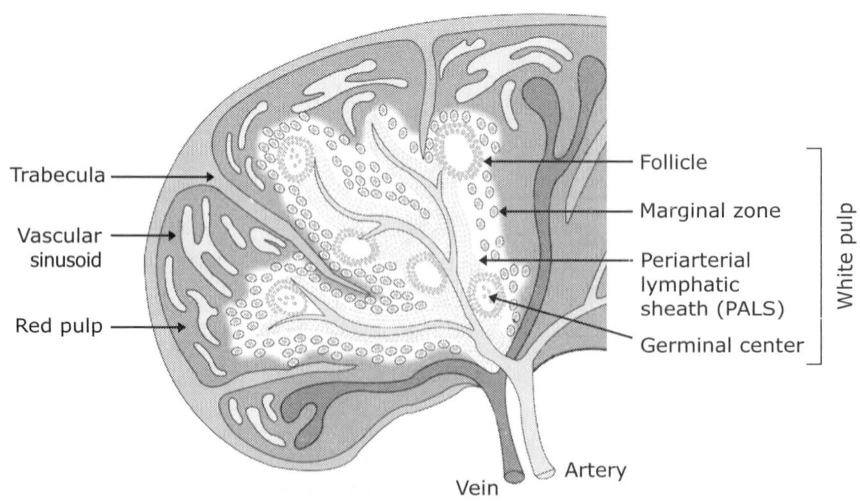

Figure 5.3 Structure of spleen.

Lymph nodes

Lymph nodes are small encapsulated bean shaped structures (normally < 1 cm in diameter) found in various regions throughout the body. The lymph nodes are composed of a **medulla** and a **cortex**, which is surrounded by a capsule of connective tissue. They are packed with lymphocytes, macrophages, and dendritic cells. Lymph nodes are highly efficient in trapping antigens and function as a type of filter. As lymph enters one end of a lymph node, foreign substances are trapped by the reticular fibers within the sinuses of the lymph node. Then macrophages destroy some foreign substances by phagocytosis while lymphocytes destroy others by immune responses. The filtered lymph then leaves the other end of the lymph node. Lymph enters lymph nodes through afferent lymphatic vessels, is filtered, and exits through efferent lymphatic vessels.

Mucosa associated lymphoid tissue

The majority of secondary lymphoid tissue in the human body is located within the lining of respiratory, digestive and genitourinary tracts. These are collectively called as *mucosa associated lymphoid tissue* (**MALT**). There are several types of MALT. Two major MALT includes *bronchial associated lymphoid tissue* (**BALT**) and *gut-associated lymphoid tissue* (**GALT**). GALT includes the tonsils, adenoids, and specialized regions in the small intestine called **Peyer's patches**.

5.5 Antigens

Adaptive immune responses arise as a result of exposure to foreign compounds. The compound of foreign origin that evokes the response is referred to as **antigen**, a term initially coined due to the ability of these compounds to cause antibody responses to be generated. An antigen is any agent capable of binding specifically to a TCR or an antibody molecule (membrane-bound or soluble). The ability of a compound to bind with an antibody or a TCR is referred to as **antigenicity**. There is a functional distinction between the term *antigen* and *immunogen*. An **immunogen** is any agent capable of inducing humoral or cell-mediated immune responses. The distinction between the terms is necessary because there are many compounds that are incapable of inducing an immune response, yet they are capable of binding specifically with antibodies or TCRs. *Thus, all immunogens are antigens, but not all antigens are immunogens.*

Requirements for immunogenicity

A substance must possess the following characteristics to be immunogenic:

Foreignness

The most important feature of an immunogen is that an effective immunogen must be *foreign* with respect to the host. The adaptive immune system recognizes and eliminates only foreign (nonself) antigens. Self-antigens are not recognized and thus individuals are *tolerant* to their own self molecules, even though these same molecules have the capacity to act as immunogens in other individuals of the same species.

Size

The second requirement for being immunogenic is that the compound must have a certain minimal molecular mass. There is a relationship between the size of immunogen and its immunogenicity. In general, small compounds with a molecular mass <1000 Da (e.g., penicillin, aspirin) are not immunogenic; those of molecular mass between 1000 and 6000 Da (e.g., insulin, adrenocorticotropic hormone) may or may not be immunogenic; and those of molecular mass >6000 Da (e.g., albumin, tetanus toxin) are generally immunogenic. The most active immunogens tend to have a molecular mass of 100,000 Da or more. In short, relatively small substances have decreased immunogenicity, whereas large substances have increased immunogenicity.

Chemical complexity

The third characteristic necessary for a compound to be immunogenic is a certain degree of chemical complexity. For example, homopolymers of amino acids or sugars are seldom good immunogens regardless of their size. Similarly, a homopolymer of poly-γ-D-glutamic acid (the capsular material of *Bacillus anthracis*) with a molecular weight of

50,000 Da is not immunogenic. The absence of immunogenicity is because these compounds, although of high molecular weight, are not sufficiently chemically complex.

Virtually all proteins are immunogenic. Furthermore, the greater the degree of complexity of the protein, the more vigorous will be the immune response to that protein. Carbohydrates are immunogenic only if they have a complex polysaccharide structure or part of complex molecules such as glycoproteins. Nucleic acids and lipids are poor immunogens by themselves, but they become immunogenic when they are conjugated to protein carriers.

Dosage and route of administration

The insufficient dose of immunogen may not stimulate an immune response either because the amount administered fails to activate enough lymphocytes or because such a dose renders the responding cells unresponsive. Besides the need to administer a threshold amount of immunogen to induce an immune response, the number of doses administered also affects the outcome of the immune response generated.

The route of administration also affects the outcome of the immunization because this determines which organs and cell populations will be involved in the response. Immunogens can be administered through a number of common routes: *Intravenous* (into a vein); *intradermal* (into the skin); *subcutaneous* (beneath the skin); *intramuscular* (into the muscle). Antigens administered via the most common route namely, *subcutaneously*, generally elicit the strongest immune responses. This is due to their uptake, processing, and presentation to effector cells by Langerhans cells present in the skin, which are among the most potent APCs. Antigens administered subcutaneously moves first to local lymph nodes. *Intravenously* administered antigens are carried first to the spleen, where they can either induce immune unresponsiveness or tolerance, or if presented by APCs, generate an immune response. Orally administered antigens (*gastrointestinal route*) elicit local antibody responses within the intestinal lamina propria.

Haptens

Substances called **haptens** (from the Greek *hapten*, which means 'to grasp') fail to induce immune responses in their native form because of their low molecular weight and their chemical simplicity. Haptens are *antigenic* but not *immunogenic*. These compounds become immunogenic when they are conjugated to high molecular weight, physiochemically complex **carriers**. Thus, a hapten is a compound that, by itself, is incapable of inducing an immune response. However, when hapten is conjugated to a carrier, an immune response can be induced against it. The hapten-carrier complex, unlike free hapten, can act as an immunogen.

Antigen-antibody interactions

Antigen-antibody interaction is highly specific and occurs in a similar way as a bimolecular association of an enzyme-substrate. The binding between antigens and immune components involves weak **non-covalent interactions**. The binding forces are relatively weak and *reversible* and consist mainly of hydrogen bonds, van der Waals forces, ionic interaction and hydrophobic forces, all of which require a very close proximity between the interacting moieties. The smallest unit of antigen that is capable of binding with antibodies is called an **antigenic determinant** or **epitope**. These two words are synonymous and are used interchangeably throughout this book. The corresponding area on an antibody molecule combining with the epitope is called **paratope**. The number of epitopes on the surface of an antigen is its *valence*. The valence determines the number of antibody molecules that can combine with the antigen at one time. If one epitope is present, the antigen is **monovalent**. Most antigens, however, have more than one copy of the same epitope and are termed **polyvalent** or **multivalent**.

Affinity and avidity

Affinity measures the strength of noncovalent interactions between an epitope and single antigen-binding site of an antibody (paratope). Low-affinity antibodies bind antigen weakly and tend to dissociate readily, whereas high-affinity antibodies bind antigen more tightly and remain bound longer. **Avidity** gives a measure of the overall strength of an antibody-antigen complex. It describes the collective binding interactions between antigen-antibody when multiple epitopes on an antigen interact with multiple binding sites of an antibody. It is dependent on two major parameters:

affinity of an epitope and an antigen binding site of an antibody and valency of both the antibody and antigen. The multivalency significantly increases the avidity of the antibody-antigen interaction.

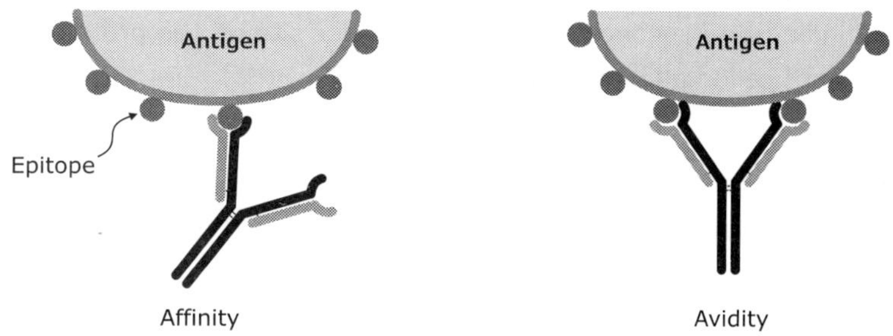

Figure 5.4 Affinity describes the strength with which single epitope interacts with an antigen-binding site of an antibody whereas avidity is the strength of antigen-antibody binding when multiple epitopes on an antigen interact with multiple antigen-binding sites of an antibody.

Cross-reactivity

Although Ag-Ab reaction is very specific, sometimes antibody elicited by one antigen can cross-react with an unrelated antigen. An immunologic reaction in which a particular antibody or T cell receptor reacts with two or more antigens that possess a common epitope is called a **cross-reaction**. Another form of cross-reactivity is seen when antibodies or cells with specificity to one epitope bind, usually more weakly, to another epitope that is not quite identical but has a structural resemblance to the first epitope.

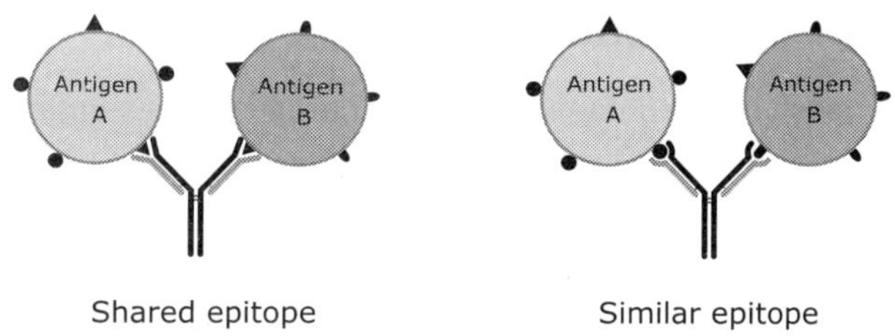

Figure 5.5 Cross-reactivity refers to the ability of an individual antibody binding site to react with more than one antigenic determinant or the ability of a population of antibody molecules to react with more than one antigen. Cross-reactions arise because the cross-reacting antigen shares an epitope in common with the immunizing antigen or because it has an epitope which is structurally similar to one on the immunizing antigen (multispecificity).

Factors affecting antigen-antibody reactions

The branch of immunology that is concerned with *in vitro* reactions involving one or more serum constituents (e.g., antibodies and complement) is called **serology**. Serological reactions are the basis for all diagnostic immunology tests. Antigen-antibody reactions depend on a number of factors.

Affinity: The higher the affinity of the antibody for an epitope of an antigen, the more stable will be the interaction.

Avidity: The overall strength of attachment between multivalent antigens and multivalent antibodies are more stable.

Antigen to antibody ratio: The ratio between the antigen and antibody influences the detection of antigen-antibody complexes because the size of the complexes formed is related to the concentration of the antigen and antibody.

Physical form of the antigen: The physical form of the antigen influences the reaction with an antibody. When the antigen is particulate, the reaction of an antibody with the antigen can be detected by agglutination (clumping) of the antigen. If the antigen is a soluble, one generally looks for the precipitation of the antigen after the production of large insoluble antigen-antibody complexes. The spatial arrangement of different epitopes on a single antigen may influence the binding of antibodies. When determinants are well separated, two or more antibody molecules can be bound to the same antigen without influencing each other; such determinants are said to be *nonoverlapping*.

When two determinants are close to each other, the binding of antibody to the first determinant may cause steric interference with the binding of antibody to the second; such determinants are said to be **overlapping**. In rare cases, the binding of one antibody may cause a conformational change in the structure of the antigen, positively or negatively influencing the binding of a second antibody at another site on the protein by means other than steric hindrance. Such interactions are called **allosteric effects**.

Adjuvant

An *adjuvant* (from Latin word *adjuvare* means 'to help') is a substance that when mixed with an immunogen and injected with it, enhances the immune response against the immunogen. Adjuvants are often used to boost the immune response in case of weak immunogens or when antigens are available in small amount. A carrier for a hapten and an adjuvant is different. A hapten will become immunogenic when conjugated covalently to a carrier; it will not become immunogenic if mixed with an adjuvant. Thus, an adjuvant enhances the immune response to immunogens but does not confer immunogenicity on haptens. How adjuvants augment the immune response has remained enigmatic.

While many adjuvants have been developed in animal models and tested experimentally in humans, only one has been used for routine vaccination. Currently, **aluminum potassium sulfate** (**alum**) is a common adjuvant used for human vaccines. Alum prolongs the persistence of antigen. When an antigen is mixed with alum, the salt precipitates the antigen. Another commonly used adjuvant is *Freund's incomplete* and *complete adjuvant*. Freund's incomplete adjuvant contains antigen in aqueous solution, oil, and an emulsifying agent such as mannide monooleate. Freund's *complete adjuvant* contains heat-killed *Mycobacteria* as an additional ingredient.

5.6 Major histocompatibility complex

Major histocompatibility complex (**MHC**) is a tightly linked cluster of genes present in vertebrate species, the products of which play important roles in intercellular recognition and in discrimination between self and non-self. MHC is located on chromosome 6 in humans and on chromosome 17 in mice and referred to as the **HLA** (*human leukocyte antigen*) complex and **H-2** (*histocompatibility-2*) complex, respectively. MHC gene is highly polymorphic i.e., many alleles exist for each gene in the population. The phenomenon of having multiple alternative forms of one gene in the population is known as **genetic polymorphism**. MHC genes are also *codominantly* expressed – that is, both alleles of MHC genes present in a cell express MHC proteins (molecules). Thus, MHC genes are polymorphic (many alleles exist for each gene in the population) and codominantly expressed (both maternal and paternal copies).

The individual genes of the MHC locus lie so close together that their inheritance is linked. A set of linked MHC genes is generally inherited as a unit from parents; these linked genes are called **haplotypes**. An individual inherits one haplotype from the mother and one haplotype from the father. Each individual expresses a distinct array of MHC molecules. This diversity comes about because different individuals within a species have different alleles of MHC genes. Because of the extensive polymorphism of MHC genes, every individual has an almost unique array of inherited MHC genes.

The MHC genes are organized into three classes – **class I MHC genes, class II MHC genes** and **class III MHC genes**. Class I and class II MHC genes encode MHC proteins that present antigens to the T cells. Class I MHC proteins present antigen to *cytotoxic T cells* (T_C cells) whereas class II MHC proteins present antigen to *helper T cells* (T_H cells). The antigen-presenting MHC molecules are encoded by *classical* class I and class II MHC genes. In both classes few MHC genes encode proteins that do not function in the presentation of peptide antigens to T cells: these are known as **non-classical MHC genes**. The concept of classical and non-classical does not apply to class III. In contrast, class III MHC genes encode a group of unrelated proteins that do not share structural similarity or function with class I and II molecules (that do not play a direct role in presenting antigen to T cells), although many of them do participate in other aspects of the immune response.

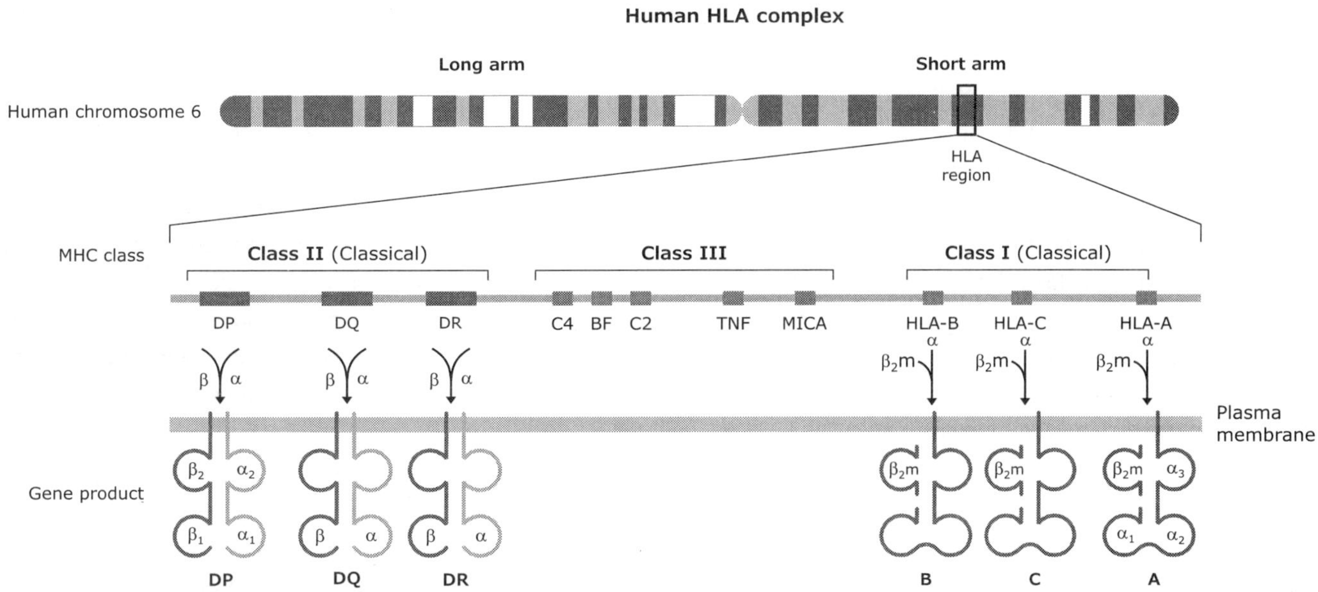

Figure 5.6 Simplified depiction of the human MHC showing regions and genes coding for polymorphic class I, II and class III MHC molecules. β_2m encoded outside the MHC. Three classical class I MHC genes called HLA-A, HLA-B and HLA-C, and three classical class II MHC loci called HLA-DP, HLA-DQ and HLA-DR. Each locus consists of one or more A and B genes. Non-classical class I and class II MHC genes are not shown. The concept of classical and non-classical does not apply to class III.

In human, there are three classical class I MHC genes called **HLA-A, HLA-B** and **HLA-C**, which encode three types of class I MHC molecules with the same names. There are three classical class II MHC loci called **HLA-DP, HLA-DQ,** and **HLA-DR**. Each locus contains A and B genes encoding α and β chains, respectively. The DR gene locus consists of a single DRA gene and up to nine DRB genes (DRB1 to DRB9). At DP and DQ loci, each has one expressed gene for α and β chains and additional unexpressed pseudogenes. The DQA1 and DQB1 gene products associate to form DQ molecules, and the DPA1 and DPB1 products form DP molecules.

Diversity of MHC molecules results not only due to multiple alleles of each gene but also from the presence of duplicated genes with similar functions. Because it includes genes with similar but not identical structure and function (for example, HLA-A, -B and -C), the MHC may be said to be **polygenic**.

Class I MHC proteins

Class I MHC genes express glycoproteins called *class I MHC molecules*, on nearly all nucleated cells. Each class I MHC gene codes for a transmembrane glycoprotein of approximately 43 kDa, which is referred to as the α (or heavy chain). It comprises three extracellular domains: α_1, α_2 and α_3. The α_3 domain is highly conserved and interacts with the glycoprotein CD8 present on T_C cells. Every class I MHC molecule is expressed on the surface of a cell forms *noncovalent* association with a small invariant polypeptide called **β_2-microglobulin** (β_2m; approximately 12 kDa), which is encoded by gene present on other chromosome (in human, chromosome 15). In the absence of β_2m; the class I MHC molecule is not expressed on the cell membrane.

In general, class I MHC molecules are expressed on most nucleated cells, but the level of expression differs among different cell types. The highest levels of class I MHC molecules are expressed by lymphocytes whereas fibroblasts, liver hepatocytes, and neural cells express very low levels of class I MHC molecules. A few cell types (e.g., neurons and sperm cells at certain stages of differentiation) appear to lack class I MHC molecules altogether.

Class II MHC proteins

Class II MHC genes code for α and β-polypeptide chains of approximate molecular mass 35 kDa and 28 kDa, respectively. Class II MHC molecules, like class I MHC molecules, are transmembrane glycoprotein molecules with cytoplasmic tails and extracellular Ig-like domains; the domains are referred to as α_1, α_2, β_1 and β_2. Class II MHC molecules are also members of the Ig superfamily. Glycoprotein CD4 present on T_H cells interacts with the invariant portion of all class II MHC molecules.

Class II MHC genes express MHC molecule *constitutively* (i.e., under all conditions) only on specialized *antigen presenting cells* (**APCs**). APCs are classified as *professional* and *non-professional antigen-presenting cells*. **Professional antigen-presenting cells** (**pAPCs**) are dendritic cells, macrophages and B cells. These cells differ from one another in their mechanisms of antigen uptake. *Dendritic cells* are considered the most powerful and most efficient of the pAPCs. These cells constitutively express high levels of class II MHC molecules. Macrophages must be activated before they express class II MHC molecules. B cells constitutively express class II MHC molecules, although at low levels, and possess antigen-specific surface receptors. Professional APCs differ by location and migratory behavior. Some circulate actively and others reside for long periods of time in specific tissues and organs. **Non-professional antigen-presenting cells** like fibroblasts, thymic epithelial cells, glial cells and pancreatic beta cells can be induced to express class II MHC molecules.

In general, in the absence of inducing factors, most cells express class I MHC molecules without expressing class II MHC molecules. Certain cells, such as B cells, constitutively express both class I and class II MHC molecules. *By convention*, cells that display peptide antigens associated with class I MHC molecules to T_C cells are referred to as **target cells** and cells that display peptides associated with class II MHC to T_H cells are called **antigen presenting cells** (but sometimes we use APC for both).

Class III MHC proteins

This class includes genes coding several secreted proteins with immune functions: components of the complement system (such as C2, C4) and molecules related with inflammation or heat shock proteins (HSP).

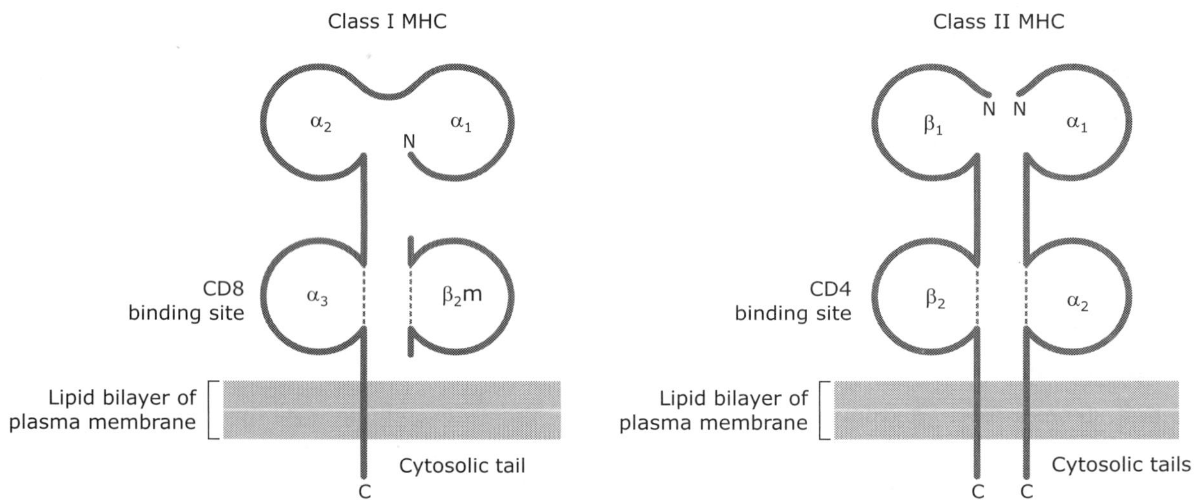

Figure 5.7 Class I MHC molecules are composed of a polymorphic α chain noncovalently attached to the nonpolymorphic β_2 microglobulin (β_2m). The α chain is glycosylated. Class II MHC molecules are composed of a polymorphic α-chain non-covalently attached to a polymorphic β chain. Both chains are glycosylated.

5.6.1 MHC molecules and antigen presentation

Both types of membrane glycoproteins (class I and class II MHC) function as highly specialized antigen-presenting molecules. The class I and class II MHC molecules present antigen to T cells. Antigen recognition is mediated by αβ or γδ T cell receptors (**TCRs**). T cells recognize only peptide antigens combined with MHC molecules. Class I molecules present processed **endogenous antigen** to T_C cells. Class II molecules present processed **exogenous antigen** to T_H cells. *Exogenous antigens* are those antigens that originate outside the organism or cell whereas *endogenous antigens* originate within the organism or cell.

Table 5.3 Feature of class I and class II MHC molecules

Feature	**Class I MHC**	**Class II MHC**
Structure	α-chain and β_2m	α- and β-chain
Polymorphic domain	α_1 and α_2 domains	α_1 and β_1 domains
Binding site for T cell co-receptor	α_3 region binds CD8	β_2 region binds CD4
Constitutive cellular expression	Nearly all nucleated cells	APCs
Peptide antigens derived from	Endogenous antigens	Exogenous antigens
Peptide antigens presented to	T_C cells	T_H cells
Nomenclature		
Human	HLA-A, HLA-B, HLA-C	HLA-DR, HLA-DQ, HLA-DP
Mouse	H-2K, H-2D, H-2L	I-A, I-E

The class I MHC molecule presents a peptide antigen of 8-10 amino acid residues long, whereas the class II molecules bind and present slightly longer peptide antigens of 13-18 amino acid residues long. Peptide binding by class I and II molecules does not exhibit high specificity. A given MHC molecule can bind to many different peptides, and some peptides can bind to several different MHC molecules.

5.6.2 Antigen processing and presentation

T cell receptor (TCR) does not recognize free antigens. TCR recognizes only antigen that is bound to *MHC molecules*. Both T_C and T_H cells can recognize antigen only when it is presented by a self-MHC molecule, an attribute called **self-MHC restriction.** T_H cells recognize antigen with class II MHC molecules on antigen-presenting cells (APCs). Thus, antigen recognition by the T_H cell is *class II MHC restricted*, whereas T_C cells recognize antigen with class I MHC molecules on target cells. Thus, antigen recognition by T_C cells is *class I MHC restricted*. The events involved in the generation of peptide antigens from proteins inside cells, the binding of peptides to MHC molecules and the display of peptide-MHC complexes on the cell surface for T cell recognition are known collectively as **antigen processing** and **presentation**.

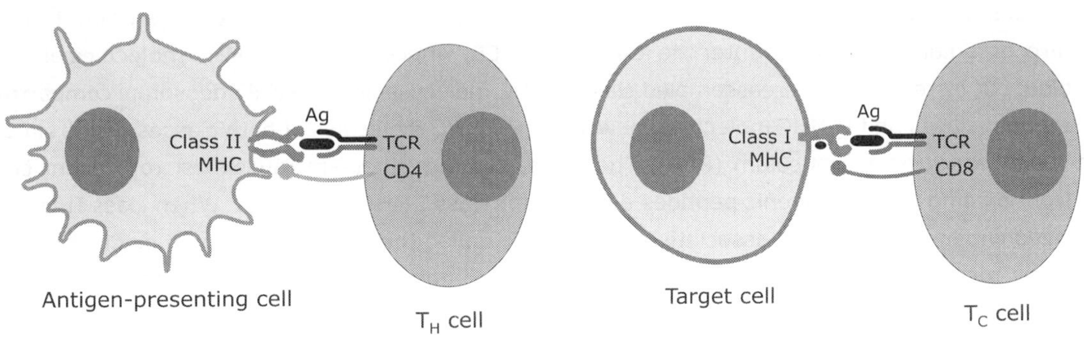

Figure 5.8 Recognition of foreign peptide antigens bound to MHC molecules by T cells. T_C cells recognize foreign peptides in association with class I MHC molecules, whereas T_H cells recognize foreign peptides in association with class II MHC molecules. In both cases, the peptide MHC complexes are recognized on the surface of an antigen-presenting cell or a target cell.

How do peptides derived from protein antigen get associated with MHC molecules? There is experimental evidence of at least two distinct routes of antigen processing and presentation that differ in their source of antigen, intracellular trafficking and MHC association. In general, *endogenous* protein antigens are presented in class I MHC molecules (**endogenous pathway**) to T_C cells while *exogenous* protein antigens are presented in class II MHC molecules (**exogenous pathway**) to T_H cells. Antigen processing and presentation in both the pathways include following steps

1. acquisition of antigen,
2. proteolysis,
3. delivery of peptides to MHC molecules, and
4. display of the peptide-loaded MHC molecule on the cell surface.

Processing and presentation of *endogenous* antigens: *endogenous pathway*

Endogenous antigens are synthesized inside a cell. Class I MHC molecules present peptide antigens derived from endogenous protein antigen. Processing of endogenous antigens occurs in the cytosol. Endogenous protein antigens are targeted for proteolysis by **polyubiquitinylation**. Polyubiquitinylated proteins are cleaved into peptide fragments by **proteasomes**. Protein synthesis, polyubiquitinylation, and proteasomal proteolysis all occur in the cytosol, whereas peptide binding by class I MHC molecules occurs in the lumen of the endoplasmic reticulum (ER). Thus, peptides must cross the ER membrane to gain access to class I molecules, a process mediated by the heterodimeric **TAP** (*transporters associated with antigen processing*), a member of the **ABC superfamily**. The specificity of the TAP is such that it can transport only a subset of all cytosolic peptides, primarily those in the length range of 5-10 amino acid residues. Once the peptides have entered the ER, they are loaded onto the class I MHC molecule, with the help of multiprotein complex referred to as the **peptide-loading complex**. This complex includes a group of *chaperone* proteins such as *calnexin, calreticulin, tapasin* and *Erp57*. Once peptide loading onto the class I MHC molecule has occurred, a conformational change releases the loaded class I MHC molecule from the peptide-loading complex. Once peptide loading is complete, the fully assembled class I MHC–peptide complex is transported to the cell surface via the secretory pathway. The part of a processed antigen that binds to the MHC molecule is termed as **agretope**. *The class I MHC pathway results in the formation of peptide-MHC complexes in which the peptides are derived from proteins synthesized by the class I MHC-bearing cell itself.*

Processing and presentation of *exogenous* antigens: *exogenous pathway*

Like the endogenous antigen presented to T_C cells, the proteins presented to T_H cells on APCs are degraded fragments of exogenous protein antigens. APCs acquire exogenous protein antigens by pinocytosis, phagocytosis, or receptor-mediated endocytosis. Proteolysis is required to convert intact protein antigens into peptides of a size suitable for binding to class II MHC molecules. Proteolysis occurs in the acidic endosomal and lysosomal compartments by various proteases. A wide range of peptide fragments is produced, including some that can bind to class II MHC molecules. Processed antigens do not enter the lumen of the ER, where the class II MHC molecules are synthesized and assembled, but instead bind to preassembled class II MHC molecules in a special endosomal compartment. Since APCs express both class I and II MHC molecules, newly formed MHC molecules of both classes reside simultaneously within the rough endoplasmic reticulum (RER). Therefore, some mechanism must exist to prevent class II MHC molecules from binding to the antigenic peptides destined for class I MHC molecules. When class II MHC molecules are synthesized within the RER, they associate with a protein called the **invariant chain** (**Ii** or **CD74**). It serves as a *chaperone*. This conserved, non-MHC protein interacts with the peptide-binding groove formed by the combination of the α and β-chains of class II MHC, blocking any endogenously derived peptides from binding while the class II molecule is still in the ER.

The invariant chain is cleaved by proteases in the late endosome. However, a short fragment of the invariant chain termed **CLIP** (for *class II-associated invariant chain peptide*) remain bound to the class II MHC. Because it is firmly lodged in the class II MHC peptide-binding cleft, CLIP is resistant to proteolytic attack. This fragment is then released (mediated by a *non-classical* class II-MHC protein called **HLA-DM**), freeing the MHC protein to bind peptides derived from endocytosed proteins. Another non-classical class II MHC **HLA-DO** may act as a negative regulator of class II antigen processing by binding to HLA–DM and inhibiting its role in the dissociation of CLIP from MHC. Finally, peptide-loaded class II MHC molecules are displayed at the cell surface by membrane fusion.

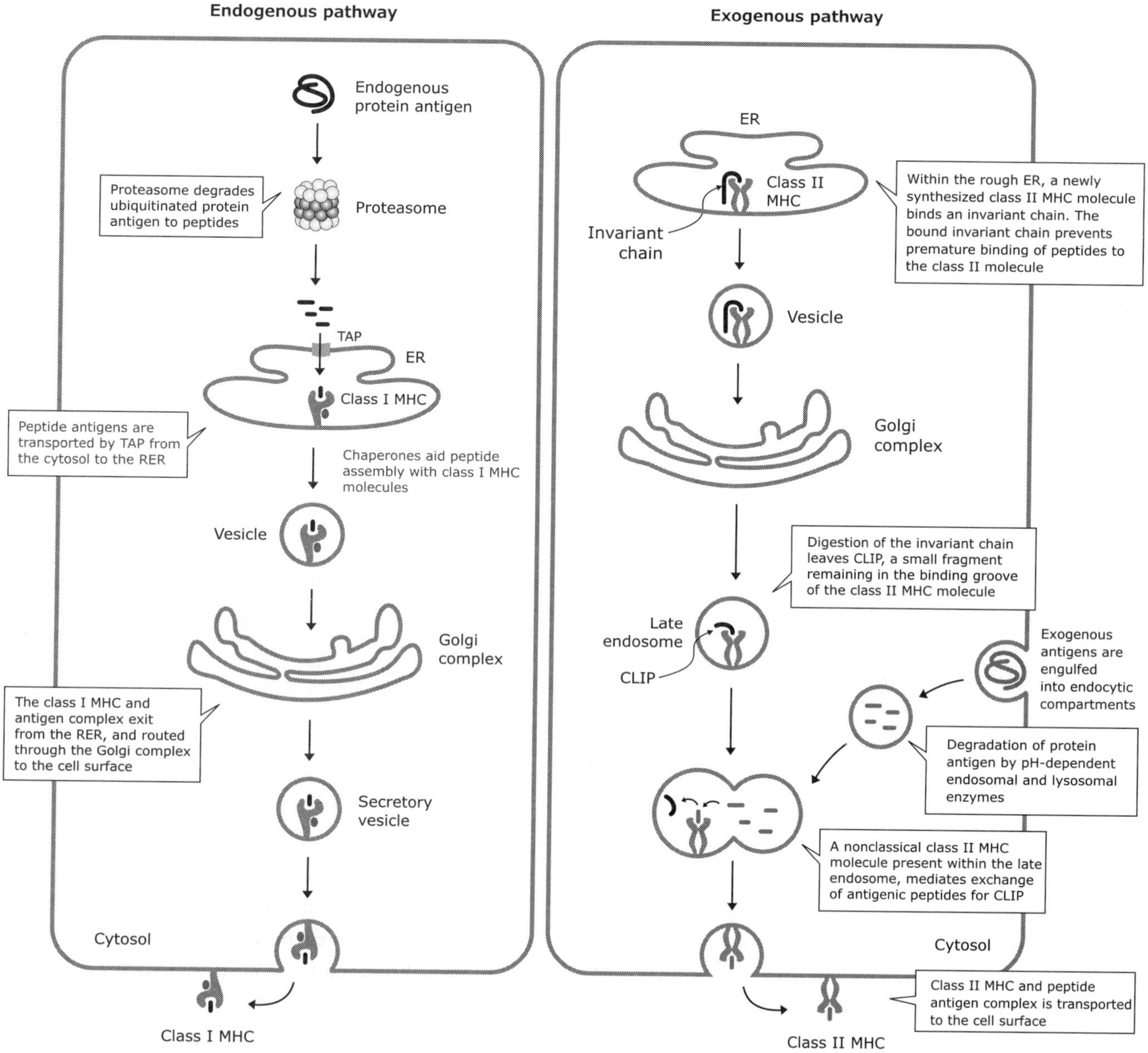

Figure 5.9 Overview of endogenous and exogenous pathways for processing peptide antigen. Whether an antigenic peptide associate with class I MHC in the rough endoplasmic reticulum or with class II MHC in endocytic compartments is governed by the mode of antigen entry into cells (either exogenous or endogenous) and the site of antigen processing. Endogenous peptide antigens are presented by class I MHC (endogenous pathway), while exogenous protein antigens are presented by class II MHC (exogenous pathway).

Presentation of *nonpeptide* antigens

Many non-peptide antigens (such as mycolic acid, glycolipid, phospholipid) are presented by members of the **CD1** family related to non-classical class I MHC. CD1 molecules share structural similarity with class I MHC molecules but function more like class II MHC molecules, presenting many non-protein (such as lipid and phosphorylated prenyl metabolites) antigens to T cells.

Box 5.2 Laboratory mice

Mice are the most commonly used mammalian research model. They are common experimental animals in biology, primarily because they are mammals, are relatively easy to maintain and handle, reproduce quickly, and share a high degree of homology with humans. Laboratory mice include several *inbred*, *outbred*, *knockout* and *transgenic mice* strains. An **inbred strain** is one that is produced using at least 20 consecutive generations of sister and brother or parent and offspring matings. The mating of two genetically related parents is called **inbreeding**. Inbreeding results in increased homozygosity. In contrast to inbred mice, outbred mice are usually heterozygous at many loci.

If mice are inbred (that is, have identical alleles at all loci), each H-2 locus will be homozygous because the maternal and paternal haplotypes are identical, and all offspring, therefore, express identical haplotypes. Inbred mouse strains are **syngeneic** or identical at all genetic loci (two strains are considered **congenic** if they are genetically identical except at a single genetic locus). Some inbred mouse strains have been designated as *prototype* strains and the MHC haplotype expressed by these strains is designated by an arbitrary italic superscript (e.g., H-2^a, H-2^b). If another inbred strain has the same set of alleles as the prototype strain, its MHC haplotype is the same as the prototype strain.

Table 5.4 H-2 haplotypes of some mouse strains

			H-2 alleles				
Prototype strain	Other strains with the same haplotype	Haplotype	K	IA	IE	S	D
CBA	AKR, C3H, C57BR	*k*	*k*	*k*	*k*	*k*	*k*
DBA/2	BALB/c, SEA, YBR	*d*	*d*	*d*	*d*	*d*	*d*
C57BL/10 (B10)	C57BL/6, C57L	*b*	*b*	*b*	*b*	*b*	*b*
A	A/He, A/Sn	*a*	*k*	*k*	*k*	*d*	*d*

5.7 Immunoglobulins: Structure and function

Immunoglobulins (also called **antibodies**) are the antigen-binding glycoproteins belong to the immunoglobulin superfamily synthesized exclusively by B cells. They constitute most of the **gamma globulin** fraction of the blood proteins. They exist in two forms: **soluble antibodies** (secreted by B cells) and **membrane-bound antibodies** (present on the B cell membrane). Secreted forms of antibodies are present in the blood plasma, in mucosal secretions, and in the interstitial fluid of tissues.

5.7.1 Basic structure of antibody molecule

An antibody is a Y-shaped molecule with two identical antigen-binding sites, one at the tip of each arm of the Y. Because of their two antigen-binding sites, they are described as bivalent. Antibody has a common structure of four polypeptide chains. It is a heterodimer and consists of two identical **light chains** (each containing about 220 amino acids residues, about 25,000 Da) and two identical **heavy chains** (each usually containing about 440 amino acids residues, about 50,000 Da). The two heavy chains of each antibody molecule are covalently linked by disulfide bonds. Heavy (**H**) and light (**L**) chains are also covalently linked by disulfide bonds. Thus, antibody is a dimer of H-L chain.

Both the light chains and heavy chains contain a series of repeating structural units, each about 110 amino acid residues in length, that fold independently in a globular motif that is called an **Ig domain**. An Ig domain contains two β-pleated sheets, each sheet composed of three to five antiparallel β-strands. The two layers are held together by a disulfide bridge. Antibody heavy chains and light chains both consist of amino-terminal **variable regions** (V) and carboxy-terminal **constant regions** (C). In the heavy chains, the V region is composed of one Ig domain, and the C region is composed of three or four Ig domains. Each light chain is composed of one V region Ig domain and one C region Ig domain. The V region of one heavy chain (V_H) and the adjoining V region of one light chain (V_L) form an antigen-binding site. The C region Ig domains do not participate in antigen recognition.

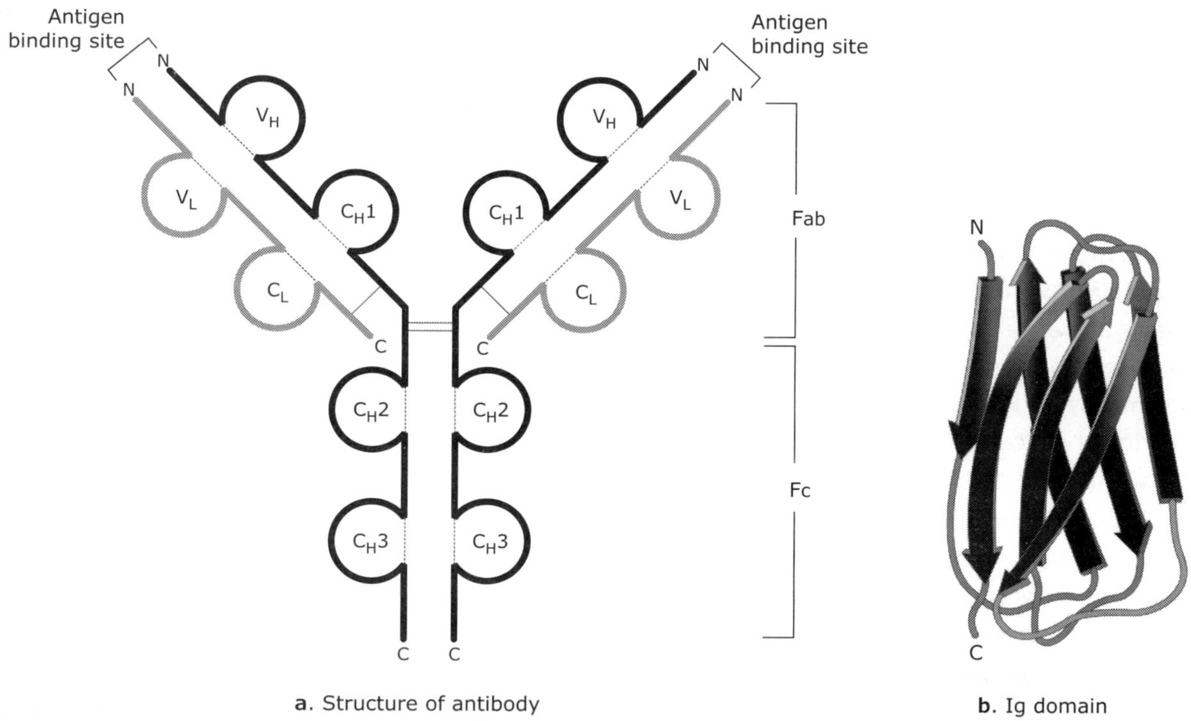

Figure 5.10 a. Schematic diagram of structure of immunoglobulins. The antigen-binding portion of an antibody molecule is the Fab region, and the C-terminal end is the Fc region. b. Structure of Ig domain.

The diversity in the variable regions of both light and heavy chains is for the most part restricted to three small *hypervariable regions* (each ~10 amino acid residues long) in each chain called **complementarity determining regions** (CDR); the remaining parts of the variable region, known as **framework regions**, are relatively constant. Proceeding from either the V_L or V_H amino terminus, these regions are called CDR1, CDR2 and CDR3. The CDR3 is the most variable of the CDRs.

All species studied have the two major classes of light chains: κ and λ. Any one individual of a species produces both types of light chain. However, in any one antibody molecule, the light chains are always either both κ or both λ, never one of each. While there are two types of light chains, the antibodies of virtually all species have been shown to consist of five different types of heavy chains– α, γ, δ, ε and μ. These five different types of heavy chains are called **isotypes**. The heavy-chains of a given antibody molecule determine the *class* of that antibody: **IgM** (μ), **IgG** (γ), **IgA** (α), **IgD** (δ) or **IgE** (ε). Each class can have either κ or λ light chains. Any individual of a species makes all heavy chains, but in any one antibody molecule, both heavy chains are identical. Thus, an antibody molecule of the IgG class could have the structure κ2γ2 with two identical κ light chains and two identical γ heavy chains. Alternatively, it could have the structure λ2γ2 with two identical λ light chains and two identical γ heavy chains.

Minor differences in the α and the γ heavy chains led to further classification of the heavy chains into subclasses. In humans, there are two subclasses of α heavy chains (α_1 and α_2) and four subclasses of γ heavy chains (γ_1, γ_2, γ_3 and γ_4). Therefore, there are two subclasses of IgA (**IgA1** and **IgA2**) and four subclasses of IgG, (**IgG1**, **IgG2**, **IgG3** and **IgG4**, listed in decreasing order of abundance in the serum). Each class (and subclass) has the characteristic properties of its own. Except for their variable regions, all the antibodies within a class have about 90% homology in their amino acid sequences, but only about 60% homology exists between classes (e.g., IgG and IgA).

Antibody molecules are flexible. This flexibility is conferred largely due to the presence of **hinge region** located between C_H1 and C_H2 in certain isotypes. The hinge region varies in length from 10 to more than 60 amino acid residues in different isotypes. The γ, δ and α-heavy chains contain the hinge region which is rich in proline and cysteine residues, giving IgG, IgD and IgA flexibility between the two Fab arms of the Y-shaped antibody molecule.

Antibody can be expressed either as *secreted* antibody or as *membrane-bound* antibody. The carboxyl-terminal domain in secreted antibody differs from membrane-bound antibody. Secreted antibody has a hydrophilic amino acid sequence at the carboxyl-terminal end. In membrane-bound antibody, the carboxyl-terminal domain contains three regions: an extracellular hydrophilic spacer sequence, a hydrophobic transmembrane sequence and a short cytoplasmic tail.

Deduction of antibody structure

Porter and Edelman elucidated the basic structure of the antibody molecule but their approaches were different. Porter found that treatment with the proteolytic enzyme **papain** split the antibody molecule into three fragments of about equal size. Two of these fragments were found of equal size, each of molecular mass about 45 kDa called **Fab fragments** (*fragment antigen binding*) because they had antigen binding activity. Each Fab fragments are considered to be univalent, possessing one binding site each and being in every way identical to each other. The third fragment, of approximately 50 kDa, spontaneously formed crystals and was therefore named **fragment crystallizable** or **Fc**. This experiment indicated that a single antibody molecule contained two antigen-binding sites and a third part of the molecule that did not participate in the binding reaction but could readily form crystals.

Edelman reduced the antibody molecule (IgG), using β-mercaptoethanol, in order to break disulfide bonds, and alkylated the reduced product so that the disulfide bonds could not spontaneously reform. Experimentally he demonstrated that each antibody molecule contained two heavy chains with a molecular mass of about 50 kDa each and two light chains of about 22 kDa each.

Another researcher, Nisonoff used **pepsin** to digest the antibody. It generated a single 100 kDa fragment composed of two Fab-like fragments and designated **F(ab′)$_2$**. Unlike Fab-fragments, F(ab′)$_2$ fragment was able to precipitate antigens. The Fc fragment was not recovered from pepsin digestion, because it had been digested into multiple fragments.

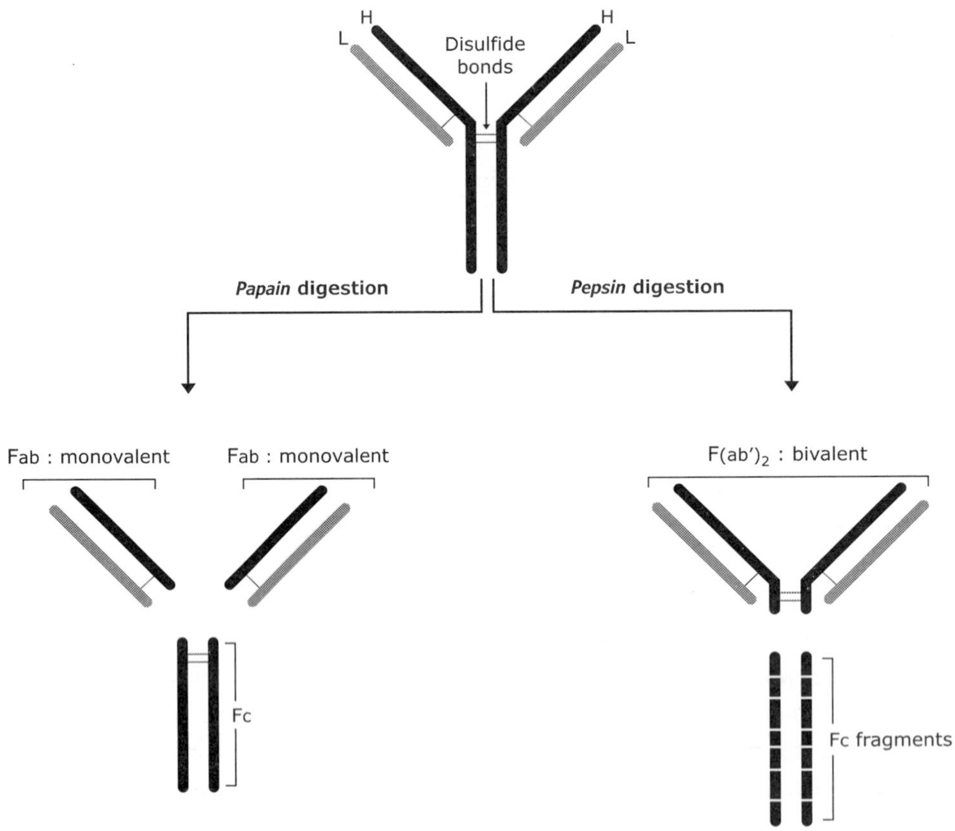

Figure 5.11 Prototype structure of IgG, showing chain structure and interchain disulfide bonds. The fragments produced by various treatments are also indicated. Light (L) chains are depicted in gray and heavy (H) chains in black. IgG molecules are cleaved by the enzymes papain and pepsin. Papain digestion allows separation of two antigen-binding regions (the Fab fragments) from the Fc fragment. Pepsin generates a single bivalent antigen-binding fragment, F(ab′)$_2$.

5.7.2 Different classes of antibody

In mammals, there are five *classes or isotypes* of antibody or immunoglobulins, IgA, IgD, IgE, IgG and IgM, each with its own class of heavy chain–α, δ, ε, γ and μ respectively. The fully assembled antibody derives its name from the heavy chain: μ chains yield IgM; α chains, IgA; γ chains, IgG; δ chains, IgD; and ε chains, IgE.

The **valency** (i.e., the number of arms available to bind antigenic determinant) of antibody refers to the number of antigenic determinants that an antibody molecule can bind. The valency of all antibodies is at least two (**bivalent**) and in some instances more (**multivalent**). Monomeric form of all antibody classes is homobivalent. Dimeric (e.g., IgA) and pentameric (e.g., IgM) forms of antibodies are multivalent.

IgG

IgG is the most abundant antibody in serum constituting about 80% of the total serum antibody. There are four human IgG subclasses, distinguished by differences in γ-chain sequence and numbered according to their decreasing average serum concentrations: IgG1, IgG2, IgG3 and IgG4. Except for the IgG3 subclass, which has a rapid turnover, with a half-life of 7 days, the half-life of IgG is approximately 23 days, which is the longest half-life of all antibody isotypes. The IgG isotype (except for subclass IgG2) is the only class of antibody that can pass through the placenta, enabling the mother to transfer her immunity to the fetus. Transcytosis of IgG antibodies from the maternal circulation across the placenta delivers maternal antibodies to the fetus. These maternal antibodies will protect the newborn until its immune system is sufficiently mature to produce antibodies on its own.

IgM

IgM is the first class of antibody made by a developing B cell. It accounts of 5-10% of the total serum Ig. IgM is also found on the surface of mature B cells together with IgD where it serves as an antigen-specific B cell receptor (BCR). Monomeric IgM, with a molecular mass of ~180 kDa is expressed as a membrane-bound antibody on B cells. IgM is secreted by plasma cells as a pentameric molecule, composed of five such units, each of which consists of two light and two heavy chains, all joined together by additional disulfide bonds between their Fc portions and by a polypeptide chain termed the **J-chain** (~15 kDa). The J-chain is synthesized in the B cell. The half-life of the IgM molecule is approximately 5 days.

IgM is the first antibody class produced in a primary response to an antigen, and it is also the first antibody to be synthesized by the neonate. IgM is more efficient than IgG in activating complement. Complement activation requires two Fc regions in close proximity, and the pentameric structure of a single molecule of IgM fulfills this requirement.

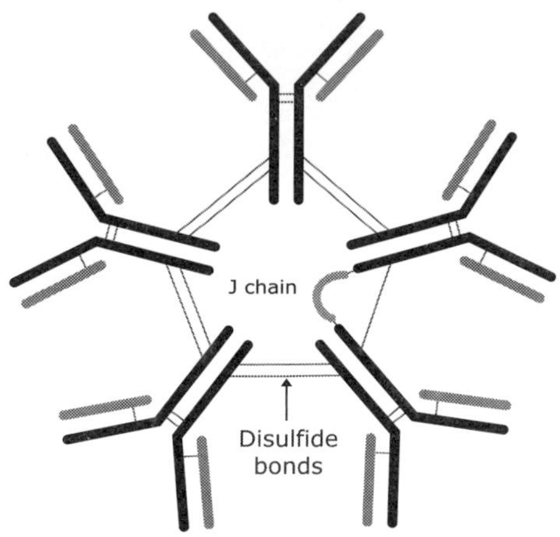

Figure 5.12 IgM forms pentamer where five antibodies are covalently linked together with disulfide bonds. Because each monomer has two epitope binding sites, a pentameric IgM has 10 binding sites. A polypeptide called J (joining) chain links the heavy chains of monomeric units of polymeric IgM. The linkage is by disulfide bonds between the J-chain and the carboxyl-terminal cysteines of IgM heavy chains.

IgA

IgA constitutes 10-15% of the total serum Ig. It is the predominant antibody class in external secretions such as breast milk, saliva, tears and mucus of the bronchial, genitourinary and digestive tracts. The IgA class of antibody contains two subclasses: IgA_1 (~93%) and IgA_2 (~7%). Serum IgA has a half-life of ~5.5 days. The IgA present in serum is predominantly monomeric. The IgA of external secretions, called *secretory IgA*, consists of a dimer or tetramer with a **J-chain** and a **secretory component**. Secreted IgA is transported through epithelial cells into the intestinal lumen (a process known as *transcytosis*) by an IgA specific Fc receptor called the **poly-Ig receptor**. It is an integral membrane glycoprotein. The secreted, dimeric IgA containing the J-chain binds to the poly-Ig receptor on mucosal epithelial cells. This complex is endocytosed into the epithelial cell and actively transported in vesicles to the luminal surface. Here the poly-Ig receptor is proteolytically cleaved, its transmembrane and cytoplasmic domains are left attached to the epithelial cell and the extracellular domain of the receptor, which carries the IgA molecule, is released into the intestinal lumen. The soluble IgA-associated component of the receptor is called the **secretory component.**

The daily production of secretory IgA is the maximum among other Ig. It is the major immunoglobulin found in the **colostrum** of milk in nursing mothers, and it may provide the neonate with a major source of protection against pathogens during the first few weeks after birth.

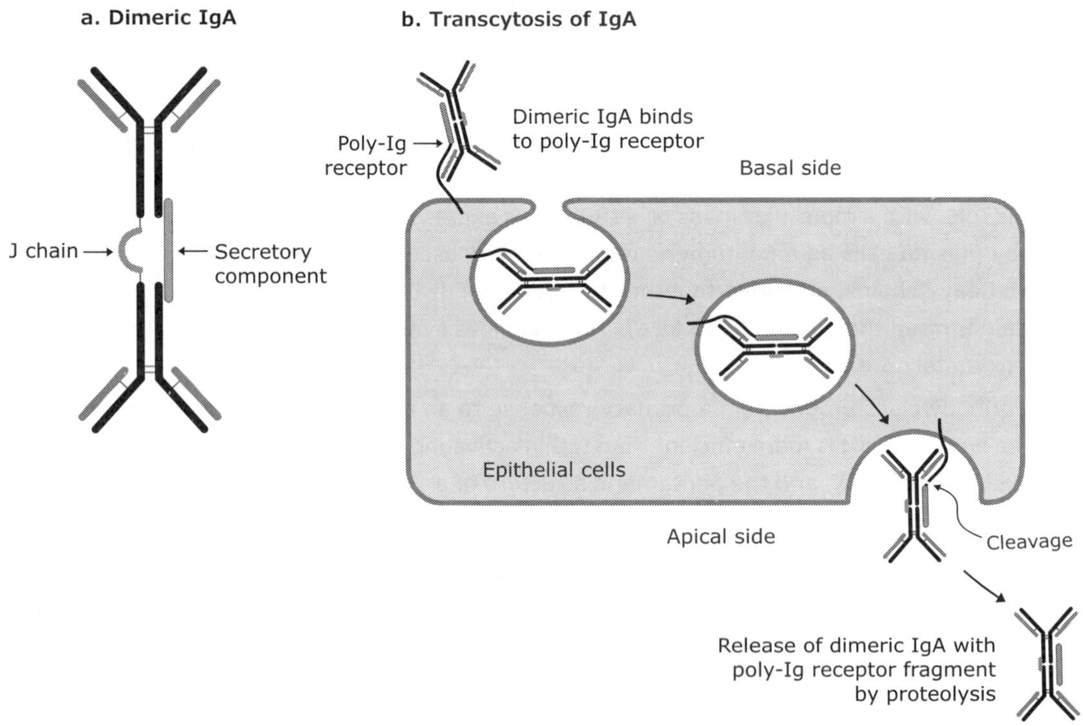

Figure 5.13 **a**. Structure of a dimeric IgA. It is composed of two monomeric IgA molecules, covalently linked through the J-chain. **b**. IgA binds to the poly-IgA receptor and is endocytosed. As the resulting complex is transported across the epithelial cell, a portion of the receptor is cleaved, and the IgA, still bound to a portion of the receptor, the secretory piece, is released at the apical side.

IgE

It mediates the immediate hypersensitivity reactions that are responsible for the symptoms of hay fever, asthma, hives and anaphylactic shock. IgE binds to Fc receptors on the membranes of blood basophils and tissue mast cells. Cross-linkage of receptor-bound IgE molecules by antigen (allergen) induces degranulation of basophils and mast cells; as a result, a variety of pharmacologically active mediators giving rise to allergic manifestations. IgE mediated degranulation is necessary for anti-parasitic defense.

IgD

It constitutes ~0.2% of the total serum Ig. IgD together with IgM, is the major membrane-bound antibody expressed by mature B cells. It is thought to function in the activation of B cells by antigen. No biological effector function has been identified for IgD.

Table 5.5 Characteristics of different antibody classes

	IgG	IgA	IgM	IgD	IgE
Molecular weight (× 10^3)	150	150, 400	900	180	190
"Y" units/molecule	1	1-2	5	1	1
Percentage of total Ig in blood	~80	10-15	5-10	<1	<1
Crosses placenta	+	–	–	–	–
Enters secretions	+	+ +	–	–	–
Agglutinates particles	+	+	+ + +	–	–
Allergic reactions	+	–	–	–	+ + + +
Activate complement	++	–	++++	–	–
Half life (days)	~23	~5.5	~5	~2.8	~2
Additional protein subunit	–	J and S	J	–	–
Binds to macrophage/neutrophils	+	–	–	–	–
Binds to mast cells	–	–	–	–	+
Percentage carbohydrate	3	7	7-10	12	11

++++ : High, +++ : Moderate, ++ : Mild, + : Low

5.7.3 Antigenic determinants on antibodies

Since antibodies are glycoproteins, they can themselves function as potent immunogens to induce an antibody response. Antigenic determinants (or epitopes) on antibody molecules are categorized into three types: *isotypic determinants*, *allotypic determinants* and *idiotypic determinants*. These are commonly distinguished serologically.

Isotypic determinants

Isotypic determinants are antigenic determinants within the constant regions of the heavy and light-chains that is characteristic of a species and present in all members of the same species. Therefore, all individuals of a species have the same isotypic determinants. But the isotypic determinants between different species are not the same. Consequently, when an antibody from one species is injected into another species, the isotype determinants of injected antibodies are recognized as foreign, resulting in the induction of antibodies (anti-antibodies) against the isotypic determinants of the injected antibodies. If human IgM is injected into a rabbit, the rabbit will recognize antigenic determinants on the constant-region of the heavy and light chains and make antibodies to them.

Allotypic determinants

It is based on genetic differences among individuals of a species. It depends on the existence of allelic forms of the same gene. All the individuals of a species have same set of genes coding for isotypic determinants. But within a species, multiple alleles exist for certain isotypic genes; consequently, individuals of a species have different antigenic determinants called *allotypic determinants*. Therefore, injection of antibodies from one individual to another individual of the same species induces anti-antibodies (anti-allotypic antibodies) formation against the allotypic determinants of the injected antibodies, provided that the two individuals differ in their allotypic determinants.

Idiotypic determinants

Antigenic determinants of the variable region are known as *idiotypic determinants* (or **idiotopes**). The unique amino-acid sequence of the variable domains of a given antibody can function not only as an antigen-binding site but also as a set of antigenic determinants. The sum of the individual idiotopes in an antibody molecule is called the *idiotype* of the antibody.

Ab Donor		Recipient	Ab produced	■ Sites recognized on Ab used as immunogen
Mouse	→	Rabbit	Rabbit anti-mouse isotypic antibodies	
Mouse (strain A)	→	Mouse (strain B)	Mouse B anti-mouse A allotypic antibodies	
Mouse 1 (strain A)	→	Mouse 2 (strain A)	Mouse A anti-mouse A idiotypic antibodies	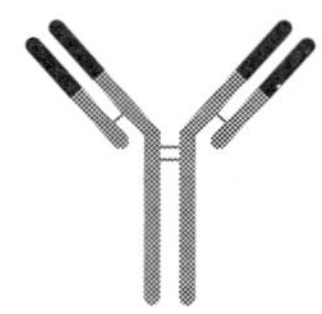

Figure 5.14 Isotype - an antibody class that is determined by the constant-region sequence of the heavy chain. Allotype - alternative allelic forms of the same isotype. Idiotype – a set of antigenic determinants (idiotopes) characterizing a unique antibody.

5.8 Organization and expression of Ig genes

One of the most remarkable features of the vertebrate immune system is its ability to respond to an apparently limitless array of foreign antigens. The genetic basis of such a remarkable diversity lies in the organization of the Ig genes. In germ-line DNA, multiple gene segments encode portions of a single Ig heavy and light chain. These gene segments are present in the germ cells but cannot be transcribed and translated into heavy and light chains until they are rearranged into functional genes. During B cell maturation in the bone marrow, some of these gene segments are randomly recombined by a dynamic genetic system capable of generating more than 10^{10} combinations.

An Ig is a tetramer of two identical light chains and two identical heavy chains. Each chain has an N-terminal variable region (V) and a C-terminal constant region (C). Variable regions and constant regions are separately coded by V gene segments and C gene segments. But V and C gene segments are not expressed as an independent unit. To construct a unit that can be expressed to form a light or heavy chain, a V gene segment must be joined physically to a C gene segment.

Germline gene organization of light chain genes

The light chains can be either **kappa** (κ) light chains or **lambda** (λ) light chains. κ and λ chains forming genes are located on separate chromosomes. Each κ and λ L-chain polypeptide consists of two major domains, a variable region and a constant region (V_L and C_L). V_L is coded by two separate gene segments: a **variable (V) segment**, which codes for the amino-terminal residues, and a small **joining (J) segment**, coding for about 13 residues at the carboxy-terminal end of the variable region.

Kappa light chain gene

The kappa (κ) locus is found on chromosome 2 in human. There are approximately 40 different V_κ gene segments, each of which can code for the N-terminal amino acids sequence of a κ variable region. These V_κ gene segments are arranged linearly, each with its own L (leader) sequence. Individual V segments are separated by non-coding sequences of 5 to 100 kb. A series of 5 J_κ gene segments are present between V_κ gene segments and C_κ gene. Each J_κ gene segment can encode the remaining amino acid residues of the κ variable region. A long non-coding region separates the C_κ gene segment—the gene coding for the single constant region of the κ chain.

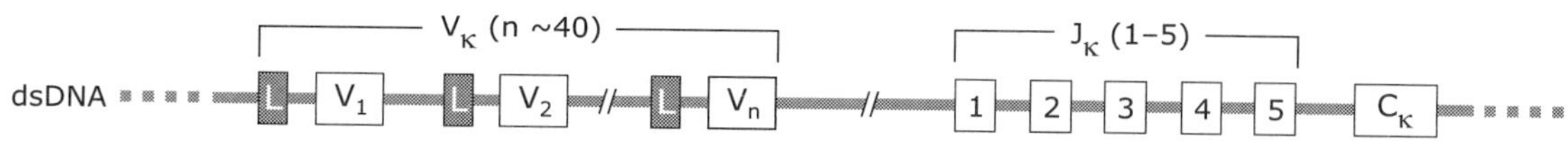

Figure 5.15 κ-light chain gene segments (in human). The κ-chain loci are arranged in groups of V and J segments that are located upstream from a single C segment.

Lambda light chain gene

The lambda (λ) locus is found on chromosome 22 in human. It is composed of 4 C_λ gene segments, one for each subtype of lambda gene segment, and approximately 30 V_λ gene segment. These V_λ genes are arranged linearly, each with its own L (leader) sequence.

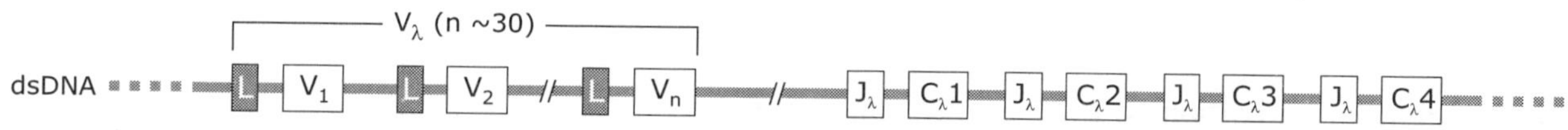

Figure 5.16 λ-light chain gene segments (in human). About 30 V_λ chain gene segments are used in mature antibody light chains. Downstream from the human V_λ locus is a series of seven J_λ-C_λ pairs, of which four or five pairs are fully functional.

V-J rearrangements in κ chain synthesis

Each B cell uses one V_κ segment coupled with one J_κ segment to create a single light-chain variable region gene. One V_κ gene segment and one J_κ gene segment are brought together in the genome to create a gene unit that, together with the C_κ gene segment, codes for an entire light chain. This unique gene rearrangement (recombination) mechanism is referred to as **V(D)J recombination** (D gene segments are discussed with H chain genes).

To make a κ chain, an early cell in the B cell lineage selects one of the V_κ gene segments from its DNA and physically joins it to one of the J_κ segments. *How this selection of V and J gene segments is made is not known but is probably a random process*. Variable-region gene arrangements occur in an ordered sequence during B cell maturation in the bone marrow. Rearranged κ gene segments contain the following regions in order from the 5′ to 3′ end: leader sequence, intron, VJ gene segment, intron and the constant region.

After a cell in the B cell lineage rearranges its DNA, it makes a primary RNA transcript. This transcript is then spliced to remove all intervening noncoding sequences, bringing the V_κ, J_κ and C_κ exons together in a mature mRNA. The mRNA is translated into the κ polypeptide chain and at the cell's rough endoplasmic reticulum, the leader sequence is cleaved off. In the lumen of the endoplasmic reticulum, it joins with a newly synthesized H chain to form an Ig molecule. *The synthesis of λ chains is similar in principle to the synthesis of κ chains*.

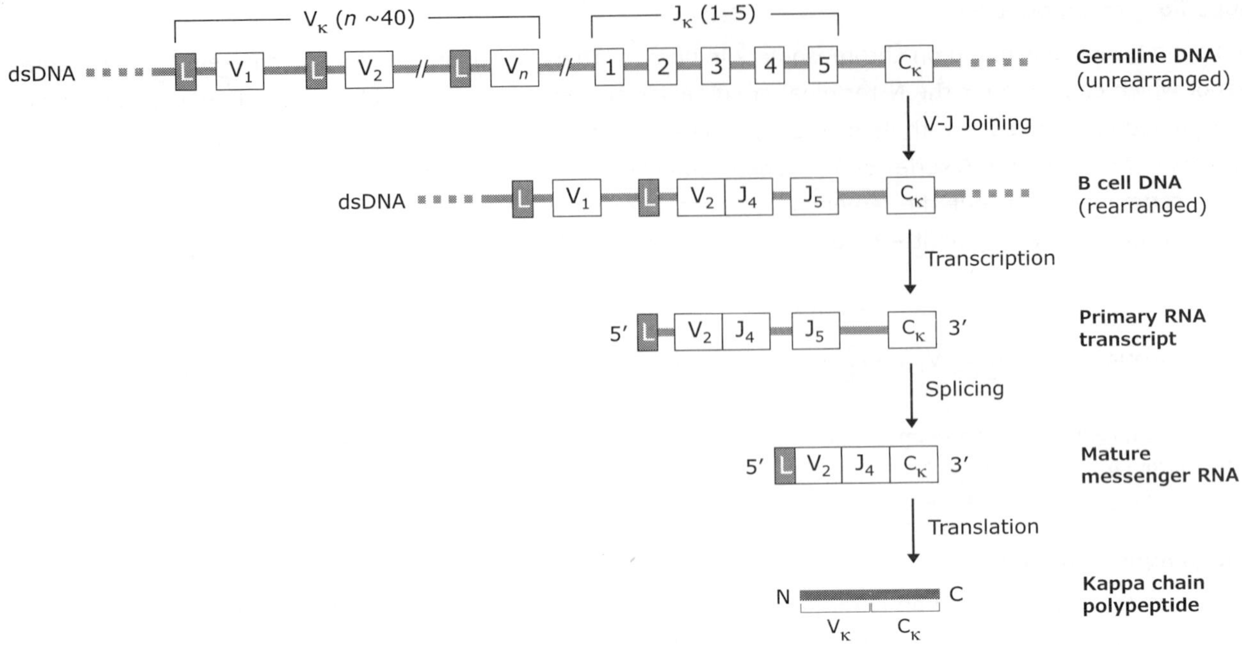

Figure 5.17 The genetic events leading to the synthesis of a kappa (κ) light chain. *Adapted and modified from Immunology A short Course, R. Coico et. al, Wiley-Liss Publication.*

Germline gene organization of the heavy chain genes

In contrast to the variable region of a light chain that is constructed from two gene segments i.e., V_L (variable) and J_L (joining) gene segments, the variable region of a heavy chain is constructed from three gene segments - V_H (variable), D_H (diversity) and J_H (joining) gene segments. Thus, in addition to V and J segments, genes coding for the variable region of a H chain also use a D segment. The human H chain locus is present on chromosome 14 includes approximately 50 V_H gene segments, approximately 20 D_H gene segments and 6 J_H gene segments.

The second key feature of the H chain genes is the presence in the germline of multiple genes coding for the C region of the H chain, one for each class and subclass of antibody. The C region determines the class of the particular antibody.

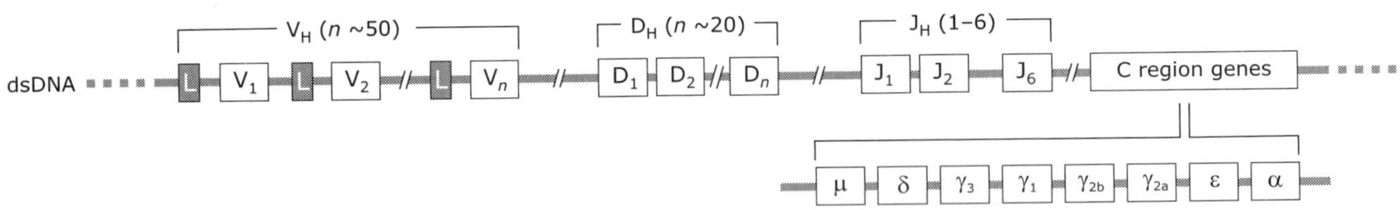

Figure 5.18 Heavy chain gene segments (in human).

VDJ rearrangement in heavy-chain DNA

Heavy chain synthesis uses the same mechanisms of rearrangement described for light chains. In the early stages of the life of a particular B cell, two rearrangements of germline DNA must occur.

The first brings one D gene segment alongside one J gene segment. The second brings one V gene segment next to the DJ unit fixing the nature of the H chain. Rearranged heavy chain genes consist of the following sequences, starting from the 5′ end: leader sequence, intron, VDJ segment, intron and a series of C gene segment. As shown in the **figure 5.19**, the rearranged DNA is then transcribed along with the closest C region genes μ and δ. This primary transcript can be spliced in two different ways (*alternative splicing*) to yield either a VDJ-μ or a VDJ-δ mRNA. Expression of secreted and membrane-bound forms of the heavy chain also depends on alternative RNA processing.

Whether secreted or membrane-bound IgM is made depends on which poly(A) site is selected during the processing of the primary transcript.

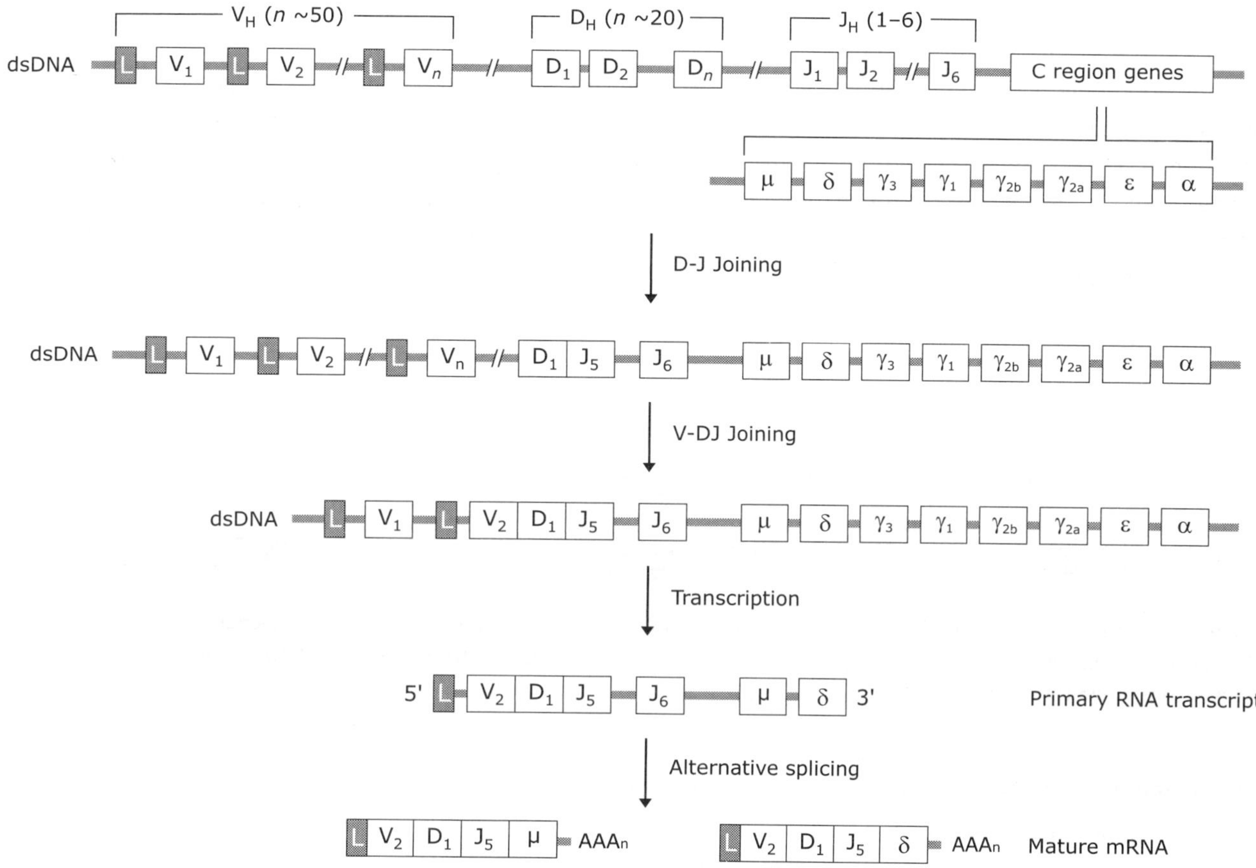

Figure 5.19 The genetic events leading to the synthesis of a human heavy chain. *Adapted and modified from Immunology A short Course, R. Coico et. al, Wiley-Liss Publication.*

Mechanism of DNA rearrangements

The germline organization of Ig loci exists in all cell types in the body. The germline genes cannot be transcribed into mRNAs that encode functional light and heavy chains of an antibody. In developing B cells, DNA rearrangement occurs through a random combination of V, D and J gene segments by a process of *somatic recombination* called **V(D)J recombination**. In the light chain forming gene, which lacks D segments, a single rearrangement event joins a randomly selected V_L gene segment to a J_L segment that is also randomly selected. The H chain forming gene contains D gene segments also, hence at these loci two sequential rearrangement events are needed, first joining a D_H gene segment to a J_H gene segment and then a V_H gene segment to the fused D_HJ_H segment.

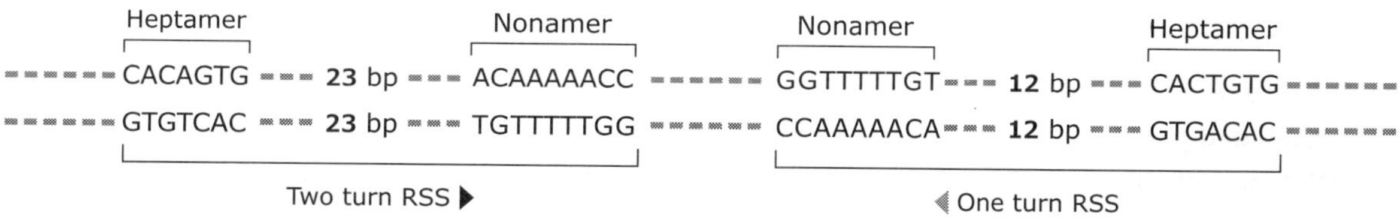

Figure 5.20 Two conserved sequences in light-chain and heavy-chain coding DNA function as recombination signal sequences (RSSs). Both signal sequences consist of a conserved palindromic heptamer and conserved AT-rich nonamer. These are separated by nonconserved spacers of 12 or 23 bp.

Flanking the V, J and D exons there are unique sequences referred to as **recombination signal sequences (RSS)**, which function in recombination. Each RSS consists of a conserved **nonamer** (a sequence of 9 bp) and a conserved **heptamer** (a sequence of 7 bp) that are separated by either 12 or 23 base pairs *spacer* as illustrated in **figure 5.20**. The 12 bp and 23 bp spacer correspond to one or two turns of the DNA helix.

Recombination only occurs between a one turn and a two turn RSS (12/23 rule). In the case of the λ-light chain, there is a one turn signal upstream of the J_λ gene segment and a two turn signal downstream of V_λ. In the case of the κ-light chain, there is a one turn signal downstream of the V_κ gene and a two turn signal upstream of the J_κ gene segment. In the case of the heavy chains there are one turn signals on each side of the D_H gene segment and a two turn signal downstream of the V_H gene segment and a two turn signal upstream of the J_H gene segment. Thus, this ensures that the correct recombination events will occur.

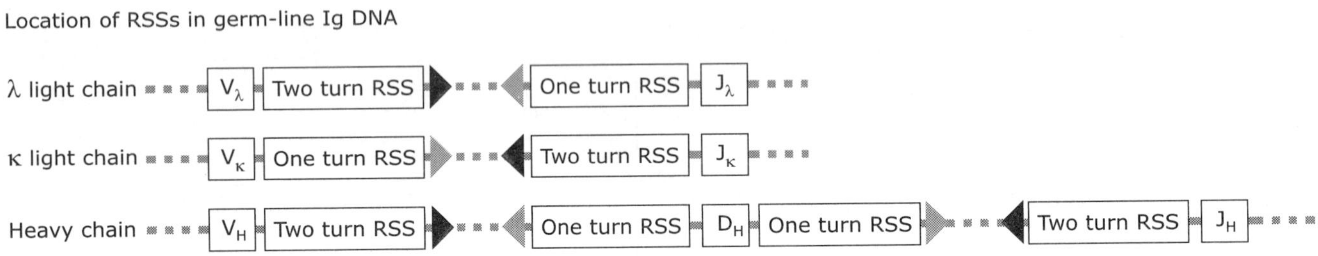

Figure 5.21 The two types of RSS have characteristic locations within λ-chain, κ-chain, and heavy-chain germ-line DNA. During DNA rearrangement of the Ig heavy and light chains, gene segments adjacent to the one turn RSS can join only with segments adjacent to the two turn RSS.

Steps involved in the process of V(D)J recombination

DNA recognition and cleavage: Recognition of the RSS by **V(D)J recombinase** (consists of two lymphoid-specific proteins, **RAG1** and **RAG2**), which work together with non-lymphoid-specific proteins, *high mobility group B protein* HMGB1 and HMGB2 to carry out DNA cleavage. HMGB1/2 act to enhance RAG1/2 binding to the RSS. RAG1 and RAG2 express exclusively in lymphocytes. RAG1 recognizes the nonamer consensus sequences for recombination. RAG2 binds to RAG1 and cleaves at the heptamer.

Generation of coding and signal ends: One-strand cleavage occurs at the junction of the coding and signal sequences (between the heptamer of the RSS and the adjacent coding sequence). The free 3′-OH end then attacks the phosphate bond at the corresponding position in the complementary strand of the duplex. This creates a hairpin **coding end**, in which the 3′ end of one strand is covalently linked to the 5′ end of the other strand and a blunt **signal end**. The intervening dsDNA, containing signal ends (the ends that contain the heptamer and the rest of the RSS), is removed in the form of an excision circle or episome.

Hairpin opening and end processing: Hairpins are opened up at the coding ends. **Artemis** is an endonuclease that randomly cuts the hairpins at the coding ends. It generates a short single strand of nucleotides at the end of the coding sequence. Addition of complementary nucleotides to this strand forms palindrome sequence (**P nucleotides**). A lymphoid-specific enzyme, called **terminal deoxynucleotidyl transferase (TdT)**, adds nucleotides to the DNA ends in a template-independent manner (**N nucleotides**). This enzyme can add up to 15 nucleotides randomly (non-genomic).

Joining: The coding ends are ligated by a double-stranded break repair process found in all cells that is called **nonhomologous end joining**. A number of ubiquitous factors participate in nonhomologous end joining. Ku70 and Ku80 are DNA end-binding proteins that bind to the breaks and recruit the catalytic subunit of DNA-dependent protein kinase (DNA-PK), a double-stranded DNA repair enzyme. DNA-PK also phosphorylates and activates artemis, which, as mentioned before, is involved in end processing. Ligation of the processed broken ends is mediated by DNA ligase IV and XRCC4, the latter being a noncatalytic but essential subunit of the ligase.

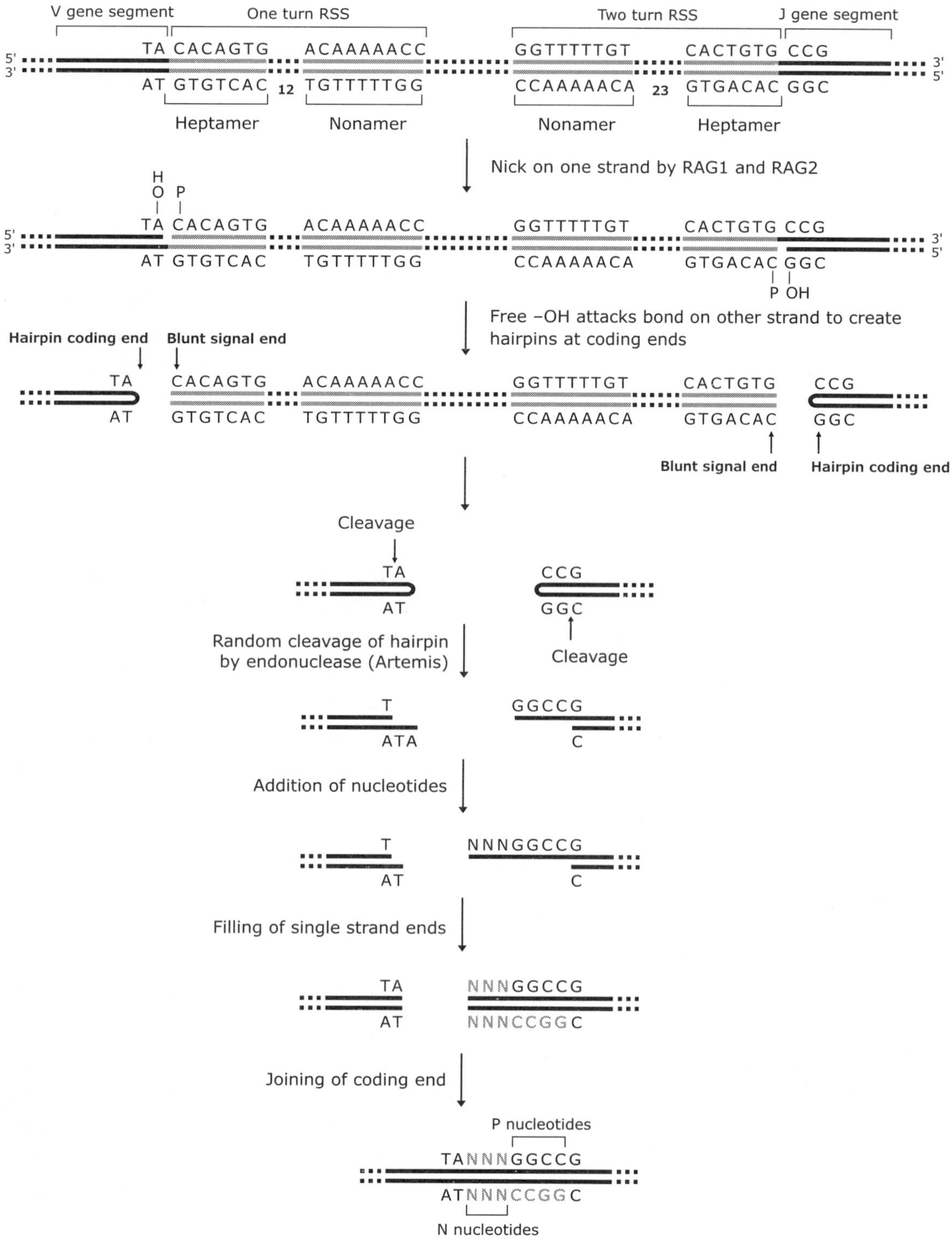

Figure 5.22 Recognition of the RSS by the RAG1/RAG2 enzyme complex. Binding of the RAG1/2 complex is enhanced by the HMGB1/2 proteins. RAG causes one-strand cleavage at the junction of the coding and signal sequences. The nick has 3′-OH and 5′-P ends. The free 3′-OH end then attacks the phosphodiester bond at the corresponding position in the complementary strand of the duplex. This creates a hairpin at the coding end, in which the 3′ end of one strand is covalently linked to the 5′ end of the other strand; it leaves a blunt double-strand break at the signal end. This second cleavage is a transesterification reaction. Next, a single-strand break is introduced into one strand close to the hairpin. This generates a single-stranded protrusion. Incorporation of complementary nucleotides to the exposed single strand then converts the coding end to an extended duplex. This reaction explains the introduction of *P nucleotides* at coding ends. Some nucleotides are added randomly further. They are called *N nucleotides*. Their insertion is catalyzed by the enzyme *terminal deoxynucleotidyl transferase*. Finally, through the mechanism of non-homologous end-joining (NHEJ) the coding ends join together.

Productive or nonproductive rearrangements of Ig gene

Due to the imprecise and random nature of V(D)J recombination, only a fraction of the resulting Ig genes is functional, i.e., they contain a productive V(D)J exon (in the correct reading frame). The recombination of V-(D)-J gene segments results in a **productive rearrangement** if all the rearranged gene segments are in the correct reading frame and lead to the expression of a functional protein. A **nonproductive rearrangement** occurs when the rearranged gene segments are not in the correct reading frame and fails to codes for a functional protein. A productive rearrangement prevents any further rearrangement from occurring. If the first rearrangement is nonproductive, the heavy chain allele on the other chromosome can complete VDJ rearrangement at the same locus. Thus, in any B cell, one heavy chain allele is productively rearranged and expressed, and the other is either retained in the germline configuration or nonproductively rearranged. As a result, an individual B cell can express an Ig heavy chain protein encoded by only one of the two inherited alleles. This phenomenon is called **allelic exclusion**, and it ensures that every B cell will express a single receptor. If both alleles undergo nonproductive rearrangements, the developing cell cannot produce heavy chains and undergoes programmed cell death.

Allelic exclusion

B cells have two sets of chromosomes, one set from each parent, so theoretically, Ig genes located on both chromosomes could synthesize antibody molecules. This does not occur. In contrast to almost all other gene products, which are derived from genes from both parental chromosomes a B cell expresses the rearranged genes for H and L chain from only one chromosome i.e., either from the maternal or the paternal chromosome. During lymphocyte development, only one allele for H- and L-chain forming genes undergoes V(D)J rearrangement at a time, and once productive rearrangement is sensed, rearrangement of the second allele is prevented. This phenomenon of using genes from only one parental chromosome is known as **allelic exclusion**.

Monoallelic expression can be divided into two subgroups, *non-random* and *random* monoallelically expressed genes. The *imprinted genes* are a well-studied example of the non-random monoallelically expressed subgroup. In this subgroup, each gene is predetermined to be expressed either exclusively from the maternal or the paternal allele in all cells in an organism. In a random monoallelically expressed gene, each cell may express either the maternal or paternal allele, and the choice of which allele of each gene is expressed varies throughout the different cells in the body.

Allelic exclusion is independent for the H- and L-chain loci. H-chain forming genes usually rearrange first. Allelic exclusion for L-chain forming genes must apply equally to both families (cells may have either active κ or λ light chains). It is likely that the cell rearranges its κ genes first and tries to rearrange λ only if both κ attempts are unsuccessful.

If DNA rearrangements occurred independently in each H-chain forming gene and each L-chain forming gene, a single cell could make up to eight different antibodies, each with a different antigen-binding site. In fact, each B cell uses only two of the six genes: one of the four L-chain forming genes and one of the two H-chain forming genes. The steps in rearrangement, allelic exclusion, and hence the synthesis of a complete Ig molecules are very tightly controlled, although all the controlling mechanisms are not yet completely clear. The mechanism of allelic exclusion ensures that every B cell and the antibody it synthesizes are *monospecific* – that is, are specific for only one epitope 'one B cell – one antibody' rule. It ensures that functional B cells never contain more than one $V_HD_HJ_H$ and one V_LJ_L unit. In this way, an individual B cell is prevented from forming and expressing Ig molecules with different antigenic specificities on its cell surface.

5.9 Generation of antibody diversity

One unique property of antibodies is their remarkable diversity. How can adaptive immune system produce lymphocytes that collectively display such an enormous diversity of receptors, including ones that recognize synthetic molecules that never occur in nature? There are several means of antibody diversification as identified in mice and humans.

Combinatorial V(D)J joining

Random association of any V gene segment with any J gene segment can occur to form an L chain variable region, and similarly, any V can associate with any D or J gene segments in the H chain gene rearrangement. These can be combined with one another to provide extensive combinatorial diversity. As there are about 40 V_κ and 5 J_κ genes coding for the κ chain variable region, assuming random association then 40×5 or 200κ chains can be formed.

Junctional diversification

Diversity generated by means of combinatorial V(D)J joining is further augmented by a phenomenon called *junctional diversification*. In most cases of site-specific recombination, DNA joining is precise. But during the joining of antibody (and T cell receptor) gene segments, a variable number of nucleotides are often lost from the ends of the recombining gene segments, and one or more randomly chosen nucleotides may also be inserted. This random loss and gain of nucleotides at joining sites is called *junctional diversification*, and it enormously increases the diversity of V-region coding sequences created by recombination. Because of junctional diversity, antibody molecules show the greatest variability at the junctions of V and C regions that form the third hypervariable region, or CDR3.

Somatic hypermutation

The variable (V) regions of germ-line DNA are susceptible to a high rate of somatic mutation during B cell development in response to an antigen challenge. This phenomenon is referred to as **somatic hypermutation** because it occurs at the rate of at least 10,000-fold higher than the normal rate of mutation. These mutations allow B cell clones to produce antibodies with somewhat different polypeptide sequences. The presence of mutations correlates with increasing affinities of the antibodies for a particular antigen that induced the response (called **affinity maturation**). Somatic hypermutation in mice and humans occurs only after antigen contact, affects only the variable regions of the antibody heavy and light chains.

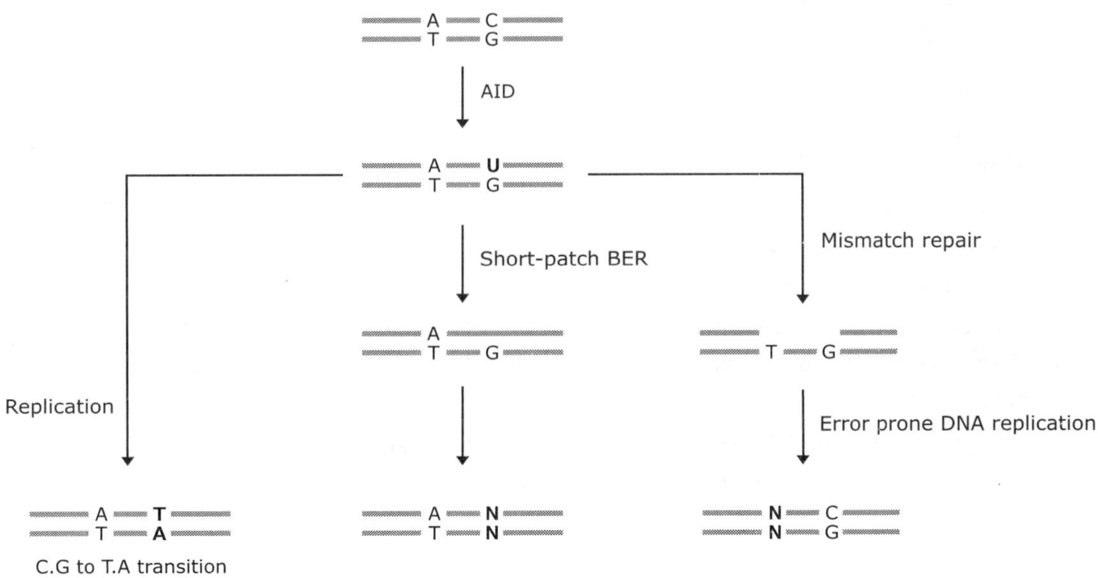

Figure 5.23 Model of somatic hypermutation. AID deaminates a deoxycytidine residue, creating a deoxyuridine: deoxyguanosine (U:G) mismatch that is resolved by several pathways that may compete with one another. AID deaminates single-stranded DNA formed during transcription. The general replication machinery can interpret the U as if it were a deoxythymidine (T). One of the daughter cells will acquire a C-to-T transition mutation (*Left*). The uracil DNA glycosylase enzyme can remove the uracil, leaving behind an abasic site. Short-patch base excision repair (BER) can fill the gap with error-prone polymerases, which can insert *any* nucleotide in place of the U, leading to transitions and transversions at G:C bases (*center*). Mismatch repair (MMR) can recognize the U:G mismatch. The U-bearing strand is excised and, at loci that undergo somatic hypermutation, proliferating cell nuclear antigen (PCNA) recruits error-prone polymerases to fill the gap, leading to transition and transversion mutations at A:T bases as well as at neighboring G:C bases (*right*).

The enzyme *activation induced cytidine deaminase* (**AID**) plays an essential role in causing somatic hypermutation. The DNA deaminase activity of AID converts C residues to U residues at specific tetranucleotide (AGCT) hotspots that are found all over the genome but are targeted primarily in rearranged V regions. The mechanism by which these rearranged V regions are specifically targeted is however still unclear.

AID introduces point mutations into V regions of the Ig genes. AID deaminates deoxycytidine residues to deoxyuridines, which are then processed by DNA replication, base excision repair (BER) or mismatch repair (MMR). A general model for the enzyme systems involved in somatic hypermutation includes a first phase that depends on the mutagenic activity of AID and a second phase that depends on the error-prone repair of the AID-induced mutations. This model has been explained in **figure 5.23**.

Combinatorial joining of H and L-chains

In addition to V(D)J combinatorial association, any H-chain may associate with any L-chain. The same heavy chain can combine with different light chains, and vice versa. The combination of different H- and L-chain pairs to form a complete antibody molecule.

Problem

Assume that an organism has 400 V and 10 J light-chain gene segments and 400 V, 10 D and 10 J heavy chain gene segments in its haploid genome. If no nucleotides are lost or gained during recombination within the heavy-and light-chain DNA, how many functional immunoglobulin light-chain genes and heavy-chain genes *theoretically* could be generated in this organism?

Solution: The variable region of each light-chain gene contains one V and one J segment. Random recombination of 400 V and 10 J regions would generate $400\times10 = 4\times10^3$ functional light-chain genes. The variable region of each heavy-chain gene contains one V, one D, and one J segment. Random recombination of 400 V, 10 D and 10 J regions would theoretically generate $400\times10\times10 = 4\times10^4$ functional heavy-chain genes.

5.10 B cell maturation and activation

B cell maturation

In adult humans, B cells originate from **hematopoietic stem cells** (HSCs) residing in the bone marrow. The main stages of early *antigen-independent* B cell development, the **pro-B**, **pre-B**, and **immature B cells**, are characterized by the expression of specific cell surface markers and by the progressive rearrangements of the Ig heavy and light chain gene segments. B cell development begins with the differentiation of common lymphoid progenitors into **pro-B cell (progenitor B cell)**. Pro-B cells are the first B-committed cells. The maturation of B cells from progenitor B cells occurs mostly in the bone marrow.

During the fetal stage (i.e., prenatally), HSCs migrate into the fetal liver, where they develop and mature to B cells. After the fetal stage (i.e., postnatally), B cell development occurs in the bone marrow. At the immature B cell stage, they migrate to secondary lymphoid tissues, where they mature.

There are two main populations of B lymphocytes, referred to as **B-1** and **B-2** B cells. B-1 cells include B-1a and B-1b subsets. B-1 cells are part of the innate immune system. In this chapter, we have referred the B-2 B-cell subset simply as 'B cells'. B-2 cells are generally considered to be mediators of adaptive immunity and are produced in the bone marrow after birth. They include a predominant population of *follicular* and a minor population of *marginal zone* B cells.

Rearrangement of the immunoglobulin heavy and light chain locus

Rearrangement of the heavy chain locus occurs prior to light chain rearrangement. In the pro-B cell stage, heavy-chain gene rearrangement occurs. Upon completion of productive heavy chain gene rearrangement, the cell is classified as a **pre-B cell (precursor B cell)**.

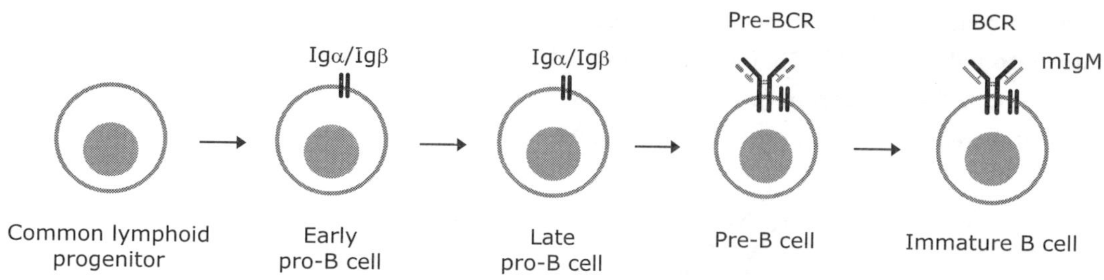

	Common lymphoid progenitor	Early pro-B cell	Late pro-B cell	Pre-B cell	Immature B cell
Gene locus **IgH**	Germline	$\mathbf{D_H \rightarrow J_H}$	$\mathbf{V_H \rightarrow D_HJ_H}$	$\mathbf{V_HD_HJ_H}$	$\mathbf{V_HD_HJ_H}$
Gene locus **IgL**	Germline	Germline	Germline	$\mathbf{V_L \rightarrow J_L}$	$\mathbf{V_LJ_L}$
Surface immunoglobulin	–	–	–	Igμ and SLC	Igμ and Igκ or Igλ

Figure 5.24 Rearrangement of the immunoglobulin heavy chain (IgH) locus is initiated at the pro-B-cell stage and, if successful, gives rise to the μ heavy chain. Pre-B cells encode VpreB and λ5, which together comprise the surrogate light chain (SLC). Two SLCs pair with two μ heavy chains, forming the pre-BCR. Rearrangement of the immunoglobulin light chain (IgL) locus starts in pre-B cells. In-frame IgL gene rearrangements in pre-B cells result in the expression of a BCR that is composed of two Igμ chains and two IgL chains on immature B cells.

A rearrangement is considered to be productive (in the correct reading frame) if it is able to correctly encode an Ig protein. If a μ heavy chain is produced from the rearranged heavy chain locus on one chromosome and forms a **pre-BCR** (pre-B cell receptor), this receptor signals to irreversibly inhibit rearrangement of the Ig heavy chain locus on the other chromosome. If the first rearrangement is nonproductive, the heavy chain allele on the other chromosome can complete VDJ rearrangement at the Ig heavy chain locus. Thus, in any B cell clone, one heavy chain allele is productively rearranged and expressed, and the other is either retained in the germline configuration or nonproductively rearranged.

Rearrangement of the heavy chain locus

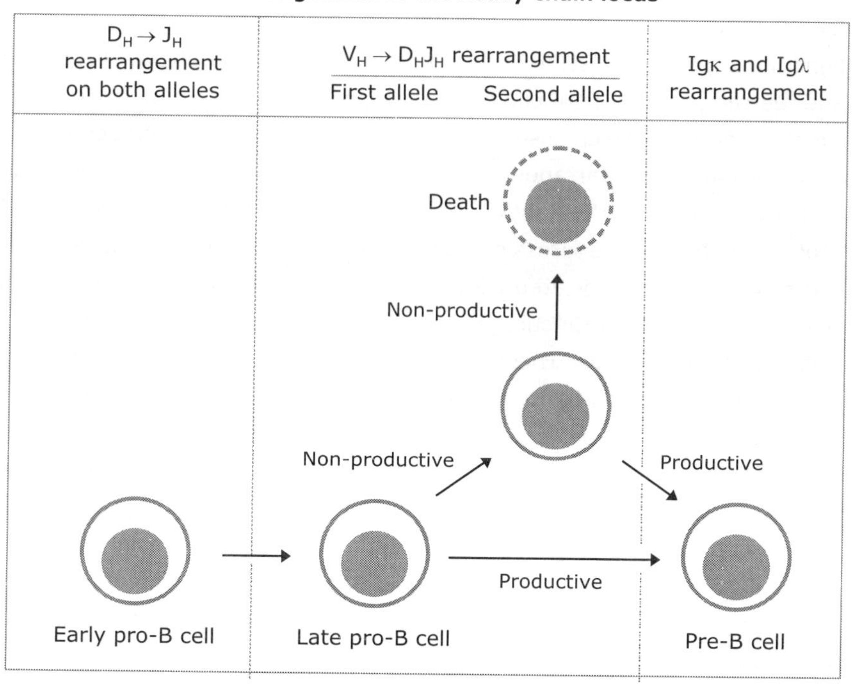

$D_H \rightarrow J_H$ D_H to J_H rearrangement
$V_H \rightarrow D_HJ_H$ V_H to D_HJ_H rearrangement
D_HJ_H rearranged D_HJ_H
$V_HD_HJ_H$ rearranged $V_HD_HJ_H$

Figure 5.25 First, if a μ chain is produced from the recombined heavy chain locus on one chromosome and forms a pre-BCR, this receptor signals to irreversibly inhibit rearrangement of the Ig heavy chain locus on the other chromosome. If the first rearrangement is non-productive, the heavy chain allele on the other chromosome can complete VDJ rearrangement at the heavy chain locus. In case of non-productive rearrangement of the one allele, cells remain at the pro-B cell stage and initiate rearrangement on the second allele.

In pre-B cells, the μ heavy chain associates with the λ5 and VpreB proteins. VpreB and λ5 together comprise the **surrogate light chain** (SLC). Two SLCs pair with two μ heavy chains and associated Igα/Igβ signaling molecules form the **pre-B cell receptor** (pre-BCR). The genes coding for VpreB and λ5 are not included in the light-chain gene families. VpreB is homologous to a light-chain V-region domain, and λ5 is homologous to λ light-chain J-C regions.

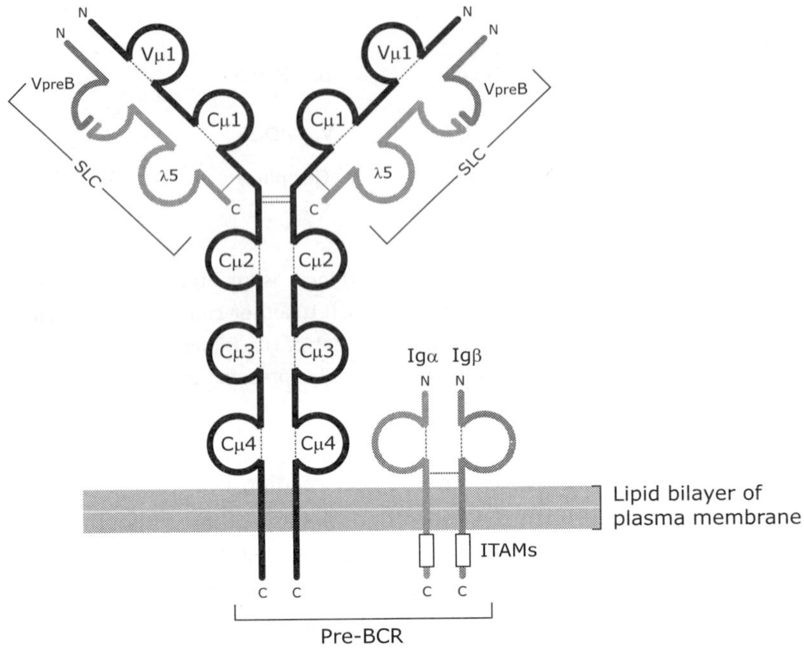

Figure 5.26 Diagram showing the composition of the Pre-B cell receptor (pre-BCR): two μ heavy chains associated with two surrogate light chains (SLCs), each made up of λ5 and VpreB and associated Igα/Igβ signaling molecules.

During the pre-B cell stage, productive light-chain gene rearrangement occurs. Pre-B cells proliferate first as *large pre-B cells*, and then shut off surrogate light chain gene expression and become nondividing *small pre-B cells* that express the μ heavy chain intracellularly and rearrange their κ light chain genes. If productive rearrangement occurs at the κ locus, the cell will produce a κ light chain protein, which associates with the previously synthesized μ chain to produce a complete IgM. If the κ locus is not productively rearranged, the cell can rearrange the λ locus and again produce a complete IgM. After productive rearrangement at the light chain locus, the cell becomes an **immature B cell** expressing membrane-bound IgM (mIgM). The first IgM-expressing cell during B cell development is called an *immature B cell*. IgM on the cell surface with two closely associated transmembrane signaling molecules Igα and Igβ, form the *B cell receptor* (**BCR**). Immature B cells bear a functional receptor in the form of membrane-bound IgM but have not yet begun to express membrane-bound IgD. These cells do not proliferate and differentiate in response to antigens. Immature B cells expressing functional IgM migrate through the circulation into the spleen and other secondary lymphoid organs where they pass the stages of **transitional B cells** and complete maturation as *follicular* or *marginal zone B cells*. The majority of peripheral B cells that reside in the spleen and other secondary lymphoid organs are known as **follicular B cells**, often referred to as 'B-2 B cells'. A second, minor population of B cells found in the spleen consists of **marginal zone B cells**, named for their predominance at the marginal zones that lie at the white pulp/red pulp junctions. Follicular and marginal zone B cells both derive from a common lineage that develops in the bone marrow and bifurcates during the final stage of B-cell maturation in the splenic follicles.

Once the functional BCR is assembled on the immature B cell membrane the receptor must be tested for whether it binds self-antigens, in order to ensure that as few as possible autoreactive (self-reactive) B cells emerge from the bone marrow. Those immature B cells that bear self-reactive receptors undergo one of three fates — **clonal deletion, receptor editing** and **anergy**. The loss of B cells bearing self-reactive receptors within the bone marrow by either clonal deletion or receptor editing is referred to as **central tolerance**. Those mechanisms of central tolerance occur when the immature B cells receive strong signals through their mIgM BCR. Self-reactive B cells that recognize soluble self-antigens within the bone marrow may survive to escape the bone marrow environment, but become anergic, or unresponsive, to any further antigenic stimuli.

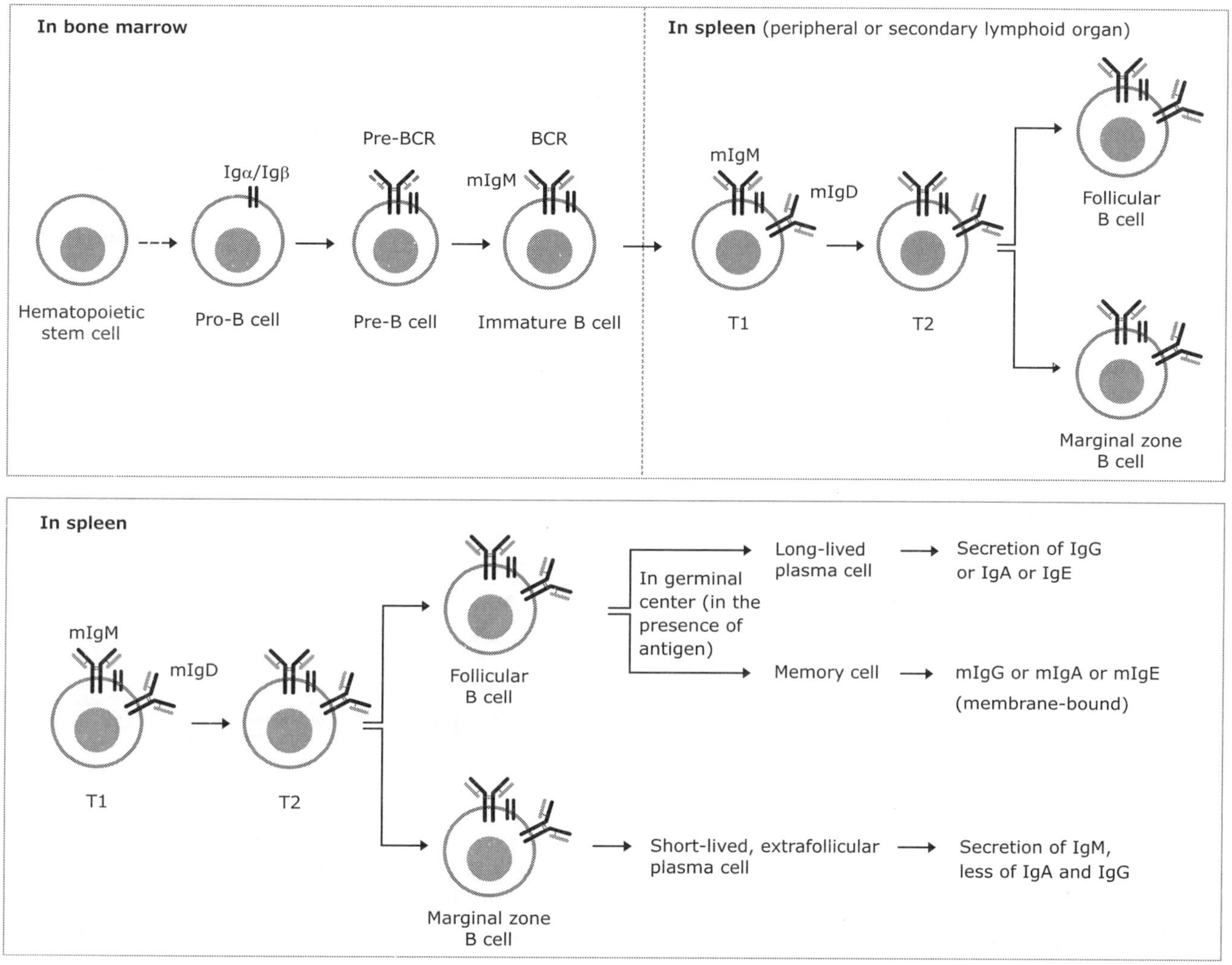

Figure 5.27 The main stages in B cell development.

Immature B cells exit the bone marrow and differentiate into transitional B cells (T1 and T2). These transitional B cells differentiate into *mature B cells* - **marginal zone B cells** and **follicular B cells**. The majority of transitional B cells that complete maturation become *follicular B cells*. A smaller proportion becomes *marginal zone B cells*, which are largely sessile and reside in the splenic marginal sinuses. Follicular B cells are also often called *recirculating B cells* because they migrate from one secondary lymphoid organ to the next.

Mature B cells are concentrated in secondary lymphoid organs. These organs include the lymph nodes, spleen, Peyer's patches, and mucosa-associated lymphoid tissue. Circulating B cells must encounter cognate antigen to fulfill their unique function of producing high-affinity antibodies to combat infection. When antigen is introduced into the body, it becomes concentrated in various secondary lymphoid organs. Blood-borne antigen is filtered by the spleen, whereas antigen from tissue spaces drained by the lymphatic system is filtered by regional lymph nodes. Secondary lymphoid organs provide an efficient meeting point for circulating B cells and antigens drained from peripheral tissues.

Mature B cells expressing both mIgM and mIgD (almost 10 times more mIgD than mIgM). The expression of mIgD along with mIgM requires carefully regulated *alternative splicing* events. Mature B cells are ready to encounter antigen, but they are considered **naïve** until they do so. All classes of antibody can be made in a membrane-bound form as well as in a soluble, secretory form. The membrane-bound form serves as an antigen receptor on the B cell surface, while the soluble form is made only after the cell is stimulated by antigen to become an antibody-secreting cell. The sole difference between the two forms lies in the carboxyl terminus of the heavy chain. Each of the heavy-chain constant regions can be synthesized as both membrane-bound and secreted proteins. Immature B cells and mature B cells (both naïve B cells that have not yet encountered their antigen and memory B cells) express only membrane-bound antibody on their cell surface. In contrast, **plasma cells**, arising from antigen-induced mature B cell differentiation, secrete large quantities of soluble antibodies. Following antigenic stimulation of a mature B cell, the cell may express a secreted form of IgM and IgD. Cells switch from the synthesis of the membrane-bound to secreted forms of IgM and IgD by alternative RNA splicing. Whether secreted or membrane-bound antibody is made depends on which **poly(A) site** is selected during processing of the primary transcript. The ability to switch between the membrane-bound and the secreted form of immunoglobulin heavy chains is controlled by alternative use of polyadenylation sites (not by *alternative splicing*).

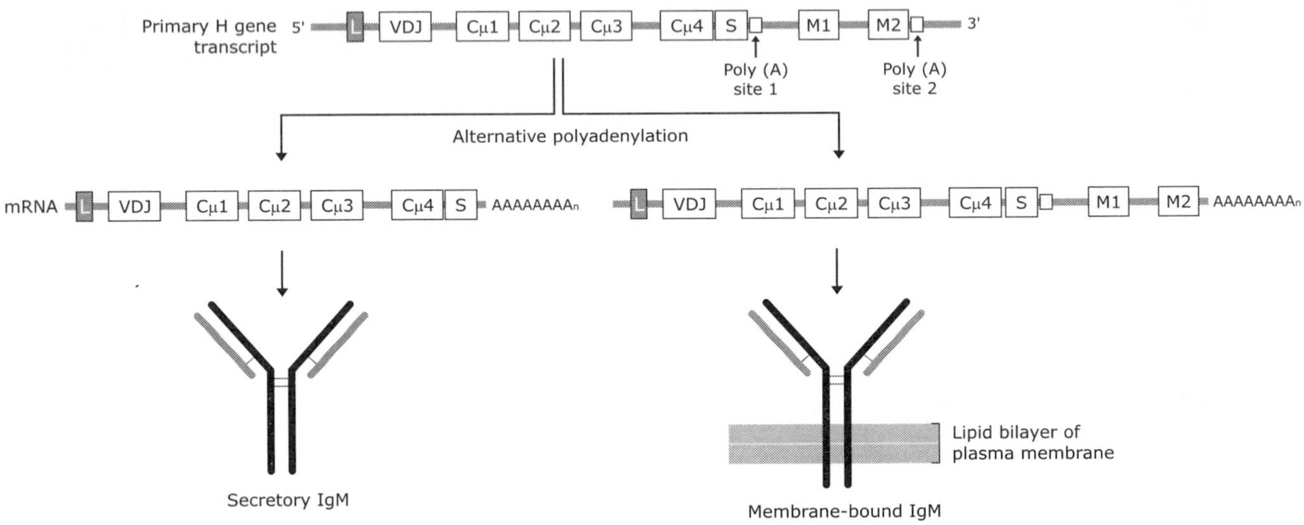

Figure 5.28 Synthesis of secreted and membrane-bound IgM. The organization of the μ heavy-chain primary transcript is shown at the top: Cμ4 is the exon encoding the fourth μ constant-region domain; S is a coding sequence unique for secreted IgM; M1 and M2 are exons that specify the transmembrane domain of the μ chain. Whether secreted or membrane-bound IgM is made depends on which poly(A) site is selected during the processing of the primary transcript. If the upstream poly(A) site is used, the resulting mRNA specifies the secreted form of the μ chain. If the downstream poly(A) site is used, the resulting mRNA encodes the membrane-bound form of the μ chain.

Immunological tolerance

Immunological tolerance is the process by which the immune system does not respond against an antigen (self or non-self). Tolerance to self-antigens is called **self-tolerance** whereas tolerance to non-self (foreign) antigens is known as *acquired immunological tolerance*. It occurs during both T and B cells development. Immunological tolerance of B cells is termed **B cell tolerance**. The B cell self-tolerance process produces a population of B cells that do not recognize self-antigens but may recognize non-self antigens. Self-tolerance is maintained by several different mechanisms that prevent the maturation and activation of self reactive B cells. These mechanisms include *clonal deletion*, *receptor editing* and *clonal anergy*.

Once the functional B cell receptor (BCR) is assembled on the immature B cell membrane, the receptor must be tested for whether it binds self-antigens. It ensures that as few as possible autoreactive (or self-reactive) B cells emerge from the bone marrow. Those immature B cells that bear self-reactive BCRs that recognize ubiquitous self-cell-surface antigens in a primary lymphoid organ are eliminated by a process known as **clonal deletion**. These immature B cells are believed to undergo apoptosis.

However, there is an interval before apoptosis during which the self-reactive B cell may be rescued by further gene rearrangements that may replace the self-reactive BCR with a new receptor, which is not self-reactive (called

receptor editing). In this condition, immature B cells are stimulated to reexpress the RAG proteins and undergo a second round of V(D)J recombination, thereby changing the specificity of the cell surface receptor they make. The loss of immature B cells bearing self-reactive receptors within the bone marrow by either of those mechanisms is referred to as **central tolerance**. It prevents B cells with strongly self-reactive receptors must be eliminated to prevent autoimmune reactions; this process of **negative selection** is one of the ways in which the immune system is made self-tolerant.

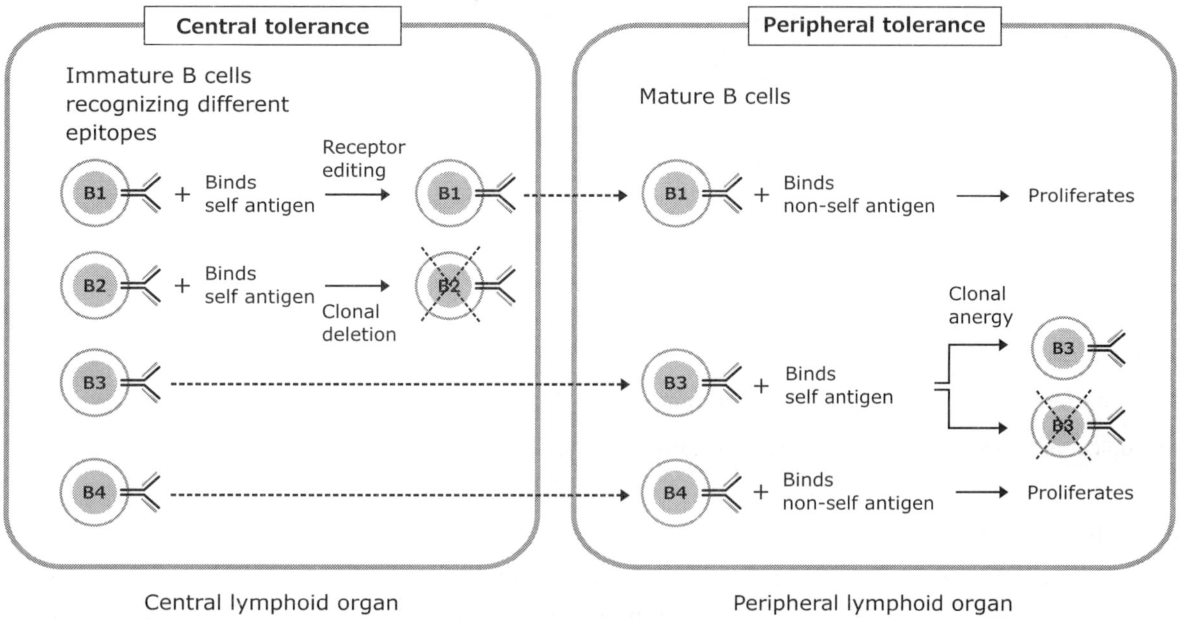

Figure 5.29 Induction of immunological tolerance to self-antigens in central and peripheral lymphoid organs.

Immunological tolerance of B cells are also mediated by the process of **clonal anergy** or *inactivation*. When a mature B cell escapes tolerance in primary lymphoid organ and binds self-antigens in the peripheral lymphoid organ, self-reactive B cell may either die by apoptosis or be functionally inactivated and cannot amplify the immune response.

Receptor editing

The receptor (i.e., antibody) present on the immature B cells that recognize self-antigens with high affinity (i.e., self-reactive or autoreactive) are often induced to change their specificities by a process called **receptor editing**. Since the receptor's binding site contains elements of both the H-chain and the L-chain, changing just one of these is often sufficient to alter the specificity. Receptor editing of L-chain (most frequently in κ chains) has been shown to occur quite frequently. Receptor editing of H-chain is less common than with L-chains.

In the process of receptor editing, if the first completed receptor in the immature B cell is found to self-reactive, the DNA rearrangement machinery is switched again. This B cell can now edit the first productive rearranged V and J gene segments (suppose, from first V3-J3 rearrangement to second V2-J4 rearrangement). Alternatively, the cell could rearrange light-chain gene segments at the second allele of same L-chain, or it can rearrange other L-chain gene segments. However, the term 'receptor editing' usually refers to the process in which a B cell rearranges the same allele more than once.

B-1 and B-2 B cells

Two populations of B lymphocytes, B-1 and B-2 cells have been described. B-1 B cells arise before B-2 B cells. B-2 B-cells are the conventional B cells involved in the adaptive immune response. B-1 B cells are part of the innate immune system. These cells are present only in low numbers in secondary lymphoid organs, and are found in large numbers in the peritoneal and pleural cavities instead. B-1 B cells are the major source of 'natural' antibodies, which are constitutively produced circulating antibodies that are secreted by these B cells prior to any infections. Unlike B-2 B cells that develop from bone marrow stem cells, the majority of B-1 B cells are generated from progenitor cells found in the fetal liver. After birth, the development of B-2 B cells predominates, and few B-1 B cells are made. They express surface IgM but little or no IgD, and are marked by the display of CD5. Most B-1 cells do not develop into memory B cells. The B-1 population responds poorly to protein antigens and undergoes much less somatic hypermutation and class switching than the B-2 B cells do.

Table 5.6 Comparison of the properties of B-1 B cells and B-2 B cells

Property	**B-1 B cells**	**B-2 B cells**
When first produced	Fetus	After birth
Primary location	Body cavities	Secondary lymphoid organs
Mode of renewal	Self-renewing	Replaced from bone marrow
Isotypes produced	Mainly IgM	All isotypes
Response to protein antigen	Poor	High
Requirement for T cell help	No	Yes
Somatic hypermutation	Little or none	High
Immunological memory	Little or none	Yes

B cell receptor and co-receptor

Igα and Igβ are associated with membrane-bound antibody molecules on all cells in the B cell lineage, from the pre-B cell to the mature B cell. Igα/Igβ are transmembrane proteins and their extracellular parts are represented by Ig domains. The complex of Igα and Igβ associated with membrane-bound antibody molecules in the B cell lineage is known as the **B cell receptor** (BCR). Igα/Igβ (CD79a/CD79b) do not bind antigen. Their function is to transmit signals to the cell nucleus, leading to a change in the pattern of genes expression; for this reason, Igα and Igβ are referred to as *signal transducing* molecules.

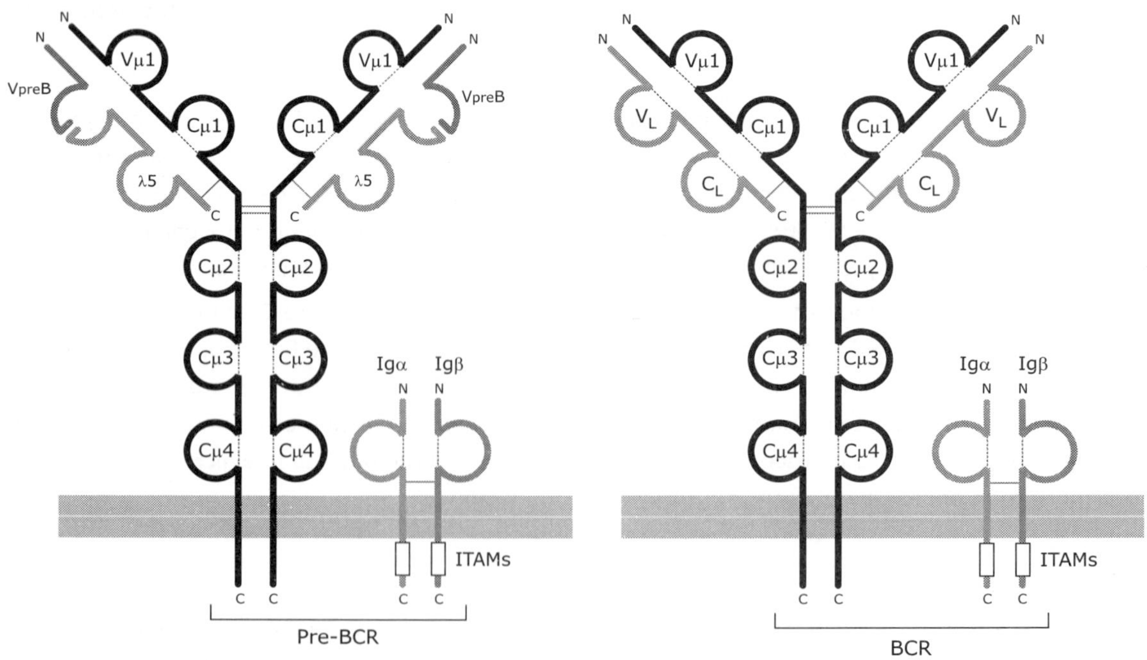

Figure 5.30 BCR is a complex comprising of membrane-bound antibody molecule and two associated signal-transducing Igα/Igβ molecules. In the pre-B cell receptor, λ5 is a polypeptide that associates with VpreB to form the surrogate light chain (SLC).

Other molecules on the B cell membrane like **CD19**, **CD81** (also known as TAPA-1) and **CD21** (CR2) are associated in a complex, known as the **B cell co-receptor**, also affect the signal that is transmitted through the BCR. CDs (*C*luster of *Differentiation molecules*) are cell surface proteins present on lymphocytes (both B and T cell) and other cells of the immune system. To date, over 300 CDs have been characterized. CDs have both biological and diagnostic significance. The presence of various CDs on the cell surface can be used to determine the cell's identity. B cells also express surface proteins known as *class II MHC molecules*. Unlike the expression pattern of many other cell types, B cell expression of class II MHC molecules is *constitutive*–that is, the molecules are always expressed. Activated B cells also express high levels of **B7** proteins (CD80/CD86), which are referred to as *co-stimulatory molecules*, because they are required in addition to antigen to activate naïve T cells. B7 proteins include two homologous proteins, named B7-1 (CD80) and B7-2 (CD86), often collectively called B7 proteins.

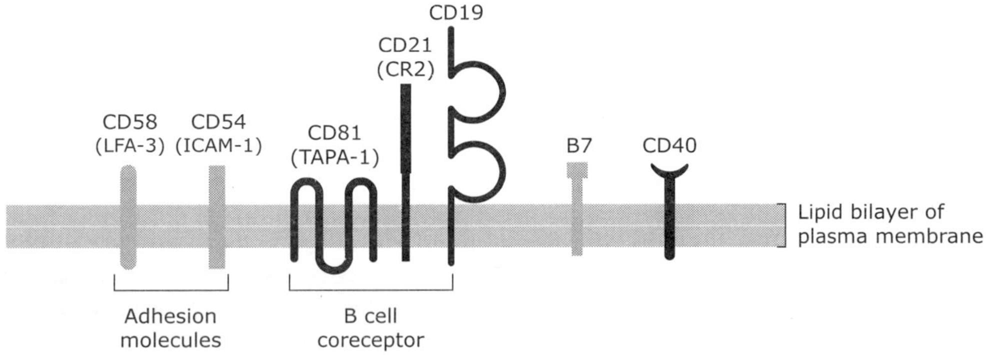

Figure 5.31 B cell co-receptor, co-stimulatory and adhesion molecules present on plasma membrane of B cells.

Naïve mature B cells express low levels of B7 and are poor APCs, whereas activated B cells are very efficient APCs. **CD40** (a co-stimulatory protein) is a member of the *tumor necrosis factor receptor* family. Interaction of CD40 with CD40L (present on T cells) is necessary for somatic hypermutation and class switching. One pair of adhesive molecules – **CD54** (ICAM-1, intercellular adhesion molecule-1) and **CD58** (LFA-3, leukocyte function-associated antigen-3) are also present on B cell membrane, which stabilize the interaction of B cell with T cell.

B cell receptor signaling

The B cell receptor (BCR) is composed of membrane immunoglobulin (mIg) molecules and associated Igα/Igβ heterodimers. The mIg binds antigen, resulting in receptor aggregation, while the Igα/Igβ heterodimer transduces signals to the cell interior. Igα/Igβ has **ITAMs** (immunoreceptor tyrosine-based activation motifs) in the cytoplasmic tails. The BCR lacks intrinsic kinase activity but couples to Src family kinases such as Lyn, Blk, and Fyn. When antigen binds with BCR, the tyrosines in the ITAMs become phosphorylated by receptor-associated Src-family tyrosine kinases Blk, Fyn, or Lyn. The phosphorylated ITAMs are then able to bind with Syk (spleen tyrosine kinase) by virtue of their SH2 domains. This initiates the formation of a '**signalosome**' composed of the BCR, the aforementioned tyrosine kinases, adaptor proteins (such as BLNK) and signaling enzymes (such as PLCγ2). Signals emanating from the signalosome activate multiple signaling cascades that involve kinases, GTPases, and transcription factors.

B cell activation

After B cells mature in the bone marrow, they migrate through the blood to secondary lymphoid organs such as spleen and lymph nodes. Activation of B cells occurs in the secondary lymphoid organs. B cells activation require antigen. Antigen binds to membrane-bound antibodies IgM and IgD on mature, naïve B cells, generating signals required for their proliferation and differentiation into antibody-secreting *plasma cells* and *memory cells*.

Antigen-driven B cell activations are divided into two major categories depending on the *nature of the antigen* and *the involvement of T_H cells* — **T-dependent** (*thymus dependent*) or **T-independent** (*thymus independent*). In both, antigen-BCR interaction yields initial activation, followed by additional signals that direct proliferation and differentiation.

In **T-dependent response,** T_H cell and B cell cooperate in presence of *T-dependent antigens* (or **TD antigens**). The responses to protein antigens require T_H cell help, so these antigens are called 'T-dependent'. B cells get help by acting as antigen-specific APCs to T_H cells. First, the B cell binds the antigenic particle which delivers an activating signal to the B cell through the BCR. For most T cell-dependent antigens, this signal is not sufficient to drive the B cell into cell proliferation. The B cell then internalizes the bound antigen, processes it into peptides, and presents it on class II MHC as a target for an antigen-specific T_H cell. When the T_H cell recognizes antigen presented on the B cell, it is activated and delivers the cytokines that provide help to the B cell.

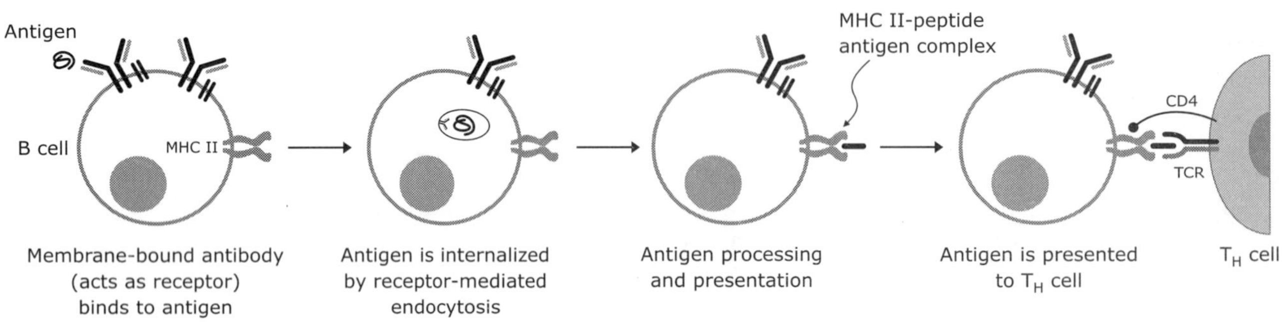

Figure 5.32 Antigen presentation by B cells to T_H cells. First, antigen-specific B cell recognizes the antigen directly with membrane-bound antibody. Protein antigens recognized by membrane-bound antibody are endocytosed and processed, and peptide fragments are presented in association with class II MHC molecules. T_H cells recognize MHC–peptide complexes on the B cells and then stimulate B cell responses. T_H cell help enables the B cell to proliferate and differentiate to form a clone of antibody-secreting cells.

Activation of B cells by T_H cells can occur at two different locations, one outside the follicles in an extrafollicular focus and the other in the germinal centers of follicles. The nature of the B cell response differs in these locations. **Short-lived plasma cells** are generated from activated B cells during T-dependent responses in *extrafollicular foci*. B cells that are activated by T_H cells in the extrafollicular foci undergo some isotype switching. In the *germinal center*, the characteristic events of T_H cell–dependent antibody responses include *affinity maturation*, *isotype switching* (or *class switching*), and generation of **long-lived plasma cells** and **memory B cells**. In T-dependent responses some activated B cells begin to produce antibodies other than IgM and IgD; this process is called **class switching** (or **isotype switching**). As the response develops, activated B cells produce antibodies that bind to antigens with increasing affinity, and these B cells progressively dominate the response; this process is called **affinity maturation**.

In **T-independent response**, antigens called *T-independent antigens* (or **TI antigens**), activate B cells without direct participation of T_H cells. Multivalent antigens with repeating antigenic determinants, such as polysaccharides, can activate B cells without T cell help. These antigens are called *T-independent*. T-independent responses to TI antigens are mediated mainly by marginal zone B cells in the spleen and B-1 cells in mucosal sites. Short-lived plasma cells are generated during T-independent responses.

The humoral response to T-independent antigens is different from the response to T-dependent antigens. The response to T-dependent antigens is stronger and involves the synthesis of memory B cells, affinity maturation and class switching to other isotypes. Responses to T-independent antigens are rapid but relatively simple, consisting mostly of low-affinity IgM antibodies, and do not give rise to memory.

Table 5.7 Properties of T-dependent and T-independent antigen

Property	T-dependent antigen	T-independent antigen
Chemical nature	Soluble protein	Lipopolysaccharides, polysaccharides
Isotype switching	Yes	No/Limited
Affinity maturation	Yes	No
Immunogenic memory	Yes	No

Role of T_H cell in B cell activation

Activation of B cells by protein antigens requires the involvement of T_{FH} cells (a distinct subset of T_H cell). First, binding of antigen to the receptor delivers first signal to the B cells that initiate the process of activation (**BCR signaling**). It leads to increased expression of class II MHC and co-stimulatory B7 proteins.

Antigen-antibody complexes are internalized by receptor-mediated endocytosis and degraded to peptides, some of which are bound by class II MHC and presented on the membrane as peptide–MHC complexes. T_H cell recognizes antigen–class II MHC on B cell membrane. This interaction also activates T_H cell. Upon antigen activation, T_H cells express CD40 ligand, which engages its receptor, CD40, (a member of the TNF receptor superfamily) on antigen-stimulated B cells. An activated T_H cell, which binds to the B cell both through its antigen receptor and via a separate interaction between CD40 on the B cell and CD40L on the activated T_H cell provides second signal to B cell (**costimulatory signaling**). In the presence of above signals, B cell begins to express receptors for various cytokines (such as IL-4, IL-21 and others) released from the T_H cell. Binding of cytokines sends third signal that support the differentiation (**cytokine signaling**).

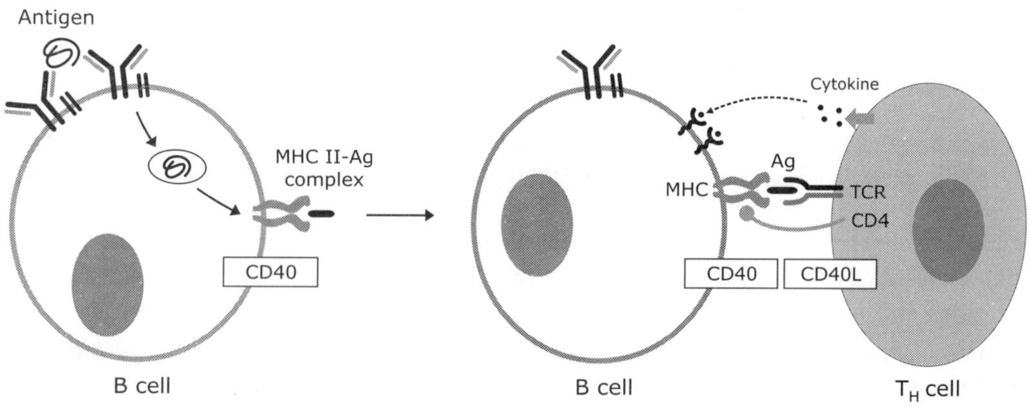

Figure 5.33 Three signals activate B cell. The first is generated when a multivalent antigen binds and cross-links mIg (signal 1). The second signal is provided by an activated T cell, which binds to the B cell both through its antigen receptor and via a separate interaction between CD40 on the B cell and CD40L on the activated T_H cell (signal 2). The bound T cell then delivers cytokines and other signals to its partner B cell to complete the activation process (signal 3).

Protein antigens are independently recognized by specific B and T cells in secondary lymphoid organs, and the two activated cell types interact with each other. Naïve T_H cells are activated in the *T cell zones* by antigen (in the form of processed, MHC-associated peptide antigens) presented by dendritic cells. Naïve B cells in the *B cell zones* (primary follicle) are activated by the same antigen (in its native conformation) that is transported there. The activated T_H cells and activated B cells migrate toward one another and interact at the interface of T and B cell zones. After the initial interaction of B cells with T_H cells at the interface between the B cell zone and the T cell zone, subsequent activation of B cells by T_H cells can occur at two different locations, one outside the follicles in an **extrafollicular focus** and the other in the **germinal centers** of follicles. The nature of the B cell response differs in these locations.

Short-lived plasma cells are generated from activated B cells during T-dependent responses in extrafollicular B cell foci. B cells that are activated by T_H cells in the extrafollicular foci undergo some isotype switching. **Long-lived plasma cells** are generated from activated B cells in T-dependent responses in the germinal center. Cells that have begun to secrete antibodies, but have not yet terminally differentiated, are called **plasmablasts**. Plasmablasts are short-lived, actively dividing, BCR-bearing cells. **Plasma cells** are terminally differentiated non-dividing cells that bear very little cell membrane BCR. Plasmablasts and plasma cells are both also called *antibody-forming* or *antibody-secreting cells*.

Memory B cells are generated during the germinal center reaction and are capable of making rapid responses to subsequent introduction of antigen. Because memory cells are generated mainly in germinal centers, they are seen in T-dependent immune responses. Some memory B cells may remain in the lymphoid organ where they were generated, whereas others exit germinal centers and recirculate between the blood and lymphoid organs.

Memory cells typically express high-affinity antigen receptors, and many have switched isotypes. The production of large quantities of isotype-switched, high affinity antibodies is greatly accelerated after secondary exposure to antigens, and this can be attributed to the activation of memory cells.

In T-dependent responses, some activated B cells begin to produce antibodies other than IgM; this process is called **isotype switching**. As the response develops, activated B cells produce antibodies that bind to antigens with increasing affinity; this process is called **affinity maturation**. Within the germinal center, the Ig genes undergo isotype switching (described in the next section), in which μ constant regions are replaced by constant regions of other isotypes. The variable regions of genes also undergo **somatic hypermutation** that result in the secretion of antibodies with increased affinity for a particular antigen due to altered sequences in their antigen-binding sites. The process that leads to increased affinity of antibodies for a particular antigen is called *affinity maturation*. It is the result of somatic hypermutation of rearranged V gene segments followed by selective survival of the B cells that produce the antibodies with the highest affinities. The mutation rate is estimated to be approximately 1000 times higher than the spontaneous rate of mutation in other mammalian genes. For this reason, mutation in rearranged V gene segment is also called *somatic hypermutation*. The presence of mutations correlates with increasing affinities of the antibodies for a particular antigen that induced the response.

Box 5.3 Lymph node

The lymph node is a secondary lymphoid organ and present throughout the body linked by the lymphatic vessels. It acts as a filter and is highly efficient in trapping and concentrating foreign substances carried in the blood. The *parenchyma* (functioning part) of a lymph node is divided into a superficial cortex and a deep *medulla*. The cortex consists of an *outer cortex* and an *inner cortex*. The **outer cortex** contains aggregates of B cells called **lymphatic nodules** (follicles). A lymphatic nodule consisting chiefly of B cells is called a **primary lymphatic nodule**. After B cells in a primary lymphatic nodule recognize an antigen, the primary lymphatic nodule develops into a **secondary lymphatic nodule**.

The center of a secondary lymphatic nodule contains a region of light-staining cells called a **germinal center**. In the germinal center are B cells, follicular dendritic cells (a special type of dendritic cell) and macrophages. When follicular dendritic cells 'present' an antigen, B cells proliferate and develop into antibody-producing plasma cells and memory B cells. The **inner cortex** does not contain lymphatic nodules. It consists mainly of T cells and dendritic cells that enter a lymph node from other tissues. The dendritic cells present antigens to T cells, causing their proliferation. The newly formed T cells then migrate from the lymph node to areas of the body where there is antigenic activity. The **medulla** of a lymph node contains B cells, antibody producing plasma cells that have migrated out of the cortex into the medulla, and macrophages. The various cells are embedded in a network of reticular fibers and reticular cells.

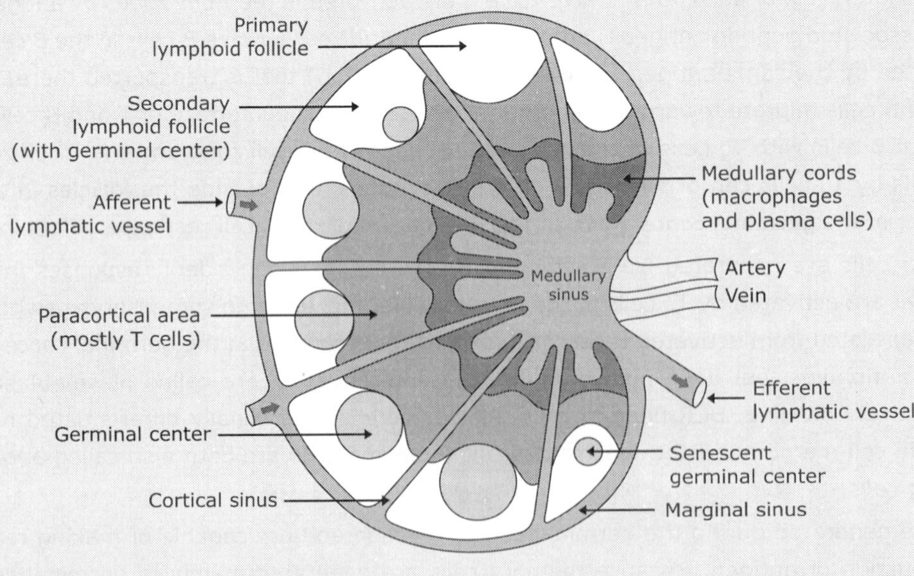

Figure 5.34 Structure of a lymph node.

Isotype switching

All B cells start productive life as immature cells engaged in the synthesis of mIgM. Mature B cells express both mIgM and mIgD. Both are encoded on the same mRNA, and the decision to translate μ (IgM) and δ (IgD) heavy chains is made at the level of RNA splicing. A B cell generally produces only a single class of immunoglobulin at any one time, but the class may change during the cell lineage. In T-dependent responses, some of the progeny of activated IgM- and IgD-expressing B cells undergo heavy chain isotype (or class) switching and produce antibodies with heavy chains of different classes, such as γ, α and ε. A switch from the expression of IgM to expression of any other classes of antibodies is called **isotype switching** (or **class switching**). It is the change in the isotype of the antibody produced by the B cell from μ to γ, α or ε. Switching involves only the C_H gene segment; the same V_H'gene segment continues to be expressed. Thus, a given V_H gene segment may be expressed successively in combination with more than one C_H gene segment.

Class switching involves DNA recombination events called **class switch recombination**. But this system is different from the V(D)J joining. In class switch recombination, the Ig heavy chain DNA in B cells is cut and recombined such that a previously formed VDJ exon that encodes the V domain is placed adjacent to a downstream C region and the intervening DNA is deleted.

Class switch recombination events involve nucleotide sequences called **switch regions**. Switch regions are located in the introns, 2 to 3 kb upstream of every C_H locus with the exception of C_δ. Switch regions are 2 to 10 kb in length and tandem repeats of GC-rich DNA sequences. These switch regions contain high densities of AID-targeting sites on both strands, such that there is a high probability of the formation of AID-induced double-strand breaks. Class switch recombination can occur anywhere within the switch regions. The enzyme *activation-induced cytidine deaminase* (**AID**) initiates class switch recombination by deaminating cytidine residues within the designated switch regions.

During class switch recombination, AID-induced cytidine-to-uridine lesions are created on both strands within a switch region, and these lesions are then converted into double-stranded breaks by members of the *base excision repair* or *mismatch repair pathway*. Switch regions contain high densities of AID-targeting sites on both strands, such that there is a high probability of the formation of AID-induced double-strand breaks. Ligation between two broken switch regions is catalyzed by proteins of the nonhomologous end-joining pathway.

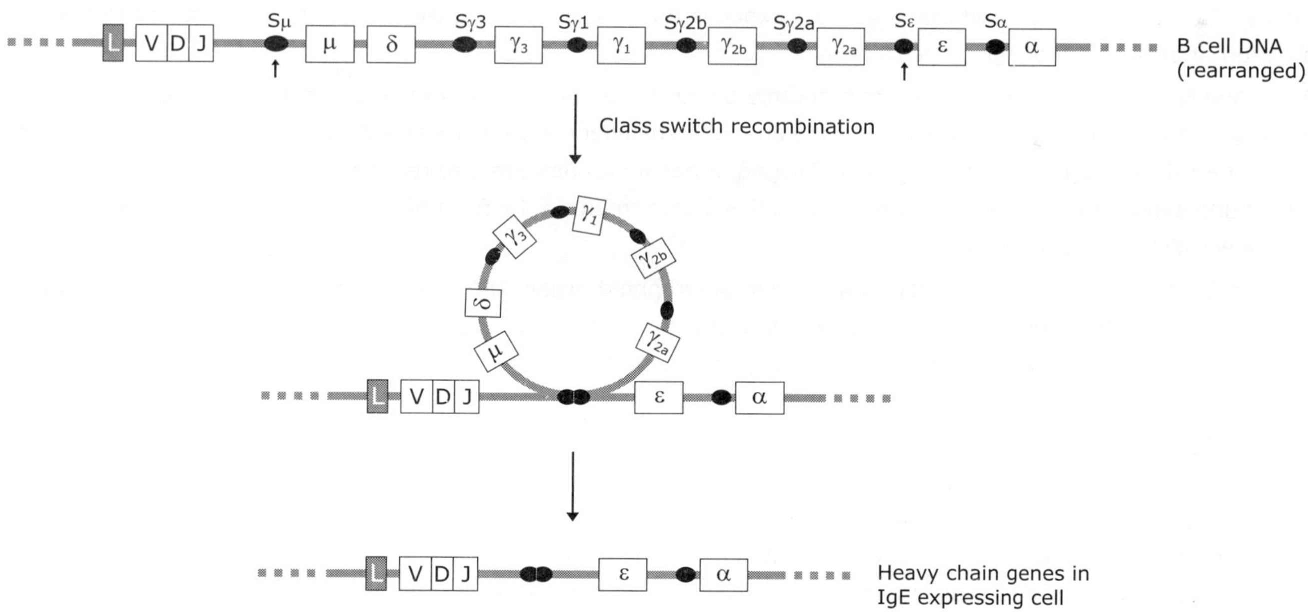

Figure 5.35 Class switch recombination from IgM to IgE. It describes a change in Ig gene organization in which the C region of the heavy chain is changed but the V region remains the same. Switch regions are involved in class switching. A switch region is typically located ~2 kb upstream of a C_H gene segment. Switch regions are indicated by circles labeled Sμ, Sγ, Sε and Sα. The switching reaction removes intervening DNA between the switch sites as a circular DNA molecule.

Class switch recombination between switch regions results in deletion of the DNA segment between the recombining switch regions. It occurs after AID deaminates dC residues within switch regions that are transcriptionally active.

In the following **figure 5.35**, class switch recombination from IgM to IgE has been shown. The DNA in between Sμ and Sε is excised from the chromosome as a circle. The intervening DNA is lost, and the VDJ exon is thus brought adjacent to Cε. The end result is the production of IgE with the same V domain as that of the original IgM produced by that B cell. Once a class switch has been made, it becomes impossible to express any C_H gene segment that used to reside between Sμ and the new C_H gene segment.

Class switching occurs in antigen-stimulated mature B cells synthesizing IgM and IgD. In addition to antigen, class switching is dependent on the presence of cytokines released by T_H cells and interaction between CD40 on the B cell and CD40L on the T_H cell. CD40 engagement induces the expression of the enzyme AID, which is crucial for both isotype switching and affinity maturation. In the presence of cytokine IFN-γ, the B cell switches to IgG2 synthesis. By contrast, in the presence of the cytokine IL-4, a B cell switches to IgG1 or IgE synthesis. There is little or no class switching by B cells in the absence of such T cell derived cytokines.

Table 5.8 Specific cytokines signal and isotypes synthesized by B cells

Cytokine signal	Isotype synthesized by target B cell
IL-4	IgG1 and IgE
TGF-β	IgA and IgG2b
IL-5	IgA
IFN-γ	IgG3 and IgG2a

Clonal selection theory

The clonal selection theory is a central paradigm of adaptive immunity. The most remarkable feature of the adaptive immune system is that it can respond to millions of different foreign antigens in a highly specific way. B cells, for example, make antibodies that react specifically with the antigen that induced their production. The clonal selection theory (formulated by Sir Macfarlane Burnet) explains how the adaptive immune system can respond to millions of different antigens in a highly specific way.

According to this theory, an animal first randomly generates a vast diversity of B cells and then those B cells that can react against the foreign antigens that the animal actually encounters are specifically selected for proliferation. As each B cell develops in a central lymphoid organ, it becomes committed to react with a particular antigen before ever being exposed to the antigen. It expresses this commitment in the form of cell-surface receptors (antibodies) that specifically fit the antigen.

When a B cell encounters its antigen in a peripheral lymphoid organ, the binding of the antigen to the receptors activates the B cell, causing it both to proliferate and to differentiate into an effector cell. An antigen therefore selectively stimulates those cells that express complementary antigen-specific receptors and are thus already committed to respond to it. This arrangement is what makes adaptive immune responses antigen-specific. According to the clonal selection theory, then, the immune system functions on the *ready-made* principle rather than the *made-to-order* one.

The term *clonal* in clonal selection theory derives from the postulate that the adaptive immune system is composed of millions of different families, or clones, of lymphocytes, each consisting of T or B cells descended from a common ancestor. Each ancestral cell was already committed to make one particular antigen-specific receptor protein, and so all cells in a clone have the same antigen specificity.

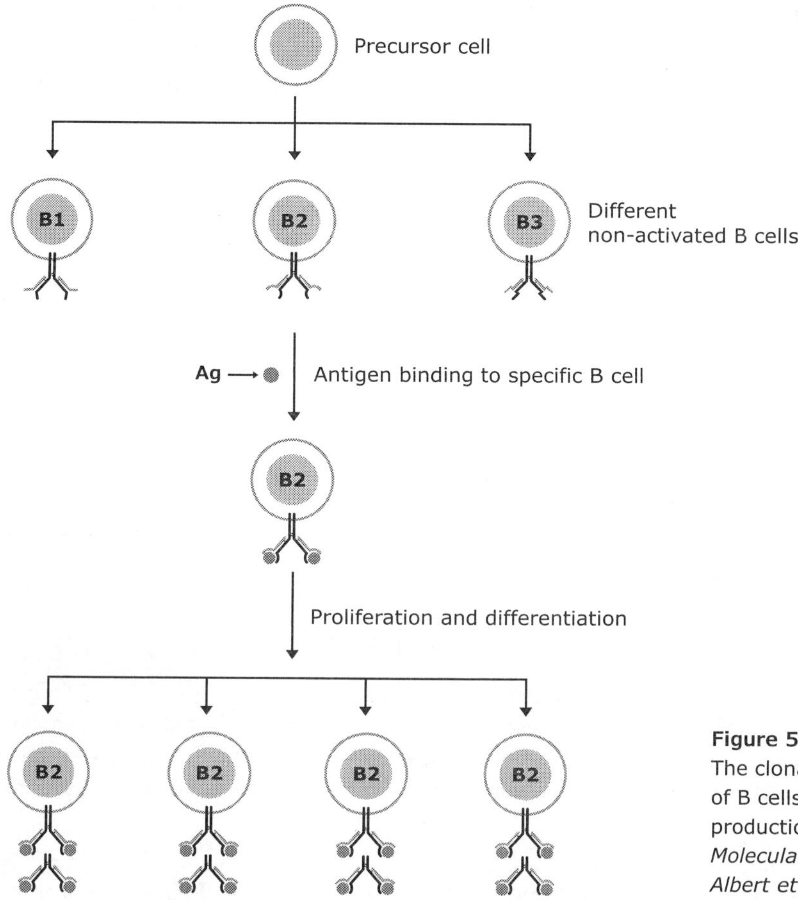

Figure 5.36
The clonal selection theory of B cells leading to antibody production. *Adapted from Molecular Biology of the cell, Albert et al., Garland Science.*

5.11 Kinetics of the antibody response

Humoral immunity is mediated by serum antibodies which are the proteins secreted by the B cells. B cells are initially activated to secrete antibodies after the binding of antigens to specific membrane-bound antibody molecules, which are expressed by these cells. Once bound, the B cell receives signals to begin making the secreted form of this antibody, a process that initiates the full-blown antibody response whose purpose is to eliminate the antigen from the host.

Primary and secondary responses

The first exposure of an individual to an immunogen is referred to as the *primary immunization*, which generates a **primary response**. The primary response may be divided into several phases, as follows:

1. *Lag* or *latent phase*: It is the immediate stage following antigenic stimulus during which no antibody is detectable in circulation. The length of this period is generally one to two weeks.
2. *Log* or *exponential phase*: In this phase, there is a steady rise in the titer of antibody and the concentration of antibody in the serum increases exponentially.
3. *Plateau* or *steady state*: During this phase, there is an equilibrium between antibody synthesis and degradation.
4. *Declining phase*: The concentration of antibody in serum declines rapidly.

A second exposure to the same immunogen results in a **secondary response**. This second exposure may occur after the response to the first immune event has leveled off or has totally subsided. The secondary response is also called the *memory* or *anamnestic* response and the lymphocytes that participate in the memory response are termed **memory cells**.

Primary and secondary responses to protein antigens differ *qualitatively* and *quantitatively*. The primary response is slow and short lived with a long lag phase and low titer of antibodies that do not persist for long. However, the secondary response is prompt, powerful and prolonged, with a short or negligible lag phase and a much higher level of antibody that lasts for long periods.

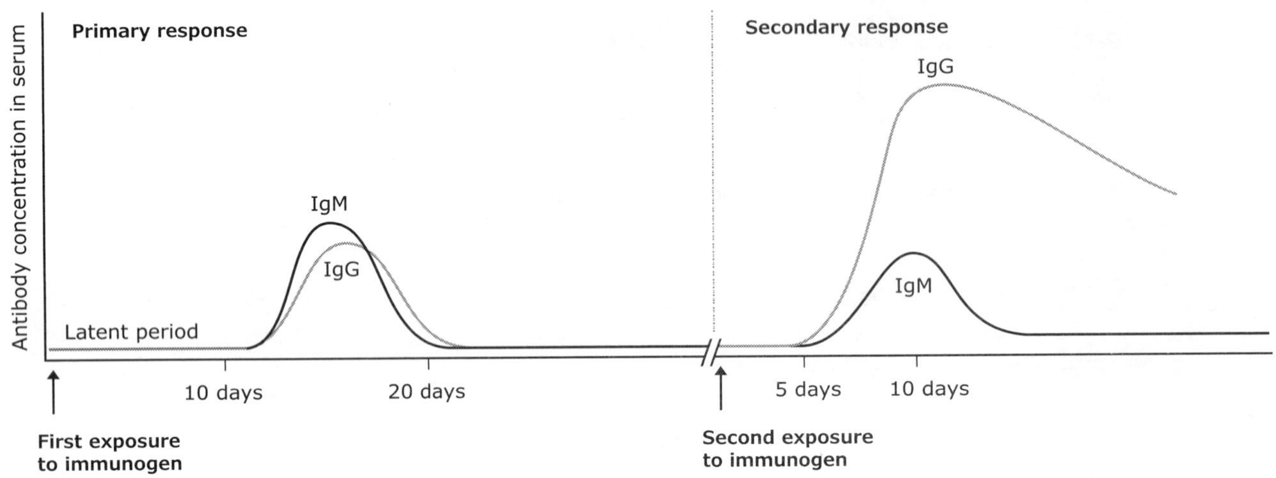

Figure 5.37 Antibody production and kinetics. In a primary response, naïve B cells are stimulated by antigen, become activated, and differentiate into antibody-secreting cells that produce antibodies specific for the eliciting antigen. A secondary response is elicited when the same antigen stimulates memory B cells, leading to production of greater quantities of specific antibody than are produced in the primary response.

In the primary response, the first class of antibody detected is generally IgM, then IgG, or another antibody class. There is a marked change in the type and quality of antibody produced in the secondary response. There is a shift in class response with IgG antibodies appearing at higher concentrations and with greater persistence than IgM, which may be greatly reduced or disappear altogether. This may also be accompanied by the appearance of IgA and IgE. The IgG, IgE and IgA molecules are collectively referred to as *secondary classes of antibodies* because they dominate secondary responses.

With the passage of time after immunization, there is usually a progressive increase in the affinity of the antibodies produced against the immunizing antigen. This phenomenon, known as **affinity maturation**, is due to the accumulation of point mutations specifically in both heavy-chain and light-chain variable region coding sequences.

Table 5.9 Features of primary and secondary responses

Feature	Primary response	Secondary response
Time lag after immunization	Usually 5-10 days	Usually 1-3 days
Peak response	Smaller	Larger
Antibody isotype	Usually IgM > IgG	Relative increase in IgG
Antibody affinity	Lower	Higher
Induced by	All immunogens	Only protein antigens
Required immunization	Relatively high doses of antigens, optimally with adjuvants	Low doses of antigens; adjuvants may not be necessary
Responding B cell	Naïve B cell	Memory B cell
Antigens	T-dependent and T-independent	T-dependent

5.11.1 Humoral immune response

Humoral immunity is mediated by secreted antibodies. It provides defense against extracellular pathogens and their toxins. Antibodies produced by B cells act to destroy extracellular pathogens and their products. This type of immunity contrasts with cell-mediated immunity, which is mediated by T cells and functions to eradicate pathogens that infect and live inside host cells. How antibodies provide protection against pathogens and their products? Antibodies provide protection against pathogens through broad range of *antibody-mediated effector functions*—that will result in removal of the antigens or death of the pathogens. Antibodies can:

- neutralize (inactivate) pathogens or toxins (**neutralization**)
- agglutinate pathogens, facilitating their clearance;
- opsonize pathogens or altered cells by binding and recruiting phagocytic cells (**opsonization**) and
- activate complement by binding to pathogen and initiating the complement cascade, which leads to several protective processes (**complement activation**).

In addition, they can cooperate with the cellular branch of the immune system by binding and recruiting the activities of cytotoxic cells, most often *natural killer cells* (**antibody dependent cell-mediated cytotoxicity**).

Neutralization

Antibodies can bind to pathogens or toxins and prevent their ability to enter cells, and therefore are thus said to *neutralize* the pathogens or toxins. Antibodies can bind to pathogens such as viruses during their extracellular phase and prevent them to infect cells by neutralizing them (**viral neutralization**). Viral neutralization prevents a viral infection due to the inability of the virus to bind to and enter its target cell. Antibodies may also bind extracellular toxins, preventing their action or ability to enter cells. This process is called **toxin neutralization**. Once neutralized, the toxin-antibody complex is either unable to attach to receptors on host target cells and is unable to enter the cell.

Antibody-mediated neutralization of pathogens and toxins requires only the antigen-binding regions of the antibodies. Therefore, such neutralization may be mediated by antibodies of any class. Neutralizing antibodies in the blood are mainly of the IgG and IgA at mucosal sites.

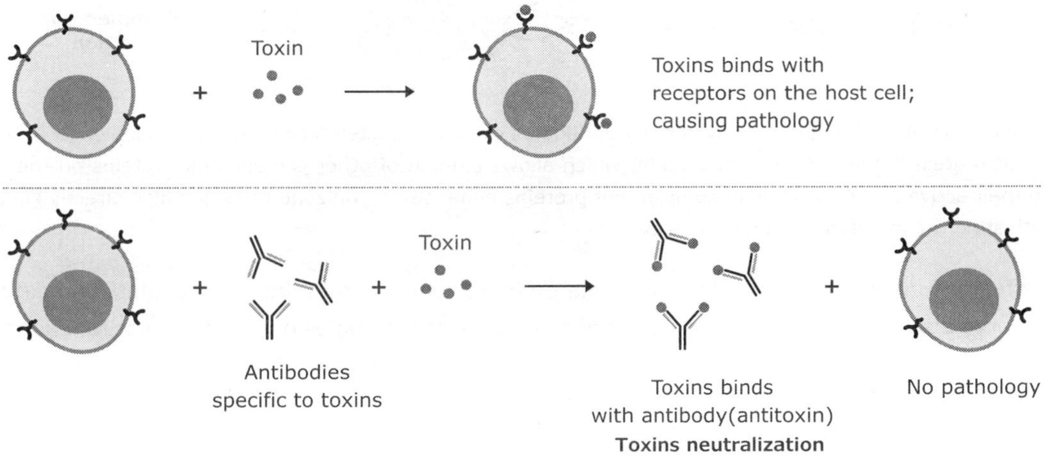

Figure 5.38 Neutralization: antibodies binding to and neutralizing a bacterial toxin, thus preventing it from interacting with host cells and causing pathology. Unbound toxin can react with receptors on the host cell, whereas the toxin:antibody complex cannot. Antibodies can also neutralize complete virus particles by binding and inactivating them.

Opsonization

Opsonization is the process by which antibodies coat (opsonize) microbes and promote their phagocytosis by binding to Fc receptors on phagocytic cells. The process of coating particles to promote their phagocytosis is called *opsonization*, and substances that perform this function, are called **opsonins.** Opsonizing antibodies, IgG, bind to

Fc receptors on the surface of phagocytic cells such as macrophages and neutrophils. These phagocytes express a variety of surface receptors that directly bind microbes and ingest them, even without antibodies. The efficiency of this process is markedly enhanced if the phagocyte can bind the microbes with high affinity. Opsonizing antibodies markedly enhance the binding of microbes with phagocytes. Binding of Fc receptors on phagocytes to multivalent antibody-coated microbes leads to engulfment of the particles and activation of the phagocytes. The IgG subtypes that bind best to these receptors (IgG1 and IgG3) are the most efficient opsonins for promoting phagocytosis.

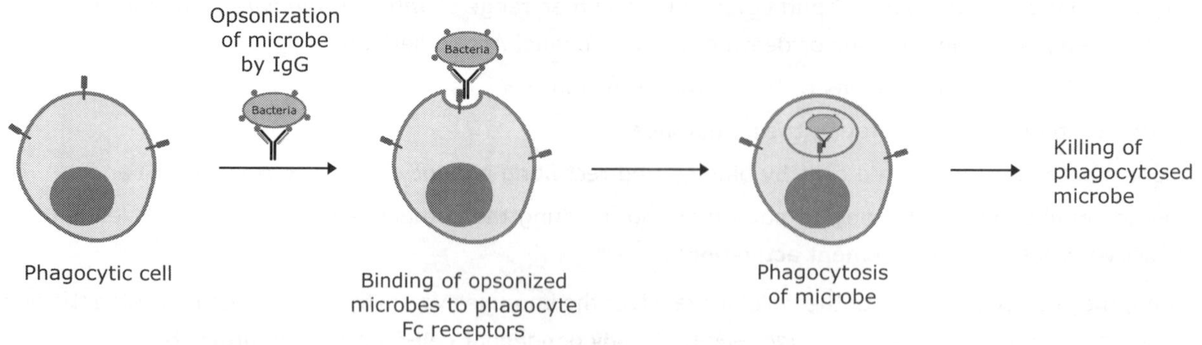

Figure 5.39 Opsonization: antibodies bind to antigens on the bacterial cell. Then the antibody's Fc region binds to Fc receptors expressed by macrophages and other phagocytes, facilitating phagocytosis. Phagocytes then ingest and destroy it.

Activation of complement

Complement is a set of plasma proteins that can be activated either by binding to certain pathogens or by binding to the antibody. Complement activation is often described as a series of cascading enzymatic events, leading to the generation of specific complement components that cause *opsonization* and *phagocytosis* of infectious agents as well as direct lysis of the invading organisms. Antibodies by forming antigen-antibody complexes can activate the complement. But not all antibody classes can activate complement. IgM and most IgG subclasses (IgG1, IgG2, IgG3) can activate the complement system.

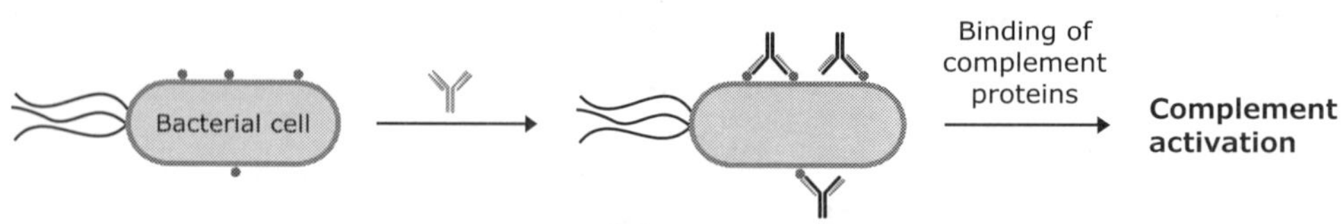

Figure 5.40 Activation of the complement system by antibodies coating a bacterial cell. Bound antibodies form a platform that activates the first protein in the complement system, which allows binding of other complement proteins on the surface of the bacterium and their activation. Deposition of complement proteins enhances opsonization and can also directly kill certain bacterial cells by activating the membrane-attack complex.

Many of the effector functions of antibodies are mediated by Fc regions of antibody molecules, and different classes of antibodies serve distinct effector functions i.e., not all classes of antibodies have the similar functional properties.

Antibody isotype (or **class**)	**Specific effector functions**
IgG	Opsonization of antigens for phagocytosis by macrophages and neutrophils
	Activation of the classical pathway of complement
	Antibody-dependent cell-mediated cytotoxicity mediated by natural killer cells
	Neutralization of microbes and toxins
IgM	Activation of the classical pathway of complement
IgA	Neutralization of microbes and toxins
IgE	Mast cell degranulation (immediate hypersensitivity reactions)
	Eosinophil-mediated defense against helminths

Antibody dependent cell–mediated cytotoxicity

Infected cells with antibodies bound to them can be killed by natural killer cells (NK cells). NK cells can recognize and destroy antibody coated target cells in a process called **antibody-dependent cell-mediated cytotoxicity** (**ADCC**). This is triggered when antibody bound to the surface of a cell interacts with Fc receptors on the NK cell. NK cells express the receptor **FcγRIII** (CD16), which recognizes the IgG1 and IgG3 antibody subclasses. Binding of antibody to this receptor activates the NK cell. The NK cells release cytoplasmic granules containing perforin and granzymes and induce death of antibody coated target cells.

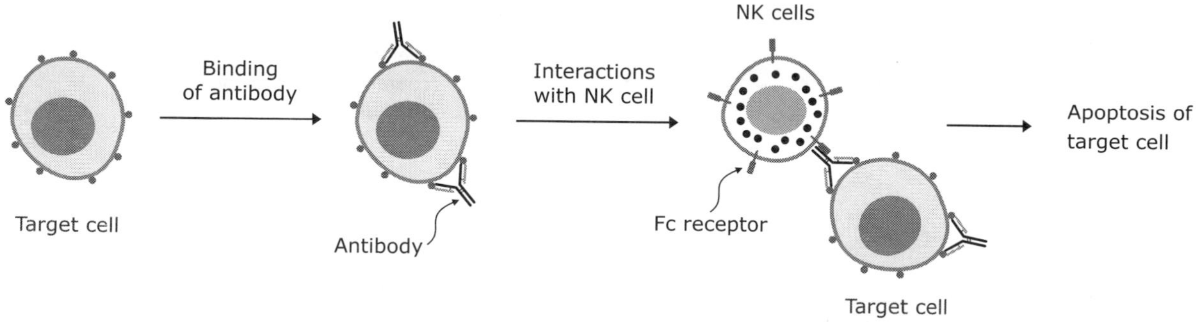

Figure 5.41 When target cell is coated with antibodies, it becomes a target of NK cells that express the Fc receptor known as FcγRIII. The interaction of FcγRIII and antibody induces the NK cell to kill the antibody-coated target cell. The NK cells release cytoplasmic granules containing perforin and granzymes and induce death of antibody coated target cells.

5.12 Monoclonal antibodies and Hybridoma technology

Antibodies produced ordinarily by infection or immunization are **polyclonal** because natural antigens have multiple epitopes, each of which generates clones of lymphocytes. This results in antisera containing antibodies from different clones of lymphocytes with specificities against different epitopes of the antigens. On the other hand, **monoclonal** *antibodies* (mAb) are monospecific antibodies. These antibodies are produced from clone of single lymphocyte directed against a single antigenic determinant or epitope. Such antibodies produced by a single clone and directed against a single epitope.

Hybridoma technology is a method of forming hybrid cell lines (called **hybridomas**) by fusing a specific antibody-producing B cell with a myeloma cell (cancerous B cell). The antibodies produced by the hybridoma are all of a single specificity and are therefore monoclonal antibodies. The production of monoclonal antibodies was invented by Cesar Milstein and Georges J. F. Köhler in 1975. They shared the Nobel Prize in 1984 for Medicine and Physiology. Hybridomas are somatic cell hybrids produced by fusing antibodies forming spleen cells with myeloma cells. Antibody-producing B cells normally die after several weeks in cell culture *in vitro*. Therefore, antibody-producing B cells are fused with B cell tumors called **myelomas**. These myelomas are capable of dividing indefinitely and are, therefore, often called immortal cell lines. The immortal cell lines that result from the B cell-myeloma fusion are hybrid cell lines called **hybridomas**. The hybridoma cell lines share the properties of both fusion partners. They grow indefinitely *in vitro* and produce antibodies. To produce a monoclonal antibody, a mouse is immunized with the antigen of interest. During the next several weeks, antigen-specific B cells proliferate and begin producing antibodies in the mouse. Spleen tissue, rich in B cells, is then removed from the mouse, and the B cells are fused with myeloma cells. Hybridomas are selected by the use of a selective medium in which the myeloma cells die, but hybridomas survive. The most widely used selective systems involve the inclusion of the antibiotic *aminopterin* in the growth medium. **Aminopterin** is a synthetic derivative of pterin. This folate analog acts as a competitive inhibitor for enzyme *dihydrofolate reductase* which catalyzes the reduction of dihydrofolate into tetrahydrofolate. Normal animal cells synthesize purine nucleotides and thymidylate for DNA synthesis by a *de novo pathway* requiring tetrahydrofolate. Thus, the addition of aminopterin inhibits the *de novo* nucleotide synthesis pathway. However, normal cells survive in this medium as they are able to use the *salvage pathway* for nucleic acid synthesis. But if the cells are unable to produce the enzyme *hypoxanthine-guanine phosphoribosyl transferase* (**HGPRT**), they are unable to utilize the salvage pathway and, therefore, die in the aminopterin-containing medium. In the procedure, myeloma cells are engineered to be deficient in enzyme HGPRT. After fusion of lymphocytes with HGPRT-negative myeloma cells, aminopterin-containing medium, supplemented with hypoxanthine and thymidine to ensure and adequate supply of substrates for the salvage pathway (HAT medium) is added, which kills myeloma cells but allows hybridomas to survive as they inherit HGPRT from the lymphocyte parent. Unfused lymphocytes die after a short period of culture, which results in a pure preparation of hybridomas.

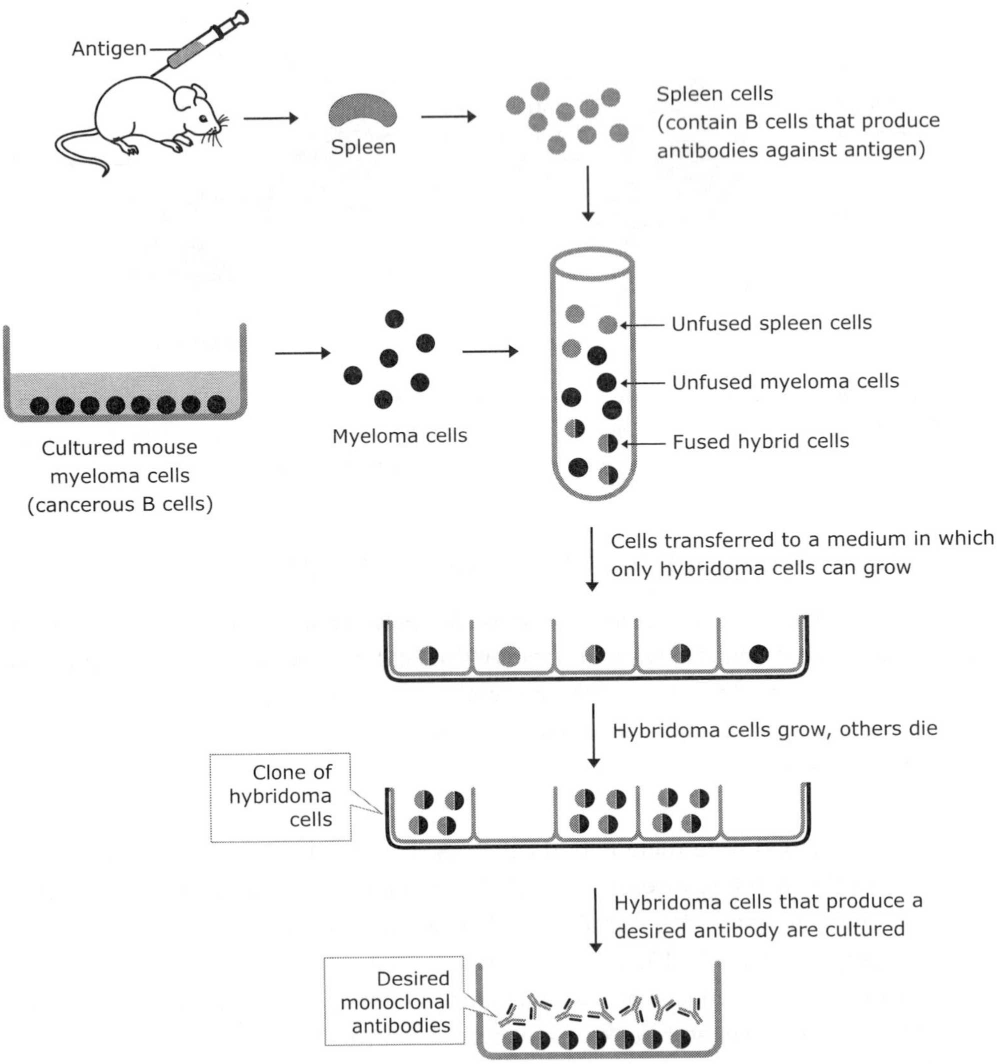

Figure 5.42 Production of monoclonal antibodies.

Box 5.4 Engineered monoclonal antibodies

Immunotoxins

Immunotoxins are protein-based drugs contain two functional domains, one allowing them to bind specific target cells (target-specific binding domain), and other that kills the cells following internalization (cytotoxic domain). An immunotoxin is prepared by replacing the target-specific binding domain of toxin with a monoclonal antibody that is specific for a particular antigen. The toxins used may be *bacterial toxins* such as diphtheria toxins or *plant toxins* such as ricin, abrin, etc. Toxins used to prepare immunotoxins include ricin, *shiga toxin* and diphtheria toxin, all of which inhibit protein synthesis.

Chimeric and humanized antibodies

Hybridoma technology generates monoclonal antibodies. Genetic engineering has fostered the generation of chimeric and humanized antibodies. It is now possible to design and construct genes that encode monoclonal antibodies in which the variable regions come from one species and the constant regions come from another. One approach to engineering a monoclonal antibody is to clone recombinant DNA containing the variable region sequences from a mouse antibody gene and the constant-region sequences from a human antibody gene. The antibody encoded by such a recombinant gene is a mouse-human **chimeric antibody**. Its antigenic specificity, which is determined by the variable region, is derived from the mouse DNA; its isotype, which is determined by the constant region, is derived from the human DNA.

Humanized antibodies are generated by the insertion of mouse complementarity-determining regions (CDRs) onto human antibody. The protein sequence of a humanized antibody is essentially identical to that of a human variant except its complementarity determining region (CDR) segments of the non-human (mouse) origin.

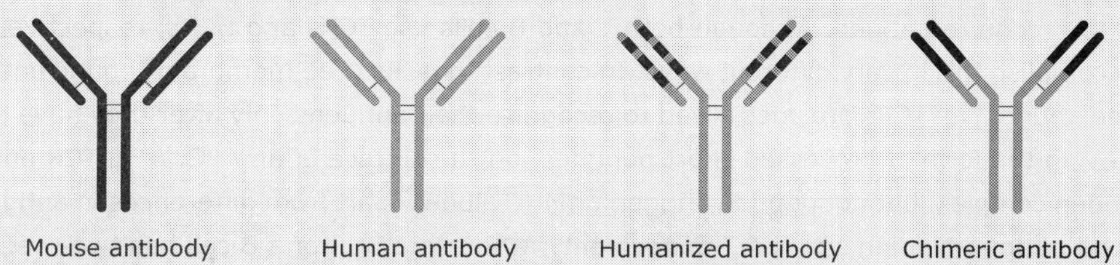

Figure 5.43 Monoclonal antibodies. Mouse, human, humanized and chimeric antibodies.

Heteroconjugates or bispecific antibodies

A natural antibody is monospecific. *Heteroconjugates* (or *bispecific antibodies*) are hybrids of two different antibody molecules. Such antibodies do not occur in nature. They can be constructed by chemically crosslinking two different antibodies or by synthesizing them in hybridomas consisting of two different monoclonal-antibody-producing cell lines that have been fused. Several bispecific molecules have been designed in which one half of the antibody has specificity for a tumor and the other half has specificity for a surface molecule on an immune effector cell, such as an NK cell, an activated macrophage, or a cytotoxic T-lymphocyte (CTL). Such heteroconjugates have been designed to activate the immune effector cell when it is crosslinked to the tumor cell so that it begins to mediate destruction of the tumor cell.

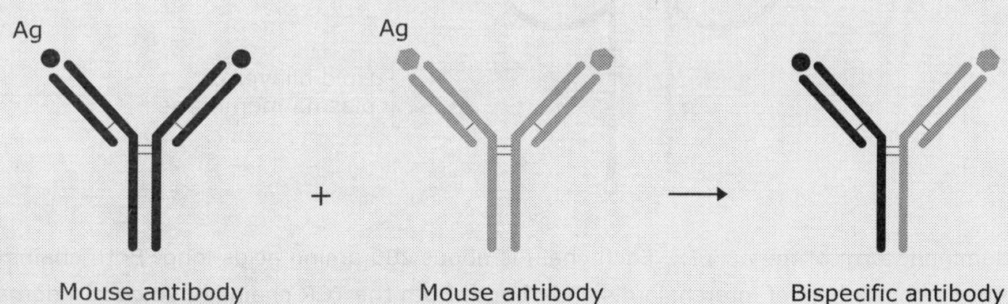

Figure 5.44 Heteroconjugates *or* bispecific antibodies.

5.13 T cells and cell-mediated immunity

Antibody molecules secreted from B cells, play a critical role in interacting with antigens when they are present *outside* the cells; for example, when viruses are encountered in blood plasma or at mucosal surfaces. Once an antigen gets into a cell however, antibodies do not generally have access to it, and so antibodies are ineffective in dealing with antigens present within the cells. T cells deal with such pathogens – such as viruses, bacteria, and parasites – that reside inside the cells of the host. T cells responses differ from B cell responses in at least two crucial ways.

First, T cells are activated by foreign antigen to proliferate and differentiate into effector cells only when the antigen is displayed on the surface of antigen-presenting cells/target cells in peripheral lymphoid organs.

Second, once activated, effector T cells act only at short range, either within a secondary lymphoid organ or after they have migrated into a site of infection. They interact directly with another cell in the body, which they either kill or signal in some way.

T cell receptor

T cells, like B cells, express antigen specific receptors. The *T cell receptor* (**TCR**) is a heterodimer and composed of two transmembrane glycoprotein chains. In humans, in >90% of T cells, the TCR consists of an α chain and a β chain, whereas in <10% of T cells, the TCR consists of γ and δ chains. Hence, there are two broad categories of T cells based on the nature of TCR: αβ T cells and γδ T cells. The extracellular portion of each chain consists of two domains, resembling immunoglobulin variable (V) and constant (C) domains, respectively. Both chains are glycosylated and connected with each other with the help of interchain disulfide bond.

T cells use TCRs to recognize antigen. Although both T and B cells use TCRs and BCRs, respectively, to recognize antigens, they accomplish this in very different ways. In contrast to BCRs (i.e., membrane-bound antibodies), which can recognize free antigen, αβ TCRs are specialized to recognize their antigens only after they have been presented by MHC molecules, in the form of processed short peptides, on the surface of an APC. A αβ TCR only recognizes a MHC-peptide antigen complex, but not peptide antigen or MHC alone. Apart from differences in antigen recognition, a TCR has only one antigen-binding site (i.e., **monovalent**), whereas a BCR of a B cell has two (i.e., **bivalent**), and TCRs are never secreted, whereas antibodies can be secreted.

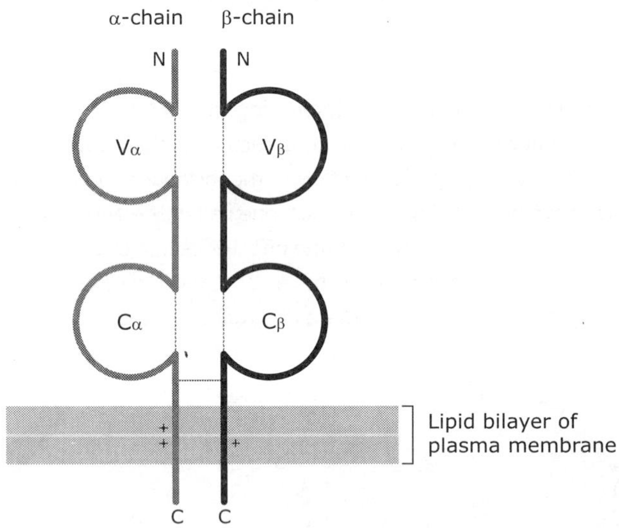

Figure 5.45 The predominant form of the αβ TCR. Each chain is about 280 amino acids long. Both chains are glycosylated and connected with each other with the help of interchain disulfide bond. Both the TCR chains have two Ig domains: one variable (V) domain at the N terminus that serves as the antigen-binding site, and one constant (C) domain. TCR V domains typically exhibit marked sequence variation. The antigen-binding site is formed by a Vα and a Vβ domain. The transmembrane helices of both chains are unusual in containing positively charged (basic) amino acid residues within the hydrophobic transmembrane segment. The α chains carry two such residues; the β chains have one. Unlike antibodies, which have two binding sites for antigen, T cell receptors have only one.

γδ T cells

Some T cells express a TCR distinct from αβ. This alternative TCR is known as γδ, and the cells expressing this receptor are referred to as γδ T cells. In normal adult humans, γδ T cells are found in much lower numbers than αβ T cells, but their numbers increase as a result of infections. In humans, γδ T cells constitute 0.5-10% of T cells in peripheral blood but are substantially enriched in epithelial tissues (e.g., in skin, lungs, intestine). Most γδ T cells have limited receptor diversity and antigen specificity. As compared to αβ T cells, γδ T cells recognize a broad range of antigens that vary much in size, composition and molecular structure. γδ T cells recognize protein or nonprotein antigens that are neither processed nor presented by a classical MHC molecule. Some $\gamma\delta$ T cell clones recognize small phosphorylated isoprenoid metabolites, commonly referred to as *phosphoantigens* or endo- and exogenous lipids and that may be presented by nonclassical class I MHC-like molecules (members of CD1protein family).

Coreceptor molecules

The TCR is expressed on the T cell surface in association with other transmembrane molecules, referred to as a **coreceptor**. These coreceptors are CD4 and CD8. CD4 is a monomeric membrane glycoprotein that contains four extracellular Ig-like domains (D1-D4). CD8 is a disulfide-linked $\alpha\beta$ heterodimeric or $\alpha\alpha$ homodimeric membrane glycoprotein. Each chain consists of a single, extracellular, Ig-like domain. The extracellular domains of CD4 and CD8 bind to conserved regions of class II MHC and class I MHC molecules, respectively. CD4 and CD8 are involved in signal transduction after antigen binds to the TCR. Specifically, the intracellular portions of CD4 and CD8 are linked to enzymes, known as protein tyrosine kinases, which are important components of the T cell activation pathways.

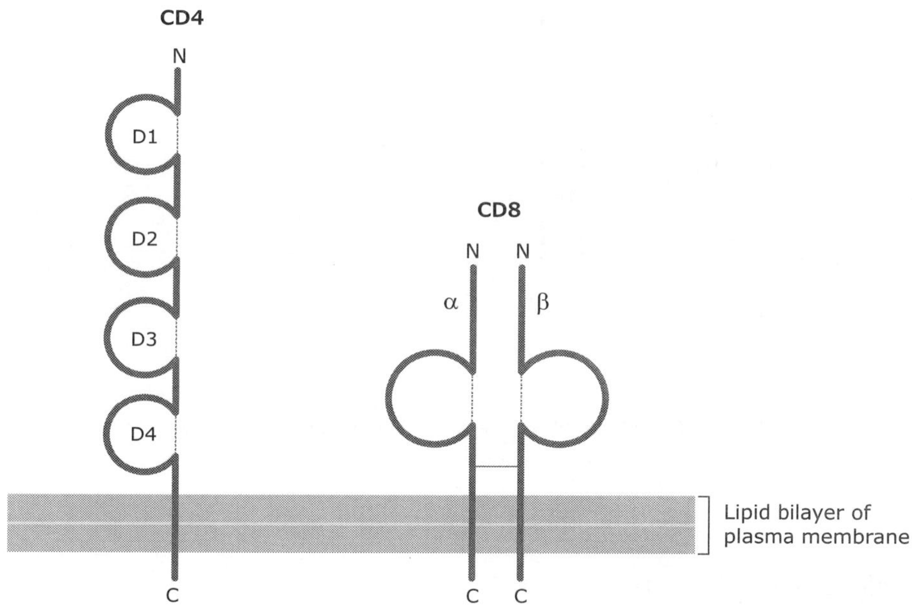

Figure 5.46 General structure of the CD4 and CD8 coreceptors. The monomeric CD4 molecule contains four Ig domains (D1-D4). The CD8 protein is either a disulfide-linked $\alpha\beta$ heterodimer or a disulfide-linked $\alpha\alpha$ homodimer (not shown in the figure). Each chain in the CD8 molecule contains one Ig domain.

Table 5.10 Comparison of $\alpha\beta$ and $\gamma\delta$ T cells

Feature	$\alpha\beta$ **T cells**	$\gamma\delta$ **T cells**
CD4	Present	Absent
CD8	Present	Present
MHC restriction	$CD4^+$: class II MHC, $CD8^+$: class I MHC	No MHC restriction
Antigen	Peptide	Phospholipid/glycolipid

TCR-CD3 complex

The antigen-recognizing α and β chains of the TCR itself does not possess signaling domains. Instead, the TCR is noncovalently associated with a conserved multisubunit signaling apparatus, the CD3 complex, consisting of CD3$\varepsilon\gamma$ and CD3$\varepsilon\delta$ heterodimers and a disulfide-linked CD3$\zeta\zeta$ homodimer. The mechanism of assembly of the TCR–CD3 complex remains unknown. CD3 is invariant – that is, it is the same on all T cells – and because it is expressed exclusively on T cells it can be used as a marker to distinguish T cells from all other cells. CD3 (*cluster of differentiation 3*) does not bind antigen. The CD3 γ, δ and ε proteins are homologous to each other. The N-terminal extracellular regions of the γ, δ and ε chains of CD3 each contain a single Ig-like domain, and therefore these three proteins are members of the '**Ig superfamily**'. The long cytoplasmic tails of the CD3 γ, δ and ε chains contain a common sequence, the *immunoreceptor tyrosine-based activation motif* (**ITAM**), which serves as docking sites for adapter proteins following activation induced tyrosine phosphorylation. There is a single ITAM in each chain. The CD3ζ chain has a short extracellular region of nine amino acid residues and a long cytoplasmic region that contains three ITAMs.

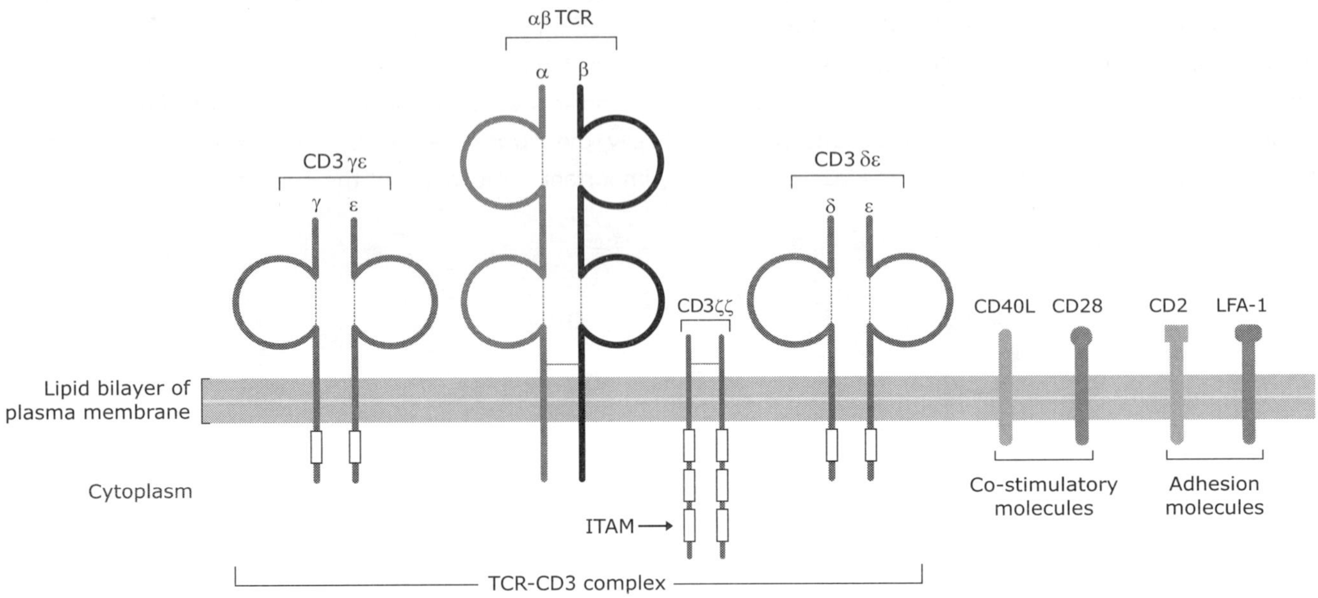

Figure 5.47 Schematic diagram of the TCR-CD3 complex. The αβ TCR non-covalently linked with three dimers: heterodimers of CD3γε, CD3δε and a homodimer CD3ζζ form TCR-CD3 complex. T cell membrane also contains co-stimulatory molecules (CD40L and CD28) and adhesion molecules (CD2 and LFA-1).

Generation of T cell receptor diversity

The mechanisms for generating diversity in T cell receptors are very similar to the mechanisms of generating diversity in B cell receptors (i.e., antibody). Like antibody heavy-chains, the T cell receptors encoding genes are arranged in clusters of V, D and J gene segments, which are brought together by somatic recombination during T cell development in the thymus. With one exception, all the mechanisms used by B cells to generate antibody diversity are also used by T cells to generate T cell receptor diversity. The mechanism that does not operate in T cell receptor diversification is antigen-driven somatic hypermutation.

Comparison of antigen recognition by T cells and B cells

The recognition of antigens by TCRs of T cells and membrane-bound antibodies (serves as the B-cell receptors, BCRs) of B cells is fundamentally different. B cells can recognize antigens in solution or on the surface of pathogens. Antigens are generally recognized in their native conformation and no processing as well as presentation is required by APCs. As compared to B cells, T cells with αβ TCRs are specialized to recognize their antigens only after they have been presented by **MHC molecules**, in the form of short peptides, on the surface of an APC. TCRs of T cells specialize to bind cell-bound, rather than soluble antigens. Thus, antigens cannot be recognized directly by TCRs unless the protein is unfolded and processed into peptide fragments and then presented by an MHC molecule. As compared to αβ T cells, γδ T cells can recognize protein or nonprotein antigens that are neither processed nor presented by a classical MHC molecule.

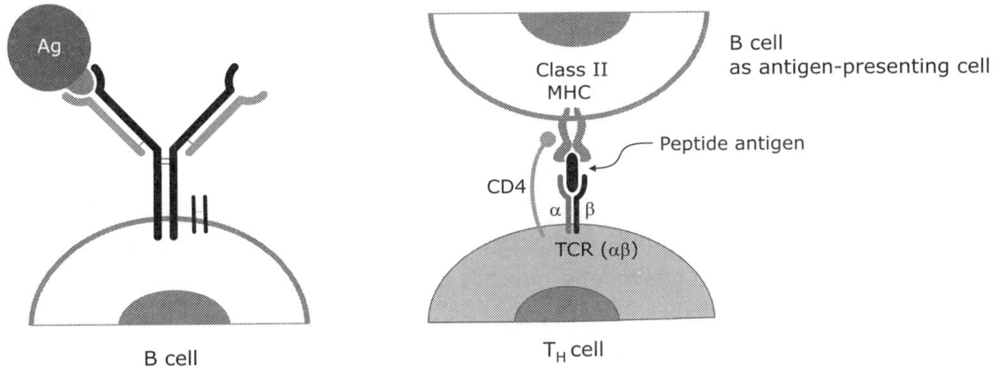

Figure 5.48 T and B cells recognize antigens in very different ways. B cells can recognize antigens (both soluble as well as surface bound) in their native conformation and no processing as well as presentation is required. Contrary to B cells, αβ T cells only recognize processed peptide antigen in the form of MHC-peptide antigen complexes positioned on the surface of APCs.

Table 5.11 Comparison between αβ TCR and mIg

Feature	**αβTCR**	**mIg** (BCR)
Components	α and β chains	Heavy and light chains
Number of V and C domains	One V domain and one C domain in each chain.	Heavy chain: one V and three or four C domains. Light chain: one V and one C domain.
Valency	Single antigen binding site i.e., *monovalent*.	Two antigen binding sites i.e., *bivalent*.
Nature of antigen	Proteins (peptides)	May be carbohydrates, lipids and proteins.
Antigen recognition	Recognize processed peptide antigens presented by MHCs on the surface of an APC	Native conformation and no processing as well as presentation is required by APCs.
Affinity for antigen	Less affinity	High affinity
Isotype switching	No	Yes
Secretory form	Does not exist in a secretory form.	Does exist in a secretory form.
Binding soluble Ag	No	Yes
MHC molecules	Required to present processed antigen.	Not required

T cell maturation

T cell development is elegantly organized, spatially and temporally. T cell maturation occurs in the thymus. Precursors of T cells travel from the bone marrow through the blood to the thymus under the influence of chemotactic factors that are secreted by the thymic epithelial cells. In the thymus, developing T cells, known as **thymocytes**, proliferate and differentiate along the developmental pathways that generate functionally distinct subpopulations of mature T cells.

Thymus is absolutely required for the maturation of T-cell precursors into mature T cells. The adverse effects of lacking a thymus and consequently not having mature T cells can be seen in children born without a thymus (**DiGeorge syndrome**) or in mice genetically lacking a thymus (known as **nude mice** because they also lack hair).

T cell maturation in the thymus is a complex multistep process. There is a precise order in which TCR genes are rearranged and in which the TCR and CD4 and CD8 coreceptors are expressed. Stages of development can be defined broadly by the expression of the coreceptors CD4 and CD8. The most immature thymocytes express neither coreceptor and are referred to as $CD4^-CD8^-$ (**double-negative** or **DN**) stage. These progress to the $CD4^+CD8^+$ (**double-positive** or **DP**) stage, which in turn mature to the $CD4^+CD8^-$ or $CD4^-CD8^+$ (**single positive** or **SP**) stages. DN thymocytes progress through four stages of development (DN1-DN4) based on the presence or absence of cell surface molecules, **c-Kit** (CD117), the receptor for stem cell growth factor; **CD44**, an adhesion molecule; and **CD25**, the α chain of the IL-2 receptor.

During the developmental process, they begin to rearrange their T cell receptor (TCR) gene loci. In DN1 stage, TCR genes present in their germline configuration and do not express TCR. During DN2 stage, the genes for the TCR γ, δ and β chains begin to rearrange. Rearrangement remains continued in DN3 stage. A decision has been taken in T cell development: whether to join the TCR-$\gamma\delta$ or TCR-$\alpha\beta$ T cell lineage. The mechanism by which T cells become committed to the $\alpha\beta$ or $\gamma\delta$ lineage is not yet fully understood. Most thymocytes become TCR-$\alpha\beta$ T cells. Those DN3 T cells that successfully rearrange their β chain gene typically commit to the TCR-$\alpha\beta$ T cell lineage. After productive (i.e., in-frame) rearrangement of the TCR β chain gene, the TCR β chain is expressed on the cell surface in association with an invariant protein called **pre-Tα** to form the **pre-TCR**. Pre-TCR signals initiate recombination at the TCR α chain locus. During transition between the DN4 and DP stages, rearrangement of TCR α chain gene completes. The α chain dimerizes with the β chain, generating a mature $\alpha\beta$ TCR. The expression of TCR $\alpha\beta$ heterodimers occurs in the $CD4^+$ $CD8^+$ double-positive cells. Double positive (or **DP**) cells undergo *negative* and *positive thymic selection* in the thymic cortex. DP cells that successfully undergo selection processes go on to mature into $CD4^+$ or $CD8^+$ T cells, which are called *single positive* (or **SP**) *cells*. During the transition from double-positive to single-positive cells, thymocytes whose TCRs recognize self class I MHC become $CD8^+$ $CD4^-$, and cells with TCRs that recognize self class II MHC become $CD4^+$ $CD8^-$. Small populations of DP cells also give rise to other T cell types, including the NKT cell and regulatory T cell. NKT cells play a role in innate immunity.

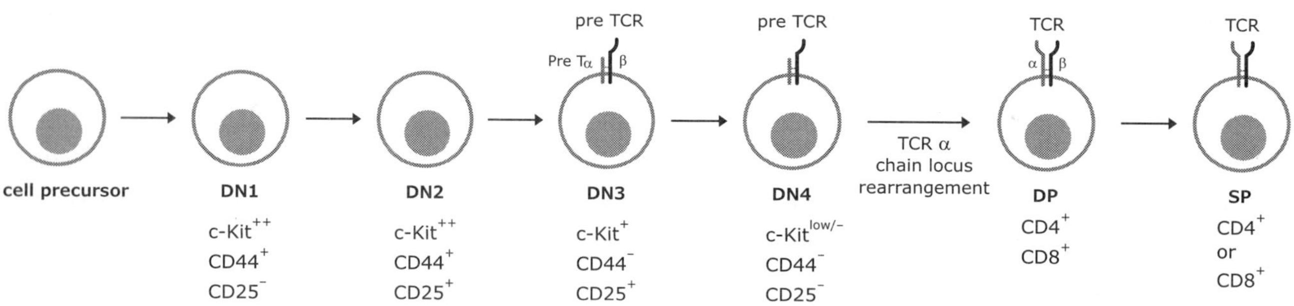

Figure 5.49 Development of T cells. T cell precursors from the bone marrow travel to the thymus via the bloodstream, undergo development to mature T cells. The most immature thymocytes are $CD4^-CD8^-$ (double-negative) and pass through several stages (DN1-DN4). Those that successfully rearrange their TCR chain proliferate, and become $CD4^+CD8^+$ (double-positive) thymocytes. Double-positive thymocytes undergo negative and positive selection in the thymic cortex. Positively selected thymocytes continue to mature and migrate to the medulla, where they are subject to another round of negative selection to self-antigens that include tissue-specific proteins. Mature T cells express either $CD4^+$ or $CD8^+$ (single-positive) and leave the thymus with the potential to initiate an immune response.

Why is thymic selection necessary? The most distinctive property of a mature T cell is that its TCR recognizes peptide antigens only when combined with self-MHC molecules. This is a phenomenon known as **MHC restriction.** The other distinctive property of the population of mature T cells is that it is largely tolerant to self-MHC/self-peptide antigen complexes. Even though T cells must recognize self-MHC with some affinity, they do not initiate a response to self-MHC/self-peptide antigen, a phenomenon referred to as **self-tolerance**. Since the TCR gene rearrangement is a random process and that the TCRs generated are unique for each cell, the probability that any given TCR will exhibit both self-restriction and self-tolerance is low. The thymic selection events that occur in the thymus effectively screen the large population of newly generated DP cells for those few cells whose TCRs have both these properties.

Thymic selection

Double positive pre T cells undergo two selection processes in the thymus – **positive** and **negative selection.** Positive selection positively selects those thymocytes that bear receptors capable of binding self-MHC molecules with low affinity, resulting in MHC restriction. Negative selection negatively selects those thymocytes bearing receptors with high affinity for self-MHC/self-peptide antigen complexes, resulting in self-tolerance.

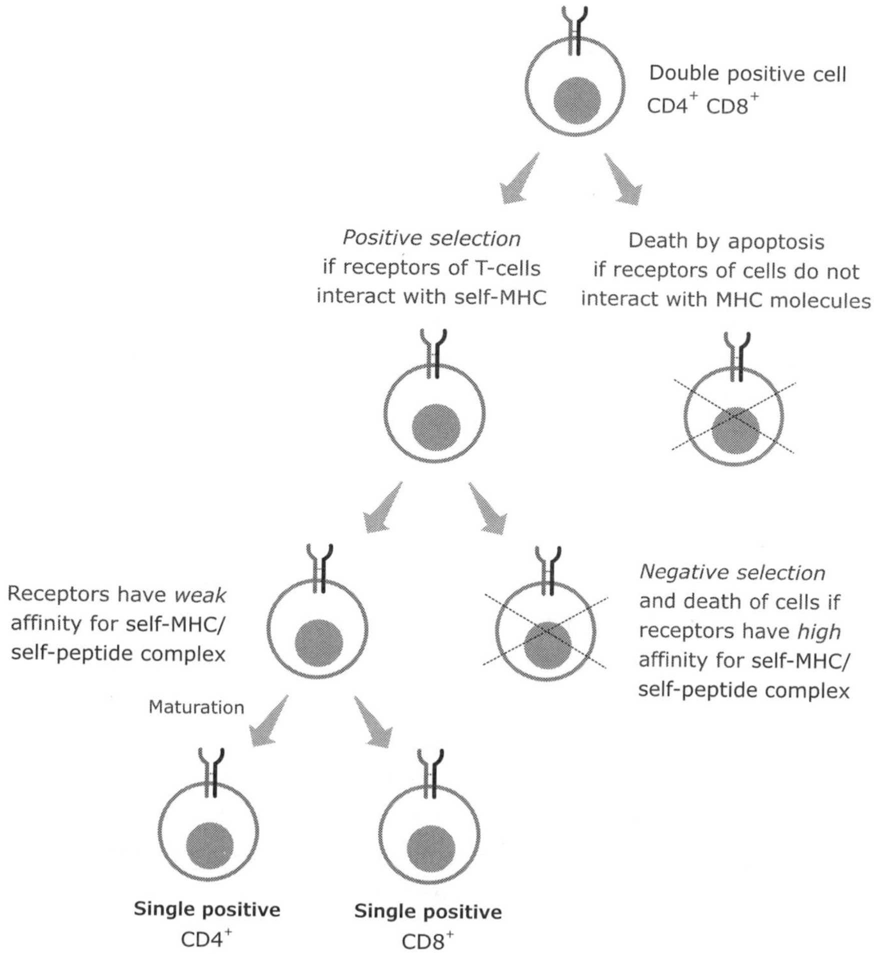

Figure 5.50 Positive and negative selection in the thymus.

Thus, in positive selection double-positive T cell becomes *educated* to the MHC molecules expressed by the thymic cortical epithelial cells. This means that for the rest of the life of the T cell, even as a mature cell when it leaves the thymus, it will respond to antigen only when the antigen is bound to the MHC molecules that the developing T cell encountered in the thymus. For this reason, the MHC molecules expressed in a person's thymus and that educate his or her developing T cells are referred to as **self-MHC**; for that person, all other types of MHC molecules are **non-self**. This is the origin of the phenomenon known as **MHC restriction**, or more specifically, **self-MHC restriction**. *Hence, T cells recognize antigens in association with self MHC molecules but not in association with foreign MHC molecules*. The bulk of double-positive thymocyte death (~95%) occurs among thymocytes that fail positive selection because their receptors do not specifically recognize self-MHC molecules, a process known as **death by neglect**.

T cells expressing TCRs specific for both foreign and self-antigens can develop in the thymus and survive positive selection. Allowing T cells with strong reactivity to self-antigens to leave the thymus and interact with these antigens in tissues could result in undesirable autoimmune response. In fact, errors in the negative selection process are responsible for a host of autoimmune disorders, including Type 1 diabetes. So, it is required to select those T cells that will be capable of responding to self MHC molecule complexed with foreign or non-self peptide antigens. To achieve this, the double-positive cell undergoes a second selection step, known as **negative selection**. Negative selection is the process in which T cells whose TCRs bind *strongly* to self-peptide antigens in association with self MHC molecules are deleted. This removes T cells expressing TCRs that are strongly autoreactive against self-antigens and develops **self-tolerance**.

Positive selection works by promoting the selective survival and expansion of T cells with self MHC-restricted TCRs whereas negative selection of T cells works by inducing apoptotic death of cells whose receptors recognize self-peptide antigen-MHC complexes in the thymus with high affinity.

Thus, double-positive thymocytes have one of three fates depending on the affinity of their new TCRs for the self-MHC/self-peptide antigen combinations that they encounter. If their newly generated TCRs do not bind to any of the self-MHC/self-peptide antigens they encounter on stromal cells, they will **die by neglect**. If they bind too strongly to the self-MHC/self-peptide antigen complexes they encounter, they will be negatively selected, and ultimately destroyed. If they bind with a low, 'just right' affinity to self-MHC/self-peptide antigen complexes, they will be positively selected and mature to the single-positive stage of development.

Positive selection is mediated exclusively by interactions between thymocytes and cortical thymic epithelial cells (**cTECs**). Negative selection, however, can be mediated by multiple cells in both the cortex and medulla, and can target thymocytes at both the double-positive and single-positive stages. Current evidence indicates that peptides expressed by cortical epithelial cells play a critical role in the positive selection step. These peptides are derived from self-antigens either expressed in the thymus or brought in the thymus. It is not currently clear, however, how these peptides derived from self-antigens select T cells with TCR specificities for non-self as well as self-antigens. In addition, it is not clear whether the peptides expressed by the cortical epithelial cells in positive selection differ from those expressed by the dendritic cell in negative selection. Coincident with positive selection, thymocytes undergo alternate commitment toward either the CD4 or CD8 lineages. Positively selected double-positive thymocytes have to decide whether to become $CD4^+$ or $CD8^+$ T cells. This process is called **lineage commitment**. Immunologists continue to debate the precise cellular and molecular mechanisms responsible for lineage commitment.

Activation of T cell

CD4 and CD8 T cells leave the thymus and enter the circulation as **naïve T cells**. Activation of a naïve T cells in a secondary (peripheral) lymphoid organ results in the generation of *effector* and *memory* T cells. Naïve T cells are mature, but they have not yet encountered antigen. Activation of naïve T cells and their differentiation into effector and memory cells require antigen recognition, costimulation and cytokines. To activate a naïve T cell to proliferate and differentiate into an effector cell, APC provides three kinds of signals.

TCR signaling: Antigen provides the first signal for the activation of naïve T cells. It is provided by a foreign peptide antigen bound to an MHC molecule on the surface of the APC (peptide antigen associated with class II MHC to T_H cells and peptide antigen associated with class I MHC to T_C cell). This peptide-MHC complex signals through the TCR-CD3 complex and its associated proteins.

Costimulatory interaction: It provides the second signal for the naïve T cell activation. It is provided by co-stimulatory proteins, especially the **B7 proteins** (CD80/86), which are recognized by the costimulatory-receptor protein **CD28** (a 44 kDa glycoprotein expressed as a homodimer) on the surface of the T cell. The expression of B7 proteins on an APC is induced by pathogens during the innate response to an infection. If a naïve T cell receives signal 1 without signal 2, it may undergo apoptosis or become altered.

Cytokine signaling: It is provided by soluble cytokines and plays a key role in determining the type of effector cell that a naïve T cell becomes. Cytokines bind surface receptors, stimulating a cascade of intracellular signals that can enhance both proliferation and/or survival. IL-2 is one of the best-known cytokines involved in T cell activation. IL-2 is produced mainly by T_H cells after recognition of antigen and costimulators. It acts in an autocrine manner, by stimulating the same cells that produce them. Cytokines can act in an *autocrine* manner, by stimulating the same cells that produce them, or in a *paracrine* manner, by stimulating neighboring cells. Even though it is often still referred to as the **two-signal hypothesis**, full T cell activation actually requires three sets of signals; third set of signal is provided by cytokines (signal 3).

Two pairs of adhesive interactions stabilize the interaction of APC and T cell. These are **CD54** (ICAM-1, intercellular adhesion molecule-1) expressed on APC and integrin **LFA-1** (leukocyte function-associated antigen-1) expressed on T cell. Similarly, CD58 (**LFA-3**) expressed on the APC and **CD2** expressed on the T cell interact with each other.

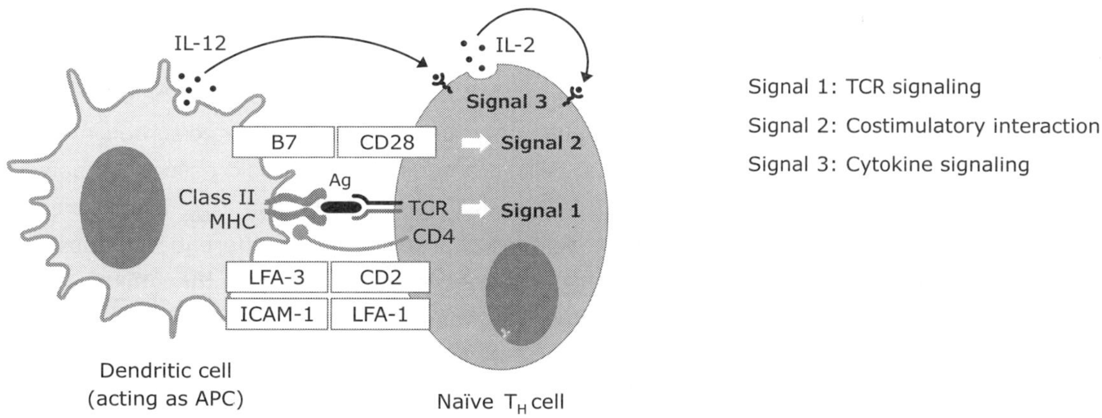

Figure 5.51 Three distinct signals are required to induce naïve T_H cell activation, proliferation and differentiation. Surface interactions between T-cell and APC are also depicted. Signal 1 is generated by the interaction of the TCR with an MHC-antigen complex on an APC. Signal 2 is a costimulatory signal provided by the interaction between B7 proteins (CD80/86) expressed by APC with the positive costimulatory molecules CD28 expressed by T cells. Signal 3 is provided by soluble cytokines and plays a key role in determining the type of effector cell that a T cell becomes.

Activation leads to clonal expansion and differentiation of the naïve cells into effector and memory T cells. Naïve cells are activated mainly in secondary lymphoid organs, whereas after activation, differentiated effector cells may respond to antigens and carry out their functions in any tissue due to their ability to migrate to any site of infection or inflammation. At these sites, the effector cells again encounter the antigen for which they are specific and respond in ways that serve to eliminate the source of the antigen. Activated T cells of the $CD4^+$ lineage secrete cytokines and express cell surface molecules that can trigger other immune cells. These T cells are classified into subpopulations (such as T_H1, T_H2, T_H17, T_{REG} and T_{FH}) on the basis of their cytokine profiles and functions. The activated cells of the $CD8^+$ lineage (called **cytotoxic T lymphocytes**, CTLs), kill infected cells and tumor cells and also secrete cytokines that activate macrophages and induce inflammation. Naïve T cells can live for months, whereas effector cells tend to be short-lived and have life spans that range from a few days to a few weeks.

Activated T cells not only differentiate into effector cells, but also into distinct memory cell subsets, which differ by their locale, their circulation patterns, and their effector function. Memory T cells (both T_H and T_C memory cells), which are more easily activated than naïve cells, are responsible for secondary responses. Memory T cells that are generated by T cell activation are long-lived cells with an enhanced ability to react against the antigen. The maintenance of memory cells is dependent on cytokines but does not require antigen recognition. The most important cytokine for the maintenance of memory T cells is IL-7.

How do memory cells arise? Although multiple explanations have been advanced to explain how memory T-cell subsets arise, several lines of evidence favor a linear, progressive model of development. According to the linear, progressive model of memory T cell differentiation, most effector cells die and some survivors develop into the memory population. At least 90% of effector cells die by apoptosis after pathogen is cleared, leaving behind a population of antigen-specific memory T cells. Memory T cells are generally longer-lived than effector cells, and are quiescent.

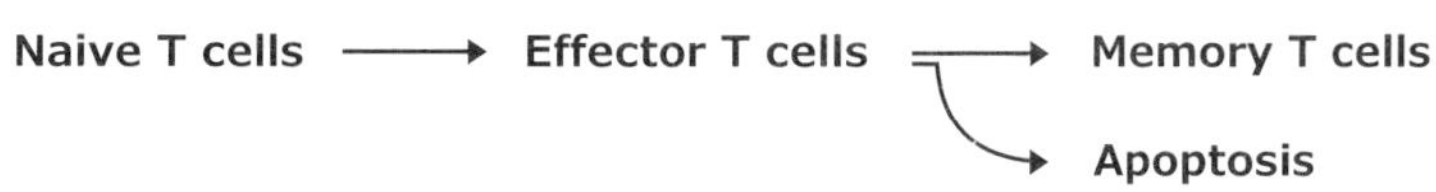

We can distinguish memory cells from naïve and effector cells, using surface markers. There are four broad subsets of memory T cells: *central memory T cells*, *effector memory T cells*, *resident memory T cells* and *stem cell memory T cells*. These differ in location, phenotype, and function. Memory T_C cells are more abundant than memory T_H cells. This is partly because T cells proliferate more robustly and therefore generate proportionately more memory T_C cells. It may also be due to differences in the life span of memory T cells: memory T_H cells are not as long-lived as memory T_C cells.

T_H cell differentiation

T_H cells are arguably the most important cells in the adaptive immune response, they not only help activate B cell to secrete antibodies and macrophages to destroy ingested microbes, but they also help activate T_C cells to kill infected target cells. T_H cells themselves, however, can only function when activated to become effector cells. When an APC activates a naïve T_H cell (also called **T_H0 cell**) in a peripheral lymphoid tissue, the naïve T_H cell can differentiate into distinct subsets of effector cells: T_H1, T_H2, T_H9, T_H17, T_H22, T_{FH} and T_{REG}. The differentiation of T_H cell subsets is regulated by **polarizing cytokines**. The defining characteristics of differentiated subsets of effector cells are the cytokines they produce. Each of the subsets produces a distinct set of **effector cytokines**. The cytokines produced by these T_H cell subsets determine their effector functions and roles in diseases.

Naive T_H cell (T_HO cell) → Under influence of *polarizing* cytokines	Signature *effector* cytokines	Effector functions
T_H1	IL-2, IFN-γ, TNF-β	Combats intracellular pathogens, activates macrophages
T_H2	IL-4, IL-5, IL-13	Combats helminth infection, activates eosinophils
T_H9	IL-9	Combats intracellular pathogens, including worms
T_H17	IL-17, IL-21, IL-22, IL-26	Combats extracellular pathogens, (bacteria, fungi) in barrier tissues
T_H22	IL-22	Combats intracellular pathogens, particularly in skin
T_{FH}	IL-4, IL-21	Induces B-cell proliferation and differentiation into antibody-producing plasma cells.
T_{REG}	IL-10, TGF-β	Suppresses immune responses

Naïve T_H cells that are activated in the presence of *polarizing* cytokines IL-12 and IFN-γ tend to differentiate, or polarize, to the T_H1 lineage. T_H1 cells synthesize and secrete signature type 1 effector cytokines such as IL-2, IFN-γ and TNF-β. IFN-γ is a particularly potent type 1 effector cytokine. It activates macrophages, stimulating these cells to increase microbicidal activity and up-regulate the level of class II MHC molecules. Its secretion also induces antibody class switching in B cells to IgG classes that support phagocytosis and fixation of complement. Finally, IFN-γ secretion promotes the differentiation of fully cytotoxic T cells.

Just as differentiation to the T_H1 subset is promoted by polarizing cytokines IL-12 and IFN-γ, differentiation of naïve T cells into T_H2 cells is promoted by a defining polarizing cytokine, IL-4. T_H2 cells synthesize and secrete type 2 effector cytokines such as IL-4, IL-5 and IL-13. IL-4, the defining T_H2 effector cytokine, acts on both B cells and eosinophils. It induces eosinophil differentiation, activation and migration and promotes B cell activation and class switching to IgE.

The major effector cytokines produced by T_H1 and T_H2 subsets (IFN-γ and IL-4, respectively) not only influence the overall immune response, but also influence the T_H cell subsets. First, they promote the growth of the subset that produces them; second, they inhibit the development and activity of the opposite subset, an effect known as **cross-regulation**. For instance, IFN-γ (secreted by the T_H1 subset) inhibits proliferation of the T_H2 subset and IL-4 (secreted by the T_H2 subset) downregulates the secretion of IL-12 by APCs, thereby inhibiting T_H1 differentiation. Furthermore, IL-4 enhances T_H2 cell development by making T_H cells less susceptible to the T_H1 promoting cytokine signals (and vice versa).

Function of cytotoxic T-lymphocytes

When naïve T_C cells bind to an MHC-peptide complex, they become activated, proliferate and differentiate into *effector cells* called **cytotoxic T-lymphocytes** (CTLs). T_H1 cells provide indirect help to T_C cells by interacting with antigen-presenting cells and producing effector cytokines, such as IFN-γ, that license the antigen-presenting cell to finalize T_C cell differentiation into CTLs. T_H1 cells also produce IL-2, which enhances T_C cell proliferation. The principal function of CTLs is to kill cells that have been infected by bacteria and viruses. In innate immune reactions, the same function of killing infected cells is mediated by NK cells. CTLs are also involved in killing of tumor cells and transplanted foreign cells during graft rejection. For this reason, CTLs are frequently referred to as **killer T cell**. The cell killed by a CTL is known as a *target*, which can be a specialized antigen-presenting cell such as a dendritic cell, or any other cell in the body. The TCR of a CTL recognizes a combination of peptide in association with a class I MHC molecule on the surface of a cell. This interaction, in the presence of appropriate second signals results in the death of the cell presenting the peptide. CTL also synthesizes cytokines; like IFN-γ, which regulates certain viral and bacterial infections, as well as TNF-β, which plays a role in the target cell killing.

As we know, effector T_H cells can differentiate into several subsets, each of which secretes a distinct panel of cytokines. Similarly, CTLs develop into two distinct subsets: **T_C1** cells and **T_C2 cells**. CTLs are biased toward becoming T_C1 cells, which secrete IFN-γ but not IL-4. In the presence of IL-4, CTLs develop into T_C2 cells, which secrete much more IL-4 and IL-5 than IFN-γ. Both subsets are potent killers, although T_C1 cells can use both perforin/granzyme- and FasL-mediated strategies, whereas T_C2 cells appear to use only perforin and granzymes.

CTL killing of target cells

Once activated, mature CTL initiates killing by attaching to the target cell. The specific signaling events involved in establishing the CTL-target interaction. The TCR-CD3 membrane complex on a CTL recognizes antigen in association with class I MHC molecules on a target cell. A CTL can kill a target in two major ways: either via the directional release of granule contents or via a Fas-FasL membrane signaling interaction. Rather than inducing cell lysis, both of these processes induce the target cell to undergo apoptosis, typically within a few hours of contact with the cytotoxic cell.

Granzyme and perforin mediated cytolysis: The first predominant pathway involves the action of the cytotoxic substances contained in granules inside the T cell. Antigen-specific CTLs interact with appropriate target cells and undergo conjugate formation. Formation of a CTL–target cell conjugate is a Ca^{2+}-dependent, energy-requiring step. After attaching to the target cell, the CTL mobilizes its granules directionally toward the target and releases the contents of these granules onto the target cell. The major constituents of the granules involved in target-cell killing are **perforin** and **granzymes** (*fragmentins*). Perforin is a pore-forming protein that polymerizes to form transmembrane channels or pores in the target-cell membrane. Polymerization of perforin is a Ca^{2+}-dependent process. The action of perforin on cell membranes is similar to the complement membrane attack complex, described later.

CTL killing via this pathway involves granzymes, a set of **serine proteases**. Granzyme-B enters into the target cell and induce apoptosis. Although granzyme B was once thought to enter into the target cell via surface perforin pores, it is now thought that it enters via endocytic processes. Regardless of the mechanism of entry, once in the cytoplasm, granzyme initiates a cascade of reactions that result in the fragmentation of the target-cell DNA into oligomers of 200 base pairs; this type of DNA fragmentation is typical of apoptosis. Granzyme proteases do not directly mediate DNA fragmentation. Rather, they activate an apoptotic pathway within the target cell.

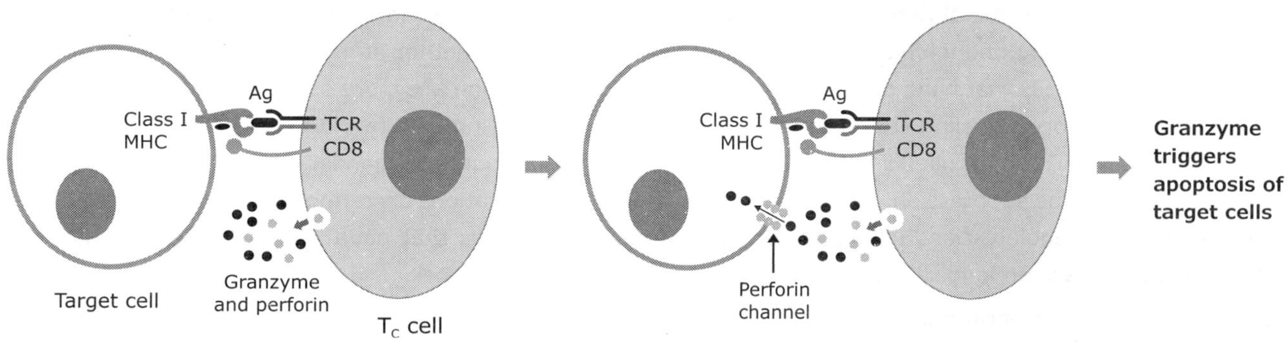

Figure 5.52 Cytotoxic granules trigger death in target cells via the action of perforin and the granule proteases, the granzymes. Granzyme B triggers apoptosis through direct activation of caspases or indirectly via mitochondrial release of cytochrome c.

Fas-FasL mediated cytolysis: A second pathway of target cell killing occurs via the interaction of the molecule Fas ligand on the CTL with **Fas** (**CD95**), a surface molecule expressed on many target cells. Transmembrane protein *Fas* is a member of the *TNF-receptor family*, can deliver a death signal when cross-linked by its natural ligand, a member of the tumor necrosis factor family called **Fas ligand** (FasL). The interaction of FasL with Fas triggers apoptosis.

Both the perforin and Fas-FasL killing strategies activate a signaling pathway in the target cell that induces apoptosis. A central feature of cell death by apoptosis is the involvement of the **caspase family** of cysteine proteases, which cleave after an aspartic acid residue. Normally, caspases are present in the cell as inactive proenzymes—**procaspases**—that require proteolytic cleavage for conversion to the active forms. Cleavage of a procaspase produces an active caspase, which cleaves other procaspases, thereby activating their proteolytic activity, which results in a cascade of events that systematically disassembles the cell—the hallmark of apoptosis.

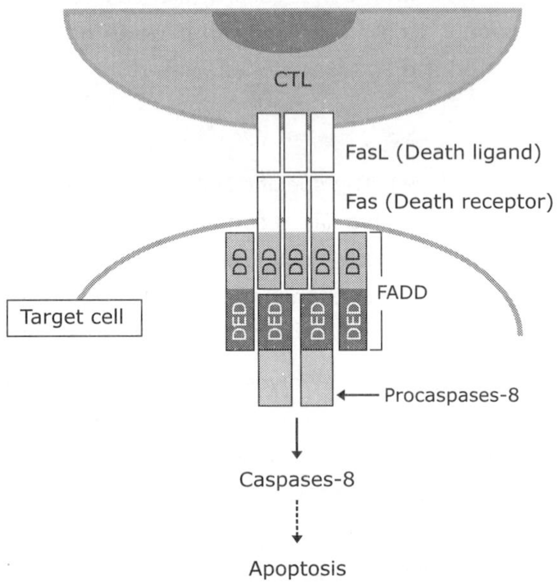

DD = Death domain
DED = Death effector domain

Figure 5.53
CTLs express Fas ligand (FasL), which binds to the death receptor Fas on the target cell. Fas then recruits the Fas-associated death domain (FADD) adaptor protein to form the death-inducing signaling complex, causing the activation of caspase-8. Caspase-8, in turn, activates the downstream caspases, such as caspase-3, culminating in apoptosis.

Antigen-nonspecific cell-mediated cytotoxicity

Cell-mediated immune responses are both *antigen-specific* and *antigen-nonspecific*. CTLs recognize the target cells for killing in antigen-dependent manner. CTLs recognize antigen–class I MHC complexes on specific target cells. As compared to CTLs, NK cells perform antigen-nonspecific cell-mediated cytotoxicity. NK cells use two different strategies to attack abnormal target cells.

The *first strategy* is to attack cells that lack class I MHC molecules. As NK cells do not express antigen-specific receptors, the mechanism by which these cells recognize tumor or infected cells are different from T cells. NK cells recognize their targets through a vast array of receptors: **cytokine receptors**, **activating receptors** and **inhibitory receptors**. Triggering of some of these receptors leads to NK cell activation while other receptors inhibit activation. The balance of activating and inhibitory signals ultimately determines whether an NK cell will respond or remain inactive. In general, cells that have downregulated class I MHC expression are more susceptible to NK cells attack due to lack of inhibitory signaling (referred to as surveillance for 'missing self' by NK cells; however, target cells expressing class I MHC can be killed if they express sufficiently high amounts of ligands for the activating receptors, which can overcome the suppression. Infection by certain viruses or mutations occurring in tumor cells often causes those cells to downregulate class I MHC. When NK cells encounter cells that have lost their class I MHC, their inhibiting receptors are no longer engaged and NK cells can kill the target cell.

Like CTLs, the cytoplasm of NK cells also has numerous granules containing **perforin** and **granzymes**. NK cells develop an organized immunological synapse at the site of contact with a target cell, after which degranulation occurs, with release of perforin and granzymes at the junction between the interacting cells. Perforin and granzymes are thought to play the same roles in NK cell-mediated induction of target cell apoptosis as they do in the CTL-mediated killing process. In addition, NK cells express FasL and readily induce the death of Fas-bearing target cells.

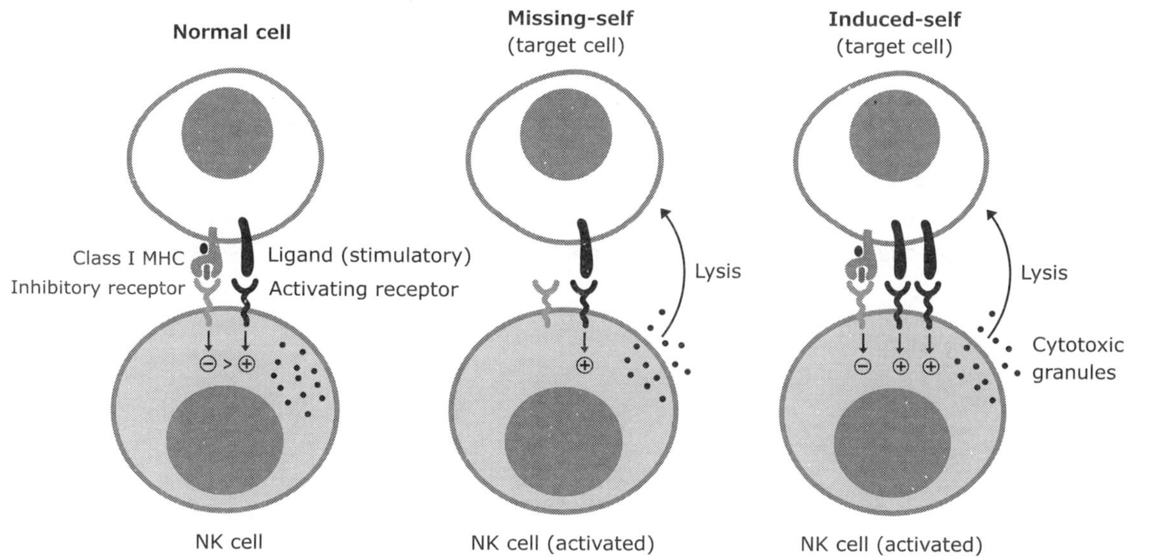

Figure 5.54 Effector responses of NK cells are regulated by inhibitory and activation receptors. An activating receptor on NK cells interacts with its ligand, inducing an activation signal that results in killing. However, interaction of inhibitory NK cell receptors with class I MHC molecules delivers an inhibition signal that counteracts the activation signal. Under normal circumstances, inhibitory receptors for class I MHC deliver signals that dominate over-stimulation through activation receptors. Hence, expression of class I MHC molecules on normal cells thus prevents their destruction by NK cells. When class I MHC is downregulated, as in 'missing-self', activation receptors stimulate NK cell the killing signal predominates, leading to their destruction. When a target is 'stressed', ligands for the activation receptor are induced, as in 'induced-self', permitting NK cell activation by overcoming MHC class I-dependent inhibition, leading to their destruction.

The *second strategy* involves **antibody-dependent cell-mediated cytotoxicity** (ADCC). NK cells express receptors FcγRIII, which recognizes the IgG1 and IgG3 subclasses of antibodies. By linking these receptors to antibodies present on the surfaces of infected cells, NK cells can arm themselves against infected cells. Binding of antibodies to Fc receptors activates NK cells to release their cytotoxic granules and induces cell death.

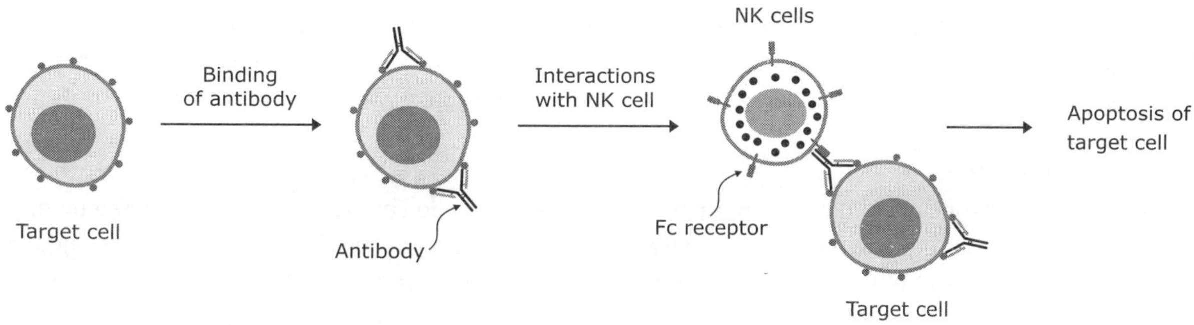

Figure 5.55 NK cells express Fc receptors. When these cells encounter cells coated with IgG antibody, they kill the target cell by releasing their cytotoxic granules.

NKT cell

A third type of cytolytic lymphocyte has been identified with characteristics shared by both the CTL and the NK cell. This cell type, designated the **NKT cell** to reflect its hybrid quality, develops in the thymus, and, strictly speaking, is a member of the adaptive immune system. Most NKT cells express an invariant TCR and markers common to NK cells. Because of limited diversity of TCR, these cells are also called **invariant NKT** (iNKT) cells. All NKT cell TCRs recognize lipids that are bound to class I MHC–like molecules called **CD1 molecules.** NKT cells and other lipid antigen-specific T cells are capable of rapidly producing cytokines, such as IL-4 and IFN-γ, after activation, and they may help marginal zone B cells to produce antibodies against lipid antigens. They exhibit both helper and cytotoxic activity and kill cells predominantly via FasL-Fas interactions.

5.13.1 Superantigens

Superantigens are viral or bacterial proteins that bind simultaneously to the variable domain of β of a T cell receptor (TCR) and to the α chain of a class II MHC molecule (i.e., outside the peptide-binding groove). Because of their unique binding ability, superantigens can activate large numbers of T cells irrespective of their antigenic specificity. Superantigens can be exogenous and endogenous. **Exogenous superantigens** are soluble proteins secreted by bacteria whereas **endogenous superantigens** are cell-membrane proteins encoded by certain viruses that infect mammalian cells.

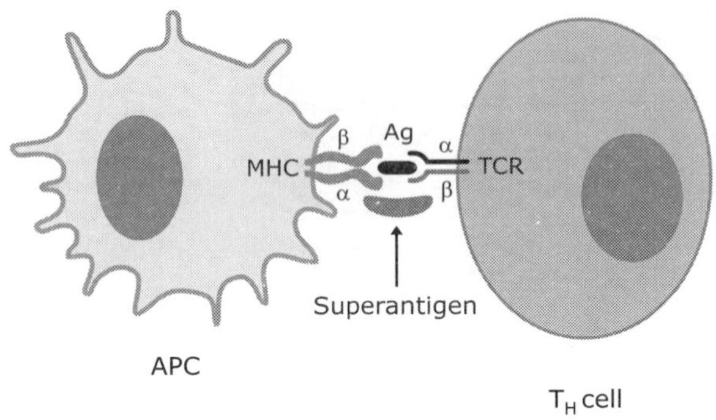

Figure 5.56 Superantigen-mediated cross-linkage of T cell receptor (TCR) and class II MHC molecules. Superantigen binds to class II MHC molecule and a part of the Vβ chain of the T cell receptor that is outside the normal antigen-binding site and this binding is sufficient to trigger T cell activation. A superantigen binds to all TCRs bearing a particular V sequence regardless of their antigen specificity.

5.14 The complement system

The complement (term coined by Paul Ehrlich) system, made up of approximately 30 serum and cell surface proteins/glycoproteins, is an important effector arm of both the innate and antibody-mediated acquired immune responses. The complement systems perform various functions. These functions include: *lysis of cells, opsonization, viral neutralization, inflammatory responses* and *solubilization and clearance of immune complexes* which remove the immune complexes from the circulation and deposit them in the spleen and liver.

Complement components

Complement components include a group of proteins/glycoproteins. These components are designated by numerals (C1–C9), by letter symbols (e.g., factor D), or by trivial names (e.g., homologous restriction factor). Designation C1, C2,...C9 denote the order in which the components were discovered, rather than their position in the activation sequence.

Complement components are synthesized mainly by liver hepatocytes. Monocytes, tissue macrophages, and epithelial cells of the gastrointestinal tract also produce significant amounts of complement components. In the circulation, the concentration of all complement proteins is about 3 mg/mL. Some complement components are found at high concentrations (e.g., C3 at about 1 mg/mL), while others (such as factor D and C2) are found in only trace amounts.

Complement activation pathways

Most complement components are present in the serum in functionally inactive forms as proenzymes or zymogens. Complement activation pathways involve the activation of one component that triggers the activation of the next component in the sequence. Upon activation, individual components are split into fragments, designated by lower-case letters. The smaller of the cleaved fragments is generally designated with a lower-case *a*, and the large fragment with a lower-case *b*; for historical reasons, however, the large cleavage fragment of C2 is usually referred to as C2a and the smaller fragment C2b. The larger fragments bind to the target near the site of activation, and the smaller fragments diffuse from the site and can initiate localized inflammatory responses. The complement fragments interact with one another to form functional complexes. Those complexes that have enzymatic activity are designated by a bar over the number or symbol (e.g., $\overline{\text{C3bBb}}$). There are three pathways of complement activation — **classical, lectin** and **alternative pathway**.

Classical pathways

The classical pathway was so named because it was the first complement pathway to be worked out. The classical pathway commonly begins with the formation of antigen-antibody complexes. Thus, this pathway is a major effector pathway of the humoral adaptive immune response. Other activators include some viruses, necrotic cells and subcellular membranes (e.g., from mitochondria), aggregated immunoglobulins, and beta-amyloid, found in Alzheimer disease plaques.

The classical pathway is initiated when C1 binds to the antibody in an antigen-antibody complex. C1 is a complex of three different proteins: C1q (made up of six identical subunits) combined with two molecules each of C1r and C1s. IgM and certain subclasses of IgG (human IgG1, IgG2 and IgG3) are efficient complement-activating antibodies. Among the human immunoglobulins, the ability to bind and activate C1 is, in decreasing order, IgM > IgG3 > IgG1 >> IgG2. IgG4, IgD, IgA, and IgE do not have C1q receptors; these antibodies do not bind or activate C1 and thus do not activate the classical complement pathway. C1q of C1 binds to the F_C region of antibodies. This activates C1r, a *serine protease* that initiates the cascade of the classical pathway. First, C4 is proteolytically activated into C4b, which in turn cleaves C2 into C2a and C2b. C4b and C2a together form **C3 convertase**.

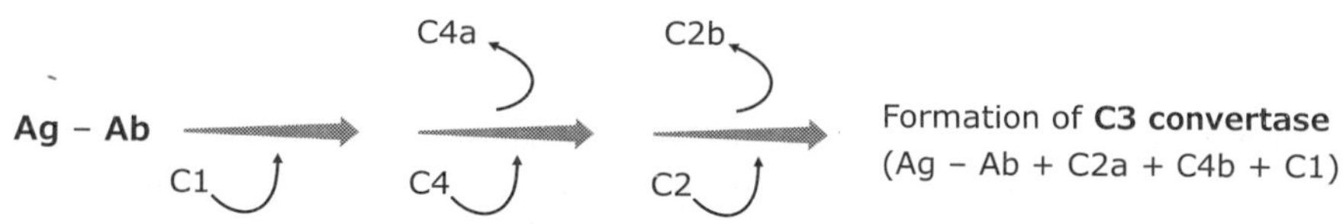

Figure 5.57 In the classical pathway, activation is triggered when the C1 complex (comprising C1q, C1r, and C1s) binds to antibodies (IgG or IgM) that are attached to antigens on a pathogen's surface. This binding leads to the cleavage of C4 into C4a and C4b, and C2 into C2a and C2b. C4b binds to the pathogen surface and associates with C2a, forming the classical pathway C3 convertase (C4b2a).

Lectin pathway

Lectins are carbohydrate binding proteins that recognize and bind to specific carbohydrate target. The lectin pathway is activated by terminal mannose residues of glycoprotein or polysaccharides found on the surface of bacteria. This pathway does not depend on antibody for activation (*antibody-independent*). It is activated by binding of **mannose binding lectin** (an *acute phase protein*) to mannose residues. These terminal mannose residues are not found on the surface of mammalian cells, and so the lectin pathway of complement activation may be responsible for discrimination between self and non-self. Because this pathway is activated in the absence of antibody, it is part of the innate immune defenses.

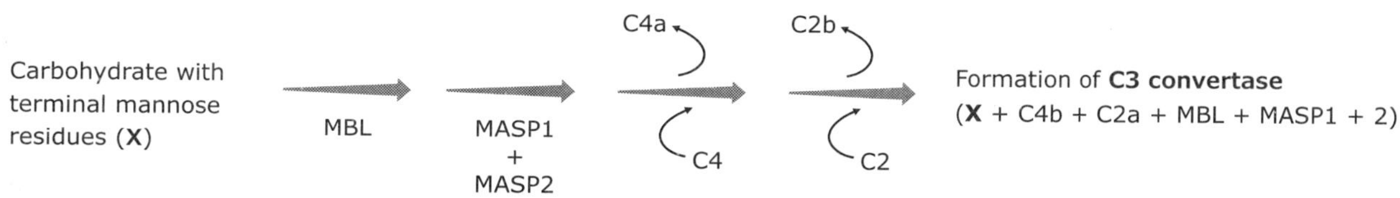

Figure 5.58 The lectin pathway is antibody-independent pathway. It is initiated when mannose-binding lectin (MBL) bind to mannose-containing carbohydrate on the pathogen surface. This binding activates MBL-associated serine proteases (MASP-1 and MASP-2), which cleave C4 and C2 in the same way as in the classical pathway, again forming C4b2a as the C3 convertase.

Alternative or properdin pathway

The alternative pathway is *antibody-independent*. This pathway of complement activation is triggered by almost any foreign substance. The most widely studied include lipopolysaccharide from the outer membrane of Gram-negative bacteria, the cell walls of some yeasts, and a protein present in cobra venom, known as cobra venom factor. Some agents that activate the classical pathway–viruses, aggregated immunoglobulins, and necrotic cells– also trigger the alternative pathway. Activation of the alternative pathway occurs in the absence of specific antibody. Thus, the alternative pathway of complement activation is an effector arm of the innate immune defenses. This major pathway of complement activation involves four serum proteins: C3, factor B, factor D, and **properdin**, also known as **factor P**.

In the alternative pathway, serum C3 is subject to spontaneous hydrolysis to yield C3a and C3b. The C3b component can bind to foreign surface antigens. The C3b present on the surface of the foreign cells can bind another serum protein called factor B to form a complex. Binding to C3b serves as the substrate for an enzymatically active serum protein called **factor D**. Factor D cleaves the C3b-bound **factor B**, releasing a small fragment (Ba) that diffuses away and generating C3 convertase. Properdin binds with C3 convertase and stabilizes it.

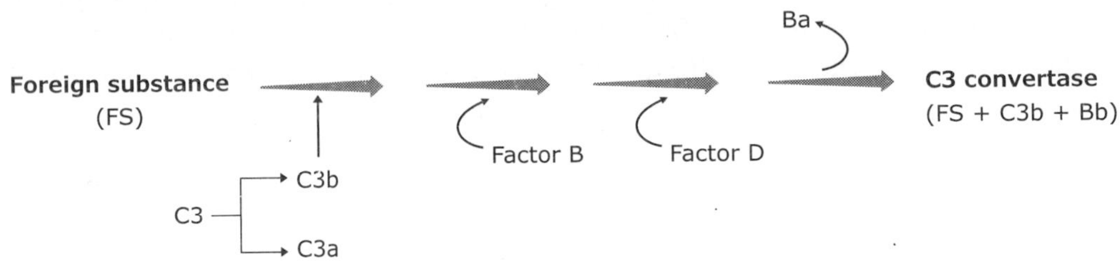

Figure 5.59 The alternative pathway is an antibody-independent mechanism. Unlike the classical pathway, it is triggered when C3b directly binds to a foreign substance. C3b then binds to Factor B, which is subsequently cleaved by Factor D into Ba and Bb; Bb remains attached, forming the enzyme complex C3bBb, known as the alternative pathway C3 convertase.

Activation of C3 and C5

C3 convertase formation is a critical step in all three complement pathways. The C3 convertase cleaves C3 into two fragments: the smaller, C3a and large fragment, C3b. C3b continues the complement activation cascade by binding to the cells surface around the site of complement activation. C3a is a fluid-phase **anaphylatoxin**. Anaphylatoxin binds to receptors on mast cells and blood basophils and induces degranulation, with release of histamine and other active mediators. Anaphylatoxin also induces smooth muscle contraction and increases vascular permeability.

C3b binding to all three complement pathways allows the next component in the sequence, C5, to bind and be cleaved. For this reason, the C3 convertase with bound C3b is referred to as C5 convertase. For the classical and lectin pathways, the C5 convertase has the composition C4b2a3b; for the alternative pathway, the C5 convertase has the formulation C3bBbC3b. The cleavage of C5 produces two fragments: C5a is released into the fluid phase and acts as potent anaphylatoxin. C5b binds to the cell surface and forms the nucleus for the binding of the terminal complement components.

The terminal pathway

The terminal components of the complement cascades are C5b, C6, C7, C8, and C9. These components bind to each other sequentially to form a macromolecular structure called the **membrane attack complex** (**MAC**) that results in cell lysis. The three complement pathways converge at the membrane-attack complex. This complex forms a large channel through the membrane of the target cell, enabling ions and small molecules to diffuse freely across the membrane. The first step in MAC formation is C6 binding to C5b on a cell surface. C7 then binds to C5b and C6 and inserts into the outer membrane of the cell. The subsequent binding of C8 to C5b67 results in the complex penetrating deeper into the cell's membrane. The final step in the formation of the MAC is the binding and polymerization of C9, a perforin-like molecule, to the C5b678 complex. C5b678 on the cell membrane acts as a receptor for C9 that binds to C8. Additional C9 molecules interact with the C9 molecule in the complex to form polymerized C9 (poly-C9). This poly-C9 forms a transmembrane channel that disturbs the cell's osmotic equilibrium:

ions pass through the channel, and water enters the cell. The cell swells, and the membrane becomes permeable to macromolecules, which then escape from the cell. The result is cell lysis.

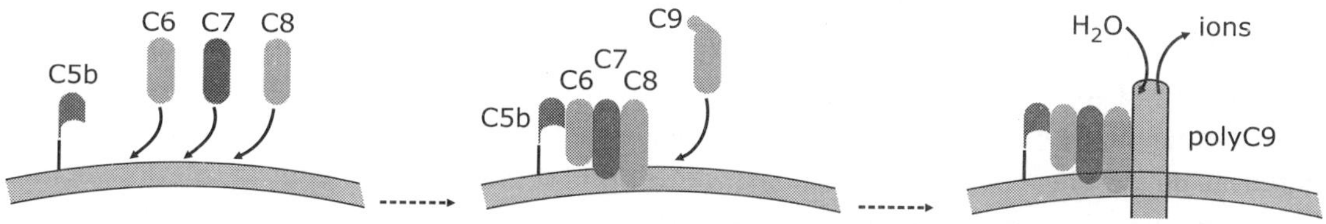

Figure 5.60 Formation of the membrane attack complex. Late stage complement components C5b-C9 bind sequentially to form a complex on the cell surface. Multiple C9 component binds to this complex and polymerizes to form poly-C9, creating a channel that disrupts the cell membrane.

Comparsion among classical, lectin and alternative pathways

Feature	Classical pathway	Lectin pathway	Alternative pathway
Trigger	Antigen–antibody complexes	Mannose-containing carbohydrates	Any foreign substance
First recognition molecule	C1 complex binds Fc portion of antibody	MBL	C3b directly binds to foreign substance
First protease	Activated C1r and C1s	MASP-1 and MASP-2	Factor D (after C3b binds Factor B)
C3 convertase	C4b2a	C4b2a	C3bBb
C5 convertase	C4b2a3b	C4b2a3b	C3bBbC3b
Antibody-dependent	Yes	No	No

Biologically active functions mediated by complement products

Activation of complement results in the production of several biologically active molecules which contribute to killing of cell, opsonization, chemotaxis, anaphylaxis and inflammation.

The most important action of complement is to facilitate the uptake and destruction of pathogens by phagocytes. This occurs by the specific recognition of membrane-bound complement components by complement receptors on phagocytes. These complement receptors bind pathogens opsonized with complement components: opsonization of pathogens is a major function of C3b and its proteolytic derivatives. C4b also acts as an opsonin but has a relatively minor role. There are several different complement receptors (CRs). CR1 and CR3 are especially important in inducing phagocytosis of bacteria with complement components on their surface.

The small complement fragments C3a, C4a, and C5a act on specific receptors to produce local inflammatory responses. When produced in large amounts they induce a shock-like syndrome similar to that seen in a systemic allergic reaction involving IgE antibodies. Such a reaction is termed **anaphylactic shock** and these small fragments of complement are therefore often referred to as **anaphylotoxins**. Of the three, C5a is the most stable and has the highest specific biological activity.

Biologically active functions	Complement component
Cell lysis	C5b–9 (membrane-attack complex)
Inflammatory response	C3a, C4a and C5a (anaphylatoxins)
Chemotaxis of leukocytes	C3a, C5a
Opsonization of particulate antigens	C3b, C4b
Viral neutralization	C3b, C5b–9 (membrane-attack complex)
Solubilization and immune clearance	C3b

5.15 Hypersensitivity

Hypersensitivity is an exaggerated immune response that results in tissue damage and is manifested in the individual on a second or subsequent contact with an antigen. Hypersensitivity has been traditionally classified into *immediate* and *delayed* types based on the time required for a sensitized host to develop clinical reactions on re-exposure to the antigen. **Immediate hypersensitivity** manifests within minutes to hours after exposure of a sensitized individual to antigen whereas in **delayed hypersensitivity** response generally occurs 2 to 3 days after T_H cells interact with antigen. Later, Gell and Coombs proposed a classification scheme which defined four types of hypersensitivity reactions.

Type I hypersensitivity

Type I hypersensitivity (also known as **allergic reaction**) is induced by antigens referred to as *allergens*. The term allergen refers specifically to nonparasitic antigens capable of stimulating type I hypersensitive responses. Type I hypersensitive reactions are IgE-mediated humoral antibody responses. These IgE-mediated reactions are stimulated by the binding of IgE (via its Fc region) to high-affinity IgE-specific Fc receptors expressed on mast cells and basophils. When cross-linked by antigens, the IgE antibodies trigger the mast cells and basophils to release **primary mediators**, vasoactive amines, stored in the granules (degranulation).

The most significant primary mediators are histamine, proteases, eosinophil chemotactic factor, neutrophil chemotactic factor, and heparin. These mediators cause all the normal consequences of an acute inflammatory reaction – increased vascular permeability, smooth muscle contraction, granulocyte chemotaxis and extravasation etc. Mast cell activation via Fc also leads to the production of two other types of mediators. These **secondary mediators**, unlike the stored granule contents, must be synthesized *de novo* and comprise arachidonic acid derivatives (prostaglandins and leukotrienes), platelet-activating factor, bradykinins, and various cytokines.

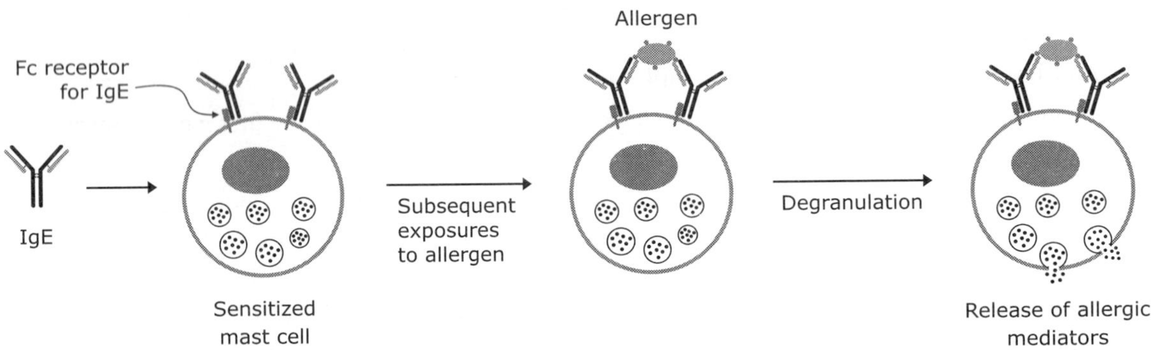

Figure 5.61 Ag induces cross-linking of IgE bound to mast cells and basophils with release of vasoactive mediators.

Type I hypersensitivity can be *anaphylaxis* or *atopy*. **Anaphylaxis** is a very rapid, life-threatening, severe whole body allergic reaction. It is caused by re-exposure to a previously encountered antigen. **Atopy** (atopic allergy) is a hereditary tendency to develop allergic reaction to substances such as pollen, food, insect venom etc.

Type II hypersensitivity

Type II hypersensitivity is generally called a *cytolytic* or *cytotoxic reaction* because it results in the destruction of host cells, either by lysis or toxic mediators. Type II hypersensitivity is caused by antibodies binding to cells or tissue antigens. Classical examples of type II hypersensitivity reactions are the response exhibited by a person who receives a transfusion with blood from a donor with a different blood group and erythroblastosis fetalis. Two different antibody-mediated mechanisms are involved in these cytotoxic reactions.

Complement-mediated: Complement-activating antibodies bind with cell membrane component and lead to the activation of classical complement pathway. This causes either to lysis of the cell or opsonization. Blood cells are most commonly affected by this mechanism.

Antibody-dependent cell mediated cytotoxicity (ADCC): In this process, antibodies mediate cell destruction, in which cytotoxic cells bearing Fc receptors bind to the Fc region of antibodies on target cells. This brings cytotoxic cells (NK cells) in contact with antibody-coated target cells. Lysis of these target cells requires contact but does not involve phagocytosis or complement fixation. Instead, ADCC lysis of target cells is analogous to that of cytotoxic T cells and involves the release of cytoplasmic granules containing *perforin* and *granzymes* that activate events leading to apoptosis. ADCC reactions involve IgG and IgG Fc receptors.

Type III hypersensitivity

Type III hypersensitivity is mediated by *immune complexes* essentially of IgG antibodies with soluble antigens. Circulating immune complexes may lodge at various tissue sites where they activate complement and subsequently cause tissue cell lysis. Normally these complexes are phagocytosed effectively by the fixed monocytes and macrophages of the monocyte-macrophage system. In the presence of excess amounts of some soluble antigens, the antigen-antibody complexes may not be efficiently removed. Their accumulation can lead to a hypersensitivity reaction from complement that triggers a variety of inflammatory process. This form of hypersensitivity has a lot in common with type I except that the antibody involved is IgG and, therefore, not prebound to mast cells.

Type IV hypersensitivity

Type IV hypersensitivity, commonly called **delayed type hypersensitivity**, is the only class of hypersensitive reactions which are triggered by antigen-specific T cells (cell-mediated immunity reactions). This is mediated by T cell dependent effector mechanisms involving T_H cells, primarily of the T_H1 subtype, but in a few cases T_C cells. Antibodies do not play a role in type IV hypersensitivity reactions. On activation, the T_H1 cells release cytokines that cause accumulation and activation of macrophages, which, in turn, cause local damage. The **tuberculin skin test** is an example of a type IV hypersensitivity. This test is done by putting a small amount of tuberculin purified protein derivative (**PPD**) under the top layer of skin. If any person has ever been exposed to the *Mycobacterium tuberculosis*, skin will react to the antigens by developing a firm red bump at the site within 2 days. It is a standard method of determining whether a person is infected with *Mycobacterium tuberculosis*.

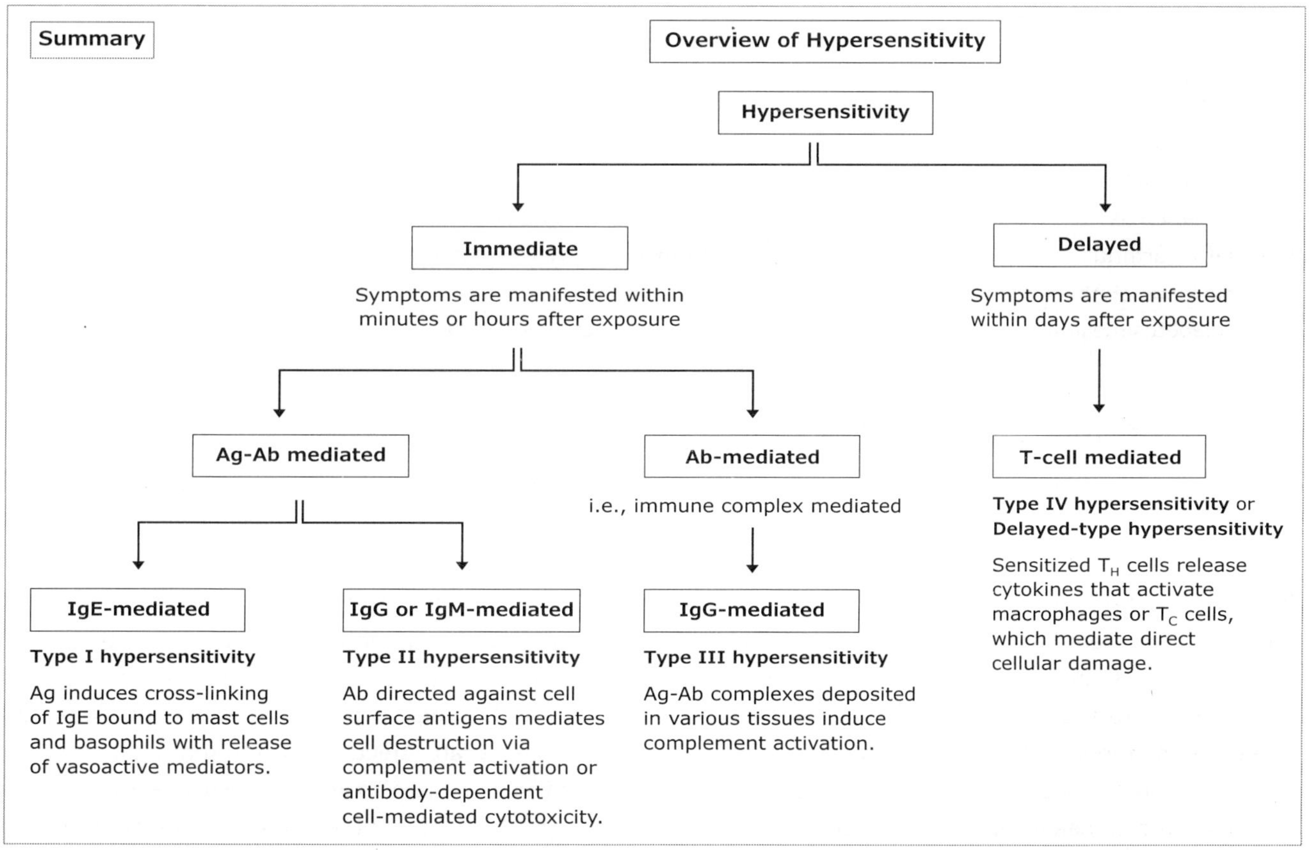

5.16 Autoimmunity

The body is normally able to distinguish its own self-antigens from foreign non-self antigens and does not mount an immunologic attack against itself. This phenomenon is called **immune tolerance**. *Autoimmunity* is a condition in which structural or functional damage is produced by the action of immunologically competent cells or Ab against self-antigen. Autoimmunity literally means protection against self, but actually it implies injury to self, and therefore sometimes the term is also under criticism. The diseases caused by autoimmunity are referred to as **autoimmune diseases**. Autoimmune diseases result from the destruction of self-proteins, cells and organs by auto-antibodies (e.g., *Hashimoto's thyroiditis*) or self-reactive T cells (e.g., *rheumatoid arthritis*).

It results from the activation of self-reactive T and B cells that, following stimulation by genetic or environmental triggers, cause destruction. Four factors influence the development of autoimmune disease. These factors are genetic, viral, hormonal and psycho-neuro-immunological (the influence of stress and neurochemicals). All four of these factors can affect gene expression, which directly or indirectly interferes with important immunoregulatory actions. Autoimmune diseases are often categorized as either *organ-specific* or *systemic*, depending on whether they affect a single organ or multiple systems in the body. Another method of categorization involves the immune component that does the bulk of the damage: T cells versus antibodies.

Autoimmunity is initiated by a combination of genetic and environmental factors. Most autoimmune diseases are polygenic and affected individuals inherit multiple genetic polymorphisms that contribute to disease susceptibility. The greatest contribution is from MHC genes; other genes are believed to influence the selection of self-reactive lymphocytes and the development of self-tolerance. Viral and bacterial infections may contribute to the development and exacerbation of autoimmunity. Infections may increase the chances of autoimmunity by several mechanisms, including enhanced expression of co-stimulators in tissues and cross-reactions between microbial antigens and self-antigens. Important examples of autoimmune diseases in human and their respective autoantigen are given below in the table.

Table 5.12 Some autoimmune diseases in humans

Disease	Autoantigen
Autoimmune hemolytic anemia	Rh antigen
Graves' disease	Thyroid-stimulating hormone receptor
Multiple sclerosis	Myelin basic protein
Myasthenia gravis	Acetylcholine receptor
Rheumatoid arthritis	Unknown synovial joint antigen
Systemic lupus erythematosus	DNA, histones, snRNP
Type 1 diabetes mellitus	Pancreatic beta cell antigen

5.17 Transplantation

Transplantation is the process of taking tissues or organs, called a **graft**, from one individual and placing them into a different individual. The individual who provides the graft is called the *donor*, and the individual who receives the graft is called either the *recipient* or the *host*. *Blood transfusion* is also a form of transplantation in which whole blood or blood cells from one or more individuals are transferred intravenously into the circulation of another individual.

The immune system has evolved as a way of discriminating between self and non-self. This discriminating power of the immune system between self and non-self is undesirable in the case of tissues or organs transplant from one individual to another for therapeutic purposes. Transplantation of tissues or organs from one individual to a genetically non-identical individual invariably leads to rejection (called **graft rejection**) of the transplant due to an adaptive immune response. Some transplanted tissues, however, do not stimulate an immune response. For example, a transplanted cornea is rarely rejected because lymphocytes do not circulate into the anterior chamber of the eye.

This site is considered an immunologically privileged site. Another example of a privileged tissue is the heart valve. Before the discussion about the immunological mechanisms associated with graft rejection, it is important to understand the special vocabulary used to describe different types of transplants:

Autogeneic graft (or **autograft**): A graft or transplant from one body part to another on the same individual.

Syngeneic graft (or **syngraft** or **isograft**): A graft transplanted between two genetically identical individuals (syngeneic). In humans, a syngraft can be performed between monozygotic twins.

Allogeneic graft (or **allograft**): A graft transplanted between two genetically different individuals of the same species.

Xenogeneic graft (or **xenograft**): A graft transplanted between individuals of different species.

Autografts and syngrafts are usually accepted, owing to the genetic identity between donor and recipient. Because an allograft is genetically dissimilar to the host and therefore expresses unique antigens, it is often recognized as foreign by the immune system and is therefore rejected. Obviously, xenografts exhibit the greatest genetic and antigenic variation, causing a vigorous graft rejection response.

Allogeneic transplantation

The molecules that are recognized as foreign on allografts are called **alloantigens**. Alloantigens elicit both cellular and humoral immune responses. The alloantigens present in allograft that stimulate adaptive immune responses are *histocompatibility proteins*, encoded by polymorphic genes that differ among individuals. The alloantigens responsible for strong graft rejection reactions are called **major histocompatibility complex** (MHC) molecules. The normal function of MHC molecules is to present peptides derived from protein antigens in a form that can be recognized by T cells. There are polymorphic alloantigens other than MHC molecules against which the recipient may mount an immune response. These alloantigens typically induce weak or slower (more gradual) graft rejection reactions than do MHC molecules and are therefore called **minor histocompatibility antigens**. Most minor histocompatibility antigens are proteins that are processed and presented to host T cells in association with self MHC molecules on host antigen-presenting cells (APCs), similar to any protein antigen.

Recognition of alloantigens: Allogeneic MHC molecules of a graft can be recognized by the recipient's T cells in two fundamentally different ways, called the *direct* and *indirect pathways*.

In the case of **direct recognition**, intact MHC molecules displayed by donor cells in the graft are recognized by recipient T cells without a need for processing by host APCs. T cell responses to directly presented allogeneic MHC molecules are very strong. In the **indirect recognition**, donor (allogeneic) MHC molecules are captured and processed by recipient APCs, and peptides derived from the allogeneic MHC molecules are presented in association with self MHC molecules. Minor histocompatibility antigens are also presented to host T cells by the indirect pathway.

Indirect presentation results in allorecognition by T_H cells because alloantigen is acquired by host APCs primarily through the endosomal vesicular pathway (i.e., as a consequence of phagocytosis) and is therefore presented by class II MHC molecules. Some antigens of phagocytosed graft cells appear to enter the class I MHC pathway of antigen presentation and are indirectly recognized by T_C cells. This phenomenon is an example of *cross-presentation* or *cross-priming*.

Activation and effector functions of alloreactive T cells

When lymphocytes recognize alloantigens, they become activated to proliferate, differentiate, and perform effector functions that can damage grafts. In the case of **direct recognition**, donor dendritic cells in the allograft migrate to secondary lymphoid tissues, where they present allogeneic MHC molecules to host T cells. In the case of **indirect recognition**, recipient dendritic cells that have entered the allograft transport donor MHC molecules to secondary lymphoid tissues and present peptides derived from these MHC molecules to alloreactive host T cells. In both cases, the T cells become activated and differentiate into effector cells. The alloreactive effector T cells migrate into the allograft, become reactivated by alloantigen, and mediate damage.

Alloreactive T_H and T_C cells that are activated by graft alloantigens cause graft rejection by distinct mechanisms. The $CD4^+$ T-cells differentiate into cytokine-producing effector cells that damage grafts by cytokine-mediated inflammation, similar to a delayed-type hypersensitivity (DTH) reaction. Alloreactive T_C cells differentiate into cytotoxic T-lymphocytes (CTLs), which kill cells in the graft that express the allogeneic class I MHC molecules. CTLs also secrete inflammatory cytokines, which can contribute to graft damage.

Only CTLs that are generated by direct allorecognition can kill graft cells, whereas helper T cells generated by either direct or indirect alloantigen recognition can cause cytokine-mediated damage to grafts. $CD8^+$ CTLs that are generated by direct allorecognition of donor MHC molecules on donor APCs can recognize the same MHC molecules on parenchymal cells in the graft and kill those cells. When alloreactive T cells are stimulated by the indirect pathway, the principal mechanism of rejection is not CTL-mediated killing of graft cells but inflammation caused by the cytokines produced by the effector T cells.

Alloreactive antibodies (or **alloantibodies**) against alloantigens also contribute to graft rejection. Most high-affinity alloantibodies are produced by T_H cell dependent activation of alloreactive B cells. The antigens most frequently recognized by alloantibodies are donor MHC molecules, including both class I and class II MHC molecules. The alloreactive antibodies produced in graft recipients engage the same effector mechanisms that antibodies use to combat infections, including complement activation and targeting and activation of neutrophils, macrophages, and NK cells through Fc receptor binding.

Pattern of graft rejection

Alloreactive T_H and T_C cells and alloantibodies all have been shown to be capable of mediating allograft rejection. These different immune effectors cause graft rejection by different mechanisms. There are three major types of graft rejection reactions:

Hyperacute rejection: Hyperacute rejection reactions typically occur within the first 24 hours after transplantation. In this case, a transplant is rejected so quickly that the grafted tissue never becomes vascularized. These reactions are caused by preexisting host serum antibodies specific for antigens of the graft and have the greatest impact in highly vascularized grafts (such as kidney and heart). Preexisting recipient antibodies bind to MHC antigens on the endothelial cells of the graft. These antigen-antibody complexes activate the complement system and result in an intense accumulation of neutrophils. The ensuing inflammatory reaction causes endothelial damage and obstructing blood clots within the capillaries, preventing vascularization of the graft.

Acute graft rejection: Acute graft rejection reactions usually begin in the first few weeks after transplantation. It is mediated by alloreactive T cells and antibodies. Although the patterns of acute graft rejection are divided into cellular (mediated by T cells) and humoral (mediated by antibodies), both typically coexist in an organ undergoing acute rejection. The principal mechanisms of **acute cellular rejection** are inflammation caused by cytokines produced by T_H cells and CTL-mediated killing of graft parenchymal cells and endothelial cells. Alloantibodies cause **acute humoral rejection** by binding to alloantigens, mainly MHC molecules, on vascular endothelial cells, causing endothelial injury and intravascular thrombosis that results in graft destruction. The binding of the alloantibodies to the endothelial cell surface triggers local complement activation, which leads to lysis of the cells, recruitment and activation of neutrophils and thrombus formation.

Chronic rejection: Chronic rejection reactions can occur from months to years after transplantation. The mechanisms include both humoral and cell-mediated responses by the recipient.

Xenogeneic transplantation

Xenogeneic transplantation is defined as the transplantation of living xenogeneic cells, tissues or organs. This transplantation process has the potential to supplement the limited supply of human material for transplantation. However, xenogeneic transplantation presents specific immunological problems for recipients. A major immunologic barrier to xenogeneic transplantation is the presence of natural antibodies in the human recipients that cause *hyperacute rejection*. Natural antibodies against xenografts induce hyperacute rejection by the same mechanisms as those seen in hyperacute allograft rejection. Even when hyperacute rejection is prevented, xenografts are often damaged by a form of *acute vascular rejection* that occurs within 2 to 3 days of transplantation. This form of rejection has been called **delayed xenograft rejection**. However, the mechanisms of delayed xenograft rejection are incompletely understood.

5.18 Immunodeficiency diseases

Immunodeficiency represents any deficiency in the immune response, whether inherited or acquired as a result of which the immune system fails to protect the host from disease-causing agents. It occurs when one or more components of the immune system are defective such as humoral immunity, cell-mediated responses, or some combination of these. Immunodeficiencies may be **primary** and **secondary**. A deficiency caused by a defect in one or more genes involved in the development or function of the immune system is called **primary immunodeficiency**. In contrast, a deficiency in the immune system that is acquired after birth, usually because of infection, and that is not related to a genetic defect, is called **secondary** or **acquired immunodeficiency**.

Examples of primary immunodeficiency diseases:

Severe combined immunodeficiency (SCID): SCID is a genetic disorder which is characterized by a very low number of circulating lymphocytes. Both arms (B cells and T cells) of the adaptive immune system become non-functional. As such patients make neither specific T cell dependent antibody responses nor cell-mediated immune responses, and thus cannot develop immunological memory. Several different defects can lead to the SCID phenotype. In X-linked SCID, which is the commonest form of SCID, T cells fail to develop because of defect in the genes code for several cytokine receptors, including those for the interleukins IL-2, IL-4, IL-7, IL-9 and IL-15. The autosomally inherited SCID occurs due to **adenosine deaminase deficiency**. Adenosine deaminase catalyzes the conversion of adenosine to inosine, and its deficiency results in accumulation of adenosine, which interferes with purine metabolism which results in an accumulation of nucleotide metabolites that are particularly toxic to developing T cells.

Chediak-Higashi syndrome: Chediak-Higashi syndrome is an autosomal recessive disease. It is characterized by recurrent bacterial infections, lack of skin and eye pigment. Phagocytes from patients with this immune defect contain giant granules but do not have the ability to kill bacteria. With time, patients develop massive infiltrates of lymphocytes and macrophages in the liver, spleen, and lymph nodes. The molecular basis of the defect is a mutation in a protein involved in the regulation of intracellular trafficking. The mutation impairs the targeting of proteins to lysosomes.

DiGeorge syndrome: DiGeorge syndrome, or *congenital thymic aplasia*, is not hereditary but occurs sporadically and is result of a deletion in chromosome 22. The syndrome is caused by defective migration of fetal neural crest cells into the third and fourth *pharyngeal pouch*. DiGeorge syndrome in its most severe form is the complete absence of a thymus. This developmental defect causes immunodeficiency along with hypoparathyroidism, and congenital heart disease. The immune defect includes a profound depression of T cell numbers and absence of T cell responses. Although B cells are present in normal numbers, affected individuals do not produce antibody in response to immunization with specific antigens.

5.19 Vaccines

An individual may be exposed to an antigen to induce immune responses, a type of immunity known as *artificial active immunity*. The material used to induce artificial active immunity is known as a **vaccine** (or an **immunogen**), and the process of generating such an immune response is **immunization**. Immunization is commonly known as **vaccination**. The term 'vaccine' has been derived from the Latin word *vaccinus* meaning *from cows*. A *vaccine* is a biological product that can be used to safely induce an immune response that confers protection against infection and/or disease on subsequent exposure to a pathogen. To achieve this, the vaccine must contain antigens that are either derived from the pathogen or produced synthetically to represent components of the pathogen.

Herd immunity

If enough people in a community are immunized against particular diseases, then it is more difficult for that disease to get passed between those who are not immunized. A type of immunity that occurs when the vaccination of a portion of the population (or herd) provides protection to unprotected individuals is termed **herd immunity**. Herd immunity does not apply to all diseases.

Type of antigens used in vaccines

Vaccines can use a variety of antigens, ranging from entire organisms to small cellular components. These antigens are classified into two main types:

Whole organism vaccines include **live-attenuated organisms** and **killed** (or **inactivated**) **organisms.**

Purified antigen vaccines (also called **subunit vaccines**) include components of a pathogen not whole organism such as toxoid (inactivated toxin), polysaccharide and recombinant antigens (proteins).

However, recent advances in molecular biology had provided alternative methods for producing vaccines such as **nucleic acid vaccines** and **recombinant vector vaccines**.

Whole organism vaccines

Whole organism vaccines are a type of vaccine that uses the whole microorganism to stimulate an immune response. These vaccines can be either:

Live-attenuated whole organism vaccines: These vaccines are prepared by attenuating pathogenic organisms by growing them in unfavorable conditions which result in gene mutations due to which organism looses pathogenicity but retains their capacity for transient growth. **Attenuated pathogenic organisms** are those that have been weakened (or attenuated) so they do not cause disease in healthy individuals. Attenuated vaccines have advantages as well as disadvantages. Due to their capacity for transient growth, these vaccines show prolonged immunogenicity and eliminate the need for repeated boosters. But a major disadvantage of these vaccines is the associated risk of reverting back to virulent form. However these days genetic engineering is also used to cause site-directed mutation causing irreversible removal of virulence genes from attenuated organisms making them safe for use.

The **Sabin polio vaccine** is an example of live-attenuated whole organism vaccines , consisting of three attenuated strains of poliovirus. Sabin vaccine in the intestines induces the production of secretory IgA, which serves as an important defense against naturally acquired poliovirus.

Killed (or **inactivated**) **whole organism vaccines**: Killed whole organism vaccines are produced by killing of pathogenic organisms by heat or chemical treatment so that organisms are unable to multiply in the host. Killing is carried out in such a way so that the structure of epitopes on surface antigens remain maintained. Hence heat treatment is generally not satisfactory since it can cause protein degradation and thus loss of some epitopes. Thus chemical inactivation using formaldehyde or other alkylating agent is more common. Killed whole organism vaccines are effective, but they are less immunogenic so often require several boosters and normally do not adequately stimulate cell-mediated immunity or secretory IgA production. In contrast, attenuated vaccines usually are given in a single dose and stimulate both humoral and cell-mediated immunity.

Table 5.13 Comparison of live-attenuated whole organism vaccines and killed or inactivated whole organism vaccines

	Live-attenuated	**Killed** or **inactivated**
Booster dose	Generally requires single booster	Requires multiple boosters
Relative stability	Less stable	More stable
Immunity induced	Humoral and cell-mediated	Mainly humoral
Reversion to virulent form	May revert to a virulent form	Cannot revert to a virulent form

Purified antigen vaccines

Purified antigen vaccines (or subunit vaccines) composed of molecules purified directly from the pathogenic microbes. Instead of the entire microbe, subunit vaccines include only specific, purified macromolecules that best stimulate the immune system. Hence, many of the risks associated with attenuated or killed whole organism vaccines can be avoided with a strategy that uses only specific, purified macromolecules derived from the pathogen. Three general forms of subunit vaccines are in current use: **toxoids**, **polysaccharide** and **recombinant antigens** (proteins).

Many exotoxins can be modified chemically so they retain their antigenicity but are no longer toxic. Such a modified exotoxin is called a **toxoid**. Toxoids are usually not as efficient as the original exotoxin for producing immunity, but they can be given safely and in high doses. Diphtheria and tetanus vaccines have been made by purifying the bacterial exotoxin and then inactivating it with formaldehyde to form a toxoid.

Some *purified antigen vaccines*, especially **capsular polysaccharide vaccines**, have one limitation - their inability to activate T_H cells. Instead, they activate B cells in a thymus-independent type 2 (TI-2) manner, resulting in IgM production but little class switching, no affinity maturation, and little, if any, development of memory cells. However, vaccines that conjugate a polysaccharide antigen to a protein carrier can alleviate this problem (termed as **conjugate vaccine**). A **conjugate vaccine** is created by covalently attaching a poor antigen to a strong antigen thereby eliciting a stronger immunological response to the poor antigen.

There are two methods for the development of purified antigen vaccines. One method involves isolation of specific, purified macromolecules from pathogens and administering this as vaccine. A second method of making a purified antigen vaccines involves cloning of gene encoding any immunogenic protein and its expression in bacterial, yeast or mammalian cells using recombinant DNA technology (called a **recombinant antigen vaccine** or **recombinant subunit vaccine**). A number of genes encoding surface antigens from pathogens have also been successfully cloned into cellular expression systems for use in vaccine development. The first recombinant antigen vaccine approved for human use is the **hepatitis B vaccine**. The immune response generated by recombinant subunit vaccines is primarily humoral. The antigens are processed via the class II MHC pathway, and therefore do not induce a cellular immune response.

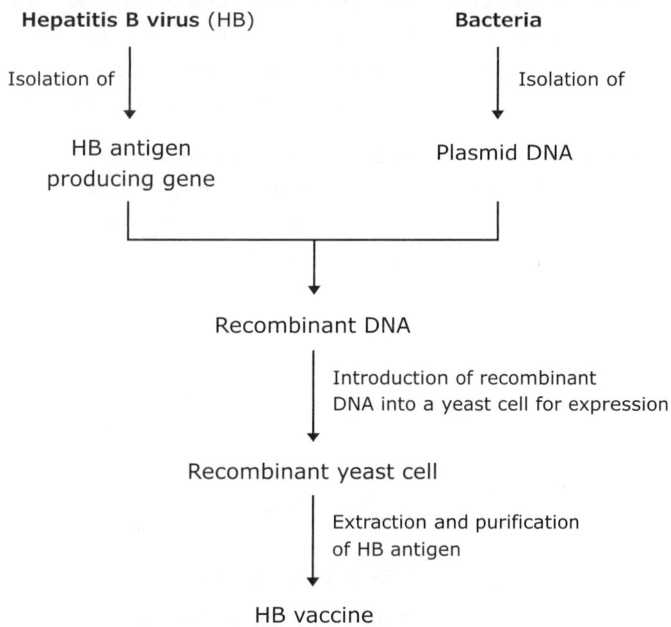

Figure 5.62 Schematic representation of the development of a recombinant antigen vaccine.

Nucleic acid-based vaccines

Nucleic acid-based vaccines use nucleic acids from disease-causing organisms to stimulate an immune response. These vaccines are engineered with either DNA or RNA that encodes the pathogen's antigenic proteins. Once inside the host cells, the genetic material utilizes the host's transcriptional and translational machinery to produce pathogen-specific antigens. The immune system recognizes these antigens as foreign and mounts a response, which includes both humoral and cellular immune responses.

DNA vaccines deliver DNA that encodes the pathogen's antigenic proteins. Once inside the cell, the DNA is transcribed into mRNA, which then instructs the cell to produce the antigen, prompting the immune system to respond. DNA vaccines utilize either a *plasmid vector-based* approach or a *viral vector-based* approach. In the plasmid vector-based approach, the sequence encoding the antigen(s) is inserted into a plasmid, which is then delivered directly to the appropriate tissue. In the viral vector-based approach, the sequence encoding the antigen(s) is delivered using a second virus as a vector.

RNA vaccines use mRNA to instruct host cells to produce the pathogen's antigenic proteins. The immune system recognizes these proteins as foreign and mounts a response against them. Unlike DNA vaccines, which introduce a DNA sequence encoding the antigen, RNA vaccines use mRNA transcribed from the DNA sequence. This mRNA is synthesized in vitro and delivered to cells via lipid nanoparticles. Once inside the host cells, the mRNA is recognized by ribosomes and translated into functional proteins.

Recombinant vector vaccines

In recombinant vector vaccines, genes that encode antigens isolated from a pathogen can be inserted into nonvirulent viruses or bacteria. Such recombinant microorganisms serve as vectors, replicating within the host and expressing the gene product of the pathogen-encoded antigenic proteins. A number of organisms have been used for vector vaccines, including vaccinia virus, the canary pox virus, attenuated poliovirus, adenoviruses and others. The antigens elicit humoral immunity as well as cellular immunity.

Table 5.14 Comparison of Recombinant vector vaccines, Nucleic acid vaccines and Recombinant subunit vaccines

Feature	Recombinant vector vaccine	Nucleic acid vaccine	Recombinant subunit vaccine
Definition	Uses a harmless virus or bacterium as a vector to deliver genes encoding an antigen into the body.	Uses DNA or mRNA that encodes the antigen, which is delivered into host cells, where it is expressed to produce the antigen.	Uses purified antigenic proteins (produced via recombinant DNA technology) directly as the vaccine.
Mechanism	Vector enters host cells, expresses the antigen, and triggers an immune response.	Nucleic acid enters host cells, directs antigen production via host machinery, and triggers an immune response.	Antigen is injected directly, allowing the immune system to recognize it and initiate a response.
Immune response	Strong cellular and humoral immunity.	Good cellular and humoral immunity.	Mainly humoral immunity; weaker cellular response.

Table 5.15 Vaccines for infectious diseases in humans

Type of vaccine	Disease
Bacterial diseases	
Live-attenuated whole organism vaccine:	BCG (Bacillus Calmette-Guérin)
Killed (inactivated) whole organism vaccine:	Pertussis, Typhoid, Paratyphoid, Typhus, Cholera and Plague
Subunit (or purified antigen) vaccine:	Pertussis, Typhoid, Meningococcal, Pneumococcal, Anthrax Diphtheria and Tetanus
Viral diseases	
Live-attenuated whole organism vaccine:	Measles-Mumps-Rubella, Varicella (chickenpox) and Polio (Sabin)
Killed (inactivated) whole organism vaccine:	Polio (Salk), Influenza, Rabies, Rotavirus and Japanese encephalitis
Subunit (or purified antigen) vaccine:	Influenza, Hepatitis A and B
Nucleic acid vaccine:	SARS-CoV-2

Self Test

Q1. Identify the *wrong* statement about B cells.

a. They can present both exogenous and endogenous antigens.

b. They can present only antigens for which they have surface immunoglobulin.

c. They can present only protein antigen.

d. They can present both protein and non-protein antigens.

Q2. All of the following are *true* with respect to IgE molecules, *except*

P. they are the principal immunoglobulin class involved in allergic reactions.

Q. they are involved in mediating anti-parasitic immune responses.

R. they will cross the placenta and fix complement.

S. they can cause the release of histamine and other chemical mediators.

a. only R
b. P and Q
c. Q and R
d. R and S

Q3. Choose the *correct* combination of statements from the following for MHC II protein

P. has α_1, α_2, β_1 and β_2 domains.

Q. α_1 and β_1 are the polymorphic domains.

R. involved in presenting antigen to cytotoxic T cells.

S. only α-chain is glycosylated.

a. Q and R
b. R and S
c. P and S
d. P and Q

Q4. For class I MHC, which of the following statements are *correct*?

P. They are expressed on all nucleated cells.

Q. They are made up of a heavy chain and a light chain.

R. They are essential for viral antigen recognition by cytotoxic cells.

S. The genes for HLA class I molecules are located on chromosome 6 and 15.

a. P and R
b. P and Q
c. Q and R
d. P, R and S

Q5. A potentially valuable therapeutic approach for killing tumor cells without affecting normal cells is the use of immunotoxins. Immunotoxins constitute monoclonal antibodies (mAb) against tumor cells conjugated to lethal toxins. Which of the following molecular approaches do you think is *not* appropriate for generating tumor cell-specific immunotoxin that will not kill normal cells?

a. Cell surface receptor binding polypeptide chain of toxin molecule should be replaced by mAb against a particular tumor cell type.

b. Constant region Fc domain of tumor cell specific mAb should be replaced by ligation of toxins.

c. Variable region $F(ab)_2$ domain of tumor cell-specific mAb should be replaced by ligation of toxins.

d. Inhibitor polypeptide chain of toxin should be conjugated to $F(ab)_2$ domain of tumor cell specific mAb.

Q6. Which of the following statements are *correct*?

P. In pro-B cells D segment is joined with a J_H segment.

Q. In pre-B cells rearranged V_H-D-J_H segment is present.

R. Heavy chain is also rearranged and transcribed in pre-B cell.

S. Immature B cell expresses antibody IgM exclusively.

a. P and S
b. Q and S
c. P, Q and R
d. P, Q and S

Q7. An ELISA designed to test for the presence of serum antibody for a new strain of pathogenic bacteria is under development. Initially, a monoclonal antibody specific for a single epitope of the organism was used both to sensitize the wells of the ELISA plate and as the enzyme-labeled detecting antibody in a conventional sandwich ELISA. The ELISA failed to detect the antigen despite the use of a wide range of antibody concentrations. What is the most probable cause of this problem?

a. The antigen is too large.

b. The antibody has a low affinity for the antigen.

c. The monoclonal antibody used to sensitize the wells is blocking access of the epitope, thus when the same antibody is enzyme-labeled, it cannot bind to the antigen.

d. The enzyme-labeled antibody used should have been a different isotype than the sensitizing antibody.

Q8. Considering complement fixation in human, what is *correct*?

P. C5 convertase is formed from C5a and C5b.

Q. C5 convertase is formed from C3b and C3 convertase.

R. C3a and C3b are formed by C5 convertase.

S. The membrane attack complex consists of C5b, C6, C7, C8 and C9.

a. P and R b. Q and S

c. Q, R and S d. R and S

Q9. A human volunteer agrees to be passively sensitized with IgE specific for a ragweed antigen (allergen). When challenged with the allergen intradermally, he displayed a typical skin reaction due to an immediate hypersensitivity reaction. If the injection with sensitizing IgE was preceded by an injection (at the same site) of Fc fragments of human IgE followed by intradermal injection with allergen, which of the following outcomes would you predict?

a. No reaction would occur because the Fc fragments would interact with the allergen and prevent it from gaining access to the sensitized mast cells.

b. No reaction would occur because the Fc fragments would interact with the IgE antibodies making their antigen-binding sites unavailable for binding to antigen.

c. No reaction would occur because the Fc fragments would interact with Fc receptors on mast cells.

d. The reaction would be exacerbated due to the increased local concentration of IgE Fc fragments.

Q10. Which of the following statements are *correct*?

P. Macrophages have the ability to process and present antigens to T cells.

Q. T-helper cells help in the generation of cytotoxic T cells.

R. Serum IgM cannot activate the complement by itself because it is planar in which complement binding sites in the Fc region are not accessible.

S. Somatic mutation of immunoglobulin genes accounts for affinity maturation.

a. P and Q b. R and S

c. P, R and S d. P, Q, R and S

Q11. Choose the *correct* match

Group I	Group II
P. IgA	1. Basophils
Q. IgE	2. δ heavy chain
R. IgG	3. Secretory component
S. IgM	4. Pentamer
	5. Crosses placenta

a. P-3, Q-1, R-5, S-4 b. P-3, Q-5, R-2, S-1

c. P-2, Q-3, R-5, S-4 d. P-2, Q-1, R-3, S-5

Q12. Which of the following is *correct* regarding cellular immunity?

a. T cells that bind too strongly or too weakly to self-MHC molecules in the thymus are deleted by apoptosis.

b. $CD4^+$ helper T cells recognized antigen bound to MHC class I molecules.

c. Full activation of T cells requires a costimulatory signal via the B7 protein on the T cell surface.

d. The T_H2 subset of helper T cells activates macrophages via the cytokine interferon-γ.

Q13. Mouse IgG is left either intact (left lane in A, B, C and D) or digested with papain or pepsin or treated with β-mercapto ethanol (β-ME) and run on non-reducing SDS-PAGE and stained with Coomassie blue. In a separate experiment, papain-digested products are immunoblotted with an anti-idiotypic monoclonal antibody. Following four profiles are attributed to each of these treatments.

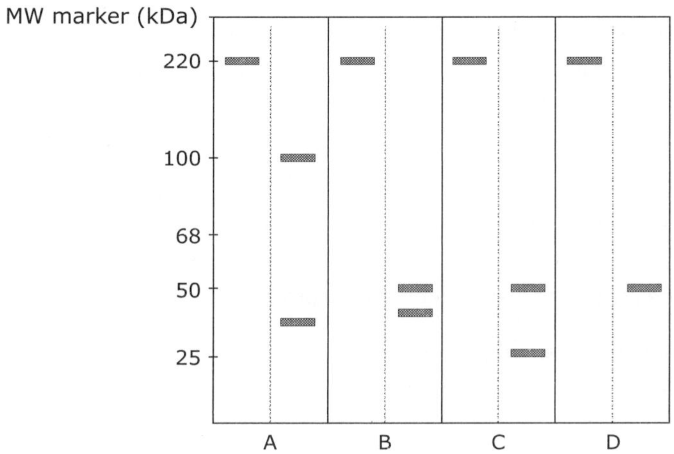

Which one of the following possibilities is *correct*?

a. A (pepsin), B (papain), C (β-ME), D (papain, followed by anti-idiotype immunoblot).

b. A (papain), B (pepsin), C (papain, followed by anti-idiotype immunoblot), D (β-ME).

c. A (papain, followed by anti-idiotype immunoblot), B (papain), C (pepsin), D (β-ME).

d. A (β-ME), B (papain), C (pepsin), D (papain, followed by anti-idiotype immunoblot).

Q14. What are *correct* steps in allergic reactions?

a. First allergen exposure → IgE production → mast cell activation → primary and secondary mediator released.

b. First allergen exposure → IgE production → second exposure to *any* allergen → IgE dimerization on mast cells → protein kinase C activation → primary and secondary mediator released.

c. First allergen exposure → IgE production → second exposure to *same* allergen → IgE dimerization on mast cells → protein kinase C activation → primary and secondary mediator released.

d. First allergen exposure → IgG and IgM production → second exposure to same allergen → IgE dimerization on mast cells → protein kinase C activation → primary and secondary mediator released.

Q15. A line of tumor cells prepared from one mouse is injected into an MHC-matched recipient. The tumor was destroyed within 5 days. When tissues from the recipient were analyzed, the animal had a negligible cytotoxic T-lymphocyte (CTL) response against the tumor. Flow cytometry revealed that the tumor cells expressed very low levels of class I MHC molecules. The *best* explanation for the destruction of the tumor cells in the recipient is that:

a. CTL had an MHC-induced alloreaction against the tumor cells.

b. CTL specific for the tumor antigens killed the tumor cells.

c. mast cells released histamine and other inflammatory mediators that clear the tumor.

d. natural killer cells recognized the absence of class I MHC molecules and killed the tumor cells.

Q16. A transgenic mouse was generated for both heavy and light chain specific for MHC molecule H-2K^m so that all the B cells in this mouse therefore had BCRs specific only for H-2K^m and made only anti- H-2K^m specific antibodies. By appropriate breeding, the H-2K^m specific immunoglobulin transgene was introduced into mice bearing different MHC genotypes H-2K^n and H-2K$^{m/n}$. With respect to selection of B cells within the bone marrow of H-2K^n and H-2K$^{m/n}$ mice, which of the following statements is *correct*?

a. In H-2K^n mice, the transgenic antibodies will not be detected on the surface of any of the B cells.
b. In H-2K$^{m/n}$ mice, the transgenic antibodies will not be detected on the surface of any of the B cells.
c. In H-2K^n mice, the transgenic antibodies will be detected on the surface of some of the B cells but not released in the serum.
d. In H-2K$^{m/n}$ mice, the transgenic antibodies will be detected on the surface of some of the B-cells.

Q17. Which one of the following statements regarding clonal selection hypothesis is *not* correct?

a. Mature B lymphocytes bear Ig receptors on their cell surface and all receptors on a single B-cell have variable specificity for antigen.
b. On antigen stimulation, B-cell matures, migrates to lymphoid organs and replicates. Its clonal descendents bear the same receptor as parental B-cell and secrete antibodies with identical specificity.
c. After immune response, more B-cells bearing receptors will remain in the host and act as memory cells for mounting enhanced secondary response.
d. B-cells with receptors for self antigens are deleted during embryonic development.

Q18. Which one of the following is *not* true for alternative pathway of complement activation?

a. Alternative pathway uses the same membrane-attack complex as the classical pathway.
b. Alternative pathway does not require antigen-antibody interactions.
c. Alternative pathway produces C3 by the same route as the classical pathway.
d. Certain microbial surfaces have physico-chemical properties that may result in activation of alternative pathway.

Q19. Major histocompatibility complex (MHC) molecules are encoded by a cluster of genes called MHC locus. There are several reasons why an MHC molecule on the surface of a cell is important. Which one of the following reasons is *incorrect*?

a. To display self class I to demonstrate that the cell is normal and healthy.
b. To display foreign-peptide in class I to show that the cell is infected and to engage with T helper cells.
c. To display a self-peptide in class I and II to test developing T cells for autoreactivity.
d. To display a self-peptide in class I and II to maintain tolerance to self-proteins.

Q20. Which of the following statements regarding B-cell receptor (BCR) and T-cell receptor (TCR) is *not* true?

a. TCR is membrane bound and does not appear as soluble form as does the BCR.
b. Unlike BCR, most of the TCR are not specific for antigen alone but for antigen combined with MHC.
c. In order to activate signal transduction, BCR associates itself with Ig-α/Ig-β whereas TCR associates with CD3.
d. The antigen binding interactions of BCR is much weaker than TCR.

ANSWER KEY

01. d	02. a	03. d	04. d	05. c	06. d	07. c	08. b	09. c	10. d
11. a	12. a	13. a	14. c	15. b	16. d	17. a	18. c	19. b	20. d

6

Diversity of Life

SUBJECT FOCUS

- **6.1 Taxonomy**
- **6.2 Five-kingdom system**
- **6.3 Protists**
- **6.4 Fungi**
- **6.5 Plantae**
- **6.6 Animalia**
- **6.7 Animal's classification**

Diversity of life can be summarized as 'variety of life on Earth.' The living world is enormously diverse. The total number of species on the Earth described so far is about 1.2 million. There are many more species that have not yet been described. Scientists are still discovering new species. Thus, we do not know for sure how many species really exist today. Current estimates of the total number of species range from 8 million to 10 million. The known species are unevenly distributed across taxonomic groups. More than 70 percent of all the species recorded are animals, while plants (including algae and fungi) comprise no more than 22 percent of the total. The variety of life on Earth plays a critical role in regulating the Earth's physical, chemical, and geological properties, from influencing the chemical and physical composition of the environment. To understand the diversity of life, it is important to organize the different kinds of organisms. Here the role of taxonomy comes which classify organisms in a way so that we can understand them better.

6.1 Taxonomy

In order to study the diversity of organisms, biologists have evolved certain rules and principles for identifying, describing, naming, and classifying organisms. The branch of science dealing with these aspects is referred to as **taxonomy** (*arrangement by the rules*). Taxonomy is often used as a synonym for **systematics**. Taxonomy can be considered as a branch of systematics. The main difference between taxonomy and systematics is that *taxonomy* is involved in the description, identification, nomenclature, and classification of organisms. In contrast, *systematics* is, in principle, broader, covering all aspects of relationships among organisms.

Levels of taxonomy: The discipline of taxonomy traditionally covers three areas: alpha, beta and gamma taxonomy. **Alpha taxonomy** is concerned with finding, describing, and naming species. **Beta taxonomy** includes the identification of natural groups and biological classes. **Gamma taxonomy** includes the study of evolutionary processes and patterns.

Organisms were first classified more than 2,000 years ago by Greek philosopher *Aristotle*. He classified organisms as either plant or animal. Modern biological classification began with the eighteenth-century Swedish naturalist *C. Linnaeus*. He established a simple system for classifying and naming organisms. He developed a hierarchy (a ranking system) for classifying organisms that is the basis for modern taxonomy.

6.1.1 Nomenclature

Nomenclature is the formal naming of a particular organism according to some standardized system. The fundamental principle of nomenclature is that each organism must have only one scientific name. In contrast to scientific names, many organisms also bear *common names* (also called *vernacular names*), which are generally used by people within a limited geographic region. Presently, the criteria for scientific naming of plants, algae and fungi are based on the rules and recommendations of the International Code of Nomenclature or ICN. It was formerly called the International Code of Botanical Nomenclature (**ICBN**); the name was changed at the International Botanical Congress in July 2011. Similarly, International Code of Zoological Nomenclature (**ICZN**) provides rules for naming animals. The scientific names of species are **binomials** (literally meaning two names). Swedish botanist Linnaeus (referred to as the *father of taxonomy*) first proposed the system of **binomial nomenclature** (or *binary nomenclature*). According to binomial nomenclature, the first name of the binomial is the **genus name** (**generic name**). The second name of the binomial is the **specific epithet** or **species epithet** (*specific name* - a term used only in zoology). The first word denoting the genus starts with a capital letter, while the specific epithet starts with a small letter. Binomial names are always either italicized or underlined to indicate their Latin origin.

Let us take the example of **mango** to understand the representation of scientific names. The scientific name of mango is written as *Mangifera indica*. In this name, *Mangifera* represents the genus while *indica* is a specific epithet. The first word *Mangifera* denoting the genus, starts with a capital letter, while the specific epithet *indica* starts with a small letter. Similarly, the scientific name for **human** is written as *Homo sapiens* (meaning 'wise man'). A genus name should be spelled out in full the first time it is used and then maybe abbreviated to an initial letter. For example, *Mangifera indica* may be abbreviated to *M. indica*. A binomial name in which the name of the genus and that of the species are identical is called **tautonym** (example, *Rattus rattus*). Tautonymy is permissible in zoological nomenclature but explicitly prohibited in botanical nomenclature.

The scientific name of an organism also includes the name of the author (the person who first validly published the name). The name of the author appears after the specific epithet and is written in an abbreviated form, e.g., *Mangifera indica* Linn. It indicates that this species was first described by Linnaeus. Although authorship is part of a scientific name but in practice, the author is not typically mentioned as part of a scientific name.

Nomenclature types: The scientific names must be associated with a physical entity, known as a **nomenclatural type** or simply **type**. It serves as a reference specimen of an organism used in scientific naming (nomenclature) of that organism. Types are usually physical specimens that are kept in a museum or herbarium, but it may also be an illustration. The type serves the purpose of acting as a reference for the name upon which the name is based. There are different types of nomenclatural type:

Holotype: A single specimen designated by the original author as the definitive reference for a newly described species.

Paratypes: Additional specimens cited in the original description that help illustrate the variability within a species. Paratypes are not holotypes but provide supporting evidence.

Isotype: An isotype is a duplicate specimen of the holotype, collected at the same time by the same person from the same population.

Lectotype: A single specimen selected later from a set of syntypes to serve as the primary reference when no holotype was designated initially.

Neotype: A specimen chosen to replace a lost, destroyed, or missing holotype when no original material is available.

Syntype: When multiple specimens were used in the original description but no single holotype was designated, all specimens used are considered syntypes.

6.1.2 Classification

There are thousands of different forms of life on the Earth. Some forms of life are very similar to each other (a rat and a mouse), and some are very different (like a rat and an elephant). How can we make sense of all of the living things that exist on the Earth? The answer that biologists have come up with is to use a classification system – a scientific method of grouping all of life in an orderly and logical manner that makes it easier to study and understand. Classification is essential to the study of organisms and is also necessary to understand the pattern of evolution. *Biological classification* is the arrangement of taxa into some type of order. It is not a single-step process but involves a hierarchy of steps. Each step represents a **rank** (or taxonomic category) and is commonly termed a **taxon**. Taxa are the plural of the taxon, which is a Greek word meaning 'group.' It is referred to as a *unit of classification*. All taxonomic categories together constitute the **taxonomic hierarchy**.

Taxonomists have defined seven ranks – **kingdom**, **phylum** (or *division*), **class**, **order**, **family**, **genus** and **species**. Each rank contains organisms with similar characteristics. The *kingdom* is the largest unit of classification. It splits into smaller units called *phyla* (singular, *phylum*). Phyla split into *classes*, classes into *orders*, orders into *families*, families into *genera* (singular, *genus*) and genera into *species*. This taxonomic system is known as **Linnaean classification system**. The most fundamental level of classification is the species. As one progresses down the hierarchy, the number of organisms in each taxon decreases, and the similarities between them increases.

Seven taxonomic ranks	Taxa
Kingdom	Plantae
Phylum (Division)	Magnoliophyta
Class	Liliopsida
Order	Arecales
Family	Arecaceae
Genus	*Cocos*
Species	*Cocos nucifera*

In the above example, *Magnoliophyta* is a taxon placed at the rank of division; Liliopsida is a taxon placed at the rank of class. As one progresses down the hierarchy, the number of organisms in each taxon decreases, and the similarities between them increase. Except for genus and species, the names must have suffix– to indicate the level of classification. In case of plants, Division names end in – *phyta*, Class names end in – *opsida*, Order names in – ales and Family names in – *aceae*. Genera and species names do not have standard ending. For animals, there are standard suffixes for taxa only up to the rank of family. In the Linnaean system, categories higher than the genus are not italicized.

As mentioned above seven ranks of the taxonomic hierarchy are known as the **obligatory ranks**. If finer degrees of classification is required, the obligatory ranks can be subdivided. For example, **subfamily** can be inserted below the rank of family, and the rank **tribe** can be inserted below subfamily.

6.1.3 Biological species concept

Biologists almost universally agree that the species is a fundamental natural unit. However, biologists have not been able to agree on exactly how species should be defined. Taxonomists practically define species by means of morphological or phenetic characters. If one group of organisms consistently differs from other organisms, it will be defined as a separate species. However, the most widely accepted species concept is the *biological species concept*. It defines species in terms of interbreeding. According to Ernst Mayr, *species are groups of interbreeding natural populations that are reproductively isolated from other such groups*. Reproductively isolated means that members of the species do not interbreed with members of other species. The biological species concept explains why the members of a species resemble one another and differ from other species. When two organisms breed within a species, their genes pass into their offspring. As this process is repeated, the genes of different organisms are constantly shuffled around the species gene pool. The shared gene pool gives the species its identity. By contrast, genes are not (by definition) transferred to other species, and different species, therefore, take on a different appearance. If two species are very similar to each other morphologically, so much so that it is difficult to distinguish but are nevertheless reproductively isolated are termed as **sibling species** (sometimes called **cryptic species**).

Subspecies

Subspecies is a taxonomic subdivision of a species often distinguished by special phenotypic characters and by its origin or localization in a given geographical region. Members of a subspecies would share a unique, geographic locale, a set of phylogenetically concordant phenotypic characters, and a unique natural history relative to other subdivisions of the species. Although subspecies are not reproductively isolated, they will normally be allopatric and exhibit recognizable phylogenetic partitioning. The terms **race** and **subspecies** are potentially misleading and are most often used synonymously. Although the term race is normally used in case of human populations. However, when a distinction is made, 'race' generally implies a lower level of differentiation. A species which consists of a single uniform population, devoid of differentiated and semi-isolated local populations (subspecies) is **monotypic** (i.e., all one basic kind). A species is **polytypic** if it is subdivided into two or more subspecies.

6.1.4 Phenetics and cladistics approaches of classification

In biology, two main methods are used to classify organisms into groups: the *phenetic*s and *cladistics*.

Phenetics

Phenetic means 'as observed in the phenotype'. Phenetics, also known as *taximetrics*, is an attempt to classify organisms based on overall similarity, usually in morphology or other observable traits, regardless of their phylogeny or evolutionary relationship. Phenetic characters refer to all the observable or measurable characters of an organism. Nothing needs to be known about evolution in order for species to be classified phenetically. Phenetic classification schemes do not distinguish between homologous characters and analogous characters. The result of phenetic relationship is often summarized with a tree-like network called a **phenogram**. Phenogram is a type of dendrogram which is based on phenetic data. Lines called *phenon lines*, drawn at right angles to the dichotomously branching dendrogram, represent lines of percentage similarity of phenetic features between organisms.

A common misconception equates phenetics with **numerical taxonomy**, but in fact most phenetic taxonomy is not numerically based. Numerical taxonomy is a classification system which developed as a part of multivariate analysis. It aims to create a taxonomy using numeric algorithms like cluster analysis rather than using subjective evaluation of their characters. The terms *phenetics*, *numerical phenetics* and *numerical taxonomy* are used almost interchangeably in modern biology.

Determination of phenetic relationship

The following operations are involved in determining phenetic relationship:

1. Selection of OTUs (operational taxonomic units) for study.
2. Selection of characters (or traits).
3. Description and comparison of character states.
5. Determine the degree of similarity (**similarity coefficient**) for each pair of OTU's
6. Constructing similarity matrix
7. Clustering and development of phenogram

'Character' refers to any heritable trait possessed by an organism. Characters are usually described in terms of their *states*, for example: 'hair present' versus 'hair absent,' where 'hair' is the character, and 'present' and 'absent' are its states. The simplest and most common type of character used by taxonomist is one that can occur as one of only two states and designated as 1 and 0. '1' might indicate the presence of a character, and '0' its absence or '1' and '0' may represent two alternative forms of a character, such as 'red' and 'white'.

Example: Let us consider six OTUs S, T, W, X, Y and Z, to determine the phenetic relationship. To provide a good indication of phenetic relationships, as many different unit characters as possible should be used, but in this example, only ten characters have been taken for simplicity. Here only characters with two states are used (e.g., red versus white flower, tall versus dwarf plant) and these are given arbitrarily numerical values of 0 for one state and 1 for another. The character states are compared from one OTU to the next.

	Character									
OTU	1	2	3	4	5	6	7	8	9	10
S	0	0	0	0	0	0	0	0	1	1
T	0	0	0	1	0	0	1	0	1	1
W	0	1	0	1	0	1	1	0	1	0
X	0	1	0	0	0	1	0	0	1	0
Y	0	1	1	0	1	0	0	1	0	0
Z	0	1	1	0	1	1	0	1	0	0

After developing a character matrix, we determine the degree of similarity (**similarity coefficient**) for each pair of OTU's. Several methods exist for determining the similarity coefficient between OTUs. One of the simplest methods is the **simple matching coefficient**. This is calculated by counting the number of character states for each character which is common between two OTUs and then dividing this number by the total number of characters used.

For example, the simple matching coefficient between S and T $= \dfrac{\text{Character states in common}}{\text{Total number of the characters}} = \dfrac{8}{10} = 0.8.$

Such calculations are done between all pairs of OTUs. The simple matching coefficients are then arranged to form a **similarity matrix**. The higher the simple matching coefficient, the more closely related are the OTUs.

	S	T	W	X	Y	Z
S	1.0					
T	0.8	1.0				
W	0.5	0.7	1.0			
X	0.7	0.5	0.8	1.0		
Y	0.4	0.2	0.3	0.5	1.0	
Z	0.3	0.1	0.4	0.6	0.9	1.0

Based on data of similarity matrix, **clustering** of OTUs is performed and a **phenogram** is constructed. The clustering based on the similarity of OTUs is performed by agglomerative methods. UPGMA is one of the agglomerative clustering methods (also used in this example). In the following phenogram, the vertical lines describing groups or clusters of OTUs having similar simple matching coefficients. Here S and T as well as W and X are linked at the 0.8 level and Y and Z are linked at 0.9 level. The level at which S-T and W-X are connected is based on an average value of the pairs S to W, S to X, T to W and T to X:

$$\frac{(\text{S to W}) + (\text{S to X}) + (\text{T to W}) + (\text{T to X})}{4} = \frac{0.5 + 0.7 + 0.7 + 0.5}{4} = \frac{2.4}{4} = 0.6$$

The relationship of Y-Z to the S-T-W-X cluster is assessed in a similar way and found to be 0.35.

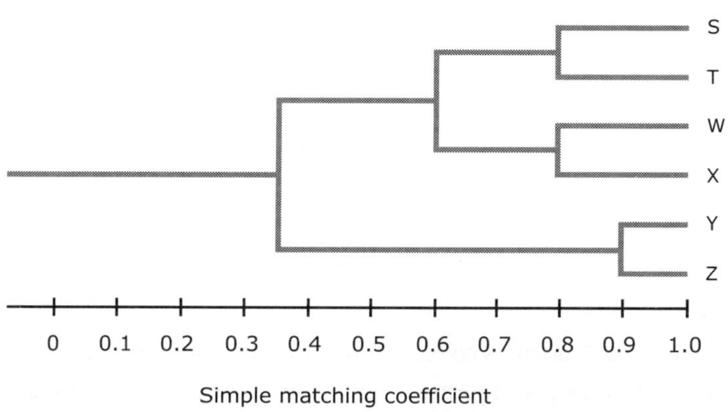

Figure 6.1
Phenogram based on simple matching coefficient. Higher the value, the more closely related are the OTUs.

Box 6.1 Measurement of similarity for binary characters

The simplest and most common type of character used by taxonomist is one that can occur as one of only two states and designated as 1 and 0. '1' might indicate the presence of a feature, and '0' its absence or '1' and '0' may represent two alternative forms of a character, such as 'red' and 'white.'

		A	
		0	1
B	0	M_{00}	M_{10}
	1	M_{01}	M_{11}

Given below are two OTUs A and B, each with n binary characters (also called *two-state characters*). The character states are compared from one OTU to the next.

M_{11} represents the total number of characters positive for both A and B.

M_{01} represents the total number of characters that are negative for A and positive for B

M_{10} represents the total number of characters that are positive for A and negative for B.

M_{00} represents the total number of characters negative for both A and B.

Many similarity coefficients have been proposed for binary data of this kind but two have been commonly used in taxonomy – simple matching coefficient and Jaccard's coefficients.

Simple matching coefficient

It is the ratio of the total number of character states for each character which are common between two OTUs to the total number of characters.

$$\text{Simple matching coefficient (SMC)} = \frac{M_{00} + M_{11}}{M_{00} + M_{01} + M_{10} + M_{11}}$$

Jaccard's coefficient (or Jaccard similarity coefficient or Jaccard index)

It is the ratio of the number of positive matches to the total number of characters minus the number of negative matches.

$$\text{Jaccard's coefficient} = \frac{M_{11}}{M_{01} + M_{10} + M_{11}}$$

When used for binary characters, the Jaccard coefficient is very similar to the simple matching coefficient. The main difference is that the *simple matching coefficient* has the term M_{00} in its numerator and denominator, whereas the *Jaccard coefficient* does not. Thus, the simple matching coefficient compares the number of matches with the entire set of the possible attributes, whereas the Jaccard coefficient only compares it to the attributes that have been chosen by at least A or B.

Cladistics

The central idea of biological evolution is that all life on Earth shares a common ancestor. Through the process of evolutionary change, the common ancestor of life gave rise to the diverse life forms. Hence, many biologists feel that classification should be based on phylogeny. The evolutionary relationship of organisms is referred to as **phylogeny**. The phylogenetic principle classifies species based on their most recent common ancestor. Species that share a more recent common ancestor are considered more closely related than species that share a more distant common ancestor.

Cladistics approach of phylogenetic classification of organisms is based on the idea that members of a group share a common evolutionary history are more closely related. These members are recognized by the presence of derived characters which were not present in distant ancestors and organisms are categorized in groups based on shared derived characters. The outcome of a cladistic analysis is a tree-shaped diagram termed a **cladogram**. This is the most widely used method of classifying organisms today.

Synapomorphies are the basis for cladistics: In cladistics, biologists collect data about the characters of each organism they are interested in. They use *shared derived characters* (synapomorphies) to identify monophyletic group. Now, first understand what is the meaning of shared derived characters. 'Character' refers to any heritable trait possessed by an organism. Biologists distinguish two different types of characters: **homoplasy** and **homology** (homologous character). To understand *homoplasy*, consider the wings of butterflies and birds. These structures look similar and serve the same function, but they are not anatomically alike. This functional similarity arises from **convergent evolution**, where different species develop similar traits independently to serve similar functions. Homoplasies are essentially **analogous structures** that exhibit similarity in function but differ in origin and structure. They are shared between species that did not inherit them from a common ancestor. These characters are not indicators of phylogenetic relationships.

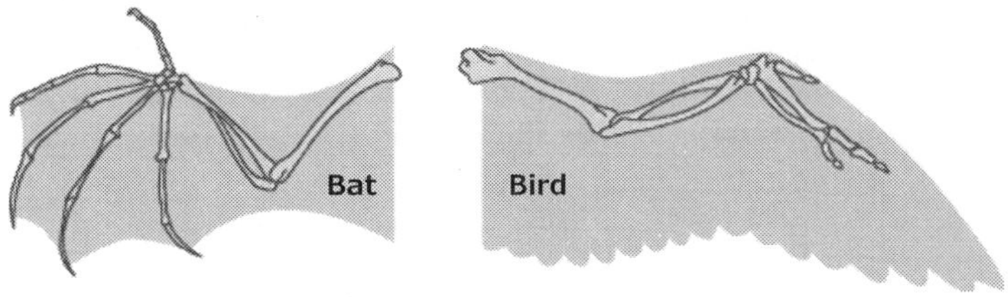

In contrast, to understand **homology** or **homologous structures**, consider the forelimbs of whales, bats, cheetahs, and humans—all of which are mammals. Despite their different lifestyles and adaptations, these species have similar anatomical structures in their forelimbs. This similarity in anatomy strongly suggests that these structures were inherited from a common ancestor. Over time, the same basic structure evolved in different directions due to adaptations to different environments and needs. Homologous structures share a common evolutionary origin but have adapted to serve different functions in different organisms, as a result of **divergent evolution**.

Homologous characters in turn are divided into *shared ancestral* (*primitive*) *characters* and *shared derived* (*advance*) *characters*. A **shared ancestral character** (or **symplesiomorphy**) is shared with the species ancestral to more than one clade or group. A **shared derived character** (or **synapomorphy**) is a character that is shared by two or more taxa and their most recent common ancestor, whose ancestor in turn does not possess the trait.

Clades and characters used to define groups in phenetics and cladistics classification

Classification	Monophyletic	Paraphyletic	Polyphyletic	Homoplasy	Symplesiomorphy	Synapomorphy
Phenetics	Yes	Yes	Yes	Yes	Yes	Yes
Cladistics	Yes	No	No	No	No	Yes

Box 6.2 **Plesiomorphy and apomorphy**

Plesiomorphy refers to a *primitive* or *ancestral* character, i.e., a character that is present from those of the ancestors and a primitive character shared by two or more taxa is called **symplesiomorphy** (shared - ancestral - character). On the contrary, an **apomorphy** (or derived character) is one that evolved in the lineage leading up to a clade and those set members of that clade apart from ancestors. A derived character shared by two or more groups is termed as **synapomorphy** (shared - derived - character). An **autapomorphy** (a uniquely derived character) is a derived trait that is unique to one group or taxon.

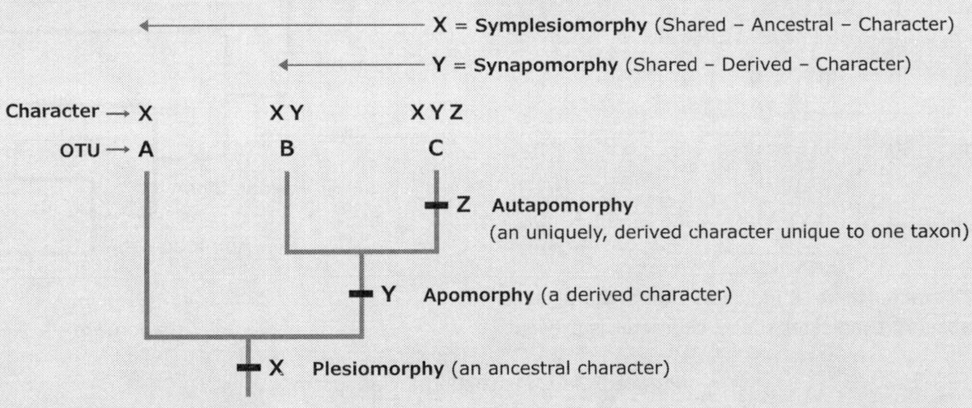

Synapomorphy can be used to group organisms into clades. Terms *synapomorphy* and *symplesiomorphy* are defined relative to a particular node on the cladogram. This means that a trait can be a synapomorphy or a symplesiomorphy if different nodes are considered.

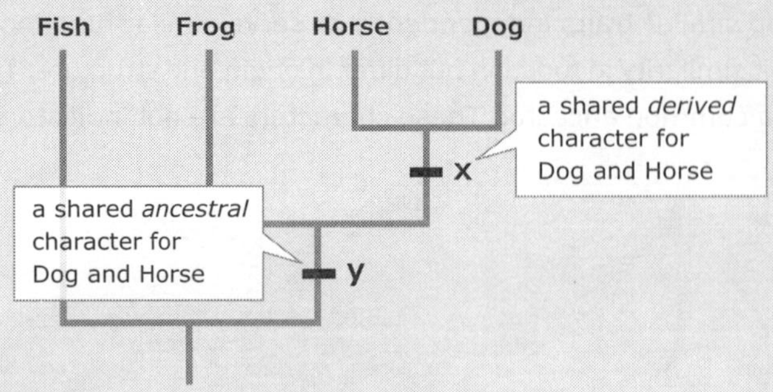

Figure 6.2 Shared ancestral and shared derived characters. **x** is a shared derived character and **y** is a shared ancestral character if we are studying the phylogeny of the dog and horse. But **y** is also a shared derived character if we are studying the phylogeny of the dog, horse and frog. The distinction between shared derived and shared ancestral character is relative to the group of species.

The basic idea behind cladistics is that members of a group sharing a common evolutionary history are recognized by sharing derived characters which were not present in distant ancestors. Hence, the first step in basic cladistic analysis is to determine which characters are *ancestral* and which are *derived*.

Let us understand this with the help of an example. Suppose in a group of vertebrates, one is mammal and rest are non-mammals. All mammals have backbones, but the presence of a backbone does not distinguish mammals from other vertebrates because all vertebrates have backbones. Thus, we say that for mammals, the backbone is a shared ancestral character. In contrast, hair is a character shared by all mammals but not found in their ancestors. Thus, in mammals, hair is considered a shared derived character, unique to a particular clade. Note that a backbone can also qualify as a shared derived character, but only at a node that distinguishes all vertebrates from other animals.

The **outgroup comparison** method is generally used to determine which characters are *ancestral* and which are *derived*. The **outgroup** is the most distantly related taxon in the cladogram which functions as a point of comparison. All the members of the group under study (**ingroup**) are more closely related to each other than they are to the outgroup, hence, the outgroup will branch off at the base of that phylogeny.

Characters ↓	Lancelet (*Outgroup*)	Lamprey	Tuna	Salamander	Turtle	Leopard
Vertebral column	0	1	1	1	1	1
Hinged jaws	0	0	1	1	1	1
Four walking legs	0	0	0	1	1	1
Amniotic egg	0	0	0	0	1	1
Hair	0	0	0	0	0	1

Character table. 0 indicates that a character is absent; 1 indicates that a character is present.

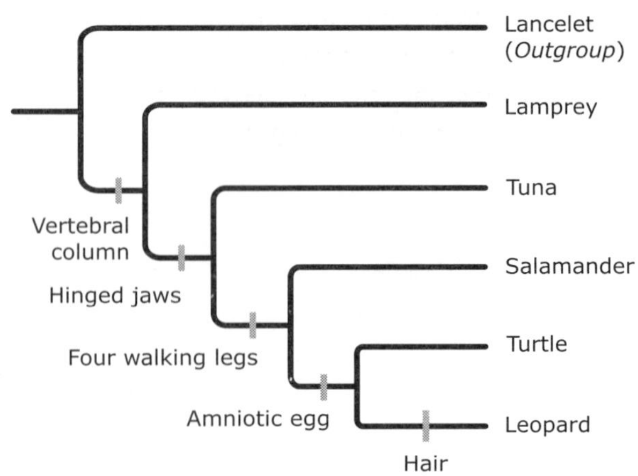

Cladogram

Figure 6.3 Constructing a cladogram.

The cladistic approach attempts to identify monophyletic groups. A group of organisms containing a single common ancestor and *all* its descendants is termed **monophyletic** (sometimes called a *clade*). Clades can be hierarchically nested within one another. The converse of monophyly is paraphyly. A group of organisms is said to be **paraphyletic** if a monophyletic group does not include all the descendants of a common ancestor. Similarly, if the group includes some or all of the descendants but not the common ancestor, it is called **polyphyletic**. The paraphyletic group contains the ancestor, whereas the polyphyletic group does not.

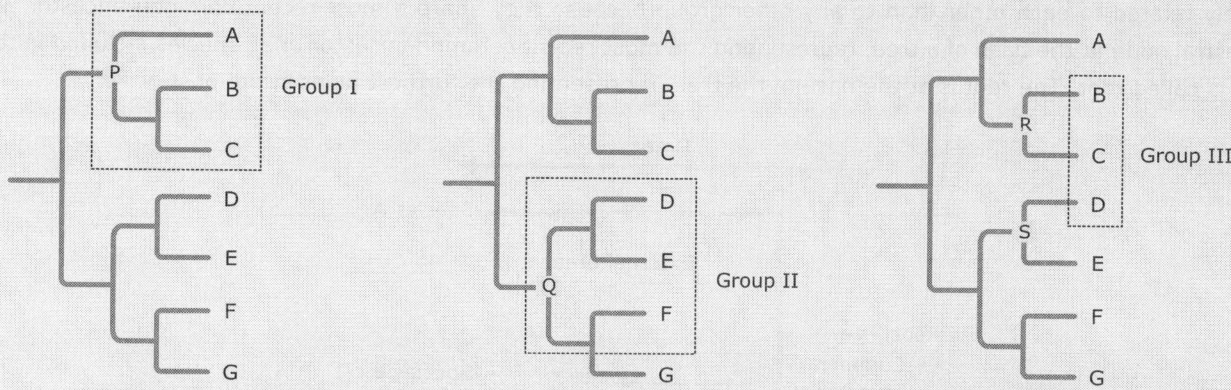

Monophyletic
Group I consisting of three species (A, B, C) and their common ancestor P, is a monophyletic group.

Paraphyletic
Group II is paraphyletic, meaning that it consists of an ancestral species Q and some of its descendants (species D, E, F) but not all of them (missing species G).

Polyphyletic
Group III is polyphyletic, meaning that its members have different ancestors. In this case, species B and C share common ancestor R but species D has a different ancestor S.

Figure 6.4 Concept of monophyletic, paraphyletic and polyphyletic. Monophyletic describes a group of organisms that form a clade (a single common ancestor and *all* its descendants). Paraphyletic describes a group of organisms that share a common ancestor but does not include all the descendants of a common ancestor. Polyphyletic describes the group includes some or all of the descendants, but not the common ancestor.

Shared derived homologies fall into monophyletic groups; shared ancestral homologies fall into both monophyletic and paraphyletic groups, and homoplasies fall into polyphyletic groups. Cladistic classifications only include monophyletic clade. It rejects *paraphyletic* and *polyphyletic* groups.

To see how this analysis is done, consider a set of characters for each of five vertebrates– a *leopard, turtle, salamander, tuna* and *lamprey*. As a basis of comparison, an outgroup is selected. An outgroup serves as a reference taxon when determining the evolutionary relationships of the ingroup (the group of taxa under study). Any trait that is present in both the ingroup and the outgroup must have evolved before the origin of the ingroup and thus must be ancestral for the ingroup. In contrast, traits that are present in only some members of the ingroup must be derived traits within that ingroup. **Lancelet** is thought to have separated from the lineage before the vertebral column arose. Therefore, we have included the lancelet as the **outgroup** for our analysis. Because derived traits are traits acquired by members after they diverged from the outgroup, any trait that is present in both the lancelet and the members of ingroup is judged to be ancestral. The species making up the ingroup display a mixture of shared ancestral and shared derived characters. The outgroup comparison enables us to focus on just those characters that were derived at the various branch points of vertebrate evolution. Note that all the vertebrates in the ingroup have backbones; this is a shared primitive character that was present in the ancestral vertebrate, though not in the outgroup.

Cladogram

A branching diagram (dendrogram) that is constructed by cladistic principle and method is called a *cladogram*, an estimate of a phylogeny. Any branching of the cladogram represents lineage divergence, the formation of two separate lineages from one common ancestor. Cladogram may be drawn with either right-angled or diagonal lines;

the information is identical. It is represented by *nodes* and *branches*. **Nodes** can be internal or external. Each **internal node** (a *branch point*) represents the last common ancestor of the two lineages. **External nodes** (also termed as *terminal nodes*) represent tip of the tree. The 'tips' of the tree branches represent the *taxa* in the study. These taxa may be called Operational Taxonomic Units (**OTUs**). The lines within the tree are called the **branches**. Branches can be internal or external. **Internal branches** (or *internodes*) connect two nodes, whereas **external branches** connect a tip and a node. The two taxa that split from the internal node are called **sister taxa**. The sister taxa must be more closely related to each other than to any other group because they share a most recent common ancestor. The ancestral node at the base of a tree, representing the most recent common ancestor of all species included in that tree is called **root**. The root is at the base of the tree, representing the furthest point in the past.

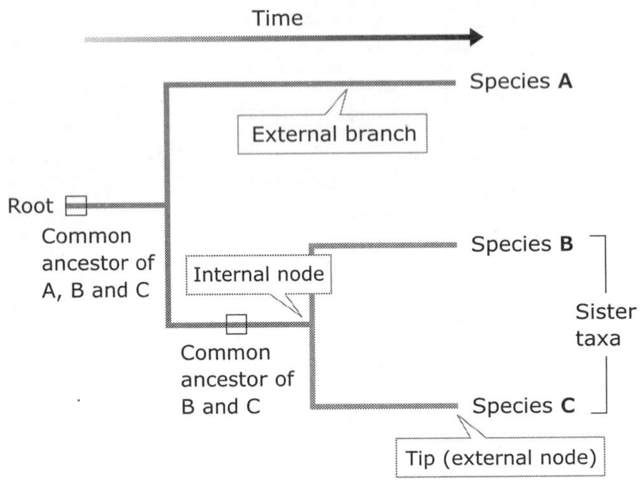

Figure 6.5 A generalized cladogram (horizontal and rectangular). The nodes represent divergences or speciation events. Root represents the most recent common ancestor of all species included in that tree.

The term *phylogram* is often used synonymously with a *cladogram*. However, phylogram and cladogram are not the same. A **phylogram** is a scaled branching diagram where the branch lengths are proportional to the amount of character changes between organisms. A **cladogram** is an unscaled branching diagram (tree) that illustrates patterns of relatedness where the branch lengths are not necessarily proportional to the amount of character changes between related organisms. In a branching tree, if branch lengths are proportional to time, it is called **chronogram**.

6.2 Five-kingdom system

In the early days of biology, all organisms were classified as either plants or animals. In year 1969, Robert H. Whittaker, an American taxonomist, described a five-kingdom classification. The five kingdoms are *Monera* (prokaryotes), *Protista*, *Fungi*, *Plantae* and *Animalia*. His classification is based on four main criteria – **cell type** (prokaryotic vs. eukaryotic), **level of cellular organization** (unicellular vs. multicellular), **mode of nutrition** (autotrophs vs. heterotrophs) and **mode of intake of nutrition** (absorption vs. ingestion). After Whittaker's original criteria, additional parameters were introduced to overcome the limitations of his scheme. These included cell wall composition, modes of reproduction, and molecular phylogeny

Monera : Prokaryotic cellular organization.

Protista : Unicellular eukaryotes.

Fungi : Multicellular eukaryotes which feed heterotrophically by absorption.

Plantae : Multicellular eukaryotes which are photoautotrophic.

Animalia : Multicellular eukaryotes which feed heterotrophically by ingestion.

Table 6.1 Characteristics of the five kingdoms

Kingdom	:	**Monera**
Cell type	:	Prokaryotic
Nuclear envelope	:	Absent
Cell wall	:	Non-cellulose
Mode of nutrition	:	Autotrophic (chemosynthetic or photosynthetic) or heterotrophic
Multicellularity	:	Absent
Genetic recombination (if present)	:	Conjugation, transduction and transformation
Kingdom	:	**Protista**
Cell type	:	Eukaryotic
Nuclear envelope	:	Present
Cell wall	:	Present in some forms, various types
Mode of nutrition	:	Autotrophic (Photosynthetic) or heterotrophic, or combination of these
Multicellularity	:	Absent in most forms
Genetic recombination (if present)	:	Fertilization and meiosis
Kingdom	:	**Fungi**
Cell type	:	Eukaryotic
Nuclear envelope	:	Present
Cell wall	:	Chitin and other noncellulose polysaccharides
Mode of nutrition	:	Heterotrophic
Multicellularity	:	Present in most forms
Genetic recombination (if present)	:	Fertilization and meiosis
Kingdom	:	**Plantae**
Cell type	:	Eukaryotic
Nuclear envelope	:	Present
Cell wall	:	Cellulose and other polysaccharides
Mode of nutrition	:	Autotrophic (Photosynthetic)
Multicellularity	:	Present in all forms
Genetic recombination (if present)	:	Fertilization and meiosis
Kingdom	:	**Animalia**
Cell type	:	Eukaryotic
Nuclear envelope	:	Present
Cell wall	:	Absent
Mode of nutrition	:	Heterotrophic
Multicellularity	:	Present in all forms
Genetic recombination (if present)	:	Fertilization and meiosis

Three domain system

The five-kingdom scheme divides living things into two fundamentally different groups – prokaryotes and eukaryotes. New data suggest that two kinds of prokaryotes diverged early in the history of life, and thus there are actually three major categories of organisms. A new classification system assigns more significance to the ancient split by creating a level of classification larger than a kingdom – a new category called a **domain**. The two domains of prokaryotes are Bacteria and Archaea. The domain Eukarya encompasses all of the kingdoms of eukaryotes. The *three-domain system* of biological classification was introduced by Carl Woese on the basis of differences in the signature sequences of 16S/18S rRNA genes of eubacteria, archaebacteria and eukaryotes.

6.3 Protists

The German zoologist Ernst Haeckel first used the term *protista*. Protists are mostly unicellular (some are colonial and multicellular) eukaryotic organisms. Most eukaryotes are single-celled organisms. Protists are difficult to characterize because of the great diversity of the kingdom. These organisms vary in body form, nutrition and reproduction. Protists are capable of sexual, as well as asexual reproduction. They can be free-living, or may live symbiotically with another organism. The symbiosis can be mutualistic, where both partners benefit, or parasitic, where the protist uses its host as a source of food or shelter while providing no advantage to the other organism. Protists are more nutritionally diverse than other eukaryote groups. Some protists are *autotrophs*. Some are *heterotrophs*, absorbing organic molecules or ingesting larger food particles. Still others, called **mixotrophs**, combine autotrophic and heterotrophic nutrition.

Despite the great diversity evident in this kingdom, scientists have been able to classify the protists into several groups. The protists can be classified into one of three main categories, animal-like, plant-like and fungus-like. Grouping into one of the three categories is based on an organism's mode of reproduction, method of nutrition and motility. The animal-like protists are known as the **protozoa**, the plant-like photosynthetic protists are the *algae*, and the fungus-like protists are the *slime molds* and *water molds*.

6.3.1 Protozoan protists

The protozoa are all unicellular heterotrophs, mostly free living. They obtain their nutrition by ingesting other organisms or dead organic materials. The word 'protozoa' comes from the *Latin* word for 'first animals'.

Features of protozoa:

- Unicellular (single celled) organisms.
- Aquatic, free-living or parasitic organisms.
- Nutrition is heterotrophic.
- Locomotion with the help of pseudopodia, cilia or flagella. The protozoans are grouped into various phyla based on their modes of locomotion. They may use cilia, flagella or pseudopodia. Some protozoans are non motile. The protozoans that use pseudopodia to move are known as **amoeboid protozoans**, those that use flagella are called **flagellated protozoans**, those that use cilia are known as the **ciliated protozoans** and those that do not move are called the **sporozoans**.
- Both asexual and sexual reproduction occur among the protozoa. One of the simplest and most common forms of asexual reproduction is *binary fission*, a mitotic process. Other forms of asexual reproduction are *budding* and *multiple fission* (or schizogony). In multiple fission, a large number of daughter cells form from the division of a single protozoan.

  Asexual reproduction is the simplest form of reproduction that does not involve meiosis, gamete formation, and fertilization (i.e., the fusion of gametes). Instead, it results in the multiplication of genetically identical individuals (clones). Sexual reproduction is a form of reproduction that involves meiosis, gamete formation, and fertilization.

Several species of protozoans infect humans and inhabit the body as commensals or parasites. Some species cause human diseases. These diseases are quite widespread, especially in the warmer climates. Many protists are transmitted to humans by arthropod vectors or in contaminated food or water. However, some protozoan diseases are transmitted by direct contact.

List of protozoan diseases in human

1. *Disease* : **Amoebiasis**
   Causative agent : *Entamoeba histolytica* (*sarcodina*)
   Transmission : Water, Food

2. *Disease* : **Giardiasis**
   Causative Agent : *Giardia lamblia*
   Transmission : Water, Contact

3. *Disease* : **Trichomoniasis**
   Causative agent : *Trichomonas vaginalis*
   Transmission : Sexual contact

4. *Disease* : **African Sleeping Sickness**
   Causative agent : *Trypanosoma brucei*
   Transmission : Tsetse fly (*Glossina*)

5. *Disease* : **American Sleeping Sickness**
   Causative agent : *T. cruzi* (Mastigophora)
   Transmission : Triatomid bug (Triatoma)

6. *Disease* : **Leishmaniasis** (Kala-azar or Black fever)
   Causative agent : *Leishmania donovani* (Mastigophora)
   Transmission : Sandfly (*Phlemotomus*)

7. *Disease* : **Balantidiasis**
   Causative agent : *Balantidium coli* (Ciliophora)
   Transmission : Food, Water

8. *Disease* : **Malaria**
   Causative agent : *Plasmodium Spp*. (Sporozoa)
   Transmission : Mosquito (*Anopheles*)

6.3.2 Photosynthetic protists

Photosynthetic protists (commonly termed as *algae*) constitute the majority of phytoplanktons. They account for about 70–80% of global photosynthesis. Examples of some important photosynthetic protists and their characteristic features are given below.

Dinoflagellates

Dinoflagellates (Phylum *Pyrrophyta*) are unicellular flagellated protists. They are found mainly in marine environments. Dinoflagellates are mostly biflagellate. Flagella have a characteristic arrangement in dinoflagellate: one long flagellum lies in a longitudinal groove with its distal end free and responsible for swimming. The other flagellum is flat and ribbon-like and lies completely within a transverse groove that encircles the cell. Flagella exhibit spinning type of locomotion hence are known as **whirling whips**. The beating of the flagella in their respective grooves causes the dinoflagellate to spin like a top as it moves.

About half of all dinoflagellates are photosynthetic and many of them are mixotrophic. Most photosynthetic dinoflagellates typically contain chlorophylls *a* and *c*. Many dinoflagellates lack a photosynthetic apparatus and hence heterotrophs.

Pigmented dinoflagellates occur as symbionts in many other kinds of organisms, including sponges, jellyfish, sea anemones, tunicates, corals, octopuses and squids, snails, and certain other protists. When they are symbionts, dinoflagellates lack armored plates and appear as golden spherical cells called **zooxanthellae**.

Reproduction in dinoflagellates is primarily asexual by longitudinal cell division, with each daughter cell receiving one of the flagella and a portion of the wall, or theca. Each daughter cell then reconstructs the missing parts in a very intricate sequence. Sexual reproduction present but is not common.

Diatoms

Diatoms (Phylum *Chrysophyta*) are the chief producers (autotrophs) in the oceans. They are found in both marine and freshwater environments. They contain a unique glass-like wall made of hydrated silica (silicon dioxide) embedded in an organic matrix. Cell wall is known as **frustule** which is divided into two halves (theca) namely *epitheca* and *hypotheca*.

There are two basic groups of diatoms – one with radial symmetry (the *centric diatoms*) and other with bilateral symmetry (the *pennate diatoms*). Diatoms contain photosynthetic pigments chlorophylls a and c and carotenoids, fucoxanthin. Diatoms energy reserves are stored as lipids and the water-soluble polysaccharide *chrysolaminarin* in vacuoles. Chrysolaminarin is similar to the laminarin found in brown algae. Although most species of diatoms are autotrophic, some are heterotrophic, absorbing dissolved organic carbon. They lack flagella, except on some male gametes.

Reproduction in diatoms is primarily asexual by *binary fission*. Each daughter cell receives half of the parental cell wall and generates a new half that fits inside it. This form of division results in a size reduction of the daughter cell that received the smaller frustule from the parent and therefore the average cell size of a diatom population decreases (a unique **shrinking division** mode of asexual reproduction). Sexual reproduction is uncommon.

Euglenoids

Euglenoids (Phylum *Euglenophyta*) are unicellular flagellated protists. They are found mainly in freshwater. They are devoid of cell wall. Instead of a cell wall, they have a protein rich layer under the plasma membrane called **pellicle** (also called a *periplast*) which makes their body flexible. Euglenoids are biflagellate. Both flagella are of unequal sizes (one short and other long one) and located at the cell's anterior end. About two-thirds of the genera are colorless heterotrophs. About one-third of the genera, including the common *Euglena*, contain chloroplasts and thus are photosynthetic. Photosynthetic euglenoids contain chlorophylls a and b as photosynthetic pigments. In contrast to the chloroplasts of green algae, euglenoid chloroplasts do not store starch. Instead, carbohydrate is stored as the glucose polymer, **paramylon** (β-1,2 glucan), in the cytosol.

Euglenoids are mainly mixotrophic. In sunlight, they are photoautotrophic, but when sunlight is unavailable, they can become heterotrophic, absorbing organic nutrients from their environment. Many other euglenoids engulf prey by phagocytosis. Reproduction in euglenoids is primarily asexual by longitudinal binary fission. Sexual reproduction is usually absent. *Euglena* is the representative example of euglenoids.

6.3.3 Slime mold

Slime molds are heterotrophic protists which exhibit characteristics of both fungi and protozoa. They resemble fungi in their production of spores and resemble protozoa in their ability to move (amoeboid movement) and ingestion and digestion of particulate foods. Slime molds can generally be divided into two main groups – *Plasmodial slime molds* (phylum Myxomycota) and *cellular slime molds* (phylum Dictyosteliomycota).

The **plasmodial slime mold** is basically a large non-cell walled, multinucleated single cell structure called **plasmodium**. Despite its size, the plasmodium is not multicellular; it is a single mass of cytoplasm and contains many diploid nuclei. This 'supercell' is multinucleated because mitotic nuclear divisions are not followed by cytokinesis.

In unfavourable conditions, plasmodium develops fruiting bodies (or sporangia). As the fruiting bodies mature, they form meiospores by meiotic division with cellulose or chitin walls. The spores germinate in the presence of adequate moisture to release either haploid non-flagellated amoeboid *myxamoebas* or haploid flagellated **swarm cells**. Myxamoebas and swarm cells act as gametes. Eventually, they fuse to form a diploid zygote. The zygote feeds, grows and multiplies its nuclei through mitotic division to form the multinucleate plasmodium.

The **cellular slime molds** exist in two forms. When nutrients are abundant, these slime molds exist as solitary free-living amoeba-like cells. Each amoeboid cell has a haploid nucleus and divides by mitosis. When nutrients become inadequate, many of these single-celled uninucleated, haploid organisms aggregate and move as a single body. The aggregated form is called a **pseudoplasmodium**, or slug. Eventually, slug forms fruiting body containing spores. After being released, each spore germinates and a single haploid amoeboid cell emerges. Cellular slime molds differ from plasmodial slime molds in being haploid organisms (only the zygote is diploid) and in having fruiting bodies that function in asexual rather than sexual reproduction. *Dictyostelium discoideum*, a cellular slime mold, is a model organism for studying the evolution of multicellularity.

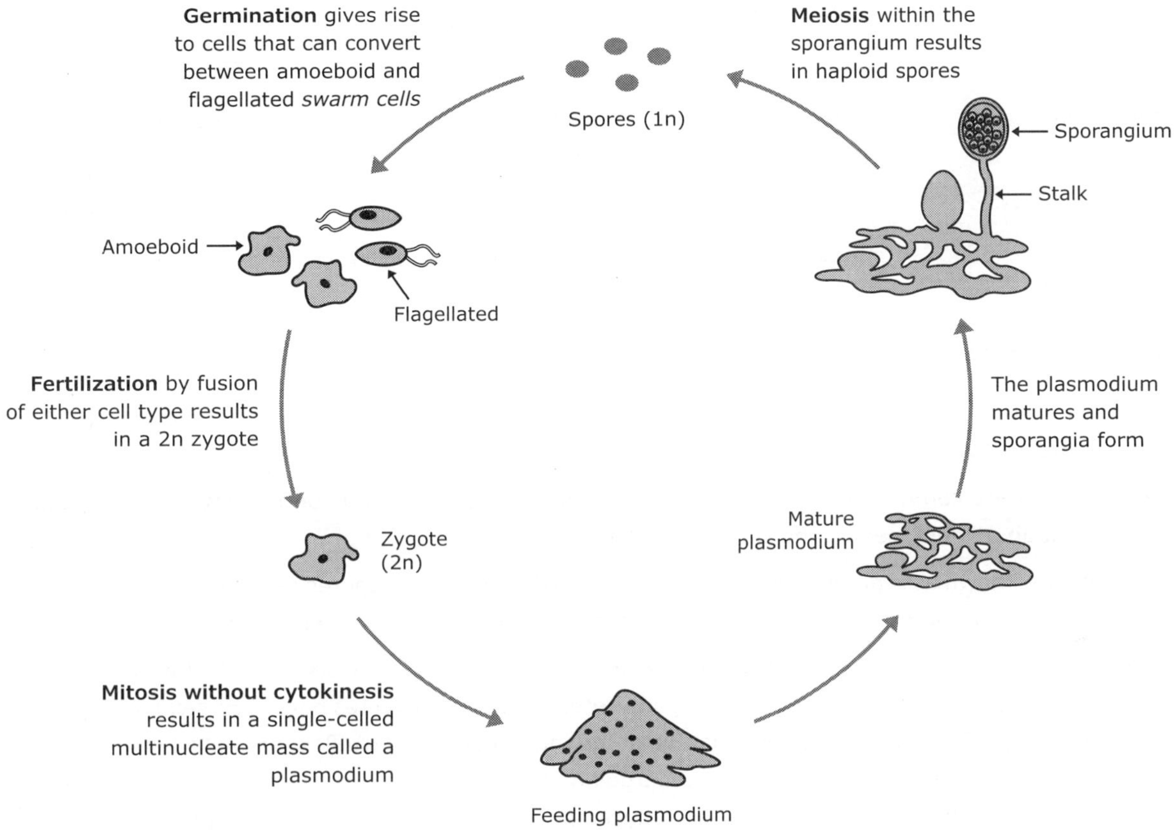

Figure 6.6 Plasmodial slime mold life cycle. Haploid spores develop into amoeboid or flagellated forms, which are then fertilized to form a diploid, multinucleate mass called a plasmodium. This plasmodium is net-like and, upon maturation, forms a sporangium on top of a stalk. The sporangium forms haploid spores through meiosis, after which the spores disseminate, germinate, and begin the life cycle.

6.3.4 Oomycetes

Oomycetes or oomycota (oomycete means *egg fungus*) include the *water molds*, the *white rusts* and the *downy mildews*. Although oomycetes have traditionally been placed in kingdom fungi and are still studied by mycologists, they are not true fungi. Unlike true fungi, the oomycetes do not have cell walls made of chitin. In the five-kingdom system, they are currently placed in the kingdom protista. Although oomycetes descended from plastid-bearing ancestors (closely related to brown algae), they no longer have plastids and do not perform photosynthesis. Instead, they typically acquire nutrients as decomposers or parasites. The most notable and best-studied oomycete species is *Phytophthora infestans*, causing late blight of potato.

6.4 Fungi

Fungi are heterotrophic, spore-bearing eukaryotes. Fungi may be single-celled or multicellular. Multicellular fungi are composed of networks of long filamentous, branched structure called **hyphae**. The hyphae often aggregate in a dense network known as a **mycelium**. The hyphae may be without cross walls (as in the case of lower fungi) or divided into compartments by formation of septa (in the higher fungi). However, even in the septate hyphae, the cytoplasm of the cells is continuous *via* a central pore in the septum. In certain stages, often during transition to the sexual or asexual reproduction phase, the mycelium forms tissue-like aggregates, called **plectenchyma**. A typical plectenchyma is the flesh of the mushroom. Although fungi lack true organs, the mycelia of ascomycetes and basidiomycetes may become organized into more complex reproductive structures called *fruiting bodies*, or *sporocarps*.

Table 6.2 Some differentiating characteristics of plants, animals and fungi

Character	Animals	Plants	Fungi
Mode of nutrition	Heterotrophy	Autotrophy	Heterotrophy
Chloroplasts	No	Yes	No
Cell wall (constituent)	Cell wall absent	Cellulose and lignin	Mainly chitin and glucans
Sterols	Cholesterol	Sitosterol/stigmasterol	Ergosterol
Food storage	Glycogen	Starch	Glycogen
Alternation of generations	No	Yes	Yes

The major divisions of fungi are mainly classified based on their sexual spores and sexual reproductive structures. Currently, four major divisions are recognized:

The **chytridiomycota** are commonly known as *chytrids*. These fungi produce zoospores that are capable of moving on their own through a liquid medium by simple flagella.

The **zygomycota** are known as *zygomycetes* and reproduce sexually with meiospores called **zygospores** and asexually with *sporangiospores*. Black bread mold (*Rhizopus stolonifer*) is a common species that belongs to this group.

The **ascomycota**, commonly known as **sac fungi** or **ascomycetes**, form meiotic spores called **ascospores**, within a special sac-like structure called an **ascus**. Unlike zygomycetes, most ascomycetes bear their sexual stages in fruiting bodies called **ascocarp**. This division includes morels, some mushrooms and truffles, as well as single-celled yeasts and many species that have only been observed undergoing asexual reproduction. Because the products of meiosis are retained within the sac-like ascus, several ascomycetes have been used for elucidating principles of genetics and heredity (e.g., *Neurospora crassa*).

Members of the **basidiomycota**, commonly known as the **club fungi** or **basidiomycetes**, produce meiospores called **basidiospores** on club-like stalks called **basidia**. The most common examples of fungi belonging to basidiomycetes are mushrooms, rust and smut fungi.

Many fungi have no sexual stage. Mycologists have traditionally called such fungi **deuteromycetes** or **imperfect fungi** (term *perfect* is referred to the sexual stages of life cycles). Imperfect fungi mostly resemble ascomycetes, or in a few instances, basidiomycetes but produce neither ascus nor basidia.

Reproduction in fungi

Fungi may reproduce sexually or asexually. In **asexual reproduction**, the offspring are genetically identical to the parent organism (they are clones). Asexual reproduction of the fungi is mostly by budding, fragmentation, or formation of asexual spores. Asexual spores like **conidiospores** are budded off at hyphal apices (*in Penicillium*, *Aspergillus*). When these arise inside sporangia, then they are called **sporangiospores** (*Mucor*, *Rhizopus*). In the lower fungi, sporangiospores are often motile by means of flagella and are called **zoospores**.

The *asexual reproduction* characteristic of yeasts (budding fungi) is *budding*; the mother cell forms an outgrowth which receives a daughter nucleus, whereupon the nucleated outgrowth is pinched off as a 'bud'. Asexual reproduction can also occur by fragmentation of the hyphae into single cells, the *oidia* or *arthrospores* (e.g., in the milk mould *Endomyces lactis*). In some fungi, these cells are surrounded by a thick wall and are referred to as *chlamydospores*. Finally, there are some yeasts (*Schizosaccharomyces*) which reproduce by *fission* in a manner similar to bacteria. During **sexual reproduction**, a mixing of genetic material occurs, as a result the offspring exhibit traits of both parents. Many species can use both sexual as well as the asexual mode of reproduction at different times, while others are apparently strictly asexual. Sexual reproduction has not been observed in some fungi of the ascomycota and basidiomycota. These are commonly referred to as **fungi imperfecti** or **deuteromycota**.

Sexual reproduction in fungi is somewhat different from that of animals or plants, and each fungal division reproduces using different strategies. Fungi that are known to reproduce sexually, all have a haploid stage and a diploid stage in their life cycles. Ascomycetes and basidiomycetes also go through a *dikaryotic stage*, in which the nuclei inherited by the two parents do not fuse right away, but remain separate in the hyphal cells.

Sexual reproduction can usually be divided into three phases. The first is **plasmogamy**, the fusion of two protoplasts. The resulting cell has two nuclei. This nuclear pair (or *dikaryon*) does not need to fuse immediately, but it can persist in the dikaryotic state during the rest of the cell division. The fusion of the two haploid nuclei (**karyogamy**) may occur later, often only after formation of a fruiting body, to give the diploid nucleus of the zygote. Following karyogamy, meiosis, the reduction division of the chromosome to the haploid number, takes place. These three processes or stages, plasmogamy, karyogamy, and meiosis, may occur in immediate sequence in some fungi, but in others they can occur during quite different stages of development.

In **zygomycetes**, the haploid hyphae of two compatible individuals fuse, forming a zygote, which becomes a resistant *zygospore*. When this zygospore germinates, it quickly undergoes meiosis, generating new haploid hyphae and asexual sporangiospores. These sporangiospores may then be distributed and germinate into new genetically-identical individuals, each producing their own haploid hyphae. When the hyphae of two compatible individuals come into contact with one another, they will fuse and generate new zygospores, thus completing the cycle.

In **ascomycetes**, when the compatible haploid hyphae fuse with one another, their nuclei do not immediately fuse. The dikaryotic hyphae form structures called *asci* (*sing*. ascus), in which karyogamy (nuclear fusion) occurs. These asci are embedded in an **ascocarp**, or fruiting body, of the fungus. Karyogamy in the asci is followed immediately by meiosis and the production of ascospores. The ascospores are disseminated and germinate to form a new haploid mycelium. Asexual conidia may be produced by the haploid mycelium. Many ascomycetes appear to have lost the ability to reproduce sexually and reproduce only via conidia.

Sexual reproduction in **basidiomycetes** is similar to that of ascomycetes. Sexually compatible haploid hyphae fuse to produce a dikaryotic mycelium. This leads to the production of a **basidiocarp**. The most commonly known basidiocarps are mushrooms, but they may also take many other forms. Club-like structures known as basidia generate haploid basidiospores following karyogamy and meiosis. These basidiospores then germinate to produce new haploid mycelia.

Table 6.3 Characteristics of the different phyla of fungi

Character	Chytridiomycota	Zygomycota	Ascomycota	Basidiomycota
Habitat	Aquatic/terrestrial	Terrestrial	Terrestrial	Terrestrial
Ploidy	Diploid	Monoploid	Monoploid	Dikaryotic, Monoploid
Motile stage	Present	Absent	Absent	Absent
Sexual spore	Not confirmed	Zygospore	Ascospores	Basidiospores
Asexual spore	Holocarpic	Sporangiospores/ Chlamydospores	Conidia	Arthrospores, oidia, conidia
Pathogenic relationship	Obligate parasites	Facultative parasites	Facultative or obligate parasites	Facultative or obligate parasites

6.4.1 Mycorrhiza

Mutualistic association between fungi and plant roots are called *mycorrhizae* (mycorrhizae means *fungus roots*). Mycorrhizal fungi (fungi that form mycorrhizae) can deliver inorganic nutrients such as calcium and phosphate. In exchange, the plants supply the fungi with organic nutrients.

There are several different types of mycorrhizal fungi. *Ectomycorrhizal fungi* form sheaths of hyphae over the surface of a root and also grow into the extracellular spaces of the root cortex. *Endomycorrhizal fungi* extend their hyphae into the root cells. When the fungal hyphae penetrate the cortical cells of the plant root, they form highly branched structures called **arbuscules**, hence these mycorrhizas commonly are called **arbuscular mycorrhizas** (AM). In many arbuscular mycorrhizae, roots harbouring arbuscules may also contain terminal balloon-like swelling called *vesicles*. Such mycorrhizas are called **vesicular-arbuscular mycorrhizas** (VAM). In ectomycorrhizas, the fungus surrounds but does not penetrate living cells in the roots. In the conifers, the hyphae grow between the cells of the root epidermis and cortex, forming a characteristic highly branched network, called the **Hartig net**.

6.4.2 Lichens

Lichens are a mutualistic association of photoautotrophic algae and heterotrophic fungi. The algal partner (**phycobiont** *or* **photobiont**) is typically unicellular or multicellular green algae or cyanobacteria. About 90% of all known lichens have a green alga as a symbiont. The most common photobionts are the green algae *Trebouxia, Pseudotrebouxia,* and *Trentepohlia,* and the cyanobacterium *Nostoc.* The fungal partner (**mycobiont**) may be a member of ascomycetes (mostly) or member of basidiomycetes (in a few cases). About 98% of the lichen-forming fungal species belong to the ascomycetes. In a lichen, the mycobiont makes up most of the thallus and plays the major role in determining the form of the lichen. There are two general types of lichen thalli based on the distribution of photobiont. In one, the cells of the photobiont are more or less evenly distributed throughout the thallus; in the other, the cells of the photobiont form a distinct layer within the thallus.

There are three major morphological types of lichen: foliose, crustose and fruticose. **Foliose lichens** are leaflike in both appearance and structure. They adhere to their substrate loosely. **Crustose lichens** are *crust-like*. They are tightly attached to or embedded in their substrate. Crustose lichens make about 75% of all lichens on Earth. **Fruticose lichens** have no distinct top and bottom and are often round in cross-section.

In a lichen which represent a mutualistic relationship, the photobiont provide carbon compounds; the cyanobacteria also fix nitrogen and provide organic nitrogen. The mycobiont provides their photosynthetic partners with a suitable environment for growth. The physical arrangement of hyphae allows gas exchange, protects the photosynthetic partner, and retains water and minerals.

6.5 Plantae

Kingdom plantae (commonly known as *plant kingdom*) includes multicellular, photoautotrophic eukaryotic organisms. It can be broadly divided into: *Algae*, *Bryophyta*, *Pteridophyta*, *Gymnosperm* and *Angiosperm*.

Bryophyta, pteridophyta, gymnosperms and angiosperms are **embryophytes** because they possess *embryo.* The embryo is *an immature sporophytic plant*. Embryophytes are usually referred to as **land plants**. Land plants may be *vascular* (or **tracheophytes**) and *non-vascular* (or **nontracheophytes**). Vascular plants contain two types of vascular tissue – *xylem* that conducts water and dissolved minerals upward from the roots and *phloem* that conducts food throughout the plant. Vascular tissues develop in the sporophytic body, but (with a few exceptions) not in the gametophytic body. Plants which do not have vascular systems are called *non-vascular* plants. Among land plants, bryophytes are non-vascular plants. Hence, non-vascular plants are often informally called *bryophytes.*

Gymnosperms and angiosperms are classified as **spermatophytes** (also known as **phanerogams**) because these plants produce *seeds*. A **seed** is an embryo packaged with a supply of nutrients inside a protective coat. The seed is a crucial adaptation to life on land because it protects the embryo from drying out. Most kinds of seeds have abundant food stored in them, either inside the embryo or in specialized storage tissue. In gymnosperms, seeds are naked i.e., are not enclosed in fruits. In angiosperms, seeds develop inside ovaries which mature into fruits. Nearly 90% of living plant species are angiosperms.

Insectivorous plants

Insectivorous plants are partly autotrophic and partly heterotrophic. These plants supplement their nutritional requirements by trapping and digesting insects. The trapped insects are killed and their proteins are digested by proteolytic enzymes secreted by the cells of the plant. They can live without insects but their growth is stimulated when they digest the insects. Some common insectivorous plants are Pitcher plants, *Drosera*, *Utricularia* and *Dionaea*.

Parasitic plants

Parasitic plants obtain their organic or inorganic nutrients from living plants. These plants are either **partial parasite** (or *hemiparasite* or *semiparasite*) or **total parasites** (or *holoparasite*). *Partial parasites* are photosynthetic plants and synthesize their organic food themselves but they depend upon the host plant for water and minerals. Partial parasites can be either *facultative* (e.g., many members of Orobanchaceae) or *obligate* (e.g., mistletoes). A hemiparasitic plant that does not require a host to complete its life cycle is facultative whereas a parasite that cannot complete its life cycle independent of a host is obligate parasite. *Total parasites* completely dependent on host and obtain food from the host. They lack chlorophylls and thus non-photosynthetic. Holoparasites are always *obligate parasites*.

Parasitic plants that attach to the host stem and root are called **stem parasites** and **root parasites**, respectively. Majority of parasitic plants target the root system of the host. All parasitic plants are dicots and with rare exception no parasitic plants are reported in other plant division.

Examples:

Partial stem parasite: *Viscum album* (commonly known as Mistletoe).

Partial root parasite: *Santalum album*

Total stem parasite: Genus *Cuscuta* (Dodder or amarbel).

Total root parasites: Genus *Orobanche* (Broomrape), *Rafflesia* and *Balanophora*.

Summary

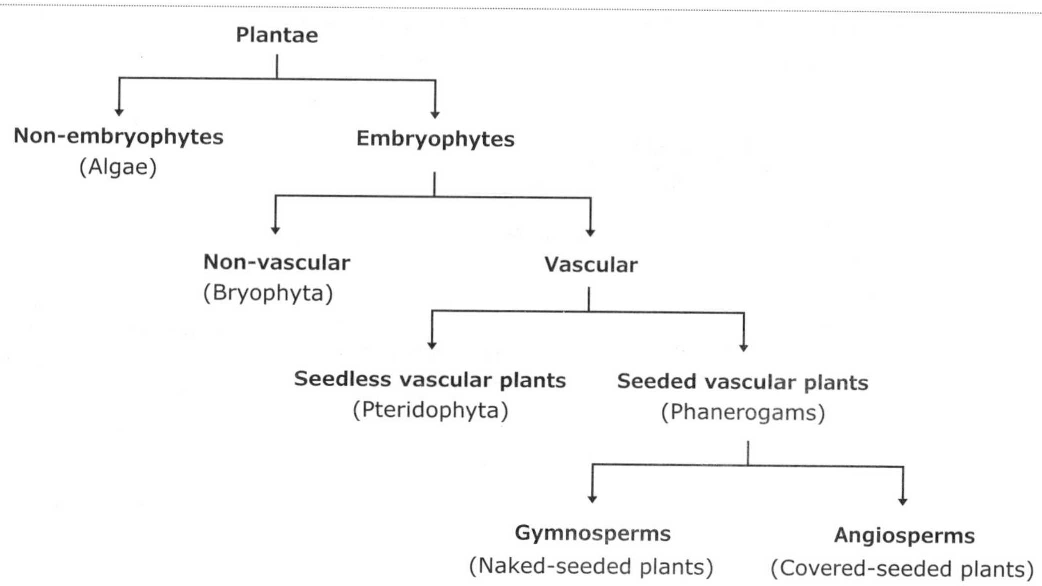

6.5.1 Plant life cycle

The sexual life cycle in plants alternate between diploid (sporophyte) and haploid (gametophyte) phases. **Sporophyte** literally means *spore-plant*, and **gametophyte** means *gamete-plant*. The haploid gametophytic body produces gametes by mitosis whereas the diploid sporophytic phase produces meiospores (sexual spores) by the process of meiosis. The diploid phase produces the haploid phase by meiosis; the haploid gametes then fuse to make a zygote that starts another diploid phase. Three distinct versions of a generalized sexual life cycle occur among plants:

Haplontic life cycle: In *haplontic* life cycle, diploid sporophytic phase is represented only by the one-celled zygote. There are no free-living sporophytes. The dominant, photosynthetic phase is the free-living gametophyte. The haploid gametophyte produce gametes by mitosis. Fusion of gametes (termed *fertilization* or *syngamy*) forms diploid zygote. Meiosis occurs in the zygote (**zygotic meiosis**) which results in the formation of haploid meiospores. These spores, in turn, germinate and divide by mitosis to form a haploid gametophyte body once again. Most green algae such as *Volvox*, *Spirogyra* and some species of *Chlamydomonas* represent this pattern of life cycle.

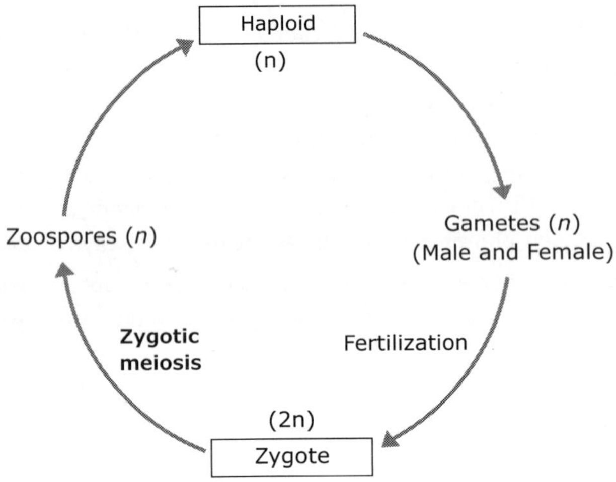

Figure 6.7
In *haplontic* life cycle, the zygote divides by meiosis (*zygotic meiosis*) to form haploid cells. Each of these cells divides by mitosis to produce a multicellular haploid individual that eventually gives rise to gametes by mitosis.

Diplontic life cycle: In *diplontic* life cycle, the zygote divides mitotically to produce a multicellular diploid individual. The diploid phase is the dominant, photosynthetic and independent phase. Certain cells of a multicellular diploid phase undergo meiosis to make gametes, not meiospores. Because meiosis produces gametes directly, it is called **gametic meiosis**. Fusion of gametes restores the diploid phase. This pattern of life cycle is not common in plants. Some brown algae such as *Sargassum*, *Fucus* follow this pattern of life cycle.

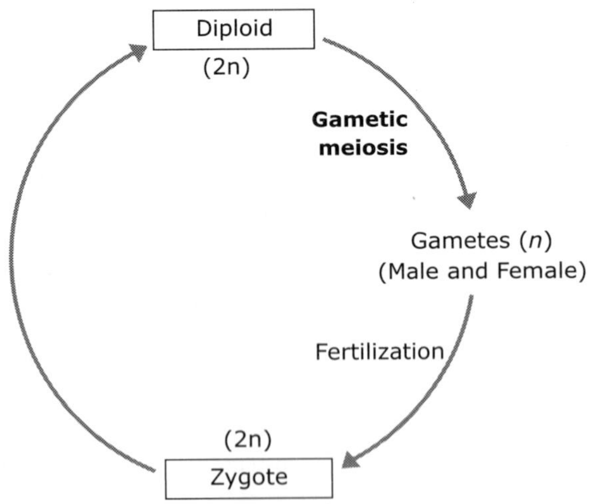

Figure 6.8
In *diplontic* life cycle, the haploid gametes are formed by meiosis (*gametic meiosis*) in a multicellular diploid individual and fuse to form a diploid zygote that divides to produce another diploid individual. This type of life cycle is characteristic of most animals and some protists, as well as some green and brown algae.

Haplo-diplontic life cycle: In the *haplo-diplontic* (also called **diplobiontic**) life cycle, diploid sporophyte produces haploid spores (meiospores) by the process of meiosis. Because meiosis produces spores directly, it is called **sporic meiosis**. The meiospores germinate and grow by mitosis into the multicellular haploid gametophytic phase of the cycle. The gametophytic bodies produce gametes by mitosis. Fusion of gametes gives diploid zygote. Fertilization restores the diploid phase. In this cycle, both phases are multicellular. However, they differ in their dominance. This life cycle is the feature of all land plants (bryophytes, pteridophytes, gymnosperms and angiosperms) and some algae like *Ectocarpus*, *Polysiphonia*.

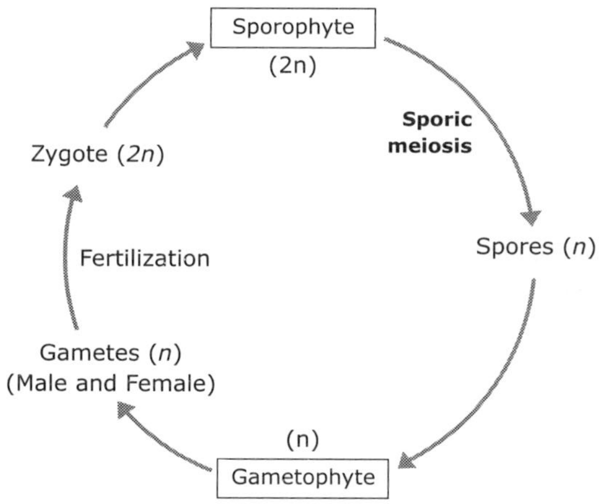

Figure 6.9
In *haplo-diplontic* life cycle, the diploid sporophyte individual, produces haploid spores as a result of meiosis (*sporic meiosis*). These meiospores do not function as gametes but germinate and grow by mitosis into the multicellular haploid gametophytic phase of the cycle. The gametophytic bodies eventually produce gametes that fuse to form diploid zygotes. These zygotes, in turn, differentiate into diploid individuals.

6.5.2 Algae

Algae are chlorophyll-bearing, thalloid, autotrophic organisms. Although the term *algae* is used for both prokaryotic such as cyanobacteria (formally known as *blue green algae*) as well as eukaryotic photosynthetic thalloid organisms. But, it should be used for eukaryotes only. The *eukaryotic algae* are part of plantae and photosynthetic protists. The algae belonging to plantae can be described as *non-vascular* (no xylem and phloem), *non-embryophytic* (no embryo development) and *thalloid* (body not differentiated into root, stem and leaf) plants. Algae belong to plantae include three main groups; *green algae*, *red algae* and *brown algae*, distinguished by the following characteristics: primary photosynthetic pigments, storage product, cell wall composition and type and location of flagella.

Green algae (Chlorophyceae)

Habitat	Mostly freshwater, some marine and terrestrial.
Photosynthetic pigments	Chlorophylls *a* and *b*, carotenoids.
Cell wall components	Cellulose (major component).
Stored food	Starch (stored inside the plastids).
Flagella	Most with two flagella per cell.
Asexual reproduction	Usually reproduce vegetatively by fragmentation or by formation of mitospores.
Sexual reproduction	The sexual reproduction shows considerable variation in the type and formation of gametes and it may be isogamous, anisogamous or oogamous.
Example	*Chlamydomonas, Volvox, Ulothrix, Spirogyra, Chara* and *Ulva* (Sea lettuce).

Red algae (Rhodophyceae)

Habitat	Mostly marine, some freshwater.
Photosynthetic pigments	Chlorophyll *a* and *d*, carotenoids, phycobilins (predominance of phycoerythrin).
Cell wall components	Cellulose (major component)
Stored food	Floridean starch (α-1,4 glucan) which is stored in cytosol outside of the chloroplasts.
Flagella	Absent
Asexual reproduction	Reproduce vegetatively by fragmentation or by formation of non-motile mitospores.
Sexual reproduction	Sexual reproduction is oogamous type and gametes are non-motile. The simplest type of sexual life in red algae involves an alternation of generations between two separate, multicellular forms of the same species—a haploid, gamete-producing gametophyte and a diploid, spore-producing sporophyte.
Example	*Polysiphonia*, *Porphyra*, *Gracilaria* and *Gelidium*.

Brown algae (Phaeophyceae)

Habitat	Almost all marine, rarely freshwater.
Photosynthetic pigments	Chlorophylls *a* and *c* and carotenoids. They vary in color from olive green to various shades of brown depending upon the amount of the xanthophyll pigment, fucoxanthin, present.
Cell wall components	Cellulose and alginic acid. Cellulosic wall usually covered from outside by a gelatinous coating of algin.
Stored food	Laminarin and mannitol
Flagella	2, unequal, lateral
Asexual reproduction	Usually reproduce vegetatively by fragmentation or by formation of motile biflagellate zoospores that are pear-shaped and have two unequal laterally attached flagella.
Sexual reproduction	Sexual reproduction may be isogamous, anisogamous or oogamous. For most brown algae, the life cycles involve sporic meiosis.
Example	*Ectocarpus, Dictyota, Laminaria, Sargassum* and *Fucus*.

Generalized life cycle of algae

The algae reproduce by both asexual and sexual means.

Asexual reproduction

Unicellular algae reproduce asexually by mitosis. Multicellular algae also reproduce asexually, either by vegetative means (by fragmentation) or by mitotically produced asexual spores called *mitospores*. These spores are either motile or nonmotile. Spores may be produced within ordinary vegetative cells or within specialized structure called *sporangia*. Some common examples of mitospores form in different algal groups are *zoospores*, *aplanospores* and *autospores*. Among different types of mitospores, the most common being the **zoospores**. They are flagellate motile spores. They vary with respect to flagellar number. Non-motile spores are called **aplanospores**. Some algal genera such as *Chlorella* produce **autospores**. These spores are nonmotile daughter cells that are released from ruptured wall of the original parent cell. They are almost perfect replicas of the vegetative cells that produce them and lack the capacity to develop in zoospore. Under unfavourable conditions, many algal groups produce thick walled resting cells, such as *hypnospores* and *akinetes*.

Sexual reproduction

Sexual reproduction involves gamete formation, fertilization (fusion of two gametes) and meiosis. Three distinct types of sexual life cycles – *haplontic*, *diplontic* and *haplodiplontic* - are reported in different groups of algae.

In algae, the sex organ (termed **gametangium**) is unicellular and non-jacketed (i.e., not surrounded by a jacket of sterile cells). The female and male sex organs are termed **oogonium** and **antheridium**, respectively. The gametes produced by the sex organs may be motile (flagellated) or non-motile (non-flagellated). In some species, the gametes are neither male nor female; all the gametes look alike. Such gametes are called *isogametes*, and reproduction by fusion of isogametes are referred to as **isogamous** (as in *Spirogyra*).

Some algae produce gametes of two different sizes. These gametes are called **anisogametes**. The reproduction by fusion of anisogametes are referred to as **anisogamous** (as in some species of *Chlamydomonas*). The smaller anisogametes is traditionally referred to as *male* and the larger one as *female*.

The most pronounced differences between the gametes are found in a situation where one gamete is large, non-motile and the other is small, motile. The large gamete is designated as the *egg* (female gamete) and the smaller one as the *sperm* (male gamete). These gametes are called **oogametes** and their fusion is referred to as **oogamous** (as in *Volvox*, *Fucus*).

6.5.3 Life cycle of land plants

The life cycles of all land plants alternate between two generations – a gamete producing haploid gametophyte and a spore-producing diploid sporophytes. Such type of life cycle is called **haplodiplontic** (also called *diplobiontic*) life cycle.

The sporophyte generation of a plant produces spores as a result of meiosis. Meiosis takes place in specialized cells called spore mother cells. The haploid spores represent *the first cell of the gametophyte generation*. Spores do not fuse with one another, as gametes do; instead, they divide by mitosis, producing a multicellular haploid individual, the gametophyte. The gametophyte generation of a plant produces gametes —*eggs* and *sperms*—as a result of mitosis. They are haploid, like the gametophyte that produces them. They fuse to form a zygote, *the first cell of the sporophyte generation*. The basic cycle involved in haplodiplontic life cycle can be summarized as:

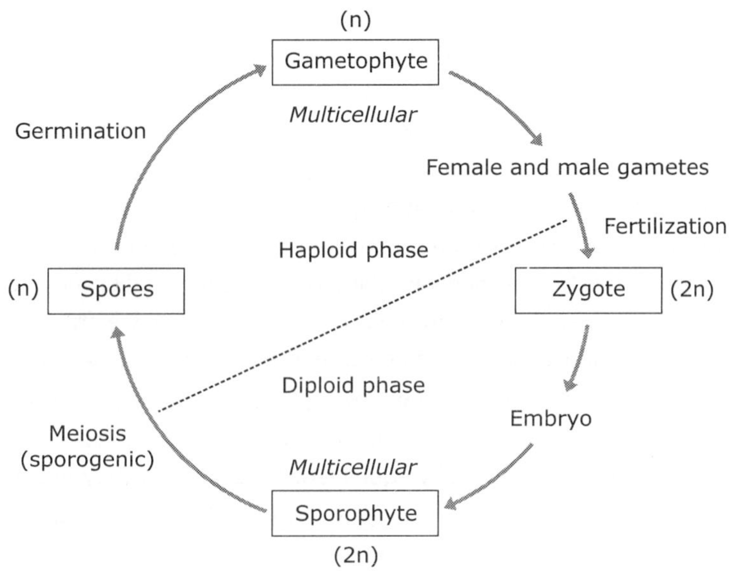

Figure 6.10 Sexual life cycle of land plants.

Such a cycle is characteristic of all land plants. In all of them, sporophyte, the diploid generation, alternates with gametophyte, the haploid generation. Although haploid and diploid conditions alternate in *all sexual* life cycles but the term **alternation of generations** applies only to life cycles in which both haploid and diploid stages are multicellular. In humans, for example, meiosis produces haploid gametes that unite, forming diploid zygotes that divide and become multicellular. The haploid stage is represented only by single-celled gametes. In contrast, alternation of generations is distinguished by the fact that the life cycle includes both multicellular haploid bodies and multicellular diploid bodies.

In gametophyte, gametes are differentiated within specialized organs called **gametangia**. Eggs and sperm are formed within different kinds of gametangia. Those in which eggs are formed are called **archegonia** (in algae it is unicellular and called **oogonia**) and those in which sperm are formed are called **antheridia**. An archegonium produces only one egg; an antheridium produces many sperms.

The antheridia and archegonia may exist together on the same gametophyte or two kinds of gametangia are borne on separate gametophytes. When one kind of gametophyte bears antheridia and another kind bears archegonia, the two kinds of gametophytes may look different from one another. One that form antheridia are called *microgametophytes*, and those that form archegonia are called *megagametophytes*.

The diploid zygote is the first stage in the sporophyte generation. The zygote divides by mitosis and develops into a multicellular *embryo*, the young sporophyte plant. Embryo development takes place within the archegonium. Eventually, the embryo grows into a mature sporophyte plant. The sporophyte bears spore-producing structure called the **sporangium**. Within the sporangium, *sporogenous cells* (or spores producing cells) divide by meiosis to form haploid meiospores. The sporophyte may produce one kind of spores or two morphologically different kinds of spores (termed *microspores* and *megaspores*). Plants that produce two different kinds of spores are called **heterosporous**; those that produce only one kind of spore are **homosporous**. If a plant forms both megaspores and microspores, each of these will be formed in different kinds of sporangium, *megasporangium* and *microsporangium*, respectively.

Among land plants, gametophyte and sporophyte differ in their dominance. In bryophytes, gametophyte is dominant, independent and photosynthetic. Whereas the sporophyte is short-lived multicellular and totally or partially dependent on the gametophyte for nutrition. In pteridophytes, sporophyte is represented by a dominant, independent, photosynthetic, vascular plant body. It alternates with multicellular, independent but short-lived gametophyte.

6.5.4 Bryophytes

General features

1. Bryophytes are *amphibians* i.e., although majority of them are terrestrial, they require lots of moisture and humidity in their surrounding. Most bryophytes are small, compact, green plants. Like green algae, they produce chlorophylls *a* and *b*, starch, cellulose cell walls, and motile sperm. Bryophytes usually grow very slowly.
2. Plant organization in bryophytes is of two types – Thalloid and Leafy. In *leafy form* the leaf and stem are simple, without vascular tissue and belong to the gametophytic generation. Thallus grows prostrate on the ground. Thallus as well as leafy form get attached to the substratum by delicate unbranched, unicellular hair-like organs called **rhizoids**. Bryophytes lack well-developed vascular tissues and lignified tissues. As a result, they grow low to the ground and absorb water by capillarity. However, not all bryophytes are strictly nonvascular. For example, some mosses have a central strand of conducting cells that are functionally equivalent to xylem and phloem.
3. Organs such as leaves and roots of vascular plants are defined by the arrangement of their vascular tissues. Since bryophytes lack true vascular tissues, they also lack true leaves and roots. However, many bryophytes have structures that are similar and functionally equivalent to leaves, so they are often referred to as such.
4. Bryophytes get their nutrients from dust, rainwater, and substance dissolved in water at the soil's surface. Tiny rhizoids (hairlike extensions of epidermal cells) along their lower surface anchor the plants but do not specialized for absorption of water or minerals. Water and dissolved minerals move by capillarity over the surface of bryophytes.
5. The gametophytes dominate the life cycle.
6. The sporophyte is short-lived and unbranched, and produces a terminal sporangium. Although photosynthetic, the sporophyte is permanently attached to and partially dependent on the gametophyte. The sporophytes of bryophytes do not have a direct connection to the ground. Spores have a cutinized coat and are usually dispersed by wind.
7. The sex organs are jacketed and multicellular. Female sex organ in the form of archegonia appears for the first time in the bryophyta in the plant world. It is a flask shaped organ. The basal swollen part of the flask-shaped body is known as venter and the narrow canal like part as the neck. There is a sterile jacket surrounding the axial canal. Antheridium is the male sex organ. It is a multicellular structure which is ellipsoidal or club-shaped in outline. The sperms are biflagellate. Both the flagella are whiplash type.
8. Fertilization takes place in the presence of water. The fertilized egg is retained within the venter of the archegonium. The zygote undergoes repeated division to form an undifferentiated structure called the embryo.

   Bryophytes are sometimes called nonvascular plants, but *nontracheophyte* is a more accurate term because some bryophytes have conducting cells other than tracheids for water and nutrients. But they lack the transport cell called, *tracheid*. The terms *bryophyta* and *bryophyte* are not synonymous. Bryophyta is the formal taxonomic name for the phylum that consists solely of mosses.

A generalized life cycle of bryophytes

During sexual life cycle, sporophyte produces spores in sporangium. Haploid spores formed by meiosis begins the gametophytic generation. The spore germinates to form a gametophyte, which is more diverse in bryophytes than in any other group of plants. The gametophyte bears antheridia and archegonia. Antheridia produce sperms, and archegonia produce eggs. Sexual reproduction in bryophytes requires free water, because the sperm must swim to the egg. Sperms released from an antheridium do not swim randomly; rather, they are attracted by a gradient of a still-unidentified chemotactic substance(s) produced by an archegonium. A sperm fertilizes an egg and forms a diploid zygote, thus beginning the sporophytic generation of the life cycle. Bryophytes have **heteromorphic** alternation of generation; that is, the sporophyte and gametophyte are distinctly different.

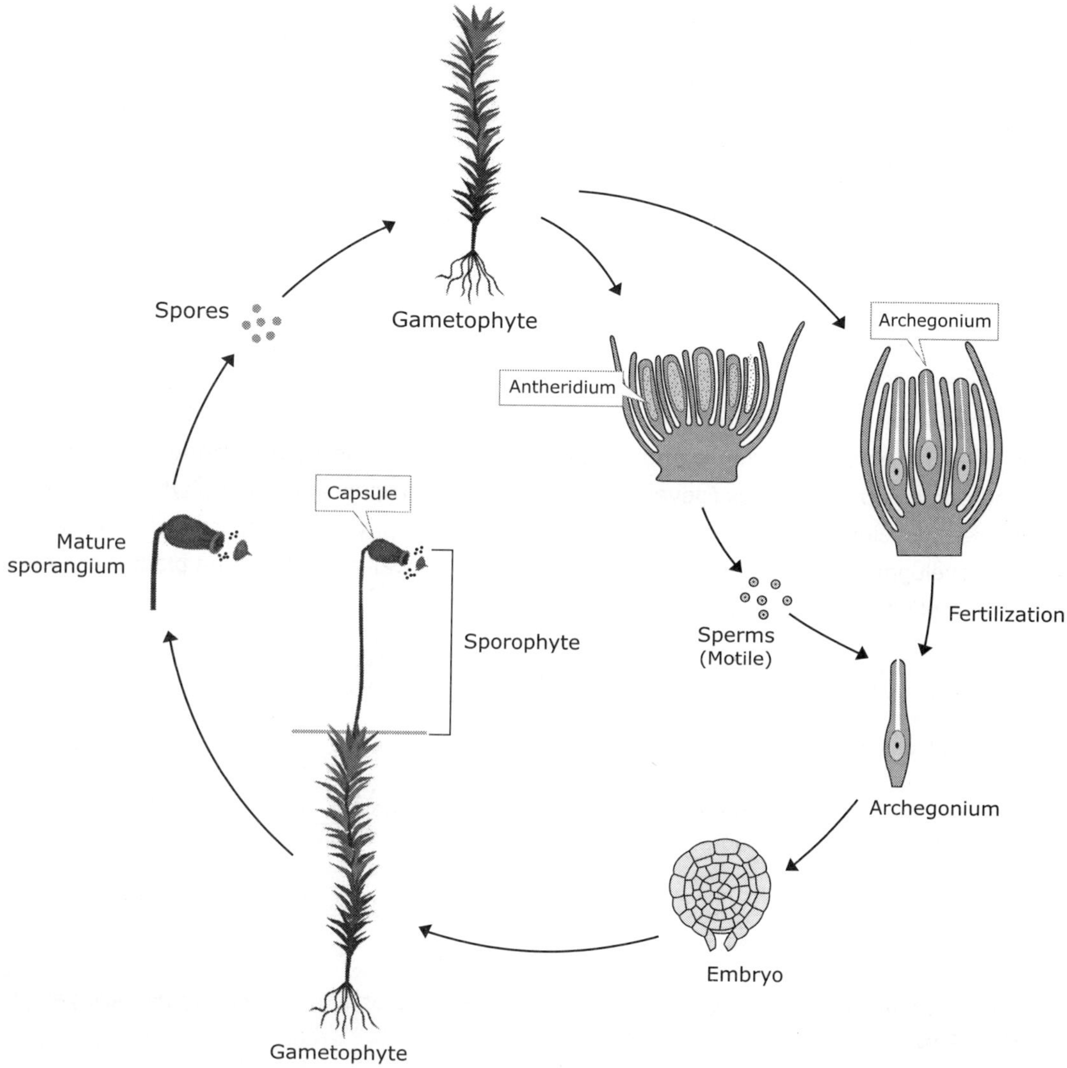

Figure 6.11 Sexual life cycle in *Funaria*. The spore germinates and produces a protonema (not shown in the figure) and the leafy stage of the gametophyte develops from the protonemal stage. The male and female sex organs, the antheridia and the archegonia respectively, are produced on the gametophytic plant. Haploid sperm are released from the antheridia and fertilize with a haploid egg present in an archegonium. The zygote develops into the diploid sporophyte. Typically sporophyte is differentiated into a foot, seta and spore forming capsule.

6.5.5 Pteridophytes

General features

1. The sporophyte of seedless vascular plants, which dominates the life cycle, is long-lived and often highly branched.
2. Sporophytes and gametophytes of seedless vascular plants are nutritionally independent of each other. Sporophytes are photosynthetic, and gametophytes are either photosynthetic or saprophytic (i.e., they obtain nutrition from dead and decaying organic matter).

3. Seedless vascular plants have a well-developed cuticle to minimize water loss. They also have stomata to allow gas exchange for photosynthesis, although bryophytes such as hornworts and mosses have stomata, but they are not well developed and do not function efficiently to prevent water loss. Most bryophytes lack a cuticle.
4. Seedless vascular plants produce chlorophylls *a* and *b*, carotenoids, starch, cellulose cell walls, and motile sperm. These features are also shared with bryophytes and many algae.
5. The life cycle of seedless vascular plants (pteridophytes) is similar to that of bryophytes and algae that exhibit sporic meiosis. The diploid sporophyte produces haploid spores by meiosis. Each spore germinates and grows into a gametophyte that produces gametes by mitosis. The gametes (egg and sperm) fuse to form diploid zygotes.
6. Eggs are produced in archegonia, and sperms are produced in antheridia.
7. Flagellated sperm swim through water to eggs. Like bryophytes, seedless vascular plants require free water for sexual reproduction.
8. The zygote germinates to produce a multicellular embryo that depends on the gametophyte for its nutrition. To complete the life cycle, the embryo grows into a mature sporophyte. A multicellular embryo also characterizes the bryophyte life cycle, but *it is absent in algae*.
9. Pteridophytes may be – **homosporous** i.e., all spores are the same, producing bisexual gametophytes or **heterosporous** - similar to flowering plants in that two types of spores are produced, which produce two types of gametophytes: *megaspores* (develop to form the egg-producing gametophyte or *megagametophyte*) and *microspores* (develop to form the sperm-producing gametophyte or *microgametophyte*). The nature of gametophyte development may be **endosporic** (within the spore wall as in flowering plants) or **exosporic** (spore germination with plant development outside the spore).

Summary

Homosporous spore production

Sporangium on sporophyll → Single type of spore → Typically a bisexual gametophyte → Egg (Female gamete) / → Sperm (Male gamete)

Heterosporous spore production

Megasporangium on megasporophyll → Megaspore → Female gametophyte → Egg (Female gamete)

Microsporangium on microsporophyll → Microspore → Male gametophyte → Sperm (Male gamete)

10. Each sporangium is protected by a multicellular jacket of non-reproductive cells. Spores are dispersed from sporangia by wind and are cutinized to resist desiccation.

A generalized life cycle of pteridophytes

The life cycle of pteridophytes is similar to that of bryophytes and few algae that exhibit sporogenic (or sporic) meiosis. The diploid sporophyte produces meiospores. Each spore germinates and grows into a gametophyte that produces gametes by mitosis. Eggs are produced in archegonia, and sperms are produced in antheridia. Flagellated sperm swim through water to eggs. Like bryophytes, pteridophytes require free water for sexual reproduction. The gametes (eggs and sperms) fuse to form diploid zygotes. The zygote germinates to produce a multicellular embryo that depends on the gametophyte for its nutrition. To complete the life cycle, the embryo grows into a mature sporophyte. A multicellular embryo also characterizes the bryophyte life cycle, but *it is absent in algae*.

A **fern** is a representative of the pteridophytes. Fern gametophytes are green, photosynthetic plants that live in relatively moist places and resemble the gametophytes of certain liverworts. They are flat, thin and heart-shaped. Rhizoids project from their lower surface. Archegonia form on the lower surface of the gametophytes near the *apical notch*. The antheridia are formed on the lower surface. When the sperm are mature, they are released from the antheridia. They require the *presence of water* to make their way to the mouth of the archegonium. The sperm probably are attracted by chemicals released from the archegonium. Inside the archegonium, a sperm fuses with the single egg, producing a zygote.

The zygote begins to divide within the archegonium of the fern. Soon the growing sporophyte becomes much larger than the gametophyte and also nutritionally independent from it. Most ferns have more or less horizontal stems that creep along below the ground; subterranean stems of this kind are called **rhizomes**.

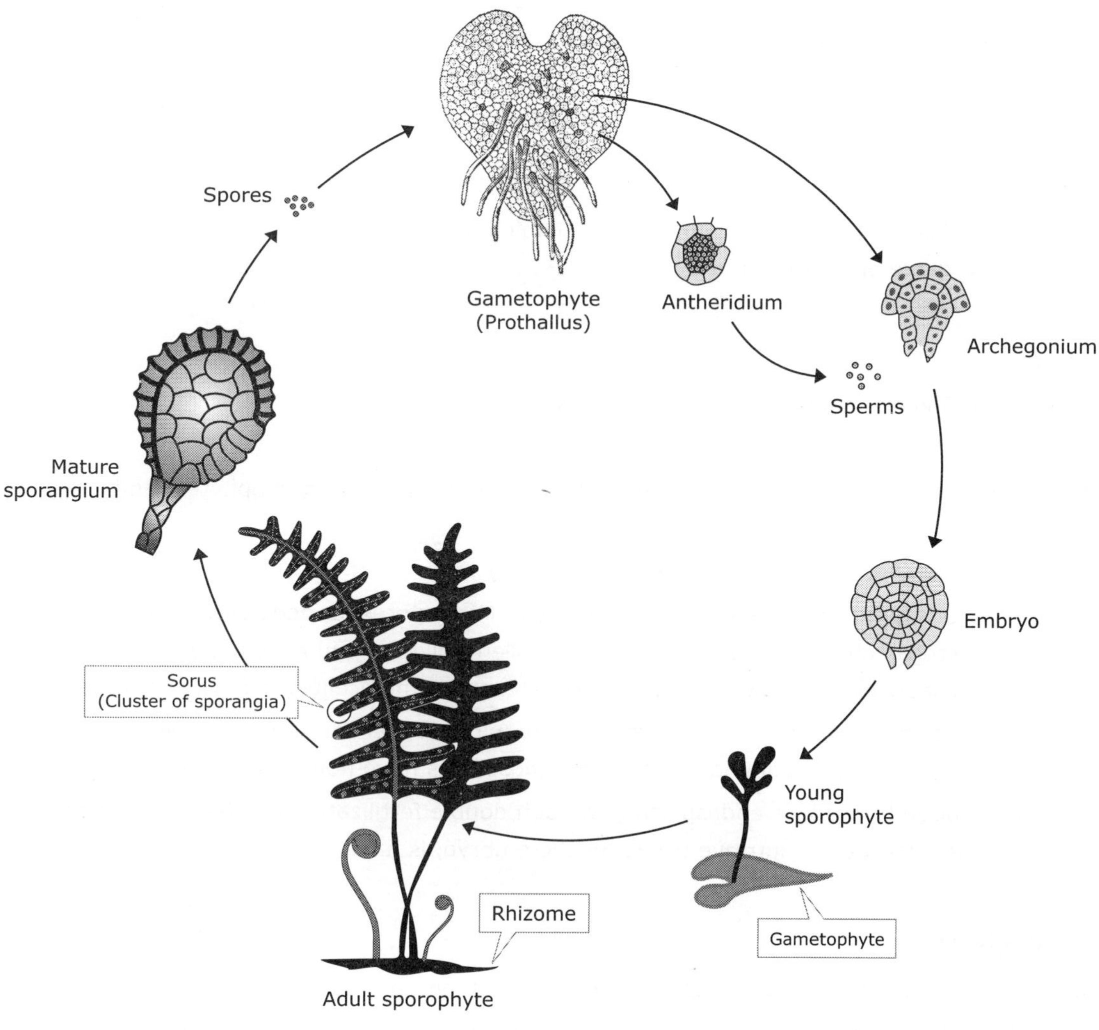

Figure 6.12 Fern life cycle.

True roots arise from these rhizomes and absorb water and nutrients from the soil in which the fern is growing. The leaves, which are called **fronds**, are borne on the rhizomes. The immature leaves are coiled and known as *croziers*. When leaves in early stage are coiled, this type of development is called **circinate vernation**. The leaves bear sporangia which differentiate on the lower surface of leaves, in clusters called **sori**. Meiosis takes place within these sporangia, followed by differentiation of the haploid spores, which ultimately are released from the sporangia. Most ferns are homosporous, producing single types of spore. Only a few genera of ferns are heterosporous producing two different types of spores – micro and megaspores. The fern life cycle differs from that of a moss primarily in the much greater development, independence, and dominance of the fern's sporophyte.

6.5.6 Gymnosperm

The gymnosperms are a group of vascular seed plants. The term *gymnosperm* derives from the Greek word *gymnos* meaning '*naked*' and *sperma*, meaning 'seed'. In these plants, the ovules are not enclosed by ovary wall and remain exposed, both before and after fertilization. Hence, the seeds that develop after fertilization from ovules remain naked. In contrast, in angiosperms the ovules are enclosed by ovary wall and thus, the seeds that develop after fertilization from ovules remain enclosed in fruit wall. Thus, gymnosperms are all fruitless plants whereas angiosperms bear fruits (which are mature ovaries). In addition to seeds, the other characteristic features of gymnosperms include:

- Heterosporous and producing **megaspores** and **microspores** that give rise, respectively, to **megagametophytes** (or female gametophytes) and **microgametophytes** (or male gametophytes).
- Reduced gametophytes and endosporic. Unlike seedless bryophytes and pteridophytes, in gymnosperms the male and the female gametophytes are very reduced and do not have an independent free-living existence.

	Bryophytes	Pteridophytes	Seed plants
Gametophyte	Dominant	Reduced, independent	Reduced
Sporophyte	Reduced, dependent on gametophyte for nutrition	Dominant	Dominant

General features

1. Terrestrial adaptation and dominant sporophytic phase.
2. Mostly woody plants.
3. Most gymnosperms lack vessels in their xylem (with the exception of the gnetophytes) and companion cells in the phloem.
4. An ovule is produced, but this is not enclosed within ovary wall.
5. All are *heterosporous* (producing mega- and microspores). Microspores termed *pollen grains* make direct contact with the ovule. Microgametophyte develops within the pollen wall (i.e., endosporic) and without male sex organ, antheridium. Megaspore bears megagametophyte which contains multicellular female sex organ (archegonium).
6. Gymnosperms differ from the seedless plants in not requiring water for sperm to swim in to reach the egg. Thus, except cycads and the maidenhair tree, all gymnosperms have non-flagellated sperms.
7. No double fertilization to produce endosperm (although double fertilization has been documented in *Ephedra* and *Gnetum*). The endosperm, nutritive tissue for the embryo, is haploid.

6.5.7 Angiosperms

Angiosperms (also called *flowering plants*) are a major group of land plants. The angiosperms, being seed plants, exhibit a life cycle that is in many respects similar to that found in gymnosperms.

General features

1. Dominant sporophytic phase.
2. Vessels present in their xylem and companion cells in the phloem.
3. The ovule develops within ovary of a carpel and enclosed by ovary wall.
4. All are *heterosporous* (producing mega- and microspores). Micro or male gametophyte develops within microspore (pollen grain) and without antheridium. Megaspores bear mega or female gametophyte and without archegonium. The gametophytes of angiosperms are much reduced in size and cell number. The mature microgametophyte within the pollen grain consists of only three cells, and the mature megagametophyte within the ovule, in most angiosperms, consists of only seven cells and eight nuclei.

5. Pollination in angiosperms is *indirect* in which pollen is deposited on the stigma of the carpel rather than directly on the ovule as is the situation in gymnosperms.
6. Double fertilization characteristically occurs in angiosperms to produce embryo as well as endosperm. The endosperm, nutritive tissue for the future embryo, is not haploid (n) but triploid (3n) and forms after fertilization.

Table 6.4 Comparative features of different land plants

	Bryophyta	**Pteridophyta**	**Gymnosperm**	**Angiosperm**
Dominant phase	Gametophyte	Sporophyte	Sporophyte	Sporophyte
Vascular system	Absent	Present	Present	Present
Embryo	Present	Present	Present	Present
Sex organ	Multicellular	Multicellular	Multicellular	Absent
Male sex organ	Present	Present	Absent	Absent
Female sex organ	Present	Present	Present	Absent
Gamete (male)	Motile	Motile	Non-motile	Non-motile

Flower

The most distinguishing feature of angiosperms is the presence of **flower**, a modified reproductive shoot of *determinate* growth. It is the reproductive unit meant for sexual reproduction in the angiosperms. Unlike a typical vegetative shoot, the flower shoot is determinate, because the apical meristem stops growth after the floral parts have formed.

The stalk of a solitary flower (or of an inflorescence) is known as a **peduncle**. The stalk of an individual flower in an inflorescence is called a **pedicel**. Based on presence or absence of pedicel, flower may be **pedicellate flower** or **sessile flower**. Flowers may be subtended by a **bract**. If the bract is present, the flower is called as **bracteate**. If the bract is absent then the flower is called as **ebracteate**. A smaller or secondary bract present on the pedicel of the flower is called **bracteoles**. If the bracteoles are present the flower is called *bracteolate* and if the bracteole is absent then the flower is called as *ebracteolate*.

Figure 6.13
A typical flower structure.
The part of the flower stalk to which the flower parts are attached is termed the receptacle. A typical flower has four whorls of appendages. From the outside in, the whorls are the sepals (collectively, the calyx); the petals (collectively, the corolla); the stamens (collectively, the androecium); and the carpels (collectively, the gynoecium).

Floral parts

A typical flower has four types of floral leaves arranged in four whorls on the **receptacle** or **torus** (an older term is *thalamus*). These are calyx, corolla, androecium and gynoecium. These four whorls are divided into two groups: *accessory non-reproductive whorls* (**calyx** and **corolla**) and *essential reproductive whorls* (**androecium** and **gynoecium**). A flower having all four floral components (calyx, corolla, androecium and gynoecium) is called **complete flower**, whereas a flower lacking one or more of the four components is called **incomplete flower**.

The accessory non-reproductive parts of the flower are called **perianth**, includes both calyx and corolla. In some flowers like lily, the perianth is not distinguishable into the calyx and corolla. The indistinguishable perianth is termed as **tepal**. Based on the presence or absence of calyx and corolla, flower may be achlamydeous, monochlamydeous and dichlamydeous. The flower without calyx and corolla is called **achlamydeous**. The flower with either calyx or corolla is called **monochlamydeous** and with both calyx and corolla is called **dichlamydeous**.

The **calyx** is the outer perianth of the flower. The individual units of the calyx are called **sepals.** It is generally green and leaf like and protects the flower bud. The calyx may be **synsepalous** (sepals united) or **aposepalous** (sepals free). The corolla is the inner perianth of the flower. The individual units of the corolla are **petals**. The petals are generally large, brightly coloured and may have fragrance and help in pollination by attracting insects. Like calyx, corolla may be also free (**apopetalous**) or united (**gamo-** or **sympetalous**).

The essential reproductive parts of flower are *androecium* and *gynoecium*. Most flowers are **bisexual** (perfect), containing both stamens and carpels, but some are **unisexual** (imperfect), having only stamens or carpels. When only stamens are present, it is said to be a **staminate flower** and when only carpels are present, it is said to be a **pistillate flower.** Each stamen consists of a filament with an anther at the tip. The anthers produce **microspores** (or pollen grains). The carpel consists of an ovary enclosing one to many ovules. The ovules produce **megaspores**. Thus, angiosperms are **heterosporous** (producing mega- and microspores). The ovules develop into seeds after fertilization.

The **androecium** is the pollen producing male reproductive organ of a flower. The individual units of androecium are **stamens** (*microsporophyll*). A stamen has two parts, the *filament* and the *anther*. In majority of angiosperm species, anthers typically consist of two lobes (thecae) and called **dithecal**. Each theca contains two microsporangia. Thus, anthers are typically **tetrasporangiate**. However, in a very few families, such as the Malvaceae, anthers are **monothecal**, having one theca with typically two microsporangia (i.e., **bisporangiate**).

Gynoecium or **pistil** is made up of one or more carpels. On the basis of a number of carpels, gynoecium may be **simple** (or *monocarpellary*) and **compound** (or *multicarpellary*). When the gynoecium is made up of only one carpel (e.g., Pea), it is known as **simple gynoecium**. When the gynoecium is made up of two or more carpels then it is known as **compound gynoecium**. Compound gynoecium may be bi-, tri-, tetra- and pentacarpellary. The multicarpellary condition may be **syncarpous** (carpels are fused, as in mustard) or **apocarpous** (carpels are free; as in lotus) in nature. If the gynoecium is apocarpous, the number of carpels is equal to the number of gynoecium. Each carpel has three parts:

Ovary: It is the swollen basal part of the carpel that contains one or more ovules which later become seeds. Ovules remain attached to the tissue called **placenta**. After fertilization, the ovules develop into seeds and the ovary matures into a fruit. A chamber within an ovary that contains the ovule(s) is termed as **locule**. Depending on the number of locules the ovary can be classified as uni-locular, bi-locular, tri-locular or multi-locular. The number of locules present in a gynoecium may be equal to or less than the number of carpels.

Stigma: It is attached to the style and receives the pollen grains.

Style: It forms the neck of the carpel to which stigma is attached. It connects the ovary to the stigma. Styles may be described as *terminal* or *apical style* (if a style is lying in the same straight line with the ovary; e.g. *China rose*), *lateral style* (if a style arises from the side of the ovary; as in members of the Rosaceae) and *gynobasic style* (if a style arising from the depression in the center of the ovary or directly from thalamus; e.g., *Ocimum*). When the base of the style is swollen to form a pad-like structure it is termed as **stylopodium** (e.g., *Coriandrum*).

Position of ovary: Depending primarily upon the apparent position of the other parts of a flower with respect to the ovary, flowers may be hypo-, peri- and epigynous. In a **hypogynous** flower, the ovary occupies the highest position on the thalamus and stamens, petals and sepals are successively inserted below it (e.g., *Citrus*, *Stellaria*). The condition is known as *hypogyny* and the ovary is termed as *superior* ovary. In **epigynous** flower, the thalamus completely covers the ovary and bears sepals, petals and stamens on the top of the ovary (e.g., *Coriandrum*, *Cucurbits*, *Guava*). The condition is known as *epigyny* and the ovary is termed as *inferior* ovary. If the thalamus grows around the ovary to form a cup and bears sepals, petals and stamens on the rim of the cup (e.g., Peach, Plum), the flower is termed **perigynous** and the condition is known as *perigyny*.

Union of flower parts: In some flowers, all the parts are attached directly to the receptacle and are entirely free from each other. Thus, there may be separate sepals (*polysepaly*), separate petals (*polypetaly*), separate stamens and separate pistils. In other, the members of a whorl may be more or less united with each other, a condition referred to as a coalescence of parts. Coalescence may involve sepals (*synsepaly* or *gamosepaly*), petals (*synpetaly* or *gamopetaly*), stamens or carpels. Stamens are named differently depending upon the parts of stamens fused. It may be **adelphous** (if the filaments of different stamens are united and anthers remain free), **syngenesious** (if the anthers of different stamens are united, but the filaments are free e.g., *Helianthus spp.*) and **synandrous** (if anthers as well as filaments of the stamens are united throughout their whole length e.g., *Cucurbita*). In adelphous condition, the stamens may be united by their filaments into one (**monadelphous**), two (**diadelphous**) or several (**polyadelphous**). The attachment of stamens with the sepals, petals or gynoecium is called *adhesion*. It may be **epiphyllous** (stamens are attached to perianth, example, *Liliaceae*), **epipetalous** (the stamens are attached to petals, example, *sunflower*) and **gynandrous** (stamens remain attached to the carpels, example, *Calotropis*).

Symmetry of flower: On the basis of symmetry, the flowers can be categorized as: actinomorphic, zygomorphic and asymmetrical. When a flower can be divided by any vertical plane into two equal and similar halves, it is called **actinomorphic** (e.g., Mustard and Brinjal). When a flower can be divided into two equal and similar halves by only one vertical division, it is called **zygomorphic** (e.g., Pea and Larkspur). When a flower cannot be divided into two equal and similar halves by any vertical plane, it is called **asymmetrical** (e.g., *Canna*).

Floral formula and floral diagram

The *floral formulas* are used to summarize the number and fusion of floral parts. In these formulas, **P** refers to *perianth parts* and is used where the perianth is undifferentiated into a typical outer calyx and inner corolla. If the perianth is differentiated into a distinct calyx and corolla, **K** represents the number of sepals and **C** the number of petals. The androecium is denoted by **A** and represents the number of stamens. The gynoecium is denoted by **G**, showing the number of carpels in the gynoecium, followed by superior or inferior to denote ovary position. The fusion of similar parts is illustrated with parentheses ( ) that enclose the number. Separate, discrete whorls of parts are separated by the sign, delimiting the number of parts per whorl; the outermost whorl is indicated by the first number, the innermost whorl by the last number. Numbers that are enclosed by brackets [ ] represent a less common or rare condition. A hypothetical example of floral formula is: $K_{(5)\ [(4)]}\ C_5\ A_{5+5}\ G_5$, represents a flower having a synsepalous calyx with five (rarely four), an apopetalous corolla of five petals, an androecium with ten distinct (not fused to one another) stamens in two whorls of five each and an apocarpous gynoecium with five carpels.

Family descriptions are also described by **floral diagrams**. These represent a diagrammatic cross-sectional view of a flower bud, showing the relative relationship of perianth, androecial and gynoecial components. Floral diagrams may show fusion of floral parts as well as things such as stamen position, placentation and perianth, calyx or corolla aestivation. They are very useful in visualizing floral structure.

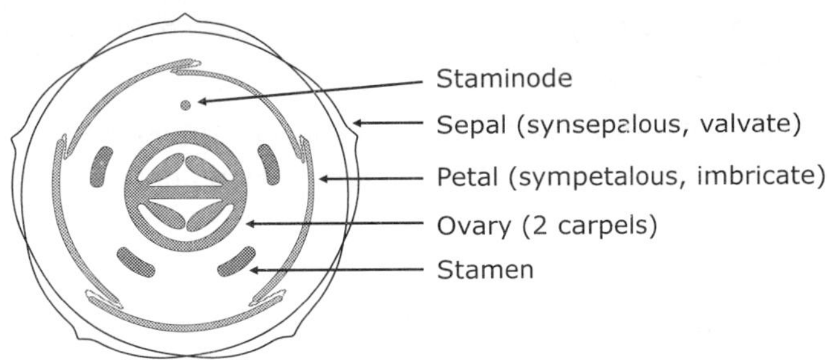

Figure 6.14 Floral diagram.

Placentation

The portion of the ovary to which the ovules are attached is known as the *placenta* and the manner in which the ovules are distributed in the ovary is called *placentation*. *Placentation* is of the following types:

Marginal : Placenta developing along the junction of the two margins of the carpel in monocarpellary and one chambered ovary; e.g., pea.

Axile : Placenta bearing the ovules developed from the central axis of a compound ovary, corresponding to the fused margins of carpels; e.g., *Citrus*, *Solanum*.

Parietal : Placenta bearing the ovules on the inner wall of the ovary and their position corresponds to the fused margins of carpels; the ovary is one chambered; e.g., *Argemone*.

Free-central : The ovules are borne on a central column without any septa, the ovary is unilocular; e.g., *Stellaria*.

Basal : Placenta present on the base of the ovary and the ovary is unilocular; e.g., *Sonchus*.

Superficial : Ovary is multilocular, carpels being numerous as in axile type but placenta in this case develop all around the inner surface of the partition wall; e.g., Waterlily.

Figure 6.15 Diagram of different types of placentation.

Fruits

A fruit is a matured or ripened ovary. It consists of *pericarp* (fruit wall) and *seed(s)*. The **pericarp** develops from the wall of ovary. It may be dry or fleshy. When pericarp is thick and fleshy, it is generally differentiated into the outer *epicarp*, the middle *mesocarp* and the inner *endocarp*. In dry fruits, pericarp remain undifferentiated. **Seed** develops from ovules after fertilization.

The fruit which develops from the ovary is called **true fruit** (*eucarp*). Most of the fruits are true fruits. If any other floral part takes part in fruit formation, it is called **false fruit** (*pseudocarp*) e.g., apple, pear. Fruits may develop after fertilization or even without fertilization. The phenomenon of development of fruits without fertilization is known as **parthenocarpy** and such fruits are known as **parthenocarpic fruits**.

Fruits can be classified into *simple*, *aggregate* and *multiple fruits* based on the number of ovary and flowers participating in the formation of fruits.

Simple fruits develop from a single carpel (unicarpellary) or multicarpellary syncarpous gynoecium of a single flower. Simple fruits may be dry or fleshy. Fleshy fruits are general adaptations for seed dispersal by animals. Fleshy fruits are generally indehiscent (not splitting open at maturity), but may rarely be dehiscent (splitting open at maturity).

Aggregate fruits are formed from multicarpellary, apocarous ovary. Each carpel develops into a fruitlet and all fruitlets together form an aggregate fruit. An aggregate of simple fruits borne, by a single flower is otherwise known as etaerio. Aggregate fruits may be *etaerio of achenes* (e.g., Strawberry) *etaerio of berries* (e.g., Custard apple) and other.

Multiple (or **composite**) **fruits** develop from the entire inflorescence that is, from many gynoecia of many flowers. These are of two types: **Sorosis** (develops from the catkin type of inflorescence, e.g., jackfruit, pineapple) and **syconus** (develops from the hypanthodium type of inflorescence e.g., *Ficus*).

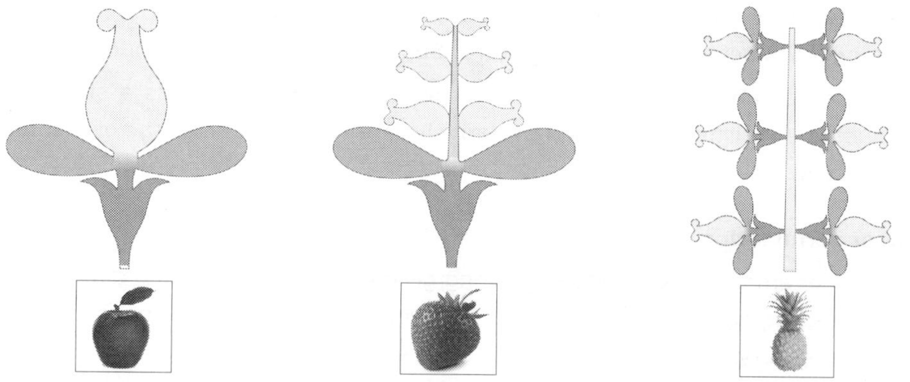

Simple fruit: Apple **Aggregate fruit**: Strawberry **Multiple fruit**: Pineapple

Figure 6.16 *Simple fruits* develop from a single carpel or from two or more united carpels (e.g., apple). *Aggregate fruits* are formed from an apocarpous gynoecium—in which each carpel retains its identity in the mature state (e.g., strawberries). The individual matured carpels, or ovaries, are called *fruitlets*. *Multiple fruits* are derived from an inflorescence, that is, from the combined gynoecia of many flowers (e.g., pineapple).

Seeds

After fertilization, the development of next sporophytic generation occurs within seed, which derives from the ovule after fertilization. Seeds are enclosed in the pericarp derived from the ovary wall. The fertilized egg (the diploid zygote) develops into the embryo, while the fertilized central cell forms the endosperm. Seed development is divided in two major phases: embryo and endosperm development and maturation. Once embryogenesis is completed, seeds enter the maturation phase. A *mature seed* consists of three genetically distinctive parts– diploid seed coat, diploid embryo and nutritive triploid endosperm.

Seed-coat is the outermost protective covering of a seed and generally made up of two layers – an outer, thick layer called **testa** and an inner, thin one called **tegmen**. In *Arabidopsis*, seed coat the outer integument consists of two cell layers and the inner integument consists of three cell layers. The innermost layer of the inner integument, named endothelium, remain in direct contact with the endosperm cells.

A scar of the funiculus on the seed coat is called **hilum**. A seed coat that is fleshy at maturity may be termed a **sarcotesta**. In addition, in some taxa an extra, fleshy layer may form outside the seed coat from the funiculus. If the fleshy layer more or less envelops the seed coat, it is known as an **aril**. A fleshy layer that doesn't surround the seed coat, but forms as a basal appendage is called **caruncle**. The caruncle and aril help in seed dispersal by animals.

Embryo is an immature sporophytic plant. It consists of an *embryonal axis* and one or two *cotyledons* attached laterally to the embryonal axis. There is a single cotyledon in **monocots** (such as wheat and maize) and two cotyledons in **dicots** (such as gram and pea). The cotyledon(s), the first leaf or leaves of the embryo, are often fleshy and full of reserve food materials. At opposite ends of the embryonal axis have the shoot and root apical meristems. The axis below (hypo-) the cotyledon(s) is known as the **hypocotyl** and above the point of attachment is the **epicotyl**. The lower end of the hypocotyl give rise to an *embryonic root* (or **radicle**). The epicotyl develops into *embryonic shoot* (or **plumule**).

Endosperm is a nutritive tissue derived from *primary endosperm nucleus*. The seeds are of two types depending on the presence or absence of the endosperm: **Endospermic** (or *albuminous*) seeds that contain endosperm and **non-endospermic** (or *ex-albuminous*) seeds that do not contain endosperm. In the **endospermic seeds**, the food is stored in the endosperm while the cotyledons are small, thin and papery. Generally, monocot seeds are endospermic but some as in orchids are non-endospermic. In cereals, endosperm comprises of two cell types: **starchy endosperm** and **aleurone**. The cells of aleurone layer contain *aleurone grains*. Each aleurone grain is enclosed by a single unit membrane. The main components of aleurone grains are protein, phytin, phospholipid and carbohydrate. In the **non-endospermic seeds** such as bean, gram and pea, the endosperm is consumed during seed development and food is stored in the cotyledons. The cotyledons become thick and fleshy. Most of the food is usually transferred from endosperm to cotyledons before the seed is mature. Seeds of dicots are non-endospermic.

Some seeds are classified as **perispermic seeds** due to presence of **perisperm** as a storage tissue. Perisperm originates from the nucellus. Perispermic seeds are relatively rare being characteristic of just few families such as Chenopodiaceae, Cactaceae.

Epigeal and hypogeal germination

The way in which the shoot emerges from the seed during germination varies among different plant groups. Seed germination may be *epigeal* or *hypogeal*. In **epigeal** germination, in which the cotyledons are carried above ground level by the elongating hypocotyl. Seed germination in the garden bean (*Phaseolus vulgaris*) and the castor bean (*Ricinus communis*) is epigeal in nature. Epigeal germination is considered evolutionarily more primitive than hypogeal germination. In **hypogeal** germination, the cotyledons or comparable storage organs remain beneath the soil while the plumule pushes upward and emerges above the ground. The hypocotyl does not elongate. It is the epicotyl that elongates, which pulls the plumule above ground. Hypogeal germination is characteristic of pea seeds and all grasses.

6.6 Animalia

Animals are multicellular eukaryotes with heterotrophic nutrition, usually ingestive. Animals are extraordinarily diverse in form and constituting millions of species (at least 4 million). The unicellular heterotrophic organisms called *protozoa* are now considered to be members of the kingdom protista. The animal kingdom includes about 35 phyla, most of which are found in the sea, with few in freshwater, and fewer still on the land.

Among the members of the animal kingdom, about 95% do not possess a backbone (or vertebral column) and hence are described as **invertebrates**. The remaining animals represent a group called *chordates*, which possess a solid supporting structure on the dorsal side of the body called *notochord*, at some stage of their life cycle.

Animal cells are diverse in structure and function. Animal cells, except for those of sponges, are organized into tissues and the tissues of most animals in turn are organized into complex structures called *organs*. With few exceptions, animals are diploid and reproduce sexually. Gametes are the only haploid cells in their life cycles.

Levels of organization

Although animals are multicellular but all of them do not exhibit the same pattern of cellular organization. Three different levels of organization exists in animals: *cellular level*, *tissue level* and *organ level*.

In **cellular level organization**, as in sponges, the cells are arranged as loose cell aggregates. This is the lowest level of organization in a multicellular organism. In coelenterates, the arrangement of cells is more complex. Here, the cells performing the same function are arranged into tissues, hence it is called **tissue level of organization**. The **organ level of organization** is exhibited by members of platyhelminthes and other higher phyla where tissues are grouped together to form organs, each specialized for a particular function. In animals like annelids, arthropods, molluscs, echinoderms and chordates, organs have associated to form functional systems, each system concerned with a specific physiological function. This pattern is called *organ system* level of organization. This is the highest level of organization.

Body plan

A set of morphological and developmental traits that are generally integrated into a functional unit is referred to as a *body plan*. There are three types of body plan in the animal kingdom:

Cell aggregate plan: The cell aggregate plan is exhibited by the simplest animals like sponges. In this body plan, body is made of mere clusters of cells which are not assembled as tissues. There are no nerve cells and, hence, there is no coordination amongst the cells constituting the body.

Blind sac plan: This type of body plan is more complex than the cell aggregate plan, as is exhibited by coelenterates and flatworms except tapeworms. They have a digestive cavity with only one opening to the outside through which ingestion as well as egestion occurs.

Tube within a tube plan: The tube within a tube plan is exhibited by animals like earthworm, cockroach, man etc. In this body plan, digestive system forms a continuous tube-like structure with an opening at each end e.g., mouth at the anterior end and an anus at posterior end. A tube within a tube plan is of two types:

Protostomic: The mouth of the digestive tract develops first in the embryo and the anus is formed later. This occurs in roundworms, annelids, molluscs and arthropods.

Deuterostomic: The anus of the digestive tract develops first in the embryo and the mouth is formed later. This occurs in echinoderms and chordates.

Body symmetry

Body symmetry is the similarity of parts in different regions and directions of the body. On the basis of symmetry, the animals are divided into the following categories:

Asymmetrical: Animals (e.g., most sponges and adult snails) which cannot be divided into two equivalent halves through any plane are described as *asymmetrical* (i.e., *the arrangement of body parts without a central axis or point*).

Radially symmetrical: Animals which can be divided into two equal halves by any longitudinal plane that passes through the central axis. Member of phylum Cnidaria (jellyfish, sea anemones and corals) exhibits radial symmetry. This symmetry allows animals to reach out in all directions from one central point. In cnidarians such as corals and sea anemones, the mouth is not circular, but oval. Thus, there are two planes that divide the body into mirror-image halves, one along the mouth and one perpendicular to it; these animals are actually *biradially symmetrical*.

Bilaterally symmetrical: Animals which can be divided into two equal right and left halves by only one plane (the **sagittal plane**) exhibits *bilateral symmetry*. Animals with this body plan are collectively termed the **bilateria**. Most animals other than sponges and cnidarians exhibit bilateral symmetry. This symmetry is present in organisms platyhelminthes to chordates except adult snail and adult echinoderms. In echinoderms (sea stars and their relatives), adults are radially symmetrical, but the larvae are bilaterally symmetrical. A bilaterally symmetrical body has, in addition to left and right halves, dorsal and ventral portions, which are divided by the **frontal plane**, and anterior (front) and posterior (rear) ends, which are divided by the **transverse plane** (in an animal that walks on all fours, dorsal is the top side).

Table 6.5 Terms of direction

Term	Description
Aboral	The end opposite the mouth.
Oral	The end containing the mouth.
Anterior	The head end.
Posterior	The tail end.
Caudal	Toward the tail.
Cephalic	Toward the head.
Distal	Away from the point of attachment of a structure on the body (e.g., toes are distal to the knee).
Proximal	Toward the point of attachment of a structure on the body (e.g., hip is proximal to the knee).
Dorsal	The back of an animal; usually the upper surface; synonymous with posterior for animals that walk upright.
Ventral	The belly of an animal; usually the lower surface; synonymous with anterior for animals that walk upright.

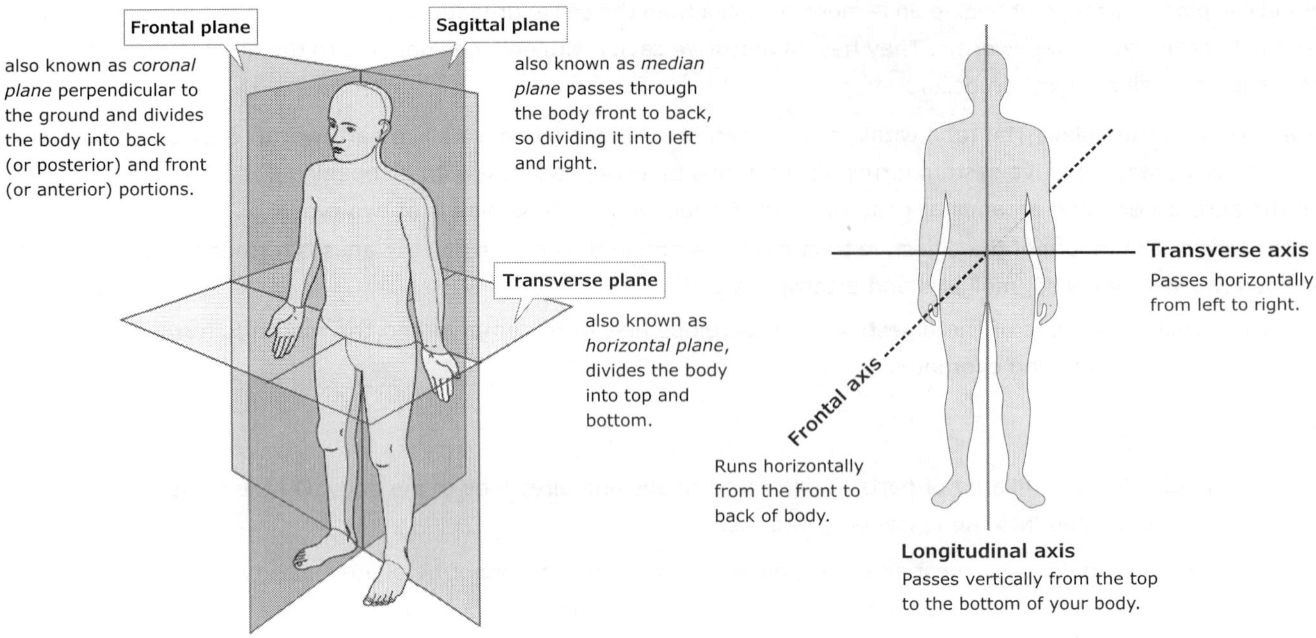

Coelom

A **coelom** is a body cavity that develops entirely within the mesoderm. A **body cavity** is a fluid-filled space in which the internal organs can be suspended and separated from the body wall. The coelom is surrounded by a layer of epithelial cells derived from the mesoderm and termed the *peritoneum*. Since diploblastic animals lack mesoderm, hence, coelom does not occur in them. Animals with coelom are termed **coelomates**. In animals like arthropods, the coelom is reduced in the adults and found to be filled with blood, hence referred to as the **haemocoel**. Animals which lack the coelom are called **acoelomates** e.g., porifera, coelenterata and platyhelminthes. A body cavity called the **pseudocoelom** develops embryologically between mesoderm and endoderm, so occurs in the adult between tissues derived from the mesoderm and those derived from endoderm; animals with this type of body cavity are termed **pseudocoelomates**. Roundworm (nemathelminthes) is an example of pseudocoelomate.

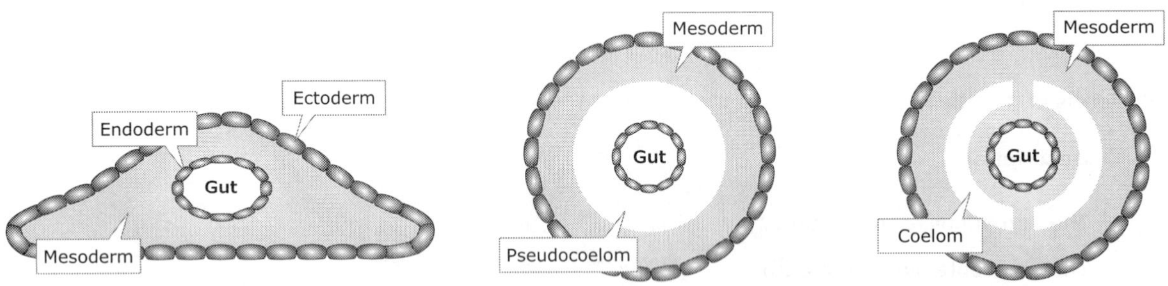

Figure 6.17 Acoelomates, such as flatworms, have no body cavity between the digestive tract (derived from the endoderm) and the musculature layer (derived from the mesoderm). Pseudocoelomates have a body cavity, the pseudocoelom, between tissues derived from the endoderm and those derived from the mesoderm. Coelomates have a body cavity, the coelom, that develops entirely within tissues derived from the mesoderm, and so is lined on both sides by tissue derived from the mesoderm.

Coelomates fall into either *protostomes* or *deuterostomes*, depending on how their embryos develop. **Protostomes** (from the *Greek* meaning *first mouth*) are coelomates whose embryonic development makes a blastopore (the first opening in the blastula) that later develops into a mouth. **Deuterostomes** (*second mouth*) are coelomates whose embryonic development produces a blastopore that later forms an anus, with a second opening forming the mouth (hence the designation of second mouth). *Vertebrates are deuterostomes.*

Germ layers

In the process of embryonic development, the cells of animals of most groups organize into three layers (called germ layers): an outer **ectoderm**, an inner **endoderm**, and an intermediate **mesoderm**. Animals with three embryonic cell layers are said to be **triploblastic**. The ectoderm gives rise to the outer covering of the body and the nervous system; the endoderm gives rise to the digestive system, including the intestine; and the skeleton and muscles develop from the mesoderm. All triploblastic animals are members of the Bilateria. The embryos of poriferans and coelenterates have two germ layers, the ectoderm and endoderm. These animals are called **diploblastic**. Ectoderm gives rise to the epidermis, the outer layer of the body wall. Endoderm gives rise to the gastrodermis, the tissue that lines the gut cavity. Between the epidermis and the gastrodermis is a noncellular layer called **mesoglea**.

Body segmentation

Segmentation (metamerism) is the repetition of organs and tissues at intervals along the body of an animal, thus dividing the body into a linear series of similar parts or segments (metameres). Most striking segmentation is seen in *Annelida* called **metameric segmentation**. Metameric segmentation occurs both externally and internally, and is a mesodermal phenomenon. The internal segmentation imposes a corresponding segmentation on the nerves, blood vessels and excretory organs. Each segment has its own excretory, nervous, circulatory organs. In some metameric animals the segmentation is visible externally (as in arthropods) but in others (e.g., chordata) external segmentation has been lost and internal segmentation is best seen in the embryo. Metameric segmentation is thought to have arisen as an adaptation to more efficient locomotion.

Body temperature

In many animals (like invertebrates, fishes, amphibians and reptiles), the body temperature varies according to the surrounding environment. They are called **poikilothermic** (or cold-blooded) animals. Body temperature of birds and mammals remains constant and does not change with the change of environmental temperature. Such animals are termed **homeothermic** (or warm-blooded) animals.

Nutrition

Heterotrophic nutrition is the characteristics of animals. The heterotrophs may be **herbivores** (eating plants), **carnivores** (eating animals) and **omnivores** (eating both plants and animals). Some animals that depend on other organisms for food are called *parasites*. The parasites that live within the body of their hosts are called *endoparasites*, while those living on the outside of the body are called *ectoparasites*.

Digestion is a mechano-chemical process which converts the macromolecules (carbohydrates, proteins, fats, nucleic acids) into micromolecules (glucose, amino acid, fatty acid, nucleotides). It is of two types: *Intracellular* (digestion occurs inside the cell as in lower animals like protozoan, poriferan) and *extracellular* (digestion occurs in the lumen of the alimentary canal as in majority of invertebrates and vertebrates). In coelenterates, digestion is both extracellular and intracellular.

Coelenterates and flatworms have a digestive tract with a single opening termed *mouth* that takes food as well as eliminates the undigested food. This type of digestive tract is called *incomplete*. Digestive tract of many animals has two openings; mouth for intake of food and anus for the elimination of faecal matter. Such a digestive tract is termed *complete*.

Respiratory system

Depending on the animal, the organs and structures of the respiratory system vary in composition and complexity. The respiratory system is composed of the organs that deliver oxygen to the circulatory system for movement or transport to all of the cells in the body. Organs or systems such as body covering, gills, lungs or trachea allow the movement of gases between the animal and its environment. These structures vary in appearance but function in a similar way by allowing gases to be exchanged.

Animals obtain oxygen in a number of ways:

1. From water or air through a moist surface directly into the body (protozoan);
2. From air or water through the skin to the blood vessels (earthworms);
3. From air through gills to a system of air ducts or trachaea (insects);
4. From water through moist gill surfaces to the blood vessels (fishes, amphibians);
5. From air through moist lung surfaces to the blood vessels (reptiles, mammals, humans).

In one-celled *aquatic animals*, such as protozoans, and in sponges, jellyfish, and other aquatic organisms that are a few cell layers thick, oxygen and carbon dioxide diffuse directly between the water and the cell. Insects, centipedes, millipedes, and some arachnids have fine tubes or *trachea* connecting all parts of the body to small openings on the surface of the animal. Movements of the thoracic and abdominal parts and the animal's small size enable oxygen and carbon dioxide to be transported from the trachea to the blood by way of diffusion.

In more complex animals, respiration requires a blood circulatory system and gills, in combination with blood, blood vessels, and a heart. Many aquatic animals have **gills**, thin-walled filaments that increase the surface area and increase the amount of available oxygen. The oxygen and carbon dioxide exchange occur between the surrounding water and the blood within the gills. The gills of some larvae and worms are simply exposed to the water, while some aquatic crustaceans, such as crayfish, have special adaptations to force water over their gills. The gills of fishes and tadpoles are located in chambers on the sides of the throat; water is taken into the mouth and forced out over the gills.

All land vertebrates, including most amphibians, all reptiles, birds and mammals have lungs that enable these animals to get oxygen from air. A heart and a closed circulatory system work with the lungs to deliver oxygen and to remove carbon dioxide from the cells. A lung is a chamber lined with moist cells that have an abundance of blood capillaries. These membranes take different forms. In amphibians and reptiles they can form a single balloon-like sac. In animals that require large amounts of oxygen, the lungs are a spongy mass composed of millions of tiny air sacs called *alveoli* that supply an enormous surface area for the transfer of gases.

In birds, a special adaptation allows for the high-energy demands of flight. The lungs have two openings, one for taking in oxygen-filled air, the other for expelling the carbon dioxide. Air flows through them rather than in and out as in the other lunged vertebrates.

Circulatory system

The majority of multicellular animals have developed a circulatory system for mass transport of nutrients and respiratory gases. Besides transport of metabolites and gases, animals need to remove the waste products formed in their tissues; to transport hormones to the target tissues and maintain homeostasis. All such functions are performed by the circulatory system. Vertebrates possess an elaborate circulatory system that includes the blood vascular system (blood, heart and blood vessels) and lymphatic system (lymph and lymph vessels).

Blood vascular system is basically of two types: *open* and *closed*. *Closed blood vascular system* occurs in annelids, some molluscs and vertebrates in which blood is circulated in the blood vessels. Arthropods and most molluscs have an *open type of circulatory system* in which the blood flows in spaces, the *sinuses*. Blood may be colorless (e.g., insects), bluish due to a respiratory pigment, **hemocyanin** (e.g., Prawn, Pila) or red due to respiratory pigment, **hemoglobin** (e.g., earthworm, vertebrates).

Excretory system

The process by which metabolic waste products are eliminated (totally or partially) from the body of animals is called *excretion*. Nitrogenous wastes (such as ammonia, urea and uric acid) are the most important metabolic waste excreted by the animals. These wastes are produced from the metabolism of amino acids and nucleic acids and are very toxic to cellular environment. The nature of the nitrogen-containing wastes (ammonia, urea and uric acid) and their excretion varies among the different species, depending on the availability of water. Most animals excrete a mixture of excretory products, but one nitrogenous product usually predominates.

The process of excreting ammonia is *ammonotelism* and organisms excreting ammonia are referred to as **ammonotelic**. Ammonia excretion is most common in aquatic animals. Ammonia, as it is readily soluble in water, is generally excreted by diffusion across body surfaces or through gill (in fish) as ammonium ions. Kidneys do not play any significant role in its removal. Most bony fish, amphibian tadpoles and most aquatic invertebrates are ammonotelic.

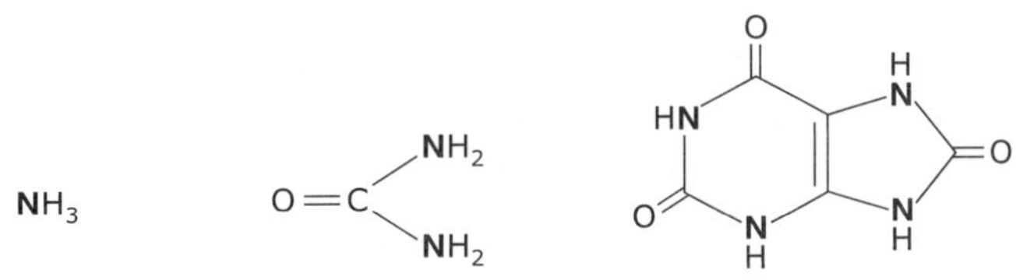

Ammonia Urea Uric acid

Although ammonia excretion works well in many aquatic species, it is much less suitable for terrestrial animals. Ammonia is very toxic, so its transportation and excretion requires large amount of water to make very dilute solutions. As a result, most terrestrial animals and many aquatic species do not excrete ammonia. Instead, they mainly excrete **urea**. Ammonia produced by metabolism is converted into urea in the liver of these animals. Urea is water-soluble and so can be excreted in large amounts in the urine. The main advantage of urea is its very low toxicity. Animals can transport urea in the circulatory system and store it safely at high concentrations. Furthermore, much less water is lost when a given quantity of nitrogen is excreted in the form of urea. The main disadvantage of urea is its energy cost. Animals use large number of ATP molecules to produce urea from ammonia. The process of excreting urea is *ureotelism* and organisms excreting urea are referred to as **ureotelic**. Mammals, most adult amphibians, cartilaginous fish and some marine bony fishes and turtles are ureotelic.

Most reptiles, birds and insects excrete nitrogenous wastes in the form of uric acid, which is very less soluble in water. As a result of its low solubility, uric acid precipitates and thus can be excreted using very little water. Uric acid is even more energetically expensive to produce than urea, requiring large number of ATP molecules for synthesis from ammonia. The process of excreting uric acid is *uricotelism* and organisms excreting uric acid are referred to as **uricotelic**.

Table 6.6 Comparison among ammonotelic, ureotelic and uricotelic

Nitrogenous wastes	**Ammonia**
Site of formation	In the liver by oxidative deamination of amino acids.
Solubility in water	Highly soluble
Examples	Most bony fishes, tadpoles of amphibian and most aquatic invertebrates.
	Organisms are referred to as ammonotelic.
Nitrogenous wastes	**Urea**
Site of formation	In the liver from ammonia and CO_2 (ornithine cycle)
Solubility in water	Highly soluble
Examples	Mammals, most amphibians, aquatic reptiles except crocodile (excrete mainly ammonia), cartilaginous fish and some bony fishes.
	Organisms are referred to as ureotelic.
Nitrogenous wastes	**Uric acid**
Site of formation	Mostly in the liver (to some extent in kidneys)
Solubility in water	Almost insoluble
Examples	Land reptiles, birds and insects.
	Organisms are referred to as uricotelic.

Mammals also produce some uric acid, but it is a waste product of the degradation of purine nucleotides, not of amino acids. Most mammals have an enzyme called *uricase*, which converts uric acid into a more soluble derivative, *allantoin*. Only humans, apes, and the Dalmatian dog lack this enzyme, and they must excrete the uric acid. In humans, excessive accumulation of uric acid in the joints produces a condition known as *gout*. It is a painful inflammation of the joints caused by deposits of uric acid crystals. In general, the kinds of nitrogenous wastes excreted depend on an animal's evolutionary history and habitat, especially the availability of water. For example, terrestrial turtles (which often live in dry areas) excrete mainly uric acid, whereas aquatic turtles excrete both urea and ammonia.

The tissues and organs associated with the removal of waste products constitute the **excretory system.** This system is also responsible for maintaining water content in the body (i.e., *osmoregulation*). The systems that perform the basic excretory functions vary widely among animal groups.

In some animals (like members of porifera, coelenterata and echinodermata), there are no specialized tissues and organs for excretion. They lose metabolic wastes by diffusion through the general body surface. Many animals have definite excretory organs, generally made up of a complex network of tubules.

Flatworms (phylum platyhelminthes) have excretory systems called **protonephridia** (singular, *protonephridium*). The protonephridia form a network of dead-end tubules which branch throughout the body into bulblike **flame cells**. These simple excretory structures open to the outside of the body (they do not open to the inside). The movement of cilia within the flame cells expels wastes outside the body through excretory pores.

Protonephridia are also found in rotifers, some annelids, mollusc larvae, and lancelets. Among these animals, the function of the protonephridia varies. In the freshwater flatworms, protonephridia serve mainly in *osmoregulation*.

Most annelids, such as earthworms, have **metanephridia** (singular, *metanephridium*), excretory organs that open internally to the coelom. Each segment of a worm has a pair of metanephridia. The metanephridia of an earthworm have both excretory and osmoregulatory functions.

Insects have **malpighian tubules** as excretory organs. The malpighian tubules are the extensions of the digestive tract that collect water and wastes from the body fluid (hemolymph). Waste products and ions (mostly potassium ions) are entered into the lumen of the tubule from the hemolymph by active transport. The uptake of ions creates an osmotic gradient that causes water to enter the tubules by osmosis. The fluid carrying waste substances then passes into the rectum. There, most potassium ions are pumped back into the hemolymph. Much of this water is reabsorbed across the wall of the hindgut. The nitrogenous wastes, mainly insoluble uric acid – are excreted from the rectum along with feces.

The excretory organs in some crustaceans (crayfish, crabs) are **antennal glands** (or *green glands*) because of their location near the antenna and their green color. In other crustaceans, the excretory organs are at the bases of the second maxillae and are termed **maxillary glands**. The excretory organs in many arachnids (such as spiders, scorpions, ticks and mites) are **coxal glands**.

In vertebrates and some other chordates, a specialized organ called the **kidney** functions in both osmoregulation and excretion. Like the excretory organs of most animal phyla, kidneys consist of tubules. The numerous tubules are arranged in a highly organized manner in these compact organs.

Animal	Excretory system
Marine invertebrate	Diffusion of ammonia through body wall.
Marine bony fish	Ammonia diffuses through gills.
Freshwater fish	Ammonia diffuses across the epithelium of gills.
Earthworm	Metanephridia remove wastes from coelomic fluid.
Insect	Malpighian tubules remove wastes from the hemolymph.
Reptile	Kidney removes nitrogenous wastes.
Bird	Kidney removes nitrogenous wastes.
Mammal	Kidney removes nitrogenous wastes.

Skeleton

Skeleton is a hard internal or external framework that supports the body. Skeletons are of two types – *exoskeleton* and *endoskeleton*, depending upon their location. **Exoskeleton** is secreted by the skin or ectoderm, e.g., calcareous shell of molluscs; chitinous cuticle of arthropods; dermal plates in echinoderm. **Endoskeleton** is formed of hard bone and cartilage tissue, and constitute the internal framework of the body of vertebrates. Skeleton may be living (e.g., cartilage and bone in vertebrates) or non-living (e.g., spicules in sponges).

Sex

When both male and female sex organs are found in one individual, it is called **hermaphrodite** (or **bisexual** or **monoecious**) e.g., liver fluke, tape-worm, earthworm, leech. The animal with either male or female sex organ, is known as **unisexual** (or **dioecious**), e.g., frog, lizard, bird, rabbit. When the male and female animals can be distinguished externally, the condition is called **sexual dimorphism**. The latter is seen in peacocks and peahen, lion and lioness. When the male reproductive organs (testes) mature earlier, the condition is termed **protandry**, e.g., earthworm and when the female reproductive organs (ovaries) mature earlier, the condition is called **protogyny** as found in amphioxus.

Reproduction

Animals reproduce asexually or sexually. **Sexual reproduction** requires two parents who donate genes to the young, resulting in offspring with a mix of inherited genes. *Sexual reproduction* encompasses the fusion of two distinct gametes to form a zygote. The gametes are haploid (containing only one set of chromosomes) while the zygote is diploid (containing two sets of chromosomes). In most cases, the male gamete, called the **spermatozoan**, is relatively motile and usually has a flagellum. On the other hand, the female gamete, called the **ovum**, is non-motile and relatively large in comparison to the male gamete. A fusion of male and female gametes is known as **fertilization**. There are two mechanisms by which fertilization can take place. The first is **external** (the eggs are fertilized outside of the body); the second is **internal** (the eggs are fertilized within the female reproductive tract).

In **asexual reproduction**, only one parent is needed, resulting in offspring that are genetically identical to the parent. These offsprings are produced by mitosis. There are many invertebrates, including sea stars and sea anemones for example, that reproduce by asexual reproduction. Common forms of asexual reproduction include: **Budding** (an offspring grows out of the body of the parent, example - Hydras); **gemmules** (a parent releases a specialized mass of cells that can develop into an offspring, example - sponges); **fragmentation** (the body of the parent breaks into distinct pieces, each of which can produce an offspring, example - Planarians); and **regeneration** (if a piece of a parent is detached, it can grow and develop into a completely new individual, example - Echinoderms).

Development

When the young ones resemble the adult it is called **direct development**, e.g., rabbit. When the young one does not resemble the adult, such young one is known as a **nymph** or **larva**, it is known as **indirect development**. The change from nymph or larva to adult is called **metamorphosis**. It is a series of abrupt structural, physiological, and behavioral changes that transform a larva into an adult.

Depending upon the site of development of zygote, followed by fertilization, the animals may be grouped into three categories – oviparous (or egg-laying animals), ovoviviparous and viviparous.

Oviparous: Oviparous (e.g., frog, reptiles and birds) are animals that reproduce by laying eggs. Fertilization may be internal or external.

Viviparous: In viviparous animals (e.g., mammals), fertilization is internal and nourishment is provided through true placenta by the uterine wall of the mother.

Ovoviviparous: Ovoviviparous animals (e.g., sharks) are similar to viviparous species in that there is internal fertilization and the young are born live, but differ in that there is *no placental connection* and the unborn young are nourished by egg yolk.

6.7 Animal's classification

Animals are extra-ordinarily diverse in form and constituting millions of species (at least 4 million). The animals are broadly classified into **vertebrates** (chordata) and **invertebrates**, based on the presence of a spinal cord and backbone. Vertebrates include classes - fish (breathe with gills and live in water), amphibians (cold-blooded and live on land and water), reptiles (cold-blooded, breathe with lungs, reproduce with eggs), birds (warm-blooded with feathers *except* penguins and ostrich) and mammals (warm-blooded). *Invertebrates* include sponges, worms, mollusks, arthropods (includes many insects), echinoderms (including starfish) and coelenterates.

6.7.1 Phylum Porifera (Pore bearing animals)

Important characters

- Sponges are primitive multicellular animals with *cellular grade of organization*. They have no fixed body shape and no plane of symmetry. A whole sponge can be regenerated from a few separated cells. Sponges can almost be regarded not as individuals but as colonies of separate cells.
- Sponges are free-living aquatic (mostly marine) and having neither nerves nor muscles. Body wall with two layers of loosely arranged cells and a mesenchyme in between (*diploblastic*).
- Reproduction occurs by asexual (external or internal buds) or sexual methods.
- The body-wall encloses a large cavity, the spongocoel and in most cases also contains numerous small canals. Either the spongocoel or canals are lined by special *collar cells* or choanocytes with flagella. The ceaseless beating of flagella maintains a steady current of water through the canals to bring in food and oxygen and remove wastes.
- Almost all sponges possess an internal skeleton. It may consist of tiny calcareous or siliceous **spicules** or of fine spongin fibres or both.
- Examples: *Sycon* (Scypha), *Spongilla* (Freshwater sponge) and *Euspongia* (Bath sponge).

6.7.2 Phylum Cnidaria (Coelenterata)

Important characters

- The coelenterates have tissues but lack an organ system. They, thus have a *tissue level of organization*.
- Usually radially symmetrical, i.e., section passing through any diameter gives two equal and opposite halves.
- The body shows two main forms, *polyp* and *medusa*. The **polyp** is cylindrical and usually fixed but may be solitary or colonial. The medusa is an umbrella-like and generally free-swimming, but always solitary. Either or both the forms may occur in a species and may have many varieties. This is called **polymorphism**. When both polyp and **medusa** forms are found in the same animal, the two forms alternate in the life-cycle. This phenomenon is termed **alternation of generation**.
- The body-wall consists of two distinct layers of cells (**diploblastic**): the outer *epidermis* and the inner *gastrodermis*. Each layer has several types of cells, which cooperate with one another as in tissues. The cellular characteristic of the cnidarians include *stinging cells* (cnidoblasts) for offence and defence, reserve *interstitial cells* to replace the worn out cells, and epithelio muscular cells to provide musculature. Between the two layers is a sheet of gelatinous material, the **mesogloea**, which may contain free cells, but is never formed of cells.
- The body encloses a single cavity, the **coelenteron**. It provides the phylum its name. It has a single aperture, the mouth. There is no anus. The mouth serves both for taking food and for throwing out faeces. Such a digestive cavity is said to be *incomplete*. Digestion is partly *extracellular* that occurs in the coelenteron and partly *intracellular* which takes place within the gastrodermal cells.

  Examples: *Physalia* (Portuguese man-of-war), *Adamsia* (Sea anemone), *Pennatula* (Sea-pen), *Gorgonia* (Sea-fan) and *Meandrina* (Brain coral).

6.7.3 Phylum Platyhelminthes (Flatworms)

Important characters

- Acoelomate, triploblastic, bilaterally symmetrical organisms.
- Possess a mouth but no anus– Blind sac body plan.
- Digestive, skeletal, circulatory and respiratory systems are absent, parenchymal gland serves as hydroskeleton.
- The body is soft and dorso-ventrally flattened. It may be leaf-like or ribbon-like. It is without segmentation.
- Possess *organ-system level of organization*.
- The organ-systems are packed in a characteristic connective tissue, called the *parenchyma*.
- The nervous system is ladder-like. It comprises the brain and two main longitudinal nerve-chords connected at intervals by transverse commissures.
- The excretory system includes characteristic **flame cells** leading into tubules that open out by one or more excretory pores.
- Hermaphroditic, often with elaborate precautions for minimizing self-fertilization.
- Fertilization is internal. Life history often includes larval stages. Asexual reproduction by transverse fission occurs in some forms.

  Examples: *Taenia* (Tapeworm), *Fasciola* (Liver fluke).

6.7.4 Phylum Aschelminthes (Roundworms)

Important characters

- Aschelminthes include **pseudocoelomates** characterized by the presence of a cavity, the pseudocoel between the gut and body wall. Cavity is not lined with mesodermal epithelium.
- The Aschelminth are triploblastic, i.e., they develop from three germ layers.
- The body-wall consists of a firm resistant cuticle, epidermis and muscle-layer. The cuticle is moulted (changed) during growth period or throughout life. The epidermis may be syncytial or cellular. The musculature generally contains longitudinal fibers only.
- A cavity is present between the body-wall and the digestive tract. It is not lined by an epithelium. Therefore, it is called the pseudocoel (or *false coelom*) instead of true coelom.
- Sexes are separate. Fertilization is internal. Life history may be simple or complex. There is no asexual reproduction.
- Amongst its various classes, class *Nematoda* is the most important. Nematodes are aquatic, terrestrial or parasitic, elongated roundworms. Body covered with cuticle, no circulatory and respiratory systems. Alimentary canal complete with muscular pharynx, anus present. Sexes are separate.

  Examples: *Ascaris*, *Enterobius* (Pinworm), Ancylostoma, *Wuchereria bancrofti* (Filaria worm), Rhabditis.

Aschelminthes was formerly known as *Nemathelminthes*. Platyhelminthes and Aschelminthes together referred to as *Helminthes* and their study constitutes a separate branch called *Helminthology*. Many helminths act as parasites and live inside their host unlike external parasites such as lice and fleas. They are worm-like organisms that live and feed off living hosts, receiving nourishment and protection while disrupting their hosts' nutrient absorption, causing weakness and disease. Those that live inside the digestive tract are called intestinal parasites. They can live inside humans as well as other animals.

List of human diseases caused by roundworms and flatworm

Disease	:	**Pinworm disease**
Causative agent	:	*Enterobius vermicularis*
Organs affected	:	Intestine
Transmission	:	Contact, food
Disease	:	**Roundworm disease**
Causative agent	:	*Ascaris lumbricoides*
Organs affected	:	Intestine, lungs
Transmission	:	Food, water, contact
Disease	:	**Trichinosis**
Causative agent	:	*Trichinella spiralis*
Organs affected	:	Intestine, muscles, eye
Transmission	:	Pork consumption
Animal host	:	Pig
Disease	:	**Eyeworm disease**
Causative agent	:	*Loa Loa*
Organs affected	:	Eye connectivity tissues
Transmission	:	Deerflies, horseflies
Animal host	:	Insects
Disease	:	**Pork tapeworm disease**
Causative agent	:	*Taenia solium*
Organs affected	:	Intestine
Transmission	:	Pork consumption
Animal host	:	Pig
Disease	:	**Blood Fluke disease**
Causative agent	:	*Schistosoma mansoni*
Organs affected	:	Liver, lungs
Transmission	:	Water contact
Animal Host	:	Snail
Disease	:	**Whipworm disease**
Causative agent	:	*Trichuris trichiura*
Organs affected	:	Intestine
Transmission	:	Food, water
Disease	:	**Hookworm disease**
Causative agent	:	*Ancylostoma duodenale*
Organs affected	:	Intestine, Lungs, Lymph
Transmission	:	Contact with vegetation
Disease	:	**Filariasis**
Causative agent	:	*Wuchereria bancrofti*
Organs affected	:	Lymph, vessels
Transmission	:	Mosquito
Animal host	:	Mosquito
Disease	:	**Beef tapeworm disease**
Causative agent	:	*Taenia saginata*
Organs affected	:	Intestine
Transmission	:	Beef consumption
Animal host	:	Cattle
Disease	:	**Intestinal Fluke disease**
Causative agent	:	*Fasciolopsis buski*
Organs affected	:	Intestine
Transmission	:	Consumption of water plants
Animal host	:	Snail
Disease	:	**Dwarf tapeworm disease**
Causative agent	:	*Hymenolepis nana*
Organs affected	:	Intestine
Transmission	:	Food, contact

6.7.5 Phylum Annelida

Important characters

- Triploblastic, coelomate, bilaterally symmetrical and metamerically segmented animals.
- In earthworm, each segment has a separate coelom which acts as a *hydraulic skeleton*. During muscular contraction, the body wall pushes against each compartment wall. This allows separate regions to contract independently and elongate during locomotion.
- The body is elongated, cylindrical or flattened. It is divided into segments by ring-like grooves, the *annuli*. This character gives the phylum its name.
- The segmented worms are triploblastic, i.e., they develop from the three germ layers.

- The body-cavity is a *true coelom*, as it is lined by a mesodermal epithelium. It is divided by vertical septa into compartments.
- A closed circulatory system present.
- Segmental *nephridia* for excretion and osmoregulation.
- Typically, there is a *trochophore larva* during development.

  Examples: *Nereis*, *Pheretima* (Earthworm) and *Hirudinaria* (Blood-sucking leech).

6.7.6 Phylum Mollusca

Important characters

- Mollusca is the *second largest* animal phylum and include snails, slugs, oysters, cuttlefish, octopuses, and many other familiar animals.
- Exhibit organ-system level of body organization
- Bilaterally symmetrical, triploblastic and coelomate animals.
- Body is covered by a calcareous shell and is unsegmented with a distinct *head*, *muscular foot* and *visceral hump*.
- Most molluscs have a rasping tongue-like radula for feeding.
- Except cephalopods, all mollusks have such an open circulatory system.
- Nitrogenous wastes are removed from the body by the **nephridium** (plural, *nephridia*).
- Mostly dioecious. Fertilization is both external and internal, oviparous with indirect development.
- Embryo develops into a free-swimming larva called a **trochophore**.

  Examples: *Pila* (Apple snail), *Pinctada* (Pearl oyster), *Sepia* (Cuttlefish), *Loligo* (Squid), *Octopus* (Devil fish), *Aplysia* (Seahare), *Dentalium* (Tusk shell) and *Chaetopleura* (Chiton).

6.7.7 Phylum Arthropoda

Important characters

- Arthropoda is the *largest phylum* of animalia.
- Exhibit organ-system level of organization.
- Bilaterally symmetrical, triploblastic, segmented and coelomate animals.
- Metameric segmentation as in annelids but segments not separated from each other by septa.
- All arthropods have an exoskeleton of chitinous cuticle. Cuticle shed periodically to allow for growth. The process of casting off of skin or integument is known as *ecdysis* or *moulting*.
- Body is divisible into head, thorax and abdomen or divisible into cephalothorax and abdomen. They have *jointed appendages* (*arthros*-joint, *poda*-appendages).
- Arthropods have an open circulatory system. Body cavity, known as *haemocoel* (*hemocoel*), is filled with fluid-hemolymph.
- Respiration takes place through the general body surface and *gills* in crustacean; through *trachea* in insects, diplopoda, chilopoda; through *book lungs* in Arachnida.
- Excretion is brought about by *green glands* in aquatic forms and *malpighian tubules* in terrestrial forms.
- Sexes usually separate; fertilization internal; oviparous or ovoviviparous; development direct or indirect.

  Examples: *Apis* (Honey bee), *Bombyx* (Silkworm), *Laccifer* (Lac insect).

6.7.8 Phylum Echinodermata

Important characters

- Exclusively marine and banthoic i.e., found at the bottom of the sea.
- Spiny skinned, free swimming, triploblastic and coelomate animals.
- Adult echinoderms are radially symmetrical but larvae are bilaterally symmetrical.
- Lack head and do not show segmentation.
- Digestive system is complete with mouth on the ventral side and anus on the dorsal side.
- Most characteristic feature in echinodermates is the presence of the **water vascular** (or ambulacral) **system**. *Tube feet* are contractile appendages of the water vascular system; serve for locomotion, food capture, respiration and attachment of the body to the substratum. They constitute glands and filtering device.
- Respiratory organs are skin gills or papulae (starfish); peristomail gills (sea-urchins); genital bursae (brittle stars); cloacal respiratory tree (holothurians).
- Perform sexual reproduction. Sexes are separate. Fertilization is usually external. Development is indirect with free-swimming larva.

  Phylum Echinodermata is divided into two subphyla – **pelmatozoa** and **eleutherozoa**. Subphylum Pelmatozoa has a single living class *Crinodiea* represented by sea lilies or feather stars like *Antedon*, *Rhizocrinus*, etc. Subphylum eleutherozoa has four living classes: *Asteroidea* (Asterias), *Ophiuroidea* (Ophiothrix), *Echinoidea* (sea urchin), *Holothuroidea* (sea cucumbers).

6.7.9 Phylum Hemichordata

The name *hemichordate* means 'half chordate,' and hemichordates share some (but not all) of the typical chordate characteristics. However, hemichordates are not classified as true chordates, although they are quite closely related. Some DNA-based studies of evolution suggest that hemichordates are actually closer to echinoderms than to true chordates. This is supported by the fact that the larvae of at least some hemichordates look very much like those of some echinoderms. Thus, hemichordata was earlier considered as a sub-phylum under phylum chordata. But now it is placed as a separate phylum under non-chordata.

Important characters

- Exclusively marine.
- Worm-like animals with organ-system level of organization.
- Bilaterally symmetrical, triploblastic and coelomate animals.
- Body is cylindrical and is composed of an anterior *proboscis*, a *collar* and a long *trunk*. Notochord present which is hollow and endodermal in origin (termed *stomochord*). Notochord occurs only in the anterior end of the body. It is called *buccal diverticulum*.
- Open circulatory system.
- Perform sexual reproduction. Sexes are separate. Fertilization is external. Development is indirect.

  Example: *Balanoglossus* (*Tongue worm*), *Ptychodera* and *Saccoglossus*.

6.7.10 Phylum Chordata

Chordates are bilaterally symmetrical, triploblastic, coelomates with organ-system level of organization. They are fundamentally characterized by the presence of a *notochord*, a *dorsal hollow nerve cord* and *paired pharyngeal gill slits*.

Dorsal hollow nerve cord, ectodermal in origin, serves for the integration and coordination of the body activities. In vertebrates, the anterior part of nerve cord is specialized to form the brain and posterior part form the spinal cord.

Notochord present beneath the nerve cord and mesodermal in origin. It may persist in some chordates; in others it is replaced during embryonic development by the vertebral column that forms around the nerve cord.

Pharyngeal gill slits serve primarily for the passage of water from pharynx to outside. The digestive tube of chordates extends from the mouth to the anus. The region just posterior to the mouth is the pharynx. In all chordate embryos, a series of pouches separated by grooves form along the sides of the pharynx. In most chordates, these grooves (known as **pharyngeal** clefts) develop into slits that open to the outside of the body. These *pharyngeal slits* allow water entering the mouth to exit the body without passing through the entire digestive tract. In vertebrates (with the exception of vertebrates with limbs, the tetrapods), these slits and the structures that support them have been modified for gas exchange and are known as *gill slits*. In tetrapods, the pharyngeal clefts do not develop into slits. Instead, they play an important role in the development of parts of the ear and other structures in the head and neck.

A *post anal tail* is present in an embryonic condition that extends beyond the anus. It is reduced or absent in many adult chordates.

There are some 42,500 species of chordates, a phylum that includes the birds, reptiles, amphibians, fishes and mammals. Phylum chordata is divided into three subphyla: *urochordata* or *tunicata*, *cephalochordata* or *acrania* and *vertebrata*. The first two subphyla are considered primitive and often referred to as **protochordates** (nonvertebrate). All of them are marine and possess a notochord but never form vertebral column. In urochordata (e.g., *Herdmania*, *Ascidia*, *Doliolum*, *Salpa*, *Ciona*), notochord is present only in larval tail; in cephalochordata (e.g., Lancelet, belongs to genus *Branchiostoma*, *formerly* called *Amphioxus*) notochord extends from head to tail region.

All the members of vertebrate contain notochord during the embryonic period. The notochord is replaced by a cartilaginous or bony **vertebral column** in the adult stage. Besides the basic chordate characters, vertebrates have a ventral two, three or four chambers heart, kidneys for excretion and osmoregulation and paired appendages which may be fins or limbs. The first vertebrates evolved in the oceans about 545 million years ago during the Cambrian period.

However, on the basis of presence or absence of jaw, the subphylum vertebrata is further subdivided into two superclass: **agnatha** (*which lacks jaws*) and **gnathostomata** (*which bears jaws*). Only one class of living members, class cyclostomata represents the superclass agnatha. Agnathans lack jaws and paired appendages, and include the lampreys, hagfishes, and extinct ostracoderms. Hagfishes (the *most primitive vertebrates known*) are scavengers in marine environments. Lampreys have a life history involving migrations from the open ocean, or large body of freshwater, to a spawning bed in a freshwater stream. All other vertebrates which possess jaws are included in the superclass gnathostomata. They are divided into six classes namely:

- **Chondrichthyes** (cartilaginous fish), includes the sharks, skates, rays and ratfishes.
- **Osteichthyes** (bony fish)
- **Amphibia**
- **Reptilia**: The earliest members of the class Reptilia were the first vertebrates to possess *amniotic eggs*. Amniotic eggs have extraembryonic membranes that protect the embryo from desiccation, cushion the embryo, promote gas transfer and store waste materials.
- **Aves**
- **Mammalia**

  The term **tetrapod** is a non-taxonomic designation that applies to all vertebrates other than fishes, and most tetrapods exhibit adaptations for life on land.

Chondrichthyans

Chondrichthyans, which means *cartilage fish*, have a skeleton that is composed predominantly of cartilage, often impregnated with calcium.

Important characters

- Marine animals having cartilaginous endoskeleton.
- *Notochord* is persistent throughout life. Gill slits are separate and without *operculum* (gill cover).
- The skin is tough, containing minute **placoid scales**.
- Mouth is located ventrally. Jaws are present. Teeth are modified placoid scales. Stomach is J-shaped.
- The swim bladder and lungs are absent and the liver is filled with oil to provide buoyancy to the body while swimming. Due to the absence of air bladder, they have to swim constantly to avoid sinking. If they stop swimming, they will sink like a stone.
- Heart is two-chambered (one auricle and one ventricle).
- Kidneys opisthonephric. Excretion ureotelic. Cloaca present.
- They are cold-blooded animals, i.e., they lack the capacity to regulate their body temperature.
- Fertilization is internal. Sexes are separate. The pectoral fins of the shark are called *claspers* and used for copulation. There are three ways in which sharks reproduce; *oviparous*, where the female lays eggs which takes a few months to develop, *ovoviviparous*, where the eggs are hatched in the oviduct and the embryo develops in the uterus and *viviparous*, in which the gestation period of the embryo is about one year.

  Examples: *Rhincodon* (Whale shark), *Carcharodon carcharias* (great white shark), *Trygon* (Sting rays), *Torpedo* (Electric rays), *Scoliodon* (Dogfish) and *Pristis* (Sawfish).

Osteichthyes

The vast majority of vertebrates belong to a superclass of gnathostomes called Osteichthyes. Unlike chondrichthyans, nearly all living *osteichthyans* have an ossified (bony) endoskeleton with a hard matrix of calcium phosphate.

Important characters

- It includes both marine and freshwater fishes with bony endoskeleton.
- They have four pairs of gills which are covered by an operculum on each side.
- Heart is two chambered (one auricle and one ventricle).
- Most fishes can control their buoyancy with an air bladder known as a *swim bladder*. Movement of gases from the blood to the swim bladder increases buoyancy, making the animal rise; transfer of gas back to the blood causes the animal to sink.
- Adult kidney mesonephric. Excretion chiefly ammonetelic.
- They are cold-blooded animals.
- Sexes are separate. Fertilization is usually external. Mostly oviparous, rarely ovoviviparous or viviparous. Development direct, rarely with metamorphosis.

  Examples: *Latimeria* (Lobe-finned fish), *Dipnoi* (Lung-fish), Hippocampus (Sea-horse), *Exocoetus* (Flying fish), *Echeneis* or *Remora* (Suckerfish), *Anguilla* (eel), *Anabas* (Climbing perch), *Catla-catla* (Catla), *Pterophyllum* (Angelfish) and *Betta* (Fighting fish).

Amphibia

Amphibians are vertebrate, that can live in both aquatic (water) as well as terrestrial (land) environment. The name *amphibian* is derived from the Greek word 'amphibios' meaning *living a dual life*. The first amphibians came into existence in the Devonian period.

Important characters

- Soft, moist (without scales) and glandular skin.
- Endoskeleton mostly bony. Notochord does not persist. The eyes have eyelids. A *tympanum* represents the ear.

- Respiration is by gills, lungs and through skin. Larvae with external gills which may persist in some aquatic adults (like salamanders).
- The heart is three chambered (two auricles and one ventricle).
- Alimentary canal, urinary and reproductive tracts open into a common chamber called cloaca which opens to the exterior.
- Kidneys are mesonephric. Excretion is ureotelic.
- They are cold-blooded animals.
- Sexes are separate. Fertilization is external. They are oviparous and development is direct or indirect.

  Examples: *Ichthyophis* (blind worm), *Ambystoma* (American salamander), *Hyla* (tree frog), *Necturus* (Mudpuppy), *Alytes* (Mid-wife toad), *Bufo* (Toad) and *Rana tigrina* (Indian Bull frog).

Reptilia

Reptiles are considered as the first animals on land with the ability to live and multiply on land, with the help of their amniotic eggs. Most of them are tetrapods, with four legs or leg-like appendages. The class name refers to their creeping or crawling mode of locomotion (*Latin*, *repere* or *reptum*, to creep or crawl).

Important characters

- They are mostly terrestrial animals and their body is covered by dry and *cornified skin*. The skin is covered with scutes or scales. The skin has high levels of keratin, which prevents water loss through the skin. Glands are usually absent. Snakes and lizards shed their scales as skin cast.
- Reptiles are considered as tetrapods with two sets of paired limbs. In some reptiles, like snakes, worm lizards, the legs are absent, but it is believed that these animals evolve from some tetrapod ancestor.
- Unlike amphibians, reptiles do not pass through an embryonic stage with gills. These animals breath with well-developed lungs, right from birth. Most of them have two lungs, except some snakes, which possess only a single lung.
- All reptiles have three-chambered hearts, except crocodiles, which have four-chambered hearts (2 atria, 2 ventricles), like mammals and birds. The three chambers in reptiles consist of two atria to receive blood and one partially divided ventricle for pumping blood.
- Reptiles do not have external ear openings. Tympanum represents ear.
- Reptiles are the first animals with amniotic eggs, that can be laid on land and not in water. These amniotic eggs can survive without water, as they have protective shells and membranes, that allow oxygen and other gases to enter. Most of the reptiles lay eggs, but some of them give birth to young ones, by hatching the eggs inside the body of the mother. Reptiles characteristics include internal fertilization, as sperm gets deposited into the reproductive tract of the female directly.
- Being cold-blooded, the body temperature of reptiles vary with the surrounding atmosphere.
- Sexes are separate. Fertilization is internal. They are oviparous and development is direct.

  Examples: *Sphenodon* (Tuatara), *Varanus* (Komodo dragon), *Draco* (Flying lizard), *Ophiophagus* (King cobra), *Hydrophis* (Sea snake) and *Crocodylus* (Indian freshwater crocodile).

Aves

Aves is the name of the class to which birds belong in taxonomy.

Important characters

- Body usually spindle shaped, with four divisions: head, neck, trunk, and tail. Skin is dry without glands except the *oil* or preen gland at the base of the tail.

- Many of the characters of birds are adaptations that facilitate flight. A bird's most obvious adaptations for flight are its wings and feathers. The forelimbs are modified into *wings*. Epidermis covered with feathers. The presence of **feather** is the most characteristic features of aves.
- Fully ossified endoskeleton and the long bones are hollow with **air cavities** (pneumatic).
- Respiration is by lungs. Circulatory system consists of four-chambered heart with two atria and two ventricles; nucleated erythrocytes. Living birds are also toothless.
- They are warm-blooded animals, i.e., they are able to maintain a constant body temperature.
- Excretory system includes metanephric kidneys; ureters open into cloaca; no urinary bladder; uric acid main nitrogenous waste.
- Sexes separate; females have left ovary and oviduct only; copulatory organ (penis) only in ducks, geese, paleognaths and a few others. Sexes are separate.
- Fertilization is internal. They are oviparous and development is direct. Amniotic eggs with much yolk and hard, calcareous shells; embryonic membranes are present in egg during development.

  Examples: Flying birds – *Corvus* (Crow), *Columba* (Pigeon), *Psittacula* (Parrot), *Struthio* (Ostrich), *Pavo* (Peacock), *Aptenodytes* (Penguin). Flightless birds– *Struthio camelus* (African ostrich), *Rhea americana* (South American ostrich), *Casuarius casuarius* (Australian cassowary), *Dromaius novaehollandiae* (Australian Emu), *Eudromia elegans* (Tinamou) and *Apteryx haasti* (Large grey kiwi).

Mammalia

Mammals are amniotes and distinguished from all other classes of vertebrates by two fundamental characteristics - hair and mammary glands (milk-producing glands). During the Jurassic period, the first true mammals arose and diversified into a number of lineages, many of which are extinct. The beginning of the Tertiary period was the start of the age of *mammals*. Modern mammals include monotremes, marsupial mammals, and placental mammals. There are two subclasses of mammals– **prototheria** and **theria**.

Important characters

- The most successful and dominant animals are mammals.
- They have sweat glands and sebaceous gland in the skin and their body is covered by hair.
- All female mammals possess mammary glands that can secrete milk.
- They have two sets of teeth viz. milk teeth and permanent teeth. Their teeth are *thecodont* (found in sockets).
- They have two pairs of limbs, adapted for walking, running, climbing, burrowing, swimming or flying.
- Heart is four chambered.
- They are warm-blooded animals.
- Breathing is by lungs and is enhanced by the muscular diaphragm.
- Only the left aortic arch is present.
- Sexes are separate and fertilization is internal. They are viviparous with few exceptions and development is direct.

Prototheria

Prototherians are **oviparous**. The only prototherians surviving today are the **monotremes**. The duck-billed platypus and two species of echidna (spiny anteaters) are the only living monotremes. Among living mammals, only monotremes lay shelled eggs.

The key anatomical difference between monotremes and other mammals is the one that gave them their name; *monotreme* means 'single opening' and comes from the fact that their urinary, defecatory, and reproductive systems all open into a single duct, the cloaca. Monotremes also lactate, but have no defined nipples, excreting the milk from their mammary glands via openings in their skin. All species are long-lived, with low rates of reproduction and relatively prolonged parental care of infants. The platypus, found only in Australia, lives much of its life in the water.

Theria

Therians make up the vast majority of mammals. Therians are **viviparous** and their young develop in the uterus. Digestive tract and urogenital ducts open by separate apertures and extra-abdominal testes, cloaca is usually absent. They are divided into two infraclasses: *Metatherians* and *eutherians*. Metatherians are more commonly referred to as *marsupials*; eutherians are typically called *placental mammals*.

Metatheria (*Pouched mammals* or *marsupials*): In marsupials, a fertilized egg is surrounded by chorion and amniotic membranes, but no shell forms around the egg as it does in monotremes. During its early development, the marsupial embryo is nourished by an abundant yolk within the egg. Shortly before birth, a short-lived placenta forms from the chorion membrane. Soon after, the embryonic marsupial is born. It emerges tiny and hairless, and crawls into the marsupial pouch, where it latches onto a mammary-gland nipple and continues its development. Today, most species of marsupials live in Australia and South America. Examples: *Didelphis* (Opossum), *Macropus* (Kangaroo), *Phascolarctos* (Koala).

Eutheria (Placental mammals): A placenta that nourishes the embryo throughout its entire development forms in the uterus of placental mammals. The **placenta** is a specialized organ that brings the bloodstream of the fetus into close contact with the bloodstream of the mother. Most species of mammals living today, including humans, are placental mammals. Examples: *Balaenoptera* (Blue whale), *Platanista* (Ganges dolphin), *Panthera leo* (Asiatic lion), *Panthera tigris* (Tiger).

Problem

What are the three basic body plans exhibited by bilaterally symmetrical animals? Describe the type of body cavity found in each. How are the internal organs arranged in the most complex plan? Which body plans are found in wormlike organisms? Which plan is found in all advanced invertebrates and vertebrates?

Solution: The three basic body plans of bilaterally symmetrical animals are acoelomates, wherein no body cavity other than the digestive tract exists; pseudocoelomates, wherein there is a cavity between the mesoderm and the endoderm; and the coelomates, wherein there is a cavity completely bounded by mesoderm. The internal organs are suspended in coelom by mesodermal double-layer mesenteries. In wormlike organisms are found acoelomate and pseudocoelomate body plans; in advanced invertebrates and vertebrates only coelomate body plan is found.

Problem

Why is it believed that echinoderms and chordates, which are so dissimilar, are members of the same evolutionary line?

Solution: Chordates and echinoderms shared a key characteristic of animal taxonomy--that of embryo growth pattern. These two groups comprise the deuterostomes whose embryological development differs greatly from the protostomes (molluscs, annelids, and arthropods). These embryological developmental patterns are guided by genetic differences in the expression of *Hox* genes, which suggests that echinoderms and chordates share a key characteristic very distinct from other animal groups. And, although the adult echinoderms look very different from the chordates, an earlier stage in their development looks more closely related to the chordates.

Self Test

Q1. Sexual reproduction in land plants

P. involve gametes formation and fertilization

Q. occurs through formation of sexual spores.

R. occurs through formation of meiospores.

S. produce genetically identical offspring.

a. P and Q

b. Q, R and S

c. P, Q and R

d. P, Q and S

Q2. In angiosperms, a spore differs from a seed in a variety of ways. Given below is a list of possible differences. Which are *correct*?

1. A spore is haploid, a seed has both haploid and diploid tissue.
2. A spore is diploid, a seed is haploid.
3. A spore is the consequence of meiosis, a seed the consequence of fertilization.
4. A spore develops into a gametophyte, a seed develops into a new sporophyte.
5. A spore develops into a sporophyte, a seed develops into a gametophyte.
6. A spore is unicellular, a seed is multicellular.
7. A spore contains little or no stored food, a seed contains stored food.

a. 2, 3, 5, 6 and 7 only

b. 1, 3, 5, 6 and 7 only

c. 1, 3, 5 and 6 only

d. 1, 3, 4, 6 and 7 only

Q3. Which of the following statements are *correct*?

P. The first eukaryotes appeared about 1.5 billion years ago.

Q. The protozoans that cause malaria in humans are sporozoans.

R. Amoebas have a flagellated phase in their life cycle.

S. Ciliates such as *Paramecium* differ from all other protozoans in having two types of nuclei.

a. P and R

b. Q and S

c. P, Q and S

d. P, Q, R and S

Q4. Choose the mismatch

Feature	Example
a. Bilateral symmetry	fish
b. First triploblastic	flatworms
c. Free-living flatworm	planaria
d. Radial symmetry	larvae of echinoderm

Q5. Which of the following statements are *correct*?

P. Polyps are fixed, sessile, cylindrical, hydra-like form of coelenterates.

Q. Spongocoel is paragastric or central cavity of a sponge.

R. Water vascular system is a unique system of radiating canals in urochordata.

S. Nephridia is a excretory structure in annelids.

a. P and S

b. R and S

c. P, Q and S

d. P, Q, R and S

Q6. The kingdom protista contains

a. prokaryotic unicellular autotrophic organisms.

b. eukaryotic unicellular photosynthetic and non-photosynthetic organisms.

c. prokaryotic multicellular heterotrophic organisms.

d. eukaryotic multicellular heterotrophic organisms.

Q7. Which of the following statements regarding plant reproduction are *correct*?

1. All seed plants do not have flagellated sperms.
2. All seed plants do not require external water for fertilization.
3. All Lycophytes are heterosporous.
4. In Pterophyta, both sporophyte and gametophyte are photosynthetic.
5. Pterophyta are better adapted to land life compared with Lycophyta.

a. 1, 3, 5
b. 2, 4, 5
c. 1, 2, 3
d. 3, 4, 5

Q8. Match the following

Column I	Column II
P. Ctenidium	1. Termites
Q. Social insect	2. Nereis
R. Triploblastic metamerically segmented	3. *Taenia solium*
S. Trochophore larva	4. Monopectinate gill
T. Mehlis's gland	5. Sea mouse

a. P–2, Q–5, R–4, S–1, T–3
b. P–4, Q–1, R–5, S–2, T–3
c. P–3, Q–4, R–5, S–1, T–2
d. P–1, Q–5, R–2, S–3, T–4

Q9. Which of the following is an accurate description of alternation of generations in vascular and nonvascular plants?

a. Nonvascular plants and seedless vascular plants have a reduced gametophyte.
b. Seed-producing vascular plants have an independent gametophyte.
c. Nonvascular plants and seedless vascular plants have dominant sporophyte.
d. Seed-producing vascular plants have a reduced gametophyte.

Q10. The following table shows the summary of characters between two taxa based on presence (1) and absence (0).

	Taxon A		
		1	0
Taxon B	1	40	18
	0	22	20

Which of the following represents Jaccard's coefficient and Simple matching coefficient respectively?

a. 0.8, 0.5
b. 0.6, 0.5
c. 0.8, 0.6
d. 0.5, 0.6

Q11. The three domain classification of life proposed by Carl Woese divides life forms on the basis of

a. mitochondrial DNA and membrane structures.
b. signature sequence of ribosomal rRNA.
c. mitochondrial DNA and protein sequences.
d. presence of single or double membranes.

Q12. Consider the following data:

P. Most ancient eukaryotes are unicellular.
Q. All eukaryotes alive today have a nucleus and cytoskeleton.
R. Most ancient eukaryotes lack a cell wall.

Which of the following conclusions could reasonably follow the data presented? The first eukaryote may have been

a. very similar to a plant cell
b. anaerobic
c. capable of phagocytosis
d. photosynthetic

Q13. For the following invertebrate structures/organs, identify their major function and the animal group in which they are found: Nematocyst (P), Protonephridia (Q), Malpighian Tubules (R), Radula (S).

a. P – Porifera, Skeletal Support; Q – Mollusca, excretion; R – Insecta, respiration; S – Anthozoa, prey capture.
b. P – Anthozoa, prey capture; Q – Planaria, excretion; R – Mollusca, excretion; S – Insecta, food processing.
c. P – Planaria, excretion; Q – Mollusca, respiration; R – Insecta, respiration; S – Porifera, prey capture.
d. P – Anthozoa, prey capture; Q – Planaria, excretion; R – Insecta, excretion; S – Mollusca, food processing.

Q14. Most members of bryophyte phylum Anthocerophyta are characterized by

a. gametophyte with single chloroplast per cell and multicellular rhizoids; sporophyte without stomata.
b. gametophyte with single chloroplast per cell and unicellular rhizoids; sporophyte with stomata.
c. gametophyte with multiple chloroplasts per cell and unicellular rhizoids; sporophyte without stomata.
d. gametophyte with single chloroplast per cell and multicellular rhizoids; sporophyte with stomata.

Q15. Identify the *correct* match between the animal (flatworm, earthworm, roundworm) and its body cavity type (acoelomate, coelomate, pseudocoelomate):

a. Roundworm – pseudocoelomate; Earthworm – acoelomate; Flatworm – coelomate.
b. Roundworm – acoelomate; Earthworm – coelomate; Flatworm – acoelomate.
c. Roundworm – pseudocoelomate; Earthworm – coelomate; Flatworm – acoelomate.
d. Roundworm – coelomate; Earthworm – pseudocoelomate; Flatworm – acoelomate.

ANSWER KEY

01. c	02. d	03. c	04. d	05. c	06. b	07. b	08. b	09. d	10. d
11. b	12. c	13. d	14. b	15. c					

7

Ecology

SUBJECT FOCUS

Ecology is the scientific study of the relationships between organisms and their environment. These relationships are complex, varied and hierarchical. The word '**ecology**' was first used by German biologist Ernst Haeckel in 1869. It is derived from the Greek words, *oikos* (meaning 'house' or 'dwelling place') and *logos* (meaning the study of). Haeckel defined ecology as '*the study of the natural environment including the relations of organisms to one another and to their surroundings*'. Ecology describes the relationships between living organisms and their environments, the interaction of organisms with each other and the pattern and cause of the abundance and distribution of organisms in nature. It is the science that attempts to answer questions about how the nature works.

7.1 The Environment

Organisms and their environments are dynamic and interdependent. The term '**environment**' etymologically means *surroundings*. It includes everything (biotic as well as abiotic) that surrounds an organism. Any factor, abiotic or biotic, that influences living organisms is called **environmental factor** (or *ecological factor* or *ecofactor*). **Abiotic factors** include factors such as temperature, sunlight levels, pH, salinity and soil composition. In contrast, **biotic factors** encompass producers, consumers and decomposers.

7.1.1 Physical environment

Soil

Soil constitutes the uppermost weathered layer of the Earth's crust. It is a mixture of weathered mineral rock particles, organic matter (i.e., both living and dead), water and air. Soil is a biologically active matrix and home of diverse organisms. The scientific discipline dedicated to the study of soil is known as **pedology**.

Soil composition

The soil is composed of *mineral particles*, *organic matters*, *air* and *water*. Mineral particles in the soil include *sand* (0.05–2.0 mm), *silt* (0.002–0.05 mm) and *clay* (<0.002 mm). The relative proportions of sand, silt, and clay in a soil are referred as **soil texture**. The soil is also composed of organic matter which includes *living biomass*, *detritus* and *humus*. **Humus** is an amorphous and a colloidal mixture of complex organic substances. It is made up of *humic* and *non-humic* substances. **Non-humic substances** include carbohydrates, proteins, lignins, lipids, organic acids etc. **Humic substances** are stable end products derived from the decomposition of plant and animal residues. It comprises about 80 to 90% of the soil organic matter and characterized by dark-colored amorphous substance. The elemental analysis of humic substances reveals that they are primarily composed of carbon, oxygen, hydrogen, nitrogen and sulfur. The three fractions of humic substances are *fulvic acid, humic acid* and *humin.* These sub-divisions are arbitrarily based on the solubility of each fraction in water at different pH. **Humins** are not soluble in water at any pH. **Humic acids** are insoluble in water under acidic conditions but are soluble in water under alkaline conditions. **Fulvic acids** are a mixture of weak aliphatic and aromatic organic acids which are soluble in water at all pH.

Summary

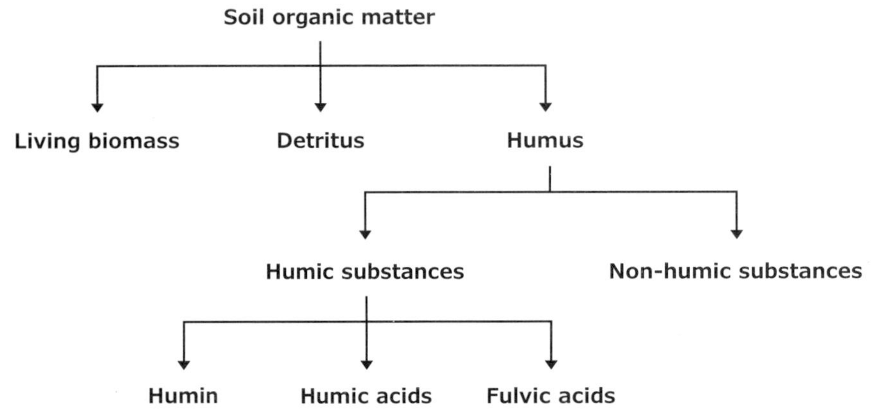

Soil air is the mixture of gases that are present in soil pores that are not filled with water. Oxygen and carbon dioxide are important constituents, and their concentration in the soil affects many processes (e.g., nitrification and denitrification).

Soil water can contribute up to 30% of soil volume, and is essential for the activity and physiological functioning of organisms in the soil. The water content in soil depends on soil type. The water-holding capacity of soil is described in terms of **field capacity**. It represents the soil profile's ability to retain water after the process of internal drainage has ceased. It is usually measured about two days after an infiltration event. The water holding capacity of a soil depends on soil texture, structure, organic matter content and arrangement of soil pores. Clay soil or soils with a high humus content have a large field capacity.

The water stored in the soil is taken up by the plant roots or evaporated from the topsoil (the topmost mineral horizon which is rich in humus) into the atmosphere. If no additional water is supplied to the soil, it gradually dries out. The dryer the soil becomes, the more tightly the remaining water is retained and the more difficult it is for the plant roots to extract it. At a certain stage, the uptake of water is not sufficient to meet the plant's needs. The amount of water soil contains at which plants wilt beyond recovery is called the **permanent wilting percentage**. The amount of water held by the soil between *field capacity* and the *permanent wilting point* is the plant available water or water that is available for uptake by plants. According to the nature of interaction between soil particles and water molecules, soil water may be classified into the following types:

Hygroscopic water: Water present as a thin film around soil particles and remains firmly attached is called the *hygroscopic water*. It is not utilized by plants hence it is unavailable to plants.

Capillary water: Water present in thin and narrow capillaries formed by soil particles and widely utilized by plants. The water present in soil, which can be utilized by plants is called **chresard** (available water).

Gravitational water: Water percolates deep into the soil due to the gravitational force of the Earth that constitutes groundwater. It is not available to plants.

Chemically bound water: Water present in the form of hydrated oxides of iron, aluminium, silicon, etc. is described as chemically bound water and is not available to plants.

Air and Atmosphere

Air is a mixture of gases that make the atmosphere. The **atmosphere** is the gaseous mass or envelope surrounding a celestial body, especially the one surrounding the Earth and retained by the celestial body's gravitational field. The atmosphere is most dense at the surface of the Earth because gravity pulls the molecules of gas toward the center of the Earth. The atmosphere is divided into four general layers:

Troposphere: More than 80 percent of the mass of the Earth's atmosphere and virtually all of the water vapor, clouds and precipitation occur in the troposphere. The troposphere extends from the Earth's surface to an altitude that varies from 8 to 18 km depending on latitude and season. At the poles, the troposphere may extend up to about 8 km, while at the equator it is about 18 km. In the troposphere, temperature typically decreases with altitude by an average of about 6.5°C km^{-1} (called the **lapse rate**). The top of the troposphere is called the **tropopause** which forms the boundary between the troposphere and the stratosphere.

Stratosphere: This layer starts from *tropopause* and goes up to 50 km. A thin **ozone layer** is present at the height of 15 to 30 km. The troposphere and stratosphere together account for about 99.9 percent of the mass of the atmosphere. Collectively, the troposphere and the stratosphere are known as **lower atmosphere**. The top of the stratosphere is called the **stratopause** which forms the boundary between the stratosphere and the mesosphere.

Mesosphere: This layer starts from about 50 km above the Earth's surface and goes up to 85 km. The boundary between the mesosphere and the thermosphere (a layer above mesosphere) is called the **mesopause**. As we move up in the mesosphere, the temperature gets colder. The top of the mesosphere is the coldest part of Earth's atmosphere (the temperature is around –90°C).

Thermosphere: It extends from about 85 km to about 600 km in the atmosphere. Within the thermosphere, temperature rises continually and goes beyond 1000°C. Within the thermosphere, there is a relatively dense band of charged particles called the **ionosphere**. The outermost layer of our atmosphere is the **exosphere**. It extends from the top of the thermosphere up to 10,000 km. The boundary between the thermosphere and exosphere is called **thermopause**.

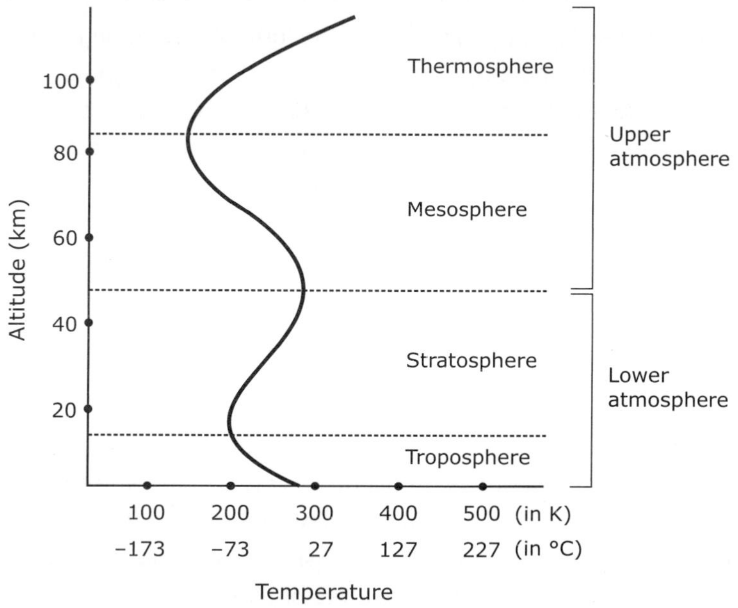

Figure 7.1
Atmospheric stratification.
Based on temperature, Earth's atmosphere is divided into four main layers – troposphere, stratosphere, mesosphere and thermosphere – moving upward from the Earth surface. The lowest region of the atmosphere, the *troposphere*, extends from the Earth surface to an altitude that varies from 8 to 18 km. The regions of the atmosphere above the troposphere are the *stratosphere* (up to ~50 km), the *mesosphere* (~50 to ~85 km) and the *thermosphere* (~85 to ~600 km). The atmosphere above 600 km is called *exosphere* (the outermost layer of Earth's atmosphere).

Table 7.1 Composition of clean, dry air

Constituent	Percent by volume	In ppm
Nitrogen	78.084%	780840
Oxygen	20.9%	209440
Argon	0.93%	9340
Carbon dioxide	0.040%	419 (Year 2021)
Neon	0.0018%	18
Helium	0.00052%	5.2
Methane	0.00018%	1.8
Krypton	0.00011%	1.1
Hydrogen	0.00005%	0.5
Nitrous oxide	0.00003%	0.3

Most commonly used units to express concentration of atmospheric gases are ppm or ppb. An carbon dioxide concentration of 419 ppm means that there are 419 carbon dioxide molecules per one million air molecules.

Light

Light is an **electromagnetic radiation.** The electromagnetic radiation is a form of energy and has both electrical and magnetic characteristics. The electric and magnetic fields in an electromagnetic wave oscillate along directions perpendicular to the propagation direction of the wave. The classification of electromagnetic waves according to frequency or wavelengths is the **electromagnetic spectrum**. Light represents a part of the electromagnetic spectrum (~400 to 700 nm). The word usually refers to **visible light** because it is visible to the human eye. The wavelengths of visible light typically range from 400 to 700 nm, between the **infrared** (with longer wavelengths) and the **ultraviolet** (with shorter wavelengths). The shorter wavelengths being the violet end of the spectrum and the longer wavelengths the red. Visible light is also called *photosynthetically active radiation* (**PAR**) because photosynthetic organisms perform photosynthesis in this region of the electromagnetic spectrum. The electromagnetic radiation with a wavelength from 100 nm to 400 nm is *ultraviolet* (UV) *radiation*. It is shorter than that of visible light but longer than X-rays. Depending upon the wavelength, three ranges in UV radiation are **UV-C** (100 to 280 nm), **UV-B** (280 to 320 nm) and **UV-A** (320 to 400 nm). Ozone layer in stratosphere have the remarkable ability to absorb UV radiation, particularly in the UV-C and most of the UV-B regions of the electromagnetic spectrum.

The Sun is the primary source of light and energy on Earth, emitting energy in the form of electromagnetic radiation, collectively referred to as **solar radiation**. The *intensity* and *duration* of solar radiation intercepted at any point on the Earth's surface vary significantly with both *latitude* and *altitude*. The **latitudinal variation** is mainly due to two factors. *First*, except at the equator, daylight hours are longest during the summer and shortest in the winter. *Second*, radiation hits the Earth's surface at a smaller angle at higher latitudes, spreading sunlight over a larger area. In addition, radiation that penetrates the atmosphere at a lower angle must travel through a deeper layer of air. In this process, it encounters more particles in the atmosphere, which reflect more of it back into space, making that sunlight much less intense. **Altitudinal variation** mainly influences the intensity of light. As elevation increases, light intensity also increases because the thinner atmosphere absorbs and disperses less light.

Effect of light on plants

Light from the Sun is the primary source of energy for ecosystems. It is captured by plants through photosynthesis and its energy stored in the chemical bonds of organic compounds. Sunlight serves not only as an energy source for photosynthesis but also as a signal that regulates various growth and developmental processes, from seed germination to fruit development. The **quality** (wavelength), the **quantity** (intensity) and the **duration** (photoperiod) of light influence photosynthesis and many growths and development features of plants.

Quality of light: The quality of light (i.e., wavelength or color) plays an important role in photosynthesis and photomorphogenesis (such as flower induction, seed germination and plant movements). In plants, photosynthesis occurs in the blue and red light. In terrestrial ecosystems, the quality of light does not change much. In aquatic ecosystems, the quality of light can be a limiting factor. Both blue and red light is absorbed and as a result, do not penetrate deeply into the water.

Light intensity: The intensity of the light that reaches the Earth varies according to the latitude, season of the year and time of the day. Variation in intensity of light affects the processes of photosynthesis, growth and reproduction in plants. Plants, in general, can be divided into two groups: **shade-tolerant species** and **shade-intolerant species**. In ecology, *shade tolerance* refers to a plant's ability to tolerate low light intensity.

Light duration: The duration of light (i.e., photoperiod) regulates many phenological process, such as flowering and fruiting, in plants. Plants use photoreceptors, such as phytochrome and cryptochrome, to sense photoperiod, which they take as signals for many growth and developmental processes.

Temperature

Temperature is the degree of hotness or coldness of a substance. Temperatures at the Earth's surface vary from place to place, from night to day, and from summer to winter. It is directly related to the duration and intensity of solar radiation. The factors which influence variation in temperatures on the Earth include latitude, altitude, topography, vegetation and others.

Temperature has a significant effect on the climatic conditions, growth response and activities of organisms. Temperature is one of the three major influences on global patterns of plant growth. Along with available sunlight and water, temperature determines whether the land will support dense forests, grassland, or nearly barren desert. On the basis of temperature conditions, world's vegetation is divided into various classes as– **megatherms** (where high temperatures prevail throughout the year and dominant vegetation is tropical rainforest), **mesotherms** (with high temperature alternating with low temperature, and dominant vegetation is tropical deciduous forest), **microtherms** (where low temperatures prevail and vegetation is of mixed coniferous forest type) and **hekistotherms** (with very low temperature and alpine vegetation being dominant).

Precipitation

In meteorology, **precipitation** refers to any product of the condensation of atmospheric water vapor that falls under gravity. This includes **rain** (precipitation in the form of liquid water drops), **snow** (precipitation in the form of ice crystals), **sleet** (precipitation in the form of transparent pellets of ice), and **hailstones** (precipitation in the form of solid balls of ice). For meteorologists, **rain** is defined as falling drops of liquid water with a diameter of 0.5 mm or greater.

Rainfall is highest near the equator in the tropics, where the strong heating by the Sun creates significant vertical uplift of air and the formation of prolonged heavy showers and frequent thunderstorms. Annual rainfall totals in the tropics usually exceed 100 inches (or 2500 millimeters) and can be as high as 400 inches (or 10000 millimeters), particularly when influenced by monsoons or when mountains enhance the uplift of air.

Within the polar regions, precipitation is low because air is too cold to contain much water vapour. In addition, the cold heavy air descends precluding much cloud formation. In fact, some parts of Antarctica and the Arctic are as dry as the hot desert climates of the subtropics, where high pressure also limits cloud formation and precipitation. Both hot and cold deserts may receive less than 10 inches (or 250 millimetres) of precipitation each year. Indeed, in some parts of the subtropics, rain may not fall for several years.

7.1.2 Adaptation to the physical environment

Every organism requires specific environmental conditions for its normal growth and development. Organisms are adapted to some environmental conditions which are necessary for them to remain alive. *Adaptations* are a product of natural selection. It involves the acquisition of genetic traits that enable an organism to survive, grow, and reproduce under the prevailing environmental conditions.

An 'adaptation' is any genetically determined heritable trait (behavioral, morphological or physiological) of an organism that has evolved over a period of time by the process of natural selection such that it maintains or increases the fitness (reproductive and survival) of an organism under a given set of environmental conditions.

The Earth's environment is heterogeneous and dynamic. Environmental conditions vary in both space and time. Each combination of environmental conditions presents a unique set of constraints on the organisms that inhabit them—constraints on their ability to survive and reproduce. The fitness of any trait is a function of the prevailing environmental conditions; the characteristics that enable an individual to maximize fitness under one set of environmental conditions generally limit its ability to do so under a different set of conditions. Therefore, as features of the environment change, so will the set of traits that increase the ability of individuals to survive and reproduce. Over the timescale of generations, natural selection favours different traits under a change in environmental conditions. This same process can occur spatially. Local populations of the same species inhabiting different environments and experiencing different selective agents will undergo differences in traits. This differentiation results in a divergence in the distribution of genotypes and associated phenotypes.

Adaptation is different from acclimatization. **Acclimatization** involves physiological, anatomical or morphological adjustments within a single organism that improve performance or survival in response to environmental change. It occurs in a short period of time (days to weeks), and within the organism's lifetime. The terms *acclimatization* and *acclimation* are widely regarded as synonymous. When an organism is subjected to changed condition in laboratory, organism shows compensatory changes to the new environment. These changes are known as **acclimation**. In other words, acclimation is adjustment to laboratory conditions. Whereas acclimatization is compensatory adjustment of the organism to change in the natural environment.

Plant's adaptation to water stress

Terrestrial plants have evolved a range of adaptations in response to variations in precipitation and soil moisture. The plants which grow in dry or xeric conditions are known as **xerophytes**, *plants of dry habitat*. Xerophytic habitat can be of different types such as: **physical dryness** (in these habitats, soil has very little water due to inability of soil to hold water or low rainfall) and **physiological dryness** (in such habitat, water is sufficiently present but plants are unable to absorb it e.g., salty soil, acidic soil).

Xerophytes have evolved many adaptive morphological and physiological features to survive and reproduce in dry environment. Xerophytes are variously adapted to conserve water. Plants with such morphological and physiological adaptations are *xeromorphic.* The xeromorphic adaptations in different xerophytic species include – surface area reduction, sunken stomata and hairs, waxy leaf surface, opening of stomata at night, CAM photosynthesis succulence (storage of water), extensive root system and other. Based on adaptive features, xerophytes are classified into three categories: *ephemerals, succulents* and *non-succulent plants.*

Ephemerals are also termed as **drought escapers** (or **drought evaders**). These plants (e.g., *Argemone mexicana*) complete their life cycle in a very short period before the approach of actual dry conditions. Ephemerals persist as seeds during periods of drought, but are ready to sprout, flower and produce seeds whenever moisture is favorable. The seeds of many such species contain a germination inhibitor that must be washed out by a certain minimum amount of water. The young plants grow rapidly following the rain. They start flowering and setting seed almost immediately. They remain small, with no elaborate stem or root systems, with all energy put into flowering and seed production.

Succulents (or **drought-enduring**) such as *Opuntia, Aloe* are xerophytes which store water in their roots or stem or leaves for the dry period. Thus, they suffer dryness externally but escape internally due to the presence of fleshy water storage tissues. In addition to *succulence* i.e., storage of water, succulent plants have other water-saving features such as CAM photosynthesis, reduction in the number of stomata, waxy and hairy, or spiny outer surface.

Non-succulent (or **drought-resistant**) such as *Calotropis procera, Casuarina equisetifolia* are the true xerophytes. These perennials plants successfully endure long and continuous dryness. These are hence called 'true xerophytes'. They face both external and internal dryness. They have many adaptations to resist dry condition.

Animal's adaptation to thermal stress

In animals, temperature plays a significant role in controlling the rate of metabolic processes and maintaining homeostasis. **Homeostasis** (literally means *same standing*) is the property of an animal to regulate its internal environment to maintain a stable, constant condition under varying external environments. Among animals, some species can regulate their body temperature and some do not have this ability. Based on this property, all animals are broadly classified into two groups: **homeothermic animals** (or **warm-blooded**) and **poikilothermic animals** (often called **cold-blooded** because they can be cool to the touch).

Homeothermic (Greek *homo* – the same, and *therme* – heat) animals like birds and mammals can maintain their body temperature at a constant level irrespective of the environmental temperature. Maintaining homeothermy (a constant body temperature) is a very energy-consuming process, and it consumes about 90% of the animal's energy intake but allows activity largely independent of environmental temperatures. They have high metabolic rates and low thermal conductance. **Poikilothermic** (Greek *poikilos* – various, and *therme* – heat) animals like reptiles, fishes and amphibians are not able to maintain their body temperature at a constant level. In these organisms, the body temperature fluctuates with changes in the environmental temperature. Poikilotherms have low metabolic rates and high thermal conductance. Environmental temperatures control their metabolic rates. Poikilotherms have an upper and lower thermal limit that they can tolerate. The range of body temperatures at which poikilotherms carry out their daily activities is the *operative temperature range.* Upper and lower limits of tolerance to temperature vary among the poikilothermic species. To maintain a tolerable and fairly constant body temperature during active periods, terrestrial and amphibious poikilotherms rely on behavioral thermoregulation such as changing position or location. To escape the long, cold winters, many terrestrial poikilotherms go into a long, seasonal torpor (dormancy) called **hibernation**. 'Torpor' is a state of decreased physiological activity in an animal. Hibernation is characterized by physiological changes such as slow breathing and heart rate and low metabolic rate. Similar to hibernation, the long-term torpor to escape hot and dry summer is termed **estivation**.

We also distinguish between **endothermic** (in Greek *endo* means 'within' and *therme* means 'heat') animals that produce sufficient metabolic heat to maintain a high body temperature and **ectothermic** (in Greek *ecto* means 'outside' and *therme* means 'heat') animals, which obtain much of their heat from the environment. *Endotherms* regulate their temperature by the production of heat within their own bodies, and *ectotherms* rely on external sources of heat. During the coldest seasons, many endothermic animals suspend their endothermic abilities and decrease the costs of endothermy by hibernating; at these times, they behave almost like ectotherms. Species that sometimes regulate their body temperature and sometimes do not are called **temporal heterotherms**.

Although it is true that many homeotherms are endotherms and many poikilotherms are ectotherms, we should not use the terms *endothermy* and *homeothermy* (or *ectothermy* and *poikilothermy*) synonymously. *Ectotherm* and *endotherm* emphasize the mechanisms that determine body temperature. The other two terms, *homeotherm* and *poikilotherm,* represent the nature of body temperature (either constant or variable).

Relationship between body size and environmental temperature: The influence of temperature is size-dependent in animals. All animals exchange heat with their external environment. A body exchanges heat with the external environment in proportion to the surface area exposed and the temperature difference. Hence, an animal with a large surface area as compared to volume exchanges more heat with the external environment. The surface area-to-volume ratio is dependent on the size, as shown in the following figure. Based on this principle, small-sized animals have a large surface area relative to volume. It decreases with an increase in size. Cold-blooded animals (ectotherms) take heat from the external environment through their body surface but must take enough heat to increase the temperature of entire body mass (volume). Therefore, the surface area-to-volume ratio is a key factor in controlling the heat uptake and the maintenance of body temperature. As an animal's body size increases, this ratio decreases. Because the organism has to absorb sufficient heat across its surface to warm the entire body mass, the amount of heat and the time required to raise body temperature likewise increase. For this reason, ectothermy imposes a constraint on body size for poikilotherms and restricts the distribution of the larger poikilotherms to the subtropics and tropics. The effect of size on homeotherms is opposite that for poikilotherms. For homeotherms, the body mass (or volume) produces heat through respiration, while heat is lost to the external environment across the body surface. The smaller the organism, the larger the ratio of surface area-to-volume and the greater the relative heat loss to the surrounding environment. Therefore, when challenged with cold, a small homeotherm loses heat more rapidly than a larger animal. If such an animal attempted to generate heat to offset the heat loss and maintain constant body temperature, it would require a relatively higher energy generation rate per unit mass. On the other hand, large animals have a relatively small surface-to-volume ratio and lose heat slowly if placed in a cold environment.

Several biological rules generalize the adaptive response of homeothermic animals to temperature due to differences in surface-to-volume ratios. Among the best known is **Bergmann's rule**, which relates body size to average environmental temperature. Bergmann's rule states that individuals of species in cooler climates tend to be larger body sizes than those in warmer climates (or species of larger body size are found in colder environments, and species of smaller body size are found in warmer areas). This relationship derives primarily because large size bodies have a small surface area-to-volume ratio. Because heat loss relates to the surface area, larger bodies can retain heat more efficiently in colder climates. In contrast, small-sized bodies (large surface area-to-volume ratio) lose heat more rapidly. An extension of Bergmann's rule is **Allen's rule** which states that endothermic animals from colder climates tend to have shorter extremities or appendages (e.g., ears and tail) than closely related species from warmer climates. Small-sized extremities have a lesser surface area, hence, dissipate less heat in a colder climate.

7.2 Shelford's law of tolerance

The existence, abundance and distribution of a species in an ecosystem are determined by the *range of tolerance* to environmental variables. Organism growth and survivorship are maximal at optimum value of the environmental factor or resource and decrease below (suboptimal) and above (supraoptimal) values. Therefore, an arbitrary optimum range, within which the organism's performance is close to the maximum value, is often defined. Tolerance characterizes organism's response to stress and is the organism's ability to grow and survive in suboptimal and supraoptimal conditions. On the earth, environmental conditions exist as gradients. The performance of an organism changes along the gradient. According to **Shelford's law of tolerance** (formulated in 1913 by Victor E. Shelford), there are upper and lower threshold values on the environmental gradient beyond which the species cannot survive. These threshold values are the *upper limit of tolerance* and the *lower limit of tolerance*. The whole range over which the species is able to survive is the **range of tolerance**. Tolerance ranges differ for one species to another. Organisms may have a wide range of tolerance for one factor and a narrow range for another. When conditions are not optimal for a species with respect to one ecological factor, the limits of tolerance may be reduced for other ecological factors.

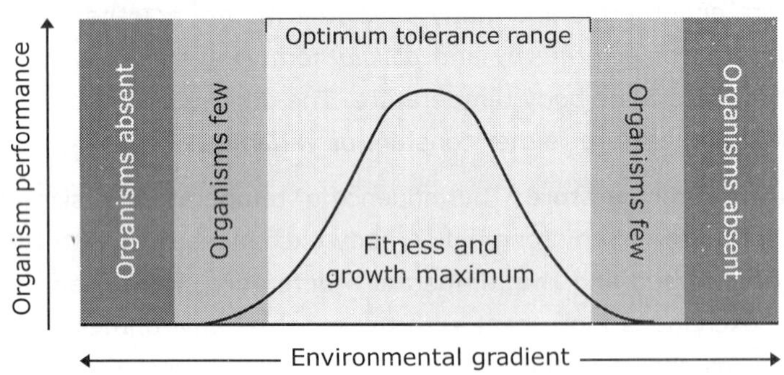

Figure 7.2
The response of an organism to a range or gradient of an environmental factors.

For example, when soil nitrogen is limiting, the resistance of grass to drought is reduced. The prefix *steno* - meaning 'narrow' and *eury* - meaning 'wide' have been used for comparing the relative narrow and wide range of tolerance, respectively of an organism to a given environmental factor. For example, **stenothermal** organisms can tolerate only a narrow range of temperature whereas **eurythermal** organisms have wide range of temperature tolerance. Similarly,

Stenohydric and **euryhydric** refer to narrow and wide tolerance, respectively, to water.

Stenohaline and **euryhaline** refer to narrow and wide tolerance, respectively, to salinity.

Stenophagic and **euryphagic** refer to narrow and wide tolerance, respectively, to food.

Stenoecious and **euryoecious** refer to narrow and wide tolerance, respectively, to habitat selection.

These terms apply not only to the organism level but equally well to the community level. For example, warm-water coral reefs occupy shallow sunlit, warm, and alkaline waters in order to grow and calcify at the high rates necessary to build and maintain their calcium carbonate structures. They are very stenothermal, in that they prosper only within a very narrow range of temperature. A prolonged 2°C drop in temperature is a stress full condition causing bleaching or loss of symbiotic algae.

7.3 Ecosystem

An **ecosystem** (or **ecological system**) is a functional unit comprising all the organisms in a particular place interacting with one another and with their physical environment and interconnected by an ongoing flow of energy and a cycling of materials. The *concept of an ecosystem* was first formally proposed by the English botanist Arthur Tansley in 1935. In the broadest sense, *'an ecosystem is the interacting system made up of all the living and non-living objects in a physically defined space.'* Ecosystems are complex, hierarchically organized, self-organizing and self-regulated systems. All ecosystems are **open systems** in the sense that energy and matter are exchanged with their surroundings. It might be theoretically possible to define particular examples of ecosystems that are *closed systems*, not exchanging matters with their surroundings, but nearly all ecosystems do exchanges of energy and matters with their surroundings.

7.3.1 Ecosystem components

Ecosystem consists of various **abiotic** (non-living) and **biotic** (living) components. The abiotic components of an ecosystem include various physical and chemical factors. The *physical factors* having the greatest effect on the ecosystem are: light, temperature, precipitation, air, fire and water. However, the *chemical factors* include pH, salinity, nutrient contents, moisture contents (for terrestrial ecosystem), amount of toxic substances and level of dissolved oxygen (in aquatic ecosystems). Organisms that make up the **biotic** component of an ecosystem are usually classified as *autotrophs* and *heterotrophs*, based on the carbon sources.

Autotrophs are organisms that primarily use carbon dioxide as their source of carbon to synthesize organic compounds necessary for growth. They are the ultimate sources of organic compounds for all non-autotrophic organisms, and for this reason, biologists refer to autotrophs as the **producers** of the biosphere. There are two kinds of autotrophs – **photoautotrophs** and **chemoautotrophs**.

Most autotrophs are *photoautotrophs* as they derive energy from the light. In most terrestrial ecosystems, green plants are the major photoautotrophs. In aquatic ecosystems, most of the photoautotrophs are phytoplanktons, consisting of various species of floating and drifting bacteria and protists. Some autotrophs, primarily specialized bacteria, derive energy from the oxidation of organic or inorganic reduced compounds. These autotrophs are called *chemoautotrophs*.

Heterotrophs are organisms that rely on organic carbon sources for their carbon needs. Unlike autotrophs, they cannot produce their own organic nutrients. Instead, they obtain these nutrients by consuming the biomass of producers or other consumers. Fungi, animals and most bacteria are heterotrophs. Heterotrophs can be classified into *consumer* and *decomposer.*

Consumers are heterotrophs, such as animals, that obtain nutrients by ingesting the biomass of producers and other consumers. There are several classes of consumers, depending on their food sources: **herbivores** (feed directly on plants), **carnivores** (feed on animals), **omnivores** (eat both plants and animals) and **detritivores** (eat detritus). *Detritus* are the dead bodies and waste product of living and once-living organisms or simply, decomposing organic material. Earthworms are a well-known example of detritivores (also known as *detritus feeders*), eating rotten plant leaves and other debris. Some detritus feeders, such as dung beetles, eat feces.

Consumers can also be classified into **primary**, **secondary** and **tertiary consumers** based on feeding level or trophic level. *Primary consumers* (i.e., herbivores) feed on producers and belong to the second trophic level. The *secondary consumers* (i.e., primary carnivores) feed only on primary consumers, and they belong to the third trophic level. Similarly, the *tertiary consumers* (i.e., secondary carnivores) feed on secondary consumers, and they belong to the fourth trophic level. *Producers* belong to the first trophic level.

Decomposers, such as bacteria and fungi, are heterotrophs that derive nutrients from dead organic matter. In doing so, they carry out the natural process of **decomposition**, breaking down dead organic material.

Both *decomposers* and *detritivores* obtain nutrition from dead organic matter. The difference is that detritivores ingest the dead organic matter directly, while decomposers secrete enzymes to digest the dead organic matter externally and then absorb the resulting molecules. Similarly, there is a difference between **parasites** and **saprophytes**. *Parasites* are heterotrophs that obtain nutrients from living hosts. In contrast, *saprophytes* are heterotrophs that obtain nutrients by digesting and absorbing nutrients from dead organic matter.

7.3.2 Productivity

Productivity refers to the rate of formation of biomass per unit area in an ecosystem. It is usually expressed in units of mass per unit area (or volume) per unit time. The term *productivity* and *production* may be used interchangeably. *Productivity differs from biomass*. Productivity is the rate at which organic matter is created by producers. **Biomass** is the amount of organic matter present at any given time. The biomass is generally expressed as *wet* or *dry* biomass. **Dry biomass** refers to the mass of living matters after it has been dried to a constant mass. **Wet biomass** refers to the mass of living matters including its water content.

The **primary productivity** is the rate at which biomass is produced per unit area by the primary producers (both **photoautotrophs** and **chemoautotrophs**). The term 'primary' indicates that we are concerned with the first trophic level in the ecosystem. It can be expressed as grams of carbon assimilated (e.g., $g\,C\,m^{-2}\,year^{-1}$) or dry weight of organic matter (e.g., $g\,m^{-2}\,year^{-1}$) or their energy equivalents (e.g., $J\,m^{-2}\,day^{-1}$). It is a fundamental ecosystem process and represents the first step associated with the capture, storage, and transfer of energy in the ecosystems. Not all primary productivity results from *photoautotrophs*. Some primary productivity also occurs through *chemoautotrophs*. In most ecosystems that receive significant light energy, chemosynthesis is only a small proportion of primary productivity. However, in ecosystems that receive very less or no light energy, chemoautotrophs can be the main primary producers.

The total amount of CO_2 fixed to organic carbon by the photoautotrophs per unit time (i.e. total rate of photosynthesis) is referred to as **gross primary productivity** (**GPP**). A proportion of this fixed organic carbon is respired away by the photoautotrophs. The total amount of organic carbon that is oxidized to CO_2 by photoautotrophs per unit time is the **autotrophic respiration** (**R_A**). The difference between GPP and R_A is known as **net primary productivity** (**NPP**). It is the amount of organic carbon produced by photoautotrophs that is not consumed by their own respiration. This is also termed *net assimilation*. NPP can be described by the following equation:

$$NPP = GPP - R_A$$

NPP represents the actual rate of production of new biomass that is available for consumption by heterotrophic organisms (fungi and animals). An ecosystem's **NPP** should not be confused with the **standing crop**. NPP is the amount of new biomass added in a given time period, whereas standing crop refers to the total living biomass, or amount of living organic matter, present in a given area at a particular point in time. It includes all the living organisms, such as plants, animals, and microorganisms, present in a given area. Primary consumers consume this organic carbon produced by autotrophs to support their growth and metabolism. Other components of the food web, such as secondary consumers, also depend directly or indirectly on primary production for their energy supply. The rate of production of new biomass by consumers is called **secondary productivity**. Secondary productivity should not be divided into gross and net productivity. Secondary productivity is dependent on primary productivity for energy. Therefore, a strong relationship exists between primary productivity in a variety of terrestrial ecosystems and the biomass of herbivores. The carbon fixed by photoautotrophs through photosynthesis can leave the ecosystem as inorganic carbon (usually in the form of carbon dioxide) via either *autotrophic respiration* (**R_A**) or, after consumption by heterotrophs, via *heterotrophic respiration* (**R_H**). The sum of R_A and R_H is called *total ecosystem respiration* (**R_E**). The difference between GPP and R_E is known as **net community productivity** (**NCP**), also termed as *net ecosystem productivity*.

Secondary productivity by herbivores is invariably less than that of the plants on which they feed. Then the question arises: where has the missing energy gone? First, not all of the plant biomass produced is consumed alive by herbivores. Second, not all the plant biomass that is eaten by herbivores (or herbivore biomass is eaten by carnivores) is assimilated and made available for incorporation into consumer's biomass. Some are lost in the form of feces. Third, not all the energy that has been assimilated is actually converted into biomass. A proportion is lost as respiratory heat. This occurs both because no energy conversion process is ever 100% efficient and also because animals do work which requires energy, again released as heat.

Patterns in primary productivity

Terrestrial primary productivity varies considerably across the surface of the Earth and among different ecosystem types. Terrestrial NPP varies latitudinally. This variation is due to gradients in plant community composition, growing season length, precipitation, temperature, and solar radiation. In terrestrial ecosystems, NPP is limited mainly by water, temperature and nutrient availability. Water is the most important factor of the primary productivity, and NPP often shows an almost linear relationship with annual precipitation in most terrestrial ecosystems. Temperature affects productivity primarily by slowing or accelerating plant metabolic rates. NPP generally declines from tropical regions to the poles because of temperature and light limitations. Tropical forests tend to be much more productive than other terrestrial ecosystems like temperate forests, tropical grassland (savanna) and boreal forests. Desert and tundra biomes, limited by precipitation and temperature respectively, contain the *least* productive ecosystems.

Table 7.2 Net primary productivity (NPP) and plant biomass of world ecosystems (Adapted from Whittaker, 1975)

Ecosystems	**Area** (10^6 km^2)	**Mean NPP per unit area**, g/m^2/yr	**Mean biomass per unit area**, kg/m^2
Continental			
Tropical rainforest	17.0	2000.0	44.00
Temperate evergreen forest	5.0	1300.0	36.00
Temperate deciduous forest	7.0	1200.0	30.00
Boreal forest	12.0	800.0	20.00
Savanna	15.0	700.0	4.00
Cultivated land	14.0	644.0	1.10
Woodland and shrubland	8.0	600.0	6.80
Temperate grassland	9.0	500.0	1.60
Tundra and alpine meadow	8.0	144.0	0.67
Desert shrub	18.0	71.0	0.67
Rock, ice, sand	24.0	3.3	0.02
Swamp and marsh	2.0	2500.0	15.00
Lake and stream	2.5	500.0	0.02
Total continental	149.0	720.0	12.30
Marine			
Algal beds and reefs	0.6	2000.0	2.00
Estuaries	1.4	1800.0	1.00
Upwelling zones	0.4	500.0	0.02
Continental shelf	26.6	360.0	0.01
Open ocean	332.0	127.0	0.003
Total marine	361.0	153.0	0.01
World total	**510.0**	**320.0**	**3.62**

Global NPP (total productivity) = Area × NPP per unit area

Relative NPP: NPP per unit area (gm/m^2/yr)

Terrestrial NPP also varies within an ecosystem with time and age. Both photosynthesis and plant growth are directly influenced by seasonal variations in environmental conditions. During cold winters or dry seasons primary productivity decreases. In the tropics, where conditions are favourable for plant growth round the year, there is little seasonal variation in net primary productivity. Disturbances due to herbivory and fire also lead to year-to-year variations in net primary productivity.

In *aquatic ecosystems*, net primary productivity is mainly limited by light and nutrient availability. The most significant nutrients affecting primary production in aquatic systems are nitrogen and phosphorus because they occur in very low concentrations.

Relationship between productivity and biomass

The standing crop biomass is a direct function of productivity. In general, there is a great difference in the total biomass that exists on terrestrial ecosystems compared to the aquatic ecosystems. But the net primary productivity (**NPP**) to biomass (**B**) ratios average 0.042 for forests, 0.29 for other terrestrial communities and 17 for aquatic communities. A very low value of NPP to B ratio for a forest is due to the fact that a large proportion of forest biomass is dead and also that much of the living support tissue is not photosynthetic. Their structure involves considerable investment in non-photosynthesizing and dead support tissues, and as a consequence, their NPP to B ratio is very low. In grassland communities, a greater proportion of the biomass is alive and involved in photosynthesis, though half or more of the biomass may be roots. The rapidly growing herbaceous species in grassland communities have relatively little support tissue. Thus, the NPP to B ratio is high as compared to the forest. In aquatic communities, particularly where productivity is mainly due to phytoplankton, there is no support tissue, there is no need for roots to absorb water and nutrients, dead cells do not accumulate and the photosynthetic output per kilogram of biomass is thus very high indeed. Another factor that helps to account for high NPP to B ratios in phytoplankton communities is the rapid turnover of biomass. The phytoplankton has a short turnover time, which means they have a small standing crop biomass compared to their production.

Measuring primary productivity

Primary productivity is usually measured as a rate of formation of biomass per unit area. Methods to measure primary productivity vary as a function of the types of autotrophs in an ecosystem—an algal population in a lake requires a different approach compared to trees in a forest. Various methods are used to estimate primary productivity. These methods include oxygen emission method, radioactive tracer method, harvest analysis method and others.

Oxygen emission method

Primary productivity is best estimated by measuring gaseous exchange—oxygen production or carbon dioxide uptake. The measurement of oxygen emission has been one of the most widely used procedures. Samples of water containing autotrophs are taken from a given depth of a pond, lake, or ocean and are distributed into pairs of small bottles. One of the paired bottles is wrapped with some material such as tinfoil so that no light penetrates. These are called the *light* and *dark* bottles, respectively. Hence, this method is also called as **light and dark bottle method**. *Light bottle* permits the photosynthesis to take place; the *dark bottle* not permits the photosynthesis but allow the respiratory activity. The oxygen concentration in each bottle is measured, the bottles are sealed and then suspended for few hours (usually 4 to 8 hours) at the same depth from which the water was originally taken. At the end of this time, the oxygen content is determined either by standard chemical titration or with an electronic sensor. A basic assumption in the light and dark bottle method is that plant respiration is the same under the two conditions. In the *light bottle*, there is photosynthesis (or GPP) as well as respiration (R). The difference between these two processes is NPP = GPP – R. In the *dark bottle*, there is no photosynthesis and only respiration.

Let us assume, initial oxygen concentration = 8 mg O_2 /L

Oxygen concentration in *light bottle* after 1 hour = 10 mg O_2 /L

Oxygen concentration in *dark bottle* after 1 hour = 5 mg O_2 /L

The oxygen increased in the light bottle compared to the initial is due to photosynthesis, and the oxygen decreased in the dark bottle due to respiration. With this information we can calculate the respiration, NPP and GPP for our system:

(Light – Initial) = (10 – 8) = 2 mg/L/hr = NPP

(Initial – Dark) = (8 – 5) = 3 mg/L/hr = Respiration

(Light – Dark) = (10 – 5) = 5 mg/L/hr = GPP

Radioactive tracer method

It is one of the most useful and sensitive methods used to estimate primary productivity in an aquatic ecosystem, especially in lakes and oceans. This method mainly measures the CO_2 uptake by using the radioisotope of carbon (^{14}C). The method involves the addition of radioactive carbon usually in the form of a bicarbonate such as $NaH^{14}CO_3$ to a sample of water. During the time of exposure both the stable carbon (^{12}C), which is present as CO_2 or HCO_3^- and the radioactive carbon (^{14}C) are assimilated into carbohydrate and incorporated in the biomass of the primary producers.

Water samples are taken from a desired level and distributed in paired light and dark bottles. A known quantity of ^{14}C, usually in the form of a bicarbonate such as $NaH^{14}CO_3$, is then introduced into the bottles, and they are resuspended to incubate, usually for about 6 hours. During the time of exposure both the ^{12}C and the unstable ^{14}C are assimilated into carbohydrate and incorporated in the biomass of the autotrophs. At the end of the incubation period the samples are filtered, and the ^{12}C and ^{14}C that has been incorporated photosynthetically is captured on the filter. The filters are dried and placed in a counting chamber to determine their level of radioactivity and hence the amount of radioactive carbohydrate produced. Calculations are then made from the photosynthetic formula, based on the assumption that the uptake of radioactive carbons is proportional to the stable carbon.

7.3.3 Energy flow

All organisms require matter for their construction and energy for their activities. Hence, ecosystems consume energy and transform matters. Organisms in an ecosystem capture solar energy, transform and transfer energy and store energy. The behavior of energy in ecosystems can be conveniently shorthanded as '*energy flow*' because energy transformations are directional in contrast to the cyclic behavior of matters. Energy flow is the key function in the ecosystem.

Energy flow and laws of thermodynamics: The behaviour of the energy in the ecosystem is based on two basic laws of thermodynamics. The **first law of thermodynamics** also known as the '**law of conservation of energy**', states that energy cannot be created or destroyed, but it can be converted from one form to another. In most of ecosystems, energy enters as sunlight and is captured by plants through photosynthesis. This solar energy is converted into chemical energy stored in organic molecules (i.e., **energy transformation**). This conversion represents the transformation of energy from one form to another. It is important to note that while energy changes form, the total amount of energy remains constant. In other words, the total chemical energy stored in the organic molecules synthesized through photosynthesis, along with the energy dissipated as heat, must equal the total solar energy intercepted by the photosynthetic organisms. Hence, energy may change form (e.g., from radiant to chemical) but not amount.

The **second law of thermodynamics** states that every energy transformation that takes place will increase the **entropy** (i.e., randomness or disorder) of the universe. In other words, energy transformations cannot be 100% efficient; some energy is always lost as heat. During the process of energy transformation, such as the conversion of solar energy into chemical energy, a certain amount of energy is converted into an unusable form that cannot be used to perform work. In most cases, this unusable energy takes the form of heat. So, every time when an energy transformation happens, some amount of useful energy is converted into an unusable form. Energy in the form of heat that does not do work goes to increase the randomness (disorder) of the universe.

Source of energy: For most ecosystems on Earth, the sun is the sole source of energy. Organisms within an ecosystem capture **solar energy**, transform it, transfer it, and store it. Solar energy is harnessed by photosynthetic organisms, such as plants, photosynthetic protists and photosynthetic bacteria, through photosynthesis, and converted into chemical energy. This energy is then passed on to other organisms in the ecosystem through the food chain. Thus, all ecosystems depend on producers, either directly or indirectly, for their food. In terrestrial ecosystems, producers are primarily photosynthetic green plants, while in aquatic ecosystems, producers are mainly phytoplankton and algae.

The fraction of incoming solar radiation that is utilized in the photosynthetic process is quite small. A specific portion of the electromagnetic spectrum necessary for photosynthesis is referred to as **photosynthetically active radiation** (**PAR**). This range includes wavelengths spanning from approximately 400 to 700 nm, which corresponds to the visible spectrum. Only 2-10 percent of PAR is actually captured through the photosynthetic process. Only a few ecosystems, such as deep-sea hydrothermal vents, rely on sources of energy other than the sun. **Deep-sea hydrothermal vents** are unique ecosystems found on the ocean floor, where hot, mineral-rich fluids are released from beneath the Earth's crust. The primary source of energy in these ecosystems is not sunlight, as is the case in most ecosystems, but rather geochemical energy. Therefore, with the exception of the deep-sea hydrothermal vent ecosystem, a constant input of solar energy is the fundamental requirement for most ecosystems to function and sustain.

Direction of energy flow: In ecosystems, energy flows unidirectionally. The conversion of solar energy into chemical energy through the process of *photosynthesis* serves as the starting point for energy flow within ecosystems. The chemical energy produced by producers is subsequently passed, either directly or indirectly, to all heterotrophs, which encompass consumers and decomposers. Because all animals rely on producers for their food needs, they are collectively referred to as **consumers**. Consumers can be further classified into *primary*, *secondary*, and *tertiary consumers*.

Decreasing trend of amount of energy: Organisms at each trophic level rely on those at the lower trophic level to meet their energy needs. As chemical energy is transferred from one trophic level to the next within an ecosystem, a significant portion of the energy is lost as heat. This means that the amount of chemical energy available to secondary consumers is considerably less than what is available to primary consumers, and the amount available to tertiary consumers is even less than that available to secondary consumers. When an organism from any trophic level dies, it is converted into detritus or dead biomass, which serves as an energy source for decomposers.

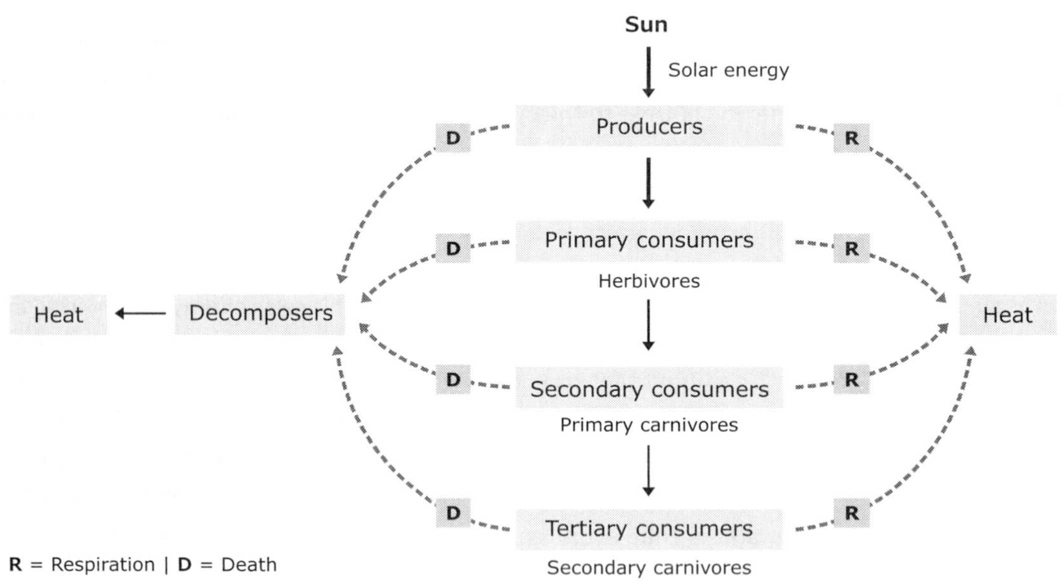

Figure 7.3 The flow of energy through an ecosystem. The energy that enters the ecosystem as solar energy (radiant energy) and is then passed along as chemical energy to successive trophic levels. At each step energy is diverted, meaning that the chemical energy available to each trophic level is less than that available to the preceding trophic level. Death at each level transfers energy to decomposers. Energy lost as heat at each level is returned to the external environment.

Why does the amount of energy decrease as it is passed from one trophic level to the next? To understand it consider the use of energy by herbivores (i.e., primary consumers) as an example. When an herbivore consumes plant biomass, it produces feces (the waste material excreted from the digestive tract). The chemical energy in the fecal matter is not passed on to the carnivore. The chemical energy assimilated by herbivores is used for various functions. A portion of this energy is released through cellular respiration and used for activities such as tissue repair, body movement, and other essential processes. This energy eventually dissipates as heat and is not transferred to carnivores. If organisms convert some chemical energy to heat, the conversion is one-way; they cannot use heat as a source of energy. Consequently, only a fraction of the assimilated chemical energy is converted into the herbivore's biomass. Additionally, some herbivores die before being consumed by carnivores, further reducing the energy transfer. As a result, a significant portion of the chemical energy in herbivores does not reach the carnivores. Ecologists estimate that, as a general rule, only about 10% of the energy available at one trophic level is passed on to the next. Ultimately, nearly all of the energy captured by photosynthesis in an ecosystem is eventually lost as heat as it is used by various trophic levels.

Concept of the trophic level

A **trophic level** refers to the organism's position in the food chain. The word '*trophic*' derives from the Greek word meaning to food (or feeding). It is simply a **feeding level**, as often represented in a food chain. Producers comprise the first trophic level, followed by the *primary consumer* (herbivores), then secondary consumers (carnivores feeding on herbivores) and so on.

It is important to note that many animals do not specialize in their diets and feed at more than one trophic level. **Omnivores** (such as humans) eat both animals and plants. Further, except for some specialists, most carnivores don't limit their diet to organisms of only one trophic level. Frogs, for instance, don't discriminate between herbivorous and carnivorous bugs in their diet. If it's the right size and moving at the right distance, chances are the frog will eat it. It's not as if the frog has brain cells to waste wondering if it's going to mess up the food chain by being a secondary consumer one minute and a quaternary consumer the next. *The number of trophic levels also varies in different ecosystems. Generally, its number is more in aquatic ecosystems than in terrestrial ecosystems.*

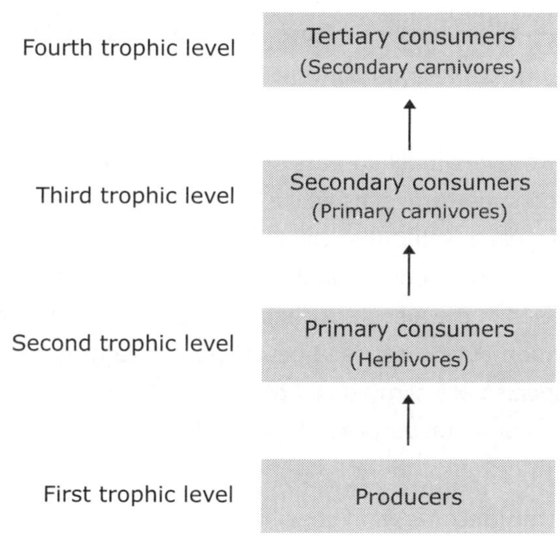

Figure 7.4
Flow of food energy through different trophic levels. Producers occupies the first level, herbivores occupy the second level (the primary consumer trophic level), primary carnivores occupy the third level (the secondary consumer trophic level) and secondary carnivores occupy the fourth level (the tertiary consumer trophic level).

7.3.4 Food chains

A classic paper by Lindeman (1942) laid the foundations of ecological energetics. He attempted to quantify the concept of food chains by considering the efficiency of energy transfer between trophic levels. The first trophic level belongs to the primary producers, the second level to the herbivores (primary consumers) and the higher levels of the carnivores (secondary consumers). Some consumers occupy a single trophic level, but many others, such as omnivores, occupy more than one trophic level. The relationship between one trophic level and adjacent trophic levels may be described by a food chain.

'*The flow of food (biomass) through a series of organisms that consume and are consumed is termed as a* ***food chain.***' A food chain shows the movement of *energy* and *matter* through a system by indicating the path of food from a producer to a final consumer. In general, food chains have 3 to 5 trophic links with 15 to 20 species. The length of food chain also may reflect the physical characteristics of a particular ecosystem. A harsh arctic landscape has a much shorter food chain than a temperate or tropical one.

Why are food chains relatively short? There are two main hypotheses. One, the **energetic hypothesis**, suggests that the length of a food chain is limited by the inefficiency of energy transfer along the chain. As we know, only about 10% of the energy stored in the organic matter of each trophic level is converted to organic matter at the next trophic level. At each transfer, a proportion (often as high as 80% to 90%) of the potential energy is lost as heat. Therefore, the shorter the food chain — or the nearer the organism to the first trophic level — the greater the energy available to that population. The second hypothesis, the **dynamic stability hypothesis**, proposes that long food chains are less stable than short chains. Population fluctuations at lower trophic levels are magnified at higher levels, potentially causing the local extinction of top predators. This hypothesis predicts that food chains should be shorter in unpredictable environments. Most of the data available support the energetic hypothesis.

Types of food chains

Within any ecosystem, there are two major food chains: the **grazing food chain** and the **detritus food chain**. The distinction between these two food chains is the source of energy for primary consumers. In the grazing food chain, the source of energy is living plant biomass (or net primary production). In the detrital food chain, the source of energy is dead organic matter or detritus.

Grazing food chains begin with photosynthetic plants (primary producers). Primary consumers (or herbivores) form the second link in the grazing food chain. They gain their energy by consuming primary producers. Secondary consumers (or primary carnivores), the third link in the chain, gain their energy by consuming herbivores. Tertiary consumers (or secondary carnivores) are animals that receive their energy by consuming primary carnivores.

Producer	→	Herbivore	→	Primary carnivore	→	Secondary carnivore
e.g. Grass		*e.g. Insect*		*e.g. Frog*		*e.g. Snake*

More often than not, such simple food chains are oversimplified versions of the reality of feeding relationships. Instead, there are often multiple and interconnecting pathways, as well as numbers of different species involved at each trophic level. These complex pathways resemble a web rather than a simple chain and are referred to as **food webs**. So, a food web is a pictorial representation of the feeding relationship between organisms in an ecosystem and consists of interlocking food chains. The species in the webs are distinguished into basal species, intermediate species, or top predators. Species that are fed upon but do not feed on others are termed **basal species**. Species that feed on others but are not prey for other species are termed **top predators**. Species that are both predators and prey are termed **intermediate species**. The fundamental purpose of food webs is to describe feeding relationship among species in a community.

Detritus food chains begin with dead organic matter (*detritus*) and goes from non-living organic matter to detritus-feeding organisms (*detritivores*) and their predators. A large amount of organic matter is generated by the death of plant's parts, animals and their excretion products in all ecosystems. Hence, the detritus food chain is present in all ecosystems.

There is one notable difference in the flow of energy between trophic levels in the grazing and detritus food chains. In the grazing food chain, the flow is unidirectional, with net primary production providing the energy source for herbivores, herbivores providing the energy for carnivores, and so on. In the detritus food chain, the flow of energy is not unidirectional. The waste materials and dead organic matter in each of the consumer trophic levels are 'recycled,' returning as an input to the dead organic matter at the base of the detritus food chain.

The flow of energy in a single food chain; either grazing or detritus, is termed the **single-channel energy flow model**. However, in nature, that is rarely the case. In all ecosystems, the grazing and detritus food chains are interconnected, not all food eaten by herbivores is actually assimilated; some (such as undigested fecal matters) is diverted to the detritus pathway. The **Y-shaped model** (or **two-channel energy flow model**) explains the connection between a grazing and a detritus food chain.

Although, most of the natural ecosystems possess both grazing and detritus types of food chains. Their relative importance, however, varies from one ecosystem to another. In terrestrial and shallow water ecosystems, grazing food chains dominate because a major proportion of the annual energy flow passes through this circuit. In case of tidal marshes, almost 90% of the primary production is routed through the detritus food chains.

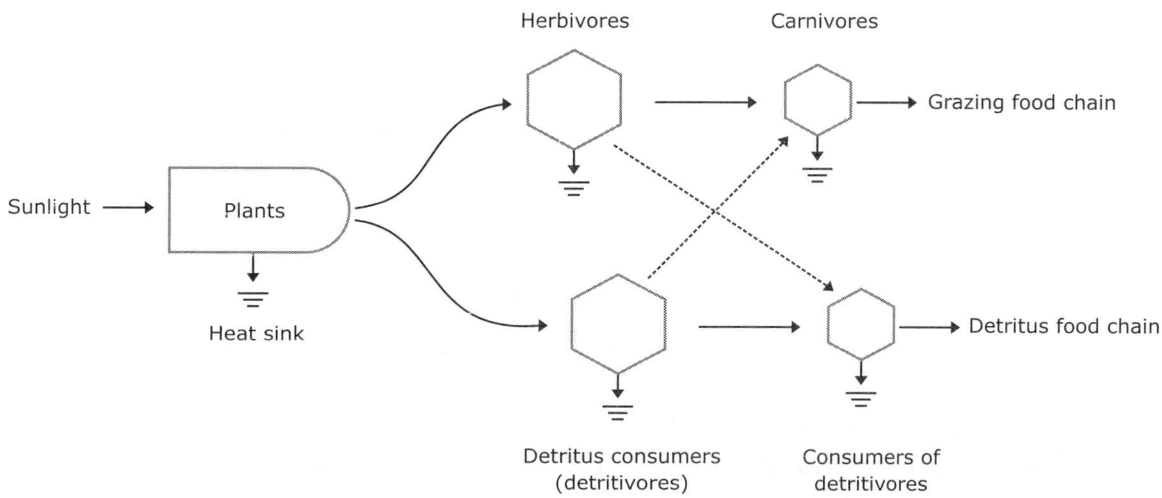

Figure 7.5 Y-shaped or two-channel energy flow diagram. Under natural conditions, the two food chains namely the grazing food chain and detritus food chain are not completely isolated from one another. The grazing food chain beginning with green plants goes to herbivores and their consumers. In the detritus food chain, beginning with dead organic matter passes to detritivores and their consumers. For instance, dead bodies of small animals that were once part of the grazing food chain become incorporated in the detritus food chain. Functionally, the distinction between the two is of time lag between the direct consumption of living plants and ultimate utilization of dead organic matter. Adapted from *Fundamental of Ecology* by Odum and Barrett.

7.3.5 Ecological efficiencies

In ecosystems, living organisms are linked together by feeding relationships. Producers (or autotrophs) have the ability to fix carbon through photosynthesis *via* chlorophylls in their leaves. Herbivores are the primary consumers of organic molecules fixed by the producers. Carnivores are secondary consumers, living on the organic molecules of the herbivores. There may be several levels of carnivores in any one ecosystem; in such cases, the ultimate level will be occupied by the top carnivore. The final groups of organisms in an ecosystem are decomposers, bacteria and fungi which can break down the complex organic chemicals of dead materials and waste products. *The amount of energy reaching each trophic level is determined by the NPP and the efficiencies with which food energy is converted to biomass energy within each trophic level.*

Percentage of energy in the biomass produced by one trophic level that is incorporated into the biomass produced by the next higher trophic level is called **ecological efficiency** (also called as **trophic efficiency** or **transfer efficiency** or **Lindeman's efficiency**).

The proportions of net primary production that flow along each of the possible energy pathways depend on transfer efficiencies in the way energy is used and passed from one step to the next. A knowledge of three categories of transfer efficiency is required to predict the pattern of energy flow. These are *consumption efficiency* (CE), *assimilation efficiency* (AE) and *production efficiency* (PE).

Consumption efficiency (or *exploitation efficiency*) is the percentage of total productivity available at one trophic level (P_{n-1}) that is actually consumed (i.e., ingested) by a trophic compartment one level up (I_n).

$$\text{Consumption efficiency (CE)} = \frac{I_n}{P_{n-1}} \times 100$$

In the case of secondary consumers, it is the percentage of herbivore productivity eaten by carnivores. Consumption efficiencies of herbivores are typically low in most ecosystems dominated by vascular plants, which are in many cases well defended against herbivores. For example, herbivores consume less than 10% of primary production in most terrestrial ecosystems. Herbivory in aquatic ecosystems is generally greater than in terrestrial ecosystems especially for algal-based ecosystems where herbivores often consume more than 50% of primary production. Similarly, in terrestrial forests, consumption efficiencies of herbivores are less as compared to grasslands where most plants are nonwoody.

Assimilation efficiency is the percentage of ingested food (I) that is assimilated (A) across the gut wall in a trophic level. The unassimilated material is lost as feces.

$$\text{Assimilation efficiency (AE)} = \frac{A_n}{I_n} \times 100$$

Assimilation efficiency depends on quality of food and the physiology of consumer. Carnivorous have a higher assimilation efficiency (approximately 80%) than herbivores (20% to 50%) because animal food is more easily digested than plant food. Assimilation efficiency also vary widely among ectotherms and endotherms. Endotherms are much more efficient than ectotherms. In aquatic ecosystem, autotrophs are mostly of small biomass but very high in digestible matters as compared to their counterparts in the terrestrial ecosystem. Hence, herbivore assimilation efficiency is higher in aquatic ecosystem than in terrestrial ecosystem.

Production efficiency is the percentage of assimilated food energy (A) that is incorporated into new biomass (P). The remainder is entirely lost as respiratory heat.

$$\text{Production efficiency (PE)} = \frac{P_n}{A_n} \times 100$$

Production efficiency (also called **net production efficiency** or **tissue growth efficiency**) varies mainly according to the taxonomic class of the organisms concerned. It is determined primarily by animal metabolism. Invertebrates, in general, have high efficiencies (30–40%), losing little energy in respiratory heat. Among the vertebrates, cold-blooded animals (*poikilotherms*) have higher values for production efficiency (around 10%) as compared to warm-blooded animals (*homeotherms*). Due to very high energy expenditure for maintaining a constant body temperature, warm-blooded animals convert only 1–2% of assimilated food energy into production. Among homeotherms, production efficiency decreases with decreasing body size because a small size results in a high surface to volume ratio and therefore a high rate of heat loss. Similarly, herbivores tend to have higher production efficiency than carnivores.

The product of the assimilation efficiency and net production efficiency is the **gross production efficiency** (production/ingestion or P/I); the proportion of food energy that is converted to consumer's biomass. For example, if a herbivore (such as a snail) was found to have an assimilation efficiency of 25% and a net production efficiency of 40%, then its gross production efficiency (A/I × P/A) is only 0.25 × 0.40 = 0.10 or 10%. Gross production efficiencies of warm-blooded terrestrial animals rarely exceed 5 percent. Herbivores tend to have higher P/A but lower A/I efficiencies than do carnivores.

Trophic transfer efficiency

Lindeman's law of trophic transfer efficiency (or simply *trophic efficiency*) states that the efficiency of energy transfer from one trophic level to the next is about 10% i.e., about 10% of the net primary productivity of producers ends up as herbivores, about 10% of the net productivity of herbivores ends up as primary carnivores, and so on. In other words, 90% of the energy available at one trophic level typically is *not* transferred to the next. This loss is multiplied over the length of a food chain. For example, if 10% of available energy is transferred from primary producers to primary consumers (herbivores), and 10% of that energy is transferred to secondary consumers (primary carnivores), then only 1% of net primary production is available to secondary consumers (10% of 10%).

After Lindeman's pioneering work, it was generally assumed that trophic transfer efficiencies were around 10% (referred to a **10 percent law**). However, there is certainly no law of nature that results in precisely one-tenth of the energy that enters a trophic level transferring to the next. It ranges from approximately 5% to 20%, depending on the type of the organisms in the ecosystem. The overall trophic transfer efficiency from one trophic level to next is simply the product of CE, AE and PE (i.e., CE × AE × PE).

7.3.6 Ecological pyramid

Ecological pyramids provide a graphical representation of the relationships between different trophic levels within an ecosystem. *Pyramid* can be based on number of individuals of different species belonging to a trophic level, total living biomass belonging to a trophic level, and energy flow in a biotic community. Any calculations of energy content, biomass, or numbers has to include all organisms at that trophic level. The base of each pyramid corresponds to the producers or the first trophic level, while the apex represents the top consumer or highest trophic level. Ecological pyramids can take on different shapes, either *upright* or *inverted*, depending on the nature of ecosystem. **Upright pyramids** indicate a decrease in numbers, biomass, or energy as we move up the trophic levels. In contrast, **inverted pyramids** indicate an increase in the number or biomass as we move up from the lower to higher trophic levels. However, there are certain limitations to ecological pyramids. It does not account for the same species belonging to two or more trophic levels. Additionally, it assumes a simple food chain and does not accommodate a food web. Moreover, there is no place for decomposers in ecological pyramids.

Pyramid of numbers: Pyramids of numbers represent the number of individuals present in each trophic level of an ecosystem and are typically measured in individuals per unit area. It is a graphic representation of the total number of individuals of different species belonging to each trophic level in an ecosystem. The length of each bar in the pyramid represents the total number of individuals present at that specific trophic level. In most ecosystems, such as grassland ecosystems, the pyramid of numbers is upright, indicating a decrease in the number of organisms at higher trophic levels. This means that there are more individuals at the base of the pyramid (producers) and fewer individuals as we move up the trophic levels.

However, it's important to note that there are certain ecological systems where the pyramid of numbers may be inverted. One example is when we consider a single tree and its associated insect population. In this case, the tree, as a primary producer, represents the base of the pyramid, and the dependent insects represent the second trophic level. However, since, at any given time, the total number of insects is higher compared to the number of trees, the pyramid of numbers would be inverted.

Pyramid of biomass: Pyramid of biomass represents the total biomass of living beings of different species at each trophic level at a particular time. It is determined by collecting and measuring the dry biomass of organisms within each trophic level. This eliminates problems arising from differences in the size and number of individuals because all types of organisms at a trophic level are weighed. Typically, the biomass of producers, such as plants, is substantially greater than the biomass of herbivores, and the biomass of herbivores is greater than that of carnivores, and so on. This pattern indicates a decrease in biomass if we move from producer to top carnivore. Therefore, the diagrammatic representation of biomass belonging to different trophic levels typically takes the form of an upright pyramid. However, it's important to note that the pyramid of biomass does not always exhibit an upright shape. In aquatic ecosystems, such as lakes and oceans, the pyramid of biomass may assume an inverted form. This is primarily because phytoplankton, the producers in aquatic systems, do not accumulate a significant amount of biomass. Consequently, at any given time, the total biomass of phytoplankton is lower compared to herbivores or other consumers. This is the reason for the base of the pyramid in aquatic ecosystem being smaller than the upper structure.

Pyramid of energy: A pyramid of energy shows the flow of energy from one trophic level of a community to the next. The units of pyramids of energy are energy/area/time, e.g., kcal m^{-2} yr^{-1}. An energy pyramid more accurately reflects the laws of thermodynamics, as energy loss occurs at each transfer from one trophic level to another. Therefore, *the pyramid is always upright*. In energy pyramids, a given trophic level always has a smaller energy content than the trophic level immediately below it. This is due to the fact that some energy is always lost as heat is going from one trophic level to the next.

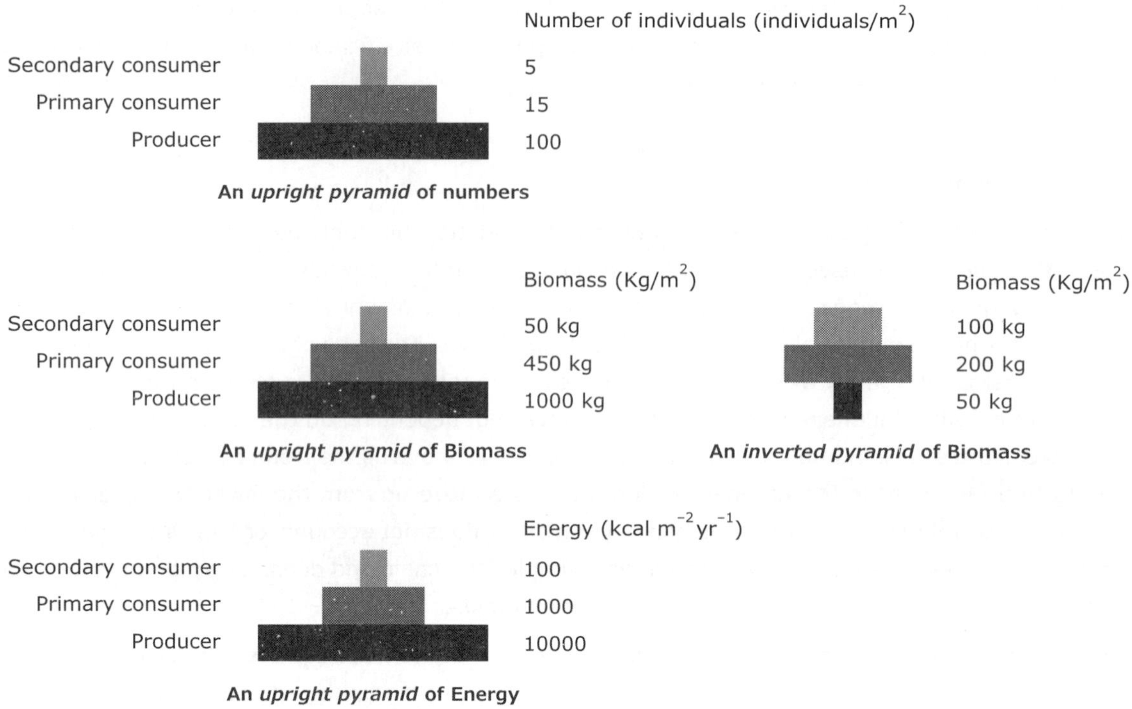

Figure 7.6 There are three types of ecological pyramid— pyramid of numbers, pyramid of biomass and pyramid of energy. The pyramid of numbers shows the total number of individuals of different species at each trophic level. The pyramid of biomass shows how much biomass is present in the organisms at each trophic level. The pyramid of energy shows that there is a decrease in energy when it moves from lower trophic level to higher trophic level.

7.3.7 Nutrient cycling

The Earth is essentially a **closed system** with respect to matter and *all matter on the Earth cycles*. Every matter that is used by living organisms passes between the biotic and abiotic components of the Earth. By 'matter' we mean *elements* (such as carbon, nitrogen, oxygen) or *molecules* (water). *Nutrient cycling* (or more precisely *element cycling*) is the movement of elements through both the biotic and abiotic components of the Earth. It is the transport and transformation of elements within and among ecosystems. It involves the incorporation of elements by living organisms and their subsequent release back into the environment via decomposition. It links biotic and abiotic parts of ecosystems. The movement of elements through atmosphere, hydrosphere, lithosphere and biosphere is generally termed as a **biogeochemical cycle**. An element's specific route through a biogeochemical cycle depends on the nature of element. All elements occurring in organisms are part of biogeochemical cycles. In addition to being a part of living organisms, these elements also cycle through abiotic components of ecosystems.

There are two basic types of biogeochemical cycles: *gaseous* and *sedimentary*. This classification is based on the primary source of element input to the ecosystem. In **gaseous cycles**, the *atmosphere* acts as a major reservoir of the element. Such cycles show little or no permanent change in the distribution and abundance of the element. Carbon and nitrogen are prime representatives of biogeochemical cycles with a prominent gaseous phase. In **sedimentary cycle***,* the major reservoir is the lithosphere from which the elements are released largely by weathering. The sedimentary cycles, exemplified by phosphorus, sulfur and most of the other biologically important elements, have a tendency to stagnate. In such cycles, a portion of the supply may accumulate in large quantities, as in the deep ocean sediment, and thereby become inaccessible to organisms and to continual cycling. Some of the elements that are characterized by sedimentary cycles do have a gaseous phase, sulfur and iodine being among them, but these phases are insignificant in that there is no large gaseous reservoir.

An element's specific route through a biogeochemical cycle varies with the particular element. Based on spatial scale, there are, however, two general categories of biogeochemical cycles: *global* and *local cycle.* In **local cycles** such as the phosphorus cycle, there are no mechanisms for long distance transfer of elements; whereas **global cycles** such as nitrogen cycle, involve atmosphere for long distance transfer of elements. Global cycles unite the Earth into one giant interconnected ecosystem. Gaseous forms of carbon, oxygen, sulfur and nitrogen occur in the atmosphere, and cycles of these elements are essentially global. Other, less mobile elements, including phosphorus, potassium and calcium, generally cycle on a more localized scale, at least over the short term. Lithosphere is the main abiotic reservoir of elements performing local cycle.

General model of nutrient cycling

Although the nutrient cycling of the various elements differ in detail, from the perspective of the ecosystem all nutrient cycles have a common pattern. A general model of nutrient cycling includes the main reservoirs of elements and the processes that transfer elements between reservoirs. Each reservoir is defined by two characteristics: whether it contains organic or inorganic materials and whether or not the materials are directly available for use by organisms. The nutrients in living organisms and in detritus are available to other organisms when consumers feed and when detritivores consume non-living organic matter. Some materials are moved from the living or organic reservoir to the fossilized organic reservoir, when dead organisms were buried by sedimentation over millions of years, becoming coal, peat. The nutrients in these deposits cannot be assimilated directly.

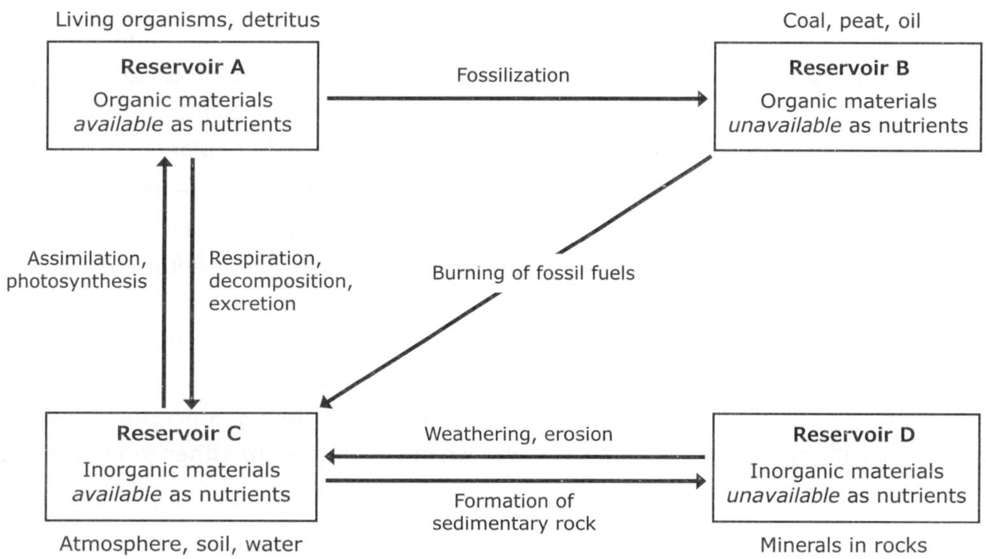

Figure 7.7 A general model of nutrient cycling.

Inorganic materials (elements and compounds) that are dissolved in water or present in the soil or air are available for use. Organisms assimilate materials from this reservoir directly and return chemicals to it through the relatively rapid processes of cellular respiration, excretion and decomposition. Although organisms cannot directly tap into the inorganic elements tied up in the rocks, these nutrients may slowly become available through weathering and erosion. Similarly, unavailable organic materials move into the available reservoir of inorganic nutrients when fossil fuels are burned, releasing exhaust into the atmosphere.

Two ecological processes – energy flow and nutrient (element) cycling – are the fundamental functions of ecosystems. These two processes proceed concurrently in ecosystems, a few generalizations can be made:

- The ultimate source of energy (for most ecosystems) is the Sun.
- The ultimate fate of energy in ecosystems is to be lost as heat.
- Energy and nutrients are passed from organism to organism through the food chain as one organism eats another.
- Decomposers remove the last energy from the remains of organisms.
- Inorganic nutrients are cycled, energy is not.

7.3.8 Decomposition

Decomposition by biological agents is a vital process that involves the breakdown of complex organic compounds into simpler forms. Dead organic matter, including the remains of plants and animals as well as fecal matter from animals, known as **detritus**, serves as the raw material for decomposition. **Decomposition**, an oxygen-requiring process, involves the active participation of biological agents known as **decomposers**, mainly bacteria and fungi. These decomposers utilize carbon compounds present in the detritus as a source of energy. Enzymes produced by the decomposers break down the detritus into simpler inorganic substances. Organisms that obtain nutrients and energy by decomposing and absorbing dead organic material are called **saprotrophs**, and decomposers are a type of saprotroph. While **scavengers** and **detritivores** may feed on detritus, they are not responsible for the complete decomposition of the organic matter they consume. It is the decomposers that ultimately carry out the decomposition process, breaking down the remaining organic matter and converting it into inorganic nutrients.

Decomposition progresses through several crucial steps, including *fragmentation*, *humification*, and *mineralization*. **Fragmentation** is the physical breakdown of organic matter into smaller pieces. **Humification** involves the formation of a dark-colored, amorphous substance known as **humus**. Humus comprises *humic substances* like fulvic acid, humic acid, and humin, as well as *non-humic* substances such as carbohydrates, proteins, lignins, and organic acids. Humus is highly resistant to microbial action and undergoes decomposition at an extremely slow rate. Due to its colloidal nature, it serves as a reservoir of nutrients. Finally, **mineralization** occurs when microorganisms break down organic compounds into simpler, water-soluble inorganic nutrients. These water-soluble inorganic nutrients move down through the soil profile, a process called **leaching**. When these nutrients leach into the soil, they can be precipitated as unavailable salts, which means they are no longer available to plants.

Decomposition rates are largely controlled both by biotic and abiotic factors. Biotic factors include mainly substrate quantity and quality and the type and size of the microbial community; abiotic factors include variables such as soil temperature, moisture and pH, which determine the soil environmental conditions. Decomposers usually grow faster and decompose organic matter more quickly in warmer climate. Hence, decomposition in a tropical rainforest is rapid, relatively little dead organic matter accumulates on the forest bed. The relatively low concentrations of some nutrients in the soil of tropical rainforests result from a faster nutrient cycling rate. In temperate forests, where decomposition is much slower, the soil may contain a large amount of the dead organic matter in the forest. Decomposition on land is also slower when conditions are either too dry for decomposers to thrive or too wet to supply them with enough oxygen.

7.4 Ecosystem services

Ecosystem services are '*the benefits which people obtain from ecosystems*'. According to **IPCC** (Intergovernmental Panel on Climate Change), ecosystem services are ecological processes or functions which have value to individuals or society. For example, forest ecosystems purify air and water, mitigate droughts and floods, cycle nutrients, generate fertile soils, provide wildlife habitat, maintain biodiversity, pollinate crops, provide storage site for carbon and also provide aesthetic, cultural and spiritual values. Ecosystem services are grouped into four broad categories. All of these services are provided by complex chemical, physical, and biological processes, powered by the Sun, and operate at different temporal and spatial scales.

Provisioning, such as the production of food and water;

Regulating, such as the control of climate and disease;

Supporting, such as nutrient cycles and crop pollination; and

Cultural, such as spiritual and recreational benefits.

Provisioning services	Regulating services	Cultural services	Supporting services
Products obtained from ecosystem. • Food • Fresh-water • Fuelwood • Fiber • Biochemicals • Genetic resources	Benefits obtained from regulation of ecosystem processes. • Climate regulation • Disease regulation • Water regulation • Water purification • Pollination	Non-material benefits obtained from ecosystem. • Spiritual and religious • Recreation and ecotourism • Aesthetic • Inspirational • Educational • Sense of place • Cultural heritage	Services necessary for the production of all other from ecosystem. • Soil formation • Nutrient cycling • Primary production

7.4.1 Control of trophic structure: top-down versus bottom-up control

We have learned about how materials and energy flow through ecosystems. Now, we can address the question of 'what controls the trophic structure'? The control of tropic structure i.e., the partitioning of biomass between trophic levels is broadly divided into two categories. The first of these categories, **bottom-up control**, emphasizes the energy inputs into the primary producers and the subsequent efficiency of energy transfer between trophic levels in determining the biomass accumulation at each trophic level. The second category, **top-down control**, emphasizes the importance of predation in influencing patterns of biomass accumulation at different trophic levels.

Bottom-up control

Bottom-up control (**abiotic control**) of trophic structure means that the production of biomass at each trophic level is controlled by inputs of nutrients, light or water that set quantity and quality of primary production. Biomass accumulated by producers then passes to higher trophic levels as a function of trophic transfer efficiency. This model proposes a unidirectional influence from lower to higher trophic levels, in which nutrients and other abiotic factors (such as light, water) are the main determinants of the biomass of primary producers. The nutrient supply controls the biomass of primary producers, which controls herbivore's biomass, which in turn controls predator's biomass. If the nutrient supply is increased, the resulting increase in production of primary producers is propagated through the food web and all of the other trophic levels will respond to the increased biomass. An important exception to this pattern occurs in aquatic food webs, where 'inverted biomass pyramids' can occur as a consequence of the extremely short generation time of unicellular producers relative to resident herbivores and predators.

Top-down control

Top-down control (**biotic control**) means that predation by higher trophic levels affects the accumulation of biomass at lower trophic levels. It suggests that biomass accumulation at any one trophic level depends on the intensity of predation from the trophic level above i.e., carnivores control population densities of herbivores directly and that herbivores control plant biomass directly. The effects of top-down control may, therefore, percolate down from predators through herbivores to plants.

A top-down control is a **trophic cascade** where the trophic structure is influenced by the removal of a top predator (a third or fourth level consumer). Top predators eat prey. By doing so predators can impact prey abundance. When the impact of a predator on its prey trickles down one or more feeding level to affect the density of prey's prey, the ecologist term this interaction a *tropic* or *feeding cascade*. Trophic cascades occur when predators limit the density of their prey and thereby enhance survival of the next lower trophic level. Trophic cascades by definition must occur across a minimum of three feeding levels.

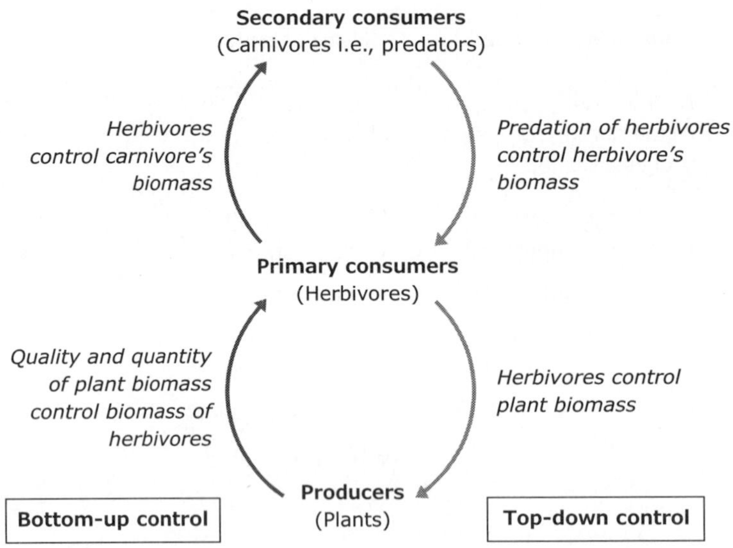

Figure 7.8 Bottom-up and top-down control. Bottom-up control proposes that plant quantity or quality limits the density of herbivores, which in turn sets limits on the abundance of predators. Top-down control proposes that plant biomass is limited by herbivores and that herbivores are limited by predators.

Thus, the top-down control postulates that the control of each trophic level comes from the trophic level above. It is mainly predation that controls the accumulation of biomass at lower trophic levels because predators limit herbivores, which in turn limit plants, which in turn limit nutrient levels through their uptake during growth and reproduction.

So, which theory is correct? While recognizing the differences between these two factors, it is also important to emphasize that both bottom-up and top-down control represent extremes along a continuum of importance for regulatory control. There is evidence from many ecosystem studies that both controls are operating to some degree, but that neither control is complete. Because both of these controls are operating in any system at any time, hence we must understand the relative importance of each control in order to help us to predict how an ecosystem will behave or change under different circumstances, such as in the face of a changing climate.

7.5 Types of Ecosystems

Ecosystems are of different types. These can be artificially categorized as follows:

A. Natural ecosystem

1. *Terrestrial ecosystem*, such as forest, grassland, desert.

   A **forest** is an ecosystem with a high density of trees and other woody vegetation.

   A **grassland** is an ecosystem where the vegetation is dominated by grasses and other herbaceous (non-woody) plants. Grasslands occur in regions that are too dry for forests but that have sufficient soil water to support a herbaceous plant canopy that is lacking in deserts.

   A **desert** is an ecosystem that receives an extremely low amount of precipitation, less than enough to support the growth of most plants. Deserts are defined as areas with an average annual precipitation of less than 250 millimeters per year, or as areas where more water is lost by evapotranspiration than falls as precipitation.

2. *Aquatic ecosystem*, which may be further distinguished on the basis of salt content as:

   Freshwater ecosystem (such as lake, pond) has very low salt content (0.5 ppt or less).

   Marine ecosystem (such as ocean, estuaries) has very high salt content (35 ppt or less).

B. Artificial or **domesticated ecosystem**

These are maintained artificially by man by the addition of energy. For example, croplands like maize, wheat, rice field etc., where man tries to control the biotic community as well as the physico-chemical environment.

7.5.1 Aquatic ecosystem

An *aquatic ecosystem* is an ecosystem in a body of water. Aquatic ecosystems are commonly categorized on the basis of whether the water is moving (streams, rivers) or still (ponds, lakes) and whether the water is fresh, saline or brackish. Aquatic ecosystems are generally divided into two major types based on salinity - the marine ecosystem and the freshwater ecosystem. *Marine ecosystems* cover over 70 percent of the Earth's surface and are largest aquatic ecosystems of the Earth. *Freshwater ecosystems* include lakes, ponds, rivers, streams and springs and cover about 2 percent of the Earth's surface. These ecosystems can be divided into **lentic ecosystems** (still water such as lake, pond) and **lotic ecosystems** (flowing water such as a river).

Marine ecosystems

Marine ecosystems are aquatic ecosystems whose waters possess a high salt content. Out of all of the types of ecosystems on the planet, marine ecosystems are the most prevalent. Scientists have classified marine ecosystems into different categories such as open ocean ecosystem, ocean floor ecosystem, estuary ecosystem; however, categories aren't always clearly defined, so some categories may overlap or envelope other categories.

Oceans represent the largest and the most diverse type of ecosystem. Oceans can be divided into numerous regions depending on the physical and biological conditions. Ocean environment is generally classified on the basis of light penetration (*euphotic, disphotic* and *aphotic zones*), distance from shore and water depth (*littoral* or *intertidal, neritic* and *oceanic zones*) and whether it is open water (*pelagic zone*; zone neither close to the bottom nor near the shore) or bottom (*benthic zones*).

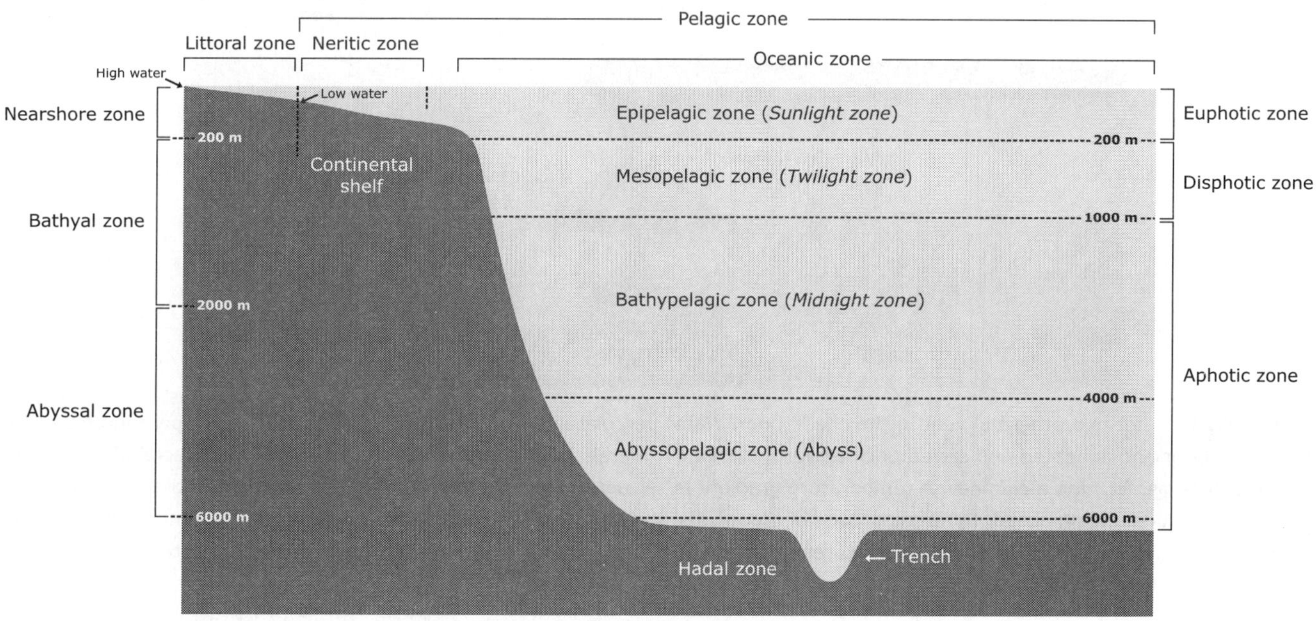

Figure 7.9 Zonation in marine ecosystem according to depth and the light availability. The benthic zone describes the bottom of the ocean, extending from the shoreline to the deep seafloor.

The **littoral zone** (or *inter-tidal zone*) is the shoreline between land and ocean. The **neritic zone** is the shallow water zone over the continental shelf, a water depth of about 200 meters. The **oceanic zone** is the deep-water zone beyond the continental shelf. The *open ocean* is called the **pelagic zone**. The pelagic zone is further subdivided into five different zones. From the surface to about 200 meters is the **epipelagic zone** (or *sunlight zone*). This is the region where the photosynthesis most commonly occurs and therefore contains the largest biodiversity. From 200 to 1000 meters is the **mesopelagic zone** (also known as *twilight zone* or *midwater zone*), where little light penetrates. Below the mesopelagic, water depth from 1000 to 4000 meters is the **bathypelagic zone** (also known as *midnight zone* or *dark zone*), where darkness is virtually complete. After bathypelagic zone is **abyssopelagic**

zone (simply as the *abyss*), down to a water depth of 6000 meters. The water temperature is near freezing, and there is no light at all. Water deeper than 6000 meters, found in deep trenches, is termed the **hadalpelagic zone.** It represents the deepest parts of the ocean.

The benthic zone describes the bottom of the ocean, extending from the shoreline to the deep seafloor. The benthic zone may include areas that are only a few meters below water surface or may be at the more than 6000 meters from water surface. It is divided into zones based on their depth from the shallowest to the deepest – **nearshore zones** (*littoral* and sub-littoral), **bathyal zone** (200 to 2,000 meters), **abyssal zone** (2,000 to 6,000 meters) and **hadal zone** (over 6,000 meters deep).

Hot hydrothermal vents

Hot hydrothermal vents are found on the ocean floor, in regions where the ocean floor is spreading and are associated with gradual upwelling of mineral-rich fluid from the Earth's interior. Moving Earth's crust creates cracks and crevices in the ocean floor. These cracks allow the sea water to percolate downwards. Seawater that percolates downward toward the hot molten rock is heated and driven back upward, carrying minerals leached from the hot rock. On ocean floor, these minerals solidify as they cool, forming *chimney-like* structures.

There are two main types of chimneys or hydrothermal vents – Black smokers and white smokers. **Black smokers** (emit a cloud of black materials) are chimneys formed from deposits of mainly iron sulfide, which is black. **White smokers** (emit a cloud of white materials) are chimneys formed from deposition of barium, calcium and silicon, which are white. A temperature gradient is set up, from more than 350°C near the core of the vent, down to 2-3°C in the surrounding ocean.

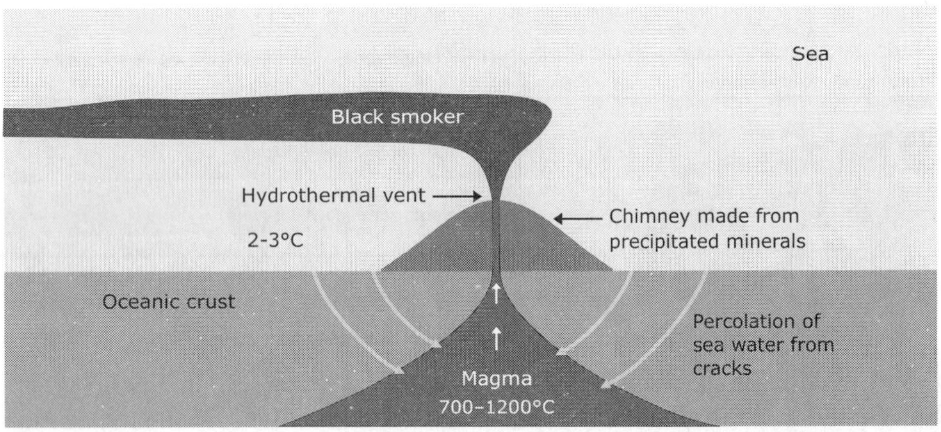

Figure 7.10 A hot hydrothermal vent in the ocean floor. Water percolates down toward the hot molten rock upwelling from the Earth's interior and is heated and driven back upward, carrying minerals leached from the hot rock. Minerals precipitate from the water as it cools, forming a chimney. A temperature gradient is set up, from more than 350°C near the core of the vent, down to 2–3°C in the surrounding ocean. Different classes of organisms, thriving at different temperatures, live in different neighborhoods of the chimney. Close to the vent, at temperatures up to about 150°C, various chemoautotrophic species of bacteria live, directly fuelled by geochemical energy.

Many types of organisms coexist near the hydrothermal vents. Close to the vent, at temperatures up to about 150°C, various chemoautotrophic species of bacteria live, directly fuelled by geochemical energy. Despite the extreme temperatures and pressures, toxic minerals, and lack of sunlight that characterized the deep-sea hydrothermal vent ecosystem, the species living there are thriving.

The basis of the ecosystems is the presence of chemoautotrophic bacteria. These bacteria use sulfur compounds, particularly hydrogen sulfide, to produce organic materials (carbohydrates) by the process of chemosynthesis. Hydrogen sulfide, found under the crust, is brought up in the vent water. Without these bacteria, the entire ecosystem of hydrothermal vents could not exist. Primary consumers in the ecosystem depend on these bacteria for food. Many animals, like the **giant tube worms** (*Riftia pachyptila*) have colonies of these bacteria inside their body and use the sugars made by the bacteria for energy. Giant tube worms have no mouth or stomach, so they are fully dependent on the bacteria.

Coral reefs ecosystem

Coral reefs are a special subtype of ocean floor ecosystem. Found only in warm tropical waters and at relatively shallow depths, coral reefs are among the most productive ecosystems on the planet. About one-quarter of marine species depend on coral reefs for food, shelter or both. Because of the diversity found in the habitats created by corals, reefs are often called the 'rainforests of the sea.'

Corals are marine invertebrates in the class **Anthozoa** of phylum **Cnidaria**. More than 6,000 species of coral are known. Most structures that we call 'coral' are, in fact, made up of hundreds to thousands of tiny coral polyps. Each soft-bodied polyp secretes a hard-outer skeleton of calcium carbonate that attaches either to rock or the dead skeletons of other polyps. Although various types of corals can be found from the water's surface to depths of 6000 m, **reef-building corals** are generally found at depths of less than 45 m. One fascinating feature of shallow water, reef-building corals is their mutualistic relationship with photosynthetic algae called **zooxanthellae**, which live in their tissues. Because reef-building corals have a symbiotic relationship with algal cells, their distribution is limited to depths where sufficient solar radiation is available to support photosynthesis. Deep-sea corals occur in much deeper or colder oceanic waters and lack zooxanthellae. The coral provides the algae with a protected environment and the compounds they need for photosynthesis. In return, the algae produce oxygen and help the coral to remove wastes. Precipitation of calcium from the water is necessary to form the coral skeleton. This precipitation occurs when water temperature and salinity are high and carbon dioxide concentrations are low. These requirements limit the distribution of reef-building corals to the shallow, warm tropical waters (20°C to 28°C).

Estuary

An *estuary* (from Latin word means *tide*) is a transition area between river and sea. It is a semi-enclosed coastal body of water where freshwater from land runoff mixes with seawater. These areas of transition between the land and the sea are driven by tides but sheltered from the full force of ocean wind and waves. When freshwater meets salty seawater, both water combines into a brackish mixture. At estuary, salinity is intermediate between salt- and fresh water. However, salinity varies spatially within estuaries, from nearly that of freshwater to that of seawater. Salinity also varies with the rise and fall of the tides. Estuaries are among the most productive ecosystems in the world and are home to unique plant and animal communities that have adapted to brackish water. However, estuaries are not only found where freshwater from rivers and salt water from the ocean meet and mix. There are also several types of entirely freshwater ecosystems that have many similar characteristics to the traditional brackish water estuaries. These freshwater estuaries also provide many of the ecosystem services and functions that brackish estuaries do.

Freshwater ecosystem

In freshwater, the average salinity is 0.5 ppt or less i.e., very low salt content. It exists in various forms such as lakes, rivers, ponds and wetlands. The study of the physical, chemical and biological properties of freshwater is referred to as **limnology**. Freshwater ecosystems include both running water (**lotic ecosystem**) or still water (**lentic ecosystem**). A lotic ecosystem (also called the **riverine ecosystem**) can be any kind of moving water, such as river, spring, channel or stream. A lentic ecosystem (also called the **lacustrine ecosystem**) entails a body of standing water such as pond or lake.

Lake

A **lake** is an inland body of standing water that is usually larger and deeper than a **pond**. Like an ocean, lake is also divided into separate zones which are defined by their distance from the shore. The **littoral zone**, which is closest to the shore, is host to a wide variety of rooted plants species due to its warm, shallow environment. In lakes and ponds, much of the species diversity is concentrated in the littoral zone, near the shore. The **limnetic zone** (pelagic zone) is the open water farther from shore and is dominated by planktons. The deeper region of a lake below the limnetic zone is called the **profundal zone** which contains only heterotrophs. The zone at the bottom of a lake is termed **benthic.** The benthic zone is occupied by communities of organisms collectively called the **benthos**. The terms benthic and benthos are derived from the Greek for *depths of the sea*, but the terms are also used in freshwater biology to refer to the zone and organisms at the bottom of freshwater bodies.

Lakes are divided into photic and aphotic zones on the basis of light penetration. The **photic zone** (*euphotic zone* or *sunlight zone*) is the uppermost layer of water in a lake that is illuminated with sunlight. The depth of the photic zone depends on light intensity and water clarity. The portion of a lake where there is little or no sunlight penetrates is called **aphotic zone.** It is formally defined as the depths beyond which less than 1% of sunlight penetrates. Light is a primary factor limiting primary productivity in aquatic ecosystems. Intensity of photosynthetically active radiation (PAR) declines exponentially with water depth in the photic zone. Hence, photosynthetic rate (production) by photosynthetic organisms declines with depth in photic zone, whereas, rate of respiration (light independent process) is relatively constant with depth. The depth of photic zone at which photosynthetic rate is equal to respiration rate ($P/R = 1$) is called the **compensation depth**. Above compensation depth, photosynthetic rate is greater than respiration rate ($P/R > 1$), whereas below compensation depth respiration rate is greater than photosynthetic rate ($P/R < 1$).

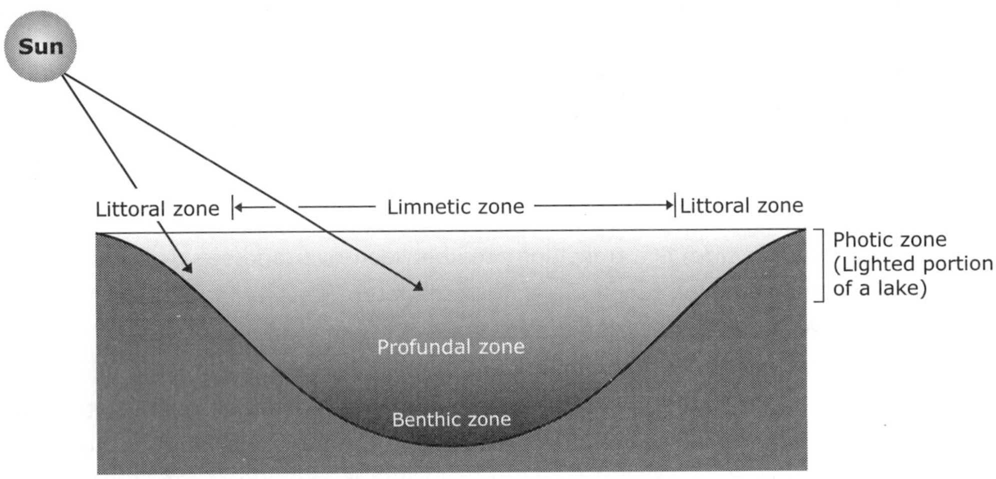

Figure 7.11 The zones in lake water are determined by gradients of light from the water surface to the bottom.

Life-forms in a lake ecosystem include *producers, consumers* and *decomposers.* The producers may be of two main types - rooted or large floating plants (**macrophytes**) generally growing in shallow water; and minute floating plants, usually algae called **phytoplankton**, distributed throughout the lake as deep as light penetrates.

Life-forms in a lake ecosystem can also be categorized as **plankton** (free-floating organisms), **nekton** (free-swimming organisms, such as fish), **benthos** (bottom-dwelling organism), **neuston** (the collective term for the organisms that float on the top of the water, **epineuston** or live right under the surface, **hyponeuston**) and **periphyton** (organisms attached to submerged surfaces).

Thermal stratification

Changes in the temperature profile with depth in an aquatic system are called *thermal stratification*. Freshwater lakes of temperate regions generally become thermally stratified due to differential heating and cooling. A well stratified temperate lake during summer has a layer of freely circulating warm surface water with small temperature gradient known as the **epilimnion**. A second layer called **metalimnion** (or **thermocline**), which is characterized by a steep decline in temperature, separates the more uniformly warm upper layer from more uniformly cold deeper waters. The third layer is the **hypolimnion**, a deep, cold layer of dense water where no temperature gradient is evident. *Thermocline checks the mixing of water* between epilimnion and hypolimnion. In freshwater lotic ecosystems, thermal stratification is not observed.

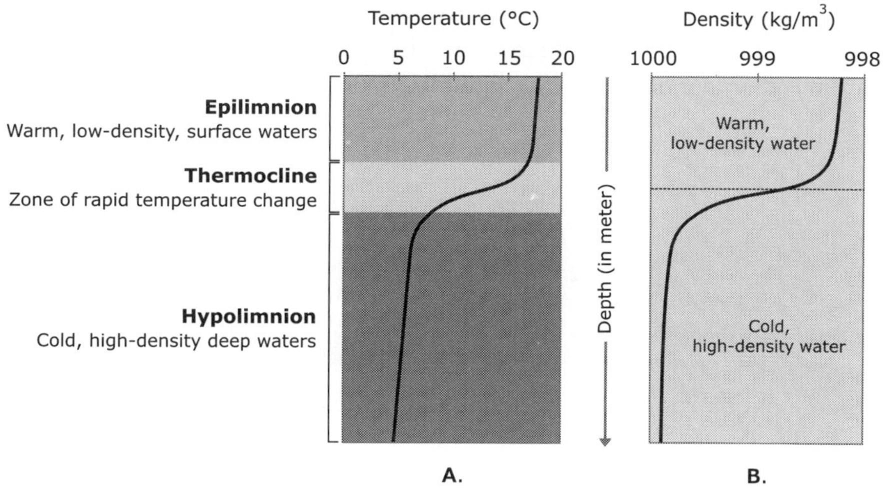

Figure 7.12 Temperature and density profiles with water depth for a temperate lake during summer. **A**. The region of the vertical depth profile where the temperature declines most rapidly is called the thermocline. The thermocline is located between an upper layer of warm, less dense water called the epilimnion and a deeper layer of cold, denser water called the hypolimnion. **B**. The rapid decline in temperature in the thermocline results in a distinct difference in water density in the warmer epilimnion as compared to the cooler waters of the hypolimnion, leading to a two-layer density profile—warm, low-density surface water and cold, high-density deep water.

Seasonal changes in water temperature

The temperature profile of a deep-water lake of *temperate region* changes from one season to the next and creates a cyclic pattern. Due to seasonal variation in the input of solar radiation to the water surface give rise to seasonal changes in the vertical profile of temperature.

Let us begin with spring season. After the ice melts on a lake, the lake water is generally has the same temperature from the surface to the bottom. It allows circulation and mixing of the lake water. Surface water can be pushed to the lake bottom and bottom water can rise to the surface. This circulation pattern allows large amounts of oxygen to reach the bottom of the lake. The mixing of the lake water at this time of year is called **spring overturn**.

As air temperature rises in summer, heat from the Sun begins to warm the lake. The layer of warm water at the surface of the lake is called the *epilimnion*. The cold layer below the epilimnion is called the *hypolimnion*. These two layers are separated by a layer of water which rapidly changes temperature with depth. This is called the *thermocline* (or *metalimnion*). Stratification during the summer acts as a deterrent to complete lake mixing. Wind circulates the surface water, but the warm water of the epilimnion is unable to move through the cold, dense water of the hypolimnion. As a result, the water is only mixed in the epilimnion.

As autumn (fall) approaches and temperature decreases, the epilimnion begins to decrease in depth. Eventually, the epilimnion gets so shallow that it can no longer be maintained as a separate layer and the lake loses its stratification. Thus, as in the spring, the lake water in the autumn has generally uniform temperatures and wind can once again thoroughly mix the lake water. In addition, surface water, which is in direct contact with the cold air, gets cooled faster than the water below. This cold, dense water sinks and further helps to mix the lake, and again more oxygen and nutrients are replenished throughout the lake. This process is called **autumn overturn**.

As winter approaches, the surface water is eventually cooled below 4°C. As water temperature at the surface reaches 0°C, ice begins to cover the surface of the lake. During the winter, ice cover prevents wind from mixing the lake water. Again, stratification occurs but the pattern is reversed (**inverse stratification**); cold water rests over warm water. A layer of water colder than 4°C, but warmer than 0°C forms just under the ice. Below this water, the remainder of lake water is usually near 4°C.

Due to the relatively constant input of solar radiation to the water surface throughout the year (the absence of seasonality), the thermocline is a permanent feature of lakes present in *tropical regions.* Similarly, ponds often show little thermal stratification during the summer due to their shallow depth, which facilitates wind-mediated water circulation.

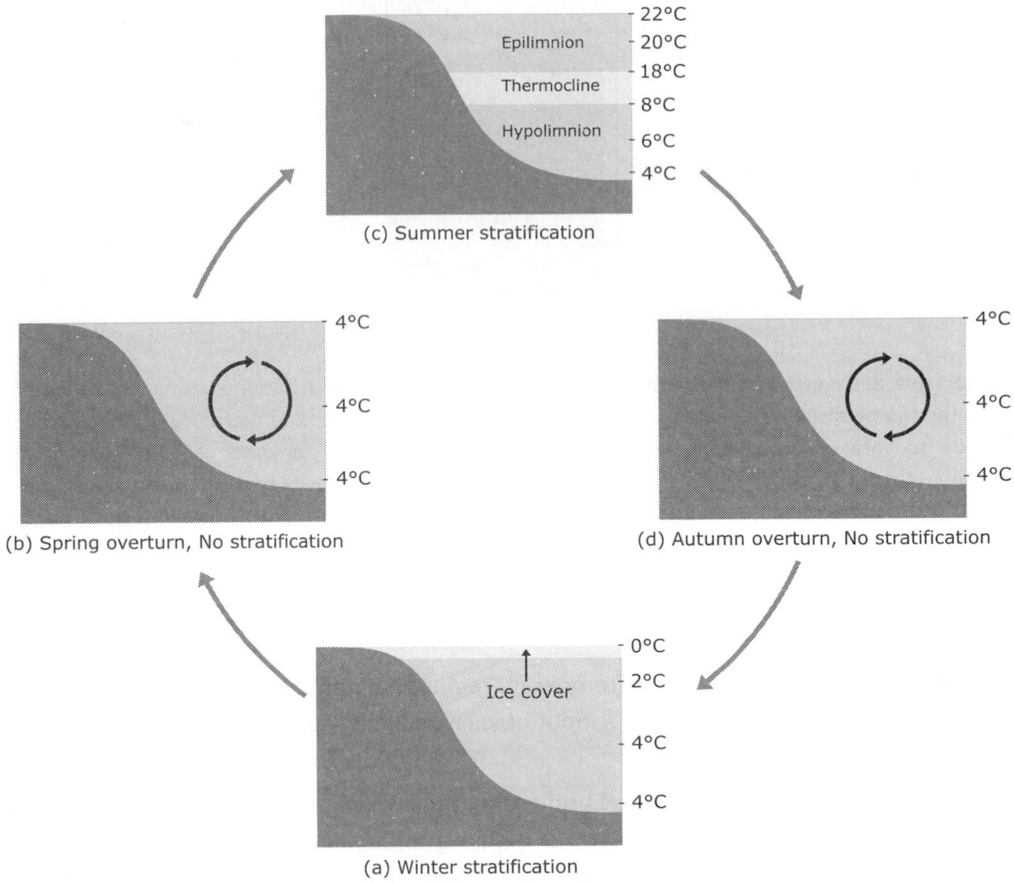

Figure 7.13 The seasonal cycle of water temperature (in °C) in a temperate lake. Cross section of a temperate lake along with temperature profiles with depth for each season. (a) The lake surface freezes in winter. (b) When the ice melts in spring, the cold water again sinks and mixes the lake. (c) In summer, the warmest water occurs at the surface, and water temperature decreases with depth. (d) Cold air temperatures in autumn cool the upper layers and this dense cold water sinks, thoroughly mixing the lake.

Eutrophication is a process in which water bodies, such as lakes and ponds, receive an excess of inorganic nutrients, primarily nitrogen and phosphorus compounds. This influx of nutrients stimulates excessive growth of plants and algae. A rapid increase in the algal population within an aquatic system is known as an **algal bloom**. It can occur in both freshwater and marine environments and are typically caused by a combination of factors, including nutrient enrichment (especially nitrogen and phosphorus), warm temperatures, light availability, and calm water conditions. Eutrophication can be *natural* or *cultural* eutrophication.

Natural eutrophication: It is a natural ageing process. It occurs as lakes and ponds age and are filled in with sediments. It is a process that occurs in all lakes over time, as the weathering of rocks and soils from the surrounding catchment area leads to an accumulation of nutrients and associated sediments in the water. Depending on climate, the size of the water bodies, the natural aging of a water body may span hundreds of years.

Cultural eutrophication: It occurs due to excessive discharge of inorganic nutrients into the water bodies due to human activities. Nutrients can come from many sources, such as fertilizers applied to agricultural fields and sewage treatment plant discharges. Excessive algal growth eventually leads to death and decomposition of algae which reduce dissolved oxygen in the water. Depending on the degree of eutrophication, subsequent negative environmental effects such as anoxia and severe reductions in aquatic animal populations may occur.

Wetlands

'Wetlands are areas that are inundated or saturated by surface or groundwater at a frequency and duration sufficient to support, and that under normal conditions do support, a prevalence of vegetation typically adapted to life in saturated soil conditions'

Wetlands are ecosystems in which the land surface is saturated or covered with standing water either permanently or seasonally. These ecosystems are transitional between terrestrial and aquatic systems where the water table is usually at or near the surface or the land is covered by shallow water. The water found in wetlands can be saltwater, freshwater or brackish. Brackish water has more salinity than freshwater, but not as much as sea water.

There are four major types of wetlands: **marsh**, **swamp**, **bogs** and **fen**. Three major features used to describe the wetlands are **hydrology**, **type of vegetation** and **type of soil**. Hydrology has two components. One involves physical movement of water: direct precipitation, flooding and groundwater. The other component is the *hydroperiod,* which involves duration, frequency and season of flooding.

Marshes are the most productive wetlands characterized by mineral soils and are typically dominated by grasses and floating-leaved plants. **Swamps** are forested wetlands characterized by mineral soil, seasonally or permanently flooded, and dominated by trees. Thus, grasses dominate *marshes*, while trees dominate *swamps*.

Bogs and **fens** are organic soil wetlands. Organic soil is produced by the accumulation of plant materials. Generally, these wetlands are referred to as **peatlands** due to their ability to form peat. **Bogs** are acidic, unproductive wetlands that develop in relatively cool but wet climates. Bogs receive water exclusively from rainfall, not from streams or groundwater. It depends on rainwater for their supply of nutrients. Since rainwater has very little nutrient content, bog has very poor nutrient level. The dominant species in bogs are mosses. **Fens** are alkaline rather than acid areas, receiving water mostly from surface and groundwater sources.

Box 7.1 Bioaccumulation, bioconcentration and biomagnification

Bioaccumulation, bioconcentration and biomagnification are distinct phenomena. **Bioaccumulation** is the intake and accumulation of a chemical in an organism by all routes of exposure including transport across respiratory surfaces, dermal absorption and dietary absorption. **Bioconcentration** is the intake and accumulation of a chemical in an organism only through its respiratory and dermal surfaces.

Biomagnification is the bioaccumulation of chemicals in organisms in increasingly higher concentrations at successive trophic levels. It occurs when the chemical is entered into the food chain. It occurs because the biomass at any given trophic level is produced from a much larger biomass ingested from the level below. Consumers at higher trophic levels ingest a significant biomass present at lower levels, along with the fat soluble pollutants stored in their tissues. Biomagnification occurs in both aquatic and terrestrial habitats. An infamous case of biological magnification that harmed top-level carnivores involved DDT, a chemical used to control insects such as mosquitoes and agricultural pests. One of the first signs that DDT was a serious environmental problem was a decline in the populations of ospreys and eagles, birds that feed at the top of food webs. The accumulation of DDT in the tissues of these birds interfered with the deposition of calcium in their eggshells. When these birds tried to incubate their eggs, the weight of the parents broke the shells of affected eggs, resulting in catastrophic declines in reproduction rates.

7.5.2 Terrestrial ecosystem

Terrestrial ecosystems are those that are found only on land. The key to the meaning of terrestrial ecosystems lies in the word '**terrestrial**', which generally means anything occurring on land. Therefore, terrestrial ecosystem refers to the interacting system made up of living organisms and non-living objects occurring on land. Only 28 percent of the Earth's surface belongs to terrestrial ecosystems.

Forest ecosystem

A **forest** is a complex ecosystem which is predominantly composed of trees and shrubs. It is defined as 'a land spanning more than 0.5 hectares with trees higher than 5 meters and a canopy cover of more than 10 percent' (UN FAO). It does not include land that is predominantly under agricultural or urban land use. Forests are the dominant terrestrial ecosystem of the Earth and are distributed across the globe. Forests account for ~75% of the gross primary productivity of the Earth's biosphere and contain ~80% of the Earth's plant biomass. Based on canopy cover, forest can be **very dense forest** (the canopy cover is 70% or more of the land area), **moderately-dense forest** (the canopy cover ranges between 40% and 70% of the land area) and **open forest** (the canopy cover ranges between 10% and 40% of the land area). The terms *open forest* and *empty forest* have distinct meanings. An **empty forest** refers to a forest that appears structurally intact, with normal tree cover and vegetation, but has suffered a significant loss of key animal species due to factors such as overhunting, poaching, or habitat fragmentation. Forest types differ widely, determined by factors including latitude, altitude, temperature, rainfall patterns and soil composition. There are three major types of forest – taiga forest, temperate forests and tropical forests.

Taiga forest (*coniferous forest* or *boreal forest*) is located at higher latitudes, close to the polar region and is dominated by needle-leaved, drought tolerant, evergreen trees. The taiga forest has a subarctic climate. Winter is long and very cold and summer is short and cool. Precipitation occurs primarily in the form of snow, 40–100 cm annually.

Temperate forests are located in the temperate climatic zone, situated between the tropics and boreal regions, in both the Northern and Southern Hemispheres. They may also be called 'four-season forests' because these forests experience four distinct seasons. In the temperate region, winters are mild and rainfall is moderate. Temperate forests are a mix of deciduous, broad-leaved and coniferous evergreen trees. They are simpler in structure than tropical forests and support a lesser number of tree species. Temperate forests can be further distinguished by weather patterns and geographical features that favour the predominance of certain kinds of trees. It can be *temperate coniferous evergreen forests*, *temperate broadleaf forests*, *temperate deciduous forests* (a subgroup of temperate broadleaf forests, consist of trees that lose their leaves every year) and *temperate rainforests* (typically have heavy rainfall and high humidity).

Tropical forests are forested landscapes in tropical regions, occurring at low altitude zones near the equator (found within 23.5° latitude of the equator). Tropical forests primarily consist of **evergreen rainforests** and **moist forests**. It also includes other forests like a **seasonal tropical forest** (also known as *moist deciduous forests*, *semi-evergreen forests*, *tropical mixed forests*, or *monsoon forests*) and **mangrove forests**. Tropical rainforests are characterized by high rainfall, with annual precipitation typically exceeding 200 cm and consistently high temperatures, with average temperatures ranging from 20°C to 25°C.

Grassland ecosystem

Grassland ecosystems are dominated by perennial grass species. Grasslands have a high primary productivity and relatively low biomass. Grazing has a significant influence on the structure and composition of grassland communities and tends to maintain high species diversity. There are two major types of grassland ecosystems – Tropical and temperate grasslands.

Tropical grassland (**Savannas**) is grassland with scattered individual trees. Savannas are always found in warm or hot climates where the annual rainfall is between 30–50 cm per year. It has a distinct wet and dry season. The dry season comes during winter. Savanna receives all its rain during summer. Plants are adapted to the long dry periods. Many plants are xerophytic in nature.

Temperate grasslands have hot summers and cold winters and the amount of rainfall (25 to 75 cm) is less than in savannas. Temperate grassland is found in all continents except Antarctica. However, a vast majority of these ecosystems are found in Africa, South America, North America and Russia. Temperate grasslands are known as the **veldts** of South Africa, the **puszta** of Hungary, the **pampas** of Argentina and Uruguay, the **steppes** of the former Soviet Union and the plains and **prairies** of central North America.

Desert ecosystem

A **desert** is a region that receives very little precipitation (an average annual precipitation of less than 250 mm or 10 inches). The amount of evaporation in a desert often greatly exceeds the annual rainfall. All deserts are *arid* and there is little water available for plants and other organisms. Humidity (water vapour in the air) is near zero in most deserts. Rain is usually the main source of water in a desert, but it occurs very rarely. Many desert dwellers rely on groundwater, stored in aquifers below the surface. Groundwater comes from rain or other precipitation, like snow or hail.

7.6 Biomes

The 'biome concept' was introduced by F.E. Clements and V. E. Shelford (1939) for broad-scale distribution of world vegetation and associated animals. A **biome** is a distinct ecological community of plants and animals living together in a particular climate. Each biome has characteristic appearance and distributed over wide geographical area defined largely by regional climatic conditions (mainly mean annual temperature and precipitation). 'Biome' is a broader term than 'habitat'; any biome can comprise a variety of habitats. It is the largest geographical biotic unit.

Biomes are defined by their characteristic *vegetational types* and *associated climatic conditions* rather than by the presence of particular plant species. A biome is the largest scale at which ecologists classify vegetation. Two regions assigned to the same biome thus may differ in the species that dominate the landscape. Tropical rainforests around the world, for example, are all composed of tall, lushly vegetated trees, but the tree species that dominate a South American tropical rainforest are different from those in an Indonesian one. Biomes are named according to their vegetation types but they also include the animals that are present.

Biome distribution

Earth's biomes are closely correlated with climate. Temperature and precipitation are the most important climatic factors affect the distribution of biomes. Temperature is largely dependent on intensity and duration of solar radiation, which is, in turn, directly associated with latitude. Similarly, precipitation pattern is strongly influenced by major wind patterns, which are associated with latitude. Because a given biome is recognized by the type of climax vegetation, besides climate, other factors such as topography, soils and exposure to disturbances such as fire also play an important role in the terrestrial biome distribution.

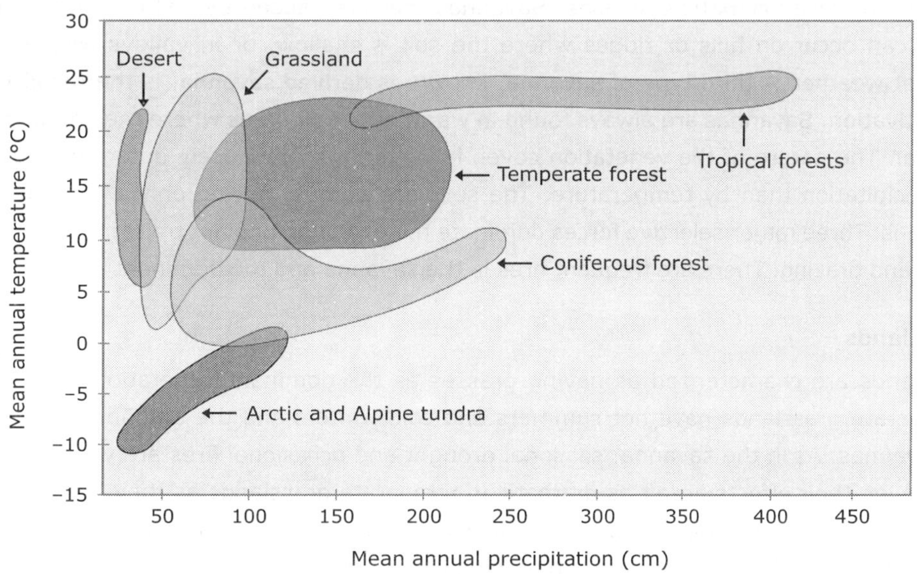

Figure 7.14 The distribution of biome types as a function of mean annual temperature and precipitation.

Biome types

Biomes are classified into *aquatic* and *terrestrial* biomes. No two ecologists seem to agree on how many biomes there are. Traditionally, biomes have been defined and classified mainly in terms of their vegetation. Some of the major terrestrial biomes in the world are tropical rainforests, deserts, tropical grasslands (savannas), temperate grasslands, temperate deciduous forests, coniferous forests (taiga or boreal forest), chaparral (shrublands) and tundra. These broad categories reflect the relative contribution of three general plant life-forms - trees, shrubs, and grasses - in their climax vegetation. The climax vegetation of the grassland biome is grass, although the species vary in grassland biomes located at different geographical regions.

Tundra biome

Tundra is a polar desert and is characterized by very extreme climatic conditions such as low temperatures, low precipitation, strong winds and long periods of shortage of liquid water. There are two main types of tundra - *arctic tundra* and *alpine tundra*. **Arctic tundra** biome is characterized by a short growing season, low precipitation and permanently frozen deeper soil (called **permafrost**). Plant life consists of grasses, sedges and lichen (Reindeer moss). Trees are absent. The **alpine tundra** is found high on the mountains. They are characterized by widely fluctuating temperatures, strong winds, snow and a thin atmosphere.

Desert biome

Deserts are found at latitudinal positions between 15° to 35° North and South of the equator and also in rain shadows. Deserts have annual precipitation less than 30 cm. Low precipitation may be due to high subtropical pressure (as in the Sahara), geographical position in a rain shadow (as in the Western North American deserts) and high elevation (as in the Gobi desert). The Sahara is the world's largest desert. There is a lot of variability in desert types, like hot deserts, cold deserts, high elevation deserts and rain shadow deserts. Consequently, there is a great deal of variation in the biodiversity, productivity and organisms found in different types of desert. Most deserts are very hot. The hot deserts generally experience hot days and cold nights. Three types of xerophytic plants are adapted to deserts – ephemeral, succulent and non-succulent.

Tropical grassland (or Savanna biome)

Savanna is grassland with scattered individual trees. The term *savanna* was originally used to describe the treeless areas of South America. Climate is the most important factor in creating a savanna. Savannas which result from climatic conditions are called **climatic savannas**. Savannas that are caused by soil conditions are called **edaphic savannas**. These can occur on hills or ridges where the soil is shallow, or in valleys where clay soils become waterlogged in wet weather. A third type of savanna, known as **derived savanna**, is the result of people clearing forest land for cultivation. Savannas are always found in warm or hot climates where the annual rainfall is between 30–50 cm per year. The nature of the vegetation cover, however, is more closely determined by the amount and seasonality of precipitation than by temperature. The soils are porous, having only a thin layer of nutrient-rich matter called humus. Three major selective forces dominate the evolution of plant traits in savannas - recurring fire, periodic drought, and grazing. There are frequent fires in the savanna and the dominant vegetation is fire-adapted.

Temperate grasslands

Temperate grasslands are characterized as having grasses as the dominant vegetation. Trees and large shrubs are absent. Temperate grasslands have hot summers and cold winters and the amount of rainfall (25 to 75 cm) is less than in savannas. As in the savanna, seasonal drought and occasional fires are very important to maintain biodiversity. However, their effects aren't as dramatic in temperate grasslands as they are in savannas. The type of grassland community that develops, and the productivity of grasslands, depends strongly upon precipitation. Higher precipitation leads to tall grasses with a high biodiversity of grasses. Temperate grasslands can be further subdivided. **Prairies** are grasslands with tall grasses while **steppes** are grasslands with short grasses.

Tropical rainforests

Tropical rainforests occur at low altitude zones near the equator (found within 23.5° latitude of the equator) and are characterized by a high temperature, high rainfall and greatest diversity of species. The average temperature is between 20–25°C and varies little throughout the year. Winter is absent. Annual rainfall exceeds 200 cm. Although, the climate of tropical rainforest regions varies geographically but is typically characterized by a mean temperature of all months exceeding 18°C and minimum monthly precipitation above 6 cm. Warm and moist conditions promote strong chemical weathering and rapid leaching of soluble materials. Soil is deeply weathered with no distinct horizons, nutrient-poor and acidic. Decomposition is rapid and most of the nutrients available for uptake by plants are a result of the rapid decomposition of dead organic matters. The vegetation of tropical rainforest is characterized by evergreen, hygrophilus, tall and rich in lianas and epiphytes. Additional characteristics of tropical rainforest include the dominance of woody plants, principally trees; high species richness; sparse undergrowth; relatively slender trunks compared to trees of temperate forests. Canopy in tropical forests is multilayered and continuous, allowing little light penetration. The dominant plants are phanerophytes – trees, lianas and epiphytes.

The largest region of rainforest in the world is in the Amazon basin of South America. The second largest is located in Southeast Asia. Tropical rainforests have a very high diversity of plant and animal species. Covering only about 6 percent of the land surface, tropical rainforests account for more than 50 percent of all known plant and animal species.

Temperate deciduous forest biome

A temperate deciduous forest (a subtype of temperate broad-leaf forest) is dominated of trees that lose their leaves every year. The deciduous leaf is characteristic of environments with a distinct growing season. Leaves are typically shed at the end of the growing season and then regrown at the beginning of the next. The temperate deciduous forest biome is characterized by a distinct seasonality that includes a long growing season together with a cold winter season in which much of the vegetation may be dormant. Temperate climate has four seasons of winter, spring, summer and fall. Precipitation (65 to 130 cm) is distributed evenly throughout the year. The temperature varies widely from season to season with cold winters and hot, wet summers. Temperatures fall below freezing each winter. The average yearly temperature is about 10°C. Temperate forests are distinguished from boreal forests by having a 4–6 month frost-free growing season with on average at least four months at 10°C or above. Located between 30° and 60°, with most forests between 40° and 55°. Soil is fertile, enriched with decaying litter.

Taiga biome

Taiga biome (**coniferous forest biome** or **boreal forest biome**) is located at higher latitudes, close to the polar region between 50° and 60° north latitudes and is dominated by needle-leaved, drought tolerant, evergreen trees. Winter is long and very cold and summer is short and cool. Precipitation occurs primarily in the form of snow, 40–100 cm annually. Soil is thin, nutrient-poor and acidic. The flora consists mostly of cold-tolerant evergreen conifers with needle-like leaves, such as pine, fir and spruce. Taiga is the largest terrestrial biome on the Earth.

Chaparral biome

'Chaparral' is the name applied to the evergreen sclerophyllous (hard-leaved) vegetation. **Sclerophyllous** vegetation possesses small leaves, thickened cuticles, glandular hairs and sunken stomata, all characteristics that function to reduce water loss during the hot, dry summer period. In North America, the sclerophyllous shrub community is known as 'chaparral'. Chaparral biome is a **shrubland** (or **scrubland**) biome, dominated of shrubs or short trees. In general, a shrub is a plant with multiple woody, persistent stems but no central trunk.

Chaparral biome is characterized by mild, rainy winters and long, hot, dry summers and is located in west coastal regions between 30° and 40° North and South latitude. Annual precipitation generally falls within the range of 30–50 cm. Plants have adapted to drought-like conditions and also adapted to fire caused by the frequent lightning that occurs in the hot, dry summers.

7.7 Population ecology

Each species in an ecosystem exists as a population. A **population**, also known as a **biological population**, is defined as a group of interbreeding or potentially interbreeding individuals of the same species that live together in a specific region. Members of a population rely on the same resources and are affected by similar environmental factors. The study of populations (especially population abundance) and how they change over time is called **population ecology**. It studies the spatial and temporal patterns in the abundance and distribution of organisms and of the mechanisms that produce those patterns. The study of population ecology includes understanding, explanation and prediction of population growth, regulation and dynamics or demography.

7.7.1 Population characteristics

Scientists study a population by examining how individuals within that population interact with each other and how the population as a whole interacts with its environment. A population has several characteristics or attributes which are a function of the whole group and not of the individual. Different populations can be compared by measuring these attributes. These attributes are *population density, natality, mortality, distributions*, etc. The study of the group characteristics of a population, their changes over time and the prediction of future changes is known as **demography**.

Population density

The size of the population is represented by its fundamental property called *density*. It is generally expressed as the number of individuals or the population biomass per unit area or volume. Two types of densities are described – *crude density* and *specific* (or ecological) *density.* **Crude density** is the density per unit of total space. Generally, populations do not occupy all the space as whole because all area may not be habitable. Hence, density per unit of habitable space is called **specific density**. It includes only that portion of total space that can actually be colonized by the population.

Determining population size

Population size (or abundance) is a function of population density and the area that is occupied (geographic distribution). Usually, population size is estimated by counting all the individuals from a smaller sample area, then extrapolated over a larger area. When the individuals are not mobile - their population size may be estimated by counting individuals within a specified area. When individuals are very mobile and frequently move from one area to another then we can count the number by applying a common method called a **mark-recapture method**. Using this method, a small random sample of the population is captured, marked, then released to disperse within the general population. The marked individuals mix freely with unmarked individuals and within a short time are randomly mixed within the population. The population is resampled and the numbers of marked and unmarked individuals are recorded. We then assume that the ratio of marked to unmarked individuals in the second sample taken is the same as the ratio of marked to unmarked individuals in the first sample. We can use a simple formula for estimating total population size (N):

$$N = \frac{\text{Total individuals marked in first sample} \times \text{Size of second sample}}{\text{Number of marked individuals recaptured in second sample}}$$

Natality

Natality refers to the birth of new individuals in a population. The **natality rate** (or **birth rate**) is expressed as the number of individuals born per female per unit of time. To accurately describe the rate, it is essential to specify the time interval (such as one year or one month) and the base population. Most commonly the base population used for calculating natality rate is **per capita** (or per individual), which is equivalent to the number of births per individual per unit of time.

Natality may be *maximum natality* or *ecological* natality. **Maximum natality** (sometimes called *absolute* or *physiological natality*) is the theoretical maximum number of individuals produced under ideal environmental conditions (i.e., no ecological limiting factors) and is a constant for a given population. **Ecological** or **realized natality** refers to the number of individuals produced under an actual or specific environmental condition. It is not a constant for a population but may vary with the size and age composition of the population and the physical environmental conditions.

In ecology, *fecundity* and *fertility* are not same. The **fecundity** can be described as the maximum reproductive output potential of an individual under ideal environmental conditions. This limit is set by the genotype. The term **fertility** differs from fecundity in that it describes the actual reproductive performance of an individual under prevailing environmental conditions and it is a generalization of the terms 'birth rate' and 'natality rate'. Both fecundity and fertility are expressed as rates. That is the mean number of offspring produced per individual in the population, per unit time.

Mortality

Mortality refers to the death of individuals in a population. Like natality rate, **mortality rate** (*death rate*) may be expressed as the number of individuals died during a given period. Mortality may be *minimum* mortality or *ecological* mortality. A theoretical **minimum mortality**, a constant for a population, represents the loss under ideal or non-limiting conditions. **Ecological mortality** (or *realized mortality*) is the loss of individuals, under a given environmental condition. Like ecological natality, it is not a constant but varies with population and environmental conditions.

Information of the death and survivor of a population with respect to age is represented in the form of table known as **life table**. It is simply 'an age-specific account of mortality'. Raymond Pearl, (1921) first used life table for *Drosophila* populations obtained under laboratory conditions. The best way to construct a life table is to follow the fate of a **cohort**, a group of individuals of the same age, from birth until all of the individuals are dead. To build the life table, we need to determine the number of individuals that die in each age class and proportion of the cohort surviving from one age class to the next.

What is really vital for the population is not which members die, but which member survives? Consequently, specific mortality rate of a population is expressed by survivorship curve. **Survivorship curves** plot the number of surviving individuals to a particular age. Survivorship curves are of three general types:

A *highly convex curve* (**type I curve**) is characteristic of the species in which the population mortality rate is low until near the end of the lifespan. It is known as the '*death at senescence*' curve. Many species of large animals such as deer, mountain sheep and man, show such curves.

A *highly concave curve* (**type III curve**) is characteristic of those species where the mortality rate is high during the young stages. Oysters or shellfish show this type of curve. In oysters, mortality is extremely high during free-swimming larval stages, but once an individual is well established on a favourable substrate, life expectancy improves considerably.

In **type II curve** which falls between type I and III, the rate of mortality is constant at all ages, so that an individual's chance of living another year is just as good at one age as another. The mortality of an individual does not depend on its age. This curve is typical of several bird's species and of human beings exposed to poor nutrition and hygiene.

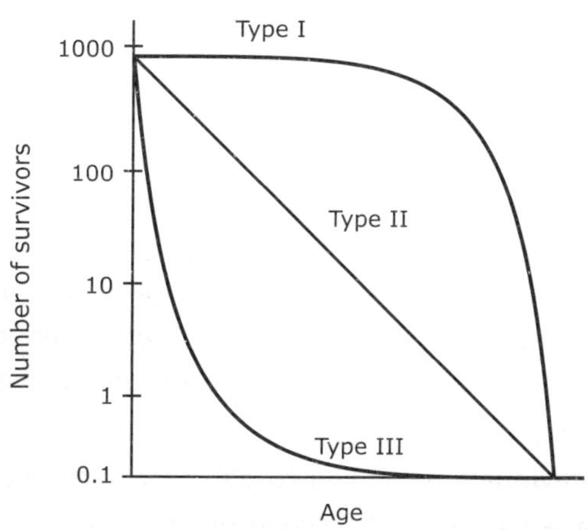

Figure 7.15
Three main types of survivorship curves. Type I – a convex curve in which mortality is low initially and most of the mortality occurs towards the end of the life. Type II – a straight line in which mortality is more or less constant throughout the lifespan. Type III – a concave curve in which mortality is extremely high initially but decreases markedly for much of the remainder of the lifespan.

Type I survivorship curves are typical of organisms which are likely to breed several times during the course of their lifespan. This strategy is referred to as **iteroparous.** Species with a type III curve are more likely to breed only once during their lifetime, a strategy referred to as **semelparous.** Note that the terms *semelparous* and *annual* are not strictly synonymous. *Semelparous* refers to the type of reproductive event, whereas *annual* refers to the lifespan. Similarly, the term perennial refers to organisms (most often plants) that live for more than one year, whereas **iteroparous** refers to the number of reproductive events in the lifespan. In plants, the terms **monocarpy** and **polycarpy** are sometimes used instead of semelparity and iteroparity.

How realistic are these three survivorship types? The three survivorship curves are generalizations, and few populations exactly fit one of the three. Some species have one type of survivorship curve early in life and another type as adults. For example, Herring gulls have a type III survivorship curve early in life and type II curve as adults.

Dispersion

Dispersion refers to the spatial and temporal distribution pattern of individuals of a population. It describes the pattern of spacing among individuals within the boundaries of the population. Individuals in a population may be distributed in three broad patterns – Regular, Random and Clumped (aggregated or contagious).

In **regular dispersion** (also called a *uniform* or *even* distribution), the individuals are more or less spaced at an equal distance from one another. Individuals are more evenly spaced than expected by chance. This is rare in nature but is common in managed systems like croplands. A regular distribution pattern may be the result of competition or social interactions.

In **random dispersion,** the position of one individual is unrelated to the positions of other individuals. This kind of distribution occurs where the environment is very uniform and there is no tendency to aggregate. This is also relatively rare in nature.

In **clumped dispersion** (also called a *contagious* or *aggregated* dispersion) individuals are aggregated into groups of varying size. Most populations exhibit this kind of dispersion. A clumped distribution pattern often results from the uneven distribution of a resource. Human population show clumped distribution due to their social behaviour, economic condition and geographic factors.

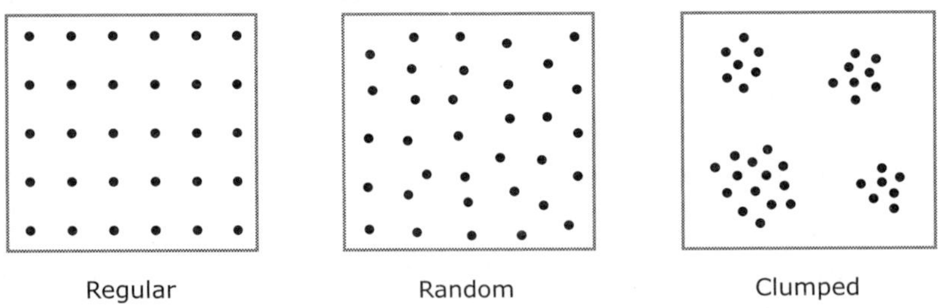

Figure 7.16 Diagrammatic representation of the spatial pattern of distribution of individuals within a population over on area.

Age structure

A population, at any given time, consists of individuals of different ages. Ecologically, individuals of a population can be categorized into three important age groups or classes: **pre-reproductive, reproductive,** and **post-reproductive ages.** The proportion of individuals in each age class is called the **age structure** of that population. The nature and character of a population are influenced by its age structure. The ratio of various age groups in a population determines the current reproductive status of the population. The relative duration of these age classes in proportion to the lifespan varies greatly with different organisms. In human, the three age classes are relatively equal in length. Many animals such as insects have very long pre-reproductive period, a very short reproductive period and no post-reproductive period.

A graphical representation that illustrates the number of individuals belonging to different age groups within a population of any organism at a specific time is called an **age pyramid.** The shape of the pyramids reflects the growth status of the population – whether it is growing (*expanding population*), stable (*stable population*) and declining (*diminishing population*).

Expanding population: It represents a population that is rapidly growing with a high birth rate. Under these conditions, the number of individuals in the pre-reproductive age class exceeds that of the reproductive age class, resulting in a **triangular-shaped** age structure.

Stable population: In this population, the number of individuals in the pre-reproductive and reproductive age classes becomes more or less equal in size. The graphical representation of this stabilized population is **bell-shaped.**

Diminishing population: This population is characterized by a low proportion of individuals in the pre-reproductive age class due to a reduced birth rate. The pre-reproductive class gradually decreases in size compared to the reproductive and post-reproductive age classes, resulting in an **urn-shaped** age structure.

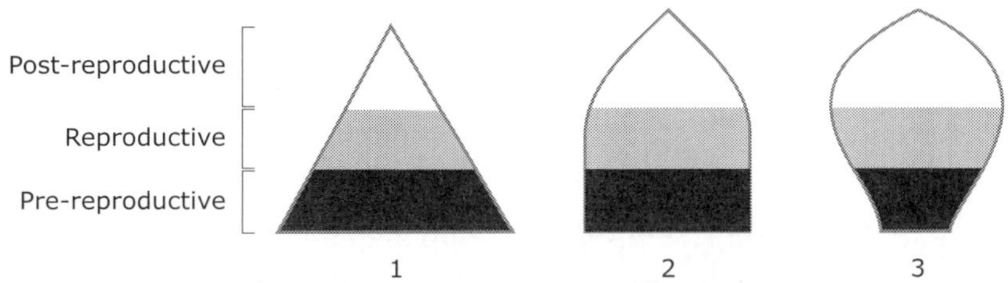

Figure 7.17 Age pyramids of different types of populations: 1. expanding population (indicating a high proportion of pre-reproductive age class individuals in a population) 2. stable population (indicating a more or less equal proportion of pre- and reproductive age classes individuals) 3. diminishing population (indicating a low number of pre-reproductive age class individuals).

7.7.2 Population growth

A population is a changing entity. The term 'population growth' refers to the change in the number of individuals in a population with time. It refers to how the number of individuals in a population increases or decreases with time. Change in population is determined by four factors: birth, death, emigration and immigration. In a **closed population**, change in population is only related to birth and death of individuals whereas, in case of **open population**, birth, death, immigration and emigration result in a change of population. Population growth is also determined by the environment, and by how sensitive the population is to changes in the environment. By environment, we mean not only the physical environment, but also interactions of the population with other species in its habitat.

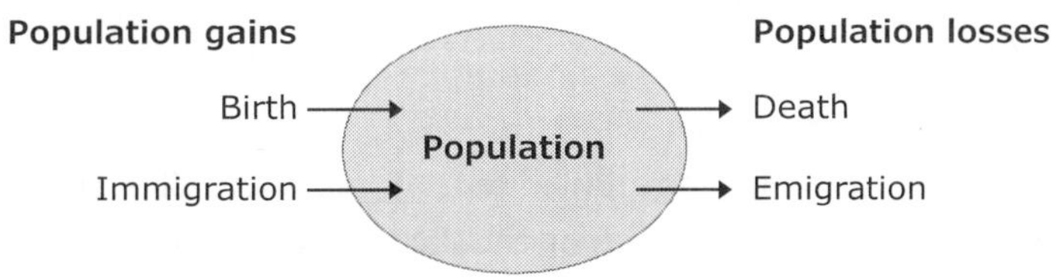

Exponential growth

A population shows *exponential growth* if there is no limitation on growth i.e. growth under an ideal unlimited environment. During exponential growth, the number increases in the geometric progression 2^0, 2^1, 2^2, 2^3,.... In **geometric growth**, the rate of increase is expressed as a constant fraction or an exponent by which a particular population is multiplied (like 2, 4, 8, 16...). By contrast, a pattern of growth that increases at a constant amount per unit of time (i.e. 1, 2, 3, 4 or 1, 3, 5, 7...) is called **arithmetic growth**. The *exponential* form of growth can be described by an *exponential growth equation*:

$$\frac{dN}{dt} = r.N \qquad \text{Equation 1}$$

$$\frac{dN}{dt} \times \frac{1}{N} = r$$

Where, N = Population size and r = Intrinsic rate of increase

The **intrinsic rate of increase** (r) represents the per capita rate of increase. It is expressed in number per unit time per individual. The maximum value of the intrinsic rate of increase (r_{max}) occurs in an ideal unlimited environment, in the absence of *environmental resistance*. The sum total of all environmental factors that together act to limit the biotic potential of an organism from being realized is called *environmental resistance*. It includes both biotic factors such as predation, competition, parasitism and abiotic factors such as drought, fire, flood etc. The intrinsic rate of increase is often referred by the less specific but widely used expression **biotic potential** (or *reproductive potential*) and it differs from one species to another e.g., deer populations can grow faster than a population of elephants.

r and r_{max}

The 'intrinsic rate of increase' can be *maximum* or *realized*. The *maximum* intrinsic rate of increase (r_{max}) occurs under an ideally unlimited environment, whereas the *realized* or *actual* intrinsic rate of increase (r) occurs under the actual prevailing environment. The maximum intrinsic rate of increase is always greater than or equal to realized intrinsic rate of increase. In exponential population growth, $r = r_{max}$.

In a **closed population**,

r is defined as the *per capita birth rate* minus the *per capita death rate*.

r = Per capita birth rate (**b**) – Per capita death rate (**d**)

Under an ideal unlimited environment, when b is maximum and d is minimum, r is r_{max}. The value of r also tells us about nature of population growth. When,

b > d	r is positive	population is increasing
b < d	r is negative	population is decreasing
b = d	r is zero	no change in the population size

Equation 1 is written as a differential equation. It tells us about the population growth rate but not the population size. However, if equation 1 is integrated, the result can be used to predict population size. Suppose, if we consider the initial population size (or we can say, population size at time zero) is N_0 and population size after time t is N_t, then the integral form of the exponential growth equation will be:

$$N_t = N_0 e^{rt}$$

Where, e is a mathematical constant, the base of the natural logarithm

$$N_t/N_0 = e^{rt}$$

By taking the natural log of both sides,

$$ln\ N_t - ln\ N_0 = rt$$

When resources (food and space) in a habitat are unlimited, all members of a species have the ability to grow exponentially. The population size that increases exponentially at a constant rate, results in a **J-shaped growth curve** when population size (N) is plotted over time (t).

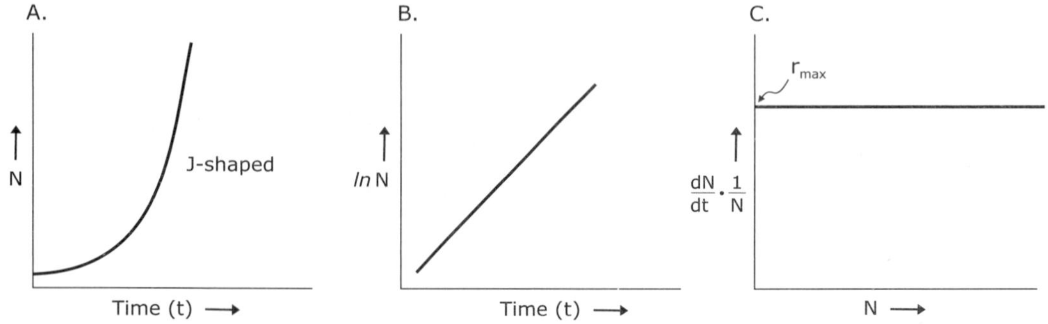

Figure 7.18 Exponential population growth. **A.** A J-shaped growth curve when population size (N) is plotted over time (t) in linear or arithmetic scale (note that a log transformation linearizes the plot). **B.** A linear growth curve when natural log of population size (*ln* N) is plotted over time (t). **C.** The relationship between dN/dt.N (i.e., r) and population size, N.

Calculation of doubling time: Doubling time indicates how long the present population will take to double from its present size. It is a measure of how rapidly a population grows. The doubling time for an exponential function N_0e^{rt} is the time t_d that gives a population of $2 \times N_0$. Thus, we can get the doubling time by solving the equation:

$$N_t = N_0e^{rt}$$

$$2 \times N_0 = N_0e^{rt_d}$$

$$2 = e^{rt_d}$$

Taking the natural logarithm of both sides gives:

$$ln\,2 = rt_d$$

$$t_d = ln\,2 / r$$

From the above equation, if we know the per capita rate of increase (*r*) we can easily find the projected doubling time of a population. The larger *r* is, the shorter is doubling time. However, we are assuming that the population is not affected by its age distribution, and that *r* is constant during this time period.

Logistic growth

The exponential growth assumes that resources are unlimited, but it is never the case in the real situation. As population density increases, each individual has access to fewer resources. It means a particular environment can only support a maximum population size. The number of individuals of a particular species that a particular environment can support indefinitely is defined as **carrying capacity** (represented by the letter **K**). Carrying capacity is not fixed, but varies over space and time with the abundance of limiting resources. It is determined by various factors including predation, competition and climatic conditions. Since such factors are many and varied, it is clear that the carrying capacity of any area for a population may vary over a period of time. So, the growth of a population eventually slows as the population reaches the carrying capacity for environment. This is known as **Verhulst-Pearl logistic growth.**

We can modify the exponential equation to incorporate changes in growth rate near the carrying capacity. If the maximum sustainable population size i.e. carrying capacity is K, then K–N is the number of additional individuals the environment can accommodate, and (K–N)/K is the fraction of K that is still available for population growth. By multiplying the exponential rate of increase r.N by (K–N)/K, we can modify the growth rate of the population:

$$\frac{dN}{dt} = r.N\,\frac{(K-N)}{K} \quad \text{or} \quad \frac{dN}{dt} \times \frac{1}{N} = r\left[1-\frac{N}{K}\right]$$

Where, N = Population size

dN/dt = Rate of change in population size

K = Carrying capacity

r = Intrinsic rate of increase

The above equation for logistic growth was formulated by Francois Verhulst in 1838, which he called the **logistic growth equation**. It is the simplest equation describing population growth in a resource-limited environment. The logistic growth equation can be written in several ways:

$$\frac{dN}{dt} = r.N\,\frac{(K-N)}{K} = \frac{rNK}{K} - \frac{rN^2}{K} = r.N - \left[\frac{r}{K}\right]N^2$$

$$\frac{dN}{dt} = r.N\left[\frac{K-N}{K}\right] = r.N\left[\frac{K}{K} - \frac{N}{K}\right] = r.N\left[1-\frac{N}{K}\right]$$

The logistic model of population growth produces a *sigmoid* (**S-shaped**) growth curve when population size is plotted over time. In sigmoid growth form, the population increases slowly at first (establishment or positive acceleration phase), then more rapidly (perhaps approaching a logarithmic phase), but it soon slows down gradually as the environmental resistance increases in percentage (the negative acceleration phase), until equilibrium is reached and maintained. The upper level, beyond which no major increase can occur, as represented by the constant K, is the upper asymptote of the sigmoid curve and has been aptly called the *carrying capacity*.

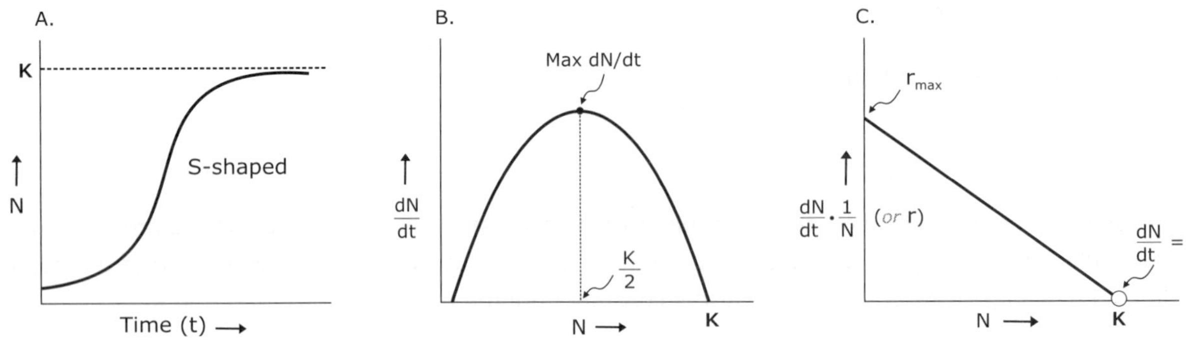

Figure 7.19 **A.** Change in population size (N) through time as predicted by the logistic model of population growth. Initially (low values of N), the population grows exponentially; as N increases, the rate of population growth decreases, eventually reaching zero as the population size approaches the carrying capacity. **B.** The relationship between the rate of population growth, dN/dt and population size, N, takes the form of a parabola, reaching a maximum value at a population size of N = K/2. The rate of population growth (dN/dt) is at its highest when N = K/2 (called the *inflection point*) and then decreases as it approaches the carrying capacity (K). **C.** The relationship between per capita rate of increase, dN/dt.N and population size, N.

In logistic growth equation, the term (K–N)/K indicates how much of the resources are still available to populations. When N is much less than K, the term (K–N)/K becomes approximately 1 and the equation becomes dN/dt = rN (equation for exponential growth). As N almost becomes equal to K, the term (K–N)/K is almost zero and dN/dt, i.e. the growth rate also becomes zero. In the logistic growth model, the greatest population growth rate is achieved at half the carrying capacity (K/2), and populations with a greater value of r will reach K more rapidly (in less time) than populations with lesser values of r.

7.7.3 Life table: Age-specific mortality and survival

The rate of population growth depends on both the survival and mortality. To obtain a clear and systematic age-specific information of survivor and mortality within a population, ecologists construct *life table*. There are two basic kinds of life tables. The one type is the **cohort** (or *dynamic* or *horizontal*) life table and other is **static** (or *time-specific* or *stationary* or *vertical*) life tables. A *cohort* is a group of same-aged individuals. In *cohort life table*, the fate of a group of same-aged individuals is followed from birth to death whereas a *static life table* is made from data collected from all ages at one particular time. Static life table is based on the assumption that each age class is sampled in proportion to its numbers in the population and the death and birth rates are constant and the population is stable.

A life table contains the following information:

x = Age.

n_x = Number alive at age x.

l_x = Age-specific survivorship (n_x/n_0).

d_x = Age-specific mortality i.e., the number of individuals dying during the age interval x to $x + 1$ ($n_x - n_{x+1}$).

q_x = Age-specific mortality rate (d_x/n_x).

F_x = Age-specific total reproductive output of entire population.

m_x = Age-specific mean number of offspring produced per individual (age-specific birth-rates or fertility). For example, if 100 females at age x produce 200 offspring, m_x = 2, which means that, on average, each female of age x produces 2 offspring in one year.

The construction of a life table begins with a cohort, a group of individuals born during the same period of time. For example, data presented below represent a cohort of 530 squirrels from a population in JNU, Delhi. The fate of these 530 individuals was tracked until all had died some 6 years later. The first column of numbers labeled *x* represents the *age* in units of years. By convention, we classify a newborn as age 0 (*not* age 1). The *ages* are 0 through 5 and *age classes* are 1 through 5. The second column, n_x represents the number of individuals from the original cohorts that are alive at the specified age (*x*). Of the original 530 individuals born (age 0), only 159 survived to an age of 1 year, while of those 159 individuals, only 80 survived to age 2. Only 5 individuals survived to age 5, and none of those individuals survived to age 6 (that is why there is no age 6).

The difference between the number of individuals alive for any age (n_x) and the number alive at the beginning of the next age (n_{x+1}) is the number of individuals that have died during that time interval represent the age-specific mortality (d_x). The number of individuals surviving to any given age (i.e., age specific survivorship) is calculated by taking ratio n_x/n_0, where n_0 is the number alive at the start of the study. The number of individuals that died during any given time interval (d_x) divided by the number alive at the beginning of that interval (n_x) provides an age-specific mortality rate (q_x).

Table 7.3 Cohort life-table from a hypothetical squirrels population

x	n_x	$d_x = n_x - n_{x+1}$	$l_x = n_x / n_0$	$q_x = d_x / n_x$
0	530	371	530/530 = 1.00	0.70
1	159	79	159/530 = 0.3	0.50
2	80	32	80/530 = 0.15	0.40
3	48	27	48/530 = 0.09	0.55
4	21	16	21/530 = 0.04	0.75
5	05	05	5/530 = 0.01	1.00

Gross and net reproduction rate

In a sexually reproducing non-hermaphroditic population, only females within the population give birth. The birth-rate of females generally varies with age. Therefore, a better way of expressing birth-rate is the number of births per female of age *x*. For example, a life-table of age-specific mean number of offspring produced per individual (m_x) of a squirrel population is given below:

Age (x)	0	1	2	3	4	5
m_x	0	2	3	3	2	0

We assume that the female survives to the maximum age of 5 years. At age 0, females produce no young, therefore the value of m_x is 0. The average number of female offspring produced by a female of age 1 is 2. For females of age 2 and 3, the m_x value increases to 3, then declines to 2 at age 4. By age 5, the females no longer reproduce, so the value of m_x is 0. The sum (represented by Σ) of the m_x value across all the ages provides an estimate of the average number of female offspring born to a female over her lifetime. It is termed as **gross reproductive rate**. In this example, the gross reproductive rate is 10. However, this value assumes that a female survives to the maximum age of 5 years. But survivorship of females also varies with age. Hence when we include both age-specific fertility and age-specific survival, it gives **net reproductive rate** (R_0).

In the following table, age-specific survivorship (l_x) in each age-class has been considered together with the age-specific fertility (m_x). Although m_x may initially increase with age, l_x in each age-class declines. To adjust for mortality, we multiply the m_x value by the corresponding l_x. The resulting value, $l_x m_x$, gives the *mean number of female offspring produced by females in each age-class*. Thus for 1 year old females, the m_x value is 2 but when adjusted with l_x, the $l_x m_x$ value drops to 0.6. For age 2 the m_x is 3, but $l_x m_x$ drops to 0.45 and reflecting poor survival of adult female.

When the values of $l_x m_x$ are summed over all ages at which reproduction occurs, it gives *net reproductive rate* (R_0). It is the average number of female that will be left during a lifetime by a new born female. If $R_0 < 1$, it indicates that the members of the population are not replacing themselves (i.e., the population is declining). Similarly, if $R_0 > 1$, it denotes an increasing population whereas, $R_0 = 1$ indicates a stationary or stable population.

Table 7.4 Life table and age-specific fertility (m_x) and average number of offspring per age class ($l_x m_x$)

x	l_x	m_x	$l_x m_x$
0	1.0	0	0
1	0.30	2	0.60
2	0.15	3	0.45
3	0.09	3	0.27
4	0.04	2	0.08
5	0.01	0	0

$R_0 = \Sigma l_x m_x = 0.0 + 0.6 + 0.45 + 0.27 + 0.08 + 0.0 = 1.40$

7.7.4 Population regulation

Are ecological populations regulated? If so, how? What does population regulation really mean? Population ecologists have identified a number of mechanisms by which populations could be regulated. Broadly speaking, the regulation of population growth is either *density-dependent* or *density-independent*.

Density-dependent regulation of population growth operates as a function of population size or density. These regulations can exhibit either a *positive* or *negative* correlation with population density. In cases of *density-dependent negative regulation*, the population's growth rate is inversely related to population density. This situation arises when either the per capita birth rate declines, the per capita death rate increases, or both occur as the population size expands.

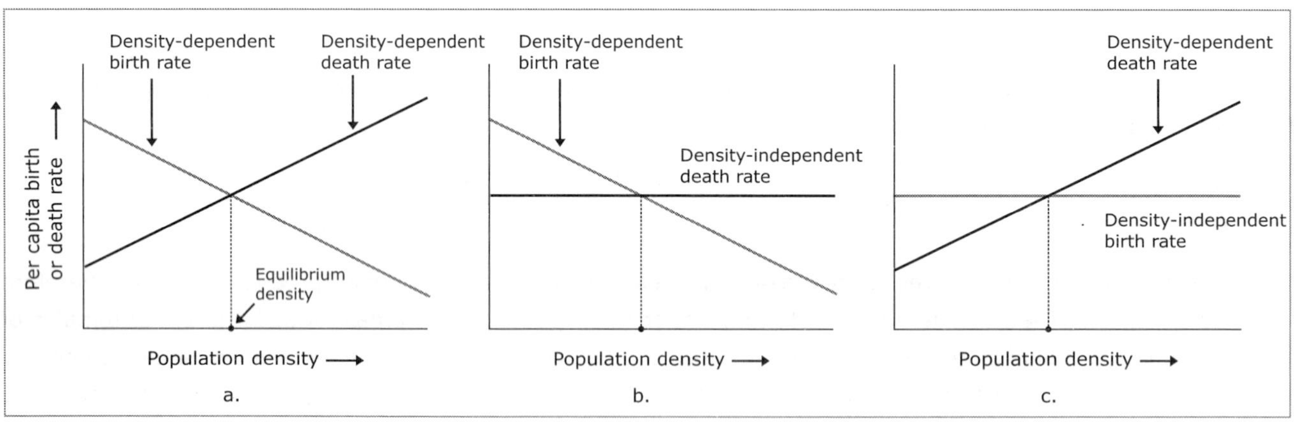

Figure 7.20 In cases of density-dependent negative regulation, the population growth rate shows an inverse correlation with its size. This situation manifests when either the per capita birth rate (b) decreases as the population size increases, or the per capita death rate (d) increases, or both phenomena occur simultaneously as the population size increases. When the birth rate equals the death rate (b=d), the population size remains constant. This equilibrium point represents the carrying capacity, K.

Negative regulation primarily involves the competition for limited resources such as space, water, and nutrients. For instance, a rabbit population might undergo exponential growth until intraspecific competition intensifies for limited resources such as space and food, causing either a decrease in the birth rate or an increase in the death rate, resulting in a reduced population growth rate.

Box 7.2 Allee effect

However, density-dependent population growth is not always negatively related to population density or size. In certain cases, the growth rate increases with population size. This phenomenon, known as the **Allee effect** (named after W. Allee, who first described it), represents a positive relationship. Generally, Allee effects are observed in small or sparse populations. Specifically, they arise from beneficial interactions among individuals that result in the per capita population growth rate increasing with the number of individuals. Allee effects come in two main types: *component* and *demographic*. **Component Allee effects** are evident in populations where there is a positive correlation between specific fitness components (such as reproduction or offspring survival) and population size. **Demographic Allee effects** occur when these component Allee effects result in a positive relationship between per capita population growth and population size.

Various mechanisms can cause a positive relationship between fitness and population size, affecting reproduction and survival. A well-established reason for the Allee effect is **mate limitation**. With sexual reproduction requiring contact between male and female gametes, mate limitation reduces reproduction in small populations. Another factor is increased vulnerability to predators. The per capita risk of predation is lower in larger prey populations compared to smaller ones. Lastly, genetic mechanisms may contribute to Allee effects. In many organisms, a small population size leads to inbreeding depression, reducing average fitness.

A special case of density dependence regulation is **undercompensating density dependence**. It refers to a situation where the effects of density on population growth do not completely offset the changes in population size. At low densities, the birth rate exceeds the death rate, leading to net increase in population size. At high densities, the death rate exceeds the birth rate, leading to net decrease in population size. At intermediate population densities, the birth rate and death rate balance each other out, leading to the highest net recruitment before density-dependent effects start to dominate and reduce the population growth rate.

Density-independent regulation of population growth operates regardless of population density. This population regulation type is usually linked to abiotic events, such as changes in the physical environment, like floods and seasonal weather variations, that either promote or hinder population growth. These effects remain independent of population density.

Relationship between intrinsic rate of increase and population size or density: The relationship between the intrinsic rate of increase and population size differs between density-independent and density-dependent regulation. In density-independent regulation, the intrinsic rate of increase remains constant regardless of the population size. Conversely, in density-dependent regulation, the intrinsic rate of increase changes in relation to the population size, decreasing as population size increases.

7.7.5 Life history

An organism's *life history* is its age-specific lifetime pattern of growth, survival and reproduction. The traits that describe the life history of an organism (termed **life history traits**) include informations like size of organism, age of first reproductive event, number of offspring produced during each reproductive event, number of reproductive events during a lifetime, size of offspring at the time of birth, reproductive life span and total life span of organism (how long do individual live?). These traits are directly associated with reproduction and survival of an organism and affect the 'life table'. Variations in these traits reflect different allocations of an individual's resources in growth, reproduction and survivorship. Combinations of these life history traits create life history strategies.

Organisms have adopted a great variety of life history strategies and these strategies have evolved to maximize their survival and reproduction fitness. How life histories of different species have evolved? The 'perfect' life history is one with maximum survivorship and maximum reproduction fitness. **Life history theory** explains how natural selection and other evolutionary forces shape organisms to optimize their survival and reproduction in the face of ecological challenges posed by the environment. The goal of life history theory is to understand the variation in life history strategies.

Life history trade-offs

The evolution of life histories involves trade-offs. As we know, each individual has finite amount of energy that it can allocate to specific tasks i.e., among growth, maintenance and reproduction. Its allocation to one task reduces the resources available for the others. Life history traits are subject to trade-offs. *Trade-offs* are caused by competitive allocation of limited resources to one life history trait versus the other within a single individual. Resources devoted to one trait are unavailable to others. A '**trade-off**' is a negative relationship between two life history traits. A trade-off exists when an increase in one life history trait (improving fitness) is coupled with a decrease in another life history trait (reducing fitness). Trade-offs can also involve more than two traits.

Organisms face trade-offs in life history traits related to growth, survival and reproduction. For example, allocation to reproduction reduces the amount of energy available for growth and survival. Because each individual has a limited amount of energy that it can allocate to specific tasks. Its allocation to one task reduces the energy available for the others. Thus, there is a trade-off between the number and size of offspring, within a given total reproductive investment. That is, a reproductive allocation can be divided into fewer, larger offspring or more, smaller offspring.

There is a trade-off between fecundity (reproduction) and survival. Individuals with higher reproductive effort have a shorter lifespan or vice versa. The energy required for reproduction is utilized for the gonad development, gametes formation, find a mate, mating activities, production of offspring and parental care. Together, the total energetic costs of reproduction per unit time are referred to as an *individual's reproductive effort*. Increased allocation to reproduction resulted in a reduction in the probability of future survival of parents, and therefore future reproduction. Therefore, allocation to reproduction at any time during the life of an individual involves trade-offs between current benefits from the production of offspring and costs in terms of potential reduction in future reproduction.

There is a trade-off between the number and size of offspring also. The number of offspring affects the parental investment each receives. If the parent produces a large number of offsprings, it can afford only minimal investment in each one. In such cases, animals provide no or very less parental care and plants store little food energy in seeds. Parents that produce few young are able to expend more energy on each.

r- and K-selection

An organism has a finite amount of energy to spend. Some must be spent for basic metabolic needs i.e., maintenance. Any energy left over can be spent in two activities: growth and reproduction. The energy required for reproduction is utilized for the gametes formation, find a mate, mating activities, production of offspring and parental care. Allocation of energy to one function must, then, reduce the amount available for the other. Allocation of energy among the various activities of an organism reflects balances between the benefits and costs of each activity. Species differ with regard to the energy available for reproduction and growth. It varies not only with life history patterns but also with the environmental conditions.

Robert McArthur and Edward Wilson proposed the idea of r- and K-selection based on environmental conditions of the habitats that species occupy. We can imagine two contrasting types of habitat's environment:

1. those that are short-lived, variable, unpredictable and uncertain.
2. those that are fairly constant or predictable environment, with few random environmental fluctuations.

The theory of r- and K-selection predicts that species adapted to these two different environments will differ in life history traits such as size, fecundity, age at first reproduction, number of reproductive events during a lifetime, and total life span. In short-lived variable, unpredictable and uncertain environment, selection favours species with a high reproductive potential. In contrast, in long-lived fairly constant or predictable environment, selection favours organisms with lower biotic potential but better capabilities for using and competing for scarce resources (greater energy investment in the maintenance and survival of the individual). The two opposing selective forces were designated '**r-selection**' and '**K-selection**'. The terms *r* and *K* used to characterize two contrasting strategies which relate to the parameters of the logistic model of population growth - r is the **intrinsic rate of increase**, and K is the **carrying capacity** (maximum sustainable population size).

A strongly variable and unpredictable environments lead to a highly fluctuating population density. These conditions select for a high intrinsic growth rate 'r' which is achieved by a distinctive life history strategy consisting of rapid development, a small body size, early reproduction, large number of offspring (with low survival), minimal parental care, semelparity and a short life-span (usually with a life-span of less than a year). Species with this reproductive pattern overcome the massive loss of their offspring by producing so many unprotected young that a few will survive to reproduce many offspring to begin the cycle again. Such species make use of temporary habitats and exploit noncompetitive situations. They are good colonizers and respond rapidly to disturbance. Species with these features are called **r-strategists** and indicates that these individuals have been favored for their ability to reproduce rapidly.

Table 7.5 Differences between r-selection and K-selection

	r-Selection	**K-Selection**
Environment	Variable and unpredictable; uncertain	Fairly constant or predictable; more certain
Mortality	Nondirected, density independent	More directed, density dependent
Survivorship	Often type III	Usually types I or II
Population size	Variable in time, nonequilibrium, usually well below carrying capacity of environment	Fairly constant in time, equilibrium, at or near carrying capacity of the environment
Rate of development	Rapid development	Slower development
r	High	Low
Age of reproduction	Early reproduction	Delayed reproduction
Body size	Small	Larger
Reproductive event	Semelparity	Iteroparity
Number of offspring	Many small offsprings	Fewer, larger offsprings
Social organization	Low level	High level
Parental care	Minimal	Usually great
Competitive ability	Usually poor	Usually high
Investment in defence	Low energetic investment	High energetic investment
Dispersal ability	Excellent	Fair to poor
Life span	Short, usually less than a year	Longer, usually more than a year
Successional stage	Early	Late, climax

Note: No organism is completely r-selected or completely K-selected; rather all must reach some compromise between the two extremes.

Synonyms for r-strategists are **r-selected species**, **fugitive species** and **opportunistic species**. Algae, bacteria, rodents, annual plants (such as dandelions) and most insects are r-strategists. Such species tend to be opportunists. They reproduce and disperse rapidly when conditions are favourable or when a disturbance opens up a new habitat or niche for invasion, as in the early stages of ecological succession.

On the other hand, long-lived fairly constant or predictable environmental conditions allow a population to reach its carrying capacity K and thus a stable population density. The concept says that these conditions select for a high K, which is achieved by slow development (associated with great competitive ability), a large body size, delayed reproduction, iteroparity and a long life-span. Species with these characteristics are called **K-strategists** (**K-selected species** or **stable species**). These species spent little energy into reproduction and put most of their energy into nurturing and protecting their young until they reach reproductive age. Among animals, parents care for the young; among plants, seeds possess stored food that gives the seedlings a strong start. Mortality relates more dependent on density than to unpredictable environmental conditions. Species are specialists, efficient users of a particular environment and cope with physical and biotic pressures.

7.8 Community ecology

An **ecological community** is a group of species that coexist in a space and time and interact with one another directly or indirectly. The term 'community' means different things to different ecologists. Most definitions of ecological communities include the idea of a collection of interacting species found in a particular place. Most communities are extraordinarily complex. However, main features of ecological communities include:

Firstly, a community represents the biotic or a living component of the ecosystem. Organisms within a community include primary producers, consumers and decomposers. In terrestrial communities, the community structure is largely defined by the vegetation.

Secondly, considering the functional aspect, communities are made up of organisms with interlocking food chains and each species depends on many other species in a community which are taxonomically unrelated.

Thirdly, a community may be of any size. It can range from small pond communities to huge tropical rainforests.

7.8.1 Community structure

The number of species, their relative abundances and their correlation of occurrence in space and time define **community structure**. Community structure varies in time as well as in space. It is first constrained by the environmental tolerances of the species, which are then modified through direct and indirect interactions with other species. Variations in the physical environment influence the distribution and abundance. Species differ in the range of conditions they tolerate. As environmental conditions change in both time and space, the possible distribution and abundance of species also change.

7.8.2 Species composition

Communities may be large or small. In each community, there are diverse species. All these species are not present in equal number (or biomass). There are few species which by their large number (or biomass) dominate the habitat and control the growth of other species of the community. These species are called the **dominant species**. The dominant species are highly successful species in a particular habitat. Generally, in most of the communities, only a single species, being particularly conspicuous, is dominant, and in such case, the community is called by the name of dominant species, as for example, spruce forest community. In other community, there may be more than one dominant species.

If the activity of a species determines community structure in spite of their low abundance or biomass, that species is called a **keystone species**. The term *keystone species* was introduced by Robert Paine (1966) to describe the importance of the predatory starfish, *Pisaster*, on the intertidal community. *Pisaster* preyed on a variety of intertidal organisms, preventing any one species from becoming very common and outcompeting the others, thus promoting species richness. Note that a keystone species is not the same as a *dominant species*, one that has a large effect in a community because of its abundance or large biomass.

Keystone species plays a vital role in controlling the relative abundance of other species. The loss of a keystone species can lead to sharp population drops and extinction of other species that depend on it for certain services and causes serious disruption in the functioning of the community. The African elephant is an example of keystone species. By their feeding habits, elephants destroy shrubs and small trees and push woodland habitats towards open grassland. As more grasses invade the woodland habitats, the frequency of fires increases, which accelerates the conversion of woods to grassland.

7.8.3 Species diversity

Species diversity is one of the most important and basic characteristic of a community. The number of species and their relative abundance define *species diversity* of a community. It includes the number of species in a community (i.e., **richness**) and the relative abundance of each species (i.e., **evenness**). Species richness is simply the number of species in a community. But, among the array of species that make up the community, not all are equally abundant. We can find the *relative abundance* by counting all the individuals of each species within a community and determining what percentage each species contributes to the total number of individuals of all species. Communities in which the species are all more or less equal in abundance exhibit **evenness**, whereas communities with one or a few abundant species (i.e., present in large numbers) show **dominance**. Species evenness is highest when all species in a sample have the same abundance. Abundance patterns in communities can be examined by numbers of individuals per species, biomass per species, or percent cover per species.

Species diversity

Species Richness
The number of different species present.

Community 1	*Community 2*
Dog	Dog
Frog	Squirrel
Elephant	Elephant
Lion	Tiger
Horse	Bear
	Leopard
	Gorilla

Number of species: Five — Number of species: Seven
Species richness: Low — Species richness: High

Species Evenness
The abundance of each species in a community.

Community 1		*Community 2*	
Dog	30	Dog	20
Frog	48	Squirrel	15
Elephant	03	Elephant	20
Lion	09	Tiger	25
Horse	20	Bear	18

Number of species: Five — Number of species: Five
Species evenness: Low — Species evenness: High

Both number of species (*species richness*) and their relative abundance (*species evenness*) define species diversity. In table 7.6, two hypothetical communities–Community 1 and Community 2–each have 5 species and 50 individuals. Species richness is the same in both communities. But the community 2 is dominated by one of the species, whereas, the community 1 has an equal abundance of each species. Although richness is same in both communities, evenness is higher in community 1 because there is an equal abundance of each species. Since species diversity depends on both species richness and evenness, the community 1 has higher species diversity as compared to community 2 because of higher evenness.

Table 7.6 Comparison of species richness and species evenness

Species	**Individuals per species**	
	Community 1	**Community 2**
Dog	10	05
Frog	10	05
Elephant	10	05
Lion	10	05
Horse	10	30
Total individuals	50	50
Total number of species	05	05

On a *spatial scale*, it has been found that there are substantial differences in species diversity among habitats. R.H. Whittaker (1972) described three levels of species diversity in term of species richness over spatial scales: alpha, beta and gamma diversity. **Alpha diversity** refers to the species diversity within a particular habitat or ecosystem (**within-habitat diversity**). It is expressed as the number of species per unit area. If we compare species diversity among habitats or ecosystems, it is called **beta diversity** (**between-habitat diversity**). It can be used to measure the change in species diversity among habitats; thus, it can reflect the extent of habitat selection or specialization. **Gamma diversity** is the total species diversity in a landscape (**regional diversity**). It combines alpha diversity and beta diversity. Unlike the alpha and gamma diversity, the exact interpretation and quantification of beta diversity varies substantially. Originally, beta diversity was defined as the ratio between gamma and alpha diversity. Today, one commonly used measure of beta diversity is the *Sørensen dissimilarity index*, which captures spatial turnover as well as differences in diversity between sites.

Let us consider a hypothetical example to understand alpha, beta and gamma diversity. Suppose there are three habitats— habitat 1, 2 and 3. The number of species in these three habitats are six, five and six, respectively. Now, we can find out alpha, beta and gamma diversity.

Let us consider a hypothetical example to understand alpha, beta and gamma diversity.

Number of species	Habitat 1	Habitat 2	Habitat 3
Species 1	+		
Species 2	+		
Species 3	+	+	
Species 4	+	+	
Species 5	+	+	+
Species 6	+	+	+
Species 7		+	+
Species 8			+
Species 9			+
Species 10			+
Alpha diversity	6	5	6
Beta diversity	1 vs 2 = 3	2 vs 3 = 5	1 vs 3 = 8
Gamma diversity	10		

7.8.4 Diversity index

A *diversity index* is a mathematical measure of species diversity in a community. It is a measure of the number of species in an area and the relative abundance of individuals among those species. That is, it takes into account the number of species present (*species richness*) as well as the abundance of each species (*species evenness*). A variety of indices have been used to estimate species diversity. We can divide them into two broad categories: *dominance indices* and *information statistic indices*. Dominance indices are more influenced by the abundance of common or dominant species. A widely used dominance index is *Simpson's diversity index*. Information statistic indices are more influenced by the numbers of rare species. Most commonly used information statistic index is the *Shannon diversity index*.

Simpson's diversity index

Simpson's diversity index is a simple mathematical measure that characterizes species diversity in a community. The term *Simpson's diversity index* can actually refer to any one of two closely related indices – *Simpson's index* and *Simpson's index of diversity*.

Simpson's index (D) is a measure of the species diversity of an ecosystem based on the concept of dominance. It measures the probability that two individuals randomly selected from a sample will belong to the same species. It is actually a measurement of dominance. There are two versions of the formula for calculating D.

$$D = \sum P_i^2 = \sum \left(\frac{n}{N}\right)^2$$

where, P_i = the relative abundance of each species (n/N), n = total number of individuals of a particular species in the sample, N = total number of individuals of all species present in the sample.

For a finite community, this is

$$D = \frac{\sum n(n-1)}{N(N-1)}$$

D is a measure of dominance, so as D increases, diversity (in the sense of evenness) decreases. The value of D ranges between 0 and 1. With this index, 0 represents an infinite diversity and 1, no diversity. That is, the bigger the value of D, the lower the diversity.

Simpson's index is usually reported as its complement 1-D called **Simpson's index of diversity**. The value of this index also ranges between 0 and 1, but now, the greater the value, the greater the sample diversity. In this case, the index represents the probability that two individuals randomly selected from a sample will belong to different species.

To understand Simpson's diversity index, let us take an example of a forest community which has five different tree species. The number of trees of each tree species are given below.

Species	Mango	Ashok	Cashew	Coconut	Amaltas
n	02	08	01	01	03

In this example, we can find the value of Simpson's index.

Species	Mango	Ashok	Cashew	Coconut	Amaltas	Total
n	02	08	01	01	03	N=15
n (n - 1)	02	56	0	0	06	64

$$D = \frac{\sum n(n-1)}{N(N-1)} = \frac{64}{15\ (14)} = 0.3$$

Simpson's index (D) = 0.3

Simpson's index of diversity (1 – D) = 0.7

Shannon diversity index

Shannon diversity index (or *Shannon-Wiener index*) is another index that is commonly used to characterize species diversity in a community. It is a measure of the species diversity of a community based on information theory i.e., on the idea that greater diversity corresponds to a greater uncertainty in picking at random an individual of a particular species. Like Simpson's index, Shannon's diversity index accounts for both richness and evenness of the species present. As the Shannon index increases, both the richness and the evenness of the community increase. It is given by the following formula:

$$H' = -\sum_{i=1}^{S} P_i \ln P_i$$

Here, S = Total number of species in the sample (species richness).

P_i = Relative abundance of each species, (n/N).

n = Total number of individuals of a particular species in the sample.

N = Total number of individuals of all species present in the sample.

How to calculate the Shannon diversity index of a community? Let us take the example of a forest community that has five different tree species. The number of trees of each species is given below.

Species	Alder	Deodar	Maple	Birch	Fir
n	06	05	01	03	12

In this example, we can find the value of *Shannon diversity index.*

Species	**n**	**n/N = P_i**	**ln P_i**	**P_i ln P_i**
Alder	06	6/27 = 0.222	−1.505	−0.334
Deodar	05	5/27 = 0.185	−1.687	−0.312
Maple	01	1/27 = 0.037	−3.297	−0.122
Birch	03	3/27 = 0.111	−2.198	−0.244
Fir	12	12/27 = 0.444	−0.812	−0.360
	N = 27			$\Sigma P_i \ln P_i = -1.372$

$H' = -(-1.372) = 1.372$

In the above example, even the rarest species, maple, contributes some value to the index. If a community had many such rare species, their contributions would accumulate. This makes the Shannon diversity index very valuable to conservation biologists, who often study rare species and their importance to the community.

Pielou's evenness index

Pielou's evenness index (J') is a diversity index, which quantifies how equal the community is numerically i.e., evenness of community. It is the ratio of observed diversity (H') to the maximum possible diversity of a community with the same species richness (H'_{max}). For any information statistic index, the maximum diversity of a community (H'_{max}) is found when all species are equally abundant.

$$J' = H' / H'_{max}$$

The observed diversity (H') is derived from the Shannon diversity index. H'_{max} is the maximum possible value of H'. The values lie between 0 and 1.

7.8.5 Disturbance and species diversity

A *disturbance*, in an ecological sense, is an event, such as a storm, fire, flood, drought, overgrazing, or human activity that changes a community by removing organisms from it or altering resource availability. It influences species coexistence and the maintenance of biodiversity. Disturbance events are characterized by their frequency and intensity. **Intensity** is measured by the proportion of total biomass, or population of a species, that the disturbance kills or eliminates. It is influenced by the magnitude of the physical force involved, such as the strength of the wind or the amount of energy released during a fire. **Frequency** is the mean number of disturbances that occur within a particular time interval.

Diversity is significantly affected by disturbance. Species diversity has been found low at low intensities or frequencies of disturbance because of competitive exclusion. In such case, competitively dominant species exclude competitively inferior species. Similarly, at high intensities or frequencies of disturbance, species diversity has been found low, because only good colonizers or highly tolerant species can persist. Both theoretically and experimentally it has been demonstrated that species diversity is higher at intermediate intensities or frequencies of disturbance due to a mix of good colonizer and good competitor species. At an intermediate intensities or frequencies of disturbance, colonization can occur, but competitive exclusion is held to a minimum and thus, diversity is at a maximum. This is referred to as the **intermediate disturbance hypothesis**, proposed independently by Michael Huston and by Joseph Connell.

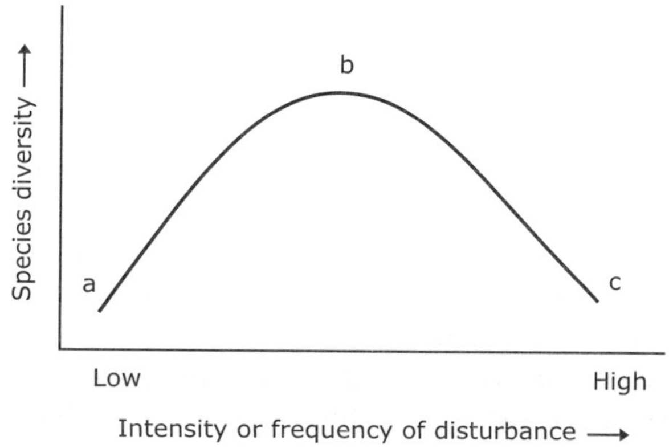

Figure 7.21 The intermediate disturbance hypothesis. **a**. Species diversity is low at low intensities or frequencies of disturbance because of competitive exclusion; **b**. species diversity is higher at intermediate intensities or frequencies of disturbance due to combination of good colonizer as well as good competitive species; **c**. species diversity is low at high intensities or frequencies of disturbance because only good colonizers or highly tolerant species can persist.

7.8.6 Diversity–Stability–Complexity relationships

Broadly, **community stability** refers to how ecological communities respond to disturbance. It can be defined as the ability of a community to resist change or recover from it. However, there is a lack of consensus about how ecological stability should be defined. In ecology, 'stability' can be analyzed by considering two parameters: *resistance* and *resilience*. **Resistance** refers to how tolerant a community is toward a disturbance before it changes. It describes the ability to resist disturbances. On the other hand, **resilience** refers to how quickly a community can return to its former state after a disturbance. It describes the ability of a community to return to its original state quickly following displacement. These two kinds of stability may be mutually exclusive; in other words, it is difficult to develop both at the same time. For example, a pine forest is quite resistant to fire, but if it does burn, it will recover very slowly or perhaps never (low resilience). In contrast, a grassland is very easily burned (low resistance) but recovers quickly in a few years (high resilience). In general, resistance is associated with the dominance of K-selected and resilience with r-selected species.

Diversity and stability

A ecological community is a set of interacting populations of different species. Its **diversity** is commonly understood to be positively correlated with the number of species it contains (**richness**), and how evenly individuals are distributed among these species (**evenness**). Are diverse communities — ones that have more species — more stable than species-poor communities? Charles Elton (1958) proposed the **diversity-stability hypothesis**, which stated that greater diversity led to greater ecosystem stability, greater resistance to invasion by exotic species, and higher productivity. He mentioned that species-poor communities (like island communities) are much more vulnerable to invading species than species-rich communities (like mainland communities).

To understand this, let us consider a community with very few species in which each predator depends on a very few prey species. The chance extinction of single prey species would then be expected to lead to the extinction of its predator. This, in turn, will lead to the extinction of that predator's predator and so on. By contrast, in a community with many species and complex food webs, we might predict that the chance extinction of a single species would have less. It might be expected to lead to changes in the population sizes of other species, but not to complete extinctions.

This view received considerable support from other influential ecologists (Odum 1953; MacArthur 1955). They reasoned that if a given species preys on several others, its population size will fluctuate less in response to environmental variations affecting one of its prey than it would if the species in question ate fewer prey species. Similarly, if a species has many predators, its population will vary less in response to exogenous changes in one predator's population size.

Diversity-stability paradox: While the common view is that ecosystems with high levels of diversity tend to be more stable, some field studies and theoretical work have challenged this perspective. In 1973, Robert May, a physicist turned mathematical ecologist, proposed a different idea, suggesting that the more diverse an ecosystem is, the less stable it becomes. He employed a mathematical model with linear interactions between the species to rigorously investigate the relationship between diversity and stability. By using linear stability analysis, May found that diversity tends to destabilize community dynamics. Therefore, it is the nature of the interactions between the species, rather than simply the diversity of species, that determines the stability of a community. In some grasslands where diversity decreases the stability of individual plant populations, it nevertheless increases the stability of the ecosystem as a whole.

Complexity and stability

Complexity is defined in terms of community dynamics and is a function of the magnitude of direct and indirect interactions between community components. These interactions can be **horizontal** (such as competitive interactions occurring among species at the same trophic level) or **vertical** (occurring between different trophic levels). The number of species alone doesn't solely determine complexity; what matters is how many species interact and how strongly they interact. In a highly diverse community, some species may interact little, resulting in low complexity, and vice versa. Ecologists have proposed various mathematical models that prioritize different properties (such as richness, evenness, connectance, etc.) when assessing *diversity* and *complexity*. In general, as the number of species in a community increases, the frequency and strength of interactions also increase, leading to greater complexity.

Intuitively, complex communities are often considered stable because the impact of sudden population changes in one species is buffered by the large number of interacting species, preventing drastic effects on the entire community. For instance, a forest ecosystem with a large biotic community can better withstand a fire compared to a grassland ecosystem with a smaller biotic community.

Nevertheless, there is a contrary perspective in ecology that argues an increase in complexity may lead to a decrease in community stability. According to this perspective, complex random systems are less likely to recover from small perturbations compared to simpler ones. This viewpoint finds support in the work of Robert May, who extensively explored the relationship between complexity and stability in random ecosystems. May's analytical results led him to the conclusion that, in general mathematical models of multispecies communities, complexity tends to foster instability. **Ecosystem complexity** was defined as $\sigma\sqrt{SC}$ where S is *species richness*, C is *connectance* (the probability that any two species will interact with each other) and σ is the *standard deviation of interaction strength*. May predicted that a system could be stable only if the criterion $\sigma\sqrt{SC} < \bar{d}$ was satisfied, where $\bar{d}$ expresses the *magnitude of intraspecific competition*. May's stability criterion $\sigma\sqrt{SC} < \bar{d}$ indirectly predicts that for complex systems to persist, interaction strength should be weaker in species-rich and highly connected systems.

7.8.7 Community gradient and boundaries

It is often difficult to determine where one community ends and the next begins. Many communities grade continuously into each other with no sharp boundaries. For example, if two forests, pine forest and spruce forest are nearby, one cannot see the boundaries between them. There are, however, instances where clear, sharp boundaries between the communities or ecosystems are seen, especially where the physical environment changes abruptly- for example, at the transition between aquatic and terrestrial ecosystems.

The *transition zone* of vegetation separating two different types of communities (e.g., between forest and grassland) is called **ecotone**.

'An ecotone is the zone of transition between adjacent ecological systems having a set of characteristics uniquely defined by space and time scales and by the strength of the interactions between the systems'.

It is a region where the influence of two different patterns of environment works together and hence the vegetation of ecotones is highly specialized. An ecotone may be narrow or wide. It has condition intermediate to adjacent ecosystems. A general characteristic of ecotone is that it has sufficiently greater number of species and high diversity as compared to the neighboring communities. The phenomenon of increased species diversity at the boundary (edge) is called the **edge effect** and is essentially due to the wider range of suitable environmental conditions. It was first defined by Odum (1958) as the tendency for increased population density and species richness at the junction between two communities. It is influenced by the area of *transition zone* (length and width) and by the degree of contrast between adjoining communities. In general, the greater the contrast between adjoining communities, the greater the diversity of species. Therefore, a border between forest and grassland should support more species than would a border between a young and a mature forest. Environmental conditions at edge enable certain species to colonize for reproduction or survival. Species that occur primarily or most abundantly at the edge for the purposes of reproduction or survival is known as **edge species**.

Box 7.3 Life forms

The form and structure of terrestrial plant communities are determined by the nature of the vegetation. Vegetation may be classified according to **life form** (or **growth form**). A life-form is characterized by the adaptation to certain ecological conditions. Its study is an important part of vegetation description. The most widely used vascular plant life-form classification system was formulated by Danish biogeographer C. Raunkiaer (called **Raunkiaer's system**). This system identifies life-forms based on a single criterion, that is, the location of **perennating buds** (shoot apical meristems) with respect to ground level. The location of buds is indicative of the degree of protection they are afforded from adverse climatic conditions. Using this single criterion, five major life-forms are recognized: *phanerophytes*, *chamaephytes*, *hemicryptophytes*, *cryptophytes* (or *hidden plants*) and *therophytes*. Cryptophytes are further subdivided into geophytes, helophytes and hydrophytes.

Table 7.7 Raunkiaer life-form classification system based on location of the perennating bud

Life form	Location of perennating bud	Plant types
Phanerophyte	>0.5 m	Trees and tall shrubs
Chamaephyte	Above the ground but < 0.25 m	Small shrubs and herbs
Hemicryptophyte	At soil surface (at ground level)	Prostrate shrubs *or* herbaceous plants
Cryptophyte	In the soil (below ground level)	Bulb forming herbs (e.g., *Allium*, *Solanum*)
Therophyte	Seed	Annuals (e.g., *Brassica*)

7.9 Island biogeography

Biogeography is the study of the geographical distribution of species and the reason for their pattern of distribution. Ecologists Robert MacArthur and E.O. Wilson, proposed the **equilibrium theory of Island biogeography**. By 'islands' we mean not only oceanic islands, but also habitat islands on land, such as the peaks of mountains and isolated springs in the desert. Any isolated habitat, totally separated from others of its kind, can be considered as an *island*. The oceanic islands can be formed in two basic ways: by the disappearance of a connecting land from the mainland (either the sea rises and floods an area in between or if joining land is eroded or sinks) or by land rising from the sea (usually form by volcanic activity on the ocean floor gradually building up igneous material until it reaches above sea level).

The theory proposes that the number of species on any island is determined by a balance between the rate at which new species colonize it (i.e., the **rate of immigration** of species from the mainland to the island) and the rate at which populations of established species become extinct (i.e., the **rate of extinction** of species on the island). The rate at which species might become extinct on the island would be related to the number that has become residents. When an island is nearly empty, the extinction rate is necessarily low because few species are available to become extinct. As more species inhabit an island, extinction rates on the island increase because of the greater likelihood of competitive exclusion. At the same time, as the number of species on the island increases, the immigration rate of new species decreases. Hence, the rate at which additional species will establish populations will be high when the island is relatively empty, and the rate at which resident populations go extinct will be high when the island is relatively full. Over time, the countervailing forces of extinction and immigration result in an equilibrium level of species richness. The **equilibrium species richness** of an island at which immigration balances extinction and which remains roughly constant.

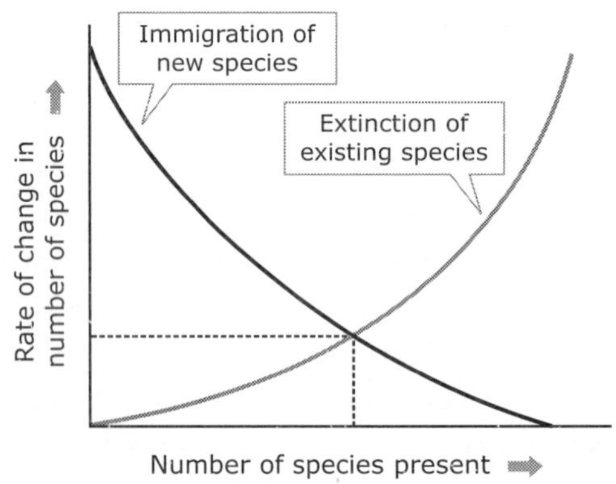

Figure 7.22 The equilibrium number of species on an island represents a balance between the immigration of new species and the extinction of species already there. According to the theory of island biogeography, immigration rate declines with increasing species richness while extinction rate increases.

Two physical features of the island further affect immigration and extinction rates: *its size and its distance from the mainland*. The **mainland** is that place where new immigrant species originally inhabited.

Effect of size: It is well established that the number of species on islands decreases as island area decreases. Small islands have higher extinction rates, as they generally contain fewer resources and less diverse habitats for colonizing species. Larger islands reduces the probability of extinction, as they contain larger habitat areas and more resources for colonizing species. The lower rate of extinction on larger islands results in a higher equilibrium number of species as compared to smaller islands.

Effect of distance: Islands that are more isolated are less likely to receive immigrants than islands that are less isolated. The greater the distance between the island and the mainland, the less the likelihood that many immigrants will successfully complete the journey. The result is a decrease in the equilibrium number of species. Thus, for two islands of equal size, an island close to mainland generally has a higher immigration rate than one farther away.

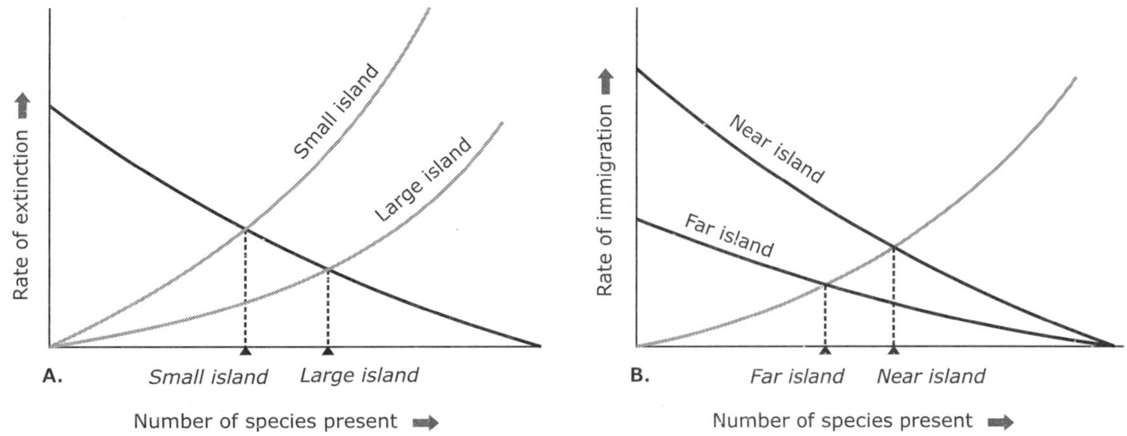

Figure 7.23 **A**. Effect of island size: Large islands have a larger equilibrium number of species than small islands because extinction rates lower on large islands. **B**. Effect of distance from mainland: Near islands tend to have larger equilibrium numbers of species than far islands because immigration rates to near islands are higher. If the island is close to the mainland, it will be easy for species to reach species will arrive quickly, so the emigration rate will be very high. If the island far from mainland, then fewer species will reach it and the rate of immigration will be much lower.

7.10 Ecological interdependence and interactions

Organisms grow, reproduce and die. They are affected by the conditions in which they live, and by the resources that they obtain. But no organism lives in isolation. Under natural conditions organisms live together influencing each other life directly or indirectly. Members of biotic community are dependent on one another. The interdependence is reflected in their interactions, mainly for food, space, reproduction and protection. These interactions are important for the survival of different species and the community as a group.

Effect of interactions between members of an ecological community can be classified within two broad categories, *direct effects* and *indirect effects*. The first of these, **direct effects**, as the name implies, deals with the direct effect of one individual on another and not mediated or transmitted through a third individual. Pollination of a flower carried out by bee is an example of direct effect. **Indirect effects** occur when the influence of one species, the **donor**, is transmitted through a second species, the **transmitter**, to a third species, the **receiver**. The observed effect is indirect because the donor influences the receiver through an intermediate species. Thus, indirect effects consist of a sequence of two direct effect steps. There are two main ways by which an indirect effect can occur. The first is known as an **interaction chain**, in which a donor species affect the abundance of a transmitter and has an effect on a recipient. The second, **interaction modification**, occurs when the donor species alters some attributes of the transmitter, such as behaviour and has an effect on a recipient.

Table 7.8 Classic categories of direct interactions in ecological communities

Interaction	Species X	Species Y
Neutralism	0	0
Mutualism	+	+
Commensalism	+	0
Predation	+	–
Herbivory	+	–
Parasitism	+	–
Amensalism	0	–
Competition	–	–

The sign (+, –, 0) represents the net effect of one species on the other species, either positive, negative, or neutral. The positive effect of one species on another as +, a detrimental effect as –, and no effect as 0.

Interactions having direct effect between populations of species in a community are broadly categorized into *positive, negative* or *neutral* interaction, depending on the nature of the effect on the interacting organisms. In **neutral interaction** (or *neutralism*), interacting species have no effect on each other. An interaction in which either both participating species or at least one of the participants gets benefits and neither is harmed is called **positive interaction** (also called *facilitation*) whereas, an interaction in which either both participating species or one of the participants gets harmed is called **negative interaction**.

Positive interaction

Mutualism

Mutualism is a symbiotic relationship between members of two different species in which both members of the association benefited. On the basis of this relationship, individuals of both species enhance their survival, growth, or reproduction. Mutualistic relationships involve diverse interactions. Mutualisms can be characterized by the degree of dependency, the kinds of benefits received, the degree of specificity and duration of the interactions.

Mutualisms can vary in the degree of dependency between mutualists. Based on this, mutualisms can be *obligate* or *facultative*. In **obligate mutualism**, both organisms benefit by living in close association, and the relationship is obligatory (i.e., neither can survive without each other). Obligate mutualists cannot survive or reproduce without the mutualistic interaction. In **facultative mutualism** (also called **protocooperation**), mutualists benefit by living in close association, but the relationship is not obligatory. The cooperating species do not depend on each other for survival. One good example is the mutualistic association between a coelenterate, sea anemone — *Adamsia palliata* and a hermit crab - *Pagurus prideaux*. The sea anemone is carried by the crab to fresh feeding sites and crab in turn is said to be protected from its enemies by sea anemone.

The term **symbiosis** is sometimes used in the same sense as mutualism. 'Symbiosis' (termed used by de Barry in 1879) simply means *living together*. In narrowest sense, it is used to describe an association in which two species are deriving mutual benefit. However, now this term is used in a broad sense to describe all types of interactions (positive, negative or neutral). So, symbiosis is a close ecological relationship between the individuals of two (or more) different species.

The duration of intimacy among mutualistic interactions and also the degree of specificity of mutualistic interactions varies from one interaction to another. The mutualistic interactions can range from one-to-one, species-specific associations (termed *specialists*) to association with a wide diversity of mutualistic partners (*generalists*). Mutualisms can also be subdivided according to the services provided, regardless of whether the participants are obligate or facultative mutualists. Based on the nature of service involved, mutualisms can be *dispersive*, *defensive* and *resource-based mutualism.* **Dispersive mutualism** involves mutualistic association in which one partner species distributing pollens or seeds of another species and in return receives resources for growth. **Defensive mutualism** involves mutualistic association in which one partner provides protection to other partner against herbivores or parasites in exchange for a place to live or for nutrients needed for growth. **Resource-based mutualism** involves interactions where resources (such as nutrients) obtained by one mutualist is made available to another.

There are many classic examples of mutualistic associations in nature. Reef-forming corals of the tropical waters provide an excellent example of *resource-based mutualism*. **Coral reefs** are a special subtype of ocean floor ecosystem. One fascinating feature of shallow water, reef-building corals is their mutualistic relationship with photosynthetic algae called **zooxanthellae**, which live in their tissues. The coral provides the algae with a protected environment and the compounds they need for photosynthesis. In return, the algae produce oxygen and help the coral to remove wastes.

Many **nitrogen-fixing bacteria** (such as *Rhizobium* and *Bradyrhizobium,* collectively called *rhizobia*) live in root nodules of legumes. The plant partners of rhizobia belong to the Fabaceae or Leguminosae family (commonly known as the legume or pea family). In this mutualistic symbiosis, the bacteria provide nitrogen sources for plant growth in return for photosynthates from the host. Depending on the host plant the symbiotic fate of bacteria can either be reversible or irreversible.

Lichens are a mutualistic association of photoautotrophic algae and heterotrophic fungi. The algal partner (**phycobiont** *or* **photobiont**) is typically unicellular or multicellular green algae or cyanobacteria. About 90% of all known lichens have a green alga as a symbiont. The fungal partner (**mycobiont**) may be a member of ascomycetes (mostly) or member of basidiomycetes (in a few cases). About 98% of the lichen-forming fungal species belong to the ascomycetes. In a lichen which represents a mutualistic relationship, the photobiont provide carbon compounds by performing photosynthesis; the cyanobacteria also fix nitrogen and provide organic nitrogen. The mycobiont provides their photosynthetic partners with a suitable environment for growth. The physical arrangement of hyphae allows gas exchange, protects the photosynthetic partner, and retains water and minerals.

Mutualistic association between fungi and plant roots are called **mycorrhizae** (mycorrhizae means *fungus roots*). About 90% of seed plants have mutualistic associations with fungi that live on or in the root tissue. Mycorrhizal fungi (fungi that form mycorrhizae) delivers inorganic nutrients such as phosphate, calcium and water to plants, which they are able to extract more efficiently from the soil than the host. In exchange, the plants supply the fungi with organic nutrients.

Commensalism

Commensalism (means '*at table together*') is a symbiotic relationship between two species in which one species benefits and the other neither benefits nor is harmed. Often, the host species provides a home and/or transportation for the other species. One very common example of commensalism is **epiphytes** (e.g., some tropical orchids) grow in branches of tropical trees. Epiphytes use other plants for support and increased exposure to sunlight and rain. Similarly, several woody climbers (**lianas**) take the support of the trees for exposing their canopy above ground without doing any harm to the tree itself.

Negative interaction

Predation

The term 'predation' is defined as the consumption of one living organism (the prey) by another (the predator) excluding scavengers and decomposers. It is an act of capturing, killing and eating. The organism which does the act of predation is called a **predator**. The second organism which is killed and eaten is called **prey**. Predation is generally linked to carnivorous animals and predator is generally larger in size compared to the prey. Although the term predator is typically associated with animals that feed on other animals, herbivory is also a form of predation in which animals prey on autotrophs. When the predator is a primary consumer (usually an animal), and the prey is a primary producer (plant), the interaction is termed **herbivory**. Predation is a direct and complex interaction rather than simply a transfer of energy. Mathematical models (differential equation model is known by the name of its originators Lotka and Volterra) suggest the interaction between prey and their predators result in coupled oscillations.

Box 7.4 Avoiding predation

As predators possess adaptations for capturing prey, prey also has adaptations that help them avoid being eaten. Any characteristic that enables individual prey to avoid being detected and captured by a predator increase its fitness. Animal species have evolved a wide range of characteristics to avoid being detected, selected and captured by predators. These characteristics are collectively referred to as **predator defenses**. These defenses include chemical defenses, cryptic coloration, warning coloration, mimicry and other defenses.

Cryptic coloration (or camouflage) includes colors and patterns that allow prey to blend into the background. This makes prey difficult to spot because the color and patterns of prey resembles to those in the visual background. Besides such advanced hiding strategies, some animals do just the opposite and appear in bright colors that are easily visible. Intensive colors are usually a warning sign of well-protected toxic organisms. Prey can avoid an attack by bright coloration as a sign of toxicity. This is termed as **aposematic coloration** (or *warning coloration*). Such warning signals are the opposite of camouflage but are also widespread.

Some prey species gain significant protection by mimicking the appearance of other species. **Mimicry** is a phenomenon whereby an individual of one species gains an advantage by resembling an individual of a different species. There are at least two types of mimicry. In **Müllerian mimicry,** named after F. Müller, several groups of organisms gain an advantage by looking like one another. This mimicry occurs among organisms in which all the mimetic species are offensive and obnoxious. The classic example is the general similarity among bees, wasps and hornets. Müllerian mimicry requires that all the species be similar in appearance and distinctly colored. In **Batesian mimicry,** a vulnerable organism (termed **mimic**) gains a selective advantage by looking like a dangerous or distasteful organism (termed **model**).

The classic example of Batesian mimicry are the **monarch** (*Danaus plexippus*) and **viceroy** (*Limenitis archippus*) butterflies. Monarch butterflies feed on milkweed plants, obtaining toxic chemicals called **cardiac glycosides**, which the monarchs store in their bodies. When a bird tries to eat a monarch, it becomes sick. Thereafter, the bird will not only avoid eating monarchs, but it will also avoid eating any butterflies that look anything like monarchs.

Many animals have developed **physical defenses** against predators. For example, the shells of tortoises are a strong means of defense against most predators. Similarly, many beetles have a tough exoskeleton that protects them from attack from other arthropod predators such as spiders.

Plants also have a variety of defenses against herbivores. These defenses include mechanical defenses (such as presence of thorns, sticky hairs), chemical defenses (presence of alkaloids, phenolics etc.) and defensive mutualism.

As prey have evolved ways of avoiding predators, predators have evolved better ways of hunting. Failure to capture prey results in reduced reproduction and increased mortality of predators. Therefore, natural selection also produces smarter and more skilled predators. As prey species evolve characteristics to avoid being caught, predators evolve more effective means to capture them.

Parasitism

Parasitism is a relationship between two organisms in which one species (**parasite**) benefits for growth and reproduction and other species (**host**) harmed. The host is the organism from which the parasite derives benefits. A **parasite** as an organism that obtains its nutrients from one or a very few host individuals, normally causing harm but not causing death immediately. In many ways, **host-parasite** and **prey-predator** relationship are similar, the parasite and predator are benefited while host and prey are negatively affected. But there are few fundamental differences. Predators live on capital whereas parasites live on interest. Parasites, like the predators, limit the population of the host species, but they are generally host-specific, and do not have choice or alternatives like predators. They are smaller in size and have higher biotic or reproductive potential compared to the predators. Parasites have poor means of dispersal and require specialized structures to reach or invade the host. Predators, on the other hand, are quite mobile and capable of capturing the prey.

Parasitoid is different from parasite. **Parasitoid** is an organism that lives the entire life attached to or within a single host. Unlike a true parasite, however, it ultimately sterilizes or kills, and sometimes consumes, the host. Parasitoids are large relative to their hosts. Parasites can be classified on the basis of size as *microparasites* and *macroparasites*. **Microparasites** include viruses, bacteria and protozoans. They are characterized by small size and a short generation time. **Macroparasites** include flatworms, roundworms, flukes, lice, fleas and ticks. They are relatively large and have a comparatively long generation time.

Parasites exhibit diverse life cycles. In a direct life cycle, the parasite completes its entire life cycle within a single host species. In an indirect life cycle, the parasite requires multiple host species to complete its life cycle. The host in which parasites reaches its sexually mature stage is called the **definitive host** (**primary host**) and other hosts where parasite complete non-reproductive stages are referred to as **intermediate hosts** (**secondary host**). The secondary host harbours the parasite only for a short transition period during which some developmental stages complete but do not perform sexual reproduction.

In some cases, an organism can serve as both a vector and an *intermediate host*. A **vector** is an organism that transmits a parasite from one host to another, while an **intermediate host** is an organism that supports some developmental stages of a parasite without reaching its full reproductive stage. In the case of the **malarial parasite**, the mosquito acts both as a vector and as an intermediate host. The primary host of the malarial parasite is the human. As a vector, the mosquito transmits the malarial parasite from an infected human to a healthy individual. When the mosquito takes a blood meal from an infected person, it ingests the malarial parasites present in the person's blood. The parasites then undergo a series of developmental stages within the mosquito, eventually reaching the infective stage. Similarly, in the case of *Trypanosomes*, humans act as the *primary host*, as they harbor the adult stage of the parasite. However, the parasite needs a **tsetse fly** as an intermediate host to undergo certain developmental stages and become infective to humans. The tsetse fly serves as a vector, transmitting the *Trypanosomes* from one human host to another.

Hosts are the habitats for parasites. Parasites can be classified into ectoparasites and endoparasites depending on either they live within the host or on the host. Parasites that live inside the body of the host are called **endoparasites** (e.g., hookworms that live in the host's gut) and those that live on the surface of the hosts are called **ectoparasites** (e.g., some mites). Endoparasite can exist in one of two forms: *intercellular* or *intracellular*. A parasite that feeds on another parasite is termed **epiparasite** and relationship referred to as **hyperparasitism.**

Parasites can be temporary parasites and permanent parasites. **Temporary parasites** are the parasites which come in contact with host for a brief period, e.g., female mosquitoes (*Culex*, *Anopheles*, *Aedes*), bedbug (*Cimex*), sandfly (*Phlebotomus*), tsetse fly (*Glossina*) whereas **permanent parasites** remain in contact with the host throughout their life, e.g., *Entamoeba histolytica*, *Ascaris lumbricoides*, *Taenia solium* etc.

Amensalism

In commensalism, one organism benefits while the other is unaffected. The opposite of commensalism is *amensalism*, where one organism is harmed while the other is unaffected. **Amensalism** takes place when one individual is negatively affected by interaction with another individual who is not affected by the relationship. A good example of this interaction is when one organism produces an antibiotic against another organism. Many molds, including *Penicillium*, secrete chemicals that kill other bacteria in their vicinity.

Amensalism is different from allelopathy. **Allelopathy** is a biological interaction in which an organism produces one or more biochemicals that influence the germination, growth, survival and reproduction of other organisms. These biochemicals are known as **allelochemicals** (or *allelochemics*) and can have beneficial (*positive allelopathy*) or harmful (*negative allelopathy*) effects on the organisms. Allelochemicals are secondary metabolites produced by plants and other organisms. For example, black walnut, *Juglans nigra*, produces a chemical called **juglone** from its roots, killing roots of neighboring plants. This phenomenon is termed as *allelopathy*, and the chemicals are known as *allelochemicals*. Although allelopathy is also a chemical effect of one organism on another through the release of chemicals into the environment, but it is different form amensalism, where one organism remain unaffected while the other a harmed (0, –). But allelopathy may also be seen has a positive interaction.

Competition

Competition occurs when two organisms compete for the same resource (such as food and space), resulting in reduced fitness in the competing individuals. In competition between two species both suffer adversely. Usually, competition occurs when resources, such as space, light and nutrients, etc. are in short supply. Competition can be *interspecific* or *intraspecific.*

Interspecific competition occurs between individuals of two different species. The strength of interspecific competition is greater between more closely related species or species in similar guilds. The strength of interspecific competition also increases with decreased resources. In this type of competition, growth and survival of one species is negatively affected either directly (e.g., *interference* or *direct competition*) or indirectly (i.e., *exploitation* or *indirect competition*).

Interference competition is observed when two species come into direct contact with each other, such as fighting or defending a territory. The most common example of interference competition is the fight over territories or food items among animals. In this case, individuals interact directly with each other, and one individual will actually prevent another from exploiting the resources. In **exploitation competition**, organisms compete indirectly (i.e., without coming in direct contact) through the consumption of a limited resource such as food, with each obtaining as much as it can. Exploitation occurs only when the resource in question is in limited supply. Interference competition and exploitation competition are categorized as *real* competition. A third form of competition is termed as **apparent competition**. It occurs when a single species of predator feeds on two prey species.

Intraspecific competition occurs between individuals of the same species. Individuals of the same species have very similar requirements for survival, growth and reproduction. Hence, intraspecific competition typically leads to decreased resource intake per individual, and thus to decreased individual growth and development. These may lead, in turn, to decrease in survivorship and fecundity. Intraspecific competition may be also either *interference* or *exploitation* competition. Generally, the intraspecific competition is more intense than interspecific competition.

7.11 Lotka-Volterra model

The Lotka-Volterra model of **interspecific competition** is a simple mathematical model representing the interaction between two competing species. This mathematical model was developed by two people working independently – Alfred Lotka (1925), an insurance actuary and Vito Volterra (1926), a mathematical physicist. On the basis of this model, the losers of competitive interactions can be predicted. The **Lotka-Volterra equation** for interspecific competition is based on the Verhulst-Pearl logistic growth equation:

$$\frac{dN}{dt} = rN\frac{(K-N)}{K}$$

In the **logistic equation**, a rate of population growth is limited by **intraspecific competition** (members of the same species competing with one another). However, this equation can be modified to include the effect of interspecific competition as well as intraspecific competition. The Lotka-Volterra model was developed to allow ecologists to predict the potential outcome when two species are in competition for the same resources. Basically, the model attempts to account for the effect that the presence of one species will have on the population growth of the other species, relative to the competitive effect that two members of the same species would have on each other.

The logistic equation and Lotka-Volterra equations for two species (species 1 and species 2).

The logistic equation for species 1 growing alone: $\frac{dN_1}{dt} = r_1N_1\left(\frac{K_1 - N_1}{K_1}\right)$

The Lotka-Volterra equation for species 1 in presence of species 2:

$$\frac{dN_1}{dt} = r_1N_1\left(\frac{K_1 - N_1 - \alpha_{12}N_2}{K_1}\right) \quad \text{or} \quad \frac{dN_1}{dt} = r_1N_1\left(1 - \frac{N_1}{K_1} - \frac{\alpha_{12}N_2}{K_1}\right)$$

Represent the negative effect of *intraspecific competition* on logistic growth (term $\frac{N_1}{K_1}$)

Represent the negative effect of *interspecific competition* on logistic growth (term $\frac{\alpha_{12}N_2}{K_1}$)

The logistic equation for species 2 growing alone: $\frac{dN_2}{dt} = r_2N_2\left(\frac{K_2 - N_2}{K_2}\right)$

The Lotka-Volterra equation for species 2 in presence of species 1:

$$\frac{dN_2}{dt} = r_2N_2\left(\frac{K_2 - N_2 - \alpha_{21}N_1}{K_2}\right) \quad \text{or} \quad \frac{dN_2}{dt} = r_2N_2\left(1 - \frac{N_2}{K_2} - \frac{\alpha_{21}N_1}{K_2}\right)$$

Where,

N_1 and N_2 = population of species 1 and 2, respectively.

K_1 and K_2 = carrying capacity of system for each species in the absence of the other.

t = time

r_1 and r_2 = intrinsic rate of increase of species 1 and 2, respectively.

α_{12} = competition coefficient representing the effect of one individual of species 2 on the growth of species 1 (the first number of the subscript always refers to the species being affected).

α_{21} = competition coefficient representing the effect of one individual of species 1 on the growth of species 2.

The **competition coefficient** (α) measures how strongly one species affects the growth of another. It compares the impact of interspecific competition to intraspecific competition. For example, if one individual of species 2 has only one-tenth the competitive effect on species 1 as one individual of species 1 has on its own population, then $\alpha_{12} = 0.1$.

When $\alpha_{12} < 1$, species 2 has a weaker effect on species 1 than species 1 has on itself.

When $\alpha_{12} > 1$, species 2 has a stronger effect on species 1 than species 1 has on itself.

Let us understand this with an example. Suppose, species 1 is a population of rabbits and species 2 is a population of sheep, both feeding on grass. One extra rabbit in the habitat reduces the growth of the rabbit population by '1 unit' (intraspecific competition). However, if adding one sheep reduces rabbit growth by only '0.2 units,' then α_{12} = 0.2. This means sheep compete with rabbits but less strongly than rabbits compete with themselves. On the other hand, if adding one sheep reduced rabbit growth by '1.5 units,' then α_{12} = 1.5, showing that sheep are stronger competitors for grass than rabbits themselves.

The Lotka–Volterra equations take a few assumptions under consideration:

1. Intrinsic rate of increase, competition coefficient and carrying capacity are all constants.
2. Every individual within each population is identical.
3. The populations are not allowed to diversify.
4. The environment (habitat) is homogeneous.

The Lotka-Volterra competition model describes the outcome of competition between two species over ecological time scale. If the values for each equation are known, then the equation can be used to predict the potential outcome of a competition (i.e., whether they can co-exist or one will eventually exclude the other). To understand the predictions of the model, it is helpful to look at graphs that show how the size of each population increases or decreases when we start with different combinations of species abundances. These graphs are called **state-space graphs,** in which the population size of species 1 is plotted on the x-axis and the population size of species 2 is plotted on the y-axis. Each point in a state-space graph represents a combination of abundances of the two species. For each species there is a straight line on the graph called a **zero isocline.**

The zero isocline for each species states that at any given point along that line the population size does not change, i.e., dN/dt = 0. The two graphs show the zero isoclines for species 1 (*black line*) and species 2 (*grey line*). Any point above the zero isocline indicates that the population of that species is decreasing; any point below the isocline that the population is increasing.

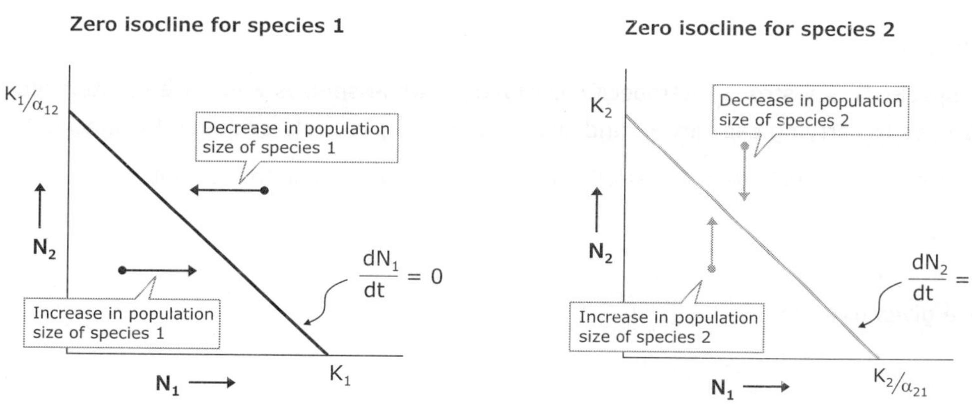

Figure 7.24 There are two lines drawn on the state-space graphs. These lines join points where there is no change in population size with time, i.e., dN/dt = 0. They are called zero isoclines and there is one for each species: the black line is for species 1 ($dN_1/dt = 0$) while the grey line is for species 2 ($dN_2/dt = 0$). Arrows indicate direction of population change.

We can map out the regions of increase and decrease in the figure for species 1 and 2 if we can draw its zero isocline.

If $\frac{dN_1}{dt} = 0$ then $r_1 N_1 (K_1 - N_1 - \alpha_{12} N_2) = 0$

This is true if, $r_1 = 0$ or $N_1 = 0$ or if $K_1 - N_1 - \alpha_{12}N_2 = 0$ then,

$K_1 - \alpha_{12}N_2 = N_1$

This equation indicates that competition has reduced the carrying capacity.

When $N_1 = 0$ then $N_2 = \frac{K_1}{\alpha_{12}}$ and when $N_2 = 0$ then $N_1 = K_1$.

Note that the zero isoclines divide each graph into two parts. Below and to the left of the isocline the population size increases because the combined abundances of both species are less than the carrying capacity of the one, while above and to the right the population size decreases because the combined abundances are greater than the carrying capacity. For the graph of the isocline of species 1, the isocline intersects the graph on the x-axis when N_1 reaches its carrying capacity (K_1) and no individuals of species 2 are present. The isocline intersects the graph on the y-axis at K_1/α_{12}, when the carrying capacity of species 1 is filled by the equivalent number of individuals of species 2 and no individuals of species 1 are present.

Similarly, based on an equivalent derivation, we can map out the regions of increase and decrease in the figure for species 2.

If $\frac{dN_2}{dt} = 0$ then $r_2 N_2 (K_2 - N_2 - \alpha_{21} N_1) = 0$ and $K_2 - N_2 - \alpha_{21} N_1 = 0$ then

$$K_2 - \alpha_{21}N_1 = N_2$$

when $N_2 = 0$ then $N_1 = \frac{K_2}{\alpha_{21}}$ and when $N_1 = 0$ then $N_2 = K_2$.

Scenarios

The two zero isoclines can be juxtaposed in four different ways, depending on the relative values of α and K for each species. The four possible competitive situations, defined by the relative positions of the isoclines, are given below.

Scenario 1: The two isoclines do not cross. The isocline for species 1 is above and to the right of the isocline for species 2.

$$\frac{K_1}{\alpha_{12}} > K_2 \text{ and } K_1 > \frac{K_2}{\alpha_{21}}$$

Rearranging these gives us

$$K_1 > K_2\alpha_{12} \text{ and } K_1\alpha_{21} > K_2$$

In this scenario, species 1 is a strong interspecific competitor, while species 2 is a weak interspecific competitor. Hence, species 1 goes to carrying capacity K_1 and species 2 is competitively excluded by species 1.

Scenario 2: The two isoclines do not cross. The isocline for species 2 is above and to the right of the isocline for species 1.

$$K_2 > \frac{K_1}{\alpha_{12}} \text{ and } \frac{K_2}{\alpha_{21}} > K_1$$

Rearranging these gives us

$$K_2\alpha_{12} > K_1 \text{ and } K_2 > K_1\alpha_{21}$$

In this scenario, species 2 is a strong interspecific competitor, while species 1 is a weak interspecific competitor. Hence, species 2 goes to carrying capacity K_2 and species 1 is competitively excluded by species 2.

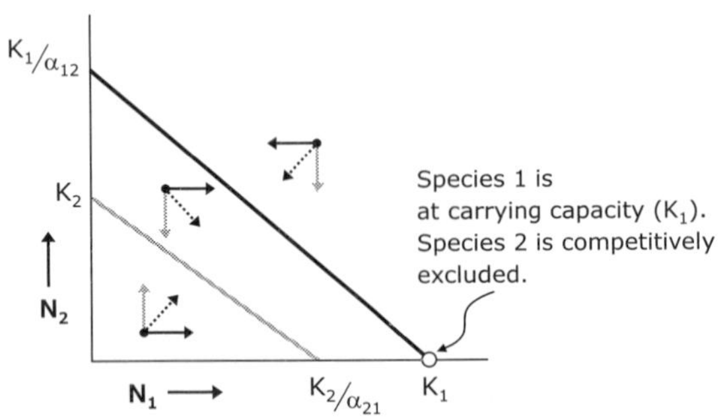

Scenario 1
Species 2 is competitively excluded.

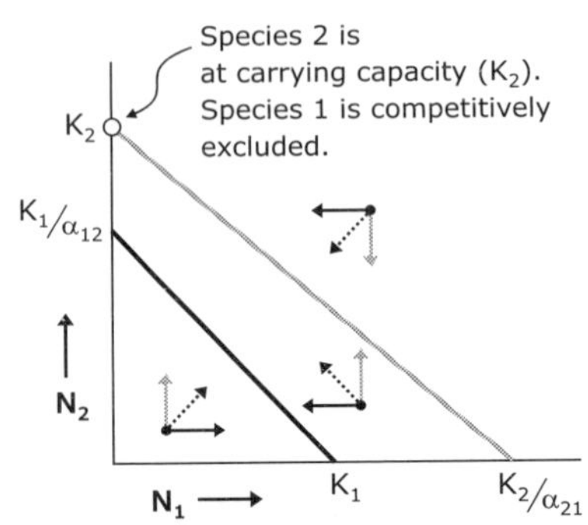

Scenario 2
Species 1 is competitively excluded.

Scenario 3: The case of stable coexistence

The isoclines cross one another, but for both species carrying capacities are lower than the other's carrying capacity divided by the competition coefficient. Rather than outcompeting one another, the two species are able to coexist at stable equilibrium point. An *equilibrium point* occurs where the isoclines cross.

$\frac{K_1}{\alpha_{12}} > K_2$ and $\frac{K_2}{\alpha_{21}} > K_1$

Rearranging these gives us

$K_1 > K_2\alpha_{12}$ and $K_2 > K_1\alpha_{21}$

In this case, both species have less competitive effect on each other i.e., weak interspecific competition. Coexistence occurs when intraspecific competition is greater than interspecific competition. The outcome of this type of competition is the *stable coexistence* of both species.

Scenario 4: The case of *unstable coexistence*

The isoclines of the two species cross one another. Here, the carrying capacity of species 1 (K_1) is higher than the carrying capacity of species 2 divided by the competition coefficient (K_2/α_{21}), and the carrying capacity of species 2 (K_2) is higher than the carrying capacity of species 1 divided by the competition coefficient (K_1/α_{12}). There is an unstable equilibrium point where the isoclines intersect.

$K_2 > \frac{K_1}{\alpha_{12}}$ and $K_1 > \frac{K_2}{\alpha_{21}}$

Rearranging these gives us

$K_2\alpha_{12} > K_1$ and $K_1\alpha_{21} > K_2$

In this case, individuals of both species have a greater competitive effect on individuals of the other species. Competitive exclusion occurs when interspecific competition is greater than intraspecific competition. The outcome of this type of competition is the *unstable coexistence* between species 1 and species 2.

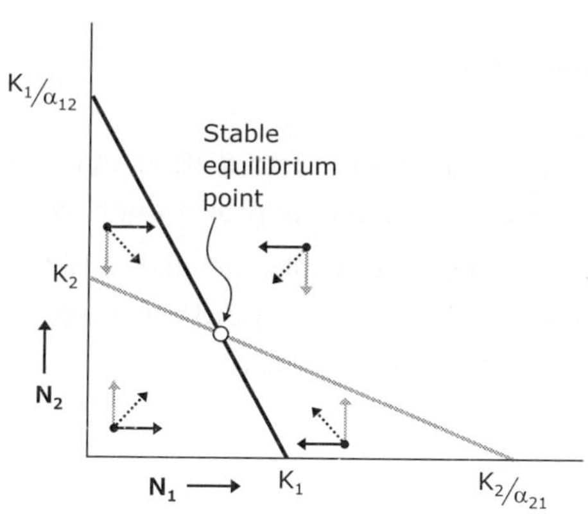

Scenario 3: Stable coexistence

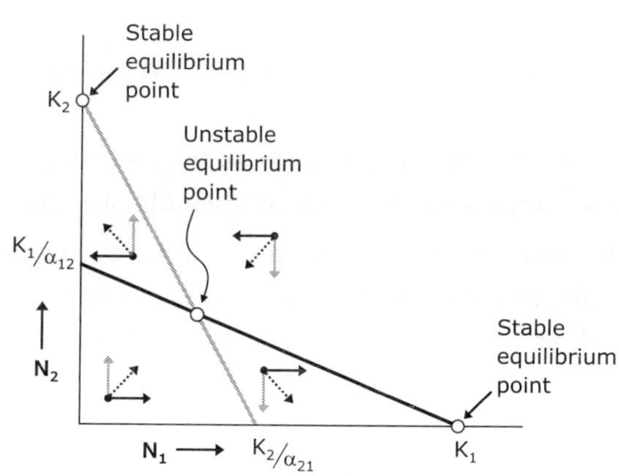

Scenario 4: Unstable coexistence
Competition can go either way

If a line is drawn between the two carrying capacities (K_1 and K_2), the position of equilibrium point either above or below that line differentiates stable from and unstable coexistence.

Dynamics of the predator–prey system

Lotka-Volterra model also explores predator-prey dynamics and tells us about the changes in prey and predator population with time. This model comprises a pair of differential equations (one for the *prey* population and another for the *predator* population) that describe predator-prey dynamics in their simplest case (one predator population, one prey population). The Lotka-Volterra equations take a few assumptions under consideration:

- No intraspecific competition in prey population.
- Predator not dependent on alternative prey.
- Predator consumption has no saturation point.
- No other environmental influence.
- No accidental death of predator.
- Prey population decrease only due to predation.

We begin by looking at what happens to the prey population in the absence of predator. The prey population will exponentially grow according to the exponential growth equation $dN_1/dt = rN_1$ (where N_1 is the size of the prey population and *r* is its *intrinsic rate of increase*).

The rate at which the prey will be consumed by the predator will depend on the frequency of predator-prey encounters and the *predator efficiency* (p). Encounters increase with the increase in the predator population (N_2) and the prey population (N_1). The *predation efficiency* is a measure of the percentage of encounters actually ending with the capture and consumption of the prey by the predator. Thus, in the presence of a predator, the growth rate of prey population will turn into:

$$\frac{dN_1}{dt} = rN_1 - pN_1N_2 \qquad \text{(Lotka–Volterra equation for \textbf{prey})}$$

The change in predator's population depends on the efficiency at which a consumed prey is converted into the production of a predator (**a**) and the natural decrease of predator population due to its intrinsic mortality rate (**d**). The predator mortality rate is assumed to be constant. The rate of change in the predator population is

$$\frac{dN_2}{dt} = apN_1N_2 - dN_2 \qquad \text{(Lotka–Volterra equation for \textbf{predator})}$$

In this simple model, parameters such as the mortality of prey population due to factors other than predation are ignored. More complex models incorporate additional parameters to obtain a closer approximation to real systems.

The Lotka–Volterra equations for predator and prey population growth therefore explicitly link the two populations, each functioning as a density-dependent regulator on the other. Predators regulate the growth of the prey population by functioning as a source of density-dependent mortality. The prey population functions as a source of density-dependent regulation on the predator population.

In the absence of predators (or at very low predator density), the prey population will grow exponentially ($dN_1/dt = rN_1$). As the predator population increases, prey mortality will increase. Eventually, the mortality rate due to predation (pN_1N_2) will equal to the inherent growth rate of the prey population (rN_1). At this point, the net population growth for the prey species will be zero ($dN_1/dt = 0$).

$$\frac{dN_1}{dt} = 0 \text{ when, } pN_1N_2 = rN_1$$

$$pN_2 = r \text{ and } N_2 = r/p$$

The growth rate of the prey population will be zero when the number of predators is equal to the intrinsic rate of increase of the prey population (r) divided by the efficiency of predation (p). If the predator population exceeds this value, the growth rate of the prey will become negative, and the population size declines. The mortality due to predation will be greater than the exponential increase of the prey population. Likewise, we can examine the influence of prey population size on the growth rate of the predator population. The growth rate of the predator population will be zero when the growth rate of predator population is equal to the rate of mortality:

$$\frac{dN_2}{dt} = 0 \text{ when, } apN_1N_2 = dN_2$$

$$apN_1 = d \text{ and } N_1 = d/ap$$

The growth rate of the predator population will be zero when the size of the prey population equals the mortality rate of the predator population divided by the product of the efficiency of predation (p) and the production efficiency of captured prey into new predators (a).

We can examine these results graphically using two axes that represent the population sizes of the prey (*x*-axis) and predator (*y*-axis). The properties of this model can be investigated by finding **zero isoclines**. There are separate *zero isoclines* for the predators and prey, both of which are drawn on a graph of prey population (x-axis) against predator population (y-axis). Each is a line joining those combinations of predator and prey population that lead either to an unchanging prey population ($dN_1/dt = 0$; prey zero isocline) or an unchanging predator population ($dN_2/dt = 0$; predator zero isocline).

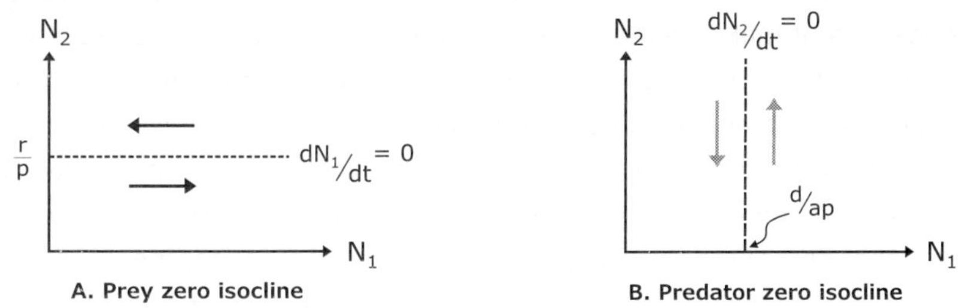

Figure 7.25 Zero isoclines (dN/dt = 0) for the prey and predator populations. Note that the zero isocline for the prey population is defined by a fixed number of predators, and the zero isocline for the predator population is defined by a fixed number of prey. Arrows show the direction of change in population size relative to the isoclines. The prey zero isocline: the number of prey increases at low predator densities and decreases at high predator densities. The predator zero isocline: the number of predators increases when prey numbers are high and decreases when prey numbers are low.

When prey and predator isoclines are combined, coupled oscillations result. When the zero isoclines are combined, the arrows can also be combined, and these joint arrows progress in anticlockwise circles. A minus sign indicates population decline, and a plus sign indicates population increase. This trajectory shows the cyclic fluctuation in the population size of both prey and predator. A fall in the prey population size determines a subsequent fall in the number of predators; this, in turn, will allow the prey population to recover, thus provides predators with a new opportunity to grow in number and so on.

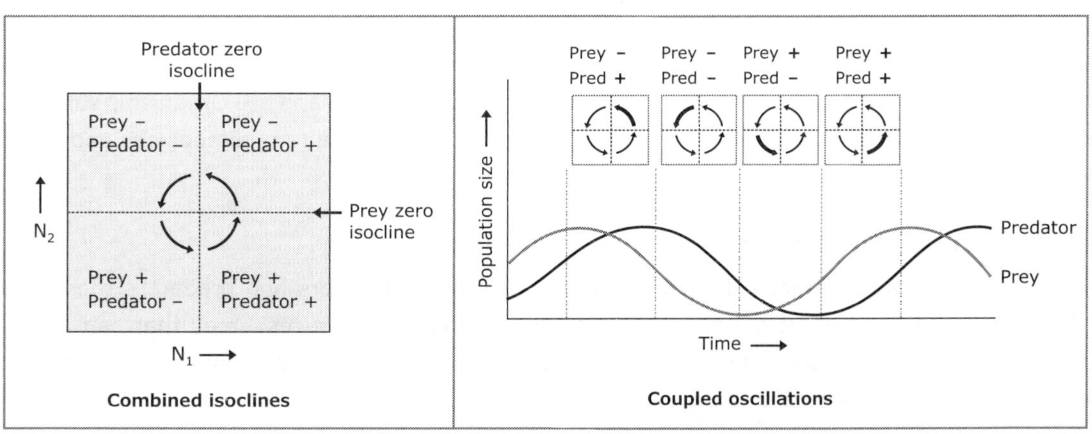

7.12 Ecological niche

All living organisms have a range of environmental conditions under which they can survive, grow, reproduce and function. This range of environmental conditions is not the same for all organisms. A set of environmental conditions and resources under which a species can survive, grow, reproduce and function define the **ecological niche**.

The term 'niche' was used for the first time by Grinnell is frequently misunderstood and misused. It is often used loosely to describe the sort of place in which an organism lives. Strictly, however, the place in which a particular organism lives is its **habitat**. Niche is different from habitat. It is not simply a place where an organism lives. *It is the sum total of all the ecological requisites and activities of a species.* It includes not only the physical space occupied by an organism but also its functional role in the community (its trophic position) and its position in environmental gradients of temperature, moisture, pH, soil, and other conditions of existence. These three aspects of the niche can be conveniently designated as the *spatial niche*, the *trophic niche* and the *n-dimensional hypervolume niche*.

Grinnell used the term *niche* in the sense of the microhabitat to describe the ultimate distributional unit, within which each species is held by its structural and instinctive limitations. Hence, his version of the concept is now called a **spatial** (or habitat) **niche**. Charles Elton used the term niche in the sense of the 'functional status of an organism in its community.' Because Elton emphasized the trophic position of an organism, his version of the concept is designated as a **trophic niche**. The concept of the ***n*-dimensional hypervolume niche** was first described by American ecologist Hutchinson (1957). He defined a niche as a multidimensional space called an *n-dimensional hypervolume*, where *n* is the number of dimensions that make up the niche within which an organism can survive, grow and reproduce. In other words, the *n* dimensions correspond to independent environmental variables that affect the survival of that organism. Temperature, for instance, limits the growth and survival of all organisms, but different organisms tolerate different ranges of temperature. This range is one *dimension* of an organism's ecological niche. An organism's environment cannot be defined by only one or two environmental variables i.e., one or two dimensions. But there are many such dimensions that determine the organism's position in the environmental gradient, an *n*-dimensional hypervolume. Clearly, the real niche of a species must be *multi*dimensional. Hence, each organism has an activity space, a range of environmental conditions and resource qualities within which it can live.

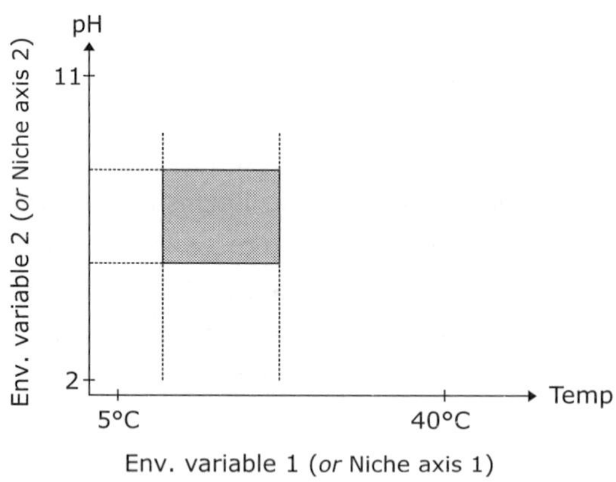

Above graph showing the 2-dimensional position of an organism in the environmental gradient considering two independent environmental variables (defining two dimensions) – temperature and pH. Organisms survive, grow, and reproduce only within certain limits. This graph shows the temperature range (one dimension) and the organism's pH range (second dimension).

Fundamental niche and realized niche

Usually, a species has a larger ecological niche in the absence of competitors and predators than it has in their presence. In other words, there are certain combinations of conditions and resources that can allow a species to maintain a viable population, but only if it is not being adversely affected by enemies. This led Hutchinson to distinguish between the *fundamental* and the *realized* niche.

The **fundamental niche** (sometimes referred to as the **physiological niche** or **pre-interactive niche**) is the maximum theoretical inhabited hypervolume which a species can occupy in the absence of interactions with other species. In other words, it is the full range of environmental variables and resources that a species can possibly tolerate and use in the absence of competitors and predators i.e., free from any sort of interference from other species. The fundamental niche is thus a hypothetical, idealized niche in which the organism encounters no interactions with other species and in which its physical environment is optimal.

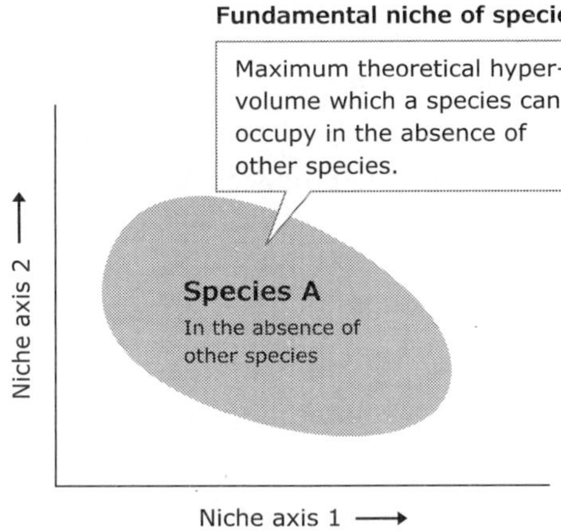

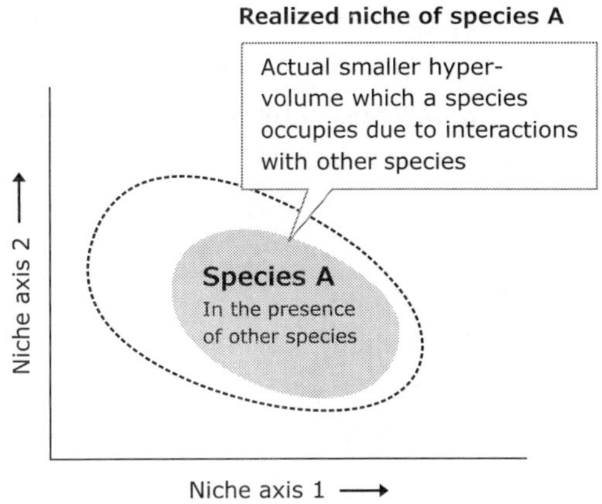

On the other hand, the portion of the fundamental niche that a species actually exploits as a result of interactions with other species as the **realized niche** (or **post-interactive niche**). It is the actual smaller hypervolume which a species occupies under interference and predation from the other species. Because of interspecific interactions, the realized niche of a species is often smaller than its fundamental niche. Realized niches (and even fundamental niches) of an organism are not always fixed. They can shift over time due to various ecological and evolutionary factors. Within a single species, different life stages (e.g., larval vs. adult) may occupy distinct niches. Additionally, in some species, niche segregation can occur between the sexes, leading to differences in resource use or habitat preference.

Ecologist uses the concept of niche to characterize species in terms of their similarity in resource use. An important measure of this includes **niche overlap**. The sharing of niche space by two or more species is called *niche overlap*. It occurs when two species use the same resources or other environmental variables. It is an index of similarity between the resource utilization of two species. The degree and type of niche overlap can be used to assess interspecific competition. Overlap is complete when two organisms have identical niches. Usually, niches overlap only partially, with some resources being shared and others being used exclusively by each species.

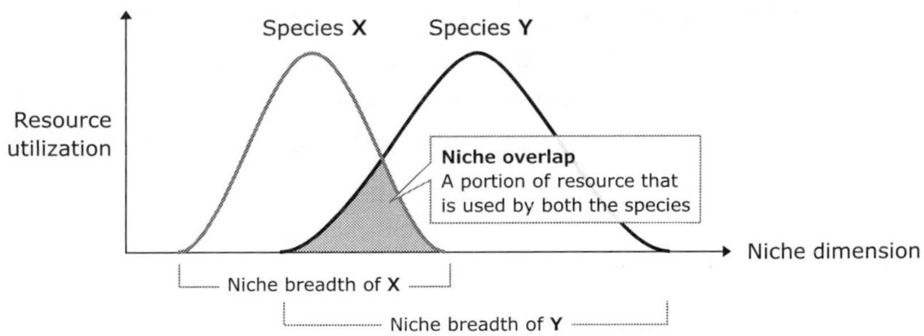

Niche width (also called **niche breadth** or **niche size**) describes the extent of the realized niche occupied by an organism. This area is defined by suitable environmental condition and available resources appropriate to that species as well as interspecific interactions. Some organisms have smaller niches than others. It is a comparative feature. We can only say that a given organism has a niche that is narrower or broader than that of some other organism. The effects of interspecific competition on niche breadth are complex and can lead to either niche contraction or expansion, depending on environmental conditions. The evolutionary process by which species adapt to increasingly specialized niches to reduce competition is known as **niche packing**.

Scientists use the *niche width* of species to classify them broadly as generalists or specialists. **Generalist species** have broad niches. They can live in many different places, eat a variety of foods, and often tolerate a wide range of environmental conditions. Flies, cockroaches, mice, rats and humans are generalist species. These species usually exploit more food types, occupy diverse habitats and build up larger populations. In contrast, **specialist species** occupy narrow niches. They may be able to live in only one type of habitat, use one or a few types of food, or tolerate a narrow range of climatic and other environmental conditions. This makes specialists more prone to extinction when environmental conditions change.

Organisms that occupy the same or similar niches in different geographical regions are called **ecological equivalents**. The idea of 'ecological equivalents' was first stressed by Grinnell in 1924. Species that occupy same equivalent niches and occur in widely separated regions are generally taxonomically much different. A grassland community develops wherever there is a grassland climate but the species of grasses (the producer) and grazers (herbivores) may be quite different especially where regions are widely separated.

Ecological compression

As more species invade a habitat, interspecific competition forces any single species to decrease the range of habitats it exploits. In the presence of a greater number of competitive species in a habitat, each species search foods on a smaller part of the total available habitat. This is termed as **ecological compression**. It means, as greater number of species make use of a habitat, the habitat used by each species shrinks. This results in species specialization in habitat occupancy and feeding habit. This consequently reduces niche overlapping. However, the range of food items eaten by each species remains constant i.e., within the reduced habitat searched by each species, a full range of food items may still be present. The actual diet may become more concentrated, but the range of items will not change. Hence, MacArthur and Pianka argued, the range of food within by a species should be independent of the number of competing species present. Ecological compression takes place on a shorter time-scale and does not involve heritable change.

7.13 Effect of competition

Competitive exclusion principle

Competitive exclusion principle (also termed as **Gause's principle**) can be stated as: 'If two competing species coexist in a stable, homogeneous environment, then they do so as a result of differentiation of their realized niches. If, however, there is no such differentiation, or if it is precluded by the habitat, then one competing species will eliminate or exclude the other.'

In the simplest form, this principle states that two species competing for the same resource cannot coexist indefinitely. Competitive exclusion principle is based on the studies carried out by Ecologist G. F. Gause on the three species of *paramecium* – *P. aurelia*, *P. caudatum* and *P. bursaria*. All three species fed on bacteria and yeast. Gause determined the growth pattern of each species by culturing separately. When cultured separately, population of all three *Paramecium* species followed a logistic growth pattern. When Gause grew *P. aurelia* and *P. caudatum* together, *P. caudatum* always declined to the point of extinction. In mixed culture, both species utilized bacteria as food occurred more in the oxygen-rich upper part of the culture tube. By contrast, when Gause cultured *P. bursaria* and *P. caudatum* (or *P. aurelia*) together, neither went extinct. However, the population of each were much less compared to when they have grown alone because some competition occurred between them. In this experiment, Gause discovered that *P. bursaria* was better able to utilize the yeast in the lower part of the culture tubes and *P. aurelia* or *P. caudatum* on bacteria in the upper part of the culture tube. From these experiments, Gause concluded that species with exactly the same requirements cannot live together for long in the same place by using the same limiting resources, that is, occupying the same niche. His conclusion later termed the **competitive exclusion principle** by Garrett Hardin (1960), essentially means that '**complete competitors cannot coexist**.' Species may avoid competitive exclusion by partitioning resources as happened in case of *P. bursaria* and *P. caudatum*. Gause's principle of competitive exclusion can be restated as:

'No two species can occupy the same niche indefinitely when resources are limiting. Two species can coexist on a long-term basis, either resources must not be limited or their niches will always differ in one or more features; otherwise, one species will out-compete the other, and the extinction of the second species will inevitably result.'

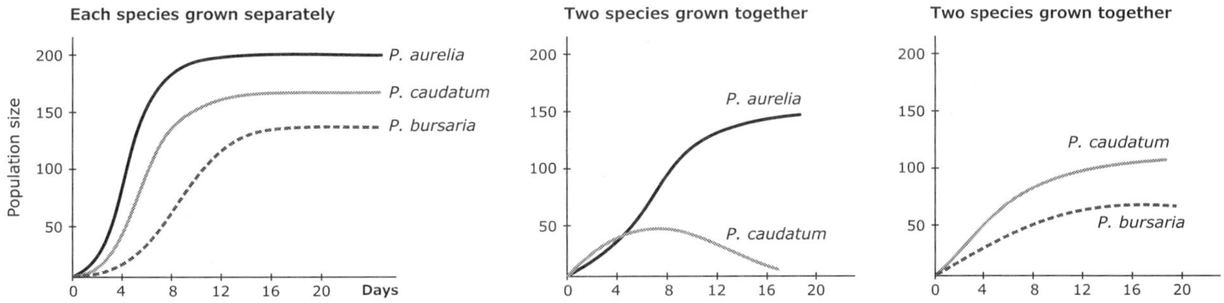

Figure 7.26 The growth of three species of paramecium in separate cultures and in mixed cultures. *P. aurelia*, *P. caudatum* and *P. bursaria*, three closely related ciliate protozoans, when grown in separate cultures, exhibited typical sigmoid population growth and maintained a constant population level in a culture medium that was maintained with a fixed density of food items. When two protozoans- *P. aurelia* and *P. caudatum* - were placed in the same culture, however, *P. aurelia* alone survived after 16 days. Neither organism attacked the other or secreted harmful substances; *P. aurelia* populations simply had a more rapid growth rate (higher intrinsic rate of increase) and thus 'out-competed' *P. caudatum* for the limited amount of food under the existing conditions (a clear case of *exploitation competition*). By contrast, when *P. bursaria* and *P. caudatum* (or *P. aurelia*) cultured together, neither went extinct. Adapted from Gause GF (1934), *The Struggle for Existence*.

Competitive exclusion and coexistence

The species coexistence is rooted in the competitive exclusion principle, which states that two species competing for the same resource cannot coexist. The species that is better at gaining the limiting resource will eventually eliminate the inferior competitor. If a superior and an inferior competitor are placed into a habitat at initially equal abundance, the former will inevitably eliminate the latter. Differences between species in their competitive ability drive the superior to dominance and the inferior to exclusion. If complete competitors drive one another to local extinction, then how two very related species will coexist?

One answer to reduce interspecific competition between species and thus competitive exclusion of inferior species is the **niche differentiation**. For example, the niche differences of the two rodent species may include differences in the size of seeds consumed – one rodent tends to consume larger seeds and other smaller seeds. By niche differentiation two rodent species can reduce competition for food and coexist.

Resource partitioning

Niche differentiation may take a variety of forms, of which *resource partitioning* is most common. Because the degree of competition is assumed to depend upon the degree of niche overlap, hence, some species evolve to reduce niche overlap through resource partitioning. The term 'resource partitioning' describes the niche differentiation, both in space and time that enables similar species to coexist in a community. It refers to the state of reduced overlap in resource use between coexisting species. By consuming slightly different forms of a limiting resource or using the same limiting resource at a different place, individuals of different species compete less with one another (interspecific competition). Through resource partitioning in temporal scale, species also able to manage to coexist by using the same limiting resources at different times. The assumption is that competition among species that are active at different times would be less intense than if the same set of species all attempted to use the same resource at the same time. Resource partitioning is often viewed as a product of the coevolution of characteristics that function to reduce competition.

Adaptations of some insect-eating bird species to reduce competition by feeding in different portions of the same tree species and by feeding on different insect species is a well-studied example of resource partitioning and coexistence. Robert MacArthur (1958) examined coexistence between five species of **warblers** (all belonged to the genus *Dendroica*) feeding in spruce trees. Each warbler species prefers to feed at a different height and portion of the tree. He found that all species vary to some degree in how they capture resources, although there is some overlap in use. MacArthur divided the trees into 16 different zones and recorded the feeding positions of the different warblers in each. He found that four of the species occupied different heights and portions in the tree and each probably fed on a different range of insects. MacArthur also recorded details of the warbler's foraging habits and discovered that they differed too.

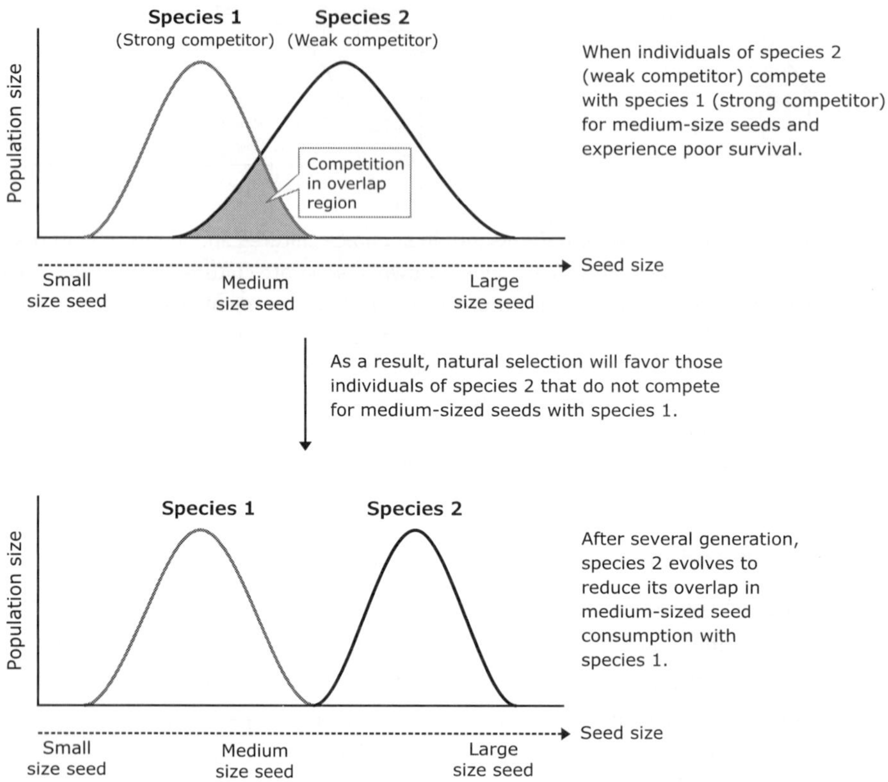

Figure 7.27 The process of competitive exclusion and resource partitioning (adapted from Friedland et al, Environmental science).

Character displacement

If complete competitors drive one another to local extinction, how can closely related species coexist in the same habitat? How different do two species have to be to coexist? Why are even closely related species often phenotypically different from one another? Answer of these questions present in the evolutionary phenomenon called *character displacement*. It is a phenomenon in which two species that live together in the same environment tend to diverge in those characteristics that overlap. As we know, interspecific competition reduces the fitness of competing individuals. Those individuals that compete less have higher fitness than individuals that compete more. Over a time, scale long enough for natural selection to occur, populations of different species competing for the same resources develop morphological, behavioural or physiological adaptations through natural selection that allow them to reduce or avoid competition and increase fitness. The result of this natural selection is a shift in the distribution of those traits that overlap within the competing population(s). Such shift in morphological, behavioural or physiological characteristics of the species is referred to as **character displacement**.

The theory of character displacement was first explicitly developed by W. L. Brown and E. O. Wilson in 1956. The idea underlying this theory is quite simple: suppose two very similar species come into contact, if resources are limiting, the species are likely to compete strongly. One possible outcome is competitive exclusion: the superior competitor will triumph and the inferior one will become extinct. But an alternative possibility is that natural selection will favour, in each population, those individuals whose phenotype allows them to use resources not used by members of the other species.

The result may be that the populations diverge in phenotype and resource use (hence the term 'displacement'), thus reducing resource competition and permitting coexistence. The phenomenon of character displacement is observed over evolutionary time scale and does involve heritable change.

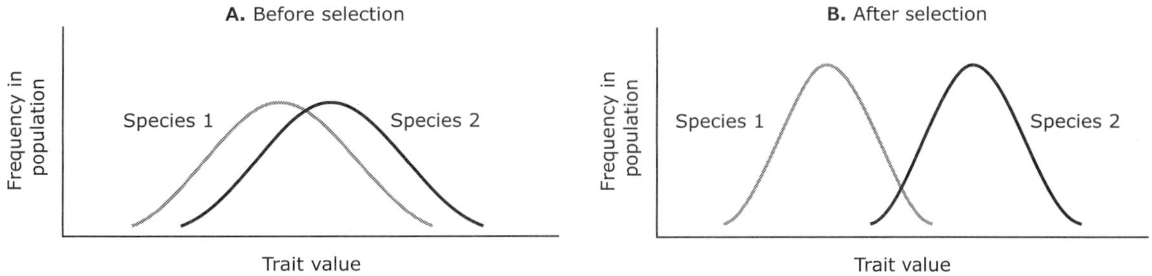

Figure 7.28 The process of character displacement. **A**. Initially, two species encounter each other and overlap in phenotypes associated with resource use or reproduction (indicated here by the two overlapping bell-shaped curves). Character displacement arises when individuals most dissimilar from the average resource-use or reproductive phenotypes of another species are more successful at acquiring resources or reproduction than other members of their population. Consequently, **B**. the most divergent individuals should experience highest fitness and the two species should tend to evolve to be less like the other.

In character displacement, competitor species can have evolutionary effects on each other that result in the divergence in resource-exploiting traits (*ecological character displacement*) or reproductive traits (*reproductive character displacement*). The **ecological character displacement** involves character displacement in traits associated with resource use e.g., morphological structures such as beaks and jaws; whereas **reproductive character displacement** involves character displacement in traits associated with reproduction e.g., sexual signals or female mate preferences).

7.14 Ecological succession

Ecological succession is a universal process of natural change in the community structure (species composition and species abundance) on an ecological time scale i.e., temporal change in community's structure. Ecological communities are dynamic and undergo a continuous change in structure and function. An important characteristic of all communities is that their structure constantly change in response to the changing environmental conditions. This change is directional and sequential, parallel with the changes in the physical environment. These changes lead finally to a community that is in near equilibrium with the environment and that is called a **climax community**. Hence, ecological succession is a gradual and fairly predictable change in the community structure in a given area. Climax community marks the end point of succession. The whole sequence of communities that replace one another in the successional process is termed **sere** (from the word *series*). It is the series of successional stages at a particular site advancing towards its climax community. The temporary successional communities in a sere is called **seral stages**.

The initial seral stage is termed the **pioneer stage** and its community as *pioneer community*. In most cases, more than one seral stage evolves until a *climax community* is attained. Each seral stage is a snapshot of a continuum that is changing over time, but each has its characteristic species composition. Eventually, succession slows as the community reaches a steady equilibrium with the environment i.e., **climax stage**.

The ecological succession can be broadly classified into two kinds on the basis of the nature of habitat from which primary succession starts - *hydrarch* and *xerarch*. Succession initiated with the establishment of pioneer community in an aquatic body is termed **hydrarch succession**. The series of aquatic communities appears in aquatic bodies leading to climax community is termed **hydrosere**. Succession initiated with the establishment of pioneer community in dry land and on the rock is termed **xerarch succession** and the whole sequence of communities that replace one another leading to climax community is called **xerosere**.

7.14.1 Pattern of succession

Ecological succession may be viewed as the development of a community from its inception (the **'pioneer' stage**), through a series of recognizable intermediate seral stages, each almost equivalent to a community in its own right, to a **'climax' stage**. It is regarded as a process resulting in the greater stability of the community, and the *climax community* is considered the most stable community that can exist in that particular environment. While ecologists today recognize that successional processes are less predictable than those proposed by Clements in the 1920s, several of his predicted patterns are generally considered to hold true for successional process. Eugene Odum, an ecosystem ecologist, described several predictable differences between early and late successional systems. For example, during succession, the **early successional species** (often referred to as **pioneer species**) are usually characterized by high growth rates, smaller size, high degree of dispersal, and high rates of per capita population growth.

Table 7.9 Trends of changes in early and late successional stages

Attribute	Early	Late
Community structure		
Total organic matter	Small	Large
Inorganic nutrients	Extrabiotic	Intrabiotic
Species richness	Low	High
Species evenness	Low	High
Biochemical diversity	Low	High
Stratification and spatial heterogeneity	Poorly organized	Well-organized
Life history		
Niche specialization	Broad	Narrow
Size of organism	Small	Large
Life cycles	Short, simple	Long, complex
Nutrient cycling		
Mineral cycles	Open	Closed
Nutrient exchange rate between organisms and environment	Rapid	Slow
Role of detritus in nutrient regeneration	Unimportant	Important
Selection pressure		
Growth form	r-selection	K-selection
Production	Quantity	Quality
Overall homeostasis		
Internal symbiosis	Undeveloped	Developed
Nutrient conservation	Poor	Good
Stability (resistance to external perturbations)	Poor	Good
Entropy	High	Low
Information	Low	High
Community energetics		
Gross production/community respiration (P/R ratio)	Greater or less than 1	Approaches 1
Gross production/standing crop biomass (P/B ratio)	High	Low
Biomass supported/unit energy flow (B/E ratio)	Low	High
Net community production (yield)	High	Low
Food chains	Linear, predominantly grazing	Weblike, predominantly detritus

Source: Odum EP (1969), *The strategy of ecosystem development*, Science.

In contrast, the **late successional species** generally have lower rates of dispersal and colonization, slower per capita growth rates, and they are larger and longer-lived. Similarly, Fakhri Bazzaz characterized early and late successional systems based on the physiology of plants associated with these stages. Early successional plants tend to have high rates of photosynthesis and respiration, high rates of resource uptake and high light compensation points, whereas late successional plants often have opposite characteristics. In the **table 7.9**, trends of changes during the early and late stages of succession are described.

7.14.2 Types of ecological succession

Primary and secondary succession

Succession occurring in new habitats developed by the processes like volcanism and glaciation, where no community existed before is called **primary succession**. In primary succession, the previously unoccupied habitat is first colonized by a few pioneer species which are often microbes, lichens and mosses. It requires species to colonize the area from outside. Soil develops gradually as rocks weather and organic matter accumulates from the decomposed remains of the early colonizers. Pioneers that initiate primary succession must be able to establish and grow on substrates that are nutrient poor and that often have unfavorable moisture conditions. The most extreme sites are exposed unweathered rock surfaces. Here, colonization may be limited to cyanobacteria, lichens and bryophytes, with no further vegetation development. Sites richer in mineral nutrients, which may contain some residual organic soil, such as the depositional zones of glacial moraines, are often colonized by herbaceous species and grasses with faster growth rates. Primary succession proceeds slowly because early colonists often must transform the environment before other species can become established.

Secondary succession occurs at a site from where an already developed community has been destroyed by some natural disturbance such as fire or flooding; or by human activity and a series of communities subsequently develop at the site. *Disturbance* starts, directs and may stop or redirect succession. It is characterized by its frequency, extent and magnitude. In this case, disturbance is defined as any process that results in the removal (either partial or complete) of the existing vegetation (community).

Hence, secondary succession is the development of biotic communities after the complete or partial destruction of the existing community. For example, the forests destroyed by fire and excessive lumbering may be reoccupied by herbs in the initial stages. The reappearance and establishment of communities in such areas is secondary succession. Primary and secondary succession are not always clearly distinguishable. There are numerous examples that are difficult to categorize as either primary or secondary succession. For example, volcanic lava clearly buries soil and biota, but the effect of volcanic eruption depend on the depth of deposition following the eruption.

The secondary succession starts on a well-developed soil already formed at the site. Hence this form of succession is relatively faster as compared to primary succession which may often require hundreds of years. Secondary succession is more common type of succession as compared to primary succession.

Some successional processes may differ from primary and secondary succession. Although ecological succession is linear in most cases extending from pioneer to climax stage. However, some succession do not exhibit linear progression, instead have a cyclic pattern. **Cyclic succession** means that community goes through several seral stages, is disturbed by some disturbance and starts over again. The community is set back to the early successional stage by some naturally reoccurring events or forces, so that the community never reaches the climax stage for that physical environment.

Autogenic and allogenic succession

The changes in environmental conditions that bring about temporal change in community structures are varied. They can, however, be grouped into two general classes: *allogenic* and *autogenic.*

Autogenic (*self-generated*) *succession* is self-driven, resulting from the interaction between organisms and their environment. In this case successional changes are brought about by the organisms themselves.

Allogenic (*externally generated*) *succession* occurs as a result of the changes brought about in the community by external agencies such as storms and fire and not by the internal interactions within existing community itself.

Autotrophic and heterotrophic succession

The succession where initially the photoautotrophs are much greater in quantity than the heterotrophs, is known as *autotrophic succession* i.e., succession begins with P > R. Such a succession takes place in a medium rich in inorganic substances. In *heterotrophic succession*, the heterotrophs, like animals and fungi are present in greater quantity in the initial stages i.e., succession begins with P < R. It begins, prominently in an organic environment, and there is a progressive decline in the energy content.

7.14.3 Mechanism of succession

According to Clements, succession is a process involving several steps. These steps or processes are*: nudation, invasion or migration, ecesis, aggregation, competition, reaction and stabilization – climax*.

Nudation: Succession begins with the development of a bare area without any form of life.

Invasion: Many species invade or reach a new site from any other area. The seeds, spores or other propagules of the plant-species reach the bare area. This process is known as *invasion* (or *migration*), and is generally brought about by air, water and various other agents.

Ecesis: After reaching the new area, the process of successful establishment of the species as a result of adjustment with the conditions prevailing there is known as *ecesis*. Ecesis is considered to be complete, if the plant is able to sexually reproduce in that particular area.

Aggregation: After successful establishment of a species as a result of reproduction, the individuals of the species increase in number. So, as compared to earlier stages, there are a larger number of individuals of a species that have aggregated in the given area.

Competition: The aggregation of individuals in an area leads to *interspecific* and *intraspecific* competition. The competition is usually for *water*, particularly when there is a shortage of water; *nutrients*, particularly when they are in short supply; *radiant energy*, if one plant grows in the shade of another plant; *carbon dioxide*; *oxygen* and *space.*

Reaction: The mechanism of modification of the environment, through the influence of living organisms on it is known as a *reaction.* As a result of the reaction, changes take place in soil, water, light conditions, temperature and many other factors of the environment. The environment thus gets modified, and becomes unsuitable for the existing community, and is eventually replaced by another community. The old occupants are ousted and fresh migrants establish themselves.

Stabilization (**Climax**): The whole process of succession results in stabilization of the vegetation which is now in complete harmony (i.e., steady state) with the environment of that place. And it is likely to persist as long as the climatic and physiographic conditions remain unchanged. The soil is fully occupied by plants and the community is closed. This final community is not replaced and is known as *climax community* and the stage as climax stage.

Concept of climax community

Succession continues until the addition of new species to the sere and the exclusion of established species no longer change in a community. When no other combination of species is successful in replacing it then it is termed as *climax community*. It is one that is self-perpetuating for relatively long periods and one in which the dynamic changes not only occur but are necessary for the maintenance of the community. A climax community is supposed to remain unchanged with time.

It was Clements who used the term *climax* to describe the idealized endpoint of succession. The climax community is in equilibrium with its environment and represents a steady state of community structure and function. Three major theories have been proposed to define, identify and interpret the climax communities. These theories are monoclimax theory, polyclimax theory and climax pattern theory.

The **monoclimax theory** (or **climatic climax theory**) was proposed by Frederic Clements. This theory recognizes only one climax, determined solely by climate, no matter how great the variety of environmental conditions is at the start. Each climax is a direct expression of its climate: the climate is the cause; the climax is the effect, which in turn reacts upon the climate. Clements's idea that a region had only one true climax forced ecologists to recognize a variety of more or less stable communities but different from regional climatic climax by giving name like:

Preclimax: In certain areas different climax communities develop under similar climatic conditions. If the community has life forms lower than those in the expected climatic climax, it is called preclimax.

Postclimax: A community that has life forms higher than those in the expected climatic climax is postclimax.

Subclimax: The stage in succession just preceding the climatic climax is subclimax.

Disclimax: When a stable community, which is not the climatic climax for the given site, is maintained by man or his domestic animals, it is designated as disclimax (*disturbance climax*).

The **polyclimax theory** was proposed by Arthur G. Tansley. The theory considers that the climax community of a region consists of not just one type, but a mosaic of climaxes controlled by several factors such as climate, soil conditions, topography, fire and animal activity. Thus, a single climatic area could easily contain a number of climax communities. Tansley recognized following climax types:

Climatic (regional) climax: A climax community, which is determined by the general climate of the region.

Edaphic (local) climax: Climax communities, which are determined by the soil properties (such as soil moisture, soil nutrients) and topography of the region.

Fire climax: A climax resulted by repeated fire is called fire climax.

R.H. Whittaker (1953) proposed a variation of the polyclimax idea, the **climax pattern theory**. This conceives a continuity of climax types, varying gradually along environmental gradients and not necessarily separable into discrete climaxes. This emphasises that a natural community is adapted to the whole pattern of environmental factors in which it exists. In addition to climatic factors, e.g., wind, there are a whole range of edaphic factors, fire, and biotic factors, including grazing, disease and mutualistic and competitive interactions. Whereas the monoclimax theory allows one climatic climax in a region and the polyclimax theory allows several climaxes in the same area, the climax pattern hypothesis allows a continuity of climax types, varying gradually along environmental gradients and not neatly packaged into discrete climax types.

7.14.4 Models of succession

J. H. Connell and R. O. Slayter (1977) outlined three different models to explain the ecological processes of community change during succession. These models are *facilitation model, tolerance model* and *inhibition model.*

Facilitation model

The classical model that explains the mechanisms of succession is the *facilitation model.* According to this model, certain pioneer species with qualities ideal for early succession can colonize the newly exposed landforms after an ecological disturbance. These initial species modify the site, making it more suitable for invasion by other species, for example, by carrying out the earliest stages of soil development. Once established, the later-successional species eliminate the pioneers through competition. This ecological dynamic proceeds through a progression of stages in which earlier species are eliminated by later species, until the climax stage is reached. This model seems to be most appropriate in explaining changes in many primary successions, but less so for secondary successions.

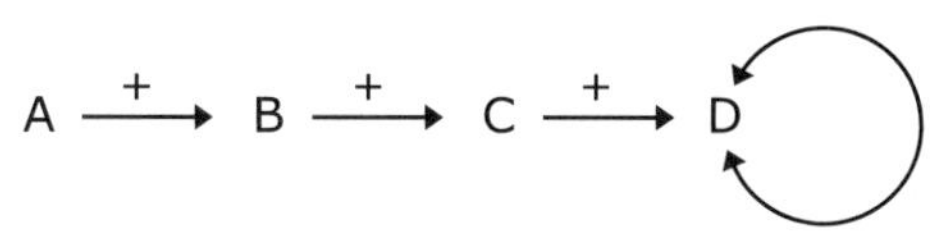

Figure 7.29 Facilitation model. It is based on the assumption that species of a previous stage are replaced by the succeeding stage. At each stage, the species modify their own environment to make it progressively less suitable for themselves and increasingly more suitable for succeeding species. ('+' indicates facilitation and circular arrow indicates that the species replaces itself). A, B, C and D represent four species.

Tolerance model

According to tolerance model, new pioneer species neither inhibit nor facilitate the growth and success of other species i.e., a species invades a new habitat and become established independently of the presence or absence of other species. All species in the succession are capable of establishing on a newly disturbed site, although with varying successes in terms of the rapid attainment of a large population size and biomass. In contrast with the facilitation model, the early occupants of the site do not change environmental conditions in ways that favour the subsequent invasion of later-successional species. Rather, with increasing time, the various species sort themselves out through their differing tolerances of the successionally increasing intensity of biological stresses associated with competition. In the tolerance model, competition-intolerant species are relatively successful in early successional stages when site conditions are characterized by a free availability of resources. However, these species are eliminated later on because they are not as competitive as later species, which eventually develop a climax community.

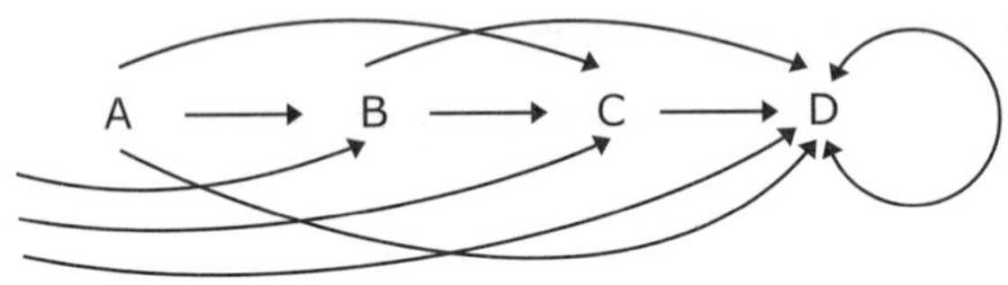

Figure 7.30 Tolerance model. In this model, the presence of early successional species is not essential, that is, any species can start succession. Some species are competitively superior and they eventually predominate in the climax community. Species that are more tolerant of limited resources, replace the other species. Succession proceeds either by the invasion of later species or by a thinning out of the initial colonists, depending on the starting conditions. In the figure, the capital letters A-D represent dominant species and circular arrow indicates that the species replaces itself.

Inhibition model

A third suggested mechanism of succession is the *inhibition model*, in which the pioneer species resist invasion and remain until they are replaced because of competition, predation or disturbance. As with the tolerance model, both early and later-successional species can establish populations soon after disturbance. However, some early species make the site less suitable for the development of other species. For example, some plants are known to secrete toxic biochemical into the soil (these are called **allelochemicals**), which inhibits the establishment and growth of other species. Eventually, however, the inhibitory species die, and this creates opportunities that later-successional species can exploit. This succession model depends on who arrives first and successional pattern is not orderly. These gradual changes eventually culminate in the development of the climax community.

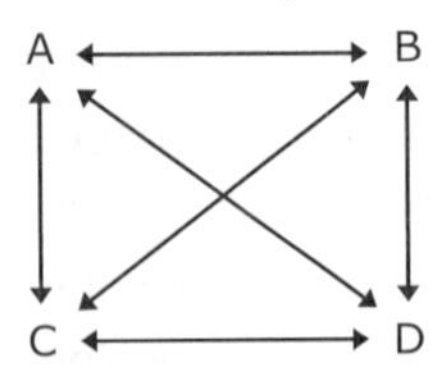

Figure 7.31 Inhibition model. According to this model, succession is very heterogeneous because the development at any one site depends on who establishes there first. Species replacement is not necessarily orderly because each species tries to exclude or suppress any new colonists. Inhibition is the opposite of facilitation - it explains the loss of species as the community changes. Inhibition can lead to communities that become resistant to invasion. In the figure, the capital letters A-D represent dominant species. In this model all replacements are possible and much depends on who establishes there first.

All three of these models – facilitation, tolerance and inhibition – can be supported by selected evidence from many ecological studies. Although these models differ significantly in their predictions about the organizing principles of successional dynamics, it appears that none of them is correct all of the time.

7.15 Biodiversity

Biodiversity, short for **biological diversity**, refers to the sum total of all the variety and variability of life in a defined area. In contrast to the more specific term *species diversity*, the term *biodiversity* was coined to emphasize the many complex kinds of variations that exist within and among organisms at different levels of the organization. It refers to the totality of genes, species and ecosystems of a region. United Nations Earth Summit defined biological diversity as:

'*Biological diversity means the variability among living organisms from all sources including, inter alia (among other things), terrestrial, marine and other aquatic ecosystems and the ecological complexes of which they are a part; this includes diversity within species, between species and of ecosystems.*'

7.15.1 Levels of biodiversity

Biodiversity includes three hierarchical levels: Genetic, species and ecosystem diversity.

Genetic diversity

Genetic diversity refers to the variation in the genetic composition of individuals within or among species. Among species level, genetic diversity can be observed at multiple levels of biological organization, including kingdoms, phyla, families, as well as among species and within species. Genetic diversity *within species* enables populations to adapt to their environments and respond to natural. It is vital because it enables species to adapt, evolve, and survive in changing environments. The extent of genetic variation serves as the raw material for speciation. What does genetic selection diversity within species mean? Let us understand with an example. Consider two populations of a particular species of butterfly present in two different habitats, **A** and **B**. Suppose the population of butterflies in habitat-A has four color variants, whereas the population in habitat-B has only two color variants. In this case, we can say that the population of butterflies in habitat-A has greater genetic diversity.

Among species, the most significant genetic diversity is typically observed between organisms from different kingdoms (e.g., plants versus animals), between phyla (e.g., arthropods versus chordates), between classes (e.g., birds versus reptiles), and so on.

Species diversity

According to the biological species concept, species are groups of actually or potentially interbreeding natural populations that are reproductively isolated from other such groups. Hence, species diversity refers to the variety of species within a region, i.e., **species richness**. However, in the broader sense, species diversity includes not only species richness but also **species evenness**.

Taxonomic (or **phylogenetic**) **diversity** is another important aspect of *species diversity*. It refers to the evolutionary differences between different species within a community. A community with high taxonomic diversity includes species that are more genetically distinct from one another, while a community with low taxonomic diversity consists of species that are closely related. For example, consider two communities, each with five species. In community A, the five species belong to different taxonomic families, such as mammals, insects, birds, and reptiles. In contrast, community B consists of five species that all belong to the insect family. Although both communities have the same species richness, community A is more taxonomically diverse because its species represent a wider range of genetic differences.

Ecosystem diversity

Ecosystems include not only all the species within them but also the abiotic factors that are characteristic of those ecosystems. For instance, in a desert ecosystem, factors like soil type, temperature range, rainfall patterns, and solar radiation shape not only the species that inhabit it, but also influence their physical characteristics, behaviours, and interactions. Ecosystem diversity is a fundamental aspect of biodiversity that describes the **habitat diversity**, **number of niches**, and **trophic levels** within an ecosystem. All of these features collectively contribute to the overall species diversity within an ecosystem. Ecosystems that exhibit high levels of diversity in these aspects tend to support a greater variety of species. This is because a wide range of habitats, niches, and trophic levels can accommodate a larger number of species, each adapted to different conditions.

7.15.2 Gradients and Magnitude of biodiversity

Gradients of biodiversity

Biodiversity varies with changes in **latitude** or **altitude**. As we move from the poles to the equator, the biodiversity increases, and vice versa. The increase in species richness or biodiversity that occurs from the poles to the tropics often referred to as the **latitudinal gradient** in species diversity, is one of the most widely recognized patterns in ecology.

In general, species diversity decreases as we move away from the equator towards the poles. With very few exceptions, tropics (latitudinal range of 23.5° N to 23.5° S) harbour more species than temperate or polar areas. For example, Colombia located near the equator has nearly 1,400 species of birds while New York at 41° N has about 105 species and Greenland at 71° N only about 56 species. India, with much of its land area in the tropical latitudes, has more than 1,200 species of birds. The tropical Amazon rainforest in South America has the greatest biodiversity on the Earth – it is home to more than 40,000 species of plants.

Several hypothesis has been proposed to explain the latitudinal gradients of species richness. Among them, the following hypotheses are predominantly addressed:

Climatic hypothesis: This hypothesis states that the climate is responsible for latitudinal gradient in biodiversity. Two reasons are mainly considered in this hypothesis. 1. Few species may able to physiologically tolerate conditions at higher latitudes. 2. Lesser climate stability at higher latitudes may increase the extinction rate.

Evolutionary history hypothesis: Tropical communities are generally older than temperate or polar communities. Over the course of evolutionary time, species diversity may increase in a tropical community as more speciation events occur. It has been calculated that speciation has occurred about five times more in the tropics as near the poles.

Species-energy hypothesis: This hypothesis suggests that the amount of available energy limits the richness of the system. Thus, increased solar energy at low latitudes causes increased net primary productivity. The higher the net primary productivity the more individuals can be supported, and the more species there will be in an area.

Biotic hypotheses: According to this hypothesis ecological species interactions such as competition, predation, mutualism, and parasitism are stronger in the tropics and these interactions promote species coexistence and specialization of species, leading to greater speciation in the tropics.

Just like latitudinal variation, **altitudinal variation** also causes changes in the biodiversity. A decrease in species diversity occurs from lower to higher altitudes on a mountain. A 1000 m increase in altitude results in a temperature drop of about 6.5°C. The drop in temperature and greater seasonal variability at higher altitudes are major factors that contribute to the reduction in biodiversity.

Magnitude of biodiversity

Our planet exhibits remarkable diversity of life. However, determining the exact number of species on Earth is a challenging task. According to the **IUCN** in 2004, approximately 1.5 million plant and animal species have been described. However, this represents only a fraction of the total number of species that likely exist on our planet. There are varying estimates regarding the total number of species, with some extreme estimates ranging from 20 to 50 million. A more conservative estimate, proposed by biologist Robert May, suggests that global species diversity is around 7 million. It's important to note that these estimates do not include prokaryotic species, as their numbers and diversity are still not fully understood by biologists. The known species are not evenly distributed among taxonomic groups. Animals account for over 70 percent of the described species, while plants (including algae and fungi) make up around 22 percent. Among animals, *insects are the most diverse taxonomic group*, comprising more than 70 percent of the total number of species. In other words, for every 10 animals on Earth, approximately 7 of them are insects.

7.15.3 Uses of biodiversity

At the ecosystem level, biodiversity provides the conditions to drive the processes that sustain the global economy – and our survival as a species. The benefits and services provided by ecosystems include:

Ecosystem services

Biodiversity is essential for the maintenance of ecosystem services and their sustainable utilization. These services include maintenance of gaseous composition of the atmosphere, climate control by forests and oceanic systems, natural pest control, pollination of plants by insects and birds, formation and protection of soil, conservation and purification of water and nutrient cycling etc.

Prevention and mitigation of natural disasters

Forests and grasslands protect landscapes against erosion, nutrient loss, and landslides through the binding action of roots. Ecosystems bordering regularly flooding rivers (floodplain forests and wetlands) help to absorb excess water and thus, reduce the damage caused by floods.

Source of economically important products

Food: About 150 crops feed most of the human population at present, but just 12 of them provide about 80% of food energy (with wheat, rice, maize and potato alone providing about 60%). Also, about 30 mammalian and bird species are used extensively, but just 15 of them account for over 90 percent of global livestock production. Biodiversity increases the range of food products suitable for human consumption. Wild biodiversity provides a wide variety of important foodstuffs, including fruits, meats, nuts, mushrooms, honey, spices and flavourings. These wild foods are especially important when agricultural supplies fail. Indeed, wild biodiversity guards against the failure of even the most advanced agricultural systems. For example, the productivity of many of the developed world's agricultural crops is maintained through the regular assimilation of new genes from wild relatives of these crops. These wild genes offer resistance to the pests and diseases that pose an ever-evolving threat to harvests.

Medicines: Biodiversity is also a rich source of substances with therapeutic properties like **morphine** (used as an analgesic), **quinine** (used for the treatment of malaria) and **taxol** (an anticancer drug). A significant proportion of drugs are derived, directly or indirectly, from biological sources. Moreover, only a small proportion of the total diversity of organisms has been thoroughly investigated for potential sources of new drugs.

Industrial materials: A wide range of industrial materials are derived directly from biological resources. These include building materials, fibers, dyes, resins, gums, adhesives, rubber and oil. There is enormous potential of obtaining economically important materials from a wider diversity of organisms.

Aesthetic and cultural benefits

Biodiversity has also great aesthetic value. Aesthetic aspects include ecotourism, bird-watching, wildlife, pet keeping, gardening etc. The beauty of nature is something many people are enthralled by. There is something within the natural environment which people really connect to, and gives them an immense sense of satisfaction when they experience nature. For some, there are cultural or spiritual meanings attached to the landscape, whereas for others it is simply the aesthetic quality of the natural environment which they enjoy so much.

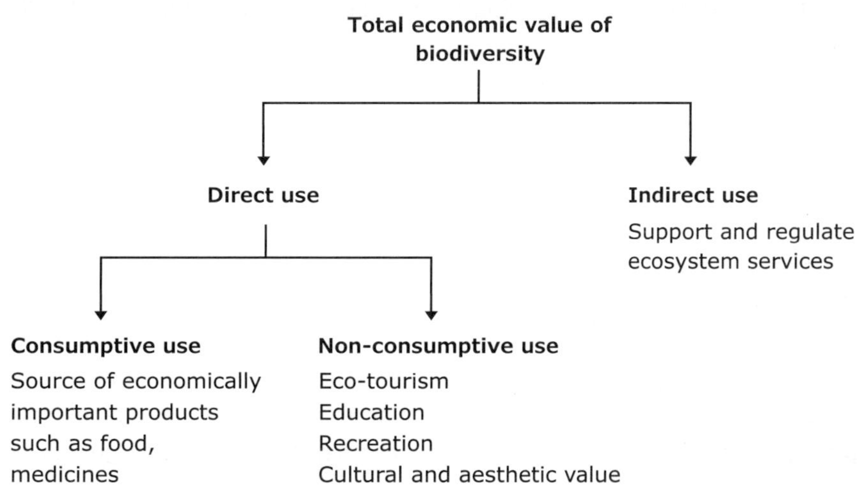

7.15.4 Threats to biodiversity

The most obvious manifestation of biodiversity loss is the extinction of species. This is a natural phenomenon: species have been going extinct since life began. Indeed, it is estimated that many more species have gone extinct than exist at present. What's worrying is the rate at which species are currently dying out. Since the total number of species on the Earth can only be estimated, the exact rate of current species loss is difficult to gauge. Working from the conservative estimate that the Earth is home to 10 million species in all, it is estimated that between 0.2 and 0.6 percent of species are being lost every year. This rate is at least 10,000 times greater than the 'background' or natural rate of species extinction, as estimated using the fossil record. The main causes of biodiversity loss are considered under the following headings:

Habitat loss and fragmentation

'Habitat' means the place or type of site where an organism or population naturally occurs. When a natural habitat, such as a forest or wetland, is altered so dramatically that it no longer supports the species it originally sustained. Plant and animal populations are destroyed or displaced, leading to a loss of biodiversity. It is called **habitat loss** or **habitat destruction**. Habitat destruction is different from **habitat degradation**. According to IUCN, a decline in species-specific habitat quality that leads to reduced survival and/or reproductive success in a population is called 'habitat degradation'. **Habitat fragmentation** is the 'breaking apart' of continuous habitat into distinct pieces. The loss of habitats is the primary reason for the loss of biodiversity. When people cut down trees, fill a wetland, plough grassland or burn a forest, the natural habitat of a species is changed or destroyed. These changes can kill or force out many plants, animals and microorganisms as well as disrupt complex interactions among the species. With the fragmentation of a large forest tract, species occupying deeper parts of forest are the first to disappear.

Introduction of invasive species

An **invasive species** (also called **introduced, exotic, non-native**) can be any kind of living organism that is not native to an ecosystem and which has a tendency to damage the ecosystem. Common characteristics of invasive species include rapid reproduction and growth, high dispersal ability, phenotypic plasticity (ability to adapt physiologically to new conditions) and ability to survive on various food types and in a wide range of environmental conditions. These species grow and reproduce quickly, and spread aggressively, with potential to cause harm. Invasive species are capable of causing extinctions of native plants and animals by competing with them for limited resources and altering habitats. Thus, leading to loss of biodiversity.

The sudden introduction of invasive species to a given ecosystem (especially on islands and in freshwater habitats) causes disastrous consequences for native species. Such introductions are usually the result of human activities. The accidental introduction of an **Atlantic comb jellyfish** species to the Black Sea is a well-known example. These invaders have out-competed native fauna, and now comprise some 95 percent of the Black Sea's total biomass. In the US, meanwhile, the introduction of exotic species has been implicated in close to 70 percent of the past century's freshwater fish extinctions.

Overexploitation

The term *overexploitation* refers to the human activities connected with excessive capturing and harvesting (hunting, fishing, farming) of organisms. According to IUCN, it is an exploitation of (removal of individuals or biomass from) a natural population at a rate greater than the population is able to match with its own recruitment, thus tending to drive the population towards extinction. Overexploitation of a particular species reduces the size of its population to the extent that it becomes vulnerable to extinction. Many species extinctions in the last 500 years, such as the **Steller's sea cow** and the **passenger pigeon**, were caused by overexploitation by humans. The decline of the Earth's largest terrestrial animal, the **African elephant**, is a classic example of the impact of overhunting. Largely because of the trade in ivory, elephant populations have been declining in most of Africa. Overexploitation can also result from incidental exploitation (catching species accidentally while harvesting other target species).

Climate change and pollution

The link between climate change and biodiversity has long been established. Although throughout Earth's history the climate has always changed but rapid climate change due to man made activities affects species ability to adapt and so biodiversity loss increases. In addition to global warming, more frequent extreme weather and changing patterns of rainfall and drought have significant impacts on biodiversity. Some species may benefit from rapid climate change but most species will not find it as beneficial as they will not be able to adapt.

7.15.5 Extinction of species

Extinction is a natural process. Extinction (the complete disappearance of a species from Earth) is an important part of the evolution of life on Earth. The current diversity of species is a product of the processes of extinction and speciation operating throughout the previous 3.8 billion years of life. It is assumed that between 5 and 50 billion species have lived at some time during the history of the Earth. The fossil record indicates that of all the species that have ever lived on Earth, about 99.9% have gone extinct. It is also reasonable to assume that those that are extant now will eventually meet the same fate. Although extinction is inevitable, but has not occurred at a constant pace through the Earth's history and also not same for all species.

The average extinction age of a species ranges from 1 to 10 million years. The **background extinction rate** (also known as the **normal extinction rate**) is about 0.1 extinction per million species per year. Scientists estimate we're now losing species at 1,000 to 10,000 times the background extinction rate. Nobody really knows how many species are in danger of becoming extinct. According to one estimate, in the past 500 years, approximately 1,000 species have gone extinct. The extinction rate has increased mainly due to human-induced habitat loss, invasive species and overexploitation and climate change. No one disputes, however, that the extinction rate for species in recent times has been far higher than this. In the past 100 years, approximately 20 species of mammals and over 40 species of birds have become extinct. The term **biodiversity crisis** is often used to describe this elevated loss of species.

Mass extinction

There have been several periods in the earth's geological history when a large number of species became extinct because of catastrophes or rapid environmental change. **Mass extinction** describes a statistically significant departure from background extinction rates. Scientists have been able to identify five major mass extinctions in Earth's history, each of which led to a loss of more than 70 percent of animal species.

Big five mass extinctions in earth's history

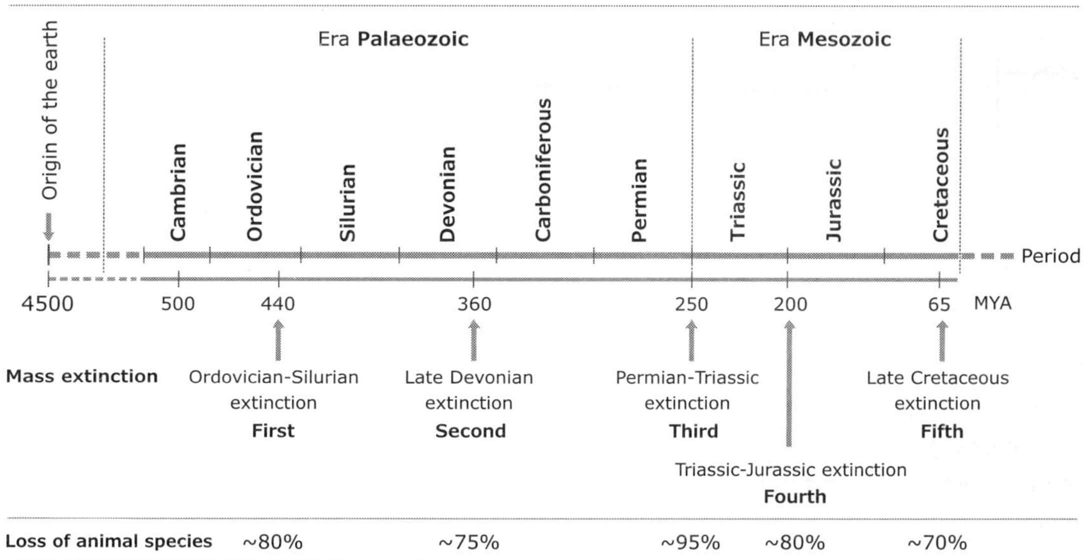

Asteroidal collisions, volcanic eruption, climatic cooling, sea-level changes and changes in habitat area caused by plate-tectonic movements are the five potentially general theories of mass extinction. The late Cretaceous extinction wiped out the dinosaurs, along with ~70% of all life on Earth. A widely accepted theory is that it was due to the collision of an asteroid. This mass extinction killed the dinosaurs. The impact would have ejected enormous amounts of debris into the atmosphere, causing global temperatures to drop. The impact may have also caused local fires, earthquakes, tsunamis, and acid rain.

Susceptibility to extinction

Susceptibility to extinction is not the same for all species. Some species are more susceptible to extinction than others. The susceptibility of species to extinction is related to various life history characteristics that influence the species' vulnerability to human activities as well as natural catastrophes. A species with a geographically widespread distribution is referred to as *ubiquitous*, whereas a species found to occur naturally in a single geographic area and no place else is said to be endemic to that location. Endemic species are particularly susceptible to extinction because a loss of habitat in one geographic region will result in a complete loss of habitat for the species. In general, the species with characteristics such as large body size, small population size, low reproductive rate, feeding at high trophic levels in the food chain, fixed migratory routes, narrow range of distribution, high specialization and poor dispersal rate are more susceptible to extinction:

7.15.6 IUCN Red List categories and criteria

The **IUCN** is an organization working in the field of nature conservation and sustainable use of natural resources. The **IUCN Red List** *categories* and *criteria* are clearly defined system for classifying species which are at high risk of global extinction. It is based upon precise criteria to evaluate the risk of extinction of thousands of species and subspecies. Species are classified by the IUCN Red List into nine groups based on criteria such as rate of decline, population size, area of geographic distribution, and degree of population distribution and fragmentation.

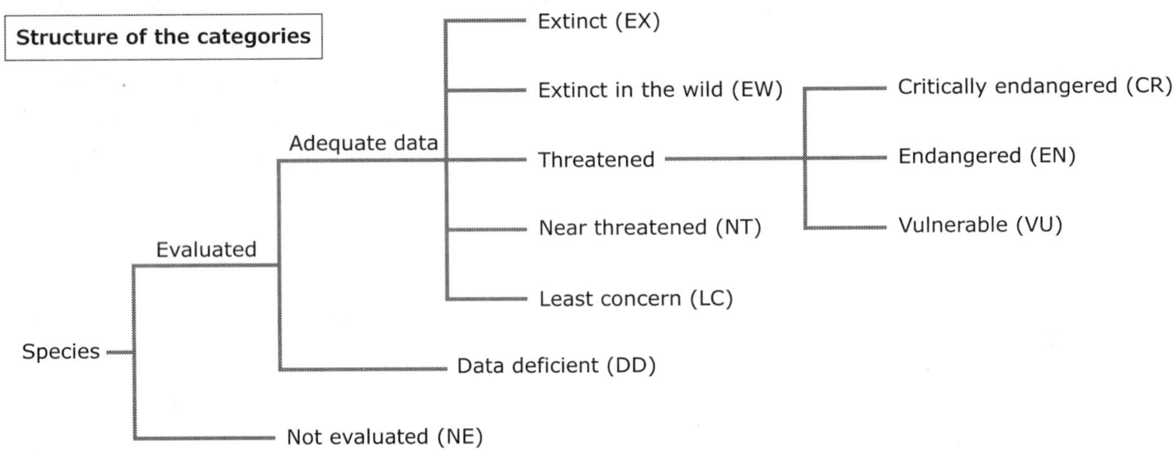

Extinct

A species is extinct when there is no reasonable doubt that the last individual has died. Example: **Dodo** (flightless bird) and **Passenger pigeon** (bird).

Extinct in the wild

A species living only in cultivation (plants) or in captivity (animals) or as a naturalized population (or populations) outside its historic range (exist solely in zoos, aquariums, botanical gardens, or seed banks). As of 2022, the IUCN listed 40 animal species as extinct in the wild. Examples: **Alagoas curassow** (bird), **Hawaiian crow** (bird), **Scimitar oryx** (mammal).

Threatened species

There are five quantitative criteria that are used to determine whether a taxon is threatened or not, and if threatened, which category of threat it belongs in – **critically endangered, endangered** or **vulnerable**. These criteria are:

Population size reduction, geographic range, population size, small or restricted population and probability of extinction. Most of the criteria also include *subcriteria* that must be used to justify more specifically the listing of a taxon under a particular category. Each species should be evaluated against all the criteria. Even though some criteria will be inappropriate for certain species. The relevant factor is whether any one criterion is met or ail are met. Because it will never be clear in advance which criteria are appropriate for a particular species, each species should be evaluated against all the criteria.

Critically endangered: A species is critically endangered when it is facing an extremely high risk of extinction in the wild in the immediate future. To be defined as critically endangered, a species must meet any of the following criteria.

- Population size reduction (A1): ≥90%
- Geographic range: Extent of occurrence (B1): <100 km^2 and area of occupancy (B2): <10 km^2
- Population size: <250 mature individuals
- Small or restricted population: <50 mature individuals
- Probability of extinction: at least 50% within 10 years or 3 generations.

Example: Gharial, Great Indian bustard, Ganges shark, Pygmy hog.

Endangered: A species, whose numbers are so small that the species is at risk of extinction. To be defined as endangered, a species must meet any of the following criteria:

- Population size reduction (A1): ≥70%
- Geographic range: Extent of occurrence (B1): <5000 km^2 and area of occupancy (B2): <500 km^2
- Population size: <2500 mature individuals
- Small or restricted population: <250 mature individuals
- Probability of extinction: at least 20% within 20 years or 5 generations.

Example: Red panda, Snow leopard, Bengal Tiger and One horned rhinoceros and Black buck.

Vulnerable: A species is vulnerable when it is not critically endangered or endangered, but is facing a high risk of becoming endangered in the near future.

- Population size reduction (A1): ≥50%
- Geographic range: Extent of occurrence (B1): <20000 km^2 and area of occupancy (B2): <2000 km^2
- Population size: <10000 mature individuals
- Small or restricted population: <1000 mature individuals
- Probability of extinction: at least 10% within 100 years.

Near threatened

A category on the IUCN Red List of threatened species which indicates that a taxon has been evaluated against the Red List criteria does not qualify for critically endangered, endangered and vulnerable status now but it is close to qualify or likely to qualify for a threatened category in the near future. Polar bears, giraffes, and white rhinos are listed as Near Threatened species because their survival depends on conservation programs.

Least concern

A category on the IUCN Red List which indicates that a taxon has been evaluated against the Red List criteria and does not qualify for critically endangered, endangered, vulnerable or near threatened. Widespread and abundant taxa are included in this category.

7.15.7 Conservation of biodiversity

Biodiversity is a source of significant economic, aesthetic, health and cultural benefits which form the foundation for sustainable development. However, there is general scientific consensus that the world is rapidly becoming less biologically diverse in terms of genes, species and ecosystems. The reason for this is clearly anthropogenic. The scale of human impact on biodiversity has been increasing exponentially primarily because of world-wide patterns of consumption, production, trade; agricultural, industrial and settlement development; and human population growth. Neither the economic nor the ecosystem value of biodiversity is as yet well understood. In particular, there is insufficient knowledge of the interdependence of species within ecosystems and the impact of the extinction of one species on others. Hence, reducing the rate of biodiversity loss and conserving still existing biodiversity as the basis of sustainable development remains a major global challenge. **Conservation** is the protection, management or restoration of wildlife and natural resources such as forests and water. Through the conservation of biodiversity, the survival of many species and habitats which are threatened due to human activities can be ensured.

Ex-situ and *in-situ* conservation

Conservation is the planned management of natural resources, to retain the balance in nature and retain diversity. Conservation efforts can be grouped into the following two categories: *in-situ conservation* (maintenance of biodiversity in natural habitat) and *ex-situ conservation* (conservation of biodiversity outside natural habitat).

In-situ ('on-site') **conservation** includes conservation of habitats and ecosystems where organisms naturally occur i.e. on-site conservation. The conservation of organisms in Biosphere Reserves (terrestrial and marine), National parks, Wildlife sanctuaries, Sacred groves, Biodiversity hotspots are all examples of *in-situ conservation*.

Ex-situ ('off site') **conservation** is a set of conservation strategies involving the transfer of a target species away from its native habitat to a place of safety, such as a **zoological garden, botanical garden** or **seed bank**. Its primary objective is to support conservation by ensuring the survival of threatened species and the maintenance of associated genetic diversity. To do so, *ex-situ* institutions preserve the genetic or reproductive material of a target species or take care of the living target species for the purpose of reintroduction. Thus, there is a fundamental difference between these two strategies: ***ex-situ* conservation** involves the sampling, transfer, and storage of target taxa from the target area, whereas ***in-situ* conservation** involves the designation, management, and monitoring of target taxa where they are encountered.

In-situ conservation strategies

The *in-situ* approach includes protection of a group of typical ecosystems through a network of protected areas. These are areas of land and/or sea, especially dedicated to the protection and maintenance of biological diversity, and of natural and associated cultural resources.

National parks are protected areas, usually declared and owned by the central government. India's first national park was established in 1936 as **Hailey National park** (now known as **Jim Corbett National park**) in Uttarakhand. At present, there are 106 national parks in India covering an area of 40,500 km^2, which is 1.23% of the geographical area of the country (National Wildlife Database, April 2015).

Biosphere reserves are a special category of protected areas of land and/or coastal environments, where people are an integral components of the system. These are representative examples of natural biomes and contain unique biological communities. The concept of biosphere reserves was launched in 1971 as a part of UNESCO's **Man and Biosphere programme** (**MAB**). The first biosphere reserve of the world was established in 1979, since then the network of biosphere reserves has increased to 531 in 105 countries across the world (MAB, 2008). Now, there are 18 biosphere reserves in India. These reserves are rich in biological and cultural diversity and encompass unique features of exceptionally pristine nature. The goal is to facilitate conservation of representative landscapes and their immense biological diversity and cultural heritage, foster economic and human development which is culturally and ecologically sustainable and to provide support for research, monitoring, education and information exchange.

Structure of biosphere reserve: Biosphere reserves have three interrelated zones that aim to fulfill three complementary and mutually reinforcing functions— core, buffer and transition zones.

Core zone: The natural or core zone represents an undisturbed or least disturbed area of representative ecosystem.

Buffer zone: The buffer zone surrounds the core zone, and is managed for research, education and training activities. It is an area peripheral to a core zone, where restrictions are placed upon resource use or special development measures are undertaken to enhance the conservation values of the area. Traditional activities including timber production, hunting, fishing and grazing are permitted.

Transition zone: The transition zone, the outermost part of the biosphere reserve, is an area of active cooperation between reserve management and the local people, wherein activities like settlements, cropping, forestry and recreation and other economic uses continue in harmony with conservation goals.

Biodiversity Hotspots

The concept of biodiversity hotspots originated with British ecologist and writer Norman Myers in 1988. A biodiversity hotspot is a relatively small area with an exceptional concentration of endemic species and a large number of endangered and threatened species. To qualify as a hotspot, a region must meet two strict criteria: it must contain at least 1,500 species of vascular plants (>0.5 percent of the world's total) as endemics, and it has to have lost at least 70 percent of its original habitat. Thus, hotspots are areas with the richest and most threatened reservoirs of plants and animals life on Earth. Norman Myers developed the hotspot concept to designate priority areas for *in-situ* conservation. A key criteria for determining a hotspot are:

1. Number of endemic species i.e., the species which are found nowhere else.
2. Degree of threat, which is measured in terms of habitat loss.

Currently, 36 biodiversity hotspots have been identified, most of which occur in tropical forests. They represent just 2.3% of earth's land surface, but between them, they contain around 50% of the world's endemic plant species and 42% of all terrestrial vertebrates. Among 36 globally identified biodiversity hotspots, four partly fall within Indian political boundaries: **Himalaya** (Includes the entire Indian Himalayan region and also regions present in Pakistan, Tibet, Nepal, Bhutan, China and Myanmar), **Western Ghats** (Includes entire Western Ghats and Sri Lanka), **Indo-Burma** (Includes entire North-Eastern India except Assam and Myanmar, Thailand, Vietnam, Laos, Cambodia and southern China) and **Sundaland** (Includes Andaman-Nicobar Islands and Indonesia, Malaysia, Singapore, Philippines).

Flagship and Umbrella species

Terms umbrella species and flagship species are used within the context of conservation goals and have no strict ecological properties. A **flagship species** is a species chosen to represent an environmental cause, such as an ecosystem in need of conservation. These species are chosen for their vulnerability, attractiveness or distinctiveness in order to generate support and acknowledgment from the public at large. Thus, the concept of a flagship species holds that by giving publicity to a few key species, the support given to those species will successfully leverage conservation of entire ecosystems.

Umbrella species are species whose habitat requirements are so large that protecting them would protect many other species existing in the same habitat. Umbrella species are species selected for making conservation related decisions, typically because protecting these species indirectly protects many other species that make up the ecological community of its habitat. Typically umbrella species are relatively large animals and thus many umbrella species are also flagship species. However, the terms are not synonymous because it is their patterns of habitat use, not popularity, that make some species good umbrellas. In particular, umbrella species usually have large home ranges, and thus by protecting enough habitat for their populations, adequate habitat for many other species will also be protected.

Self Test

Q1. Which of the following statements about energy flow are *correct*?

P. The amount of energy decreases as we move from lower to higher trophic levels.

Q. Only net primary productivity is available to consumers.

R. About 90% of the energy at one trophic level does not transfer to the next.

S. The length of the food chain is limited by the inefficiency of energy transfer along the chain.

a. P and Q

b. P, Q and S

c. Q, R and S

d. P, Q, R and S

Q2. What is the fundamental difference between flow of *matter* and *energy*?

a. Matter is cycled through ecosystems; energy is not.

b. Energy is cycled through ecosystems; matter is not.

c. Energy can be converted into matter; matter cannot be converted into energy.

d. Both energy and matter are cycled through ecosystems.

Q3. A *type I survivorship curve* is characteristic of species with increased mortality in old age. This type of curve is

a. typical of many invertebrates that produce a large number of offspring.

b. typical of humans and other large mammals.

c. almost never found in nature.

d. typical of all species of birds.

Q4. Which of the following statements is correct with reference to *ecotones*?

a. Ecotones are rich in endemic species and contain only species not found in surrounding ecosystems.

b. Ecotones are degraded habitats that harbor endangered species absent from nearby communities.

c. Ecotones are species-poor habitats due to a scarcity of soil nutrients and limited resource availability.

d. Ecotones are transition areas between two ecosystems and have a greater number of species than either of the neighboring communities.

Q5. Consider the following statements:

P. Genetically adopted local population is referred as ecotypes.

Q. Ecotypes differ from each other on the basis of morphological and physiological characters.

R. Ecotypes are interfertile.

S. Ecotypes are found in sessile animals.

Identify the true statements.

a. P and Q

b. P, Q and R

c. R and S

d. P, Q, R and S

Q6. *Biodiversity hotspots* are recognized on the basis of

a. their proximity to national parks and reserves.

b. the number of endemic species they contain.

c. Degree of threat, which is measured in terms of habitat loss.

d. both b and c

Q7. Which of the following statements regarding the *efficiency of energy transfer* in an ecosystem is *false*?

a. A trophic level can support more herbivores than carnivores.

b. Birds and mammals have low production efficiency.

c. The efficiency of energy transfer depends on the total production at a particular trophic level.

d. Herbivores are less efficient with respect to assimilation efficiency than carnivores.

Q8. Group I lists relationships that can exist between two organisms. Their descriptions are given in Group II. Find the correct set of matches between Groups I and II.

Group I	Group II
P. Ammensalism	1. one population is benefited and the other is harmed
Q. Commensalism	2. two dissimilar species living together in close association
R. Mutualism	3. heterotrophic organisms that ingest other organisms
S. Parasitism	4. one population is inhibited but the other is not affected
	5. one population is benefited but the other is not affected

a. P-4, Q-1, R-2, S-3
b. P-3, Q-5, R-4, S-1
c. P-1, Q-4, R-3, S-5
d. P-4, Q-5, R-2, S-1

Q9. A *biomes* represents a distinct ecological community of plants and animals living together in particular climate. Which of the following statements are *correct* about different biomes?

1. Tundra biome is a polar desert, with very low temperature and low precipitation.
2. Savanna is grassland with *scattered* individual trees.
3. Temperate grasslands are characterized as having grasses as the dominant vegetation.
4. Chaparral biome is characterized by mild, rainy winters and long, hot, dry summers.

a. 1, 2 and 3
b. 2 and 4
c. 1, 3 and 4
d. 1, 2, 3 and 4

Q10. Which of the following are *correct* statements about the *regulation of populations*?

1. Logistic equation reflects the influence of population density and stabilizing populations around the carrying capacity.
2. Density-independent regulation experiences greater effect as a population's density increases.
3. High densities in a population may cause physiological changes that inhibit reproduction.
4. Because of the overlapping nature of population-regulating factors, it is often difficult to precisely determine their cause-and-effect relationships.

a. 1, 2 and 3
b. 2, 3 and 4
c. 1, 3 and 4
d. 2, 3 and 4

Q11. In Lotka and Volterra's two species competition model:

$$\frac{dN_1}{dt} = r_1N_1\left(\frac{K_1 - N_1 - N_2\alpha_{12}}{K_1}\right) \text{ and } \frac{dN_2}{dt} = r_2N_2\left(\frac{K_2 - N_2 - \alpha_{21}N_1}{K_2}\right)$$

Where *N* represents population size, r growth rate and *K* maximum carrying capacity for species 1 and 2. The inter specific competition coefficient $\alpha_{12} < 1$ will mean:

a. individuals of species 2 have less inhibiting effect on individuals of species 1 than individuals of species 1 on others of their own species.

b. individuals of species 2 have a greater inhibiting effect on individuals of species 1 than individuals of species 1 on others of their own species.

c. individuals of species 1 have less inhibiting effect on individual members of species 2 than individual of species 2 on others of their own species.

d. individuals of species 1 have a greater inhibiting effect on individuals of species 2 than individuals of species 2 on others of their own species.

Q12. Suppose you discovered a new species about which you know only two facts: it is small-sized (<10 cm) and short-lived (<20 d). Which of the following reproductive strategies is most likely to be *true* for this species?

a. Breeds early and more than once in life and produces large number of small-sized offspring.

b. Breeds late and only once in life and produces large number of small-sized offspring.

c. Breeds early and only once in life and produces large number of small-sized offspring.

d. Breeds early and only once in life and produces a small number of large-sized offspring.

Q13. Primary production in aquatic ecosystem is measured using Light-and-Dark-Bottle technique. In this method, as an indirect measure of photosynthetic production, dissolved oxygen concentration of the pond water enclosed in a BOD bottle is measured initially (I) and after a fixed duration of incubation in a light bottle (L) and a dark bottle (D). Then, the gross and net primary production are estimated as

a. (L-D) and (L-I), respectively

b. (L-I) and (L-D), respectively

c. (L-I) and (I-D), respectively

d. (L-D) and (I-D), respectively

Q14. According to MacArthur and Wilson's *equilibrium theory*, which of the following is *true*?

a. Larger islands and islands closer to mainland are expected to have more species than smaller and isolated islands.

b. Smaller islands and islands far from mainland are expected to have more species than larger and isolated islands.

c. Smaller islands and islands closer to mainland are expected to have more species than smaller and isolated islands.

d. More species are expected on all islands irrespective of their size and distance from the mainland.

Q15. Which of the following statements are *true* for an *r-selected species*?

1. They invest little energy in parental care of young.
2. Reproductive energy is put into producing many offspring, rather than a few well-developed offspring.
3. They exhibit type III survivorship.
4. They live in a stable environment where resource availability is predictable.
5. They are primarily regulated by density-dependent factors.
6. They exhibit type I survivorship.
7. Density dependent factors (such as competition for food, disease) control population size and growth.

a. 1, 2 and 3
b. 4, 5 and 6
c. 3, 5, 6 and 7
d. 1, 2, 3, 4 and 7

Q16. A forest fragment in an agricultural landscape can be viewed as an island. MacArthur and Wilson's island biogeography model can be used to predict patterns of species richness in these forest fragments, as represented in the graphs below:

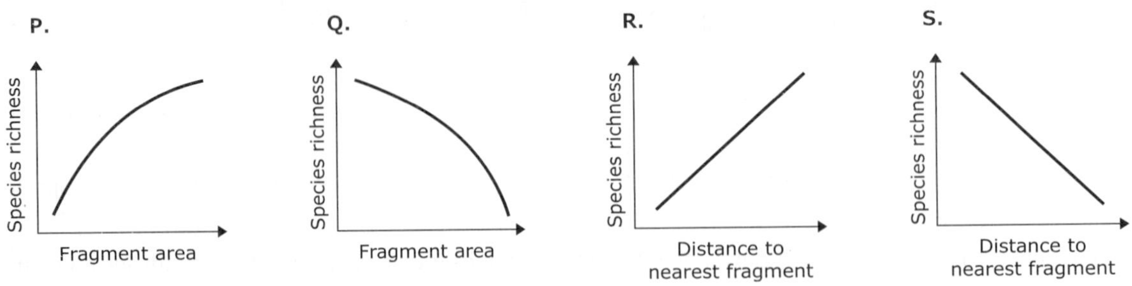

Which one of the following combinations of the graphs *correctly* represents predictions from the model?

a. P and R
b. P and S
c. Q and R
d. Q and S

Q17. Following table shows the number of individuals of five tree species in a community:

Tree species	Number of individuals
A	50
B	20
C	20
D	05
E	05

Based on the above, the *Simpson's index* of the community will be

a. 0.552 b. 0.335

c. 0.435 d. 0.345

Q18. Which of the following is *not* true for a *critically endangered species*?

a. Reduction of population breeding ability due to increased relatedness through the action of incompatibility mechanisms in plants or behavioral difficulties in animals.

b. Individuals of the species, which have declined to low numbers, are still a genetically open system.

c. Loss of some alleles from the species, causing a loss of genetic diversity and inability to respond rapidly to selection.

d. Expression of deleterious alleles and increased homozygosity raise the mortality of young, and inbreeding depression leads to reduced offspring fitness.

Q19. The population size of a bird increased from 600 to 645 in one year. If the per capita birth rate of this population is 0.125, what is its *per capita death rate*?

a. 0.25 b. 0.15

c. 0.05 d. 0.02

Q20. A grasshopper population is being assessed by *capture-mark-release-recapture method*. On the first day, 100 grasshoppers were captured from a given area in 1 hour time, marked and released. On the next day during recapture, 10 marked and 90 unmarked grasshoppers could be found in the same time period from same area. What will be the estimated population size in the given area?

a. 80 b. 100

c. 1,000 d. 10,000

Q21. The diagram below depicts energy flow within a single trophic level, where I = amount ingested, NA = amount not assimilated, R = respiration, and P_n = biomass production at trophic level.

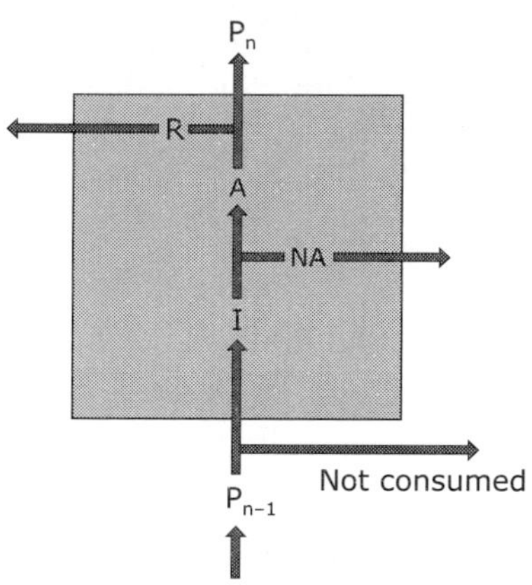

Which one of the following options represents *correct* values for P_n, NA, R and I in kcal respectively, if P_{n-1} = 1000 kcal, I/P_{n-1} = 20%, A/I = 35% and P_n/A = 20%?

a. 56, 14, 130, 200

b. 14, 130, 56, 200

c. 200, 130, 56, 14

d. 56, 130, 200, 14

Q22. A population is growing logistically with intrinsic rate of increase (r) of 0.15 per week, in an environment with a carrying capacity of 400. What is the *maximum growth rate* (number of individuals/week) that this population can achieve?

a. 15

b. 30

c. 22.5

d. 60

Q23. Given below are the possible reasons of high probability for extinction of species. Choose the *correct* statements.

1. Increased homozygosity of alleles.
2. Increased heterozygosity of alleles.
3. Decreasing population sizes.
4. Increasing demographic stochasticity i.e., greater random fluctuations in population size.
5. Decreasing environmental stochasticity.

a. 2, 3 and 5

b. 1, 3 and 4

c. 1, 2 and 3

d. 2, 3 and 4

Q24. Following are a set of statements about various models of succession:

A. In the inhibition model, strong competitive interactions are present, and no species is completely superior, meaning each species can inhibit the others' establishment, preventing any single species from dominating.

B. In tolerance model, later successional species are neither inhibited nor aided by the species of previous stages. They are able to tolerate the conditions created by earlier species.

C. In inhibition model, competitive interaction is weak as no species is completely superior.

D. In facilitation model, later successional species are neither inhibited nor aided by species of previous stages.

Which one of the following options represent *correct* statements?

a. A and D

b. B and C

c. A and B

d. C and D

Q25. Which of the following life history traits is *most* likely in a rodent species when snakes prefer to prey upon large, older individuals of the rodent species that grow continuously over their lifespan?

a. Early reproduction and slow growth rate.

b. Delayed reproduction and fast growth rate.

c. Delayed reproduction and slow growth rate.

d. Early reproduction and fast growth rate.

ANSWER KEY

01. d	02. a	03. b	04. d	05. d	06. d	07. c	08. d	09. d	10. c
11. a	12. c	13. a	14. a	15. a	16. b	17. b	18. b	19. c	20. c
21. b	22. a	23. b	24. c	25. a					

Index

A

B

C

D

E

F

G

H

I

J

K

N

O

P

Q

R

S

T